The 47th Indiana Volunteer Infantry

ALSO BY DAVID WILLIAMSON
AND FROM McFARLAND

*The Third Battalion Mississippi and the 45th Mississippi Regiment:
A Civil War History* (2004)

The 47th Indiana Volunteer Infantry

A Civil War History

DAVID WILLIAMSON

McFarland & Company, Inc., Publishers
Jefferson, North Carolina, and London

LIBRARY OF CONGRESS CATALOGUING-IN-PUBLICATION DATA

Williamson, David, 1942 Nov. 21–
The 47th Indiana Volunteer Infantry : a Civil War history / David Williamson.
　　　　p.　　cm.
Includes bibliographical references and index.

ISBN 978-0-7864-6595-8
softcover : 50# alkaline paper ∞

1. United States. Army. Indiana Infantry Regiment, 47th (1861–1865)
2. United States — History — Civil War, 1861–1865 — Regimental histories.
3. Indiana — History — Civil War, 1861–1865 — Regimental histories.
4. United States — History — Civil War, 1861–1865 — Campaigns.
I. Title.
E506.547th.W55 2012　　　973.7'4772 — dc23　　　2011045865

BRITISH LIBRARY CATALOGUING DATA ARE AVAILABLE

© 2012 David Williamson. All rights reserved

*No part of this book may be reproduced or transmitted in any form
or by any means, electronic or mechanical, including photocopying
or recording, or by any information storage and retrieval system,
without permission in writing from the publisher.*

On the cover: Soldiers from Company A,
47th Indiana (courtesy of Keith Hudson)
Front cover design by TG Design

Manufactured in the United States of America

*McFarland & Company, Inc., Publishers
Box 611, Jefferson, North Carolina 28640
www.mcfarlandpub.com*

To the memory of my grandfather, Harvey Keagy Rose, who was the initial inspiration for this project, and to my grandmother, Josephine Kirkbride Rose, who knew more about the war and its aftermath than she was willing to tell an inquisitive little boy.

To the memory of my father, David, and my mother, Mary Kathryn Rose Williamson, who passed on to me my grandfather's interest in family history.

To the memory of my great-grandfather, Private Eli E. Rose, and great-grandmother, Mary Keagy Rose, and to all the soldiers of the 47th Indiana Volunteer Infantry and their descendants.

And, to my dear wife, Brenda, without whose help this book could not have been written.

Table of Contents

Preface and Acknowledgments   1

    I. Constitutional Crisis (August–December 1861)   3
   II. New Madrid and Island No. 10 (January–April 1862)   16
  III. Memphis (April–July 1862)   45
  IV. Helena, Arkansas (August–December 1862)   63
    V. White River, Arkansas (January 1863)   78
  VI. Yazoo Pass, Mississippi (February–April 1863)   82
 VII. Port Gibson, Mississippi (April–May 1863)   97
VIII. Champion Hill, Mississippi (May 1863)   124
  IX. Vicksburg (May–July 1863)   146
    X. Jackson, Mississippi (July 1863)   172
  XI. Natchez, New Orleans and Bayou Teche (July 1863–January 1864)   190
 XII. New Orleans and the Red River Campaign (January–June 1864)   207
XIII. Morganza, the Atchafalaya and New Orleans (May–September 1864)   233
XIV. St. Charles, Arkansas (September–December 1864)   245
 XV. New Orleans and Mobile (January–June 1865)   261
XVI. Shreveport and the Rio Grande (June–November 1865)   285

Epilogue   299
Appendix A. The McLaughlin Story   311
Appendix B. Zent's Regimental Song   316
Appendix C. The Flags of the 47th Indiana   318
Appendix D. Roster of the 47th Indiana Volunteer Infantry   321
Notes   357
Bibliography   418
Index   431

Preface and Acknowledgments

The gift of Lossing's *A History of the Civil War, Illustrated with Reproductions of the Mathew Brady War Photographs*, by my grandfather, Harvey Keagy Rose, to my mother, Mary Kathryn Rose Williamson, and her passing it on to me as a young boy, led to my interest in the Civil War and curiosity about what my ancestors who fought in it had experienced.[1]

Grandpa Rose had done some research on his father's Civil War experiences, but only enough to know that he had left Summit County in northeast Ohio as a young man of twenty-two, signed up with the 47th Indiana Volunteer Infantry at Huntington, Indiana, lost his left leg at Spanish Fort, Alabama, and fought in "some of the most sanguinary battles of the Civil War."[2]

I never took what limited opportunity I had to question my grandfather about his family research, although he did leave some of his papers to my mother and she passed them on to me while I was still very young. With many questions left unanswered, however, I determined to find out what my great-grandfather had gone through in the war.

Having found no letters, diaries, or memoirs written by Eli, I wondered why he, born and raised in Ohio, had gone to Huntington, Indiana, to sign up with the 47th Indiana Volunteer Infantry. Eli's father (Eli E. Rose, Sr.) and mother (Hannah Jenkins Rose) had come to Ohio from New Jersey and had no known family ties in Indiana.[3] In addition, the 1860 Census for Summit County, Ohio, has young Eli working as a farm laborer for Elihu Griswold near Hudson, Ohio, where his parents lived. A possible explanation came from an unverified family story that had him carrying the mail on horseback from northeastern Ohio westward to Indiana. A more plausible explanation arose with the discovery that an older brother, Walter B. Rose, leased a farm in Huntington County, Indiana. Sometime after the 1860 Census, Eli apparently moved to Indiana to help Walter on the farm until he left in December 1861 to join then Colonel James R. Slack's 47th Indiana, listing his home as "Clear Crick," Indiana.[4]

My wife Brenda and I had discovered in previous research efforts that two of our direct ancestors had been shooting directly at each other at the Battle of Franklin, Tennessee.[5] In our current research, we also discovered that Brenda's great-great uncle, Abner Wilkes of the 46th Mississippi Infantry, came into relatively close contact with Eli at the Battle of Port Gibson and would have come into close contact at the end at Fort Blakely had Eli not been seriously wounded at Spanish Fort. Uncle Abner had some pithy comments to make about the war and we have included a few of them in this book.[6]

I would like to acknowledge and thank Mrs. Sara Firehammer for her early help and encouragement. I would also like to thank Jeff T. Giambone and Gordon Cotton of the Old Court House Museum, Vicksburg, Mississippi; Grady Howell; Ted and Teresa Lofton; Joe Means; Thomas and Charlotte Rose Freitag; Merrill Lewis; Maureen Frei; Mark Davis; James Manning; Bob Cooper; Keith Hudson; Dewey Jones; Commander Roger L. Johnson, U.S. Navy (retired); Dan Nelson; Terry C. Smith and Kevin Lindsey.

I also appreciate the Indiana Historical Society and the Huntington County Historical Society for their generosity to long-distance researchers, the resources and assistance of the Indiana State Library, the Indiana War Memorials Commission, the Lilly Library of Indiana University, the Cook and McCain Libraries of the University of Southern Mississippi, the Index Project (a computerized database of Civil War courts-martial), and Carol Ryan, Interlibrary Loan Specialist (retired), of the Library of Hattiesburg, Petal, and Forrest County, Mississippi. Finally, my thanks to graphic designer Katherine Stanley for her skill in making my line maps readable; and to my wife, Brenda, for expertly proofreading and editing the manuscript.

I

Constitutional Crisis (August–December 1861)

By the time Colonel James R. Slack began organizing the 47th Indiana Volunteer Infantry in the fall of 1861, South Carolina, Mississippi, Florida, Alabama, Georgia, Louisiana, Texas (where U.S. forces surrendered), Virginia, Tennessee, Arkansas, and North Carolina had formed the provisional government of the Confederate States of America; selected former U.S. senator Jefferson Davis of Mississippi as their provisional president; ratified a constitution, moved their capitol from Montgomery, Alabama, to Richmond, Virginia, organized an army, and won several key battles.

Back in March, with the secession of the first seven southern states and the formation of the Confederate States of America well underway, newly inaugurated President Abraham Lincoln, acting to quell the disintegration of the United States, justified his naval blockade of southern ports and call to arms by citing his solemn oath "to preserve, protect, and defend" the Union. The real underlying question, however, was not whether the Union could or even should be preserved, but whether constitutional democracy, the ostensible basis of that Union, could survive civil war. Differences of opinion on this question created an ideological divide in the North that quickly erupted into violence.[1]

The first serious challenge to the administration's war policy in the North occurred on 19 April 1861 in Baltimore, Maryland, five days after Fort Sumter, South Carolina, surrendered to Confederate forces and the same day President Lincoln declared the blockade of southern ports. In what came to be known as the Baltimore Riots, Confederate sympathizers attempted to block the passage of Federal soldiers being sent from Philadelphia to Washington to reinforce the southern defenses of the Federal capital. Violent clashes erupted on Baltimore city streets as soldiers attempted to transfer on foot to the Washington depot, with casualties on both sides.

Baltimore Mayor George W. Brown called an emergency session at his house that evening attended by, among others, Governor Thomas H. Hicks, a guest of the mayor at the time, the police marshal, and the president of the police commission. Apparently believing that state sovereignty gave them authority to block Federal troop movements through Baltimore, they authorized the burning of the two railroad bridges leading into the city from the north. Although Federal troops quelled the riot the next day, the bridges of the Philadelphia, Wilmington & Baltimore and the North Central Railroads were burned overnight, forcing the Federal military to rely on steamers from the northern end of Chesapeake

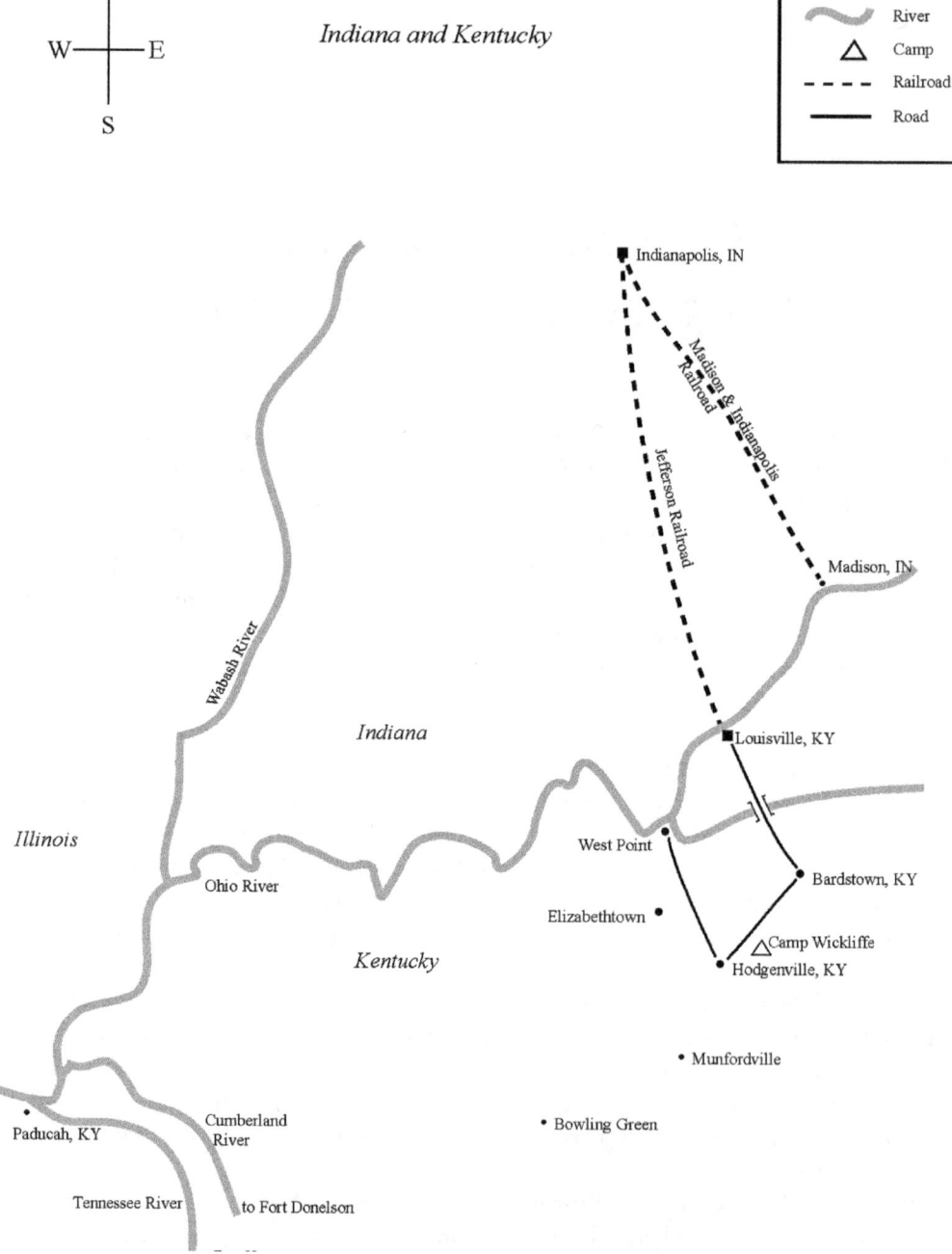

From Atlas Plate CLI and Google Maps

Bay and the Elk Ridge Railroad from Annapolis, Maryland, to supply the Federal capital.[2]

In order to deal with this mini-insurrection, on 27 April 1861 President Lincoln directed Lieutenant General Winfield Scott, then commander-in-chief of the army, to suspend the writ of habeas corpus between Washington and New York City, shortly thereafter extending the suspension to the Florida coast, Key West, the Dry Tortugas, and Santa Rosa Island. The president's proclamation essentially authorized the military to suspend the writ of habeas corpus if they encountered either resistance or persons they deemed suspicious or dangerous, "either by the commander personally or through the officer in command at the point where resistance occurs."[3]

The notion of state sovereignty quickly dissipated as troops under Brigadier General Benjamin Butler occupied Baltimore on 13 May, followed by the first test of the president's suspension of habeas corpus. At 2:00 A.M. on 25 May, John Merryman, a citizen of Maryland and reportedly a member of the Maryland militia suspected of having taken part in the Baltimore bridge burnings, was arrested at his home on orders issued by Major William H. Keim of the Pennsylvania militia. He was taken to Fort McHenry in Baltimore Harbor, where he was kept in close confinement. Merryman immediately sued for a writ of habeas corpus.

On 27 May, the Supreme Court's aging Chief Justice, the Hon. Roger Taney, then sitting as a circuit judge in Baltimore, received Merryman's petition, issued the writ to Bvt. Major General George Cadwallader, commander of the Department of Annapolis and Fort McHenry, and ordered Cadwallader to release the prisoner. Under orders from Winfield Scott, however, Cadwallader refused to accept the writ or produce the prisoner and refused Taney's subpoena to appear in the assigned courtroom at the Masonic Hall in Baltimore. Understanding that his subpoena was unenforceable without compliance of the military, Taney fired a symbolic shot across the administration's bow by issuing an opinion and having a copy sent to the president, to wit: "The privilege of the writ of habeas corpus can not be suspended, except by act of congress." And, noting that Merryman had been arrested "on vague and indefinite charges, without any proof, so far as it appears," Taney opined that holding Merryman in military custody was illegal and that the actions of Generals Keim, Scott, and Cadwallader constituted a usurpation of judicial power by the military. Chiding Lincoln to uphold the laws of the land, Taney concluded that because of Lincoln's unconstitutional suspension of habeas corpus, "the people of the United States are no longer living under a government of laws, but every citizen holds life, liberty and property at the will and pleasure of the army officer in whose military district he may happen to be found."[4]

The president ignored Taney's opinion but indirectly answered the chief justice in a 4 July message to a special session of Congress in which he reminded the legislators that there was an emergency at hand. "Now," the president argued, "it is insisted that Congress, and not the Executive, is vested with this power. But the Constitution itself is silent as to which, or who, is to exercise the power; and as the provision was plainly made for a dangerous emergency, it cannot be believed the framers of the instrument intended that, in every case, the danger should run its course until Congress could be called together; the very assembling of which might be prevented, as was intended in this case, by the rebellion." Although there was no widespread lawlessness in the North, Congress had not been interrupted, and all the civil courts were open and functioning, the president insisted "the whole of the laws" that he was required to faithfully execute were being resisted. Lincoln posed his now-famous rhetorical question to justify the suspension of the writ: "Are all the laws *but one* to go unexecuted, and the government itself go to pieces, lest that one [habeas corpus and due process of law] be violated?"[5]

Indicted in July for conspiracy to commit treason, Merryman was released on bail and, largely due to Taney's efforts, discharged. Undeterred, President Lincoln, concerned about the possible secession of Maryland and buoyed by the opinion of his attorney general, Edward Bates, that his suspension of habeas corpus in order to suppress insurrection or ensure public safety was constitutional, ordered the military to make widespread arrests of civilian opponents and pro-secession legislators. With "the great writ of liberty" suspended, the battle over civil rights in the North was joined.[6]

In Maryland, the State and War Departments issued large numbers of arbitrary arrest warrants for secret, middle-of-the-night arrests of those suspected of disloyal activities, including the mayor, the police chief, the police commissioners of Baltimore, and, in order to fend off the probable secession of the state, large numbers of state legislators. In addition, the military closed two Baltimore newspapers, *Daily Exchange* and *The South*, for their antiwar views and imprisoned their editors (W.W. Glenn and F. Key Howard of the *Daily Exchange*, and Thomas W. Hall and S.S. Mills of *The South*) for calling Lincoln a despot, calling the war unconstitutional, and complaining that the military had unconstitutionally closed their newspapers. The four newspapermen refused on constitutional grounds to sign an Oath of Allegiance and were imprisoned with other political prisoners from Maryland and elsewhere at Forts Lafayette and Columbus in New York Harbor.[7]

Political arrests occurred in New York City as well as hostility against the war, and fear of military dictatorship spread. In a move that created more suspicion and hostility in the North than its intended purpose of suppressing antiwar ideas achieved, Secretary of State Seward and Postmaster General Montgomery Blair, ignoring the constitutionally guaranteed freedom of the press, arbitrarily began attempting to curtail the circulation of antiwar newspapers by issuing orders not to allow them to be sent through the mails. Among the papers targeted were the *New York News*, the *New York Journal of Commerce*, the *Republican Watchman* of Greenport, Long Island, and the *National Zeitung* of New York. And in an attempt to censor the news, the Lincoln Administration pressured the American Telegraph Company to prohibit any telegram about the military to be sent to any newspaper without the consent of the military.[8]

The attempt to suppress antiwar ideas moved west rapidly as the *Circleville (Ohio) Watchman* and the *Plymouth (Indiana) Democrat* also became government targets because of their political opinions. A *Watchman* editorial had drawn the ire of the Deer Creek, Ohio, postmaster, who dutifully sent a copy to Secretary of War Simon Cameron, when it called the editors of the *Cincinnati Commercial* "nameless boobies" who supported "military despotism" and a "damnable abolition war" against "all those who do not shout hosannas to Abe Lincoln and his unconstitutional and unholy war upon the people of the South." To say the least, Republican newspapers did not rush to support the right of their rival Democratic newspapers to dissent against that war. What might be considered the Republican mood was expressed in an editorial in the 15 July 1861 *Indianapolis Daily Journal* entitled "What is Free Speech?" To the *Daily Journal* editorialist, whatever free speech was, it was not the freedom to express opinions favorable to secession or criticism of the war against it. Equating opposition to the policies of the Lincoln Administration with treason, the *Daily Journal* labeled those opinions "disloyal" and called for them to be suppressed by force if necessary. Those who held such views were to keep quiet or leave the country.[9]

In deeply divided Indiana, county political conventions were being held by both parties to take positions on these issues. Huntington County Democrats met at the courthouse in Huntington where three prominent attorneys, James R. Slack, John R. Coffroth, and Lambdin P. Milligan, held forth. Slack had come to Huntington County in 1840 as a young attorney, the county's first, when it was still a "howling wilderness"; Coffroth and Milligan arrived a few years later. The three quickly established themselves among the preeminent attorneys in northern Indiana as well as friends, colleagues, and fellow Democrats. In the mid–1840s all three became charter members of the La Fontaine Lodge, No. 42, of the Huntington Odd Fellows fraternal order.[10]

Secession, however, split not only the country but also the Indiana Democratic Party and other voluntary organizations, including the Huntington Odd Fellows, who disbanded due to differences of opinion on the war and on President Lincoln's policies. The Democratic convention, which met in Huntington on 1 June, one of many held by both parties around the country that month, presented a microcosm of the issues that divided the country. Milligan and Coffroth proposed a series of resolutions in which they essentially asserted that the framers of the Constitution never intended for the country to be held together by force; that although they did not agree that the Confederates had just cause to secede, they had the right to do so and a peaceable separation and a treaty of amity should be signed with them as an independent nation. The problem, they argued, was President Lincoln's unconstitutional usurpation of power, including, among other acts, the suspension of the writ of habeas corpus, denial of due process in the courts, subjugation of the press, and abridgement of the freedom of speech. They maintained their loyalty to the government but asserted that they "would never be prostituted to a sycophantic adulation of a tyrant or a quiet submission to his usurpations." This epitomized what came to be known as the "Peace Democrat" or "Copperhead" position.[11]

Slack, on the other hand, who had just resigned his state senate seat, submitted resolutions to that same convention in which he called the conduct of the secessionists "illegal, unconstitutional, outrageous and treasonable" and said secession should be stopped by force of arms. He added a state sovereignty and thinly veiled pro-slavery caveat that prosecution of the war should not interfere with the domestic institutions of any state of the Union. Following a debate with Milligan, the convention adopted Milligan and Coffroth's "Peace Democrat" resolution and rejected Slack's, which epitomized what came to be known as that of the "War Democrat" faction. Slack's position was, in fact, not much different from the position adopted by the Indiana Republican Convention to "sustain the Government in the present war to put down rebellion and sustain the supremacy of the Constitution," with the same caveat "disclaiming all desire to interfere with the domestic institutions of any State" and opposing "all enemies of our Constitution, be they Rebels, Rebel Sympathizers, or," notably, "Garrisonian Abolitionists."[12]

Slack took to the hustings and during a particularly heated Democratic meeting at Warren, came to blows with Sam F. Winter, editor of the *Huntington Democrat*. In the scuffle, Slack, no shrinking violet, reportedly wounded Winter slightly in the side with his penknife and was thereafter referred to in the *Democrat* as "the Pen knife General."[13]

In what would become a typical broadside against Slack, the editor of the *Democrat* wrote in the 12 September 1861 edition:

The Pen knife General we are informed, held a Wood Picking some night last week, in Clearcreek township. On mounting the "rostrum" and taking a survey of his audience, he found about 40 Republicans and one or two Democrats. For the moment he was non plussed, but, stung to madness, he quickly rallied and introduced his rebellion harangue in substance thus,— "I do not see before me the kind of a crowd I would like to address. I came here to speak to sinners. I find but few here." (Immense applause) So Democrats are *sinners* and Republicans *saints*—eh, Jim?[14]

Meanwhile, except to staunchly antiwar Democrats, the Constitution and Bill of Rights took a back seat to worry about the fate of the Union as Confederate forces won the first two major battles of the war at Bull Run, Virginia, near Washington, D.C., on 21 July, and at Wilson's Creek, near Springfield, Missouri, on 10 August 1861.

In Missouri, the State Convention opted to remain in the Union, set up a new state government and, for greater security, moved the capital from Jefferson City to St. Louis. Following Wilson's Creek, however, pro-secessionists under Benjamin McCulloch and Sterling "Old Pap" Price controlled enough of southern and western Missouri to establish a separate Confederate state government at remote Neosho. Unable to cope with McCulloch, Price, or the numbers they were recruiting to Confederate service, Brigadier General John C. Fremont, then at St. Louis in command of the Union Department of the West (all states and territories west of the Mississippi River), declared martial law in Missouri. On 30 August he proclaimed, among other orders, that the property of all persons in Missouri who took up arms against the United States, or aided those who did, would be confiscated and their slaves "declared freemen." President Lincoln, noting that the confiscation order and liberation of slaves would be impolitic (it would "alarm our Southern Union friends"), immediately ordered Fremont to rescind the proclamation.[15] Fremont, whose earlier training as a topographical engineer and glory days as an explorer in the West had not converted into military leadership or expertise, finally, due largely to his inability to drive McCulloch and Price out of Missouri, lost the confidence of the War Department and the president. On 12 September, with Price holding the western Missouri town of Lexington under siege, President Lincoln began looking for Fremont's replacement.[16]

Problems in the West escalated as Confederate forces also took control of western Tennessee and now posed a credible threat to Cairo, Illinois, as well as to Kentucky. The threat manifested itself on 3 September 1861 when Episcopal bishop and Confederate Brigadier General Leonidas Polk violated Kentucky's neutrality by moving his troops into the Mississippi River town of Columbus. Although ill-prepared to meet the challenge, three days later a Federal force under U.S. Grant, then commander of the District of Southeast Missouri, crossed the Ohio River and occupied Paducah.[17]

By mid–September, with Confederate troops pouring into Kentucky by railroad from Mississippi and Tennessee, Confederate Brigadier General Simon Buckner of Kentucky, leading the advanced division of General Albert Sidney Johnston's Confederate Army of Central Kentucky, occupied Bowling Green, as Johnston, also a native Kentuckian, established a defensive line running from the Mississippi River at Columbus, through Bowling Green, all the way to the Cumberland Gap.[18]

A worried Governor Oliver P. Morton of Indiana had written on 29 August to Assistant Secretary of War Thomas A. Scott in Washington that civil war in Kentucky was inevitable and that he wanted a large force concentrated at Evansville to defend Indiana's border counties. Four days later (2 September 1861), Morton wrote Scott that the Tennessee Confederates lining the southern border might strike a blow "at any moment," and added, "If we lose Kentucky, God help us."[19]

I. Constitutional Crisis (August–December 1861)

Ten days later (12 September 1861), Governor Morton wrote an urgent letter directly to Secretary of War Simon Cameron informing him that the "war in Kentucky [had] commenced" and Indiana's borders were "nearly defenseless." To make matters worse, Brigadier General Anderson wrote Morton on 15 September to warn him that he might be compelled to take the field against Johnston's advance before his troops were ready.[20]

Increasingly desperate, on 22 September Morton wrote to Fremont in St. Louis that reliable information showed a Confederate advance on Louisville by "not less than 10,000 men, and Anderson has not more than 3,000." Noting that they were out of arms and that Louisville was in great danger and probably could not be saved, he urged Fremont, who had more troubles of his own in Missouri than he could handle: "Please send us arms by special train."[21]

Morton also telegraphed President Lincoln that Owensboro, Kentucky, an Ohio River town forty miles above Evansville, had fallen to the "secessionists." The president replied to Morton by telegraph on 22 September, informing the governor that he had relayed his message to Fremont in St. Louis and had told Fremont to consider sending a gunboat from Paducah, if feasible, to help recapture Owensboro, adding: "Perhaps you had better order those in charge of the Ohio river to guard it vigilantly at all points."[22]

At about this time, as part of Morton's buildup of Indiana troops, Huntington's own James R. Slack was appointed colonel of the 47th Indiana Volunteer Infantry and began to recruit volunteers from the Eleventh Congressional District in northeastern Indiana.[23]

In early October, Grant, continuing to move Federal troops into northern Kentucky, occupied Paducah, Louisville and Covington, and temporarily checked Albert Sidney Johnston's Confederate advance toward the Ohio River. Ill-prepared and in a rush to get competent officers in the field and their largely volunteer army ready to defend against Johnston's move into Kentucky, the Federal forces in the West went through a series of reorganizations.

On 8 October 1861, Brigadier General William T. Sherman replaced Robert Anderson as commander of the Department of the Cumberland. The aging and weary former commander at Fort Sumter, unable to persuade Washington of the dire need for troops in the department to defend against the Confederate buildup, resigned for health reasons.[24]

The next day, Secretary of War Simon Cameron and Adjutant-General of the U.S. Army Lorenzo Thomas, accompanied by newspaperman Sam Wilkeson of the *New York Tribune*, who was acting as Cameron's confidential advisor, left Washington ostensibly for an inspection tour of the Department of the West, but with orders relieving Fremont of command.[25]

Cameron's entourage found Fremont at Tipton, Missouri, but Cameron delayed handing him his dismissal on Fremont's word that he had a major victory in the works. Cameron told Fremont he would withhold the order until he returned to Washington in about two weeks, giving Fremont sufficient time to win a battle against Price or McCulloch. With that, on 14 October, Cameron moved with his entourage to Indianapolis to spend two days interviewing Governor Morton. Adding General Thomas J. Wood at Indianapolis, Cameron's entourage headed for Louisville to interview Sherman at the Galt House Hotel in Louisville.[26]

Knowing that Sherman would not talk candidly in the presence of a newspaperman, Cameron, who urged Sherman to speak freely, did not tell him that Wilkeson was from the *Tribune*, introducing him only as his trusted friend and that the meeting was confidential.

Sherman, thus assured of confidentiality, bluntly spelled out the difficulties they faced in the Department of the Cumberland, insisting that they needed 60,000 troops immediately to defend Kentucky and would need some 200,000 more to take the offensive. Cameron, reportedly taken aback by Sherman's assessment of Federal chances in the West, left Louisville on 16 October for Washington, muttering that Sherman must be "unbalanced" or "crazy." Before leaving Louisville with Cameron that day, Wilkeson told Henry Villard of the *Cincinnati Commercial* about Cameron's feelings; Villard in turn sent the sensational story to Murat Halstead, his editor at the *Commercial*.[27]

Gen. James R. Slack (CivilWarIndiana.com/ Craig Dunn Collection.)

On 30 October, the *New York Tribune* published excerpts from Lorenzo Thomas's report of the western tour (possibly written by Wilkeson for Thomas), which was especially critical of Fremont, but included Cameron's mistaken official assessment that Sherman's call for more troops in Kentucky was exaggerated and overly "gloomy." Moreover, the day before he resigned on 7 October, Anderson, in a conciliatory effort to keep the support of reluctant Kentuckians, had requested the civil authorities, and ordered the military, to stop arresting civilians for merely voicing approval of secession. Arrests were to be made only where evidence existed that the person had attempted to join or had given aid and information to the Confederates, and then the evidence was to be submitted only to the federal district court where the alleged offenses occurred. Upon taking command, Sherman had implemented Anderson's order and, following publication of Lorenzo Thomas's report, the influential *Chicago Tribune* accused him of encouraging treason and espionage.[28]

In the meantime, the president ordered the first major reorganization of the Federal army by naming Major General George B. McClellan to succeed the aging Winfield Scott as commander-in-chief of the Federal armies and commander of the Army of the Potomac, the main Federal force in the East. McClellan then proceeded with a major reorganization of the western armies.[29]

In the first week of November, Fremont, with no major victory at hand and deemed incompetent, was relieved of command and the Department of the West divided into three separate departments.[30] Major General David Hunter took command of the new Department of Kansas (Kansas and the Indian Territory west of Arkansas); Colonel E.R.S. Canby took command of the Department of New Mexico; and Major General Henry W. Halleck came to St. Louis to take command of the new Department of the Missouri (Missouri, Iowa, Wisconsin, Illinois, Arkansas, and Kentucky west of the Cumberland River). On 9 November, Sherman[31] was relieved of command and the Department of the Cumberland was placed within the new Department of the Ohio (Ohio, Michigan, Indiana, Kentucky east of the Cumberland River, and Tennessee), commanded by Brigadier General Don Carlos Buell.[32]

In mid–November, Sherman was assigned to Halleck's department and relegated to inspector of troops at Sedalia, Missouri. (His knowledge of the South's war preparations in the 1850s and their potential military prowess, downplayed by nearly everyone else, came from his early military career in Missouri and the South and a stint from August 1859 until his resignation in 1861 as the first superintendent of the new Louisiana Seminary of Learning and Military Academy).[33] Understandably upset and even disheartened, not by his demotion, which he had essentially requested, but by the inept leadership in the War Department and the poor performance of the officers and troops in Missouri, Sherman remained an outspoken critic of the Federal war effort. In late November, Halleck, in order to help Sherman cool down, granted him a 20-day leave to visit with his family in Lancaster, Ohio; on 2 December, Halleck told McClellan that Sherman was physically and mentally unfit for duty.[34]

On 11 December, Murat Halstead, after learning Sherman had been relieved of command of the Department of the Cumberland and had gone or been sent home from Missouri, apparently felt safe to publish Villard's story of Sherman's "insanity." Sherman's well-known antipathy toward newspaper reporters (he thought their reports aided and abetted the enemy[35]) and occasional arrest or banishment of them from his department, accompanied by his seemingly unrelenting criticism and unkempt appearance, at least by military standards, led many reporters who disliked him to pick up the story and spread the rumors of his "insanity."[36]

By the time the story broke about Sherman's "insanity," even Halleck had begun to echo Sherman, complaining to McClellan about the "total disorganization" and "general lack of discipline" among his officers and troops in Missouri, and a lack of arms for those Federal regiments that were ready for the field. Anyone with knowledge of these facts would have been at least somewhat despondent, if not "agitated."[37]

Nevertheless, both Northern and Southern newspapers ran stories of Sherman's "insanity," notwithstanding his (as well as Anderson's and Governor Morton's) legitimate concern about the Confederate move into Kentucky, and his (and Halleck's) concerns about the Federal army in Missouri. Although Anderson was called "old and tired" and Sherman "insane," Oliver Morton, the powerful Republican governor of Indiana, who had voiced the same concerns as Anderson and Sherman, was praised in the Republican press. The Republican *Indianapolis Daily Journal*, for example, scathing in their attack on Sherman, was unabashed in their praise for Morton.[38]

On 18 November, Confederates, supported by General Albert Sidney Johnston's occupation of southern Kentucky, established George W. Johnson as governor of the Provisional Government of Kentucky, with their capital at Bowling Green; and, on 10 December, the Confederate Congress in Richmond admitted Kentucky to the Confederacy. But, hampered by a lack of money and supplies, Johnston was unable to take full advantage of his incursion into Kentucky before the Federal response began in earnest early in December.[39]

In the vanguard of that Federal response, Slack's 47th Indiana Volunteer Infantry mustered in their last three companies (E, H, and K). They departed from Camp Sullivan on 13 December 1861 with 936 newly enlisted men and 41 commissioned officers on the night train to Louisville, a trip of about eight hours on the Jeffersonville Railroad.[40]

Crossing the Ohio River by ferry at Jeffersonville, Indiana, the following morning, the 47th Indiana encamped several miles south of Louisville on farmland owned by Confederate General Simon Buckner, whose force was about 110 miles south at Bowling Green. Near the old Oakland Race Course, which was then being used as Federal cavalry stables, their camp was located between the planked Louisville and Nashville Turnpike Road and the Louisville & Nashville Railroad. To Buckner's chagrin, his well-located property was now being used as a staging area and drill field for the new Union regiments.[41] The 47th Indiana remained in camp near Louisville from 14 to 16 December before beginning a three-day march southeastward down the Louisville and Nashville Turnpike Road to Bardstown.

With mobilization in full force in Indiana, many newspapers used soldiers in the field to act as war correspondents and add a more personal, hometown touch to the war stories. The staunchly Republican *Indianapolis Daily Journal* used Chaplain Samuel Sawyer of the 47th Indiana as one of their war correspondents. Sawyer, an ardent abolitionist, graduate of Princeton University and Union Theological Seminary in New York City, had served as minister of the Second Presbyterian Church of Rogersville, Tennessee, until he was forced to resign in 1857 after publicly criticizing an influential church elder, a Colonel Netherland, for abusing his slaves. His criticism of Col. Netherland appeared in the *New York Times*, along with a rebuttal by Col. Netherland, and an attack on Sawyer by the iconoclastic East Tennessee publisher/editor, William G. "Parson" Brownlow. Faced with such formidable opposition, Sawyer left East Tennessee to become president of the College of Indiana. He resigned his post at the outbreak of the war and reportedly brought 85 of his 485 College of Indiana students with him when he became chaplain of the 47th Indiana Volunteers.[42]

Writing from Camp Wickliffe, Bardstown, Kentucky, on 23 December 1861, Chaplain Sawyer wrote the first of his series of letters to the *Indianapolis Daily Journal*, this one describing their movement from Indianapolis to Louisville and their three-day, 40-mile march from Louisville to Bardstown down the Louisville and Nashville Turnpike Road. The weather in Kentucky had been warm and balmy until a cold front on 22 December brought in heavy rain, followed the next day by freezing weather.

LETTER FROM THE FORTY-SEVENTH
CAMP WICKLIFFE, BARDSTOWN, KY.,
DECEMBER 23, 1861

Ed. Journal: The 47th regiment, Colonel Slack, have reached the headquarters of Gen. Dumont, at the county seat of Nelson county. We have a beautiful encampment on the grounds of Gov. Wickliffe,[43] now a member of Congress.

After we left Camp Sullivan, Indianapolis, we hurried on to Louisville, where we spent three days [14–16 December], and at two o'clock last Tuesday morning [17 December] we were wakened by the reveille, and at half-past five we were on our road to Bardstown. The first day we marched 18 miles, the second day 15, and the next morning 7 miles farther to our camping ground, stopping to give three rousing cheers for Gen. Dumont. The General came to the door and bowed gracefully, and the regiment moved onward, and had their tents spread and dinner ready by twelve o'clock.

There was but one regiment here when we arrived, the 49th Indiana, commanded by Col. Ray, encamped at the Fair Ground, two miles from town. In the front of their encampment is a magnificent amphitheatre, some nine hundred feet in circumference where the beauty and chivalry gather once a year to witness the Agricultural Fair.

The 11th Michigan regiment, the 46th, commanded by Col. Fitch[44]; the 51st, commanded by Col. Streight, and the 48th, I believe, commanded by Col. Carr, and another regiment, are encamped near the town.

Word has just reached us that the enemy, in considerable force, are within a few miles of us, and a Captain and ten men from each regiment, have just been sent out as a scouting party to ascertain the facts in the case, and report at headquarters.

While the Colonel was engaged in battalion drill this afternoon, the Major arrested two suspicious looking men, who seemed to be spies, moving around our camp. The boys felt like putting them through on the fast line. The Major, attended by a small squad, has just taken them over to Gen. Dumont.

Last Sabbath [22 December] was a most disagreeable day, as it rained steadily from morning till night, but at 2 o'clock, by the kindness of the Presbyterian church, our boys were tendered the use of their house of worship, and a good congregation turned out, attended by the Chaplain. At light it cleared off, the wind blew a hurricane, and to day it is freezing weather.

A few of our men, fifteen in all, troubled with measles, have just been sent to the hospital. We are using the large Presbyterian Seminary buildings for a brigade hospital.

Bardstown claims to have fifteen hundred people. Formerly she had a splendid bar.—The first men of the State "practiced law" at this point, such as Clay and Crittenden and Marshall, and even James Buchanan once hung out his legal sign along her streets. But alas her glory has departed. The place has lost much of its importance. There are four churches here — Presbyterian, Methodist, Baptist and Roman Catholic, and four schools once flourished here. The schools are dwindling down and some of them may never be revived.

I could write much more, but prefer to be brief.
Yours very truly,
Samuel Sawyer
Chaplain of 47th Reg.

P.S.— Your old friend P. McNaught, our Sutler, is with us, busy as a beaver, and hearty and good natured as ever. The boys are eager for the conflict, and you will hear a good account of the 47th.[45]

Although vehemently antiwar, the *Huntington Democrat* also used a number of Indiana soldiers to provide their readers with the enlisted man's account of the war. One such correspondent, Private Joseph "J.Z." Scott of the 46th Indiana, was among the first enlisted men to act as war correspondents.[46] Marching with the 46th Indiana about a day behind the vanguard 47th, he described their encampment and enthusiastic reception both at Louisville and later on their march to Bardstown:

Letter from the 46th
Camp Nelson, Near Bardstown, Kentucky
December 22d, 1861

Messrs. Editors: I arrived in Logansport the day I left Huntington, in time to leave for Indianapolis with the 46th regiment. They started about 11 o'clock, arrived at Indianapolis at 7, and set up their tents in Camp on Saturday. We found the 47th encamped near Indianapolis; they left on Friday evening [13 December], for Ky. We left Indianapolis on Saturday, Dec. 17th [*sic*: 14th] and arrived at Louisville on Sunday. We encamped at a place called Oakley, about two miles from Louisville, on the land of General Buckner, the notorious secession commander, who is now intrenched in Bowling Green, waiting for the arrival of the U.S. army. He has a splendid farm near Louisville, but now it looks desolate and deserted, and is used for drilling U.S. soldiers. There were five regiments of Infantry encamped near Louisville after we arrived, and three or four of Cavalry, one consisting of twelve hundred men. Several passed through there while we remained. The 46th Indiana was encamped there.

There is great enthusiasm in favor of the Union about Louisville. The Stars and Stripes are floating from nearly every house, and as we passed along the streets we were cheered at every corner by the citizens, while at the same time, the windows were full of the heads of the *beauty* and fair of Louisville, waving flags and handkerchiefs, an indication by their smiling faces, that they were also in favor of the Union, as well as most all ladies are. We packed our tents and baggage on last Wednesday, started for this place by way of the Louisville and Nashville, Tennessee, Pike. The first day we marched ten miles through a splendid country, and encamped at a place called Camp Louis on Farren Creek, and started from there at 10 o'clock the next morning, and marched ten miles, encamped at a place called Camp Porter. The citizens along so far appeared to be as enthusiastic for the Union as any place I have been. — We would frequently see flags waving, and nearly every place along the road, we were greeted with waving handkerchiefs and "Hurrah for the Union," when a shout would raise from the whole regiment, such as Indiana boys well know how to give. We left Camp Porter on the morning of the 20th, encamped at a place eight miles from here. The 11th Michigan passed us here, as also the 51st Indiana. We have taken up our abode here for awhile, and I suppose will remain here for three or four weeks, unless we are called away to pitch into some secesh army. There are eight or ten regiments encamped around here. The 47th Indiana is here. I don't think there are many secessionists about here; the presence of the army may have a tendency to keep them quiet. The country through here is very hilly, and the soil very productive. I saw the largest corn here I ever saw anywhere; many places through here would be a bad place to meet an enemy; choosing their own ground, they could rake us fore and aft.

I like camp life very well; it agrees with me, so far, to sleep on the ground, although we have had no bad weather yet; it is raining to-day, but warm. Last week was as hot here, as it is in July, at home. More again.

J.Z. Scott [47]

At Camp Wickliffe, the 47th Indiana came under the command of Brigadier-General Ebenezer Dumont. In charge of the troops in and near Bardstown at the time, Dumont told the newly arrived soldiers that, having come "as friends ... of the loyal and law-abiding citizens," they were "not to interfere or tamper with any of the institutions of the State, or rights, or property of the people." They had come "to maintain the law and the Constitution of the State of Kentucky, and of the Federal Union." Ordering his troops to respect "private rights" and "private property," Dumont, by now familiar with the area around Bardstown, also emphatically outlawed "the sale or gift of liquor, or intoxicating drinks, of any kind, to any non-commissioned officer, musician, or private." Officers, on the other hand, were only warned not to get drunk, or to be an accessory to getting a soldier drunk, or they would be "court martialed and cashiered."[48]

Sergeant P.D. Caverly, the *Huntington Democrat*'s correspondent from the 47th Indiana, writing on Christmas Day, described the 47th Indiana's first Christmas in camp. Unlike Chaplain Sawyer, he pointed out that the cases of measles in the 47th originated at Camp Sullivan:

Letter from the 47th
Camp Wickliffe, Near Bardstown, Kentucky
December 25, 1861

Dear Democrat: According to promise when I was last in your town, I sit down to pen you a few lines from this beautiful camp, located about one fourth of a mile east of Bardstown, the county seat of Nelson county, about 43 miles S.E. of Louisville, on the Louisville and Nashville Pike, which place we reached after two and a half days' march from the city of Louisville, making 17 miles the first day, 16 the second, and 7 miles the third. The march was accomplished with but little difficulty otherwise than fatiguing a few boys who had been down with the measles previous to leaving our first camping ground in your State. We are now here under General Wood's Division, who has been appointed to supercede General Dumont, our first Brigadier. We had the pleasure of his presence for the first time on battalion drill, this P.M., and the boys were remarkably well pleased with his appearance as a military man, in every respect. To-day being Christmas, the boys all feel happy and jovial over their dinners, which consisted of Turkies, Pies, Corn Dodgers &c. This P.M., we had battalion drill as usual, and in the evening a dance in the camp, in which the boys had considerable amusement, as they opened it out with the privates and non-commissioned officers and closed the entertainment by introducing their staff and field officers (even to Chaplain.) How long we will remain here, I am unable to say, or in what direction we will move. We believe that if we are called into action, that we have a leader in Gen. Wood, who knows and fears no danger, and he has not a man under his command but will sacrifice his life for his country. The boys in our company are as a general thing well — in good spirits and anxious for a scratch with some of the Southern rebels — let it come when it may. Our camp is situated upon a high elevation, owned by ex-Governor Wickliff, with plenty of water and fuel at our disposal. The town on our east is rather an old village, with a population of about 1,500 souls which is said to be equally divided, as regard politics, and is under strict martial law, being guarded by our forces. The 47th sent out a scouting party on Saturday, which returned with one prisoner — a Post Master, who was court martialed and found guilty of conveying news from our forces to the rebel army. We also arrested two men in our camp, on suspicion of being rebel spies, but they were honorably discharged upon their recognition after proving themselves to be good Union men. Nothing more at present but remain, Yours, truly,

P.D. Caverly

P.S. Brinkerhoff is well, but out on a lark, in company with Corporal Carle.[49]

Back in Indianapolis on Christmas Day, ads in the *Indianapolis Daily Journal* noted that Santa Claus had arrived at J.H. Baldwin's Fancy Bazaar and that a "Celebrated Tragedian" would perform that night at Metropolitan Hall[50]:

METROPOLITAN HALL!

Lady and Gentleman, Dress Circle............75 cents
Each Additional Lady..........................25 cents
The Celebrated Tragedian
Mr. J. Wilkes Booth
will appear on Christmas Night as
Richard III.
Miss Marion Macarthy
as Lady Anne.
Mr. Felix A. Vincent
In the Happy Man.
Thursday Evening
M a c B e t h,
By Mr. J.W. Booth
Favorite Farce
Miss Marion Macarthy and Mr. Fellix A. Vincent, Dec. 25.

II

New Madrid and Island No. 10 (January–April 1862)

Back on 8 November 1861, the irascible sixty-three-year-old Captain Charles Wilkes, U.S.N.,[1] renowned navigator, scientist, explorer, and "firebrand" (or to some, loose cannon[2]) of the Union Navy, acting on his own and against legal advice, used his gunboat, the USS *San Jacinto*,[3] to forcibly intercept the British mail packet *Trent* as it plied the old Bahama Channel off the north coast of Cuba on its passage to St. Thomas, West Indies.

A week or so earlier, Wilkes had learned that two Confederate commissioners, James M. Mason and John Slidell, would be aboard the *Trent* when it left Havana on 7 November on their way to England and France, respectively, to urge recognition of the Confederacy. Wilkes, who considered Mason, Slidell, and their papers to be "contraband of war," intercepted the *Trent*, searched the boat, and seized Mason, Slidell, their papers, and their two secretaries, George Eustis and J.E. McFarland. Wilkes permitted the *Trent* to proceed with the rest of its passengers and crew, but hauled away the four hapless Confederates aboard the *San Jacinto*, and on 24 November delivered them to their new quarters at Fort Warren Prison in Boston Harbor.[4]

By entering the murky waters of international maritime law and acting on his own authority, Wilkes managed to brew more than just a tempest in a very large teapot. The ensuing flap over interference with British maritime rights, which came to be known as the "*Trent* Affair," very nearly caused a war between the United States and Great Britain that could have changed the political geography of North America. For the United States, that war probably would have ensured the success of the Confederate secession; for the British, it probably would have resulted in the loss of their weakly garrisoned Canadian provinces, not to mention that siding with the South and its slave-based economy would have put Prime Minister Lord Palmerston's Liberal government at odds with the rising tide of public opinion at home.[5]

In the end, after a month and a half of military saber rattling and diplomatic huffing and puffing on both sides, cooler heads prevailed and a face-saving agreement was reached. On the British side, Queen Victoria, with advice from the gravely ill Prince Albert, proposed an agreement that effectively scuttled Lord Palmerston's gunboat diplomacy. (Prince Albert died of typhoid on 14 December, two weeks after helping to craft the agreement.) On the American side, a pragmatic President Abraham Lincoln, assisted by able Secretary of State William Seward and United States Minister to Great Britain Charles Francis Adams,

II. New Madrid and Island No. 10 (January–April 1862)

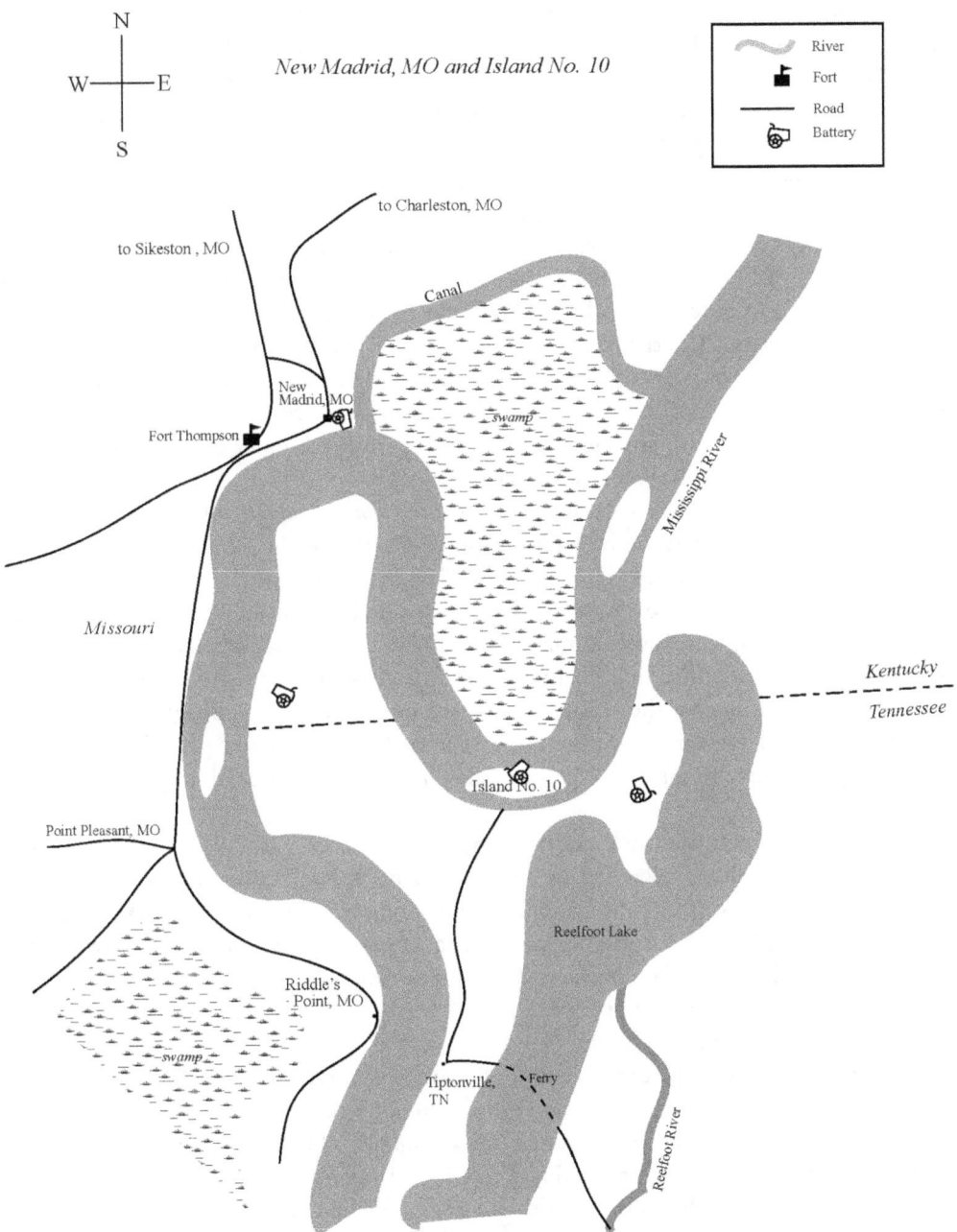

From Atlas Plate X, No. 1

accepted and agreed to release the prisoners. British Foreign Minister Lord Russell calmed British sensibilities by pointing out that they had made the upstart Americans stand down, which they had, although they never received a formal apology. Secretary of State William H. Seward, on the other hand, calmed American sensibilities by asserting that, although they conceded the seizure of the four men was wrong, they had finally forced the British to acknowledge the American concept of neutrality rights on the high seas over which they had fought the War of 1812 — and which, he left unsaid, Captain Wilkes had violated by not taking the *Trent* and all its passengers and crew, including the four arrested Confederates, to the Key West prize court for adjudication. The two wily diplomats sealed the deal and on the first day of 1862 the four Confederates steamed out of Provincetown, Massachusetts, for England aboard the HMS *Rinaldo*.[6]

That same day, before news of a peaceful resolution reached them, the *Indianapolis Daily Journal*, concerned about President Lincoln's failure to "soothe British sensibilities," noted, "British warlike activities continue unabated" and reported ominously that "a portion of the British Mediterranean fleet at Gibraltar is in preparation to cross the Atlantic."[7]

Three days later and still feeling bellicose about the British, the *Daily Journal* was pleased to announce, in what turned out to be a slightly exaggerated report, that the U.S. gunboat *Ottawa*, after fighting off a "rebel mosquito fleet" commanded by Commander Tatrall, captured the British steamer *Fingal* and a Spanish schooner out of Havana as they attempted to run the Federal blockade of Savannah.[8]

More belligerent in their 6 January edition, the *Daily Journal* appeared ready to take on Canada. Even after learning of the peaceful resolution of the "*Trent* Affair," the *Daily Journal* reported with a touch of regret that Canadians, whom they felt were too pro–Confederate, were "jubilant" over the peaceful resolution because "however much a war with England might damage us, it would make the Canadian lake coast a blazing ruin, and they know it." In fact, bellicose editorials in northern newspapers like these helped turn Canadian public opinion against the North and toward tolerance, if not outright support of the Confederate cause. Nevertheless diplomacy trumped war and set a precedent for future maritime agreements. Resolved peacefully, the "*Trent* Affair" soon disappeared from the news.[9]

Back at Bardstown, Kentucky, on Sunday, 5 January, the 47th Indiana dedicated their regimental flag, which was donated by the "Ladies of Wabash county," and selected Sergeant Henry Lindsey of Company I as their color sergeant.[10] The weather in Kentucky had turned rainy and cold, and the next day they began a two-day march from Bardstown toward a new camp near Hodgenville, President Lincoln's birthplace, about 25 miles to the south. Riding to the summit of Muldraugh's Hill, Slack, although not a particularly religious person, reportedly dismounted and sang "Am I a Soldier of the Cross" as he led his troops past the schoolhouse where President Lincoln had learned to read and write.[11]

Although he made no mention of hymn singing on the march, Chaplain Sawyer wrote to the *Indianapolis Daily Journal* from their new "Camp Wickliffe" in La Rue County, about two miles northeast of Hodgenville. Here the 47th Indiana was assigned, along with the 46th Indiana, the 41st Ohio, and the 6th Kentucky, to then-Colonel William B. Hazen's brigade in Brigadier General William "Bull" Nelson's division.

Letter from the 47th Regiment
Camp Wickliffe, La Rue Col, Ky.,
January 8, 1862

Ed. Journal: The 47th Regiment Indiana Volunteers has moved from the supervision of Gen. Wood to the headquarters of General Hazen, to form a part of his brigade. Camp Douglas had become so muddy that we did not object to the change. Col. Fitch and his regiment [the 46th

Indiana] being near the road, had orders to march at 7 o'clock on Monday morning [6 January], Col. Slack at 8, and the Kentucky Sixth at 9 o'clock.[12]

We found the road much better for traveling than many of us supposed it would be, and the men journeyed on in fine spirits. Col. Fitch pitched his tents about 2 o'clock, but as our men felt pretty brisk we marched forward till we came to the place where President Lincoln was born, and there we chose our encampment.

The land now belongs to Mr. Rapier, a Union member of the Kentucky legislature. In the Presidential canvass Mr. Rapier was a strong Douglas man, but from attachments felt for Mr. Lincoln, he found it difficult to get some of his neighbors to vote against him. The boys made good use of some of the rails, which may have been rived by the Great Rail-splitter, supposing that they were appropriating them properly to add to the personal comfort of the volunteer defenders of the Union.

47th Indiana Regimental Flag. The "Shillito" flag, an early flag manufactured by the Shillito Department Store in Cincinnati, Ohio (Indiana War Memorials Commission).

Mr. Rapier's hostility towards Gen. Buckner is most intense. He regards him as the blackest-hearted of all the infernal traitors warring upon the country. He expressed his great desire to be present when Buckner should be caught and killed, and he wanted them "to be a week a killing of him." He said his plan of the campaign against Buckner was to move on a column of 80,000 men to Munfordsville [sic], halt 30,000 and move 50,000 straight to Nashville. Simultaneously he would move on our division of 20,000 due east of Bowling Green, and 20,000 from Cairo due west. This would put Buckner in a regular bull-pen, and his Gibraltar at Bowling Green would be of little service to him.

At 6 o'clock Tuesday morning [7 January] we were on the road. On the top of Muldraugh's Hill we passed the school-house ground where President Lincoln was first sent to school. We passed but one school-house in coming from Louisville to Camp Wickliffe, a distance of sixty-five miles. The cause of common school education must be "a great way back" in the Corn Cracker State.

Gen. Hazen, our Brigadier General, is a graduate of West Point, and as a gentlemanly and energetic military man, he has no superior, it is thought in the Division. Our brigade consists of the 41st Ohio, 6th Kentucky, and the 46th and 47th Indiana.

General Nelson visited our camp yesterday. He is a large man, and is very pleasing. We hear him complimented for courage, but complained of for what many regard as unnecessary harshness. The boys say that in size he is a man, but they wish he was more gentle.— Some of the volunteers in the 34th dropped him a line, I have just learned, conveying the intelligence that they were not slaves, but free-born, and animated with the feelings of freemen! And yet I suppose there is not a single man in any regiment of General Nelson's Division who would not freely risk his life in obedience to any reasonable or legitimate order he may give.[13]

We have a pleasant encampment. The ground is dry, the men contented and generally well. As to-day is the 8th of January we have been released from drill by an order from General Nelson. Three cheers were given for General Nelson as our Adjutant read his patriotic order.

All day yesterday cannonading was heard in the direction of Munfordsville [sic].

Yours very truly, Samuel Sawyer Chaplain 47th Ind. Vol.[14]

Upon taking command of his brigade, Hazen, referring in his memoirs to his colonels as "men of high character," and their regiments as "composed of admirable material," also noted that they lacked adequate instruction. To remedy this, Hazen established a school of instruction at Camp Wickliffe. Using Winfield Scott's *Infantry Tactics*, he assigned then-Captain Emerson Opdycke of the 41st Ohio to instruct the 47th Indiana.[15]

The 47th Indiana would spend one very cold and rainy month at Camp Wickliffe, described by Hazen as "beset with camp diseases, especially diarrhea and measles,— the latter singularly fatal."[16]

Also complaining about the unsanitary conditions in camp in a letter to his wife Lucy, dated 31 January 1862, then-Captain Emerson Opdycke described his daily routine as the 47th Indiana's drill instructor at perpetually waterlogged Camp Wickliffe:

> At half past seven or eight A.M., your most obedt, marches through mud half way up to his knees to the camp of the 47th Ind about a quarter mile distant; drills the officers of that same regiment for one and a half hours, then superintends those officers drilling their companies, till half past eleven A.M., then wades back to dinner; but stop, before dinner I recite for Col. Hazen, or in his absence, I hear others recite, *then* dinner, and at one P.M. I wade back again, and drill the battalion, (unless they send a horse for me) until four P.M., return and at six P.M., recite to Col. H till seven, when I *wade again*, to hear the officers of the said 47th Ind recite for two hours.[17]

Meanwhile, reporting on the western front, the 11 January 1862 edition of the *Daily Journal* indicated a general disgust with the Federal inaction in Kentucky and what they called "the mismanagement of affairs there."

The next day, Chaplain Sawyer wrote the *Daily Journal* regarding the Federal "inaction" in Kentucky:

Letter from Bardstown
Camp Wickliffe, La Rue Col, Ky.,
January 12, 1862

> Ed. Journal: We have made no forward movement since I wrote you last, except in the military improvement of our men. Col. Slack at the head, all our staff, with the Captains and Lieutenants, are drilled every day. They have lessons assigned them each day in the tactics of war, and every night they are assembled as a school of instruction, and go through a regular recitation. Considerable emulation has been excited amongst them, and both officers and men are greatly benefited by the system.[18]
>
> Col. Hazen is rigid in discipline, and yet a mild and gentlemanly commander. Having been religiously trained, he honors his teachings by a genuine respect for morality and Christianity. By repressing vice and profanity he very properly thinks he can increase the efficiency of his brigade.
>
> He was invited to our headquarters yesterday, to attend a dinner given by Lieut. Col. Robinson. The dinner "came about" in this wise: The father-in-law of Col. Robinson, Mr. Ballard, of Knightstown, was entrusted with a box of provisions to bring to Camp Wickliffe. On arriving at Louisville, he called on Gen. Buell, and requested a pass to our division of the army. The General very politely sent him back home, but forwarded the box. The box reached its destination, and when the Lieutenant Colonel opened it, his good wife had put in everything to remind him of a Thanksgiving dinner at home. There were nice biscuits and bread, and two rolls of golden butter, a fine boiled ham, a turkey just ready to be carved, two chickens, cheese, tomatoes, pickles, pound cake and white cake, and "round" cake two layers deep, and canned cherries and peaches, with two quarts of the richest kind of cream. Of course there was plenty or a table full. Extemporizing a table and a tablecloth, and spreading out the plentiful supply, Col. Robinson, with Col. Hazen, Capt. Updycke [*sic*: Opdycke], Lt. Col. Cotton, of the 6th

Kentucky regiment, Col. Slack, Maj. Mickle, Quartermaster Nichol, Mr. Lemon, and myself, as invited guests, sat down to enjoy the good cheer before us. Craving the Divine blessing, with humble and thankful hearts, we discussed the dinner with hearty appetites. It was one of the pleasantest camp "episodes" we have had since we entered the service. Voting our thanks to Mrs. Robinson for her handsome entertainment, we went to our respective quarters, wondering when such another occasion would call us together.

Mr. Ballard will no doubt be glad to learn that the good things he started with were well disposed of even though Gen. Buell sent him back to Indiana.

Gen. Nelson, who has been quite unwell, is to-day much better.

The resignation of Col. Steele, and the request that Dr. Ryan would take his place, have probably been published in your columns.—Many of the friends of Col. Steele hoped he would lead the regiment on to Tennessee. He will carry back with him the kind regards of a large portion of his men.

The sight of a Journal in the 47th would be good for sore eyes. I will write you again, as we draw nearer the great enemy of Kentucky.

Yours truly, Samuel Sawyer,
Chaplain 47th Regiment.[19]

The first break in the Confederate defensive line in Kentucky came on 19 January 1862 at the Battle of Logan's Cross Road (or Mill Springs) in eastern Kentucky, in which Federals under George H. Thomas drove Brigadier General George B. Crittenden's Confederates south across the Cumberland River. Confederate Brigadier General Felix Zollicofer, whose troops from East Tennessee had helped Johnston establish his defensive line by defeating the Federals at Barboursville, Kentucky, on 19 September 1861, was killed in the action.[20]

Continuing pressure on Johnston's army came early in February as Federal troops and gunboats under U.S. Grant steamed out of Cairo, Illinois, and up the Tennessee River to attack the Confederate garrison at Fort Henry. Heavy shelling from Grant's gunboats forced the Confederates to surrender Fort Henry on 6 February, opening the Tennessee River for Federal troop movements south into the Confederacy.

Writing about one month later, after heavy and persistent rains had turned the camp into a muddy quagmire, J.Z. Scott, who also now referred to their Bardstown camp as "Camp Morton," gave the *Huntington Democrat* a Hoosier infantryman's view of Kentucky and Kentuckians.

Letter from the 46th
Camp Wycliffe, Ky.,
Feb. 6th, 1862

Messrs Editors:—It has been so long since I last wrote to you, that I scarcely know where we were when I did write last, but if my recollection serves me right, it was at Camp Morton. Since that time we have advanced near twenty-five miles further South, and now find ourselves encamped in the woods, in a place called Camp Wyckliffe, Larue county, Ky., with mud around our tents so deep that it almost pulls our boots off to go into it. If a Hoosier, or any other man, wishes to be relieved of ever again complaining of mud and rain, let them enlist in some regiment, and take a trip through this part of Ky., in this season of the year, and if he is not satisfied that his lot on this round sphere is cast in a pleasant place when compared with this part of Kentucky, there is no place on God's green earth will satisfy him.

The country from Bardstown to this place is very broken, and the land poor. There are but few inhabitants, and they are mostly stuck on the sides of the hills, in old log huts, in which a Northern back woodsman would consider himself disgraced to live.

On our march from camp Morton to this place, we encamped on the farm on which A. Lincoln, President of the United States, was born. It is about as forbidding as the principles which his devotees advocate. The remains of the old house in which the little circumstance occurred, was pointed out to me by Col Fitch, who remark'd at the same time, "He had got some sound Democrats on his old rough farm now."

The inhabitants of this part of the State partake very much of the nature and appearance of the country. A few vendors of tough chickens, musty slap-jacks, and corn bread, come around the guard lines of our camp every day, dressed in butternut cloths, and draggle-tail dresses, who sell their articles at a price that would astonish an Indianian not posted in their exorbitant prices. They seem to think Uncle Sam's soldiers have plenty of money, and arrange their prices accordingly.

We have had but little cold weather here this winter, and about snow enough to remind us that it is near the season of the year for that article to make its appearance. Our winter has consisted of principally in rain and abundance of mud.

The 46th regiment is for the present attached to a temporary brigade, composed of the 46th and 47th Indiana, 41st Ohio, and 6th Ky., regiments, all commanded by Col. Hazen, and encamped here together. The country is dotted over with camps, and at reveille, or guard mounting, there is a constant roar of drums and bugles in every direction. The health of the soldiers in our camp is generally good. Three have died in camp, since we came here, and were buried with honors of war, in the desolate looking woods adjoining.

Col. Fitch is very attentive to the sick, and leaves nothing undone which can in any way relieve them, in consequence of which, we can turn out more men on dress parade than any other regiment in the regiment [*sic*: brigade].

We have orders for marching, on Saturday, Feb 9th. Our destination is Green River, and perhaps, Bowling Green. The proceedings in our several camps, looks like there was a storm ahead. Our sick have all been sent back. The commissary stores have all been brought back from the advance, and placed in the rear. Each man has 40 rounds of ammunition distributed to him. We are constantly kept under the strictest kind of military drill, from six to eight hours per day. The enemy is posted but a few miles in advance of us. Col. Bridgeland's cavalry had a small fight with them last Sunday; don't know the particulars. News came to our camp to-day that Col. B., was about dying.

My opinion is, that you will hear of sharp work in Kentucky, soon.

J.Z. Scott.[21]

With the fall of Fort Henry, Johnston's Kentucky line became indefensible. In order to avoid being intercepted by Grant's Federal force now beginning to penetrate behind his line of retreat, Johnston began moving his army south from Bowling Green to Nashville, sending reinforcements to Fort Donelson on the Cumberland River, less than ten miles east of Fort Henry, to help defend it against Grant's advance.

Grant's infantry, who held Fort Donelson under siege within a week after the fall of Fort Henry, waited for the gunboats to move back to the Ohio River and up the Cumberland before attacking the fort. The main Federal attack commenced on 15 February and the fort was surrendered unconditionally the next day, earning Grant the sobriquet, "Unconditional Surrender." Confederate generals John B. Floyd, commander at Fort Donelson, and Gideon Pillow, second in command, fled across the Cumberland, leaving Kentuckian Simon Buckner to surrender their force to his old friend Grant. Floyd's fear of having treason added to the charges against him if he were captured and returned to Washington may account for his quick exit from Fort Donelson in the face of Grant's Federals. Floyd's C.S.A. superiors apparently did not appreciate his quick exit either, relieving him, and Pillow, of command shortly thereafter.[22]

On Friday, 14 February 1862, while Grant was at Fort Donelson, Halleck assigned him

II. New Madrid and Island No. 10 (January–April 1862)

to command the new, as yet ill-defined District of West Tennessee; William T. Sherman, his career as a field officer still in limbo from the false "insanity" charges, was given Grant's old command of the District of Cairo, putting him in charge of directing troop deployment at Paducah.[23]

That same day, the 47th Indiana left Camp Wickliffe with the remainder of Hazen's brigade (the 6th Ohio, 45th Ohio, 6th Kentucky, and 46th Indiana) and "Bull" Nelson's division of Buell's Army of the Ohio to take part in the Fort Donelson fight. Marching northward toward the Ohio River, they covered fifteen or sixteen difficult miles through deep mud and snow and camped without tents near Elizabethtown, the baggage wagons having bogged down in the mud. The next day they marched another four to six miles and waited for the wagons to come up. Camping that night in the frigid cold with only fence-rail fires to keep them warm, Captain Opdyke told his wife that he awoke the next morning surprised to find he "was not frozen stiff;" and on Sunday they marched about twenty-two miles, reaching the Ohio River at West Point, Kentucky, near the mouth of the Salt River, in the late afternoon and early evening.[24]

It took all of the next day (17 February) to march the mile and a half from camp to the landing and load the fleet of steamers. Confusion reigned as men piled aboard the steamers while large squads of soldiers helped the teamsters back the loaded supply wagons down the steep riverbank and pile the unsorted equipage on the decks. (The "Right Wing" of the 47th Indiana boarded the steamer *Glendale*; the "Left Wing" boarded the *Lady Pike*.) Steaming downriver that evening in misty rain and fog, they learned at Evansville, Indiana, that Fort Donelson had already surrendered. Ordered to "ship about," the next morning they steamed back up the Ohio River some twelve miles to the mouth of the Green River. Continuing upriver on Tuesday morning, they returned to their starting place at West Point, Kentucky, before being ordered back downriver to Paducah the next morning. Taking on coal at Cannelton, Indiana, they arrived at Paducah at dawn on Friday, 21 February.[25]

Writing from Paducah, Sgt. P.D. Caverly described the 47th Indiana's march and Ohio River cruise:

Letter from the 47th
Paducah, Ohio River, Feb. 21, '62

Dear Democrat:— Here we are waiting orders from General Halleck for future movements. We left Camp Wickliffe on the 14th inst., and after three days hard marching, made the Ohio river and embarked aboard the steamers composing our fleet, nineteen in number, and occupying one day to accomplish the distance of one and a half miles and get our trains safely aboard of the steamer. We left West Point about 10 o'clock [P.M.] on the 17th, and moved down the river as far as Evansville, where we successively came to, and remained there until morning when we received orders to "about ship" and retreat up to the mouth of Green river — a distance of 12 miles. After lying at Green river over night, we received orders to keep on up the Ohio to our starting point at the mouth of Salt river. After proceeding as far up as Cannelton, where we took coal we were again ordered down the river to Paducah, which point we reached about daylight this (Friday) morning. There is a boat lying here with about 250 wounded from the siege of Ft. Donelson. Our boys are not permitted to go ashore unless they are of the red tape grade. We have no privileges granted, therefore cannot describe to you the town. We can see the stars and stripes wave over some of the buildings. May they wave there henceforth forever.

How long we will remain here it is impossible for me, or any other man, to say; but I do not believe we will remain here long. You may expect to hear of some great deeds of valor from the boys of the 47th and 34th, for I know when they come to be weighed in the balance they will not be found wanting.

Our boys had the pleasure of seeing for the first time, this morning, a gunboat, of a rather small class, mounting only three guns on a side.

Two boys of the 34th, I understand, were drowned since we have been on the river. I did not learn their names.

Our boys are all in good health and spirits, and eager for the dance.

Yours, P.D.C.[26]

At Paducah on 21 February, Sherman detached the 34th, 46th, and 47th Indiana from Hazen's brigade over "Bull" Nelson and Buell's objections, transferring them and the 43rd Ohio to Cairo, Illinois, to join John Pope's new Army of the Mississippi, which was being organized in Missouri to open the upper Mississippi River to navigation. Their first task would be to silence Confederate guns at New Madrid, Missouri, and Island No. 10. Other troops, including Buell's Army of the Ohio and the remainder of "Bull" Nelson's division, were diverted to Grant's force on the now-open Tennessee River. Their first task would be to push Albert Sidney Johnston's army out of Tennessee.[27]

Opdyke wrote his wife Lucy that Nelson's division had been split, but averred that with the opening of the Tennessee they had seen "the beginning of the End of the Rebellion." And, giving an idea of the feelings the *Trent* Affair had aroused in the army, he noted: "But when we have settled up our own little domestic affair, I hope we shall teach England a dear lesson for her impudence and hypocrisy towards us, such conduct from such a nation, under such circumstances, ought to be the overthrow of English power on this continent, this, I think, is the feeling of the Army generally."[28]

At Cairo the 34th, 46th, and 47th Indiana, and the 43rd Ohio, left Hazen's brigade and boarded the steamer *Glendale* to join Pope's army at Commerce, Missouri, a small Mississippi River town in the southeastern corner of the state about 30 miles upriver from Cairo.

Back in Indiana, as Federal troops began occupying more slave-state territory, the pro-slavery *Huntington Democrat* worried that fanatics in Congress and in the Republican press would succeed in changing the purpose of the war from restoring the Union to "a mighty John Brown raid."[29] And in early March, disarray in the West continued as "Old Brains" Halleck accused "Unconditional Surrender" Grant of misconduct and put Brigadier General C.F. Smith in command of the expedition up the Tennessee River. The *Huntington Democrat*, although it neglected to point out that it was solely Halleck's decision to suspend Grant, railed in an editorial about an abolition conspiracy:

> The Juggernaut of Abolitionism is, like John Brown's soul, "marching on." Another Democratic General's head is rolling in the dust. The gallant Grant, the hero of Fort Donelson, has been suspended. The charge against him is not specified. It is unquestionably the work of abolition malignity. The Democratic Generals stand in the way of making this an abolition war, and, apparently short work is to be made of them. We expect to hear that Halleck and Burnside have been suspended, next.[30]

At Commerce, Slack was assigned temporary command of what would soon become Brigadier General John M. Palmer's division, which consisted of the 34th, 43rd, 46th, 47th and 59th Indiana regiments, Lt. Col Milton Robinson taking command of the 47th Indiana. On 24 February they were sent ahead on an "easy march" on a ridge road to the town of Benton, about eight miles southwest of Commerce and about thirty-eight miles north of New Madrid. At Benton they set up camp south of town at or near a place General Pope referred to as "Col. Hunter's farm," which had been the camp of Brigadier General Meriwether Jeff Thompson of the Confederate Missouri State Guard.[31]

At Benton, Slack and his Hoosiers, apparently considering the townspeople to be "secessionists," treated them accordingly, including a raid and sacking of the local courthouse and the home of an unnamed colonel in the Confederate service — possibly the Col. Hunter on whose farm they were encamped. Tongue in cheek, an anonymous soldier from the 46th Indiana wrote the *Logansport* (Indiana) *Journal* calling for "the lawyer officers" of Slack's brigade to be as impartial in their judgment of soldiers who stole chickens and pigs as they were of officers who stole law books[32]:

A soldier of the 46th Indiana, writing from New Madrid to the Logansport *Journal*, says:

> Our old brigade (or the second one rather) is broken up. We are now with the 43d Indiana, with Col. Fitch as ranking Colonel.
>
> The same correspondent tells the following good one on the lawyer soldiers of Col. Slack's Brigade:
>
> The behavior of the soldiers towards the secession inhabitants is generally in accord[ance] with orders from headquarters. The [only] deviation from them noticed was the [confis]cation of all the law books found in the [Court] House at Benton and in the rebel Col[onel's] before mentioned, by the lawyer officers [of] the brigade. Over a hundred volumes [were] brought into camp, but they were con[veyed] back again under orders from General [Palmer] our immediate commanding general. [___] to have this to say about our legal [opi]nions, but justice to other solders who [have] had a weakness for chickens and pigs, [comm]ands that the record shall be impartial.[33]

Echoing the anonymous soldier of the 46th Indiana, two officers of the 46th Indiana wrote in their history of the regiment:

> There was a large bar, according to the Record, but the members of it were absent, following the fortunes of General "Jeff" Thompson. The 46th filled the bench, the bar, the witness and jury boxes, and members cried, "O yes! O yes!" from the sheriff's desk. The seats were fully occupied by the less ambitious members of the regiment. There was a great influx of law books in regimental quarters. General Palmer collected about a hundred volumes of reports and statutes and returned them to the Court-house. It was remarked that stray law books were found only about the quarters of ex-attorneys. Nothing was discovered in the other tents except chickens and an occasional pig.[34]

General Palmer, who arrived in Benton to take command of his division after the sacking of the courthouse, ordered all the law books be returned and assigned Slack command of the 46th and 47th Indiana. Fitch, who arrived there on 25 February, was assigned command of the 34th and 43rd Indiana; the 59th Indiana transferred to Hamilton's division.[35]

Although Palmer, an Illinoisan, was generally held in high regard by his troops, his only fault, according to "Raw Recruit," a soldier-correspondent from his all-Indiana division, was not being a Hoosier. Although given very high marks, Palmer did not quite measure up to the approbation given Hoosiers Slack and Fitch. Their down-to-earth openness and informality in dealing with the needs of the lowly enlisted man, "Raw Recruit" noted, made them "idols of their men, and worthy of higher positions."[36]

Their leadership would soon be tested, as Pope was about to initiate their march through the Great Mingo Swamp to the Confederate fortifications at New Madrid and their first taste of battle.

The Mississippi River at Island No. 10 and Madrid Bend

The Mississippi River flowed southward several miles below the Kentucky/Tennessee state line and curved abruptly westward past Island No. 10, an island about three miles long and a mile wide, which at the time sat nearly in the middle of the river. About a mile west of the island the river curved sharply northward and ran about ten miles, forming an upper peninsula, before it again curved abruptly westward and ran about five miles past the right bank town of New Madrid, Missouri. The river curved abruptly southward several miles past New Madrid and ran another twelve miles or so past the village of Point Pleasant, Missouri. About six or seven miles below Point Pleasant the river formed a promontory on the Missouri side called Riddle's Point. The town of Tiptonville, Tennessee, sat slightly downriver from Riddle's Point on the left bank several miles below the western neck of a roughly twelve-mile long horseshoe peninsula below New Madrid called Madrid Bend.[37]

The Confederate Fortifications

Back in September 1861, Leonidas Polk, commanding Confederate troops on the Mississippi, had been searching for a northernmost position from which to blockade the river. Taking Gideon Pillow's advice that Island No. 10 sat too low in the water to be useful, Polk sent Pillow's division north into the town of Columbus, Kentucky. (This was the move that initially violated Kentucky's untenable neutrality and triggered the Federal move into the state.) Perched a bit too high on bluffs overlooking the river, the steep downward or plunging trajectory made hitting transports on the river difficult for Polk's artillery, so it proved to be a poor choice to blockade the river. At the same time, however, Confederate Chief Engineer A.B. Gray brought up some five hundred slaves from Fort Pillow to work on fortifying Island No. 10, the town of New Madrid, and Madrid Bend.[38]

With the collapse of Albert Sidney Johnston's Kentucky line in February 1862, Columbus, now vulnerable on the landside, could no longer be held. Prior to evacuating Columbus, however, and heading to Corinth, Mississippi, where Albert Sidney Johnston was assembling a new and larger army, Polk sent Major General John P. McCown's division to Island No. 10 and the town of New Madrid to garrison the river. Well situated for a blockade except that it was prone to flooding, Island No. 10, so named because it was the tenth island below the confluence of the Ohio River, was about forty-five miles south of Columbus via the river and ten miles south (upriver) from New Madrid, surrounded by swampland on each bank of the river.[39]

Although Island No. 10 was so low in the river that one of its batteries became inoperable due to high water, it was, nevertheless, well protected by swampland and river overflow on each bank: Engineer Gray fortified it with nineteen heavy guns including 8-inch Columbiads, smoothbore and rifled 32-pounders and 24-pounder Dahlgrens. In addition, the floating battery *New Orleans* was anchored off the upper end to command the north or upper channel past the island with eight 8-inch Columbiads and one 32-pounder rifled gun. The winding Mississippi and the swampy and now flooded upper peninsula across from its right bank also provided some protection by preventing the Federals from placing a large force or planting heavy batteries there.[40]

The battery above Island No. 10 covered its northern river approach with eight earthworks and twenty-six guns, including 8-inch Columbiads and rifled and smoothbore 32-pounders. Other batteries of 8-inch Columbiads and 32-pounders were scattered down the western side of the peninsula from just beneath the flooded upper end to just above Tiptonville, where they had a battery of four 24-pounder siege guns and four 8-inch siege howitzers or siege mortars.[41]

On the downriver side of New Madrid on the right bank stood Fort Thompson, a heavily armed, bastioned earthwork constructed by slave labor in November. Commanded by Confederate Colonel E.W. Gantt, it was garrisoned by troops from the 11th and 12th Arkansas regiments and had two companies of artillery—R.A. Stewart's Point Coupee (Louisiana) Battery and Upton's Tennessee Battery—mounting 14 heavy guns, mostly 24- and 32-pounders. Brigadier General A.P. Stewart, in charge of the New Madrid line, also utilized slave labor to place another smaller earthwork for Capt. Smith P. Bankhead's Tennessee Battery at the upper end of the town. Commanded by L.M. Walker, it had seven pieces of 24- and 32-pounders and with abatis-lined rifle pits connecting them. Originally designed to blockade the river, all the guns of the right-bank land batteries were hurriedly turned to face northward on reports that a large Federal force was heading their way by land from Commerce.[42]

McCown, replaced at the end of March by Brigadier General William W. Mackall, commanded the entire Madrid Bend and Island No. 10 force from his headquarters at Tiptonville; A.P. Stewart commanded at New Madrid with E.W. Gantt at Fort Thompson and L.M. Walker at Fort Bankhead. Although the numbers are imprecise, McCown's entire force totaled an estimated 5,000, including a reported 1,256 inside Fort Thompson.[43]

Confederate Flag Officer George N. Hollins's fleet of six wood gunboats, only two of which carried thin iron plating over their engines, were incapable of withstanding even light artillery. Nevertheless, carrying four to six heavy guns each, they patrolled the river from Tiptonville to Island No. 10; and because the land was so flat and the river so high, Hollins's gunboats looked directly over the riverbank and could sweep the approaches to the New Madrid fortifications for several miles.[44]

Tiptonville, several miles below the western neck of the Madrid Bend peninsula, was only about fourteen miles south of Island No. 10 by land, but the road connecting them passed around now flooded cypress swamps and the overflowed western bank of Reelfoot Lake and was incapable of heavy traffic, making it necessary to supply the upriver posts by steamer on a nearly thirty-mile upriver trip around the bend.[45]

Reelfoot Lake, more a flooded cypress swamp than a lake, was created in 1811 when the New Madrid earthquake uplifted land and dammed Reelfoot Creek as the land behind it sank. Full of trees, limbs and other snags, it was navigable only by flatboat or canoe. Fed by cypress swamps at the Kentucky state line, it stretched to near Tiptonville with depths varying to eighteen feet. Discharging into Reelfoot Creek and the Obion River, its waters passed through more cypress swamps to the Mississippi about forty miles below. Although the lake and swamps kept the Federals from sweeping around on the Tennessee side, it potentially trapped the Confederates within the Madrid Bend peninsula.[46]

POPE'S PLAN

New Madrid and Tiptonville were therefore the keys to driving the Confederates off Island No. 10 and breaking the blockade. Capturing Tiptonville would cut the supply line to Island No. 10, necessitating its abandonment; and, if the decision to evacuate came too late, the entire force risked being trapped and captured.

To get to New Madrid, Pope's troops had to march down an old, deteriorated corduroy roadway that ran from Benton to New Madrid following what is roughly today U.S. Highway 61. Essentially a causeway through the 30-mile-wide alluvial bottomland called the Great Mingo Swamp that extended westward from Commerce and southward to New Madrid, it was in very poor repair to the town of Sikeston, about eighteen miles south of Benton, where the destroyed tracks of the old Cairo & Fulton Railroad passed through town. The Mississippi was overflowing its banks and the whole area was under water from one to ten feet deep.[47]

On 28 February, Schuyler Hamilton's division marched from Commerce in the vanguard of Pope's march to New Madrid, bivouacking at midnight on "Col. Hunter's farm" in the mud and rain.[48]

Later the next morning (1 March), after Col. Josiah W. Bissell's engineers had cleared the roadway of obstacles including trees recently felled by Jeff Thompson's troopers. Hamilton's division marched to Sikeston. Stanley and Palmer's divisions followed, marching about twelve miles from their camps and bivouacking from four to six miles above Sikeston.[49]

Pope, now realizing that the rising water would close his line of communication with Commerce, sent word to Halleck that he wanted Brigadier General E.A. Paine's infantry division[50] to move from Bird's Point, Missouri, the Mississippi River town across from the Federal supply depot at Cairo, to Sikeston, Missouri, to repair the old Cairo & Fulton Railroad that ran between those two towns.[51]

Pope also sent a cavalry detachment from Bird's Point down the broken railroad toward Sikeston in pursuit of Jeff Thompson. Thompson, who had been forced to abandon his camp near Benton, moved north from New Madrid to harass the Federal advance by felling trees and damaging bridges in Pope's path. Known as the "Swamp Fox," Thompson, an inveterate partisan ranger, objected to fighting from inside forts (although he had supervised the slaves who had constructed the fort at New Madrid that carried his name), opting instead to operate out of the Great Mingo Swamp between New Madrid and Commerce.[52]

Thompson and his troopers also helped protect the shadow Confederate state government[53] as well as to maraud and harass Federal posts and transports on the river. Their efforts included a failed attempt to capture or sink the steamer *Glendale* carrying Slack and the 47th Indiana to Commerce. Thompson's Plan was reportedly foiled by a warning signal from a Union woman as the steamer approached town.[54]

Surprised by Pope's pursuit force coming down the old Cairo & Fulton tracks, Thompson split his troopers, sending most into the swamp on a road he claimed was known only to his guides, where they were to wait until he returned from New Madrid with reinforcements. The Federals, however, pursued Thompson's troopers into the swamp to a point about three miles south of Sikeston and routed the "Swamp Fox" when he returned from New Madrid, sending him and his troopers fleeing once again into the swamps and back to New Madrid. The Federals captured six pieces of very light artillery (1-pounders) that had been specially made for Thompson's use, and a number of prisoners including two engineering officers, Captain James T. Hogane and Lieutenant D.B. Griswold.[55]

The next day (2 March), Kellogg's 7th Illinois Cavalry and Colonel J.L. Kirby Smith's 43rd Ohio Infantry from Stanley's division reconnoitered into New Madrid to within three-quarters of a mile of the Confederate works. Pope's troops, Stanley's division in the vanguard, followed by Hamilton's and Palmer's, resumed the march at 7:00 A.M. in a cold drizzle that before noon turned into a torrential thunderstorm that lit the sky with lightning and soaked the troops. Arriving at Sikeston at 5:00 P.M., about twenty miles north of New Madrid, after two days of slogging through muck and mire, Pope temporarily halted the march during what Slack referred to as "one of the most terrific thunder-storms" he had ever witnessed: "It was terrifically sublime. The water ran down my neck until my boots were filled. We were all drenched to the skin, and that night I had to sleep in a wet bed, in wet clothes. The next day we went into a fight at Madrid. That was the first I ever saw of genuine, real, active war."[56] Pope, who referred to it as "the most disagreeable days I ever passed," permitted all those who regarded themselves as unfit to continue to step from the ranks. Those who could continue were ordered to leave their knapsacks at Sikeston to lighten their load. Below Sikeston the road improved and the rain stopped, enabling them to go another ten miles before bivouacking for the night at 8:00 P.M. about ten to twelve miles from New Madrid. That night, however, temperatures plummeted and iced over their wagons and field guns.[57]

The next day (3 March), Stanley's division, followed by Hamilton's and Palmer's, arrived near New Madrid at about 1:00 P.M. caked in mud. Kellogg's cavalry and Stanley's division moved toward town, followed by Hamilton's and Palmer's divisions, driving in the Confederate pickets while drawing fire from the Confederate forts and gunboats, which, due to the high level of the river, were nearly level with and commanded the surrounding countryside. Pope's gunners returned fire as he withdrew his troops out of range of the Confederate guns, bivouacking about two miles from New Madrid in cornfields at the edge of the swamp.[58]

Pulling back, however, had also taken Pope's smaller caliber guns out of range. Hoping to avoid a bloody assault, he laid siege to the fort while appealing to Halleck for heavy siege guns from Cairo, which he believed could be transported to New Madrid if Paine's troops could repair the railroad line to Sikeston.[59]

While awaiting the arrival of the heavy siege guns from Cairo, Pope sent Colonel Joseph B. Plummer's brigade (the 11th Missouri, Lt. Col. William E. Panabaker and the 26th Illinois, Col. John M. Loomis; three companies of cavalry and a field battery of 10-pounder Parrott and rifled guns from Hamilton's division) downriver to Point Pleasant to make a lodgment of batteries and a line of rifle pits for 1,000 troops on the right bank of the river to harass and blockade Hollins's gunboats. The beginning of the end came for the Confederate blockade when Hollins's gunboats failed to dislodge Plummer's isolated batteries (Hollins reporting that although he could temporarily drive them from their position, his wooden-hulled gunboats could not stay for long near the Federal guns on the right bank) and McCown failed to send an infantry force across to accomplish the task. McCown and Hollins apparently felt secure that Pope could not get the heavy siege guns he needed through the swamps to Point Pleasant by land. Indeed, in spite of Plummer's lodgment, Confederate gunboats and packets continued to steam from Tiptonville to New Madrid with relative impunity from the Federal 10-pounders by hugging the mile-and-a- half-wide river's left bank.[60]

The railroad repairs to Sikeston were completed on or about 9 March and the siege guns sent across the river from Cairo to Bird's Point, Missouri. On 11 March they were transported on the repaired tracks of the Cairo & Fulton Railroad to Sikeston, where they were mounted on carriages and hauled to New Madrid over the corduroy road now much improved by Bissell's engineers, arriving at sunset the next evening. Placed northwest of town about eight hundred yards from Fort Thompson, artillerymen immediately began constructing two redoubts as Stanley's division moved to their support. The 10th and 16th Illinois regiments of Col. James D. Morgan's brigade worked through the night digging rifle pits and connecting curtains for the redoubts. McCown, who had learned of the repaired railway and the probability that the Federals could now bring heavy siege guns to New Madrid, and belatedly concerned about Plummer's position, moved two 24-pounder guns across from Point Pleasant and began preparations for a possible evacuation to Fort Pillow.[61]

Meanwhile, as Pope's army moved into southeast Missouri, Samuel L. Curtis's Federal Army of the Southwest moved into northwest Arkansas, where they defeated a Confederate force under Earl Van Dorn at the Battle of Pea Ridge or Elkhorn Tavern, Van Dorn's Confederates escaping into the Boston Mountains. Back at New Madrid, on the day before their evacuation, a Confederate soldier, referring to overly hopeful rumors about the battle at Pea Ridge and describing the siege and impending onslaught at Fort Thompson, wrote:

Fort Thompson, New Madrid, Mo
March the 12/1862

Miss Pink Willis
Dear Pink,
Your kind letter was received about Fifteen days since and since that time old Nick [the Devil] has been to pay. About the time I received your letter the Yankees came down on us by thousands and we were only 600 strong and the Lincolnites were at least 15000 strong. They have been continually skirmishing with us for the last fifteen days and we have had some beautiful cannonading; we have 5 gunboats each mounting 5 guns (32 pounders and some larger) and after all our pickets skirmishing and cannonading we have lost only 4 or 5 men, and it is reported that one of our shells killed 30 or 40 of the enemy. However I don't know that the latter report is true. But true or not it is official and official reports are generally true. The Lincolnites have been in sight of our barrack 12 or 13 days but they haven't sufficient bravery

to make a decisive attack on our almost impregnable little force and Fort. But we certainly will not be held in suspense much longer. The Yankee force is so vastly superior to ours that they will certainly attack us in a few days. Our company is on picket guard now. They have been firing at the Yanks all day and the Yankees have not been idle. They have generally returned the fire and then run like Blue Blazes.

***

Pink I suppose Jimmie and David have smelt powder before now for it is rumored that Price

has gained a great victory at Boston Mountains and is now closely pursuing the scamps. You must forgive me for not writing sooner, for I dident have any paper, and I dident wish to write no way until the anticipated fight was o'er but alas it ain't over yet. For the present I must close. Pink I hear heavy cannonading at Point Pleasant 7 miles below here warm times there. We are almost intirely surrounded by the enemy and scarcely no chance to get out, but I don't care. My love to all, uncle Brice and Sallie, and the rest. Kiss Mollie for me.
Yours with profound respect.
D.A. Turren[62]

With their siege guns in place at 3:00 A.M., the Federals opened fire on Fort Thompson at dawn on 13 March, the morning after D.A. Turren wrote his letter. Driven downriver, Hollins's wooden-hulled gunboats still returned enough fire to prevent Pope's infantry from moving on the fort. The 10th and 16th Illinois, supporting the siege guns, came under heavy fire but held fast; Slack's brigade (the 34th and 47th Indiana), which had been moved forward to the river, came under such heavy fire that they were ordered to withdraw to the rear of Hamilton's division to prepare for an assault the next morning.[63]

With aim difficult in the morning fog and heavy smoke, many of the balls from each side bounded over the heads of the batteries they were aimed at, were retrieved by the gunners, and sent back whence they had come. At about midday and faced with overwhelming Federal firepower, McCown and Stewart agreed to an overnight evacuation of their New Madrid fortifications. To provide a diversion for the evacuating troops, the two Arkansas regiments remained in the rifle pits and the artillery gunners continued to fire away. The evacuation fell into chaos later that night when a thunderstorm hit and some of the transports failed to arrive or refused to approach New Madrid. Nevertheless, most of the troops were evacuated to Tiptonville and Island No. 10, although the heavy guns could not be hauled through the mud and were left behind with much equipment and abandoned supplies.[64]

At 2:00 A.M. on 14 March, Slack's brigade moved in the dark through the rain and knee-deep pools of water with Schuyler Hamilton's 2nd division to relieve Stanley's troops in the waterlogged rifle pits in front of Fort Thompson. Believing that they were in for a bloody assault against Fort Thompson, Slack ordered his flag bearer to leave the 47th Indiana's flag in camp and bring his rifle and bayonet instead. At 6:00 A.M., however, several men carrying a flag of truce informed the Federal batteries that the Confederates had evacuated during the night and had retreated downriver some twenty miles to Tiptonville, Tennessee.[65]

Hamilton then ordered Slack to send his brigade into the fort and troops from the 47th Indiana were the first to enter, without their flag, followed by Captain Joseph Mower and twenty of his artillerists, who also did not bring their flag. Finally, the 34th Indiana entered and planted their flag in the captured Confederate fort. Most of Gantt's troops had escaped from Fort Thompson except for two killed, one wounded and thirteen soldiers (principally men from the 11th Arkansas Infantry who had left their rifle pits during the storm seeking shelter in unoccupied tents in the rear) who were captured when they fell asleep and missed the evacuation.[66]

Describing the march of the 47th Indiana to New Madrid and the subsequent capture of Fort Thompson from a soldier's viewpoint, Sgt. P.D. Caverly of the 47th Indiana wrote the *Huntington Democrat*:

Camp Near New Madrid, Mo.,
March 14th, 1862

Dear *Democrat*:—I take pleasure in writing you once again. We reached here on the 3d inst., at about 1 o'clock, in a disagreeably cold rain storm. The 2d is a day that will long be remembered by our men, as we received a soaking on that "memorable" day that penetrated to the skin. We took it decidedly *cool*, and with a soldier's fortitude and courage, scarcely a murmur being heard. We encamped within 2½ miles of this place, when, after partaking of a cold collation by a warm fire (we captured a quantity of rails along the road, for miles, for the purpose of building fires), we were ordered to fall into line and march into the town. Each regimental color being struck, and our bands striking up Yankee Doodle, the boys picked up fresh courage and we started on our mission, and accomplished our object. The 39th Ohio, and one of the Iowa regiments entered the town under a fire of shot and shell from the enemy's gunboats, which did but little damage to our forces. After skirmishing around for about two hours in the town, we withdrew our forces and went into camp about 1½ miles north of town with a loss of three killed and about fifteen wounded on our side, as near as I could learn. The boys in the 46th picked up a few of their shells as they came near to us for examination—they proved to be 12 pound conical shells and none that came out to where we were halted would act manly enough to explode. It appeared they were sent in an unjust and unholy cause. We have been here now about 11 days, part of the time drilling, and doing picket duty keeping the enemy's forces of infantry within their fortifications until the arrival of some heavy ordnance which we had to have before making another attack upon them, as the ordnance we had was nowhere in comparison with the enemy's gunboats. Our ordnance arriving on Wednesday, they were planted and the fortifications thrown up the same night, and an order given to prepare one day's rations, and be ready for an attack yesterday (Thursday) morning. Our Brigade was in readiness at the time set, but the morning being dark and foggy, we did not get under way until half past 5 o'clock. The large guns from our new fortifications opened on the rebel gun boats with 32 and 64 pound shot, while our infantry were skirmishing around from one position to another, accompanied by a battery of Flying Artillery which occasionally would return a shot or two at the enemy, but to no effect as their infantry forces kept close in their fortifications.

Our heavy guns disabled two of their gunboats by 12 o'clock, M. A heavy cannonading was kept up all the time till 3 o'clock in the afternoon, when our brigade withdrew and returned to camp with orders to be in readiness this (Friday) morning for another attack on the devils at 3 o'clock. Three o'clock came, everything was in readiness, and the brigade got under headway at the time set for the action. It had rained during the night, and the morning was cloudy and cool, which was regarded as favorable for our forces, as it had been uncomfortably warm the previous day. Our boys went out and commenced to work on the entrenchments until 6 o'clock this A.M., when the discovery was made that the enemy had evacuated the fortifications, spiking their guns and leaving all their stores behind, consisting of mules, wagons, and beef, pork, sugar, corn, and all kinds of goods appertaining to a commissary department, besides a heavy magazine, valued at over $150,000.

Our regiment was the first to enter the fortification but the 34th had the honor of planting the first color, as the 47th left their colors in camp, it being too nice, I suppose, to use on so important an occasion.

The loss in killed and wounded on our side does not exceed 75. The loss on the rebel side is not known to us.

The houses around here are all deserted, the rebels leaving everything behind, with instructions to their slaves to protect the property.

Our next destination is as yet unknown, but presume we will remain here for some time to come. I must close, as it is getting late, by saying: give my best respects to all Unionists of Huntington, and vicinity. Yours, truly,

P.D. Caverly

P.S. Announce the deaths of Robert Hilderberger, of the 34th reg., and Robert Brown, of Rock Creek, also of the 34th.[67]

Giving his view of the capture of Fort Thompson, on 14 March 1862 Chaplain Sawyer of the 47th Indiana wrote to the *Indianapolis Daily Journal*:

THE INDIANIANS AT THE TAKING OF NEW MADRID
NEW MADRID, MO., MARCH 14

Ed. Journal: We no longer date our letters "Near New Madrid," at a safe distance from the rebel gun-boats, for the town and fortifications are ours. When Gen. Pope found that his command had not guns of equal caliber to those of the enemy, he resolved to take the place with as little loss of life as possible, and therefore he ordered several heavy guns and a 68-pound mortar from Cairo. These arrived on Wednesday evening. The next morning, to their great amazement, we had our guns planted, and from behind breastworks nearly half a mile in extent, we opened two batteries upon the fortifications of the enemy.

The First and Second Divisions were in advance of us, but Gen. Palmer, at break of day, had his men marching towards the river. With one of his Aids the General, pushing bravely on through the fog, rode close to the rebel pickets, and his whole column was pressing on after him. As the balls and shells began to fall around us we drew back, under orders, in the rear of Gen. Hamilton's Division, to await the result of the cannonading. The gun-boats and forts played on our batteries their "level best," thinking they could easily demolish them; but hour after hour passed away, and our batteries seemed to be as threatening and formidable as at first. One of their largest balls struck the embankment and our artillery-men picked it up and fired it back. It dismounted one of their heaviest cannon and killed several of their gunners.—Just afterwards, however, one of their balls, a 36-pounder, entered the muzzle of our best gun; breaking off six or eight inches of its mouth, killing two of our men, and wounding several. For an hour or two it was serious work.

I went over to the hospital, where ambulances were arriving at short intervals with the wounded. With the aid of chloroform five brave soldiers had each a leg amputated and others more or less severely injured were treated with the best surgical skill and attention. The amputated limbs were decently interred.

During the day Gen. Palmer's force changed its position several times; and in the middle of the afternoon we found ourselves within range of the gun-boats, a mile from the river. As the enemy seemed not a little alarmed by our driving in their pickets, by the numbers we presented, and by our bold and skillful cannonading, Gen. Pope felt assured that they would make no attempt to storm our batteries, and we were ordered back to camp.

At night we learned through Gen. Palmer that our loss in killed was eight, and about twenty were wounded. There were various speculations as to the programme for the next day. Some thought it was idle for us to talk of taking the fortifications without a further supply of heavy cannon, and we might be under the necessity of waiting a week, more or less, until we received them. The gun-boats and the cannon on the forts were deemed too strong for us. As yet we had heard nothing of the fatal precision of our shells and balls. We did not know that the Captain who had been sent from Memphis to command the fort had been killed by our batteries; that several other officers had fallen; that Dr. Bell on one of the gun-boats had been instantly killed by a ball that took off the pilot house, upper deck and chimneys; and that the bursting of shells in the fort and among the barracks had made a fear and trembling among the rebels.

On our part, we heard that the number of gun-boats had been increased and the fortifications reinforced.

At 11 o'clock at night orders were received at our headquarters that the 1st brigade of the Third Division should be ready to march to the entrenchments at 3 o'clock Friday morning [14 March]. At 10 minutes before 3 o'clock our guide appeared, and the brigade commenced its march under Acting Brig. Gen. Jas. R. Slack. The night was rainy, the road muddy and dismal, but the men pushed on quietly through the open country and long woods, running against each other, stumbling over roots and stumps, dashing against trees, or stepping down into deep mud holes or rifle-pits, in the thick darkness relieved only by an occasional lightning flash. At length we reached the extemporized entrenchments. Those coming away hailed us, as we passed, with such expressions as these: "You'll catch it to-day boys," "They'll give it to you, but Indiana is good for them." If the enemy opened their fire on us as the day dawned, desperate work was before us. In that case, our brigade was ordered to advance in the face of the forts and gun-boats, exposed to all their murderous fire, throw up new breast-works, replant our batteries five hundred yards nearer the foe, and be prepared to storm the fortifications at the point of the bayonet. The First Brigade seemed the forlorn hope, and the known coolness and courage of Indiana troops were to be once more tested in the face of danger and of death. Col. Slack felt this very sensibly, and when the color bearer came out in the morning with the flag, the Colonel told him to take it back and get his rifle and bayonet. He wanted every man to carry his gun to-day. He felt that in all human probability, should the enemy hold their ground, one half of his command ere the setting of the sun, would be borne out for burial. His Aids, Adjutant De Hart and Lieut. Daily, were near him to bear his orders over the field. Lieut. Col. Robinson had command of the 47th, and, well aware of the bloody work which might be before us, he was ready to go bravely with his men wherever duty might call. All of the officers and men seemed animated with one purpose, to sell their lives as dearly as possible, and if destined to fall on the field, to die fighting manfully for the honor of Indiana and the glory of the Union. Not a man there would have flinched in the hour of peril.

Just as our artillerymen were loading their cannon to fire upon the enemy, Gen. Hamilton rode up and announced to Col. Slack that a rumor had come that the enemy had spiked their guns and disappeared, and he ordered him to send out two companies from his command as skirmishers to visit the fort, and ascertain whether it was evacuated. Others were detailed to follow them with the national flag. Then Col. Slack regretted that the national banner was left in camp, as the 47th was upon the right and had the post of honor but the flag of the 34th was used, for the time being, instead. In a few moments we saw the stars and stripes waving from the fort, and loud cheering went up from the entire brigade. Lieut. Colonel Cameron was left in temporary command of the fort, and companies A and B of the 47th Regiment were ordered forward to take possession. In advance of company A, with Aid-de-Camp Daily and Capt. McLaughlin, I entered the fort and took a survey of its strength. Several of the heavy cannon were dismounted; one brass piece was broken by our shot, the rest were uninjured. Everything indicated that the enemy had fled in haste. We found the guns poorly spiked. — There were three magazines full of ammunition. One of our shells or shot felled their flag, and they had cut down the staff, as our gunners took delight in aiming at it, and every shot in their direction took effect. Several rebel flags were found, and plenty of canteens and knapsacks. We found one knapsack marked "Vermont Second Regiment" — captured, perhaps, in the Bull Run engagement. A gunboat was seen at a distance coming up the river, and we commenced mounting our guns. From our batteries to the fort, with the help of ropes, every gun was drawn by the brave-hearted and willing men, and under the direction and energizing help of Col. Slack, the cannon were ready to play all round the fort, and in thirty-five minutes, by the watch, the river was effectually blockaded in favor of the Union. Several boats appeared in sight, caught a glimpse of the stars and stripes, and veering around, disappeared. The pulling of the cannon from our batteries, and mounting them on the fort in a little over half an hour, so as to be ready to bear on the enemy, was a feat almost without a parallel in history, and was due to the energy of the Colonel commanding the First Brigade.

We found an officer of the artillery from McNairy county, Tenn., who had been shot in the back of the head. We lifted the canvass from his face, and saw a vigorous frame and an intelligent countenance. His fall struck the gunners with terror. Gen. Hamilton ordered that he should be decently buried, that the three prisoners we had taken should be accompanied by their guards and dig his grave and bury him. At Col. Cameron's request I conducted the religious services at the grave.

Two of the prisoners were from Arkansas. One of them was a waggoner. He was sleeping in the wagon, and his confederates forgot to wake him. He had been in the service eight months. He was much agitated when arrested, until assured that he would be treated well. His Arkansas companion was a youth of eighteen. They both had squirrel guns, and so had most of their companions in the service. The third prisoner was a shrewd Irishman. He had tried to come North, but the blockade had stopped him, and thrown him into the fort. He had no wish to get away, and having slipped though the lines into the town the night before, he came down in a friendly way, he said, to give us welcome. The prisoners stated that the enemy had been very much alarmed by the fearful work of our cannon, and felt certain if they stayed another day they would all have to surrender. This was the decided opinion of their commander, Col. Gantt, of Arkansas, and hence their abrupt departure. As we passed through their barracks we saw evidence of their hasty flight everywhere. In one tent we found a Major's uniform, sword, sash, and all. In another we saw the table spread, meat served on the plates, partly eaten. The sugar and spoon dropped between the bowl and cup, the chairs upset, their trunks and looking glasses and spurs and likenesses and letters left behind, and the candles burning; flour and meal in abundance, and molasses and sugar and mace, and barrels of beef and pork and potatoes in large supplies, were on hand. They had not only the necessaries, but many of the luxuries of life. Violins and accordions, and books of poetry, and law books, and blooded dogs were all left for the "Yankees." We captured one hundred and twenty mules, fifty horses, with their wagons, and hundreds of other things, of which more particular mention may be made by the reporters for the press.

In our rounds we discovered a clear outline map of the fort, which we sent to Gen. Pope. It was called Fort Thompson, and an immense amount of labor has been bestowed upon it. Five hundred Negroes were at work, under skillful directors, until it was complete. It is now ours, and we feel strongly entrenched. The universal wonder is why the rebels abandoned such a position. Col. Slack said, after our guns had been planted, that it was all owing to the fact that "they had a bad cause, and that the God of battles was on our side," that the fort fell into our hands without a fearful sacrifice of life, and that was the feeling of all of us. I have given you a brief sketch of Fort Thompson. Gen. Pope took possession of the other fortification, half a mile above. I had no time to examine its condition before our brigade was ordered back to camp. We returned feeling that our officers and men had done some good service to their country by driving the rebels from their last stronghold in Missouri, and in planting upon these fortresses the glorious stars and stripes. Yours very truly.

Samuel Sawyer Chaplain 47th Regiment Ind. Vols.[68]

On 15 March, reluctant Flag Officer Andrew H. Foote's Federal flotilla, which included the flagship *Benton*[69] and the city-class gunboats *St. Louis, Mound City, Carondelet,* and *Pittsburg,* finally arrived above Island No. 10. Nicknamed "Pook Turtles,"[70] the city-class gunboats quickly drove back the CSS *Grampus* ("Dare-devil Jack"), a small and fast light-draft stern-wheeler that Hollins used as a scout boat. But Foote, whose powerful although somewhat underpowered gunboats would be fighting downstream and subject to be carried into the enemy's possession if disabled, was content, to Pope's chagrin, to lurk upstream and fire mortars and shells ineffectively at Island No. 10 from long range.[71]

Safe passage of his troops across the river at Tiptonville required Foote's ironclads below Island No. 10 to drive off Hollins's vulnerable gunboats and silence Confederate land batteries. Frustrated at Foote's unwillingness to run the gauntlet past the Confederate guns, Pope, on advice from Hamilton and Bissell, decided to bypass Island No. 10 by cutting a channel from the river just below Island No. 8 eastward across the swampy upper peninsula and back to the river at New Madrid via Wilson's and St. John's Bayous. And, at 9:00 o'clock on the night of 16 March, in order to push Hollins's Confederate gunboats below Tiptonville and further prepare the trap for McCown's Confederates inside Madrid Bend,

Pope sent Palmer's division on another, even more grueling mud march. Moving at night to avoid Hollins's gunboats, each brigade hauled by hand one 24-pounder gun "mounted upon wheels ... hitched to by a hundred men each," and dragged through woods and swamps to Riddle's Point, about five miles below Point Pleasant, about one mile above Tiptonville.[72]

The 47th Indiana was assigned the task of hauling one of the 24-pounders, which they dubbed "Betsy," along with a wagonload of ammunition. (The other 24-pounder made it only three miles below New Madrid where it was left temporarily.) Guided that night by "a young colored boy who had escaped from the Rebel works and had come to camp" to offer his services, Palmer moved his troops inland to avoid the shells of Hollins's gunboats. "Wading half the distance" and stopping frequently to haul "Betsy" and the ammunition wagon out of deep mud, they reached Point Pleasant at daybreak on 17 March. At 1:00 P.M., still avoiding Hollins's gunboats and the Confederate batteries at Tiptonville and wanting to keep their presence a secret to the Confederates, they marched five more miles through woods and swamps to just above Riddle's Point, where they bivouacked at 4:00 P.M., inland from the river about one mile above Tiptonville. During the night they constructed an emplacement for "Betsy" on the bank of the river flanked by rifle pits dug in the sand for the 47th Indiana troops armed with Enfield rifles.[73]

In his memoirs, Palmer related an anecdote about reconnaissance in the unfamiliar and flooded bottom lands around his Riddle's Point camp. Palmer needed skiffs or flatboats so his small reconnaissance parties could move in the overflowed bottom lands and across flooded creeks and sloughs, but he was unable to find any. The young escaped slave who had guided them from New Madrid introduced Palmer to a middle-aged slave preacher. With the only stipulation that he was anxious to keep his identity concealed for fear of retribution against him by local whites, the slave preacher merely asked Palmer what he needed and in what direction he desired to go. "The next day," Palmer wrote, "one of my scouting parties found no difficulty in crossing streams or bayous. The necessary means of crossing were ready when needed; where they came from no one seemed to know, and I was informed that after the parties had used them they disappeared as if by magic."[74]

Palmer said that he had "rarely met a more remarkable person," adding, "his manner was grave almost to sadness." Palmer continued:

> He was a pure negro, beyond doubt, and, as almost all the ambitious negroes were, he was a preacher. I found all over the South that, as the only thing resembling a profession open to the slaves was the ministry, a very large number of them became preachers, and, by virtue of the position, leaders of their people.
>
> As a class the preachers were regarded with jealousy by the slave owners, but they were often useful to them as teachers of the religious duty of the slave to obey his master. The man to whom I refer had often no doubt (especially in the hearing of white people) preached to his race from the choice texts of the slaveholder's gospel: "Servants, obey your masters," etc., but he furnished evidence by his language, and more forcibly by his conduct, that the iron of hopeless servitude had entered his soul, and that he would be prepared, if ever the hour should come when it was necessary, to shed blood to rid himself from bondage.[75]

RIDDLE'S POINT: BATTLE WITH THE GUNBOATS

At 7:00 the next morning (18 March), Hollins discovered the new Federal battery, manned "by a detachment of Iowa volunteer artillerists" (possibly from the 2nd Iowa Cavalry); and, hoping to silence "Betsy" at point-blank range, sent his fleet of six gunboats steadily up and around the bend past the peach orchard toward the awaiting 47th Indiana sharpshooters in their rifle pits dug in the sand. Two intense one-hour battles ensued that filled the air with smoke and iron shot.[76]

As one soldier from the 43rd Indiana, calling himself "Kizer," reported:

LETTER FROM NEW MADRID
CAMP AT RIDDLE'S POINT,
FOUR MILES BELOW POINT PLEASANT, MO.,
MARCH 22D, 1862

...There has not been a more daring or hotter contest during this war than this was, upon the part of the brave boys who manned that solitary gun. The three boats were driven back, but only to come again, with two others, and a revenue cutter, mounting seven guns of large caliber. Then came the tug of war. Our gun was planted in a large pit, and for two hours stood the unceasing and galling fire of the six vessels of war, and absolutely drove three of them back in crippled condition. The cutter and another of the boats followed soon thereafter, and the remaining boat made a desperate attempt to come ashore. Then it was that two hundred rifles popped up from the ground along the shore, followed by two hundred human heads. Two hundred reports, mingled to one, rang out, and every rebel gunner in sight fell a corpse upon the deck. During the contest our gunners were compelled to crouch down behind the banks for ten minutes at a time, and yet they fired their gun one hundred and fifty six times. The only inconvenience they experienced was from the dirt thrown upon them by the shot and shell, and improbable as it may seem, not a single man was injured on our side.

Shots have been exchanged ever since we have been here, but the enemy kept at a respectable distance, and have killed but one of our men....[77]

Raining 32- and 64-pounder shells on the Palmer's "nest" of Hoosiers, Hollins attempted a landing to capture "Betsy." But the soldiers of the 47th Indiana, who when bombarded had disappeared into their rifle pits like sand crabs, popped up and opened fire with their Enfield rifles, reportedly killing a number of Confederate gunners and preventing the landing. In short order, "Betsy" disabled one of the boats, which retreated downriver. Then a second boat was disabled and retreated when "Betsy's" gunner "sent a shot which made a new port hole in her side." Iron continued to fly in two separate one-hour attacks as the four remaining gunboats returned fire. One dropped downstream, taking aim but rolling its shots over the heads of the riflemen of the 47th Indiana. Shortly thereafter, due to their vulnerable wooden hulls, Hollins withdrew his damaged flotilla six miles below Tiptonville and out of harm's way, ending the intense two-hour battle. Remarkably, although there were many narrow escapes, only one man was killed in Palmer's division "in or near the magazine," possibly when "Betsy's" muzzle was hit and slightly damaged. Hollins reportedly lost three sailors killed and eight wounded.[78]

Describing the 47th Indiana's part in the action as they marched down the west bank of the Mississippi from New Madrid to Riddle's Point, Chaplain Sawyer wrote the *Daily Journal* on 21 March about their "Battle with the Rebel Gunboats":

LETTER FROM GEN. POPE'S ARMY
THE BATTLE WITH THE REBEL GUNBOATS
FOURTEEN MILES SOUTH OF NEW MADRID,
MISSOURI, MARCH 21ST, 1862

Ed. Journal: In my last letter I gave you an account of our taking Fort Thompson, at New

Madrid. As the river had been blockaded at Point Pleasant, eight miles from the fort, we were puzzled to find out in which direction the rebels had fled. From the testimony of one of the Tennessee prisoners, and from all circumstances, we became satisfied that they had gone up the river and effected a landing not far from No. 10, and with their fugitive companions in arms were making special haste to get below us on the way to Fort Pillow or Memphis. Word reached us on Sunday [16 March] that a part of their force was endeavoring to land on the western bank of the Mississippi, and at nine o'clock, P.M., General Palmer's Division, consisting of the 43rd, 46th, 34th and 47th regiments, struck tents, and with a guide marched all night through the rain and mud. Daylight found the column at Point Pleasant, within the destructive range of two batteries of 32-pounders of the enemy. General Slack filed the column to the right, and, wading through a desperate swamp, the men moved on to a place of safety. Resting awhile for their tents and camp equipage to overtake them, the men were just beginning to feel comfortable, when General Palmer ordered them forward to our present encampment. The 47th Indiana regiment was detailed to bring one of the cannon by hand from the battery above, and plant and defend it, from their rifle pits, against the rebel gunboats which were stalking up and down the river at all hours, night and day. The rifle pits were noiselessly dug, by men who had marched all the night before, the cannon placed, and with some solicitude, but with undaunted courage, the regiment awaited the issues of the day. Colonel Robinson was in command. As the day dawned hundreds of tents could be seen near Tiptonville, on the Tennessee side of the river, and two gunboats, afterwards increased to seven, hove in sight, and opened a most fearful fire upon our lone cannon and our sheltered men.

Gen. Palmer, Gen. Slack, and Aid-de-Camp Daily, drew near the regiment, but the 32 and 64 pound shot and shell literally rained around them. They protected themselves as well as they could by the large sycamores which were near, dodging the balls as they flew right and left around them. Lieut. Purviance, of Huntington, was nearly buried in his rifle pit, by the bursting of a shell. At one time during the cannonading the gunboats adopted a plan, apparently, of landing their men to capture our guns. They moved up very near the shore, when Col. Robinson gave command to the men to fire. The 47th rose up in their rifle-pits, and taking steady aim, their bullets flew amongst the gunners, who fell in every direction. The roar of musketry came like a thunder-clap upon the rebels, and one of the boats, as she turned her course, received a shot from our cannon in the stern which sent her rolling down the river double quick, in a disabled condition. The rest of the gunboats then renewed the fire with redoubled fury. From the shore their officers could be heard distinctly berating the gunners as cowards for not standing to their posts. Exasperated by these taunts, they would pour their terrific fire upon our solitary gun, until they drew near enough to test the virtue of our good Enfield rifles — and as another wheeled back into the middle of the channel, our gunner sent a shot which made a new port hole in her side, and from the smoke which rose up, left the impression that the boiler had been reached. Thus a second boat was laid aside. Three of the others continued the firing. One of them dropped down stream, took the range of our rifle pits, and rolled her shot and shell right over our men. Some of the men thought they had heard cannonading before, but they acknowledge with one accord that they never heard anything to compare with this. Some one, not belonging to our regiment, proposed that we should spike our cannon and abandon the ground. "Never, be jabers," said our Irish gunner. Colonel Robinson told the men they must stand by the gun and never surrender.

Col. Slack almost feared, at one moment, that some of the men would lose their presence of mind and run away from the place of danger, and resolved if they did to rally them and lead them back in the face of the enemy's fire. But the volunteers of Indiana have gone in for victory, and not for defeat. Believing in the justness of their cause, and the favorable providence of God, they know no such words as fail. This was the feeling of the 47th Regiment during the entire contest. Every gunboat disabled by our solitary but well aimed gun augmented the enthusiasm of the men, and nerved them to stand their ground like heroes. Frequent firing heated our cannon, again and again, but our cannonier was cool and self-possessed, and often taking deliberate aim, he hurled his balls with crushing effect upon the enemy until three, if not four, of the gunboats which had engaged us were disabled, and giving up the contest they went down the river, out of our range. The enemy had fired over seven hundred times with their shot and shell, poured from five of their gunboats, and we had returned their fire over one hundred and twenty times. The single cannon which colonel Slack had planted amid the cheers of his men, upon Fort Thompson, kept at bay, and, finally, "whipped out" seven of the enemy's gunboats.

The fact stands out almost unparalleled in the history of warfare. It was a splendid day's work, courageously and brilliantly executed. The commanding officers feel proud of the unflinching bravery of their men.

As an instance of cool self-possession and daring, I may mention that, during the heat of the battle, our color bearer, Sergeant H. Lindsey of Wabash county, fearing that the beautiful banner, which the ladies of Huntington presented to Captain Shearer's company, might be shot down, and fall into the river, removed it from the battery and planted it in the rear of the rifle pits, where it waved proudly throughout the day.

I might add other interesting incidents for the same spirit ran through the ranks.

General Palmer complimented the heroic courage of the men, and feels that he can confide in them in any future engagement.

While I am writing, the cannon are still thundering at Island No. 10.

Yours very truly, Samuel Sawyer

Chaplain 47th Reg. Ind. Vols.[79]

Describing the capture of Fort Thompson and the march from New Madrid to Riddle's Point from a soldier's standpoint, on 27 March a correspondent, probably a soldier in the 47th Indiana who identified himself only as "A. Hoosier," wrote the *Indiana State Sentinel*:

OUR ARMY CORRESPONDENCE—THE 47TH INDIANA ON THE MISSISSIPPI.
CAMP NEAR RIDDLE'S POINT, ON THE MISSISSIPPI,
47TH INDIANA VOLUNTEERS, COL. SLACK,
MARCH 27TH, 1862.

Editor Sentinel: Sir—Should the 47th manifest a little pride in coming before the public, and having a few words to say about itself, we don't think there should be any to find fault, for we would not in the least infringe upon the rights, or in any manner whatever do an act of injustice to anybody else. Our career has not been paraded in the newspapers with such brilliancy as some of the other regiments with which we have been co-mingling since our leave-taking of Hoosierdom, or, I might say, the soil of Kentucky, but still we have certainly won for ourselves a reputation no less enviable, of knowing no higher duty than that of at all times obeying orders.

During the three months' stay in Kentucky, it was deemed necessary that we should endure many long marches through mud and rain, and that without any inclination to murmur, being anxious, to meet the rebels. After finding the rebels growing beautifully less daily within the boundaries of Kentucky, we were ordered to Missouri, where we safely landed at Commerce with our brigade, including the 46th, 43rd and 34th Indiana regiments, and were immediately ordered forward to New Madrid, where, it was understood, the rebels were lying in wait for us.

The time was short until we were being paraded back and forth from battery to battery, in presence of the gunboats of the rebels, at the above mentioned place, where, by times, the shot flew thick and fast, we not at this time, having guns of sufficient caliber to compete with them. However, we answered as targets, and escaped without losing many Hoosier lives, miraculously. Soon came to hand the desired 24 pounders so anxiously wished for—and then came the tug of war.

The same evening of the day the guns arrived, they were planted in a masterly manner, and on the morning of the 13th opened up, much to the great surprise of the enemy, with telling effect, upon their boats, also upon their fort, which was returned by them in thunder-tones, as much as to say, we are with you.

During the day the firing was continued thick and close, the 10th and 16th Illinois regiments occupying the intrenchments, and losing a number of men — not knowing the fatality produced upon the enemy, but disabling several of their gunboats, also having a desirable effect upon their fort.

On the same evening, the 47th and 34th Indiana regiments received orders from headquarters to prepare twenty-four hours' rations, and be ready to march by 10 o'clock A.M. for the battery, which order was cheerfully complied with. Accordingly we set out through mud and rain and the darkness of the night for the intrenchments, a distance of perhaps two and a half miles from camp, where, upon arriving, we without reluctance, took our several places in the intrenchments, awaiting the break of day to renew the conflict of the day previous, *with the slight addition* of being possessed with the knowledge of there being an order issued from headquarters that before the dawn of another day we were to lead the way of the forces which were this day to melt before the fire of the rebels, or have the glory of planting upon the ramparts of Fort Madrid [*sic:* Thompson] the glorious old flag, but to our great surprise, as the day opened, what did we behold but that which sent forth a shout making the welkin ring, informing us of the evacuation of the fort, which was, in twenty-five minutes afterwards, occupied by the 47th and 34th Indiana regiments.

On the 16th we received orders to take up the march at 9 o'clock P.M., which we did, during the whole night, making our way to this point, bringing by hand our beloved old 24-pounder, which the boys have chosen to call "Betsy," and by the side of which they have since closely remained, defending it against the united force of five gunboats, consisting of perhaps forty or fifty guns, some of which are pieces throwing balls of immense size — we coming off more than victorious. The rebels, after making one grand move for our single gun in full force, attempted a landing of forces, but were completely routed after losing a number of men, being picked off by our riflemen as fast as they make their appearance.

More anon. A. Hoosier.[80]

Following the battle with the gunboats on 18 March, the other 24-pounder and two 10-pounder Parrott guns were reportedly brought down by the 63rd Ohio. Although having successfully run off Hollins's now damaged flotilla, Palmer had planted the battery at Riddle's Point a little too high on the river to command either Confederate embarkations from, or Federal embarkations to the landing below Tiptonville. Pope had Palmer move the battery downriver about a mile and a half to just below Riddle's Point, as far as they could get before reaching more swampland, in order to control the lower Tiptonville landing.[81]

On the night of 4 April, Henry Walke, intrepid commodore of the *Carondelet*, ran his "Pook Turtle" past the guns on Island No. 10 during a violent thunderstorm, the Confederate gunners having been unable to see "the little black looking monster" well enough between lightning flashes to take accurate aim. Bissell's engineers finished the channel, and the next day four steamers transported Paine's division through it to the mouth of Bayou St. John at the river near New Madrid.[82]

Meanwhile, the *Carondelet* continued down to Riddle's Point and back to New Madrid, bombarding the Confederate batteries on the west bank of the Madrid Bend peninsula. Although he got the dates wrong, in his memoirs Palmer related that Walke invited him to come aboard at Riddle's Point on Sunday, 7 April, to witness the gunboat in action. Steaming back upriver to finish off a battery made up of one 32- and one 24-pounder across from Point Pleasant that it had almost completely cleared out on its way down, the *Carondelet*, with Palmer aboard to watch, took it out in about twenty-five minutes. In Palmer's account (he remembered only the 24-pounder gun, perhaps the only one still being operated after the earlier attack), the *Carondelet* "moved up in short range, and with a few shots, which sent earth around the ears of the artillerists, drove them from their gun."[83]

On the night of 6 April, Lt. Commander Egbert Thompson, taking advantage of another torrential storm (and the fact that Confederate artillerists were spiking their guns in preparation to escape across Reelfoot Lake), ran the gunboat *Pittsburg* past Island No. 10. Captain of Artillery A. Jackson Jr. and Lt. Col. W.D.S. Cook of the 12th Arkansas Infantry, having been assigned at the last minute to command the mainland and Island No. 10 batteries respectively as Mackall moved his infantry into Madrid Bend, withdrew their troops to the left bank. Escape across Reelfoot Lake for the entire force being impracticable, when steamers carrying Paine's Federal division were seen steaming out of the mouth of St. John's Bayou, and knowing that two Federal ironclads were already downriver, most realized it was over and surrendered Island No. 10 the next day (7 April).[84]

On 7 April, protected by the gunboats *Carondelet* and *Pittsburg*, Paine's division crossed to the landing below Tiptonville, followed by Stanley's and Hamilton's divisions. Moving forward, Paine's troops pushed Mackall's Madrid Bend force back into the swamps and forced their surrender. At 2:00 o'clock the next morning, Mackall sent Paine a flag of truce, surrendering his remaining Madrid Bend force, estimated at about 3,900 troops—5,000 including those already captured. Palmer's division remained at Riddle's Point.[85]

A number of artillerists, infantrymen and cavalrymen, however, escaped with Jackson and Cook off Island No. 10 that evening. Throughout the night, Hudson's cavalrymen rode and the infantrymen and artillerists slogged and waded on the flooded road around Reelfoot Lake for about ten miles, those on foot arriving at Stone's Ferry at the southern end of the lake the next day (8 April) at about noon, the cavalrymen earlier in the morning. At Stone's Ferry it began to snow and the escaping Confederates fought each other for the few remaining flatboats and canoes available to cross there. Those who made it across moved onward to Dyersburg the next day. Aided by citizens, on 11 April they made it to Bell's Station on the Memphis & Ohio Railroad, where they stayed for two days before moving on to Memphis, arriving there three days later. Jackson claimed that 244 of his artillerists had arrived in Memphis with him and Cook claimed that 300 of the 12th Arkansas and 150 of the 1st Alabama had arrived with him, both mentioning that stragglers were still coming in.[86]

The *Indiana State Sentinel*, not relying entirely on soldiers' reports, also sent a reporter to cover the action of Hoosier troops on the Mississippi. Describing very well the gunboat battles and the role of what he called the "Hoosier Brigade" at the capture of Island Number 10 and New Madrid, their anonymous correspondent wrote[87]:

OUR ARMY CORRESPONDENCE—FROM THE MISSISSIPPI.
RUDDLE'S [*SIC*: RIDDLE'S] POINT, MO., APRIL 9, 1862.

J.J. Bingham, Esq.—*Dear Sir*— Before we were positive of the fact here, the telegraph doubtless informed you of the fall of the rebel stronghold at Number Ten. It is a fact well known that in extended military operations, the participators, particularly upon the wings or flanks of an army, are frequently left for days in doubt of the result of their labors. While their friends at home were rejoicing at the victory, the Hoosier Brigade of Gen. Palmer, which formed the extreme right of General Pope's army, was watching the rebel gunboat fleet, the vessels of which would saucily poke their noses around a bend some three or four miles below our batteries, and snort defiance, with steam up, however, ready to run at the first shot.

On Friday night [4 April] the Carondelet ran the blockade, and made her appearance in front of New Madrid, with the stars and stripes waving from her stern. The fact was known here early in the day, and we knew then that Number Ten was doomed to fall in a few days. On Sunday she engaged the rebel batteries opposite New Madrid, silencing them after a few rounds. The day was fine, and a large party rode up from here to see the fun. It was a glorious sight. The little black looking monster, looking really diminutive at the distance of a mile, under the large volume of smoke, like the tail of a comet, that rolled lazily from behind her chimneys, would quarter across the river, paying no attention to the enemy's fire until she obtained a position to suit her above the enemy, when she would float quietly by and rake the batteries fearfully as she passed. A few movements of this kind drove the enemy from the guns of the two upper works, when she steamed down to Point Pleasant to attend to a work opposite that place, which for a week had been playing upon that town and annoying the troops and trains as they passed. One round was sufficient. The gunners fired at random and fled, all but one man who stood to his gun and kept blazing away with an old shot gun as she ran to the shore, and the party who landed to spike the cannon had reluctantly to cripple the gallant fellow—they did not try to kill him—and let him hobble away. The Carondelet then ran down to Ruddle's Point to coax a shot from the battery above Tiptonville, where the enemy seemed to be encamped in force, but she could not provoke a response, and it afterwards appeared that the guns had been hastily removed from there the night before.

It was understood in camp that on Monday Number Ten and its dependencies was to be forced to come down. Troops were to cross the river but what divisions were to be the favored ones was not published. General Palmer's command, and I presume others, were ordered to be in readiness to move at a moment's notice. The "Hoosier's nest" was gleeful at the prospect of a close fight; but yet the boys were fearful that if there were no earthworks to build they would be left behind. They had been so long listening to the thunder of cannon, sleeping in pits and dodging shell, that they feel like going in at short range. They had made the gunboats skedaddle from Ruddle's Point when they had the temerity to attempt a landing and they wanted to try their muskets and rifles on the secesh land. Long before reveille Col. Slack commanding the first brigade in Palmer's division, was on horseback and W.W. Hatcher of Lafayette and myself were dashing through the mud with him as volunteer aids. The duty of a volunteer aid is to be with the General on all trying occasions, help him eat his dinner if he gets any extra, and try the whisky, and see at what range it will kill, and on the field to carry all orders &c. The selection for this occasion I am sure you will pronounce most excellent. At early dawn, we were on a point near New Madrid anxiously peering through the grey mist for the first appearance of the gunboats. Another one had run the gauntlet of the rebel fire the night before, and we felt assured that the upper batteries, which had been silenced on Sunday without spiking the guns would have to be reduced again. Sure enough as the drums and trumpets of the several camps gave out their distant calls, the gunboats moved from the moorings on the Missouri shore and the rebel batteries opened.

We moved up the shore until the dull and almost indistinct roar of the guns assumed the sharp distinct sound of close action, and from the river bank we witnessed the final fight which sealed the fate of the Gibraltar of the Mississippi. The guns at Fort Thompson took part in the fight, and for an hour or more the thundering was terrible. One rebel battery fought with great gallantry and finally succumbed to a perfect avalanche of shot and shell hurled at it by the gunboats and our fort doubling on it. By nine or ten o'clock two or three divisions were in motion to cross—cavalry, artillery and infantry hurrying up in hot haste. A large force was soon landed in admirable order and were shortly concealed from our view. A reconnoitering party was thrown forward until it reached the pickets around the bend, and at midnight without further fighting—without loss, the Island and its dependencies was ours. The number of prisoners who, by the way, seemed to be a better class of troops than those taken at Fort Donelson, say that the plunder lost by them will count up millions.

Transports have been plying up and down the river freely to-day, and this evening Col. Fitch's brigade is ordered to cross to Tiptonville, and as I write the boys are busy packing up.

II. New Madrid and Island No. 10 (January–April 1862)

To-morrow Col. Slack's brigade will follow, and a new Hoosier's nest will be formed on the ground where General Gant's rebel force lay, as the rear guard of Number Ten.[88]

Back on the Tennessee River, on 6 April 1862, Albert Sidney Johnston's reorganized and resurgent Army of the Mississippi, bolstered by Leonidas Polk's "Grand Division" that had evacuated Columbus, Kentucky, surprised and nearly defeated a Federal force, under the "rehabilitated" William T. Sherman, and the exonerated U.S. Grant, at Sherman's camp near Shiloh Church. Overrun and pushed back to the river at Pittsburg Landing after the first day's fight, Grant's army, now known as the Army of the Tennessee, aided by the arrival of Don Carlos Buell's Army of the Ohio from Nashville and Lew Wallace's late-arriving division, turned the tide on the second day and drove the Confederates back to Corinth, Mississippi.

With the capture of Island No. 10, and Grant's victory at the Battle of Shiloh, Halleck moved his headquarters from St. Louis to Pittsburg Landing and took charge of his armies in the field. Reorganizing immediately, Halleck again took away Grant's command, this time relegating him to second in command with no clear authority.

On 12 April 1862, Slack was placed in command of Federal forces at New Madrid, Island No. 10 and Tiptonville, where he established headquarters — the 47th Indiana remaining at Tiptonville to collect and take charge of all public property there, and the 34th Indiana returning to New Madrid to garrison the town. Fitch's brigade (the 43rd and 46th Indiana) broke camp at Riddle's Point, Missouri, and crossed the river to Tiptonville.[89]

Describing the activity at New Madrid and Tiptonville in preparation for the move down the Mississippi to Fort Pillow and Memphis, as well as mentioning the effects of the 47th Indiana's 24-pounder "Betsy" against Hollins's Confederate gunboats at Riddle's Point, the *Indiana State Sentinel*'s anonymous war correspondent wrote:

NEW MADRID, MO., APRIL 14, 1862

J.J. Bingham, Esq: From the day the river above was opened until the present time, what is left of this miserable little muddy village has been like a bee-hive. The bank has been lined with steamers, and the puddle-holes and deep mud have been in constant commotion, men, horses and mules dashing knee deep to and fro. No time has been lost by either Commodore Foote or Gen. Pope in following up their bloodless victory. The gunboats and mortar fleet left on Saturday morning, and in the evening, or rather at midnight, Gen. Pope, with the 1st Division, sailed also for Dixie.

The 59th Indiana, Col. Alexander, is with the advance under Gen. Hamilton, of whom, by the way, the Hoosier boys speak in the highest terms. The 59th is a splendid body of men, and their Colonel is every inch a soldier, and I have no doubt the honor of the State will be safe in their hands "away down South."

Yesterday and to-day boats have been leaving every hour. Gen. Granger's Division was the last to embark, as it embraced the cavalry, of which there is a large force. The 43rd Indiana, Col. McLean, and the 46th Indiana, Col. Fitch's brigade, embarked at Tiptonville. The 47th Indiana, Col. Slack, remains at Tiptonville, and the 34th, Lieut. Colonel Cameron, stays here. Col. Cameron is now in command of the post, and an active, energetic and efficient one he makes. Col. Slack, acting Brigadier, will be in command of the District of New Madrid, embracing the territory and military posts from Columbus to Tiptonville. Gen. Slack would rather go below with the advancing army, but the troops necessarily left behind are well pleased at the selection made for them. Col. Slack is a good officer, and takes gracefully to the roughing and privations of military life as he did to the rough and tumble of Senatorial debates, and is always just as prompt and good-humored as he was when seated with his back to the railing in our old Senate Chamber.

We have rumors here from the fleet below, but as they are only rumors I will not give them. The facts officially you will hear in all probability before we will. The prisoners who are still here, chiefly belonging to the Medical Department of the army, say they do not expect any strong opposition to our advance at Fort Pillow, as the heavy guns were removed from there to Island No. 10; but they seem to look upon Commodore Hollins and his fleet as the very devil in our way. As a few hundred Hoosiers with one 24 pounder whipped Hollins and his entire fleet some days ago, and with three guns kept them at bay for a week after, the scareism held up by these Southern gentlemen, does not alarm any one. Lord help poor Hollins if Foote gets in easy range of him with his iron-heeled boot, say the knowing ones here.

Yesterday I was all over and around the fortifications at Island No. 10. They are truly formidable—as much so as earth works and big guns and the convenient windings of a large river could make any position. And the rebels had fixed to stay there—there can be no doubt of that, whatever their reports or papers may say to the contrary now. There are acres of ammunition and everything that a garrison force would require to hold a post. The army of the Mississippi will go through to the Gulf—the good people at home may bet on that.

It has been impossible to obtain transportation up the river—everything that floats going down, except Commodore Foote's express boat, and it is uncertain when I can leave here. You may hear from me again from Memphis or from Pittsburg, it is uncertain which.[90]

Two days later (16 April), Pope's Army of the Mississippi was transported downriver to near Osceola, Arkansas, to cooperate with Foote's attack on Fort Pillow, only to be called back the next day when the attack was called off. Halleck then ordered Pope to transport his army to the Tennessee River town of Hamburg, Tennessee, to take part as the left flank in his campaign against Beauregard's Confederate forces at Corinth, Mississippi. (Most of Grant's old Army of the Tennessee, now commanded by George Thomas, made up Halleck's right flank, Buell's Army of the Ohio the center.)

Although Palmer went with Pope to Hamburg, his division (Slack's 34th and 47th Indiana; and Fitch's 43rd and 46th Indiana) was detached and remained on the Mississippi River to continue the Mississippi River Expedition, now under the command of Brigadier General Isaac F. Quinby, and Slack was placed in command at New Madrid and Island No. 10. A week or so earlier Slack had told his wife, Ann, that he thought the war would end with the imminent capture of Memphis, but later noted with some annoyance at being left behind to "straighten ... out" the "unallowable confusion" at New Madrid while the rest of the army continued on toward Memphis.[91]

III

Memphis (April–July 1862)

With the Mississippi River now open southward to just above Fort Pillow, about 60 miles above Memphis and some 150 miles below Tiptonville, the Confederate hold on the river continued to weaken. Next to fall were the southern defenses near the mouth of the river, which fell on 24 April 1862 to Admiral Farragut's Federal fleet. Anchored off New Orleans the next day, Farragut found the waterfront ablaze, his boats anchored in the midst of burning debris, and a recalcitrant mayor who refused to surrender even as Confederate troops evacuated the city. Mayor John Monroe held out for five more days until, with all the forts defending the city captured and threatened with bombardment, he reluctantly surrendered the city on 1 May 1862 to Major General Benjamin F. Butler. Announcing the capture in their 30 April edition, the *Indianapolis Daily Journal*'s headline blared: Latest By Telegraph. Night Dispatches. Evacuation of New Orleans. The City in Possession Our Troops.[1]

In Huntington, on the same day that Admiral Farragut's fleet broke through the Confederate defenses at the mouth of the Mississippi, the *Democrat*'s headline, taken from the *Portsmouth (Ohio) Times*, warned: Ohio Becoming Africanized. The *Times* editorial had announced the arrival of fifty-five "negros" from Western Virginia on the steamer *Piketon* with the warning that "it was high time for the Legislature of Ohio to follow the example of other States and enact a law prohibiting the negros from coming into the State." The *Democrat*, concerned about the increased immigration of blacks, slave or free, into Indiana, added, "Indianapolis is rapidly filling up with strange Africans, and the same thing, I am credibly informed, is observable in the cities and villages along the Ohio river."[2]

Back at Pittsburg Landing, Tennessee, Halleck began his slow march toward Corinth in pursuit of what was now Beauregard's Army of Mississippi. On the upper Mississippi, river flooding and well-placed Confederate batteries at Forts Pillow and Randolph slowed preparations for a Federal expedition downriver to Memphis.

Describing the flooded Mississippi and a visit with Colonel Slack and the 47th Indiana, then in camp about one mile below Tiptonville, the *Indiana State Sentinel*'s war correspondent, now with the byline "B," accompanied by a Mr. Holloway, and with permission of the "Naval Commandant at Cairo," wrote on 16 and 17 April 1862 from on board the steamer *Shingiss*:

> We left Cairo at 2 P.M., and at 4 o'clock, the present writing, have just passed Hickman, a distance of forty miles, against a strong head wind that sends the waves in spray clear over the cabin. The river is very high and rising. The rise is from both the Ohio and the upper Missis-

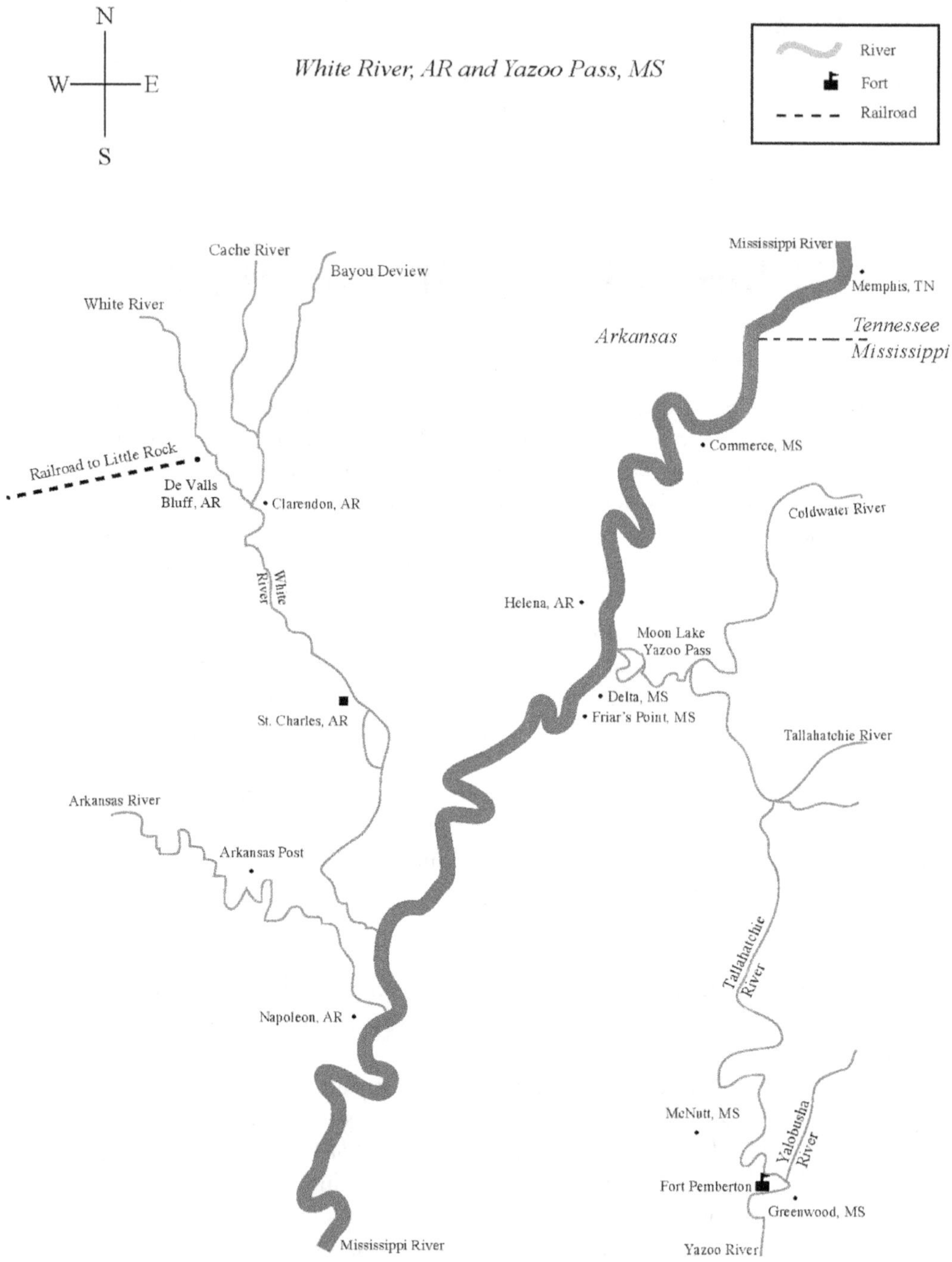

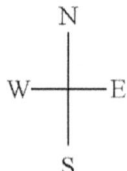

White River, AR and Yazoo Pass, MS

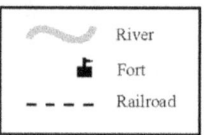

From Atlas Plate CLIV

sippi, and it is feared it will make against the operations of the land forces below. Yesterday morning, as I passed up, there was quite a little bank visible at Columbus, and now the water is over the streets and lots of the town....

At Tiptonville.

We passed New Madrid about dusk.... It was dark and raining when we reached Tiptonville. A regular New Madrid thunder and lighting earthquake storm was brewing. The orders of the

III. Memphis (April–July 1862)

Captain were to run directly to the fleet, but to keep out in the stream if such a storm as was raging, would be certain destruction to the craft, and the Captain determined to lay up until the fury of the storm was passed. Gen. Slack's brigade, in which was the 47th Indiana, was encamped about a mile below, and we determined to visit them. Getting ashore in such a hurricane was a matter of some danger and difficulty, and groping our way through the horses and teams of a large body of cavalry, was no less difficult; but guided by the vivid lighting which lit up the entire encampment every few moments, we contrived to get through without a kick or a scratch. We found Gen. Slack still up with his aids Lieutenants DeHart and Daily, making himself master of his situation, receiving reports from scouts, &c. While the rain fell in torrents on the canvas covering, and the thunder roared as it only can bellow in this region, and the lighting flashed blindingly, we passed a very pleasant hour with our Indiana friends. By the way, the Indiana troops in the Mississippi division of the army are badly clad. The State is anxious to supply them, but red tape is somewhere at fault. Let it be cut at once, and not have our poor boys, as I have often seen them, searching for old coffee sacks in which to wrap their feet for want of shoes when ordered at night to the trenches.

Our intrepid correspondent "B" continued down river on board the *Shingiss* to the Federal flotilla then at Plum Point, Tennessee, across the river from Osceola, Arkansas, and about twenty-five miles above Fort Pillow via the winding Mississippi[3]:

By midnight the storm had slowed itself out, and one of those dull, hot, foggy calms peculiar to this region had succeeded it. The Captain resolved to take the chances and run anyhow, as he had dispatches for Commandant Foote and a large mail for the fleet. It was a dangerous business.... The fog was so thick that the green trees of the shore were not visible at over one hundred feet, and then very indistinctly. The bends had to be guessed at, but the pilots were familiar with the river and calculated the distance made, working out the situation of the craft in the same manner that marines do when an "observation" is not to be had.

At daylight, we were met by a steamer with a peremptory order from General Pope to put back. The reply was that the "Shingiss" belonged to the Navy, and received orders from the Commodore only. In an hour more we were in the midst of General Pope's transports just above Plum Point bend. They were all afloat and such a rapid succession of shrill whistles as our arrival created was never heard before. It was like turning a fresh hog in a pen of old porkers. Every fellow had a grunt at us, and as we could only see their black smoke slowly winding up and back in the thick white mist, and they could only see our smoke, it completely mystified us. Presently the signal from the flag boat was heard to report. We ran close up, and General Pope and Assistant Secretary of war, Colonel Scott, with other dignitaries, became visible on the afterguard of the "Perry." They wanted to know what the devil we were doing there. Told them, and inquired where Commodore Foote was to be found, and was told he had not changed his position since the Shingiss left him....

While rounding Florence Island and making for the Tennessee shore the mist lifted, so that the low black mass of the "Benton" was distinctly visible, Flag Officer's signal to "round to and report" was heard ... in a few moments we were on board the flag ship. Her iron-clad deck was scrupulously clean and order reigned above and below. The finest cambric handkerchief might sweep her gun-deck without being stained, and the crew grouped about cheerful without being noisy, and in point of cleanliness presentable in any society....

Invited to accompany a reconnaissance of the Confederate batteries downriver, "B" continued on a tug with Captain Henry C. Maynadier, chief of the mortar fleet, to observe the bombardment of the Confederate batteries at Fort Pillow:

For two days the big guns on both sides have been sullenly silent. The rebels only stir themselves when our folks wake them up, and this was one of the days appointed to pitch a few shells into their nest. The defenses are at the first Chickasaw bluffs, on the Tennessee shore. On all maps that I have seen it is called Fort Randolph, and Fort Pillow is placed below. [Fort Pillow sat on the first Chickasaw bluffs, Fort Randolph below at the mouth of the Hatchie River.] The river just above the bluff makes one of those abrupt bends so common on the Mississippi—the Arkansas shore running out like a promontory, the tall timber of which hides the bluff.... From the Tennessee shore, however, where the flag ship lays, the high land is to be seen, dotted with tents which the rebels have been moving since yesterday. The river narrows at the point; the bluff is bristling with cannon, so that a vessel rounding the point would run into their jaws....

Shortly after meridian Captain Myndlers [Maynadier] of the army, the chief of the mortar fleet, announced all ready. The tug boat came alongside and Cols. Fitch and McLean, Mr. Holloway and myself with the naval and military gentlemen immediately interested, stepped on board. The active little craft ran down by the mortar fleet, Captain Myndlers [Maynadier] giving his orders to the several mortars as she passed the boats, and then she headed for the opposite shore, the pilot having orders to place her directly opposite the bend. As she passed it (the bend) the bluffs lifted to view and when we reached the middle of the river the upper rebel battery was to be seen distinctly with the naked eye. The tug headed up stream and kept steady while the officers swept the hill with their glasses. Presently the signal was give to the first mortar boat to open fire. A volume of smoke rose slowly up, a heavy roar so loud that I have not language to describe it succeeded and this was followed by a rumbling as of distant thunder as the shell sped through the air. These immense shells do not scream or screech in their progress as lesser missiles do—they rumble and reverberate almost beating nature in their imitation of thunder. Every eye was strained to note the effect of the shot. Moments elapsed, the thunder rolling on and on, when a small white cloud was seen immediately above the cliff which sent back a sound like a twenty-four pounder. The shell had burst—the range was right. Another and another succeeded in rapid succession from the other boats, followed and mixing up the thunder in such confusion that earth and water seemed to quake. They all had range. The rebel gunboats below steamed up to get out of the way, for we could see the black smoke from their stacks getting blacker and swaying in large clouds above them. The reconnaissance was over—the fight was opened, and Capt. Myndlers [Maynadier] gave orders to run for the mortar boats. The rebel batteries were slow to respond, but when they did open they kept up the fire briskly and with their heaviest guns. Their shells mostly burst in the woods on the promontory and their solid shot went clear over the mortar boats. The boats were hid from their view by the timber and they aimed for the smoke of the guns as it rose above the trees. In half an hour the fight was hot and the constant roar of such heavy artillery was deafening. The rebels evidently have some fine guns in position and of heavy caliber. A one hundred and twenty pound shot struck with a few feet of the Carondolet, dashing the water over Mr. Fishback of the St. Louis *Democrat*, as he stood, one of the group on her deck. The sight was grand. The decks of all the vessels were crowded with spectators and the panorama of the broad bay with its infinite variety of craft and the many thousands witnesses was exceedingly beautiful, if such a word can be appropriately used amidst such a stormy cannonade. For two hours the mortar boats thundered and the rebels replied, when orders were given to throw our shell every fifteen minutes and keep it up at that.

The trip to the fleet paid well if only to witness the bombardment of a few hours which I have so feebly described. B.[4]

About a week later, the Mississippi River spilled over its banks, and the *Indianapolis Daily Journal*, quoting a dispatch of 1 May 1862 from Cairo to the *Chicago Tribune*, reported:

The packet Diligence, from Tiptonville, reports an alarming stage of water in the Mississippi. Hundreds of houses at Tiptonville and New Madrid are submerged and thousands of sheep, cattle, and hogs have been washed away. Everywhere along the river there is great suffering in consequence of the unprecedented flood.

The whole of Columbus [Kentucky], up to the foot of the fortification, is overflowed, the water running into the windows of houses.

III. Memphis (April–July 1862)

Hickman is also suffering greatly.

The fortifications of Island No. 10, and upon the mainland opposite, are still above the water, excepting the upper battery. A large amount of cannon and heavy ordnance stores captured from the rebels on the main shore, are still lying in the bayou, and cannot be removed until the water subsides.

Point Pleasant is entirely drowned out.[5]

On 21 April, "B" alerted the *State Sentinel* that the steam pumps at Cairo had broken down. "The foaming flood of river," he reported, "is even with the top of the levee," had flooded the town and its railroad supply lines in water "six inches to six feet" deep, and the ground on the Missouri side was flooded from Bird's Point "for miles back." Noting that the 47th Indiana was in the advance with Fitch's 46th and 43rd Indiana below Tiptonville, "B" opined that, although land forces could not operate in the flood, Fort Pillow would be taken as soon as the water subsides because "our Indiana boys ... can live like alligators if necessary."[6]

With Federal plans to take Fort Pillow stymied by the flood and their Army of the Mississippi comrades on the march with Halleck toward Corinth, Chaplain Sawyer, with a little time on his hands and apparently chomping at the bit lest there be a surrender before the 47th Indiana saw more action, railed against secessionists:

Letter from the Mississippi
Tiptonville, Tenn., May 3, 1862

Mr. Editor: The 47th Indiana regiment seems to be fixed here for the present, much against the wishes of most of us, as we prefer to share the honor of the great victories just before us. The rebellion, so wicked and causeless, throwing in the shade the black conspiracy of Cataline against which the thunders of Cicero were hurled, and surpassed only by the grand meeting of the "Dragon and his angels" against the hosts of the almighty, is becoming more effectually girdled and must soon be laid in its grave. Many of the secessionists around us acknowledge that they have failed in their purpose, and that things have turned out contrary to their wishes and hopes. They now concede that the Government is too strong for them, and unless the Federal forces are utterly routed at Corinth and Yorktown, they will be constrained to take the oath of allegiance to the old Government of their fathers, or choose some other land for their home. Some talk earnestly of removing to South America. Others say if the war should result in an entire sweeping of the State of Tennessee of the institution of slavery, they would cheerfully give up all the slaves they have, because the enhancing value of their lands in five years would amply repay them for the temporary loss.

Several changes have taken place recently in this regiment. Captain Dent, of company C, has resigned on account of his health, and Lieutenant Crabbs, of Decatur, taken his position. Sergeant Major Jennings has been appointed First Lieutenant of the same company. Lieutenants Williams and Emery, of company I, have resigned, and Messrs. John Martin and H. Lindsey, of Wabash county, take their places. Major Mickle has resigned on account of his health, and John A. McLaughlin, of company A, is now Major of the regiment, and Lieutenant Morehouse, of Indianapolis, is in command of company A.

The morning the Major left, the regiment assembled, and he addressed them a few parting words. His heart was full, so that his tongue could scarcely express, he said, the emotions he felt at the idea of leaving them. He thanked them all for their kindness to him in his official position, and for obedience to all his orders, and it was with deep regret that he was constrained by reason of his health to return home. He would gladly have gone with them to the end of the war, and his prayers should go up for their prosperity and success. His heart swelled with deep emotions, and his voice trembled as he bade them good-bye. Many eyes moistened as they took him by the hand and said farewell. A committee was appointed to prepare suitable resolutions respecting his leaving us, and the following were adopted:

[Excerpted in brief, the committee resolved that his] *urbane manner and kindly bearing ... had won the regard of all*; [that he was] *a faithful officer*; [that] *... he ... uniformly cheered and encouraged his men ...* [and was] *only leaving but for the precarious condition of his health.* [They therefore resolved to] *gratefully remember him for his kind offices ...* [and to] *follow him with the hope that his life may be spared ... and, that when* [they] *succeeded in crushing out this wicked rebellion ... he may be among the happy number to welcome back to Indiana the 47th Regiment of her Volunteers.*

Milton J. Robinson, Lieut. Col.
John A. McLaughlin, Major.
E.C. Hill, Capt., Co. K.
Samuel Sawyer, Chaplain.
Committee.

Yesterday evening our camp was agreeably surprised by two visitors from Huntington in the persons of Mrs. Slack and Mrs. Mills.—They left home the morning before, and made very good time. Since the boat *Diligent* has been chartered by Gen. Strong to bring us a daily mail we hear oftener from home, though the men complain that they do not receive as many letters as they have a right to expect.—We get a hundred daily papers in camp, receiving them one day after publication. Last night two dozen "Frank Leslie's Pictorial" for May 3rd made their appearance, and as Tiptonville was fully represented as it looked on the day of the surrender, there was quite a "rage" among the boys to get a copy. The supply could not satisfy the demand.

This afternoon we have had some rare sport leading the mules and horses captured from the rebels to be shipped to Cairo. Some of the boys thought we had some rare specimens of pull back, kicking, perverse mules, which might furnish a side illustration of the truth of total depravity. Col. Robinson, with his men, hugely enjoyed the sport of getting them on the boat, and he made a full hand.

The secessionists are very confident that the Federal army will be worsted by Beauregard at Corinth. They have no idea that their favorite General will leave Corinth without a battle. But time will determine.

Col. Slack has command of the District of New Madrid, comprising the three posts, New Madrid, Tiptonville and Island No. 10—His headquarters, by order of Gen. Pope, are at the latter place. The health of the regiment is good, though we have several very sick men. We have buried two since we came to Tiptonville. Aid-de-Camp Dellart has been furloughed for thirty days. He was hurt seriously by a fall from his horse, and he is quite unwell. He is much respected by the regiment. But I am writing at greater length than I designed and must close.

Yours very truly,
Samuel Sawyer, Chaplain 47th Reg. Ind. Vols.[7]

The flooding subsided on the Mississippi River and the Federal expedition to Fort Pillow got underway. The Federal gunboat fleet, now commanded by Flag Officer Charles H. Davis, waited until Quinby's land force could place shore batteries on the Arkansas shore to protect his gunboats. Starting on 19 May, Quinby's force of about 2,500 men, including eight companies of Slack's 47th Indiana, four companies of Cameron's 34th Indiana, two companies of the 54th Illinois, four companies of Hogg's 2nd Illinois Cavalry, a section from each two companies of the 2nd Illinois Artillery; three pieces of DeGolyer's Michigan battery, one-half of the Missouri company of Volunteer Sappers and Miners, and Fitch's brigade (the 43rd and 46th Indiana), moved to the Arkansas side, repairing the levee in preparation for building the shore batteries. Within range of the guns of Fort Pillow, Quinby's force was discovered when his pickets mistakenly shot and killed one of their own men who had ventured too far from camp and neglected to give the signal. Hearing the shots, the Confederates sent a small force across the river and drove in Quinby's pickets. On 22 May, having also heard that a small Confederate force was threatening the Federal posts upriver, Quinby withdrew his force to their various posts on the east bank of the river; Davis's gunboats and Ellet's ram fleet remained near Plum Point.[8]

The same day that Quinby's land force moved toward Fort Pillow, the *Liverpool (England) Post*, noting the recent Southern defeats and the "dark slave spot ... upon their cause," proclaimed the war to be virtually over:

> The civil war in America is virtually at an end. In a few days peace, in all probability, will be proclaimed; and then a rush of prosperity, of which the most sanguine have but a faint idea.
> We have never, from the first, denied the right of the South to revolt, if assured of two things—first, that it was competent to obtain independence, and next, that it would benefit by separation....
> We said a few weeks ago, that the secessionists had been used badly. Their apparent friends were their worst enemies. The British and French
> Governments encouraged them in the belief that at least their independence would be recognized.... The French Minister at Washington was an avowed advocate of secession; and if Lord Lyons did not agree with M. Mercier, the Southerners certainly believed that he did.
> Then the English press, with half a dozen exceptions, indulged in Southern "proclivities" ... and in consequence, the southern element in Liverpool had no difficulty in giving an early direction to public opinion in favor of the South. Naturally enough, the secessionists derived encouragement from all this, and fondly suffered themselves to be deceived. But the dark slave spot was upon their cause, and European governments dared not to face the popular indignation that was sure to be evoked by anything stronger than sympathy for the South.[9]

Lending some credence to the *Liverpool Post*'s opinion that the war was virtually over, on 28 May 1862 at Corinth, Beauregard ordered Brigadier General John B. Villepigue to abandon all forts above Memphis, and to burn all the cotton, sugar, and other goods in the vicinity of Memphis that they could not carry to Grenada, Mississippi, about ninety miles south on the Mississippi & Tennessee Railroad. Two days later, Beauregard, now nearly surrounded by Halleck's armies, retreated from Corinth to Tupelo, about fifty miles south on the Mobile & Ohio Railroad. At Corinth, Halleck reassigned U.S. Grant command of the Army of the Tennessee; Buell the Army of the Ohio; and Pope the Army of the Mississippi.[10]

Back on the Mississippi, while Flag Officer Davis of the Federal gunboat fleet and Colonel Charles Ellet of the recently arrived ram fleet argued over whether or not to run past the fort and attack the Confederate fleet, Villepigue abandoned both Forts Pillow and Randolph, and the Confederate force at Memphis abandoned the city. On reconnaissance the next morning (5 June), Fitch's brigade discovered that Fort Pillow had been abandoned.[11]

Describing not only the 47th Indiana's part in Quinby's land force, the Confederate threat to their upriver post at Tiptonville, and an earthquake, in his 7 June 1862 letter to the *Daily Journal*, Chaplain Sawyer also availed himself of the opportunity to preach against the evils of slavery:

> Ed. Journal: Just after my last communication eight companies of the 47th regiment, four companies of the 34th, under Col. Cameron, and some cavalry and artillery, all under command of Gen. Quinby, moved down the Mississippi to beleaguer Fort Pillow, with what success your readers have doubtless all heard. We may have excited the fears of the enemy, we may have revived the hopes of our friends at Memphis, we may have renewed our own courage and faith,

but beyond this little was achieved. We cut out a road and selected a point to plant a battery four miles below the fort, but the pickets of the enemy crowded upon us and endangered the safety of some of our men. A private of the 34th regiment was killed, and another wounded.—Lieut. Graham, of the 46th, received a bullet through the hips, and others narrowly escaped with their lives. By a proper and efficient co-operation of the fleet with the land forces it seemed to us that the rebels would have soon left the fortification in our possession, as they did those of Fort Thompson and Island No. 10. But Com. Davis thought the risk of life might be too great and as the surrender of the fort was a mere question of time we turned our transports up the river again and came back to our camps.

During our absence the guerilla bands had come unpleasantly near to Tiptonville, led on by a marauder named Caldwell from the direction of Trenton, Tenn. Had it not been for the depth of the lake [Reelfoot Lake] our whole camp and what equipage and stores we had might have been captured.

Immediately on his return Col. Slack set about strengthening his position. It was reported that some man from the Bend had used his pass to visit Corinth, and bring back, as was supposed, cavalry enough to retake the position. The enemy had approached within a few miles of us, and had already sounded the lake for the best crossing. A number of friends of the Union were alarmed, and brought us various information, urging us to be ready for any emergency.

A company of cavalry and a battery were soon landed here from up the river, and those of the citizens who love our cause and are praying for its success, are reassured again. The officers are drilling our men six hours a day, in skirmish, battalion and company drill, that the regiment may give a good account of itself should we be called to engage the enemy again. Col. Slack is an early riser, and before sun rise has his men under arms for the morning drill. Col. Robinson frequently accompanies the men in this exercise, and especially since the battle with the gunboats at Riddle's Point, he has been much respected and liked by the regiment. Major McLaughlin is performing the duties of his station to general acceptance, and he is counted, on all hands, an efficient officer.

Geo. Nichol, of Anderson, is acting Quartermaster again. This is agreeable to all of us, not that we had any complaints against Lieut. Brinkerhoff, but because we did not wish to lose Mr. Nichol from the regiment. He is so prompt and accommodating, so respectful and gentlemanly in his bearing, and of such business qualifications, that it would be difficult to find another so well fitted for the position.

The Sutlers, Slack and Jones, are holding on the even tenor of their way. They have a dry goods store just beyond the lines, which is quite an accommodation to the citizens.—Your old friend Peter McNaught is acting as chief merchant, and is quite a favorite with the natives. They admire his good humor, his keen wit, his exhaustless fund of anecdotes, and they enjoy an hour with him very much. Some of them even crowd around him on the Sabbath, and Mac complains that they interfere with his devotions. Anthony Slack[12] is managing the Sutler business within the lines, and is making things sprightly and agreeable. Mr. Jones is absent laying-in supplies, and it is hoped that he will bring the paymaster back with him. Our men are beginning to need money again, and they will be much disappointed if they do not soon receive it.

The boat dispatched by Gov. Morton to take away our sick men, called a few days since and we sent several soldiers who had been suffering from jaundice and camp fever, homeward, rejoicing. The Governor will always be gratefully remembered by the invalid soldier, and by his many friends.

Our mails have been coming to us irregularly for ten days, which is quite an annoyance and trial, but we are looking for an improvement in this particular. The Mail Agent is a very gentlemanly man, and takes great pleasure in trying to get fresh news from home. We get a hundred daily papers each day, from Chicago, St. Louis and Cincinnati, but the Indianapolis *Journal* seldom reaches us.

Corinth, we learn, is ours, and now we are rapidly nearing the hour when the navigation of the Mississippi will be uninterrupted, and the Federal forces march anywhere and everywhere with the stars and stripes, and in the name of the government, they can throw it to the breeze—

The monarch of all we survey,
Our right there are none to dispute.
From the center all round to the sea,
We are lords of the fowl and the brute.

A friend on my left suggests that if the fowl be omitted, the rest of the quotation will be very permitted.

The 47th regiment of Indiana volunteers has neither women or negroes within its lines. The officers and privates approve of the arrangement. The natives of Tennessee respect us a little more, perhaps, but hate us none the less, for our determination to avoid the negro question. We have occasional discussion in the camp, and now and then a man inquires why the negro is not suffered to rest, and why there is so much talk about him. The intelligent answer from all who have no sympathy with Abolitionism is, "No people, since time began, have ever suffered so much from oppressive legislative enactments — no other people, by law, has been so stripped of its natural and inalienable, God-given rights and this by a usurping power, and in plain violation of divine authority. Marriage has been abolished, adultery legalized, and the culture of the immortal mind by legislation absolutely prohibited among them. And as there is a holy and righteous God in heaven, the party, by the section or nation which commits itself to the defense of such atheistic principles, and such gigantic wrongs, will in the end reap the bitter fruit of its own folly, and by a retributive Providence be made to drink the cup of trembling and wo to its very dregs. But the Almighty has already begun to speak, and all will do well to heed his voice.

Yours very truly,
Samuel Sawyer,
Chaplain 47th Regiment Indiana Volunteers.

P.S. The camp has just been rocking with an earthquake. There was a deep, rumbling noise, and a trembling and shaking of the earth, lasting nearly thirty seconds, which greatly alarmed some of our men. Ground, trees, and houses all quivered as though Nature had a shake of the ague.[13]

On 6 June 1862 at Memphis, in the last great river battle of the war on the Mississippi, Davis's gunboats and Ellet's rams virtually destroyed the Confederate fleet as crowds watched from the bluffs during the morning battle, which lasted about two hours, the Hon. John Park, mayor of Memphis, surrendering the city at 11:00 A.M.[14] In their edition on that evening, the *Memphis Evening Argus* announced:

The hour of trial has come, and, perhaps, before another issue of this paper, Memphis will have passed from Confederate to abolition rule. The evacuation of Fort Pillow, announced yesterday, and the inability of our fleet to withstand the overwhelming numbers of the enemy's, as witnessed from the bluff early this morning, have virtually placed Memphis in the enemy's power....

...Let the demeanor of the people show to our boasting enemy, and the world, that Unionism is as dead and loathsome in Memphis as in New Orleans; that our people possess as much of that spirit which can never be conquered as the brave men and women of those cities; and that they *yield to brute force,* and to *nothing else.*

Stand firm! As certain as a just God exists, the day is not far distant when not only Memphis, but Tennessee and Virginia, will be freed from the presence of the invaders. Let the enemy enjoy *his* triumph now; *our* day of rejoicing will yet surely come.[15]

Arriving one week later from Tiptonville on board the steamer *J.D. Perry,* the 47th Indiana and Nolen's cavalry occupied Memphis.

Upon arrival, Slack, who had seniority, replaced Fitch in command of the troops there, immediately prohibited the circulation of Confederate Treasury notes, and required all residents to receive permits to pass the guard stations around the city. The *Indianapolis Daily*

Journal reported that the two pro-secession newspapers remaining in Memphis, the *Argus* and the *Avalanche*, objected. The *Avalanche*, lamenting Fitch's replacement, noted in particular their belief that the order would be "modified, as it conflicts with the expressed views of Col. Fitch in his interview with the bankers of the city." The correspondent for the *Indiana State Sentinel* noted, however, "Rebel sympathizers are beginning to wince under the vigorous policy of the new commandant."[16]

Describing the surrender and occupation of Memphis by the Federal forces, including an example of the effect of Slack's suppression of Confederate currency, and perhaps responding to the sentiments expressed earlier by the editor of the *Evening Argus*, on 18 June 1862, Chaplain Sawyer wrote the *Daily Journal*:

LETTER FROM MEMPHIS

The 47th at Memphis—Scenes at the Provost Marshall's Office—Post Office—Refugees—General Wallace.
Memphis, June 18, 1862.

Mr. Editor: The long agony is over, and the stars and stripes wave above the city of Memphis. She has long resisted the Federal power, and again and again threatened to burn her houses and her wealth to ashes, before the "vandal hordes of the North should pollute her sacred soil." But the presence of the gunboats and the Hoosier boys have brought her to better frame of mind. She still stands, beautiful yet, though half deserted. Colonel Fitch kept his command on the transports until Colonel Slack arrived. The 47th regiment left Tiptonville on the 12th, on board the *John D. Perry*, and Colonel Slack, with Major Sharp, on the morning of the 13th, selected a camping ground a mile and a half east of the river, and bright and early the men, by pontoons, to the tune of Yankee Doodle, with head erect and step steady, marched through the proud city of Memphis, bearing the national flag and our beautiful regimental colors thrown to the breeze. Thousands lined the streets to witness the scene—and then passed to their counting rooms and houses, to brood over their "humiliation," or to exult that the hour had come when they could breathe more freely and express that devotion to the Union which had been for a twelve month smothered, but not subdued. Two or three flags waved us welcome as we passed, and hundreds of citizens have come to the camp to greet us and to tell of the outrages to which they had been subjected during the reign of terror.

The leading secessionists were quite pleased with the executive ability and the course of policy displayed by Col. Fitch. As he was a Breckenridge man, they deemed him quite a gentleman. Others doubted the wisdom of his administration, fearing that it would weaken the confidence of the Union men here, and strengthen the hands of those who had done everything in their power to destroy the Government. These eulogies and complaints, however, though general, might have been hasty and somewhat captious.

Colonel Slack established his headquarter in the Planter's Bank building, on Main street. The Provost Marshal's office is on the first floor—the Colonel's home above. Without witnessing the scene for themselves, your readers can have a very imperfect idea of what transpires in and around the offices of the Provost Marshal, under the circumstances which surround us. Having been requested by Capt. Gould, the gentlemanly and efficient Marshal, to give what aid I could in expediting business, I send you a brief synopsis of some of the incidents connected therewith. On Saturday, we had but one entrance to the office, and the throng clamorous for passports was so great it was found necessary to employ more clerical force. Two men were detailed from the 47th regiment for that purpose, and a third subsequently joined them.

It is Monday morning—breakfast is over, and at least five hundred men and not a few women need passports. Headquarters are almost surrounded; guards with fixed bayonets can scarcely keep them back. Some have been waiting a week to get away from the city, are nearly out of money and must leave. Let us pass through the entrance on Main street; ascending a flight of steps, and turning to the right, we are in the Provost Marshal's office. Some citizen is talking to Capt. Gould about a pass to go to Mississippi to get rid of several thousand dollars of Confederate money. He is afraid to take the oath till he returns, lest he should be killed. The Captain tells him it is his misfortune to have so much of the bogus currency on hand, but he cannot get through our lines without taking the oath. He says he will study on it and steps out.

Here is a man who wishes to go a-fishing; another who wishes to cross the river; another wishes to go over into McNairy and Marshall to buy cattle; another who wishes to go after his sister, ten miles in the country. They have all been stopped by the pickets and have a repugnance to taking the oath. They are told there is no possibility of getting through our lines without takng the oath of allegiance. All but one came to terms and are sworn.—Here is a lady who wished to pass to St. Louis; another to Cairo. The passes are given, and they are gone. A gentleman appears and makes complaint that some citizens broke into his store last night; he knows the whereabouts of the burglars and wants help to secure them. A guard is detailed to arrest them and hold them subject to further orders. Some pickets have just come in with some prisoners—soldiers flying from Beauregard's army; others had come before. They are all called in and about fifty of them take the oath of allegiance and are passed to St. Louis. A man enters who has one hundred fifty bales of cotton, which he had buried out of sight of the Southern confederacy; he wishes to pass with cargo to Cincinnati. Another has twenty bales, another seven bales and thirty hogsheads of sugar, another ten hogsheads of sugar and fifty bales of cotton; they, also, wish passes with cargoes to Cairo. Here comes a man from Cincinnati asking authority to open out a quantity of goods for sale; another has brought and sold a lot, and wishes to return for more. Here is a man who lived in Memphis; he was a Union man; he had a $200 gold watch and a new piano taken from him, and he was constrained to leave. He came back, unexpected by the guilty parties, and found the piano and is on the track of the watch; he wishes a passport now to go up the river and to return with family. Men, too, who have been railroad hands and boat hands are out of employment and wish to leave the city to find labor at Cairo or Saint Louis by which to earn their daily bread.

But where shall I stop; Jews and gentiles of every hue and calling are pressing on and falling back, each imagining his a special case, demanding the immediate attention of the Provost Marshal.

Colonel Markland, Military Postmaster of Memphis, wished my services part of Monday, with one permanent clerk, detailed from the regiment. The first mail sent out was quite small, yet it went to twenty-one different States. Yesterday we sent out two full sacks of letters and in a few days this office will receive and distribute more letters than any other office in the Mississippi valley. Col. Markland is a native of Maysville, Ky., a pleasant and gentlemanly man, and eminently fitted to conduct the mail department at this post. He brought with him $15,000 worth of postage stamps. The way they are going off of his hands he will soon need more.

Major Sharp, an old railroad manager, has captured five locomotives and one new passenger car, and with a force from the 47th regiment, repaired some of the bridges which were broken down or burnt; in a week's time we hope the locomotive and the telegraph will bring us fresh news and the Northern papers daily.

Our pickets are bringing in prisoners almost every hour, some of them infantry and some of them cavalry. Yesterday Major General Lew Wallace, with several thousand of his command, reached Memphis. His old friends gave him a cordial welcome to the city. His men are encamped three-quarters of a mile from us; a part of them are to go down the river to land at some point below. The General looks well and is as frank and agreeable with his friends as ever. His men all look hearty and they have learned how to deal with rebels. They brought a citizen last night into the office of the Provost Marshal for talking "secession doctrine." Col. Robinson put him under guard till this morning when he gave him a lecture and let him go. The clerk of the Gayoso House was arrested yesterday for suffering a man to register C.S.A. after his name. Gen. Wallace had him placed under guard in his room. The effect will be wholesome.

There were four papers in Memphis—the *Bulletin*, *Avalanche*, *Argus* and *Appeal*. The first was against secession, the last was an advocate of rebellion, and the first to run away. The editor of the *Bulletin* is now associated with the *Avalanche* and gives that paper a semi-loyal aspect. The

Argus ought not to appear any more without a more thorough conversion, though it is modifying steadily. The *Appeal* office is still here, and Colonel Slack may take possession of it in the name of the Government.

There are thousands of Union people in Memphis and in a short time public sentiment in the city will be definitely and irresistibly developed in favor of the Constitution and the Union. The work goes bravely on. Let the friends of the Government be of good cheer, for we are drawing, each day, nearer to the end of the war. The rebel sympathizers talk differently and hope differently, but they are losing heart themselves.

A hundred items are crowding upon my pen for record, but I must bid them wait for further orders; meanwhile, I remain

Truly yours,
Samuel Sawyer
Chaplain 47th Indiana Regiment

P.S. — Some scalawag with a flag of truce came into town on Saturday, accompanied by a Chaplain. Lieutenant Davis stopped them, mounted their buggy, took the reins, and drove to headquarters. Colonel Slack read the communication, and, satisfied that it was an attempt to impose upon him ordered the Lieutenant to take them in the buggy and hurry them beyond our lines on the *double quick*.

The 34th and 43rd Indiana are encamped by our side. Colonel Ryan is at New Madrid, troubled by some serious charges which have been forwarded against him. What will be the result of the judicial investigation none of us can tell. It is to be hoped for the honor of the army that it may be favorable.

We have about the most suitable house in Memphis for a hospital — called the Overton House. It is said to contain over two hundred rooms. The 43rd has one hundred sick there, the 46th has forty, and the 47th has four.

The Sanitary condition of our regiment is excellent. Dr. Dickson is Post Surgeon. He reports that we have not a man in the 47th who could not shoulder his rifle and take part in battle.
S.S.[17]

The editors of the staunchly pro-Confederate *Memphis Daily Appeal* did, indeed, flee southward to Grenada, Mississippi, announcing tersely to their readers: "The occupation of Memphis by the Federal forces has convinced us of the necessity of removing our office of publication to Grenada, Mississippi." Unlike the other prewar Memphis papers, they continued to publish independently as a pro-Confederate newspaper. Forced out of Grenada at the end of November 1862, editors Benjamin F. Dill and John R. McClanahan and a small staff of printers and reporters continued to publish, moving ahead of Sherman's army to Jackson, then Meridian, Mississippi, and on to Montgomery, Alabama.[18]

On 12 April 1865, James H. Wilson's Federal cavalry captured Montgomery and forced Dill, McClanahan and company to pull up stakes for the last time, their publication odyssey finally ending when troopers from Col. John H. Noble's 3rd Iowa Cavalry detained them at Columbus, Georgia. Having chased the intrepid newspapermen across the South, Noble proudly announced with grudging admiration that his 3rd Iowa troopers had finally captured the "defiant rebel sheet" in the basement of the Perry House. Then, as part of Wilson's final orgy of destruction, Noble ordered his troopers to destroy the remaining equipment.[19]

With nothing left (even the Appeal Building had been sold out from under them), Dill and McClanahan returned to Memphis to resume publication. Although McClanahan died tragically in a fall from a window at the Gayoso Hotel in Memphis in July and did not live to see it, by November, Dill, through the largesse of friends and admirers, resumed publication of the *Daily Appeal* in Memphis, the paper having long since earned the sobriquet "Bible of the Confederacy." Due largely to his travail during the last few years of the war, Dill fell ill and died several months later, his wife and a new editor continuing his and McClanahan's work.[20]

Back in Memphis, Slack took control of the *Daily Appeal*'s office on Union Street and quickly used the facility to publish a pro-Union newspaper controlled by the military, putting Pvt. Joseph K. Davisson of the 24th Indiana Infantry, a soldier with some newspaper experience, and Chaplain Sawyer of the 47th Indiana in charge. First dubbed the *Union Reveille*, they quickly, in a thinly veiled attempt to co-opt the *Daily Appeal*'s readers, renamed it the *Union Appeal*.[21]

Following the surrender of Memphis and the withdrawal of Confederate forces southward to Grenada and Tupelo, Mississippi, accompanied by hundreds of civilian refugees from Memphis, Halleck ordered Buell to move his Army of the Ohio into eastern Tennessee and to repair the tracks of the Memphis & Charleston Railroad as they marched.[22]

About a week later, on 17 June 1862, Brigadier General Isaac Quinby, commanding the District of the Mississippi from Columbus, Kentucky, wrote to Slack in Memphis that he understood the problems Slack was having in garrisoning the city without a sufficient force, given all the "rebel sympathizers" in the city and the threat of Forrest's Confederate cavalry. On 18 June 1862, Brigadier General Lew Wallace, who had arrived with an infantry division, wrote that a heavy body of Confederate troops under Forrest and Jackson were marching from Holly Springs, Mississippi, and other points toward Memphis, either to attack his division at the railroad depot, or to attack and burn the city, and that Slack had no means to stop it. The attack on Memphis, however, never materialized.[23]

That same day (17 June), a flotilla of Federal gunboats (the ironclads *Lexington*, *Mound City*, *St. Louis*, and *Conestoga*, and the tug *Tiger* carrying a 24-pounder howitzer)[24] accompanied by Fitch's brigade (the 43rd and 46th Indiana) on three transports, set out in pursuit of the few remaining Confederate gunboats. Moving up the White River, the Federal flotilla was forced to halt near St. Charles, Arkansas, when the *Mound City* encountered the gunboat *Maurepas* and two transports scuttled in the river to obstruct passage and a small Confederate blockading force on a bluff overlooking the river. A heavy battery of two 32-pounders taken from the CSS *Pontchartrain* and manned by some of its sailors controlled the river from atop the bluff. In addition, a light battery of three rifled 8-pounder Parrotts and a 12-pounder howitzer taken from and manned by some sailors from the scuttled *Maurepas* was positioned four hundred feet below, along with thirty-five sharpshooters in position along the bluff.[25]

That morning, after Fitch's troops landed and the gunboats drove the Confederate sharpshooters back up the bluff, the Confederate land batteries opened on the flotilla. After an exchange of fire at about 10:30 A.M., shortly after the *Mound City* had moved forward close under the heavy battery, a 32-pounder shell penetrated its port casemate and exploded the steam chest, killing eight sailors at the port gun; only fifty sailors from the 175-man crew survived the scalding steam, and only twenty-five of them were uninjured. One hundred twenty-five were killed, eighty-two in the casemate from wounds or scalding, and forty-three killed in the water either by drowning or by being shot by Confederate sharpshooters. Fitch's 46th Indiana moved up and took out the Confederate batteries while those from the small Confederate force who could, escaped.[26]

Describing the explosion on the *Mound City*, as well as life in occupied Memphis, John Hardesty, a soldier in the 34th Indiana, wrote the *Daily Journal*:

> ### LETTER FROM MEMPHIS
> ### OUR TROOPS THERE—APPEARANCE OF THE CITY—
> ### *DEFACING JACKSON'S MONUMENT BY THE REBELS.*
> ### MEMPHIS, TENN., JUNE 21ST, 1862
>
> Dear Journal: Occupying Memphis is rather a pleasant job, just now. General Lew Wallace is here, and it is supposed will assume the command of all the forces here and below, on the river. The 34th, 24th, 47th and 43rd Indiana regiments are here, and the 46th Indiana is at St. Charles, about sixty miles up White River, where offensive operations are going on successfully against the rebels.
>
> The only remaining rebel gunboat, after the fight in front of Memphis, sought refuge at a bluff near St. Charles, on White River. It is said that they transferred the guns, six in number, from the boat to the shore, and sunk the boat, and when our boat came steaming along in pursuit, the land battery opened on them, striking the *Mound City* in the steam-chest and heater, the shot lodging in the pantry on the starboard side, killing outright and scalding a large number. Many of the men leaped into the water, but were shot by the enemy's sharpshooters. Col. Fitch's regiment of infantry immediately landed and took the battery at the point of the bayonet. None of his men were killed, and but seven wounded.
>
> Memphis is almost a deserted city. Fifteen thousand will cover the entire number of citizens in the place. The large and magnificent residences that grace the outer edges of town are left standing without an occupant, thus showing that it is the aristocratic and wealthy who have gone to "parts unknown." Almost everywhere your eye will see placards posted up, bearing the inscription, "to rent," "to sell," and "to lease." Property sells very low, with more sellers than buyers
>
> Last evening I took a stroll through the city, and among other places went to see Jackson's monument. It is a beautiful piece of marble, bearing on each side an appropriate motto — on the north side being the immortal words of the old hero: "The Federal Union — it must be preserved." The word "Federal" has been effaced. A Col. Brant, of Price's army, took a chisel and cut the word out. Such a miscreant and god-forsaking *rebel* should be hung higher than Haman.
>
> Capt. J.H. Gould, of the 46th Indiana, is Provost Marshal of this city, and does up the business of his office with commendable alacrity. I will write again in a few days.
>
> Yours, etc. John Hardesty, 34th Indiana Regiment[27]

A week later (23 June), following more guerrilla attacks on his troops and gunboats from the woods across from St. Charles, Fitch issued a proclamation to citizens of Monroe County, Arkansas, that, in retaliation, all personal property of those caught in guerrilla activity would be seized and destroyed.[28]

Upon learning of Fitch's proclamation, Brigadier General T.C. Hindman, commanding the Confederate District of Arkansas, responded to Fitch that the partisans in Monroe County had been authorized by him to form companies of volunteer citizens not within the age of conscription, from ages ten to eighty, to "cut off Federal pickets, scouts, foraging parties, and trains, and to kill pilots and others on gunboats and transports." They were to be paid as Confederate soldiers by the Confederate government and were therefore in the Confederate service. If Fitch carried out his threat, Hindman warned that he would retaliate man for man against any Federal officer or soldier in his custody.[29]

Fitch replied that Hindman's orders were uncivilized; that they would lead to "rapine and murder"; that this policy had led Hindman's men at St. Charles to shoot at scalded sailors of the *Mound City* who were helpless in the water (whereas Federal sailors had helped rescue Confederate sailors in the water at Memphis); and that Hindman's "captains of ten" (referring to the size of the companies he had authorized) would "soon become little else than highway banditti."[30]

Shortly after Fitch's proclamation, the *Indianapolis Daily Journal* erroneously noted in an editorial that Fitch had "hung two citizens of Arkansas, promptly, and publicly, because the guerrillas murdered one of his soldiers," adding, "Good for Colonel Fitch."[31] Elaborating on the story two days later, and making their approbation all the worse, the *Daily Journal* added:

> Colonel Fitch had captured seven of the prominent residents of St. Charles, and held them as hostages for the good behavior of the guerilla bands known to be on the river banks. They had been paraded on the decks of the Federal transports dressed in Federal uniforms. Gunfire on the transports from the river banks stopped until someone fired on the Lexington, killing the first engineer. Fitch immediately selected two of the most rabid rebels of the seven [civilian] hostages and hung them by the neck until dead, in sight of the Arkansas shore, and undoubtedly in view of their own neighbors and friends.[32]

The *Daily Journal's* erroneous report helped fuel a firestorm of controversy that had already erupted over the alleged murder of civilians and captured Confederate officers by Federal military.[33]

In addition to the correspondence between Fitch and Hindman, in August, the Federal commander at Baton Rouge, Colonel H.E. Paine, responding to Confederate General John C. Breckenridge's complaint about Federal forces burning and destroying private property, also brought up the *Mound City* incident, reminding Breckenridge that "while we saved your drowning men at Memphis, you shot ours on the White River."[34]

In fact, much more correspondence passed between Federal and Confederate officials regarding the treatment of civilians in Arkansas. Indeed, as late as October 1862, officials on both sides were exchanging accusations — the Confederate officials in the District of Arkansas justifying the use of any means possible, including guerrilla warfare, to fight the invaders; the Federals countering that the Confederates were making a civil war in Arkansas more desperate by arming civilians, adding that they would seize and destroy the property of anyone caught aiding or participating in guerrilla activity. None of this correspondence mentioned any executions of hostages having taken place there.[35]

In a letter to Halleck dated 22 August 1862, Fitch, who resigned his commission shortly thereafter, denied the *Daily Journal's* story and appears to have put to rest Confederate concerns about the execution of hostages in Monroe County, Arkansas:

> Sir: To-day for the first time a letter from General Lee, C.S. Army, dated near Richmond, 2nd instant, fell under my observation charging Brigadier General G.N. Fitch with having murdered in cold blood two peaceful citizens. I have no claim to the title, being plain colonel, but am doubtless the officer alluded to. Some journal lauded me during the late White River Expedition for the alleged hanging of two hostages. General Lee censures me for the same supposed act.
>
> The praise and censure are alike underserved and the charge in both cases without the shadow of foundation in fact. However many of them may have deserved different treatment not a man was killed by the troops under my command except in fair action.
>
> I am, very respectfully, your obedient servant,
> G.N. Fitch, Colonel Forty-sixth Indiana Volunteers.
> Commanding Brigade and late White River Expedition.[36]

Back at Memphis, Union rule also occasionally flared into violence. In a letter to Ann, Slack, who described the city as "a hotbed of treason,"[37] noted: "This city is filled with a terrible set of robbers and cut throats. Men are knocked down & robbed without any notice, but they are now becoming more shy. Are afraid of our soldiers."[38] With good reason, it appears. Pvt. John B. Ridgley of Co. B, 47th Indiana, for example, was court-martialed for the murder of a Memphis citizen named "Bully" Fagan. Fagan, apparently living up to his nickname, reportedly provoked a quarrel with Pvt. Ridgley, and Ridgley responded by shooting and killing him. The court-martial ruled that Ridgley's actions were justifiable and acquitted him on both murder and manslaughter charges.[39]

Meanwhile, U.S. Grant, commander of the District of West Tennessee, arrived at Memphis on 23 June and the next day granted Brigadier General Lew Wallace a leave of absence, replacing him with Brigadier General Alvin P. Hovey of Indiana. Brigadier General John A. McClernand was named commander of all forces south of Union City to the Memphis & Charleston Railroad line, and Slack's 47th Indiana, along with the 34th and 43rd Indiana, camped east of town, were assigned to garrison the city. All other troops were ordered to camp along the railroad line that ran southward to Grenada, Mississippi. A week later, in a move to supply and reinforce Samuel Curtis's Army of the Southwest, Grant ordered all troops in the Memphis area except Slack's brigade to move with Fitch's brigade and flotilla, already on the White River in Arkansas.[40]

The action shifted quickly to Kentucky as Confederate Colonel John Hunt Morgan of the 2nd Kentucky Cavalry began his first raid into that state. Starting from Knoxville, Morgan's cavalry defeated some Federal cavalry at Burksville, Kentucky, and successfully raided Tompkinsville, Glasgow, and Cave City. In Tennessee, Confederate cavalry under Brigadier General Nathan Bedford Forrest captured the garrison at Murfreesboro.[41] Back in Indiana, the *Daily Journal*'s editor, having earlier in the week warned that a "secret treasonable organization" was operating in the state, reacted to Morgan's Kentucky raid by warning its readers on 15 July 1862: To Arms!! To Arms!! Nashville Threatened! The Indiana Line in Danger. Morgan Advancing to the Ohio.[42]

The next day, the nervous editor, wondering how Morgan and Forrest were able to successfully raid Middle Tennessee and northern Kentucky — and wondering what Don Carlos Buell's 40,000-man Army of the Ohio was doing in Tennessee — asked: "Where is General Buell?" Knowing full well that Buell's army had been ordered into southeastern Tennessee and had left Kentucky and northern Tennessee open for Morgan's Kentucky and Forrest's Middle Tennessee lightning raids, he opined that for all the good he is doing us, "he might as well be in Brazil."[43]

Roaming freely in northern Kentucky, on 18 July Morgan sent a detachment across the river at Newberg, Indiana. After capturing some arms and supplies and creating a little havoc that night, Morgan's raiders returned to the Kentucky shore. The next day, headlines in the *Daily Journal* blared: Indiana Invaded. Newburg Taken. Evansville Threatened. Rebels in Possession of Henderson, Ky. Up Hoosiers and Defend Your Homes.[44]

That same day, U.S. Grant assumed command of all the troops in the Armies of the Tennessee, the Mississippi, the District of the Mississippi, and Cairo; two days later (20 July), Grant put William T. Sherman in command at Memphis; and, four days later, on 25 July 1862, Sherman ordered Slack to move his 47th Indiana, now part of Hovey's division, from Memphis to Helena, Arkansas, to report to Curtis and his Army of the Southwest.[45]

On 24 July, only days after taking command in Memphis, Sherman, disturbed by an article Chaplain Sawyer had written in a recent edition of the *Union Appeal* titled "City Council — General Sherman and Colonel Slack," replied with a blistering letter warning Sawyer to stop writing about "personalities" in the newspaper.

HEADQUARTERS, MEMPHIS, JULY 24, 1862

Samuel Sawyer, Esq., Editor *Union Appeal*, Memphis

Dear Sir: It is well I should come to an understanding at once with the press as well as the people of Memphis, which I am ordered to command; which means, to control for the interest, welfare, and glory of the *whole* Government of the United States.

Personalities in a newspaper are wrong and criminal. Thus, though you meant to be complimentary in your sketch of my career, you make more than a dozen mistakes of fact, which I need not correct, as I don't desire my biography to be written until I am dead. It is enough for the world to know that I live and am a soldier, bound to obey the orders of my superiors, the laws of my country, and to venerate its Constitution; and that, when discretion is given me, I shall exercise it wisely and account to my superiors.

I regard your article headed "City Council — General Sherman and Colonel Slack," as highly indiscreet. Of course, no person who can jeopardize the safety of Memphis can remain here, much less exercise public authority; but I must take time, and be satisfied that injustice be not done.

If the parties named be the men you describe, the fact should not be published, to put them on their guard and thus to encourage their escape. The evidence should be carefully collected, authenticated, and then placed in my hands. But your statement of facts is entirely qualified, in my mind, and loses its force by your negligence of the very simple facts within your reach as to myself: I had been in the army six years in 1846; am not related by blood to any member of Lucas, Turner & Co.; was associated with them in business six years (instead of two); am not colonel of the Fifteenth Infantry, but of the thirteenth. Your correction, this morning, of the acknowledged error as to General Denver and others, is still erroneous. General Morgan L. Smith did not belong to my command at the battle of Shiloh at all, but he was transferred to my division just before reaching Corinth. I mention these facts in kindness, to show you how wrong it is to speak of persons.

I will attend to the judge, mayor, Boards of Aldermen, and policemen, all in good time.

Use your influence to reestablish system, order, government. You may rest easy that no military commander is going to neglect internal safety, or to guard against external danger; but to do right requires time, and more patience than I usually possess. If I find the press of Memphis actuated by high principle and a sole devotion to their country, I will be their best friend; but, if I find them personal, abusive, dealing in innuendoes and hints at a blind venture, and looking to their own selfish aggrandizement and fame, then they had better look out; for I regard such persons as greater enemies to their country and to mankind than the men who, from a mistaken sense of State pride, have taken up muskets, and fight us about as hard as we care about. In haste, but in kindness, yours, etc.

W.T. Sherman, *Major-General*[46]

Chaplain Sawyer's stint as editor of the *Union Appeal* ended abruptly about a month later when Sherman, acting on a complaint from Curtis that a letter written anonymously by the Rev. Charles Fitch, chaplain of the 24th Indiana, and published by Sawyer in the 22 August 1862 edition of the *Union Appeal*, accused Osterhaus's "barbarian" forces, then under Curtis's command, of wanton destruction of property in Clarendon, Arkansas. Sherman, responding to Curtis's complaint, had Sawyer, as publisher, arrested and charged with "uttering that which is false and libelous." His bail set at $1,000, he was ordered "to appear and answer whenever duly notified of formal charges against him." Truth being the ultimate test in libel cases, at least in civilian courts, not to mention Sawyer's political connections as an ardent Republican abolitionist, which would have been useful in his appearance before a military tribunal, no formal charge was ever filed against him, although his tenure ended as editor/publisher of the *Union Appeal*. Leaving the newspaper business, Sawyer resumed his role as chaplain of the 47th Indiana at Helena, Arkansas.[47]

IV

Helena, Arkansas (August–December 1862)

Back in Indiana, with Morgan's raiders back across the Ohio River, life returned to normal, albeit with greater concern for security along the Ohio River and the loyalty of antiwar Democrats in the Ohio River counties. Governor Morton, making some political hay out of the raid in this election year, charged that a secret organization, the Knights of the Golden Circle, was being organized in Indiana and all of the "North-West" in order to, among other things, resist the collection of the war tax recently increased by Congress, discourage enlistment, and overthrow the Lincoln government. Morton targeted one of his key Democratic political opponents, former congressman, unsuccessful Democratic candidate for governor in 1860, and then Peace Democrat candidate for the United States Senate, Thomas A. Hendricks, with trying to foment secession of the "North-West" states from the eastern seaboard in order to form a union with the South.[1]

An astute politician, Oliver P. Morton had become governor of Indiana in 1861 in a political deal with Henry Smith Lane. Both Lane and Morton were influential members and founding fathers of the Republican Party; both, however, had gubernatorial aspirations in 1860 with roughly equal claims to the party's nomination. Republican Party politicos worked out the impasse with a deal contingent on Republicans winning control of the state legislature. Believing Lane would bring the Old Line Whigs into the party, the party bosses convinced a reluctant Morton to run for lieutenant governor and let Lane head the ticket. In the deal, if Lane and Morton were elected and the Republicans won control of the state legislature, Lane would be given the U.S. Senate seat vacated by Graham N. Fitch (who had resigned to accept a commission as colonel in the U.S. Volunteer Infantry), and Morton would then become governor. The deal worked. Fitch, as already noted, led the 46th Indiana Infantry in a short and somewhat tumultuous military career until his resignation in September 1862; Lane became U.S. Senator from Indiana, serving until his term ended in 1867; and Morton became governor. In spite of Morton's, and the *Daily Journal*'s, best efforts, Thomas A. Hendricks would be elected to the United States Senate as a Democrat from Indiana in the upcoming November elections and serve from 4 March 1863 to 3 March 1869.[2]

The tide of war began to shift as Major General Braxton Bragg took command of the Confederate Army of Mississippi from the ailing P.G.T. Beauregard. After their disastrous defeats at Shiloh and Corinth, Bragg, resuming the Confederate offensive, boldly planned to take the war back to Kentucky. Near the end of July, he began an unprecedented 800-mile flanking movement around Buell's Army of the Ohio, then in the vicinity of Murfreesboro, Tennessee, by moving his troops rapidly by rail from Tupelo, Mississippi, to Chattanooga, Tennessee, via Mobile and Atlanta. From Chattanooga, he would bypass Buell and march his army into Kentucky to reclaim the state for the Confederacy.[3]

Trouble also erupted back on the Mississippi River on 5 August 1862 when a Confederate force at Baton Rouge, Louisiana, led by Major General John C. Breckenridge, defeated a Federal force under Brigadier General Thomas Williams and reopened the river for the Confederates from Baton Rouge to Helena, Arkansas.

Back in Arkansas, the water level rose on the White River; and, on 4 August 1862, A.P. Hovey led another expedition up the White River to Clarendon, Arkansas. By mid–August, Hovey's expedition had pushed the remaining Confederate troops back to Little Rock, where Thomas Hindman had his Confederate District of Arkansas headquarters.[4]

Although assigned to Hovey's division, the 47th Indiana remained at Helena following their arrival from Memphis, and Slack took a leave of absence to visit his family in Huntington. Shortly after the 47th Indiana arrived at Helena, a squad of forty-five soldiers from Company A and a small contingent of cavalry were sent across the Mississippi River to guard confiscated cotton at a place known as Brown's Plantation, Mississippi. While there, on the night of 11 August 1862, one of their guard posts was surprised and attacked by Confederate raiders.[5]

Of the action at Brown's Plantation, Mississippi, the 20 August 1862 *Indianapolis Daily Journal* announced:

Massacre of Indianians in Mississippi.

The Memphis *Union* gives the following account of the surprise and massacre of a company of Indiana men in Mississippi the other day.

Lieutenant Morehouse [Hiram Moorhous], company A, 47th Indiana, had been sent out with a squad of nineteen men to guard cotton, twelve miles from Helena, in Mississippi, and was surprised by guerrillas. He had cavalry for pickets, to give warning of approaching danger, and, feeling secure, the 47th boys laid down upon the bales and fell asleep. While sleeping, the guerrillas, in force sufficient to capture them, came noiselessly upon them and fired. Elijah Thrailkill and Isaac Johnson were instantly killed; John W. Higgins and Thomas Rowney mortally wounded. Smith Johnson received two balls in his leg, Allen Miller was wounded in the arm, Michael Hodgson was shot in the neck, Isaac Hodgson was also wounded, Smith Ralston was hit by bullets in the thigh and shoulder blade, Saml. Tate was wounded in the thigh, John Thomas and Jonas Ingle were also slightly wounded.—Charles Morgan was taken prisoner. Lieut. Morehouse was slightly wounded, captured, and carried off by the murderers. Only six escaped unhurt. From their account but one rebel was shot. Company A was recruited by Major Jno. A. McLaughlin.

A few weeks later, the *Daily Journal* published Captain Albert Moorhous's account of that action:

Skirmish Near Helena, Ark.

Ed. Journal: Having a chance to send this communication by a friend, I wish to correct a false statement in regard to a skirmish that occurred on the night of the 11th of August, ten miles south-east of Helena, in the State of Mississippi, while guarding some cotton, between my company and a band of cotton burners. I was sent with my company of 45 men, two miles from the main camp, and having followed a brainless negro around for a guide until 9 o'clock at night, we finally got to the cotton where it was piled up in the woods; three hundred yards further was the cotton gin to guard, and another pile of cotton, making three posts to guard with 45 infantry and 13 cavalry. I left 12 cavalry and 21 infantry at the first post, under command of a lieutenant, and divided the remaining force at the other posts, the men all sleeping with their cartridge boxes on and guns by their sides. The cavalry took their turn on picket duty; the infantry coming off and cavalry going on at 3 o'clock in the morning. In three-quarters of an hour after changing guard at the post where the lieutenant had command, the enemy came over two of the posts where the cavalry was posted. They gave no alarm, and are supposed to have been asleep. Advancing until within twenty feet of our men they fired one gun to alarm them, and as the men rose to their feet they gave them a terrible fire from double barrel shot-guns, loaded with rifle bullets, nine in each barrel, killing and wounding sixteen men in three minutes. I called the other two parties together of only twenty-four men, and hurried to their rescue. I was there in five minutes from the firing of the first gun. The enemy saw us coming prepared to fight, and commenced running. We had to let them run some distance for fear of killing our own men when we gave them a volley; but being dark, and the men fearful of killing their comrades, did not do much damage. They carried off five prisoners in their flight. Whether they were wounded or not cannot be known. The whole affair was over in ten minutes.

I tried to send the account to you for publication as soon as it was over, and have failed to get a letter through to Indianapolis for friends or anybody else. There is some worthless postmasters somewhere on the route.

Capt. A. Moorhous, Co. A, 47th Regt. Ind. Vols.[6]

Following the action at Brown's Plantation, Private Evan Phillips of Company A filed charges against 2nd Lieutenant Hiram Moorhous (the lieutenant referred to by Captain Albert Moorhous in his article in the *Daily Journal*) for "neglect of duty to the prejudice of good order and military discipline" for the part he played there. Although Private Phillips gave a detailed specification of the charge against Lieutenant Moorhous, the military court rejected it as "improper" simply because it had been "preferred by a private directly against an officer."[7]

Back in Kentucky, Federal control, which had been considered secure following Albert Sidney Johnston's withdrawal earlier in the year, suddenly began to weaken. On 14 August 1862, Confederate Brigadier General E. Kirby Smith, reinforced with some troops from Bragg's army at Chattanooga (now known as the Army of Tennessee), marched around the Federal garrison at Cumberland Gap and into Kentucky. Two weeks later, Bragg began marching his army north from Chattanooga, feinting toward Nashville in hopes of delaying Buell there. Federal control began to unravel at the end of August when E. Kirby Smith's Confederates routed a Federal force led by "Bull" Nelson, sending Nelson "howling back to Louisville with a bullet in his leg." (Following the battle, Nelson would blame Indiana Brigadier General Mahlon D. Manson, as well as Manson's green Indiana troops, for the disaster.)[8]

In Indiana, the *Daily Journal* noted that the situation in Kentucky was becoming desperate as Bragg's and Smith's Confederate forces converged on the state. Referring to Smith's force, the *Daily Journal*'s headline warned: "Kentucky News! Lexington Occupied Tuesday! Six o'clock Tuesday rebels occupied Lexington 6,000 strong." The next day their headlines blared: "Great Excitement in Cincinnati! The Rebels at Paris, Ky," as they warned their readers that the Confederates could advance on Louisville or Cincinnati, and that "Citizens [of Cincinnati] were being armed and hurried across the river."[9]

Smith's army continued to Frankfort, forcing the state legislature to "adjourn" to Louisville, while Bragg's army entered the state in a race with Buell to reach that city. Headlines in the *Daily Journal*, whose editor considered both Don Carlos Buell and "Bull" Nelson to be incompetent, reported the capture of "over 5,000 Indiana troops" at Munfordville and warned their readers: "Bragg nearing Louisville! Women and children ordered to leave. Gen. Nelson in command!! An attack expected!!"[10]

Three days later, the *Daily Journal* reported that Nelson had suspended Indiana General Jeff C. Davis, angrily protesting "another Indiana general was suspended for nothing" and that it was "pretty nearly time this sort of thing was ended." To make matters worse, the next day the *Daily Journal* reported that the "rebels" had seized Suit's Salt River Distillery near Louisville. The reporter noted with relief, however, that "most of the stock had been removed to Louisville."[11]

Although Buell beat Bragg to Louisville, the Federal command there was in disarray, delaying an offensive against Bragg and Smith. Not only were orders awaiting Buell in Louisville for his replacement as commander of the Army of the Ohio, but, following an argument on the morning of 29 September at the Galt House Hotel in Louisville, Davis shot and killed "Bull" Nelson. The *Daily Journal* editorialized that the shooting was justifiable, "provoked by Nelson's unbearable insolence." The editors hoped the army would not prosecute Davis — and they did not.[12]

The Confederates under Bragg and Smith made a few missteps, too. Bragg's delay to capture the Federal garrison at Munfordville on 17 September, not to mention Smith's failure to join him for an attack on Louisville, enabled Buell to arrive in Louisville in time to protect the city. Bragg then turned northeastward toward Lexington to unite with Smith.

In spite of the command problems, including Nelson's death and his own near removal from command, Buell moved his army eastward in pursuit of Bragg and Smith; on 4 October 1862, in a diversionary move, two divisions from Alexander McCook's corps disrupted the inauguration of Richard Hawes as the short-lived Confederate governor at Frankfort. Four days later, the rest of McCook's corps, primarily in search of water in drought-stricken central Kentucky, encountered Bragg's main force, led by the "fighting bishop" Leonidas Polk, near the town of Perryville. In a near disaster for the Federals, Bragg's Army of Tennessee drove McCook's corps off the field of battle, McCook's troops holding on only enough to save their supply train and give Buell and his other two corps, out of position on the first day, time to move up and unite with his badly beaten corps.

Bragg, having won the field of battle but aware that he was greatly outnumbered, pulled back to a better defensive position at Harrodsburg. When Buell did not pursue, Bragg and Smith, having failed to find much support for their cause or recruit many troops in Kentucky, retreated into East Tennessee. Governor Morton, however, wrote to President Lincoln that Bragg's bloody incursion into Kentucky had created "distrust and despair" in the Northwest and urged speedy and decisive action.[13]

Recently returned from his leave, Slack had also become depressed by the recent Confederate successes in Kentucky and on the eastern front, where Robert E. Lee had moved his Army of Northern Virginia northward across the Potomac and into Maryland. In a letter to his wife, Slack, who felt the war should have been over by now, asserted that the campaigns in the East were being conducted stupidly, even treasonably, by some of the commanding officers.[14]

A few days later, Slack wrote Ann again, this time about a proposed expedition down the Mississippi to the mouth of the Yazoo River and candidly expressed his negative opinion of West Point Academy ("a little petty contemptible aristocracy which is entirely inconsistent with the genious and spirit of the institutions of our country"), as well as West Point graduates, especially all those in the Confederate Army. "All the prominent officers in the South are graduates of West Point. West Point is the basis of this rebellion, and I shall never cease my clamor against that institution until it is wiped out of existence."[15]

Due to the crowded, unsanitary conditions at Helena, disease began to take a toll in the army, the *Daily Journal* reporting, "nearly 2,000 had died since Gen. Curtis's army reached Helena." Regretfully, the *Huntington Democrat* announced that one of their correspondents, Sergeant Philip D. Caverly, Co. F, 47th Indiana, was one of the soldiers who had succumbed to "camp fever" there on 13 September 1862. In memoriam, the *Democrat* wrote: "We regret to announce the death of Philip D. Caverly, a member of Captain Shearer's company, in the 47th regiment. He was a brave soldier and a whole-souled, sociable comrade. He died of a camp fever. Peace to his manes."[16] At about this time, Slack replaced Brigadier General Cadwallader C. Washburn as commander of the post at Helena due to Washburn's ill health.[17]

Discussing, among other things, the boredom of camp life, illness among the troops, and a particular "blackamoor quack" from Lagro, Indiana, who was in camp exploiting the sick soldiers, Joseph Z. Scott of the 46th Indiana wrote the *Huntington Democrat*:

ARMY CORRESPONDENCE
CAMP NEAR HELENA,
ARKANSAS, OCT. 16TH, 1862

Messrs Editors:—All quiet on the Potomac has within a few weeks become obsolete, and we how frequently see at the heading of newspaper articles, "all quiet at Helena." The peace on the Potomac has been considerably broken of late, and the rebels, judging from accounts, have been walking rough shod over all opposition. I see a report to-day, stating they have got into Pennsylvania. I think they will have to call on the western boys yet to square accounts with the rebels about Washington City. Let Indiana, Illinois in there and all quiet on the Potomac will soon be restored.

We have but little fighting to do here now, our business is preparing for fight and defense.— Aside from an occasional wayside shot from a bushwhacker, and some little skirmishing with guerrillas, "all quiet about Helena," and in Arkansas too. Our advance pickets have lately had several little fights with rebel cavalry, which amounted to nothing more than a few being killed, wounded and taken prisoners on both sides.— Some suppose our post here will be attacked, and it seems to be the wish of all to have them attack us; are anxious for a fight. But judging from appearances, there is no such a thing as fight apprehended by our officers. A considerable part of our army, I think one half, has been ordered to prepare winter quarters. Whether we will all be kept here to garrison this place or not is hard to tell. We were in hopes of wintering in Little Rock or some place in the interior of Arkansas.— The place of attraction west of the Miss. seems now to be in Missouri. From what we can learn of the rebels in this State, there is not much danger of a very extensive invasion of Mo., from this State, neither will they attack us here. If they can save their State, it is as much as they desire, and probably more than they can accomplish. From what we can learn their whole force in Arkansas is not more than Twenty or thirty thousand with but few cavalry, and very inefficient artillery, and they in different parts of the State. If this should be the strength of their army, they would have a gloomy prospect ahead, should they attempt to invade Missouri.

Contrabands are at work here erecting fortifications which are beginning to make considerable appearance. The soldiers are cutting the timber around, and I apprehend if the rebels should attack this place they would have a sorry time of it.

Cool, pleasant days and cold nights, have taken the place of the very hot weather we had some time ago.

A boat load of Corinth prisoners passed down the river yesterday for Vicksburg, to be exchanged. They were a sorry looking set of fellows.—Some of them had no shoes others no coats. They were dirty and ragged, and were dressed in shirts and pants of all colors, the butternut predominating. As the boat lay at the wharf here, they and our boys had a merry time throwing jokes back and forth at each other, which were not very complimentary to either side, but which was all done in a jovial manner. They were nearly all from Arkansas and Mississippi.

The health of the army is not very good, but better, I think, than it was some time ago, a great many are homesick, which is a disease that don't often kill. An ignorant blackamoor quack from Lagro, Ind., was here last week and the week before, who went around putting mischief in the boys heads from that part of Ind. He intruded his black carcass amongst us by presenting that he had been sent here by Gov. Morton to look after the sick, when in truth, like many other brawling cowards, he sneaked away from Ind., to avoid being drafted, and to smuggle rebel mules through to the north; being slightly acquainted with Capt. Thomas, he quartered in our tent one night and kept us awake all night scratching his rough scaly hide where the mosquitoes would bite him. Said blackamoor quack, is the same, who, with his rowdy companions, went through the country a year ago last spring raising and exciting mobs.

We understand here that the prospect of a draft caused a great many to become deaf, lame, ringboned, spavined, or the end of a finger taken off. Hurrah! for the war uncompromising, home patriotic, brave gentlemen, who were going down south some morning before breakfast and wipe out these rebellious sotherners from the face of the earth at one fell blow. Come gentlemen; lay aside your cowardice and to war, or else keep off the corners of the streets, dealing out your poisonous principles to every gaping list'ner you can get. Show your pluck and go, you advocated war from the beginning, and if you refuse you are no better than the most ____ rebel in the south.

I hope those young gentlemen north of Huntington who could not "stand the fatigues of camp life" would not become further diseased from the thoughts of a draft. Poor fellows; the ladies ought to form some kind of a society, say Home Protection Society, and guard the delicate chaps from all exposure and for fear some terrible bloodthirsty southerner might suddenly come upon them.

Politics are not much talked of here. I hear it mentioned occasionally about the time the election should have come off. We have enough of other things to think about aside from politics, although we would like to hear how the rulers and would be rulers of the land are getting along too.

Yours &c.,
Jos. Z. Scott.[18]

The soldiers in the field may not have been talking politics, but in Indiana, the election was hotly contested. Nervousness about the near invasion of the state, and anger at the aid received by the Confederates, especially in the southern counties, was accompanied by an increased crackdown on civil liberties. In fact, only a few months earlier, the *Daily Journal*, giving its peculiar spin on the First Amendment, asserted: "Thought is free, but speech is not." This twisted definition of the First Amendment by an influential Republican newspaper, led, in turn, to a deepening political division and increased hostility in the state.[19]

By October, Lincoln's suspension of the privilege of the writ of *habeas corpus* and the added provision for military trial not only for "Rebels and Insurgents" but all those who aided and abetted the rebellion in almost any way had taken effect and led to the arrests of many anti-war activists who dared to voice their dissent at peaceful political meetings in the state. Reacting to the assault on the right to free speech and peaceful assembly, the *Huntington Democrat* reported the arrest of "Dr. Huston of Wells County, Harris Reynolds of Fountain, and a number of the citizens of Blackford County," who had been charged with unspecified "disloyal practices" and were now political prisoners in the "Federal Government Building" in Indianapolis. Not mincing words, the *Democrat* said "all [were] charged with 'disloyal practices'; all kidnapped at the midnight hour, by the scullions of the pimps of the administration; and all incarcerated in defiance of law, and without knowledge of the charges on which they were arrested, as well as a speedy trial denied them."[20]

Possibly referring to the same incident, the *Indiana State Sentinel* reported the arrest of seventeen citizens in October following a political meeting in Nottingham Township, Wells County, who were also being held without bail at the "Government postoffice building" in Indianapolis, solely for having voiced dissenting opinions on the Federal war effort. An affidavit had been filed against the seventeen by John Phipps of Company A, 34th Indiana, also known as "Morton's Rifles," of Slack's Brigade, who had attended the political rally, purportedly to recruit volunteer soldiers. When no volunteers came forward, Phipps filed an affidavit charging Dr. Theodore Horton of Wells County and sixteen others with having "discouraged enlistments." After his arrest and incarceration, Horton filed an affidavit denying the charges, claiming that he had not even spoken until after Phipps had concluded his unsuccessful efforts to recruit any volunteers.[21]

Perhaps due to the slow progress of the war and the ever-increasing death notices, perhaps due in part to resentment against the Republican assault on the Bill of Rights, the election of 1862 showed a great gain for the antiwar Democrats. Indicative of the deep political split in the state, and lack of full support for Lincoln's war effort, the *Huntington Democrat* happily announced that the state elections had gone overwhelmingly Democratic, the Democrats winning seven out of eleven of the state's congressional races. In the Eleventh Congressional District, the 47th Indiana's home district, Democrat James F. McDowell defeated the incumbent Republican, John Peter Cleaver Shanks, whom the *Democrat* called "Fremont's Man Friday," by about 1,000 votes — Shanks's margin of victory in 1860 was reported to have been about 2,000. The state legislature also went Democratic. In the Senate, 27 Democrats were elected and 21 "Abolitionists" (the *Democrat*'s term for Republicans); in the House, 62 Democrats and 38 "Abolitionists."[22]

The Republicans denied that their losses had anything to do with a voter backlash against the increasing numbers of political prisoners that followed the president's general suspension of the writ of habeas corpus. Rather, in traditional post-election rhetoric, the Republican newspapers, most notably the *Huntington Herald* and the *Indianapolis Daily Journal*, accused the Democrats of "ballot-box stuffing." The Lincoln administration apparently felt otherwise. On 22 November 1862, the War Department released all prisoners who had not taken up arms against the United States or had not used force of arms to resist, or attempt to resist, the draft.[23]

Back in Arkansas, accusations and denials continued to be hurled back and forth about each side's conduct of the war in that state, but the animosity between the Confederate and Federal forces simmered down enough for some prisoner exchanges.[24]

Discussing one such exchange, as well as the dedication of the newly completed "Fort Curtis" (which Brigadier General Frederick Steele called a "humbug" due to its weak defensive position, being commanded as it was by several hills), and the replacement of Lieutenant Colonel Milton Robinson by Lieutenant Colonel John McLaughlin in command of the 47th Indiana,[25] Chaplain Sawyer wrote:

Letter from Helena
Helena, Ark., October 30th, 1862

Ed. Journal: It has been an important day with us at Helena. The dedication of the Fort was in yesterday's programme, but a boat arrived from Little Rock bearing a flag of truce, and one hundred and three prisoners for exchange. They had been captured by the guerrillas, forwarded to the capital, and thence, by water, sent back to their regiments again. The clothing of our returned captives, all tattered and torn, looked forlorn, but the boys seemed in good spirits, and were glad enough to get back to their comrades again.

Not wishing the rebels to ascertain the number and caliber of our guns the dedication was deferred till to-day. The morning was bright and beautiful — the weather mild and pleasant. At 10 o'clock the music sounded, and each regiment in front of its quarters took its stand, as on dress parade. The 47th Indiana, as they had the Fort under their special charge, were marched before the entrance and formed into line. At length Gen. Hovey, who, owing to the sickness of General Clark, is in temporary command, with his staff rode up to the Fort and entered it in true military style. The artillerymen saluted his entrance and then passed to their guns. As the engineer of the fort loosened the flag, and Gen. Hovey raised it to the top of the flagstaff, the cannon belched forth their thunders of joy. As the echoes died away, and the National banner floated to the breeze, one gunboat after another sent out its glad salutation. Then the batteries which covered the hills to the west of us sent forth their answering peals. Then the batteries six miles southwest of us took part in the rejoicings of the day. "Curtis," by general agreement, was the name given to the Fort, and three hearty cheers, proposed by Gen. Hovey and Col. Slack, were given with a will in honor of Gen. Curtis. Again the music sounded, and officers and men returned to their quarters to discuss the viands of the dinner hour.

A rumor has reached us that we must part with one of our valued officers. I send you a copy of the resolutions unanimously approved by the officers of the regiment. The testimonial is just to Col. Robinson, and will be grateful to his many friends:

Resolution adopted by the Officers of the 47th Regiment of Indiana Volunteers at Helena, Ark., Oct. 29th, 1862.

Whereas, Information has reached us that Lieut. Col. Milton S. Robinson has been commissioned Colonel of the 75th Indiana Regiment,

Resolved, That we recognize in Milton S. Robinson an officer of merit, well worthy of his promotion to a higher command.

Resolved, That he has won our confidence as a man of unquestioned courage on various occasions, and pre-eminently in the famous battle with the rebel gunboats at Riddle's Point, Mo.

Resolved, That while we acquiesce in the call which requires us to part with him, we commend him most cordially to the 75th Regiment as one who will prove himself true and faithful in the day of trial, and who will aid them in making an honorable history.

Resolved. That in terminating his official relation to the 47th Regiment, Col. Robinson has not severed the ties of friendship and esteem which bind us to him, and we follow him with our best wishes that he may be crowned with abundant success in his new position.

Major McLaughlin of Indianapolis is now Lieut. Colonel of the 47th. The regiment has confidence in him as a soldier, and officer and a gentleman, and though they regret the loss of Col. Robinson, they rejoice in the Major's promotion.

Yours very truly, Samuel Sawyer, Chaplain 47th Ind.[26]

On 16 November 1862, A.P. Hovey's division, made up of a force of 6,000 infantry, including the 47th Indiana, and 2,000 cavalry, embarked on steamers at Helena on an expedition to Arkansas Post. They intended to disembark on the White River and march to

Arkansas Post, but the White River proved to be too low for the transports, and the expedition returned to Helena on the night of 21 November 1862.[27]

On the Confederate side, in early October, a force under Brigadier Generals Earl Van Dorn and Sterling "Old Pap" Price, operating temporarily east of the Mississippi to help defend Vicksburg, and now the main Confederate force opposing Grant at Memphis, attacked Rosecrans' Federal force at Corinth, Mississippi. Defeated, the Confederates retreated westward to Holly Springs, Mississippi, where Major General John C. Pemberton superseded Van Dorn in command. Rosecrans did not pursue, and Pemberton moved his force south about fifteen miles, establishing his defensive line along the upper Tallahatchie River.[28]

Back at La Grange, Tennessee, U.S. Grant, commanding the Department of the Tennessee since Halleck's move to Washington in July, had since early November been casting a wary eye on Major General John A. McClernand, who was in the Midwest recruiting volunteers and sending them south to Memphis. McClernand, an Illinois Democrat, had traveled to Washington, D.C., in September to court Lincoln for an independent command on the Mississippi River. McClernand succeeded in his quest and received confidential orders from Lincoln, which granted him command of an expeditionary force against Vicksburg to open the Mississippi if he could raise his own troops. As a quid pro quo, McClernand would use his influence in Ohio River towns, where antiwar sentiments were running high, to gain support for Republican or pro-war candidates in the upcoming elections.[29]

Although McClernand's orders were "confidential," his recruiting activities and troop shipments to Memphis were very public, and by November had created speculation, much of it inaccurate, about what he was up to. It appears, however, that Grant first became aware of McClernand's quest for independent command on the Mississippi in early November when Lt. Col. James H. Wilson, Grant's topographical engineer and aide-de-camp, reported to him after being told by McClernand about the expeditionary force while he was in Washington the previous month.[30]

Attentive to the complications that could arise if McClernand were granted an independent command on the Mississippi, Grant wrote Halleck on 10 November requesting that his status as commander of the department be clarified, and asking if Halleck wanted him "to push as far south as possible." Halleck replied the next day, telling Grant that he had complete command of his department "and have permission to fight the enemy where you please." With these orders, Grant took the initiative by beginning the campaign against Vicksburg before McClernand could arrive from his recruiting trip through the Midwest.[31]

Acting quickly, Grant ordered Sherman to march his troops to Holly Springs, Mississippi, for a movement against Pemberton's Tallahatchie line. In conjunction with this operation, Frederick Steele would send a force from Helena southeastward to Grenada, Mississippi, while Porter would move his gunboat fleet downriver to the mouth of the Yazoo, about six miles above Vicksburg.[32]

Several days later, under Steele's orders, A.P. Hovey, with 5,000 infantry from the 2nd and 4th divisions of the Army of the Southwest and a cavalry division of 2,000 under Cadwallader Washburn, departed from Helena on sixteen steamers. On 27 November, Washburn's cavalry disembarked at Delta (Friar's Point), Mississippi. Supported by the 11th and 24th Indiana regiments under William T. Spicely, they led the expedition down the ridge road to the junction of the Coldwater and Tallahatchie Rivers, crossed, and drove some of

Pemberton's force from the east bank. Bridging the Tallahatchie near Panola on the first day of December, Spicely's infantry skirmished with the retreating Confederates on the north bank of the Yoknapatalfa (Yocona) River and drove them toward Coffeeville with the help of Washburn's light artillery. That night, Spicely's infantry bivouacked at Mitchell's Cross-Roads.[33]

Besides Spicely's force, the remainder of Hovey's infantry marched through mud and slept in cold rain without tents while providing support for Washburn's cavalry as it moved across country. Cutting telegraph lines and burning bridges on the Mississippi & Tennessee and the Mississippi Central Railroads north of Grenada, they destroyed one locomotive and thirty freight cars, and took forty prisoners. The 1st Indiana Cavalry proceeded down the Tallahatchie and burned the Confederate steamer *New Moon*.[34]

Col. John A. McLaughlin (CivilWarIndiana.com/Craig Dunn Collection).

At the end of the first week in December, Hovey's infantry and Washburn's cavalry returned to Helena on steamers with some 300 freed slaves, the captured Confederates, and a number of wagons, arms, and other supplies. Their return to Helena was unopposed except for a minor night raid on the 28th Iowa's rear guard camp on the Coldwater River about five miles from the main column.

While some newspapers relied on reports from soldiers and occasionally chaplains in the field, the larger New York City newspapers like the *Times, Herald,* and *Tribune,* as well as other larger newspapers in the interior like the *Indiana State Sentinel,* sent paid reporters to the front as war correspondents. Many were sent west to cover Fremont and stayed on to cover Grant. These reporters, who came to be known as the "Bohemian Brigade," dispatched stories via telegraph that were quickly disseminated among the various associated newspapers.[35]

One such member of the "Bohemian Brigade," *New York Times* reporter Franc B. Wilkie, accompanied the raid and reported on it under the pen name "Galway."

> Friday night the whole expedition left Coldwater, and reached here [Delta] this morning without further adventure than an attack upon the rear-guard by a small party of guerillas. Last night the Twenty-eighth Iowa encamped some five miles back from the main column. They had just lighted their camp fires, when about thirty mounted Confederates dashed boldly through

the camp, blazing away right and left as they passed, but hitting no one save one individual, who was straggling away from the regiment, and who was shot dead while running in. Two teams and wagons were run off, and along with the rebels, disappeared into the recesses of the swamp.[36]

In his report to the *Times*, Wilkie pronounced the expedition a "brilliant" success, but added the caveat:

> There is only one thing to mar the effect of their efforts and that is, that on their return, everything en route was destroyed. Charleston, Oakland, and Panola were sacked, and everything destroyed that fell into their hands. Stores were broken open, houses plundered, citizens insulted — in short, the country was reduced to wilderness.

Wilkie added a poignant account of the trek of the newly freed slaves to Helena

> What shall we do with them? Along with our forces on the return, came some three hundred negroes of all ages, sexes, colors, sizes and conditions. Trampling eagerly through the deep mud, came old, paralytic, bent with age and infirmity who bore the pelting rain and the discomforts of camp without complaint, their faces and souls all aglow with the thought that they were bound for the North and Freedom. Mothers waded through mud and water, carrying babies in their arms, sustained by the thought that they had at length obtained that wonderful blessing — Freedom. Barefooted children, ragged adults, young women clad in hermaphrodite suits of half petticoats and pantaloons, all came budging on, grinning over the sublime thought that they had obtained that priceless boon — Freedom.

He also included some thoughts about the meaning of freedom and an eye opening account of how the newly freed slaves were treated at Helena.

> Freedom in the abstract is a fine thing, and will do to fight, preach, pray, suffer, starve for; but when freedom amounts to no more than what the negroes obtain at Helena, it is a different affair. There it simply means the freedom to starve, rot, die, and the sooner the better. Since I reached that place the average daily mortality among the contrabands has been from ten to twenty. Nobody takes any further interest in them than to kick them out of the way whenever they get in it, and to curse them upon all occasions as a source of the most serious demoralization in the army. Their condition is not a single remove above that of brutes — a more degraded, helpless class of people exists no where on the Continent. If our philanthropy is to end in taking them away from their masters, we had better, in mercy to them, decree that as fast as emancipated they shall be shot.[37]

Wilkie was correct that the raid was successful from a military standpoint. The penetration behind Pemberton's upper Tallahatchie line, in conjunction with Sherman's move southward from Holly Springs, forced Pemberton to retreat southward to the Yalobusha River at Grenada. His main force was already constructing breastworks south of the river to block passage when Washburn's cavalry and infantry support arrived, but did not attempt to cross and engage Pemberton's main force.[38]

In the meantime, Grant moved his force south from La Grange to Oxford, Mississippi, leaving Col. R.C. Murphy of the 8th Wisconsin to guard the supply depot at Holly Springs. Having forced Pemberton southward, Grant ordered Sherman to take his corps, including the new troops McClernand was recruiting and sending to Memphis, and sail with Porter's gunboat fleet downriver to the Chickasaw Bluffs just above Vicksburg to probe Pemberton's northern defenses.[39]

From Oxford on 17 December, Grant, apparently attempting to get his department in order, and perhaps responding to a complaint made by A.P. Hovey several weeks earlier that "unprincipled sharpers and Jews" were supplying the enemy at Delta and Friar's Point, Mississippi, complained to C.P. Wolcott, Assistant Secretary of War, that "Jews and unprincipled traders" were selling goods to the enemy. That same day, Grant issued an order expelling all Jews (without mentioning the other "sharpers" or "unprincipled traders") from the Department of Tennessee, igniting a storm of protest. An embarrassed President Lincoln soon canceled the order.[40]

The next day (18 December 1862), Halleck formally organized Grant's Department of the Tennessee into a four-corps army. McClernand, still in the Midwest gathering volunteers, was assigned command of the 13th, William T. Sherman the 15th, Stephen A. Hurlbut the 16th and James B. McPherson the 17th Army Corps. Three days later, Halleck also officially notified Grant that McClernand, under Grant's direction, was to lead the Mississippi River expedition when he arrived.[41]

On 20 December, Confederates counterattacked. Moving up from Grenada, Van Dorn raided Holly Springs, captured prisoners and destroyed Grant's Mississippi supply depot. In southwestern Tennessee, Nathan Bedford Forrest's cavalry, roaming through the countryside, cut the railroad at Trenton and Humboldt and disrupted Grant's Memphis supply line. Forrest's raid also forced Grant to move his headquarters back to La Grange and derailed his plan for an overland campaign against Vicksburg in conjunction with the Sherman/Porter expedition to the Chickasaw Bluffs before McClernand could take charge.[42]

In the meantime, Brigadier General Willis A. Gorman arrived from the eastern front to supersede Frederick Steele in command of the District of Eastern Arkansas. On 22 December, Gorman's command was transferred to McClernand's 13th Army Corps to participate in the "down-river expedition." Appalled by what he saw of the Federal troops in Missouri and Arkansas, a month later Gorman reported that Sherman's army had "wantonly burned much property" on their march down the Mississippi from Memphis; that at Helena the army had "acquired the unenviable reputation for plundering, robbing, and burning property"; and, at Helena, was "the most undisciplined mob [he] ever came in contact with." Pointing to what he saw as the source of the problem, Gorman noted, "the material is splendid, but the political demagogues among the line officers are enough to damn the best army on God's footstool."[43]

Not long after taking command at Memphis in July, Sherman had established the policy to expel ten families for each boat attacked by partisans, adding that, as insurance against attack, he would "see that a fair proportion of secesh travel in each boat." More tellingly regarding partisan attacks, Sherman stated, "we cannot undertake to chase them through the country, but must hold the neighborhood responsible." Once the official order to burn the homes of civilians started, however, it was difficult to stop the troops or army stragglers from continuing the practice.[44]

Although claiming to be appalled by the actions of the Federal army along the Mississippi River, in mid–December, following several partisan attacks on Federal mail boats in which three people were killed, Gorman adopted Sherman's policy of "holding the neighborhood responsible" by sending Colonel James R. Slack with three companies of the 47th Indiana, part of the 11th Indiana, and the Peoria Battery to Commerce, Mississippi, to, as Chaplain Sawyer said, "burn the town and all the houses within a circuit of five miles."[45]

Slack, describing the sacking of Commerce to a friend or relation in Newtown, Bucks County, Pennsylvania, wrote:

IV. Helena, Arkansas (August–December 1862)

The day Mrs. Slack left me at Helena, I took part of the 11th and part of the 47th Indiana, and one gun of the Peoria (Ill.) battery, and escorted her to Memphis. We went up about midnight, landed at Commerce, in this State, and took all the white men prisoners, and burnt every house for three miles around. It was to me a horrible sight, yet the chastisement had to be given, and I did it as tenderly as possible. Fine palatial residences, furnished in the most costly manner, beautiful pianos, costly parlor ornaments, magnificent paintings, splendid wardrobes — all crumbled into ashes. This was done to chastise them from firing into the steamer Mill Boy, and killing three citizens who were Union men. There has not been a boat fired into since in that neighborhood. The next day we started on an expedition up the White river, in Arkansas.[46]

Chaplain Sawyer, mentioning Gorman's assumption of command at Helena, Slack's expedition to Commerce, Mississippi, and the brutal treatment of sick or invalid former slaves by local hospital personnel in Helena, wrote:

LETTER FROM THE 47TH REGIMENT.
HELENA, ARK., DEC. 22, 1862

Mr. Editor — The river has been alive with boats for a few days, loaded with soldiers on their way southward bound. Some of the new regiments were with the expedition, and our boys were happy to meet an old acquaintance here and there, fresh from home. We have our opinion where the blow will fall, and as the rise of water is favorable, we shall look for a brilliant success.

Gen. Gorman, who superseded Gen. Steele in command at this post, is working some thorough changes. He is passing all who wish to leave without our lines, and allowing none to enter. The necessity for this is generally conceded. Men claiming to be peaceable and loyal citizens have come in on the plea of trading to supply family wants, and a night or two afterwards our pickets have been shot or captured, and some of our scouting parties worsted. Last night a company of the 6th Missouri were fired into as they were passing along the road by a lot of guerrillas lying on the ground, and over 20 badly wounded. A force was immediately sent out to capture the guerrillas, but they had done their work and escaped. — The General commanding promises himself that he will succeed in effectually guarding the entire army here against similar surprises in future. He is energetic and wide awake.

Col. Slack, at his own request, has been relieved of his police command and returned to active duty as Brigade commander. His brigade comprises the 43rd, 46th and 47th Indiana regiments, with artillery and cavalry attached. Our mail boat was stopped on her trip towards Memphis last week, at a little town on the Mississippi side named Commerce. — Three men had been killed on another boat, and the mail boat narrowly escaped capture. Col. Slack took three companies, C, D and H, went to Commerce, burned the town and every house within a circuit of five miles, captured some prisoners and returned without the loss of a man. He brought back some buggies and some valuable horses. Thorough work was required, and his orders were executed with a will.

Major Goodwin makes an efficient officer. Lieut. Col. McLaughlin has charge of the regiment, and his energy and military spirit are infused, more or less, into all the officers and men. Lieutenant Vance makes an excellent Adjutant. Our Quartermaster, Geo. Nichol, has been a most gentlemanly and worthy officer, and we would not exchange him for any Quartermaster in the service. Spicer Jones is still sutler.

The Chaplains' Association has been doing some good work during the past week in visiting the various hospitals and distributing religious and valuable reading to the army.

The hospitals are in good condition and the sick well cared for, with the exception of the hospital of the contrabands, which is under the immediate supervision of Doctor Jack, a physician from Helena. We found it in a wretched condition, and the inmates were brutally whipped with leather straps for trivial offences, or for not doing what they were unable to do. For sometime the Doctor had been the editor of the Helena *Shield*, and is quite ambitious, it is said, to represent Arkansas in the U.S. Congress.

The camp was startled a few moments ago by the announcement that one of our regimental teamsters had been suddenly killed. He was hauling a load of wood, and was jarred from the wagon under the horses' feet; the fore-wheel ran over his head and crushed it. His name was Martin Railing, from Adams county. He belonged to Company C, and has a brother here who grieves much over his loss. The deceased was a good soldier, and much respected.

The river continues to rise, and boats continue to come down. The preparation has been grand, and the execution, we hope, will not be less so. The weather is most favorable.

What rejoicing there would be if by January 1st the entire Mississippi river and its southern tributaries were under our control! The whole army is panting for progress. It gives fresh vigor and hope to our men to hear of an advance movement. I will keep your readers apprised of any changes in this department.

I sent to the State Library, a few days since, some of the rebel Memphis papers, in which you may find some items of interest. In the size and quality of their issues you may obtain a good idea of the effect of the blockade upon the confederates. The papers will, of course, be open to the inspection of the press.

The death of Lieutenant [John A.] Martin, of Co. I, was quite unexpected. He died below Cairo, and was buried at Memphis. He was much respected in the regiment.

Yours, Samuel Sawyer, Chaplain 47th Reg. Ind. Vols.[47]

Back in Indianapolis on Christmas Day 1862, J.N. Sweetser, the City Attorney, ran an ad in the *Daily Journal*: "Look Out Boys! The ordinance against shooting in the street will be rigidly enforced."[48]

Appearing that night on streets presumably free of gunfire, Matilda Heron, the highly acclaimed actress from the New York stage, performed her celebrated if not somewhat scandalous role as Camille[49]:

> Metropolitan Hall!
> Second night of the great actress.
> Matilda Heron.
> Thursday Evening, December 25, 1862
> Only time of the thrilling play of
> C A M I L L E.
> Camille..........................Matilda Heron
> The Belle of the Season!
> Florence Upperton..........................Matilda Heron
> Molly Bardtiel......................Miss Marion Macarthy
> Prices of Admission
> Dress Circle and Parquette........................50 cents
> Lady and Gentleman...............................75 "
> Each Additional lady..............................25 "
> Private Boxes...$4.00
> No seats sold in Private Boxes
> Doors open at 7 o'clock. Performance commences
> At 7½ o'clock. Dec 25

And, for those who preferred their entertainment a little less highbrow, popular comedian and minstrel Billy Arlington and "Leon," the "dean of minstrel female impersonators," held forth at the Masonic Hall[50]:

> Masonic Hall!
> For Four Nights Only.
> Commencing Monday, December 22.
> Arlington, Leon & Donniker's Minstrels.

IV. Helena, Arkansas (August–December 1862)

Excelsior Troupe of the World
From 585 Broadway, New York
Will have the honor of appearing before the citizens
of Indianapolis in all their new and original styles
Ethiopian Minstrelsy,
Who challenge the profession to compete with them.
Doors open at a quarter before 7 o'clock. Concert
commences at a quarter before 8. Admission 25 cents.
A Grand Matinee will be given on Thursday, Dec.
25th, commencing at 3 o'clock. Doors open at 2 P.M.
Admission 25 cents; children 15 cents.
R.S. Dingess, Agent

V

White River, Arkansas (January 1863)

President Lincoln's Emancipation Proclamation became effective on New Year's Day 1863. Although it included only those areas where the people were "in rebellion against the United States," the 3 January 1863 *Chicago Tribune* headline trumpeted:

>THE PROCLAMATION!
>A New Year's Gift to Humanity.
>A Nation Born in a Day.
>Over Three Millions of Freedmen.

In that same edition, the *Tribune* published the statement of the Federal Military Governor of South Carolina, Brigadier General Rufus Saxton, which read in part:

> *A Happy New Year's Greetings to the Colored People in the Department of the South*:
> In accordance, as I believe, with the will of our Heavenly Father, and by direction of our great and good friend, whose name you are all familiar with, Abraham Lincoln, President of the United States, and Commander-in-Chief of the army and navy, on the 1st day of January, 1863, you will be declared "forever free."...
> I ... call upon all the colored people in this Department to assemble on this day at the headquarters of the 1st Regiment of South Carolina volunteers, there to hear the President's Proclamation read, and to indulge in such other manifestations of joy as may be called forth on this occasion. It is your duty to carry this good news to your brethren who are still in slavery. Let all your voices, like merry bells join loud and clear in the grand chorus of liberty—"We are Free," "We are free"—until listening, you shall hear its echoes coming back from every cabin in the land—"We are free," "We are free."[1]

On that same day, the *Indianapolis Daily Gazette* described the celebration of freed slaves in Norfolk, Virginia:

> Considerable excitement was created in Norfolk today by a negro celebration. Contrabands collected together, with their Marshals, formed a procession of at least 4000 negros of all kinds and colors, headed by a band of music, drums and fifes, and paraded through the principal streets of the city. They carried several Union flags, and cheered loudly for the downfall of African slavery. It is understood they were celebrating the day the emancipation proclamation was issued.[2]

In a less charitable New Year's Day editorial, the pro-slavery *Huntington Democrat* argued that the emancipation of slaves was unconstitutional and that the war was now being prosecuted, not "to subject the South to the Constitution and laws of the land," but to advance the cause of Abolition.³

In another irate New Year's Day editorial, the *Democrat* called radical Abolitionist Congressman Thaddeus Stevens of Pennsylvania "the greatest villain this country was ever cursed with," for having, among other things, submitted a bill in the new session of Congress to invest the president "with the power to declare a suspension of the writ of habeas corpus at such times and places ... as in his judgment the public safety may require," and for indemnifying the president and others who would enforce the suspension. Warning that the bill would grant the president "the prerogatives of a dictator," the *Democrat* added "Old Thad" was "out–Heroding Herod."⁴

At about the same time that the political and philosophical battle lines were being hardened in the North, the war resumed in frostbitten Middle Tennessee on 31 December when Bragg's Army of Tennessee routed Rosecrans's Army of the Cumberland at Murfreesboro, Rosecrans averting disaster only after his reformed battle line held on the Nashville Pike. Two days later Rosecrans's regrouped army soundly defeated Bragg's second assault, forcing Bragg to withdraw his army south through cold rain and mud to the vicinity of Tullahoma, Tennessee.

Back on the Mississippi, Grant sent Sherman's infantry with Porter's gunboats to the mouth of the Yazoo River to penetrate the northern defenses of Vicksburg, forcing Pemberton to hurriedly withdraw from his defensive line at the Yalobusha River southward to the city's fortifications. At Chickasaw Bayou, about 215 miles below Helena and several miles above Vicksburg, Pemberton's well-posted infantry and artillery turned back Sherman's expeditionary force with heavy loss, closing that route to Vicksburg. Private Abner Wilkes of the 46th Mississippi put it succinctly after the war when he wrote about meeting the Yankees at Chickasaw Bayou: "We met them and gave them Hail Columbia; we made them get back in due time from whence they came."⁵

Sherman's defeat at Chickasaw Bayou was not Grant's only problem. Forrest's raids on his railroad supply line and Earl Van Dorn's raid on his advanced depot at Holly Springs, Mississippi, forced him to withdraw back to La Grange, Tennessee, and give up the idea of a land campaign through Mississippi. And now, about 108 miles below Helena and about 8 miles below the mouth of the Arkansas River, Confederates captured the supply boat *Blue Wing*, which had steamed out of Helena several days before, carrying ammunition and towing two barges of coal for the Mississippi fleet. Hit by artillery fire from the Arkansas shore, the *Blue Wing* ran aground at Cypress Bend and was captured. Slack believed the *Blue Wing*'s captain ran it aground intentionally so that the Confederates could tow it and its cargo up the Arkansas River, which they did.⁶

On 4 January 1863, McClernand finally arrived downriver at Milliken's Bend, Louisiana, to take command of what he dubbed the Army of the Mississippi. (It comprised his 13th Army Corps, commanded by Brigadier General George W. Morgan; Sherman's 15th Army Corps; and gunboats from Rear Admiral Porter's fleet.) Following the debacle at Chickasaw Bayou, Sherman and Porter had determined to take a gunboat flotilla and some infantry about fifty miles up the Arkansas River to attack Arkansas Post, where the Confederates had established a fort to control the Arkansas River and harass Federal transports on the Mississippi, as they had done in the capture of the *Blue Wing*.⁷

McClernand assumed command and on 11 January attacked. His troops faced stiff

Soldiers from Company A, 47th Indiana. Front row, left to right: 1st Lt. Eli Arnold, b. 29 Sep 1829, d.1927; Cpl. William Anderson, b. 1834; Pvts. Aaron Custard, b. 1830; Peter Runkle, b. 1834, d. 20 May 1911; Joseph Jones, b.1840; John Tate, b. 1836, d. Helena, AR, 5 Mar 1863; Michael W. Hodgson, b. 1843; Samuel Tate, b. 1830; and Pvt. Simeon Crosby, b. 1840. Back row, left to right: Privates Elijah Alspack, b. 27 Apr 1840, d. 1886; Elbridge Johnson, b. 1838; John Custard, b. 1834; Zebedee Craig, b. 1833; William H. Tharpe, d. Helena, AR, 2 Feb 1863; Daniel Alspack, b.10 Aug 1842, d. 5 May 1893; Isaac Crosby, b. 1844; and Charles H. Morgan, b.1824, d. 9 Feb 1902 (courtesy of Keith Hudson).

resistance and suffered casualties until Porter's gunboats reduced the fort and forced the two-brigade garrison of nearly 5,000 to surrender. Shallow water upriver prevented the gunboats and troop transports from proceeding to Little Rock.[8]

At the same time, in a coordinated effort to gain control of the state of Arkansas, Porter sent the ironclads *Baron De Kalb* and *Cincinnati* up the White River to destroy the Confederate defenses at St. Charles and De Valls Bluff, the terminus of the Little Rock & Memphis Railroad. The two "Pook Turtles" were to clear the way for the transports carrying W.A. Gorman's District of Eastern Arkansas expeditionary force, which consisted of A.P. Hovey's 2nd division and Brigadier General Clinton Fisk's infantry brigade, sent to Gorman by Curtis about a week earlier from Columbus, Kentucky. From De Valls Bluff, they hoped to recapture or destroy the errant *Blue Wing* before moving westward across Grand Prairie to make a junction with McClernand at Little Rock.[9]

Meanwhile, although the move against Arkansas Post had been Sherman's idea in the first place and Grant would later call it a good idea, on 11 January, Grant complained to Halleck that McClernand had gone on a "wild goose chase" in Arkansas. The next day, Grant got his wish and Halleck authorized him to take command of the expedition against Vicksburg, officially subordinating McClernand to Grant's overall Department of Tennessee command. Grant then ordered McClernand to cease his movements in Arkansas and return his troops to Milliken's Bend.[10]

Although McClernand's movements up the Arkansas River had been terminated, Gorman's expedition up the White River continued. Due to the upper White River having a depth of less than 6 feet, too shallow for the two 512-ton "Pook Turtles," the light-draft "tinclads" *Signal*, *Romeo* and *Forest Rose*[11] were added to the fleet. Arriving at St. Charles, Arkansas, on 14 January, they discovered that the Confederate garrison had used the *Blue Wing* to evacuate and transport themselves and two 8-inch Columbiads upriver to De Valls Bluff. The *Cincinnati* remained at St. Charles, and two days later at 3:00 P.M. the remainder of the flotilla arrived at Devall's Bluff. They found the abandoned Columbiads still awaiting shipment to Little Rock, the small garrison having fled about fifteen minutes earlier with their suppers still cooking, some escaping upriver in the elusive *Blue Wing*. Gorman's troops captured the two guns along with the flatcars, 90 new Enfield rifles and 25 prisoners.[12]

The narrow, winding White River also prevented Gorman from sending the larger gunboat *Baron De Kalb* and coal barges farther upstream, although the *Romeo* and the *Forest Rose*, accompanied by infantry under Colonel W.T. Spicely of the 24th Indiana, including Slack's brigade, made it to Des Arc, thirty-four miles upriver, where they took the post office, captured and paroled 39 prisoners from a hospital, several thousand bushels of government corn, 70 small arms, and recaptured 200 rounds of 6-pounder ammunition, which the Confederates were believed to have taken a few weeks earlier from the *Blue Wing*. Also taken back to Gorman at Devall's Bluff aboard the *Forest Rose* were James Warren and his family, who wanted to get back to Illinois.[13]

Gorman reported that some planters and farmers were moving southwestward with their slaves and livestock toward Texas, leaving all the Confederate forces "except two, or possibly three, companies of bushwackers" under a Major Chrisman, east of the Arkansas River. The marshy and bayou-laced country westward between Devall's Bluff and the Arkansas River, especially Bayou Meto, became impassable when the four or five inches of snow that had fallen began melting, flooding the roads and preventing pursuit.[14]

Slack's 47th Indiana joined Walker's tinclad flotilla (the *Forest Rose* and the *Romeo*) to pursue the *Blue Wing* and any other boats that "might be stowed away on the various bayous along the river." But orders from McClernand to return to the Mississippi arrived that same day, and they were called back before they left.[15]

As Gorman withdrew his forces from the White River and returned to Helena, all troops in Arkansas within reach of Grant's orders, including Gorman's, were placed under Grant's Department of the Tennessee command. Although considered a minor success (Slack claimed Gorman's force "captured 75 prisoners, two heavy siege guns, and three of four hundred stand of arms"[16]), the White River Expedition, at least in Clinton Fisk's brigade, resulted in heavy losses back at Helena due to diseases spread by the filthy conditions and close quarters on the White River transports.[17]

Reporting from Grenada, Mississippi, on 29 January 1863, Confederate Major General William W. Loring noted optimistically that Gorman's expedition on the White River in Arkansas had failed; that Grant's army was falling back toward Memphis on the Charleston Railroad; and that "all accounts agreed to their demoralization." Van Dorn, however, had been unable to hold Holly Springs, and Pemberton had been forced back to Vicksburg. Grant did move his headquarters back to Memphis with Hurlbut's and McPherson's corps, but Sherman's and McClernand's corps, and Porter's gunboat fleet, remained downriver some one hundred miles or so above Vicksburg, biding their time, awaiting Grant's order to move forward.[18]

VI

Yazoo Pass, Mississippi (February–April 1863)

In mid–January, Grant, now in full charge of operations, but concerned about defensible supply lines, began studying alternate routes to Vicksburg. Shades of New Madrid, and against Porter's advice, he searched for a route that his gunboats and troop transports could use to bypass the Confederate guns at Vicksburg.

Grant set up headquarters at the Mississippi River village of Young's Point, Louisiana, opposite the mouth of the Yazoo, several miles above Vicksburg. Young's Point sat at the head of a sharp bend in the river that created a five- or six-mile-long promontory of land west of Vicksburg that gave the village its name. In 1862, a mile-long canal had been cut across Young's Point to eliminate the bend in the river. Grant, believing that it could be used to bypass Vicksburg's guns, put his chief engineer, Captain Frederick Prime, in charge of a crew of 550 freed slaves and about 4,000 soldiers to do the heavy work of clearing trees and excavating the bed to widen and deepen the canal. On 6 March, after strenuous labor, as Porter predicted, the Mississippi rose suddenly, broke the dam at the upper end that had been built to keep the water out, and flooded the excavation work already done. Belatedly, Grant stopped the project when he realized that the canal was untenable because Confederate batteries on the Warrenton Bluffs controlled the area where the canal entered the river below Vicksburg.[1]

At about the same time, Grant, maintaining his headquarters at Young's Point, continued his search for a water route to bypass Vicksburg. Grant had McPherson's 17th corps, primarily Josiah Bissell's engineer regiment, open another cut in the Mississippi River levee at Lake Providence, Louisiana. Lake Providence had been part of the old river channel and was now about one mile inland, but with an outlet into Bayou Baxter. Grant believed that with water from the Mississippi flowing through the lake, a navigable stream could be dug and trees cut to connect Bayous Baxter and Macon with the more reliably navigable Tensas, Washita and Red Rivers. Bypassing the Vicksburg batteries, Grant's forces could conceivably reach the Mississippi below Warrenton for possible cooperation with Major General Nathaniel Banks in an attack on Port Hudson, Louisiana, opposite the mouth of the Red River. Banks had replaced Benjamin "the Beast" Butler in command of the Department of the Gulf and was to help Grant open the Mississippi from below. This route proved untenable as well, the waterway being too shallow for gunboats or steam transports and too easy for the Confederates from Port Hudson to obstruct.[2]

Back at Lake Providence, as his engineers tried to alter the flow of the Mississippi at two different points, Grant reorganized the Army of the Tennessee, detaching the District of Eastern Arkansas from Curtis's Department of the Missouri and attaching it to McClernand's 13th Army Corps in two divisions (the 12th and 13th) under newly arrived Brigadier General Benjamin Prentiss. Earlier, Rear Admiral Porter had complained to Grant that Gorman had expropriated navy coal for army use. Grant used the opportunity on 15 February to replace Gorman in command of the District of Eastern Arkansas with Prentiss, who had been exchanged in October following his surrender at Shiloh and was looking for a suitable command. Gorman, however, retained field command of the troops in Helena.[3]

To add to the confusion, Brigadier General Leonard F. Ross arrived from west Tennessee, where he had commanded a division guarding the Mississippi Central Railroad. Ross outranked A.P. Hovey by three days, and with Prentiss and Gorman in command of the troops at Helena, Hovey was temporarily reduced to brigade command. At the same time, Cadwallader C. Washburn, who was Hovey's junior, was assigned command of a division of cavalry. Hovey, according to Gorman, was bitter about being reduced to brigade command and complained to Grant. Grant, to soothe Hovey's slightly ruffled feathers, had Prentiss send him north to St. Louis and Cincinnati "on a flying trip to secure small boats" that would be needed to ply the inland streams Grant was thinking about using to bypass the Vicksburg batteries. (Hovey would regain command of the 12th division upon his return in late March).[4]

In the meantime, Ross assumed command of the 13th division, which now consisted of Brigadier General Frederick Salomon's 1st and Clinton Fisk's 2nd brigade. Salomon, a Prussian by birth and another exile from the European revolutions of 1848, had been commanding a brigade in Kansas prior to being sent to the 13th corps. The 47th Indiana was assigned to his brigade along with the 43rd and 46th Indiana, and the 28th Wisconsin. Fisk, now detached from Curtis's command, was assigned command of the 29th, 33rd, and 36th Iowa, and the 33rd and 35th Missouri.[5]

THE YAZOO PASS EXPEDITION

As the arduous work of cutting and dredging new channels through the bayous on the west bank of the Mississippi commenced, Grant looked to the Mississippi Delta for another water route to Vicksburg. At first, before realizing how navigable the streams actually were, Grant just hoped to get into the Yazoo River from above to destroy Confederate transports plying the inland rivers of the Mississippi Delta and to destroy the navy shipyard at Yazoo City, where gunboats were being built. Realizing that the streams were more navigable than originally thought, Grant opted for a more ambitious plan to use the Yazoo to gain a major foothold above Vicksburg on the high ground at Haynes' Bluff. This route also required laborious levee breaching, tree cutting, and channel dredging. McPherson's corps and a division or two from McClernand's and Sherman's corps were selected to follow Lt. Commander Watson Smith's gunboats through Yazoo Pass, down the Coldwater, Tallahatchie and Yazoo Rivers to Yazoo City and below to the northern defenses of Vicksburg. Ross's division of McClernand's corps, at Helena and closest to the pass, was to lead the expedition behind Watson Smith's gunboats while Quinby's division, at the van of McPherson's corps, waited for transports at the entrance to the pass.[6]

Prior to the construction in 1856 of a levee across its approximately 75-foot-wide entrance, the Pass had served as an inland route in Mississippi for small or light-draft boats to Yazoo City, Greenville, and Vicksburg. From its entrance into the Mississippi River, Yazoo Pass emptied into Moon Lake, a crescent-shaped lake formed from the old Mississippi River channel about one mile inside the levee. From Moon Lake, the pass twisted eastward about twelve miles through dense forests to the Coldwater River. The Coldwater wound southward through wilderness about forty miles before emptying into the Tallahatchie River below. The Tallahatchie continued southward about ninety miles until merging with the Yalobusha near Greenwood to form the Yazoo River. From Greenwood, the Yazoo River wound southward about forty-five miles to Yazoo City, southwestward another thirty miles to Haynes' Bluff, and another fifteen before entering the Mississippi about ten miles above Vicksburg.[7]

On 3 February, Federal engineers blew open two cuts in the nearly 100-foot-thick and 18-foot-high levee across the entrance to Yazoo Pass and water poured through the two cuts "like ... Niagara Falls," carrying "logs, trees, and great masses of earth" over the 8½-foot drop down to Moon Lake. By the next day, water was pouring through an opening 75 to 80 yards wide, although it took several more days for the water level to rise in Moon Lake sufficiently to allow boats to pass through. On 7 February, the U.S. gunboat *Forest Rose* (Captain George W. Brown) entered Moon Lake, and three days later Cadwallader Washburn brought the first troops in from Helena (the 34th Indiana, 33rd Iowa, and 16th Ohio Battery) on three small steamers to begin clearing the pass of felled trees and driftwood.[8]

When it became apparent in late 1862 that the Federals might try to reopen the levee at Yazoo Pass, after reconnoitering the area, Captain Isaac N. Brown, C.S. Navy, recommended that trees (mostly sycamore, oak, and elm) be felled across the waterway to obstruct travel on the Coldwater River. Brown's plan was implemented and the narrow waterway was obstructed with felled trees. In February 1863, with news that the Federals had blasted open the levee, Confederate sailors under Lt. Francis E. Sheppard and partisan rangers under Lt. Ed E. Porter moved upriver from Yazoo City to harass the Federals, along with engineers, overseers, and a crew of slaves who worked to fell more trees into the pass ahead of the Federal movement. After a week or so sniping at Federal soldiers and felling trees, on the morning of 14 February, Lt. Sheppard sent a message to Brown, his commander at Yazoo City, who forwarded the message to Pemberton at Grenada, that his men had "worked under their noses" until the Federals finally drove them off, adding with some urgency "hasty obstructions with fortifications may save Yazoo City."[9]

On 16 February, however, partisan rangers continued to harass Federal troops clearing the waterway, prompting Washburn to send a dispatch to Prentiss that Confederate cavalry were still "hovering around" and he needed about 200 more cavalry to clear them out.[10]

A soldier identifying himself as "Morton Rifles" wrote the *Daily Journal* describing the role of the 34th Indiana in clearing the Yazoo Pass. The "guerillas" he referred to were most likely Ed E. Porter's partisan rangers or, perhaps, Sheppard's sailors.

FROM THE YAZOO PASS
CAMP OF THE MORTON RIFLES
YAZOO PASS, 7 MILES ABOVE COLDWATER
FEBRUARY 19, 1863

Eds. Journal: Since my last to you, we have had some changes, both in the weather and the army. Gen. Gorman has been superceded in the command of the forces at Helena by Gen.

Prentiss, of Ill., which has caused a pretty general reorganization of our command. Gen. Gorman now commands a Division under Prentiss.

On Friday last [13 February] Col. Cameron was ordered to take his regiment and report for duty in Yazoo Cut-Off, to Gen. Washburn, for the purpose of cleaning out a lot of large trees which had been felled across the Bayou by the guerrillas, to prevent our transports from passing through. To get into this pass, the State Levee had to be cut.

Yazoo Pass, or Cut-Off, is about eighty or one hundred feet wide, and about fifteen or twenty deep. It leaves the Mississippi about 10 miles below Helena, on the Mississippi side, runs about 18 miles and empties into Cold Water. This empties into the Tallahatchie, which flows into Yazoo river. Thus you will see that if we succeed in clearing this Pass out and obtain a passage through for our transports and gunboats, it will give us possession of Yazoo City, and from thence a good road to the rear of Vicksburg. We have already succeeded in clearing out 12 miles of the pass.

Col. Cameron, contrary to the example of most of our Colonels when their regiments are ordered on *fatigue duty*, accompanied us down here, and has worked as faithfully through mud and rain as any of his men. He is emphatically a working Colonel.

On the 16th, when about eight or ten miles down the Pass, a small detachment of the Morton Rifles, composed of portions of companies H, D and A, under command of Capt. Ferrel, while on picket were attacked by two companies of guerilla cavalry. The enemy had dismounted and posted themselves in a piece of heavy timber, from which they fired on our men, who were coming up from the front. After the third volley had been fired our men fell back, and deployed out as skirmishers on both flanks; they advanced and drove the rebels from their position, though not till they had had time to carry off all their dead and wounded. Our loss was three wounded—Noah Stoner, in the thigh; Amos Slane, just below the knee; James M. Cunningham, just above the knee, all of company D. They are all doing well and are well cared for. The surgeon thinks, with proper care, they will all recover.

We have not been paid off yet, but I understand there is a paymaster at Helena ready to pay us two months' pay. This is glorious news if correct, provided we can be relieved long enough to go up and get it and pay off some old scores and get some new duds, &c.

Speaking of pay I think the Government is paying unnecessarily a large number of surplus regimental as well as general officers. Almost all of our old regiments are now reduced to about one-half their original number of men, but still have their complement of field, staff and line officers, thus continuing an enormous unnecessary expense. This matter should be looked after by our public men, by the Secretary of War, and if these old regiments cannot be filled up they ought to be immediately consolidated. It might cause some little trouble as to who should retain the commissions, but I think they would either find enough who are either tired of the service, sick or incompetent, to rid the service of all the excess, thus leaving only those in command who are earnest and zealous in the cause, and render our army ten times as effective as it now is.

Will not some of our leading journals call attention to this matter as one worthy of immediate consideration.

Morton Rifles.[11]

Although Pemberton did not think the Federals could "effect anything serious" by attempting to bring a flotilla of steamers and gunboats down the Coldwater, when news came that the levee had been breached and Grant's troops were clearing the obstructions, he sent a detachment from Jackson under Major General William W. Loring to Yazoo City to find a place above on the Tallahatchie to obstruct the river. Arriving at Yazoo City on 17 February, Loring selected a small peninsula of land between the Tallahatchie and the Yazoo Rivers near Greenwood that commanded the mouths of the Tallahatchie and Yalobusha rivers above Greenwood as they converged to form the Yazoo. Establishing Fort Pemberton (or Fort Greenwood), Loring's engineers, directing a work crew of slaves, constructed a defensive line made of cotton bales and piles of dirt and sand that extended about 500 yards across the neck of the peninsula between the Tallahatchie and the Yazoo, with artillery emplacements on the river bank about eight feet above the river to provide good plunging fire against the oncoming ironclads. Work also began on a raft to be swung across the Tallahatchie upriver on the right. Waul's Texas Legion garrisoned the fort with troops and a few field pieces as detachments and supplies came down from Grenada on the Yalobusha and up from Yazoo City on the Yazoo. By the time Smith's ironclads arrived, the artillery inside Fort Pemberton consisted of at least one 18-pounder and one 32-pounder rifle and some smaller field guns.[12]

Back at Helena, a soldier who identified himself only as "H" of the 11th Indiana, part of the Federal forces remaining in Helena and not involved in the expedition, wrote the *Indianapolis Daily Journal* complaining that Indiana troops were "rusting out" there. Informing the newspaper that Chaplain Sawyer of the 47th Indiana had been put in charge of the "contraband" camp of freed slaves at Helena, he added somewhat bitterly that an ungrateful Grant had ignored the Indiana troops, specifically his own and the 24th Indiana, who had been with Wallace's division at Shiloh and had saved Grant from being "cleaned out."

Letters from Helena.
Camp 11th Indiana, Helena,
February 15, 1863.

We are all quiet here at Helena, and again fixed apparently to stay. A portion of the Helena forces are still engaged in clearing out "Yazoo Pass," or rather Yazoo *blockade*, and a half dozen gunboats are lying here, I suppose ready to enter the Pass when it is opened.

The gunboat "Chillicothe," under the command of Lieut. Foster [Lt. Com. James D. Foster], of the U.S. Navy, is among the fleet. She is armed with guns of tremendous caliber.

Paymasters

The paymasters are here at last, but we are informed are prepared to pay the soldiers but two months' pay, instead of four. At the end of this month there will be six months due, and to some of the soldiers eight months.

Another Movement on Little Rock

It is reported that there is to be a move upon Little Rock soon from this point. Then all Arkansas will be in our possession, so far as the soil or territory is concerned.

Illinois vs. Indiana

Gen. Hovey has gone down to Vicksburg, rumor says, to beg Gen. Grant to give our division an opportunity to win some laurels at Vicksburg or elsewhere. So far as I can see we have done nothing for the government or for ourselves since the "little brush" we had at Shiloh. It is reported in certain quarters that Grant is partial to the Illinois delegation, and is disposed to hold Indiana soldiers in the background, even to our Major generals.—This is most ungrateful if true, for we saved him from being completely "cleaned out" at Shiloh. But be this as it may, without desiring to be too inquisitive, some of us, indeed Indiana soldiers everywhere, would like to know what has become of Major Gen. Lewis Wallace.

Payment of Soldiers

Gov. Morton's proposition to secure the prompt payment of Indiana soldiers, has excited the interest and attention of our regiment and, if possible, has increased the esteem and regard which are entertained towards him by officers and privates.

Deceased

Elijah Cox, of company I, died yesterday, of chronic diarrhoea.

Changes at Helena, Etc.

Gen. Prentiss has assumed command of the district, but Gen. Gorman still acts in command of the forces here, and has the entire military direction and control of affairs.

There are now four Brigadier Generals here, viz: Prentiss, Gorman, Ross and Hovey — entirely too many for a mere post. Some of them will doubtless soon leave for active service in the field. I know that active service is what Generals Gorman and Hovey desire ardently. Our regiment, however, are nearly ready to conclude that the Fates have assigned us to this desolate, do-nothing hole, as a "fixed institution," to remain until the close of the war, or to the close of our respective mortal careers.

Col. M'Ginnis

Our old colonel, McGinnis, was addressed the other day, by Gen. Grant, as "Brigadier General," and regularly assigned to a new brigade, but, as he has received no papers to justify such an address, he declined accepting the honor, and, I am informed, has asked to be permitted to resume the command of his regiment. He will not put on the stars until he gets the "documents" authorizing it, and I am inclined to think that he is right, for "there's many a slip," &c.

Silly Critics, and Ignorant

Those papers that abuse Gen. Gorman for making an expedition up White river, and of taking possession of Friar's Point, &c, ought to know that in all these movements he acted in obedience to orders from his commanding officers. Moreover, the cry of "*the great cost*" of these expeditions, and of the "*little profit*" to us, is foolish and deceptive. These boats were in the service of the Government before this expedition was made, and have been every day since, though many of them apparently doing nothing.

I most earnestly wish that these boats were more frequently going forth on "*expeditions*" in search of an enemy, instead of lying all the year idle at the landings. Moreover, I wish that we had more Generals with the nerve and energy sufficient to prompt them to go where *rebels* are, to do, or at least to try. *Action* now is what we most need, and with more will and purpose. The army is actually rusting out, and wasting away from mere *ennui*.

Contrabands cared for

Brother Sawyer, Chaplain of the 47th Ind., has been acting here as superintendent of the "contrabands" of this post. He has been laboring zealously in behalf of these unfortunate sons of Africa, and in all his efforts to discipline, elevate them, and ameliorate their condition, he has had the hearty co-operation and approval of Gen. Gorman, who appointed him for these purposes. Gen. Gorman is a Democrat, and has all the vulgar prejudices to an eminent degree against the negro. Yet he is a true patriot, and his patriotism and loyalty, and his love of the Union and the Government, rise superior to all lesser things. Those anonymous letters which have lately appeared in the papers charging him with opposing the President's proclamation and sacrificing the interests of his country upon the altar of prejudice and selfishness are slanderous and unjust. Gen. Gorman most unreservedly and unconditionally indorses the President's proclamation, and has done so from the beginning. H.[13]

On 25 February, with Yazoo Pass cleared, Leonard F. Ross's division (about six thousand troops) entered Moon Lake on twelve transports (the *Volunteer, Lebanon No. 2, Cheeseman, Diana, L. Logan, Saint Louis, Mariner, Moderator, Ida May, Citizen, John Bell,* and *Emma*[14]) to join Watson Smith's gunboat flotilla awaiting them in the pass. Smith's flotilla included the *Chillicothe* (an ironclad side-wheeler that drew about four feet of water, carried two 11-inch Dahlgrens and 2.5-inch armor plate), the 512-ton "Pook Turtle" *Baron De Kalb*; and five light-draft tinclads.

With their less-than-an-inch thick iron plating and their batteries of mainly 12- and 24-pounder Dahlgren boat howitzers, northern wags had by this time dubbed the tinclads the "Mosquito Fleet." They included the 165-ton flagship *Rattler*, which carried two 30-pounder Parrotts and four 24-pounder howitzers; the 260-ton *Forest Rose*, which carried six guns; the 207-ton *Marmora*, which carried eight guns; the 226-ton *Petrel*, which carried eight guns, and the 190-ton *Signal,* which carried six guns. Two rams, the *Lioness* and the *Fulton*, a light-draft mortar boat, and three coal barges pulled by the towboat *S. Bayard* completed Smith's flotilla.[15]

Writing to a friend back home from on board the steamer *Henry Von Phul*, Milt Shaw, a young infantryman from the 5th Iowa, reflected on their impending voyage into Mississippi's mysterious and seemingly impenetrable Yazoo Delta.

> Dear Alf
> I wrote to you from Louisiana. But as we are just on the point of going into the Yazoo Pass, from thence the deuce & Mr Grant only know. I hope you will consider it no intrusion to drop you these few lines. The reports tell us that we go into the pass thence into Moon Lake, thence into Coldwater, thence the Tallahatchie, thence into Sunflower into the Yazoo river, by a kind of overland steamboat, mud puddle route unheard of but in the philosophy of modern warfare. Can you imagine the consternation which our advent into this unexplored part of Dahamy[16] will create amongst the bulfrogs & Alligators whose peaceful streams have hitherto been undisturbed since this mass of clay was sent on it voyage around the sun. But excelsior is our mottoe and with the slight variation onward & downward we dive into the ubiquitous swamps of Miss without so much as saying by your leave....[17]

Writing to Ann from deep inside the Yazoo Pass about his lack of faith in the expedition, although with less trepidation than the Iowa soldier, Slack also mentioned what, at first blush, appears to be an oddly sociable relationship with Confederate General James L. Alcorn: "Last night we laid alongside of the plantation of Genl Alcorn. In the evening I went up to see him, having formed his acquaintance at Helena last fall." Alcorn's plantation was about nine or ten miles east of Friar's Point.[18]

After five days plying the sixteen-mile Yazoo Pass, the flotilla reached the Coldwater River on 1 March. The next day, Confederate partisan ranger Captain Ed. E. Porter sent a message to Loring at Fort Pemberton that the Federals had left General Alcorn's farm that morning and had come down the pass with thirteen small transports carrying about 400 or 500 men each and five gunboats.[19]

In a last-ditch effort, on 8 March, Captain Isaac N. Brown, C.S.N., took the steamers *Thirty-fifth Parallel* and *St. Mary's* upriver on the Tallahatchie to purchase enough cotton to finish protecting the steamer *Magenta* with cotton bales.[20] As his little flotilla approached the descending Federals about seventy miles upriver from Greenwood, Brown switched to the *St. Mary's* and sent the *Parallel* on ahead. With the narrow but overflowed Tallahatchie's current making navigation as difficult for the Confederates who knew the river as it was for the Federals who did not, the *Thirty-fifth Parallel* became disabled when it "ran into the woods" bordering the river. Before returning to Greenwood, Brown ordered the *Thirty-fifth Parallel* and her prized cargo of cotton burned to keep it out of the hands of the slowly approaching Federals. The Federal flotilla arrived at the Tallahatchie on the evening of 6 March and passed the burning steamer four days later. On the night of 10 March, it took all hands to save the boats from conflagration as "a constant stream of burning cotton floated past the fleet." Ross reported that the Confederates burned some 3,000 bales of cotton on their boats and that he believed as many more were on fire on the plantations they had passed.[21]

Giving a vivid account of the movement of Ross's fleet down the wider and more navigable, although still flooded, Coldwater and Tallahatchie Rivers, a correspondent calling himself "W.C.F." wrote the *Indiana State Sentinel*:

VI. Yazoo Pass, Mississippi (February–April 1863)

From the Mississippi Squadron
Mississippi Squadron (Tallahatchie River), Yazoo Pass Expedition

March 9, 1863

Editor State Sentinel: We are rapidly drawing to our destination, and twenty-four hours will in all probability determine for us the extent of forces and fortifications that we will have to encounter. We have been a very long time on the route, but it would have been impossible to have come any faster and kept up the order of sailing, for we have literally made a river through a country densely overgrown with cane, cottonwood, sycamore, birch, &c. We have, with a large fleet of boats, gone where a year ago one would have been considered insane to have even contemplated the attempt. But such are the daring projects that war produces, and if we but succeed after we get into the Yazoo river, we will have accomplished more than any expedition of the war; but if we fail, we will have but opened a good route for the Rebels to attack us from above, as well as have furnished them with a fleet of transports, tin-clads, (musquito boats,) mortar boats and iron-clads to do it with, besides furnishing ourselves with a locality somewhere in the vicinity of the Railroad Depot Hotel at Vicksburg, with a very polite sentinel to usher us in and out. The Rebels are very polite, and I don't doubt for a moment but they will be very hospitable and generous, but before they will get the opportunity I am much mistaken if they don't get entertained by the guns of the Chillicothe, &c., with 198-pounder solid shot, 168-pounder shell, besides, to assist the operation, a few 140-pounder grape, canister and shrapnel.

So far we have had nothing of interest to occur in the Yazoo Pass Expedition, save the loss of a steamboat sunk, a pilot house or two carried away, some dozen wheel houses staved in and smashed up, the hog-chains of the ram Lioness twice broken from trees falling on her. It may be well to remark that the transports have lost all their ginger bread work, but their guards and hulk were in an especial manner preserved, so that they will give a good account of themselves in the way of cotton when they return.

The health of the army and navy is good. Spring has opened beautifully, and the woods are redolent of sweet odors and sweet music. But soon these delicious good things will give way, and instead of balmy airs we will have oven like hotness — instead of sweet odors we will have miasm and instead of the music of the mockingbird, the song of the mosquito and gallinipper.

W.C.F.[22]

Continuing his account of the expedition and the plantation fires noted by Ross, "W.C.F." wrote:

Mississippi Squadron (Tallahatchie River), Yazoo Pass Expedition, March 10, 1863

Editor State Sentinel: For two days and nights, it has done nothing but rain. Our route is one presenting a scene of vast, untold destruction on the part of the Rebels. Since we entered the Tallahatchie, every plantation has presented a huge conflagration. Millions of dollars' worth of property, more especially cotton, has been most foolishly and recklessly destroyed by the Rebels, under the idea that we were in search of their *king*. Today, I witnessed the destruction of a fine bridge, a saw mill, a barge heavily ladened with household furniture, and the burning of a Rebel steamboat *Thirty-fifth Parallel* with 3,500 bales of cotton aboard. In one hour, I saw a million, or more, of dollars worth of property — all destroyed by its owners. People in alarm, flee the country and leave nothing behind. The Rebels, high water, and the Yazoo Pass Expedition, will leave Northern Mississippi a more desolate place than the land of Edom. In Edom, I believe, bats and owls do inhabit; but in the district I am now going through, it will barely be possible for a bat to live. Such is social or civil war.

Yesterday, an intelligent physician told me that quinine was worth $40 per ounce; morphine, $15 per draghm; whisky, $40 to $58 per gallon; and so of everything else.

Perhaps, tomorrow, we will have our first fight with the Rebels at Clayton's Landing, seventeen miles from here and three miles above the mouth of the Tallahatchie River. Our next fight, if successful at this point, (and this is said to be a strong one) will be near Yazoo City. If again successful, we will then strike in the rear at Vicksburg; but if failure is our lot — what? Your correspondent can form no conception.

It is now midnight. An immense conflagration is seen down the river. We suppose the Rebels are burning up their boats and fortification at Clayton's Landing. Daylight will tell. W.C.F.[23]

On 11 March, Watson Smith's gunboat fleet and Ross's troop transports reached the Curtiss plantation, about twelve miles' above Greenwood via the Tallahatchie and five miles marching distance to Fort Pemberton across soggy, overflowed land. Moving forward at 10:00 A.M, just after Loring's troops had blocked passage by swinging their unfinished raft across the Tallahatchie and scuttling the steamer *Star of the West*, the *Chillicothe* rounded the bend in view of Fort Pemberton. As she approached to about 800 yards, Confederate gunners opened fire and a well-aimed 32-pound shell struck the *Chillicothe*'s turret with enough force to splinter its 9-inch pine backing and move it four inches, followed by several solid 18-pound shots that damaged its iron plating. Foster prudently backed the now heavily damaged *Chillicothe* upstream behind the protection of the bend and lobbed five shells before withdrawing out of range.[24]

That same morning (11 March), Ross, who had accompanied Watson Smith on the *Chillicothe*, sent Bringhurst's 46th and Slack's 47th Indiana on a land reconnaissance, the 46th moving westward, the 47th southward toward Fort Pemberton in conjunction with the gunboat attack. The 46th Indiana encountered Colonel T.N. Waul's Texas Legion and skirmished briefly before both sides withdrew. Unable to advance in force across the inundated countryside, Ross bivouacked his troops on the Curtiss Plantation.[25]

At about 4:00 P.M., the two ironclads returned to attack. The *Chillicothe*, in advance of the difficult-to-maneuver stern-wheeler *Baron de Kalb*, opened fire from about 800 yards, but within seven minutes Lt. Com. Smith ordered both ironclads to withdraw after a well-directed shell penetrated the *Chillicothe*'s open No. 2 gun port while an 11-inch shell was being loaded. Both shells exploded and destroyed the port, killing four and wounding sixteen. That evening, Smith's sailors repaired and strengthened both boats with cotton bales, covering their casemates and turrets. On land, Federal troops erected a cotton-bale battery of two 30-pounder Parrott guns and one 12-pounder howitzer in thick woods in front of Fort Pemberton, which Loring noted his gunners could not prevent because of the scarcity of their ammunition. The next day during a lull in the fighting, both sides strengthened their positions.[26] On 13 March, supported by the land battery and mortar boat, the *Baron De Kalb* and the *Chillicothe* abreast at about 800 yards, each now cotton-clad and tethered by lines to trees and light-draft gunboats to prevent them from drifting into Confederate hands if disabled, opened fire. In a fight that "raged furiously the entire day," iron filled the air as Confederate gunners heeded Loring's call to "Give them blizzards, boys! Give them blizzards!" and returned shot and shell "in showers over the boats and batteries."[27]

One of the *Chillicothe*'s 165-pound shots from an 11-inch Dahlgren passed through the fort's parapet, blew cotton bales into the air, ignited a tub of Whitworth cartridges, slightly wounded the commander of the gun, and burned fifteen gunners from the Pointe Coupee Artillery, although there was no explosion and no irreparable damage. Another shell burst over a Confederate gun, killing one of the gunners and wounding three others.[28]

In spite of these shots, both the *Chillicothe* and the *Baron de Kalb* had great difficulty in bringing their 9- and 11-inch Dahlgrens to bear on the fort, the *Chillicothe* forced to rely on its 5- and 10-second shells, which it expended in about an hour and a half. Struck thirty-eight times primarily by 68-pound solid shot and 64-pound (6½-inch) conical rifle shell, the *Chillicothe* took the brunt of the Confederate barrage and was forced to withdraw when its port slides were either blown away or otherwise damaged and all the cotton bales set on fire, the crew saved by "a squad of negro firemen [who] went up with hose and extinguished the flames."[29]

The *Baron de Kalb* was struck six times. One shot penetrated the forward casemate and imbedded in the timber; another entered between two ports and cut away a dozen beams, killing three and seriously wounding one. The *Baron de Kalb*, the mortar boat, and the land battery, neither of which were damaged, continued to exchange shots with the fort until sunset with surprisingly few casualties on either side.[30]

Describing the battle, "W.C.F.," overly impressed by the effect of cannon fire on cotton bales, gave the *Sentinel* readers a detailed and colorful report:

MISSISSIPPI SQUADRON (TALLAHATCHIE RIVER), MARCH 13, 1863

Editor State Sentinel: We engaged the enemy again today with terrible effect on their fortifications, which are composed of cotton bales, wood, and dirt. The *Chillicothe* silenced one of their largest guns, and she and the *Baron De Kalb* and a 13-inch mortar with two navy guns ashore, threw their cotton bales thirty and forty feet high. The *De Kalb* was struck twice, killing two men, and wounding, perhaps mortally, two more.

The *Chillicothe* had two wounded and was struck thirty-four times. The *Chillicothe* is terribly riddled to pieces, turret and all. The enemy penetrated her 3-inch iron casemates in many places with ease, after penetrating cotton bales that were placed before them. The *Chillicothe* sustained perhaps the most terrible fire of this or any other engagement of this war. Her officers and crew behaved with unflinching and noble heroism. The action lasted one hour and thirty-eight minutes, on the part of the *Chillicothe*. The *De Kalb*, the mortar and the mortar and shore navy guns, kept up a fire for several hours at long intervals after the *Chillicothe* withdrew from the action to repair damages and get a fresh supply of ammunition.

The *Chillicothe* fired fifty-three 11-inch shells into Fort Greenwood. She will engage the fort again to-morrow along with the *De Kalb* and others, and, I hope, successfully. If we fail to-morrow the expedition will be a failure for the want of ammunition, &c.

I would like to give you a description of the heroic conduct of the Captain, officers and crew of the *Chillicothe*, and so of the *De Kalb* and others engaged, but my duties will not allow me to take the time. Col. Slack is a splendid officer and elegant gentleman. So is the Colonel of the 46th Indiana. The Colonel of the 43rd Indiana is at Helena. His regiment is here. W.C.F.[31]

On 14 March, in preparation for a renewed gunboat attack on Fort Pemberton, Ross sent Slack's 47th Indiana and Col. William A. Pile's 33rd Missouri to reconnoiter both sides of the Tallahatchie River. On the east side of the Tallahatchie, the 33rd Missouri encountered and skirmished with a detachment of Confederates from Colonel Ashbel Smith's 2nd Texas Infantry.[32] Describing their reconnaissance in a letter to Ann, Slack wrote:

In the forenoon I made a reconnaissance with my Regt between our front picket line and the Yazoo River. I sent but thirty men to the advance. They had to wade in water up to their breasts. It was a pretty severe job. On the east side of the Tallahatchie we had a little skirmish yesterday. It was done by the 33rd Missouri. They killed one, wounded another, and took one prisoner. They were Texas troops. The wounded man died soon after they brought him in.[33]

Another effort was made on 16 March to take Fort Pemberton by assault, the ironclads *Chillicothe* and *Baron De Kalb* to open in conjunction with the land batteries. If successful in silencing the batteries in the fort, the infantry was to be brought forward on board the tinclads to assault the fort. In about fifteen or twenty minutes, however, the *Chillicothe* was disabled and withdrew when her hull was again penetrated by a reported 68-pound shot that hit and jammed the front port and starboard running plates, effectively silencing the guns. The *De Kalb* withdrew as well, ending the idea of an assault, although the land batteries and sharpshooters continued until sunset. The beleaguered Smith relinquished his command to Lt. Com. James P. Foster of the *Chillicothe* and returned to Helena, claiming his health had failed "under the influences of climate."[34]

Ross's infantry remained in front of the fort the next several days, reconnoitering the countryside without success to find a feasible point of attack across the overflowed countryside against the "island" fort. Meanwhile, in a futile attempt to flood the Confederates out of Fort Pemberton, Grant, believing the fort was lower in the water than it actually was, had a second cut made in the Mississippi levee across from Helena.[35]

Grant's second cut failed to deliver enough water into the Tallahatchie, and the Confederate fort held on well above the water line. On the Federal side, the expected reinforcements were nowhere in sight, and fear arose that a Confederate movement up the Mississippi & Tennessee Railroad from Grenada to Panola (Batesville) and down the Tallahatchie on steamers to the mouth of the Coldwater would block their return upstream. Having done little irreparable damage to the fort in spite of heavy bombardment, on 20 March Ross and Foster (Smith had already departed) withdrew the flotilla, the *Chillicothe* miraculously still afloat. Loring, who would earn the sobriquet "Old Blizzards" for his defense of Fort Pemberton, breathed a sigh of relief, boasting that the Federals had been "forced to an ignominious retreat ... a check which will undoubtedly prevent a further invasion of the State of Mississippi by the way of the Tallahatchee and Yazoo Rivers."[36]

Although it would turn out to be true, unbeknownst to Loring, Brigadier General Isaac Quinby's division from McPherson's corps was moving down the Tallahatchie to reinforce Ross's division in front of Fort Pemberton. The next day, Ross's fleet, retreating up the Tallahatchie, met Quinby's reinforcements coming down. Surprised at the encounter, Quinby, who was senior to Ross, took command and ordered Ross to return with his force to their recently abandoned position in front of Fort Pemberton. At about this time, a worried Halleck warned Grant of the danger that McPherson's isolated column would be attacked, and advised him, since steamers on the western waters were scarce, not to let his boats be caught on the upper Yazoo in case the water fell.[37]

Moving back upriver on 20 March with Ross's force, Slack, aboard the steamer *Moderator*, wrote to Ann about their meeting with Quinby's force coming down:

> Well we started back to Helena yesterday morning at daylight. I was up nearly all night. My Regt was picketing the front line. About midnight I was directly in front of the rebel fort when a terrible fire of rifles was opened from the rebel fort. We for a few minutes expected an attack, but in the course of a half hour it quieted down and we heard no more of it. At 3 o'clock we withdrew our picket line and went on board transports, and at daylight started up the river....
>
> Well we came up the river at this point, about eighty miles above the point we left yesterday, and here met Genl Quinby with his Division coming to reinforce us, and turned us back, and now we are on our way back again to our first point of attack. Will get down there day after tomorrow. What the movement will be, I cannot yet say.[38]

On 23 March, Quinby's flotilla began arriving back at the Curtiss plantation. That afternoon Quinby sent the *Chillicothe* and *De Kalb* ahead to draw fire, camping his division across on the east bank of the Tallahatchie. The *Chillicothe* fired three shots; none were returned, and both gunboats withdrew.[39]

Ross's division arrived the next day in a hard rain, returning to their old Curtiss plantation campground on the west bank. Two days later, Slack wrote to Ann:

> Here we are at our old camping ground, at the Curtis farm. We reached here day before yesterday. As soon as we struck the shore the 46th Regt immediately jumped ashore and went down to reconnoiter the old location of our battery, and in doing so came upon a party of 14 Secesh cutting timber. They took them all in and we now have them under guard. I am now quite well. Stand it much better than most of the officers of the Regt....
>
> Wm. T. Delvin [Co. K] died on Sunday morning at 10 o'clock. We buried him Monday in a beautiful mound, near where we are now lying.[40]

Writing on 28 March in anticipation of the arrival of the remainder of McPherson's corps and the planned assault scheduled for the next day, Slack noted that the day before four companies from the 47th Indiana and 28th Wisconsin had traveled upriver about twenty miles on a foraging expedition to the town of McNutt.[41] There they captured fifteen "Butternuts, destitute of intelligence or any other redeeming trait," whom he identified as "part of Forrest's guerilla band" who had been firing into their boats on the Tallahatchie.[42]

After the initial reconnaissance, Quinby determined that, due to west-bank flooding, an assault on the fort was only practicable down the east bank of the Tallahatchie. Lt. Com. Foster, now commanding the gunboat fleet, told Quinby that by 1 April, he was taking the gunboats back to the Mississippi. On 28 March, however, Quinby discovered that the Confederates had placed a battery to cover the east bank of the Tallahatchie that he had planned to use. Heavy Delta rains came, making the east-bank roads nearly impassable and preventing the establishment of a Federal battery to silence the new Confederate battery on the east bank. With the Confederates apparently prepared to meet them, the elements against them, and the navy disinclined to continue the fight, Quinby called off the assault.[43]

As for the 47th Indiana, their luck ran out in the predawn hours of 29 March 1863, when a violent Mississippi Delta thunderstorm spawned strong winds that uprooted a tree and blew it onto a tent, killing five members of Company F, and causing the regiment more damage than either Loring's artillery or Confederate skirmishers had done.[44]

While the 47th Indiana was on picket in front of Fort Pemberton, fires were set on the picket line on the nights of Tuesday, 31 March and Friday, 3 April, which drew fire from the fort as the Confederates commenced steady shelling on the evening of 2 April. Later, Slack would file charges against Lt. William H. Hayford of Company K for setting the fires and failing to place videttes in front of his picket line as ordered. Hayford, however, would be acquitted of these and several other subsequent charges.[45]

Inside Fort Pemberton, a now apprehensive Loring reported on 3 April that the Federals had been reinforced by "at least 3,000," that he anticipated a "desperate" fight, and that they were using up their ammunition just trying to prevent the Federals from erecting batteries in their front. He ended with an urgent request for "one hundred rockets."[46]

That same day, looking toward Loring's fortress-moat, a somewhat fatalistic, if not disheartened, "W.C.F." wrote the *Sentinel*:

From the Mississippi Squadron
Tallahatchie River, Miss.,
April 3, 1863

Editor of State Sentinel: "*Che sara sara*" is an Italian proverb which means "what is to be, is to be" and so it is, as I suppose that we are still before Fort Pemberton. [Greenwood.]

There is little of a head, or of generalship here. When at the mouth of the Yazoo, it used to be said that we were going to h__l by the way of Vicksburg; but we can now say, with truth, that we are going to Vicksburg by the way of h__l.

Fort Pemberton is situated on the Tallahatchie River — about three miles from its intersection with the Yalobusha to form the Yazoo. It is so situated that it commands the Tallahatchie River in an approach from above; and it also commands the Yazoo in an approach from below. It is now entirely surrounded by water.

To day, the Rebels have been firing at half-hour intervals upon our men engaged in throwing up fortifications opposite Fort Pemberton. I can't see what these fortifications will accomplish, unless at long range with incessant cannonade. There is unfordable water between the enemy's works and those, which are being erected by us. However, the river will soon fall, when the gunboats will return to the Mississippi River, or be gobbled up; and, when the gunboats leave, good bye to the vaunted Yazoo Pass Expedition.

The army seems to have come for no other purpose than to look on, with the solitary exception of Gen. Ross. Gen. Ross can't well fight the Rebels and grog-shops and cotton speculators at the same time.

The gunboats have the river in advance — the transports in their rear. Generals Ross, Fisk and Solomon, have the right shore of the Tallahatchie, and General Quinby has the left shore.

Large reinforcements are on their way here; but unless this shall be our future base of operations, I do not see their purpose.

Since we have been here, we have captured about fifty prisoners, and filled our hospitals. Here, the sanitary arrangements so boasted of, in the Army of the Potomac, are not enforced. I have doubted the propriety of dispensing medicines in the army — there are so many rare birds in the profession of physic. It is suggested that some old ladies with herb teas could fairly supply the places of our *surgeons* for everything except the discipline with which they put through hospital stores.

The weather is delightful. The buffalo gnats are as voracious as an ostrich, and the musquitoes — well, I can't do justice to the subject.

W.C.F.

10 o'clock P.M. — The Rebels are still firing away, without doing any hurt, at our workmen. We don't condescend to notice them. We are like the Dutchman at the battle of Horse-shoe — laying low for a big fight, may be.

W.C.F.[47]

Two days later (5 April), Quinby, unaware of Grant's orders to bring all the Yazoo Pass Expedition troops back to the Mississippi, realized that it was futile to try to assault the fort under such flooded conditions and ordered a retreat up the Tallahatchie.[48]

Following Quinby's withdrawal, a somewhat relieved Loring was able to report accurately, except for his estimation of the effectiveness of their shells on the Federal camps: "The enemy are moving up the Tallahatchee, toward the mouth of the Coldwater. The information is not sufficient yet to make certain that they are going to the Mississippi River. The probability is that it is their intention to do so. We are certain that our shells and shot did great execution in their crowded camps before leaving."[49] In the meantime, on 14 March, while Ross's expedition was attacking Fort Pemberton, Grant, out of touch with Ross for about two weeks, received reports from Mississippi newspapers of a gunboat fight at Fort Pemberton and that several thousand troops from Vicksburg had gone up the Yazoo River.

VI. Yazoo Pass, Mississippi (February–April 1863)

With the outcome of the fight in doubt, Grant and Porter decided to use Steele's Bayou, which entered the lower Yazoo near its mouth on the Mississippi, to bypass the Confederate guns at Haynes' Bluff and get Porter's gunboats and Sherman's troops to the Yazoo above the bluff to create a diversion for Ross and "hem in the enemy on the Yazoo." If successful, the Sherman/Porter expedition would become the main operation against Vicksburg.[50]

Two days earlier, Porter had made a partial reconnaissance of Steele's Bayou, but had learned that several other streams also running north and south through the delta could be reached via Steele's Bayou and used to get to the Yazoo well above Haynes' Bluff. About forty miles up Steele's Bayou, a winding four-mile passage called Big Black Bayou connected it to Deer Creek, which descended about thirty-five miles to Haynes' Bluff. A little over thirty miles up Deer Creek, however, a seven-mile passage called the Rolling Fork connected Deer Creek to the navigable Little Sunflower River, which descended fifty miles from the Rolling Fork and entered the Yazoo twenty miles above Haynes' Bluff.[51]

On 15 March, Porter's flotilla (the *Louisville, Mound City, Cincinnati, Pittsburg* and *Carondelet*, with four tugs, four mortar boats, and coal barges), accompanied by Grant on the gunboat *Price*, cut their way up Steele's Bayou. That same day, at the entrance to Big Black Bayou, Grant, promising Porter infantry support, returned to his headquarters at Young's Point, where he ordered Sherman to proceed up Steele's Bayou on two troop transports. The flotilla turned into Big Black Bayou, which was even more densely choked with cypress, willow, oak, cottonwood, and sweetbriar vines than Steele's Bayou. Flooded on the north bank, the cultivated cane fields of Hill's Plantation on the south bank of Big Black were the first dry land the sailors had seen. Some of its astonished residents watched the ironclad behemoths push cypress trees out of the way while some sailors grappled with snags in the channel and others helped to heave the boats around the bayou's sharp bends. On the morning of 17 March they entered Deer Creek, whose higher banks provided a depth of from ten to twenty feet, but whose channel was narrow with overhanging trees and choked with willow saplings that snagged the hulls of the boats, making navigation more difficult than expected.[52]

Working slowly up Deer Creek the next four days, "at times barely half a mile an hour," past cotton plantations, farms, cleared fields, and stretches of woods, Porter's flotilla ground to a halt on 20 March in the sapling-choked channel. The *Carondelet*, only several hundred yards from the Rolling Fork, found its entrance blocked with felled trees and a small Confederate force to dispute their passage. Sherman's supporting troops had not been able to keep up and were not there to prevent Colonel Samuel W. Ferguson's small force of 250 sharpshooters, 6 pieces of light artillery, and 50 troopers from the 28th Mississippi Cavalry from blocking the Rolling Fork on 19 March before Porter's gunboats could get through. Having received word of Federal gunboats entering Deer Creek, Ferguson sent his cavalry on a forced march and took his sharpshooters and artillery on board a steamer to the Rolling Fork, some forty miles below their camp on upper Deer Creek (near present-day Leland). At the Rolling Fork, they rounded up slaves from nearby plantations to fell trees into the stream. The next day, as Porter's gunboats cut their way slowly up Deer Creek, skirmishing some with Ferguson's troopers, Brigadier General Winfield S. Featherston moved up from Haynes' Bluff to the Rolling Fork via the Little Sunflower with two regiments (the 22nd and 23rd Mississippi) and one section of artillery (Co. C., 1st Mississippi Light Artillery) and took command of the combined Confederate force of about 1,300 men.[53]

On 21 March, faced with the obstructions, a firefight with Confederate sharpshooters and artillery, and attempts by Featherston's men to fell trees into Deer Creek below, Porter's gunboats began to back down the creek until one of Ferguson's artillerists hit the tug *Dahlia*, killing Assistant Engineer Henry Sullivan and sinking the coal barge that the *Dahlia* was towing, which blocked Porter's retreat. His entire fleet now trapped in Deer Creek, Porter sent an urgent dispatch to Grant for infantry assistance. Sherman, already on his way with Giles Smith's brigade, moved up from Big Black Bayou and the lead regiment skirmished with Featherston's combined force. The flotilla remained trapped until sailors from the *Louisville* blew up the coal barge and enabled the gunboats to back down Deer Creek as Sherman and the remainder of Giles Smith's brigade came up. The next day (22 March), having trailed Porter's flotilla down Deer Creek for about six or seven miles, the Confederates pulled back rapidly after a sharp skirmish near Moore's Plantation, an officer of the *Cincinnati* crediting the 8th Missouri (U.S.) with driving them off. Some sporadic rearguard skirmishing continued as Porter's flotilla escaped through Big Black Bayou and Sherman's troops boarded transports at Hill's Plantation and followed the gunboats back to Young's Point.[54]

Porter would later write on being trapped in Deer Creek: "I never knew how helpless a thing an ironclad could be when unsupported by troops. Our guns were three feet below the level, the woods stood just far enough back to enable the sharpshooters to pick off our men without our being able to bother them except with mortars, which kept them off."[55] Halleck, worried about Grant's division of his forces into small expeditions and the possible loss of Porter's gunboats in the Yazoo Delta, ordered Grant to concentrate his troops to cooperate with Banks's planned attack on Port Hudson, Louisiana. If Banks could not get to Port Hudson, Grant and Porter were to destroy Grand Gulf, Mississippi, before it became too strong. "The President," Halleck added, "is impatient about matters on the Mississippi."[56]

With his troops stretched out on the Mississippi about seventy-five miles from Lake Providence to Young's Point, Louisiana, and concerned that returning his army to Memphis or northern Mississippi for a land campaign against Vicksburg, as Sherman and Porter suggested, would risk the appearance of another retreat, Grant chose instead to combine his forces as ordered and move them southward from Milliken's Bend past Vicksburg on what he considered to be the best available, albeit waterlogged, land route on the Louisiana side. McClernand, his headquarters already at Milliken's Bend, would lead the way, followed by McPherson from Lake Providence and Sherman from Young's Point.[57]

Porter's gunboats and transports carried Sherman's troops back to Young's Point, where they disembarked on 27 March; McClernand's 13th corps formed above at Milliken's Bend; and farther upriver at Lake Providence, Louisiana, McPherson's 17th corps prepared to march down to the Milliken's Bend rendezvous. The Yazoo Pass Expedition forces returned to Helena, Arkansas, where the 46th and 47th Indiana, while still on board their transports, were detached from Salomon's brigade and immediately sent down to Milliken's Bend to join Hovey's new division in McClernand's 13th corps as Porter readied his gunboat fleet for the run past Vicksburg and Grant readied his infantry for the march through Louisiana.[58]

VII

Port Gibson, Mississippi (April–May 1863)

BACK HOME IN INDIANA

Governor Morton, anticipating trouble prior to the opening of the Democratic-dominated General Assembly on 8 January 1863, wrote to Secretary of War Stanton that antiwar sentiments were growing. He asked that Brigadier General Henry B. Carrington, who had been supervising recruitment of volunteers in Indiana, and had been credited with the arrest of some 2,600 deserters and stragglers, be permitted to remain: "He is the man for the emergency and there are great signs of trouble here." Those troubles included, according to Morton, a threat by the Indiana legislature, which he based on their political rhetoric in the previous fall's campaign, "to pass a joint resolution acknowledging the Southern Confederacy," and a movement to urge the States of the Northwest to "dissolve all constitutional relations with the New England States." Morton got his wish and Carrington remained in command of the post at Indianapolis.[1]

Striking early, on 14 January the Indiana House of Representatives condemned the Lincoln Administration for using "the tyrant's plea of military necessity" to unconstitutionally usurp power and establish a military dictatorship, adding the charge that the president had suspended the writ of habeas corpus in order to "[cripple] free speech and discussion [of] his hellish scheme of emancipation." The previous day, the Senate had presented a similar preamble and a series of resolutions regarding the unconstitutionality of the war.[2]

The idea fueled by Morton that there was movement afoot in Indiana to support a Northwest Confederacy motivated Alvin Hovey to write an address to the Democracy of Indiana, published in various newspapers in February, urging Indiana Democrats not to support or give aid and comfort to the Southern rebellion, and certainly not to entertain the idea of a coalition of the Northwest with the South. Among other things, he noted ominously, "separation on either side, with peace in the future, is impossible." Colonels William T. Spicely of the 24th Indiana, William E. McLean of the 43rd Indiana, George F. McGinnis of the 11th Indiana, and James R. Slack of the 47th Indiana signed Hovey's address. The *Huntington Democrat* denounced Hovey's address and those who signed it as "pampered hirelings ... that ... have grown to assume dictatorial powers over the Democracy of Indiana." The editors saved their most vitriolic attack for their former friend and

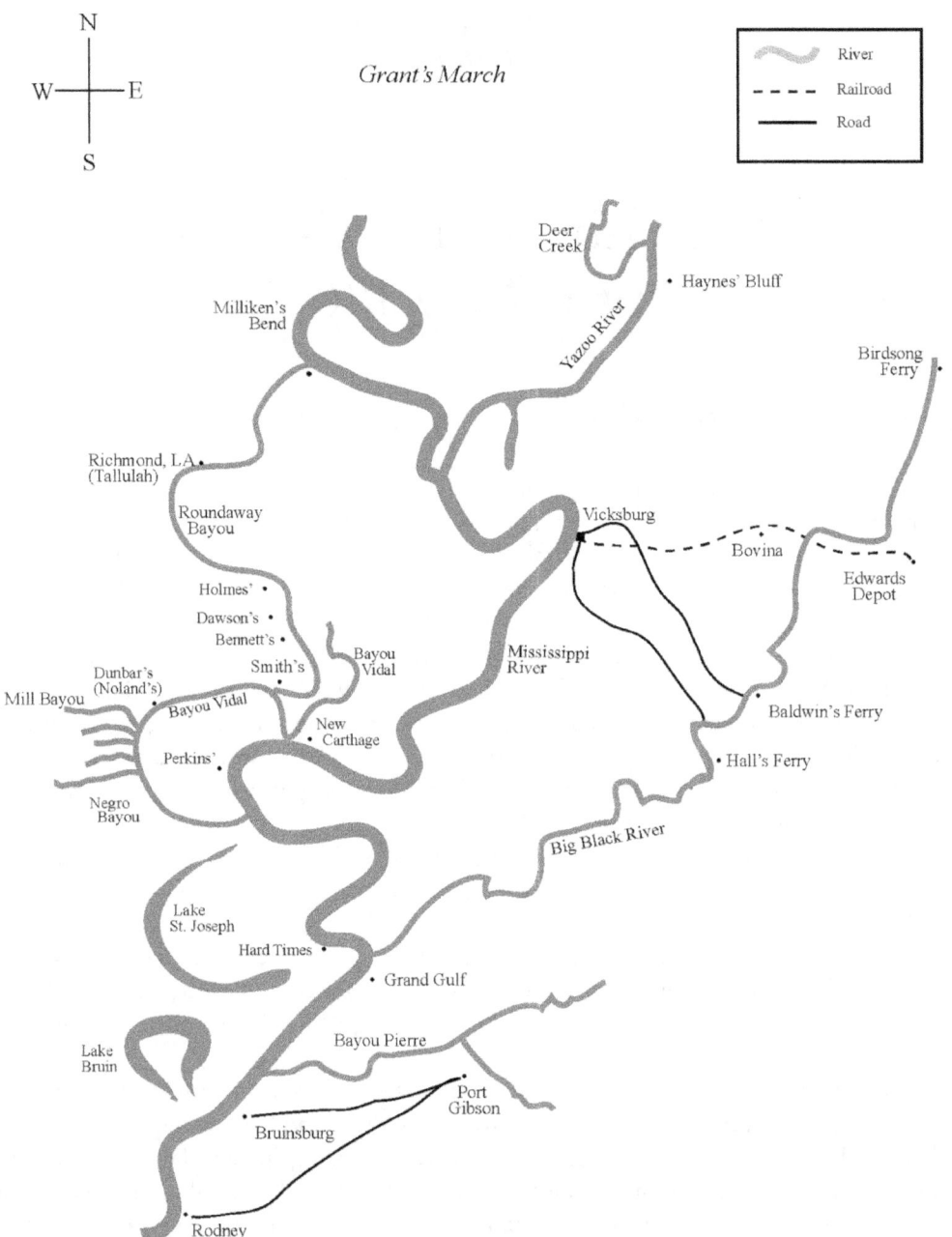

Based on O.R., Ser. I, Vol. XXIV, pt. 1, p. 188, and Atlas Plates XXXVI, No. 1 and CLV

colleague Slack, whom they called, among other things, "an enemy to his country's Constitution; a renegade to party and principle; and ... a contemptible political trafficker, beside whom Simon Cameron is pure as an angel.... We produce the Address, that it may stand in these columns as a monument to the debasement of Jim Slack. It here follows."[3]

To the Democracy of Indiana: Having a deep interest in the future welfare and glory of our country, and believing that we occupy a position in which we can see the effects of the political struggles at home upon the hopes and fears of the rebels, we deem it to be our duty to speak to you openly and plainly in regard to the same.

The rebels of the South are leaning upon the Northern Democracy for support, and it is unquestionably true that unjustifiable opposition to the Administration is "giving aid and comfort to the enemy." Whilst it is the duty of patriots to oppose the usurpations of power, it is alike their duty to avoid captious criticisms that might create the very evils which they attempt to avoid.

The name *Democrat*, associated with all that is bright and glorious in the history of the past, is being sullied and disgraced by demagogues, who are appealing to the lowest prejudices and passions of our people. We have nothing to expect from the South and nothing to hope, without their conquest. They are now using their money freely to subsidize the press and politicians of the North, and with what effect, the tone of some of our journals and the speeches of some of our leaders too plainly and painfully testify.

We see, with deep solicitude and regret, that there is an undercurrent in Indiana, tending towards a coalition of the Northwest with the South against the Eastern States. Be not deceived! Pause, for the love you bear to your country, and reflect! This movement is only a rebel scheme in disguise; that would involve you, alike with themselves, in the crime of rebellion, and bring to your own hearthstones the desolation of a French revolution. Separation on either side, with peace in the future, is impossible, and we are compelled by self-interest, by every principle of honor, and every impulse of manhood, to bring this unholy contest to a successful termination.

What! Admit that we are whipped? That twenty-three millions of Northern men are unequal to nine millions of Southerners? Shame on the State that would entertain so disgraceful a proposition! Shame upon the Democrat who would submit to it; and raise the cowardly voice and claim that he was an Indianian! He, and such dastards, with their offspring, are fit "mud sills," upon which should be built the lordly structure of the Southern aristocracy! And with whom would this unholy alliance be formed? With men who have forgotten their fathers, their oaths, their country, and their God — with guerrillas — cotton burners — with those who force every male inhabitant of the South, capable of bearing arms, into the field, though starving wives and babes are left behind! Men who persecute and hang, or drive from their lines, every man, woman and child who will not fall down and worship their Southern God! And yet freeborn men of our State will sympathize with such tyrants, and dare to even dream of coalition! Indiana's proud and loyal legions number at least seventy thousand effective men, in the field, and as with one great heart, we know they would repudiate all unholy combinations tending to the dismemberment of our Government.

In this dark hour of our country's trial, there is but one road to success and peace, and that is, To be as firmly united for our Government as the Rebels are against it. Small differences of opinion amount to nothing, in this grand struggle for a nation's existence. Do not place even one straw in the way, and remember that every word you speak to encourage the South, nerves the arm that strikes the blow which is aimed at the heart's blood of our brothers and kindred.

Alvin P. Hovey, Brig. Gen.
William T. Spicely, Col. 24th Ind.
William E. McClean, Col. 43rd Ind.
Geo. F. McGinnis, Col. 11th Ind.
Jas. R. Slack, Col. 47th Ind.

Facing similar problems, on 1 March 1862, President Davis, authorized by the Confederate Congress, declared the privilege of habeas corpus suspended in cities of the Confederacy threatened by invasion, including Richmond and ten miles of the surrounding countryside. Two days later in Washington, acting to remedy Justice Taney's ruling in the Merryman case that only Congress could suspend the privilege of habeas corpus, the United States Congress passed a new Habeas Corpus Act by a party-line vote of 75 to 41 that authorized the president, "during the present rebellion," to suspend the privilege of the writ of habeas corpus anywhere in the United States or any part thereof,[4] "whenever in his judgment, the public safety may require it."

The act recognized the president's authority to suspend the writ of habeas corpus without the approval of Congress; it relieved military commanders from their obligation to answer the writ; and soldiers or officers who followed the president's orders were protected against future lawsuits or other legal action in Federal courts. The act, however, did attempt to regulate and control the rising number of arbitrary arrests. In a rule that applied to future as well as previous arrests, the Secretaries of War and State were required to furnish Federal circuit and district courts with the names of prisoners. If grand juries found no indictment against the prisoners, they were to be released by judicial order upon taking the oath of allegiance. Judges were also authorized to release prisoners when no list of names was supplied. And, on the petition of any citizen, prisoners detained more than 20 days without being listed were to be discharged upon taking the oath of allegiance. Nevertheless, as James Madison warned at the time Congress passed the Bill of Rights, "words written on paper cannot always prevent determined government officials or intolerant majorities from abusing the rights of unpopular citizens." Indeed, in spite of the limitations included in the new Habeas Corpus Act, the president and military commanders continued to ignore court mandates and political arrests increased dramatically after its passage on 3 March 1863.[5]

In the North, the Lincoln Administration used the suspension of habeas corpus and military imprisonment, even after the 3 March 1863 Habeas Corpus Act, to stamp out dissent and close down antiwar newspapers. In spite of this governmental and military harassment, including some sixty recorded cases of extra-judicial mob violence against the Democratic newspapers or their editors, many led by soldiers home on leave, most antiwar newspapers continued to publish, albeit carefully, throughout the war.[6]

In the South, a compliant press and extra-judicial intimidation sufficed to silence pro-Unionists or "peace agitators." Even before secession, abolitionists and other opponents of secession were driven out of the South or into silence if they stayed at home. Speaking or publishing anything about freedom for the slaves or advocating an end to slavery was outlawed, considered tantamount to fomenting insurrection, and the penalty was jail, the lash, or, for the second offense, death.[7]

The same day that the Habeas Corpus Act passed (3 March 1863), President Lincoln signed the Conscription Act, which called for a quota of troops from each state that could be filled by either conscripts or volunteers. Within days of the passage of the Conscription Act, protests erupted in the North over Section 13, which specified that a conscript would be discharged of his obligation to serve if, on or before the day of his scheduled appearance, he either furnished an acceptable substitute or paid the government a fee, capped at $300, to procure a substitute. Protesters immediately claimed, with reason, that it had now become "a rich man's war and a poor man's fight." The *Indiana State Sentinel*, quoting the *Providence (Rhode Island) Post*, editorialized: "The rich man is allowed to stand back by paying the Government three hundred dollars. The poor man, who cannot raise three hundred dollars, must shoulder his musket and march." In that same edition, the *State Sentinel* reported that the German Workingmen's Association in Chicago had unanimously passed a resolution, signed by over one thousand members, which condemned Congress for placing "$300.00 on par with the life blood of a poor man."[8]

In Detroit, violence erupted against the war and against the people who were, in a twisted way, seen as the cause of it. On 6 March, the *Chicago Tribune* reported, "a depraved Copperhead mob fell upon the colored people of Detroit the other day, and murdered and burned many in their homes, and destroyed by fire the humble dwellings of scores of negro families." In what became known at that time as the Detroit Riot, a mob reported by victims to be mostly German (referred to colloquially as "Dutch") and Irish working-class whites armed with guns, axes and cudgels, many of them young men of draft age and boys as young as ten years old, roamed the streets of the city. They attacked and burned a black-owned and -operated cooperage, and attacked vulnerable black men, women and children wherever they encountered them on the street. At least one person was killed, many injured, and some thirty houses of black citizens burned before the military intervened and dispersed the mob. The police of Detroit, known as a "Democratic" city, did virtually nothing to stop the attacks, which were quelled only when the military intervened. The Michigan state legislature "encouraged" the City of Detroit to compensate the victims, but the Detroit City Council voted against it. In response, the Reverend S.S. Hunting of the Lafayette Street Unitarian Church in Detroit noted perceptively in a sermon following the so-called riot, printed in the *Detroit Advertiser & Tribune*, "That Government is of little value which does not hold the rights of its poorest subject as sacred as those of the richest.... [W]hoever lifts the brickbat or cudgel to beat him down or ... slanders him and talks of his extermination — is putting a torch to his own house."[9]

Indeed, violence on both sides continued as antiwar Democratic newspapers were attacked by mobs, in many cases soldiers on leave or recently paroled. On 10 March, the *Chicago Tribune* reported that the editorial rooms of *The Crisis* of Columbus, Ohio, were destroyed by a mob of soldiers. On 15 March in Indiana, the office of the *Richmond Jeffersonian* was destroyed by a sledgehammer-wielding mob identified as recently paroled soldiers from Illinois and Wisconsin who were on their way home after having been captured at Murfreesboro. The *State Sentinel* noted, however, that the soldiers' rampage was decried by the Republican *Eaton (Ohio) Register* in their 19 March edition.[10]

Carrington, backed by findings of a circuit court grand jury, claimed that "secret oath-bound organizations," referred to explicitly in the *Indianapolis Daily Journal* as the "Knights of the Golden Circle," existed in Indiana who were encouraging soldiers to desert with their arms. In one Indiana case he had to send troops to dislodge seventeen deserters holed up in a log cabin behind defensive works to make the arrests. On 16 March, the *Daily Journal* printed a report by one of Carrington's soldiers (Adam J. Cook, Co. E, no regiment named) who, on assignment arresting deserters in the state, claimed that "Butternuts" in Shelby and Decatur counties were resisting the draft, and that in the town of Milford, armed with revolvers and shotguns, they drilled and performed mock battles a half mile from town.[11]

The Knights of the Golden Circle was perhaps the last of the filibustering empire and slavery-expansion schemes of the 1850s: a secret military society and filibustering scheme concocted by a clever, self-educated con artist named George Washington Lafayette [or Lamb] Bickley to raise funds for a purported invasion and annexation of Mexico.[12] Born in Virginia in 1819, Bickley moved to Cincinnati in 1852 and successfully passed himself off as a physician and lecturer at the proprietary Eclectic Medical Institute, where, from 1852 through 1854 and 1857 to 1860, he was a member of the faculty and an editor of the Institute's newsletter, the *Eclectic Medical Journal*. An inveterate schemer, while on sick leave in

1855 he gave a series of lectures on biblical revelation at the Broadway Tabernacle in New York City, a series titled "The Doomed Cities of Antiquity," to promote and finance what he hoped would be a money-making expedition to Mesopotamia. The scheme failed for lack of support and he returned to the Eclectic Institute in Cincinnati.[13]

Back in Cincinnati, Bickley, apparently bored with eclectic medicine, concocted his grandiose filibustering and slavery-expanding scheme, along with an elaborate set of secret rituals and symbols. (The "golden circle" referred to the circle of Caribbean and Gulf of Mexico countries, with Cuba at its center, to be annexed to the United States as slave states.) During this period, Bickley used Texas as his model, itself an example of a very successful slavery-expanding land grab, to convince Kentucky slaveholders to finance his scheme and recruit members for the initial phase, which was to colonize, then gain control of, and reintroduce slavery into what was left of Old Mexico, then badly weakened by civil war.[14]

Bickley's scheme was also aided by the fact that another freebooter, William Walker, who had failed in an attempt to take over territory in northwestern Mexico in 1853, had, with the support of Southern slave interests, succeeded in taking over Nicaragua in 1856, where he established himself as president and reintroduced slavery in the year that he held power. Walker was overthrown a year later but returned to New Orleans as a conquering, albeit displaced, hero, and he continued to attempt to raise funds from southern slave-expansionists for another assault. Following in Walker's footsteps in 1859 and attempting to tap into that same source of funds, Bickley was given free publicity by major Southern newspapers as well as the *New York Times* to finance his slavery-expanding venture. In one case, Bickley asked each slave owner to send him one dollar for each slave he owned in order to expand slave territory or, better yet, five dollars for each slave to ensure that "no more negroes will be spirited away on the famous underground railway." Oddly, Bickley seemed to be saying that conquering new slave territory was less costly than blocking the underground railway escape route.[15]

Bickley gained both national and international notoriety and even financed a short-lived Baltimore newspaper called the *American Cavalier*. After John Brown's raid at Harpers Ferry, Virginia, however, interest in expanding Southern slavery into the Caribbean gave way to talk of secession. This development essentially scuttled his money-raising and recruitment efforts until he moved to Texas in October 1860, where, even at this late date, his plans to invade Mexico continued to resonate. He recruited perhaps several hundred followers or "knights," and his planned invasion began to take shape until Governor Sam Houston, who had been lobbying Washington for permission to invade Mexico and apparently did not want to be upstaged by a ragtag band of misfits, broke up their plans.[16]

The outbreak of civil war ended Bickley's grandiose scheme, although 150 of his "knights" mustered into Confederate service and became part of then Colonel Ben McCulloch's force that helped drive the Federal garrisons out of Texas. Bickley would later take credit for this and for triggering "the greatest war of modern time." Not wanting to get involved in a real shooting war, however, "General" Bickley moved back to Tennessee and Kentucky to try to revive the K.G.C. and aid secession in the Border States.[17]

Abolitionist secret orders had emerged in the turbulent 1850s as well. A semi-secret and quasi-military order of young men known as the "Wide Awakes" was organized in 1856, ostensibly as a mutual protection society to serve as poll watchers for the new Republican Party and their presidential candidate John C. Fremont. Especially prominent in Abraham

Lincoln's 1860 presidential campaign, where they were also known as the "Rail Maulers," they paraded, did military drills and, if necessary, intimidated or defended against attacks by their opponents. When war broke out, most, but not all, Wide Awakes disbanded when their younger members joined the Union Army. Some groups with older members kept the name, although where the Wide Awakes disbanded, they were generally replaced by secret "Union" or "Liberty" Leagues that served the same purpose.[18]

Although the K.G.C. essentially ceased to exist with the onset of war, the name lived on, even internationally, in the public's imagination, largely due to Republican newspapers like the *Indianapolis Daily Journal*, politicians like Morton, and military officials like Carrington. Morton, in an attempt to defeat his Democratic opponents at the polls, associated the name with the rise of antiwar sentiment in Indiana and as a specter of a vast, secret, well-organized and traitorous Democratic conspiracy to subvert his administration and the war effort. The *Daily Journal* eagerly promoted this idea.[19]

Many antiwar and anti-draft secret orders emerged independent of the K.G.C. as "mutual protection associations" to resist the draft and military arrests, and to protect what they considered to be their basic constitutional rights. Although most were nameless local groups of disaffected Democrats, one in particular emerged in St. Louis with pretensions almost as great as those of the old K.G.C.

Much like Bickley's defunct K.G.C., the Order of American Knights originated as the filibustering fantasy of one man, Phineas C. Wright, a New York-born lawyer who dreamt it up while he lived in New Orleans in the 1850s. New Orleans, however, was overrun with filibusters and lawyers, and Wright, essentially a failure at both occupations, moved to St. Louis in 1859. There he joined forces with Charles L. Hunt, former United States Consul to Belgium, who, with several others, had formed a local antiwar, anti–Republican, secret society with the grandiose name of "Corps de Belgique." Their actual membership existed largely on paper, but they counted as presumptive members the large number of pro-slavery partisans in the state. These few men, having joined "forces" with Wright, adopted Wright's name, the "Order of American Knights," and named Wright their "Supreme Commander" and Hunt the "Grand Commander" in Missouri. Early in 1863, Wright would attempt to recruit and organize cells or "lodges" of the O.A.K. in Illinois, Indiana, and New York.[20]

Although Morton's claims about a vast, well-organized conspiracy were greatly exaggerated, at the time, especially in rural southern Indiana, many people had joined local, independent, secret anti-draft and antiwar groups. As Churchill points out, most of the people of southern Indiana were yeoman farmers and laborers who worked family farms and relied heavily on their own free labor, and, especially at harvest time, help from their neighbors. The military conscription of able-bodied adult males seriously threatened this economy as well as their communal sense of autonomy from governmental interference. Not unimportantly, the idea of a war of emancipation and the entry of free blacks into the Indiana work force did not sit well with them either. In this context, many independent, local, anti-draft, mutual protection societies formed from which Wright hoped to organize his all-encompassing O.A.K. Anticipating problems, Morton asked Carrington to begin recruiting "confidential agents" to infiltrate the antiwar secret societies.[21]

Concerned about the rise in antiwar sentiments and militant antiwar groups regardless of their names, the editors of the *Daily Journal* noted with contempt that their counterparts at the *Cincinnati Enquirer* had admitted to the existence of the secret societies, but had, according to the *Daily Journal*, disingenuously argued that they were not trying to disband the Union Army or forcibly resist the draft. The editors of the *Enquirer* had argued that the federal government's attack on the Bill of Rights, notably freedom of speech and press, had given rise to the secret societies. The *Indiana State Sentinel* called the military investigations and arrests "The Inquisition," and pointed out that Abolitionist Unions or Liberty Leagues were not being investigated. Earlier, the *State Sentinel* had listed a number of violations of the Constitution including the rights of freedom of speech and press, the right to security from arrest and detention without charge, the right of trial by jury, and not least, the right of property, including slaves, that had been abrogated by the Emancipation Proclamation. Republican newspapers denounced this view.[22]

Antiwar agitation and draft resistance in the North, certainly in Indiana, Illinois, and Ohio, had in early 1863 become so widespread that Brig. Gen. Alexander Asboth advised that Illinois regiments, especially new ones, be kept as far from their homes as possible to prevent desertion. Brig. Gen. William Rosecrans, commanding the Department of the Cumberland, asserted that political agitation to encourage desertion had become so great that those three states had become havens for thousands of skulkers and deserters and appealed to the War Department for authority to send officers "to arrest and collect them, and bring them to duty."[23]

In one notable case, Carrington sent troops from Indiana into Illinois to arrest and place in military detention a sitting judge of the Fourth Judicial Circuit, then at Marshall, Clark County, Illinois, thus exposing a still potentially volatile Constitutional conflict between civil and military authority not dealt with in the newly signed Habeas Corpus Act. On 6 March, acting on orders to track down and arrest deserters, the authority for which was provided in the new Conscription Act, Sgt. John McFarland of the 31st Indiana Infantry and Sgt. Thomas Long of the 1st Indiana Cavalry, operating out of a recruiting station at Terre Haute, crossed the Wabash River into Clark County, Illinois. They tracked down and arrested four deserters from the 130th Illinois and the 31st Indiana regiments, placing them under arrest in a hotel in Livingston, about fifteen miles east of Marshall, prior to taking them back to Indiana.

That night, Elizabeth Gamron, mother of one of the arrested deserters, James Gamron, hired a local attorney who advised her to obtain a warrant to arrest McFarland and Long for kidnapping. The following morning (Saturday), as McFarland and Long were about to leave with their prisoners for Terre Haute, they were arrested by the Clark County sheriff and taken to Marshall, where they obtained an attorney and a hearing before Judge Charles H. Constable of the Fourth Judicial Circuit.

Judge Constable, however, citing "state rights," refused to recognize the authority of the military officers from Indiana to arrest persons in Illinois, or to take them out of the state against their will (much as Chief Justice Taney had argued in *Ex parte Merryman*), and ordered them to appear in court the following Thursday to face the charge of kidnapping. They were both released on $500 bonds, and Judge Constable set the deserters free.

Carrington learned quickly of the arrests and contacted his immediate superior, Horatio Wright, commander of the Department of the Ohio, as well as Secretary of War Stanton in Washington and Governor Oliver P. Morton in Indianapolis. With explicit military orders from Wright and the tacit approval of the War Department and Gov. Morton, Carrington took a force of 200 infantry from the 63rd Indiana and 40 troopers from the 5th Indiana Cavalry to Marshall to free the sergeants, rearrest the deserters, and to arrest Judge Constable "for harboring and protecting deserters."

At 9:30 A.M. on Thursday, 12 March, Carrington's force surrounded the Clark County Courthouse. Carrington arrested Judge Constable while court was in session to hear the charges against McFarland and Long. At 3:00 P.M., Carrington, with Judge Constable in custody, returned to Terre Haute and on to Indianapolis the next day. There Judge Constable, free to roam the city, was kept at the Bates House Hotel to await trial by a military commission for releasing the deserters.

On 25 March, after considerable legal and political deliberation from the president and the War Department on down about the consequences of this military action, that could, at least potentially, unleash violent civil strife in this deeply split region, a decision was made to turn Judge Constable over to civilian authorities. On 2 April, Constable was taken to Springfield, Illinois, where a hearing of his case was scheduled before the U.S. District Court for Southern Illinois. Constable was then released on parole until the hearing. On 7 April U.S. District Judge Samuel H. Treat, after hearing both sides, dismissed the charge and released Constable, who returned to the Fourth Circuit bench after his release. Although officials in Washington breathed a sigh of relief that a Constitutional crisis had been averted, both Judges Constable and Treat were well-known antiwar Democrats, and the decision in turn exacerbated the partisan dispute at home.[24]

While the Constable case was still proceeding, Carrington was promoted to brigadier general and assigned command of the newly established Military District of Indiana, a part of Horatio Wright's Department of the Ohio.[25]

On 30 March the Democratic *Indiana State Sentinel* published Carrington's address to the people. Referring to him as "the Military Governor of Indiana," they bemoaned that Indiana had, for the first time in its history, been placed under military rule: "This is a new feature in the history of our State. Never before has Indiana been placed under military rule. It is a dangerous delegation of power. General Carrington is not amenable to the civil power of the State. He is above it. He is not responsible to the people of Indiana for the discharge of the trust confided in him.... In that regard this new department in the Federal Government overrides the sovereignty and independence of the State."[26]

In the meantime, Major General Ambrose Burnside, relieved of command of the Army of the Potomac in January following his disastrous defeat at Fredericksburg in December, superseded Horatio Wright as commander of the Department of the Ohio. Embarrassed by his defeat at Fredericksburg and seething over the antiwar speeches of Clement L. Vallandigham, Burnside issued General Order Number 38. (Vallandigham had been defeated in November in his bid for reelection to the U.S. Congress but remained a leading Copperhead spokesman.) Although the order pertained largely to spies in the department, it included a challenge to Vallandigham and other Copperheads: "The habit of declaring sympathy for the enemy will not be tolerated in this department." And, a week later, Burnside established a military commission at Cincinnati to try those persons found in violation of General Order Number 38.[27]

Vallandigham accepted the challenge. On 1 May, he excoriated the Lincoln Administration and the war against the South in a speech at a large public gathering in Mount Vernon, Ohio. In response, Burnside ordered Vallandigham arrested on 5 May in the middle of the night at his home in Dayton and taken into military custody at Cincinnati essentially for "uttering disloyal sentiments" in violation of General Order Number 38. Brought quickly before the military commission, whose authority and jurisdiction he denied, Vallandigham was convicted on 16 May and sentenced to prison at Fort Warren, Boston Harbor, for the duration of the war.[28]

An outcry against this military arrest and violation of Vallandigham's constitutional right to freedom of speech (the *Daily Journal* referred to the protest as the "Dayton Riot") validated what the Copperheads had been saying all along, and assisted Phineas Wright's floundering efforts to recruit for the O.A.K. Three days later, a somewhat embarrassed President Lincoln commuted Vallandigham's sentence to banishment south beyond the Federal military lines. George E. Pugh, Vallandigham's counsel, appealed immediately to the U.S. Circuit Court in Cincinnati that the military commission lacked jurisdiction in this case under the Habeas Corpus Act of 1863 and applied for a writ of habeas corpus. Judge Humphrey H. Leavitt ruled that the circuit court lacked authority and denied the writ. In a somewhat surprising ruling, in December, the Supreme Court denied Vallandigham's writ of certiorari, stating that the Constitution gave the Supreme Court no authority to review or revise the results of a military commission.[29]

Vallandigham's arrest and conviction by a military commission brought widespread condemnation and an outcry that he should have been tried in a civilian court. According to Lincoln's secretaries and biographers, John Nicolay and John Hay, "No act of Government has been so strongly criticized, and none having relation to the rights of an individual created a feeling so deep and widespread."[30]

If the Constable and Vallandigham cases were not enough, on 20 April, Ambrose Burnside, in a portent of things to come, removed Carrington from command of the Military District of Indiana and replaced him with Brigadier General Milo Hascall, reportedly because of Carrington's belief that indicted civilians should be tried by the circuit courts rather than by military commissions. Upon arrival in the state, Hascall issued General Order Number 9, in which he affirmed that he would enforce Burnside's General Order Number 38 in Indiana and would go after any newspapers or public speakers that encouraged resistance to the draft or any other war measure passed by Congress. A firestorm of protest ignited, however, when he added that all who "endeavor to bring the war policy of the Government into disrespect will be considered as having violated [General Order Number 38] and treated accordingly." Once again, only this time by military edict, opposition to the Lincoln Administration's war policy was equated with treason.[31]

Newspaper editors around the state and elsewhere protested the order and published their intention not to obey General Order Number 9. In response, Hascall threatened to suppress any such newspaper which did not immediately print a retraction. Three Indiana newspapers (the *Columbia City News*, the *South Bend Forum*, and the *Warsaw Union*) and one from New York (the *New York Express*) are recorded as having received threats of suppression for publishing articles critical of the order or their intention to violate it. Even Governor Morton had had enough. Impressed by the outcry that ensued from angry voters and irritated by what he considered to be Hascall's attempt to usurp his authority as governor (at least Carrington had consulted him prior to Judge Constable's arrest), Morton asked President Lincoln to remove him from command. United States Supreme Court Justice David Davis also urged the president to remove Hascall.[32]

In the meantime, Burnside, supported by the *Daily Journal*, also went on the attack against freedom of the press, which had thrived in spite of earlier attempts by the Postmaster General to stop the circulation of antiwar newspapers through the mails and the military takeover of the telegraph system. On 1 June, he issued an order to suppress the publication of Wilbur Storey's *Chicago Times* and to prohibit the circulation of the *New York World* in the Department of the Ohio because of what he considered to be their disloyal antiwar and anti-administration editorials. A military detachment from Camp Douglas took possession of the *Times*, which in turn led to a mass meeting of a reported 20,000 in Chicago to protest the military suppression of the freedom of speech and press. Troops from Springfield were on the way to Chicago when President Lincoln issued an order to Burnside to revoke the order.[33]

Responding to Morton's request for Hascall's removal, and speaking on behalf of the president, Secretary of War Stanton told Burnside to remove Hascall from command because of Morton's "familiarity with the temper of the people." He added that the president understood the harm done by "an indiscreet or foolish military officer, who is constantly issuing military proclamations and engaging in newspaper controversies upon questions that agitate the public mind." In a postscript, Stanton mentioned that President Lincoln had also become aware of Burnside's suppression of the *Chicago Times*, and, because "the irritation produced by such acts is in his opinion likely to do more harm than the publication would do," ordered Burnside to rescind his suppression orders. Weary of "indiscreet and foolish" military officers, Stanton added: "On questions such as the arrest of civilians and the suppression of newspapers not requiring immediate action the President desires to be previously consulted." About a week later, Hascall was given thirty days' leave and superseded by Brigadier General Orlando B. Willcox, whose new command now included the state of Michigan. Hascall was sent off to command the 3rd division in Major General George L. Hartsuff's newly organized Army of the Ohio.[34]

Back east, "Fighting Joe" Hooker, now in command of the Army of the Potomac, sat stalemated across the Rappahannock from Fredericksburg; Rosecrans, who had survived a near defeat at Murfreesboro at the beginning of the year, was now ensconced in Middle Tennessee, although not moving; and, on the Mississippi, Grant was seen as stymied in his attempt to take Vicksburg.

GRANT'S MARCH

While the political split in Indiana deepened, back on the Mississippi, Grant organized his forces for the march southward through Louisiana. A.P. Hovey's 12th division joined Peter J. Osterhaus's 9th, Andrew J. Smith's 10th, and Eugene A. Carr's 14th divisions in McClernand's 13th corps. Benjamin Prentiss remained in command of the District of Eastern Arkansas; Willis Gorman retained command of the Post of Helena; and Leonard Ross remained at Helena in command of the 13th division. Frederick Salomon and Clinton Fisk remained as well, commanding the 1st and 2nd brigades, respectively.[35]

Also joining the Vicksburg Campaign, the 46th Indiana transferred from Salomon's brigade to McGinnis' 1st brigade of Hovey's 12th division, joining the 11th, 24th, and 34th Indiana and the 29th Wisconsin. Slack was again given command of the 2nd brigade of

Hovey's division, and command of the 47th Indiana again reverted to Lt. Col. John A. McLaughlin. Joining the 47th Indiana in Slack's brigade were the 87th Illinois (Col. John E. Whiting), the 24th Iowa (Col. Eber C. Byam); the 28th Iowa (Col. John Connell); and the 56th Ohio (Col. William H. Raynor). Hovey's 12th division artillery consisted of Battery A, 1st Missouri (Capt. George W. Schofield), the 2nd Ohio (Lt. August Beach), and the 16th Ohio (Capt. James H. Mitchell).[36]

Porter and Sherman had recommended Grant move against Vicksburg on an inland route through Mississippi. But, with his troops stretched out on the Louisiana side of the river about seventy-five miles from Lake Providence to Young's Point, he chose not to return to Memphis or northern Mississippi to begin the campaign and risk the appearance of a retreat. Rather, he chose to move from Milliken's Bend, Louisiana, on what he considered to be the best available land route. McClernand's corps, headquartered there, would lead the way, followed by McPherson's corps down from Lake Providence and Sherman's up from Young's Point.[37]

On 29 March, Osterhaus's division led the advance of McClernand's 13th corps. Marching southward about twelve miles from Milliken's Bend to Richmond, Louisiana, a detachment of infantry, cavalry, and artillery under Colonel James Keigwin of the 49th Indiana drove Major Isaac F. Harrison's 15th Battalion Louisiana Cavalry out of town. At Richmond, Captain William F. Patterson's independent company of Kentucky pioneers bridged Roundaway Bayou and Osterhaus's troops wound their way southward to Smith's Plantation, which sat at the junction of Roundaway Bayou and Bayou Vidal. At Smith's, the two bayous formed a two-mile channel, referred to as a continuation of Bayou Vidal, which continued southward to the Mississippi River levee at New Carthage. New Carthage, however, originally thought to provide a good troop staging area by Grant because it was the first point below Vicksburg that could be reached by land, had become an island accessible only by boat due to breaks in the Bayou Vidal levee and the high level of the Mississippi.[38]

From its junction with Roundaway Bayou, Bayou Vidal also flowed in a westward arc behind a natural levee around the extensive Perkins's Somerset Plantation land and reentered the Mississippi River about five or six miles below the upper end. Confederate cavalry still held the high ground from the site of Judge Perkins's[39] mansion on the Mississippi River, about halfway between the upper and lower ends of Bayou Vidal, along a narrow eight-mile ridgeline that ran westward to Dunbar's Plantation on the outermost point of Bayou Vidal. Osterhaus's division moved down and took control of Roundaway Bayou from Richmond to Smith's Plantation as the remainder of McClernand's 13th Corps (A.J. Smith's, Carr's, and Hovey's divisions) gathered at Milliken's Bend.[40]

The next day (15 April), in a token effort to stop the Federal advance in Louisiana, Pemberton sent three Confederate infantry regiments from Grand Gulf across the river to James's Plantation, several miles downriver from New Carthage and adjacent to Perkins's Plantation, to support Harrison's attack on Keigwin's force, which had moved to Dunbar's Plantation near the confluence of Mill Bayou and Bayou Vidal. In a brisk skirmish, Keigwin's Federals (the 2nd Illinois Cavalry) drove Harrison's 15th Battalion Louisiana Cavalry troopers and the 1st Missouri Infantry (CS) from Cockrell's brigade, who had waded across Mill Bayou and splashed across an overflowed field in thigh-deep water, back across Mill Bayou and Bayou Vidal. The Confederate troops at James's plantation withdrew without a fight upon learning of Harrison's retreat on their left flank.[41]

VII. Port Gibson, Mississippi (April–May 1863)

By 16 April, McClernand had begun concentrating his corps on Roundaway Bayou. Osterhaus's vanguard division occupied Smith's Plantation, Carr's the area close behind, and A.J. Smith's troops occupied Holmes's Plantation, about twelve miles from Richmond.[42]

Slack's brigade reached Richmond before dark and bivouacked, but not before burning many of the plantations they passed. Colonel William H. Raynor of the 56th Ohio recorded in his diary that on the march to Richmond more than a dozen buildings were set ablaze by troops primarily from the Methodist minister-laden 24th and 28th Iowa.[43]

That night (16 April), seven gunboats and a ram from Porter's fleet, along with the steamers *Silver Wave* and *Forest Queen*, ran past the Vicksburg batteries. Losing only the steamer *Henry Clay*, Grant now had the means to ferry at least some of his troops to Hard Times Landing just above the Confederate fortifications at Grand Gulf; and, if Grand Gulf could be taken, or at least silenced, he had the means to ferry them across the river below Vicksburg.[44]

Describing the one-and-a-half-hour running of the eight-mile gauntlet of batteries from Vicksburg to Warrenton by Federal gunboats from the perspective of a soldier in Osterhaus's division, Private Owen Johnston Hopkins of the 42nd Ohio wrote:

> A little before midnight, when most of the lights had disappeared from Vicksburg, and silence reigned over both camps, the gunboats were to pass down in a single file, and when opposite the batteries were to open on them a terrific fire. Under cover of this fire and protected by the gunboats, the transports were to endeavor to run by unseen. The gunboats — huge masses of blackness — emerged from their concealment and moved silently down the stream. Breathlessly, the army at Young's Point watched the movements of these clouds of darkness from which War's most awful thunders were soon to burst.
>
> Three-quarters of an hour of silence elapsed, when two flashes from one of the Vicksburg batteries, followed by a roar that shook the hills, announced the opening of the grand drama. In an instant, the whole line of bluffs was ablaze with fire. The three transports — the *Forest Queen*, *Henry Clay*, and *Silver Wave*— were now on the most impetuous rush down the stream. The ironclads lay squarely before the city, from twenty-five guns pouring their storm of shell and shrapnel directly into the streets. Suddenly a gleam of light appeared, and an immense bonfire blazed from one of the hills of Vicksburg, converting night into day. The beacon flames lit up the hills so brilliantly that every boat was exposed to the careful aim of the batteries.
>
> The *Forest Queen* was disabled and was taken in tow by a gunboat and carried without further injury down the stream. The cotton on the *Henry Clay* ignited from a bursting shell, and that steamer burned to the water's edge. The crew in both escaped to the western shore. The *Silver Wave* was not touched, and reached our lines below in safety.[45]

Describing the running of the Federal gunboats from the perspective of a Confederate soldier viewing it from Vicksburg, Sgt. William Pitt Chambers of the 46th Mississippi wrote:

> Between three and four o'clock next morning I witnessed an impressive scene. Being aroused by the pickets firing I knew another battery-running enterprise was afoot. Hastily climbing a high hill I obtained a pretty fair view of the splendid panorama. Across the river two or three buildings were on fire, the flames leaping madly upward, lighting up the sky and the dense curtain of smoke that swung over the river with a livid glow. The whole surface of the stream was lighted up and far out on its broad bosom was a fleet of five or six steamers and two gun-boats. The latter were firing as rapidly as their guns could be worked, while our batteries were sending forth a stream of shot and shell. The dense smoke that partially concealed the flashes of sulphurous flame added to the weirdness of the scene.[46]

On 17 April, after listening all night to the sound of artillery fire in the direction of Vicksburg, Hovey's division marched down Roundaway Bayou in the footsteps of Osterhaus, Carr and A.J. Smith's troops. Marching twelve miles past deserted and now ransacked plantations, they camped at Dawson's Plantation, which was about two miles below A.J. Smith's camp at Holmes's Plantation, three or four miles above Carr's division, and about five miles above Osterhaus's camp at Smith's Plantation.[47]

That day, Slack wrote to Ann about their march to Dawson's Plantation through land "rich beyond conception." Other than calling it "a hard days' travel," Slack, unlike Raynor, did not mention that any of his brigade's troops burned plantations on the march to Richmond. Nor did he mention that most of the plantations on Roundaway Bayou had already been ransacked by McClernand's vanguard troops.[48]

That same day (17 April), in a move to divert attention from Grant's march, Colonel Benjamin H. Grierson's cavalry brigade left La Grange, Tennessee, with 1,700 troopers from the 6th Illinois, the 7th Illinois, and the 2nd Iowa Cavalry on a raid through the heart of Mississippi.[49]

On the evening of 19 April, with McGinnis's brigade remaining at Dawson's, Slack's brigade moved several miles farther down Roundaway Bayou ("the alligator swamp") to adjoining Bennett's Plantation.[50]

With the channel via Roundaway Bayou and Bayou Vidal navigable from Smith's Plantation to the Mississippi, Grant sent Osterhaus and Carr's divisions forward to the Perkins's Plantation rendezvous, where he set up his headquarters. Quickly realizing that transporting the entire army to Perkins's via steamers would be, as he put it, "exceedingly tedious," he assigned Hovey's division the task of opening a military road around Bayou Vidal to bring the remainder of his army to Perkins's Plantation by land.[51]

Acting on their new orders, at 6:00 A.M., Hovey's division broke camp at Dawson's and Bennett's Plantations, marched several miles down Roundaway Bayou, turned westward on the right bank of Bayou Vidal, and continued ten more miles to Dunbar's and Noland's Plantations. That day, the men camped on the plowed plantation fields without tents, sweltering in the midday heat until drenched by a late afternoon thunderstorm, which continued intermittently all night and turned the fields into a muddy quagmire.[52]

Slack wrote Ann that they arrived at "Noulen's Plantation" on 21 April after a ten-mile march on a "passable road." The men camped at the plantation and he established his headquarters in the parlor of the mansion, which had been gutted by the troopers from the 2nd Illinois Cavalry, who were apparently angry because a party that reportedly included the mansion's owner had killed one of their troopers.[53]

A mile or so beyond this point, Bayou Vidal curved southward and a series of four or five bayous bounded by Mill on the north and Negro on the south entered it from the west. Now overflowed, they made several miles of the road from their camps to the river impassable and forced Hovey's pioneers to bridge to the heavily timbered and swampy but not inundated left bank.[54]

The next day (22 April), Hovey's pioneers, led by Lieutenant Peter C. Hains of the engineers, Patterson's Kentuckians, and a squad of pioneers under Captain George W. Jackson of the 34th Indiana, began constructing the bridge. That night, six transports towing two barges each loaded with forage and rations ran past the Vicksburg batteries. Only the steamer *Tigress* sank on the Louisiana shore after passing the batteries. Almost all of the supplies and half of the barges made it through in usable condition, thus helping to seal Vicksburg's fate.[55]

Describing this run past Vicksburg, Pvt. Hopkins of the 42nd Ohio wrote: "On the 22nd of April six more transports were sent down the stream, towing twelve barges loaded with forage. One of these transports, the *Tigress*, received a shot below the water line and sank on the Louisiana shore. The rest, with one half the barges, got through with but trifling damage."[56]

Mississippi soldiers in Vicksburg at the time appeared to be more worried about reports of Grierson's raid through their state than they were of Grant's imminent crossing of the river below them. Describing their feeling at that time, Sgt. Chambers of the 46th Mississippi wrote: "On the night of the 22d one gun-boat and five transports succeeded in running past our batteries.... About this time our regiment was greatly excited over reports of a Federal raid led by Col. Grierson, which passed nearly through the entire state."[57]

Back at Hovey's camp, pioneers spanned Bayou Vidal with a 100-foot-long and 24-foot-wide floating raft. Anchored by a cable and chain and tethered by ropes tied to notches cut in trees, it could withstand a rise or fall of 18 inches of water, and was extended southward another 240 feet on immovable trestles. Cutting southward through heavy timber, the troops constructed a corduroy road of split logs and a 150-foot-long trestle bridge over a deep slough. A third bridge, 550 feet long, 12 feet wide, and made of sixteen rafts secured to trestles at either end and supported in a manner similar to the Bayou Vidal bridge, curved westward around the mouth of Negro Bayou to the right bank of Bayou Vidal.[58]

The road continued down Bayou Vidal on the natural levee that curved southeastward around Perkins's Plantation land to the rendezvous point on the Mississippi River. By 26 April they had constructed about five miles of road, two miles of which were in heavy timber; over one thousand feet of bridges, much of it done in neck-deep water; and opened a military road over which could now move thousands of Federal troops from Milliken's Bend to the rendezvous point at Perkins's Plantation.[59]

On 26 April, still awaiting the arrival of Hovey's division and the opening of the military road, Richard Yates, Republican Governor of Illinois and staunch Lincoln supporter, visited Grant at Perkins's Plantation on what was essentially a political campaign tour. Yates was embroiled with a Copperhead legislature and a rising tide of antiwar sentiment in Illinois at the time and was at least thinking about running for the United States Senate seat as a "Union Republican." Charles Dana, "special commissioner" to the War Department, would write to Stanton and blame McClernand for causing a delay in the departure of troops.[60]

With Grant's troops continuing to assemble at Perkins's Plantation, on Monday, 27 April, starting at daybreak on Bayou Vidal, it took McGinnis's vanguard brigade four or five hours to cross the three bridges, which could support only one company, one cannon, or one wagon at a time. Slack's brigade followed later in the morning when another severe thunderstorm, which lasted most of the day, blew in and again turned what there was of dry ground into three or four inches of mud. The rear guard of Slack's brigade crossed and entered the Perkins's land sometime after 7:00 P.M. Hovey's troops continued marching by moonlight another two or three miles and camped in the wet grass about three miles from the river. The wagon train did not make it across until about midnight.[61]

While Hovey's pioneers were opening the military road through the swamps around

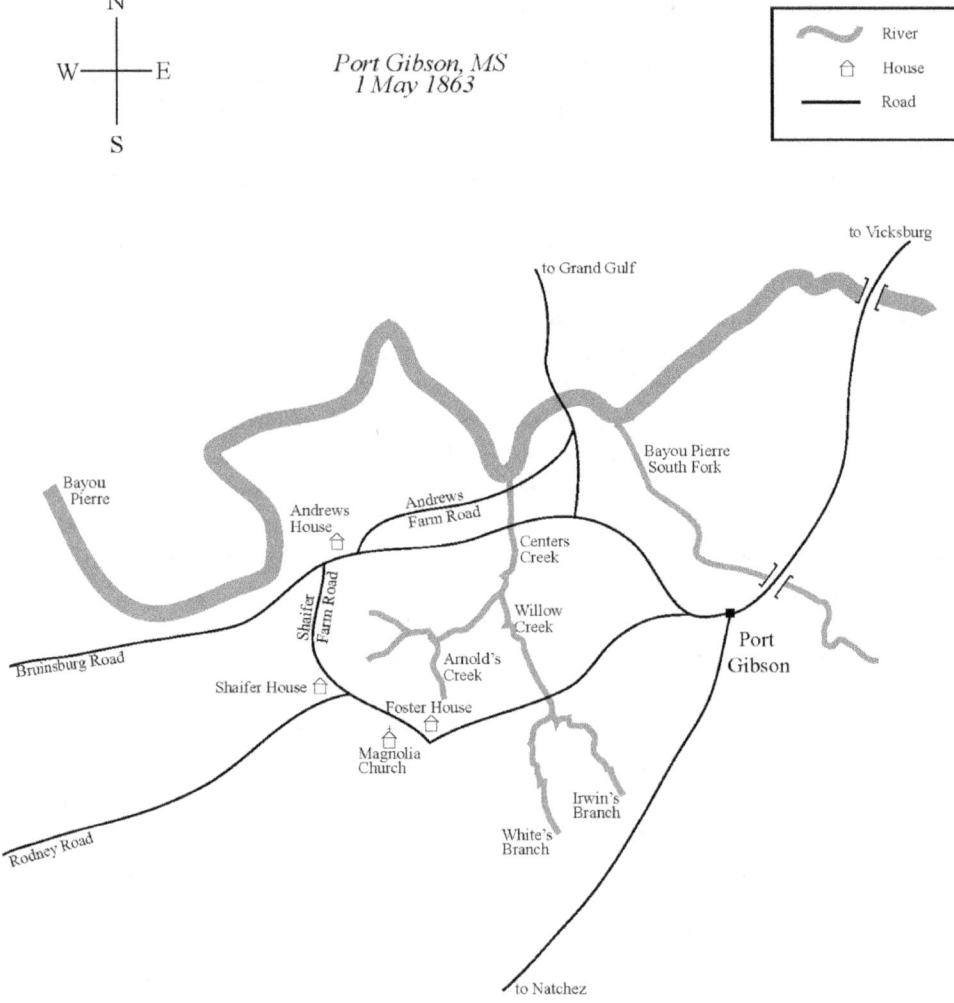

Expanded version of Terry Winschel's maps in "The Battle of Port Gibson, May 1, 1863," in *Blue & Gray Magazine*, February 1994, and Google Maps

Bayou Vidal, sporadic skirmishing continued as Keigwin's detachment continued in pursuit of Harrison's 15th Battalion Louisiana Cavalry, which had been ordered to save itself by retreating southward while offering token resistance and burning bridges to slow the Federal advance. On the morning of 26 April, Keigwin, clearing the way to Hard Times Landing, encountered Harrison's troopers on a point of land between Phelps and Clark's Bayous near where they entered Lake St. Joseph, dispersing them with a few shells and about an hour's skirmish between two companies Keigwin sent across to drive off Harrison's dismounted rear guard. On 28 April, after building two bridges in two days, Keigwin again encountered Harrison's cavalry and artillery at Choctaw Bayou on an angle of land where the bayou connected with Lake Bruin. After another artillery duel of about an hour, Harrison's force retreated and the Federals finally secured control of the road around the west side of Lake St. Joseph. The troops for whom there were no river transports could now march to Hard Times Landing, opening the way for Grant's attack on the Confederate batteries at Grand Gulf, Mississippi.[62]

That same day (28 April), Osterhaus's and Carr's divisions and Burbridge's brigade from A.J. Smith's division embarked from Perkins's Plantation on steamers and barges for Hard Times Landing. Due to a lack of transports, the remainder of A.J. Smith's division marched around Lake St. Joseph to Hard Times Landing. Hovey's division (McGinnis's and Slack's brigades), marched at noon toward the river. Slowed by the hot sun and the road filled with troops, they arrived that evening and embarked for Hard Times Landing on the returned transports.[63]

In Mississippi, Grierson's Federal raiders bypassed Meridian, where W.W. Loring's division now protected the Mobile & Ohio Railroad, and attempted to seize the town of Enterprise, several miles south on the railroad. At Enterprise, however, they found the city and railroad protected by Goodwin's 35th Alabama Infantry, stationed behind bales of cotton. Reconsidering the importance of Enterprise, Grierson turned his raiders westward with only token pursuit from Loring's command, and tore up track, destroyed locomotives and cars, and burned several bridges on the Southern Mississippi Railroad around the town of Newton.[64] A dispatch from the *Mobile News*, written while Grierson's raiders were in the vicinity of Meridian, although printed about two weeks later in the *Natchez Weekly Courier*, advised Mississippians: "From all we can learn, their motions have been too rapid to commit very extensive depredation. Wherever they could mount negroes they carried them off. Many escaped and returned to their homes. The Yankees said they did not expect to do much more fighting, their policy being to make raids and starve us out — in other words to plunder and steal."[65]

At Newton, Grierson's raiders turned southwestward toward Hazlehurst and the New Orleans, Jackson & Great Northern Railroad, cutting telegraph wires as they rode. At this point, Pemberton was forced to weaken his army by sending Wirt Adams's cavalry from Grand Gulf to intercept the Federal raiders. Skirmishing and brushing aside Adams's cavalry at Union Church on the road from Hazlehurst to Natchez, Grierson's raiders continued southward, forcing Pemberton to send cavalry, infantry and artillery from Frank Gardner's command at Port Hudson, Louisiana, to intercept the raiders. Grierson, whose troopers were exhausted and now under some pressure, crossed the Amite River at midnight 31 April, about two hours ahead of Gardner's column, and headed for the safety of Nathaniel Banks's force at Baton Rouge, Louisiana.[66]

On the morning of 29 April, while Grierson's raiders skirmished at Brookhaven, Mississippi, on the New Orleans, Jackson & Great Northern Railroad, Porter's Federal gunboat flotilla steamed toward the Confederate batteries at Grand Gulf, Mississippi, manned by troops from Brig. Gen. John S. Bowen's Confederate division, followed by steamers and barges carrying an assault force comprised of Osterhaus's, Smith's, and Hovey's divisions. Hovey's troops, who were to follow and support Osterhaus's and Smith's in the assault, were assigned five transports and two coal barges, at least one of which was badly in need of repair and "in almost sinking condition," and the steamer *Horizon*, to transport them to Grand Gulf while Carr's division remained at Hard Times to await transports.[67]

The upper battery at Grand Gulf was just above the town on a precipitous bluff called Point of Rocks, just below the mouth of the Big Black River, estimated at from 60 to 75 feet above the water level at the time of the battle. According to then Capt. Henry Walke of the USS *Lafayette*, the upper battery mounted two 100-pounder rifles, one 64-pounder shell gun, and one 30-pounder rifle. About ¾ of a mile downstream, the lower battery was about 60 feet above and 400 yards from the river. It mounted one Blakely 100-pounder rifle, two 8-inch shell guns and two 32-pounders. A covered road and a double line of rifle pits, with a middle battery of six to eight smaller caliber guns mounted on high points in between, connected the upper and lower batteries.[68]

ATTACK ON GRAND GULF

At 7:30 A.M., an hour after sunrise, the Federal assault force, which had been waiting on the river for several hours, watched from their barges and transports while Porter's gunboats weighed anchor and maneuvered into position. Following the signal from the flagship *Benton*, they moved upriver about a mile, then swung downstream at four-minute intervals, the *Pittsburg* in front, followed by the *Louisville*, the *Carondelet*, the *Mound City*, the *Benton*, the *Lafayette*, and the *Tuscumbia*. At about 8:00 A.M., the *Pittsburg* rounded on the upper Point of Rocks battery and opened fire, remaining until the *Benton*, the *Lafayette* and the *Tuscumbia* rounded and took up position at Point of Rocks. The remainder of the flotilla passed below the lower battery, raking the range of the Grand Gulf embrasures and rifle pits before turning about with some difficulty in the strong 6-knot current, firing continuously from their bow, starboard and port guns, many of them 100-pounder rifled shot and shell, as they struggled to come to bear against the Confederate batteries. The *Pittsburg* concentrated on the middle battery, the *Carondelet*, *Mound City*, and *Louisville* on the lower. Confederate artillerists and sharpshooters answered in kind with their 100-pounders, smaller caliber guns, and musketry fire.[69]

Back upstream, struggling in an eddy north of Point of Rocks, the *Lafayette* attacked the Confederate position primarily with its stern guns from about 600 yards out, swinging around occasionally to fire broadsides. The *Benton* and the *Tuscumbia*, however, firing from the west, were hit severely by the Point of Rocks artillery. Both gunboats fired from port, starboard and bow guns as they came to bear while they circled and struggled to maintain their positions in the strong current. Sometimes they moved close to shore, where they received heavy musketry fire from the rifle pits, which were responded to in kind from their portholes by infantry sharpshooters from Companies F and G of the 58th Ohio on board the *Benton* and Company D of the 29th Illinois, on board the *Tuscumbia*.[70]

Early on, a number of shells penetrated the *Tuscumbia*'s iron hull. At 8:35 A.M., a shell entered the midship forward port, killing four and wounding several others; another penetrated the starboard wheelhouse, killing 1st Lt. Samuel Bagsby, commanding the 29th Illinois sharpshooters, and disabling the entire crew of the starboard gun. The *Tuscumbia* finally dropped out of action at 12:35 P.M. and tied on the Louisiana side to repair the engine. In this fight, at 9:00 A.M. a shell penetrated and exploded in the *Benton*'s starboard quarter; about an hour later another shell penetrated the *Benton*'s pilothouse and disabled her wheel. Trying to turn about, the *Benton* drifted downriver about 1,500 yards to the lower battery, where the wheel was repaired while she fired on the lower fort. Just as the *Benton* was hit and temporarily disabled, the *Pittsburg* moved up to take her place at Point of Rocks and "for a short time bore the brunt of the fire" from the Confederate artillery and musketry

VII. Port Gibson, Mississippi (April–May 1863)

there. Sharpshooters from Company H of the 58th Ohio on board the *Pittsburg* participated in the action when she maneuvered close to shore.[71]

Her wheel repaired, the flagship *Benton* returned upriver to Point of Rocks. At 12:30 P.M., Admiral Porter moved the *Benton* above to consult with Grant, who was observing the fireworks from a small tug in the river, presumably out of the line of sight of Confederate artillery; otherwise they would truly have been sitting ducks if Confederate artillerymen had known of the lowly tug's important passengers. Aboard the *Benton*, Grant and Porter agreed that the Point of Rocks could not be taken by assault from the river. Grant decided to land the troops and march them below; the gunboats and transports would run past Grand Gulf that night. At 1:00 P.M., after about five hours of heavy shelling, the firing stopped, and the *Benton* signaled for the other gunboats, and the transports and barges carrying McClernand's troops, to move upstream to Hard Times Landing. The most heavily damaged boats with most of the serious casualties in the battle were the *Tuscumbia*, the only one completely disabled (5 killed, 24 wounded), the flagship *Benton* (7 killed, 19 wounded), and the *Pittsburg* (6 killed, 13 wounded).[72]

Due to the "skillful and scientific arrangement of the embrasures" and rifle pits, the tonnage of iron fired at the Confederate positions did relatively little damage, although ironically Bowen's Chief of Artillery, Colonel William Wade, who designed the works, was killed in the barrage at the lower battery. Unable to reduce the batteries, at 1:30 P.M. the Federal gunboats withdrew three miles above to Hard Times Landing, forcing Grant to look for a crossing farther downriver. McClernand's troops, who had spent much of the time struggling to keep the barges afloat while watching the fireworks, disembarked at Hard Times Landing, where they rejoined Carr's division.[73]

From his perspective in the Confederate rifle pits at Point of Rocks, Corporal Ephraim Anderson of the 2nd Missouri Infantry (C.S.A.) recalled in his memoirs that at the outset, two of the Federal gunboats "did not seem inclined to form in line with the others." According to Anderson, these gunboats (he may have been describing the action of the *Tuscumbia* and the *Benton*) circled the upper battery at close range and created "a perfect storm of iron" by "ploughing" the upper battery with broadsides of shot and shell while "hurling" grape and canister into the rifle pits.[74]

Anderson, perhaps referring to the return of the *Pittsburg* to Point of Rocks and her replacement of the temporarily disabled *Benton*, continued his description:

> We now discovered that the iron-clads, which had kept such a respectful distance from our guns, were not afraid to come to close quarters. The two already mentioned, which were steaming up and down in every direction, determined to try the strength of our works at the closest possible range, and one of them, the Pittsburg, understood to be under the command of Captain [William R.] Hoel, ran immediately under the upper battery, within ten steps of the guns, and fired a tremendous broadside up immediately upon them. She lay so close under the bank that the muzzles of the guns in the battery could not be brought to bear upon her; but the smoke-stacks were riddled, and one of them shot almost entirely off, and she was soon forced to leave her position by our sharp-shooters, who poured a destructive fire into her port-holes whenever opened. She also had sharpshooters aboard, who fired upon our artillerymen with some effect.
>
> As the Pittsburg moved off to a more respectful distance, a shot from one of our guns penetrated a port-hole, and, I afterwards learned, killed and wounded thirteen of the crew.[75]

Describing the experience of being transported to watch the gunboat battle at Grand

Gulf from a barge "in almost sinking condition" similar to that provided Hovey's division, Colonel Theodore Buehler of the 67th Indiana of A.J. Smith's division, wrote:

> On the 28th at 9 A.M., we went on board a hay barge, towed by the transport *Silver Wave* to a point in Hard Times Bend, Louisiana, opposite Grand Gulf. Remained on board the barge in about 7 inches of stinking water, and keeping the pumps steady at work to keep the barge from filling, until after the unsuccessful attempt of our gunboats to silence the rebel batteries at Grand Gulf on the 29th, when we disembarked about 4 pm, marching 3 miles across the bend to a point below the Gulf, encamping for the night.[76]

Describing in his memoir the gunboat battle from a slightly more comfortable vantage point than Colonel Buehler, and noting the disappointment among the soldiers at the failure of the Federal gunboats to reduce the Confederate batteries at Grand Gulf, Private Hopkins of the 42nd Ohio of Osterhaus's division, wrote:

> The army embarked on transports and barges, and moved down toward the batteries on the 29th of April, while Admiral Porter's gunboats opened a heavy fire upon the rebel works, continuing the bombardment for four or five hours. On the steamboats, hardly out of range of the enemy's shots, we watched the grand sight, which but few witness in a lifetime. The ironclads often moved up to within but pistol shot of the batteries, and poured their deadly hail right into the enemy's embrasures. The attempt, however, proved a failure. The gunboats, having exhausted all their energies of valor and skill, a little after noon were compelled to withdraw, leaving the principal batteries apparently uninjured.
>
> During the bombardment, the army impatiently awaited upon the transports the moment when our advance should be ordered. The withdrawal of the fleet caused general disappointment, for it seemed the whole expedition had been a failure. Our commander, however, was prepared for this emergency as he had been for all others. The troops disembarked and continued on the march down the western bank of the river three or four miles.[77]

At about 5:00 P.M., McClernand's troops disembarked at Hard Times Landing and marched across swampy Coffee Point to Disharoon's Plantation. There they were joined by the remainder of A.J. Smith's troops, who had marched to the landing around Lake St. Joseph just ahead of John Logan's division of McPherson's 17th Corps. Uncertain whether to cross the river ten miles below at Bruinsburg or eight miles farther downriver at Rodney, that night Grant decided on Bruinsburg after learning from "a negro man" of a good road from Bruinsburg to Port Gibson.[78]

At 6:00 P.M., the *Lafayette* returned downstream and opened fire on Point of Rocks. About two hours later, the remainder of Porter's gunboats steamed downriver, formed a line of battle in front of Grand Gulf, and exchanged fire with the Confederate batteries while the transports, led by the *General Price* (formerly the C.S. ram *General Sterling Price*), with two disabled transports in tow, ran past the batteries. At about 9:45 P.M., with the last transport having safely passed the batteries, Porter's gunboats dropped downstream to join them at the Disharoon's Plantation rendezvous. Only one transport, the *Horizon*, was disabled in the run, and the gunboat *Mound City* was struck on the starboard side, killing 1st Sgt. Fritz Verwold of the 58th Ohio instantly. (Cpl. Anderson of the 2nd Missouri, C.S.A., probably after having taken a careful glance from his rifle pit as exploding shells lit the night sky, saw the *General Price* towing two transports and recalled incorrectly in his memoirs that the transports were securely fastened by cable on the opposite side of each ironclad as they ran past the batteries.[79])

In order to gain a foothold in Mississippi and perhaps make it to the bridge over Bayou

VII. Port Gibson, Mississippi (April–May 1863)

Pierre at Port Gibson before it could be burned, Grant began the crossing to Bruinsburg the next morning (30 April) with all the supply wagons and horses, except for the artillery, held back. On board the *Benton* that morning, accompanied by Porter and carrying the 24th and 46th Indiana, he observed the two Indiana regiments disembark at Bruinsburg without opposition and returned to Disharoon's with Porter on board the *Benton* as a parade of transports steamed up and down the river from Disharoon's to Bruinsburg, disembarking most of McClernand's 13th corps by noon.[80]

Halting only long enough to draw three days' rations, Carr's vanguard moved out on the Bruinsburg Road (the direct route eastward to Port Gibson), followed by Osterhaus's, then Hovey's between 2:00 and 3:00 P.M. with "such haste that many companies [of the 46th Indiana] were obliged to roll their provisions along the road as they marched." (Members of the 22nd Iowa of Carr's division reportedly solved the problem by impaling their extra ration of meat on their bayonets.[81])

Marching about three miles from Bruinsburg up into the bluffs, the troops halted at Windsor Plantation, where McClernand established his temporary headquarters as A.J. Smith's division completed the crossing. In the late afternoon at Windsor, with all his troops across, McClernand determined to surprise the Confederates with an overnight forced march to Port Gibson. Moving out before sunset, Carr's vanguard division, instead of moving directly eastward from Windsor, detoured southward for three or four miles before they turned northeastward at Bethel Presbyterian Church on the Rodney Road about ten miles from Port Gibson, followed by Osterhaus's and Hovey's divisions, whose troop "snatched a few minutes and got supper" at 8:00 P.M. before marching all night.[82]

Private Owen Johnston Hopkins of the 42nd Ohio described the crossing to Bruinsburg from the perspective of a soldier in Osterhaus's division:

> April 30th. This morning we cross the Father of Waters and draw five days rations Preparatory to a long march Who knows where. 3 P.M.— Take up our line of march toward the interior of the State of Mississippi on the road leading to Port Gibson. Continue on the march until the Morning of the 1st of May, when we halt and prepare a cup of the Indispensible, everlasting, and never-ending Coffee. Add to this the Unconquerable hardtack and slice of "sowbelly," our breakfast is finished, and amid the noise or rattling wheels, the Clarion notes of the Bugle, and the Neighing of War horses, we move onward.[83]

The Bruinsburg Road approached Port Gibson from the west, the Rodney Road from the southwest. As the two roads approached within several miles of Port Gibson, the ridges on which they ran were separated by impassible cane thickets and creek-filled ravines until they converged about a half-mile west of town.

On the evening of 29 April, Bowen hurriedly sent Martin E. Green's brigade-the 15th and 21st Arkansas, the 12th Arkansas Sharpshooter Battalion, the 6th Mississippi, and four guns from Alfred Hudson's Battery (Mississippi Pettus Flying Artillery)— from Grand Gulf to Port Gibson, about eight miles to the southeast, to block the roads entering Port Gibson from the west and south and the bridge across Bayou Pierre east of town. At 3:00 A.M. on 30 April, Green initially set up his command at the junction of Bruinsburg and Rodney Roads. Because the rough terrain made it ideal for defending against numerically superior forces, Green moved his skirmishers westward from Port Gibson three and a half miles to a ridge near the Magnolia (or Union) Church that was bisected by the Rodney Road, with a few thrown forward another third of a mile to near the Shaifer farmhouse and the intersection of the farm road that wound northward to the Bruinsburg Road. Green, awaiting reinforcements, established his main line several miles back (about a mile and a half west of town) on a fenced ridge near the Foster farmhouse that ran parallel to and about two hundred yards east of the Magnolia Church ridge. Edward D. Tracy's Brigade (the 20th, 23rd, 30th, 31st, and 46th Alabama regiments) and six guns from Botetourt's Virginia Artillery arrived that evening, and Green sent them from Port Gibson to block Bruinsburg Road at its junction with the Shaifer farm road.[84]

BATTLE OF PORT GIBSON: THE MORNING FIGHT

In the predawn darkness of 1 May 1863, Stone's 2nd brigade of Carr's division led the way toward Port Gibson. At 1:00 A.M., four companies of the 21st Iowa Infantry and one howitzer from the 1st Iowa Battery encountered Confederate skirmishers in advance of Green's Magnolia Church line. Green's advance opened fire and Stone quickly brought up the remainder of his brigade and the remainder of Griffith's 1st Iowa Battery, as well as Klauss's 1st Indiana Battery from Benton's brigade. Green's skirmishers fell back, Federal artillery moved up, and a nearly two-hour artillery duel with Hudson's Battery, posted on Green's main line just north of the road several hundred yards east of Magnolia Church, lit the night sky. It ended at about 3:00 A.M. when both sides, hit hard by the accurate artillery fire, ceased firing and held their positions. Stone's Federals, unable to advance in the dark, lay on their arms covered by the rough terrain to await daylight, the chance to reconnoiter the area, and the arrival of Osterhaus's division.[85]

With the arrival of daylight (about 6:00 A.M.), Carr sent four companies from the 33rd Illinois of Benton's 1st brigade to reconnoiter and hold the Shaifer farm road. Encountering some of Tracy's Confederates posted there, they skirmished until Osterhaus's division arrived and moved up to secure McClernand's rear and push Tracy's Confederates back toward Port Gibson on Bruinsburg Road.[86]

After marching all night, Hovey's troops arrived on the heels of Osterhaus's division and took position in reserve on the right of Rodney Road on the crest of two hills opposite the Shaifer farmhouse, where McClernand established his headquarters. McGinnis' 1st brigade took the first hill; Slack's 2nd brigade, and the 47th Indiana, took the second, which Slack referred to as Thompson's Hill, a little to the rear of McGinnis's position on what was then the extreme right of McClernand's line.[87]

With his rear secured by Osterhaus's move up the farm road, Carr ordered Benton's 1st brigade forward on the right side of Rodney Road while Stone's 2nd Brigade, held in place on the left, fired artillery and musketry in support. Struggling through cane and vine-choked ravines, Benton's brigade forced Green's skirmishers to fall back from the Magnolia Church ridge to Green's main line near the Foster house about 200 yards east. To meet the Federal movement, Green pulled the 23rd Alabama and Botetourt's Virginia Artillery (called "Anderson's Battery" in Confederate reports) from Tracy's uncertain position on Bruinsburg Road. Forced by the terrain to bring them around through Port Gibson, Green placed them on his main line on the right of Rodney Road near Hudson's Battery.[88]

Although having taken the Magnolia Church ridge, as they approached Green's main line, Benton's troops were hit hard and pinned down by down by fire from Hudson's and

Anderson's Confederate batteries. At 7:00 A.M., McClernand ordered Hovey to send McGinnis's and Slack's brigades to reinforce Benton. McGinnis's brigade moved toward Benton's right through a ravine described by Hovey "as being about 40 rods wide, and filled with vines, cane, deep gulches, and exceedingly difficult of passage." As Slack's brigade moved around the left side of the ravine near Rodney Road toward Benton's left flank, the 47th Indiana was detached and sent across the road to support Schofield's Battery A of the 1st Missouri Light Artillery. In position north of the road on the Magnolia Church ridge, Schofield's Battery held what was then, with Stone's brigade holding its position on the extreme left, the left front of McClernand's advancing column.[89]

Bowen, recognizing the need to retake the Magnolia Church ridge from whence his troops were being bombarded by Federal artillery and musketry fire, ordered Green to send the 6th Mississippi and the 23rd Alabama on his extreme right to charge the Federal batteries and attempt to retake the ridge. Hit hard by Schofield's artillery and checked by fire from the 47th Indiana, the Confederates failed in their attempt to regain the ridge.[90]

Describing the 47th Indiana's position in Slack's brigade and their movement to the Magnolia Church ridgeline to support Schofield's Battery while under heavy fire from Green's Confederates (including the attempt by the 6th Mississippi and 23rd Alabama to retake the ridge), Lt. Col. John A. McLaughlin of the 47th Indiana wrote:

> At about 6:30 A.M. we formed line of battle on the extreme right of the Second Brigade, where the battle immediately opened upon the part of the infantry. At about 7:30 A.M. we were ordered to the left and front, to support the First Missouri Battery, Captain Schofield, which position, upon the height to the left of the road leading to Port Gibson, and about 1 mile in advance of our first line of battle, we occupied for more than two and a half hours, where we delivered three effective volleys at the enemy maneuvering upon our right. In this position the enemy's bullets fell among us thick and fast, but as we were well sheltered under the brow of the hill, we only lost 1 man from Company B and 1 man belonging to the ambulance corps of the Fifty-sixth Ohio Volunteers, both killed.[91]

With the arrival of A.J. Smith's division, which was kept in reserve near the Shaifer house, and with the failure of Green's attempt to regain the Magnolia Church ridge, McClernand moved up Stone's brigade to form a two-division front line that, although broken by the rough terrain, now extended beyond both flanks of Green's Confederate position. At this point, Hovey ordered the 34th Indiana and 56th Ohio to charge Hudson's and Anderson's Confederate batteries in their front. Leaping a fence and "rushing with loud shouts and fixed bayonets, toward the battery," the 34th Indiana and 56th Ohio were hit hard by grape and canister from the Confederate batteries and forced to take cover under the brow of a hill.[92]

Recovering quickly from the failure of the initial charge, the 11th and 46th Indiana from McGinnis's brigade, along with the 18th Indiana and 99th Illinois of Benton's brigade and the resurgent 34th Indiana and 56th Ohio, resumed the charge against the Confederate batteries in their front. With Green's artillery low on ammunition, the second Federal charge completely overran Green's line. Hudson's Battery was able to withdraw, but Anderson's, with its horses killed and about half of its gunners killed or wounded, could not. Overrun and captured, the guns of Anderson's Battery were turned on the fleeing Confederates. The 56th Ohio "captured a large number of prisoners and the battle flag of the 23rd Alabama."[93]

Meanwhile, Baldwin's brigade (the 17th and 31st Louisiana and the 4th and 46th Mississippi) arrived at Port Gibson after a forced march from Vicksburg to find a scene of confusion where "men with pale faces were running hither and thither, some with arms and seeking a command, women sobbing on every side, children in open-eyed wonder clinging to their weeping mothers, not understanding the meaning of it all, and negroes with eyes protruding like open cotton bolls were jostling each other and everybody else, continuously asking about 'dem Yankees.'"[94]

Moving out about two miles on the Rodney Road, they encountered Green's troops "falling back from all points" and Baldwin formed a new line on separate ridges between the White and Irwin branches of Willow Creek. The 31st Louisiana was placed on the right, separated from the remainder by "a deep wooded hollow" north of Rodney Road, the 17th Louisiana in the woods on the left of the road, the 4th Mississippi to the left, separated from the 17th Louisiana by a deep ravine. The 46th Mississippi was posted in reserve on a hill on the left of the road just under a half-mile in rear of the front line. Green's troops passed through Baldwin's new line and on to Port Gibson, where they were regrouped and sent to support Tracy's beleaguered troops on the Bruinsburg Road. Tracy had been killed in the fighting and replaced by Col. I.W. Garrott.[95]

BATTLE OF PORT GIBSON: THE AFTERNOON FIGHT

Shortly after Baldwin's line was established, Francis M. Cockrell's veteran brigade arrived from Grand Gulf with the 3rd, 5th, and 6th Missouri, and artillery from Guibor's (4 guns) and Landis's (2 guns) Missouri Batteries. Landis's Battery was placed on a salient in the line to the left of the 4th Mississippi; Guibor's Battery, commanded by Lt. William Corkery, was posted in reserve with the 46th Mississippi. The 5th Missouri was placed on the extreme left of Bowen's new Confederate line, with the 3rd Missouri behind it in reserve. The 6th Missouri was detached and sent to support M.E. Green's regrouped command, now with Garrott's troops on the Bruinsburg Road. (The 1st Confederate Battalion, the 1st and 2nd Missouri Infantry regiments, remained at Grand Gulf to guard the batteries.[96])

During a short lull in the fighting, A.J. Smith's division was brought forward, Landram's brigade in advance, Burbridge's in supporting distance. At about noon, Grant, who had been on the scene for about two hours, ordered McClernand to resume the advance. Carr's, Hovey's and A.J. Smith's troops moved forward, clambering through the ravines and tangled vines until crossing Arnold's Creek and climbing onto a plateau in range of Landis's and Guibor's Missouri (C.S.A.) artillery. Under fire, McClernand halted the advance and called for more support. Logan's division of McPherson's 17th Corps had recently arrived, and Grant sent Stevenson's brigade to McClernand, accompanied by Logan, while McPherson went with John E. Smith's brigade to support Osterhaus on the Bruinsburg Road.

McClernand's new Rodney Road line had, from left to right, Carr's division (Stone's brigade, supported by Benton's); A.J. Smith's division (Landram's brigade, supported by Burbridge's); and Hovey's division (Slack's brigade, supported by McGinnis's and Stevenson's). Temporarily stymied but determined to break the center of Bowen's line, McClernand brought the 24th and 28th Iowa from Slack's brigade to Landram's brigade in the center. Moving forward under fire, they took shelter along the banks of White's Branch, where they exchanged fire for about ninety minutes with Baldwin's and Cockrell's troops and the Missouri batteries.[97]

Although he had them pinned down, Bowen saw the extended Federal line as a real danger to his left flank. As McClernand strengthened his center by weakening his right flank, Bowen, in a desperate but timely move, took the offensive by sending Cockrell's 3rd and 5th Missouri through the woods, skirting Irwin's Branch to a position on a knoll several hundred yards beyond Slack's weakened position on the Federal right flank.[98]

Discovering Cockrell's move, Hovey rushed four batteries from his division (24 guns from the 2nd and 16th Ohio batteries, Company A, 2nd Illinois Light Artillery, and Company A, 1st Missouri Light Artillery), to a point overlooking White's Branch and ordered the 47th Indiana and 56th Ohio from Slack's brigade on the extreme right flank, supported by the 24th Indiana and 29th Wisconsin of McGinnis's brigade, to counter Cockrell's threat.[99]

The 47th Indiana and 56th Ohio moved over a ridge and across White's Branch of Willow Creek into an open field on top of a hill, where they exchanged fire for about half an hour with Cockrell's 3rd and 5th Missouri and Landis's Battery. Holding their own until they saw Cockrell's troops moving fast around the right flank of the 56th Ohio, the 47th Indiana countered by moving back to the left along the ravine to form a right angle with their former position, which was filled on the run by the 24th Indiana and 29th Wisconsin from McGinnis's brigade.[100]

Cockrell's troops charged up out of the creek bottom, the 24th Indiana and 29th Wisconsin taking the brunt of the charge. The 29th Wisconsin, an untested regiment under fire for the first time, held on in spite of heavy casualties until relieved by the 8th Indiana, sent to their aid from Benton's brigade. "A terrific and jarring fire" from Hovey's artillery and the 47th Indiana and 56th Ohio in their front, and from McGinnis's troops and the 8th Indiana on their flank, finally checked Cockrell's charge, although they recovered and "returned fire with great spirit and pertinacity for about two hours" until many of Cockrell's Missourians had fallen. With the prospects of more Federal reinforcements and a virtual hailstorm of canister fire from the Federal artillery, Cockrell's surviving troops fled, "leaving their dead and wounded on the field," as Bowen's entire line collapsed.[101]

Describing the 47th Indiana's part in this fight and their relief by the 19th Kentucky of Landram's brigade, McLaughlin reported:

> At about 11 o'clock we were ordered to the front. We then proceeded to the Port Gibson [Rodney] road, up which, toward Port Gibson, we advanced about 2 miles, and crossed to the right of said road, and formed in line of battle upon the crest of the hills. Here we ordered forward Company D, of the Forty-seventh, as skirmishers, and advanced to the extreme front over a ridge and across Willow Creek, and to the top of the hill beyond, where we formed in line of battle in the open field, our skirmishers being engaged in front with the Third and Fifth Missouri (rebel) Regiments, a rebel battery playing upon us at the same time. We here engaged the enemy, who opposed us hotly for half an hour. We were holding our own to good purpose, when we discovered that the rebels were advancing in line at double-quick at our right, and in a position favorable to taking us upon the right flank and in our rear. As we were a long way in advance of our main body when we took this position, and supposing ourselves entirely unsupported at our rear, we changed position, retiring by the left flank along the ravine through which we had gained the summit of the hill, and formed in line of battle at right angles with our former position, our left resting upon it. And immediately opened a brisk fire upon the enemy's lines, which were in full charge upon us. Here the battle raged furiously for over two

hours, during which time the pieces of our men became so heated from rapid, continuous firing as to make it impossible for them to continue firing longer with safety to themselves. We were relieved at this position by the Nineteenth Kentucky, the Forty-seventh retiring a few paces to the gully formed by Willow Creek.

The firing having entirely ceased, and the enemy routed at this point, the Forty-seventh stacked arms in the hollow a few paces to the rear of Willow Creek, and, being exhausted by the previous night's march and the heat and fatigues of the day, was resting, when suddenly a well directed volley from the enemy, who had skulked up under cover of the bushes upon the crest of the hill, informed us that the battle was not yet over. We immediately formed a few paces to the rear, under cover of the ravine. We were then ordered to advance to the same position (the bed of the stream), which position we held for the remainder of the day without hearing further from the enemy.[102]

Recounting Cockrell's charge in his memoirs (as told to him by Cockrell and several others who had been on the field), including their encounter with Slack's and McGinnis's troops, Cpl. Anderson of the 2nd Missouri, Cockrell's brigade, wrote:

A Federal battery of Parrott guns was in position upon an eminence some distance upon the left of the road, on which our force was posted, and shelled its line with considerable effect. Cockrell was ordered by General Bowen to take two of his regiments, the Third and Fifth, and make a circuit in the woods to the left, beyond the battery; then, by a rapid attack from the flank, either to try and take it or drive it from the field.

The colonel, with the two regiments, proceeded to obey the order by making the required movement; but, upon coming up at a point which he considered far enough to the left to flank it, or any support it was likely to have, and debouching from a ravine and dense cane-break into open woods, he found himself confronted, about two hundred yards from the battery, by the angle of a heavy body of troops, formed in the shape of two sides of a square. Upon seeing his approach, the Federals waved their caps and cheered, and about the same time he gave orders to his command to charge. For about twenty minutes the struggle was hot and furious, but the resistance was so determined, and maintained with such superior force, he was unable to capture the battery. He threw everything into confusion around, and finally retired, when nearly surrounded by a legion of blue-coats.[103]

Following what was essentially his first real combat, Slack gave a somewhat caustic account of Cockrell's charge against his two batteries:

During this engagement the two batteries in my command [Schofield's 1st Missouri Battery and Fenton's Peoria Battery] located on the hill to our right and rear threw shell and shrapnel into the enemy's ranks, which created great havoc. In this engagement the Fifth Missouri (rebel) Regiment was almost totally annihilated, there being but 19 of them left, who were taken prisoners. With this contest closed the battle on the right, and it was a fair, square fight of regiment against regiment, of about equal numbers and equally armed, resulting in the complete triumph of the troops of Indiana and Ohio over the chivalric braggarts and flower of the Southern Army.[104]

With Cockrell's rout, Bowen ordered Baldwin to bring up the 46th Mississippi from reserve to a position north of the Rodney Road to attempt, with the 17th Louisiana, and the 4th Mississippi positioned south of the road, to ascertain the Federal strength. The ground these regiments covered was "too much intersected by hollows, woods, and deep ravines to admit a simultaneous action"; and before they could get into position, the Federals swept their line with deadly fire, enfilading Baldwin's troops from the right and center, forcing them back. The Federals then pulled six guns of De Golyer's 8th Michigan Light Artillery to the crest of the hill, which gave them command of the Irwin Branch, from whence they unloaded a heavy and destructive fire of shell and canister, forcing the Confederate line to again retreat in some disorder.[105]

By 5:00 P.M., Garrett's Confederates had been forced to withdraw from Bruinsburg Road; and, at 5:30 P.M., Bowen, to avoid becoming trapped, ordered a retreat of his entire force up the Andrews farm road to Bayou Pierre. Baldwin's brigade was cut off from Andrews farm road by John E. Smith's Federal brigade that had been operating against Garrott's troops on the Bruinsburg Road, and was forced to retreat in confusion eastward through Port Gibson and across the south fork of Bayou Pierre, sometimes referred to as "Little Bayou Pierre."

Sgt. Chambers of the 46th Mississippi, Baldwin's brigade, remarked after the war: "Such confusion as the road presented! Whole families were flying they knew not where, while delicately nurtured ladies implored us by endearing epithets to save them from the hands of the foe."[106] Leaving Port Gibson behind them, Baldwin's brigade turned north across Bayou Pierre as troops from Cockrell's brigade, Bowen's rear guard, set fire to the bridges. The Federals did not pursue in the darkness.[107]

Perhaps, for all the spin in the official reports, Corporal Abner James Wilkes of the 46th Mississippi, Baldwin's Brigade, provided the best summary of the battle from a Confederate soldier's standpoint when he wrote: "We met them two miles below Port Gibson; they gave us a few shot and shell that certainly made us look wild, you bet. We gave them some grape and canister to think on, and we generally gave them as good as they sent, but we had to fall back in bad order to Vicksburg."[108]

Grant had finally established a foothold in Mississippi south of Vicksburg with about 40,000 troops to face Pemberton's 28,000, and an army that, by the end of the campaign, would total about 75,000 troops. The Confederates, including Joe Johnston's force, may have totaled about 50,000. The next day, Grierson completed his two-week raid through the state, arriving at Baton Rouge, Louisiana, on the afternoon of 2 May, diverting sorely needed cavalry from Pemberton's defensive force while leaving in his wake destroyed railroads, locomotives, cars, and telegraph lines, and capturing arms, ammunition, and prisoners, over 500 of whom were paroled.[109]

After the Battle of Port Gibson, Hovey's troops "slept upon the field" before moving into town the next day. Slack wrote Ann: "My [brigade] loss was 89 killed, wounded and missing. The 47th lost 6 or 8 killed, none from Huntington. Jim Dougherty was shot through the hand. Had not an officer killed. No more severe battle has been fought during the war." On 2 May, they assisted in building a bridge over Bayou Pierre and the following day marched to Willow Springs, about eight miles northwest of Port Gibson, and bivouacked that evening.[110]

VIII

Champion Hill, Mississippi (May 1863)

Back at Grand Gulf, W.W. Loring's division, which had moved across the state from Meridian, linked with Bowen's division. The two were ordered by Pemberton to destroy the magazines and evacuate Grand Gulf as he deployed his forces on a roughly thirty-eight-mile defensive line around Vicksburg. Carter L. Stevenson's division held the roughly sixteen-mile line from Warrenton to Bovina on the Southern Railroad of Mississippi, where Loring's division was posted. Bowen's division (Cockrell's and Green's brigades) occupied the trenches guarding the railroad at the Big Black River about three miles east of Bovina, with a small force from Green's brigade at Edwards Depot, about six miles east of the Big Black. Gregg's brigade arrived from Port Hudson and occupied the town of Raymond, some thirteen miles southeast of Edwards Depot and seventeen miles west of Jackson.[1]

An optimistic editorial in the 13 May 1863 edition of the *Natchez Weekly Courier*, quoting a dispatch from the *Vicksburg Whig*, assured their readers about the Confederate retreat from Port Gibson and Grand Gulf: "The troops moved up the road towards Big Black where they still remain, and in which vicinity the Yankees will find an army, when they advance, that will render their campaign in Mississippi as disastrous as that of McClellan in front of Richmond."

In spite of the *Weekly Courier*'s assurances, Grant moved his supply depot to Grand Gulf and sent McPherson's corps northward in pursuit of Pemberton. On 4 May at Hankinson's Ferry, about fifteen miles north of Grand Gulf, Crocker's division pushed Pemberton's rear guard across the Big Black and Grant set up his headquarters there to await the arrival of Sherman's corps, which he had sent to Haynes' Bluff to divert attention from his Bruinsburg landing.[2]

Sherman's corps arrived at Grand Gulf on 6 May and the next day Grant sent McPherson northeastward toward Jackson via Rocky Springs, Utica, and Raymond, to destroy the railroad, telegraph, and public stores, McClernand and Sherman moved northeastward a little to the west of McPherson's line to cut the railroad between Bolton and Edwards Depots, twenty and thirty miles west of Jackson, respectively. McPherson was to turn westward at Jackson and rejoin Grant's main force near Bolton Depot.[3]

That night, McClernand's corps camped at Rocky Springs, ten miles east of Hankinson's Ferry. Hovey's division camped about two miles west of Rocky Springs on Little Sandy Creek, and the 2nd Illinois Cavalry of Osterhaus's division skirmished with and dispersed

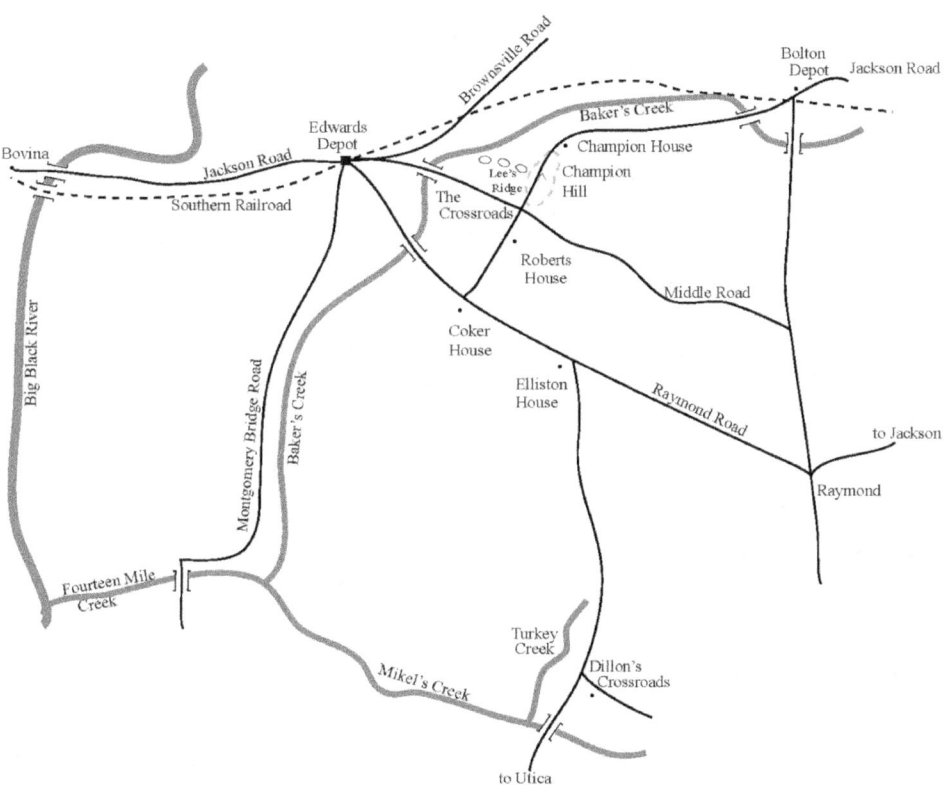

From Atlas Plate XXXVI, No. 1

Confederates at Hall's Ferry, about ten miles north on the Big Black. On 8 May, McClernand's corps moved several miles northeastward to Big Sandy Creek and Sherman's corps marched to Hankinson's Ferry. On 10 May, McPherson's corps moved eastward five or six miles to Utica on the main road to Raymond; Sherman's corps moved to Big Sandy Creek near McClernand's corps. On 11 May, McPherson's corps marched five miles and camped about twelve miles from Raymond; McClernand's corps continued northeastward five or six miles and camped on Five Mile Creek, about fourteen miles south of Edwards Depot and twenty-two miles southeast of Vicksburg. Sherman's corps moved several miles above McClernand's camp.[4]

SKIRMISHES AT FOURTEEN-MILE CREEK: 12 AND 13 MAY 1863

The next day (12 May), Hovey's division in advance followed Sherman's corps about five miles in the direction of Fourteen-Mile Creek. The 2nd Illinois Cavalry in the vanguard of Hovey's division encountered Elijah Gates' 1st Missouri Cavalry C.S.A (dismounted) from Bowen's division, who, with a section of artillery, held the creek where the road from Port Gibson crossed four miles south of Edwards Depot. Hovey brought up Slack's brigade on the "double-quick" to form two lines in support of a battery. Following a sharp skirmish of about an hour with Gates's artillery and dismounted troopers, Gates pulled back two miles to his reserve. Slack's troops secured the crossing and camped on both sides of the creek that night. Back at Edwards Depot, Bowen used some seventy-five wagons to move all their commissary stores from the depot as Pemberton began shifting some of his force toward Edwards Depot.[5]

That same day (12 May), Sherman's corps drove off Wirt Adams's Mississippi Cavalry and seized the crossing of Turkey Creek, about ten miles east of McClernand's position on Fourteen-Mile Creek, while McPherson's corps, in heavy fighting about eight miles east of Sherman's position, drove Gregg's brigade from Raymond back to Jackson, about fifteen miles to the northeast.[6]

The worried editors of the *Daily Mississippian* in Jackson, reporting on erroneous early reports of Wirt Adams's success, reviewed the movement of Grant's army for their readers in their 12 May edition:

> Skirmish on Fourteen-Mile Creek
> We learn, by a gentleman from Edwards' Depot last night, that our cavalry pickets attacked the pickets of the enemy six and a half miles from Edwards' on Fourteen-Mile Creek, yesterday morning, driving them back. Loss not known.
> The enemy was reported 1,800 strong at Utica. Utica is eighteen miles south of Edwards' Depot, in Hinds (this) county.
> It is reported that six companies of Wirt Adams' regiment attacked three regiments of infantry, four miles of the Port Gibson College, on Thursday or Friday last, and drove them to the river under the protection of their gunboats.
> Position of Grant
> Scouts from Adams' cavalry have ascertained that the two main divisions of Grant's forces are entrenching at Willow Springs and Rock Springs. The first place is about 13 or 15 miles from Port Gibson, and the last about the same distance from the first, both situated on Big Black, with the Bayou Pierre on the south. He has established military stations from Grand Gulf to the present scene of his entrenchments for the protection of his military stores in their transit from the river.
> We have information deemed correct, that Gen. Osterhaus has occupied Utica, in the southwestern part of this county, with a heavy force of infantry, cavalry and artillery, and is fortifying his position. The enemy will not, surely, be allowed to entrench himself that near Jackson without an effort to hustle him off howling, by General Pemberton.[7]

A notice in the same edition of the *Daily Mississippian* alerted foreigners living in the state of the fate of their "disloyal" counterparts in Louisiana:

> The *Shreveport Gazette* recently published a card signed by about a hundred foreigners, who, fearing that they might be drafted in the militia, adopted that course to notify the people that they are French subjects, and owed no allegiance to Louisiana. The News says that Mr. B. Courtade, one of the signers of the card, was taken out of his bed and "tarred and cottoned" the same night, and the rogue's march was played before the business houses of the balance.

On 13 May, with Grant concentrating his three-corps force (reportedly 43,000 effective troops) on Jackson, Pemberton, who had been admonished by President Davis to hold

Vicksburg and Port Hudson at all costs, and whose own theory of warfare centered on protecting strategic locations, believed he should keep his roughly 25,000-man army between Grant and Vicksburg, which he considered "the most important point in the Confederacy." Opting to protect Vicksburg, Pemberton left Martin L. Smith's and John Forney's divisions (about 7,500 troops) to garrison Vicksburg and moved his headquarters to Bovina, about eight miles east of Vicksburg and a few miles west of the Big Black River railroad crossing. He placed Vaughn's brigade at the railroad bridge where Loring's and Stevenson's troops earlier had set up nearly indefensible works on the east bank with their backs to the deep river. He deployed his remaining force of about 17,500 (Bowen's, Loring's, and C.L. Stevenson's divisions) around Edwards Depot to control the southern and eastern approaches to town — Bowen's on the right, Loring's in the center, and Stevenson's on the left — and sat and waited for the arrival of Grant's army.[8]

In the meantime, Joe Johnston was on his way from Tullahoma, Tennessee, to take command of the Confederate forces in Mississippi. Gregg's brigade, in Jackson after their retreat from Raymond, and W.H.T. Walker's brigade, just arrived from P.G.T. Beauregard's Department of South Carolina, Georgia, and Florida, made a force of 6,000 at Jackson. Maxey's brigade, expected in from Port Hudson, Louisiana, and Gist's brigade, expected from the east in a day or two, would add another 5,000 to Johnston's force at Jackson with more expected.[9]

Johnston, whose theory of warfare differed radically from Davis's or Pemberton's, believed that a smaller and hopefully more mobile army could, by selecting the battlegrounds and using strategic retreats, harass and annoy a larger occupying force until the occupiers wearied of the fight and left. Johnston's strategy was not unlike the "retreat to victory" principles of American Revolutionary War hero General Nathanael Greene, who used a smaller, more mobile army and strategic retreats to defeat Lord Cornwallis in North Carolina. Operating from this viewpoint, Johnston cautioned Pemberton not to let his army get trapped in Vicksburg and urged him to attack McPherson's corps, which his reports indicated was detached and in the vicinity of Clinton.[10]

That same day (13 May), as part of his concentration on Jackson, Grant ordered McClernand's corps to withdraw from Bowen's front on Fourteen-Mile Creek and move to Raymond. In a reasonably adept move from a somewhat precarious position, McClernand slipped his corps away without incident. Osterhaus's and Carr's divisions marched to Raymond while Hovey's rear guard division (about 4,500) feigned an attack on Edwards Depot to cover the flank and rear of the corps as it withdrew from Bowen's front. Bowen, who could have caused Hovey's rear guard some problems if he had attacked in force, especially with the remainder of Pemberton's force either already nearby or on the way, sent only a token force of sharpshooters under Captain W.S. Catterson of the 1st Battalion Arkansas Cavalry (dismounted) to reconnoiter and harass Hovey's troops on Fourteen-Mile Creek. Slack took the 28th Iowa (with the 56th Ohio and 47th Indiana in reserve), easily repulsed Catterson's sharpshooters, and, as Bowen waited for an attack, followed Hovey's rear guard division eastward across winding Baker's Creek, which at that point flowed southward into Fourteen-Mile Creek, and on toward Raymond. They camped that night at Dillon's Crossroads on Turkey Creek, where Sherman's troops had fought the day before.[11]

That evening, General Joseph E. Johnston, having just arrived at Jackson to take direct command of the Confederate forces in Mississippi, telegraphed Confederate Secretary of

War J.A. Seddon with some ominous news: "I arrived this evening, finding the enemy in force between this place and General Pemberton, cutting off the communication. *I am too late.*"[12]

On 14 May, Johnston evacuated Jackson and moved his force northward to the town of Canton with as much of his military stores as he could transport and ordered Maxey and Gist to rendezvous there. McPherson's and Sherman's corps, after skirmishing with Johnston's rear guard, occupied Jackson later that day. That evening, Johnston, with reinforcements coming in from the east and hoping to defeat Grant's divided army near Jackson, sent a message to Pemberton to attack Grant's force near Clinton, and then to move north to make connection with his own small force as reinforcements arrived from the east.[13]

That same day (14 May), Hovey's division moved forward eight miles in a severe thunderstorm that again required his pioneers to drain parts of the flooded roadway, which, in places, had water up to the men's knees. Passing through Raymond, they camped near upper Baker's Creek four miles southwest of Clinton.[14]

Meanwhile, Pemberton, following President Davis's admonition that Vicksburg and Port Hudson must be held, replied to Johnston that he believed Johnston did not "fully comprehend" the hazards of attacking Grant's force near Clinton "or the position Vicksburg [would] be left in" if he complied with Johnston's orders to attack. Pemberton did not move.[15]

Johnston, who never quite got over being told by Pemberton that he did not "fully comprehend" the situation, later claimed that Pemberton had disobeyed orders by sitting at Edwards Depot for two days when time was of the essence instead of moving against the Federal supply line from Port Gibson or joining his forces to fight Grant at or near Jackson. With Pemberton sitting for two days at Edwards Depot, the possibility of concentrating the Confederate forces was lost when Grant, then in Jackson, turned his force westward toward Edwards Depot to block just such a junction. In fact, when Grant established a foothold in Mississippi, it was only a matter of time, as Johnston knew, before Vicksburg fell; and Johnston was correct when he telegraphed Secretary of War Seddon that by the time he arrived in Mississippi it was too late to save Vicksburg.[16]

On the afternoon of 15 May, Pemberton, who argued that he was complying with Johnston's orders of the day before, albeit slowly and reluctantly, began marching his force southward from Edwards Depot toward Dillon's Crossroads to attempt to cut Grant's supply line from Port Gibson, which Grant, however, had already abandoned. Now in receipt of Johnston's orders to move eastward and attack the rear of Grant's army at Clinton, Pemberton chose instead to redirect his line of march southeastward toward Raymond. Moving eastward from Edwards Depot on the Jackson Road to avoid the washed-out Baker's Creek Bridge on the Raymond Road, Pemberton turned his column southward at Ratliff Plantation Road and reconnected with Raymond Road. That night, Loring's vanguard division bivouacked for the night on the property of a Mrs. Elliston, about six miles from Raymond, with his troops strung along the Ratliff Plantation and Raymond Roads.[17]

Grant, in the meantime, went on the offensive. Having learned at Jackson that Johnston had ordered Pemberton to attack his force from the rear near Clinton, he immediately ordered McClernand and McPherson to turn back toward Edwards Depot to attack Pemberton. Sherman's corps, minus Blair's division, which was detached to accompany McClernand's corps, remained in Jackson to destroy the Vicksburg supply line, including all railroads, military factories, arsenals, or supply depots. Thus, prior to a confrontation with Pemberton's dangerous force, Grant left his best general on the sidelines.[18]

At 5:00 A.M. on 15 May, Slack's brigade began their four-mile march to Clinton with Hovey's division. At Clinton they learned that McPherson and Sherman had taken Jackson, and Grant ordered Hovey to turn his division westward on the Jackson Road in order to get into position ahead of McPherson's corps. Marching about eight more miles, Hovey's troops camped that evening near Bolton Depot, about ten miles east of Edwards Depot on the railroad, seven miles north of Raymond via the Raymond/Bolton Road, and some twenty-two miles east of the Vicksburg fortifications.[19]

That same day (15 May), reconnaissance by Colonel John J. Mudd of the 2nd Illinois Cavalry, Chief of Cavalry in McClernand's corps, indicated that three roads (the Jackson, Middle, and Raymond) converged on Edwards Depot from Raymond and Bolton. A few miles west of Bolton, the northern or Jackson Road, which to that point paralleled the tracks of the Southern Railroad of Mississippi, turned abruptly southward at the Champion House. Running about three-quarters of a mile to the south through cultivated fields, the road began its ascent up a wooded ridge that ran north to south and was known as "Champion Hill" because of its location on the Champion property, or as "Midway Hill" because it was midway between Jackson and Vicksburg. A quarter-mile farther south, the road made short jogs to the east and back south, passing about 15 or 20 feet below the 75-foot crest. Jackson Road continued sloping gradually southward another half-mile to the southern foot of the ridge, where it took a sharp turn to the west toward Baker's Creek and Edwards Depot.[20]

The Middle Road (today's Billy Fields Road) ran roughly westward from the Raymond/Bolton Road about a mile and a half to two miles south of and parallel to the Jackson Road, the two roads merging where the Jackson Road turned sharply westward. At this point the Ratliff Plantation Road (today's D.J. Johnson Road), ran southwestward and connected the Jackson and Middle Roads with the Raymond Road (today's S.R. 467) and formed the geographical area known as "the crossroads."[21]

Later that morning, McClernand's corps led the westward advance toward Edwards Depot along the Raymond and Middle Roads. Starting at 5:00 A.M., A.J. Smith's division (Burbridge's and Landram's brigades, with the 17th Ohio Battery and Chicago Mercantile Battery), supported by Blair's division of Sherman's corps (Giles Smith's and T. Kilby Smith's brigades, with Companies A and B, 1st Illinois Light Artillery), marched from Raymond up the Raymond Road. One hour later, Osterhaus's division (Garrard's and Lindsey's brigades, with the 7th Michigan and 1st Wisconsin Artillery) began marching westward on the Middle Road from its junction with the Raymond/Bolton Road several miles north of Raymond, followed by Carr's division (Benton's and Lawler's brigades, with the 1st Indiana Artillery and Company A, 2nd Illinois Light Artillery).[22]

In the meantime, Hovey's division (McGinnis and Slack's brigades, with the 2nd and 16th Ohio Batteries, and Company A, 1st Missouri Light Artillery), detached from McClernand's corps, marched westward from Bolton Depot on the Jackson Road in the vanguard of McPherson's corps and ahead of disgruntled John "Black Jack" Logan who was reportedly sore, at least for the moment, that his division (John E. Smith's, Leggett's, and John Stevenson's brigades, with Company D, 1st Illinois Light Artillery, Company L, 2nd Illinois Light Artillery, the 8th Michigan and the 3rd Ohio Artillery) was not in the vanguard.

Isaac F. Quinby's division (Sanborn's, Holmes,' and Boomer's brigades, with Company M, 1st Missouri Light Artillery, the 11th Ohio, 6th and 12th Wisconsin Batteries), commanded by Marsellus M. Crocker in Quinby's absence due to illness, followed Logan. Sherman's corps, after completing their work in Jackson, marched westward, north of the railroad, to block any attempted junction of Pemberton's and Johnston's forces.[23]

Sylvanus Cadwallader, war correspondent for Wilbur Storey's[24] *Chicago Times*,[25] accompanied Logan on the march, and related in his memoirs that Logan believed his division should be in the vanguard and became incensed when he encountered Hovey's division entering Jackson Road ahead of his column. Although Cadwallader would later misinterpret the fighting done by Hovey's and Logan's men and report incorrectly that "the real battle began" when Crocker's division "came into line," his eyewitness account of Logan's outburst on the march that morning may have some merit. According to Cadwallader:

> Logan was compelled to halt till Hovey had passed this intersection, and then start on squarely in Hovey's rear. I rarely ever witnessed such an exhibition of rage, profanity and disappointment as Logan then gave. The air was just blue with oaths, till speech was exhausted. McPherson's arrival a few minutes after was the signal for another outburst. But there was no apparent remedy. Hovey had the road by right of prior occupation, but Logan's division was avenged before nightfall.[26]

That same morning, Pemberton, now in compliance with Johnston's orders to form a junction of their forces near Canton via the Brownsville Road, ordered his chief engineer, Samuel H. Lockett, to replace the washed-out lower bridge over Baker's Creek on the Raymond Road and ordered a countermarch back to Edwards Depot. Reynolds's brigade was detached from Stevenson's division to guard the supply train as it crossed the upper bridge over Baker's Creek on Jackson Road and headed for Edwards Depot. The 42nd Georgia of Barton's brigade, and Sharkey's section of Company A, 1st Mississippi Artillery, guarded the Jackson Road bridge over Baker's Creek. Just as the movement began, however, Pemberton's cavalry pickets, reconnoitering between the Middle and Raymond Roads early in the morning, encountered A.J. Smith's column on the Raymond Road and opened up with long-range artillery fire.[27]

A.J. Smith's appearance on the Raymond Road, and Osterhaus's on the Middle Road shortly thereafter, indicated a major Federal advance. Pemberton, who had not ordered reconnaissance to the north and was unaware of Hovey's approach on the Jackson Road, ordered his division commanders to form in line of battle facing eastward behind the Ratliff Plantation Road on the wooded Coker House Ridge. Loring's division (Tilghman's, Buford's, and Featherston's brigades), having continued to fall back about a mile and a half from the Elliston property in the face of the Federal advance on Raymond Road, formed on the right astride the Raymond Road; Bowen's and Stevenson's divisions moved back up the Ratliff Plantation Road, Bowen's division (Cockrell's and Green's brigades) in the center, and Stevenson's division (S.D. Lee's, Cumming's, and Barton's brigades) on the left at the crossroads.[28]

Surprised by Hovey's appearance beyond his left flank at about 10:00 A.M., Pemberton sent S.D. Lee's and Cumming's brigades from Stevenson's division northward on Ratliff Plantation Road to the crest of Champion Hill with Bowen's division moving up and Loring's continuing westward on the Raymond Road in concert with Stevenson in order to continue the Middle and Raymond Road blockade. In the shift, Pemberton moved his headquarters to Isaac Roberts's house on Ratliff Plantation Road, about a quarter mile southwest of the crossroads. Pemberton accomplished his move to the left while exchanging heavy artillery fire with Osterhaus's and A.J. Smith's Federal artillery on his right because McClernand, following Grant's initial order to proceed cautiously, remained essentially stationary after driving in Pemberton's pickets.[29]

From the crest of Champion Hill, the north slope of which had been cleared of trees for about fifty yards, Lee's brigade (the 20th, 23rd, 30th, and 31st Alabama) turned roughly northwestward along a line of disconnected ridges, leaving the two remaining guns of Captain John W. Johnston's Botetourt Virginia Battery on the crest west of the Jackson Road (four guns had been captured at Port Gibson), one 6-pounder on the right and a 12-pounder Napoleon on the left, facing north. Shortly thereafter, S.D. Lee sent a section of two 12-pounder Napoleons commanded by Lt. T. Jeff Bates from Waddell's Alabama Battery and they formed on the right of Johnston's Battery with a view commanding Jackson Road as it ascended the hill, although "only by peering through little open spaces." Johnston's and Bates's artillerist, however, could not see to the rear (south) at all across a "deep ravine which had its head near the Jackson Road," and which made limbering and retreating with the guns difficult at best.[30]

Cumming's brigade followed Lee northward. Although unable to see Lee's position in the dense woods, Cumming turned the 39th Georgia and four companies of the 34th Georgia sharply to the left at the crest, positioning them to the right of the Confederate batteries facing north. (Because this was his second position, Cumming referred to it as his new or "second front.") The remainder of the 34th Georgia and the trailing 36th Georgia followed onto the crest but remained east of the road facing roughly to the east on what Cumming continued to call his "first" or original front. The 56th and 57th Georgia remained in place on Cumming's lower "first front" at the crossroads in support of the remainder of Waddell's Alabama Battery, which faced eastward down the Middle Road toward Osterhaus's approach. Barton's brigade (the 40th, 41st, 42nd, 43rd, and 52nd Georgia) continued Stevenson's line to the right. Facing eastward, they filled the gap between the 36th Georgia and Waddell's Battery at the crossroads.[31]

Bowen's division (Francis M. Cockrell and Martin E. Green's brigades) remained in position between the Raymond and Middle Roads and Wade's Missouri Battery faced eastward some 600 yards south of Waddell's guns at the crossroads. They faced the approach of Garrard's brigade in the vanguard of Osterhaus's column on the winding Middle Road. Several miles south, Loring's division (Buford's, Tilghman's, and Featherston's brigades) fell back to the Coker House Ridge astride the Raymond Road at its intersection with the Ratliff Plantation Road, facing Burbridge's brigade in the vanguard of A.J. Smith's column, which gave Pemberton's repositioned line of battle roughly the shape of a figure "7."[32]

Lee's and Cumming's Confederate brigades were just getting into position (Lee's on the series of ridges west of Champion Hill, Cumming's at the salient of Pemberton's line on the crest of Champion Hill) when Hovey's division, led by 1st Lt. James L. Carey's 1st Indiana Cavalry and the 24th Indiana of McGinnis's vanguard brigade arrived on the Champion property at about 10:00 A.M. (Lee's skirmishers had followed the brigade northward and were in position south of the Champion House and in front of Lee's line on the ridge; Cumming's nine companies of skirmishers remained essentially out of position at the crossroads; and, with two regiments on detached service, Cumming was left with only about 1,000 men on the crest, the equivalent of two regiments, to support the four-gun battery.)[33]

HOVEY'S POSITION (MCGINNIS'S AND SLACK'S BRIGADES)

Facing Cumming's troops and artillery on Champion Hill, Hovey posted McGinnis's 1st brigade on the right flank in a rye field south of the Champion House and west of the Jackson Road and posted Slack's 2nd brigade in the field on the left, east of Jackson Road. On McGinnis's line the 11th Indiana held the left, the 46th Indiana and the 29th Wisconsin the center, and the 24th Indiana the right, with the 34th Indiana in reserve and skirmishers from the 24th Indiana out front.[34]

Slack formed his 2nd brigade into two lines, the 28th Iowa on the left front and the 47th Indiana on the right, with the 56th Ohio and the 24th Iowa on the second line, their exact positions not specified by Slack. Companies B and G of the 47th Indiana under Capt. John F. Eglin, companies A and F of the 56th Ohio under Capt. Manring, and two companies of the 24th Iowa (their leader not named) were sent forward as skirmishers.[35]

As Hovey's line moved forward, they drove in skirmishers from Lee's Alabama brigade, in position in rear of the Champion House and in front of Lee's line on the detached ridges west of Champion Hill. In this movement forward, the 46th Indiana was crowded out of line about a half mile south of the Champion House near the wooded northern slope and was placed in reserve to support the 11th Indiana and the 29th Wisconsin. The 34th Indiana remained at the time in reserve supporting the 24th Indiana on McGinnis's right flank.[36]

LOGAN'S POSITION (M. LEGGETT, J.E. SMITH, AND J. STEVENSON)

Grant arrived and established his headquarters at the Champion House, immediately positioning Logan's division (Mortimer Leggett's and John E. Smith's brigades) on line to McGinnis's right, facing across an open field toward S.D. Lee's Confederate brigade, posted behind a fence on the wooded ridges on the Confederate extreme left.[37]

Leggett's troops formed on the left with Manning Force's 20th Ohio in front on the left, Warren Shedd's 30th Illinois in front on the right. Smith's brigade moved to the right of Leggett's brigade with the 23rd Indiana, 20th Illinois, and 31st Illinois posted in front. Samuel De Golyer's 8th Battery, Michigan Light Artillery, was posted in rear of Leggett's and Smith's brigades; Henry A. Rogers's Battery D, 1st Illinois Light Artillery was posted on Smith's right. John D. Stevenson's brigade (the 8th Illinois, 32nd Ohio, and 81st Illinois) was kept in reserve, with the 7th Missouri posted as rear guard behind William S. Williams's 3rd Battery, Ohio Light Artillery.[38]

THE BATTLE OF CHAMPION HILL, 16 MAY 1863

At about 10:30 A.M., Grant ordered Hovey and Logan forward. On the right, Logan's troops (Leggett's and Smith's brigades), unable to charge across the open field in the face of S.D. Lee's troops firing from behind fences on the wooded ridges running westward from the crest of Champion Hill, remained in place and exchanged fire.[39]

On the left, however, Hovey's line, which had become "crescent-like" as it conformed to the shape of the hill, moved up to the wooded foot of Champion Hill and, as one soldier of the 24th Iowa wrote, "darted into the woods as eager as houns for the chase," Slack's on the left of the road and McGinnis's slightly advanced on the right.[40]

Describing the onset of the fight against Lee's skirmishers, Slack reported:

> Skirmishing soon began and continued for about one hour, when I advanced the whole line, with the Forty-seventh Indiana on the right and the Twenty-eighth Indiana on the left. The thick growth of underbrush and vines, ravines, and hills made it very difficult to advance, but it was accomplished with little disorder, until we reached the crest of the hill, where we found the enemy in very heavy force about 200 yards in front of us, and under cover of a wood beyond a field.[41]

Slack's skirmishers had difficulty advancing through brush and vine-choked gullies and up ravines on the wooded eastern slope. Due to the difficult terrain, the 28th Iowa, beginning on the left of the 47th Indiana, was forced to move farther to the left around the eastern slope, and the 56th Ohio moved up to fill the gap created between the 28th Iowa and the 47th Indiana. The 24th Iowa moved up and the 47th Indiana, in turn, moved to the right across the road "under a galling fire," continuing forward up the northern slope in support of the 11th and 46th Indiana of McGinnis's brigade. (During the battle the 34th Indiana moved to the right and fought with Logan's and Crocker's troops, participating in the capture of the M.L. Wood's 46th Alabama of S.D. Lee's brigade.)[42]

McGinnis's line, slightly in advance of Slack's brigade and now including the 47th Indiana, faced the Confederate artillery and "almost immediately sharp and rapid firing was commenced between the skirmishers" in their front. Advancing slowly and cautiously up through the woods, the 11th Indiana were on the left of the road, the 29th Wisconsin to their right on the right of the road and the 24th Indiana on the right of the 29th Wisconsin. The 46th Indiana, which had been squeezed out of position, and McLaughlin's 47th Indiana, now detached from Slack's brigade, supported the 11th Indiana and the 29th Wisconsin.[43]

Farther to the Federal right, S.D. Lee's line began to waver as Logan brought up Stevenson's brigade to extend his line past the Confederate left flank. To counter Logan's move, Pemberton pulled Barton's brigade from Cumming's right flank and sent them to the left to extend the Confederate line toward the upper Baker's Creek Bridge.[44]

Back on the Federal left, in order to avoid the barrage of grape and canister from the Confederate artillery in his front, McGinnis ordered his troops to lie down and fix bayonets before moving forward again at his signal when the barrage stopped, falling to the ground at his signal when it resumed. Hidden about seventy-five yards from the batteries, McGinnis's front-line troops (the 11th Indiana, the 29th Wisconsin, and the 24th Indiana) rose up and charged out of the woods against Johnston's Botetourt Virginia Battery, firing one round before moving in with fixed bayonets. The 46th Indiana moved up simultaneously on the left of the 11th Indiana and, supported by McLaughlin's 47th Indiana, charged out of the woods toward Bates's section of Waddell's Alabama Battery.[45]

Apparently surprised by the suddenness and ferocity of the assault, after some five minutes of hand-to-hand fighting, Cumming's "second front" west of the road collapsed. The Botetourt Battery's horses were killed and the battery captured by the 11th Indiana and 29th Wisconsin. The 46th Indiana charged and captured Bates's two 12-pounder Napoleons as the surviving gunners and soldiers of the supporting 39th Georgia who did not surrender fled down the ravine, up through the canebrakes, and down the southeastern slope of the hill as McGinnis's troops struggled to pursue in the confusion of dense smoke and thick underbrush.[46]

The 47th Indiana, pushing forward just west of the road in support of the 46th, formed on the crest and exchanged fire with the 34th Georgia, which had fallen back and taken shelter behind a slave cabin, outbuildings, and heavy timber on the south slope. Slack's brigade, moving up the northeastern slope where Barton's brigade had been, enveloped Cumming's right flank and forced them to retreat down the southern slope.

As Cumming's line on the crest collapsed, Slack's brigade pursued down and around the southeastern side to a cornfield that sloped down to the crossroads where Cumming's skirmishers and the 56th and 57th Georgia supported the remainder of Waddell's Alabama Battery on Cumming's "first front." With Osterhaus's advance on the Middle Road stalled about 600 yards east, the Georgians were able to turn northward and, from behind a strong rail fence, pour deadly fire into Slack's line. Unwavering, Slack's troops overlapped the Confederate line and drove the Georgians from the fence while sharpshooters from the 24th Iowa firing Enfield Rifles killed Waddell's horses before they could be limbered and harnessed. The remainder of the 24th Iowa charged and captured Waddell's battery as the Georgians retreated down Ratliff Plantation Road and regrouped in the fields near Pemberton's headquarters at the Roberts House, while Slack's weary, depleted, and now somewhat disorganized brigade rested on their arms at and beyond the crossroads.[47]

Overcoming the smoke and confusion, McGinnis's brigade remained intact on the southwestern slope of Champion Hill, and the 29th Wisconsin and 24th Indiana swung to the right to attack the 20th Alabama on the extreme right of S.D. Lee's line. Hit by enfilading fire, the 20th Alabama retreated south about 600 yards to a ridge north of Jackson Road, which at that point ran to the northwest, where they reformed, followed shortly thereafter by the 31st Alabama. Under pressure from Leggett's attack, S.D. Lee, after failing to rally his two right regiments, prudently moved his three remaining regiments (the 46th, 30th, and 23rd Alabama) back and formed a new line on the ridge with the regrouped 20th and 31st Alabama.[48]

As S.D. Lee's troops were reforming Pemberton's left flank on the upper or northwestward segment of Jackson Road, Barton's troops arrived and temporarily held the line, even pushing back John E. Smith's Illinois brigade on the Federal right flank until Smith's troops recovered and held the line. Logan then ordered John D. Stevenson's Federal brigade (the 8th and 81st Illinois and the 32nd Ohio) to sweep around the Confederate left flank. Barton's Georgians now found themselves too far forward and unsupported as skirmishers commanded by Colonel Herman Lieb of the 9th Louisiana (African descent) checked their forward movement. In a counterchage, John Stevenson's three regiments on the field, and the 124th Illinois from A.J. Smith's brigade, swept Barton's entire brigade from the field. John Stevenson's charge resulted in the capture of Max Van Den Corput's Cherokee (Georgia) Battery and Battery A of the 1st Mississippi Artillery, about 1,100 troops, and blockaded Pemberton's Jackson Road line of retreat as Pemberton's line began to collapse.[49]

BOWEN'S COUNTERATTACK

With the Confederate left flank turned and the crossroads in Federal hands, had McClernand moved his troops aggressively forward on the lower roads, Pemberton's army could have been defeated and large parts of it captured much earlier in the fight, which, in fact, would most likely have ended the need for a Vicksburg siege. Miscommunication between Grant and McClernand, miles apart and in unknown territory, ended this possibility.[50]

McClernand, obeying his initial orders to proceed cautiously, kept his troops stationary on the lower roads, content to fire long-range artillery. With S.D. Lee's brigade barely holding what remained of the Confederate left on Jackson Road and with both of Lee's flanks exposed, McClernand's failure to move aggressively, and Grant's inability to send timely and clear orders for him to attack, enabled Pemberton to avoid losing his army. With no movement against his right flank on the Middle or Raymond Roads, the now desperate Pemberton sent Bowen's division (Cockrell's and Green's brigades) northward from his headquarters on Ratliff Plantation Road to regain Champion Hill and sent couriers in search of Loring to get him to bring up his division. Only able to find Buford's brigade (the 27th, 35th, 54th and 55th Alabama, the 9th Arkansas, the 3rd and the 7th Kentucky, and the 12th Louisiana), Pemberton sent them to support S.D. Lee's struggling troops.[51]

In Bowen's counterattack, Cockrell's Missourians (the 1st, 2nd, 3rd, 5th, and 6th Missouri regiments) arrived first. Initially, the 3rd and 5th Missouri encountered the 24th Iowa at Waddell's captured battery at the crossroads and were driven back. In the fields just north of the Roberts House, Cockrell, reportedly holding the reins of his horse and a magnolia blossom in one hand while waving his sword in the other, quickly rallied his two leading regiments and brought up the remainder of his brigade, including Guibor's and Landis's batteries, Guibor's going to the left and Landis's to the right toward the crossroads. In the meantime, Green's Arkansas brigade (the 15th, 19th, 20th, 21st Arkansas regiments; the 12th Arkansas Sharpshooter Battalion; the 1st Arkansas Cavalry Battalion, dismounted; the 1st and the 3rd Missouri Cavalry, dismounted) began forming to move forward on Cockrell's right.[52]

Cockrell's brigade struck first, west of the Jackson Road, moving up against McGinnis's brigade ensconced in the woods on the southwestern slope, the 1st Missouri on Cockrell's right flank hitting the 47th Indiana on McGinnis's left, just west of the road. Slack's troops, holding on east of Jackson Road at the crossroads, hit Cockrell's right flank until the rallied 56th and 57th Georgia moved up on Cockrell's right. About ten minutes later Green's Arkansas brigade moved up on the Georgians' right and completely enveloped Slack's line, forcing them back across the open cornfield with heavy casualties.[53] Reporting on this part of the fight, Slack wrote:

> A new rebel line, which had not been in action [Martin Green's Arkansas brigade and the regrouped 56th and 57th Georgia] appeared in treble our force, and opened a most murderous fire upon our lines, which the unflinching and determined braves of the Twenty-fourth [Iowa] resisted for fifteen minutes, but, because of the overwhelming force brought to bear upon them, reluctantly retired from the battery, but kept the rebel re-enforcements at bay by their incessant fire and stubborn resistance.[54]

East of the Jackson Road, survivors of Slack's brigade reached the wooded ravines north of the field and fell back fighting, contesting every ridge and clinging "to every tree stump and log" against a hailstorm of minie balls, bursting artillery shells, and "falling branches of trees." Dockery, reporting for Green, acknowledged that because of the rough terrain on the southeastern slope beyond the cornfield "the troops could scarcely advance faster than a walk, and many of the hills were ascended with great difficultly."[55]

West of Jackson Road, McGinnis called the first half-hour of the fight up the southwestern slope of Champion Hill "one of the most obstinate and murderous conflicts of the war ... each side [taking] their turn in driving and being driven." On the Confederate side, Cockrell referred to the entire duration of the conflict as "fearful strife ... kept up uninterruptedly for two and a half hours." In this uninterrupted strife, McGinnis ordered two pieces of the captured artillery hauled away from the original Confederate line on the crest, spiked the remainder, and brought up a section of the 16th Ohio Battery to turn on Cockrell's advancing troops. Briefly effective, the Ohio battery, in danger of being captured, was hauled off, although its commander, Captain J.A. Mitchell, was killed. McGinnis's troops fell back fighting "contesting every inch of ground" and also took position on the crest near the captured Confederate battery.[56]

Meanwhile, with the sounds of gunfire moving back up the hill, Hovey, realizing that his troops were being pushed back from the crossroads, alertly positioned sixteen pieces of artillery (Schofield's Battery A, 1st Missouri Light Artillery; Murdock's 16th Battery, Ohio Light Artillery; and Dillon's 6th Battery, Wisconsin Light Artillery) on a rise in a graveyard west of Jackson Road in position to enfilade Bowen's entire line if they broke through and came down the northern slope into the cleared fields.[57]

With Hovey's division faltering at the crest, Grant sent his last reserves from Marcellus M. Crocker's division (Sanborn's, Boomer's and two regiments from Holmes's brigades) and recalled John Stevenson's brigade from the upper Baker's Creek Bridge on Jackson Road to relieve Hovey's embattled division. Pemberton's troops on that front were too weak to take advantage of the opening, but it did inadvertently leave a line of retreat temporarily open.[58]

Sanborn's brigade, the first to arrive, moved off to the right to support Logan's division, the 59th Indiana and 4th Minnesota in support of DeGolyer's battery, then pounding the remainder of Lee's line on the upper Jackson Road. The 48th Indiana and the 18th Wisconsin were sent back 100 rods (about one-third mile) to the western slope of Champion Hill to support McGinnis's desperate fight with Cockrell's Missourians at the crest.[59]

Boomer's brigade (the 93rd Illinois, 5th Iowa, 10th Iowa, and 26th Missouri) followed up the northern slope in support of McGinnis and temporarily thwarted Cockrell's attempt to break through and move down the northern slope. The arrival of the 17th Iowa and 10th Missouri from Holmes's brigade prevented Green's Arkansans from overrunning Slack's embattled brigade and enabled them to withdraw down the northeastern slope to regroup in the fields below.[60]

In the ebb and flow of the fighting on Champion Hill, Bowen made one last thrust as both sides began to run out of ammunition, a situation more dangerous for Bowen's troops because their supply wagons had left the field. Outflanking McGinnis's brigade at the crest and Boomer's and Holmes's reinforcements on both sides of the road on the southern slope, Cockrell's and Green's troops forced most of the Federal line up and over the crest and down the northern slope to the fields below. Before Bowen's troops could break through the woods at the base of the slope, however, Hovey spotted the clear separation of the two lines, ordered his troops who were still in the line of fire to lie down, and ordered his artillery (Schofield's 1st Missouri, Murdock's 16th Ohio, and Dillon's Wisconsin batteries) to open fire on Bowen's troops. The barrage of grape, canister, and shell zipped and whistled over the heads of Hovey's troops and stopped Bowen's surge cold. The thick timber and underbrush of the northern slope "was mowed," according to an account Hovey gave to the *Indianapolis Journal* years later, "almost as with a scythe." In his official report, he said "the cheers from our men on the brow of the hill told of the success." Some of Cockrell's and Green's troops held on in the wooded ravines of the northern slope with what ammunition they could gather while those who could retreated back up the hill.[61]

Boomer's and Holmes's reinforcements, the regiments of Slack's brigade who could, and McGinnis's regrouped and rearmed troops, including the 47th Indiana, once again charged into the woods of the northern slope in what Hovey referred to as "the ground which had been hotly contested for the third time that day" and drove Bowen's troops back to the crest.[62]

Meanwhile, as Green's front line moved forward, then faltered, Pemberton detached the 12th Louisiana and 35th Alabama from Buford's brigade and sent them to support Green's right flank against the appearance of McClernand's troops (Osterhaus's column) who had inched up the Middle Road and now posed a real threat to the Confederate right flank, especially to Bowen's troops on Champion Hill. The 35th Alabama moved to the support of Wade's battery, still some 600 yards south of the crossroads firing at Osterhaus's essentially stationary division. The 12th Louisiana moved to the crossroads near Waddell's recaptured guns and Landis's Missouri Battery where, according to their commander, Colonel Thomas M. Scott, they "found General Green's brigade (or at least the right of it) retiring from the field in great confusion."[63]

Forming his line "at right angles to the line occupied by Green's forces," Scott's 12th Louisiana moved eastward toward Osterhaus's column of brigades on the Middle Road, where Colonel James Keigwin's 49th Indiana and Major William H. Williams' 42nd Ohio had moved in advance on the right of Garrard's vanguard brigade. Scott's 12th Louisiana moved forward and charged the 42nd Ohio with fixed bayonets. Although the 42nd Ohio gave way on the right, Keigwin's 49th Indiana held on in the hand-to-hand fight and retired to a small elevation where they turned and fired on Scott's troops, driving them back.

Scott claimed that the 12th Louisiana "charged an entire brigade and caused them to flee in great confusion," that he held his troops in place because he "did not consider it prudent to pursue the enemy, as a heavy line was advancing on my left flank—the same force that General Green had engaged," and that he withdrew only under orders from Buford. The 42nd Ohio had broken, but Keigwin's 49th Indiana held and Keigwin claimed they made Scott's troops fall back "faster than they had approached." In any case, while the fighting raged on Scott's left on Champion Hill against Green and Cockrell's line, Scott withdrew the 12th Louisiana to the crossroads "without any further engagement" when ordered to do so by Buford, and continued on to the lower bridge where they deployed to protect what was soon to be the retreat across Baker's Creek.[64]

Colonel Edward Goodwin's 35th Alabama, after being detached from Buford's brigade, had supported Wade's artillery for about an hour as it fired eastward against Osterhaus's column until the battery ran out of ammunition and was ordered off the field. The 35th Alabama stayed in position but changed front to the north when hit by fire from that direction. Goodwin reported:

> The enemy, being driven off [referring to Osterhaus and Carr's timid approach on the Middle Road], the battery [Wade's] retired from the field having exhausted its ammunition. Just as the battery drove off, the enemy had moved around to the left, and were giving me an enfilading

fire. I therefore changed my front [northward] to meet him, in the meantime sending a courier to General Green for further orders.⁶⁵

When S.D. Lee's line began to give way to Logan's Federals on the Confederate left flank at the same time that Osterhaus's Federals approached their right flank on the Middle Road, Pemberton called retreat. Bowen's troops (Cockrell's and Green's brigades), now in danger of being trapped on Champion Hill, collapsed to the rear. Cockrell apparently believed that his brigade was still in good position and delayed relaying Pemberton's order to retreat, hoping that Loring's division "might still arrive in time." "In the meantime," Cockrell reported, referring to Osterhaus's approach on the Middle Road, "the enemy were rapidly advancing on the right, in order of battle almost perpendicular to our own, and I was thus forced to withdraw, which was done in good order." Dockery, writing the report for Green's brigade, also claimed that they withdrew "slowly and reluctantly." Landis's and Guibor's batteries did help delay the slow Federal advance on the Middle Road and enabled many to get away.⁶⁶

Colonel Goodwin of the 35th Alabama viewed the retreat from Champion Hill in a different light, however. Referring at least to Green's retreat if not Cockrell's, Goodwin reported:

> At this time our friends gave way and came rushing to the rear panic-stricken. I rushed to the front, and ordered them to halt, but they heeded neither my orders nor those of their commanders. I brought my regiment to the charge bayonets, but even this could not check them in their flight. The colors of three regiments passed through the Thirty-fifth. Both my officers and my men, undismayed, united with me in trying to cause them to rally. We collared them, begged them, and abused them in vain. At length I received orders from General Green to follow the battery. I accordingly moved out in rear of the Twelfth Louisiana, and at my urgent solicitation was permitted to rejoin the brigade.⁶⁷

Earlier in the day Hovey's division had made a remarkably successful charge up and over Champion Hill to the crossroads. Later in the day Bowen's Confederates, albeit coming in fresh against Hovey's then weary and depleted troops, made a remarkable counterattack of their own. In the end, however, Hovey's regrouped troops made the final sweep of Champion Hill.

CONFEDERATE RETREAT

Although Pemberton, while looking for Loring, had found and sent Buford's brigade northward to support his beleaguered left flank, and to support Bowen's countercharge up Champion Hill, Loring remained out of communication with, or ignored, Pemberton's order. Loring did, however, keep Tilghman's brigade in position on the Coker House ridge that commanded Raymond Road. When McClernand's troops (Osterhaus's and Carr's divisions) finally broke through on the Middle Road, Pemberton had already called for retreat across the newly constructed lower Baker's Creek Bridge on Raymond Road and at a now fordable point below.⁶⁸

Osterhaus and Carr, delayed somewhat by the 12th Louisiana and 35th Alabama, but mostly by McClernand's inertia, finally moved forward following Bowen's and Lee's rout and captured many of the fleeing Confederates, including Lt. Henry B. "Harry" McLaughlin of the 35th Alabama Infantry, brother of Lt. Col. John A. McLaughlin of the 47th Indiana. (See Appendix A.[69])

Tilghman's brigade, assisted by Bowen's regrouped troops, was able, even in the confusion of the precipitous retreat, to form an effective rear guard for Pemberton's shattered army at the lower bridge and ford on Raymond Road because A.J. Smith's and Frank Blair's divisions had also remained inert on Raymond Road, content to fire long-range artillery. Meanwhile, whatever glory McClernand thought he would gain from this battle evaporated in the hot afternoon sun.[70]

John D. Stevenson's Federal division, accompanied by De Golyer's battery, pursued fleeing Confederates across the upper Baker's Creek Bridge on Jackson Road and used long-range artillery fire to disrupt Pemberton's crossing at the lower ford and bridge. Meanwhile, Burbridge's brigade of A.J. Smith's Federal division, which had belatedly moved up, attacked Tilghman's rear guard at the lower bridge on Raymond Road. At 5:20 P.M., Tilghman was killed by a shell from either the 17th Ohio Battery or the Chicago Mercantile Battery, brought up to assist Burbridge's brigade.[71] Loring, finding that Burbridge's Federal infantry and artillery now commanded the lower crossing, turned his division southward instead of following Pemberton's line of retreat across Baker's Creek.[72]

The Federal pursuit stopped at nightfall around Edwards Depot on Jackson Road east of Big Black River. Osterhaus and Carr proceeded to Edwards Depot with the remainder of Grant's army, while Holmes's brigade and Hovey's troops remained on or near the field of battle, the 47th Indiana pushing on about two miles until ordered to camp for the night.[73]

Giving an infantryman's shorthand, if not somewhat inaccurate account of Hovey's division (they numbered only 4,180), Joseph Z. Scott of the 46th Indiana of McGinnis's brigade wrote the *Huntington Democrat*:

> *Messers. Editors*: ...On the morning of the 16th we learned the rebels had been greatly reinforced, and were preparing to give us fight, about six miles to the front. We started early, and arrived about 9 o'clock near the enemy. We found them stationed on the hills around, on ground of their own choosing. At ten we advanced to meet them, and were soon engaged in deadly conflict with the John rebels.
> Our division was placed in the center and front, and had to do the fiercest of the fighting. The rebs, after fighting for some time, began to give ground; we followed them closely, sometimes shooting them down, sometimes punching them up with the bayonet. We followed them in this way about half a mile, when they were reinforced. Our little division was then 15,000 or 20,000 men, and were in turn compelled to run; we did so fighting as we went. We lost all the ground we had gained. When we had got to the top of the hill where the fight commenced, the rebels close after us, Gen. McGinnis rode along our line and halloed, "Boys, for God's sake hold out fifteen minutes longer, reinforcements are coming"— at the same time telling us to look back. The hills to the rear were almost covered with our men, coming at double quick to our assistance. We rallied, gave a yell, fixed bayonet and charged, completely checking the rebels and holding them, until sometime after, when the reinforcements arrived, who filed in before us, and, in an hour afterward the rebs were in full retreat. It was then about five o'clock.
> We had been living on one-third rations for some time, and on that day had nothing to eat; we, of course, were well satisfied to let others take up the chase, and we remained on the battle field. Our brigade was pretty well cut up, being the worst used up of any in the division, which lost a little over thirteen hundred in the action. We remained on the field two days after gathering up the arms and burying the dead. In places they lay so thick that we could walk on dead men every step. I slept but little the first night on the field; the groans of the wounded were awful.[74]

In fact, Hovey's division took the heaviest casualties in the Federal army with 211 killed (5 percent of the division and over one-half of Grant's total of 410 killed), 872 wounded (21 percent), and 119 missing (2.8 percent), for a total of 1,202 casualties or almost 29 percent, about one-half of Grant's total casualties of 2,441. Of Hovey's two brigades, Slack's lost 108 killed, 365 wounded, and 93 missing, for a total of 566, or 31 percent of the 1,809 engaged. McGinnis's brigade lost 103 killed, 507 wounded, and 26 missing, for a total of 636, or 27 percent of the 2,371 men engaged. Boomer's brigade of Crocker's division, which came in relief, was the only other brigade that took comparable casualties with 111 killed, 388 wounded, and 11 missing.[75]

These numbers are, of course, subject to some error. The Official Records lists 32 killed, 91 wounded, and 17 missing from the 47th Indiana. The 47th Indiana's roster, however, lists 37 killed and 10 mortally wounded, for a total of 47 deaths. Four days after the battle, Slack wrote Ann: "In my brigade I lost 677 — in the 47th Regt. 143." If, as estimated, the 47th Indiana took 450 men into battle, they lost a little over ten percent killed or mortally wounded; counting the wounded survivors and missing, they suffered thirty-two percent casualties. Slack's brigade, at 677, lost thirty-seven percent. In a letter to Ann the day after the battle, Slack noted poignantly: "Many of the poor boys from Huntington are laid low."[76]

Although Confederate reports vary, they indicate that Cumming's, Green's, and Cockrell's brigades suffered similarly heavy casualties. Cumming, who took 2,500 men into battle, lost, according to his official report, 142 killed (5.7 percent), 314 wounded (12.6 percent), and 539 missing or captured (21.6 percent) for a total of 995 (39.8 percent). Neither Cockrell's nor Green's brigades list the total number of men engaged, but reports indicate that Cockrell lost between 61 and 65 killed, 290 to 293 wounded, and 238 to 242 missing or captured, for a total between 589 and 600. One report indicates that Green's brigade lost 66 killed, 137 wounded, and 65 missing or captured, for a total of 268. Although he gave no numbers, Dockery, who wrote the report for Green, provided a vivid picture of the slaughter when he noted that they were "terribly cut to pieces" and forced to fall back "leaving our dead and wounded on the field."[77]

Hovey did not exaggerate in his report when he dubbed Champion Hill "The Hill of Death:"

> I cannot think of this bloody hill without sadness and pride. Sadness for the great loss of my true and gallant men; pride for the heroic bravery they displayed. No prouder division ever met as vastly superior foe and fought with more unflinching firmness and stubborn valor. It was, after the conflict, literally the hill of death; men, horses, cannon, and the *debris* of an army lay scattered in wild confusion. Hundreds of the gallant Twelfth Division were cold in death or writhing in pain, and, with large numbers of Quinby's gallant boys, lay dead, dying, or wounded, intermixed with our fallen foe. Thus ended the battle of Champion's Hill at about 3 P.M., and our heroes slept upon the field with the dead and dying around them.
>
> I never saw fighting like this. The loss of my division, on this field alone, was nearly one-third of my forces engaged....
>
> It is useless to speak in praise of the Eleventh, Twenty-fourth, Thirty-fourth, Forty-sixth, and Forty-seventh Indiana and Fifty-sixth Ohio. They have won laurels on many fields, and not only their country will praise, but posterity be proud to claim kindred with the privates in their ranks. They have a history that Colonel Macauley, Colonel Spicely, Colonel Cameron, Colonel Bringhurst, Lieutenant-Colonel McLaughlin, and Colonel Raynor, and their children's children will be proud to read.[78]

The next morning, an angry Stephen G. Burbridge, whose brigade was in the vanguard of A.J. Smith's column on Raymond Road, complained, with some justification, that if McClernand had ordered Smith forward rapidly, they "could have captured the whole rebel force opposed to us, and reached Edwards Station before sunset." Smith's column lay on their arms that night and the next day Burbridge reported that there was "abundant evidence that the rebels had skedaddled most hurriedly, leaving arms, ammunition, etc., strewn by the roadside."[79]

From the crossroads, Carr's Federal division moved about six miles westward toward the Big Black River in pursuit of Pemberton, followed by Osterhaus's division; Hovey's division remained on or near the battlefield. That night, Loring circled back from near the lower Baker's Creek ford, destroyed the artillery that could not be moved on the old plantation roads, and marched past Hovey's campfires on the battlefield. Finding Edwards Depot in Federal hands, Loring turned and marched southeastward between the towns of Raymond and Utica, reaching Crystal Springs on the evening of 17 May, some twenty-five miles south of Jackson on the New Orleans & Jackson Railroad. Two days later, he reunited with Johnston's force at Jackson, which had been reoccupied following Sherman's withdrawal.[80]

Although criticized by Pemberton for his failure to support Stevenson's and Bowen's troops that day, Loring, having remained on the Raymond Road, had probably helped delay Pemberton's inevitable retreat, and possibly the loss of his entire force, by fooling McClernand into believing a much larger force was in his front on Raymond Road than really was. As Grant pointed out later, if McClernand had moved aggressively as ordered, it was quite possible that Pemberton's entire force could have been wrapped up that day. Of course, if Grant had taken charge on the lower roads and left the presumably able and trusted West Pointer McPherson in charge on Jackson Road, all of that could have been avoided and the battle ended earlier and with better results. On the Confederate side, Johnston, who did not want Vicksburg occupied, approved of "Old Blizzard's" behavior at Champion Hill.[81]

The 25 May 1863 *Indianapolis Daily Gazette* trumpeted:

> The Battle at Baker's Creek!
> Gallantry of Our Men!
> Complete Victory!![82]

A few weeks later, the *Indianapolis Daily Journal* printed a poignant story originally sent to the *Cincinnati Commercial* of the 47th Indiana at Champion Hill:

> "Mack" writes to the Commercial that in the battle of Baker Creek, near Vicksburg, May 15th, "Lieutenant Perry, of the 47th Indiana, was with his company under the hottest of the engagement. His regiment occupied such a position that his command was very much exposed and was suffering dreadfully. One of his comrades suggested to him that he ought to avail himself of a little cover immediately in his rear. Perry looked at him calmly but resolutely, and said: 'No sir. The 47th never gives back an inch.' A moment afterward he was shot through the heart and fell without a groan. Two of his men, on seeing him fall, wept like children.[83]

Although his official report was somewhat vague on their retreat from the crossroads, Slack did briefly recount the adventures of Maj. Edward Wright of the 24th Iowa and Capt. George Wilhelm of the 56th Ohio. During the "terrific charge" against Waddell's Battery, Slack reported, "Maj. Edward Wright, of the Twenty-fourth, was wounded in the abdomen, immediately after which he captured a stalwart rebel prisoner and made him carry him off the field." According to Slack, Maj. Wright and Maj. L.H. Goodwin of the 47th Indiana, who had also been seriously wounded, were both "rapidly recovering," and in fact did return to active duty.[84]

In another dramatic capture, Slack reported that Captain George Wilhelm "of Company F, Fifty-sixth Ohio, was badly wounded by a shot through the left breast, left on the field and also taken prisoner. After being removed about 6 miles from the field," Slack continued, "he was left in charge of a rebel soldier as a guard. The rebel laid down his gun, for the purpose of taking some observations, when Captain Wilhelm grabbed hold of it and took his guard prisoner, marched him into camp, and delivered him over to the provost marshal." Wilhelm received the Medal of Honor for his actions and Slack's succinct report mirrors Wilhelm's postwar account. (Although their actions were similar, Edward Wright received no Medal of Honor for his action.[85])

Some thirty-four years after the battle, William Aspinwall, who adapted to civilian life by becoming a tramp known as "Roving Bill," recounted his memories of the battle as a young private in Company H of the 47th Indiana. Although his recollection of the specifics of the battle are hazy, as were it seems everyone else's — the 1st Missouri Battery was on Hovey's artillery line, not at the crossroads — his memory of being shot and its aftermath seems plausible from what is known about the battle. Arriving with the 47th Indiana at the Champion property on the morning of 16 May 1863, "Roving Bill" recalled:

> We turned off the road into a vacant field. I should judge about 9 o'clock A.M. and marched across the field to a ravine which was thick with timber and underbrush. There we formed in line of battle the 1st brigade, General McGinnis on the right, and the 2nd brigade, Colonel Jas B. Slack on the left.
>
> Skirmishers were ordered out and went into this ravine and soon found the Johnnies. The firing became brisk, and a rebel battery opened fire on us from the bluff beyond the ravine. An advance of the division was ordered, and the gallant 1st brigade charged the battery and took it with our brigade following. They drove the advance lines of Pemberton across a field where his whole army was massed. We halted where the battery was taken on the side of the bluff and they flanked our 1st brigade which fell back to our position. The Johnnies came for us at least ten to one; but we gave them a warm reception, both with musketry and artillery using the battery of the guns we had just captured from them, and the 1st Missouri battery of our brigade was to the front. These batteries threw death and destruction into their ranks in a fearful way. The last words I remember hearing before being shot were uttered by some of our officers who were begging our men to fall back as the rebels were flanking us. As I had my gun up to my shoulder three buck-shots, coming from the right flank, struck me in the right shoulder. My arm fell helpless by my side and not more than a second afterward a minie ball plowed across the top of my head cutting the scalp and chipping the skull, and cutting the hair across the head as neatly as it could have been done with a sharp pair of shears. I fell to the ground and our orderly sergeant, J.W. Whitmore, said I bounced around like a chicken with its head cut off. John E. Sturgis, one of our sergeants and now a druggist and a prominent citizen of Bluffton, says he saw five of us boys, of our company, all wallowing around together in our own blood like stuck hogs.
>
> When I came to my senses I was inside the rebel line, the bullets falling around me like hail. It was some little time before I could make out my surroundings. A Confederate officer came and sat down on a little bank of earth beside me. He looked at the wound in my head and said, "My boy, I am afraid you are done for." He gave me a drink of water out of his canteen, raising my head very gentle with one hand, so I could drink.
>
> He asked me what State I was from. I replied, "Indiana," proudly. He made some other remarks about my youth, and what a shame it was to see me in that condition. I will never forget his kindness. I think he was an officer of General Pemberton's staff as the general was near

by, himself and staff on foot, taking observations. After he left me I got up and started towards our lines, passing the retreating Johnnies, and almost rubbing clothes with them. Andersonville prison being constantly in my mind, I preferred death to going there. I succeeded in getting into our lines and finding my captain, who got me in an ambulance and I was taken to the hospital which was in a corn field. The wounded were made as comfortable as possible under shades made by driving forked poles cut from the woods in the ground across which poles were laid and these covered with brush. By this means the boys were protected from the hot sun. There were rows of the wounded with aisles between, and the surgeons worked on their rude dissecting tables in these aisles. What horrible sights, and what pitiful cries and groans. I never want to experience it again. Let some of our later-day soldier-haters have the experience, if the necessity should occur again.

I merely walked through the hospital and after that I was content to stay on the outside, for I could not endure to witness the misery of my comrades. Many a noble boy of my regiment would never see mother or home again; their bones were to be left on the battleground of Champion Hill.

In the evening some of my comrades brought me blankets, doing without themselves, and made me a bed in a fence corner outside of the hospital. In a little while a Confederate soldier came along. He had been shot somewhere in the bowels and was in great pain. I said — "Here, partner, I will share my bed with you," — and he laid down beside me. He told me that he was from Savannah, Georgia, and that he could not get well. He wanted me to write to his wife and children and gave me a card with their address. I was to tell them that I had seen him and what had become of their beloved husband and father. Being weak and exhausted from the loss of blood, I dozed off to sleep and left him talking to me.

In a little while I awoke and spoke to him two or three times, but he did not answer. I put by hand over on his face; he was cold in death. My foe and friend had crossed the river. I laid there with him until daylight, then found a sergeant who dressed my wounds and a comrade who wrote two letters for me, one to my mother in Bluffton, Indiana, and one to this poor confederate's family in Savannah, Georgia. I took the letters over to the Confederate hospital which was a short distance from ours in an adjoining cornfield. They had no brush sheds. The poor fellows were laying around between the corn rows and there was a large number of them. I found a Confederate officer to whom I stated the circumstances and gave him the letter. He said I could rest assured that he would see to it that the dead soldier's family got the letter and he complimented me on my kindness and said that if he ever saw me in trouble he would assist me with all his power. A number of ladies had assembled from the surrounding towns and country waiting on the Confederate wounded and they looked daggers at me; not a one of them spoke to me. They did not like the color of my blood-spattered uniform.

During the night while laying beside my dead companion I heard loud singing and shouting. The next morning I made inquiries and found it was the 24th Iowa holding a Methodist revival camped on the battlefield among the dead and wounded. This gallant regiment was largely composed of members of the Methodist church and was called the Methodist regiment. It belonged to our brigade. How strangely their singing and shouting sounded on that unhappy night above the groans of the wounded and dying and the sounds of distant musketry and artillery firing.

Thus wound up the battle of Champion Hill, the first decisive of the war, for it was a complete defeat to the Confederates, and finally giving us the boasted Southern Gibraltar, Vicksburg and Port Hudson, and opening up the Mississippi River from St. Paul to the sea, cutting the confederacy in twain.[86]

THE SKIRMISH AT BIG BLACK RIVER BRIDGE

With Loring's division circling toward Jackson, Stevenson's division retreated westward across the Big Black and bivouacked at Bovina. Acting as rear guard, Cockrell's and

Green's, brigades of Bowen's division, "after marching under cover of darkness through plantations, along and across ravines, and leaving Edwards Depot to the right," joined Vaughn's brigade already stationed on the east bank of the Big Black in Pemberton's mile-long line of cotton bale-and-dirt rifle pits and field artillery.[87]

Pemberton failed to utilize the bluffs on the west bank to protect his line of retreat, choosing instead to set up his battle line across the narrowest part of the river's horseshoe bend in the bottomlands of the east bank. The river crossings of the deep and swift Big Black had been prepared by flooring and covering the railroad bridge for passage of wagons and men and at the dirt road by swinging the steamer *Dot*, which had had its machinery removed, across as a foot bridge. Pemberton's line was fronted by what Grant called "an open, cultivated bottom of nearly one mile in width, surrounded by a bayou of stagnant water, from 2 to 3 feet in depth and from 10 to 20 feet in width, from the river above the railroad to the river below." As one of Cockrell's astute Missourians said after the war: "This position would have been a good one, if the fortifications had been on the other side of the stream."[88]

Green's Arkansas brigade held the extreme left of the Confederate line from the northern bend of the river; Vaughn's East Tennessee brigade held the center from Green's right to the railroad, both brigades in rifle pits facing east, looking from behind abatis across the shallow bayou and a roughly quarter-mile clearing to a copse of wood that stretched from the river above to the railroad. Cockrell's Missouri brigade completed the line on the right, running southward from the railroad "as far toward [their] right as the bayou," actually an oxbow lake left behind when the river changed course. The oxbow lake and a swampy cypress break protected Cockrell's right flank, and his line, with almost a mile of cleared fields in front, contained most of the Confederate artillery.[89]

In the predawn hours of 17 May, Osterhaus's, Smith's, and Carr's Federal divisions from McClernand's 13th corps moved in pursuit to the Big Black some six miles distant while Hovey's division remained on the battlefield to help collect the wounded and bury the dead. Early that morning, Carr's division, leading the pursuit, formed on the Federal right in the woods, largely out of view of Green's and Vaughn's Confederates. Osterhaus's and Smith's divisions followed, forming south of the railroad facing Cockrell's troops across the open field.[90]

Following a long-range artillery bombardment of the Confederate line, Brigadier General Michael Lawler, commanding the 2nd brigade of Carr's division, on the Federal right, moved his troops to the left through the woods in front of Green's position under the protection of an old "meander scar" (the old riverbed of the meandering river). Acting on the suggestion of their colonel, W.H. Kinsman, Lawler sent the 23rd Iowa to attack the right of the Confederate line and brought the 49th and 69th Indiana regiments over from Osterhaus's division to support the charge on Lawler's left in front of Vaughn's position.

As the 22nd Iowa peeled off to the right toward the safety of the riverbank, the 23rd Iowa led the 21st Iowa and 11th Wisconsin on a mad dash out of the woods and across the quarter-mile clearing, splashing across the obstructed bayou in a hail of bullets. As soon as Lawler's troops moved forward, Keigwin's 49th Indiana followed on the left against Vaughn's Confederates. On Lawler's front, although Kinsman was killed leading the charge, his 23rd Iowa was first to gain a foothold inside the Confederate works. Simultaneously on the left of Lawler's line, the 49th Indiana, led by Captain James C. McConahay of Company A, stormed out of the woods toward Vaughn's right flank. Sergeant William Wesley Kendall took charge after McConahay was wounded and reportedly led the 49th Indiana through the bayou at its deepest point, leaped across a ten-foot wide ditch into a pile of rails being used as abates, and laid the rails across the ditch so that Keigwin's men could follow more easily. Thanks to Kendall, the 49th Indiana was the second regiment to break through the Confederate works. He would be awarded the Medal of Honor for his efforts.[91]

As the remainder of Lawler's troops poured into and behind the Confederate works, Pemberton's line collapsed. Vaughn's troops gave way without much resistance, fleeing across the swollen Big Black over the railroad and boat bridges, pulling Green's and then Cockrell's troops with them.[92]

At the last minute, Confederate engineers burned the railroad bridge with turpentine-soaked cotton and fence rails. Chief Engineer Samuel H. Lockett, aboard the *Dot* and aided by a lieutenant, waited until all the soldiers in sight had crossed before setting the steamer alight by igniting a barrel of turpentine and tipping it over. Within moments both bridges were ablaze, preventing Federal pursuit as the fleeing Confederates joined the remainder of Pemberton's force now trapped inside the Vicksburg fortifications. Not all Confederates could escape, however, and the Federals captured about 1,800 prisoners, some Confederates drowning in the swollen Big Black while trying to escape.[93]

That same day, 17 May, Johnston, who later lamented that he had been too ill to take command when he first arrived, dispatched yet another futile warning to Pemberton: "If Haynes' Bluff is untenable, Vicksburg has no value, and cannot be held. If, therefore, you are invested in Vicksburg, you must ultimately surrender. Under such circumstances, instead of losing both troops and place, we must, if possible, save the troops. If it is not too late, evacuate Vicksburg and its dependencies, and march to the northeast."[94] But with Pemberton's entire force now trapped inside Vicksburg, it was too late.

IX

Vicksburg (May–July 1863)

Pemberton's army fell back into Vicksburg's fortifications on 17 May 1863. M.L. Smith's division formed on the left from Fort Hill overlooking the river where Vaughn's brigade, along with Harris's Mississippi State Troops, were posted behind Fort Hill Road looking north. Baldwin's brigade continued on the ridge behind Fort Hill Road facing north. Shoup's brigade continued in the line of works, curving across the Graveyard Road, including the Stockade Redan that guarded that entrance to the city. Forney's division continued the line with Hebert's brigade extending from Shoup's right to both sides of the Jackson Road that was guarded by the 3rd Louisiana Redan and the Great Redoubt. Moore's brigade extended from just south of Hebert's position on Jackson Road to the 2nd Texas Lunette, which guarded the Baldwin's Ferry Road, and rifle pits covering the railroad. Stevenson's division covered Pemberton's right flank. S.D. Lee's brigade, with Waul's Texas Legion in reserve, extended from the Railroad Redoubt, which covered the tracks of the Southern Railroad of Mississippi as it entered the city, southward on the meandering ridgeline to the Square Fort. Cumming's brigade extended from the Square Fort to Hall's Ferry Road; A.W. Reynolds's brigade continued the right-center of the line from Hall's Ferry Road; and Barton's brigade formed the extreme right flank in the fortifications covering the southern approaches and the Warrenton Road. Bowen's division (Cockrell's and Green's brigades), which had been decimated by heavy losses in killed and captured at Port Gibson, Champion Hill, and Big Black River, was placed in reserve closer to the city in rear of Moore's brigade, his troops to be sent to various points on the line as needed.[1]

On 18 May, Sherman's corps, the advance columns of Grant's Army of the Tennessee, began forming outside Vicksburg's fortifications, taking control of the Walnut Hills and the Yazoo River north of town (facing Vaughn's, Baldwin's, and Shoup's brigades of M.L. Smith's Confederate division). That evening, McPherson's corps began forming on Sherman's left flank, their line facing westward toward the Vicksburg defenses. Grant also sent Brigadier General John McArthur with one brigade from his division to Warrenton to guard the Federal depots and to close access to Vicksburg from the south via Warrenton Road. In addition, George Neeley's brigade was detached from Elias Dennis' District of North East Louisiana to assist McArthur.[2]

Osterhaus's division (Albert L. Lee's and Daniel W. Lindsey's brigades) led McClernand's corps toward its position on McPherson's left flank. Turning south from the Jackson Road at Mt. Albans, they bivouacked that night across the Baldwin's Ferry Road, about two miles from the city and in sight of its fortifications. The next day, as Grant's invest-

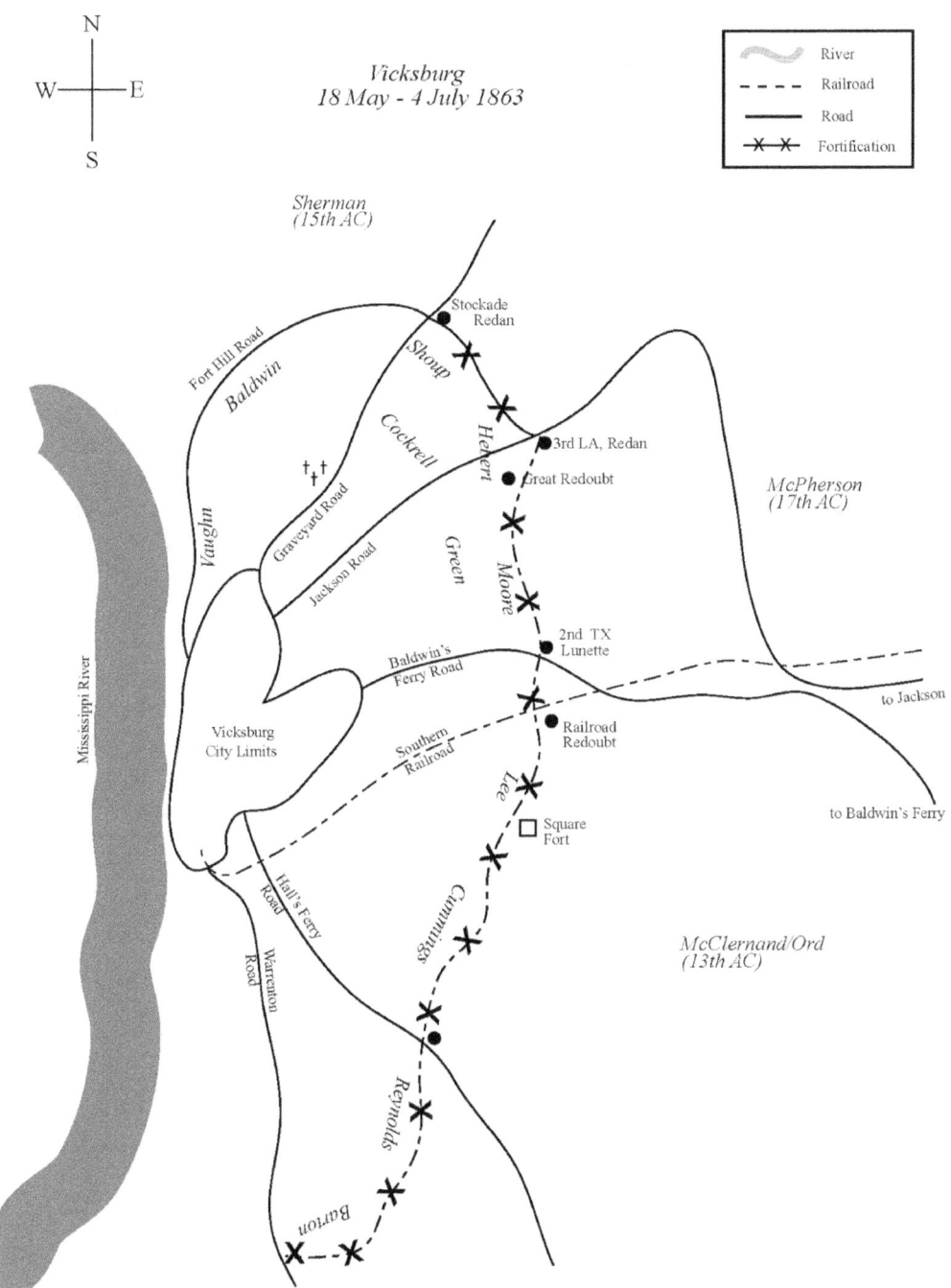

From Atlas Plate XXXVII, No. 1

ment of the city continued, Osterhaus's division moved southward to cover the approach to the city along Hall's Ferry Road and A.J. Smith's division (Stephen G. Burbridge's and William J. Landram's brigades) moved in to fill the gap created by Osterhaus's move southward with Carr's division (William P. Benton's and Michael K. Lawler's brigades) in reserve.[3]

Grant also brought Brigadier General Jacob G. Lauman's division from Cadwallader

Washburn's 16th corps in Memphis to Haynes' Bluff. At this time, Grant's line stretched some fifteen miles from Haynes' Bluff above the city to Warrenton below, although not continuously, with a gap between the Hall's Ferry and Warrenton roads. Hovey's division (George F. McGinnis's and James R. Slack's brigades) remained at Big Black River guarding the bridge and river crossings.[4]

First Assault on Vicksburg, 19 May 1863

Back at Vicksburg, Grant hoped to catch Pemberton's soldiers demoralized and unprepared. On 19 May, with only Sherman's corps in proper position, Grant ordered a general assault on Pemberton's line. Following a morning of artillery shelling, at 2:00 P.M. Frank Blair's division (Giles A. Smith's, T. Kilby Smith's, and Hugh Ewing's brigades) attacked vigorously across the fields astride the Graveyard Road toward abatis made of tangled brush and fallen timber that protected the parapet called Stockade Redan, called by one soldier of the 93rd Indiana on approach, "the monster work looming up in front of us." The regulars of the 1st Battalion, 13th United States Infantry managed to plant their flag on the outside slope of Stockade Redan, but heavy Confederate fire along the entire line forced most of Blair's troops to find shelter in the ravines and behind tree stumps, with many of the Federals remaining there until darkness allowed them to pull back safely. McPherson's and McClernand's corps, both of which were still coming in, did not attack as vigorously and suffered many fewer casualties, although Albert L. Lee, commanding the 1st brigade of Osterhaus's division, was wounded and replaced by Colonel James Keigwin of the 49th Indiana. Grant's frontal assault was easily repulsed along the entire line, causing the loss of about 1,000 of his men—a "dreadful sight," according to one Indiana soldier.[5]

Grant spent the next two days bringing the remainder of his troops into line and resting them while building up supplies. On the 20th, McGinnis's brigade of Hovey's two-brigade division arrived from Big Black River and was placed in support of Osterhaus's division on the extreme left, while Carr's division moved up and relieved A.J. Smith's troops on the front line.[6]

Second Assault on Vicksburg, 22 May 1863

On 22 May, Grant, still believing he could take heavily fortified Vicksburg by frontal assault, ordered another general assault to commence at 10 o'clock that morning.[7]

On the right, Sherman sent Steele's 1st division to attack Baldwin's position from the north and Blair's 2nd division again attacked the northeast salient near Stockade Redan.[8]

In the center, McPherson sent John E. Smith's 1st brigade of "Black Jack" Logan's 3rd division down the Jackson Road to attack just north of the 3rd Louisiana Redan.[9]

On the left, McClernand sent Lawler's brigade (the 21st and 22nd Iowa and 11th Wisconsin) of Carr's division, and Landram's brigade (the 77th, 97th, and 108th Illinois, 19th Kentucky, and 48th Ohio) of A.J. Smith's division down the Baldwin Ferry Road to attack the Railroad Redoubt just left of the railroad in front of their position. They were to be supported by Benton's brigade of Carr's division and Burbridge's brigade of A.J. Smith's division. Osterhaus's division was to assault on their left, then the extreme left of the army, supported by McGinnis's brigade of Hovey's division. Slack's brigade, including the 47th Indiana, remained on Big Black River.[10]

Remembering Sherman's assault against Baldwin's Confederate brigade, Sergeant William Pitt Chambers of the 46th Mississippi wrote: "Column after column was hurled against our works, only to be driven back in confusion and leaving the ground in front of our lines literally blue with dead and wounded Federals." Both Sherman's and McPherson's assaults were stopped with heavy losses, although Grant merely reported that Sherman's corps made a "vigorous assault."[11]

The left of McClernand's corps line received a similar reception, and his attack stalled when Osterhaus's troops were hit by enfilading fire. McGinnis's brigade of Hovey's division, temporarily commanded by William T. Spicely of the 24th Indiana, did not get into the action.[12]

On the right of McClernand's line, the four brigades of Carr's and A.J. Smith's divisions had more success attacking the Railroad Redoubt and the 2nd Texas Lunette.

ATTACK ON THE RAILROAD REDOUBT

Lawler's brigade, supported by Landram's, led the assault on the Railroad Redoubt, the small fort held by the 20th and 30th Alabama Infantry of S.D. Lee's brigade. It was situated on a salient angle in the Confederate line atop a steep, sloping ridge that commanded the approaches via the railroad. As Colonel William M. Stone of the 22nd Iowa and Lt. Col. Cornelius W. Dunlap of the 21st Iowa watched from a hill overlooking the Railroad Redoubt, Lt. Col. Harvey Graham led the 22nd Iowa's assault on the redoubt, supported by the 21st Iowa.[13]

Earlier in the day, firing 30-pounder Parrot siege guns from about five or six hundred yards, Major Maurice Maloney's 1st U.S. Infantry gunners opened a breach in the sloping twenty-foot wall at the southeast angle of the Railroad Redoubt. As McClernand's line moved forward along the line and Graham's Iowans charged the Railroad Redoubt, most of the Alabamans, having had their fill of 30-pounder Parrot shells, unable to withstand Federal sharpshooter fire on their parapet, and their relatively ineffective use of hand grenades (typically loaded 10-pound shells with short fuses) tossed over the side when the Iowans filled the ditch below, scurried back to the Confederate second line and took refuge with the remainder of S.D. Lee's brigade in the rifle pits near the redoubt. Although the grenades injured a number of Graham's troops, fewer exploded than expected, some even caught "on the fly" by Graham's troops and extinguished in puddles of water before they could explode.[14]

Led by Sergeants N.C. Messenger and Joseph E. Griffith, a squad of from fifteen to twenty soldiers (some reports say as many as fifty) from the 22nd Iowa stormed up and over the breach and captured the few remaining Alabamans inside the fort. The Iowans took possession of the Railroad Redoubt and planted the U.S. flag and the regimental flag of the 77th Illinois, who were not in the initial assault, but whose flag was brought over on Stone's orders until the 22nd Iowa's regimental flag could be brought up and planted as well. Messenger was killed, but Griffith was credited with capturing thirteen prisoners.[15]

Attack on the 2nd Texas Lunette

Shortly after the attack on the Railroad Redoubt began, A.J. Smith's division (Benton's and Burbridge's brigades) assaulted the well-entrenched but thin Confederate line just north of the railroad and made it to the wall of the 2nd Texas Lunette.[16]

The 2nd Texas Lunette guarded Baldwin's Ferry Road, one of the two principal entrances to the city, the other being the Jackson Road farther north. It was described by Colonel Ashbel Smith of the 2nd Texas as "an irregular lunette ... with a parapet about 4½ feet high on the inside ... surrounded by a ditch in front nearly 6 feet deep, with an irregular glacis made by the natural slope of the earth to the ferry road." Situated on a salient ridge with a line of rifle pits and two embrasures for cannon with a traverse between them, the lunette was held by the 42nd Alabama Infantry on the right and the 37th Alabama Infantry on the left. Following the ridgeline, it angled back sharply on the right and left, with a one-hundred-yard gap between the lunette's left flank and the continuation of the Confederate line. Baldwin's Ferry Road passed through this gap, leaving their left flank somewhat exposed. It was therefore considered by Smith to be the key to this portion of the works and, indeed, the most assailable point on the entire Confederate line.[17]

Burbridge's Federal troops had some early problems fighting Smith's Texans and Alabamans at the lunette until Federal artillery fire nearly destroyed the lunette's cotton sack and dirt embrasures, pinned down the Texans inside and drove the Alabamans out of their rifle pits. Safe from enfilading fire because the lunette was so far forward, and safe from above because the walls of the lunette were so steep that the Texans could not shoot down at them without risk of being picked off by Federal sharpshooters, Burbridge's Federals placed a number of their flags on the slopes of the lunette while a squad from the 23rd Wisconsin Infantry pulled one gun from Capt. Patrick H. White's Chicago Mercantile Battery up to a point held by the 16th Indiana only twenty-five feet from the lunette. White's gunners "double-shotted" the cannon and fired it directly at the lunette, destroying an embrasure and disabling a 24-pounder siege gun inside. Virtually destroying the lunette, the cannon and musket fire ignited the cotton scattered from the exploded embrasure and filled the air with smoke.[18]

Describing the initial attack on the 2nd Texas Lunette, Colonel Ashbel Smith of the 2nd Texas reported:

> In one of the furious assaults the enemy mounted the parapet to near its superior slope. Numbers of them were pouring a murderous fire through our right embrasure, amid the smoke of the burning cotton, which enveloped and almost blinded the men in this angle of the fort, and they were apparently on the eve of dashing in. I shouted, "Volunteers to clear that embrasure!" Four men sprang to the platform — Sergeant [William T.] Spence, of Company B, and Privates [T.E.] Bagwell, [A.S.] Kittridge, and [J.A.] Stewart, of Company C — and, discharging their guns within 5 paces of the muzzles of the assailants, hurled them back headlong into the ditch outside. The repulse was decisive. Bagwell fell dead on the platform; Spence fell by his side, shot through the brain. He lingered a few days.[19]

While Graham's squad was holding on inside the redoubt, the 130th Illinois, the 48th Ohio and the 77th Illinois apparently moved into the ten-foot-wide and six-foot-deep ditch below with the remainder of the 21st and 22nd Iowa and planted their flags on the slope while still subject to some crossfire from the extended line of Confederate rifle pits.[20]

Seeing the flags on the parapet of the Railroad Redoubt and on the slope of the badly damaged and smoke-filled 2nd Texas Lunette, and having been urged by many of his commanders for reinforcements (especially by Graham in the ditch at the Railroad Redoubt), at noon McClernand sent a dispatch to Grant calling for help. He claimed in effect, that Landram's and Lawler's troops had partial possession of the Railroad Redoubt and that Benton's and Burbridge's troops had carried the ditch and slope of the 2nd Texas Lunette, including the destruction of an embrasure and gun inside.[21]

Grant had taken position near McPherson's front north of the Jackson Road, over a mile and a half from the railroad. In spite of the fact that his view would have been obscured by the Jackson Road ridge and smoke of battle, Grant made the dubious claim that he could see all of McPherson's line and a part of each of Sherman's and McClernand's. Grant also claimed that by the time he received McClernand's three dispatches calling for assistance (between noon and 1:00 P.M.) he could see Federal flags from a portion of each of his three corps planted on the outer slopes of the Confederate bastions where no break in the line existed, so he was highly skeptical of McClernand's claim to have taken even partial control of two forts. Slow to make a decision, asserting that he did not want to risk being wrong about McClernand's claim and thus lose an opportunity to break the Confederate line, Grant waited until later in the afternoon to send Quinby's division (Sandborn's, Boomer's, and Holmes's brigades) down from McPherson's front, and ordered McArthur's division up from Warrenton to assist McClernand. Sherman and McPherson were to resume their attacks as a diversion to help McClernand.[22]

Late Afternoon Attack at the Railroad Redoubt

Meanwhile, at the Railroad Redoubt, S.D. Lee's Confederate brigade was in trouble. A sortie had been made earlier in the afternoon by a detachment from the 30th Alabama under Captain Henry P. Oden that was cut down inside the fort, all reported lost in the attack. Subsequently, soldiers of the 20th and 30th Alabama refused orders to retake the redoubt and Federal flags flew on its parapet and walls for three hours before Lee was able to rally his troops and put together a force made up of thirty-five volunteers from Col. T.N. Waul's Texas Legion. Familiar with the approaches to the redoubt, Lt. Col. E.W. Pettus (minus his recalcitrant 20th Alabama) volunteered to lead Waul and his men into the redoubt. While McClernand and Grant dawdled in the late afternoon, Waul's Texans charged and drove the Iowans through the breach and recaptured the redoubt, killing, wounding, and capturing half of the Iowans who had remained inside. The Iowans who were not killed or captured escaped into the ditch below. (Prior to Waul's attack, Sgt. Griffith and a few others had marched their prisoners out of the ditch and over the hills to their brigade, division and corps headquarters before finally turning them over at Grant's headquarters "with the compliments of Col. Graham." Some of those who remained in the fort and anticipated Waul's assault leapt from the parapet and took the Stars and Stripes and the 22nd Iowa's regimental flag with them[23]).

Even with Waul's recapture of the redoubt, the stalemate continued as the Federal troops in the ditch below, although subject to crossfire, remained protected from rifle fire in their front by the steep walls of the redoubt. Some of Waul's men mounted the parapet and fired into the ditch, but in so doing, also put themselves in the line of fire from below and from sharpshooters on the Federal main line. The stalemate ended near dark when Waul's troops again tossed a few hand grenades over the wall onto the Federals below. The brave but prudent Graham surrendered with nineteen of his soldiers.[24]

At this point, Lt. Col. James Wrigley's 2nd Battalion of Waul's Texas Legion sallied from the redoubt in cautious pursuit of the remaining Federals. As darkness fell, Wrigley's Texans returned to the redoubt and the remainder of Graham's contingent in the ditch escaped back to the Federal line, taking the flags of the 48th Ohio and 21st Iowa with them.[25]

Late Afternoon Attack at the 2nd Texas Lunette

At about the same time Waul's Texas Legion was retaking the Railroad Redoubt, the embattled Forney, relying on their heavy fortifications to hold off McPherson's and Sherman's renewed assaults, pulled troops from M.L. Smith's division (the 17th Louisiana from Baldwin's brigade and half of the 28th Louisiana from Shoup's brigade) and sent them south to assist the struggling 37th and 42nd Alabama.[26]

In the meantime, some Arkansas and Missouri troops from Martin E. Green's reserve brigade came up to assist Ashbel Smith's beleaguered 2nd Texas as Moore's brigade regrouped around the 2nd Texas Lunette. Rallying against Burbridge's Federals, who had earlier pushed them from their rifle pits, Moore's Confederates retook the rifle pits on either side of the lunette where the 2nd Texas continued to hold on in spite of Federal artillery and the burning cotton bale embrasure.[27]

Describing this part of the fight, Col. Ashbel Smith of the 2nd Texas reported:

> To clear the outside ditch, spherical case were used as hand-grenades, and, it is believed, with good effect. After the repulse of this assault, which was about 3 P.M., there was for an hour or more a great slackening of the enemy's fire. He despaired, as it appeared, of being able to carry our works by an unsupported assault in front, and ordered an attack to be made on our left. A heavy column came marching up the valley already described as debouching in the interval on our left.[28]

The heavy column reported by Smith were Sanborn's and Boomer's brigades sent by Grant from Quinby's division to assist Carr's assault. Arriving at his headquarters at about 4:00 P.M., Carr sent Sanborn's brigade (the 38th and the 48th Indiana, the 4th Minnesota, and the 18th Wisconsin) to the right (north) to support Burbridge's brigade, then still holding on in front of the 2nd Texas Lunette.

As Sanborn's troops arrived in support of Burbridge's brigade, Moore's and Green's regrouped Confederates opened fire and Burbridge's line collapsed. Burbridge and Carr blamed the collapse on Sanborn's troops, whom they claimed were quickly scattered by Confederate fire as soon as they arrived. Sanborn, on the other hand, claimed that as soon as his brigade line was formed, it was Burbridge's troops that gave way, forcing him to pull his troops back from the lunette's wall when some of Moore's Confederate troops left their works and threatened to turn his right flank. Sanborn added that it was his troops, Company C of the 4th Minnesota in particular, who, when darkness fell, retrieved White's cannon, abandoned when Burbridge's troops fled to the rear. In any event, by nightfall Moore's and Green's troops succeeded in pushing Sanborn's and Burbridge's Federals back about a quarter mile from the 2nd Texas Lunette on Baldwin's Ferry Road.[29]

Just south of the 2nd Texas Lunette and north of the railway, Carr sent Boomer's brigade (the 93rd Illinois, 5th Iowa, 10th Iowa; and 26th Missouri) to attack the rifle pits that angled severely from the right flank of the 2nd Texas Lunette and followed the ridges and rough terrain north of the railroad. Boomer's brigade also suffered heavy casualties in the assault, including the death of Colonel George B. Boomer, who was replaced by Colonel Holden Putnam of the 93rd Illinois. Shortly after Boomer's death, and with the resurgence of S.D. Lee's troops at the Railroad Redoubt and Moore's troops at the 2nd Texas Lunette, Putnam was ordered to halt his advance against the Confederate rifle pits, held by Forney's thin line, and to withdraw after dark. Farther south, Holmes's brigade, the last of Quinby's troops to arrive, moved to support Osterhaus, but their attack was countermanded due to the lateness of the hour. McArthur's division, coming up from Warrenton, did not arrive until the next day.[30]

Describing the late afternoon and early evening attack from inside the 2nd Texas Lunette, Col. Ashbel Smith reported:

> Early in the day I had observed our exposed condition on this side, and had asked for support from the reserves. It was now at hand and opportunely, for my numbers were so reduced by killed and wounded that I could ill spare any considerable body from my front. It was now about 5 P.M. The reserve, some Arkansas and Missouri [troops], under General Green, hesitated for a moment, and allowed a most gallant lieutenant to get some 20 paces in advance of his company. I ordered instantly Captain [J.J.] McGinnis' company, which was in the rifle-pits to the right, to march to the left, crossing the gorge of the fort, to their aid, but as this company was coming into position, the Missourians dashed forward, and, after half an hour's sharp fighting, they repulsed the enemy most gallantly. This approach of the enemy's column on the left and the fighting was the signal for the renewal of his attack in front. The firing was very brisk, but the assault was feeble compared with the fierce onslaughts earlier in the day. The day was now drawing to a close. As the shades of the night were setting in, the enemy's fire slowly and sullenly slackened. It ceased with the dark. The enemy returned to their covers in the hollows and valleys.[31]

The assault had now failed all along the line, with many Federal casualties — double what they would have been, according to Grant, if McClernand had not misled him into believing that he had captured two Confederate forts and needed more support. McClernand, on the other hand, claimed he had not misled Grant and had, in fact, reported accurately to Grant that his troops had gained "partial possession of two forts" (the Railroad Redoubt and the 2nd Texas Lunette) and had taken prisoners from both.[32]

McClernand's claim was at least partially correct. The Railroad Redoubt had been taken; but the 2nd Texas Lunette had not — although McClernand's troops early on had effectively destroyed the parapet, planted their flags on the slope, and pinned down the Confederates inside. In fact, Confederate Brigadier General John C. Moore, the brigade commander of that position, called it the weakest part of Pemberton's line with barely sufficient troops to fill the trenches; and Ashbel Smith, 2nd Texas, commanding in the lunette, called it the most assailable point on their line.[33]

McClernand argued that Grant had misled him by not informing him that Sherman's and McPherson's assaults had been halted, leaving his corps to continue the attack alone and unsupported. Grant, however, claimed that he could see the Railroad Redoubt from his position at McPherson's headquarters and saw no sign of is having been taken by McClernand's forces. In support of McClernand's assertion, a number of his subordinates, including the captured Harvey Graham of the 22nd Iowa, indicated later that they did not believe Grant could have seen McClernand's operations from his viewpoint at McPherson's headquarters, which was at least a mile and a half away. They were correct. The Jackson Road ridgeline and heavy smoke would have obscured Grant's view of the Railroad Redoubt or the 2nd Texas Lunette from McPherson's headquarters.[34]

Grant, on the other hand, admonished McClernand to bring up his own reserves to support the attacks near the railroad. In turn, McClernand's response that he had no reserves to send because all his troops were too heavily engaged was somewhat disingenuous since McGinnis's reserve brigade, which did not get into the fight when Osterhaus's attack stalled, was available.[35] In any event, whether or not they could have broken Pemberton's line at Baldwin's Ferry Road or the railroad if Grant had properly supported McClernand's attack, or if McClernand had thrown McGinnis's reserve brigade into the fight in that sector, the responsibility for the great Federal losses rested on Grant's shoulders, not McClernand's. Grant had ordered the ill-conceived general assault, the second in three days, against the length of Pemberton's heavily fortified line, and was therefore totally responsible for the unnecessary loss of life.

Pvt. Owen Johnston Hopkins, 42nd Ohio (Osterhaus's division) understood Grant's culpability in ordering the general assaults when he wrote in his diary:

> Friday, May 22nd. (Bad luck to _____ !) Will ever be remembered by the Soldiers of Grant's Army as one of the Bloodiest of the campaign. In ordering the Charge on the entrenched Position of the Enemy, May 22nd, General Grant Sealed the fate of Hundreds of his best Soldiers. It was not a charge; it was not a Battle, nor an assault; But a Slaughter of Human Beings in cold Blood. We done our best; we struggled manfully; we fought desperately; all would not do, we were repulsed and with fearful loss.[36]

THE SIEGE: 23 MAY TO 4 JULY

Pemberton's Confederates, "neither idle nor dispirited" following the second Federal assault, worked hard to add about two feet to the thickness of their parapets. All along the Confederate line that night work was conducted to repair and strengthen the works, and the morning found them in as good a condition as at the beginning of the Federal assaults. Prepared to build countermines, the Confederate engineering force included twenty-six sappers and miners; eight mechanics and foremen; four overseers for 72 slaves hired from the owners; three 4-mule teams, and twenty-five oxen.[37]

Following his two disastrous assaults and renewed defensive efforts by Pemberton's troops, Grant finally decided that he would have to "out camp the enemy."[38]

On 24 May, Grant sent Osterhaus with one brigade (Keigwin's) to replace Slack's brigade at Big Black River, with Lindsey's brigade remaining under Hovey's command. Slack's brigade rejoined Hovey's division line at Vicksburg, their first view of the Vicksburg fortifications. Hovey's line, which extended Grant's left flank to Hall's Ferry Road, faced S.D. Lee's and Cumming's Confederate brigades, Lindsey's brigade on the right, just south of the Railroad Redoubt; Slack's in the center, facing the Square Fort; and McGinnis's on the left.[39]

Grant's siege began in earnest two days later. Using pioneer troops and escaped slaves who had been hired for $10 a month after crossing into Federal lines, as well as occasional details from his infantry, Grant put his army to work moving his line forward toward the Confederate parapets. To protect themselves from flanking fire as they inched forward, Grant's troops dug a series of zigzag offensive trenches or "saps." To protect the soldiers ("sappers") from frontal fire, shields were placed at the head of each sap. The most common type shield was the "gabion," usually wicker baskets woven from saplings, cane, or grape vines and filled with dirt.[40]

The strangest devices used to shield the Federal sappers and miners from frontal fire were the "sap rollers." Due to a scarcity of trained engineers, these contraptions were made largely by trial and error and had varying degrees of success. The idea was to roll them ahead of the sappers to protect them from direct gunfire while they dug—the successful ones able to protect the men from six and twelve-pound shot. One sap roller was described as being between eight and ten feet long and four and a half to five feet wide, made of wire mesh that was filled with cane and reinforced by wooden pork barrels; some were made of a wicker mesh of woven vines filled with cotton; and one, on the Jackson Road, consisted of a large pile of cotton bales on a flat bed railcar on iron wheels.[41]

When sap rollers failed or were destroyed near the Confederate line, "fascines," or bundles of cane bound together, were used as roofs over the roughly six-foot-deep trenches to at least give the men some protection from musketry and rifle fire, although not from hand grenades dropped on them from the parapets above, or fire balls (18-pounder shells wrapped in turpentine-soaked cotton) bowled at them. Where available, railroad ties were laid across the trenches to form a stronger gallery to protect the sappers and miners as they dug closer to and under the Confederate line.[42]

THE APPROACHES

On Sherman's line north of the city, Thayer's brigade (from Steele's division) moved forward from the crest of a ridge toward the Confederate position on a parallel ridge of about the same elevation that was held by Baldwin's brigade and the left of Shoup's brigade. Due to a shortage of manpower, the Confederates were unable to occupy that ridge. The Confederates also had less artillery than the Federals and were very conservative in expending ammunition, enabling Thayer's Federals to move down the slope of the ravine and up the opposite side toward the center right of Baldwin's and left of Shoup's Confederate brigades under the protection of heavy Federal artillery fire. The lack of Confederate artillery fire at this point enabled Thayer's pioneers to advance hidden from view and somewhat protected from musketry fire by cane fascines placed across the top of the six-foot-deep trenches. By 14 June, Thayer's troops were able to approach within 100 paces of Baldwin's parapet, where work on the saps was halted and mining began when they heard what they thought was Confederate countermining efforts.[43]

Ewing's brigade (from Blair's division) provided Sherman's main thrust, pushing forward astride the Graveyard Road toward Stockade Redan, held by the center of Shoup's Confederate brigade. By 4 June, the Federals had established a third line of parallels at about 150 yards from the Confederate salient works and double-saps commenced against the Stockade Redan on Graveyard Road, the 3rd Louisiana Redan just north of Jackson Road, and the 2nd Texas Lunette on Baldwin's Ferry Road.[44]

Protected by Federal artillery and sharpshooters, Ewing's troops pushed forward toward Stockade Redan behind gabions and sap-rollers to within 75 yards of the redan. On 14 June, Federal artillery fire destroyed the redan's parapet and disabled its 12-pounder gun. But as the Federal sappers moved closer to the Confederate ditch, Shoup countered by organizing his artillerists into a "hand grenade and thunder barrel corps," using the rampart to drop 6- and 12-pound loaded shells onto the sappers below. At that point, Ewing's troops, who had moved up behind gabions and a sap roller, protected themselves from the hand grenades by placing rails over their saps to create a gallery and began mining operations under the Confederate works. Shoup countered with a gallery and countermine of his own.[45]

Giles A. Smith's brigade (from Blair's division) pushed forward from a ravine parallel to the Confederate line about two hundred yards southeast of Ewing's Graveyard Road approach against heavy resistance from Hebert's and Green's brigades on Forney's Confederate line.[46] On McPherson's line, Ransom's brigade (from McArthur's division) started from the same ravine as Giles A. Smith's brigade, and by 20 June was able to approach to within 100 paces of the Confederate works north of the Jackson Road.[47]

Logan's division, in the center of McPherson's line, followed a little farther south on the Jackson Road ridge, referred to by the Federals as "Fort Hill," toward the "3rd Louisiana Redan" perched above the Jackson Road on a salient in the Confederate line defended heartily by Hebert's brigade.[48] Logan's troops pushed forward to within sixty feet of the 3rd Louisiana Redan behind the sap roller devised from a flatbed railway car and stacks of cotton bales that could be pushed forward at will. To stop this cotton-bale juggernaut, on 8 June, at the suggestion of one of his soldiers, Lt. Col. S.D. Russell of the 3rd Louisiana had his troops fire "pieces of port-fire and cotton balls steeped in turpentine into it from muskets." These "fireballs" ignited the cotton bales while Confederate sharpshooters prevented the Federals from extinguishing the flames or pulling the sap roller back to safety, thus destroying the sap roller and forcing the Federals to temporarily fall back to a safer distance. It also caused Grant to complain later that the Confederates had resorted to the "barbarous" use of "explosive musket-balls." After the war, Confederate Chief of Engineers S.H. Lockett asserted that they never had exploding musket balls and cited their having fired port-fire and turpentine-soaked cotton from muskets as "the origin of General Grant's notion that we had explosive shells."[49]

McClernand's line, whose trench line was led by Lieutenant Peter C. Hains of the U.S. Corps of Engineers, had A.J. Smith's division on the right approaching the 2nd Texas Lunette; Carr's division in the center, approaching the railroad cut; and Hovey's division on the left, converging on the Square Fort.

A.J. Smith's division (Burbridge's and Landram's brigades) approached the 2nd Texas Lunette astride the Baldwin Ferry Road. Impeded by heavy artillery and musket fire from Moore's Confederate brigade, Smith's Federals moved forward erratically, straying temporarily from their assigned approach on the Baldwin Ferry Road because the ground was too hard to dig and the terrain too rough for sap rollers. By 15 June, Smith's troops, still unable to use sap rollers due to the roughness of the terrain, had approached the lunette so closely that they had to proceed with "the greatest caution" against the Texas sharpshooters, who prevented them from working in the day, but allowed them to work at night.[50]

Just to the south, Carr's division (Brig. Gen. Wm. P. Benton and Col. Charles C. Harris's brigades) dug two approaches toward the Railroad Redoubt, the right approach starting in the railroad cut about 350 yards east of the Railroad Redoubt, the left approach starting in a hollow about 280 yards southeast of the Railroad Redoubt. By mid–June (the 15th) Carr's troops had reached the top of the hill nearest to the Railroad Redoubt, the right approach about 150 yards from the redoubt, the left approach to within 80 yards.[51]

Hovey's division converged on the Square Fort held by troops from Isham Garrott's 20th Alabama of S.D. Lee's brigade. With the terrain in front too rough for sap rollers, and with a scarcity of entrenching tools on McClernand's entire line, Hovey's troops pushed forward digging rifle pits on the crests of hills in front of the Confederate line held by both S.D. Lee's and Alfred Cumming's brigades. Lindsey's brigade (the 54th Indiana, 22nd Kentucky, 16th, 42nd and 114th Ohio) approached on the right, just south of Carr's approach on the railroad. Sharpshooters from Slack's brigade (the 87th Illinois, the 47th Indiana, the 24th and 28th Iowa, and the 56th Ohio) occupied rifle pits on Hovey's line 275 yards northeast of the Square Fort, facing troops from Col. F.K. Beck's 23rd Alabama of S.D. Lee's brigade. McGinnis's brigade (the 11th, 24th, 34th and 46th Indiana, and the 29th Wisconsin), facing troops from both Lee's and Cumming's brigades, converged on the Square Fort from the east and south.[52]

Referring in part to the advance of Slack's brigade and the 47th Indiana, S.D. Lee reported:

> As each of their ditches was completed, it was filled with sharpshooters, who kept up a continuous fire upon our lines. The enemy had also from fifteen to thirty pieces of artillery in front of my line, which kept up a heavy fire during both night and day. The fire from their small-arms commenced generally about half an hour before daylight, and continued until about dark in the evening. There was no relief whatever to our men, who were confined for forty-seven days in their narrow trenches without any opportunity of moving about, as there was during the day a perfect rain of Minnie balls, which prevented any one from showing the least portion of his body, while at night, in consequence of the proximity of the enemy, it was impossible for the men to leave their positions for any length of time. After about the tenth day of the siege the men lived on about one-half rations, and on even less than that toward its close.[53]

On 25 May, Slack wrote Ann to describe the siege of S.D. Lee's position:

> We go into the fight today to relieve the 1st Brigade, and stay on duty two days. It is very queer sort of fighting. Our men take position directly under the rebel forts, and prevent them from loading their guns. We have them afraid to approach their heavy guns to load them. Every time the men attempt it, our sharpshooters pick them off. There is no general fighting, every one has to fight on his own hook. We are now laying siege to the place, and expect to continue it until they surrender.[54]

At about this time, Grant brought Lauman's division from Haynes' Bluff to relieve McArthur's detachment on Warrenton Road and to help close the gap between there and Hovey's division above Hall's Ferry Road. Without a heavy Federal force below Hall's Ferry Road, Reynolds's and Barton's Confederate troops were not as tightly penned in as Cumming's and Lee's troops were in front of Hovey's division. As a result, they were able to sally out of their fortifications to harass the limited Federal force that had been posted on Warrenton Road.

At 9:30 P.M. on 25 May, only three days after Grant's disastrous general assault, troops from Barton's Confederate brigade sallied out of a skirt of timber in the swampy land between the river and Warrenton Road, which the Federals considered impassable, surprising and capturing a large portion of the 46th Illinois regiment from Cyrus Hall's brigade of Lauman's division. The 46th Illinois had been sent specifically to relieve the 63rd Illinois of Neeley's brigade on picket and were probably the 107 enemy pickets reported captured by Col. W.E. Curtiss's 41st Georgia Infantry from Barton's brigade.[55]

Back on Hovey's line, still the extreme left of Grant's continuous line, the Federal position was much stronger and Hovey's sharpshooters and artillerists continued to harass S.D. Lee's Confederates. Describing their life as sharpshooters in those trenches, Captain S.J. Keller of Company H of the 47th Indiana recorded in his diary:

> May 26th — Ordered out as sharpshooters and are in trenches within 200 yards of the enemy's forts. No enemy dare show his head. We shoot so close, or pick them off, as to warn them to keep hid. Had heavy artillery firing on both sides. A flag of truce went out to bury the dead and bring in the wounded. The men from both sides came together and talked friendly. Our boys jollied them and advised them to give up and save their city and many lives. They replied that they still had hopes General Johns[t]on would come to their relief.[56]

On the Confederate side, "the usual work of repairs and improvements went on; the rifle pits on the river front were pushed ahead; the battery in rear of General Lee was finished, and a 30-pounder Parrott put in position." Confederate chief of engineers Samuel Lockett also noted: "On this night [26 May] the enemy for the first time fired on our working parties, and wounded a lieutenant commanding a fatigue party."[57]

The next day (27 May), Porter's gunboats joined the mortar boats in bombarding Vicksburg. At the behest of Sherman to demonstrate the capability of the Federal gunboats in front of his position, the USS *Cincinnati* steamed upriver to the upper Confederate battery at Fort Hill and was promptly sunk.[58]

On 28 May, back from two days of duty as sharpshooters in the rifle pits, Captain Keller noted that they "had only one man wounded ... but some of the men had narrow escapes."[59]

That same day, Slack wrote Ann about the action of his brigade and the 47th Indiana and the interaction between his men and the Confederates opposite them.

> Well we are entrenched in rifle pits along the crest of a hill directly opposite their rebel forts and a string of rebel rifle pits.
> My line is nearly a mile in length. It is very amusing to sit down in their trenches & hear the men talk. The rebels are from 150 to 300 yards distant from our men, and they shoot at each other as deliberately as though they were hunting & shooting birds. They resort to all kinds of strategy to get each other to show their heads above the entrenchments, and woe to the fellow that does it.
> Our boys now have the advantage of them. They have logs put up in front. One log is put down on top of the entrenchment with notches cut in it, then another log put on top which leaves a hole between just large enough to shoot through, which makes it an almost impossibility to hit them. They stand and watch, and as soon as a head is shown bang it goes from perhaps fifty guns at once. We are worrying them most terribly. Monday afternoon a flag of truce was sent over & hostilities were suspended from about three o'clock in the afternoon for the balance of the day. I had one man shot in the calf of the leg after the order "cease firing" was given. Presume it was a mistake.
> As soon as the firing ceased the rebel forts & our hills in a line parallel with them were literally swarming with soldiers. They very soon began to hallow at each other & very soon began to

visit shake hands and talk, trade knives, exchange papers &c &c. Our boys gave them some crackers, whiskey, &c. They acknowledged that we had them whipped, and their only hope rested in holding their fortifications sufficiently long to let Genl Johns[t]on get in our rear, and thus relieve them. They are short of provisions. I think there is no hope of Johns[t]on helping them out, they must come down.[60]

The next day (29 May), Confederates put in a new battery in rear of their line on Hall's Ferry Road, and added an 18-pounder to the battery in rear of S.D. Lee's position. This came to be known as "Whistling Dick" because of the sound its shells made as they flew through the air. Closer to the center, Federal sharpshooters drove off a working party attempting to start a new battery in rear of Moore's position.[61]

On 3 June, Slack told Ann that the Confederates attempted to plant a battery to the left of his position overnight, but that his men drove them back and took their rifle pits. He added three days later: "Our sharpshooters are located directly under the rebel fortifications, so near that they have scarcely any use at all of their artillery. The moment they attempt loading their guns, our boys concentrate a fire upon them which puts a veto upon the whole thing. It is very amusing to sit in the rifle pits and hear the boys communication."[62]

Across the Mississippi, Lt. Gen. Edmund Kirby Smith, commander of the Confederate Department of the Trans-Mississippi, ordered Maj. Gen. Richard Taylor, commander of the District of West Louisiana, to lead an expedition to the Mississippi to cut what he mistakenly thought was Grant's supply line from Lake Providence to Young's Point, Louisiana, and to relieve the siege of Vicksburg. Taylor sent Brig. Gen. J.G. Walker's division to accomplish the task.

In the predawn hours of 7 June, Brig. Gen. Henry E. McCulloch's brigade moved to attack the Federal garrison at Milliken's Bend commanded by Brig. Gen. Elias Dennis, commander of the District of North-East Louisiana, and garrisoned by a brigade of newly recruited and inexperienced black troops and detachments from the 23rd Iowa Infantry and 10th Illinois Cavalry. Grant's supply line on the Louisiana side having been long since abandoned, the Federal troops were posted there primarily to guard Federally controlled cotton plantations and the riverside camps of freedmen who cultivated them.[63]

Notified that a Confederate force was moving toward them on the road from Richmond, Dennis sent two companies of the 10th Illinois Cavalry and Col. Herman Lieb's 9th Louisiana Infantry African Descent to reconnoiter, with two companies of the 9th Louisiana leading the way mounted on mules. Accompanied by the two companies from the 10th Illinois Cavalry, they skirmished with Harrison's cavalry in McCulloch's vanguard and, in the face of a much larger force, fell back to their line along the levee at Milliken's Bend, which had from left to right: the 9th Louisiana Infantry African Descent, the 1st Mississippi African Descent, the 13th Louisiana African Descent, the 23rd Iowa detachment, and the 11th Louisiana African Descent.

Due largely to the difficulty that the inexperienced and untrained black troops had in handling their old Belgian rifles, McCulloch's Confederates broke through the Federal line at the levee. The fighting quickly became a desperate hand-to-hand struggle with clubbed muskets and bayonets until the Confederates moved around the Federal left flank on the levee and poured in a deadly enfilading fire, aiming especially at the white officers and killing many of the black troops.

The Federals were forced to fall back to their last line of defense at the riverbank and an old levee on the extreme right where two companies of the 11th Louisiana Infantry African Descent were posted in reserve behind cotton bales. The soldiers of the 11th Louisiana held off the charging Confederates, now exposed on the flat open ground between the levee and the riverbank, enabling the retreating Federals to regroup behind the steep riverbank, which served as a natural breastwork behind which they could safely stand and shoot. The attack at Milliken's Bend ended after several hours of intense fighting when McCulloch's troops, stopped by the determined Federal defense at the river, were hit by broadsides from the gunboats *Lexington* and *Choctaw* of Admiral Porter's fleet. His troops scattered in confusion McCulloch decided to withdraw.[64]

Later that day down at Young's Point, when Confederate Brig. Gen. J.M. Hawes learned that McCullough's troops had withdrawn from Milliken's Bend without carrying and holding their position, he withdrew his troops without making an attack, causing Taylor to lament that the results of the expedition against Milliken's Bend and Young's Point were less than they should have been simply because the soldiers of Walker's division had suddenly developed a "dread of gunboats."[65]

Two days later (9 June), Bartlett's 13th Louisiana Battalion and Crawford's 13th Texas from Walker's division made a mounted attack on Goodrich's Landing near Lake Providence and were driven off by a Federal force of 800 commanded by Brig. Gen. Hugh T. Reid, including 300 soldiers of Col. Hiram Scofield's 8th Louisiana Infantry African Descent, as new black recruits began to show their worth as soldiers in the Federal army. Following these setbacks, Taylor gave up the attempt to relieve the Vicksburg siege from the opposite bank. Leaving Walker's division opposite Vicksburg at E. Kirby Smith's insistence, Taylor moved the remainder of his force into the bayou country of southern Louisiana, where he hoped to draw Banks away from Port Hudson.[66]

Across the river at Vicksburg on the morning of 10 June, heavy rain forced Slack out of his tent: "I laid down in my cot, and when I woke up the water was about a foot deep in my tent, and running like a mill tail. I had to wade out. It continued to rain till afternoon, when I had to move my tent." Capt. Keller of the 47th Indiana noted that it was a little tougher on the men in the rifle pits. After it "thundered and lightened and poured as if the earth and sky were coming together," the riflemen came into camp from the pits "wet, muddy and half dead."[67]

The next day, 11 June, was also the day that Maj. Gen. F.J. Herron's division (Vandever's and Orme's brigades) arrived from the Department of the Missouri, brought down by Grant to complete the investment of Pemberton's forces from the river above the city to the river below. Herron's division was put into position on the extreme left, south of the city along Warrenton Road, and Lauman's division was moved to Herron's right across the Hall's Ferry Road, between Herron and Hovey. Three days later the 1st division of the 9th corps, Maj. Gen. J.G. Parke commanding, arrived and was posted at Haynes' Bluff along with William Sooy Smith's and Nathan Kimball's divisions of Washburn's 16th corps detachment, recently arrived from Memphis. Mower's brigade of Tuttle's division was sent across the river to Young's Point to reinforce the Louisiana side as Grant's army now completely invested Vicksburg on the land side, with Federal gunboats controlling the river and a constant barrage of rifle and artillery fire along the entire line.[68]

On 13 June, "P," the *Daily Journal's* anonymous correspondent in the 47th Indiana, sent the latest news from Vicksburg, including the unfortunate notice that Pvt. Robert Thomson of Company C had been killed by a stray bullet while asleep in his tent that morning:

VICKSBURG NEWS

From a number of letters from the army at Vicksburg, we glean some points of interest. Under date of June 13th, a correspondent writes:

The siege is still progressing, with no perceptible change, except the strengthening of our lines. The chain of artillery is being slowly advanced, and in many places is within three hundred yards of their works — quite short range for artillery. The line of "sharpshooters" have advanced their lines until in many places they are immediately under their works.

Our forces are not suffering, as the protection is good. The troops are in fine spirits — confident that, with General Grant to lead them, victory will be the reward.

We go on duty every fourth day in the pits; the other three days we lie in supporting distance, and do such fatigue duty as is required.

The loss in the 47th has been but three since the commencement of the siege — John Martin, company I, wounded in head; William Porter, company C, in leg and, this morning, Robert Thompson, private, company C, was mortally wounded while yet asleep. The wounded left at Champion Hills have all been brought up. About one-half have been paroled. Yours P[69]

Continuing his description of the siege on 16 June, "P" of the 47th Indiana wrote the *Daily Journal*:

A LETTER OF LATER DATE.— THE DAILY ROUTINE OF THE SIEGE
REAR OF VICKSBURG, JUNE 16, 1863.

Mr. Editor: To-day is the twenty-eighth day of the siege of Vicksburg, with fine rains filling our "tanks." Glorious weather, cold and pleasant; plenty of supplies — a healthy army — all in fine spirits. We still invest the "Southern Gibralter."

The "wood-choppers" are chopping more earnest than ever, (the term is applied to the "sharp-shooters," the report of their guns resembling chopping timber) and are unusually active, while ever and anon, the "heavy timber falling," (discharges of cannon and bursting bombs) gives evidence that "the work goes bravely on" and must soon be finished.

It cannot last much longer. From deserters, we learn that their fare is indeed meager. Peas and beans mixed, (what bread!) and a little bacon, and not half rations at that furnished. Men cannot subsist upon such fare and perform duty, and as they report, which we believe, large numbers of them are being daily taken to the hospitals, whilst a large proportion of those on duty are too weak to escape far, even if an opportunity were offered.

They may be holding out, trusting to be reinforced, but it will be to them a vain delusion. There are no reinforcements for them within many miles of this place. Our cavalry have and are scouring the country in every direction. Even were it otherwise, it would be just what is wanted; their approach would be known to us some days before they could reach here, having blockaded the roads and destroyed the bridges, hence would welcome them upon ground of our own selection, and it would soon be settled who would be victors. We would rather fight them here than elsewhere. This is the usual feeling. Let them come.

Our casualties since we have been here has been light, although our batteries are so near, and trenches in some places but a few hundred feet form their works.

The whistling balls, in countless numbers, pass over our heads with a *scipp* and a *whis*, but little harm is done. Occasionally they open a battery, but are soon silenced. Fifty of our guns are brought to bear at once. Nothing can withstand that storm of shot and shell.

During the night quiet reigns, except the bursting of bombs and firing from our siege guns at regular intervals.

All quiet in the trenches, on both sides, when dark approaches, each apparently satisfied with their day's work. Yours, P.[70]

After about a month in Vicksburg with supplies dwindling and confined in narrow entrenchments and small forts, not to mention daily harassment by Federal sharpshooters and artillery fire, Pemberton's troops began to feel the effects of Grant's siege. According to one Confederate private, Abner Wilkes of the 46th Mississippi Infantry, they felt "penned up like so many hogs in a pen." [71]

On 17 June, Col. Isham W. Garrott of the 20th Alabama Infantry, also apparently tired of being penned up like a hog inside the Square Fort, borrowed an infantryman's rifle, went to the skirmish line to find some action and was shot and killed almost immediately by one of Hovey's sharpshooters. The Confederates renamed Square Fort "Fort Garrott" in his honor.[72]

On 18 June, the battle of egos between McClernand, Grant, Sherman, and McPherson came to a head in the Federal camp when Grant fired McClernand, replacing him with Brigadier General E.O.C. Ord.

McClernand's dismissal followed a steady deterioration in his relationship with Grant, ranging from their initial dispute over command of the Mississippi Expedition to their dispute over who was to blame for the disastrous 22 May assault at Vicksburg. It was, however, McClernand's 30 May "General Orders, No. 72," also known as his "congratulatory address" to his troops, that precipitated his rapid departure from the Army of the Tennessee.

McClernand's congratulatory address to his troops included, not unlike many written during the war, praise for the great effort of his troops, who had indeed operated in the vanguard of Grant's army, opened the military road through the swamps and bayous of Louisiana, crossed the river, and had fought and won the battles of Port Gibson, Champion Hill and Big Black River Bridge. In the address, however, he implied, and not without some merit, that if Grant on 22 May had provided assistance "by massing a strong force" at the Railroad Redoubt and the 2nd Texas Lunette as called for, his troops could have penetrated and broken the Confederate line. Adding fuel to the fire, he implied, unfairly, that Sherman and McPherson's lack of a "simultaneous and persistent attack" on their fronts also contributed to the failure of his men to penetrate the Confederate line. To top if off, he failed, of course, to mention in his list of accomplishments that his own slow, cautious movement on the lower roads nearly cost the Union victory at Champion Hill and had certainly added to the number of casualties in Hovey's division there.[73]

Both Sherman and McPherson exploded in anger when they learned of the contents of the address in which McClernand had at least indirectly impugned their leadership at Vicksburg. Sherman learned of the address in the 13 June 1863 edition of the *Memphis Evening Bulletin* and reported immediately to Grant, with some justification, that what McClernand had written was "humbug," a vainglorious and hypocritical account of the Vicksburg Campaign that was "manifestly designed for publication for ulterior political purposes." McPherson read McClernand's address in the 10 June 1863 edition of the *Missouri Democrat* and complained to Grant about a week later that McClernand had depicted himself in northern newspapers as "the hero, the mastermind" of the military operation at Vicksburg. Both Sherman and McPherson had a point about McClernand playing politics, although McPherson's accusation about McClernand claiming to be the hero or mastermind of the entire campaign was untrue.[74]

McClernand, however, had overplayed his hand. Grant knew that neither Sherman nor McPherson could stand McClernand; and, if he, himself, were killed or disabled,

McClernand would be next in line to succeed him in command of the Army of the Tennessee. To avoid certain disruption of command under those circumstances, Grant, using the pretext that McClernand had violated an earlier order of his that all official documents were to be submitted to his office before publication, fired McClernand. McClernand, realizing his gaffe, apologized for the oversight, although, true to form, he blamed his adjutant for the misstep. Grant, of course, could not pass on the opportunity to rid himself of the troublesome McClernand and ordered his dismissal on 18 June 1863.[75]

Upon receiving his letter of dismissal, McClernand, who believed that only Lincoln could fire him, immediately wrote Lincoln, Stanton and Halleck to have his dismissal rescinded. In this battle of egos, however, Lincoln, who had originally appointed "War Democrat" McClernand to help keep Copperhead-laden southern Illinois pro-Union before the election, knew very well which of his generals he could ill afford to lose in the field and quickly approved of Grant's order of dismissal. McClernand, with only enough time to fire off a few letters of protest, packed his bags and headed back to Springfield, Illinois, where he arrived on 27 June.[76]

Grant and company won this battle. But McClernand was no slouch as a politician, and seven months later, after considerable lobbying, he was reinstated to his old 13th Corps command, then part of Banks's Department of the Gulf, replacing E.O.C. Ord, who had replaced him. Arriving in New Orleans on 15 February 1864 to take command, Banks, prompted from Washington, assigned him to lead an expedition to Texas.[77]

When Grant heard of McClernand's reinstatement, he feared that Banks might place McClernand in charge of the Red River Campaign and wrote to Sherman on 18 February 1864 that he "had little or no confidence in his ability for command." On 8 March 1864, Sherman, referring to McClernand's reinstatement and assignment to Banks's Department of the Gulf, reassured Grant that "General McClernand has been ingeniously disposed of by being sent to command in Texas." Indeed, Lincoln had sent McClernand as far away from Grant as he could, while, at the same time, he had removed the disgruntled McClernand from southern Illinois, where he could have become politically troublesome in the upcoming elections.[78]

On 20 June, with McClernand out of the way and Pemberton's force effectively penned in, Grant put Sherman in charge of a force to chase after Joe Johnston. During this time, Slack wrote Ann that on the night of 18 June one of his batteries had thrown "red hot shot till midnight" at the city. "The balls," he wrote, " were plainly seen as they flew from the guns. Looked like a ball of fire ... as they went on their scorching mission. We are trying to burn the town." Three days later, optimistic but impatient, Slack wrote Ann that despite all the red-hot shot that the Federals had thrown into Vicksburg and the "destitution & starvation" of Pemberton's troops, they continued to "hang out with as much pertinacity as ever."[79]

In the Trans-Mississippi, E. Kirby Smith, commanding that Confederate department from his desk in Shreveport, continued to feel obliged to help relieve Vicksburg from the west bank. Richard Taylor, on the other hand, seeing the futility of operating opposite Vicksburg, moved his District of West Louisiana headquarters to Alexandria, Louisiana, on the Red River. Leaving Walker's brigade behind opposite Vicksburg at Smith's insistence, Taylor sent Mouton's and Green's brigades southward to raise havoc among the Federal garrisons in the bayou country of south Louisiana.[80]

Starting on 15 June, Col. James P. Major's Confederate cavalry brigade swept eastward from Morgan's Ferry on the Atchafalaya River to Hermitage and Waterloo, where they demonstrated against Banks's pickets from Port Hudson. They withdrew westward to Gross Tete Bayou and moved south to Rosedale. From Rosedale, Phillips's regiment raided eastward to Plaquemine on the Mississippi, where they took 87 prisoners, burned three steamboats, and captured commissary stores. Major's cavalry then crossed Bayou Plaquemine and moved down the west bank of the Mississippi to Bayou Goula, where they took more commissary stores, destroyed Federal plantations and recaptured over 1,000 freed slaves who were working there. Bypassing the Federal fort at Donaldsonville, they moved southward along Bayou La Fourche through the swamps, arriving at Thibodeaux at 3:30 A.M. on 21 June, where they cut the telegraph wires on the New Orleans, Opelousas & Great Western Railroad.[81]

On the night of 22 June, Major, having raided through bayou country, was moving westward from Thibodeaux to cooperate with Mouton's attack on Brashear City, arriving at Chacahoula Station just before dawn the next day, about twenty miles to the east. That same night, Mouton's and Green's Louisiana and Texas troops, including the Valverde and Nichols batteries, moved under the cover of darkness toward the eastern fortifications of Brashear City as Hunter's intrepid little flotilla gathered at the mouth of Bayou Teche above the city.[82]

The Valverde Battery opened fire at dawn, awakening the Federals, who concentrated their land batteries on them as the Federal gunboats retreated. Their whole attention paid to the Confederate batteries, the Federals missed Hunter's raiding party coming down the Atchafalaya above the city. The intrepid flotilla of skiffs landed above the city and Hunter's raiders charged through the city, capturing one gun after another until the garrison of 1,200 surrendered without much resistance. Mouton's force captured thousands of dollars in commissary stores, ordnance, small arms and eleven heavy guns along with 1,200 prisoners.[83]

Although Mouton's raid on Brashear City was very successful, it did nothing to break Banks's siege of Port Hudson. Mouton turned his force eastward toward Donaldsonville, Louisiana, and Federally held Fort Butler on the Mississippi River. Filled with confidence from the success of the night attack at Brashear City the week before, at 1:30 A.M. on 28 June, Green's force attacked Fort Butler, commanded by Major Joseph D. Bullen of the 28th Maine Volunteer Infantry and a contingent of 225 inexperienced men from companies C, G and F of the nine-month 28th Maine and Maj. Henry M. Porter's 7th Vermont Volunteer Infantry.[84]

Bullen left his sick quarters to lead the defense inside the fort. They were, however, greatly aided by Capt. M.B. Woolsey's gunboat, *Princess Royal*, which shelled Green's troops in the woods, joined by the gunboats *Winona* at 4:00 A.M. and *Kineo* a half an hour later. In a four-and-a-half-hour fight, Green's troops penetrated the fort but, in the confusion of the night fight, were trapped below and hit hard by musketry fire from above in desperate fighting. Green's force lost some 350 killed or wounded and about 120 captured, including Col. Joseph Phillips, Lt. Col. D.W. Shannon, and Major Alonzo Ridley.[85]

On the Federal side, losses were slight: 8 killed and 13 wounded in the fort, and 1 killed and 1 wounded on board the *Princess Royal*. Maj. Bullen, however, was murdered two days later following a quarrel with a private from the 1st Louisiana Volunteers (U.S.), who was among the reinforcements who arrived at the fort the day after the battle.[86]

Even with the failure at Donaldsonville, Taylor's forces continued to harass the Federals in bayou country, occupying the area around Thibodeaux and Bayou La Fourche as Banks withdrew his forces on the New Orleans, Opelousas & Great Western Railroad to the town of Algiers across the river from New Orleans. Banks reported confidently that the "fall of Port Gibson will enable us to settle [with Taylor's forces] very speedily."[87]

Back at Vicksburg, the siege continued with the most active Confederate forces continuing to make sallies against the southern approaches. Herron's recently arrived troops moved slowly up the Warrenton Road toward Barton's Confederate position, and Lauman's troops moved toward Cumming's along the Hall's Ferry Road as the Federals crept closer to the southern end of Pemberton's line of defenses.

Lauman's line near Hall's Ferry Road had the most difficulty. On 22 June a sortie by the 57th Georgia of Cumming's brigade resulted in the capture of Lt. Col. William Cam of the 14th Illinois and nine guards in the working party, plus the loss for a night and day of their advanced trenches, which the Georgians filled in. Problems on Lauman's line led C.A. Dana, Secretary of War Stanton's representative at Vicksburg, to write to his boss, "The night before last [Lauman] had a lieutenant colonel and 9 men captured by the enemy. Lauman is a brave man, but an ox is just as fit to command as he is."[88]

Three days later, on Sherman's northern approach, Baldwin's Confederate brigade made sorties against Thayer's troops on the Graveyard Road, including sharpshooters, a 3-inch rifle, and a 24-pounder howitzer placed on the site of the Riddle House that had a plunging line of fire 150 yards from the Federal frontline works near the Graveyard Road. Although it was a standoff, it was a case of too little Confederate artillery used too late. Baldwin's howitzer, with its plunging fire, could have easily destroyed the cane fascines covering the Federal works at that point, although overwhelming Federal artillery fire would most likely have knocked it out of action had Pemberton not surrendered first.[89]

The greatest progress was made on McPherson's line. According to Grant, as the sap reached the 3rd Louisiana Redan on the Jackson Road: "The soldiers of the two sides occasionally conversed pleasantly across this barrier; sometimes they exchanged the hard bread of the Union soldiers for the tobacco of the Confederates; at other times the enemy threw over hand-grenades, and often our men, catching them in their hands, returned them."[90]

Late afternoon on 25 June the camaraderie ended and the lobbing of hand-grenades and heavier artillery began in earnest as the Federals exploded a mine under the 3rd Louisiana Redan with 2,200 pounds of powder. The night before, Hickenlooper's Federal miners had become frightened and evacuated their mine when they heard the picks of Confederate miners edging toward them. The Confederates in their countermine also heard "the picking, picking, picking" of the Federal miners. Hickenlooper rushed them back into the mine to plant charges to spring their mine. The force of the explosion was greatly weakened, however, when its force was vented up the shaft of the Confederate countermine and it blew up only a portion of the outer rampart, creating a small crater. Six enlisted men from the 43rd Mississippi who were at work in their countermine were killed and several men on the rampart were blown into the air, some of them coming down on the Federal side still alive.[91]

Hebert's troops, along with Cockrell's reserve brigade, were able to regroup behind a retrenchment line prepared for such an emergency. The Federals, led by the 45th Illinois and 100 volunteers from the 23rd Indiana of Mortimer Leggett's brigade, entered the crater and brought with them loophole timber for their sharpshooters, but were unable to hold the crater. Hebert's artillery (Lt. C.C. Scott's Appeal Battery) splintered the timber, and Hebert's troops tossed a barrage of 6- to 12-pound hand grenades down upon the Federals, mangling those remaining in the crater and forcing the rest to fall back to the outer slope behind sandbags. The parapet of the 3rd Louisiana Redan was too high to return the grenades by hand, so Leggett's Federals used "coehorn" batteries, which were mortars fashioned out of cylinders of wood skirted with iron bands with an effective range of 100 to 150 feet, to return fire. In a bloody standoff, Leggett's coehorn mortars rained "a terrific shower of hand-grenades" (the 6- and 12-pound shells) down on Hebert's troops huddled in their retrenchment line.[92]

Following the explosion under the 3rd Louisiana Redan, Capt. S.J. Keller of the 47th Indiana recorded in his diary that a "heavy artillery duel" followed, which lasted two hours.[93]

Before dawn (2:00 A.M.) the next day, Shoup's Confederates exploded two countermines on the Graveyard Road, destroying a Federal sap roller in front of Stockade Redan and crushing the Federal mine gallery, which forced Ewing's pioneers to detour about thirty feet around the collapsed gallery. On 27 June, Brig. Gen. Martin Green of Bowen's division, whose brigade was stationed in the gap between Shoup's brigade on Graveyard Road and Hebert's brigade on the Jackson Road, was shot in the head and killed by a Federal sharpshooter while looking over the parapet in front of a sap only sixty yards away.[94]

Just south of Ewing's approach, Giles A. Smith's sappers had been able to move close to the Confederate line, but had to halt their sap rollers due to a 6-pound rifled gun in the Confederate ditch that had perforated their line three times. Close in, Colonel Oscar Malmborg's 55th Illinois were "served so copiously with hand grenades that he had to cover the head of his sap."[95]

Mining and countermining efforts continued on both sides. By the end of June, A.J. Smith's division had pushed forward to about fifteen feet from the ditch in front of the 2nd Texas Lunette, although with heavy resistance from Moore's Confederates along Baldwin's Ferry Road in and near the lunette.[96]

Ashbel Smith's Texans inside the lunette succeeded in burning two sap rollers, described by Smith in his 2nd Texas report:

> Various attempts were made by us to burn them; at length successfully. The sap on the right was now [late June] within 18 feet of our ditch. Fire-balls of cotton soaked in spirits of turpentine were thrown against the sap-roller. These fire-balls were drawn into the sap and extinguished. At length an 18-pounder shell wrapped with the soaked cotton was bowled against the sap-roller. Its explosion, as one of the enemy was seizing it, made them wary of our fire-balls. The sap-roller was ignited and thoroughly consumed. The other sap, protected by its roller, was pushed within 20 feet of our left. The core of this sap-roller was two cotton bales placed end to end. A fuse fired from a smooth-bore musket ignited one end of the core of cotton. An incessant shower of Minies from our works make it perilous for the enemy to attempt to extinguish it. This sap-roller, too, was wholly consumed.[97]

Not to be left out, an occasional Confederate cannon ball would pass through the camp of the 47th Indiana. On 30 June, Capt. S.J. Keller noted in his diary that they were busy working on their payrolls when "a cannon ball from the enemy's guns struck my tent and threw dirt all over us."[98]

The main action was north on the Jackson Road at the 3rd Louisiana Redan. Unable to drive Hebert's Louisiana and Cockrell's reserve Missouri troops from the other side of the crater created by the explosion on 25 June, Logan's troops resumed mining three days later and ran a new gallery under the left wing of the fort. On 30 June, Confederate Chief of Engineers S.H. Lockett discovered the new mine under the redan, its gallery entrance covered with heavy timber that his 13-inch shells could not damage. To remedy this, Lockett, lighting the fifteen-second timed fuse himself, had two of his sappers roll a barrel containing 125 pounds of powder over the parapet. The exploding barrel destroyed the heavy timber screen, hurling pieces of timber, gabions and fascines into the air, killing a number of Federal sappers.[99]

The next day (1 July), however, Logan's miners reentered the mine and returned the favor by lighting 1,800 pounds of powder. The explosion created a crater up to 50 feet in diameter and 20 feet deep, completely destroying the redan and damaging its interior works. Federal artillery and musketry opened simultaneously with the explosion, which Confederate Chief Engineer S.H. Lockett called "the deadliest fire of musketry ever witnessed by any of us there present." But Col. Francis M. Cockrell, leading the Confederate Missouri brigade, said that a wooden (coehorn) mortar had their exact range and exploding 12-pound shells did the worst damage. Logan's troops, given their failed attempt on 25 June, did not enter the new crater.[100]

One overseer (a private named Owen) and seven or eight slaves were killed while at work in the countermine. In addition, "a large number" of the 6th Missouri from Cockrell's brigade "were blown up and thrown over the brow of the hill." It was in this explosion that chief Federal engineer Fredrick Prime reported that six Confederates were blown into the Federal works and Federal engineer Andrew Hickenlooper reported seven or eight thrown into the Federal works. Chief Confederate engineer S.H. Lockett reported that he had been down in their countermine only a few minutes before the explosion "and had left seven men there, only one of whom would ever be seen again; he a negro, was blown over into the Federal lines but not seriously hurt."[101]

Although in his memoirs he recalled that it resulted from the 25 June explosion at the 3rd Louisiana Redan, Grant related the story of the "negro" miner who Confederate engineer Lockett said was blown into Federal lines alive on 1 July:

> I remember one colored man, who had been under ground at work, when the explosion took place, who was thrown to our side. He was not much hurt, but was terribly frightened. Some one asked him how high he had gone up. "Dunno, Massa, but t'ink 'bout t'ree mile," was the reply. General Logan commanded at this point, and took this colored man to his quarters, where he did service to the end of the siege.[102]

The 1 July explosion of the mine at the 3rd Louisiana Redan effectively ended hostilities on the Jackson Road portion of the line, but heavy firing along the rest of the line continued through 3 July as the temperature soared to over 100 degrees Fahrenheit. By this time, Slack's brigade had dug their trench "almost into the enemy's works" and the 47th Indiana participated with Slack's brigade in a two-hour firefight on the night of 2 July, holding their position against S.D. Lee's troops near Fort Garrott.[103]

On the morning of 3 July, however, Maj. Gen. John S. Bowen carried Pemberton's surrender terms, which included a proposed meeting of commissioners, to Brig. Gen. A.J. Smith, who in turn passed it on to Grant. Grant declined, telling Smith to relay the message that unconditional surrender meant there was no need for commissioners. Under a flag of truce at about 3:00 P.M. at the Confederate trenches on Jackson Road, Grant, accompanied by Ord, McPherson, Logan, and A.J. Smith, met briefly with Pemberton, Bowen, and Col. L.M. Montgomery.

Firing continued on the rest of the line all day, however, as the truce applied only to the Jackson Road area. As negotiations proceeded that day, Grant, in order to take advantage of what he thought was the war-weariness of the Confederate troops and their desire to go home, ordered his corps commanders to "permit some discreet men on picket tonight to communicate to the enemy's pickets the fact that General Grant has offered, in case Pemberton surrenders, to parole all officers and men, and to permit them to go home from here."[104]

That same night, to stop the grenade attacks on Malmborg's position near the Graveyard Road, Ewing sent Giles Smith sixteen veteran coal miners from the 4th West Virginia to begin a mine under the Confederate works. Working through the night, they discovered that the Confederates had a countermine only eight feet away on the same horizontal plane.[105]

Grant sent his final proposal to Pemberton at 10 o'clock that same night. While the West Virginians worked on their mine, Pemberton met with his aides and generals to discuss Grant's unconditional terms. Just before dawn of 4 July, just one half hour before Malmborg was set to detonate the 200 pounds of powder sent him by Captain William Kossack of the Engineers, Pemberton replied to Grant that he accepted the terms and would surrender the city and garrison at 10:00 A.M. that day.[106]

Ironically, the surrender of Vicksburg posed something of a dilemma for Grant. It would leave him with about 30,000 prisoners; and, due to the lack of adequate prison facilities and the cost of guarding and feeding them or sending them north, came the question of what to do with them. To relieve his army of this burden, Grant chose parole, believing that most of Pemberton's troops were war-weary southwesterners, who, if treated with respect and granted paroles would simply go home, leaving his troops unencumbered to chase after and drive Joe Johnston out of Mississippi.[107]

HELENA

At dawn on 4 July, however, upriver at Helena, Arkansas, a Confederate force of about 7,600 Trans-Mississippi troops, commanded by Lt. Gen. Theophilus Holmes and Maj. Gen. Sterling Price, attacked Fort Curtis in a late and vain attempt to relieve the Vicksburg siege and maintain the blockade of the Mississippi River.[108]

Brig. Gen. Benjamin Prentiss, who commanded a force of about 4,000 at Helena, had returned to the army and had been assigned by Grant to command the District of Eastern Arkansas in February 1863 following a stay as a guest of the Confederate government pursuant to his surrender at Shiloh in April 1862. Fort Curtis, which protected Helena from the west, had been dubbed a "humbug" of a fort by its then commander, Brig. Gen. Frederick Steele, when it opened in October 1862 because of its weak defensive position. But Old Ben apparently learned his lesson well at Shiloh, and he heavily fortified the bluffs on the perimeter of the fort and the town with four separate batteries, all protected by rifle pits and breastworks, not to mention Parrot guns on the levee, siege guns inside the fort and the gunboat *Tyler* in the river.[109]

The town of Helena, just under a mile long and about three-quarters of a mile wide, sat facing due east on the west bank of the Mississippi River. The Lower Little Rock Road approached town from almost due south passing by Hindman Hill and entering town at the southwest corner; the Upper Little Rock Road approached from the southwest; the unmarked graveyard road ran due east into town; the Upper St. Francis Road approached from the northwest; the Old St. Francis Road converged on Helena from about a mile north of the upper road; and the Sterling Road approached town from almost due north.[110]

Prentiss's batteries and breastworks roughly arced from north to south of town, with a series of rifle pits dug across the main roads approaching town. Battery A (called Fort Righter by the Confederates) was placed on a bluff on the Sterling Road about a mile north of town; Battery B was located on a bluff on the north side of Upper St. Francis Road, about a mile from town; Battery C (called Graveyard Hill by the Confederates) was placed on a bluff between an unnamed road skirting the northern edge of the hill and the Upper Little Rock Road, about a half mile west of town; Battery D (called Fort Hindman by the Confederates) was on a bluff about a quarter mile due south of Battery C between the Upper and Lower Little Rock roads, with breastworks covering the approaches from the Lower Little Rock Road to the levee south of town. Fort Curtis was on the lower ground on the northwestern edge of town. All the perimeter batteries and the guns in Fort Curtis were manned by troops from the 33rd Missouri Infantry. The Federal infantry was made up of Brig. Gen. Frederick Salomon's 13th division of the 13th Army Corps, former comrades-in-arms of Slack's brigade and the 47th Indiana.[111]

Holmes planned to hit batteries A, C and D in a concerted dawn attack. The rough, wooded terrain and darkness made bringing up artillery and maneuvering troops difficult, but Holmes planned to send Brig. Gen. J.F. Fagan's brigade of Arkansans from the south against Battery D (Fort Hindman); a division commanded by Maj. Gen. Sterling Price consisting of Brig. Gen. M. Monroe Parsons's brigade of Missourians and Brig. Gen. Dandridge McRae's brigade of Arkansans against Battery C on Graveyard Hill; and Brig. Gen. J.S. Marmaduke's Missouri and Brig. Gen. L.M. Walker's Arkansas cavalry divisions against Battery A (Fort Righter) from the north.[112]

Predawn firefights erupted on these approaches in which Federal pickets were driven in, but some of Marmaduke's guides lost their way, and when the picket fire got hot, some of them deserted. With his commanders floundering in unfamiliar, ridge-lined territory in the dark, Holmes's task of launching a coordinated attack was doomed from the start. Holmes's troops nevertheless made a determined, albeit uncoordinated, morning attack with their now familiar yells and whoops. Federal sharpshooters and artillery, including exceptionally accurate fire from the gunboat *Tyler*, checked the Confederate attack at all points except on Graveyard Hill. McRae's and Parsons's troops, facing "murderous fire," overran infantry pickets from the 33rd Iowa and drove off the hill troops from the 43rd Indiana Infantry and the 1st Indiana Cavalry (dismounted) who were supporting Battery C and the gunners from the 33rd Missouri.[113]

The Federal gunners, however, had the presence of mind to spike one of their guns and run off with the firing mechanisms of the others, leaving their guns unusable by McRae's and Parsons's Confederates, whose own artillery was unable to be brought up due to the rough terrain. Although McRae's and Parsons's troops had captured Graveyard Hill, their position was barely tenable. Enfiladed from the south by the guns of Battery D and musketry fire from Fort Hindman, they were also hit especially hard from the north by the guns of Battery B, which no one had attacked. When Holmes called for support for Fagan's thwarted attack on Battery D, McRae began moving his battered troops off Graveyard Hill. At the same time, Parsons claimed that he was ordered to attack Fort Curtis; and, with McRae's move off the hill, mistook it to be a general movement toward town. Parsons's troops, apparently happy to leave their precarious position on the hill, advanced and were quickly hit by enfilading fire and surrounded, although some of Parsons's men made it all the way into town, even to the levee. Most of the prisoners reported captured by the Federals were from the 7th and 10th Missouri Infantry (CSA) from Parsons's brigade who had taken refuge in a ravine from Federal artillery fire. Parsons lost heavily here in killed, wounded and captured, and the Federals regained Graveyard Hill. McRae's troops soon learned that Graveyard Hill had been retaken and, realizing the hopelessness of their position, retreated. The battle now lost, at 10:30 A.M., Holmes called a general retreat and withdrew his force toward the White River.[114]

VICKSBURG SURRENDER

At 10:00 A.M. that same day, Pemberton surrendered Vicksburg to Grant.

The terms were simple: rolls were to be made out and paroles signed by every officer (2,166) and enlisted man (27,230) promising "not to take up arms against the United States until exchanged by the proper authorities." Officers were permitted to take their side arms and clothing; field, staff, and cavalry one horse each. The rank and file was allowed no other property than their clothing, rations sufficient to last them beyond Federal lines, and cooking utensils to be taken from the remaining Confederate stores in thirty 2-mule or horse-drawn wagons.[115]

Grant was right about at least some of Pemberton's troops. Although many protested that Pemberton had "sold out" to the Yankees, they were not interested in languishing in Confederate parole camps and merely went home. According to Sgt. William Pitt Chambers of the 46th Mississippi Infantry, after his regiment signed their paroles and left on 11 July, "once outside the intrenchments, the two Louisiana regiments [the 17th and 31st Louisiana of Baldwin's Brigade] turned to the right in the direction of their native state, and were never connected with the Brigade any more."[116]

Corporal Abner Wilkes, also of the 46th Mississippi, was one of those who felt that Pemberton had sold them out and recorded in his memoirs, "We never could have been wiped out there, but General Pemberton sold us to the Yankees at some price."[117]

Abner signed his parole on 10 July:

VICKSBURG, MISSISSIPPI, JULY 8TH, 1863
TO ALL WHOM IT MAY CONCERN, KNOW YE THAT:

I [signed]: *A.J. Wilkes* a *Corpl* of Co. *B 46* Reg't *Mississippi*
Vols. C.S.A., being a Prisoner of War, in the hands of the United States Forces, in virtue of the capitulation of the City of Vicksburg and its garrison, by Lieut. Gen. John C. Pemberton, C.S.A., Commanding, on the 4th day of July, 1863, do in pursuance of the terms of said capitulation, give this my solemn parole under oath —
That I will not take up arms again against the United States, nor serve in any military, police,

or constabulary force in any Fort, Garrison or field work, held by the Confederate States of America, against the United States of America, nor as a guard of prisons, depots or stores, nor discharge any duties usually performed by Officers or soldiers, against the United States of America, until duly exchanged by the proper authorities.
[Signed]: *A.J. Wilkes*
Sworn to and subscribed before me at Vicksburg, Miss, this *10th* day of July 1863.
[Signed]: *Sam Roper, 56th* Reg't *Ill Inf Vol*
Captain and paroling officer[118]

Abner was also one of those Confederate soldiers who, having signed his parole and having given his solemn word not to take up arms against the United States, considered himself to be out of the war:

> Now, we surrendered on the fourth of July, and started for parole camp at Raymond, Mississippi, but all got home that were able to walk home. Some of our boys were sent around by New Orleans, and never have been heard from since.
> I was home a few days when the news came that we were all exchanged, which was a lie. We were never exchanged, but we went back to the front. You bet it went against the grain, thinking we were not exchanged and were violating the war regulations.[119]

The Confederate authorities, of course, disagreed. They did furlough the paroled soldiers for thirty days, forty days for Texas troops, although most had already dispersed by the time the furloughs were issued.

Not all had abandoned the cause, however. The first of the paroled soldiers of the 46th Mississippi arrived in camp at Enterprise, Mississippi, in early September, although they were not officially exchanged until 16 October 1863. They, along with many others paroled at Vicksburg, were sent in November from Enterprise to Dalton, Georgia, to join Joe Johnston's Army of Tennessee. Abner, holding firm to his belief that he was legally out of the war, was forced to report to duty after the parole camp at Enterprise had been disbanded, and he did not show up at Dalton until early spring 1864, just prior to the start of the Atlanta Campaign. Referring to his arrival at Dalton to join his regiment he wrote, "The enemy was in close pursuit of them when I got with them."[120] Although reluctant, Abner, and many others like him from Pemberton's army, fought with the 46th Mississippi and their other units to the bitter end, through the Atlanta and Tennessee campaigns to their surrender at Fort Blakely, Alabama, at the end of the war.

As Pemberton's troops dispersed and the Federals occupied Vicksburg, Grant turned his attention to Joe Johnston's force near Black River and sent Sherman on the first of his many attempts to chase down the elusive Confederate general — adding ominously, "I want you to drive Johnston from the Mississippi Central Railroad; destroy bridges as far as Grenada with your cavalry, and do the enemy all harm possible." E.O.C. Ord and Frederick Steele joined Sherman's expedition to drive Johnston out of Mississippi.[121]

X

Jackson, Mississippi (July 1863)

While the Vicksburg siege dragged on, the political battle intensified back home. In June 1863, Governor Richard Yates of Illinois, faced with a state legislature dominated in both houses by Peace Democrats who threatened to pass antiwar and especially antidraft legislation, used his authority under the Illinois Constitution to prorogue the legislature when the two houses could not agree upon a fixed day for adjournment. In complicity with the minority Republicans, Yates adjourned the legislature until "the Saturday next preceding the first Monday in January 1865." Sustained by the Illinois Supreme Court, Yates governed from that point by edict and military support until near the end of the war.[1]

Although his actions intensified the political animosity in the state, he was able to scuttle Democratic antiwar and antidraft legislation, such as plans to make it unlawful to apprehend or return deserters in the state to their regiments in the field, the ruling that had gotten Judge Constable in trouble with the Indiana military authorities. Illinois Democrats, unable to do anything about Yates's proroguing of the legislature, turned their efforts, as did the Republicans, to political rallies, often festive occasions in the rural Midwest, to get their ideas out and candidates elected in this hotly contested presidential election year.[2]

In Indiana, Governor Morton also faced a hostile and dominant Democratic majority in the state legislature. The minority Republicans walked out when the Democrats threatened their own antiwar and antidraft legislation, including threats to nullify Morton's power as chief executive and to take control of the state militia. The Republican walkout deprived the legislature of a quorum and forced an adjournment before an appropriations bill was passed.

The Democrats believed that Morton would be forced to call a special session on appropriations in which they could pass their antiwar legislation, but Morton foiled their plans by not calling a special session. Instead, he bypassed the Democratic state treasurer and established his own "Bureau of Finance" (his office safe) with funds raised from private sources, including wealthy individuals, the Terre Haute & Richmond Railroad, the W.R. McKeen Bank of Terre Haute, Republican-controlled counties, and the state arsenal, from which he sold weapons and munitions to the federal government. Morton amassed well over $200,000 in mostly personal recognizant loans from these sources and another $250,000 loan from Secretary of War Stanton's War Department funds that were designated for use in states

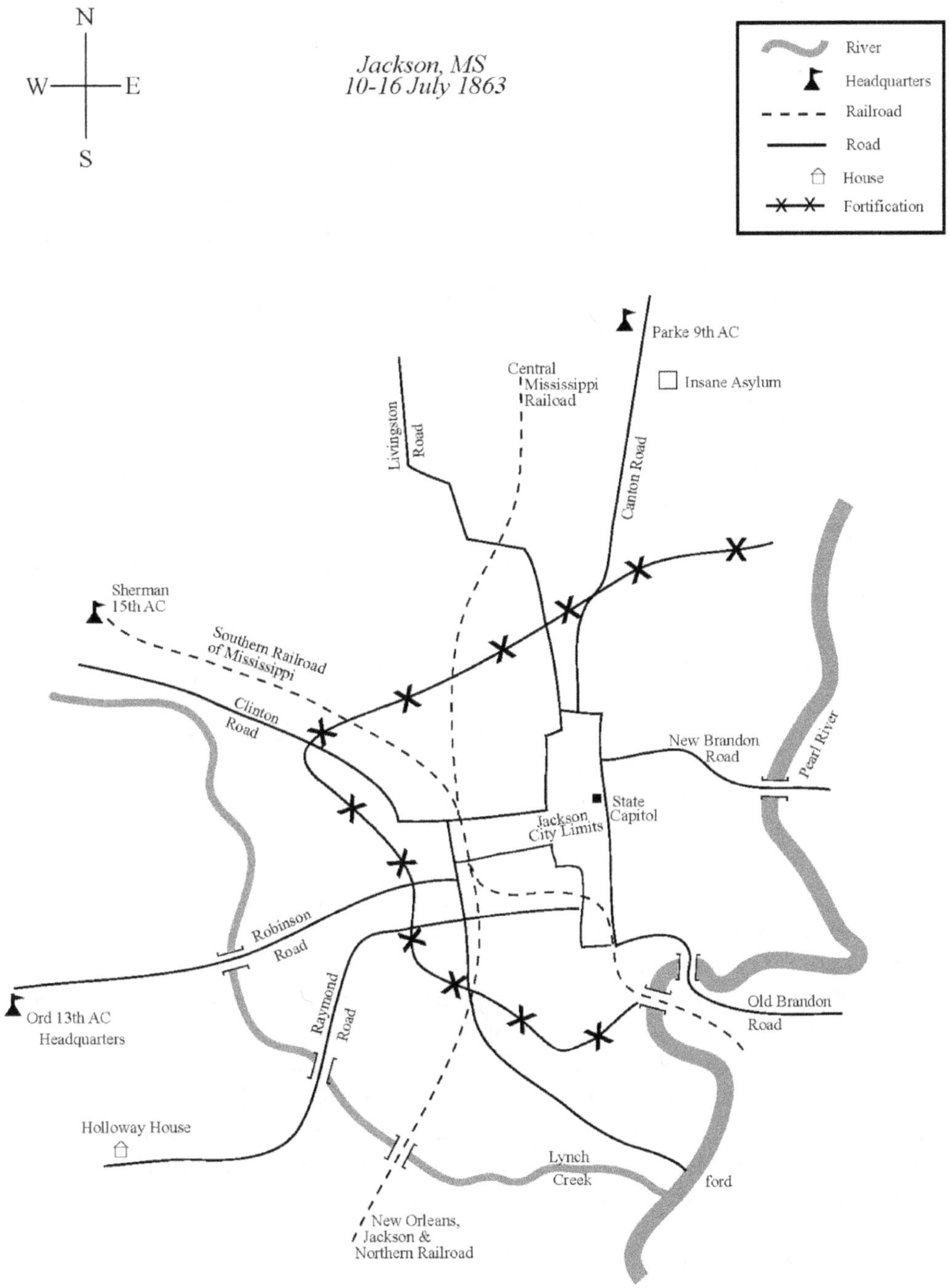

X. Jackson, Mississippi (July 1863)

From Atlas Plate XXXVII, Nos. 2, 3, and 5

under threat of rebellion — after his requests had been rejected by President Lincoln and Treasury Secretary Salmon P. Chase.³

In addition, in order to keep the state from defaulting on interest payments on the state debt, Morton received a $160,000 loan from a New York bank. Based on objections by the state treasurer, the Indiana Supreme Court ruled that it was illegal for Morton to pay the interest on the debt without a specific legislative appropriation. Morton, backed by Carrington's Military District of Indiana troops, simply ignored the court's ruling. Like Yates in Illinois, Morton, who would eventually disburse about one million dollars, was able to keep the state legislature adjourned for the remainder of the war; as his critics alleged, he was able to govern Indiana from that point as a virtual military dictator. This, of course, brought political animosities in the state to the boiling point and the Democrats threatened to prosecute Morton.⁴

Unsupported by the Indiana Constitution, Morton's actions were extralegal at best. He understood that if he lost his bid for reelection in 1864, and if the Democrats maintained control of the legislature, he could be prosecuted for his actions and a jail cell would likely await him upon leaving office. From this point on, Morton, who had already enlisted Carrington to set up a spy network to infiltrate the various local antiwar groups and tie them to the mysterious and essentially nonexistent Knights of the Golden Circle, would work tirelessly to discredit his Democratic opposition and attempt to tar them with the brush of domestic treason.⁵

Making Morton's task easier, on 8 July 1863, the same day that the *Daily Journal* announced the surrender of Vicksburg as well as a break-in of the Huntington Depot (where two or three boxes of guns and ammunition were stolen, allegedly by members of the K.G.C.), John Hunt Morgan and his Confederate cavalry crossed the Ohio River at Brandenburg, Kentucky, and into Indiana about forty-five miles downriver from New Albany. Governor Morton would call up the militia and suspend habeas corpus as Morgan's raiders crossed the southern part of the state, bypassed Cincinnati and rode up the Ohio River Valley before being captured on 26 July by cavalry detachments under Major G.W. Rue of the 9th Kentucky and Major W.B. Way of the 9th Michigan about eight miles east of Salineville in northeastern Ohio near the Pennsylvania state line.⁶

To add to the appearance of a great conspiracy, George W.L. Bickley, who had received a pass from Rosecrans to cross over to his old home in Cincinnati, was arrested on 18 July when he violated his pass by going instead to New Albany, Indiana. Although no connection was ever proven, he was dubbed a spy for Morgan by the Republican press and imprisoned by military authorities. With Morgan's raid, besides calling up the militia, Governor Morton had also suspended habeas corpus and Bickley was held in military custody in various prisons without charge or trial until released from Fort Warren, Massachusetts, at the end of the war.⁷

In spite of Morgan's raid into the state, the editors of the *Huntington Democrat* complained that the governor was arming the home guard of Indiana, who, they asserted, were "members of secret abolition societies" and was preparing a "reign of terror" against his unarmed political opponents.⁸

At the same time, the 1863 Conscription Act was beginning to be implemented in the northeast in areas that could not otherwise fulfill their quotas with volunteers. On Saturday, 11 July 1863, without much publicity, military officials began the draft lottery at the

Ninth District Provost Marshal's office on 3rd Avenue and 47th Street in lower Manhattan by drawing names of the draftees from a rotating wooden barrel. On Sunday, the *Herald* and the *Times* published the 1,246 names drawn on Saturday (the *Tribune* published the names on Monday) and word spread rapidly among the antiwar and anti-abolition population that the government was, in fact, going to carry out the draft.[9]

Leading up to the draft lottery in New York City, opposition to the war and to compulsory military service had become highly volatile issues inflamed by proslavery Democratic politicians like former Mayor of New York Fernando Wood and newspapermen like John Gordon Bennett, editor of the *New York Herald*. Wood, a supporter of the Southern states and the constitutionality of slavery, is perhaps best known for his January 1861 recommendation to the aldermen of New York City's Common Council that if the South seceded, New York City should secede as well and become an independent city. Running later that year against the "abolition war," Wood lost his bid for reelection to Republican George Opdyke. And Bennett, who used his newspaper to denounce Horace Greeley's ardent abolitionism and support of the employment rights of blacks, had been warning unskilled white workers since October 1862 that Greeley's policy would bring "hordes of darkeys" to the North who would take their jobs by working for "half wages."[10]

Greeley, on the other hand, blamed Bennett and the proslavery press for provoking periodic violence against black workers, including an incident on 13 April 1863 in which a gang of about three hundred longshoremen attacked black laborers working on the barges of the Swiftsure Line that were lying at Pier No. 4 on the East River. Greeley asserted that this violent attack against black workers had been provoked, just as the violence in Detroit had been, by the persistent bigotry of the proslavery press that had worked diligently "to strengthen the prejudices, and embitter the hatred of its readers, and the rest of the more ignorant part of the populace against the negro" by printing "malignant falsehoods ... that white men were to be cheated out of work by an immigration of negroes." On the right of blacks to work, Greeley noted: "This is not Richmond, but New York — a fact which seems occasionally to be forgotten, and here at least the negro is a citizen, with rights which white men are bound to respect."[11]

Ironically, the tension between Irish and black workers had been building for the past two decades with the arrival in the mid– to late 1840s of a wave of extremely poor and uneducated Irish peasants, who, unlike earlier and better educated Irish immigrants, were escaping starvation. They had come to America destitute, and by the mid–1850s, working for even lower wages, had undercut and replaced black longshoremen, who had to that point dominated work on the waterfront. Frederick Douglass had often noted correctly since the 1850s that it was the flood of unskilled Irish immigrants that had originally "elbowed" blacks out of the job market, not the reverse. Nevertheless, as Greeley charged, Bennett used his newspaper, especially popular among Irish longshoremen, to inflame the animosity that existed between them and black workers.[12]

By the mid–1850s, the Irish, now dominant on the waterfront, began to organize and strike for well-deserved higher wages and shorter workdays. Faced with walkouts, the shippers, in a classic example of how to create class and ethnic conflict, broke the strikes by replacing Irish strikers with black workers. In the year leading up to the draft riots, Irish longshoremen had struck on a number of occasions for modest pay increases and shorter workdays, only to find the shippers, who were becoming very rich in wartime trade, replacing them in many cases with desperately poor recently liberated slaves ("contrabands"). In January 1863, in fact, in spite of wartime inflation, the pay of many longshoremen, who lived in overcrowded and squalid tenements and were working essentially as "wage slaves," had been reduced from an already low $1.50 for a nine-hour day to $1.12, lending some credence, at least in the minds of white longshoremen, to Bennett's demagogic warning about the likely effects of abolition.[13]

Tensions continued to rise in June 1863, just a month before the draft riots, when the United States Army broke a longshoremen's strike for these reasonable and modest increases by using some 160 deserters in custody to load and unload military cargo in port. With the army providing stevedores for military shipments and protection on the docks from violence against strikebreakers, shippers hired unemployed workers, white and black, at $2.00 for a 9-hour day, with $0.25 per hour overtime. In an attempt to break the longshoremen's organization efforts, shippers not only pitted striking whites against their white and black replacements, but against each other as well by rehiring some strikers while blackballing the leaders.[14]

Two additional factors added to the tension in New York. The $300 exemption rule (Section 13 of the Conscription Act of 1863), which applied to this draft lottery only and which no poorly paid worker could afford, and President Lincoln's 8 May proclamation that all foreigners who had applied for citizenship were eligible for the draft, made avoidance of military service if drafted seem impossible not only to poor white workers but to poor immigrants who had applied for citizenship.[15]

With this in mind, anger boiled over after the names of draftees were published on Sunday, 12 July. Indeed, before the resumption of the draft lottery on Monday morning, hundreds of workers left the shipyards and foundries and converged on the provost marshal's office, closing other shops, cutting telegraph lines, damaging tracks, and gathering more workers as they marched, many carrying "No Draft" placards. By the time the draft lottery resumed at 10:30 that Monday morning, hundreds of protesters had converged on the provost marshal's office with perhaps up to 10,000 filling the streets of lower Manhattan.[16]

Among the crowd of protesters that morning were the mostly Irish lads of the oddly if not ironically named "Black Joke Engine Company No. 13," one of New York City's many competing volunteer fire companies. Opposed to the war and expecting that firemen would be exempt from the federal draft, when the name of one of their members was called in the Saturday lottery, the lads of Engine Company No. 13 determined to shut down Monday's draft. After about fifty names had been called on Monday, the "Black Joke" firemen, dressed in their uniforms, broke into the essentially unguarded office, drove off the draft officials, smashed the lottery barrel, set fire to the provost marshal's office, and triggered several days of mob violence in what would become known as the New York City Draft Riots.[17]

With most New York City units at Gettysburg, the only troops on duty and readily available in the city for the unexpected attack were seventy invalid soldiers in the 1st Battalion of the Invalid Corps commanded by Colonel Robert Nugent, Assistant Provost Marshal of New York City. Following the burning of the provost marshal's office and the movement of the mob into the streets of lower Manhattan, Nugent divided the battalion into three units and sent one up 3rd Avenue to quell the disturbance at the Ninth District headquarters. At 42nd Street, about four or five blocks from headquarters, protesters showered the invalid soldiers with bricks and paving stones. The soldiers replied "with one volley of ball-cartridges," killing and wounding a number of people. Undaunted, the crowd turned and routed the invalid soldiers before they could reload, killing several soldiers and wounding a few. The remainder fled and regrouped to help guard the State Arsenal at the corner of 7th Avenue and 35th Street. Following the rout of the invalids, the crowd moved through Manhattan in roving packs. Their numbers soon overwhelmed the city police, who could barely protect their own headquarters at Mulberry and Bleeker Streets. Rioters burned and looted stores, sacked and burned several hotels and a number of private homes, and brutally attacked and in many cases killed any black person who appeared on the streets.[18]

Topping off an afternoon of murder and mayhem, at about 5:00 P.M., one of the roving packs, including many women and children, ransacked and burned down the nearby Colored Orphan Asylum on 5th Avenue between 43rd and 44th Streets. Some 237 children and staff barely escaped with their lives thanks to the efforts of the city's Chief Engineer John Decker and six of his men, who, under threat of death, held off the mob and attempted, albeit unsuccessfully, to extinguish the numerous blazes they set.[19]

That night another roving pack of fairly well organized rioters regrouped and turned toward Printing-House Square in search of Horace Greeley, who was, thanks in large part to James Gordon Bennett of the rival *Herald*, perhaps the publisher most despised by white workers for his outspoken advocacy of abolition and the employment rights of all blacks. The evening staff at Greeley's *Tribune* fled in search of police assistance as the mob ransacked and set fire to the first-floor offices. The prompt arrival of a company of policemen under a Captain Thorne of the Nassau Street Station drove off the attackers and, with help from the *Tribune's* staff, extinguished the fire and saved the *Tribune* building from total destruction. To assist Greeley and the other vulnerable publishers on Printing-House Square from further attack, Rear Admiral Hiram Paulding sent a midshipman from the navy yard with a howitzer and deadly, crowd-killing canister ammunition. As the *Tribune* put it, in spite of the sacking of their first-floor offices, they continued to publish, protected by "Mr. Steven D. Adams, a midshipman in the United States Navy, who had charge of a howitzer located at the Spruce Street corner of *The Tribune* office." The howitzer, the *Tribune* noted, "was loaded with canister, and would have done fearful execution if it had been used."[20]

Across the square from the *Tribune* building, Henry J. Raymond, editor of the *New York Times*, armed his staff with U.S. Army rifles and three of the army's new Gatling guns. Raymond and financier Leonard W. Jerome, a major *Times* stockholder, reportedly manned two of the Gatling guns at the windows of the *Times'* first floor business office, with the third gun strategically placed on the roof to sweep in any direction — including toward Greeley's *Tribune* building. With the wealthier neighborhoods downtown also organizing for self-defense, firing the Navy howitzer or the army Gatling guns became unnecessary as the roving packs turned elsewhere in search of the defenseless.[21]

Tuesday morning, with military reinforcements at least a day away, roving packs continued to rule the streets. Some of the more militant protesters gathered at Gramercy Park and battled all afternoon with police for control of the cache of guns stored at the Union Steam Works at 2nd Avenue and 22nd Street. By late afternoon, a little farther uptown, other rioters constructed barricades along 9th Avenue from 36th to 42nd Streets. The police finally retook control of the Union Steam Works later that evening after killing some two dozen rioters.[22]

On Wednesday morning, however, small contingents of cavalry and infantry arrived and began to take control of the city. Led by Colonel Thaddeus P. Mott of the 14th New York Volunteer Cavalry and supported by Captain Henry R. Putnam's detachment of the 12th United States Infantry, they used howitzers to dislodge the barricades and disperse the crowd on 9th Avenue, killing twenty-eight people in the process, although seven cavalrymen were killed and several wounded. Sporadic fighting continued into the evening as snipers fired from windows and from around corners, holding their own against the soldiers.[23]

On Thursday, New York National Guard regiments began arriving from Gettysburg, although fighting continued that evening in the Gramercy Park neighborhood, where Mott's dismounted cavalry was being bested by snipers on the streets and from rooftops until several companies of Putnam's infantry and police arrived to rescue them and drive the snipers from the neighborhood.[24]

The military finally took control of the city on Friday with the arrival of more New York militia regiments from Gettysburg, and the dispersed rioters returned to work. All told, between 105 and 119 people were known to be killed and 128 seriously wounded. Three hundred and fifty-two people were identified as rioters out of an estimated two or three thousand, perhaps more, participants. Most of the 352 whose country of origin could be determined were unskilled working-class Irish immigrants, none of whom could afford the $300 fee which would, in any case, have exempted them only from this and not future drafts.[25]

The *Tribune* concluded that the riots were an attempt by northern supporters of the Confederacy to "remove the seat of war to the banks of the Hudson"; the *Times*, on the other hand, viewed the riots as class warfare — "a proletaire outbreak ... a movement of the abject poor against the well-off rich"; and the *Herald*, although they characterized the rioters as acting more like "fiends than human beings," maintained its sympathy for them and asserted that "the principal cause of the outbreak was the idea that the draft was an unfair one, inasmuch as the rich could avoid it by paying $300, while the poor man, who was without 'the greenbacks,' was compelled to go to the war."[26]

THE JACKSON EXPEDITION AND SIEGE

Back on the war front, following the fall of Vicksburg, Sherman's troops prepared to move eastward in pursuit of Joe Johnston's "Army of Relief."

Johnston had learned of Vicksburg's surrender on the evening of 4 July about the time that Sherman began putting Grant's plan to drive him out of the state in motion. Johnston had been under pressure from Richmond to relieve Pemberton, but reluctant to risk losing his army in what he considered an impossible and foolhardy task. Nevertheless, he had planned to "create a diversion south of the railroad to help Pemberton cut his way out" of Vicksburg; that plan was called off when he learned of Pemberton's surrender. Using his cavalry division, commanded by Brigadier General William H. "Red" Jackson, to slow the Federal advance, Johnston pulled his troops back from the east bank of the Big Black to his fortifications at Jackson. Loring's, French's and Walker's divisions fell back from their bivouac along a four-mile stretch on the east bank of the Big Black between Birdsong Ferry and Messinger's Ford; and Major General John C. Breckenridge's division, which had just marched from Jackson on the main Jackson Road for the planned attack, turned back at Edwards Station. Col. John W. Whitfield's cavalry brigade protected Johnston's retreat from Birdsong's Ferry and Messinger's Ford; Col. George B. Cosby's cavalry brigade, with "Red" Jackson present, protected the southern line along the main Jackson Road and the tracks of the Southern Railroad of Mississippi, which ran eastward from Vicksburg to Meridian.[27]

The day Vicksburg surrendered, Col. Wirt Adams, commanding a Mississippi regiment attached to Cosby's cavalry brigade, reported intelligence gathered from citizens inside the Federal lines at Vicksburg that Grant's troops were suffering greatly and had lost many soldiers from disease and from their unsuccessful assaults. The belief expressed to Adams was that the climate alone would cause the siege to be raised, if Pemberton's garrison could hold out for three more weeks.[28]

Although Vicksburg surrendered that very day, with no rain in sight and the temperature continuing to hover around 100 degrees, Johnston decided to lure Sherman into making a rash assault on the Jackson fortifications before his water supply ran dry and his soldiers started to die of heat stroke. The roughly ten-mile area between Fleetwood Creek at Bolton and the town of Clinton, just west of Jackson, would be especially difficult on Sherman's troops due to the lack of spring water, which caused residents in the area to rely largely on cisterns for their water supply. To delay the pursuing Federals, Johnston's retreating troops poisoned cisterns and left the carcasses of dead livestock in nearly every pond and water source still available on the roads to Jackson, which forced the Federal cavalry, even before they reached Bolton, to send parties out to confiscate mules, horses and carriages to collect water and forage from distant sources.[29]

While on the march, Slack told Ann: "The rebels are burning the corn in the country to prevent us using it, and are killing hogs, cattle, and sheep, and throwing them into the water along the road to poison it so we cannot use it." The remaining citizens also complained of "serious depredations" by hundreds of stragglers from Breckenridge's and other commands retreating toward Jackson, which prompted Breckenridge to warn his troops that unless the depredations were stopped at once, "the presence of the army will be regarded as a curse instead of protection."[30]

On 5 July, Steele's 15th corps, spearheading Sherman's pursuit, rendezvoused at Messinger's Ford on the Big Black, where Tuttle's advanced troops had constructed a bridge using lumber taken from buildings on the Messinger Plantation. Pickets from Whitfield's Confederate cavalry brigade, camped on Queen's Hill, slowed the crossing at Messinger's Ford.[31]

That same day, Parke's 9th corps, on the northern prong of Sherman's advance, moved to Birdsong's Ferry, about ten miles north of Bovina on the railroad, and found the bridge gone. Upriver rains had also caused the river to rise four feet, slowing their progress. Originally picketed by two regiments from French's division, that day a detachment from Whitfield's cavalry set up pickets at Birdsong's Ferry as French's troops marched toward Jackson.[32]

On the southern prong, Ord's 13th Corps (A.J. Smith's 10th, Hovey's 12th, and William P. Benton's, formerly Carr's, 14th divisions) moved from Vicksburg toward Big Black

River Bridge, where Osterhaus's 9th division awaited their arrival. Benjamin H. Helms's brigade picketed the tracks of the Southern Railroad of Mississippi, and Daniel W. Adams's brigade picketed the main Jackson Road at Champion Hill as Breckenridge's Confederate division retreated to Jackson, protected on their flanks by Wirt Adams's cavalry.[33]

At daylight on 6 July, Steele's 15th corps began crossing the Big Black at Messinger's Ford with McMillan's brigade of Tuttle's division in advance. They skirmished most of the day with Confederate pickets (probably from Whitfield's cavalry brigade) before driving them off. McMillan's brigade moved southeastward about three and a half miles to the Bridgeport-Jackson Road, making camp that evening several miles east of Bridgeport. Pioneers from Parke's 9th corps, upriver at Birdsong Ferry and Jones' Ford, spent the day building a bridge and repairing a ferry found sunken in the river. Ord's corps, Osterhaus's division in advance, crossed the Big Black on the main Jackson Road at 2:00 P.M. Only one mile beyond the Big Black, Major Hugh Fullerton's cavalry encountered pickets from Cosby's mostly Mississippi cavalry led by "Red" Jackson himself. Driving them eastward, Fullerton's troopers bivouacked at Edwards Station.[34]

On the morning of 7 July, Johnston's army arrived in Jackson and immediately began strengthening the earthworks surrounding the city on the west bank of the Pearl River. Loring's division was placed on the right, or northern end of Johnston's line, defending the area from the Pearl River to the northbound Canton Road. On Loring's left, Walker's division extended southwestward from Canton Road, across the tracks of the Southern Railroad of Mississippi to the Clinton (or main Jackson) Road. French's division continued the line angling southeastward to near the tracks of the New Orleans, Jackson & Great Northern Railroad, which ran from Jackson to New Orleans via Hazlehurst and Brookhaven. Breckenridge's division defended the southern end of Johnston's line, crossing the tracks of the New Orleans, Jackson & Great Northern Railroad and extending to the Pearl River.[35]

That same day (7 July), Blair's division, marching only in the morning and the early evening to avoid the scorching midday sun, led the 15th corps toward Bolton. Forced to deal with the heat and scarcity of water, they bivouacked that evening at Fleetwood Creek, one mile northwest of Bolton.[36] Late that afternoon, Parke's 9th corps crossed the Big Black at Birdsong Ferry and Jones' Ford, heading southeastward toward Queen's Hill Church with Sooy Smith's division, detached from the 16th corps, leading the way. Infantrymen from the 48th Illinois and 6th Iowa of Sanford's brigade skirmished with Whitfield's cavalry, driving them off Queen's Hill and capturing some camp equipage and several sick troopers from the 6th Texas Cavalry. That night they bivouacked at Robertson's Plantation near Queen's Hill Church, about six miles northwest of Bolton.[37]

On the southern approach, sweeping across country from the main Jackson Road to as far south as Fourteen Mile Creek, Fullerton's cavalry encountered "Red" Jackson with Cosby's cavalry brigade about two miles west of Bolton. In a spirited fight utilizing the 2nd Illinois Cavalry dismounted as skirmishers and the mountain howitzers of the 6th Missouri (U.S.) Cavalry, Fullerton's cavalry pushed Jackson's troopers back across Baker's Creek and out of a plantation one mile east of the bridge at Bolton, where Fullerton's cavalry bivouacked for the night. The remainder of Ord's 13th Corps, marching "through dust and heat, without water ... most of the way," although not being shot at, stretched out on the road behind them.[38]

The long drought ended that night when a line of thunderstorms drenched the parched and sweltering troops, flooded the creeks, and turned the dusty roads to mud. So severe were the winds that at 9:00 o'clock that night near Robertson's Plantation, a falling tree killed Major Robert Parrett of the 100th Indiana.[39] Meanwhile, the news of the surrender of Vicksburg spread to Port Hudson, Louisiana; and, on 8 July, the Confederate garrison surrendered to Federal General Nathaniel Banks, which opened the entire length of the Mississippi River to the Federals and cut the Confederacy in two.

That same day in Mississippi, Sherman, unaware of Parke's position only about six miles northwest of Bolton, postponed the march to Clinton scheduled that day. When he learned that Parke's troops were in position, he ordered his cavalry forward toward Clinton. Early that evening, Col. Cyrus Bussey, commanding Sherman's cavalry, turned at Bolton onto the Clinton Road and proceeded about two miles until encountering pickets from Whitfield's Texas cavalry. In a series of sharp skirmishes, Bussey's troopers drove Whitfield's Texans eastward about five miles. Late in the day they encountered Whitfield's main force in line of battle two miles west of Clinton. Following a severe skirmish, Whitfield, whose task was to slow the Federal advance, withdrew his force. As darkness fell, Bussey's troopers camped there for the night at the head of the 15th corps' column.[40]

From Queen's Hill Church that day, Parke's 9th corps proceeded to the Bridgeport-Jackson Road until they encountered the rear of Steele's 15th corps on the same road. Parke moved his corps north of Steele's line of march on what he called a side road, bivouacking that night a few miles from Clinton.[41]

Starting out at 4:00 P.M. from their camp near Baker's Creek on the southern approach, Osterhaus's division and Fullerton's cavalry encountered "Red" Jackson and Cosby's cavalry brigade defending the hills and ridges along the Jackson Road. The 6th Missouri Cavalry (U.S.), supported by their mountain howitzers, charged Jackson's line, dispersed his troopers, and the remainder of Fullerton's cavalry drove the Confederates to within three miles of Clinton as Ord's 13th corps camped for the night.[42]

On 9 July, Ord's troops, having resumed their march at 4:00 A.M., arrived at Clinton at 5:30 A.M., where they had a "tenacious" fight with "Red" Jackson and Cosby's cavalry about one mile west of Clinton. Fullerton's troopers drove Jackson's men through the woods with Sharpe's rifles and their mountain howitzers. On emerging from the woods, Fullerton's troopers encountered a Confederate battery with rifled and 12-pound shell artillery. Jackson's artillery (Clark's Missouri Light Artillery, CSA) stationed at the intersection of the Bridgeport-Jackson and the main Jackson roads on the western outskirts of Clinton and out of range of the Federals' mountain howitzers, forced Osterhaus to bring up one section of the 7th Michigan Battery to dislodge Clark's artillery. Osterhaus also brought up Keigwin's brigade to support the 7th Michigan Artillery and sent the 2nd Illinois Cavalry to turn Jackson's left flank. Osterhaus's move succeeded, and the 6th Missouri and 2nd Illinois Cavalry regiments pursued the retreating Confederates.[43]

Parke's 9th corps, moving on a "side road," again came up on the rear of Steele's 15th corps and once again diverged to the north, this time cutting trees and building a new road through plantation land nearly parallel to Steele's line of march. Steele's 15th corps, in the meantime, moving on the Bridgeport-Jackson Road and screened by Bussey's cavalry, turned at Clinton onto the main Jackson Road. Marching past Ord's resting troops, they pushed forward another mile and camped for the night.[44]

On 10 July, Steele's 15th corps advanced on the main Jackson Road until 8:00 A.M., when they drew fire near the Deaf and Dumb Asylum, only a mile and a half from the State House, from a 32-pounder rifled gun using solid shot. Blair deployed his division on the left of Jackson Road and around the asylum grounds; Thayer's division deployed on the right of the road, with Tuttle's division held in reserve. In a two-and-a-half-hour exchange, four 20-pounder Parrotts from Battery H, 1st Illinois Light Artillery, went into action and silenced the Confederates' 32-pounder.[45]

That same day on the northern approach, Sooy Smith's and Thomas Welsh's divisions swept across plantation fields until they hit the Livingston Road and began skirmishing with Confederate cavalry, who turned south at the Canton Road roughly two miles above Johnston's northern defensive line. Parke's force followed in pursuit with Sooy Smith's division moving down the west side of Canton Road. Welsh's division moved down the east side with Henry Bowman's brigade in advance; Robert B. Potter's division followed in reserve. Led by the 45th Pennsylvania skirmishers, Bowman's brigade took possession of the State Lunatic Asylum on the east side of Canton Road about a mile north of Johnston's northern line whence Parke's 9th corps line extended westward. Welsh's division held the left flank from near Pearl River, passing through the grounds of the State Lunatic Asylum and across the Canton Road. Sooy Smith's division on the right covered the line west of Canton Road, across the tracks of the Mississippi Central Railroad to Livingston Road.[46]

Meanwhile, Osterhaus's division continued in the vanguard of Ord's 13th corps on the southern approach, followed by A.J. Smith's, with Hovey's and Benton's divisions lagging behind in reserve to guard the supply train. Ord's column moved southeastward through the woods until Ord turned his column due eastward on Robinson Road, which Ord, Osterhaus and A.J. Smith all mistook for the Raymond Road. It was an easy mistake to make. Ord's line of march brought them to the eastward-running Robinson Road, which, although it was several miles north, ran parallel to the Raymond Road. Their target, Raymond Road, approached Jackson at an angle from the southwest before turning eastward about a mile west of Jackson and a mile or two south of Robinson Road. At 2:00 P.M., about two miles west of Jackson, Osterhaus's division encountered Confederate pickets from French's division at the bridge over Lynch Creek on Robinson Road, which Osterhaus referred to as Anderson's Creek.[47]

At the crest of a small rise, Fullerton's cavalry with their trusty mountain howitzers drove the Confederate pickets back to a ridge in front of their works, which contained a strong line of infantry. Keigwin's brigade, backed by artillery, charged the ridge and into the nearby houses, driving the Confederates back into their line of works. Osterhaus established his line about 250 yards west of the Confederate fortifications and exchanged artillery fire as A.J. Smith's division moved into position along the ridge on the right. Smith, concerned about reports of a heavy Confederate cavalry force on their right, refused his line to the right with Col. Richard Owen's 60th Indiana to protect from an attack from the south. Skirmishers from the 60th Indiana pushed the Confederates back and captured a house with a cistern of good water. The Confederate skirmishers regrouped and drove the 60th Indiana from the house, but Owen sent the 67th Indiana to their support and they retook the house and cistern. The good water was important in that five soldiers of Owen's brigade, two of whom died later, had already been prostrated with sunstroke. That evening, Smith brought up Benton's division from reserve and placed it on his refused right flank. Fullerton's cavalry was sent to the right to guard the area west of the Pearl River from attempts by the Confederate cavalry force to get in the rear of the Federal right flank. A.J. Smith's, Benton's and Hovey's divisions followed on Robinson Road, and by the end of the day the entire town of Jackson was vulnerable to crossfire of shot and shell from Federal artillery.[48]

At dawn on 11 July, on Parke's line north of the city, Welsh's and Sooy Smith's infantry divisions moved closer to Loring's Confederate works, Welsh's on the east side of Canton Road, Smith's on the west. At 7:00 A.M., due to some confusion in orders, all but the three left companies (C, H and F) of the 2nd Michigan, which had met stiff resistance during an hour of skirmishing, unexpectedly charged. The Confederate skirmishers fell back to a dry-run ravine just north of the Confederate works, where their main line of support was positioned on the south bank. The 2nd Michigan charged into and over the ravine, driving the Confederates into Loring's position on their main line. Sherman, however, without knowledge of the near breakthrough, ordered his northern line to halt to consolidate their position. The 2nd Michigan, having charged unexpectedly, was therefore left unsupported and isolated, forcing them to withdraw to their original position, and the near break in Loring's line was not exploited.[49]

Meanwhile, on his southern line that same day (11 July), having discovered a force of Confederate cavalry south of Jackson and west of the Pearl River, Sherman ordered Ord to move his troops to the right (southeastward) across the actual Raymond Road and swing eastward to the river. Benton's division successfully wheeled to the right from its refused position, pivoting on its left toward Raymond Road while skirmishing with Confederate pickets from French's division.[50]

Later that day, Slack's and Spicely's brigades of Hovey's division, followed by Lauman's division (temporarily attached from the 16th corps), moved in on Benton's right. Slack's and Spicely's brigades, having to move from the main Jackson Road to the Raymond Road on a road built by pioneers, took most of the day to arrive at Raymond Road in their attempt to connect with Benton's right. Reaching the Raymond Road at Holloway's farm, about two miles from town, Slack and Spicely swung their brigades eastward on the Raymond Road, Slack's brigade on the left of the road, Spicely's on the right. Advancing three-quarters of a mile on the left of Raymond Road, Slack's brigade skirmished with Confederate pickets from Lt. Col. D.H. Reynolds's 1st Arkansas Mounted Rifles (dismounted) of McNair's brigade, French's division.

Reaching Lynch Creek, Slack sent two companies of the 47th Indiana as skirmishers across the creek. Lying in wait, the Arkansans opened fire as soon as they crossed, halting the advance on Slack's part of Hovey's line until, at twilight, Slack moved his entire line across Lynch Creek. They fought for about half an hour before the outnumbered Arkansans fell back to a line just in front of the Lynch house, and Slack's brigade bivouacked for the night on the bank of Lynch Creek.

Advancing on the right of Raymond Road, Spicely's troops skirmished with the 2nd and 4th Arkansas from McNair's brigade and the 4th Louisiana from Maxey's brigade, all of French's division. With assistance from a section of the 16th Ohio Battery, they drove the Confederate pickets back across the New Orleans, Jackson & Great Northern tracks toward their fortifications and bivouacked for the night. Lauman's division bivouacked that night behind Hovey's division west of the railroad, Ord's right flank still out of alignment.[51]

In his official report, which he misdated "the 9th of July," Slack described his brigade's crossing of Lynch Creek:

> On the 9th [10th] of July, we took up our line of march and advanced toward the enemy's line. When within 2 miles of the enemy, the advance of the First Brigade encountered the rebel pickets, immediately after which the action commenced.
>
> General Hovey, commanding, directed me to form my brigade to the left of the Raymond road and forward the whole column, which was speedily executed, and we advanced to Lynch's Creek. Here I advanced two companies [A and F] of the Forty-seventh Indiana Infantry as skirmishers across the creek. As soon as they crossed the creek, the enemy opened fire upon them, to which the skirmishers spiritedly replied, and, after a contest of about thirty minutes, drove the enemy from the field. While the skirmishers were contesting the ground, I advanced the whole command over the creek and formed directly on the bank. We advanced no farther that night, the men lying upon their arms all night, with a strong picket line in front.[52]

On 11 July, protected by heavy Federal artillery fire, Hovey moved his division forward on Ord's southern line to connect with Benton's division at Raymond Road, while Lauman swung his line eastward across the tracks of the New Orleans, Jackson & Great Northern Railroad. Johnston had prepared for this eventuality by burning several houses near Raymond Road to open a line of fire for their artillery. Hovey countered by placing a section of the 1st Missouri Battery on Raymond Road, about 500 yards from the Confederate battery, which enabled Slack's and Spicely's brigades to adjust their lines to the right by about a brigade's length, both moving forward now between Raymond Road and the railroad, Slack on the left, Spicely on the right, while skirmishing sharply with McNair's brigade of French's division.[53]

In his official report, Slack described the 11 July movement and establishment of their siege line:

> On the morning of the 10th [11th] instant, I advanced a line of skirmishers, consisting of one company from each regiment, and my brigade in line in the rear across a field, but met no obstacle until we reached the high ground through the woods in advance of the field, when the rebel pickets were again encountered, but, after a few well-directed volleys from my line of skirmishers, the enemy was sent howling behind their fortifications.
>
> During the advance of the line, Lieutenant Harper, then in command of the Second Ohio Battery, shelled the woods in our front, and contributed greatly to drive the enemy back. The whole line was immediately advanced to within 500 yards of the enemy's works, where we formed a line, threw out a line of skirmishers covering my whole front, and at once began constructing intrenchments. In the afternoon of the advance of my line, in pursuance to the order of Brigadier-General Hovey, I ordered up Lieutenant Callahan, with his section of artillery, who took position in the Raymond road, and opened on the rebel line with very fatal effect.[54]

The next morning (12 July), the Federal siege line opened with an artillery barrage from the six guns of the 5th Ohio Battery on Lauman's line, which was immediately responded to with good effect by two 12-pounder Napoleon guns from Cobb's Kentucky Battery and Slocomb's 5th Company of the Washington, Louisiana, Artillery. Well-supported by the 19th Louisiana and 32nd Alabama, they got the 5th Ohio's range on their first shot. In the meantime, on Lauman's left, Hovey's line, supported by the 1st Missouri Battery, moved forward between Benton's division on their left and Lauman's on their right. In about an hour and a half fighting, Benton's and Hovey's troops drove the Confederates back and occupied the woods within short range of the Confederate works, where they were forced to halt.

On the far right flank, however, Lauman, facing across an open field toward Breckenridge's abatis-protected breastworks, ordered Isaac Pugh's 1st brigade (over Pugh's objection) to charge. In spite of his better judgment, Pugh obeyed Lauman's order and led the 41st and 53rd Illinois, the 3rd Iowa, and the unlucky 28th Illinois, sent over from the 3rd brigade, into a firestorm of grape, canister and musketry, some of them while moving directly toward the Confederate battery.

Caught in the open and in clusters trying to get around the abatis, Pugh and his men were forced to withdraw from the killing field, leaving over half their force of 880 men and officers dead and wounded on the field. Skirmishers from the 47th Georgia, the 1st, 3rd and 4th Florida from Marcellus A. Stovall's brigade of Breckenridge's division, moved up and captured 200 mostly wounded infantrymen and the regimental colors of the 28th, 41st and 53rd Illinois.

Threatened by Stovall's skirmishers, the 53rd Indiana came up from reserve and saved the six guns of the 5th Ohio Battery, whose men and horses were badly disabled by the accurate fire of the Confederate battery. (Capt. C.H. Slocomb, commanding the 5th Company of the Washington, Louisiana, Artillery, reported that he picked up a sergeant's diary belonging to the 5th Ohio Battery, which was in position on the railroad about 800 yards from his left piece.) Ord dismissed Lauman from command when he learned of the blunder, Sherman approved, and Hovey took command of Lauman's division.[55]

In spite of Lauman's blunder and the ensuing Federal losses, Sherman's artillery barrage on the remainder of the Federal line reached all parts of Jackson, reminding Johnston, in spite of pressure from Richmond, of the impossibility of maintaining his position in Jackson.[56]

As Federal reinforcements continued to arrive from the depot at Big Black,[57] Johnston made a last-ditch effort "to postpone at least the necessity of abandoning the place" by sending William H. "Red" Jackson's cavalry (Cosby's and Whitfield's brigades) to intercept Sherman's ammunition train. Whitfield's brigade rode north from Jackson about 12 miles on the east bank of the Pearl River, crossed at Grant's Mills, and united with Cosby's brigade, which had come down from Canton, before swinging south through Livingston and Brownsville to attack the Federal ammunition trains at Clinton and Bolton.[58]

Having learned of Jackson's move, on the night of 15 July Sherman telegraphed Col. Greenburg F. Wiles of the 78th Ohio, whose regiment was near Clinton guarding the train. In the predawn hours the next morning, Jackson's Confederate cavalry force attacked Wiles's outpost. After a spirited skirmish of about an hour, Wiles's Buckeyes and a relief brigade under Brigadier General Charles H. Matthies, all from McPherson's 17th corps, drove off Jackson's troopers, but not before they succeeded in cutting Sherman's telegraph wires.[59]

Some of Jackson's force attacked the train at Bolton and succeeded in capturing eight wagons belonging to a pioneer company of Ord's 13th corps, but did not attempt to capture the principal train, which was guarded by Col. Alexander Chambers's brigade from McArthur's division of the 17th corps. Both of Jackson's brigades retreated toward Canton and Sherman sent Col. Charles R. Woods's brigade, Landgraeber's battery of four light guns and Bussey's cavalry to intercept them. Operating with Woods's infantry, Bussey's troopers destroyed the pontoon bridge over the Pearl near Madisonville (Grant's Ferry), several miles southeast of Canton. They encountered Jackson's returning cavalry near Madisonville, and, in a brisk skirmish, drove the Confederate troopers northward through Canton and beyond. Woods's infantry spent the day in and around Canton destroying the Mississippi Central Railroad, including two miles of rail, three hundred feet of trestle and bridgework, thirteen railroad buildings—everything connected to the railroad.[60]

Johnston, who had been reporting daily by telegraph to President Davis in Richmond about his precarious position in Jackson, finally told Davis on 15 July, to Davis's consternation, that his army could neither resist a siege nor attack Sherman's force, and that he would abandon the place. Early on, the owners of the Mississippi Central Railroad had sent some of their surplus rolling stock up the railroad to Grenada for safekeeping. The next day, after learning that "Red" Jackson had failed to destroy Sherman's ammunition train, Johnston quickly put in motion his planned withdrawal. Utilizing pontoon bridges constructed earlier by Chief Engineer Samuel H. Lockett, Johnston moved all the sick and wounded, and all the public property that could be moved, across the river to Brandon. He then used cars of the Southern Railroad of Mississippi, which was still open east of Brandon, to send stores and rolling stock to Meridian and Mobile.[61]

Meanwhile, that same day, Sherman responded to a letter signed by a delegation from the City of Jackson requesting that he spare the city. Sherman replied:

> Gentlemen: Your communication is received. The city of Jackson will be occupied by a division of troops, commanded by General Blair. His orders will be to protect private property. I can make no terms, because resistance has been made with artillery until it became hopeless, and terms would compromise the Government of the United States, but I assure you that all citizens acting in good faith will be respected by me and my command, and that all families will be encouraged to get home, stay there, and resume their peaceful vocations.[62]

That night, in the first of many impressive "skeddadles" in the face of an overwhelming force commanded by his then nemesis and later friend Sherman, Johnston put the plan for his army's "retrograde movement" from Jackson into action with explicit instructions, including street directions. Stuck with munitions and other supplies that could not be moved, Johnston ordered the warehouse on the railroad tracks burned. Spreading rapidly, the fire consumed a city block and several civilian homes.[63]

In preparation for the move, that evening Johnston had his brass band serenade the Federals. Corporal Louis Bir of the 93rd Indiana described the effect of the music:

> But on the night Johnston Sent one of his Brass Bands out on or near the Fortification & Surenaded us with Some of the finest music I thought that I ever herd one of the Pieces that captured my Soul was the Bony Blue Flag & while we were charmed by thir musick Johnson was Withdrawing his army and crossed Purl River & Burnt the Bridge Leaving only Enough men to hold the fort until morning. And on the morning of the 16 [17] we Had No trouble to take the work for we taken only a few Prisoners and the town was ours. But we did not get as much Whisky & Tobaco & Provisions as we had got in May of same year.[64]

With the Federals lulled to sleep, Johnston cautioned his men to move "as rapidly and noiselessly as possible." To accomplish this, the artillery in or near the trenches was moved by hand and dragged a half-mile or more before they were limbered up. The artillery led the way across the Pearl River at 9:00 P.M. One hour later the infantry followed, Loring's and Walker's divisions on the right moving on the new or upper road to Brandon, crossing the Pearl River on the pontoon bridge at Carson's Ferry; Breckenridge's and French's divisions on the left moving on the old Brandon Road on pontoon bridges across the Pearl River at the lower end of town.[65]

Not only did Johnston serenade the Federals with his brass band, he also apparently used the town fire bells to call in his pickets, or perhaps to hide the intentional firing of the warehouse. The next morning Col. Richard Owen of the 60th Indiana reported:

> Friday, July 17 — An evident change in the enemy's position was discovered at dawn this morning, and it was soon ascertained that they had evacuated the town during the period between the ringing of the fire-bells, to call in their pickets, as we afterward learned, and the dawn of morning. The men were now permitted to take some rest, and a few at a time to visit town.[66]

Some of Potter's troops on Parke's northern line reported "the enemy in motion"; but Potter on reconnaissance found the enemy pickets still in place and did not raise an alarm. Sherman himself reported that wagons could be heard in Jackson, "but nothing that betokened an evacuation." Betokened or not, Johnston got his entire force across by daylight. In fact, some of his stragglers who had fallen asleep and missed the skedaddle left Jackson about seven or eight o'clock the next morning and reported that the Federals had not yet discovered their departure.[67]

Potter's division from Parke's 9th corps was the first to enter the city, but was quickly replaced, as Sherman had promised, by Blair's division from his 15th corps. In spite of Sherman's assurances to the civilian delegation, his troops and others who entered the city, including at least some from Slack's brigade, sacked and burned much of what remained of the city. Sherman, although admitting that his troops did some of the damage, blamed Johnston for most of it and reported tersely: "The place is ruined."[68]

With Jackson in ruins and the citizens destitute, both Sherman and Johnston lobbed accusations at each other about who destroyed Jackson. Johnston accused Sherman of burning Jackson to the ground; Sherman countered that Jackson had been partially destroyed by the Federals in their first occupation in May but that Johnston had more recently burned houses to open a field of artillery and musketry fire and had finished the job when he set fire to the warehouse prior to his evacuation.[69]

Sherman had only halfheartedly considered trapping Johnston's army inside Jackson. Satisfied to have run them across the Pearl River, he reported confidently that Johnston was "retreating east, with 30,000 men who will perish by heat, thirst, and disappointment." Instead, Johnston led his army through Brandon to Morton, a station on the Southern Railroad of Mississippi about thirty-five miles east of Jackson, where many went home on furlough.[70]

STEELE'S EXPEDITION TO BRANDON AND 19 JULY SKIRMISH

Grant wanted Sherman not only to destroy the railroad north and south of Jackson, but also to pursue and harass Johnston's retreating force. With Bussey's cavalry busy wrecking the Mississippi Central Railroad north of town and Fullerton's busy wrecking the New Orleans, Jackson & Great Northern Railroad south of town, Sherman sent a mounted infantry expedition from his old 15th corps on a halfhearted pursuit to Brandon. Steele commanded the force made up of Col. Milo Smith's Iowa brigade (the 4th, 9th, 26th and 30th Iowa) from Thayer's division and a composite brigade made up of two regiments from each of the 1st and 3rd brigades of Tuttle's division, accompanied by Capt Allen C. Waterhouse's Battery E, 1st Illinois Artillery, and their six 12-pounder Napoleon guns.[71]

To slow any pursuit, Johnston's men "placed loaded shells with torpedoes in the roads leading out from the river." These early land mines killed a civilian and wounded two soldiers from Lightburn's brigade; but, after a two-hour skirmish, Steele's Federal pursuit force drove "Red" Jackson's cavalry eastward through Brandon. After burning the jail and courthouse, the next day Steele's Federals returned to Jackson due to the intense heat and scarcity of water and forage.[72]

Federal Evacuation of Jackson

On 20 July, Parke's 9th corps left Jackson for their old position at Haynes' Bluff north of Vicksburg after tearing up tracks of the Mississippi Central Railroad north of Jackson. The next day, Ord's 13th corps started for their old camp at Vicksburg via Raymond as Sherman's 15th corps remained in Jackson.[73]

While in Jackson, and after both Johnston's and Sherman's armies had stripped the countryside of almost everything the civilian population needed for subsistence, Sherman received a plea from Jackson Mayor C.H. Manship for food and supplies for the now destitute citizens of the area. Sherman replied the next day:

> Yours of July 20 is received. I will cause 200 barrels of flour and 100 barrels of mess pork to be delivered at Big Black River Bridge, to the order of any committee you may accredit who will undertake to distribute the same to people in want, living in and near Jackson. Let the committee be appointed at once, and I will furnish them safe conduct to and from the river.[74]

Mayor Manship formed a committee composed of Judge William Yeager; D.N. Barrows, Esq.; J.H. Boyd, Esq.; Dr. W.Q. Poindexter; F.S. Hunt, Esq.; Fulton Anderson, Esq.; J.A. Kausler, Esq.; J.M. Coats, Esq.; and the Hon. W.L. Sharkey. The committee promised to distribute fairly and equitably to the inhabitants in proportion to the number of family members the "200 barrels of flour and 20,000 pounds of pork, or its equivalent in hard bread and bacon." Two days later from Clinton, a letter to Sherman signed by M. Tanner, W.W. Dunton, and W. Hillman acknowledged receipt "from the United States of fifteen thousand rations for subsistence for destitute people of Clinton and vicinity" and pledged that it would be "equitably distributed" and that none would be converted "to the use of the troops of the so-called Confederate States."[75]

Back in Vicksburg, Slack wrote Ann that, contrary to Sherman's protestations to Johnston, Federal troops moved in and "almost literally burned the town to ashes." Optimistic that the war was now almost over, he also noted that Hovey had returned to Indiana on a thirty-day furlough and that he would have temporary command of the division in Hovey's absence.[76]

On 28 July, Sherman wrote to Grant that the Confederates in Raymond needed medicines and provisions for the 150 sick left there: "Having stripped the country thereabouts, of course we can do no less than supply them, but they have brought no teams, the country having been stripped of them also. Send captured teams and carriages to Big Black if you have some."[77]

Declaring that all organized bodies of the enemy had been driven from those parts of Kentucky and Tennessee west of the Tennessee River, and from all of Mississippi west of the Mississippi Central Railroad, Grant admonished civilians not to support partisan irregulars if they wanted to live in peace and regain their prosperity.[78]

In the meantime, however, Joe Johnston rendezvoused the paroled prisoners from Vicksburg and added them to his army at Enterprise, Mississippi, on the Mobile & Ohio Railroad about 80 miles east of Jackson. At Enterprise he put plans in motion to repair the railroads and bridges in order to move as much railroad stock from north Mississippi to Mobile, which was about 110 miles south of Enterprise by rail. Lt. Gen. William J. Hardee transferred east from the Army of Tennessee to assist Johnston at Enterprise while Johnston traveled to Mobile to supervise the defenses of that city against what appeared to be an imminent attack by Grant's forces.[79]

Back at Jackson, as soon as Sherman pulled his troops out, "Red" Jackson moved his Confederate cavalry division back into what was left of it and John L. Logan moved his Confederate cavalry up from the Port Hudson area to the town of Terry, about twenty miles southwest of Jackson on the New Orleans, Jackson and Great Northern Railroad. Logan wrote Johnston from Terry that he believed that he could hold the area southwestward from the railroad at Terry to Natchez and could, as requested, collect "beeves between here [Terry] and Port Hudson" to supply Johnston's army at Enterprise.[80]

XI

Natchez, New Orleans and Bayou Teche (July 1863–January 1864)

Federal prospects looked much better in mid–to late summer 1863. The capture of Vicksburg and Port Hudson had opened the entire length of the Mississippi River to Federal shipping and effectively cut the Confederacy in two; Jackson and central Mississippi had been destroyed as a military hub; and Pemberton's army at least temporarily broken up. In Middle Tennessee, Rosecrans's Army of the Cumberland was driving Braxton Bragg's Army of Tennessee southeastward toward Chattanooga in what came to be known as the "Tullahoma Campaign." And, on the eastern front, Robert E. Lee's foray into Pennsylvania had been stopped cold at Gettysburg sending his Army of Northern Virginia in hasty retreat to the defenses around Richmond.

On the other hand, Joe Johnston's force had escaped into eastern Mississippi, where he regrouped and slowly began to add paroled Vicksburg prisoners to his army. After the fall of Port Hudson and Vicksburg, Col. John L. Logan's cavalry brigade continued to operate for Joe Johnston between southeast Louisiana and Jackson, Mississippi. And, although supplies to and from the Trans-Mississippi fell dramatically with Federal control of the Mississippi River, arms and equipment continued to flow into the Confederacy through the port of Mobile.

Mobile had, in fact, been so heavily supplied from Europe via Havana that in 1863 it was a reasonably prosperous city and home to reportedly 15,000 civilian non-combatants, many of whom were homeless war refugees. To stop this inflow of supplies, before moving into north Georgia to help Rosecrans wrap up Bragg's Army of Tennessee, Grant proposed an amphibious expedition from Lake Pontchartrain (New Orleans) against the port of Mobile.[1]

The Lincoln Administration, however, had what it considered to be greater problems in the Trans-Mississippi. Up to this time, arms and supplies from Europe and Mexico had flowed across the Rio Grande to Kirby Smith's Confederate Department of the Trans-Mississippi, with Texas cotton the primary medium of trade. The flow of goods between Matamoros, Mexico, and Brownsville, Texas, was so great that by spring 1862 Leonard Pierce Jr., United States Counsel at Matamoros, had already dubbed it "the great thoroughfare" of trade from Europe to the Confederacy. So great had the flow become, in fact, that Bag-

XI. Natchez, New Orleans and Bayou Teche (July 1863–January 1864) 191

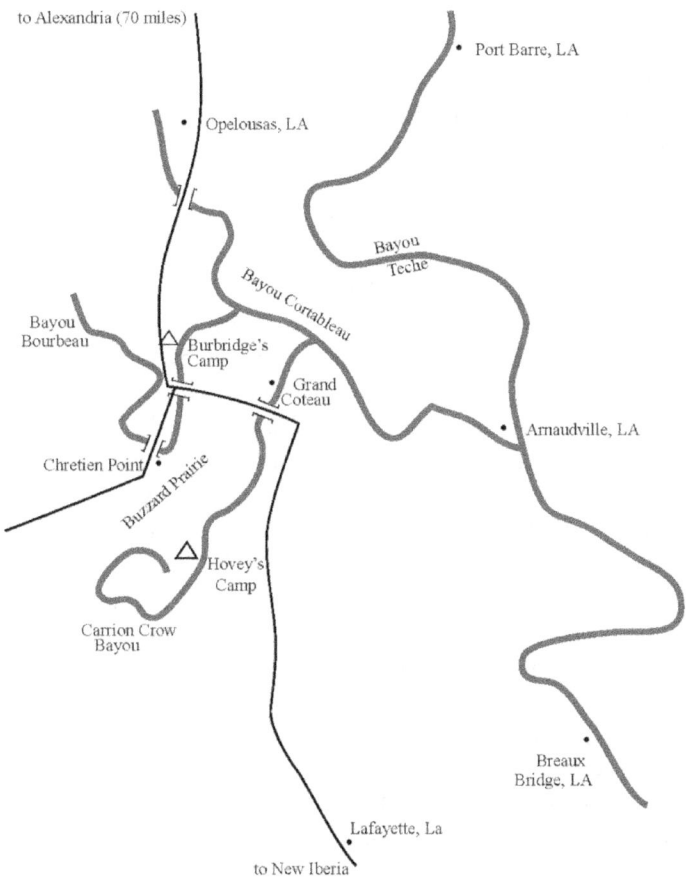

Expanded version based roughly on Map 5, "The Battle of Bayou Bourbeau, November, 1863," in Richard Lowe, *Walker's Texas Division, CSA: Greyhounds of the Trans-Mississippi* (Baton Rouge: LSU Press, 2004), p. 138, and Google Maps.

dad, Mexico, a sleepy fishing village at the mouth of the Rio Grande (Boca del Rio), had been turned into a major trans-Atlantic shipping center. Not surprisingly, Lincoln had been receiving diplomatic advice to interdict those supplies.[2]

The Lincoln Administration also felt increasing pressure from New England textile manufacturers and politicians to capture Texas and use its cotton-producing capacity to regain the British market and a more stable supply for their own faltering mills. By mid–1862,

New England faced a cotton shortage and a decline of about seventy-five percent in textile manufacture. By mid–1863, even more spindles were idle, and New England politicians and textile manufacturers pressured Lincoln to invade Texas and capture the extensive cotton and sugar lands so they could establish, using New England technology and workers, plantations to supply a steady stream of cotton for their mills. To the argument that those crops could be commercially successful only under slave labor, they noted that there had been limited free labor production of cotton and sugar cane in Texas by German immigrants prior to the war and that New England capital, technology and free labor could be used to "emancipate the world from the delusion that slave labor [was] necessary to the production" of these staples.[3]

Added to this pressure was the French invasion of Mexico in May 1862 and their threatened alliance with the Trans-Mississippi Confederates. The situation in Mexico that troubled Lincoln had been building since the early 1850s when President Antonio Lopez de Santa Ana seized power in a *coup d'état* rather than give up the presidency as mandated by the constitution. Santa Ana, in turn, was ousted in the Liberal revolution of 1855 and replaced by Liberal Juan Alvarez, who appointed Benito Juarez, recently returned from exile in New Orleans, as Chief Justice in the Ministry of Justice and Ecclesiastical Affairs.

In 1857 the Liberal congress enacted a new constitution, which reduced the power of the military and separated church and state both politically and economically. Liberal Ignacio Comonfort was elected president (by Congress, not by plebiscite); Juarez was elected president of the Supreme Court and ex-officio vice-president.

The passage of the new reformed constitution plunged Mexico into a civil war (the "War of the Reform"), and in June 1858 a Conservative *coup d'état* ousted Comonfort. Juarez succeeded to the presidency as constitutionally mandated, but Conservative Roman Catholic Church forces under Gen. Felix Zuloaga drove him and his government from Mexico City. Juarez, supported by most of the Mexican states, established the rival Liberal government at Vera Cruz on the Gulf of Mexico. In February 1859, Gen. Miguel Miramon replaced Zuloaga as the head of the Conservative government, whose territory at the time was confined primarily to Mexico City; and, in April 1859, the Buchanan administration recognized the legitimacy of the Juarez government. By 1861, victories by Liberal forces enabled Juarez to return with his government to Mexico City.[4]

With the Mexican treasury nearly bankrupt, Juarez unilaterally suspended interest payments on loans from Britain, France and Spain that had been incurred by his and previous Mexican governments. In 1861, those three countries intervened to protect their interests in Mexico by occupying Vera Cruz. In 1862, after coming to realize that Louis Napoleon (Napoleon III) of France had colonial ambitions, Britain and Spain reached settlements with the Juarez government and pulled out. In May 1862, the French Army moved inland; and, on 5 May (Cinco de Mayo), was defeated at the town of Puebla by Juarez's Mexican Army, led by Gen. Ignacio Zaragoza.[5]

The victory, however, was short-lived. French reinforcements poured into Mexico; and, in June 1863, Louis Napoleon's Imperial Army, supported by Mexican Roman Catholic Church Party Royalists, succeeded in driving the Juarez government out of Mexico City. Escaping north with a small army, Juarez continued his battle with the French and Mexican Royalists while maintaining a government-in-exile recognized as legitimate by the United States. Back in Mexico City, the French set up a provisional government, proclaimed

Mexico to be an empire, and Napoleon III offered the crown to Archduke Maximilian of Austria. Maximilian accepted, although he would not arrive in Mexico and be crowned Emperor Maximilian I until 1864.[6]

This raised concerns in the Lincoln Administration not only about allowing an American republic to be replaced by a European monarchy, but by a potential alliance between the French and E. Kirby Smith, whose Confederate Trans-Mississippi forces still controlled Texas and the Rio Grande. In fact, Texas Confederates were anxious for official recognition by the French, who at least initially were anxious for help from the Confederates in defeating Juarez's Mexican government, which, with his loyal army, was then operating as a mobile government-in-exile in northern Mexico. Juarez, of course, hated the French invaders and their Mexican Royalist allies perhaps as much as he hated Anglo-Texans for what he considered their 1836 land grab, their imported slave system, their desire to expand slavery into Central America and the Caribbean, and their persistent violation of Mexican sovereignty while chasing escaped slaves.[7]

Rumors ran rampant that the French, who were moving toward the Rio Grande, were willing to cooperate with the Trans-Mississippi Confederates in return for the reannexation of Texas and Arizona to Mexico. More realistically in the short term, the Confederates offered Napoleon III aid in defeating the Republican forces of Juarez, many of them operating as guerrilla units along the Rio Grande, in exchange for duty-free transshipments to Matamoras.[8]

Indeed, since the French invasion and resurgence of their Mexican Royalist allies in 1862, Juarez had tried to close the border to the Confederates. Although the flow of goods into Texas essentially never stopped, it was occasionally interrupted by Juarez's partisan forces, who attacked and seized on occasion both Confederate cotton bound for their European suppliers and military arms and equipment brought upriver in return. To the Confederates, Juarez partisans such as Octaviano Zapata on the upper Rio Grande, and Juan Nepomuceno Cortina on the lower end near Matamoras, were "banditti." To the Lincoln Administration, however, they were anti–Imperialist freedom fighters in what, by 1863, had become a heated border war.[9]

The Confederates, in fact, with only a small force in Texas, had their hands full on the Rio Grande frontier and were vulnerable to a Federal invasion. Major General John Bankhead "Prince John" Magruder commanded the 6,500-man Army of Texas from his headquarters in Houston, all the force he had to cover the entire state and its 400-mile Gulf Coast. Brigadier General Hamilton P. Bee, who had no military experience, commanded the 1st division (two brigades of cavalry) at Brownsville. Bee's cavalry patrolled the Rio Grande border, crossing occasionally to fight "banditti," while Bee, a former Texas legislator, brokered deals and administered the exchange of cotton for armaments between Brownsville and Matamoras.[10]

United States diplomats in Mexico advised Lincoln that pro-Union Texans would assist an invasion force against the Confederates, many of them having organized into secret pro-Union peace parties not unlike what the pro-Southern Copperheads had done in the North. They were primarily, although not exclusively, German immigrants and Mexican United States citizens living in Texas and in exile in Mexico. One of the leading pro-Union Texas refugees was former judge of the 12th Judicial District at Brownsville, Edmund J. Davis, forced into Mexico after secession under threat of death. Davis organized the 1st Regiment

Texas Volunteer Cavalry (U.S.) from among dissident Texas refugees in Mexico and as far away as New York City. A Confederate force crossed into Mexico and captured him in Matamoros on 15 March 1863 while he attempted to bring his family across the river to safety. H.P. Bee, who was attempting to maintain trade ties with increasingly hostile officials in Tamaulipas, relented to pressure and returned Davis to Mexican territory. Davis went on to command a small cavalry brigade attached to the 13th corps in the Bayou Teche Campaign.[11]

In addition, Charles Francis Adams, the United States Minister to Great Britain, had reported a plan hatched by wealthy European merchants and capitalists in London to smuggle goods into Texas via the Rio Grande as a way to recoup their private loans to the Confederate government. Adams argued that nothing short of occupation of the east bank of the Rio Grande could prevent it.[12]

Given this context and buoyed by Rosecrans's and Meade's recent successes in Tennessee and Pennsylvania, on 29 July 1863, Lincoln wrote to Stanton:

> Sir: Can we not renew the effort to organize a force to go to Western Texas?
> Please consult with the General-in-Chief on the subject.
> If the Governor of New Jersey shall furnish any new regiments, might not they be put into such an expedition? Please think of it. I believe no local object is now more desirable. Yours truly. A. Lincoln[13]

A week later, Lincoln wrote to Grant:

> I see by a dispatch of yours that you incline quite strongly toward an expedition against Mobile. This would appear tempting to me also, were it not that, in view of recent events in Mexico, I am greatly impressed with the importance of re-establishing the national authority in Western Texas as soon as possible. I am not making an order, however; that I leave, for the present at least, to the General-in-Chief. Yours truly, A. Lincoln[14]

Lincoln's wish became Halleck's command. Grant's plan to attack Mobile was shelved temporarily and he was forced to sit idly by in Vicksburg to oversee the dismantling of his vast expeditionary force and to co-operate with Banks, who was assigned command of the Texas Expedition. Grant, who blamed Halleck for shelving his Mobile plan, sent, under Halleck's orders, a division of 5,000 troops to Schofield in Missouri, who was having some trouble with raids from Sterling Price's Confederates; 4,000 men to Banks in New Orleans; and returned the 9th Corps to Kentucky. Grant's remaining troops around Vicksburg "were busily and unpleasantly employed" fighting small detachments of Confederate cavalry "and in destroying mills, bridges and rolling stock on the railroads."[15]

Grant detached Brigadier General Thomas E.G. Ransom's brigade from McPherson's 17th corps in mid–July and sent them to Natchez to occupy and secure the area of southwestern Mississippi. They landed at Natchez that same day without any military opposition, and city officials surrendered the town to Ransom. Federal troops immediately seized 5,000 head of Texas cattle bound for Johnston's army in east Mississippi. Crossing to the Louisiana side, Federal troops also captured ordnance being shipped to Kirby Smith's Trans-Mississippi forces.[16]

Several weeks later, on 30 July, Ransom sent troopers under Major Asa Worden to sweep the area south of Natchez. Finding no opposition and a population anxious for peace, they moved to Liberty, Mississippi, where they destroyed sugar, 150 saddles, an artillery carriage and wagon, and 50 small arms. At Woodville they burned a large, 40-loom cotton factory, which supplied cloth for making Confederate uniforms and destroyed 14 freight cars, 2 passenger coaches, a railroad machine shop, 2 locomotives, 250 barrels of CSA molasses, army clothing and 25 small arms. Ransom also reported that Worden captured a French-made 6-pounder gun "said to have been used by General [Andrew] Jackson at [the 1815 Battle of] New Orleans." Worden noted that the people of the area were discouraged with the rebellion and anxious for peace on any honorable terms. Ransom, on the other hand, noted that Worden's raid had caught the attention of Confederate mounted infantry and cavalry under Colonel J.L. Logan of the 11th Arkansas Infantry (mounted). Logan's force operated out of the 3rd Military District of Joe Johnston's Confederate Department of Mississippi and East Louisiana and was part of Johnston's planned harassment of Grant's forces in Mississippi. They were heading north toward Natchez from Bayou Pierre with 1,500 well-armed troopers.[17]

Logan's task, besides harassing Federals, was to transship ordnance from Mississippi to E. Kirby Smith's force on the west bank in Louisiana, and to collect Texas beef cattle shipped across from the Louisiana side (among which were the 5,000 head captured by Worden). Logan's mounted troopers were part guerrillas and part cattle drovers until Ransom's Federals put a stop to them.[18]

At the end of July, Grant sent Ord's 13th corps to join Banks's Department of the Gulf Texas expeditionary force, although under protest, as he still hoped to convince Halleck of the wisdom of attacking Mobile instead.[19] Slack's brigade[20] led Ord's corps to Natchez, which was now a Federal post commanded by Ransom. Arriving on the evening of 2 August, two days later Slack wrote Ann: "Here we are in the very heart of Dixie, in the midst of the most beautiful section of the southern Confederacy, indeed the most magnificent county I ever saw in any portion of the Union.... It is the aristocratic resort for all this wealthy region. Wealthy planters, retired merchants and the rich nabobs of all classes concentrate here and spend their time in ease & luxury." Slack set up camp on the outskirts of town, "on a hill 200 feet above the river" overlooking "Mr. Brown's" residence "under the hill ... the most beautiful place I ever saw." He noted, however, that their foraging parties were being harassed by "a gang of about 1500 rebels under command of Genl Logan," but believed they would "succeed in capturing some in a day or two, or drive them out of the country."[21]

On 10 August, Slack received his orders to leave Natchez for New Orleans with the 13th corps. Although uncertain, he still believed their destination would be Mobile. Writing to Ann on 16 August from their camp near the river at Carrollton, Louisiana, some six miles upriver from New Orleans, Slack described New Orleans somewhat surprisingly as one of the healthier places to live and took the time to rant against Copperheads in the North.[22]

Moving their camp downriver to Greenville[23] while awaiting orders, Slack continued his description of New Orleans and his rant against anti-war Democrats in Huntington. He added his displeasure at being sent to Banks's Department of the Gulf, where some trouble was brewing between the eastern or "Yankee" troops, as Slack called them, who were stationed there and the newly arrived western troops from the 13th corps.[24]

Banks, given the choice to invade north Texas via Alexandria and Shreveport on the Red River, or south Texas via the Gulf of Mexico, chose the latter, deciding to send an amphibious force to Sabine Pass, where Confederate Fort Griffin guarded the mouth of the Sabine River on the Louisiana and Texas border. Banks selected Major General William B.

Franklin, recently arrived to command the 19th corps, made up of New England units, to lead an amphibious expedition to Sabine Pass that consisted of four light-draft gunboats, commanded by Lt. Frederick Crocker of the navy, and seven troop transports. Franklin had been relieved of command by Ambrose Burnside after a dispute over who was to blame for the debacle at Fredericksburg, Virginia, on 13 December 1862. Banks assigned Franklin command of the 19th corps after the fall of Port Hudson in July.[25]

Crocker's gunboats were to reduce the fort, and the troops were to land and move as far inland as the railroad that connected Beaumont with Magruder's headquarters at Houston. Although Magruder was hard pressed to get troops to Fort Griffin to defend the pass, on 8 September, a small force inside Fort Griffin, which consisted of the Davis Guards and Cook's Texas Artillery, and on water, the CSS *Uncle Ben*, assisted by a shallow sand bar and strong current, defended the fort. Cook's artillerists, who had heart and good aim, almost immediately sank the lead light draft Federal gunboats, the *Clifton* and the *Sachem*, and disabled the *Arizona*. The officers and crew of the *Clifton* and *Sachem* were captured, although the crippled *Arizona* and the fourth gunboat, the *Granite City*, were able to turn around and flee. Seeing the gunboats flounder, the lead troop transport, which had crossed the shallow bar behind the *Clifton*, turned and fled as well, and Franklin, unable to find a safe landing place for his infantry, ordered the expedition to return to New Orleans.[26]

That same day, believing they would follow Franklin's troops to Sabine City, Slack wrote Ann about their prospective movement to Texas and the possibility of war with France. He also mentioned that Grant had come to visit the troops in New Orleans and was seriously injured when a locomotive caused his horse to bolt and he was thrown and seriously injured when it crashed into a carriage. Grant was incapacitated in New Orleans for about one month.[27] Two days later, 10 September, Frederick Steele, recently appointed to command the Federal troops in Arkansas, forced Sterling Price's Confederates out of Little Rock, threatening Kirby Smith's entire Trans-Mississippi operation. Price and his army retreated southwest to Arkadelphia.[28]

With the failure of his amphibious Sabine Pass Expedition, Banks, still dubious about Halleck's favored Red River route, chose to send Franklin to lead his 19th and Ord's 13th corps on an overland expedition to the Sabine via Bayou Teche in south Louisiana. On 12 September, Slack wrote Ann that they had received orders and were "off in the morning" for Sabine City and Galveston, Texas.[29]

Franklin moved his force across the river to Algiers and loaded them in boxcars of the New Orleans, Opelousas & Great Western Railroad, along with boxes and barrels and of provisions for an eighty-five mile ride westward to Brashear City (present-day Morgan City), which sat on the east bank of the southerly-flowing Atchafalaya River near its confluence with southeasterly-flowing Bayou Teche. About fifteen miles north of the Gulf of Mexico, the wide Atchafalaya was known at this point as "Berwick Bay."[30]

The 47th Indiana and 28th Iowa left Algiers on Sunday morning, the remainder of Slack's brigade (the 24th Iowa, 56th Ohio, and 87th Illinois) on a later train, followed by Slack and his staff on the midnight train from Algiers. Slack and his staff arrived at their camp on Berwick Bay just above the city at 7:00 o'clock Monday morning. There they awaited the arrival of Franklin's 19th corps "Yankees," whom Slack now referred to as "the Nutmegs," who were, he presumed correctly, to take the advance up Bayou Teche in about a week's time.[31]

XI. Natchez, New Orleans and Bayou Teche (July 1863–January 1864)

Writing from the camp of McGinnis's division on 25 September, correspondent "Snacky" of the *Indianapolis Daily Journal* sent home news about Cameron's 1st and Slack's 2nd brigades. In this article, "Snacky" mentioned that the rancor between the eastern and western troops was at least beginning to diminish, and noted his respect for the military discipline and competence of the Corps d'Afrique soldiers. He also pointed out, as did Slack, that following the advance of the French Imperial Army in Mexico, rumors were rife in camp on the prospect of war with France.

From Gen. McGinnis' Division — Things at Brashear City
Correspondence of the *Daily Journal*
Brashear City, La., Sept. 25, 1863

From Vicksburg to Natchez, from Natchez to Carrollton, La., and from thence to this city of few houses and fewer inhabitants, has the old division removed since my last epistle. And so long a time has elapsed since so doing that it will hardly interest you for me to enter into particulars as to the trip to this place.

Brashear City, on Berwick Bay, is not a place of much importance, save in a military point of view. It is connected by railway with New Orleans, distant ninety miles.

As to the 3rd division, the general health is good. We have, by long exposure, become acclimated, and do not suffer from excessive heat any more than we did as citizens from unusual heat in the North.

Gen. Hovey is yet North. Rumor has it that he has been assigned to some other command. All here would be sorry to lose him.

Brig. Gen. McGinnis is now in command of the Division, vice Lee assigned to the cavalry service.

The 1st Brigade is commanded by Col. N.T. Spicely, of the 24th Indiana, a brave and true man, and what is better, a war Democrat. The 2nd Brigade is under command of Col. Slack, of the 47th Indiana....

My dear sir, did you ever go "crabbing?"—the regular salt water crab. That is all the rage here. Crabs for breakfast, crabs for dinner, and crabs for supper—nothing but crabs. Does a man prove missing at roll call? He is sure to have gone "crabbing."

An officer proposes something for amusement, and to while away time. It is nothing more than "going a crabbing." No vagrants here. All have "visible means of support" as long as the crabs bite. It does not require a great amount of skill nor a vast outlay of capital to "rig up" the crab-catching apparatus. All to be done is to take a small line, affix thereto a chunk of fresh beef or "sowbelly," with a small dip [k]not. Let down the string until the meat rests upon the bottom. The crab soon "lays along side" to take in supplies. When he has a good hold draw in the string; the meat follows the string, and the crab still retains his grip upon the meat. When near the surface, sink under the net and lift the gentleman out. There it is—the whole programme of crab catching. Not much skill required; no mystery about the matter in the least. In handling them, look out for their claws. They are more dangerous than a lobster, and a crawfish nowhere in comparison with them. They are armed with terrible claws, and woe unto the unlucky individual who is foolish enough to allow them a hold upon his fingers. They pinch outrageously as the writer can testify to, to his sorrow. It is all humbug, though, about their being such great luxuries. It is rather more shell than meat when it comes to eating.

Fresh oysters in the shell are also to be had here by paying one dollar per hundred. Cheap enough.

One can live here. We have plenty of "rations," and add thereto occasionally by confiscating some poor "hog," "sheep," or "fowl," that may be caught straying around "without a pass." And occasionally onions, potatoes and other vegetables are "went for," causing much grumbling among the good Union planters who live around.

We are under Eastern rule now, and with them the "oath of allegiance" has not yet lost its coloring.

Here we had our fist glimpse of "salt water." Vast were the "cussings" at first, when the boys not knowing of its flavor, would gulp down a mouthful, too saltish to quench thirst. The only way to obtain water here is by sinking wells, and even then the water has a strong, brackish taste.

An expedition into Texas seems to be the order of the day. The 19th Army Corps has already crossed the Bay and started on the march. The 1st Division, 19th Army Corps is crossing today. The 3rd division goes over tomorrow.

The Bay at this point is not more than half a mile wide. A little town called Berwick is situated on the other side.

Corps d'Afrique are numerous here, and for drill and military discipline present a fine appearance. Negroes make good soldiers, and there is no use disguising the fact; and under the lead of proper officers will do good service.

Eastern and Western men at first did not agree. They did not like one another. But this useless and unnecessary rancor is fast dying away. This is as it should be. Soldiers fighting together in the same cause should work together harmoniously.

Much speculation is rife as to the prospect of a war with France, on account of her "doings" in Mexico. The French are reported as fortifying at Matamoras. It might be possible that this expedition would turn up somewhere near there.

I see by a late paper that Dan. Voorhees, the man of Copperhead principles, come near being hung by the 63rd Indiana. It is only regretted here that the officers interfered to save his worthless life. Better for Indiana, in time to come, had that rope been allowed to do its work.

Governor Morton has recently had another Agent from Indiana here to look after the welfare of his soldiers. Mr. Kimball is said Agent.

Wm. Sayre, Company G, 11th Indiana, died in the hospital at Carrollton, Louisiana, Aug. 28th, 1863.

Clay Moore, Company C, 46th Indiana, died at Natchez, nearly a month since, of camp diarrhea. He was from Clay township, Carroll county, Ind.

A great many soldiers have been transferred to the Invalid Corps, also a good many promoted to positions in negro regiments. This is thinning out the ranks of veteran regiments.

Yours, Snacky[32]

As he wrote from camp on Berwick Bay on 20 September while waiting to cross, Slack's Dutch ancestry showed in a cure for ague that he sent to Ann: "Drink hot tea, and then top off with about three glasses of Lager beer for a month, and I think you will effect a permanent cure, and can count yourself free for another year. I have no doubt that I am very greatly indebted to the use of beer from my uninterrupted good health for the last eight or ten years." He also boasted of his, and the army's, ability to withstand the heat and humidity of south Louisiana and again cited rumors he believed to be credible that they would not go through Texas, but would turn and strike Mobile instead.[33]

Around this time, however, earlier Federal successes began to unravel. Rosecrans' Army of the Cumberland, which had successfully maneuvered Bragg's Army of Tennessee into north Georgia, was nearly trapped in the region's difficult hills and coves. And, on 20 September, his Army of the Cumberland was defeated at Chickamauga Creek, George Thomas's troops holding the line long enough for Rosecrans's routed army to escape into Chattanooga, where they immediately came under siege by Bragg's victorious Army of Tennessee. Bragg had Rosecrans penned inside Chattanooga from atop Lookout Mountain to the south and west, from Missionary Ridge to the east, and by Wheeler's cavalry in the Sequatchie Valley to the north, blocking the road across Walden's Ridge, the only remaining supply route open to Chattanooga. In Arkansas on 22 September, Joseph O. "J.O." Shelby's cavalry, part of Price's Confederate force at Arkadelphia, began a successful lightning raid against Fed-

XI. Natchez, New Orleans and Bayou Teche (July 1863–January 1864)

eral outposts in Arkansas and Missouri that would cover about 1,500 miles and last until early November.[34]

Even before the news of Rosecrans's defeat at Chickamauga, Halleck had ordered Grant, still recuperating in New Orleans, to send all his available forces to Memphis and eastward to assist Rosecrans at Chattanooga. Grant sent Sherman's corps and a division from McPherson's. By the time Grant received his orders on 27 September, Rosecrans' army had already been badly defeated at Chickamauga and was under siege in Chattanooga.

In the meantime, the War Department frantically sent "Fighting Joe" Hooker with the 11th and 12th corps of the Army of the Potomac to help break the siege and save Rosecrans's troops. Grant himself was summoned by the War Department to Nashville and given command of the Military Division of the Mississippi, "composed of the Departments of the Ohio, the Cumberland, and the Tennessee, and all the territory from the Alleghenies to the Mississippi River" north of Banks's Department of the Gulf command. Department commanders remained the same, except that Rosecrans was relieved of command of the Army of the Cumberland and replaced by Major General George H. "Rock of Chickamauga" Thomas. Later in the month, Grant would proceed to Chattanooga, along with Sherman, who was now in command of the Army of the Tennessee, to help break the siege of Chattanooga. Banks's Texas Expedition, no longer quite so urgent in Washington, was put on the back burner, and Grant refused to send Banks the additional troops he requested.[35]

Back on Berwick Bay, however, it had become clear to Slack that Texas was their destination. He wrote his daughter Sallie on 29 September from their camp on the west bank near the mouth of Bayou Teche that he expected "a most miserable march of about two hundred miles" to Texas, but that he hoped to get "a nice Mexican mustang pony" before he left there. Unlike the officers, the enlisted men were to travel light, without tents. Each regiment had four wagons for provisions and ammunition and each soldier was provided "with hard bread, coffee and salt." All other provisions were to be "procured" on the march.[36]

On 4 October, Franklin's vanguard 19th corps troops, marching up a good road that followed Bayou Teche, skirmished with about 250 infantry under Alfred Mouton and a portion of Thomas Green's cavalry division from Richard Taylor's Western Louisiana forces, and drove them from Nelson's Bridge near New Iberia, about fifty miles above Berwick Bay and the mouth of the bayou. That same day, Slack's brigade, part of Ord's 13th corps three-division rearguard detachment, arrived at the town of Franklin, Louisiana, at noon, about twenty-five miles below New Iberia.[37]

On 9 and 10 October, the vanguard skirmished about fifteen miles above New Iberia at Vermillion Bayou, near Vermillionville (present-day Lafayette). From 14 to 19 October, between Carrion Crow Bayou and Grand Coteau, several miles apart on the road from Vermillionville to Opelousas, which ran northward for about twenty miles. Mouton's Confederate infantry and Green's cavalry division continued to fall back after these skirmishes as Franklin's troops continued up the Teche toward Opelousas. On 11 October, Landram's 2nd brigade from Burbridge's 4th division of the 13th corps arrived in Franklin and remained to garrison the town. Four days later (15 October), Burbridge's 4th division moved to the vanguard and the next day established a camp at Barre's Landing on Bayou Teche, about eight miles east of Opelousas.

On 20 October, Ord's illness became severe enough for him to go on sick leave, and

Cadwallader Washburn replaced him in command of the 13th corps detachment, Michael Lawler replacing Washburn in command of the 1st division of the 13th corps. In turn, that same day, Washburn moved Bringhurst's 46th Indiana to the vanguard alongside a regiment of engineers from the Corps d'Afrique who marched up the Bayou Teche road "in perfect order" singing "John Brown." The next day (21 October), Burbridge's division drove the Confederates out of Opelousas and Franklin's 19th corps moved in and occupied the town while the 46th Indiana and the Corps d'Afrique detachments continued to Barre's Landing in search of forage. Finding that no supplies could be taken from the bayou, they returned to the main column, which was now in Opelousas, about fifty miles north of New Iberia.[38]

Indeed, not only had frequent rain made the already difficult roads to the west across south Louisiana impassable, the prospects of forage on those roads looked bleak as well. On 27 October, the 1st division of the 13th corps began the retreat back to New Iberia, signaling an end to the Sabine Pass Expedition. After a brief skirmish on 31 October with Mouton and Green's force several miles up the Teche near the town of Washington, Franklin withdrew his force from Opelousas and began the retreat to New Iberia.[39]

Franklin's force, the 19th corps in the lead, followed by the 13th corps detachment, moved down Bayou Teche about eleven miles and encamped near Carrion Crow Bayou. Burbridge's division, and Col. John G. Fonda's mounted infantry brigade, followed as the rear guard. Heading southward to Grand Coteau, they camped on winding Bayou Bourbeau seven miles below Opelousas and three or four miles north of the main camp on Carrion Crow Bayou. As Franklin pulled his expeditionary force from Opelousas, Mouton deployed Green's cavalry division and three infantry regiments (the 11th, 15th, and 18th Texas) under Col. O.M. Roberts, with a rifled section from Daniel's Battery and two sections of the Valverde Battery under Lieutenants Samuel M. Hamilton and P.G. Hume, to "pursue and harass" Franklin's rear guard as they withdrew down the Teche.[40]

At its head, about seven miles south of Opelousas, the shallow and muddy Bayou Bourbeau, at most points less than waist-deep, snaked southward through a ravine bordered by a 150-yard skirt of timber before it curved sharply eastward and crossed the Bellevue Road that ran from Opelousas southward to Vermillionville. Following the ravine, Bayou Bourbeau turned abruptly northward at Chretien Point, flowing northward for several miles before entering Bayou Courtableau, which wound eastward to Bayou Teche. Burbridge's rear-guard 4th division camped on the north bank prairie near Chretien Point, where the eastward-running bayou turned abruptly northward. They faced northwestward, their right flank rested on the skirt of timber and their left extended about one hundred yards into the prairie. Across the bayou and another wide skirt of timber, "Buzzard Prairie" extended three to four miles southeastward to the roughly parallel Carrion Crow Bayou along which the remainder of the 13th corps, including Slack's brigade, and Franklin's 19th corps camped.[41]

THE BATTLE OF BAYOU BOURBEAU (GRAND COTEAU)

After sporadic skirmishing on the first and second day of November, Green chose to launch an attack on Burbridge's somewhat isolated position. Early in the morning of 3

November, a portion of Green's cavalry drove in Burbridge's outposts on the Bellevue Road. Realizing his vulnerable position, Burbridge sent for assistance to Washburn, some three or four miles away at Carrion Crow Bayou. Green's Confederate cavalry then withdrew and Burbridge rescinded his request, saying that the enemy had disappeared from sight. Believing, as did Franklin and Washburn, that there was no large Confederate force nearby, Burbridge sent the 83rd Ohio and 200 troopers from John G. Fonda's mounted infantry on a foraging expedition eastward toward Grand Coteau. In addition, two paymasters in camp set up tables to pay off the troop and a polling place for the 23rd Wisconsin soldiers to cast absentee ballots in the Wisconsin state elections.[42]

Shortly thereafter, sometime between 11:00 A.M. (according to the Confederates) and noon (according to the Federals), Green returned with his cavalry division and three regiments of infantry (the 11th, 15th, and 18th Texas) under Colonel O.M. Roberts of the 11th Texas. Green and Roberts led their men down the Bellevue Road and into the timber toward Burbridge's right flank, where they hit the 60th Indiana with musketry and artillery fire. The Hoosiers returned fire as the 23rd Wisconsin, whose exercise in democracy ended abruptly, quickly got into position with the 83rd and 96th Ohio, along with four pieces of artillery from the 17th Ohio Battery. The forage expedition arrived at about the same time that the attack began, and Fonda ordered his men to quickly unload the forage, load the camp equipage, and get the wagons to the main camp on Carrion Crow Bayou. Fonda, with most of his cavalry brigade, moved across the bayou bridge and into Buzzard Prairie, where his troopers formed a line of battle. According to Green, the Federals put up very stubborn resistance until he sent his cavalry and infantry support sweeping westward around the Federal camp to turn Burbridge's left flank.[43]

Obviously in trouble, Burbridge sent another plea for help to Carrion Crow Bayou, and Washburn ordered McGinnis's division (Cameron and Slack's brigades, led by Cameron due to McGinnis's illness) forward. Green's cavalry, A.P. Bagby's brigade in the center supported by artillery (the rifle section of Daniels's Battery) and the 4th and 5th Texas Cavalry (dismounted), opened up in front, while Major's cavalry with the Valverde Battery swept around the western prairie and attacked the 67th Indiana on Burbridge's left flank. Burbridge ordered his line to move to the right to what he thought would be a better position, but Lt. Col. Theodore E. Buehler of the 67th Indiana failed to comply, and his regiment was quickly surrounded by Major's cavalry and surrendered without a fight. One section of Nims's 2nd Massachusetts Battery (six 6-pounder rifles) and one section of the 17th Ohio Battery (10-pounder Parrotts) opened up, but with the 67th Indiana gone, they were forced to withdraw, losing one of Nims's 6-pounder rifles after its horses were killed attempting to cross the bayou. Fonda's cavalry and the 83rd Ohio charged across the bridge and drove the Confederates from their camp, but were forced to retreat back across the bridge when the 67th Indiana surrendered en masse and Major's Confederates rolled up Burbridge's left flank.[44]

With their left flank entirely gone and now finding themselves greatly outnumbered, Burbridge's right flank retreated into the timber, and his artillery and wagons fled across the bridges that the Federals had constructed across the bayou. Lieutenant William Marland of Nims's 2nd Massachusetts Battery reported that following a hot skirmish with Confederate cavalry in which they were fired upon by two pieces of artillery, they were forced to limber up. With revolvers drawn, they then had to "charge through" the Confederate cavalry then in possession of the bridges, and did so without loss, some Confederate pursuers getting mired in the muddy bayou.[45]

Burbridge avoided a complete rout only by the timely arrival of Bringhurst's 46th Indiana from Carrion Crow Bayou. Forming a line on the ground, the 46th Indiana opened fire and checked Green's troopers as they charged into Buzzard Prairie in hot pursuit of Nims's 2nd Massachusetts Battery, which enabled Marland to form on Bringhurst's right and turn his 6-pounder rifles on the charging Confederate cavalry. Accompanied by rapid fire from the 46th Indiana, they drove Green's troopers back into the woods and beyond. Burbridge's remaining troops then formed a line with Nims's Battery and the remainder of the 17th Ohio Battery as Cameron and Slack's brigades arrived. Federal accounts differ, but at this point Harai Robinson's 1st Louisiana Cavalry (U.S.) charged up the ravine while troops from Burbridge's new line fixed bayonets and drove Roberts's Texans out of the woods; chasing them a mile or two, they captured sixty-five. Back at Carrion Crow Bayou, Confederate cavalry attacked Washburn's camp but were driven off by the 11th Indiana, 29th Wisconsin and 24th Iowa left behind to protect the camp.[46]

Casualties reported officially on both sides were about even except for the number of captured or missing. The Federals reported 25 killed, 129 wounded, and 562 captured or missing; the Confederates reported 22 killed, 103 wounded, and 55 missing.[47]

Of his retreat in the face of Cameron's reinforcements, Green, who had already sent his 562 prisoners north to his camp near Opelousas, reported: "Deeming it imprudent to fight this large additional force, after a warm skirmish, I withdrew slowly and without loss, the enemy not attempting to follow me." Roberts also claimed that his infantry "withdrew in good order" up the Bellevue Road with the 15th Texas acting as rear guard.[48]

On the Federal side, Bringhurst and Swigart agreed with the Confederate account. They noted that the 46th Indiana had arrived first and, with the regrouped 2nd Massachusetts Battery, had effectively driven the Confederates back into the woods. Ordered to await the arrival of Slack's brigade, however, they did not pursue. By the time Slack arrived, they claimed that the Confederates had already escaped up the road to Opelousas.[49]

On the other hand, Slack, in a letter to Ann, wrote:

> In about two hours word came to us that he [Burbridge] was attacked driven across the bayou and most of his command captured or killed. Immediately we formed and moved to his aid. When within a half mile of him I formed and moved up directly to his left and in his line, or rather in a line with him, and just to the left of his battery. His Battery was belching forth on the enemy very rapidly. The moment I struck his left we all moved forward most gallantly. We were then about a half mile from the woods skirting the bayou, when within about 400 yards I moved at double quick, the skirmishers about 100 yards in advance firing as they ran.
>
> Our effort was to get possession of the skirt of woods for protection. The men met it with a yell. With fixed bayonets they looked irresistible. As soon as we struck the woods, the rebs about 200 yards in front, broke and ran. Then the foot race began. We ran them about a mile, and took about 100 prisoners. They were very fleet. Our [Burbridge's] loss was about 450; killed 25, wounded 100, prisoners 325. I did not have a man touched in my Brigade. Genl Cameron had three wounded. The loss occurred to Genl Burbridge before we reached him. Had we went out when first formed in the morning would have saved him entirely.
>
> The rebel force was about 5000, as near as could be estimated. The 67th Indiana was almost wholly captured. They lost their flag which I recaptured with my own hands. Have it yet. Will send it to them the first opportunity. Burbridge had most of his camp burned. As we were advancing to his relief, his wagon train came over the prairie in a perfect stampede, wagons

filled with great healthy men with their guns in their hands, teams in a full run, negroes eyes nearly all white, looking back over their shoulders. I abused the cowardly pups as much as I had time and ability to do, but they took no offence at it. Our boys jeered them a great deal. It was a novel sight indeed. I do not believe we will have a fight here amounting to anything. How long we will remain in this camp is a matter of uncertainty. Am inclined to the opinion we will go to Texas, but when or which route is yet wrapped in mystery and uncertainty. Think myself we will go by the gulf, but in that may be mistaken.[50]

Lending some credence to Slack's account, Marland of the 2nd Massachusetts Battery wrote that after forming on the right of Bringhurst's 46th Indiana and checking Green's cavalry advance, he led his light horse artillery "back through the woods with General Cameron's command, driving the enemy in disorder." They, he added, "left their dead and wounded on the field."[51]

Also supporting Slack's account, Dr. T.J. Woods, surgeon of the 96th Ohio, agreed with Bringhurst and Swigart that the 46th Indiana had saved them, but agreed with Slack about the pursuit and capture of fleeing Confederates. He closed with a sentiment that probably best summarized the Federal view of the battle:

> To our delight and surprise it is the Forty-sixth Indiana, whose colonel [Bringhurst], hearing the roar of battle, instantly formed his command, and waiting for no orders, with the instincts of a true soldier, had marched at double-quick, and halting for a moment to take breath, found the opportunity to save us from utter annihilation. We join these brave comrades and charge upon the line of gray and steel, with a cheer. A short sharp struggle with the bayonet, they flee through our camp so swiftly that they find no time to disturb anything.
>
> For two long miles we pursue them, then return to our camp, both humiliated by defeat and exultant by victory.[52]

A truce was called after the battle and captured enlisted men who were wounded and hospitalized at a Mrs. Rogers's plantation near Opelousas were returned to their units. The truce over, Franklin withdrew his force and headed south for the breastworks at New Iberia; Green's cavalry continued to dog their footsteps, capturing or killing the occasional forager.[53]

Back in New Orleans, Banks understood that his failed attack at Sabine Pass and Franklin's foray into south Louisiana had at least forced Magruder to shift most of his available troops to east Texas and had left the mouth of the Rio Grande virtually unprotected. In perhaps his best military move, on 27 October, the same day Franklin ended his failed Bayou Teche Campaign, Banks set sail from the mouth of the Mississippi on over twenty transports, both sail and steam, convoyed by the gunboats *Monongahela*, *Owasco*, and *Virginia*, for the town of Brazos Santiago, Texas, on the island of the same name at the mouth of the Rio Grande, just below present-day South Padre Island. Banks had with him an infantry force of about 4,000, commanded by Major General Napoleon J.T. Dana and made up of Dana's 2nd division of the 13th corps, the 13th and 15th Maine Volunteers, Col. Edmund Davis' 1st Texas Cavalry (U.S.), and the 1st and 16th Regiments, Corps d'Afrique.[54]

Notified by Magruder that a Federal flotilla was heading his way, Hamilton Bee, left with only several regiments of cavalry, evacuated Fort Brown. Heading north to King's Ranch, his troopers burned all the cotton and equipment they could not haul away. Unfortunately, embers from the fire ignited 8,000 pounds of powder in the garrison and sparked an explosion and fire that destroyed several blocks in Brownsville.[55]

Accompanied by the three gunboats, a gale and rough seas gave Dana's troops more opposition than Bee's remaining cavalry. Arriving off the Rio Grande on 1 November, they spent the next several days landing the troops on Brazos Island in rough waters. On 6 November, after crossing to the mainland and driving Capt. Richard Taylor's cavalry regiment from Point Isabel, Dana's 2nd brigade marched upriver about thirty miles and occupied now evacuated and partially burned Brownsville.[56]

Meanwhile, on 4 November, the Federal gunboats surprised and seized four British trading vessels (the schooner *Matamoras*, the brig *Volante*, the bark *Science*, and the brig *Dashing Wave*) anchored off the mouth of the Rio Grande in American waters. They were found to be carrying Confederate uniforms, gray cloth, boots, shoes, and blankets, much of which was hidden inside cotton bales, and all bound for Bee's command at Brownsville. Seized as blockade-runners, they were taken to Commodore H.H. Bell, U.S. Navy, commanding the West Gulf Blockading Squadron on board the U.S. Steam Sloop *Pensacola* at the mouth of the Mississippi River and escorted upriver to the U.S. Prize Court in New Orleans for adjudication.[57]

Banks's unexpected arrival on the Rio Grande and occupation of Brownsville also upset the political situation across the river in Matamoros and led to a takeover of Matamoros by Juan Cortina.

With the French invasion of Mexico in 1862, Cortina had joined Juarez to fight the French Imperialists and their Mexican Royalist allies. By late summer 1863, he had risen to the rank of lieutenant colonel of cavalry and was sent to Matamoras in command of a cavalry force. A fight erupted between the Juarez republicans and Mexican royalists at Matamoros, and the arrival of the U.S. Army at Brownsville opened the door for Cortina to take control of the town and the Mexican side of the river. The combination of the U.S. Army in Brownsville and Cortina in Matamoros temporarily shut down those two towns as a transit point for Confederate trade with Europe and forced the Confederates to rely on Gov. Santiago Vidaurri of Coahuila and Nuevo Leon to keep upriver sites open to them at Eagle Pass and Laredo. The U.S. consul in Matamoros was also now able to relay covert information to guerrilla bands supporting Juarez so they could attack and hopefully seize arms shipments or other goods heading to Eagle Pass and Laredo.[58]

Banks also sent Cadwallader Washburn, recently arrived from Bayou Teche via Algiers, Louisiana, aboard the steamer *Clifton*, to occupy the Texas coast as far as Pass Cavallo. Washburn brought with him aboard the *Clifton* Col. Henry D. Washburn's 1st brigade of the 1st division. Brig. Gen. T.E.G. Ransom followed with the 3rd brigade of the 2nd division, also from the 13th corps. Not part of the Teche Campaign, Ransom's brigade had been stationed at the Mississippi River town of Morganza, Louisiana. On 17 November, facing little opposition, Ransom's brigade, operating in cooperation with the gunboat *Monongahela*, captured Mustang Island and the Confederate battery on the northern end at Aransas Pass, which guarded the entrance to Corpus Christi Bay, and five days later assisted Washburn's brigade in the capture of Fort Esperanza at Pass Cavallo on the northern tip of Matagorda Island, which guarded the entrance to Matagorda Bay. A land force with wagons moved upriver to Rio Grande City and captured 82 bales of cotton.[59]

Banks, in fact, accomplished the task that Lincoln, Stanton, and Halleck had deemed so important—he now occupied the lower Rio Grande; he had interdicted at least some supplies entering the Confederacy; and he had driven Bee's Confederates inland. Hamilton Bee himself reported from Corpus Christi in November that he believed a recent mutiny among Texas cavalry on the Rio Grande had the stamp of the U.S. consul in Matamoras, which felt more secure now that the U.S. Army occupied Brownsville, and was also connected to Cortina's takeover of Matamoras. "The worst condition imaginable," Bee reported, "now exists on the Rio Grande."[60]

Back on the failed Bayou Teche Campaign, on 15 November, Franklin ordered McGinnis to move his 3rd division of the 13th corps to New Iberia. On 17 November at New Iberia, the 7th Texas Cavalry attacked a detail of two wagons and ten men from the 47th Indiana who were out about a mile and a half from camp foraging for wood. The Texans captured "seven of the men and the two teams," although three men escaped.[61]

In retaliation for the attack on their foraging detail and the capture of five foragers from the 46th Indiana, on 20 November Albert L. Lee led two brigades of cavalry and the horse artillery of Nims's 2nd Massachusetts Battery in a predawn raid on the 7th Texas Cavalry's camp near Spanish Lake, about six miles north of New Iberia. After a "lively skirmish" Lee's troopers captured "12 commissioned officers, 101 enlisted men, 100 horses and equipments, and about 100 stand of arms of all kinds." Cameron's infantry brigade moved in support, but the cavalry attack was so quick they did not arrive in time to take part in the action.[62]

Four days later from New Orleans, Slack notified Ann that he had received his orders to report to Indiana for recruiting service and would be coming home via Havana and New York on the steamer *Evening Star*. She was to meet him in Philadelphia.[63]

Meanwhile, the winds of war shifted again in late November as Grant's force at Chattanooga drove Bragg's Army of Tennessee off Missionary Ridge and into north Georgia, Hooker's pursuit and near capture of Bragg's retreating Confederates stopped only by the determined stand of Cleburne's division at Ringgold Gap. A few days later, Sherman's force entered Knoxville, ending Longstreet's siege there. With that, Grant moved his headquarters to Nashville and both armies went into winter quarters: the Federals in east Tennessee and the Confederates in north Georgia, where Joe Johnston arrived to take command of the Army of Tennessee.[64]

Slack's brigade remained with McGinnis's division in New Iberia; and, with both Slack and McLaughlin in Indiana on recruiting service, Maj. Lewis Goodwin took temporary command of the 47th Indiana.

Slack's detail of recruiters arrived at Indianapolis on 18 December 1863 and the next day the *Daily Journal* reported their arrival, including a description of life on Bayou Teche:

Our 47th Regiment

A detail of some ten or twelve officers, commissioned and non-commissioned, from our 47th regiment, Col. James R. Slack, arrived in this city yesterday, on recruiting service, under the immediate direction of Lieut. Col. McLaughlin. Capt. Harding and Lieutenant Johnson of the party called upon us, while they were in the city, and from them we learn that this regiment is in excellent condition, delightfully situated, and in high spirits. It is encamped near Iberia, Louisiana, in the region of Bayou Teche, where the climate is so nearly tropical that when the party left camp roses were in bloom, and everything showed the verdure and beauty of spring. The health of the men was so good that but one dose of medicine had been issued by the Surgeon in the last ten days, and *every* man was fit for duty. There were no sick at all. This is a pleasant showing for those who want to join this veteran and gallant regiment, which bears on its flag the names of as many victories as any in the Army of the Gulf. Col. Slack, who is also at home, will, we understand, give all his efforts to recruiting, and we trust he may speedily fill his ranks full. Recruits can't well find a better regiment, a better location, or a more competent and kindly set of officers.[65]

With most of the 13th corps on the Rio Grande and the lower Texas coast, McGinnis' 3rd division (Cameron's and Slack's brigades) remained on Bayou Teche. From their camp near New Iberia in early December, a soldier of the 11th Indiana wrote a letter to the *Indianapolis Daily Gazette* in which he described the beauty and richness of the countryside and, perhaps inadvertently, explained why the residents along Bayou Teche disliked the Hoosiers at least as much as they disliked the Nutmegs.

LETTER FROM THE GULF

A friend has kindly shown us an interesting letter from a member of the 11th Ind. dated "New Iberia, La, Dec. 12, 1863," from which we take the following extracts:

Our Division, the 3rd, is all that is left of the 13th army corps. The 19th army corps is with us. Some of the boys who have been down to New Orleans say the river Teche is just lined with sugar and molasses. Our regiment went out five miles yesterday and got 90 hogsheads of sugar and 80 barrels of molasses. This was last year's crop. How sullen the old planters looked when we took it!

This is beautiful country — nature has done a great deal for it; the ground is very level and rich and pasture in any quantity. The streams here are nearly all navigable. You would think a man crazy to hear him talk of running a steamer in the Teche if you did not see it. It is not wider than Fall Creek and so full of what is called Pond reed that it is entirely covered in some places, and Vermillion Bayou is still smaller, but they are very deep and straight and navigable. There is only one place within thirty miles of here where a steamer can turn round.

I can hardly imagine that it is winter — it is warm and the birds sing in the morning as if it were spring. The timber here is principally live oak and evergreen. The trees are covered with Spanish Moss, which hangs down in large bunches. I believe the live oak is the most beautiful tree I ever saw. I saw one, the branches of which were sixty and seventy feet long, and I could reach the lower limb any where, it grew so close to the ground. All the regiment could sit under the tree.

Our brigade captured a lot of rebs the other day and I tell you they looked more like a lot of ragamuffins than any thing else. We have a splendid Brass band with us — Earl Reid, of the old Indianapolis City Grey's Band is the leader, and he is a good musician. Our regiment is getting a new Zouave uniform made in New York City — blue instead of red pants. Major George Butler has command of the Regiment. Col. Dan Macauley is in command of the brigade. The health of the troops here is better than ever before — all the men are fit for duty.

A happy New Year to you all and don't forget me when you are carving the turkey.
Your Soldier Friend.[66]

On 16 December 1863 at New Iberia, 409 soldiers of the 47th Indiana, most of the regiment, re-enlisted as veteran volunteers. Moving to Algiers three days later, they were paid $402 and officially mustered in as veterans on New Years' Day 1864 while awaiting their 39-day veteran furloughs home.[67]

XII

New Orleans and the Red River Campaign (January–June 1864)

Back in Indiana at the beginning of the presidential election year, politics had heated to a boil. Illustrating the political divide that existed not only in Indiana but in the rest of the North as well, the antiwar *Indiana State Sentinel* cited what they considered to be the Lincoln administration's violations of the Constitution.

Among the violations cited were arrests being made in the state for "utterances of sentiments distasteful to the men of power" in violation of freedom of speech; the suppression of newspapers for publishing dissenting political views in violation of freedom of the press; suspension of habeas corpus and violations of the right to security from arrest without charge or trial; unlawful search and seizure; and the replacement of civilian courts and juries with military tribunals. The *State Sentinel* also complained that the 1863 Conscription Act had violated the right of states to manage their own militias; and, in support of their Southern brethren, that the Emancipation Proclamation had violated property rights. One month later, President Lincoln, acting under the congressional conscription act, ordered 500,000 new troops to be drafted for three years or the duration of the war, guaranteeing that the draft, despised especially in the rural counties, would be an election issue in this presidential election year.[1]

Riding the tide of antiwar and antidraft sentiments, earlier in 1863 Phineas Wright had succeeded in recruiting Harrison H. Dodd, an Indianapolis printer and publisher, and Dr. William A. Bowles, a wealthy French Lick, Indiana, physician and well-known Southern sympathizer, to set up lodges of the O.A.K. In January 1864, leading antiwar publisher Benjamin Wood hired Wright as an editor of the *New York Daily News*, although by this time Wright had fallen out of favor with leading midwestern antiwar Democrats, who had come to view him and his organization as a "humbug." Dodd attempted to fill the void by concocting his own secret organization based on the old O.A.K. cells he and Wright had set up in Indiana and whose purpose, as a faction of the Democratic Party, would be to nominate a more antiwar or "peace" candidate than the favored moderate General George B. McClellan, as well as to counter the electoral activities of the secret Republican Union or Liberty Leagues. Hoping to evoke the patriotic spirit of 1776 image, he chose to call his organization the "Sons of Liberty."[2]

At a 22 February 1864 meeting of leading antiwar Democrats in New York City, the leading antiwar Democrats discarded Wright and his O.A.K. for Dodd's Sons of Liberty

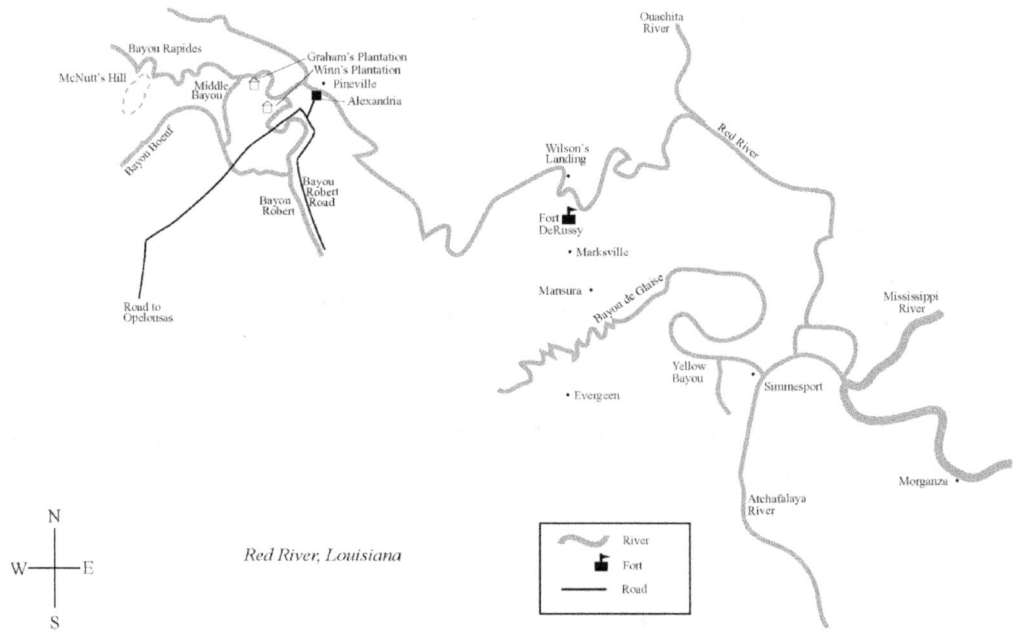

From Atlas Plate LII, No. 1 (lower half)

concept. On his way back to Indianapolis, Dodd stopped off at Windsor, Canada, and persuaded Clement Vallandigham, still in exile in there, to be the nominal "Supreme Commander," with Dodd the "Grand Commander" in Indiana. In Indiana, Dodd was able to recruit antiwar radicals into his largely paper organization, then made up a "military arm" and named Dr. David T. Yeakel, Bowles, Andrew Humphreys and Lambdin P. Milligan, Esq., as "major generals." Only Yeakel and Bowles ever admitted knowledge of the military arm, and John C. Walker soon replaced Yeakel; Milligan and Humphreys swore they knew nothing of their appointments as "major generals."[3]

As they entered the new year, Morton, increasingly worried about his reelection chances and the prospect of being prosecuted for his extralegal maneuvers as governor if he lost, ordered Carrington to recruit more "confidential agents" and to step up his surveillance of Dodd, Bowles, and the others who were outspoken opponents of the war and of his administration. Samuel P. Heintzelman, commanding the Northern Department, which included the Districts of Indiana, Michigan, and Ohio, had assembled a motley crew of spies to infiltrate the various antiwar societies, and he and his district commanders like Carrington were usually tipped off in advance of any move or plan. Wright, ostensibly traveling to Detroit for the *New York Daily News,* was arrested on 27 April 1864 by the military at Detroit and remained in military custody for the remainder of the war without charge or trial.[4]

Back in Louisiana, the lucky homeward-bound soldiers of the 47th Indiana waited in camp at Algiers for their veteran furloughs. Their less fortunate comrades from Slack's old 2nd brigade (the 24th and 28th Iowa and 56th Ohio), whose veteran furloughs had been postponed, moved from Carrollton to Madisonville on the north shore of Lake Pontchartrain. All they could do there was sit and wait with the 46th Indiana, the only regiment remaining from the 1st brigade, while Halleck devised his ill-conceived plan to send Banks's army on a land and river expedition up the barely navigable Red River.⁵ Writing from their camp at Algiers, Chaplain Sawyer described how both the citizens of New Orleans and the area sugar and cotton planters were coping with the novel free labor system. And the forthcoming statewide elections, he noted, indicated that progress was being made on the president's request to "re-construct" Louisiana and bring it back into the Union as soon as possible.

THE FORTY-SEVENTH—AGRICULTURAL SLAVERY AND FREEDOM—POLITICS
CORRESPONDENCE OF THE *INDIANAPOLIS JOURNAL*
ALGIERS, LA., FEBRUARY 6, 1864

Our letters from home bring us word that you are having weather intensely cold in Indiana, but here it is delightful. It may sound odd, yet it is fine weather for gardening, and for two weeks the people of the city have a run at it. The spade and the hoe are in great demand. Many of the contrabands having left their old homes, their white and Creole owners must take up their trade and "do" their own horticulture. They work awkwardly, like all new beginners, but they will doubtless improve under good practice. The Gordian knot has been effectually cut by the sword, and the question of the last half-century, "What shall be done with the Negro?" is answering itself. The condition of the colored people in this Department is as prosperous as could be expected under all the circumstance. In the main they are sober, peaceable, industrious and thrifty. The men find no difficulty in getting remunerative employment. The women, toward whom the former slaveholders are particularly spiteful, by washing, cooking, street vending, and in various ways, earn a comfortable support. Sugar and cotton planters adjacent to the city pay from eight to fifteen dollars per month for male and female hands, and in consequence the Superintendent of Freedmen informed me that he seldom had over two hundred contrabands, all told, drawing rations from the government. He is unable to supply the growing demand for plantation hands. Capital and labor are thus adjusting themselves to the confusion of rebels and copperheads.

With the exception of a dozen or two, the entire 47th Indiana Volunteers have enlisted into the veteran service. It was most gratifying to see the unanimity with which the officers and men came forward at the country's call to serve during the war. General Ord ordered the regiment to report to Governor Morton for furlough, and they are now awaiting transportation "homeward bound." The paymaster has paid us his bi-monthly visit, with plenty of the "needful," and in excellent health and spirits, the men are waiting, on the *qui vive*, for the boat to bear them to their beloved State.

Some secession rebel fired the premises adjoining the building where the paymaster was paying the regiment, hoping, no doubt, in the confusion, to make a handsome thing of it, but veterans know how to handle traitors, and the flames were extinguished after two or three small frame houses had been burned.

Quartermaster Nichol feeling that his present interest and duty required his presence at home, sent in his resignation, which has been accepted. He has been a most faithful and exemplary officer. One or two others have tendered their resignations, but their papers have returned "disapproved."

The boat upon which we expected to embark has been taken by the Medical Director for the sick, but hope to be at Cairo in ten days, and thence, soon as practicable, to Indianapolis. The officers of the regiment sent home to gather recruits will doubtless be there with many others to greet us.

The Free State men of Louisiana could not agree in their nominees. The bolters, though in the minority, nominated a ticket of their own. It is thought that a third ticket, brought out by the "unimpassioned" conservatives, will be put in the field. But in the present condition of things division is strength, for the friends of each ticket will rally as many as possible to the support of their respective candidates, and thus perhaps several thousand additional voters will take the oath of allegiance and commit themselves to the policy of Freedom, that they may take

part in the re-construction of the State under the most favorable auspices for themselves and the men of their choice. Mr. Hahn, the choice of the Free State Convention, will address the citizens of Algiers tonight. If elected he says that with his consent there shall not be a slave in Louisiana after the 22d of February next. He is the people's man, and will no doubt be chosen.
Yours, very truly, Samuel Sawyer
Chaplain, 47th Indiana Vols.[6]

As Sawyer noted, three candidates contested the race for governor in the 22 February elections. Michael Hahn, Esq., ran on the "Free State" ticket. A native of Bavaria, Germany, Hahn graduated from the University of Louisiana (now Tulane University) with a law degree, served one term as a "Unionist" representative in the 37th U.S. Congress, and was the "prize commissioner" in New Orleans when he ran for governor. Benjamin Franklin Flanders, a partisan of the Secretary of the Treasury Salmon D. Chase faction of the Republican Party, the candidate of the "bolters" as Sawyer called them, ran on the "Radical" ticket. A graduate of Dartmouth College, Flanders studied law at the University of Louisiana, served one term as the other "Unionist" representative from Louisiana in the 37th U.S. Congress, and in 1863 returned to New Orleans and was appointed special agent of the U.S. Treasury Department for the southern district. After the war, Flanders was military governor of Louisiana in 1867 and 1868 and mayor of New Orleans from 1870 to 1872. The third candidate, New Orleans attorney John A.Q. Fellows, Esq., ran on the "Conservative" or "Copperhead" ticket. Reflecting the proportion of the state under Federal control, 10,218 votes were cast in a contest that would have normally drawn about 40,000. Hahn won by a landslide, garnering sixty percent (6,153); Fellows came in second with twenty-one percent (2,144); and Flanders finished third with nineteen percent (1,921).[7]

On 9 February 1864, the 47th Indiana's orders arrived to report to Gov. Morton in Indianapolis on veteran furlough. Embarking on the steamer *Continental*, they reached Indianapolis on Friday, 19 February, where the public greeted them, and Col. John A. Keith's 21st Indiana Volunteers (1st Heavy Artillery), as heroes. Hahn's National Band played "patriotic airs" and led the way up Washington and New Jersey Streets to the Soldier's Home, the 21st Indiana behind the band pulling three cannons they had captured, followed by the 47th Indiana and the six-month volunteers of the 118th Indiana, all with their banners flying in a stiff breeze on the bitterly cold day. Following a huge dinner at the Home, the column of soldiers followed Hahn's Band and the captured artillery down Washington Street to the Metropolitan Theater on Jay Street for a formal reception attended by Governor Morton, Mayor Cavan, and A.P. Hovey.[8]

Describing their departure from Indianapolis the next day, the *Daily Journal* noted: "The Forty-Seventh Regiment left the City on Saturday for home [Huntington, Wabash, Bluffton, and their other 11th Congressional District towns in northeastern Indiana], going over the Bellefontaine road. They were escorted to the depot by Hahn's excellent band, and marched to the music of 'Home, Sweet Home,' 'Hail Columbia,' etc., making a splendid appearance and drawing hundreds in the street to see them."[9]

Meanwhile, on the military front that month, McClernand's career was temporarily resuscitated and he was ordered to report to Banks at New Orleans. About a week later he was ordered to Pass Cavallo, Texas, to replace E.O.C. Ord in command of the 13th corps, or at least the two divisions that remained there, and to "assume control of military affairs on the coast and frontier of Texas." In January, Ord, who had resumed command of the

13th corps in Texas following his illness, objected to McClernand's return and was reassigned to the War Department in Washington. Napoleon J.T. Dana assumed command of the 1st division at Pass Cavallo and Francis T. Herron the 2nd division at Brownsville. In March, Cadwallader C. Washburn left Texas to take temporary command of the post at Annapolis before moving to Memphis a month later to assume command of the District of Western Tennessee.[10]

Brig. Gen. Thomas E.G. Ransom, who had been in command of the 4th division at Decrow's Point (Pass Cavallo), Texas, on the tip of Matagorda Peninsula, was ordered to Louisiana to take part in Banks's Red River Campaign in command the 13th corps detachment (the 3rd and 4th divisions) in William B. Franklin's largely 19th corps column. In Ransom's 13th corps detachment, Brig. Gen. Robert A. Cameron was assigned command of McGinnis's old 3rd division, whose unlucky veterans had had their furloughs postponed. Lt. Col. Aaron Flory commanded the 1st brigade, which consisted of only the 46th Indiana and 29th Wisconsin. Col. William H. Raynor of the 56th Ohio commanded Slack's old 2nd brigade, which consisted of the 24th and 28th Iowa, and 56th Ohio. The 3rd division's artillery was made up of Battery A of the 1st Missouri Light Artillery (Lt. Elisha Cole), and the 2nd Ohio Artillery (Lt. William A. Harper). Col. William J. Landrum of the 19th Kentucky replaced Ransom in command of the 4th division.[11]

Back at Vicksburg in February, Sherman, who had returned following the year-end campaign in east Tennessee, turned his attention to driving what remained of Joe Johnston's old army out of the state and to breaking up the Southern and the Mobile & Ohio Railroads "at and about Meridian." Leonidas "Warrior Bishop" Polk commanded the remaining two infantry divisions in Mississippi, one under "Old Blizzards" Loring at Canton, the other under Samuel G. French at Brandon, a cavalry division under Stephen D. Lee, and Nathan Bedford Forrest's semi-independent cavalry force of about 2,500 in north Mississippi.[12]

Sherman's column, which consisted of two divisions each from the 16th and 17th corps, had no problem pushing Polk's infantry and Lee's cavalry across the state. Facing only minor resistance from Lee's troopers, Sherman's column arrived at Meridian on the afternoon of 14 February. French's division had evacuated the night before, Loring's that very morning, both crossing the Tombigbee River covered by Lee's cavalry; and Polk himself skedaddled to Demopolis, Alabama, at 10:30 A.M. on the last rail car out. Federal troops destroyed the town and Sherman was able to report: "Meridian, with its depots, store-houses, arsenal, hospitals, officers, hotels, and cantonments no longer exists."[13]

It was a different story for Sooy Smith's 7,000-man 16th corps cavalry division, which included troopers under the vaunted Benjamin Grierson. Moving southeastward from Memphis, they were to turn southward at Okalona and destroy the Mobile & Ohio Railroad and bridges before rendezvousing with Sherman's column at Meridian and a possible pursuit of Polk. Smith's column started about a week late, however; and, on 22 February a detachment ran into Forrest's cavalry near West Point, Mississippi, some thirty miles south of Okalona and ninety miles north of Meridian. Forrest's troopers routed the detachment, although they were able to recover and reunite with the remainder of Smith and Grierson's much larger Federal force, which had been unconcerned about attack and carelessly overextended. The entire Federal force retreated northward in a fiercely contested running battle and staved off disaster in the hills between Okalona and Pontotoc when Forrest withdrew for want of ammunition and fresh horses.[14]

Returning to Memphis, Smith left Forrest free to roam the countryside from north Mississippi to the Ohio River and left Sherman sitting in now-ruined Meridian, irritated by Smith's failure to appear and his own inability to pursue Polk without cavalry. Although frustrated, Sherman wrote his wife to say famously that he had at least "scared the Bishop out of his senses."[15]

Disgusted with Smith's slowness and ineptitude, Sherman returned to Vicksburg and traveled to New Orleans to confer with Banks about Henry Halleck's planned joint expedition up the Red River with Rear Admiral Porter's Mississippi Squadron. Halleck, who had remained focused on Texas, remained convinced that Shreveport was the key to that state, in spite of the fact that Banks had already established a base at Brownsville from which new troops could have taken control of the entire Rio Grande Valley and effectively blocked trade between Kirby Smith and the Europeans without another expedition and without risking the loss of Porter's gunboat fleet on the barely navigable Red River.[16]

Banks, at the president's request, remained in New Orleans to assist the transition to a civilian government, and he placed William Franklin in charge of the march to Alexandria. Sherman, who agreed that a "quick dash" up the Red River was a good idea, sent Andrew J. Smith with a detachment from his Army of the Tennessee (the 1st and the 3rd divisions of the 16th corps under Joseph Mower and Thomas Kilby Smith's division from the 17th corps) to move up the Red River from its mouth on the Mississippi on transports protected by Porter's gunboat fleet. Franklin's column (the 1st and 2nd divisions of his 19th corps; the 1st brigade and engineers, an infantry and an engineer brigade from the Corps d'Afrique; Albert Lee's cavalry division, and the reduced 3rd and 4th division detachment from the 13th corps commanded by Thomas E.G. Ransom) was to retrace their steps up Bayou Teche and on to Alexandria, where they would link with A.J. Smith's column and move to Shreveport under Banks's command. In Arkansas, Frederick Steele would complete the sweep of Kirby Smith's Trans-Mississippi Confederates by moving against Sterling Price's force in southwest Arkansas before linking with Banks at Shreveport.[17]

On 12 March, Porter's flotilla of gunboats convoyed A. J. Smith's troops onboard transports up the Red River to Simmesport, Louisiana, on the Atchafalaya River about ten miles from the Mississippi and five miles from its junction with the Red, where the troops disembarked and the gunboat crews began removing obstructions placed in the river by the departing Confederates. Two days later on the Red River, about thirty miles above Simmesport, Mower's 16th corps division captured Fort De Russy and opened the river to Porter's flotilla, which, having to deal with obstructions in the river, did not participate in the attack. With the obstructions cleared and Fort De Russy captured, however, Porter's gunboats moved up to Alexandria the next day and A.J. Smith's troops occupied the town on 16 March as Richard Taylor's Confederate District of West Louisiana troops continued to fall back to Shreveport under orders from Kirby Smith, who called up what few reinforcements he had from Arkansas and Texas to meet the threat.[18]

Franklin's column, which had gathered at Berwick City, set out on 14 March on its return trip up Bayou Teche, with Albert Mouton and Thomas Green's Louisiana Confederates falling back toward Kirby Smith's headquarters at Shreveport without offering resistance. Albert Lee's cavalry, at the head of Franklin's column, arrived at Alexandria on 16 March without opposition.[19]

As Banks's Red River Campaign got underway, the War Department announced a

XII. New Orleans and the Red River Campaign (January–June 1864)

major shift in command and military strategy. On 12 March 1864, Halleck stepped aside to become the top aide to Stanton in the War Department and was replaced by Grant, who received a commission as Lieutenant General and commander of all the armies of the United States. With that, all the Federal armies in the field came under one commander for the first time. Now completely in charge, Grant took direct command of Meade's Army of the Potomac, which was reinforced by Burnside's 9th corps, and Butler's Army of the James. On 17 March, he assigned Sherman to command of the Military Division of the Mississippi, which included the Armies of the Cumberland, Ohio, Tennessee, and Arkansas, or all the territory north of Natchez and east of the Alleghenies.[20]

No longer looking to encircle and strangle the Confederacy as envisioned in the old "Anaconda Plan," Grant planned instead to directly attack the two principal Confederate armies in the field: Robert E. Lee's Army of Northern Virginia, which still guarded Richmond on the south bank of the Rapidan in essentially the same position they held when the war began; the other, the Army of Tennessee, now commanded by Joe Johnston, which, ensconced in the hills of north Georgia, guarded the approach to Atlanta from Chattanooga. Grant would spearhead the attack against Lee's defense of Richmond; Sherman the attack on Johnston's army in Georgia.[21]

Although Grant had opposed Halleck's plan to send Banks and Porter up the Red River (as did Banks initially), by the time that he took command of all the armies on 17 March, the campaign had already gotten underway successfully. Expecting Banks to make quick work on the Red, he told Banks to proceed with all dispatch, and, as soon as he arrived in Shreveport, to return A.J. Smith's troops to Sherman, who needed them for his upcoming campaign against Joe Johnston in Georgia. In fact, Grant added with some urgency that Banks was to return Sherman's troops as soon as possible "even if it leads to the abandonment of your expedition." On return, Banks was to take his own troops to New Orleans and prepare for an operation against Mobile. Frederick Steele would remain in Shreveport in command of the defense of the Red River.[22]

Early Federal success on the Red River continued on the evening of 21 March at Henderson's Hill, about twenty-four miles above Alexandria on Bayou Rapides, when Mower's 16th corps infantry and Lee's cavalry surprised and captured most of the 2nd Louisiana Cavalry (CSA), Taylor's only cavalry until Thomas Green's division arrived from Texas, and Edgar's Texas Battery, including some 250 prisoners, four pieces of artillery with caissons, and 200 horses.[23]

Three days later Banks arrived in Alexandria via steamer and took command of the expedition. The next day, 25 March, Franklin's infantry arrived, having retraced its steps up Bayou Teche and beyond. On 28 March, Banks, his entire command overconfident from lack of resistance from Taylor's Confederates, remained behind and sent Franklin's column northwestward toward Monett's Ferry, which was about thirty-six miles above Alexandria on the Cane River, just above its lower mouth on the Red River. (Cane River was the name given to the old, narrow channel that formed when the Red River changed course at Grand Ecore, its "upper" mouth, and bypassed Natchitoches about five miles below. It paralleled the Red River from Natchitoches and reentered the Red at a point about thirty miles downriver, its "lower mouth," a few miles below Monett's Ferry.) From Monett's Ferry, they continued up the Cane another thirty miles to Natchitoches, arriving there on 1 April, almost seventy miles above Alexandria. That same day, Porter's navy pulled in at Grand Ecore.[24]

On 23 March in Arkansas, Steele began his march southward from Little Rock with his column of about 13,000, which included the 47th Indiana's old comrades in Frederick Salomon's 3rd division; John M. Thayer's Frontier Division, which included Arkansas and Kansas troops and the 1st and 2nd Kansas U.S. Colored Troops; and a division of cavalry led by Eugene A. Carr. They faced Sterling Price's force they had earlier driven into southwest Arkansas, which, following the withdrawal of Walker, Churchill, and Parsons's infantry divisions to join Taylor on the Red River, was made up of from 6,000 to 8,000 troopers from Maxey's, Marmaduke's, and Fagan's cavalry divisions.[25]

Back in Indiana at about this same time, the soldiers of the 47th Indiana, their veteran furloughs over, gathered at Indianapolis for their return to New Orleans and assignment to duty in the Defenses of New Orleans, commanded by Major General Joseph J. Reynolds.

Meanwhile, on 28 March 1864 in eastern Illinois, tensions between soldiers, especially Coles County soldiers from the 54th Illinois home on furlough, and Coles County Peace Democrats (Copperheads) erupted into violence. Although the heckling went both ways, at various times during the past year, soldiers of the 54th Illinois had been involved in a number of acts of harassment and violence against antiwar citizens in Coles County, primarily in the towns of Mattoon and Charleston. The harassment by soldiers included dragging known Peace Democrats off their wagons, making them kneel on the ground and swear allegiance to the United States. Two notable Peace Democrats, Circuit Court Judge Charles H. Constable, the same judge arrested in Illinois and taken into custody in Indiana by Col. Henry B. Carrington back in March 1863, and a Dr. J.W. Dora, both thoroughly disliked by county Republicans, were reportedly humiliated in this manner on 29 January 1864.[26]

Violence erupted the day after Judge Constable and Dr. Dora's humiliation at the hands of soldiers when a member of the 17th Illinois Cavalry reportedly shot and killed one Edward Stevens, a known Peace Democrat, on the streets of Mattoon. The 54th Illinois, in Mattoon since 12 February at the end of their veteran furlough, had also reportedly beaten two Peace Democrat citizens to death solely for their political views. Although the Republican *Mattoon Gazette* denied the charges, the editors admitted: "Soldiers have occasionally knocked down and dragged out a Copperhead, but none have ever been seriously injured with the exception of a common thief [Stevens] who was shot, sometime since, by a drunken soldier."[27]

In early March, two Charleston Peace Democrats had been severely beaten by soldiers; and, on 26 March, there had been another incident of violence by soldiers against two other known Peace Democrats only two days before "Court Day," which celebrated the opening of circuit court in Coles County. People came to town on Court Day to eat, drink, and listen to political speeches, in this case a Democratic Party rally. Unfortunately, the drink of choice was corn whiskey, a Coles County specialty. In anticipation of Court Day and with news that at least some of the 54th Illinois soldiers, whose furloughs had ended, would be in town to "clean up [Judge Constable's] Butternut Court," rumors spread rapidly that the Peace Democrats, or at least the more extreme Copperheads, would retaliate for the previous attacks.[28]

The cast of characters on Court Day included presiding Judge Charles H. Constable; John O'Hair, the county sheriff and noted Peace Democrat, whose duty had him in court to maintain order; Democratic Congressman John Eden, who was scheduled to speak at the Democratic rally; soldiers from the 54th Illinois; armed citizens from both parties, especially some Peace Democrats who had come to town with shotguns hidden under straw in their wagons; and plenty of corn whiskey.

With the whiskey flowing freely, by late in the afternoon an encounter between a Peace Democrat named Nelson Wells and a 54th Illinois soldier named Oliver Sallee, both armed with pistols, led to shots being fired. Who started the fight depends on whether the witness was a Republican or a Democrat. Words were said, a scuffle started, and both men drew pistols, although Wells apparently shot first, mortally wounding Sallee. Sallee, however, returned fire and killed Wells, sparking a widespread shootout, mostly among the armed citizenry of both parties.

The soldiers in the two companies of the 54th Illinois, not expecting trouble, had stacked arms and were at a decided disadvantage when the gunfire erupted, much of it aimed at them as they scurried for cover. Sheriff O'Hair exited the courthouse, ostensibly to help quell the disturbance, but quickly sided with the Peace Democrats in the melee and was said by Republican witnesses to have been seen shooting at soldiers. Colonel Greenville M. Mitchell of the 54th Illinois, who was in the courthouse when the shooting erupted, was wounded by gunfire when he exited the courthouse, and Major Shuball York, surgeon of the 54th Illinois, was shot and killed at close range as he exited behind Col. Mitchell in what was possibly a targeted assassination or revenge killing. (Conjecture that Maj. York had been targeted for assassination came from the fact that he was a member of a known Abolitionist family of Paris, Illinois, in adjacent Edgar County, and was reported by the *Chicago Tribune* to have been considered by the Republicans to be a likely candidate for Congress in the 7th District to run against John R. Eden, the incumbent Democrat who was to speak at the political rally on Court Day. York and Eden had allegedly exchanged some "heated remarks" a few days prior that had angered Peace Democrats. In addition, York's son Milton, of the 66th Illinois, had been involved in fight in Paris on 23 February and had shot and wounded a Copperhead named Cooper.[29])

Colonel Mitchell wired Lt. Col. Augustus H. Chapman, at Mattoon with the remainder of the 54th Illinois, for reinforcements. Assisted by armed citizens, Mitchell gathered what guns he could and rallied his small squad of soldiers. The gunfire was over in a matter of minutes, however, and the not-so-peaceful Democrats, including Sheriff O'Hair, dispersed across the courthouse square and fled northeast of town. At about 5:00 P.M., Chapman arrived with a squad of 250 soldiers; with assistance from citizen vigilantes, they gathered all the guns and horses they could find and chased after the supposed ringleaders.[30]

Many of the actual participants escaped, and some, including Sheriff O'Hair, reportedly fled to Canada. Nevertheless, squads of soldiers and vigilante Republican citizens rounded up over fifty Peace Democrats in a sweep of the Charleston and Mattoon areas and reportedly ransacked Sheriff O'Hair's home and the homes of other known Peace Democrats in the process. Mitchell reported twenty-seven rounded up near Charleston and the remainder at Mattoon. To his credit, Lt. Col. James Oakes of the 4th U.S. Cavalry, Assistant Provost Marshal-General of Illinois, released all but fourteen of those arrested at Charleston and all but two arrested at Mattoon for lack of evidence. The remaining sixteen were placed in military custody, sent to Mattoon and forwarded to Camp Yates in Springfield. One died in custody at Camp Yates and the remaining fifteen were quickly transferred to military prison at Camp Delaware in the State of Delaware.[31]

With Sheriff O'Hair's apparent complicity in the riot, rumors spread quickly that the disturbance had been part of a grand conspiracy to aid Nathan Bedford Forrest's Confederates. Forrest, after disposing of Sooy Smith's Federals in north Mississippi the month before, had come north and was now operating along the Ohio River, including a raid on Paducah, Kentucky, that same day.[32]

With their veteran furlough over, the 47th Indiana departed from Indianapolis on the railroad on 30 March at 4:00 P.M. At Terre Haute, Slack received word of the troubles in eastern Illinois and that his men were needed in Mattoon, where the citizenry were "in a state of excitement" over a supposed imminent attack on the town by a large body of armed Copperheads ostensibly to release the prisoners being held there. The 47th Indiana arrived in Mattoon at midnight and was joined by Col. Isaac C. Pugh's 41st Illinois, which had come down from Camp Butler at Springfield. Both regiments, under command of Col. James M. True of the 62nd Illinois, commander of the recruiting station at Mattoon, fanned out in the dark in search of the "rebels" who were supposedly south and southwest of town in great numbers. In the sweep, which also included citizen vigilantes, the 47th Indiana took the Terre Haute & Alton Railroad about twelve miles west, disembarked near Windsor, and marched three miles south to Price's Mill. On their sweep, Slack wrote Ann that they "found no enemy of any kind." Not surprisingly, Oakes reported that no "rebels" were found in their roughly twelve-mile sweep of the area, that they must have "dispersed." In fact, there was no grand conspiracy with Forrest and no proof that a raid had been planned to rescue the prisoners at Mattoon. The crisis over, the 47th Indiana returned to Mattoon that morning (31 March); and, with the Illinois troops garrisoning the town, they were permitted to continue onward to Cairo en route to New Orleans.[33]

Exact numbers of those rounded up in the two sweeps are difficult to determine, but it is known that most were released for lack of evidence and that fifteen were transferred to Fort Delaware, where a writ of habeas corpus, issued by the U.S. Circuit Court for their release to civil authorities, was refused by the military. They were held without charge or trial until 4 November 1864, when President Lincoln, still highly troubled by the civilian-versus-military judicial and jurisdictional conflicts that had followed his suspension of habeas corpus, ordered their release.

Replying to a 26 July 1864 query from Acting Judge Advocate General Addison A. Hosmer, President Lincoln ordered, not without a touch of irony: "Let these prisoners be sent back to Coles County, Ill., those indicted be surrendered to the sheriff of said county and the others be discharged." (It would, of course, have had to be to an acting sheriff since Sheriff O'Hair had fled.) Although the military had refused to turn over the prisoners prior to the president's orders, in June a Coles County grand jury, authorized by "Butternut" Judge Constable, had, in fact, handed down fourteen murder indictments. Only two people, however, were ever brought to trial and they were acquitted in court at Effingham on 7 December 1864. Most, including Sheriff O'Hair, returned to Coles County after the war without ever being prosecuted, although O'Hair was later murdered, apparently in retaliation for his part in the riot.[34]

The Republican newspapers blamed the Democrats. The *Chicago Tribune*, whose dispatches were widely circulated to Republican newspapers, blamed the riot on the brothers O'Hair. Warning that local offices could not be safely entrusted to Peace Democrats, the *Tribune*, in a special dispatch to the *New York Times*, added: "Two meaner tools of the rebellion cannot be found in Illinois than the two infamous brothers, Williams S. O'Hair, Sheriff of Edgar County, and John S. O'Hair, Sheriff of Coles County. Their father is the ex-Sheriff Mike O'Hair of Edgar, and both are 'chips off the old block.'" The *Tribune* editorial concluded that the three O'Hairs would be "far less dangerous to us in the rebel service" than in public office in the state.[35]

The next day, 31 March, an *Indianapolis Daily Gazette* editorial fueled the rumors that the riot at Charleston had been planned cooperation between "the Copperhead-Vallandigham Democracy of Southern Illinois" and Forrest's movements in Western Kentucky, which, they claimed, included a planned invasion of Illinois and Indiana. The *Daily Journal's* headlines also served to fuel the rumors of further Copperhead raids when they announced: "Copperhead War. Insurgents Entrenched. The Veterans Closing in on Them. Another Raid Threatened." That day, both newspapers published the same news dispatches from the *Chicago Tribune* that troops were assembling to prevent any further attacks. The *Daily Journal* noted more specifically that the 47th Indiana and the 41st and 54th Illinois were heading to Charleston to quell the riot; the *Daily Gazette* noted that the 47th Indiana had been ordered by Gen. Carrington to report to Col. Oakes at Mattoon "to assist in quelling the outbreak in that place."[36]

On 1 April, the *Daily Journal* published a 28 March "Extra" from the *Charleston Plain Dealer*, also widely distributed, which, in a detailed although one-sided account, blamed the riot on "squads of Copperheads" who had come to town "armed and determined upon summary vengeance against our soldiers." Although the *Plain Dealer's* dispatch admitted that the soldiers "were somewhat excited by liquor, and subsequently rather boisterous," they were "more disposed for fun than fight" and the belligerency was entirely the fault of the Copperheads. In a separate editorial in the same edition, the *Daily Journal*, acting essentially as Morton's mouthpiece, again raised the specter of a KGC conspiracy and its ties to the Democratic Party: "The miscreants are rebels, Knights of the Golden Circle, followers of Vallandigham and [Congressman Daniel W.] Voorhees and though they are not the Democratic party, they are a large part of it, and the most active part of it."[37]

The Democratic papers, of course, looked at the events differently. The *Chicago Times* referred to it only as a "row between drunken citizens and drunken soldiers." The *New York World* opined: "The troubles in the West are clearly due to an unhealthy public sentiment among Republicans countenancing drunken soldiers in insulting peaceable citizens." But the *Dayton Daily Empire*, Vallandigham's paper, called Sheriff O'Hair's actions "a legitimate effort of civil authority to protect against the encroachment of military usurpation."[38]

Shortly after steaming out of Cairo for New Orleans aboard the *Madison*, Slack was ordered to take the 47th Indiana back upriver to Paducah, where a week earlier, on 25 and 26 March, Forrest's Confederate cavalry had attacked Fort Anderson. Slack wrote Ann that, although "Col. Hicks & his command made a most gallant defence" of the fort, the town was "terribly shot up, nearly every house on the river front has a cannon shot through it." The "rebels," he explained, "got into those buildings and attempted shooting our gunners on the gunboat, when they [the gunboats] opened on the buildings, killed a great many, and drove them out," but not before "all the buildings within range of the fort were burned" as well as "a number of fine residences." Finding "no enemy ... nearer than thirty miles," Slack and his 47th Indiana troops resumed their trip to New Orleans.[39]

Back on the Red River by 3 April, Franklin's column was concentrated near Natchitoches. That same day, after struggling to get over the rapids at Alexandria, Porter's light-draft gunboats and twenty-six transports carrying A.J. Smith's troops and supplies arrived at Grand Ecore. Three days later, Albert Lee's cavalry led Franklin's column forward from Natchitoches on a narrow road through the piney woods toward Shreveport. In a blunder they would soon pay for, Franklin, not expecting any resistance until Shreveport, insisted that Lee place his 300-wagon supply train behind the cavalry and in front of the infantry column, which was led by Ransom's 13th corps detachment. On 7 April, A.J. Smith, with Mower's two 16th corps divisions, followed the 19th corps and the brigade of Colored Troops and remained a day's march behind. That same day, Kilby Smith's division moved up the Red River on transports convoyed by six of Porter's light-draft gunboats to link with Banks's infantry at Springfield Landing near Mansfield.[40]

In the meantime, Green's cavalry arrived from Texas, upping Taylor's total to about 11,000 troops, with 6,000 more troops from Churchill's and Parsons's divisions sent by Price from Arkansas within a day's march. Taylor quickly deployed his force (Walker's, Mouton's, and Green's divisions) in a good defensive position across the road at Sabine Cross Roads, just south of Mansfield. A detachment from Green's cavalry, sent out on reconnaissance, encountered Lee's Federal cavalry and skirmished on 7 April at Wilson's Farm near Pleasant Hill before pulling back to Taylor's Sabine Cross Roads line.[41]

On 8 April, Lee led his cavalry division forward and encountered Taylor's line at Sabine Cross Roads. Instead of falling back to a good defensive position, Banks, who had just arrived at the front and whose line stretched for twenty to thirty miles, called up Landrum's brigade of Ransom's 13th corps detachment to assist Lee in driving Taylor's force back. Taylor pulled back skirmishing to a well-selected defensive position that spanned both sides of the road and covered both flanks of Banks's advanced line. At about 4:00 P.M., Banks faced Taylor's line with his cavalry and their infantry support too far forward and their supply train blocking the path of his infantry column. Mouton, who was killed in the action, charged abruptly against the Federal left flank. As Landrum's brigade faltered on the left, Ransom called up Cameron's brigade, but was wounded and carried to the rear at about the same time that the left collapsed and teamsters, followed by Lee's troopers, stampeded down the road and through the woods to the rear. Cameron's brigade came up, but became entangled with Lee's routed troopers and was quickly wrapped up by Mouton's charging Confederates. Walker's Confederates finished the job by attacking and rolling up Banks's now isolated right flank. Total disaster was averted when Franklin's troops held the Confederates in check three miles in rear of the line of battle and darkness ended the fight, although Banks lost some 1,400 captured, including over 80 officers, and scores killed and wounded.[42]

Banks pulled his column back and concentrated in a good defensive position at Pleasant Hill. The next day, Taylor moved forward to finish the job with Churchill's and Parsons's newly arrived divisions added to his command. When Taylor attacked at 5:00 P.M., Banks's line (Emory's 19th corps division and A.J. Smith's 16th corps troops) held after an initial break in Emory's line. Emory counterattacked, supported by Smith's troops, and broke Churchill's and Parsons's line, causing them to scatter in confusion and forcing Taylor to fall back and end the battle. The next day, however, Banks, under some pressure to return to New Orleans by 10 April, in spite of the victory at Pleasant Hill, ordered a retreat to Grand Ecore.[43]

Bringhurst and Swigart, who understood Halleck's admonition to Banks to keep his column concentrated to avoid being attacked in detail (Banks had assured him about a week earlier that his line was not too extended), called it "one of the great blunders of the war." Banks's army, they wrote, "was defeated and destroyed with the loss of material inestimable, and a sacrifice of life terrible to contemplate, through a plan of battle which threw in the fight detachments of troops only as fast as they could be destroyed." Banks's retreat also left Porter's gunboat fleet isolated and vulnerable on the "narrow and snaggy river." Porter ordered his heavy gunboats below and kept six light drafts to convoy Kilby Smith's transports back to Alexandria. His vessels could move at twenty to thirty miles a day at best, which enabled the Confederate cavalry to ride downriver and attack the fleet from several points below, which they did following Banks's retreat. Taylor regrouped at Mansfield following his defeat at Pleasant Hill and sent Green's cavalry and Mouton's infantry division, now commanded by Camile de Polignac, to harass Banks and Porter's retreat. Taylor took his Texas, Arkansas, and Missouri divisions to reinforce Sterling Price in Arkansas, who now had only some 6,000 to 8,000 cavalry to stop Frederick Steele's move toward Shreveport.[44]

In Arkansas, after struggling on bad roads and being harassed by Sterling Price's cavalry at Elkin's Ferry and Prairie d'Ane, Steele turned his line of march southward to Camden, on the upper Ouachita River, where he arrived on 15 April. While at Camden, with forage difficult to find in southwestern Arkansas and supplies running low, Steele sent a forage party about twenty miles up the Praire d'Ane to Camden Road to seize the contents of a Confederate storehouse on White Oak Creek. On their return, Confederate cavalry (Marmaduke's and Maxey's divisions) attacked the long Federal wagon train at Lee's Plantation (Poison Springs) about fifteen miles from Camden and captured some 200 wagons and teams, all the seized corn, and four pieces of artillery. The Federal cavalry rode off and the infantry dispersed into the woods, as did the few prisoners captured by Marmaduke and Maxey's cavalry. Busy with their recaptured supplies and newly captured Federal wagons, the Confederates did not pursue. A week later at Marks' Mills, Steele's supply train, which was escorted from Little Rock by Lt. Col. Francis Drake's brigade, was attacked and routed by Maxey's and Fagan's divisions. Four more pieces of artillery were captured along with another 200 supply wagons and teams, including forty more burned in the fight. At about that same time, a courier brought Steele the news that Banks had been turned back near Mansfield and was in retreat. With that news, Steele, who was unable to find forage in the depleted lands of southwestern Arkansas and unable to protect his supply trains against Confederate cavalry raids, turned his expeditionary force back toward Little Rock. Price's Confederates accomplished their purpose, but were unable to stop Steele's retreat. Steele, on the other hand, had at least caused Kirby Smith to unnecessarily divert Walker's division back to Arkansas.[45]

Although Steele complained about lack of support by Federal gunboats on the upper Ouachita River, Rear Admiral Porter, after entering the Red River on 12 March, did send the 1000-ton gunboat *Lafayette* up the Ouachita, which wound its way from southwestern Arkansas, curving almost due south at Hot Springs and flowing through Camden to its mouth on the Red River about thirty-five miles above the Red's mouth on the Mississippi. The *Lafayette* made it to Monroe, Louisiana, about 130 miles from the mouth of the Red, where they burned the courthouse, railroad depot, and bridge. They moved on to Ouachita City, Louisiana, 20 miles farther upriver, but turned back about 100 miles below

Steele's position at Camden, Arkansas. The *Lafayette* brought back between 2,500 and 3,000 bales of cotton and nearly 800 freed slaves.[46]

On the Red River, with Banks's army in retreat, Green sent his cavalry down both sides of the river with muskets and artillery to harass Banks and to capture or destroy if possible Porter's gunboats and transports. They attacked first from the bluffs on the left bank near Coushatta, then, on 12 April, Green led a detachment on the right bank that attacked and attempted to capture the gunboat *Osage*, hard aground at Blair's Landing, with the transport *Black Hawk* alongside attempting to pull her off. According to Porter, Green and his men, who appeared suddenly on the road that led eastward to the landing from Pleasant Hill, were "flushed with victory or under the excitement of liquor." Attempting to capture the vessels, Porter said their "hootings and actions baffled description" as they attacked the *Osage* in waves, "only to be cut down by grapeshot and canister" from both the *Osage*'s guns and from the musketry fire of soldiers aboard the *Black Hawk*, who were protected by cotton bales. When the ironclad *Lexington* arrived, she opened crossfire on Green's troopers, who continued to fight, according to Porter, with "such desperation and courage against certain destruction" that it could only be accounted for by intoxication. This was later verified, according to Porter, when they found the bodies of the slain Confederates "actually smelled of Louisiana rum." Green was killed in the action when hit by a shell from one of the gunboats. Green's surviving troopers retreated and Major General John A. Wharton replaced the fallen Green in command of Taylor's cavalry.[47]

In the meantime, the 47th Indiana arrived at New Orleans at sunset on Thursday, 14 April, and camped at the Crescent Cotton Press, which Slack located "pretty well uptown" and said they were "very comfortable all under roof," although the officers were "keeping close," and the men not allowed to "go round town."[48]

A steamer arrived at New Orleans five days later carrying rumors that Nathan Bedford Forrest had captured Memphis and that he had ordered the massacre of the garrison at Fort Pillow, which was manned by 295 hated, in some cases for good reason, "homemade Yankees" from Major H.F. Bradford's 1st Battalion Tennessee Cavalry, and 262 reviled and feared black troops and their white officers from the 1st Battalion, 6th U.S.C.T. Heavy Artillery (formerly the 1st Regiment Alabama U.S.C.T.). The rumor about Memphis was false, the rumor about a massacre at Fort Pillow true, and Slack wrote Ann regretfully: "This looks to me like the beginning of the end, that the war would result in one of extermination."[49]

The Fort Pillow massacre was essentially a continuation of the cycle of personal violence and revenge that was all too common in border areas, and was perhaps one of the more egregious examples of it. Forrest's men, reacting at least in part to recent acts of murder and mayhem committed by Federal Tennessee cavalry units, and acting under the presumption that black Federals would show them no quarter if the tables were turned, overran the fort in heated fighting, then killed most of the garrison's soldiers in an orgy of violence inside the fort, and some at the river, after the garrison's soldiers had thrown down their arms.[50]

Personal accounts from Forrest's men and the reports of survivors immediately after the incident told of rampant and savage attacks on black and white soldiers and their white officers. These early accounts from both sides clearly show that Forrest's troopers showed no quarter and killed most of the Federal soldiers in the garrison after they had surrendered. Some eyewitness accounts, including statements attributed to Brigadier General James R. Chalmers, who led the attack, suggest that Chalmers and Forrest attempted to, and eventually did, stop the massacre after their men had begun the killing frenzy inside the fort and at the river. Forrest, in his first report dated 15 April, denied ordering the massacre but could not resist boasting "that negro soldiers cannot cope with Southerners." Chalmers, showing the true source of the frenzied violence, proudly added that his men had "taught the mongrel garrison of blacks and renegades a lesson long to be remembered."[51]

A Joint Committee of the U.S. Congress quickly assembled eyewitness testimony, including a sworn statement from W.R. McLagan that he had been unwillingly conscripted into Confederate service prior to Fort Pillow. McLagan said he was on the march between Brownsville and Jackson, Tennessee, on 14 May with Colonel William L. Ducksworth's 7th Tennessee Cavalry (CSA) of Forrest's command when he saw Bradford led into the woods by guards and shot, and that he later saw Bradford's unburied body in the woods. He added that he escaped from his 7th Tennessee Cavalry "recruiters" shortly thereafter. Acting Master William Ferguson, who had brought the steamer *Silver Cloud* to Fort Pillow as part of a rescue mission and had visited the garrison under a flag of truce, testified that the soldiers of the garrison had been killed "with a furious and vindictive savageness" and "cold-blooded barbarity" after they had surrendered. This coincides with written eyewitness accounts from Forrest's own soldiers, including one soldier who wrote home that, under Forrest's orders, they had turned the garrison into a "slaughter pen." Initially, Confederate newspapers like the *Memphis Appeal*, then published out of Atlanta, boasted about the capture of Fort Pillow and the slaughter of the Federal troops there.[52]

Faced with scathing accusations in the Northern press, however, and a real threat of retaliation from the Lincoln administration, Forrest and the higher Confederate authorities quickly changed their tune. In what became the cleaned-up Confederate version, clearly contradicted by the firsthand accounts of his own men, Forrest, in his 26 April report, written in response to the reports in Northern newspapers, claimed that the garrison's soldiers were merely battlefield casualties. They were, he said, soldiers who refused to surrender and were killed initially when his troopers "poured into the fortification" and subsequently when they enfiladed the Federals as they retreated to the river "arms in hand and firing back, and their colors flying."[53]

Regardless of what actually transpired that day, "Remember Fort Pillow" became a battle cry that would rally Federal soldiers, black or white, thenceforth wherever they went into action, but now with approval of the Federal authorities to "show no quarter" to those Confederates like Forrest and his men who had shown no quarter to them. Forrest was a fine tactician, and indeed the "Wizard of the Saddle" (two retaliatory expeditions sent out against him failed), although his harassment of vulnerable garrisons and outposts in western Tennessee and Kentucky had almost no impact on the outcome of the war. He would, however, spend the rest of his life trying to erase the stain of Fort Pillow from his name.[54]

Back on the Red River, on 22 April, Banks moved his column from Grand Ecore toward Alexandria. At Monett's Ferry (Cane River Crossing) the next day, Emory, leading the 19th corps in Banks's advance, encountered Hamilton Bee's cavalry blocking their path across the Cane River. Avoiding the trap, Emory outflanked Bee and forced him to retreat. The road to Alexandria now open, Emory's pioneers laid pontoons; Banks's entire force crossed the next day, and the first troops entered Alexandria on 25 April.[55]

Banks had called up McClernand's 13th corps detachment from Texas a few weeks earlier, and they arrived in New Orleans on 21 April. Two days later they were ordered to Alexandria along with Slack's 47th Indiana on what would be a roughly two-day boat trip, McClernand on board the flagship *Emma*, Slack and the 47th Indiana on the *Starlight* and *Universe*, and the remainder of McClernand's detachment on the *Polar Star* and the *John H. Groesbeck*.[56]

Chaplain Sawyer, who apparently came to New Orleans about a week later aboard the steamer *Missouri*, sent the account of his arrival in New Orleans, commentary on the political affairs of the city, and news of his embarkation with the 47th Indiana for the Red River aboard the *Starlight*, and included an amusing story about Col. Slack's handling of some "derelict" musicians on the trip:

FROM THE TWENTY-SEVENTH [SIC: FORTY-SEVENTH]
MISSISSIPPI RIVER, NEAR MORGANZA
BEND, APRIL 25, 1864

Correspondence of the *Indianapolis Journal*

We reached New Orleans last Friday [22 April], after a most pleasant trip on the new steamer *Missouri*, from Cairo down. It has seldom been our lot to find more agreeable officers, or more sumptuous fare. Everything was done up in princely style, and to general satisfaction. A series of resolutions were drawn up complimentary to the Captain and crew, and commending the *Missouri* to the traveling public, which were unanimously adopted.

The 47th Regiment was quartered in the Crescent City Cotton Press. Few people have any proper conception of the number of buildings, from twenty to forty rods square, erected in New Orleans to meet the former necessities of the cotton trade. An officer in the army remarked the other day that 100,000 soldiers could be camped in them with all ease.

The Churches of the city are still sparsely attended by the natives.

The "Noon-day Prayer Meeting" seems thinned from the absence of many Christian soldiers with General Banks in Western Louisiana. The new government of the State is in successful operation. The Constitutional Convention is in session, but little real progress has been made. The city press in the main stands by the Union in our great struggle, and accepting as a fact that slavery has been overthrown by Confederate madness, the various papers labor almost with a single purpose to complete the revolution which sets in so resistlessly in favor of freedom throughout the State.

With several regiments under command of General McClernand, we were ordered up Red River and six companies of the 47th embarked on the steamer *Starlight* and left New Orleans yesterday morning. The rest of the men expect to overtake us at Alexandria. I distributed 100 Testaments, 100 hymn books and 400 tracts, papers and pamphlets yesterday, it being the Sabbath, to the new men, and we held religious services in the cabin, which were well attended.

This morning we had a novel time. Several of the musicians had repeatedly failed to come to time, and for these derelictions of duty Col. Slack made up his mind to administer a rebuke. By order, Adjutant Vance had four of them arrested and brought into the cabin under guard. The Colonel had spoken to the Chaplain to select some chapter for them to read and to follow the reading with suitable admonitions. A Testament was handed to each of the four, and they were requested to turn to the 27th chapter of the Acts of the Apostles. The officers of the regiment, some of their fellow soldiers, and some of the officers of the boat and citizen passengers were around them, and in their confusion and embarrassment they could scarcely find the place. One looked a considerable time for the book of "Acts" in the middle of Matthew. At length they had found the place, and reading five verses each in turn, they finished the chapter.

The chaplain [then] reminded [them] of the shipwreck about which they had been reading, and called their attention to the fact that it was by obedience to orders that all on board were saved — told them why they had been put under arrest, and expressed the hope we all had, that this would be the last time they would be found disobedient to orders or remiss in the performance of their duties. Colonel Slack enforced what had been said by some practical and telling remarks, and the musicians marched out of the cabin in single file, looking as serious and solemn as if going to a funeral. The boys are amusing themselves over the Colonel's case, and expressed the opinion that in future the musicians will be very likely "to come to time." Yours very truly,

Samuel Sawyer
Chaplain 47th Reg't Ind. Vols.

P.S.—The 47th regiment now numbers nearly eight hundred men. The men were quite successful in rallying recruits.[57]

Back on the Red River, Banks's army had little trouble retreating southward from Grand Ecore to Alexandria. On the other hand, Porter's detachment of light draft gunboats, left behind without infantry support by the army's retreat to Alexandria, became easy targets for Taylor's sharpshooters and artillery. Without Banks's army to hold them back, Confederate cavalry could now roam freely down the left bank, and to a lesser extent, down the right bank above Alexandria as well, and were able to set up good artillery and sharpshooter positions to attack the errant wooden and cotton-clad vessels.[58]

On 15 April, the 700-ton ironclad *Eastport* had been sunk by a torpedo about six miles downriver from Grand Ecore. It had been raised by pump boats sent up by Porter from Alexandria and had continued downriver after being repaired, her guns removed and placed on a barge, but was again grounded on a sandbar on 25 April several miles farther downriver, about twenty miles above the lower junction of the Cane and Red Rivers. Porter sent the larger gunboats to Alexandria and retained only his light-draft gunboats upriver to protect the remaining transports and attempt to save the *Eastport*. Without army protection and with Confederate cavalry on both banks, however, Porter ordered the valuable ironclad blown up. The light-draft gunboats, *Cricket*, *Fort Hindman*, and *Juliet*, drove off the harassing Confederate sharpshooters and enabled the officers and crew to transfer to the *Fort Hindman*, which continued downriver with the pump boats *Champion No. 3* and *Champion No. 5*.[59]

Later that same afternoon, however, Colonel John H. Caudill's sharpshooters from Polignac's division and the four guns of Captain Florian O. Cornay's Louisiana Battery (two twelve-pound brass guns and two howitzers), posted on De Loach's Bluff near the lower junction of the Cane and Red Rivers, opened up on Porter's light-draft flotilla as it steamed downriver. The wooden gun and pump boats were shredded, and Porter himself barely escaped injury or death aboard his flagship, *Cricket*. Tragically, in what the Chief of Confederate Artillery, Col. Joseph L. Brent, called "probably the most fatal single shot fired during the war," a 12-pound shot penetrated the starboard boiler of the unlucky pump boat *Champion No. 3* and exploded, enveloping the boat in scalding steam and water and killing most of those on board, including the captain, three engineers, and nearly two hundred recently freed men, women, and children taken from Red River plantations. (Federal reports indicated that the blacks killed on board were members of the crew.) The *Fort Hindman*, the *Juliet* and the *Champion No. 5* were forced back upriver to avoid the battery, although the heavily damaged *Cricket* made it past. The next day (27 April), the *Fort Hindman* and the *Juliet* ran past, but the *Champion No. 5* was sunk; like *Champion No. 3*, it was captured and later put into Confederate service. Shrapnel and canister from the gunboats did some damage to the Confederate battery, and Cornay was killed in the action. In testimony to the action of Cornay's 4-gun battery, however, Porter reported that he thought he had faced eighteen pieces of artillery.[60]

Due to the heavy action upriver and the fact that the Confederate cavalry had not yet discovered that they could bypass Banks's army and block the river below Alexandria, McClernand arrived at Alexandria without incident, followed by the fleet carrying his 13th corps detachment, and took command of the 13th corps in the field on 26 April. The *Starlight* arrived at Alexandria the next day, also without incident. Slack and the 47th Indiana, numbering 650 men, veterans and new recruits, arrived as part of the 2nd brigade of the 1st division under Michael K. Lawler's command, along with the 16th Ohio (480 men), the 34th Iowa (367), the 49th Indiana (404), the 69th Indiana (422), the 114th Ohio (345), and the 1st Wisconsin Battery with six rifled guns (94 men). A reorganization at Alexandria placed Slack in command of the 1st brigade of Cameron's 3rd division with the 11th, 24th, and 47th Indiana, the 24th and 34th Iowa, the 87th and 118th Illinois, and the 114th Ohio.[61]

At Alexandria, Banks discovered what his engineers had warned him about: the river had fallen about six feet and had exposed the rocks in the rapids, trapping ten gunboats and two tugs above. The level at the foot of the rapids was only a little over three feet and the gunboats needed at least seven feet to pass; Banks could not continue his retreat until they were either saved or destroyed. Forced to protect the trapped vessels, the ironclads were especially needed to keep the Mississippi River open to Federal shipping, Banks formed his camps around the outskirts of Alexandria, placing A.J. Smith's 16th and 17th corps detachment on the left, stretching about eight miles south of town and west of the river, across the railroad to the Opelousas Road. Troops from McClernand's 13th corps, including Slack's 47th Indiana who spent their first night in camp on 27 April, continued the camp line that curved northward from the Opelousas Road to the bridge on Bayou Rapides Road and up the Shreveport Road, about six miles north of town. Emory's 19th corps troops were held in reserve and Lee's cavalry on picket.[62]

On 28 April, Taylor brought his force to the outskirts of Alexandria and the Federal camps, about three and a half miles from town, where detachments of his cavalry and artillery skirmished with Lee's cavalry and McClernand's 13th corps troops on the Bayou Rapides Road and A.J. Smith's 16th and 17th corps detachment on the Bayou Robert Road. Unprepared for Taylor's Confederates, McClernand's troops were forced to abandon their camps and build a more secure line of breastworks closer to Alexandria. That night, a nervous Banks ordered the burning of houses on the Opelousas Road leading south from town.[63]

At Alexandria on 26 April, Lt. Col. Joseph Bailey of the 4th Wisconsin, the 19th corps Chief of Engineers, had proposed building a dam at the foot of the lower rapids to raise the water level high enough so the gunboats trapped above could be floated over. In consultation with Bailey, Col. George D. Robinson of the 3rd Engineers, Corps d'Afrique (the 97th U.S.C.T.) and Lt. Col. Uri B. Pearsall of the 5th Engineers, Corps d'Afrique (the 99th U.S.C.T.), proposed building another dam at the head of the rapids to alleviate the pressure on the lower dam. Bailey turned down Robinson and Pearsall's suggestion and opted for one dam, which Banks, skeptical but with little choice, approved.[64]

The monumental task began on 30 April when crews (some 3,000 men and 200 to 300 wagons) were assembled, and work collecting material for ballast on the right bank and cutting trees on the left bank began. On the right bank, Robinson supervised the work of troops from Col. William H. Dickey's Corps d'Afrique brigade as they disassembled local steam mills and abandoned brick buildings, and collected rocks and old iron rails for ballast, which the 3rd Engineers (97th U.S.C.T.) hauled to the river by the wagonload. On the forested left bank, troops from the Maine regiments of the 19th corps went to work felling trees. Actual construction work began on 2 May, supervised on the right bank by Pearsall with the 5th Engineers (99th U.S.C.T.) placing, loading, and bracing the four barges in the center of the river in roughly three feet of water and constructing a "crib dam" of logs and stone on the right bank. On the left bank, protected by infantry outposts, the 29th Maine, detachments from the 110th and 116th New York, and pioneers from the 13th corps went to work on a "wing dam" of large trees and crossties tied together and weighed down with rocks.[65]

In the meantime, Taylor, with dreams of capturing Porter's gunboat fleet, or causing it to be destroyed, moved his force of about 6,000 to the outskirts of Alexandria. On 1 May, having discovered the ease of movement around the Federal line, he sent Major's Texas and Arizona cavalry (commanded by George W. Baylor) downriver about twenty to twenty-five miles on the right bank to Wilson's Landing and David's Ferry to blockade the river between Fort De Russy and Alexandria. That same day, even before their artillery arrived, two regiments of Baylor's cavalry captured and burned McClernand's former flagship *Emma*. Baylor reported that Chisum's 2nd Texas Partisan Rangers and Smith's Arizona Scouts captured her "after an exciting chase of 2 miles" and took her captain, quartermaster and crew prisoner before burning the vessel. The Federal account said the *Emma* was "in at the bank" without guard when it was captured and blamed it on McClernand's quartermaster, who reportedly "would not permit the depot quartermaster to give her any orders." At any rate, all that was found near the burnt hull of the *Emma* "were the remains of a few official envelopes."[66]

Two days later, Baylor had Lt. John Yoist's section of West's Battery in place, and a shot from a Parrot rifle hit the boiler of the transport *City Belle*, which carried the 120th Ohio upriver to Alexandria. About half of the 700 soldiers of the 120th Ohio jumped overboard and escaped to the left bank and made it to Alexandria; about 270 were taken prisoner and the others died on board. An unnamed gunboat and another transport were reportedly damaged and driven off in the fight. Baylor's men sank the *City Belle* across the river channel.[67]

On 4 May, the transport *John Warner*, convoyed downriver by the gunboats *Covington* and *Signal*, and carrying Col. William H. Raynor and 250 soldiers from the 56th Ohio going home on leave, was fired on by some of Baylor's sharpshooters while passing Wilson's plantation. Several miles farther downriver, the three vessels tied up for repairs with the two gunboats firing intermittently all night toward the Confederate positions on the right bank. Heading for Fort De Russy the next morning, the *John Warner* was hit by artillery from Lt. W.H. Lyne's section of West's Battery as it rounded a bend near Dunn's Bayou. Its rudders disabled, it drifted downriver and ran hard aground on the left bank, where it was fired on by infantry and artillery from the opposite shore, only one hundred yards away. The soldiers returned fire but lost some 125 men killed and wounded in the action. Ordered to abandon ship, a small portion of the *John Warner*'s crew was captured, but the remainder escaped into the woods on the left bank and made it back to Alexandria; Col. Raynor, however, was wounded and captured. In the fight, the *Covington* lost her water when struck under the boilers and was scuttled by the crew when their ammunition gave out. Most of the officers and men also made it into the woods on the opposite shore and back to Alexandria, although they lost five officers and thirty-nine men missing. The *Signal* was unable to withstand the fire that was now concentrated on her and surrendered. A portion of the crew was captured along with a quantity of ammunition and stores on board. With this, Taylor effectively blockaded the river and cut off communications between Alexandria and Fort De Russy.[68]

Back at Alexandria, while Bailey, Pearsall, and Robinson were overseeing the construction of the dams, McClernand fell ill with the malaria he had contracted on his Texas sojourn and placed M.K. Lawler in temporary command of the 13th corps. (At about the same time, Franklin, who had been wounded, relinquished command of the 19th corps to William H. Emory.) In the next several days, Lawler led Cameron's 3rd division and Keigwin's 2nd brigade from the 1st division out to disperse Taylor's force west of town. Encountering resistance several miles out from Wharton's cavalry, primarily from Brig. Gen. William Steele's cavalry detachment (the 12th, 19th, and 21st Texas Cavalry and Moseley's Texas Battery), they skirmished the next several days and brought up Landrum's 4th division.[69]

On 5 May, Keigwin's brigade and Cameron's division drove Steele's Confederates westward beyond Graham's Plantation and up Bayou Rapides Road (some four or five miles out), killing 8, wounding 20, and taking 3 prisoners, while losing 1 killed and 10 wounded, and fell back to Winn's Plantation, where they bivouacked for the night. Of the fight at Graham's Plantation, Slack told Ann: "It was a very spirited running fight of about five miles. The rifle balls and cannon shot came in fearful proximity some times, but the men pressed on with cheers and drove them constantly. We lost eighteen men altogether. The 47th lost four, all wounded only, one probably mortally, he belonged to Co. C. Co F was not in the fight." Slack, who had been ill, moved to the rear to recuperate and turned temporary command of his brigade over to Lt. Col. John Q. Wilds of the 24th Iowa. Under Wilds, they pushed farther west without opposition and bivouacked for the night on Middle Bayou, which ran between Bayou Rapides on the north and Bayou Boeuf on the south, about eight miles out.[70]

On the morning of 7 May, in a heated skirmish about twelve miles west of Alexandria, Cameron's division drove Steele's Confederates across the Bayou Rapides Bridge near McNutt's Hill. Late that afternoon Cameron's pickets from Company A of the 28th Iowa shot and killed Major George W. McNeil of H.P. Bee's staff, who, while serving temporarily with Wharton's cavalry, was reconnoitering their lines close to Bayou Rapides Bridge. Finding important papers on McNeil that indicated the weakness of their opposition, Cameron attacked and drove them southward across Bayou Boeuf before withdrawing back to Middle Bayou to bivouac for the night. There they remained in line of battle while Bailey's team worked on the dam.[71]

Bailey's dam was completed on Sunday, 8 May, the water rising from three feet to eight or nine feet, enough to float the boats over. At 5:00 o'clock the next morning, however, as Robinson and Pearsall predicted, Bailey's dam broke under the tremendous pressure and the two barges in the center washed away. Fortuitously, in washing downstream, the two barges grounded and, in effect, created a new sixty-feet wide chute with the barges acting as "fenders" to keep the gunboats in line as they passed. Taking advantage of the temporary rush of water, the *Lexington* steamed through, followed by the *Neosho, Fort Hindman,* and *Osage.* That left six gunboats and two tugs above the rapids, and the immediate need to tighten and repair the lower dam. More importantly, it demonstrated Robinson and Pearsall's point about the need for another dam about a mile and a quarter upriver at the head of the rapids, to relieve pressure on the lower dam.[72]

That morning (9 May), Bailey designed wing dams ("light log cribs lashed together by rope and filled with brush and bricks") and placed Pearsall in charge of construction and placement. By the next day (10 May), these cribs raised the water level at the head by about fourteen inches, enabling the *Chillicothe* to work her way through, but she got aground on the rocks above the lower dam. The *Carondelet* attempted to follow but the rapidity of the current and the poor placement of these wing dams forced her aside and turned her stern downstream and diagonally across the channel. The *Mound City,* whose side iron and guns had been removed by the crew, entered but grounded abreast of the *Carondelet.*[73]

Faced with disaster, and with only four of the six gunboats through the lower dam, Bailey let Pearsall select the site and the work crew to build a dam that would float the *Chillicothe, Carondelet,* and *Mound City* as well as the remaining vessels over the rapids. Pearsall selected Capt. John B. Hutchens's 13th corps pioneers, which included crews from the 47th, 11th, 24th, and 46th Indiana, the 56th and 83rd Ohio, the 24th and 28th Iowa, and the 29th Wisconsin from Cameron's division, as well as crews from a number of other 13th corps regiments. Hutchens himself was a member of the 24th Indiana. Pearsall designed and Hutchens's men constructed "bracket dams" made of two-legged trestles and waited for the 10,000 feet of two-inch wooden planks needed to complete the dam.[74]

Upriver at daylight the next day (11 May),[75] Pearsall and Hutchens's crew entered the swift water of some four and a half feet in depth to place and set the trestles. (Several men were swept away, but none were drowned.) After the trestles were in place, it took about an hour to set and anchor the two-inch planks. Shortly thereafter the water rose enough for the gunboats to position themselves, the heavier boats needing to be hauled over the rocks into position. The water rose in the channel created by the bracket dams; and, on 12 May, the *Mound City, Carondelet,* and the *Pittsburg* passed through beautifully and over the lower dam to the cheers of the onlooking troops, although the *Mound City* struck hard crossing the lower dam and got aground. Pearsall's improvement worked; the lower dam held; and on 13 May, the *Louisville,* the *Ozark,* the two tugs, and finally the *Chillicothe* passed over without incident except for one man swept overboard from one of the tugs. The *Carondelet* and *Fort Hindman* pulled the *Mound City* off the rocks and, by 3:00 P.M., all of Porter's fleet were coaled and steaming downriver. A fire raged near the coal pile on the river at Alexandria as the last of Porter's fleet coaled, and by 4:00 P.M., the town was in flames.[76]

That same day, A.J. Smith led Banks's retreating column down the river road and the levee, Lawler's 13th corps troops following in the afternoon from Middle Bayou. As the fire in Alexandria spread from the levee, Banks, his staff, and Grover's soldiers attempted to put out the blaze. Richard Taylor, who had moved most of his force downriver and was still uncertain about the condition of Porter's gunboats at Alexandria, reported heavy explosions and thick smoke at Alexandria and that "twenty-three transports and two gunboats had up steam and the river was full of floating masses of cotton." Banks's column, he noted, reached about twenty miles below that night with 313 wagons.[77]

Banks's dispirited troops, however, were, noted the *New York Times* correspondent

"Union," cheered "by the news that Grant had whipped Lee" in Virginia. On the morning of 16 May at Mansura (Belle Prairie), Smith's column found Taylor's force arrayed in line of battle across the roads leading southeastward to Simmesport, about sixteen miles away. A.J. Smith moved his newly energized 16th corps detachment by column to the front before daybreak "ready," according to the *Times* correspondent, "to jump to arms at the first tap of the drum." The artillery battle commenced almost immediately. "I was anxious to see a battle on a prairie," he wrote, "all the movements could be discerned, and when the general went to the front, it looked more like an immense military review than anything else, although the shells were ploughing through the air for some time, making hideous sounds." Taylor's artillery dueled with Smith's for about four hours until Smith extended his left flank by bringing up Emory's 19th corps detachment and, on his extreme left, Cameron's division. His left flank now threatened, Taylor prudently retreated southward on the road to Evergreen, where his trains were parked, leaving the road to Simmesport open.[78]

On 17 May, Cameron's division marched down Bayou de Glaise Road beside the wagon train and behind William H. Dickey's Corps d'Afrique brigade. Five miles from Simmesport, Yager's cavalry and the 2nd Louisiana Cavalry (C.S.A.) attacked the train. Lt. Col. John C. Chadwick's 92nd U.S.C.T., out in front as skirmishers and flankers, met the attack, and, in their first engagement as a regiment armed with inferior and unreliable Springfield smooth-bore muskets, protected the train from damage and drove off the two Confederate cavalry regiments, who left nine dead on the field. The 92nd U.S.C.T. lost two killed, four wounded, and six missing.[79]

True to Kirby Smith's policy that his soldiers execute captured or wounded black soldiers and their white officers on the battlefield, at least one of the two black soldiers killed, Sgt. Antoine Davis of Co. E, was shot and wounded, then shot again two more times at point-blank range while helplessly prostrate on the ground, the pistol's muzzle to his chest. In his Confederate report, Taylor greatly exaggerated the success of his troopers, boasting falsely that they had "dispersed the negro guard and killed many white officers."[80]

The encouragement to execute captured black soldiers and their white officers came directly from E. Kirby Smith. In two 13 June 1864 letters, he directed Richard Taylor to show no quarter to either when taken in arms. If they were brought in alive, warned Smith, they must be turned over to the state authorities where they would be subjected to civilian judicial proceedings for inciting servile insurrection. This would, according to Smith, absolve the Confederate military from blame for their execution and the Federals would not be justified in retaliation against Confederate prisoners, although these odious prisoners would be a great encumbrance until they could be turned over to the civil authorities. Smith averred that the simplest solution was summary execution on the field, where they would be listed as battlefield casualties.[81]

Confederate Secretary of War Seddon's recommendation that black soldiers and their white officers not be executed (though, "a few examples might perhaps be made") did not reach Smith for another month or so. As a result, at least some black soldiers captured in the Trans-Mississippi in late July 1864 were not executed. Instead, they were imprisoned at Trinity, Louisiana, on the Ouachita River about thirty miles west of Vidalia, under threat of a return to slavery.[82]

In an exchange on this matter, Col. William P. Hardeman (CSA), commander of the post at Trinity, replied on 30 July 1864 to a request from Lt. Col. Hubert A. McCaleb,

XII. New Orleans and the Red River Campaign (January–June 1864)

commander of U.S. Forces at Vidalia, for information on the condition of Pvt. Wilson Wood of the 6th U.S.C.T. Heavy Artillery. Stating the revised Confederate position very clearly, Hardeman wrote:

> Sir,
> In the skirmish of the 22nd July 1864 a negro man named Wilson was captured by the Confederate forces. He is wounded in the calf of the leg (flesh wound) and is receiving such medical attention as we have. When he is well if his owner lives in the Confederate lines he will be delivered to him, if not he will be held to slavery by the Government. I have to inform you that negroes are not considered prisoners of war, but all who surrendered to us are treated as property and either delivered to their original owner or put at labor by the Government. I am very respectfully your obedient servant. Wm. P. Hardeman, Col. Comd'g Post.[83]

On 31 July 1864, Brig. Gen. J.M. Brayman, commanding U.S. Forces at Natchez, wrote to McCaleb with instructions on what to tell Hardeman about the Federal policy of retaliation:

> Sir,
> I have through you this day the communication of Col. Wm. P. Hardeman ... in reply to your inquiry concerning the treatment of Private Wilson of your command, captured by the enemy of the 22nd instant. Please advise him in reply that when the Government of the United States made negroes soldiers, it assumed towards them the same obligations as were due to any others who might wear its uniform and bear its flag.... As the matter is understood by me, the Government will, for every black soldier reduced to slavery, put a rebel soldier in like condition, and will, for every violation of the usages of war respecting the men, exact ample retaliation. Respectfully yours Etc. M.M. Brayman, Brig. Gen, Comd'g."[84]

Back on the retreat down Red River, the 13th and 19th corps followed Banks's vanguard into Simmesport that evening. They went into camp to await the building of a bridge to cross the Atchafalaya, which was about six to seven hundred yards across, at that point. Describing the unusual steamboat bridge, Bringhurst and Swigart wrote: "The pontoon was laid on steamers anchored close together. String pieces were bolted down across the decks and, upon them, a floor of the flat cypress rails of the country was laid. It made a good bridge, but exceedingly crooked from the unequal height and length of the boats. Wagons, mules and men crossed on it. The artillery was ferried over."[85]

While the bridge was being constructed, A.J. Smith's 16th corps detachment was left in the rear to guard Banks's line. Two miles west of Simmesport, where the northward-flowing Yellow Bayou entered the eastward-flowing (at that point) Bayou de Glaise, Taylor attempted one last effort to harass Banks's unstoppable retreat. A.J. Smith sent Mower to clear them out; and Mower, with about 1,000 men from three infantry brigades, some artillery, and initially Richard Arnold's (formerly Albert Lee's) cavalry, moved across Yellow Bayou and encountered a force two or three times their size. Taylor opened with twelve pieces of artillery and advanced his infantry, initially driving back Mower's left flank. Mower's right flank held near Bayou de Glaise, however, and Mower changed position to meet the threat. In the ebb and flow of battle, which included several distinctive charges and countercharges in the thickets, Mower's troops "severely repulsed" Polignac and Baylor's Confederates, forcing Taylor to stop the movement of his troops on the right. In the process, the tinder-dry prairie thicket caught on fire and gave Taylor, whose position had become precarious, the opportunity to withdraw westward to Evergreen, where his trains were parked, ending his part in the Red River Campaign. With a fire in his front and no further support from Banks or Smith, Mower withdrew his detachment eastward and back to their original position protecting the river crossing.[86]

On 19 May, Lawler's 13th corps troops, with Arnold's cavalry, crossed Yellow Bayou at the dike three miles below Simmesport in pursuit of Taylor, but were ordered to return unless Taylor attacked. That afternoon, with Taylor gone, they returned to Simmesport and camped for the night; the next day all the troops were across "the bridge of boats." Lawler's troops marched all night and arrived at Red River Landing on the Mississippi River, twenty miles above Morganza, by 6:00 A.M. on 21 May. They continued the march the next day at 7:00 A.M. and were all in camp at New Texas Landing on the Mississippi, just above Morganza, by 9:00 o'clock that night.[87]

In his 22 May correspondence, Chaplain Sawyer provided the *Daily Journal*'s readers with a good description of their adventures, from Coles County, Illinois, to the conclusion of the disastrous Red River Campaign:

THE FORTY-SEVENTH INDIANA IN THE RED RIVER EXPEDITION

Correspondent of the *Indianapolis Journal*
Camp in the Field,
Morganza Bend, La., May 2 [*sic*: 22], '64

As many of your readers are interested in whatever concerns the welfare of the 47th Indiana V.I., I send you a few lines form this point. After our brief furlough home, as you are already aware, we were ordered to Coles County, Illinois, to quiet the Knights of the Golden Circle led by an Irish Sheriff to deeds of violence and blood. The sheriff and his traitorous crew lost courage as the Veterans approached and as no enemy confronted us, we moved on to Cairo. From Cairo we were thrown forward to Paducah to beat back Forest [sic] and his rebel horde, and having returned from this mission, we embarked for New Orleans. Tarrying there ten days, we were ordered to join the forces of General Banks at Alexandria, and reached that place just four weeks ago today. The army we found in a peculiar condition — it had just whipped the enemy severely two days out of three and yet instead of being allowed to hold its ground, or to advance and rest the well earned fruits of victory, it had been ordered to fall back on Alexandria, its base of supplies. The enemy finding no disposition on our part to pursue them, at length rallied and from fifteen to twenty thousand strong, they threw themselves in our rear and toward the mouth of Red river. They commenced firing upon boats and soon succeeded in blockading the river, and by cutting off our supplies, they had us in a state of siege, our gunboats and transports were above the falls, and it became a necessity to get them down. General Banks, with some Yankee shrewdness of a Lieut. Colonel to plan the work, commenced building a dam across the river. Night and day the men worked cheerfully — the red jackets, as they call our boys, among them, and when some of the dam gave way, it was forthwith repaired and another constructed higher up the river, so that gradually the water in mid channel was raised and the boats floated down the tide, stopping at Alexandria to be loaded for the Mississippi.

Meanwhile the enemy became very bold in his attacks from the west. The 13th Army Corps was ordered eight miles out to Middle Bayou to hold him in check, and to drive him back without bringing on a general engagement. The order was admirably executed. — The rebel sharpshooters filled the woods before us and their cannon opened fire, but column after column of our men moved magnificently on to engage them. We charged on them twice, once for nearly half a mile across an open field and through thick thorn hedges. — Bullets fell like hail all around us. Except at the 4th of July battle at Helena, Arkansas, I never had so many bullets fall around me in so short a time, and yet strange to tell only six of the 47th were wounded, all of whom, it is thought, will recover. A soldier of the 49th was killed by the bursting of a shell. A bullet came whizzing by Colonel Slack, and a shell burst near his horse, and another burst close by General Cameron, but the column made no halt, and the rebels gave back precipitately before us. We returned to Middle Bayou and encamped for the night. The next day we were ordered out again and passing over the field a rebel shell struck Milton Sloan, of Company H, in the leg, shattering it horribly. Mr. Carnes and some of his comrades bore him from the field. We put him carefully in the ambulance and sent him on to the hospital. His leg was taken off, and on Tuesday morning, May 8th, he died. One hundred and two dollars were found upon his person, which the surgeon sent to the Assistant Medical Director at New Orleans, payable to his parent on call.

We moved forward without wavering till we reached the twelve-mile bridge, driving the foe before us. Here we camped, threw out our pickets, and lay down to rest. A shot from the pickets startled us, and presently word came that Major McNeill, an accomplished rebel officer, had been shot by the men of Company A, 28th Iowa, while venturing too close to ascertain our position. Upon his person were found important dispatches revealing the position and force of the enemy, and in a few minutes the camp was routed up and we fell back to Middle Bayou again.

We remained here until Friday, May 13th, when marching orders came and we struck out for the river. From some cause Alexandria had been fired and two-thirds of the town burned; the boats however had cleared and the army was gone. Saturday afternoon the rebels began to hover on our rear, and skirmished some with our men. The next day we passed by the place where the rebels stockaded the river, and strange enough quite a number of the 47th picked up parts of letters they had written to their friends at home. The rebels had read them and they lay scattered around us by the bushel. The trunk of Col. Raynor, 56th Ohio Vet. Vol., captured by the blockaders, was found in a house by the way, along with steamboat chairs and other furniture. Monday, May 16th, the enemy 15,000 strong, confronted us in line of battle, and Gen. Banks marshaled his army of 40,000 in a prairie field containing about 10,000 acres, and moved them forward. Over 100 pieces of artillery were thundering death to the foe, and the cavalry and infantry ready to charge at the word. I never witnessed a more imposing military array. The rebels were afraid to risk an engagement and we went on with our train. During the day, however, the train was fired on, several colored soldiers and cavalry were wounded, and a bullet struck Capt. Keller, Co. H, of the 47th, in the leg. Tuesday we reached Atchafalaya Bayou which had to be crossed on a pontoon bridge. On Wednesday the enemy assailed our rear with five thousand men. We lost over 200 men killed, wounded and missing, and besides killing many of the rebels we captured 200. They could not stand the resistless charge of our men. Had the 13th Army Corps been ordered out in time to support the 6th [*sic*: 16th] Corps it is thought the whole 5,000 might have been disposed of in a most summary manner.

The pontoon bridge completed, the army crossed the bayou and marched ten miles to the mouth of Red river, where we received a heavy mail from home, which encouraged the men. Sunday, May 22nd, we reached Morganza Bend, where we were thrown into camp and where we are likely to remain for some time to come.

The army is in good fighting trim. It is indulging in a variety of criticism upon the management of the recent expedition, much after the general spirit of the press, and expressing the hope that a better day is before us.

The most intense interest is felt in the movements of General Grant. The soldiers have confidence in his generalship, and are most sanguine in their belief that he will succeed. God grant that he may. There are other things worthy of record connected with our recent march, some of which I reserve for another communication.

Yours very truly, Samuel Sawyer
Chaplain 47th Indiana Regiment.[88]

With the Red River Campaign over, Grant, now in command of all the Federal armies, finally looked toward Mobile. And now that Banks had shown his incompetence in leading a major expedition, Grant acted quickly to remove him from command without dismissing him outright with all the political ramifications that would entail in this presidential election year. In early May, Grant created the Military District of West Mississippi and brought Major General Edward R.S. Canby in from the west to lead the expedition against Mobile from New Orleans. The new military district put both Steele's Department of Arkansas and Banks's Department of the Gulf under Canby's command, deftly removing Banks from the military decision-making structure without firing him outright. In the meantime, Slack and the 47th Indiana remained at Morganza.[89]

XIII

Morganza, the Atchafalaya and New Orleans (May–September 1864)

In Virginia, Grant's army, although sustaining terrible losses at the Wilderness and Spotsylvania, pushed relentlessly toward Richmond. In fights from 23 to 26 May, Grant, unable to turn Lee's right flank on the North Anna River, moved southeastward twenty miles behind Sheridan's cavalry toward the crossroads at Cold Harbor Tavern, only about ten miles east of Richmond. In the meantime, closing out the month of May in Georgia, Sherman pushed to within thirty miles of Atlanta before running into stiff resistance from Johnston's army at New Hope Church and Pickett's Mill. Along the Mississippi River, Banks returned to New Orleans; A.J. Smith's 16th corps detachment, too late to join in Sherman in Georgia, returned to Memphis; and Slack's brigade, along with the remainder of Lawler's 13th corps detachment, sat with Emory's 19th corps at Morganza, Louisiana, waiting for transportation downriver.

Back in Indiana, when the public's eyes were not on Grant's movements, or lack thereof, in what seemed to be an endlessly bloody stalemate, they were following Sherman's progress against Joe Johnston in Georgia. Closer to home, attention shifted to Kentucky, where John Hunt Morgan, having escaped from the Ohio Penitentiary after being captured on his previous raid, reentered Kentucky to try to relieve Sherman's pressure on Johnston.

Locally, of course, eyes were also on the upcoming nominations for the fall elections. Commenting on the report that some Democrats wanted to nominate James R. Slack for governor of Indiana, the editors of the *Huntington Democrat*, continuing to throw barbs at their former friend, exclaimed: "When the Democratic State Convention makes a nomination, they will elect a *Democrat*, and not a dog with Lincoln's collar around its neck."[1]

Down in New Orleans on 27 May, in what appeared to be an act of sabotage, a destructive fire broke out on the riverfront at the foot of Canal Street. A strong breeze on the river that night quickly spread the fire from the steamer *Black Hawk* to seven other steamers and two schooners. A large crowd gathered to watch the fire and exploding ordnance stored on board until the steamer *Fawn* blew up and rained burning debris down on the onlookers. Henry Thompson, correspondent for the *New York Herald* sent a dispatch to his paper, in which he praised the bravery of the Pelican Hook and Ladder Company who faced fire and exploding shells in their attempt to save the vessels moored at the Canal Street wharf:

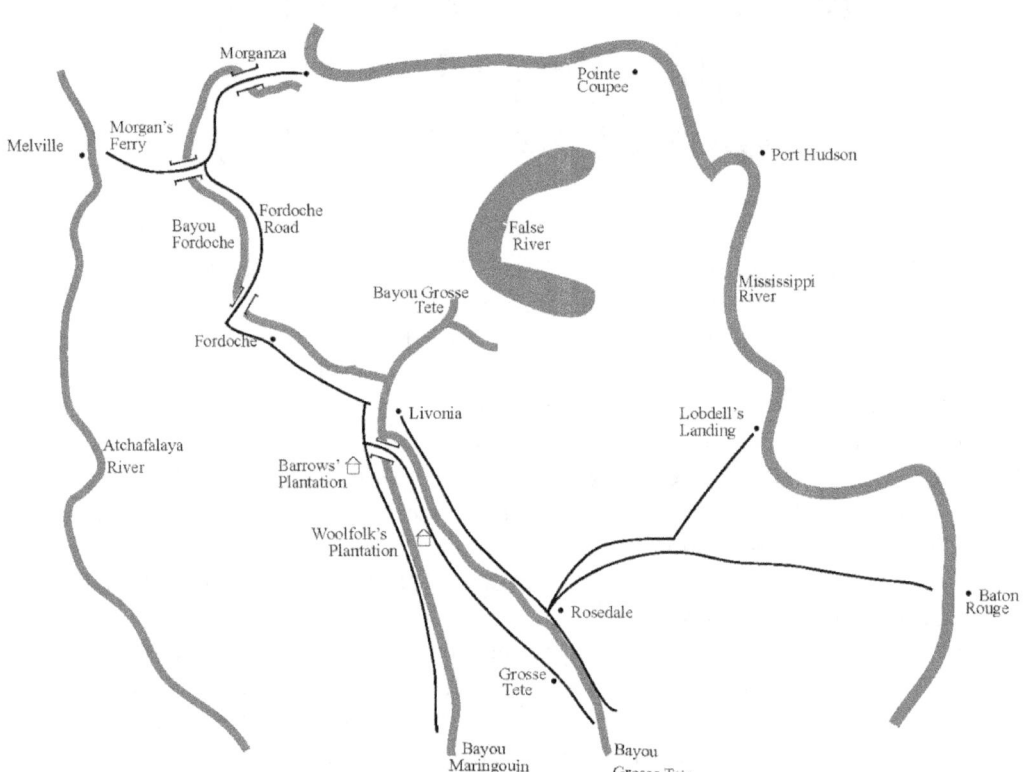

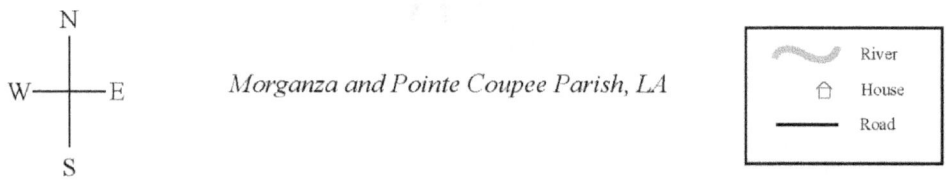

From Atlas Plate CLVI and Google Maps

Mr. Henry Thompson's Dispatch.
New Orleans, May 28, 1864
Large Fire in New Orleans—Eight Steamers Burned.

About nine o'clock last night a fire very mysteriously broke out in the ladies' cabin of the steamer *Black Hawk*, lying a short distance below Canal street.

The flames spread rapidly, and when first observed, had made such headway that it was found impossible to extinguish them. The city bells sounded the alarm, and in a short time the entire force of the Fire Department was present, and bravely set to work to extinguish the flames, though they were informed that powder and shells were on board in large quantities.

A strong breeze was blowing down the Mississippi at the time, and before the steamers adjoining could be unmoored and moved into the center of the river, the fire communicated to them also, and the consequence was that eight were destroyed....

Explosion—Gallantry of the Fire Department

Soon after the *Fawn* caught fire a terrible explosion occurred. Shells now and then exploded on the *Empire Parish* and other boats, without occasioning much alarm; but when the earth and buildings fairly shook from the explosion of the *Fawn*, and the air was filled with pieces of the wreck, a panic seized the thousands who had assembled to witness the conflagration, and all started a bee line and a full run from the neighborhood, many, I believe, not stopping until they reached their homes.

Fortunately no persons were injured.

The Fire Department deserves especial praise, as even before and after the explosions they worked their engines, throwing several streams of water upon the burning boats. At the time, the Pelican Hook and Ladder Company were the nearest to the *Fawn*, and were not more than two hundred feet distant. Total loss, about $275,000.

SUSPICIOUS

Lieutenant J.F. Moussier, in charge of the *Black Hawk*, stated that, hearing the alarm of the fire, he ran towards the *Black Hawk*; that he was about to go on board, and before he had crossed the gangway plank, a man, running with great speed, brushed by him. He called after him, but he ran at such speed that he was soon out of reach. He was dressed in black, with a yellow duster, a black slouch hat, and was of medium size.[2]

Back at Morganza on 29 May, angry at being alluded to as Lincoln's dog by the "miserable traitors" at the *Huntington Democrat*, Slack wrote Ann that the burning of the steamers in New Orleans would probably delay their transfer to Carrollton a few days, adding: "This war is fast turning into one of extermination. If it continues a short time, or very much longer, there will be no prisoners taken. The Federal forces will be driven into slaughtering all that fall into their hands by way of retaliation. All ready we cannot pass a plantation without the buildings being burned, unless we place a guard over the premises. Our road from Alexandria here was lighted by fires from burning buildings."[3]

At camp that same day and concerned with more mundane issues, Private Bert of the 47th Indiana wrote his sister, Ann, that they had been in camp for a week about a quarter mile from the Mississippi River but had "moved down close to the river so we could be handy to the watter." He added that they had walked about a mile to the woods to collect brush for shade and green corn for their beds. Satisfied that they had fixed up their Morganza camp as if they were going to stay awhile, he added the infantryman's timeless caveat that he and the other soldiers "don't know anything about it."[4]

While Emory's force encamped at Morganza, Kirby Smith sent Walker's division back to the Little River in southwest Arkansas, left Polignac's infantry division at Fort De Russy, and returned the Texas troops, except Wharton's cavalry, to Texas. Wharton's cavalry, armed primarily with Enfield rifles, camped along Yellow Bayou and the west bank of the swollen and rising Atchafalaya. In an ill-advised move, Wharton, who had already sent a company known as McNelly's Scouts across the Atchafalaya and southward to scout Federal movement in Pointe Coupee and Iberville Parishes, sent Madison's 3rd Texas Cavalry (CSA) across the Atachafalaya at Morgan's Ferry to picket Emory's camp at Morganza.[5]

In response, on 30 May, Emory sent Lawler with some 6,000 infantry from the 13th corps detachment, Sharpe's brigade, a 19th corps battery, and 1,700 Federal cavalry under Texan Edmund J. Davis to attack and disperse Madison's Texans and prevent any further crossings. Davis's cavalry led the pursuit as Lawler's troops followed on the Morgan's Ferry Road.[6]

The Morgan's Ferry Road (present-day LA-10) followed Bayou Fordoche westward from Morganza for about four miles and followed the bayou southward another four or five miles before turning westward at the junction of the Morgan's Ferry and Bayou Fordoche roads. At this point, referred to in official reports as the "junction," the Morgan's Ferry road ran westward some six miles to the ferry on the Atchafalaya (across from present-day Melville, Louisiana) and the Bayou Fordoche Road (present-day LA-77) continued southeastward along the bayou about fifteen miles to the town of Livonia on Bayou Grosse Tete. The Grosse Tete, which wound southwestward from near False River before turning due south, split about a mile or so south of Livonia, Bayou Maringouin on the west and Grosse Tete on the east. Running parallel about a mile or two apart, they diverged some six miles farther south and were about five miles apart at the town of Rosedale on the Grosse Tete.[7]

By the time Davis's cavalry arrived at the junction of the two roads at 7:00 A.M., Madison's Confederate cavalry (estimated at 200 to 400) had retreated down the Bayou Fordoche Road. Two hours later, Lawler established his headquarters at the junction and deployed his troops along the bayou. With Lawler's arrival, Davis sent Colonel Morgan H. Chrysler with the 6th Massachusetts, 2nd New Hampshire, and the 3rd Maryland to reconnoiter the Morgan's Ferry area. Chrysler returned at 3:00 P.M. without encountering Madison's cavalry but after having discovered a working sawmill on the Atchafalaya River and a ferry with five flatboats two miles above the mill. About an hour later Davis sent Colonel John M. Crebs with the 1st Louisiana, the 87th Illinois, and the 2nd New York down Bayou Fordoche Road ahead of the infantry. Crebs's cavalry encountered some of Madison's troopers and artillery at the Fordoche Bridge, another four or five miles south of the junction, and exchanged artillery fire. A section of Lt. Hardman P. Norris's 1st U.S. Artillery, Battery F silenced their gun and drove them off. The Confederates left Lt. James R. Leavy and three enlisted men dead on the field and several wounded. Lawler's infantry followed Crebs's cavalry down the Fordoche Road to Livonia.[8]

Crebs's cavalry moved on to Livonia, arriving between 8:00 and 9:00 P.M., followed by the vanguard of Lawler's infantry an hour later. The only trouble on the night march down Bayou Fordoche occurred when some Confederates concealed in the brush on the west bank opened fire into Slack's brigade line. Captain Benjamin G. Paul of the 24th Iowa of Slack's brigade was killed and eight others slightly wounded. Slack's troops quickly returned fire and dispersed the hidden bushwhackers.[9]

Learning at Livonia that the False River country was flooded and impassable for his infantry, Lawler changed his plan to have them sweep the area to the east and north and at 5:00 o'clock the next morning (Tuesday, 31 May), turned his troops around to retrace their steps back to Morganza on the Bayou Fordoche and Morgan's Ferry Roads. They camped that night at the junction of the two roads.[10]

Describing their part in the two-day action to Ann, Slack wrote:

> On Monday last [30 May] we marched over or about twenty miles. Was very hot and dusty. Did not go into camp until ½ past ten at night. About 9 o'clock at night the rebels ambushed me along Bayou Fordoche and fired perhaps a hundred shots into my ranks. Could not see them, and could not get at them because of the Bayou being so swampy we could not cross it. Very few of our guns were loaded, but we returned their fire immediately with what were loaded, and one shot of canister from the 1st Missouri battery. We moved on and they opened fire upon a Brigade in my rear, from the 19th Corps. Our men returned the fire immediately and thus it ended. They fired on us at about fifty yards distance. They killed one Captain in my Command, Captain Paul, 24th Iowa, and wounded four men. You cannot imagine how startling such an attack is. It is the first time I was ever fired upon after night whilst marching. The attack was made close by where I was riding. For a moment I did not know

XIII. Morganza, the Atchafalaya and New Orleans (May–September 1864)

hardly what to do, but soon recovered the surprise and drove them. Capt Paul was shot through the chest. Was riding in the ambulance when shot. Got out & fell dead immediately upon stepping on the ground. Was a first rate man and officer, brave as a man could be.

...We killed about eight of the fellows fighting us on Monday and Tuesday, and wounded about twenty. Our loss was eight, one killed and seven wounded. We recaptured a large lot of Commissary stores and Sutlers goods, taken from the boats they destroyed on Red river, and ran the rebels all out of the country, and also destroyed a saw-mill, at which they were making lumber to build boats.[11]

Meanwhile, Lawler sent Crebs's cavalry in search of Madison's Confederates. Reconnoitering down the Grosse Tete some four or five miles below Livonia and finding no Confederate cavalry, Crebs returned up the Grosse Tete, crossed over to Bayou Maringouin, at that point about one mile to the west, and encountered Madison's troopers camped on the west bank "in the woods in the rear of David Barrow's plantation." In a running fight, Crebs's cavalry quickly scattered Madison's troopers into the canebrake and on toward the Atchafalaya and captured a considerable quantity of commissary stores and clothing at the camp. Destroying what they could not carry away, they returned that afternoon to Lawler's headquarters at the junction of the Bayou Fordoche and Morgan's Ferry Roads.[12]

In his report, Davis identified David Barrow as "the uncle of Ratcliffe [Ratliff], the guerilla" and noted that the commissary stores and clothing on Barrow's plantation had most likely been smuggled upriver by New Orleans or Baton Rouge merchants because they bore New York brands, which "negroes and others" claimed were landed on the Mississippi at Plaquemine and hauled to Barrow's plantation.[13]

On Wednesday, 1 June, Lawler sent Davis with 500 troopers, Sharpe's infantry brigade, and a section of the 7th Massachusetts Battery to destroy the sawmill on the Atchafalaya two miles below Morgan's Ferry. The battery destroyed the mill's machinery on the opposite bank, but Wharton's Confederate sharpshooters on the west bank kept them from getting the artillery close enough to the ferry to destroy the flats moored on the west bank. On their return to Lawler's headquarters, however, they destroyed several bridges on the Morgan's Ferry Road.[14]

The next day, Lawler received orders from Emory to send Davis's cavalry to Rosedale, twelve miles south of Livonia on Bayou Grosse Tete and some thirty miles south of Morganza, with orders to return to Morganza via False River country. Leaving the 3rd Maryland Cavalry with Lawler's infantry, at 10:00 A.M., Davis rode south with the remainder of his cavalry about twenty-four miles to Woolfolk's Plantation (Mound House), where they camped for the evening. That afternoon, Lawler's infantry returned to Morganza.[15]

Back at camp, Slack wrote Ann optimistically about news of Grant's progress on the eastern front. Several days later, however, Grant's troops were badly mauled in yet another disastrously bloody charge, this time at Cold Harbor, the rural crossroads about ten miles northeast of Richmond. Meanwhile, Atlanta remained in Confederate hands as Sherman and Johnston maneuvered through northwest Georgia.[16]

On their final sweep of Pointe Coupee Parish, on Friday, 3 June, Davis's cavalry moved three miles south, crossed the Rosedale drawbridge over the Grosse Tete, and swung fifteen miles northeastward on the very waterlogged plank, road to the Mississippi River at Lobdell's Landing, about ten miles below the lower end of False River. The next day, Davis sent Crebs with what he called "300 of his best horses" to sweep around the outside of False

River and Chrysler with the same number to sweep the inside. Chrysler found only poor small farms; but, about six miles out, Crebs's cavalry encountered McNelly's Scouts. In the ensuing skirmish, Crebs's troopers killed and wounded four and took a lieutenant and seven men prisoners while losing one man killed and two wounded, although Crebs reported that his horses were too used-up to pursue and take the remainder of McNelly's Scouts. They returned to Morganza the next morning.[17]

A week later, Slack's brigade and the 47th Indiana bade farewell to Morganza with a cow captured on their Bayou Fordoche expedition: "She supplies our mess with all the milk we want. Will take her to New Orleans with us ... and keep her so long as we can get transportation." Steaming toward New Orleans aboard the *N. Longworth*, cow on board, they disembarked at Kenner, Louisiana, several miles upriver from Carrolton.[18]

With the creation of E.R.S. Canby's new Military District of West Mississippi, the 13th corps was temporarily disbanded and Slack's brigade and other former 13th corps troops were assigned to E.R.S. Canby's command. Toward the end of June, Slack's brigade (the 47th Indiana, the 24th and 28th Iowa, and the 29th Wisconsin — the 56th Ohio was home on furlough) moved to the town of Thibodaux, about fifty miles southwest of New Orleans. Sitting four miles north of the tracks of the New Orleans, Opelousas & Great Western Railroad, Thibodaux was connected to New Orleans via steamers on Bayou Lafourche. "A point," Slack noted, "where all the rebel women of the surrounding country concentrate & live whose husbands are in the rebel army. They are said to be very hostile & bitter." At Thibodaux they became part of Brig. Gen. Robert A. Cameron's District of Lafourche. Cameron went on temporary leave and Slack took command of the district as Colonel William A. Greene of the 29th Wisconsin assumed temporary command of his brigade.[19]

By the beginning of July, Cameron had returned to his command of the District of Lafourche and Slack returned to command his brigade. He was ordered back to Algiers, Louisiana, on the west bank of the Mississippi across from New Orleans, to report to Major General Joseph J. Reynolds, who that month replaced William H. Emory in overall command of the 19th corps. Emory continued to command a detachment that consisted of the 1st and 2nd divisions of the 19th corps, bringing them from Morganza to New Orleans in preparation for their transfer to Virginia.[20]

Arriving at Algiers on 7 July, the next day, uncertain about future orders and referring to the breakup of the 13th corps, Slack wrote to Ann that his brigade had not yet been assigned to a division but correctly presumed that it would be placed somewhere in what was now Joseph Reynolds's 19th corps. He noted, alas, that at Thibodaux their cow proved to be "Secesh" and had run off at the first opportunity.[21]

While languishing at Algiers, most members of Slack's brigade, including Slack himself, looked forward to the prospect of being transferred east to the Army of the Potomac. On 21 July, Private Henry Bert noted that the 8th Indiana and 24th Iowa of Slack's brigade were on board a Gulf steamer heading east to Join the Army of the Potomac, mistakenly assuming the 47th Indiana would soon follow them eastward.[22]

Back in Texas, with the return of Texas Confederate troops to the state following the end of the Red River Campaign and the approach of the French Imperial Army to the Rio Grande, Francis J. Herron, commanding the last of Banks's partially successful but fading Texas Expedition, decided to withdraw from Brownsville. Although urged by Juan N. Cortina,[23] then in tenuous control of the State of Tamaulipas, not to withdraw from

Brownsville, Herron feared that he would be unable to hold the outpost and withdrew, satisfied to be "cooped up" on the coast at Brazos Santiago Island. Herron left Col. H.M. Day in command of the remaining Federal force on the island and departed to take command of the District of Baton Rouge.[24]

Confederates under John S. "Rip" Ford reoccupied Brownsville on 22 July and immediately reopened trade with Matamoros after tough negotiations with Cortina, an old antagonist of Ford and normally hostile to Confederate interests. Since the outset of the war, the sleepy fishing village of Bagdad, Mexico, at the mouth of the Rio Grande had become a major international seaport as supplies poured into Kirby Smith's Trans-Mississippi from Europe. Now, however, Smith's Trans-Mississippians were having trouble with the collapse of Confederate currency west of the Mississippi and the need to pay for supplies with scarce gold or silver specie or else barter with a now-uncertain supply of cotton. With the Federal withdrawal from Texas except for the detachment at Brazos, they were at least able to hire Mexicans, by paying them with a portion of the cargo, to haul what cotton and supplies they had to Laredo, Eagle Pass, or Brownsville, which was now devoid of forage for their livestock.[25]

Back in Algiers on 25 July, Chaplain Sawyer wrote to the *Daily Journal* about religious interest in Slack's brigade as well as the health of the men of the 47th Indiana. Sawyer also noted that one battalion of the 8th Indiana had left Algiers along with the 24th and 28th Iowa regiments from Slack's brigade, which he also believed signaled that the 47th Indiana would soon be heading to the Army of the Potomac. At the end of his letter he included the signed statement of the officers of the 47th Indiana in support of Colonel Slack against charges of cotton speculation and silverware stealing that the *Huntington Democrat* had gleefully published in their 9 June 1864 edition:

THE 47TH INDIANA—STATEMENT OF OFFICERS.
CORRESPONDENCE OF THE *INDIANAPOLIS JOURNAL*.
ALGIERS, LA., JULY 25, 1864

Morganza is left by us, and Carrollton and Kennersville and Thibodaux, and the 47th Indiana is just ready to leave Algiers and embark on ocean steamers for another Department. The men are cheerful and in high hopes. They enlisted to do service wherever they are most needed, and at a moment's notice they are ready to obey orders. One battalion of the 8th Indiana, now brigaded under Colonel Slack, has already gone with the 24th and 28th Iowa Regiments, and the rest of the brigade will soon follow them.

The fourth of July was duly celebrated at Thibodeaux. The oration of the day, delivered by the Chaplain of the 47th Indiana Volunteers, was published, a copy of which is herewith forwarded. Colonel Slack, General Cameron, and Chaplain Simmons were called out in impromptu addresses, and with eloquent and patriotic words they richly entertained the vast assembly. The day will be long remembered by the soldiers who enjoyed it so far from home.

Considerable religious interest prevails in several regiments. Out door meetings have been held, night after night for the brigade, and some of the Chaplains have preached every night at the Algiers Methodist Church for the last fortnight. Last night Rev. Dr. Newman, of New York, preached on Personal Influence. He is a man of intellect and force, an impressive speaker, of superficial theology, but of earnest patriotism.

The health of the regiment is good. The veterans stand the season and climate admirably. Like other troops from Indiana, they are anxious to be where they can strike some telling blow against the rebellion. It will be a fortnight, probably, before I can write you again.

The enclosed document in reference to Col. James R. Slack was drawn up and signed by every officer in the regiment. They all have but one opinion of the manner and baseness of those who will lie and lie willfully against the absent. You will, of course, take pleasure in publishing the document.

Yours very truly,
Samuel Sawyer
Chaplain 47th Indiana.

UNANIMOUS STATEMENT OF THE OFFICERS OF THE FORTY-SEVENTH REG'T IND. VOLS.

Certain professed abstracts of the report of the McDowell Investigating Committee charging Colonel James R. Slack, of the 47th Regiment Indiana Volunteers, with speculation in Cotton and embezzlement of Silver Ware at Helena, Ark., having been published, and such statements — as far as Colonel Slack in concerned — having been authoritatively denied by the Representatives of the State of Indiana in the United States Senate;

That the matter may go still more fully before the public, and the reputation of a most valuable officer of the army receive no injury from the misrepresentations and calumnies of the enemies of the Government — based, as they are, upon garbled extracts of *ex parte* testimony — this document, without the instigation or knowledge of Colonel Slack, is drawn up and signed by all the officers of the 47th Indiana Regiment.

We were with the regiment at Helena, Arkansas. We were intimate with Colonel Slack, and well acquainted with his acts as a military commander, and of our own personal knowledge we most positively affirm, over our own signatures, that the charge of his being connected with, or implicated in, any manner whatever in any cotton speculation at Helena, Arkansas, or anywhere else, is utterly and absolutely false. There is not one iota of evidence to sustain the accusation, and no man can make the charge without uttering a falsehood, or repeat it without being a calumniator and traducer. We use the same strong language with reference to the charge respecting the silverware taken from Mrs. Cogswell, of Commerce, Mississippi, all of which, she says, was not returned. Of our own knowledge, we assert that the box of silverware was passed by the officer who had it in charge to Colonel Slack, and by Colonel Slack, through A.R. Cooledge, merchant of Helena, to Mrs. Cogswell, exactly as he received it. As living, competent witnesses, we testify to this. So far as colonel Slack is concerned, the whole transaction was straightforward and upright. Nothing, in our judgment, can be more so.

We sign this document, unanimously, as a matter of justice to Colonel James R. Slack, that the public may know the facts. We do not believe there is an officer in the service whose entire official career in the army has been more free from all venality or corruption.[26]

As Chaplain Sawyer noted, one battalion of the 8th Indiana, and both the 24th and 28th Iowa regiments, were all transferred with William H. Emory's 19th corps detachment to the Army of the Potomac, along with their comrades in the 11th Indiana, and would eventually become part of Sheridan's force in the Shenandoah Campaign. The remainder of Slack's brigade (the 47th Indiana and 29th Wisconsin) returned upriver to what Private Bert referred to as the "miserable hole of Morganza."[27]

Having arrived at Morganza on 27 July, at 1:00 o'clock the next morning, Slack's troops moved with Daniel Ullmann's U.S. Colored Troops and E.J. Davis's cavalry on an expedition down the Morgan's Ferry Road, where, at about 10:00 o'clock, they encountered some 200 of Wharton's cavalry who had crossed to the east bank of the Atchafalaya. Wharton's troopers retreated under fire back across the river, but Federal gunners were unable to bring their artillery to bear on the three Confederate guns positioned on the west bank. Unable to cross the river, Ullman returned his force to Morganza, arriving at camp that evening after what Private Bert called "an awful hard day's march being very muddy coming in for it rained all afternoon." Lawler reported that Ullmann's expedition lost two men killed and several wounded while killing five Confederates and capturing two. Bert reported seven wounded in the 47th Indiana. Two days later, the 2nd New York Cavalry reported that the Confederates had disappeared from the west bank of the Atchafalaya and were moving north toward Alexandria.[28]

In his letter to the *Daily Journal*, Chaplain Sawyer, relying as so many did on the words of poet Robert Burns to explain the confusion about troop movements, described the place of the 47th Indiana and the disappointment that the men and officers felt about not being transported to Grant's army in the east. Sustaining Pvt. Bert's opinion of Morganza, Chaplain Sawyer also described the skirmish on the Atchafalaya at Morgan's Ferry Road and their narrow escape from poorly aimed Confederate artillery.

FROM THE 47TH INDIANA.
CORRESPONDENCE OF THE *INDIANAPOLIS JOURNAL*
MORGANZA BEND, LOUISIANA

July 28, 1864

It is just as true now as when the poet Robert Burns first wrote it, that—
"The best laid schemes of mice and men Gang aft aglee."

Ten days ago the 47th Indiana Regiment expected by this time to be near Petersburg or operating somewhere with the Eastern army. Ten regiments of us had been assigned as a division of Gen. McGinnis, and a part of Colonel Slack's brigade, the 24th and 28th Iowa, and one battalion of the 8th Indiana embarked on an ocean steamer and in a day or two we expected to follow them. The boat *Matanza* was assigned us, and many letters had been sent home telling the friends to write hereafter to Grant's army. The men were all anxious to go there, for they believe Gen. Grant has his heart set upon his work and they love to be under such men. But Tuesday morning one o'clock, the camp was roused and three transports were loaded with troops, and at two o'clock Wednesday morning we were at Morganza Bend.

We encamped between the levee and the river, the residue of Col. Slack's brigade forming the extreme right of the forces.

The camp presented a busy scene until tents were spread and bunks and tables made, and we began to feel quite at home, when orders came to Col. Slack to have his men ready at one o'clock this morning with two days' rations for active service.

It is now dark and the regiment have just returned after a most fatiguing march of thirty miles. The day too was misty and rainy and the roads heavy. They went to the Atchafalaya Bayou, the cavalry driving the rebels before them in most gallant style. At length the rebels opened on us, firing buckshot, bullets and shell across the bayou. The fire was briskly returned, and had not the bayou been in our way, the battery of the enemy could have been taken and their whole force captured. One man in the 29th Wisconsin was killed and two wounded. Three of the 8th Indiana were wounded. William Doll, Co. G, wounded in the elbow, and D.M. Coppic, Co. I, in the face. Sergt. Goodlander, Co. F, is missing; Clifton Brown, Co. F, was shot through the thigh and putting him under the influence of chloroform Dr. Bigelow amputated his leg. The men seem to be doing well.

The following soldiers of the 47th Regiment were wounded:

Sergeant Isaac Haynes, Co. C, slightly in the foot with a bullet; Samuel Heinel, Co. F, was wounded in the right fore-finger; Thomas J. Wohlford, Co. F, wounded with a piece of a spent shell in the face and a spent ball in the breast; Michael Hey, Co. G, with buckshot in the hip.

Jesse Pronty, Company A, was struck with a piece of spent shell on the arm; Humphrey Morrison, Company K, was run over by a caisson of the 21st New York Artillery; Edmond Cope, Company K, was shot through the left hand; and Solomon Phares, Company K, was hit with a piece of spent shell on the left shoulder. C.C. Parker, Company K, after he came back to camp, received a flesh wound in the hip, by the accidental discharge of a gun in Company G.

A Colonel of the 2nd New York Cavalry was shot in the shoulder.

The men think they have never been in a much more dangerous position than they were in to-day. If the rebels had not overshot us they might have killed hundreds.

Various opinions have been expressed with regard to the object of the scout. Two large wagon loads of cotton, comprising sixteen bales, were met coming in, and several loads of provisions, consisting of flour, hams, &c, were met going out of our lines. The presumption is it was all right, but the men did not understand it. General Ulmann,[29] of New York notoriety, had charge of the expedition. To-morrow another force will make a reconnaissance in the same direction.

Yours very truly,
Samuel Sawyer
Chaplain 47th Indiana Volunteers[30]

At the end of July, E.R.S. Canby brought Major General Gordon Granger from the Army of the Cumberland to the Military District of West Mississippi in New Orleans to help direct the expedition to Mobile Bay in cooperation with Admiral David G. Farragut's fleet. The long-awaited Mobile Campaign began on 3 August when Granger, with 1,800 men from New Orleans, landed on Dauphin Island, Alabama, and captured Fort Gaines. Protected by Farragut's fleet, they proceeded across the mouth of the bay to Fort Morgan and began a siege.

On 18 August, Joseph J. Reynolds's 19th corps troops at Morganza, part of E.R.S. Canby's Military District of West Mississippi, were reorganized into two divisions, one commanded by Elias Dennis, the other by George F. McGinnis. Dennis's two-brigade 2nd division consisted of Colonel Benjamin Dornblaser's 1st and Slack's 2nd brigade, which now consisted of the 47th Indiana, the 21st Iowa, the 120th Ohio, the 99th Illinois and the 29th Wisconsin. McGinnis commanded the three-brigade 3rd division.[31]

Four days later (22 August) on the Gulf Coast, Fort Morgan surrendered to Granger's besieging force following a heavy bombardment, and the Federals gained control of the entrance to Mobile Bay.

THE CLINTON EXPEDITION

Meanwhile, in an effort to disrupt the shifting of Federal troops to the Gulf Coast, a Confederate force under Colonel John S. Scott of the 1st Louisiana (CSA) Cavalry began harassing Federal outposts in the area of Clinton, Louisiana, about thirty miles north of Baton Rouge and about twenty miles northeast of Port Hudson. Although the Federals controlled the major cities in Louisiana, Confederates continued to control large areas of the countryside in southeast Louisiana and southwest Mississippi. The Confederate District of Southwest Mississippi and East Louisiana extended from the Homochitto River in southwest Mississippi on the north to the Gulf of Mexico on the south and from the Pearl River on the east to the Mississippi River on the west.[32]

Scott's troops were headquartered at Woodville, Mississippi, and there were various small Confederate forces scattered across the district with large stores at Monticello, Mississippi, on the Pearl, and at Mt. Carmel, about thirty miles east of there. They had been sending cotton to Bayou Sara in exchange for wagonloads of flour and were smuggling other contraband goods, including carbines and percussion caps, from New Orleans across Lake Pontchartrain and up the various bayous and rivers on the north shore.[33]

On 5 August at Doyal's Plantation, Scott's force (about 700 or 800 men from the 9th Louisiana Infantry Battalion and the 9th Louisiana Cavalry), then operating out of Clinton, Louisiana, surprised and surrounded a Federal outpost manned by four companies of Major S. Pierce Remington's 11th New York Cavalry. Remington escaped by charging through the Confederate line, although horses, mules, sick Federals and those who had failed to follow Remington's lead were captured. In order to clear Scott's Confederates from the area, the Federal commander at Baton Rouge, Major General Francis J. Herron, recently arrived from Texas, organized a force led by Albert L. Lee's cavalry division and Dennis's infantry division from Morganza. Lee's cavalry was to ride to Clinton from Baton Rouge on an approximately thirty-mile trek; Dennis's infantry, after steaming down from Morganza to Port Hudson, was to march approximately twenty miles to Clinton, where, in cooperation with Lee's troopers, they were to surround and capture Scott's troopers.[34] Both Slack and Lt. Col. John A. McLaughlin of the 47th Indiana were absent on leave in New Orleans. In their absence, Col. William A. Greene of the 29th Wisconsin assumed command of the detachment from Slack's brigade, which was made up of the 47th Indiana, the 120th Ohio, and the 29th Wisconsin. Major Lewis H. Goodwin assumed command of the 47th Indiana. Dornblaser's brigade consisted of the 8th, 11th, 46th and 76th Illinois, the 30th Missouri, and a detachment of the 7th Missouri. Dennis's infantry embarked on steamers from Morganza on the night of 23 August "with seven days' rations and forage and 100 rounds of ammunition per man," arriving at Port Hudson at 5:00 A.M. the next day.[35]

Lee's cavalry, except for the 11th New York, which remained on outpost duty near the Mississippi River, consisted of the 118th Illinois Mounted Infantry, the 6th Missouri, the 14th New York and the 2nd Illinois Cavalry. They rode out of Baton Rouge on the afternoon of that same day (24 August) and encountered Scott's Confederate troopers (estimated by Lee as about 1,800 men; Slack, in his 25 August letter quoted below, estimated Lee's cavalry force at 2,000) at Redwood Creek, about seventeen miles from Baton Rouge. Skirmishing sharply from midnight to 2:00 A.M., Lee's cavalry drove Scott's Confederates some seven or eight miles to the Comite River.

On 24 August at about 9:00 A.M., Scott's Confederates were dislodged from their position and a running fight ensued for about four miles until Scott's troopers made another stand one mile from Clinton. Here the 118th Illinois Mounted Infantry dismounted and, with the remainder of the Federal cavalry, drove Scott's troopers through Clinton. Lee's Federals pursued a few miles and Scott escaped with most of his command northward toward Liberty and Osyka, Mississippi. Although Scott's force remained at large, Lee's Federals captured, depending on whose report, twenty or thirty-five prisoners, including a Captain Bradford of Scott's staff and a Captain Thompson, if he survived his wounds; they also freed a number of slaves, destroyed a workshop in Clinton, and hauled off a few bales of cotton and a few cows.[36]

Dennis's infantry force of 3,000, not leaving Port Hudson until 5:00 P.M. that same day, missed the fight and the chance to capture Scott's force. With Dornblaser's brigade in the lead followed by Green's detachment from Slack's brigade, they marched all night and arrived at Clinton on the afternoon of 25 August after Lee's cavalry had already driven Scott's troopers through town. Resting in Clinton, Dennis's infantry started back to Port

Hudson in the late afternoon the next day. Arriving back at Port Hudson at 8:00 A.M. on 28 August, they boarded steamers later that afternoon and arrived back at Morganza the next morning. With only one man wounded from the 26th New York Light Artillery, the remaining thirteen casualties in Dennis's infantry came from exhaustion as men fell out on the march in the oppressive heat and humidity and were captured by Confederate cavalry that dogged their withdrawal. The 47th Indiana lost one man missing.[37]

Kirby Smith's Trans-Mississippi Confederates, in spite of their success on the Red River in Louisiana and at Camden, Arkansas, in April and the Federal withdrawal from Brownsville to Brazos Island in July, found themselves in an untenable stalemate with Federal forces. In still deeply divided Missouri, although sporadic partisan warfare continued, the Confederate Army had long since been driven out and William Rosecrans's Federals essentially controlled the key areas of the state. In Arkansas, in spite of his failure to drive Price from Camden, Frederick Steele's Federals controlled the entire length of the Arkansas River from its mouth on the Mississippi to Fort Smith and the area eastward from Little Rock to Memphis, including the lower White River. And, in Louisiana, Department of the Gulf troops essentially controlled a corridor of about twenty-five to fifty-miles wide between the Mississippi and Atchafalaya Rivers that was dotted with productive plantations, some owned by people forced by circumstances to declare their loyalty to the United States, and some owned or operated by Northern planters.

On the Confederate side, Kirby Smith still held Shreveport, the Red River Valley, the area west of the Atchafalaya, and all of Texas except Brazos Island; Sterling Price, operating out of Camden, held southeastern Arkansas; and J.O. Shelby's cavalry roamed freely in largely deserted northeastern Arkansas. Their problem was that the economy of the Confederate Trans-Mississippi had collapsed. The U.S. dollar was the paper currency in Louisiana bayou country in spite of Dick Taylor's effort to stamp it out. Confederate currency and bonds had become worthless and were not in use west of the Atchafalaya. In Texas, although Confederates had been able to reopen more of the border for arms shipments after the Federal withdrawal from Brownsville, they were unable to pay in anything except increasingly scarce gold or silver specie or bales of cotton, which were in short supply since the Federal expedition up the Red River and as western planters became unwilling to accept virtually worthless Confederate bonds in payment.[38] Nevertheless, with reports coming in that indicated Lincoln and the Republicans were vulnerable to defeat in the upcoming October and November elections, Price, at least, believed that an independent Confederacy was still possible. If McClellan and the Peace Democrats won the elections, the war-weary North, he believed, would sue for peace and open boundary negotiations with the Confederacy. The problem for Price was that the Confederate Army held no territory in his home state of Missouri and it would therefore be left out of inclusion in any Confederate boundary settlement.

To avoid this, Price believed that he could successfully raid and occupy key parts of Missouri, notably St. Louis and Jefferson City, and hold it until the presumptive start of peace and boundary negotiations. (In late August, one B.P. Van Court of the Order of American Knights, still operating a largely paper organization out of St. Louis, assured him that thousands of new recruits would flock to his banner if he invaded the state.) Kirby Smith, skeptical of Price's ambitious claims, nevertheless agreed to permit the raid, believing at least that it would provide a good diversion for their now somewhat beleaguered armies in the east.[39]

XIV

St. Charles, Arkansas (September–December 1864)

While Slack and his troops sat in camp at Morganza, Louisiana, and E. Kirby Smith and Sterling Price contemplated a move into Missouri, back in Indiana, politics reached the boiling point. In fact, by early summer, Harrison H. Dodd and his handful of Sons of Liberty cronies were busy making lucrative deals with Confederate agents in Chicago and Toronto, Canada, where Jacob "Jake" Thompson ran a small network of Confederate spies and saboteurs. Thompson and his agents had contact with Dodd and other antiwar Northerners, including Democratic politician Clement Vallandigham, then in exile in Canada, and apparently expected substantial support from the Sons of Liberty.[1]

Dodd, an inveterate schemer and con artist like the filibusters before him, had come to the attention of Thompson after he gave a speech in Hendricks County, Indiana, in which he railed against the Lincoln Administration's interference with the activities of the Democratic Party in Indiana and called for the creation of a Northwest Confederacy, Vallandigham was about to return to Ohio from his Canadian exile to participate in the upcoming elections.[2]

Northern newspaper accounts of the activities of the Sons of Liberty, and assurances by rabidly antiwar Peace Democrats like Vallandigham and Dodd who spoke for the secret society, apparently deluded Thompson and his spies into believing that the North was overrun with opponents of the war who would be willing to assist them in armed revolt. Impressed with the idea that the Sons of Liberty controlled a vast "army" of followers who would heed the call for armed rebellion and separation from the Union, Thompson held out large sums of money, $300,000 in total according to his own figures, closer to one million dollars in gold according to Confederate documents, to arm Northerners for a rebellion. Such an uprising would, if nothing else, help liberate prisoners of war held in Ohio, Indiana, and Illinois; if highly successful, it would take those old Northwestern states out of the Union, with Missouri and Kentucky to follow shortly thereafter.[3]

As one of the beneficiaries of Thompson's largesse, Dodd allegedly received an estimated $10,000 and a promised shipment of arms on the stipulation that he would lead the Sons of Liberty in an uprising immediately prior to the upcoming Democratic National Convention scheduled to open on the 4th of July. (A planned uprising scheduled for 15 June, reportedly to begin with Vallandigham's anticipated arrest when he returned to the United States, had already fizzled when Secretary of State Seward ordered that he not be arrested.) Dodd accepted the money, apparently without telling Thompson that most of his so-called members did not know of his military scheme or that newspaper stories on the strength of the Sons of Liberty, not to mention Vallendigham's personal assurances before he left Canada, were greatly exaggerated.[4]

In the meantime, Morton, increasingly worried about his chance for reelection in the October state elections and about Lincoln's reelection in November (even Lincoln believed he was going to be defeated at this time), pressured Carrington to gather more incriminating evidence on his Democratic opponents and to arrest Dodd and Dr. Bowles. Carrington's "confidential agents" had already infiltrated the few active cells of Dodd's Sons of Liberty in southern Indiana, Illinois, and Kentucky, and the Confederate plans soon became known to military authorities and the governors of those states In fact, in March 1864, while Slack was home on veteran leave in Huntington, he recruited Huntington physician and fellow War Democrat, Dr. Henry L. Zumro, to become one of Carrington's "confidential agents." Zumro, in turn, was assigned to spy on Slack's former Huntington friend and colleague, Lambdin P. Milligan, Esq.[5]

Felix Stidger, another of Carrington's "confidential agents" and perhaps the most notorious, was assigned by Carrington in May 1864 to pay particularly close attention to Dr. Bowles and his activities in southern Indiana. Stidger, in fact, became "Grand Secretary" of the Sons of Liberty in Kentucky, which was headed by Judge Joshua Bullitt of the Kentucky Court of Appeals, and was one of the few active members in Kentucky. Paid by the Sons of Liberty in Kentucky for recruiting new members, Stidger could, in fact, be considered one of its founders. Judge Bullitt introduced Stidger to Bowles and Dodd, thereby giving him intimate access to all the Sons of Liberty plans and records.[6]

Stidger, in turn, handed over to Carrington a load of papers and pamphlets on the Sons of Liberty published by Dodd, which included their purpose (essentially a states' rights platform), secret rituals, and a list of prominent officers and members, including Lambdin P. Milligan, Esq.,[7] then "Peace" candidate for governor in the Democratic primary, and J.J. Bingham, publisher of the *Indiana State Sentinel* and chairman of the Democrat Party State Central committee. Both Stidger and Carrington added unverified and exaggerated claims that Dodd's Sons of Liberty had been in cahoots with Forrest in his attack on Paducah and with Morgan on his raid into Indiana and Ohio. Carrington used the papers and pamphlets along with Stidger's and his own unverified claims to write a report to Governor Morton dated 28 June 1864 in which he detailed what he called the treasonable activities of Dodd and the Sons of Liberty. Morton delayed publication of the report for about a month, apparently to gather as much information as possible before tipping his hand that his detectives had infiltrated the Sons of Liberty, and to provide maximum damage or embarrassment to the Democratic Party, which was about to select a candidate to oppose him.[8]

Meanwhile, the Democratic National Convention at Chicago, originally scheduled for the 4th of July, was postponed until 29 August 1864, which disrupted and delayed Thompson's plans for a pro-Confederate uprising and prison break. Then, at the Indiana State Democratic Convention on 12 July, well-respected moderate and former state attorney general Joseph E. McDonald easily defeated radical peace candidate Lambdin P. Milligan for the Democratic Party gubernatorial nomination. The Democrats closed their state convention with resolutions condemning the actions of the Republican legislature and Morton's extralegal financial maneuvers; decrying the suppression of freedom of the press, habeas corpus, and the Bill of Rights in general; promoting states' rights; and calling for a more stringent "negro exclusion" law to protect jobs for white laborers from a feared influx of free blacks and mulattos looking for work in the state. McDonald immediately hit the campaign trail, assailing Morton for his usurpation of power and contempt for the Constitution and laws of the state. By the end of the month Morton struck back and the two agreed to a series of debates to begin on 10 August at La Porte.[9]

With the debates arranged, on 29 July Morton released Carrington's exaggerated expose to the *Indianapolis Daily Journal*, which used some fourteen columns to publish it in full the next day. Within several days it appeared in all the major Republican newspapers, usually under the headline: "Treason in Indiana." Morton's timing was good, and Carrington's now widely published report transformed Dodd from a mere "humbug" into a total pariah among Indiana Democrats, sending McDonald, Bingham, and other Democratic leaders scurrying to disassociate themselves from him. Morton did his best to tie McDonald to the exaggerated version of the Sons of Liberty; but McDonald would hold his own in their debates by continuing to hammer Morton on his illegal usurpation of power as governor.[10]

Carrington's expose effectively ended the Sons of Liberty as a viable organization. Apparently enraged, Dodd brought together his few remaining rabidly antiwar cronies, changed the name to the "Order of the American Cincinnatus," and metamorphosed into a dangerously loose cannon on board the Democratic ship of state by concocting a scheme to release prisoners at Camp Morton in conjunction with Thompson's planned Chicago insurrection. Neither Bingham nor Milligan nor anyone else from the Democratic State Central Committee was part of Dodd's new organization.[11]

Nevertheless, events began to unfold rapidly as Stidger, who was in Indianapolis with Judge Bullitt when he learned of Dodd's insurrection plan, had Bullitt and Dr. Henry F. Kalfus, his former superior in the 15th Kentucky and sponsor in the old Sons of Liberty, arrested upon their return to Louisville on 30 July, along with thirty-three others. Stidger, his cover still intact, returned to Indianapolis, where Dodd outlined for him his entire plan, which Stidger passed on to Carrington.[12]

Four days later, following information that Dodd frequented the Terre Haute law office of Congressman Daniel Voorhees, another outspoken critic of Morton and the Lincoln administration, Assistant Provost-Marshall Colonel Richard W. Thompson's troops in Terre Haute raided the congressman's then-unoccupied law office. They seized Sons of Liberty papers and personal correspondence, including a letter to Voorhees from former Senator James W. Wall of New Jersey dated 21 August 1863, in which Wall vouched for "the excellent quality and great efficiency of the rifles" that Voorhees had written him about. An enclosed letter dated 14 August 1863, from a supplier named E.W. Carr, said that he had "twenty-thousand rifles" available for sale. Although no record of Voorhees's having ordered or received a large shipment of rifles was produced, the *Daily Journal* trumpeted the raid and seizure of Congressman Voorhees's personal papers as proof of his, the Sons of Liberty's, and by extension, the Democratic Party's treasonable activities.[13]

On 6 August, at a council meeting of the Order of Cincinnatus in Chicago, Dodd proposed the uprising scheme which, due to the change in schedule of the Democratic National Convention in Chicago to 29 August, he rescheduled for 16 August. By now, however, with the Kentucky arrests, even his most radical cohorts who followed him into the Order of Cincinnatus realized the folly of his scheme and rejected it outright.[14]

Undaunted, Dodd visited Bingham at the *State Sentinel* office and proposed the uprising scheme. Astonished, Bingham rejected it and rounded up other fellow moderate Democrats to warn them of Dodd's crackpot scheme. Gathering the Democratic State Central Committee at the house of Morton's rival, Joseph E. McDonald, Bingham and other high-ranking Democrats warned Dodd and his partner John C. Walker to immediately drop the 16 August scheme, which they agreed to do. The Democratic State Central Committee, however, worried about what they believed would be a Republican attempt to use the military to take over the polls, urged Democrats to arm themselves and organize to protect the polls.[15]

Meanwhile, Dodd informed Bowles in southern Indiana of the scheme's rejection, and Bowles passed the news on to Stidger. Stidger, however, reported back to Carrington with the false information that the order's "Supreme Council" had approved an insurrection in the event that "a Confederate force crossed the Ohio" or "opened up in Kentucky." Carrington then reported the planned insurrection to Samuel P. Heintzelman, his Northern Department commander in Columbus, Ohio, and added his own exaggeration that one Andy Humphreys, a candidate for state representative, was responsible for guerrilla raids in Sullivan and Green Counties.[16]

Meanwhile, under pressure from Morton to arrest Dodd, Carrington put Dodd and his Indianapolis printing and publishing company under surveillance. When a shipment of boxes arrived at Dodd's shop on 20 August, a squad of Carrington's military police raided and seized-to the great dismay of Dodd, not to mention the consternation of McDonald, Bingham, and the Democratic State Central Committee-an unusually large shipment of arms and ammunition for a bookbinder ("400 large navy revolvers and 135,000 rounds of fixed ammunition for that same arm") that had arrived from New York that afternoon. Papers from Dodd's office were also seized, primarily his mailing list, the "Great Seal of the Order of the Sons of Liberty," and several hundred copies of their printed ritual. Based on this evidence, William H. Harrison, secretary of the Sons of Liberty, was arrested and incarcerated. Charles P. Hutchinson and J.J. Parsons, Dodd's partners in the printing business, were also arrested, but released on their affidavits that they were not members of the secret order. Dodd, a delegate to the Democratic National Convention, was in Chicago for the convention at the time of Carrington's raid and was not immediately arrested.[17]

Meanwhile, Captains Thomas H. Hines and John B. Castleman, two Confederate agents from Jake Thompson's Canadian spy network, came to Chicago to lead an uprising and release of prisoners at Camp Douglas during the Democratic National Convention. Both Hines and Castleman were former members of John Hunt Morgan's cavalry and had come to Illinois with about sixty or so former Confederate soldiers who had escaped from northern prisons and wanted to return to the Confederate Army. Hines, who led the expedition, had persuaded Thompson that, even after the 16 August cancellation, the Sons of Liberty were still reliable. With all the money and arms Thompson had sent to the Sons of Liberty, he and his small band of soldier/spies, using the Democratic National Convention as a cover, could lead the supposed Sons of Liberty "army" in the uprising and liberation of prisoners from Camp Douglas, if not Rock Island as well, without any undue risk to the prisoners. Traveling in small groups intermingled with conventioneers, they rendezvoused in Chicago shortly before the convention.[18]

Upon their arrival in Chicago, Hines and Castleman not only discovered Federal soldiers swarming the city, but that their Sons of Liberty contacts, including Dodd himself, had no "army," had never seriously organized for an uprising or release of prisoners from Camp Douglas or any other prison, and were disinclined, and most probably never intended, to become involved in any sort of armed uprising to bring down the government. With that, Hines, Castleman, and their two small bands of provocateurs left the city and headed into southern Illinois, where they avoided capture with help from friendly Copperheads who were not involved in any grand conspiracy, but who ran what was, in effect, a reverse Underground Railroad.[19]

Hines and Castleman made grand claims of burning boats at St. Louis and Federal installations at Mattoon and Marshall, Illinois, although the record shows that no incendiary sabotage that could be attributed to them took place at those locations in September and October. Rather, Hines and his squad continued on to Kentucky via Cincinnati, while Castleman and his squad remained quiescent in southern Illinois. They appear to have dispersed when Castleman was arrested at Sullivan, Indiana, in early October by Carrington's troops and held in close quarters at Camp Morton and the Old Capital Prison in Washington, D.C., for the remainder of the war.[20]

In Chicago, the Democratic National Convention proceeded without disruption, the party split between the "War Democrats," who believed that recognition of the Union by the Confederates should be an indispensable precondition for peace talks, and the "Peace Democrats," represented by Clement Vallandigham, who believed that cessation of hostilities should proceed without any preconditions. The convention concluded on 31 August 1864 with the nomination of "War Democrat" General George B. McClellan but with a "Peace Democrat" platform that essentially called for immediate cessation of hostilities and return to the antebellum status quo with "the rights of the States unimpaired." This of course included the reinstitution of slavery in the South as well as the resumption of constitutionally protected freedom of speech and press, and citizens' right to bear arms. To assuage the Peace Democrats who did not trust McClellan to follow their platform, the convention then nominated staunch Vallandigham supporter George H. Pendleton of Ohio as vice president. The Republican press quickly dubbed the duo the "War Horse" and the "Peace Horse."[21]

McClellan's nomination and the virtual disappearance of any support for insurrection ended Jake Thompson's plans for an uprising and massive prison break in the Northwest, although Thompson remained hopeful that the large sums of money he had spent on draft resistance, arson, and other individual acts of sabotage would eventually pay off. In the end, Thompson blamed the large Federal military force, and the large bounties paid by the swarms of Federal detectives to informers, for the failure of his operatives to liberate any prisoners or foment a successful insurrection in the Northwest.[22]

In the meantime, on 29 August, Alvin P. Hovey, apparently at Morton's request, replaced Carrington in command of the Military District of Indiana. Both Carrington, who had done most of the investigation, and Heintzelman, Carrington's Northern Department commander, believed the prisoners should be tried in the federal circuit court. Morton, on the other hand, preferred a military tribunal. The matter was settled when Secretary of War Stanton telegraphed Morton on 21 August and asked him, "How would you like to have General Hovey assigned to command the Military District of Indiana?" To which Morton responded on the same day, "Gen. Hovey will be satisfactory. Order him here at once."[23]

With that, in what would become a precedent-setting case in constitutional law, Hovey, who, like Morton, believed strongly that any alleged conspirator should be tried by military commission, replaced Carrington in command of the Military District of Indiana. Carrington turned his investigation over to Hovey, and when Dodd returned to Indianapolis from the Democratic National Convention in Chicago on or about 3 September, Hovey arrested him and placed him in military custody. Dodd's partner, John C. Walker, who had also taken money from Thompson, avoided arrest by fleeing to Canada.[24]

Back at Morganza in early September, Slack and the 47th Indiana, "ready to move at a moment's notice," had seen little action except taking occasional potshots at Confederate scouts on the east bank of the Mississippi.[25]

In the meantime, about three hundred miles north, Sterling Price led Marmaduke and Fagan's cavalry divisions out of the southern Arkansas town of Princeton on the first leg of his Missouri raid. Although about one-third of his troopers were unarmed, he believed he could move northward, capture arms and ammunition from the isolated Federal garrisons on the Arkansas River, cross the river near Little Rock, and swing northeastward to rendezvous with Shelby's cavalry at the small, deserted town of Pocahontas in northeastern Arkansas. From there, they would take a force of 12,000 in three columns into southeastern Missouri, their primary objective the Federal Arsenal at St. Louis.[26]

Shelby's cavalry, which numbered about 2,500 and had been operating relatively freely along the Mississippi River, had reportedly been supplied with arms and ammunition by smugglers from Memphis. Operating in eastern Arkansas, Shelby raided near Helena in early August to divert attention from Price's planned movement northward from Princeton. Later in the month, to divert attention from Price's movement west of Little Rock, Shelby attacked several Federal posts on the Memphis & Little Rock Railroad, between eight and fifteen miles west of De Valls Bluff on the White River and some forty to fifty miles east of the capital. They destroyed some ten miles of track, surrounded and captured post guards from the 54th Illinois Cavalry at three posts on the railroad (Shelby claimed 577 prisoners), downed telegraph wires, tore up track, burned 3,000 bales of hay and farm equipment, and captured 500 stand of small arms, horses, blankets, and shoes before the Federal cavalry reinforcements from the 8th Missouri, a detachment of the 9th Missouri Cavalry (U.S.), and the 9th Iowa Cavalry arrived to chase them off. Steele telegraphed Canby for reinforcements.[27]

On 6 September, A.J. Smith's veteran 4,500-man 16th corps detachment (the 1st and 3rd divisions), then passing Cairo on their way to reinforce George Thomas's garrison at Nashville, were diverted to St. Louis to help Rosecrans's inexperienced Department of Missouri militia volunteers defend the city against Price's raid.[28]

Slack wrote Ann that same day from aboard the steamer *Laurel Hill* that he and his troops were being sent up the White River to reinforce Steele's beleaguered troops in Arkansas, although when he wrote her two days later from their camp in a large, mosquito-infested cotton field at the mouth of White River, he noted with some foresight that Price and Shelby would probably bypass Little Rock and raid Missouri instead. Describing the trip from Morganza, he told Ann that the *Laurel Hill* was so packed that it was almost impossible to move around. Although he did not mention the incident, which may have occurred on another of the overcrowded steamers, Pvt. Eli E. Rose of Company F was accidentally shot in the right arm near the shoulder by Pvt. Harvey Oats of his company. Fortunately,

XIV. St. Charles, Arkansas (September–December 1864)

it was only a flesh wound, and Pvt. Rose recovered as the overcrowded troops debarked and set up camp.[29]

In the meantime, in the first several days of September, Sherman's forces defeated Bell Hood at Jonesboro and Lovejoy's Station and now occupied the city of Atlanta. (General John Hood had been given command of the Army of Tennessee, replacing Joe Johnston, who was relieved of command for his seeming inability to stop Sherman. News that Sherman had taken Atlanta first appeared in the *Indianapolis Daily Journal* on 3 September, and Slack noted in his 8 September letter that they had just received word of it in camp at about the same time they learned of McClellan's nomination for president by the Democrats. Both events, he said, were received favorably in camp. He did not find the Democratic Party platform objectionable, considered it a big defeat for the Copperheads, and predicted that McClellan would "get a strong army vote." That same day, McClellan, after waffling between the two factions, formally accepted the Democratic nomination but insisted on the "conservative" view that "re-establishment of the Union" (presumably under Federal terms) was an "indispensable condition for peace."[30]

On Saturday, 10 September, they started up the White River to St. Charles, Arkansas, and arrived there Sunday evening after "a very tedious and unpleasant trip." At 3:00 P.M. on Saturday, "a log got into one of [the] wheels and broke out four brackets and six arms." Unable to run with one wheel, they had to lay up five hours for repairs; and unable to run the snag- and sand bar-filled river at night, they were forced to wait until morning to continue. But, before departing early on Sunday, the *Pringle* sprang a leak, forcing them to turn on the pumps and hoist out the ammunition and other stores. Slack proceeded to St. Charles aboard the steamer *Mittie Stevens*, leaving the disabled *Pringle* under charge of John McLaughlin. The steamer *Melenotte* took some of the 47th Indiana troops and helped lighten the *Pringle*'s load so she could get over the bars. Slack reached St. Charles on Sunday afternoon at about two o'clock, the *Melenotte* at about five, and the *Pringle* at about eight. The remainder of Slack's brigade, the 21st Iowa, the 87th Illinois Mounted Infantry, and one section of the 7th Massachusetts Battery, had arrived at six o'clock in the evening.[31]

With "very fine camping grounds" at St. Charles, Slack placed the 47th Indiana on the right, the 99th Illinois on the left, and the 21st Iowa in the center, inside the outer line of works, with the 29th Wisconsin and the 120th Ohio in reserve on the inside of the inner line of works. Four artillery pieces were placed in the outer works, and two in the inner; the 87th Illinois Mounted Infantry camped to the right and rear of the 47th Indiana near the river; and two light-draft tinclads patrolled the riverfront. Slack established his headquarters inside the outer works in the house of a Mr. Hennant, a Union man reportedly threatened with death by Confederate partisans.[32]

Meanwhile, Shelby had moved north following his raid on the Memphis & Little Rock Railroad west of De Valls Bluff and was waiting to link with Price at or near the deserted town of Pocahontas, Arkansas, about 160 miles north of St. Charles. With Shelby no longer in the area and unaffected by Price's move toward Missouri, Slack was able to set up his brigade headquarters and administer to the ever-mounting needs of the impoverished people in Federally occupied Arkansas, many of them destitute widows. Aside from occasional encounters with bushwhackers who infested the area, garrison duty at St. Charles was relatively easy.[33]

On 27 September, Chaplain Sawyer submitted his resignation. Several months later, the *Daily Journal* published Sawyer's farewell letter, in which he wrote: "[T]he revolution almost ended, the General Assembly of the Presbyterian Church have directed me here [Knoxville], as Missouri Agent, to re-organize our churches, which have been decimated or broken down in the progress of the war." Somewhat surprisingly, he concluded by praising "Parson" Brownlow, his prewar nemesis who had played a leading role in forcing him out of East Tennessee back in 1857: "Of Dr. Brownlow nothing need be said. The country knows his unyielding loyalty, and the world will yet read the story of his patriotism with admiration."[34]

Back in Indiana, Harrison H. Dodd's trial before Hovey's military commission began on 22 September in the Post Office Building at Indianapolis. Dodd, originally incarcerated in the military prison at Indianapolis, requested, and was granted, on his word of honor that he would not escape, a transfer to what military officials called "mitigated confinement" in a room on the second floor of the Post Office Building where his trial was being held.[35]

Dodd faced five charges: Conspiracy against the government of the United States; affording aid and comfort to the rebels against the authority of the United States; inciting insurrection; disloyal practices; and violations of the laws of war. Essentially, Dodd was charged with treason, the charges generally specifying that he was an organizing member and Grand Commander in Indiana of the Sons of Liberty, whose purpose was the overthrow of the government; he had communicated with the enemy; he had conspired to seize munitions of war and to free rebel prisoners in the north; and he had attempted to establish a Northwest Confederacy. In spite of the incriminating evidence that Carrington claimed had been collected from Dodd's Indianapolis office (the 400 revolvers and 135,000 rounds of ammunition, the seal and membership list, the printed "Ritual" of the organization, as well as a roll of 400 Confederate prisoners said to be members of the order), Dodd pleaded not guilty to all the charges and specifications.[36]

The trial began with Major Henry L. Burnett, Judge Advocate of the Northern Department, presenting the government's witnesses, the first and principal one being none other than Henry B. Carrington's "confidential agent," Felix G. Stidger. Although Carrington had offered no direct evidence of any overt act of treason, Stidger's inside information, albeit somewhat tainted, accompanied by testimony from other former associates that he had communicated with Confederates, made Dodd's hope of acquittal look quite remote.[37]

Meanwhile, as Dodd's trial progressed in the first week of October and as the crucial state elections approached, Hovey ordered the arrests of nine more alleged conspirators: J.J. Bingham, editor of the *State Sentinel* and chairman of the State Democratic Central Committee, after he criticized the trial and the political motives behind it in his newspaper; Dr. David Yeakel; Dr. James B. Wilson; Lamdin P. Milligan, Esq.[38]; Horace Heffren; Andrew Humphreys; Stephen Horsey; Dr. William A. Bowles; and William H. Harrison. With the new wave of arrests and the evidence piling up against him, the worried but ever-resourceful Dodd escaped from his third-floor cell in the Post Office Building in the wee hours of 7 October. One version, Klement's "twine-in-the-pie" story, has Mrs. Dodd bringing him a pie on the evening before his escape in which she had concealed a length of twine. Dodd is said to have used that twine "to draw up to his window a large rope furnished by some parties outside who assisted in the escape." Whether or not this version of the story is accurate, Dodd did escape with help and fled to Canada via Minnesota.[39]

Dodd escaped only four days before the state elections, and Republican newspapers made hay of the story and helped the Republicans regain the seats in the legislature lost to the Democrats two years before, not to mention aiding Lincoln's reelection bid a month later. With Dodd on the lam, Judge Advocate Henry Burnett rested the case against him and recessed the trial until 10 October, one day before the state elections, so that he could prepare for the prosecution of the other prisoners and the commissioners could review the evidence and return their verdict.[40]

On 10 October, the commission reconvened the Dodd trial and both sides presented their final arguments. The prosecution asserted they had proven conclusively that Dodd was guilty on all charges and specifications; Dodd's attorneys, on the other hand, argued that the military court lacked jurisdiction and that the evidence presented by the government before Dodd's sudden departure amounted to nothing more than hearsay and supposition. The military commission rejected the defense arguments and ruled that Hovey had convened the commission within his military jurisdiction and that martial law was therefore in effect. Dodd was found guilty on all charges and specifications and sentenced *in absentia* to death by hanging. The remaining defendants remained incarcerated for their military trial.[41]

The voting in state elections began the next day (11 October) in Indiana, Ohio, and Pennsylvania, the other state elections to be held on national Election Day, 8 November. With Sherman's timely occupation of Atlanta and the trial, escape and conviction *in absentia* of H.H. Dodd, the Republicans swept to victory in all three states. In Indiana, Morton defeated McDonald, who had run a credible race, by about 20,000 votes and thereby made it unlikely that the Democrats would ever be able to prosecute him for his extralegal actions as governor. On the national level, Indiana picked up four Republican congressional seats, Ohio eight, and Pennsylvania six, assuring the Republican Party a strong enough majority in the next Congress, regardless of the outcome of the other congressional races, to prevent McClellan, if he were elected in November, from conceding anything "to the rebels."[42]

Back in Arkansas, during a three-day conference with Frederick Steele at Little Rock, Slack learned that if Price's raiders were to pass near there on their retreat from Missouri, his brigade would be involved in the action. On 19 October from his headquarters at St. Charles, Slack reassured Ann, again with some foresight, that Price would be defeated in Missouri and forced to retreat through Kansas and Indian Territory, although, he added, "the old thief" would not be caught.[43]

At the time Slack wrote the letter, Price's raiders were nowhere near Little Rock. Price had encountered almost no citizen support upon entering Missouri, and realizing that his cavalry could not take St. Louis with A.J. Smith's veterans blocking the way, he had veered westward.[44] Forced to bypass Jefferson City as well, and now attempting to avoid direct confrontation with the Federals, Price opted to inflict as much structural damage as he could before he left the state. He had raided successfully along the Missouri River and the Pacific Railroad west of Jefferson City, tearing up track, downing telegraph lines, looting homes and farms, and temporarily taking over the towns of Glasgow and Sedalia, where he picked up a few recruits and some reluctant conscripts. But the Federals finally gathered an effective pursuit force and his time ran out.[45]

In western Missouri on the day Slack wrote his letter, Price encountered a hastily organized three-brigade force of Kansas militia under James Blunt from Curtis's Army of the Border that had moved into Missouri to stop them. Although pursued from the east by Alfred Pleasanton's four-brigade cavalry division and A.J. Smith's infantry, over the next several days Price easily pushed Blunt's militia westward some thirty miles from Lexington to the Little Blue River and on to the Big Blue at Independence, where Curtis formed a battle line with the remainder of his Kansas troops.[46]

Had Curtis been able to hold the front at any one of those locations between Lexington and Independence, Pleasanton's cavalry and A.J. Smith's slower-moving infantry might have caught them from behind and destroyed them. At Independence on 22 October, Curtis's troops put up a stiff resistance but were forced to fall back late in the day against superior numbers just as Pleasanton's cavalry hit Price's rear guard from behind and routed them. Curtis's withdrawal from his front and some confusion in Pleasanton's command in his rear enabled Price to escape southward while under pursuit. As evening fell, Price was able to form a line along Brush Creek just south of Westport, although he lost two pieces of artillery and some 300 to 400 men captured in the retreat. The next day at Brush Creek (Westport), Pleasanton's cavalry, with support from Curtis and Blunt's Kansans, continued to push Price and the remainder of his three-column force southward, nearly capturing Price's loaded wagon train.[47]

On the morning of 25 October, the Federals shelled Price's camp on the Marais des Cygnes and drove them across Mine Creek and the Little Osage River, capturing Marmaduke, Cabell, and several other officers along with at least 500 more prisoners, Price's artillery, and his plunder-laden wagons. As Price continued to retreat, on 28 October he was forced to make one last stand at the town of Newtonia in southwest Missouri by a portion of Blunt's Kansas militia (two brigades and the 1st Colorado Battery). Although Blunt's militia was greatly outnumbered, he believed that support was closer than it was and attacked Price's camp in the late afternoon. During the two-hour battle Blunt's militia, protected from a bluff in the rear by canister fire from the 1st Colorado Battery, was forced back about 500 yards.

Near sundown, just as they were about to be flanked, Sanborn's veteran cavalry brigade arrived, dismounted, and routed the flanking force. The flankers and the remainder of Price's raiders escaped under cover of darkness, leaving their dead and wounded on the field. Pursuit ended the next day when Rosecrans recalled his troops to St. Louis, and Curtis, left with only 3,500 troops who wanted to go home, returned to Kansas. Price continued southwestward through Indian Territory to northern Texas, and moved with a few remaining troopers back into southwestern Arkansas after having lost his wagon train, some rustled cattle, his artillery, half his horses, and most of his Missouri recruits.[48]

On 24 October, after conferring with Elias Dennis[49] at the mouth of the White River, Slack began moving his brigade from St. Charles to the railhead at De Valls Bluff to be in position to assist Steele. By the next day, while Price's raiders were being defeated on the Marais des Cygnes, they were encamped at De Valls Bluff. As Slack predicted, Price's defeated raiders fled through Indian Territory and "the old thief" was not caught.[50]

Back home in Indianapolis, on 21 October the second treason trial began with only Lambdin P. Milligan, Esq., Stephen A. Horsey, Dr. William A. Bowles, Andrew Humphreys, and Horace Heffren indicted. Three of the other prisoners, J.J. Bingham, Dr. James B. Wilson, and William H. Harrison were released and given immunity from prosecution in exchange for testimony against the other five. The fourth to be released was Dr. David T.

XIV. St. Charles, Arkansas (September–December 1864)

Yeakel, reportedly because he had firsthand knowledge of key government witness Felix Stidger's activities in the Sons of Liberty and was eager to rebut his testimony.[51]

With the exception of Bingham, Wilson, and Harrison, the government witnesses in the second trial were basically the same as those available for Dodd's before his sudden departure abruptly ended the first trial. Drawn from a varied assortment of people, they included "confidential agents" such as Stidger, Confederate prisoners of war who would gain their freedom by testifying, deserters from the U.S. Army who would gain immunity from prosecution if they testified that they were induced to desert by members of secret organizations, and other citizen prisoners linked with those secret organizations who would be released if they testified for the government. All were either paid informants or those with vested interests in testifying for the government.[52]

One witness who was paid to testify specifically against Milligan was Huntington physician Henry L. Zumro, one of Carrington's "confidential agents" who had been recruited back in March by Slack while he was home on veteran furlough. Assured he would be protected, and with the approval of the Provost Marshall's office, Zumro agreed to work for $100 per month. He was to make public anti–Lincoln statements, join the local Sons of Liberty, be "arrested" for "disloyal" activities, and hire Milligan as his legal counsel to defend him against these charges in hopes of luring and entrapping Milligan into committing or at least admitting specific treasonable Sons of Liberty activities.[53]

Milligan was too smart a lawyer to be entrapped in this manner, whether or not he had inside information on treasonable activities, and gave Zumro nothing with which to indict him. As a result, Zumro's testimony amounted to nothing more than supposition and hearsay about Milligan's "disloyalty."[54]

In fact, as the trial proceeded into its second week, Yeakel's testimony proved to be unnecessary as both Bingham and Harrison, testifying for the prosecution, contradicted Stidger's testimony, which was, if not full-blown perjury, based almost entirely on second-hand information at best and was full of unproven assumptions. In fact, Harrison and Bingham's testimony placed the alleged conspiracy solely in Dodd's hands and was far more favorable to the defense than it was to the prosecution. To counteract this unforeseen turn of events, Judge Advocate Burnett dropped all charges against defendant Horace Heffren in return for Heffren's turning state's evidence and testifying for the prosecution.[55]

The turning of Heffren by the prosecution just days before the presidential election came as a major surprise to Heffren's attorney, Cyrus L. Dunham, Esq., who stated in court that he had no prior knowledge of the deal between his client and the prosecution and that he first learned in open court that Heffren was to become a government witness when Burnett called Heffren to the stand. Under cross-examination, Heffren stated that one evening during the trial, while having dinner with Governor Morton and General Hovey, General Hovey suggested that he become a witness for the prosecution. Both Heffren and Burnett denied any deal was made, although Burnett acknowledged that he could not have called Heffren, or any other defendant, to the stand without first having dropped all charges and specifications. Burnett defended his actions by arguing that the government could quash any charges or specifications against a defendant at any time.[56]

In their 3 November edition, the editor of the *Huntington Democrat* charged that hundreds of draft resisters and protesters were being arrested in Indiana and that the sweeping midnight raids had the state in the grips of a "Reign of Terror."

The arrests are invariably made at midnight, with the utmost stealth, and when the victim least suspects that his safety is endangered. To such a pitch have the fears of the people been aroused, that the galloping of a horse at midnight past a house brings the family to their feet; the growling of a watch dog sets them to trembling, and a tap on the door throws them into despair. Neighbors distrust each other, and social intercourse seems entirely destroyed.[57]

Lending some credence to the *Huntington Democrat*'s charge of a "Reign of Terror," in a transparent attempt to influence the national elections, on the night of 7 November, Colonel Benjamin J. Sweet, commandant of Camp Douglas, sent his soldiers along with Chicago police on an all-night raid to arrest conspirators in an alleged plot to release prisoners from Camp Douglas and sack and burn Chicago. Over one hundred citizens were dragged from their homes that night and imprisoned at Camp Douglas.[58]

There, of course, had been a "Camp Douglas Conspiracy" directed by Jake Thompson in Canada to coincide with the 29 August Democratic National Convention in Chicago, but it had been aborted by Hines and Castleman for lack of support from Dodd's presumptive "army." In October, however, as Klement points out, a new Camp Douglas conspiracy was concocted by newspaperman William "Deacon" Bross, president of the *Chicago Tribune*, who presumably wanted to increase newspaper sales and influence the election, and by Colonel Benjamin J. Sweet, who reportedly desired to rejuvenate his declining military career.[59]

Bross had picked up rumors of the planned August attack on Camp Douglas; and, when it did not take place, he, with the help of Colonel Sweet, invented a story that an uprising was planned for the eve of the presidential election. In a conspiracy of their own, Sweet and Bross hired or recruited a number of highly dubious and untrustworthy characters to dig up evidence of a new plot. One who would figure prominently was Isaiah W. Ayer, a civilian con artist/hustler who worked with Bross. At the time, shades of George Bickley, Ayer, who apparently had attended Harvard periodically for several years but had received no degree, was posing as a doctor of eclectic medicine in Chicago. Two of the others were John T. Shanks and Maurice Langhorne, both of whom had served with Morgan's cavalry. Shanks had been captured with Morgan and imprisoned at Camp Douglas; Langhorne had come with Hines to Chicago in August but stayed behind when Hines and the others left the city and reportedly approached Sweet with information for sale. Sweet hired him, smuggled Shanks out of Camp Douglas, and put them together, in exchange for pay and full pardons, if they provided Sweet with the "evidence" he needed to justify his sweeping pre-election raids. They did their part by attempting to entrap a number of prominent antiwar Democrats, and by providing false information against them when that failed; Bross did his part by publishing the "exposé" in the 6, 7, and 8 November editions of the *Tribune*. About fifty more citizens were arrested as the sweep continued in the days following the election, but only eight were actually indicted by Judge Advocate Burnett on two charges: conspiracy to release prisoners from Camp Douglas and conspiracy to lay waste and destroy the city of Chicago.[60]

In Indiana and elsewhere on 8 November, Lincoln swept to victory. As results came in the next day, the *Indianapolis Daily Gazette*, citing Copperhead conspiracies and Democratic dupes as the reason for the sweeping Republican victory, ran the headline "The Union Forever! Old Abe Vindicated," and boasted: "The reply to the Dodd conspiracy has been emphatic and Indiana has been redeemed from Copperhead factions. The majority will be much greater than that for Governor Morton. The Confessions of Bingham and Heffren have had their effect upon the men who had been duped by them and their partners in villainy, the Democratic leaders of the State."[61]

Back at the Indianapolis treason trials, John R. Coffroth, Slack's good friend and colleague from Huntington, defended Milligan. He asserted that Milligan had been targeted for arrest shortly after he gave his anti–Lincoln political address to a large audience of preconvention Democrats at Fort Wayne on 13 August 1864. Milligan had, Coffroth noted, spoken out against the control New England states exerted over national politics and the agricultural economy of the northwest, but he had never conspired to bring about a secession of the northwestern states. That had been solely the "insane and hellish" scheme of Dodd and a few others who had not been indicted, but that it had been scuttled when the Democratic State Central Committee, meeting at Joseph McDonald's office, rejected the idea.[62]

Coffroth argued that Milligan's address at Fort Wayne was constitutionally protected political speech that had been misrepresented in the press by William S. Bush of the politically partisan *Cincinnati Gazette*, who had been "paid a penny a line" for an article written to embarrass or assail the Democratic Party prior to the election. Bush, who acted as a court reporter and government witness during the proceedings, was permitted to give hearsay testimony about what he recalled that Milligan had said without introducing the full text of the speech.[63]

Coffroth also noted that, unlike government witness Joseph J. Bingham, who had learned of the planned uprising but had failed to report it to the authorities, Milligan had no knowledge of any such scheme. Even government secret agent Felix Zumro, posing as Milligan's client, had been unable to entrap him into admitting complicity or providing any other information pertaining to the conspiracy. Without mentioning his friend Jim Slack's part in recruiting Zumro, Coffroth said that he was "compelled to give its authors credit for the completeness of their plan," but noted that it had failed to find treasonable activity on the part any of the accused. Felix Zumro's attempt to entrap Milligan, he argued, was proof that any conspiracy that may have existed was, in fact, a government conspiracy. Another key government witness, secret agent Felix G. Stidger, while under Carrington's pay and direction, had assisted in recruiting new members and extending the order in Kentucky and Indiana. And, Coffroth noted, the testimony of the other key government witnesses, Joseph J. Bingham, Dr. James B. Wilson, and Horace Heffren, also fell under a "cloud of suspicion" because they were, by their testimony, purchasing their own immunity from prosecution.[64]

Jonathan W. Gordon, Esq., representing both Bowles and Humphreys, argued, as did the other defense attorneys, that Hovey's military commission had no jurisdiction in this case; that the civilian courts in Indiana were open and that jurisdiction belonged there. Martin M. Ray, Esq., also representing Bowles and Milligan, defended them with arguments similar to Coffroth's defense of Milligan, impugning the government witnesses and noting that no direct evidence of treasonable activity against his clients had been presented at trial; that membership in the Sons of Liberty, in and of itself, did not constitute a treasonable conspiracy.[65]

In his closing argument for the government, Judge Advocate Henry L. Burnett, of course, asserted that General Hovey had the right under his military authority to make the arrests and establish a military commission to try the defendants, and that he had "proved beyond question" that a "thoroughly organized" and "partially armed" conspiracy existed "in almost every town and county" of Indiana as well as in the States of Missouri, Illinois, Kentucky, and Ohio.[66]

The trial ended on 1 December following the closing arguments. Following an adjournment until 6 December, the four defendants were quickly found guilty on all charges, although Andrew Humphries and Stephen Horsey were acquitted on several of the specifications. Humphreys was found not guilty on the 2nd Specification of Charge III, "Inciting Insurrection" (i.e., he was not guilty of arousing sentiments hostile to, or attempting to induce people to revolt against, the Government of the United States), and on the 1st Specification of Charge V, "Violations of the Laws of War" (i.e., he was not guilty of engaging in rebellion against the United States while the United States was at war, or of attempting with enemies of the United States to overthrow and destroy the authority of the United States). He was sentenced to imprisonment at hard labor for the duration of the war. Horsey was found not guilty on the 5th Specification of Charge IV, "Disloyal Practices" (i.e., he was not guilty of being an officer in the military forces of an "unlawful secret society" in Indiana). Nevertheless, he was sentenced to death along with Lambdin P. Milligan, Esq., and Dr. William A. Bowles, who were convicted on all charges and specifications, and the three were remanded to their cells at the Soldiers' Home prison. The findings and sentences, which were not made public, were sent to President Lincoln for final approval.[67]

On 23 December, Judge Advocate Henry Burnett, now free to prepare a second political show trial, transferred thirteen of the over one hundred people arrested and incarcerated at Camp Douglas on his pre-election sweep, including the Hon. Buckner S. Morris and his wife Mary, to the McLean Barracks military prison in Cincinnati in preparation for what would become known as the "Cincinnati Treason Trials."[68]

While the military arrests and trials garnered headlines, back in Arkansas and far from the action on the eastern fronts, on 16 November, the 47th Indiana and the 29th Wisconsin were sent by rail to Little Rock. Private Bert noted that the 47th Indiana arrived at 9:00 A.M. without shelter, at about 1:00 P.M. they were deluged by a heavy downpour that lasted until 10:00 o'clock the next morning, drenching the men and turning their camp into a sea of mud. The next day, Bert noted, they finally "got into some houses which some other soldiers," who had been transferred to Fort Smith, "had built and left." Meanwhile, Slack and the remainder of his brigade embarked for Memphis, the 99th Illinois and the 120th Ohio on board the steamer *John H. Dickey*, and the 21st Iowa on the steamer *Rose Hambleton*. At Memphis, Slack was appointed brigadier general and headed home on furlough.[69]

About a week later, the 47th Indiana and 29th Wisconsin were ordered to rejoin Dennis's division at Memphis, where the army reorganized. The old 19th corps was designated the Reserve Corps of the Military Division of West Mississippi, commanded by J.J. Reynolds with headquarters in New Orleans. M.K. Lawler took command of Slack's old brigade, which was designated the 1st brigade of the Reserve Corps. The 28th and 29th Illinois were added, and the 120th Ohio was consolidated with the 114th Ohio and transferred to the 3rd brigade of the Reserve Corp. N.J.T. Dana was assigned command of the new Department of Mississippi with headquarters at Memphis, where Lawler's brigade and other reserves remained "in readiness to move out an any moment and in any direction required."[70]

In the meantime, following the fall of Atlanta in September, in an audacious, last-gasp move on an even larger scale than Sterling Price's raid in Missouri, John Bell Hood turned his Army of Tennessee northward to attack Nashville and bade farewell to Sherman's immense Federal army.

To counter Hood's move, and with A.J. Smith's detachment from his Army of the Tennessee still in western Missouri following Price's raid and unable to reach Nashville in time, Sherman detached John Schofield's Army of the Ohio and David Stanley's 4th corps and sent them under Schofield's command to Nashville to reinforce George Thomas's green garrison troops. Sherman, in the meantime, garrisoned Atlanta, and, without opposition, began his march to the sea.

On 29 November, Hood nearly corralled Schofield's army at Spring Hill, Tennessee, but let them slip northward that night to the breastworks at Franklin. The next day, in a folly even greater than Pickett's at Gettysburg, he ordered a disastrous charge that effectively cost him nearly two-thirds of his army and his best generals. That night Schofield withdrew his force to Nashville. Hood, whose army, except for S.D. Lee's division, lay in ruins, nevertheless pushed on to Nashville, where, in the bitter cold of 16 December, after a blunder or two by the Federals the day before, he was routed by Thomas's Federals, which now included Schofield's troops, James Steadman's detachment from Chattanooga, and A.J. Smith's 16th corps detachment from Missouri.

Retreating southward, the remnants of Hood's army began crossing the Tennessee River the day after Christmas with the help of the seemingly ever-present Forrest and his cavalry who, aided by the inclement weather, checked the pursuit by James H. Wilson's Federal cavalry.

In late December, while the remnants of Hood's army were still retreating southward to the Tennessee River, Dana sent Benjamin Grierson from Memphis to break the Mobile & Ohio Railroad between Corinth, Mississippi, and Mobile. Dana, believing that the Confederates still had strong forces in north Mississippi, ordered Lawler on 20 December to move with his six regiments, including the 47th Indiana,[71] and three regiments detached from Dennis's 2nd brigade, to Moscow, Tennessee, on the Wolf River some forty miles east of Memphis. Lawler's infantry was to feint making repairs on the Memphis & Charleston Railroad Bridge at Moscow to mask Grierson's move across the state and to tie down any pursuit forces that Dana feared might chase after Grierson.[72]

With Forrest north of the Tennessee River holding off the Federal pursuit of Hood's defeated army, there were essentially no Confederates in north Mississippi willing or able to challenge Grierson. His 3,500 troopers had no trouble except for the cold and rainy weather in cutting the railroad at Verona, Mississippi, about fifty-five miles south of Corinth, on 25 December, and at Egypt, Mississippi, on 28 December, about twenty miles south of Verona. Several miles below Egypt, however, Grierson ran into some 500 well-entrenched Confederates on the railroad who persuaded him that his mission was accomplished. Leaving the Mobile & Ohio, Grierson's troopers galloped westward through Houston to the Central Mississippi Railroad at Winona and on to Vicksburg, where Grierson reported proudly that his raid was a success.[73]

Although it was technically a success, Grierson had nevertheless left the Mobile & Ohio open from West Point, Mississippi, to Mobile. And with no Federal cavalry south of the Tennessee River to round them up, Hood's weary and battle-scarred troops crossed the Tennessee River and went into camp around Corinth. Marching southward gradually about fifty miles to Tupelo, they continued around Grierson's breaks in the railroad another fifty miles to the Mobile & Ohio railhead at West Point, Mississippi. From there, many of Hood's surviving troops traveled by rail to reinforce their garrison at Mobile. Some even continued east to the Carolinas, where old Joe Johnston had returned to command and was struggling to hold off Sherman's advance into the Carolinas.[74]

Even with these reinforcements, however, Mobile's number had finally come up. With Grant closing in on Lee in Virginia, Sherman closing in on Johnston in the Carolinas, Hood's army defeated at Franklin and Nashville, and Kirby Smith's Trans-Mississippi neutralized, Federal forces under E.R.S. Canby began to rendezvous in New Orleans for the long-awaited campaign against Mobile.

Back in Indiana on Christmas Eve, Baldwin's Fancy Bazaar at 6 East Washington Street, Indianapolis, advertised "Toys! Toys! Toys! For Boys and Girls," including "Rocking Horses" and "Fine Doll Babies, in Wax, China, Wood, Rubber, Sleeping, Crying, Laughing and Walking — every style." For dear old Dad, "Fine Traveling Cases, Rich Shaving Cases, Willow Smoking Chairs (For husbands, attractive — sure to induce evenings at home); Beautiful Canes, Embroidered Slippers (Rich patterns — select early that his shoemaker may finish them), Cigar Cases & Stands, Pocket Books, Knives, [and] Meerschaum Pipes."[75]

Hasheesh Candy continued to be a big hit: "A most delightful exhilarant confectionized.... Produces the most perfect mental cheerfulness.... The writer, the speaker, the student and the business man, seem to gather new inspiration and new energy, a readiness and keenness of perception unknown before ... one of the most wonderful and efficient medicines ever known.... It imparts a vigor and strength to the mind and body truly marvelous, and will rejoice the hearts of thousands.... Imported only by the Gunga Wallah Company, 36 Beekman Street, New York. Brown & Sloan, Agents."[76]

If Hasheesh Candy were not enough, one could turn to Wahoo Bitters: "Nature's Great Restorative ... entirely vegetable, being compounded from different Roots, Barks and Herbs.... They cure Dyspepsia, Liver Complaint, Dropsy, Asthma, Sour Stomach, Sick Headache, warm and strengthen the Bowels, are a preventive of Dysentery, Summer Complaints, Cholic, Cholera, Morbus, Chills, Intermittent Fever, Fever and Ague, &c, &c.... The Spirits used to preserve these Bitters is a PURE RYE WHISKEY, distilled in Copper under my direction and personal attention and is the only Spirits recommended by the Medical Faculty for its medicinal qualities. Put up only by myself, the Inventor and Patentee ... E. Dexter Loveridge, Buffalo, NY."[77]

And appearing on Christmas Eve at the Metropolitan Theatre in Indianapolis was "the great American Tragedian, Mr. Joseph Proctor," in the play, "The Robbers ... to conclude with a dance by Fanny Merrill."[78]

XV

New Orleans and Mobile (January–June 1865)

As the New Year dawned, Federal successes in the field raised hope that this would be the war's decisive year, Ben Butler's failed Christmas Day attack on Fort Fisher, North Carolina, notwithstanding. On the home front in Indiana, the preliminary results of the treason trial began to emerge as Andrew Humphreys's sentence was reduced to parole within the confinement of Wright and Stockton Townships in Greene County, with the stipulation that he "not participate, either directly or indirectly, against the prosecution of the war by the United States against the rebels in arms."[1]

The sentences of the other three prisoners, Milligan, Horsey, and Bowles, were not announced, and they remained in limbo in their Soldiers' Home cells, although with Humphreys' parole, word leaked that they had all been sentenced to death, the supposed time and place subject to rumor and conjecture. According to Stampp, the *Indiana State Sentinel* and the *Indianapolis Daily Journal* published sketchy results in their 2 and 3 January editions, respectively, although the *Chicago Tribune* complained editorially on 4 January that rumors about the sentences were rife since nothing official had been released by the Commission.[2]

On 11 January, Judge Advocate Burnett convened the military court and opened the Cincinnati Treason Trial. Eight of the now fourteen prisoners who had been transferred from Camp Douglas were charged with two crimes: conspiring to release rebel prisoners of war at Camp Douglas, and conspiring to lay waste and destroy the city of Chicago, Illinois. Captain Thomas Hines of the Confederate army, the actual organizer of the scheme, was named as a conspirator on both charges, but was not indicted.[3]

On the military fronts, Grant's army, although stalled in wintry Virginia, invested Lee's army from Petersburg to Richmond. In North Carolina, Alfred Terry replaced Ben Butler and prepared a second amphibious attack on Fort Fisher. In Georgia, Sherman, having reached Savannah, prepared to move northward into the Carolinas. In the Trans-Mississippi, isolated skirmishes and the pursuit of bushwhackers continued. And with word that some of Hood's badly defeated Army of Tennessee had moved around Grierson's December breaks in the Mobile & Ohio Railroad and were now with Dabney Maury's troops in Mobile, E.R.S. Canby sent troops under Gordon Granger to establish a base at Pensacola, Florida, and began gathering his scattered forces in New Orleans for a move against Mobile and a thrust into the heart of Alabama.[4]

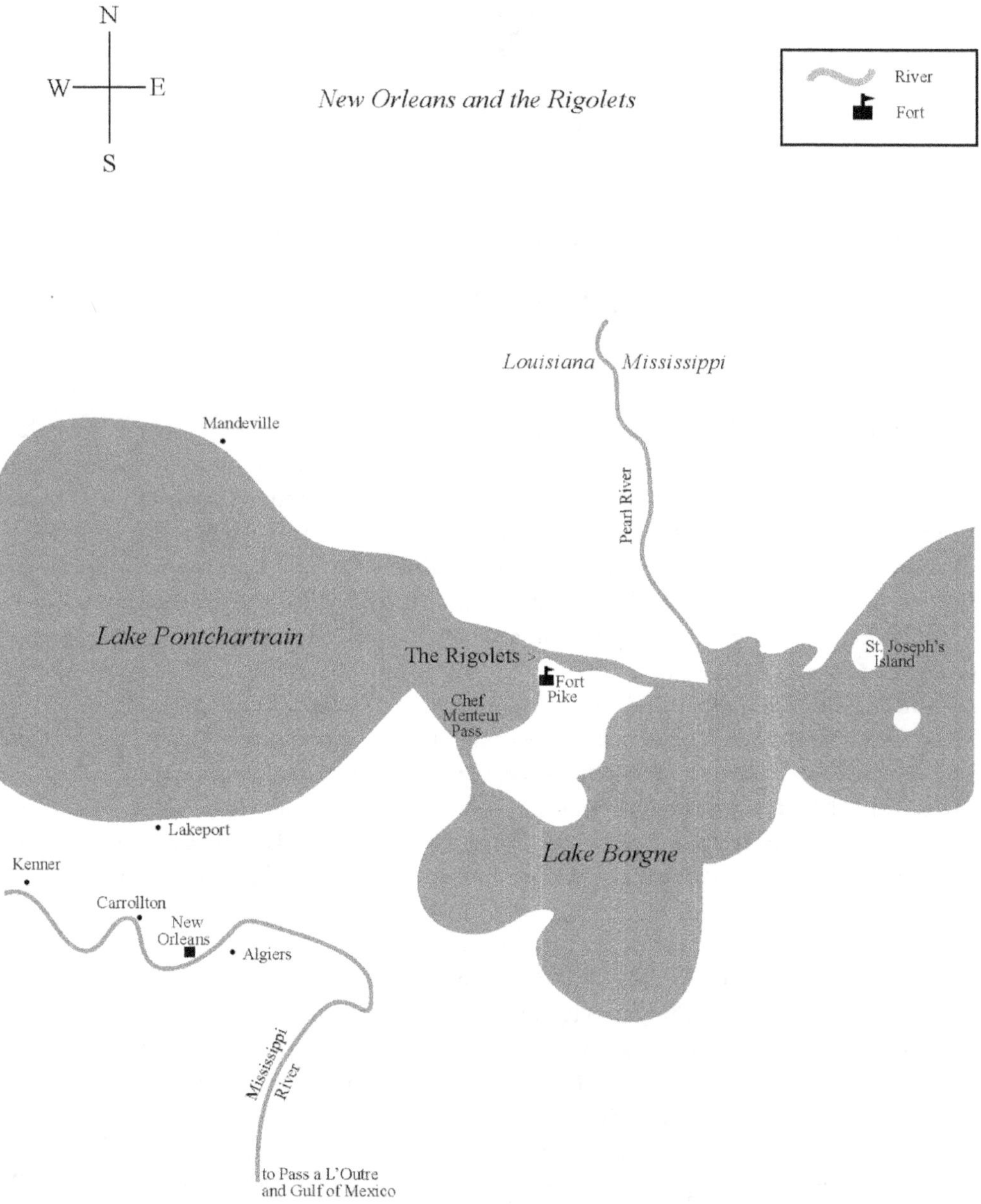

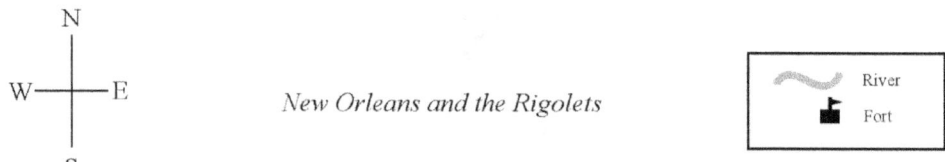

New Orleans and the Rigolets

From Atlas Plate CLVI and Google Maps

On the Confederate side, although Braxton Bragg, then in charge at Wilmington, North Carolina, had held off Benjamin Butler's 25 December 1864 attack on Fort Fisher, his command was in disarray. Due to their dire military situation, on 23 February 1865, Richmond officials reluctantly returned Joe Johnston to command the remaining troops in the Department of South Carolina, Georgia, and Florida to stop Sherman's relentless move northward through the Carolinas. Johnston was joined by P.G.T. Beauregard and William Hardee, who had avoided capture by slipping out of Savannah with his small force while

Sherman sat at the gates of the city. Incredibly, the remainder of Hood's remnant force, being sent on from Mobile to the Carolinas on what remained of their dilapidated railway system, showed up to assist Johnston's attempt to "drive back Sherman" from the southern approach to Lee's besieged army at Petersburg, Virginia.[5]

Back in Tennessee, Lawler's reserve troops returned to Memphis, and in the first two days of the New Year 4,262 reserve troops began shipping out for New Orleans. On 2 January the 47th Indiana, the 21st Iowa, a detachment from the 28th Illinois, and the 15th Massachusetts Battery (1,437 troops) steamed out of Memphis aboard the U.S. Marine Boat *Baltic*, the fifth transport to depart. Observed passing Morganza on 4 January at 3:40 P.M., they arrived at the Canal Street wharves in New Orleans early the next morning. Due to confusion about landing sites, they laid at the wharf until noon, when they were sent back upriver to report to Frederick Steele's camp at Kenner.[6]

On Friday, 13 January, the *New York Times*' correspondent in New Orleans, who called himself "M," wrote that there had been "a prolonged season of cold damp weather, much colder and damper than expected." There had been frost on the ground on several successive mornings so thick, he wrote, that it appeared to have snowed. It would melt with the afternoon sun, but it was so cold that in the homes "good large fires are requisite, day and evening." He also noted that the river had fallen three inches in the last twenty-four hours after having risen to five and a half feet below the high water mark of 1862 and had kept all steamers in port since last Saturday.[7]

That same day at Kenner, Private Henry Bert of the 47th wrote his sister that the "very muddy water" of the Mississippi was all they had to drink, but "it was the purest water" they had had in Louisiana. The weather had turned pleasant and Bert, with time on his hands and impressed with the number of well-educated men in camp, told his sister Annie, who was in school in Indiana, that "when I get my money I intend to go to the city and get me some school books if I can and try to learn something too for there are a great many men in the camp that can give me lessons in all kind of school books and if I don't learn anything I will try and keep from forgetting everything I did know."[8]

Meanwhile, having been instructed by Grant to select a plan that he deemed best, Canby prepared to move against Mobile, seated on the upper western shore of Mobile Bay. Choosing to attack the city from its weaker eastern shore fortifications at Spanish Fort and Fort Blakely, Canby would utilize a flotilla of steamers and light-draft gunboats to lead one column of 32,000 from New Orleans to the staging area at Dauphin Island, several miles south of the western shore and three or four miles west of Mobile Point Peninsula, a twenty-mile-long peninsula that jutted westward into the Gulf and formed the eastern entrance to Mobile Bay. From there, Canby would utilize his flotilla to move his vanguard force northeastward across the bay and up the Fish River to about twenty miles below Spanish Fort; the remainder would be transported to Mobile Point for a long march across the peninsula and up the eastern shore to their Fish River rendezvous. Frederick Steele would lead a second column of 13,000 northward from Fort Barrancas and Pensacola, Florida, and feint toward Montgomery and Selma before turning westward to join in the attack on the Confederate eastern shore fortifications.[9]

By early February, Canby's mobilization had begun in earnest. On 3 February at Kenner, the 1st division of the Reserve Corps was reorganized in anticipation of their immediate embarkation for Mobile Point Peninsula. M.K. Lawler was assigned command of the

1st brigade (the 47th Indiana, 21st Iowa, 29th Wisconsin, and the 99th Illinois), Elias S. Dennis command of the 2nd brigade (the 8th, 11th, and 46th Illinois), and Loren Kent[10] command of the 3rd brigade (the 29th Illinois, 30th Missouri, 161st New York, and 23rd Wisconsin.) The 1st division artillery included the Massachusetts Light Artillery, 4th Battery (D) and 7th Battery (G). Lawler's brigade was to travel by steamer from the Lakeport pier at the terminus of the Jefferson & Lake Pontchartrain Railroad (also referred to as the Jefferson & Carrollton Railroad), Dennis's and Kent's brigades by sea via the Mississippi River. With Slack not yet available and with Lawler having received a leave of absence, the command of the 1st brigade transferred to Lt. Col. John A. McLaughlin of the 47th Indiana, along with the task of transferring the brigade to Mobile Point Peninsula via Lake Pontchartrain aboard the steamers *George Peabody* and *Belvedere*.[11]

Unfamiliar with the area and anxious to get started, McLaughlin, who saw the wide expanse of Lake Pontchartrain as easily navigated, complained in his report about the reticence of the captain of the *Peabody* to travel at night with overloaded boats.[12] The lake's depth, which ranged from eight feet at the Lakeside pier to about ten feet farther out, did make it relatively easy to navigate in good weather, but what McLaughlin failed to realize when he wrote his report was that daylight would be required to navigate the twists and turns that connected the lake with the Gulf of Mexico, hence the captain's reticence. For the roughly 136-mile trip from Lakeside (New Orleans) to Fort Gaines on the eastern tip of Dauphin Island, the boats would have to steam about thirty miles across the southeastern corner of the lake to Fort Pike on the eastern shore, maneuver through a narrow winding channel about eight miles long known as "The Rigolets,"[13] in places only seven feet deep, and then steam another eight miles across the top of Lake Borgne, which had an acceptable depth ranging from nine to ten feet, but which required navigation around shoals at its eastern mouth created where the Pearl River emptied into it. Beyond the shoals, they would proceed through a channel a little over a mile wide between the Saint Joseph's Island lighthouse on the north and Grand Island on the south before entering the Mississippi Sound[14] from whence, if the weather held, there would be about ninety miles of relatively clear sailing to Fort Gaines. For those traveling via the Mississippi River, it would be a roughly 200-mile trip, requiring navigation of ocean-going vessels through the labyrinthine delta channels from "Head of Passes" just below the present-day town of Venice, into eastward-running "Pass a l'Outre,"[15] and out into the open Gulf for a 100-mile trip northeastward to Dauphin Island.[16]

Dennis's 2nd brigade left Kenner on 4 February. Sailing via the Mississippi River and the Gulf of Mexico, they landed on Dauphin Island on 8 February and went into camp. McLaughlin's 1st brigade was to start across Lake Pontchartrain at about 3:00 P.M. on 5 February, but due to overcrowding was forced to leave behind some of their transportation. It is unclear when they finally left Kenner, but they would make it to Dauphin Island on or about 10 February, where they joined Dennis's brigade in camp. Kent's 3rd brigade followed on 6 February aboard two ocean-going steamers, bringing with them the transportation left behind by McLaughlin's (Lawler's) brigade.[17] Back in New Orleans on 8 February, Slack was assigned command of Lawler's 1st brigade and Lawler, when he returned from furlough, was assigned to command the post of Baton Rouge, Louisiana. Slack, in turn, was ordered to report immediately to Major General Gordon Granger, then commanding the District of West Florida and South Alabama at Fort Gaines.[18]

XV. New Orleans and Mobile (January–June 1865)

Arriving at Dauphin Island on the morning of 15 February following a thirty-six-hour voyage, which he said should have taken twelve, Slack, now in command of the 1st brigade, described the fourteen-mile-long island as "a bed of white sand, covered in part by yellow pine, and the balance with a small growth of spruce. The whole is surrounded with an oyster bed from which the men gather them by the wagon load."[19]

Three days later, the Reserve Corps was renamed the 13th corps, reviving the old designation, and Gordon Granger assigned command. The next day A.J. Smith's peripatetic Army of Cumberland detachment began to arrive at New Orleans from Memphis. Going into camp on the old 1815 battlefield site at Chalmette, about six miles downriver from Canal Street, New Orleans, they were designated the 16th corps. On 25 February on Dauphin Island, Hoosier Brigadier General James Veatch assumed command of 1st division of Granger's 13th corps. Brigadier Generals Christopher C. Andrews and William P. Benton commanded the 2nd and 3rd divisions, respectively.[20]

Canby began his movement on 17 March, and, over the next several days, sent 16,000 troops from Smith's 16th corps on a flotilla of fourteen transports and six light-draft gunboats across the southern end of Mobile Bay into Bon Secours Bay, a cove on the southeastern shore formed by Mobile Point Peninsula, and up the narrow, winding Fish River, which emptied into Bon Secours Bay about eight nautical miles north of Navy Cove. Winding northward up the Fish River another seventeen miles, Smith's flotilla arrived at the Dannelly's (or Danby's) Mill rendezvous point, a steam sawmill on the right bank of the river, between 19 and 21 March to await the arrival of Granger's land column.[21]

That same day (17 March), Benton's 3rd division, with Henry Bertram's brigade detached from Andrews' 2nd division in the advance and acting as pioneers, led Granger's 13th corps column of almost 17,000 on their march from Navy Cove eastward on Mobile Point Peninsula. Veatch's 1st division followed Benton's column from Dauphin Island, McLaughlin and the 47th Indiana on board the steamer *Mustang*. Remaining in camp at the Navy Cove rendezvous, two days later at 5:00 A.M., Veatch's division began the difficult eastward trek on sandy Mobile Point Peninsula, Slack's rear guard brigade starting an hour later.[22]

Their dry sandy trek ended abruptly at Shell Bank Bayou, an arm of Bon Secours Bay about eight miles east of Navy Cove, when they were forced to wade in about thirty inches of water. Back on sand, they continued another five or six miles before going into camp late that afternoon near the eastern tip of Mobile Point Peninsula after a march of about twelve miles. On 20 March, torrential rains brought Benton's column to a halt as swamps and streams overflowed the eastern shore roadways. Bertram's pioneers, who had been corduroying roads, watched as their work floated off in the high water and teams of one hundred men replaced exhausted horses to drag supply wagons, artillery and caissons out of the mud and mire. That day Veatch's column crossed Muddy Bayou and came up on the rear of Benton's stalled column. Veatch sent 1,200 men, including details from the 47th Indiana, forward to help build bridges over the swamp and to repair or lay new corduroy roads.[23] That same day, Steele's column, setting out from Pensacola, marched northward up the west bank of the Escambia River, on the road to Pollard, Alabama.[24]

McLaughlin, describing the 47th Indiana's trek from Dauphin Island and up the eastern shore toward Dannelly's Mill, reported:

On the morning of the 17th of March I received orders to embark my regiment on the steamer Mustang for Navy Cove, which point was reached at 1 P.M. of the 17th, where with but trifling delay the regiment debarked and marched a distance of three or four miles up the peninsula, going into camp for the night. March 18, lay in camp. March 19, received orders to move at 5 A.M., reaching an arm of Bay Bon Secours at 10 A.M., which was forded, the men wading. Went into camp at 5 P.M., having marched a distance of fourteen miles. March 20, broke camp at 5 A.M.; marched in rear of the brigade. Came upon the train of the Third Division, Thirteenth Army Crops, which was unable to move forward on account of the roads being impassable, about 9 A.M., when a halt was ordered and 200 detailed from the regiment, by order of General Slack, for the purpose of bridging, to enable the columns to pass over the swamps that lay in our way. After several hours' labor were enabled to move forward a distance of two miles, going into camp about dark, soon after which it commenced raining, and continued during the entire night. March 21, were engaged the entire day in bridging and getting trains forward. Detail of 100 men from the regiment relieved hourly during the day. March 22, moved at 4 A.M., going into camp at 12 m., having marched about four miles. Detail of 200 men to work at bridging. March 23, ordered to move at daylight. Marched three miles, bridging as before.[25]

With A.J. Smith's 16th corps encamped at Dannelly's Mill and Granger's 13th corps column moving slowly toward the rendezvous point, on the afternoon of 21 March Bertram's vanguard brigade arrived at Fish River, crossed a 320-foot-long bridge that had taken Capt. J.J. Smith's pontoniers three hours to lay, and bivouacked on the left of the 16th corps. According to a *New York Times* correspondent who accompanied the 16th corps, Granger's line now extended "from 'Donnelly's Mills' on the right to 'Tom Danton's' on the left, a distance of about six miles."[26]

Meanwhile, as it became apparent that Canby intended to attack either the eastern shore fortifications or move against Montgomery or Selma, Confederate Major General Dabney H. Maury, in command at Mobile with a force of about 9,000 and referred to affectionately after the war as General "Puss-in-Boots,"[27] sent some 6,000 veterans, remnants of Hood's former Army of Tennessee (from Gibson's, Holtzclaw's, Cockrell's, Ector's and Sears's brigades), to Brig. Gen. St. John Liddell, who, from his headquarters near Blakely, commanded a force on the eastern shore that consisted of a small contingent of artillerists at Blakely and Brig. Gen. Bryan M. Thomas's young, untested Alabama Reserves (the 1st, 2nd, and 21st Alabama Reserves). Liddell's eastern shore cavalry consisted of Col. Charles C. Armistead's two-regiment cavalry "brigade" (Ball's 8th Alabama, Spence's 16th Confederate and Lewis's Battalion) and Col. Henry "Harry" Maury's "Command" (the 15th Confederate Cavalry and Capt. Thomas F. Tobin's Battery); and Brig. Gen. James H. Clanton's brigade (the 3rd, 6th, and 8th Alabama and Keyser's detachment).[28]

Originally a water battery that guarded the northern end of the bay, Fort Blakely stood at the junction of the Tensas and Blakely Rivers on a bluff north of Bay Minette. From the river at the former village of Blakely Landing the woods rose gradually eastward about a mile to a point about sixty feet above the water level where a substantial fortress had been constructed to defend the landward approaches along a roughly three-mile semi-circular line extending from the marshland of Bay Minette northward across several ravines to the Tensas River bottomland. Blakely consisted of nine artillery redoubts and forty-one pieces of artillery connected by palisades and two rows of rifle pits set fifty yards apart. Prepared by slave labor (Liddell had about 1,000 slaves at his disposal for this work), the line in rear was protected by slashed timber and brush and in front by marshy, briar-filled ravines, slashed timber and pikes strung with telegraph wire and, shades of Vicksburg, mined with

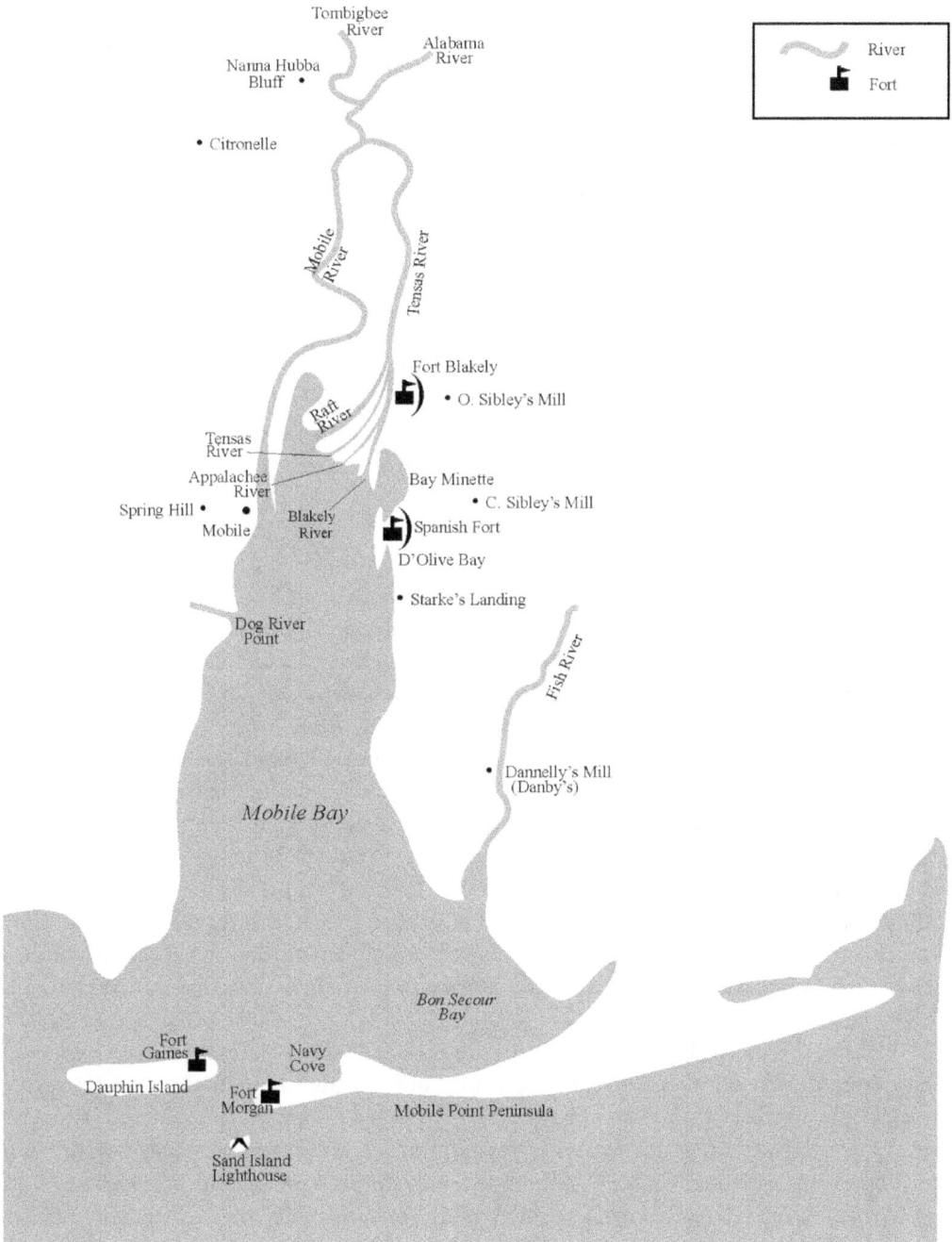

From Atlas Plate CX

"subterra torpedoes" made of buried 12- and 24-pound cannon balls set with pressure triggering devices.[29]

At its junction with the Blakely, the Tensas veered southwestward around a marshy island and entered Mobile Bay several miles east of Mobile. With depths from ten to twelve feet, both rivers provided water communication with Mobile as well as northward up the

Tensas to the Alabama and Tombigbee Rivers and enabled the five Confederate gunboats (the wooden *Morgan*; the ironclad floating batteries *Tuscaloosa* and *Huntsville*; the ironclad *Nashville*; and the ironclad ram *Baltic*) to operate above and near Fort Blakely.[30]

The Blakely River continued southward three or four miles past Blakely Landing until it forked at a sandbar island shaped like an inverted "V." Both forks continued another three or four miles before emptying into Mobile Bay. The western fork was called the Appalachee River; the eastern fork was a continuation of the Blakely River and emptied into Mobile Bay several miles below Spanish Fort. Fort Huger, a water battery of eleven heavy guns (Brooke rifles, Columbiads, and mortars) manned by 200 artillerists from the 22nd Louisiana artillery and the 1st Mississippi Light Artillery, sat at the tip of the inverted "V" about a mile or so above and in rear of the northern end of Spanish Fort. Fort Tracy, a smaller water battery of five 7-inch rifled guns manned by 120 artillerists from the 22nd Louisiana, sat about a half-mile north on the right bank of the Blakely at its junction with the Appalachee River. Both batteries commanded the northern end of Spanish Fort and the water approaches from Mobile Bay.[31]

As Canby's force gathered at Dannelly's Mill, Liddell sent Randall L. Gibson[32] southward to take command at Spanish Fort, its left flank situated on the marshland south of Bay Minette, some three or four miles south of the lower end of Fort Blakely. Gibson's force consisted of his own Louisiana brigade of 500 commanded by Colonel Francis L. Campbell, as well as Thomas's Alabama Reserves (950 "boy reserves"), Col. Isaac Patton's artillery (360 gunners), and the consolidated 32nd and 58th Alabama under Col. Bushrod Jones, giving Gibson initially some 1,800 troops inside Spanish Fort.

In addition, with Clanton's three-regiment brigade at Pollard, Alabama, at the junction of the Mobile & Great Northern and Florida & Alabama Railroads about fifty miles north of Pensacola and about sixty miles northeast of Blakely, in position to monitor Steele's possible northward movement to Selma or Montgomery, Liddell detached Spence's 16th Confederate Cavalry from Armistead's two-regiment "brigade" and sent them to monitor both Canby's movements up the eastern shore and possible northwestward turn by Steele up the Pensacola Road to Greenwood and Blakely. The remainder of Armistead's cavalry moved eastward to Canoe Station on the Mobile & Great Northern Railroad about fifteen miles west of Pollard.[33]

Making the most of what little cavalry he had, Liddell also detached Lt. Artemus O. Sibley from Maury's 15th Confederate Cavalry and assigned him to command a special force of thirty or forty picked men, including Lt. Origen Sibley Jr., to scout and harass the rear of Canby's column, which was still struggling through the swollen marshes on the eastern shore toward Dannelly's Mill. Although their familial relationship is uncertain, both Artemus and Origen Jr. were born and raised on the eastern shore, and Liddell, who referred to them collectively as "the Sibleys," relied on their knowledge of the eastern shore to guide and maneuver his forces through the area's maze of streams and marshes.[34]

On 24 March, as Veatch's division began arriving at the Dannelly's Mill rendezvous, Artemus Sibley's special force moved south to scout Canby's rear guard, which was guarded by Slack's brigade, and to "retard his progress in every possible manner." Sibley's scouts had no trouble getting around the Federal line and at 3:00 P.M. "made a dash" on the stationary 1st division supply train, which was bogged down between the East and North Branches of Fish River. According to Brig. Gen. C.C. Andrews in his postwar history of the campaign, Sibley's scouts surprised and captured five resting men from Slack's brigade, including two from the 29th Wisconsin and a drummer boy. Slack himself, according to Andrews, "was sitting not far off" and therefore narrowly avoided being captured. Turning southward, Sibley's scouts charged the train a few hundred yards below, capturing a few wagoners and ten mules before troops from the 99th Illinois came up and drove them off.[35]

Slack made no mention of his supposed near capture and reported only that a "dash" had been made against Benton's train, not his own: "Friday, 24th, left camp at 9 A.M.; took the rear of the division; was much delayed by the third Division's train; had to help them through. About 3 P.M. of this day a squad of rebel cavalry made a dash at General Benton's train, close to our advance, and captured 8 of the drivers and 14 mules. Crossed Fish River and came up with the advance, and went into camp at 8 P.M., having made 13 miles."[36] Granger and Veatch accepted Slack's brigade report of 8 teamsters and 14 animals captured from Benton's 3rd division train. McLaughlin, however, reported that the 47th Indiana, starting at 6:00 A.M., marched sixteen miles to Fish River with little delay except that they "lost three men ... captured by guerillas in a dash made upon the train of [Veatch's] 1st division."[37]

Of Slack's three other regiments, the 21st Iowa reported one soldier captured and a delay of about one hour, the 29th Wisconsin reported two captured, and the 99th Illinois reported one captured. Artemus Sibley, on the other hand, reported capturing twenty-one prisoners, plus ten mules in harness, and having killed eight mules they could not take with them "as the only means to destroy their transportation."[38]

Moving on the next day (25 March), Canby's column, Smith's 16th corps in advance, marched eight miles north-northwest from Dannelly's Mill to Deer Park, about fifteen miles or so south of D'Olive's Creek. Slack's brigade marched nine miles that day and arrived at Deer Park at sunset. Meanwhile, Gibson sent out parties to establish a battle line on the north bank of D'Olive's Creek and in a futile attempt to "dispute the passage," or at least slow down the overwhelmingly larger two-corps, 32,000-man Federal force, Gibson set extra campfires along his line to give a false impression of his strength and opted to aggressively defend his D'Olive's Creek line to inspire and encourage the untested young militia troops in Thomas's Alabama Reserve.[39]

That same day, Lucas's Federal cavalry division (Chrysler's and Spurling's brigades)[40] encountered and overwhelmed Clanton's Confederate cavalry at Bluff Springs near Pollard, Alabama. Led by the successful charge of Lt. Col. Algernon S. Badger's 1st Louisiana Cavalry (U.S.), Lucas's troopers routed Clanton's Confederates and captured 120 prisoners, including Clanton, Lt. Col. Washington T. Lary of the 6th Alabama Cavalry, 17 other officers, and the 6th Alabama's battle flag.[41]

The next day, Steele's infantry column occupied Pollard, but found that, upon learning of Clanton's defeat, alert local citizens had carried off the Confederate supplies Steele had hoped to find there. Unable to get shipments over the bar and up the Escambia River by steamer and running short of supplies, Steele turned his column westward on the Mobile & Great Northern Railroad. Marching about fifteen miles to Canoe Station, he discovered that citizens, aided by Armistead's cavalry, had also carried off much of the Confederate supplies stored there. They were able, however, to capture a supply of corn left in haste at the depot and several teams of oxen, which they used for beef. In the meantime, Spurling's cavalry continued its raid on the Florida & Alabama Railroad, and about thirty-five miles north of Pollard captured "the up and down trains (2 locomotives and 14 cars loaded with stores) and 100 officers on their way to Mobile," cut telegraph wires to Greenville, Alabama, and destroyed the Sparta, Alabama, depot.[42]

Back at Mobile Bay on Sunday, 26 March, A.J. Smith's 16th corps column separated from Granger's and moved up and around to the northern end of Spanish Fort. Skirmishing lightly, Smith's troops had little trouble taking position at Cyrus Sibley's Mills, about four miles east of the northern end of Spanish Fort. That same day, Granger, with Slack's brigade of Veatch's 1st division in the vanguard, marched his 13th corps column northwestward toward the southern end of Spanish Fort. At about 2:00 P.M., about a mile and a half south of Spanish Fort, Van Anda's 21st Iowa hit Gibson's D'Olive's Creek line and skirmished with Gibson's Louisianans until near dark. Moving forward again at 8:00 P.M., they skirmished past 9:00 o'clock as Gibson's troops fell back and Canby's troops began their investment of Spanish Fort.[43]

Spanish Fort at this time consisted of five redoubts on an approximately two-mile semi-circular line that curved out about 700 yards from 400 yards above the marshland of D'Olive's Bay and extended to the deep marshland about 100 yards south of Bay Minette. The landward redoubts were connected by a continuous line of rifle pits extending to Redoubt No. 5, covered in front from a quarter to a third of a mile out by an abatis of felled trees, telegraph wire, and buried torpedoes. Beyond the salient, however, the rifle pits and bastions were left incomplete and for the last six hundred yards had no works of any kind due to a lack of time and tools, and to the fact that the party of slaves who had been working to fell trees and build the bastions "ran in" and refused to work after Canby's army began closing in on Gibson's skirmishers. Liddell prudently ordered their removal to Fort Huger. Gibson's troops frantically tried to complete the works and plant more torpedoes, but the extreme left of the line remained protected only by a few disconnected rifle pits, the seemingly impenetrable marshland south of Bay Minette, the batteries of Forts Huger and Tracy, and the gunboats plying the waters of northern Mobile Bay.[44]

Redoubt No. 1 had been the original 18th century Spanish water battery (Old Spanish Fort) and mounted four heavy guns (7-inch Columbiads and 30-pounder Parrotts) manned by 120 artillerists from the 22nd Louisiana. About eight miles east of Mobile, it overlooked the eastern shore of the bay from a sixty-five-foot bluff that commanded the water approaches to Forts Huger and Tracy.[45]

On the Confederate right, about 400 yards south of Redoubt No. 1, the eastern or inland side of the bluff rose to about 100 feet before sloping another 400 yards through marshland and felled trees to the water's edge at D'Olive's Bay. Here Redoubt No. 2, known as "Fort McDermott" to the Confederates and "Fort Alexis" to the Federals, mounted 15 heavy guns (a Brooke Rifle, six 6-pounder smoothbore rifles, two 24-pounder howitzers, and six mortars) manned by 200 artillerists from the 22nd Louisiana, Owens's Arkansas Battery, and Massenberg's Georgia Light Artillery, and commanded the land approach from D'Olive's Creek. About 800 yards north across a ravine and on another lower bluff sat Redoubt No. 3, manned by 90 artillerists from the 5th Washington Artillery of New Orleans, mounting an 8-inch Columbiad, two Napoleons, one 3-inch rifle and four cohorn mortars. Six hundred yards farther north sat Redoubt No. 4, called the "Red Fort" by Granger, which was manned by 60 artillerists from Phillips's Tennessee Battery and covered the extreme left flank of the eastern-facing line, which, at this point, angled sharply westward and formed a ragged but nearly right-angled salient, the incomplete and disconnected rifle pits running another 600 yards westward, ending about 100 yards south of Bay Minette. Sixty artillerists from Lumsden's Tuscaloosa Battery manned redoubt No. 5, which covered the northern or upper end of the salient (Gibson considered Redoubts 2, 3, and 4 his only landward redoubts, and Redoubt No. 5 merely a hastily constructed battery.)[46]

In addition, a narrow plank treadway only eighteen inches ("two planks") wide, 1,200 yards long, and set several feet above the marshland, had also been constructed as an escape route from Spanish Fort. It ran from the water's edge on the left or northern flank up a small peninsula through tall grass, across the mouth of Bay Minette and over a broad marsh to the junction of the Blakely and Apalachee Rivers opposite Battery Huger. A direct pathway had also been scouted and staked out by engineers and several soldiers from the 9th Texas through the marshland between Spanish Fort and Fort Blakely.[47]

Since August of the previous year, Maury's chief engineer, Lt. Col. Victor von Sheliha, had protected the approaches to Forts Huger and Tracy with "frame torpedoes," which he referred to as "chevaux-de-frise," or outward-pointing wooden pikes anchored in the bay to protrude just above the water line with torpedoes fastened to their tips.[48] Sheliha used the frame torpedoes to create a narrow channel for picket boats to move between the forts and into Bay Minette. Mobile Bay had an average depth of ten feet, in places as deep as twelve feet, and along with the chevaux-de-frise, was also laced with submerged "floating torpedoes," which carried from 70 to 120 pounds of gunpowder, and were designed to keep water communications open with Mobile and to keep Federal gunboats away from Spanish Fort. Made primarily of beer barrels, they were anchored two or three feet below the surface of the water and set to blow out the bottom of vessels that struck them.[49] If Sheliha's water defenses held, Confederate steamers plying the upper bay could rescue evacuees from Spanish Fort and transport them to Batteries Huger and Tracy, Fort Blakely, Mobile or points north on the inland waterways that flowed into Mobile Bay.[50]

Bertram's brigade held the extreme left of Canby's line near the bay and the marshes of D'Olive's Creek, followed on the right by Veatch's division (Kinsey's 3rd, Slack's 1st, and Dennis's 2nd brigade, in that order), past Redoubt No. 2 (Fort McDermott or Alexis) to Redoubt No. 3. Benton's 3rd division continued the line to the right and connected near Redoubt No. 4 (the "Red Fort") with McArthur's division of A.J. Smith's 16th corps. Carr's division completed Canby's line, which angled westward at the "Red Fort" and Redoubt No. 5 salient and extended into the marshland on the south shore of Bay Minette about four hundred yards from the northern end of Spanish Fort. Carr's troops, not facing any redoubts or other bastions, were nevertheless hit hard by enfilading fire from Forts Huger and Tracy and from Confederate gunboats above on the Blakely River.[51]

Granger's and Smith's troops threw up a line of works and that evening two hundred men from the 23rd Wisconsin were sent from Kinsey's 3rd brigade, then in reserve on the left to Veatch's battle line, to Veatch's picket line, which had Slack's 1st brigade pickets on the left and Dennis's 2nd brigade pickets on the right. At midnight, Slack threw forward companies I, F and C of the 47th Indiana on the left to relieve the 21st Iowa and to join the pickets from Henry Hadley's 23rd Wisconsin on his 1st brigade picket line.[52]

At daybreak on 27 March, Gibson, now reporting 2,325 men armed with muskets, kept up his aggressive stance. Hoping, apparently, to at least delay the inevitable, Gibson sent a 550-man detachment, commanded by Lt. Col. Robert H. Lindsay, to charge Veatch's line. According to Andrews, Lindsay's men moved carefully to within musket range of Veatch's picket line, fired a volley, charged with a yell, and drove back skirmishers from the 161st New York in position on the left of the 47th Indiana skirmishers. McLaughlin reported that when Lindsay's Confederates hit, the regiment on the left of the 47th Indiana's picket line (the 161st New York) fell back and enabled the advancing Confederates to enfilade his skirmishers, killing one, mortally wounding another, and seriously wounding six. (Slack reported two killed and five wounded.) Veatch's entire battle line quickly moved up as Lindsay's troops retreated to Spanish Fort.[53]

According to McLaughlin in his 47th Indiana report:

> The enemy advanced on the morning of the 27th about daylight and attacked the pickets. The regiment on the left gave way, allowing the enemy to advance upon the flank of the line occupied by the Forty-seventh Indiana, who seeing their situation formed in line and charged the enemy, regaining the ground and driving the enemy from the field, with a loss to the Forty-seventh Indiana of 1 killed and 6 wounded, 1 mortally, and who died on the 27th.[54]

In a letter to Ann, Slack noted: "George Risor of Co. F, 47th Ind was killed instantly by rifle ball through the head. George Dillon of Co. F ... was shot through the hip outside of the bone. Eli Rose of Co. F, had his thigh shattered, and had to be amputated above the knee. James Beal of Co. F, flesh wound in the thigh. Two or three others of Co. F were wounded whose names do not now occur to me. They did not belong to Huntington. The 29th Wis had one killed & two others wounded, the 99th Ill one or two wounded, one mortal."[55]

Gibson reported that Lindsay's sortie surprised and captured "a few prisoners and a large number of arms and accouterments" before falling back in the face of "a heavy and extended order of battle." Although Lindsay's daring dawn sortie undoubtedly surprised Veatch's picket line, none of Veatch's brigade and regimental commanders reported any pickets captured and only Slack and McLaughlin reported any specifics of the morning attack. Faced with the rapid arrival of that extended order of battle, they could and probably did take some arms and accouterments from the 161st New York if they fled precipitously, or more likely, from the few wounded and killed on Veatch's picket line, before they retreated back to Spanish Fort, although not the "large numbers" claimed by Gibson.[56]

While the artillery and firefights continued, Acting Rear Admiral H.K. Thatcher, commanding the West Gulf Blockading Squadron on the U.S. Flagship *Stockdale*, attempted to bring a flotilla of gunboats from Ship Island and Pensacola up Mobile Bay for a bayside bombardment of Spanish Fort. Sheliha's crude but effective beer-barrel torpedoes effectively blocked passage and Federal gunboats moving up Mobile Bay could make only about five knots behind light-draft picket boats that were trying to scoop up the torpedoes with drag nets or drag ropes, some even trying to push them aside with poles or saplings. By 28 March, the monitor-class gunboat *Milwaukee*, one of the lead gunboats in Thatcher's flotilla, had made it to the mouth of the Blakely River, about a mile and a half below Fort Huger, when it struck a torpedo and sank.[57]

After the war, P.D. Stephenson, stationed with the Washington Artillery (New Orleans) inside Spanish Fort's Redoubt No. 3, remembered the appearance of the Federal gunboat fleet, which for those inside the fort was their first view of the approaching Federals, and the sinking of the *Milwaukee*:

> At last the enemy were in sight. Farragut's [Thatcher's] fleet appeared first. How gallantly ship after ship came up the bay and how we watched them! But suddenly the foremost was hid in a dense cloud of smoke and water. When she came to view again her bow was up in the air and she was evidently sinking. From where we were we could hear no report, but we knew that she had struck one of our torpedoes. The channel was full of them. This is why our leaders left us so exposed, apparently, in our rear. This stopped the advance for the time on the water side.[58]

The next day while at anchorage near the mouth of the Blakely, the gunboat *Osage* hit a torpedo and sank while maneuvering to avoid a collision with the *Winnebago*; and on 1 April, while towing a scow with equipment to raise the *Milwaukee*, the tinclad *Rodolph* struck a torpedo and sank. With the loss of three gunboats in five days, Admiral Thatcher kept his fleet in cleared water a mile or so below Spanish Fort and, while his gunboats lobbed shells from a distance, prepared a shore battery of the navy's heaviest guns to operate in conjunction with the army.[59]

From inside Spanish Fort, Stephenson recalled:

> But soon after the appearance of the Federal gunboats the pop, pop of our pickets' guns drew our attention to our immediate front. The firing grew into volleys, our men came into view through the woods, slowly falling back and finally retiring to the line already marked for them as their permanent fighting posts. The blue waves of the Federal forces circled around us and by nightfall we were invested.[60]

By 28 March, batteries were thrown up on Granger's line and his troops were digging saps and parallel approaches while under fire. With Federal land batteries in place in their front and with Federal gunboats hanging back about a mile or so to avoid the torpedoes but still in range from their rear, Stephenson noted that Federal gunboat shells could "plump into our backs" while the Federal land batteries "raked us fore and aft."[61]

Although now completely invested on the landside, Maury's Confederates still controlled upper Mobile Bay and used four former blockade-runners, the steamers *Red Gauntlet*, *Virgin*, *Heroine*, and *Mary*, to remove wounded troops and nonessential personnel from Spanish Fort. They were also able to use the guns of Forts Huger and Tracy and fire from the gunboat *Morgan*, until it temporarily grounded on a sand bar near the junction of the Blakely and Apalachee Rivers, and fire from the partially ironclad ram *Nashville*, to slow Smith's investment of the Confederate left flank at Spanish Fort. Anchored on the Tensas River near its junction with Raft River over 3,000 yards above Smith's right flank, fire from the *Nashville*'s two 7-inch Brooke rifles, in conjunction with fire from Forts Huger and Tracy, proved very effective in slowing down Smith's investment of the left flank of Spanish Fort until Smith was able to establish a battery of eight 30-pounder Parrotts and two Whitworth guns on a bluff overlooking the south shore of Bay Minette.[62]

Describing action that was very similar to what was happening all along the Federal line through 29 March, including Gibson's dawn sortie against Veatch's line, McLaughlin reported:

> On the morning of the 27th, at 10 A.M., moved forward in line of battle within a short distance of Spanish Fort, where fortifications were erected, and one company was thrown forward, by order of General Slack, as skirmishers, intrenching as they advanced. March 28, were on the advance line; shelled by the enemy at regular intervals during the day, the skirmish line advancing about 100 yards. Casualties, one man of Company E wounded while in the main line, not seriously. March 29, engaged in fortifying main line and advancing skirmishers, which the

enemy attempted to check. Regiment ordered into line about 11 o'clock to support skirmishers. Remained under arms during the night.[63]

Continuing his aggressive defense with artillery and occasional night sorties, near midnight on 29 March, Gibson sent another sortie out "with a yell" against Elias Dennis's 2nd brigade line. Although Gibson's sortie was driven back, the 47th Indiana had to be called over from Slack's brigade line to relieve Dennis's skirmishers from the 8th, 11th, and 46th Illinois, and they remained under arms all night.[64]

That same day, Steele's column left the Mobile & Great Northern Railroad and marched northwestward to Weatherford. Arriving there on 29 March, Steele sent scouts eastward to Montgomery's Landing on the Alabama River to communicate his position and his lack of supplies to Canby. Finally hearing from Steele, Canby ordered him to move southward to Holyoke Mills, about ten miles east of Fort Blakely. The next day (30 March), Canby withdrew Veatch's division from the Spanish Fort line and sent them with a seventy-five-wagon supply train to Holyoke Mills, about eight or nine miles northeast of Spanish Fort, to rendezvous with Steele's force. For want of forage, instead of heading for Holyoke Mills, Steele turned his column southwestward to Stockton on the Tensas River (downstream from the Alabama River on the maze of waterways flowing into Mobile Bay), about twenty miles north of Blakely.[65]

Late in the afternoon of 30 March, Veatch's division pulled out from Spanish Fort and marched about two miles before going into camp for the night, their place in the line digging trenches and saps taken up for the next four days by Marshall's 16th corps brigade (the 12th and 35th Iowa, 7th Minnesota, and 33rd Missouri).[66] Leaving early the next morning, Veatch's column continued the remaining six or seven miles to Holyoke Mills, the lead wagons arriving at about noon, where upon they encamped awaiting Steele's arrival.[67]

The next morning (31 March), Smith's Battery quickly silenced the guns of Huger and Tracy and drove off the Confederate gunboats. With their batteries established, Smith and Granger were able to continue their Vicksburg-like siege by moving sharpshooters forward slowly via saps and parallel trenches. At about this time, Liddell withdrew the Alabama Reserves from Spanish Fort and sent Ector's and Holtzclaw's brigades to Gibson at Spanish Fort.[68] Later that afternoon, Gibson kept up his aggressive defense in spite of Federal artillery, utilizing smoke from burning brush to mask an attack on Benton's line. On Gibson's last sortie, seven or eight of his men emerged from the smoke and surprised a section of the 7th Vermont regiment in their advanced trenches, capturing Captain Riley B. Stearns and twenty-two of his men before retreating back to Spanish Fort.[69]

At Fort Blakely, Francis M. Cockrell, commanding French's old Army of Tennessee division that had survived Franklin and Nashville and had made it to Mobile in spite of Grierson's efforts to destroy the Mobile & Ohio Railroad in December, formed on the left and center. Col. Thomas N. Adaire, commanding Sears's old Mississippi brigade, took position on the extreme left, facing Hawkins's Federals. Cockrell's Missouri brigade, now commanded by Col. James McCown, formed in the center; and Thomas's Alabama brigade of "Boy Reserves" held the right.[70]

The next day (1 April), as Steele's column moved due south from Stockton toward Fort Blakely, Spurling's cavalry (the 2nd Maine, 2nd Illinois, and 1st Florida) reconnoitered to find the best route to Holyoke Mills. At noon, Spurling's troopers encountered Confederate pickets about seven miles north of Blakely. The Confederate pickets fell back skirmishing about two miles to where their main picket outpost had barricaded the road with fence rails from an abandoned farm. Dismounting, the 2nd Maine Cavalry engaged in a brisk running firefight with the Confederate pickets, who fell back behind fences and whatever shelter they could find as the 2nd Illinois Cavalry, still mounted, went around their flank and charged, routing them and capturing seventy-four men and three officers, mostly from the 46th Mississippi, as well as the 46th Mississippi's flag, although a large number escaped capture by fleeing through the woods and ravines. Spurling reported that several companies of the 2nd Illinois Cavalry pursued to within a half-mile of Blakely.[71]

Among the Confederate pickets who escaped back to Blakely and were inside the earthworks as Hawkins's troops invested their line, Private Abner Wilkes of the 46th Mississippi recalled that they "had been penned up once before at Vicksburg," and "now," at Blakely, "began to feel sort of squally."[72]

On 2 April, the day Grant's forces entered Petersburg and Richmond, Virginia, Steele's column pushed past Origen Sibley's Mill on Bay Minette Creek, about three miles east of Blakely, where Pile's and Drew's brigades from Hawkins's U.S.C.I. division, having relieved Spurling's cavalry, encountered more Confederate pickets and drove them back to Fort Blakely. Drew's brigade formed on the extreme right of Steele's line, their right on the bottomland swamp on the east bank of the Tensas River; Pile's brigade, extending leftward, continued the line to the Stockton Road. C.C. Andrews's division came up on Pile's left, turning the line southward from the Stockton to the Pensacola Road as Steele's army began the investment of the upper end of Fort Blakely.[73]

That same day, Steele sent his wagons back about six miles to Holyoke Mills for supplies, arriving there at 3:00 P.M. That evening at dark, Slack's brigade moved out from Holyoke toward Steele's line. Marching about four miles, they encamped between 10 o'clock and midnight near Origen Sibley's Mill. At midnight Canby ordered Veatch to march the remainder of his division to support Steele at Blakely, and at 1:00 A.M. on 3 March, Veatch put his column in motion. In the van of Veatch's division, Slack "roused camp at 3 A.M." and led his troops to Steele's Fort Blakely siege line. Arriving at daylight, that morning they formed on the left of C.C. Andrews's division and extended Steele's line across the Pensacola Road, followed by Dennis's and Kinsey's brigades. Kenner Garrard's division from the 16th corps followed and formed on Kinsey's left, completing the investment of Fort Blakely with their left extending to the Blakely River swamps just north of Bay Minette.[74]

With Garrard's arrival, Slack's and Kinsey's brigades moved to the rear in reserve while Dennis's brigade remained on the front line between Garrard's and Andrews's positions. On 4 April, a small force from the 47th Indiana and 29th Wisconsin was sent out to reconnoiter the Confederate skirmish line and fix the line of investment. Remaining in camp the next two days, at 7:00 P.M. on 6 April the 47th Indiana and 29th Wisconsin relieved Dennis's brigade in the rifle pits in front of the Confederate fortifications. That night and most of the next day they advanced the saps and trenches another 100 yards until relieved at 7:00 P.M. the next night by the 21st Iowa and 99th Illinois.[75]

Back at Spanish Fort, sharpshooting and artillery exchanges kept apace as the Federals pushed forward their saps and parallels. By 5 April, after ten days of siege, Canby's overwhelming firepower had taken its toll. The heavy and accurate artillery bombardment made it so difficult for Gibson's gunners to man their guns that it effectively silenced them. Heavy rains in the first several days of April made the roads impassable for heavy ammunition trains and Canby's supply ran low, causing him to slow the artillery bombardment somewhat for the next several days. Confederate gunners did manage to do some damage with their short-range coehorn mortars and "the picket fights waxed hotter and hotter" until the Federal ammunition trains loaded with heavy artillery rolled in again on 7 April to supply Canby's fifty-three siege guns and thirty-seven field pieces.[76]

THE CAPTURE OF SPANISH FORT, 8 APRIL 1865

At 5:30 P.M. the next day at Spanish Fort, Canby ordered his replenished artillery to open up along their entire line. About forty minutes later, under cover of this bombardment, Col. William B. Bell's 8th Iowa Infantry (from Col. James L. Geddes's brigade) of Carr's division of A.J. Smith's 16th corps, led by companies A and G, splashed and slogged through the muddy marshland and over slashed timber on the southern edge of Bay Minette against Holtzclaw's veteran Alabama troops who manned the unconnected and greatly separated rifle pits on the extreme left flank of the Confederate line. In a spirited firefight, Bell's Iowans gained the crest of a commanding hill and quickly turned Gibson's left flank by attacking and wrapping up each position in detail. Some of Holtzclaw's troops were killed and wounded in the action, some chose to die in what was truly their "last ditch," and 450 surrendered, some after first taking their last pot shot at "Billy Yank" before throwing down their rifles, as resistance ended on this section of Gibson's line.[77]

Bell, describing this action, reported: "We here witnessed the spectacle of dying in the last ditch, as quite a number of the rebels refused to surrender and were shot in their ditches, and on the other hand quite a number of them who were taken prisoners ought, in justice to our men, to have been killed, as they would first fire at our men after being ordered to surrender, then throw up both hands and surrender."[78] Having carried some five hundred yards of Gibson's left flank, the Iowans were unable to continue due to incoming artillery fire from the Federal left. Geddes's troops, with Carr's approval, dug in and ran trenches that enfiladed the entire northern defenses of Spanish Fort.[79]

On the Confederate side, although some of Gibson's remaining troops continued to move up and harass Geddes's troops, Holtzclaw, his line having collapsed, advised Gibson that they had an insufficient force to counter the Federal penetration on their extreme left. At sunset, with Geddes's Federals entrenching on the north, Gibson ordered his gunners to open all batteries and called on the skirmishers of his own brigade, commanded by Col. F.L. Campbell, to protect the withdrawal by keeping up a brisk fire on the well-entrenched and now stationary Federals on all their fronts.[80]

Describing the Federal assault from behind the Confederate breastworks at Spanish Fort, P.D. Stephenson, Fifth Company, Washington Artillery wrote:

> The main attack was on our left. They penetrated through that dense marshy jungle, which we looked upon as almost impenetrable, and pushing back the feeble picket line we had there, got to the bay between us and Blakeley, thus cutting us off. There, as we afterwards found out, they planted a battery. From that point they came on down our line driving our slender force before them until they got to the fort on our left, which they captured. It was only a few hundred yards from us and we could see them there moving about in the moonlight. Why they did not

come right on and take us, too, we could never understand. It was one of those curious blunders which happened so often on both sides during the war.[81]

Gibson and his remaining troops, choosing not to die unnecessarily and hoping to avoid imprisonment on Ship Island or anywhere else, spiked their few remaining guns and slipped out of Spanish Fort at nightfall. Clinging to vines and rocks, they descended the steep bluff to the narrow plank treadway on the beach fifty feet below that Federal gunboats had been unable to reach and Federal batteries had overshot. Concealed in the moonlight by tall grass on the water's edge, they followed the treadway up the peninsula walking "just above the water's surface." Crossing the narrow entrance to Bay Minette, they continued up the marshy peninsula to the junction of the Blakely and Apalachee Rivers, where they gathered on the muddy bank at the end of the treadway and watched Federal shells pass overhead as they awaited transport to Fort Huger on the light-draft blockade-runners sent to rescue them. About 200 troops chose to follow Col. Bushrod Jones on the moonlit path to Blakely that had been staked out through the marsh west of Bay Minette. But with a Federal attack on Fort Blakely imminent, the steamers were ordered to turn around and carry Gibson's men, including Jones's contingent when they arrived at Blakely, on to Mobile via the Tensas River for a temporary respite. Back at Spanish Fort, out of the 2,888 aggregate that Gibson reported under his command, 556 officers and men, 350 of them wounded, remained in Spanish Fort and were taken prisoner by Bertram's brigade.[82]

Permitting Gibson's troops to escape may have been a "blunder" earlier in the war, but Carr, knowing that Gibson's men had nowhere to run and not wanting to risk lives unnecessarily, held his line in check. Carr's "blunder" in fact resulted in far fewer widows and orphans than otherwise would have been produced by a continued all-out assault. There were also fewer prisoners to have to ship to and guard at Fort Massachusetts on Ship Island, Mississippi.[83]

After dark that evening (8 April), with Carr's troops stationary but in control of the left flank of Spanish Fort and unaware that Gibson was evacuating the fort, Canby ordered Slack's brigade to support Carr's attack at Spanish Fort. All of Slack's regiments except the 21st Iowa, who were still in the trenches, were in camp resting that day after being relieved from grueling front-line duty the night before. Moving from the lower end of the Blakely line at about 10:00 P.M., after the 21st Iowa came in, they arrived at Spanish Fort after a night march of about three miles. Told by A.J. Smith upon arrival that they were not needed, they rested on the south shore of Bay Minette about a quarter-mile east of Gibson's treadway and escape path up the west shore of Bay Minette. They turned around and marched back to Blakely, arriving at their camp at 2:00 A.M.[84]

THE CAPTURE OF FORT BLAKELY, 9 APRIL 1865

After having heard of the evacuation of Spanish Fort, Canby ordered an assault on Fort Blakely to commence the next day at 5:30 P.M. and sent Carr's and McArthur's brigades from A.J. Smith's Spanish Fort line to support Garrard's division on the Federal left flank.

Only hours after Lee surrendered to Grant at Appomattox Court House, Virginia, but unbeknownst to them, at about 5:00 P.M. on the Federal right, skirmishers from Lt. Col. Henry Merriam's 73rd U.S.C.I. of Pile's brigade, Hawkins's division, pushed forward under fire about 100 yards beyond Andrews's division line on their left and waited for orders. Within forty-five minutes the entire three-mile-long Federal line with some sixteen thousand troops in thirty-five regiments (Garrard's division on the left, Veatch's and Andrews's line in the center, and Hawkins's Colored brigade on the right), with regimental colors flying, charged nearly simultaneously with a yell through a minefield of torpedoes and abatis-filled ravines toward the Confederate parapets. Confederate riflemen and artillerists fired their last desperate rounds as the "stormy wave" of blue surged over their parapets.[85]

On the Federal right, Merriam's slightly advanced troops, upon hearing Andrews's division charging on their left, had charged as well. Within minutes Confederate artillery and musketry fire was silenced as Pile's brigade under heavy fire went up and over the parapets and disheartened Confederates threw down their arms to surrender. Merriam's 73rd U.S.C.I. were the first on Hawkins's line to plant their flag on the Confederate works and many of Cockrell's Missourians and Adaire's Mississippians, to avoid capture by blacks, ran to their right to surrender to white troops from Vifquain's 93rd Ohio and Baldwin's 83rd Ohio, the first of Andrews's division to pour over the parapets.[86]

As Pvt. Abner Wilkes of the 46th Mississippi, one of Adaire's Mississippians on the extreme Confederate left flank who was unable to reach and surrender to Andrews's white troops, put it: "The woods were full of those 'blue bellies.' There were so many that they overpowered us and took all our army prisoner. Oh! I felt so bad to think that I had to go to Ship Island to prison, and to be guarded by negroes at that."[87]

On the Federal left, Kinney's 119th Illinois led the charge of Garrard's division up and over the parapets as Thomas's youthful Alabama Reserves fell back in disorder.[88]

On Garrard's right, the 8th Illinois led Dennis's brigade on Veatch's one-brigade front. Supported by Kinsey's brigade and Storer's section of the 7th Massachusetts Light Artillery, Dennis's troops charged through wire-and torpedo-laced abatis while under fire from the Confederate skirmish line and a battery on their right firing canister. With the 8th Illinois in advance, the 11th Illinois trailing on the left and the 46th Illinois trailing on the right, Dennis's troops overran the skirmish line and captured the 4-gun battery on their right that had been firing canister with deadly effect. As on other parts of the line, Confederates manning the parapets surrendered while those who could streamed the mile or so to the rear to seek rescue from Confederate gunboats and steamers that still plied the Blakely and Tensas Rivers.[89]

The CSS *Nashville*, which was anchored at the mouth of the Tensas River, and other boats from the Confederate squadron moved as close to shore as they could and rescued between 150 and 200 men from Blakely "who could float themselves off." When it was reported to Lt. John W. Bennett, the commander of the *Nashville*, that Liddell was waiting on the beach to escape, Bennett sent a gig to pick him up, but Federal sharpshooters drove it off before it could reach shore. Abandoned on the beach, Liddell surrendered to Garrard's troops.[90]

Slack's brigade, having only returned to camp at 2:00 o'clock that morning, remained in reserve. Hearing the "yelping" later that day, they would watch the charge as spectators and, as Pvt. Bert noted, were lucky not to get into it.[91]

Bertram's brigade was assigned to guard and transfer the 232 commissioned officers and 3,386 enlisted men captured at Spanish Fort and Fort Blakely to prison on Ship Island, Mississippi.[92]

A few Confederate soldiers managed to escape in the post-battle confusion. Among them was Pvt. Abner Wilkes of the 46th Mississippi, who wrote after the war:

> Myself and ten more of the boys were on the extreme left of the army, which reached close to a large swamp. We had not given up our guns, and concluded that we would make a break. We shot the guard, who were on horseback. We shot them about two or three feet from the muzzle of our guns. I don't know whether we hit them; they were off their horses, and I noticed one hung to his stirrup and his horse jumping and "a-sousing." Oh! My God, I have seen that man a good many times since in my sleep; still I don't know whether we hit them or not. But I know one thing: we got from that place through mud and water and briars and everything that is bad. I suppose that we went about three miles in that mud and water before we got on a big pine log and began to whistle like partridges and got the boys together.[93]

The next day (10 April), Slack's brigade moved their camp three miles north to the upper end of Fort Blakely, while on Mobile Bay, the Confederate gunboats *Nashville* and *Morgan* and several light-draft blockade-runners rescued the garrisons from Forts Huger and Tracy and blew up the forts. That same evening, with the Tensas now under Federal control and the Alabama River at Selma held by Maj. Gen. James H. Wilson's Federal cavalry, the floating batteries *Huntsville* and *Tuscaloosa* were scuttled twelve miles above Mobile in the Spanish River. The gunboats *Nashville* and *Morgan*, the ram *Baltic*, and the river transport *Black Diamond*, carrying the crews of the two scuttled floating batteries and the rescued garrisons of Forts Huger and Tracy, steamed 230 miles up the Tombigbee River to Demopolis, Alabama. Nevertheless, the Federal gunboats *Octarora*, *Sebago* and *Winnebago*, now able to ply the waters of the upper bay, followed up the Mobile River and blockaded the Tombigbee.[94]

Before daylight on 11 April, Canby received the "preconcerted signal" indicating that Maury was evacuating the city and assigned Granger the task of occupying Mobile with Veatch's 1st and Benton's 3rd divisions. That evening, as part of Granger's 13th corps occupying force, Slack's brigade left camp at 7:00 P.M. and marched twelve miles south to Starke's Landing (present-day Daphne, about four miles south of Spanish Fort), arriving at 4:00 A.M. the next morning.[95]

After sending Gibson's brigade and remnants of his other units of infantry and artillery, about 4,500 or half his original number, toward Meridian that same day, Maury assured the mayor of Mobile that if he met the Federal convoy with a flag of truce, the city would not be attacked. He then followed his troops early the next morning, the same day that Wilson's Federal cavalry occupied Montgomery, Alabama.[96]

THE OCCUPATION OF MOBILE

Granger and Thatcher's convoy of gunboats and transports departed from Starke's Landing before daylight on 12 April for Dog River Point[97] some five to six miles below downtown Mobile, Granger on the steamer *General Banks*, Thatcher on the flagship *Stockdale*. About a half-mile from shore, the *Metacomet* fired one shot, spotted a large white flag waving on shore, and sent a boat carrying Lt. Col. Robert G. Laughlin of Granger's staff, Lt. Com. Samuel R. Franklin of Thatcher's staff, and Generals Veatch and Benton to meet Mayor Robert H. Slough and the city council, who, following Maury's advice, had come down the Bay Shell Road to the Magnolia Race Course in carriages to surrender the city.

Giving Mayor Slough Granger's surrender demands, the four federal officers rode back to the city with the mayor's entourage, and the first troops began disembarking at 10:30 A.M. at the temporary, single-file Magnolia Race Course Pier. After the entourage arrived in downtown Mobile at the Custom House and Post Office on Royal Street between St. Francis and Dauphin, a United States flag was hoisted and Mayor Slough gave a short speech. The civilian/military entourage then moved several blocks south on Royal Street to City Hall, on the block between Government and Conti Streets, where, at 12:30 P.M., the mayor formally surrendered the city.[98]

Slack's brigade weighed anchor from Starke's Landing at 7:00 A.M. that day, the 47th Indiana aboard the steamer *Landis*, the 99th Illinois and 29th Wisconsin aboard tinclad *No. 41*, and the 21st Iowa aboard the steamer *Warrior*. Instead of using the unsteady single-file racecourse pier, Slack's brigade made an amphibious landing in small boats at about the time that the city was being formally surrendered. Arriving at the southern city limits at about 8:00 P.M., they encamped near the bay but were soon ordered to move to the north end of town. Marching through town with the bands playing, the 47th Indiana encamped for the night at about 10:00 P.M. in the Mobile & Ohio Railroad depot on the northern end of Royal Street, about ten blocks above Government Street, the other three regiments encamping in nearby cotton sheds. Slack and the other generals (Veatch, Benton, Dennis, Granger, and Canby, among others) bedded down seven blocks below at the Battle House Hotel on Royal Street next to the Custom House.[99]

The next day, Veatch's division was assigned to man the outer works of Mobile and to garrison the city. At 5:00 P.M., as part of Veatch's division, Slack's brigade marched eight miles to what Slack called the "beautiful village of Spring Hill" seven miles west of Mobile, "occupied," he noted, "almost wholly by retired merchants and businessmen of the city." According to Pvt. Bert, their "beautiful camp" was situated "on top of a nice hill," surrounded by "the beautifulest springs" he had ever seen. Benton's division moved to the town of Whistler about six and a half miles northwest of downtown Mobile to guard the Mobile & Ohio Railroad.[100]

Back in the Confederate Trans-Mississippi, on 21 April at Shreveport, Kirby Smith had to give a morale-boosting speech to his now dejected troops, who were beginning to talk of quitting and going home after news was published from Shreveport to Houston of Lee's surrender to Grant.[101]

With Lee's Army of Northern Virginia now history, on 26 April at the Bennett House near Durham Station, North Carolina, Joe Johnston surrendered his army to Sherman and Grant on the same terms that had been given to Robert E. Lee. On 4 May at Citronelle, Alabama, about thirty-five miles north of Mobile, Lt. Gen. Richard "Dick" Taylor, who had slipped across the Mississippi River to take command of the remnants of the Army of Tennessee after Hood's disastrous Tennessee Campaign, surrendered his remaining forces, most of whom were scattered throughout Alabama, Mississippi and East Louisiana, to E.R.S. Canby.

That same day at Citronelle, Confederate Commander Ebenezer Farrand signed an agreement to surrender the remaining Confederate fleet at Nanna Hubba Bluff on the Tombigbee River just above its junction with the Alabama River (near the town of Calvert) about eighteen miles east of Citronelle. With the *Morgan*, *Baltic*, *Nashville* and *Black Diamond* at Demopolis, some 185 miles north via the river, the last vessels of the Confederate river fleet would not be formally surrendered at Nanna Hubba Bluff until 10 May, the day that President Johnson (who had taken office after Lincoln's assassination) declared that hostilities were now at an end. On 8 May at Meridian, Mississippi, having been included in the surrender at Citronelle and as news of Joe Johnston's surrender came in, Gibson bade farewell to his troops before they dispersed to their homes, and Maury gave up his aspirations of joining Johnston in North Carolina with those troops.[102]

On the Rio Grande, however, on 11 May the militarily inexperienced Col. Theodore H. Barrett, who had recently taken command of U.S. forces at Brazos Santiago following the resignation of veteran Col. Robert B. Jones of the 34th Indiana, sent Lt. Col. David Branson with 250 men from the 62nd U.S.C.I. and 50 new and yet-to-be-mounted men from the 2nd Texas Cavalry (U.S.), across the Boca Chica Inlet with two 6-mule wagon teams on an expedition of dubious necessity, ostensibly to capture a Confederate outpost upriver on the Rio Grande. The next day, near White's Ranch, about 10 miles upriver from Boca Chica, Branson's force encountered Gidding's Battalion of cavalry (180 men) from "Rip" Ford's command who were picketing the road from Boca Chica. Ford's command had been somewhat diminished by furloughs that were given after it appeared to Ford and his Western Sub-District of Texas commander at Brownsville, Brig. Gen. James Slaughter, that an unofficial truce with Federal forces at Brazos Santiago would, in spite of its rejection by their superiors, remain in effect.[103]

Branson's troops drove Gidding's Battalion back upriver about five miles to their outpost at Palmetto (Palmito) Ranch, capturing the outpost. At about 3:00 P.M., however, while Branson's men rested, "Rip" Ford counterattacked with reinforcements from Fort Brown, forcing Branson to pull back to a more defensible position and send for reinforcements of his own.[104]

Barrett arrived at daybreak the next day (13 May) with 200 veterans from Lt. Col. Robert G. Morrison's 34th Indiana, who had just returned to camp following several exhausting days rounding up cattle on Brazos Santiago Island. With Barrett now in command, the Federal expedition again moved forward skirmishing and retook Palmetto Ranch. After burning the remaining Confederate supplies, Barrett ordered a return to Brazos Santiago and the Federal expedition fell back about a mile and a half to a bluff on the river. At about 4:00 P.M., "Rip" Ford mounted a more effective counterattack with some 270 mounted troopers and 30 artillerists manning six pieces of field artillery, including one manned by volunteer French artillerists from Maximilian's Imperial Mexican Army.[105]

Nearly flanked by Ford's cavalry, and now outgunned, the teamsters turned their wagons and fled southward when Barrett called "quick time" retreat. Morrison's troops guarded the front of the retreating column, including the flying wagons, while Branson's guarded the rear against cavalry charges. As Barrett's wagons flew back toward Boca Chica, Ford's cavalry quickly cut off and captured forty-eight skirmishers from the 34th Indiana. The remaining 34th Indiana troops, trying to keep up with the flying wagons, created some confusion when they broke through the 62nd U.S.C.I. rear guard line at "double-quick time." The 62nd U.S.C.I. troops held their position, however, and, falling back while protecting the rear to near Boca Chica, parried each of several charges made by Ford's troopers and fired in effect the last volley of the war. Near sunset, Ford, his men "greatly fatigued" and his cavalry horses "jaded," called off the pursuit and turned back toward Brownsville.[106]

Reportedly learning that the war in the east was over after returning to Brownsville,

Slaughter and Ford's cavalry troopers went home and the two Confederate commanders began plans to move to Mexico. As news spread about the disaster in the east, Confederate troops all over Texas began to desert. The next day at Galveston (14 May), the garrison troops mutinied. Col. Ashbel Smith was able to restore order there, but the disintegration of other Confederate forces in Texas continued rapidly as most soldiers chose to return home to protect their families.[107]

In spite of the problems in Texas, Kirby Smith flatly rejected the terms of surrender presented to him by Col. John T. Sprague on behalf of Major General John Pope, commander of the Military Division of the Missouri at St. Louis. Sprague had traveled to Shreveport, where he presented the terms to Smith on 9 May. While Sprague waited his answer in Shreveport, Smith held a conference of Trans-Mississippi governors at Marshall, Texas, in which the governors urged him to accept the terms. In spite of this, Smith returned to Shreveport on 15 May and rejected them, informing Sprague that he had more than 50,000 troops who would fight to the end. Returning to St. Louis, Sprague informed Pope of Smith's bravado.[108]

With the French gaining a foothold on the Rio Grande and Kirby Smith having rejected the surrender terms, not to mention Barrett's blunder at Brazos, Grant ordered Frederick Steele to take a force of 12,000 troops to Brazos Santiago to take control of the Rio Grande and assigned Phil Sheridan command west of the Mississippi and south of the Arkansas River with orders "to restore Texas and that part of Louisiana held by the enemy to the Union in the shortest practicable time"—and in effect to get Kirby Smith.[109]

Meanwhile, the death of President Lincoln on 15 April brought into office the more belligerent Andrew Johnson and eliminated any hope that the convictions or death sentences against Milligan, Horsey, and Bowles would be vacated. Perhaps remembering the H.H. Dodd fiasco, Judge-Advocate Burnett, who, following the end of the Cincinnati Treason Trial[110] on 18 April, had returned to Washington, D.C., to aid in the investigation of the president's murder, quickly relayed War Department orders to Hovey to have Milligan, Horsey, and Bowles put in irons and their guard increased to prevent their escape or rescue.[111]

On 2 May, President Johnson officially approved the military court-martial death sentences, which arrived at Indianapolis on 9 May. Hovey quickly ordered that the death sentences by hanging be carried out on 19 May 1865 at Indianapolis on the parade grounds between Camp Morton and Burnside Barracks between noon and 3:00 P.M. In response, counsel for the three defendants filed writs of habeas corpus in federal court in Indianapolis, claiming the military commission had no jurisdiction in their cases.[112]

The death sentences shocked many including, as Klement points out, staunch death penalty advocates like the Republican *Indianapolis Daily Journal*, edited by Governor Morton's brother-in-law, William R. Holloway, who called for a stay until the question of jurisdiction could be tested in federal court. Even Morton himself, who had pronounced all four defendants guilty of treason and had clamored for their blood before the trial began, lobbied for commutation of the death sentences. (Morton's newfound prudence coincided with a meeting in Indianapolis he had with U.S. Supreme Court Justice David Davis.[113])

On 16 May, President Johnson relented somewhat and commuted Horsey's death sentence to life in prison at hard labor at the state penitentiary at Columbus, Ohio, and postponed the execution of Milligan and Bowles until 2 June 1865.[114]

Meanwhile, as mutiny spread through the Confederate Trans-Mississippi, and shortly after he rejected Pope's surrender terms, Kirby Smith put Simon Buckner in charge at Shreveport and moved his headquarters to Houston. With Smith en route to Houston and without his knowledge, on or about 23 May, Buckner, along with Generals Sterling Price and J.L. Brent, headed down the Red River for New Orleans to confer with E.R.S. Canby about the surrender of the Trans-Mississippi.[115]

Before Smith arrived at Houston, however, Governor Pendleton Murrah and General John B. Magruder commissioned Col. Ashbel Smith and citizen W.P. Ballinger, Esq., to travel to New Orleans to seek a separate surrender for the State of Texas. Granted permission to travel by Admiral Thatcher, the two Texas commissioners steamed out from Galveston toward New Orleans aboard the USS *Antona*.[116]

Buckner's party reached New Orleans first and on 25 May conferred with Canby's representative, Major General Peter J. Osterhaus, at the St. Charles Hotel. The next day they officially surrendered the Trans-Mississippi on the same terms granted Lee and Johnston. Arriving at New Orleans several days later, Ashbel Smith and Ballinger ended their mission upon learning that Buckner had already surrendered the Trans-Mississippi.[117]

While the two separate commissions were steaming toward New Orleans, Kirby Smith, having finally learned that widespread mutiny had left him a "commander without an army — a general without troops," told the few soldiers who had remained to return to their families.[118]

Back at Mobile at about the same time, the city's luck in avoiding the devastation of war ran out at 3 o'clock on the afternoon of 25 May when careless handling of ordnance accidentally ignited tons of powder and shells stored at the main ordnance depot on Hunt Street (present-day Beauregard Street) near the Mobile & Ohio Railroad station. The explosion destroyed eight city blocks in the Warehouse District north of downtown, the heaviest damage occurring on Water Street above St. Michael and on the upper part of Commerce Street, which at the time paralleled Water Street one block to the east and ran along the Mobile River wharfs. Brick warehouses and cotton sheds in the epicenter of the blast lay in ruins and several boats were destroyed on the waterfront. Effects of the blast radiated out as buildings on Royal Street from the railroad station south to Conti Street suffered varying degrees of structural damage. The *Mobile News* building at 59 St. Michael Street between Water and Royal Streets had its north and east fronts blown out, as did the Customs House a block south on the southeast corner of Royal and St. Francis Streets, about 1,000 yards from the explosion. An estimated three hundred people were killed.[119]

Slack had come into the city and was just awaking from a nap at a boarding house about four blocks away when the explosion blew out the windows of his room and showered him with glass. Describing the aftermath to Ann, he wrote:

> About eight squares of the city were literally blown into one confused wrecked mass. You can form no conception of the appearance of the buildings, the terrible wreck. The walls of those immense cotton sheds were thrown out and the immense roofs fell in, crushing everything underneath. Immediately following the explosion the buildings began to burn. A great many persons underneath the rubbish, unable to get out, were roasted alive. Shells were constantly exploding, men crying most piteously for help, the fire approaching them, and no helping hand could save them. Five or six steamers lying at the wharf were shattered into atoms, and two of them burned. I walked through the destroyed district this morning before breakfast. It cannot be described, has to be seen to be fully appreciated.[120]

On 27 May, Slack, having returned to Spring Hill, brought his brigade back to Mobile under orders to embark them that same day with the rest of Veatch's division on boats for Shreveport. He, in turn, was relieved of command of his brigade and ordered to report to Gordon Granger for assignment.

With the surrender of the Trans-Mississippi, Philip Sheridan was ordered to restore Federal control in Texas and western Louisiana. To accomplish the task, Sheridan sent Frederick Steele with Steele's and Benton's divisions to the Rio Grande, Major General Godfrey Weitzel's 25th corps to follow shortly from the east coast.[121]

In Washington on 30 May, President Johnson commuted the death sentences of Milligan and Bowles, although for reasons known only unto himself, ordered via a coded and strictly confidential letter that the commutations be kept secret until 2 June, the day of their scheduled hanging. On that day, all three prisoners, Bowles, Milligan, and Horsey, were transferred to the penitentiary at Columbus, Ohio, where they began serving their life terms at hard labor. Undeterred by offers of pardon if he would withdraw his petition, Milligan insisted he had violated no laws and his case became known as *Ex parte Milligan* as it wended its way to the Supreme Court.[122]

XVI

Shreveport and the Rio Grande (June–November 1865)

The war over, on 29 May President Johnson issued his first Amnesty Proclamation, which granted amnesty and pardon and returned all property rights "except as to slaves" to all ex-Confederates upon taking an oath to henceforth support the Constitution and obey all laws. Exceptions included many notable ex-Confederates, including all those who had taxable property of over $20,000, those who held civil or diplomatic offices, former Confederate officers above the rank of colonel in the army or lieutenant in the navy, those who resigned commissions in the U.S. Army or Navy, all those educated at West Point or the Naval Academy, all who left seats in the U.S. Congress, all governors of the "pretended Confederate states," and all who made raids into the U.S. from Canada, among a few others.[1]

Although President Johnson permitted anyone to apply for clemency and promised a liberal clemency policy, many notable ex-Confederates who fell outside the amnesty and pardon guidelines chose not to rely on Johnson's liberality and scrambled to leave the country. Kirby Smith, in fact, had had his eyes on Mexico since February, when he first persuaded Shreveport businessman Robert Rose, a former U.S. diplomat who was ostensibly on his way to Mexico on business, to act as his personal emissary to offer his services to Maximilian's Imperial Army. Three months later, and about three weeks after Lt. Col. John Sprague first presented him with the surrender papers at Shreveport, Smith wrote Sprague that he was ready to sign but would "go abroad until the further policy of the United States Government toward the South is announced, and will return to my family only when I can do so with security to my life and person." When the steamer *Fort Jackson* arrived at Galveston harbor on 2 June 1865, Smith and Magruder went on board and signed the Trans-Mississippi surrender agreement, and shortly thereafter both left for Mexico via San Antonio and Eagle Pass.[2]

On the Rio Grande, "Rip" Ford[3] took his family across the river to Matamoras, where he and James Slaughter delivered their remaining six pieces of field artillery and transport wagons to Tomas Mejia, commander of the Mexican Royalist force at Matamoras. They also carried and sold to brokers a large supply of cotton from the Brownsville warehouse. Slaughter, who did not cross at Matamoros, was reported in some accounts to have been arrested and held by his former soldiers until he could come up with their back pay. According to Sheridan and Brigadier General Egbert B. Brown, who had replaced Theodore Barrett in command of the garrison on Brazos Santiago, Slaughter won his freedom by distributing the proceeds of his armament and cotton sales, reportedly some $20,000 in specie, before he traveled upriver to cross into Mexico at Eagle Pass. According to others, Slaughter was released after he opened Confederate stores so that his ex-soldiers could take whatever they wanted in lieu of back pay. In any event, on 30 May, E.B. Brown moved his force upriver and occupied Brownsville in anticipation of the arrival of Steele's 12,000.[4]

Back at Mobile, after seeing his old brigade and his baggage put aboard steamers bound for New Orleans, Slack received orders to accompany the first flotilla of Steele's troops to Texas. While he steamed to the Rio Grande, his old brigade steamed from New Orleans up the Mississippi and the now somewhat more hospitable Red River to Shreveport.[5]

Francis J. Herron arrived at Shreveport in late May to take command of the Northern Division of Louisiana and garrison the Red River. Upon arrival at Shreveport, he reported that there had been, especially among what he identified as the Texas troops, "a general pillage and destruction of property from the time it was known that General Buckner had gone to New Orleans until our arrival." Referring in effect to Sterling Price, J.O. Shelby and their Texas and Missouri troops, he reported that "a number of officers who have been thieving have largely gone to Mexico." Many destitute ex-Confederates marauded their way through Missouri and Texas, some on their way home, others following their more affluent former officers and officials on their way to Mexico. Many citizens on their pathway formed vigilante committees to protect themselves and, as in northern Louisiana, peace was restored only upon the arrival of Federal troops.[6]

From his headquarters in New Orleans, Sheridan turned his attention to garrisoning the Trans-Mississippi to restore order and the authority of the United States — and to his unofficial orders from Grant to pressure the French to withdraw from Mexico by supporting the Liberal/Republican forces of ousted President Benito Juarez. Grant's orders were necessarily unofficial since both President Johnson and Secretary of State Seward, fearful of bringing on a war with France, insisted on at least the appearance of neutrality in the dispute between Juarez and Maximilian.[7]

Back at Shreveport on 3 June 1865, Herron informed the citizens of northern Louisiana that slavery no longer existed: "There are no longer any slaves in the United States; all persons heretofore held as such became free by virtue of the Executive proclamation of January 1, 1863, commonly known as the Emancipation Proclamation."[8] What it meant to be free, however, had yet to be determined. Due to a workforce problem created by former slaves leaving the plantations, Herron ordered newly freed slaves to stay home and work the crops. To ensure this, he ordered that they could not leave the area without a military pass or congregate at military posts, adding that any former slaves found wandering would be arrested and punished. On the other hand, planters were required to make definite and binding contracts with their former slaves, treat them kindly, and pay them reasonable wages for the balance of the present season with assurances that their free status would not be compromised by working for wages on the plantations. Agents of the Freedmen's Bureau, he assured them, would have all the pertinent information when they arrived. Until then, the post commander and provost marshal's role was to see that his order was enforced.[9]

Slack arrived at Brazos Santiago Island, Texas, on 5 June in the first wave of Steele's force of 12,000. Assigned command at Brazos Santiago, Slack was charged with establishing a deployment base for troops from Weitzel's 25th corps, coming in from the east, and William P. Benton's division from Mobile. To house the new Federal troops pouring in, lumber and other building materiel was sent to Brazos Santiago Island to construct a "town" on its southern tip at Boca Chica Inlet, about nine miles south of the town of Brazos Santiago. New construction included a hotel or rooming house run by a Mrs. Clark, who may have given the town its name, "Clarksville," not to be confused with the town of Clarksville in northeastern Texas.[10]

Meanwhile, on 16 June in New Orleans, Sheridan assigned Gordon Granger command of Federal forces in Texas and ordered him to proceed to Galveston and to direct Steele at Brownsville to demand the return of all arms and munitions of war "taken to Matamoras by the rebels, or obtained from them ... since the surrender of General E. Kirby Smith."[11]

From his headquarters at Galveston three days later, Granger, speaking to the citizens of Texas, issued General Orders No. 3:

> The people of Texas are informed that, in accordance with a proclamation from the Executive of the United States, all slaves are free. This involves an absolute equality of personal rights and rights of property between former masters and slaves, and the connection heretofore existing between them becomes that between employer and hired labor. The freedmen are advised to remain quietly at their present homes and work for wages. They are informed that they will not be supported by idleness either there or elsewhere.[12]

Accordingly, June 19 is observed to this day as "Juneteenth."

As noted in Louisiana, the problem of what to do with the newly freed slaves and who would harvest the crops created a number of problems in the Trans-Mississippi, not the least of which was what it meant to be free. On 23 June 1865 from Camden, Arkansas, Brig. Gen. George F. McGinnis wrote, "Many negroes are leaving home; former masters anxious to keep them at home to assist with crops, promising to feed, cloth[e] and pay them whatever wages the Superintendent of Freedmen decides." McGinnis added, "Being free, I cannot insist on their returning unless I have instructions to do so." McGinnis received word from Joseph J. Reynolds, commanding the Department of Arkansas, that his actions were approved; former slaves were free to choose their employers, but they were cautioned to respect their contracts.[13]

Many newly freed slaves, risking arrest if they were found on the road without work and without a military pass, left the plantations in droves, choosing instead to try the road to freedom. For those who left, as well as for those who remained on the plantations, it would turn out to be a grueling and treacherous quest for freedom and full citizenship lasting through the next century.[14]

Back on Brazos Santiago Island, Texas, the 35th Wisconsin and 46th U.S.C.I. regiments arrived at Clarksville (the 46th from the town of Brazos on the northern end of the island). The 46th U.S.C.I. would move on to Brownsville as soon as the swollen Rio Grande abated, leaving the 7th Vermont, the 77th Ohio, the 27th, 28th and 35th Wisconsin, the 28th Illinois, the 26th New York Battery, and the wagon train, all from William P. Benton's division, at Slack's Clarksville post.[15]

Sheridan arrived from his headquarters in New Orleans on an inspection tour, and Slack tried to get the 47th Indiana transferred to Texas so that he could consolidate them with the 34th Indiana. There had been some troop movement from Shreveport to Texas, but the 47th Indiana's luck held out. By 18 June, they were the sole infantry regiment at the Shreveport garrison, along with some cavalry, which probably saved them from being transferred to the Rio Grande.[16]

In a major postwar reorganization of military departments and divisions, Sheridan's command, with headquarters in New Orleans, was dubbed the Military Division of the Gulf and encompassed the Departments of Mississippi (Henry W. Slocum), Louisiana and Texas (E.R.S. Canby), and Florida (John G. Foster). Gordon Granger commanded troops in Texas, including troops under Frederick Steele that had been sent to the Rio Grande to secure the frontier with Mexico. Slack's new command was part of Steele's Western District of Texas, which covered the area between the Rio Grande and the Nueces Rivers.[17]

Slack's old brigade remained in Shreveport as part of Francis J. Herron's Northern Division of Louisiana. Earlier in the year at Baton Rouge, Herron had worked with Captain W.B. Ratliff, C.S.A., and Alexander Barrow to allow Ratliff's troops ten days, commencing on 26 March, to stamp out "jayhawking and plundering" by Confederate troops, presumably deserters, without interference from United States troops in the territory on the west bank of the Mississippi between Bayou Plaquemine, about eighteen miles south of Baton Rouge by land, northward about fifty-five miles to Morganza. Ratliff accomplished his mission as promised and Herron moved his headquarters to Shreveport to continue the task of convincing former Confederates that the war was over. His troops, including the 47th Indiana, were used to keep the peace on the Red River and track down recalcitrant Confederates in northwestern Louisiana.[18]

Back in Texas, with the river crossing at Brownsville closed, the upriver roads to Eagle Pass became crowded with ex-Confederates bound for exile in Mexico, ready to try their luck with either the Liberals or, as in most cases, Maximilian's French Imperialists. Among other notable ex-Confederate officers who chose exile in Mexico were Sterling Price and J.O. Shelby, who left Shreveport for Mexico with about four or five hundred armed troopers from Shelby's Missouri brigade and a wagon train of arms and ammunition, including several pieces of artillery.

At the unofficial San Antonio rendezvous site for notable ex-Confederates, Shelby and Price met and escorted safely through to Mexico a number of former officers and civilian officials, including ex-Governors Pendleton Murrah of Texas, Henry W. Allen and Thomas O. Moore of Louisiana, and Thomas C. Reynolds of Missouri. At busy Eagle Pass on or about 4 July, Shelby's Missourians reportedly weighed down their old battle flag with rocks and sank it in the Rio Grande before they crossed over to Piedras Negras and sold their artillery and ammunition for much-needed specie to the Liberal Governor of Coahuila, Andres Viesco. Turning down Viesco's offer to join Juarez's Liberals, they were nevertheless allowed to proceed to Imperialist-held Monterrey.[19]

Downriver near Matamoros on 6 July, Sheridan reported that Cortina drove in Mejia's pickets and captured the steamer *Senorita*, adding, "Affairs on the Rio Grande are getting beautifully mixed up." Four days later, ignoring admonitions from Washington, Sheridan noted that Cortina's small skirmish victories over Mejia had embarrassed the French and "little irritations which I have encouraged along the river have alarmed them so much that there is a perfect exodus from Matamoras."[20]

In two separate telegrams dated 10 and 14 July from his headquarters in New Orleans, Sheridan relayed to Grant Frederick Steele's reports from Brownsville that the "Franco-Mexicans" (Mexican Royalists) were bitter and anxious to bring on difficulties with the United States. The Royalists had abandoned their garrison at Camargo and taken their Confederate-supplied cotton to Matamoros, where Mejia's Royalists maintained control, although Cortina now controlled the roads around Matamoros. Indeed, meeting with Steele in Brownsville, Cortina, acting as the Liberal governor of Tamaulipas State, gave Steele permission to bring United States forces into Mexico. Sheridan added that Shelby had escorted an entourage of notables into Mexico including Governors Murrah of Texas and Allen of Louisiana, and Generals Kirby Smith and Magruder, along with "three pieces of artillery, forty wagon loads of Enfield rifles, and a large wagon train." Maximilian, however, had already directed Mejia to turn over to the United States authorities at Brownsville the armaments and cotton that Shelby and others had brought over. Cortina made application for the three pieces of artillery then at Brownsville and Sheridan directed that it "be quietly turned over to him."[21]

French and Austrian troops, however, began arriving at Vera Cruz on their way to bolster the faltering Royalists on the Rio Grande. With events moving fast, Sheridan, having difficulty commanding Federal troops in Texas and maintaining control of the Mexican border from his headquarters in New Orleans, informed Grant on 18 July that he was heading for the Rio Grande in two days and that he would watch Maximilian's Imperial troops and Mejia's Mexican Royalists at Matamoros very closely.[22]

On the Rio Grande, Slack gave Ann his opinion of what he called the Mexican government, presumably referring to Mejia's Royalists in Matamoros: "Day before yesterday, at 6 o'clock in the morning the Mexican authorities executed a Mexican soldier for stealing a sack of corn. I heard the volley that shot him. They only give their soldiers a shilling a day, and require them to find their boarding out of that, then shoot them for taking something to eat." His opinion of Cortina was not much better: "He is nothing more or less than a mere brigand, a robber and murderer. Was formerly a resident of Texas, born here, and now there are three or four indictments in the Court at Brownsville against him for murder, horse stealing, &c &c."[23]

Although Slack and many others dismissed Cortina as, essentially, a criminal, he had been by some accounts a respected rancher in Texas until about 1850. An increasing number of land disputes between Anglo and Mexican Texans had been brought about by Anglo developers hungry for land following the Mexican War, and the Treaty of Guadalupe Hidalgo, which ended the war, did not include protection of Mexican land rights in the ceded territory.[24]

Although not part of the ceded territory, the same was essentially true in Texas following the so-called revolution in the Mexican State of Coahuila y Tejas, in which Anglo-Texan settlers (immigrants primarily from the southern United States) and their descendants, ostensibly fighting President Antonio Lopez de Santa Ana's usurpation of power, successfully removed Tejas and a part of Coahuila from Mexico and established the Anglo-dominated, slave-labor Republic of Texas. Even though much of the Anglo land in Texas had originally come through Spanish land grants, the new Anglo-Texan rulers challenged the land rights of Mexicans in newly independent Texas and welcomed land developers from the United States.[25]

This inevitably led to anger among Mexicans living in the now-independent republic whose families had owned land for generations while it was Mexican territory, but who now found themselves in title disputes with Anglo developers. In one case, Rafael Garcia Cavazos, a relative of Cortina, won a land title lawsuit against Charles Stillman, an importer/exporter turned land developer who was one of a number of businessmen, also included in the lawsuit, who had operated their businesses on the Mexican side of the Rio Grande until high tariffs imposed on exports after the war with the United States induced them to move their businesses across the river to Texas. As part of this movement, Stillman began a trading center on the river adjacent to Fort Brown that he called Brownsville.[26]

Stillman and the Cavazos family, heirs to an 18th-century Spanish land grant in Coahuila y Tejas across the river from Matamoros, came into conflict when Stillman attempted to acquire land for his new town by taking advantage of the uncertainty, if not outright denial, of Mexican land rights north of the Rio Grande. The Cavazos family, who owned extensive lands and had lived in the area for generations, had problems after the war with the United States ended in 1848 with squatters crossing the river and settling on their land with so-called labor or squatter's titles. Taking advantage of this situation, Stillman bought these "squatter's" titles to acquire land for his new town.[27]

In 1849, Cavazos, alleging that the former republic and now State of Texas aided the illegal usurpation of property ownership based on Spanish land grants by issuing "pretended titles" and "illegal grants or claims," sued Stillman and his partners in the U.S. District Court of Texas. The Federal court ruled in favor of Cavazos's claim that the original Spanish land grant titles were valid and the State of Texas titles illegal. Stillman and the others, alleging bias and improper judicial conduct, threatened to appeal and petitioned the House Judiciary Committee to bring impeachment charges against Federal District Judge John C. Watrous, who had ruled against them. In 1852, Cavazos, undoubtedly impressed by the power of the businessmen and their lawyers to bring impeachment charges against the judge and unable to afford continued litigation, agreed to sell the land to Stillman for $33,000. Brownsville was incorporated the next year.[28]

Cortina's mother, Dona Estefana, also heir to a large 18th-century Spanish land grant, owned a ranch about six miles upriver from Brownsville that also had been subject to several lawsuits in the Federal District Court of Texas challenging her ownership of the land. She was reportedly forced to give up a league of land in order to establish title to the property that had been in her family for generations. Cortina saw this essentially as an Anglo land grab, a form of theft or usurpation of Mexican real estate by the Anglo rulers in Texas that made Mexican Texans "foreigners in their native land."[29]

Cortina's anger reportedly boiled over on 13 July 1859 after, according to at least one version, he witnessed the Anglo city marshal of Brownsville pistol-whip a Mexican who had been employed by his family. Armed and on horseback, he reportedly wounded the marshal, rescued the Mexican prisoner and rode to safety in Matamoros, where he was welcomed as a defender of Mexican rights. Shortly thereafter, he put together a band of an estimated four hundred or more armed men at his, or his mother's, ranch that he called "Rancho del Carmen" some six miles upriver from Brownsville. (Rancho del Carmen was accessible only by one road leading to it, flanked on either side by dense chaparral and protected in front by two pieces of light artillery.) Two months later (28 September 1859), Cortina and some forty to eighty of his men attacked the city of Brownsville, killed three Anglos, and released prisoners from the city jail before withdrawing upriver to Rancho del Carmen. Two days later from Rancho del Carmen, Cortina issued his first proclamation asserting his right to defend Mexican property from usurpation by Anglo lawyers and developers.[30]

Reprisals, including deadly attacks against Mexican Texans in the lower Rio Grande, many of them indiscriminate, and counterattacks by Cortina's men in the months following the Brownsville raid became known as "Cortina's War." In November, Cortina's men subsequently drove off a militia force of Brownsville citizens as well as a party of Texas Rangers under Capt. William G. Tobin, who had attacked his Rancho del Carmen stronghold. Following this unsuccessful attempt to defeat him, on 23 November Cortina issued a second proclamation that complained about lawyers and land speculators who were denying Mexican property rights and called on Gov. Sam Houston to defend those legal rights.[31]

His pleas ignored by Houston, Cortina held off attacks against his stronghold at Rancho del Carmen until December, when troops under Col. Robert E. Lee of the U.S. Army arrived, having been sent to Texas to secure the border. Lee sent Maj. Samuel P. Heintzelman with an expeditionary force of infantry, cavalry and artillery, along with Capt. John S. "Rip" Ford's company of Texas Rangers, to drive Cortina out of Texas. Unable to cope with such a force, Cortina retreated across the Rio Grande but continued to harass the Federal cavalry and Ford's rangers, including a failed attempt to capture the cargo of a steamboat on the Rio Grande.[32] Indeed, for many Mexicans in Texas and in Mexico, Cortina was a "Robin Hood of the Rio Grande" or even a "social revolutionary" fighting against injustice and for Mexican property rights in Texas. To Anglo-Texans and Texas land developers, of course, he was a bandit, a horse thief, and a murderer.[33]

Having been driven from the United States, Cortina subsequently got involved in the labyrinthine and often deadly world of Mexican politics. With the secession of Texas in May 1861, Cortina invaded Carrizo, Texas, on 23 May, was defeated by Texas troops under Santos Benavides, and retreated back to Mexico, where he operated as an independent caudillo (loosely translated as a political boss with armed followers on horseback). At Puebla he joined with Juarez's army, which was largely a coalition of the forces of various independent caudillos who supported the republican cause or at least opposed the French invasion. In late August or early September 1863, Cortina, then a lieutenant colonel in Juarez's army, was sent to Matamoros in command of a cavalry force to fight against the French Imperialists and their Mexican Royalist allies on the Rio Grande.[34]

In November 1863, when H.P. Bee, facing the arrival of Banks's Federal force on Brazos Santiago Island, abandoned Brownsville and accidentally burned part of the city, Mexican Royalist General Jose Maria Cobos, who had been living in exile in Brownsville, turned the city over Banks on 5 November, then crossed over to Matamoros with his small force, arrested the pro-U.S. Liberal military governor of Tamaulipas, Don Manuel Ruiz, and took possession of the city. Cortina, operating very loosely as a lieutenant colonel in Juarez's cavalry, arrested Cobos when he refused to swear allegiance to Juarez and the next day summarily executed Cobos and two of his subordinates. Offered protection by Cortina, Ruiz chose to leave Matamoras. Cortina then lifted the state of siege in Tamaulipas, which Juarez had instituted several years earlier to calm the civil unrest that followed the elections in that troubled state, and restored Don Jesus de la Serna to the governor's office. In all this, the French Embassy accused Francis J. Herron, then in command of Federal forces at Brownsville, of sending arms and recruits to Cortina, which Herron denied, noting that Cortina had complained about his not having helped him.[35]

Considering Cortina's unauthorized lifting of the state of siege in Tamaulipas dangerous insubordination, Juarez sent a brigade from his own soon-to-be-evacuated headquarters at San Luis Potosi to assist Ruiz. Ruiz met the brigade on the road, took command and led it back to Matamoros to oust de la Serna and restore Juarez's authority. A violent confrontation was avoided when, on advice from Juarez, de la Serna abdicated and retired to his ranch, while Ruiz, with assent from both Juarez and Cortina, reclaimed the governorship of Tamaulipas. On 12 January 1864, however, with the ink hardly dry on the agreement, one of Cortina's officers insulted Ruiz; and Ruiz, apparently now feeling very secure in his position, had the offending officer arrested and shot that very afternoon. Considering the summary execution a deal breaker, that evening Cortina ordered his troops to open fire on Ruiz's headquarters at Matamoros, driving the hapless Ruiz and his top officers across the river to Brownsville. That same month, from his new headquarters at Monterrey, Juarez appointed civilian Andres Trevino to replace Ruiz, but Cortina refused to accept Trevino and proclaimed himself the acting governor of Tamaulipas.[36]

Juarez, however, had greater problems than Cortina's insubordination. Having already been driven out of San Luis Potosi in December 1863 by French Imperial troops under Marshal Francois Achilles Bazaine, Juarez was now forced northward to Monterrey in the state of Nuevo Leon and Coahuila, ruled by yet another independent caudillo, erstwhile Liberal turned Royalist Don Santiago Vidauri. Just upriver from Tamaulipas, Vidaurri had cobbled Nuevo Leon and Coahuila together in 1857 by force of arms. Although he initially supported the Republican fight against the French Imperialists, he soon broke with Juarez in a power struggle. After the outbreak of the U.S. Civil War, Vidaurri traded heavily with the Texas Confederates through the "House of Milmo," his son-in-law's import/export business in Monterrey, about 200 miles west of Matamoras. By the time the French army had pushed Juarez northward to Monterrey, Vidauri had thrown his support to Maximilian's effort to create an empire in Mexico.[37]

In February, as Cortina began his stint as self-proclaimed governor of Tamaulipas, troops loyal to Vidauri forced Juarez to move his headquarters to Saltillo, about fifty miles west of Monterrey. Vidaurri persuaded several of Juarez's generals to abandon the Republican cause, including an unsuccessful attempt to recruit Cortina, and even suggested to Juarez that he abdicate. Instead of abdicating, however, Juarez, using his enormous popular support to gather recruits, defeated Vidauri in early April, captured armaments and forced him to flee to Laredo, Texas, to seek protection from Santos Benavides for what turned out to be temporary exile.[38]

On 7 April 1864, with Bazaine's French army still moving north toward Juarez's headquarters at Saltillo and a column heading toward Matamoros, Cortina worked out a deal with the U.S. forces at Brownsville to close the Mexican border to trade with the Confederates in exchange for refuge from the advancing French and Mexican Royalists.[39]

At the same time Cortina, hedging his bets, worked out a deal with his old adversaries, Col. Santos Benavides (C.S.A.) and Col. John S. "Rip" Ford (C.S.A.), to protect Confederate cotton crossing at Laredo in exchange for refuge in Texas if the need should arise. With Vidauri in Texas and faced with the possible closure of their lucrative trade routes through Mexico, Major General John B. Magruder (C.S.A.), commander of the District of Texas, and Governor Pendleton Murrah of Texas developed newfound appreciation for Cortina (a marriage of convenience if there ever was one) and approved the deal, even offering Cortina sanctuary in Texas with immunity from prosecution for "any former complications" he may have been involved with in Texas.[40]

Maximilian arrived in Mexico in May 1864 and the next month was crowned Emperor of Mexico. By July, Bazaine's army was on the move, threatening Juarez's position at Saltillo, and a force under Du Pris was at Victoria, the capitol of Tamaulipas, about 100 miles south of Matamoras. To make matters worse, at the end of July at Brownsville, Banks, from his headquarters at New Orleans, believing that Herron's Federal troops could not adequately defend their isolated garrison, ordered them to withdraw to Brazos Santiago and the Confederates reoccupied Brownsville. Herron, transferred to command the District of Baton Rouge, was replaced by Col. Henry M. Day of the 91st Illinois Infantry in command of the remaining Federal forces on Brazos Santiago Island.[41]

With the U.S. forces pulling back and the likelihood of interference or intervention thus reduced, Bazaine, in a near-total defeat of Juarez, forced him out of Saltillo and northwest through the desert plains of Coahuila and Chihuahua to remote Paso del Norte (now Ciudad Juarez) on the upper Rio Grande. Shortly thereafter, in early September, a contingent of the French army under A. Veron, accompanied by Mexican Royalists under Gen. Tomas Mejia, moved by sea toward Bagdad while another column approached by land from Monterrey. His empire at high tide, Maximilian's armies took control of large parts of Mexico. Juarez, in retreat, regrouped and resupplied, with unofficial U.S. assistance, in remote Paso del Norte while his armies, defeated in battle but with great popular support, were forced to resort to guerrilla warfare.[42]

Back in Matamoras and facing Maximilian's onslaught, on 8 September Cortina asked Day for assistance against and refuge from the approaching French and Mexican Royalist armies in exchange for closing the border at Matamoras to Confederate trade. Although Day granted Cortina refuge, Cortina, still hedging his bets, made another agreement, or reiterated the old one, with "Rip" Ford for free and unrestricted Confederate commerce with Mexico in exchange for safe refuge in Confederate Texas.[43]

Fighting Veron's French and Mejia's Mexican Royalist forces as they moved up from Bagdad, and apparently no longer interested in exile in Confederate Texas, Cortina fired on "Rip" Ford's Confederate position in Brownsville, causing orders to go out that if he was caught, he was once again to be treated as a robber and murderer, not a prisoner of war. On 29 September 1864, however, the cautious French, pushing aside Cortina's troops but not wanting to overplay their hand and do anything to endanger their understanding of neutrality with the United States, permitted Mejia and his Mexican Royalist army to enter and take command in Matamoros while they withdrew to Bagdad.[44]

Mejia quickly established friendly relations with the Texas Confederates, and Cortina, instead of fleeing to Brazos Santiago, surrendered to Mejia but avoided execution by swearing allegiance to Maximilian. A brigade of Cortina's troops commanded by Col. Miguel Echarzaretta did cross over to Brazos Santiago carrying with them a large supply of armaments, but all of the officers and most of the men petitioned for, and Mejia is believed to have granted, safe return to Mexico as peaceable civilians. Some, however, remained on Brazos Santiago and mustered into Day's U.S. forces to be used, or so U.S. Consul at Matamoros, Leonard Pierce Jr., hoped, as rangers or "beef hunters" whose knowledge of the area would help keep the frontier clear of Confederates. (Twelve Mexican troopers from Echarzaretta's "Exploradores del Bravo" who had enlisted in the U.S. service were acknowledged by Day to have been captured by "Rip" Ford's cavalry in skirmishes between 6 and 12 September.[45])

Although his activities after surrendering to Mejia in September 1864 and submission to the Empire are somewhat obscure, on or about 1 April 1865, Cortina renounced his association with Maximilian's Imperialists and made arrangements to move his family to Brownsville as soon as U.S. troops could reoccupy the place, which they did on 31 May 1865. Accepted back into the Liberal fold by Juarez, Cortina's force was able to drive in Mejia's pickets with ease, and he soon controlled all the roads around Matamoros. Santos Benavides even reportedly pledged to cross with his now or soon-to-be ex-Confederate command to join Cortina in his fight for the Mexican Republic. By June, the ebb tide of Maximilian's empire had begun.[46]

With the end of the U.S. Civil War, and Sheridan's veterans occupying the Rio Grande, U.S. Secretary of State Seward began pressuring the French to withdraw from Mexico and warned them against reintroducing slavery into the Americas by replacing French, Austrian and Belgian volunteers with Nubian slaves from the Sudan sent to them by the Pacha of Egypt in forced military servitude. The French replied that the recruitment from the Pacha had been suspended due to an uprising in Egypt, but it was their prerogative to recruit and make arrangements with any foreign power for military aid — and they did not know, nor apparently care, how the Pacha recruited his soldiers. Seward reiterated that "compulsory civil or military servitude in this hemisphere" would not be tolerated.[47]

Seward, although he publicly called for neutrality, privately looked the other way as Sheridan, with Grant's unofficial approval, supplied arms and ammunition to Juarez, some of which the French had confiscated or purchased from fleeing Confederates and returned to the U.S. By leaving the arms and ammunition "at convenient places" along the river where it could be easily retrieved, Sheridan helped to revive Juarez's army in northern Mexico. Threats from Sheridan that he would cross the river, and Juarez's resurgent army now under the reliable General Mariano Escobedo, persuaded Marshal Bazaine to begin withdrawing his now beleaguered and overextended French army from the Rio Grande.[48]

Due to Cortina's well-known shifting loyalties, Slack, like prewar Texans, viewed him as a murdering brigand. On the other hand, the more pragmatic Sheridan felt that Cortina had at least "suspended his free-booting for the nonce" and was useful in the fight to drive Maximilian's Imperialists from Mexico. His loyalty and reliability were improved, according to Sheridan, by "coaxing or threats," not only from Sheridan himself but from Juarez's resurgent army under Escobedo, who continued to hold Mejia's Royalists in check in Matamoras, the only town still held by Maximilian on the Rio Grande.[49]

With the French withdrawing from the Rio Grande near the end of July, tranquility reigned at Clarksville. Slack, with Benton's departure, now in command of the 3rd division of the 13th corps, and still trying to get the 47th Indiana transferred to Texas, mentioned to Ann that his friend, Lt. Col. Robert L. Morrison of the 34th Indiana, had been court-martialed and wanted him to serve as his defense counsel at Brownsville. (Based on the rout of a portion of the 34th Indiana at Palmetto Ranch, Texas, in May, Morrison was charged with disobedience of orders, neglect of duty, abandonment of his colors and failure to discipline or properly instruct and drill his men.[50])

Back at Shreveport, James C. Veatch replaced Francis J. Herron in command of the Northern Division of Louisiana, and Elias S. Dennis took command of the Shreveport garrison. Continuing the policy of pacifying the region, the 47th Indiana served the Provost Marshall by going out on "scouts" to serve warrants on recalcitrant ex-Confederates in the area between Shreveport and Mansfield, Louisiana. Corporal John M. Ray of Company C, for example, noted in his diary on 16 July that a detail of twenty men from the 47th Indiana went out on a "skout" to serve warrants. Three days later his company was ordered to prepare thirty days' rations for a longer "skout" toward Mansfield, about thirty-five miles south of Shreveport, led by Capt. Ira A. Blossom.[51]

Ray described the 30-day "skout" briefly in his diary:

> Wednesday 19 [July 1865]
> We got orders in for thirty days rations ready for skout.
> Thursday 20
> We started for Mansfield and after 30 mile march my horse died about three miles before we went into camp.
> Friday, July 21, 1865
> A elegant day and Capt. Ira A. Blossom pressed an old gray mare for me and we marched 25 miles and camped for the night and got one man.
> Saturday 22
> A nice day and a reg't of negroes came in.[52]

On 28 July Cpl. Ray noted the death of Pvt. W.I. Jones at the hospital in Shreveport, without mentioning the cause of death.

Back in Texas, by the first of August the French and Austrian troops were withdrawn from the entire Rio Grande Valley; the Mexican Royalists held only Matamoros and Monterrey, with Juarez's Liberals holding the remainder of the Rio Grande Valley. "Maximilian," according to Sheridan, "holds but little in Mexico, except the towns occupied by Franco-Mexican troops, and in some of these towns only the ground their troops are encamped upon." And Sheridan, who wanted permission to go into Mexico after Shelby and the other ex-Confederates who had allied themselves with Maximilian, or at least to go to Eagle Pass to support Juarez's troops, reported: "I am also happy to state that the rebels who went into Mexico have been defeated in their calculations and have been forced to join the losing side."[53]

About a week later Sheridan noted that Cortina had captured and disarmed some six to seven hundred ex-Confederates under "Judge Terry, of California notoriety," perhaps the last armed band of ex-Confederates to cross into Mexico.[54] Terry and most of the notable ex-Confederates like Smith, Moore, Reynolds, Price and Shelby would return to the United States within a year or two and take the amnesty oath.[55]

Back in Shreveport with the 47th Indiana, on 1 August, Corporal Ray reported another "fine day and the squad came in with one prisoner and went on dress parade." Four days later, however, he noted a little discontent and a small mutiny among the boys of Company C. "A fine day and we were ordered to have Co. Drills, but the boys refused to go out and did not go but went on battalion Drill and Dress parade."[56]

Peace and tranquility appear to have returned to Company C, and the next day (5 August) Ray reported that he went out on another scout to serve warrants on seventeen apparently recalcitrant ex-Confederates.

> Saturday, August 5
> A fine day and I went out on a skout with a warrant for 17 men and notified Angus Nicholson.
> Sunday 6
> A fine day and I read the warrants to R.G. Bonez, Thos. R. Fullilove, D.S. Wells.
> Monday 7
> A fine day and we got back to camp and everything right.

> Tuesday, August 8, 1865
> A fine day and I reported my success to the Provost Marshall.[57]

The remainder of Ray's time seems to have been spent on guard duty at the corral and stables, at the nearby spring, and going on drill, dress parade and inspection. The monotony of camp life was mitigated on 30 August when he reported: "Showery and seven men and I took a hunt." The next day he noted that they came back without mentioning what they brought back: "A wet showery day and we got back from the hunt." Following that came monotonous days of inspection, drill, dress parade, guard duty, and more rain.[58]

Back on the Rio Grande, on 31 July, Slack began moving his troops on a hot and arduous two-day march to Brownsville, although, with Morrison's court-martial already in progress, he was too late to participate in Morrison's defense. Morrison, nevertheless, was soon acquitted on all charges.[59]

At Brownsville on 23 August, Slack mentioned to Ann having received a letter from Shreveport regarding the attitude of Louisianans, especially the girls of the Minden Female College, toward blacks and Yankees:

> Ed [Kessler] went over to Minden to see Dr Bright[60] & family. He admires them very much, but says some of the young lady borders at the school [Minden Female College] insulted them very much by the use of slang expressions, such as "nigger lovers," "Yank," "Abolitionist," &c &c. Minden is garrisoned by Negro troops, which Ed says takes them down terribly.[61]

Back at Shreveport, besides suffering taunts from the young ladies of Minden Female Academy, the soldiers of the 47th endured a wet and monotonous September of guard duty, inspection, drill, and dress parade. On top of that, orders to cut logs for winter quarters made prospects of being home by Christmas look bleak. Good news arrived on Tuesday, 3 October, however, when orders came to report to Baton Rouge to be mustered out. The war was finally over for the boys of the 47th Indiana.

Corporal Ray provided their itinerary home:

> Tuesday, October 3
> A fine day. Orders came for us to report to Baton Rouge to be mustered out.
> Wednesday, October 4, 1865
> Four Cos [companies] packed up.
> Thursday 5
> Co. A went aboard with them that were sick.
> Friday 6
> We went aboard the Jennie Whipple.
> Saturday, October 7, 1865
> We left Shreveport 2 P.M. and moved down the river 45 miles and laid up.
> Sunday 8
> Moved down the river 45 miles [illegible] for the night.
> Monday 9
> Still down the river.
> Tuesday, October 10, 1865
> Down the river.
> Wednesday 11
> We landed it the boat was about to sink.
> Thursday 12
> The boiler burst and put out the fire five miles above Alexandria and we disembarked and marched below town went in camp.

XVI. Shreveport and the Rio Grande (June–November 1865)

> Friday, October 13, 1865
> A wet day and we towed the boat to Alexandria with a ___ and marched below town and went into camp.
> Saturday 14
> Five Cos [companies] left for down river.
> Sunday 15
> Still at Alexandria
> Wednesday 18
> We moved on the Steamer Navigator and started down the river.
> Thursday, October 19, 1865
> Arrived at Baton Rouge and our papers were made out.
> Monday 23
> Was mustered out and in the evening moved everything to the landing.

Continuing his diary, Ray provided an idea of the time it took to travel up the Mississippi River from Baton Rouge to Cairo, Illinois:

> Tuesday 24
> We got aboard the John Kilgore and [remainder of sentence is illegible]
> Wednesday, October 25, 1865
> Passed Vicksburg
> Thursday 26
> Passed the mouth of White River
> Friday 27
> Passed Memphis
> Sunday 29
> We disembarked at Cairo, Ill and got aboard the [railroad?] to Mattoon, Ill.
> Monday 30
> We arrived at Indianapolis and went to the Soldiers Home.
> Tuesday, October 31, 1865
> We turned over our guns.
> Wednesday, November 1
> We had a recetion [reception] dinner and speatch. I & K were paid off and discharged.
> Thursday 2
> We were discharged and started for home.
> Friday, November 3, 1865
> We got home. Enlisted in the U.S. Ser[vice] Oct 8th 1861. Re-enlisted Dec 15th 1863. Discharged Nov 3d 1865. 4 years & 95 days service.

Sent home from Texas at about the same time, Slack was with the 47th Indiana at Indianapolis on 1 November 1865 for their reception dinner, eliciting this comment from the *Indianapolis Daily Gazette*: "The City. We saw the round, rubicund face of General Slack in the street, several times yesterday. He is as handsome as ever."

Describing the reception of the 47th Indiana, the *Indianapolis Daily Evening Gazette* reported:

> Indianapolis, Thursday, November 2, 1865.
> Reception of the 47th Regiment. — The unpleasant weather of yesterday did not prevent the ceremony of receiving this gallant body of men in becoming style. Speeches were made by Governor Morton, General Slack, Colonels Morrison and McLaughlin, and Captain Peyton. The remarks of the Governor were well timed, and delivered in his usual earnest manner. He extended the usual thanks of the State, and complimented the regiment very highly and justly for their services, and the many manifestations of patriotism they had exhibited. He expressed

himself highly gratified in being able to refer to the record of Indiana troops generally and prove to the world, that they were not a whit behind those of any State in the Union. They had done as "well as the best." He paid a high compliment to the officers, asserting that no disaster had befallen us through their imbecility or inefficiency.

General Slack followed in a witty and humorous speech. He was received with great enthusiasm by his old command. Our paper was issued too early yesterday for any extended report, and as those in the morning papers are quite full it is not necessary for us to give much space to this reception. The exercise wound up by three cheers for the Union, three for Gen. Slack, three for the officers and men of the 47th, and three time three for Governor Oliver P. Morton. At the close of the exercises, the Governor announced that by the request of the regiment the sum of $1,169, contributed by the regiment for the erection of a monument to the memory of President Lincoln, had been transferred to the board of Control of the "Indiana Soldier's and Seamen's Home." This is a most princely donation, and should serve to shame or incite the people of Indiana, to contribute to this noble institution, certainly as generously as those who have braved all the storms, and borne the burnt of the great battles of the war.

The next day, the *Daily Gazette* reported: "Very few of the 47th Regiment remain in town. After receiving their pay we presume the boys were anxious for the comforts and delights of 'home, sweet home.' The boys are right."[62]

Epilogue

For six days in March 1866 the Supreme Court heard the arguments in *Ex parte Milligan*. Attorney General James Speed, Henry Stanbery (a prominent Republican attorney and successor to Speed as Attorney General), and General Benjamin ("the Beast") Butler, argued the government's case, which was essentially that the president, due to the necessity of wartime, had the right to suspend the Bill of Rights. The Constitution, they argued, authorized the president in wartime or other emergency to suspend habeas corpus and to organize military commissions to try civilians even where the civil courts were open and functioning.[1]

Milligan's defense team included James A. Garfield, former Civil War general, Republican congressman, and future president; David Dudley Field, noted New York attorney and brother of Supreme Court Justice Stephen J. Field; Joseph E. McDonald, former attorney general of Indiana and unsuccessful gubernatorial candidate; Addison L. Roache, McDonald's law partner; Jeremiah S. Black, former justice of the Pennsylvania Supreme Court; and John R. Coffroth, Milligan's friend and original counsel.[2] They held essentially that under the Habeas Corpus Act of 1863 the military had no jurisdiction to arrest and try civilians not connected in any way to the military service of the United States who resided in states where the civil courts were open and functioning.[3]

On 3 April 1866, the Court, agreeing unanimously with Milligan, ordered that his petition be granted and that he be released from custody as required by the Habeas Corpus Act of 1863. The Court then entered a like order for William Bowles and Stephen Horsey.[4]

The Court split five to four,[5] however, in its ruling that Congress itself did not have power to authorize the trial of civilians by military commission. The dissenters worried that without such power Congress would not be able "to indemnify the officers who composed the commission against liability in civil courts for acting as members of it." Without comment, Chief Justice Salmon P. Chase announced that majority and minority opinions would be read at the beginning of the next term in December.[6]

Six days later (Monday, 9 April 1866), John R. Coffroth came to Columbus, Ohio, with a writ of habeas corpus for Milligan and another for Bowles and Horsey. Milligan's writ was issued and served the next day — the same day President Johnson, under pressure from the Court's decision, independently issued an order to the warden of the Ohio Penitentiary for the release of all three prisoners. Milligan was released from prison at 3:00 P.M., Bowles and Horsey two hours later, followed by a reception at the Neil House Hotel in

Columbus. Milligan, accompanied by Coffroth and George R. Curlew, who had originally been asked to bring Milligan's remains back to Huntington, boarded the train in Columbus at noon on 12 April for the trip back home. Arriving at Peru, Indiana, Wednesday evening (18 April) they were met and accompanied to Huntington by friends Charles H. Lewis, John Roche, Samuel F. Day, John Ziegler, and the Reverend R.A. Curran. On arrival at the Huntington Depot early Thursday morning, Milligan, viewed as a hero, was met by Mayor William C. Kocher and the town Common Council, a brass band, a crowd waving their handkerchiefs, and a cannon fire salute, reportedly "one of the greatest ovations ever given to any man in the State."[7] Although arrested later, Milligan was released under Coffroth's guarantee and the indictment against him was dropped, as were the indictments against Bowles, Horsey, and those still pending against H.H. Dodd and other leaders of the Sons of Liberty.[8]

In December, Judge David Davis, writing the majority opinion, concurred with Milligan's assertion that his arrest, incarceration, trial and conviction by a military commission were all illegal acts in and of themselves. Military law, Davis asserted, "can never be applied to citizens in states which have upheld the authority of the government, and where the courts are open and their process unobstructed," as was the case in Indiana. "No usage of war," Davis continued, "could sanction a military trial there for any offence whatever of a citizen in civil life, in no wise connected with the military." Triggering the dissent, Davis added, "Congress could grant no such power."[9]

Writing the dissent, Chief Justice Salmon P. Chase argued essentially that Congress did indeed have the power, although not exercised in the Milligan case, to authorize military commissions for the trial of civilians. Chase based the minority opinion primarily on the Fifth Amendment: "No person shall be held to answer for a capital, or otherwise infamous crime, unless on presentment or indictment by a grand jury, except in cases arising in the land and naval forces, or in the militia, when in actual service, in time of war or public danger." Chase argued that this exception authorized the president in time of war or public danger to suspend the writ of habeas corpus and to arrest and detain citizens deemed to pose a danger. Indiana, he noted, had been both invaded and made into a military district by the time Milligan was arrested, and therefore the president, facing "a controlling necessity," was authorized to suspend the writ of habeas corpus and order the arrest and detention of soldiers or civilians. Congress, he asserted, was authorized to sanction the organization of military commissions for the trial of these soldiers or civilians, even where the civil courts were open and functioning because those courts "might be open and undisturbed in the execution of their functions and yet wholly incompetent to avert threatened danger, or to punish with adequate promptitude and certainty, the guilty conspirators." The president and Congress, according to Chase, had the authority to declare martial law in time of war or public danger and temporarily abrogate the Bill of Rights by replacing due process in civil courts with military trials for both civilians and soldiers alike.[10]

"The government," Davis countered, "had no right to conclude that Milligan, if guilty, would not receive in [civil] court merited punishment; for [the Indiana civil court] records disclose that it was constantly engaged in the trials of similar offences, and was never interrupted in its administration of criminal justice." There was "no unwritten criminal code," Davis added, that could be used as a source of jurisdiction for the military. If the minority's opinion on the scope of martial law were sound, he continued, "and the country subdivided into military departments for mere convenience," as was done in the North during the Civil War, then the commander of one of them could, if he so chose, "on the plea of necessity, with the approval of the Executive, substitute military force for and to the exclusion of the laws, and punish all persons, as he thinks right and proper, without fixed or certain rules."[11]

Summarizing the majority opinion's doctrine of "one law in war and peace," Davis wrote:

> The Constitution of the United States is a law for rulers and people, equally in war and in peace, and covers with the shield of its protection all classes of men, at all times, and under all circumstances. No doctrine, involving more pernicious consequences, was ever invented by the wit of man than that any of its provisions can be suspended during any of the great exigencies of government. Such a doctrine leads directly to anarchy or despotism, but the theory of necessity on which it is based is false; for the government, within the Constitution, has all the powers granted to it, which are necessary to preserve its existence; as has been happily proved by the result of the great effort to throw off its just authority.[12]

The Supreme Court ruling in April 1866 had caused some consternation in Republican circles, but it was not until the majority opinion and minority dissent were read in December, accompanied by President Johnson's lenient policy toward ex-Confederates, that feelings became highly agitated. The Democratic press, of course, applauded the Court's ruling as vindication of their right to dissent during the war. On the other hand, the more radical Republican newspapers[13] feared that the *Milligan* decision would derail their plans for military rule in the South.[14]

What the Milligan ruling did establish, at least outside the unreconstructed South, was that the government could not use a plea of necessity ("the tyrant's plea") to arbitrarily suspend the Bill of Rights or due process of law. They remained in effect for civilians, even in time of public danger, where the courts remained open and functioning. Adherence to the "one law in war and peace" doctrine would nevertheless prove to be fleeting.[15]

Feeling vindicated, Humphreys, his travel restrictions lifted following the release of Milligan, Bowles, and Horsey, was the first to turn to the civil courts for revenge against those who had arrested him. On 1 February 1866, he filed a complaint in heavily Democratic Sullivan County, Indiana, against Captain Samuel McCormick of the U.S. Army, who had arrested him, and ten others accusing them of "assault and battery and false imprisonment." A favorable venue for Humphreys, Sullivan County remained heavily Democratic and the circuit court was presided over by wartime Copperhead Judge Delana R. Eckles. The jury found McCormick and the others guilty and awarded Humphreys the tidy sum of $25,000 in damages. The defendants, of course, appealed, and the case bogged down in the courts. In the end, Humphreys never collected the money he had been awarded, although he retained a good measure of respectability and stature in southern Indiana.[16]

In March 1867, however, the heavily Republican Indiana state legislature quickly closed the door that Humphreys had opened by passing tort reform legislation to protect state and federal officials from such lawsuits and to provide those officials free legal representation. The act also limited the damage awards, excluding court costs, to five dollars, especially, as Klement notes, "if the plaintiff were associated with 'any society or organization ... in sympathy with the rebellion.'"[17]

On 13 March 1868, Milligan filed a complaint in the Huntington County Common

Pleas Court against Slack, Henry Zumro, and twenty-two others, including Governor Oliver P. Morton, General Alvin P. Hovey, Benn Pitman, and James M. Bratton, who, in 1864, was the Huntington County Sheriff and marshal of the draft board who had arrested him. Milligan charged all the defendants essentially with false imprisonment, but added that they had "purposely and maliciously [intended] to murder and destroy" him, and that Benn Pitman, who had acted both as court reporter and government witness during the trial, had libeled him in a rather biased book he had edited on the trial, which was published in 1865. Milligan complained that Pitman's book had reappeared in Huntington in 1867 in two versions (the original Milligan referred to as *Indiana Treason Trials*; the other he referred to as a "similitude" or copy titled *Trial for Treason at Indianapolis*), and in so doing the defendants had once again libeled and slandered his otherwise good name with the intent to ruin him. For the various instances of false imprisonment, brutal treatment, libel and slander, Milligan asked for cumulative damages of $850,000.[18]

Presented at the May 1868 term of the Huntington County Court of Common Pleas, *Milligan v. Slack, et al.*, wound its way through the court system and finally went before a jury in the federal circuit court at Huntington in 1871, Judge Thomas H. Drummond presiding. The court dismissed the charges against Slack and all the other defendants[19] except General Hovey, the members of the military commission (Charles D. Murray, Benjamin Spooner, Richard P. De Hart, Thomas W. Bennett, and Ruben Williams), Henry Zumro, and James M. Bratton.[20]

With charges against Slack dropped, the case became *Milligan v. Hovey, et al.* Judge Drummond ruled, however, that by waiting to file, Milligan had missed the two-year statute of limitations and that the law did not recognize imprisonment or any other cause as an impediment to filing suit. Drummond's ruling meant that the defendants would only be liable for any acts done after 13 March 1868.[21]

Although the jury ruled for Milligan against all the defendants, due to the hastily passed March 1867 Indiana tort reform, they were only able to award him five dollars for damages and about one thousand dollars in court costs. Following his victory in court, Milligan continued his legal career in Huntington and went on to regain some of his lost fortune. Perhaps not surprisingly, he supported his former defender, Republican James A. Garfield, for president in 1880, but astonished many when he switched to the Republican Party and became, according to his friend and Democratic politician Thomas R. Marshall, "the most virulent, vindictive and caustic of the critics of the Democratic party that we had in Northern Indiana." Following his death on 21 December 1899, no less than the *Huntington Herald* lauded his latter-day Republican epiphany, calling him "a good citizen ... an honorable and upright businessman" and "a credit" to the Huntington bar.[22]

As for some of the earlier major players, George W.L. Bickley, originator of the Knights of the Golden Circle, received a conditional release from Fort Warren on 14 October 1865. His practice of eclectic medicine now a distant memory, Bickley left for England to try to profit from his notoriety by going on a lecture tour. His notoriety, alas, had faded to obscurity; and, not unlike his attempts to raise money in New York City before the war, he found that people willing to pay to hear him speak were scarce at best. His tour a failure, his health failed and he returned to the United States. He died in Baltimore on 10 August 1867.[23]

Phineas C. Wright, founder of the Order of American Knights, attorney, failed filibuster, and briefly, before his arrest in Detroit in April 1864, editor of the *New York Daily*

News, was released from Fort Warren in August 1865. He returned to St. Louis and reportedly headed for exile and obscurity in Central America.[24]

H.H. Dodd, one of the actual accomplices in the Chicago or Camp Douglas conspiracy, at least on the Confederate side, left exile in England for Windsor, Ontario. In 1869, he moved to Fond du Lac, Wisconsin, to work for his two brothers-in-law at their Fond du Lac office of the American Express Company. Joined there by his wife and children, Dodd reentered Democratic politics, eventually served two terms as mayor of Fond du Lac, and supported Democrat Samuel J. Tilden for president in 1876. The year after Tilden lost to Republican Rutherford B. Hayes in the controversial 1876 election, he, like Milligan, with Hayes officially ending Reconstruction and the "Black Republicans" by then virtually extinct, switched to the Republican Party.[25]

One of the actual masterminds, Confederate spymaster Jake Thompson traveled through Europe in 1866 and 1867 before returning to Memphis, Tennessee, in 1868, to manage his extensive holdings. He died a wealthy man in Memphis on 24 March 1885.[26]

Confederate spy Thomas H. Hines, who was never captured, returned north undetected and escaped to Canada at the end of the war. Although mentioned in the Cincinnati Treason Trial as a conspirator and essentially found guilty in absentia, he was never sentenced. He studied law in Toronto under the exiled John C. Breckenridge and returned to Kentucky in May 1866, about one year after President Johnson's first proclamation of amnesty and pardon, which, although it excluded those who had acted as foreign agents, was becoming increasingly liberal. He passed the bar exam in Memphis in June 1866 and went on to have a distinguished legal career. Elected to the Kentucky Court of Appeals in 1878, he served for eight years, the last two as chief justice, after which he resumed his law practice in Bowling Green. He died at Frankfort in 1898.[27]

Hines's partner, John B. Castleman, avoided execution when President Lincoln, as a personal favor to Judge Samuel W. Breckenridge of St. Louis, reprieved his death sentence. (Judge Breckenridge was also the husband of Castleman's sister, Virginia, who had asked him to contact the president on her brother's behalf.) Released and banished from the United States following Lincoln's assassination, Castleman also went to Canada. Since President Johnson's first amnesty proclamation clearly excluded him, he traveled with Jake Thompson to Europe, where he remained until receiving a presidential pardon in 1866. He returned to Kentucky, graduated from the University of Louisville School of Law in 1868, founded the insurance company Barbee and Castleman, was a founder and first president of the American Saddlebred Horse Association, and served as a volunteer colonel in the U.S. Army during the Spanish-American war. Promoted to brigadier general, he served for a time as the military governor of Puerto Rico. He died in Louisville in May 1918.[28]

After their return from exile, Hines and Castleman collaborated on a greatly exaggerated and fictionalized version of their lives as Confederate spies, which they offered up as a nonfiction account of their adventures. Their fictionalized version, titled "The Northwestern Conspiracy," was written at the request of former Confederate General Basil Duke, who had recently revived the magazine *Southern Bivouac* and wanted to publish an account of their exploits. The story first appeared in June 1886 under Hines's name, although Castleman and W.W. Cleary reportedly wrote it by relying heavily on a greatly exaggerated version titled "The Chicago Conspiracy" that appeared anonymously (reportedly written by James R. Gilmore) in the July 1865 edition of the *Atlantic Monthly*. Hines and Castleman also relied on official federal reports, full of misinformation and outright falsehoods, to embellish their exploits, which, although daring, had largely ended in failure. In 1917, Castleman published an exaggerated account of his own in a book titled *Active Service*. As Klement pointed out, some historians have accepted the Hines-Castleman version as true and correct, and their writings continue to be a source of controversy about what actually happened in Chicago in the last half of 1864.[29]

Of the three actually convicted and sentenced at Cincinnati, only wealthy and connected Englishman George St. Leger Grenfell, a self-styled soldier of fortune and general gadfly, remained in custody.[30] On the night of 6 March 1868, however, following eighteen months of appeals on his behalf by influential friends and the denial of a final jurisdictional appeal based on the *Milligan* decision, the colorful but hapless Grenfell, now about sixty years old but perhaps at his swashbuckling best, made a daring escape from Fort Jefferson with three other prisoners and one apparently very disgruntled sentry guard. With one of the prisoners still carrying his ball and chain, they piled into a small, open sailboat that the sentry had stashed away and rowed out into the pouring rain and pitch-black darkness of Garden Key Harbor. Catching a northerly wind and apparently hoping to reach Cuba, they sailed out into the Straits of Florida never to be seen again, all five presumed drowned when their boat was swamped in the high seas.[31]

As for James R. Slack, his subdued (compared to Milligan's) but heartfelt welcome home with the 47th Indiana was tempered somewhat by Milligan's May 1868 complaint naming him as the principal in his lawsuit for wrongful arrest and imprisonment. That same month, however, Slack, who unlike Milligan remained a Democrat, was appointed circuit court judge in the newly created Twenty-eighth Judicial Circuit. He subsequently won reelection in 1872 and 1878, but was defeated in 1880 by Republican George W. Steele in the race for a congressional seat. He died in Chicago on the "28th day of July, 1881, when while waiting for a street car on the corner of Fifth Avenue and Madison Street ... he was seized with a stroke of paralysis and died within an hour." Survived by his wife Ann and their three living children, he was buried in Huntington.[32]

In March 1868, John A. McLaughlin moved to Topeka, Kansas, with his wife, Louisa (Morehouse) McLaughlin of Huntington, and five children: Mary, twins Ida and Emma, James, and John G. Reestablishing his prewar gunsmith trade, he owned and operated a sporting goods store in Topeka, where their sixth child, Lulu, was born. He died circa 1888.[33]

An ad appearing in the 18 June 1868 *Topeka Weekly Leader* read:

> J.A. McLaughlin,
> Manufacturer of and Dealer in
> Guns, Pistols, Ammunition,
> Fishing Tackle & Sporting Apparatus
> No. 231 Kansas Avenue
> Topeka, Kansas[34]

Little is known of John's brother Harry, a 2nd Lieutenant in the 35th Alabama Infantry when captured at Champion Hill, Mississippi, but he appears to have returned to his farm and family at Florence, Alabama.

Milton Stapp Robinson (1832–1892) enlisted as a lieutenant colonel and served with the 47th Indiana for about one year before being promoted to colonel of the 75th Indiana

Volunteer Infantry on 29 October 1862. After the war, he served in the Indiana State Senate from 1866 to 1870 and was elected as a Republican to the Forty-forth and Forty-fifth Congresses (4 March 1875–3 March 1879). Not a candidate in 1878, he resumed his law practice and was appointed associate justice of the Indiana appellate court in March 1891, and subsequently as chief justice, serving until his death in 1892.[35]

For enlisted men, the transition was not always that easy. "Roving Bill" Aspinwall, like many other returning soldiers physically and mentally stressed by their war experiences, adapted to postwar civilian life on the margins of society. Unlike some who became vagrants and petty criminals, however, Roving Bill relied on survival skills learned in the army, going "on a tramp" that lasted the next forty years or more. Born in Ohio in 1845, reasonably well-educated and literate, Roving Bill became part of the large homeless population of former soldiers that emerged after the war. He lived on the road as an itinerant tinker and mechanic, repairing umbrellas, clocks, and sewing machines, even leaving the road for a time to work as a woolen mill machine operator and mechanic, and later lived off his small military pension, reportedly six dollars a month.[36]

In the meantime, Connecticut social reformer and college professor, the Rev. John James McCook, concerned about the plight, and reform, of the many homeless vagabonds he encountered, began an early sociological study of tramp life. In 1893, as part of this study, McCook asked a tramp called Connecticut Fatty to return postage-paid postcards with stories about his life on the road. Connecticut Fatty, a reluctant correspondent, in turn handed the postcards over to Roving Bill.[37]

Perhaps really a Bohemian at heart, after nearly thirty years on the road, Roving Bill gladly accepted the offer. Describing himself as a nomad and gentleman of the road, over the next twenty-four years (18 May 1893 until 1917) he not only gave interviews about his life during the war, as in his story about the Battle of Champion Hill, but also wrote several hundred pages of stories for McCook about his life on the road, including some scathing social commentaries. McCook edited Roving Bill's writings, took them on the lecture circuit, and published a nine-part series in 1901 and 1902 in *The Independent* called "Leaves from the Diary of a Tramp." The old Bohemian died in a war veterans' home circa 1917.[38]

Other soldiers, who were also undoubtedly stressed by their experiences, but had better circumstances, avoided life on the margins. Some adapted to civilian life by resuming their prewar occupations, those with the background and wherewithal began new ones, some returned to their families, and some started families of their own.

William Ralph Myers enlisted as a private in Company G and was promoted through the ranks to captain. After the war he taught school and, in 1869 and 1870, served as superintendent of public schools of Anderson, Indiana, before being admitted to the bar in 1871 and establishing his practice in Anderson. Elected as a Democrat to the Forty-sixth Congress (4 March 1879–3 March 1881), he was unsuccessful in his bid for reelection in 1880, but served as Secretary of State of Indiana from 1882 to 1886. He purchased the *Anderson Democrat* in 1886 and was its editor. An unsuccessful Democratic candidate for governor, he again served as secretary of state from 1892 to 1894 and then resumed his law practice. He died in Anderson in 1907.[39]

The 47th Indiana had three known sets of father/son recruits. Thomas Paul, of Co. K, enlisted in 1861 as a 1st sergeant, rose through the ranks, and mustered out as a 1st lieutenant in 1865. His son Charles enlisted in 1861 and mustered out in 1865 as the company's

Eli E. Rose and Mary Keagy Rose, from their Marriage Certificate, 18 November 1868 at the Franklin Hotel, Newry, Blair County, Pennsylvania (photographed by Brenda Perrott Williamson).

principal musician. Athaniel Reed Sr. and Athaniel Reed Jr., of Co. G, both enlisted in 1861. Athaniel Sr. was discharged on 23 February 1863, and Athaniel Jr. mustered out with the regiment in 1865.[40] Private Abraham Cooper of Company B enlisted in 1861 and mustered out with the regiment in October 1865. His father, Pvt. John H. Cooper, joined in 1862 and mustered out in July 1865.[41]

Sergeant Docter B. Davis of Company G married Matilda E. Eads on 6 October 1867 in Madison County, Indiana, and farmed and manufactured tile in Stoney Creek Township. Private William Carmany, apparently listed erroneously as having died in New Orleans in June 1864, married Ida M. Reynolds on 17 June 1869 and became assessor of Adams Township.[42]

After the war, Private Albert Augustus Manning of Company H moved back to Indiana and taught school before moving to Iowa and, later, South Dakota, to take up farming. He died in Miller, South Dakota, on 16 November 1913 and is buried in the G.A.R. cemetery there. His brother, William Ziba Manning, farmed in Reno and Kingman Counties, Kansas, after his service in the war. He died 22 July 1864 at Murdock, Kansas.[43]

Eli E. Rose (b. 15 July 1841, Columbiana, Ohio), son of Eli and Hannah Jenkins Rose (the daughter of Zacharia and Rhoda Penn Jenkins, Burlington County, New Jersey), worked as a farm laborer for Elihu Griswold in Northfield Twp., Summit County, Ohio, before moving at age nineteen to Clear Creek Township, Huntington County, Indiana, where, on 3 December 1861, he enlisted as a private in Company F of the 47th Indiana Infantry. After he was wounded by a musket ball to his left knee on 27 March 1865 at Spanish Fort, Ala-

bama, his left leg was amputated just above the knee about two hours later at the 1st division, 13th corps field hospital. He was transferred on 1 April 1865 to Sedgewick U.S.A. General Hospital, Greenville (New Orleans), Louisiana, to recuperate.

Honorably discharged from Sedgewick Hospital on 26 July 1865 with a Surgeon's Certificate of Disability, Eli moved to Limaville, Stark County, Ohio, with a disability pension of $8.00 a month. In March 1867, he moved to Bedford County, Pennsylvania, where he taught school and, on 18 November 1868, married Mary Keagy, daughter of John B. and Anna Maria Keagy, owners of the Keagy Woolen Mill at Potter's Creek, near Woodbury, Pennsylvania.

In spite of being hobbled by his wooden leg, Eli worked for seven years at the Keagy Mill, including three on the road as a driver for the woolen mill. Their five children were all born in Woodbury. The first, Rozella Maria, was born 6 November 1870 and died at age two. Charles Warren was born 20 July 1873, Eliza Edna on 17 November 1876, Harvey Keagy on 8 July 1878, and James William on 18 October 1879. In 1880 the family lived in Woodbury while Eli learned tailoring and barbering. In 1892 they moved to Portage County, Ohio, then, in 1898, to Newton Falls, Trumbull County, Ohio,

Top: The Eli E. and Mary Keagy Rose Family, taken at the Beard Gallery, Newton Falls, Ohio, circa 1895. Front row, left to right: Charles Warren Rose, b. 20 July 1873, d. 30 December 1959; Mary Keagy Rose, b. 22 Aug 1843, d. 1 May 1927; and Harvey Keagy Rose, b. 8 June 1878, d. 7 March 1964. Back row, left to right: James William Rose, b. 18 Oct 1879; Eli E. Rose, b. 15 July 1841, d. 9 June 1915; Henry Sutcliffe, b. 1874; and Eliza Edna Rose Sutcliffe, b. 17 Nov 1876 (courtesy of Thomas R. and Charlotte Rose Frietag). Bottom: Private William Lindsey, Co. H, taken by S. Anderson, Photographer, No. 61 Camp Street, New Orleans, Louisiana, ca. March 1864 (courtesy of Kevin Lindsey).

Left: Sergeant Benjamin Jones, Co. A (courtesy of Dewey Jones). *Right:* Private Daniel Hilton, Co. A (courtesy of Commander Roger L. Johnson, U.S. Navy, retired).

where Eli worked as a barber, mechanic, and tailor. Eli died on 9 June 1915 at Youngstown, Ohio, at age seventy-three; Mary died at Youngtown on 1 May 1927 at age eighty-three.[44]

Mustering in as a private in Company A on 25 September 1861, Eli Arnold was promoted to corporal on 12 April 1862, to 1st lieutenant on 19 October 1862, and was discharged on 30 December 1864 due to illness. Eli and Hannah Nixon Arnold had five small children when Eli enlisted, the oldest seven years old. They would have nine children in all, five surviving to adulthood. His three brothers, Samuel, Thomas, and Daniel, and his three brothers-in-law, including John Custard of Company A, all served with Indiana regiments. After Hannah's death in 1874, Eli married Lurinda Hart. They had four children, three surviving to adulthood. A farmer both before and after the war, he also ran a mercantile business in Montpelier, Roll, and Mt. Zion, Indiana, was a notary public and an enumerator for the 1880 census. Eli died in 1927 at the age of ninety-eight.[45]

Born in Ohio in 1839, William Lindsey enlisted in Company H in March 1864 and mustered out with the regiment on 23 October 1865. Moving west after the war, he traveled from Texas to Washington and worked as an Indian Agent, a cowboy, and a pioneer. He finally settled in Medicine Lodge, Kansas, and in 1879 married Sarah Swank. They had three children: Rhoda, Sybil, and William E. Sarah died in 1891 and William, a member of the Grand Army of the Republic, returned to Indiana in the 1890s. He died at the Soldiers Home at Marion, Indiana, in October 1899 and is buried there.[46]

Enlisting as a corporal in Company A on 2 November 1861, Benjamin Jones survived a skull fracture from a spent shell at Vicksburg and an injury to his leg in a barge accident at New Orleans before mustering out with the regiment as a sergeant on 1 November 1865.

He moved to Van Wert, Ohio, after the war and on 24 December 1865 married Mary Dailey. They had thirteen children: Emma, Eva, Dailey, Esaias, Oscar, James (died in infancy), Charles, Harry, Anna, Harlen, Clyde, Fred, and Clara. Benjamin worked as a progressive farmer in Willshire Township, Van Wert County, Ohio, and eventually purchased land in North Carolina, Alabama, and Iowa that was farmed by his sons. He died on 27 January 1903 at the age of sixty-six. (Captain Esaias Dailey of Company C was Mary's uncle; 2nd Lieutenant William Dailey of Company C was Esaias's nephew and Mary's cousin.[47])

On 3 May 1859, Daniel Hilton married Jane Clendenen in Adams County, Indiana. One year later, Daniel leased twenty-five acres of land, built a small cabin, and cleared five acres for livestock. Their first child, Lydia Ann, was born on 13 March 1860, and twins,

Top: Corporal Henry S. Adams, Co. E (courtesy of Dan Nelson). *Bottom:* Henry S. Adams's cannon, unknown type; appears to be Mexican War vintage.

who died in infancy, were born on 4 August 1861. Persuaded by his father-in-law to volunteer for the army, he sold his lease, left his wife and child with his father-in-law and enlisted as a private in Company A on 25 November 1861 at Indianapolis. After the war, Daniel reunited with Mary, built a new house in the spring of 1866, and resumed farming until buying property and moving to Pennville in November 1890. Mary, who had become invalid thirty years prior, died on 18 June 1909; Daniel died at Geneva, Indiana, 13 July 1914 at the age of seventy-eight.[48]

Born into a farming family on 2 May 1836 in Parke County, Indiana, Henry S. Adams, as a young man of seventeen, moved to Iowa and two years later to Leavenworth, Kansas, where he, as a government employee, drove a U.S. Army supply wagon across the plains to Salt Lake, Utah, for General Albert Sidney Johnston and then Colonel E.R.S. Canby. After leaving government employment in 1858, he returned to Indiana and married Mary L. Small on 11 March 1860.

Enlisting as a private in Company E on 24 October 1861, he lost his right eye to a Minie ball at the Battle of Champion Hill, was taken prisoner, paroled, and sent from the hospital in St. Louis to parole camp at Indianapolis. Assigned to the 91st, 2nd Battalion, Veteran Reserve Corp at Camp Morton, he was honorably discharged as a corporal in 1864.

In 1865, he and Mary moved with their two children, Martin Luther (b. 2 June 1861) and Olive May (b. 17 May 1865) in a covered wagon from Farmington, Indiana, to Dallas, Iowa. Daughter Mary Matilda was born there on 3 November 1867, and two years later they moved to Donaphan County, Kansas. In 1868 they traveled in a prairie schooner with their three young children to Johnson County, Texas, and later into Indian Territory, pulling a pre–Civil War era cannon behind them. Their fourth child, Daniel Livingston, was born in Texas on 15 September 1879. Having secured land under the Tree Homestead Act, they moved back to Kansas and built a two-room sod house in which their twins, Anna Florence and Alvin Lawrence were born on 23 February 1876. Two years later Henry bought a 168-acre farm near Powhattan, which became the family home where their seventh child, James Harvey, was born on 27 January 1878. On 27 December 1917, Mary died at their farm at age seventy-five; shortly thereafter, Henry moved to the Kansas home of his daughter, Annie Walters, where he died on 3 March 1926 at age eighty-nine.[49]

Appendix A

The McLaughlin Story

On 16 May 1863, Federal forces at the Battle of Champion Hill captured 2nd Lieutenant Henry B. "Harry" McLaughlin of the 35th Alabama Infantry. Sent to the officer's prison at Johnson's Island, Ohio, Harry, the brother of Lt. Col. John A. McLaughlin of the 47th Indiana, and the other prisoners of war were held over at Indianapolis, Harry's hometown. Getting wind of the story, the *Daily Journal* wrote excitedly, if somewhat exaggeratedly, of their "almost face to face" combat. Without elaboration (he probably encountered him after the battle among the captured or surrendered Confederates), John McLaughlin only mentioned their "singular meating" [sic] on the battlefield. Upon learning of Harry's plight, both of their sisters Eliza and Susan went to work immediately to secure his release. The following letters trace their efforts.

On 3 June 1863, the *Indianapolis Daily Journal* announced the arrival of Confederate prisoners of war in the city:

> ARRIVAL of Prisoners — The trains of Rebel prisoners arrived here yesterday afternoon and evening. The first train reached Terre Haute Depot a little after two o'clock, and had on board about 900 men, mostly Missourians, of Price's army. The guard in charge were portions of four companies of the 39th Ohio, and the officer commanding the escort was Col. Spaulding of an Ohio regiment. The second train arrived about 7 o'clock and brought some 1100 prisoners. The third train came in between 9 and 10 o'clock, and had at least 900 more on board. The prisoners resembled the Fort Donelson prisoners in dress and general appearance, except that they are more healthy and hardy. This is probably owing to the season of the year. Nearly all were captured at the battle of Big Black River. They were marched to Camp Morton well guarded by details of Companies from the 71st Regiment. Our streets were crowded in the afternoon with people to witness the somewhat novel procession.

The next day the *Daily Journal* reported:

> Ed. The balance of 4,400 rebel prisoners arrived here about 2 o'clock yesterday after noon and were marched to Camp Morton. About 3 o'clock a train of three passenger cars arrived from Cairo with 165 rebel officers on board. They were all taken out and placed in the Soldier's Home for safe keeping. They will be sent to Johnson's Island near Sandusky City, Ohio, this morning. These officers are composed of all grades, from Colonel down to 3rd Lieutenant. There are three Colonels and a few other field officers.
>
> We learn form one of the guards that as the train was running along at its usual speed in some part of Illinois, during Tuesday night, one of the officers of high rank jumped out of an open window and secured to light safely upon the ground and was seen to take to the woods in double-quick time. He is said to have formerly resided in Illinois where he still has a family whom it is supposed he has gone to visit.

Among the rebel prisoners that arrived here yesterday was Lieut. Henry McLaughlin of an Alabama regiment, formerly of this city. He is a brother of Lieut. Col. John A. McLaughlin, of the 47th Indiana. Both brothers fought almost face to face in one of the fiercest battles near Vicksburg, one in command of a regiment and the other in command of a company. Lieut. McLaughlin removed from here some years ago, and married at Florence, Ala., where he has a wife and child. He was visited at the Soldiers Home last evening by his relatives here, who conversed with him freely for some time.[1]

On 15 June 1863, Lt. Col. John A. McLaughlin of the 47th Indiana, referring to the 4 June 1863 article in the *Daily Journal*, wrote to one of his sisters (unnamed) confirming his "singular meating" with their brother Henry on the battlefield:

HEAD-QUARTERS 47TH IND INFTY
REAR OF VICKSBURG JUNE 15TH 1863

Dear Sister I received yours of the 3rd Inst and take this opportunity to answer. I was glad to get a letter from you once more. it has seamed to me that all my sisters might write oftener than they do, but if they think not, then I canot complain, *or wont*.

I have letters from Lou as late as the third of this Month they wer all well then. I have bin fortuneate in getting letters of late date from them of late through private sources and otherwise. Last evening I got a letter from Cousin John B. McLaughlin written at Murfreesboro Tenn. he tells me that his brother James is with him in the same Co which is Co. G, 89th Ill. Infty in Gen Willich's Brigade which is the 1st Brigade, 2nd Division Army of the Cumberland, they have bin in several hard battles but came through all right so far. he tells me that cousin Amanda died in Sept 1862, that all the family is well that he had a letter only a few days before from his sister Hannah. I answered it at considerable length immediately, for it had bin a long time since I had heard from aney of them.

he made inquiry if I new aneything of Henry. I told him of our singular meating on the battle field and that the last I heard from him was from the Indps Journal of the 4th when he was receiving visits from his friends and relatives at his *old home Indianapolis*. I fancy this will be rather startling news to the boys. Dock Mitchell [Dr. T.G. Mitchell, husband of Eliza Kimberly McLaughlin] has bin down here as you sayd but I did not get to see him. I saw Dr. Bullard while he was here, but I could not get away to go to see Tom G [?] for I am the only Field officer with the Regt and have bin for a long time and the consequence is I am tied down here with the Regiment all the time and Gen Grant's lines are closed to citizens and have bin ever since we invested this place and it is proper that it should be so, or there would be more of them than there is soldiers, and in various ways impede the armeys operations. this is the 26th day of the Siege and how much longer it is going to last you know as much as I do. the impression is that the end is not maney days off, but what to base an opinion of this kind on I cannot see. Of cource it is 26 days nearer a close than when it comenced, and there supplies must nesisarily be getting short. But there may be hard fighting before the close. there certainly will be if Johnson attempts to attack our rear, but in no event do we expect defeat, or the loss of Vicksburg. This army don't know what defeat means. they have yet to learn the application of that term. we feel confident that we could hold this garrison in its work and send out enough to whip Johnson with fifty thousand of his best troops before they get in hearing of this place. you may think that we feel too invincible. I tell you that invincible feeling is what makes an invincible army. you once get an army impressed with the belief *fully* that they can whip the enemy and they will do it shure. and then let them whip them five or six times in succession and they think of nothing els than being able to repeat it. the career of Gen Grant's army since the 28th of April has bin one of the longest and most brilient in the history of the war *by far*, and we intend to ad one more, and the crowning star to the already long list of victoreys. Vicksburg yes it must and shall be ours. This is not only my feelings but the determined feelings of this vast army surrounding us with a thribble line of bayonets the entire rear of the besieged place.

let god and justice be our motto and right will be on our side, and victory perch upon our banners. *Union and liberty now and forever our reward.* write soon and often dear sister and be assured that your letters will ever be most thankfully received.

I remain *as ever*, your affectionate brother
Jno. A. McLaughlin
Lt. Col. 47th Ind Vols[2]

On 24 June 1863, Lieutenant Henry (Harry) B. McLaughlin of the 35th Alabama Volunteer Infantry wrote one of his sisters, Eliza Kimberly McLaughlin Mitchell [wife of Dr. T.G. Mitchell] to ask her help in getting him released from prison.

Prison Johnsons Island Ohio June 24th 63
Dearest of sisters, donot think for a moment that I have forgotten you although political convultions and contending armies have even prevented correspondence but now that I am situated so that I can write short letters I imbrace with pleasure the opportunity although it is from a prison cell. the ties of nature as well as those of affection still bind my sisters dear to me. They may censure me for the past but if they do I cannot help it. I know that my life has bin mingled with eror, but you will remember that I have had a lonesome time in this world, with no one to whom I could go for councel but my own judgement. I had earley learned to think the world quite honest and kind, but sad experience proved the eror and then I doubted all, and my feelings were chilled toward society but in my lonelyest hours and my deapest sadness I have sat and watched your minature faces and they seamed like guardian Angels sent to gard my steps, and I remember as tho it was but yesterday when last I saw you how I watched your laboured breathing and how my hart ached to think that I might never see your face again. years have past and strange things have ocured, and we have not met but I still believe we will. Donot think hard of me for being a rebel officer we all have to be governed by circumstances when they are unavoidable, and to you Dear Eliza I will say that my hart is tru to the union as that of my Brother but we was differently situated. the circumstances that surrounded me I cannot give you now as I have written as much as the regulations alows. Write to me Eliza and give me all the news. Give my respects to Dock and tell him to write.

Ever your affectionate Brother
Lieut — Harry B. McLaughlin[3]

Apparently any efforts on his behalf that Eliza may have tried did not succeed. About a year and a half later, Harry asked Lt. Col. Edward A. Scovill, superintendent of the Johnson Island prisoner of war camp, to write to his sister Susan [Susan Louise McLaughlin Brown, wife of Dr. S. Clay Brown] on his behalf. Colonel Scovill agreed and sent a letter to Susan dated 1 January 1865, from the Depot of Prisoners, near Sandusky, Ohio:

Mrs. S.M. Brown
Huntington, Ind.
Madam,
I write this note at the request of your brother Henry B. McLaughlin a prisoner of war confined at this post. Upon his arrival here some 16 months ago he stated his case to me and made immediate application to take the Oath of Allegiance. [F]rom what I have observed I am perfectly satisfied his is a sincere application and in my opinion he should be released. [I]f it was in my power I would do it immediately.

Very Respectfully Yours
[Edward A. Scovill]
Lt. Col. 128th Regt. O.V.I.
Supt. of Prison[4]

On 7 January 1865, Governor Morton wrote to President Lincoln to introduce Susan, who was to go to Washington to petition the president for her brother's release.

His Excellency
   Abraham Lincoln
   President
   Dear Sir,
This will introduce Mrs. Susan M. Brown, wife of Surgeon Brown, who desires an interview with you in relation to release of her brother now held as a prisoner. I shall be under many obligations if you will grant her an interview.
Very Respectfully Yours,
   Your Obedient Servant
   O.P. Morton
   Governor of Indiana
   Let this man take the oath of Dec. 8, 1863 & be
   discharged. A. Lincoln, Jan. 12, 1865.[5] [Note attached]

Years later, Susan recounted her quest for Harry's release in an undated letter (ca. 1919) to the editor of the *National Tribune*:

Editor National Tribune:
I read, with much interest, the notice in your paper a few weeks ago of the death, at Beacon, N.Y. of Mrs. Anna Priscilla Erving, an ex-army nurse of the Civil War. I had an experience very similar to hers. I was also an Army nurse in the Civil War. For some time before the beginning of the war, my youngest brother had been living in the south. He had bought a small tract of land in Alabama and was living on it with his wife and one child. He thought the war would soon be over and he was not anxious to lose his home and all he had invested in it, so he continued in the south.

Very soon his life was threatened if he refused to go into the Confederate Army. He enlisted with the intention of escaping to the Union lines at the first opportunity. In one of the battles in the rear of Vicksburg he came face to face with his eldest brother who was Lt. Col. of the 47th Ind. Infy. The Ind. Reg. captured the Ala. Reg. My brother was sent as a prisoner of war to Johnson's Island near Sandusky, Ohio, where he remained a prisoner for twenty months. Early in January 1865 he wrote to me asking if I couldn't do something to secure his exchange. At that time my husband was with the 18th [Indiana] near Winchester, Va. He had written to me to come on and make him a visit. They had gone into winter quarters and the Colonel's wife was to be there for the winter, so why not I? I concluded to kill two birds with one stone, see what I could do for my brother and visit my husband. As I was one of the nurses appointed by Gov. Morton and I had interviewed the Governor on several occasions, I asked him for a letter of introduction to President Lincoln and told him my object in visiting the White House. He very kindly gave me the letter, in which he stated that a brother and also my husband were officers in the Union Army and that I wanted to do what I could to secure the exchange of another brother who was a prisoner on Johnson's Island. With this letter, I went to Washington and to the White House on the morning after my arrival. The President received callers only in the afternoon from two to four. I was there promptly at two o'clock only to find at least fifty others waiting in the hall outside the door. I secured a position as near the door as possible and was one of the first to be admitted.

I walked down the middle of a long room. The President sat at a table, alone at the very farther end of the room. The members of his Cabinet were ranged on either side of the long room, from front to back. I stopped in front of the President and handed him Gov. Morton's letter. He took it and read it through very carefully. Then looking up at me he asked, "upon what grounds do you ask for the release of this prisoner?" I answered, "upon the grounds that we believe him to be a loyal man who was forced into the Confederate Army against his will." He turned Gov. Morton's letter over and wrote on the back of it his instructions to the Secretary of War. Then he gave me explicit instructions how to find the right room in the War Dept. building, even to what door to enter, what stairs to go up and which way to turn at the top, to find the right room. In this room some further instructions were written on the back of Gov. Morton's letter and the letter was returned to me with very minute directions how to find the office of the Commissioner of Exchange. I found the place, and presented my, now very valuable document. "That" said the officer in charge, "is all that you can do. Your brother will be in Indianapolis before you are." And he was. But I wanted that letter of introduction from Gov. Morton, with President Lincoln's instructions on the back and also the instructions of the Sec'y. of War, on the back. I asked the Commissioner of Exchange if I could have it and what do you think he said? "I would be delighted to let you have it but we have to put it on file."

I returned to Harper's Ferry and called upon the Commander of that Post and asked him where the 13th Army corps was located. He gave me an odd glance as he answered, "I don't know. They passed through here four days ago, with sealed orders. No one but the General who issued the Order knows where they were going." Not until they were out on the Atlantic ocean did they know that they were on the way to take the place of Sherman's Army at Savannah, Ga. when Sherman marched up the coast.

Mrs. S. Clay Brown[6]

Appendix B

Zent's Regimental Song

Sergeant Henry W. Zent, Company E, of Huntington County wrote this song on 22 July 1862 while they were stationed at Memphis, Tennessee. The song gives the names and ranks of all the staff and company officers except for lieutenants, and even includes the regimental sutlers "who," as an anonymous commentator typed at the bottom of the lyrics page, "were generally unloved by the common soldier." Sergeant Zent listed the companies by the way they stood in line of battle, left to right, the lead companies being A, F, D, and I.[1]

"THE FORTY-SEVENTH INDIANA VOLUNTEERS"
BY SERGEANT H.W. ZENT, CO. E, 47TH REGIMENT INDIANA VOLUNTEERS

Come all ye Forty-Seventh, brave Hoosiers, come in time.
We'll sing about our Regiment, we'll put it all in rhyme;
We'll tell you of each Company, truly rehearse its fame,
We'll mention all the Captains, we'll tell you each one's name.

Company A is first, they're brave and true you know,
When Captain Morehouse leads the van they'll surely make things go,
They have good help right by their side, its Company F I mean,
When Captain Shearer leads his boys, they do the thing up clean.

Then on we come to Company D, Captain Brewer's not behind,
He'll call his men, they'll follow him, and whip the Secesh blind,
Then little Company I is there, its little Captain too,
When Bruner whips the secesh Blind, Henley'll beat them black and blue.

Now Company C is next, they bring the Colors on,
Young Captain Crabs says "spring, boys," they're quickly out and gone,
No sooner than Captain Keller though, I never saw him halt,
With Company H, he'll "pepper" rebels, then lay them up in salt.

Then Company E we next shall name, when in those "rifle pits";
Captain Wintrode cried, "up, boys," they gave the gunboats "fits";
Bold Company K is always right, for they have Captain Hill,
To lead them on, if in a fight, the traitors sure they'd kill.

Now Company G is next, Captain Robinson's their choice,
They'll follow him into the fray, with one united voice,
Now comes the last, its Company B, it never faltered yet,
Captain Goodwin's good as any, on that we'll stand a bet.

Our Colonel — who'd dare to say, there is another one

To equal him, in any land beneath the shining sun,
Old Colonel Slack — we've tried him, he makes the traitors fly,
He'll stand up for his boys, stand by them till they die.

Then there's the Lieutenant Colonel, in every fight he's dipped,
The worst fault that he has, he "don't know when he's whipped";
If that's a fault at all, Colonel Robinson's not to blame,
You know, to flinch, give up, or turn, why that is not his name.

Major McLaughlin's in his tent, we'll just step in and see,
He's brave — we know he is, he made the rebels flee.
At New Madrid you know it was, they took unto their heels,
They're real afraid of cannon balls, they dance such curious reels.

Our Adjutant, where's better? Mr. Evans is his name,
He reads us all our orders, he glories in our fame;
Chaplain Sawyer, too, is not excelled, very kind he is to us,
He shouldered his old rifle too, when we got into a fuss.

Next Sergeant Major Rumsey, just mention in the song,
He is a jolly fellow, he's just as broad as long.
But that is not his fault; Dame Nature made him so,
But notice when he moves, he'll surely make things go.

There's Quartermasters Nichols and Wallace, we will station
Down near the sutler's tent, to deal each man his ration
Of bacon and potatoes, hard crackers, beans and corn,
With a few "and so forths" thrown in, which the boys like "in a horn."

We next into the hospital, where physic "cures or kills,"
Will ask your friendly visit to see Doctors Dickens and Jim Mills,
They're busy 'mong the sick, they do their best to save,
But old death oft is master, and lays men in the grave.

We've made the rounds almost, there's Dr. Crosby every morning
Deals out blue pills, and quinine, and gives the sick good warning,
To take good care, be careful, take a little exercise,
Which is sufficient you all know, "a hint unto the wise."

And now comes Slack and Jones, the regimental sutlers,
There're clever men no doubt it, but like old Pharoah's butlers,
Or like the leech of which Solomon speaks, you've read in days of yore,
They cry give, give, oh give again, then ask for something more.

We now have passed all o'er the list, and to Memphis we have come,
In honor of her "loyal" sons we'll "fire the parting gun,"
Exhorting all to firmly stand by Freedom's holy cause,
And ne'er falter in supporting the Constitution and the Laws.

We'll close now by drinking healths to all our gallant men,
Our Colonel and his officers, but halt my nimble pen,
Here's a health unto our gallant wives, the "dear loved ones at home,"
The last line of my song, they claim it for their own.

Appendix C

The Flags of the 47th Indiana

According to the Indiana Adjutant General's Report of 1869, the 47th Indiana is known to have carried seven flags during the course of the war, three national and four regimental. Six of these flags, three national and three regimental, are preserved at the Indiana War Memorial in Indianapolis.

Based on the Stars and Stripes and carried on a staff nine feet ten inches long, the National Flag was six feet six inches on the fly and six feet on the hoist. It had thirteen painted horizontal stripes, seven red and six white, and a dark blue canton with thirty-three to thirty-five stars, depending on the year of manufacture, painted in the upper left corner. Each canton on the 47th Indiana's three nationals varied in size. All three cantons reached down the hoist a little over three feet to the top of the fourth white stripe, but each differed in length along the fly, ranging from a little over two feet to almost three and a half feet. The stars have worn off all three flags, and one, probably the earliest, has lost its regimental designation. Of the other two, one has "47th Regt. Ind. Vols." stenciled in black across the third white stripe from the bottom; the other has the same designation stenciled in gold across the third red stripe from the bottom. In 1869, the adjutant general described one of the nationals as "silk, worn, torn and faded; staff good"; another as "silk, nearly worn out; staff good"; and the third as "bunting, full of bullet holes; staff shot through center and near the top."[1] The Regimental Flag, also six feet six inches on the fly and six feet on the hoist, had a regulation blue silk field trimmed with gold fringe on all but the staff side; and, depending on who manufactured the flag, had variations of the United States Coat of Arms embroidered on its center.[2]

The Indiana War Memorial in Indianapolis holds three such flags in its collection. Although the dates of issue are unknown, the earliest Regimental Flag in the collection appears to be one manufactured by the John Shillito Company of Cincinnati, Ohio.[3] An eagle with its wings spread is embroidered in gold on the center of the flag under an arc of dark storm clouds behind which shine rays of sunlight. The eagle bears a small shield on its breast with 13 vertical stripes, seven red and six white, surmounted by a wider horizontal blue stripe. The eagle's right talon clutches an olive branch and its left a cluster of seven arrows. The eagle's head is shot away, but it would have been turned toward the olive branch and its beak would have clutched a ribbon with the motto, "E Pluribus Unum." Beneath the eagle, "47th Regiment Ind. Vol. U.S.A." is stenciled in gold on a blue ribbon outlined in gold.

This may have been the flag donated by the ladies of Wabash, although many donated

The Flags of the 47th Indiana 319

Top left: 1347th Indiana Regimental Flag. The "Spanish Fort" flag. (Indiana War Memorials Commission). *Top right:* 47th Indiana Regimental Flag. The "Shillito" flag, an early flag manufactured by the Shillito Department Store in Cincinnati, Ohio (Indiana War Memorials Commission). *Bottom left:* 1447th Indiana National Flag. (Indiana War Memorials Commission). *Bottom right:* 1547th Indiana National Flag with "47th Regt. Ind. Vols." stenciled on the third white stripe from the bottom. (Indiana War Memorials Commission).

Shillito flags had "Presented by the Ladies of" painted on the flag and this one does not. The missing flag described by the adjutant general in 1869 as "Regimental Flag; blue silk, faded, embroidered, soiled, torn; inscribed '47th Indiana Regiment' in gold thread letters; staff good," could also have been that flag, although the adjutant general did not specify that it had been donated by anyone. The flag presented by the ladies of Wabash in all likelihood would have been a Shillito of similar design.[4]

On 30 December 1862 at Helena, Arkansas, Col. Slack, Lt. Col. McLaughlin, and Maj. Goodwin certified that the 47th had been engaged in the battles at New Madrid and Riddle's Point, Missouri; and, on 19 February 1863 at Helena, Col. Slack submitted a Requisition for Flags. On 2 June 1863 at Vicksburg, he certified that the 47th had been, in addition to New Madrid and Riddle's Point, engaged at Fort Pemberton, Port Gibson,

Fourteen Mile Creek, Champion's Hill and Vicksburg. All battle honors requested were accepted except Fort Pemberton.⁵

Sometime during or after the siege of Vicksburg, they received another Regimental Flag, but of different manufacture and design. A bald eagle is embroidered in natural colors on the center of the blue field under a double arc of gold stars. Although its shield and part of its beak are shot away, it clutches a bunch of arrows in its right talon and an olive branch in its left. Its white head is turned toward the olive branch and its beak clutches a white ribbon with the motto, "E Pluribus Unum." Beneath the eagle, "47th Regt. Indiana Volunteers" is stenciled in gold on a red ribbon. In 1869, the adjutant general described this flag as: "Regimental Flag; blue silk; eagle nearly all torn out by a shell; bullet holes through flag; inscribed: '47th Regiment Indiana Volunteers;' 'Fourteen Mile Creek;' 'Vicksburg;' 'New Madrid, Mo.;' 'Champion Hill;' 'Port Gibson;' 'Riddle's Point, Mo.;' staff good."⁶

164 47th Indiana National Flag with "47th Regt. Ind. Vols." stenciled in gold on the third red stripe from the bottom. (Indiana War Memorials Commission).

The last Regimental Flag in the collection was of the same manufacture and design as the previous flag, but with their complete battle honors listed. The adjutant general described this flag as: "Regimental Flag; blue silk; worn, torn and ragged; inscribed '47th Regt. Ind. Vols.;' 'New Madrid, Mo.;' 'Riddle's Point, Mo.;' 'Port Gibson, Miss.;' 'Vicksburg, Miss.;' 'Fourteen Mile Creek;' 'Spanish Fort;' 'Blakely;' 'Mobile;' 'Atchafalaya;' 'Champion Hills;' 'Jackson, Miss.;' 'Muddy Bayou;' staff good."⁷

Appendix D

Roster of the 47th Indiana Volunteer Infantry

Regimental Officers

Colonel:

Slack, James R.; Huntington; commissioned 25 Sep 1861; mustered in 13 Dec 1861; promoted Brigadier General 31 Dec 1864.
McLaughlin, John A.; Indianapolis; commissioned 1 Mar 1865; mustered out as Lt. Colonel with regiment.

Lieutenant Colonel:

Robinson, Milton S.; Anderson; commissioned 25 Dec 1861; mustered in 13 Dec 1861; promoted Colonel, 75th [Indiana] Regiment.
McLaughlin, John A.; Indianapolis; commissioned and mustered in 22 Oct 1862; promoted Colonel.
Shearer, Sextus H.; Huntington; commissioned 4 Mar 1864; mustered out as Major with regiment.

Major:

Mickle, Samuel S.; Decatur; commissioned 25 Sep 1861; mustered in 13 Dec 1861; resigned 12 Apr 1862.
McLaughlin, John A.; Indianapolis; commissioned 15 Apr 1862; mustered in 12 Apr 1862; promoted Lt. Colonel.
Goodwin, Lewis H.; Wabash; commissioned and mustered in 22 Oct 1862; honorably discharged 3 Dec 1864.
Shearer, Sextus H.; Huntington; commissioned 1 Jan 1865; mustered in 20 Jan 1865; promoted Lt. Colonel.
Vance, William H.; Jay Court House; commissioned 25 May 1865; mustered out as Adjutant with regiment.

Adjutant:

Evans, Marion P.; Kokomo; commissioned 29 Nov 1861; mustered in 13 Dec 1861; resigned 4 Sep 1862.
Vance, William H.; Jay Court House; commissioned and mustered in 5 Sep 1862; promoted Major.
Stockham, David M.; Knightstown; commissioned 1 Sep 1865; mustered out as Sergeant Major with regiment.

Quartermaster:

Nichol, George; Anderson; commissioned 25 Sep 1861; resigned 20 Jan 1864.
Ballard, Warren F.; Knightstown; commissioned 5 Mar 1864; mustered in 29 Apr 1864; mustered out with regiment.

Chaplain:

Sawyer, Samuel W.; Marion; commissioned 20 Oct 1861; mustered in 13 Dec 1861; acquitted of being absent without leave by Military Commission of Inquiry 1 Apr 1863; resigned 9 Oct 1864.[1]

Surgeon:

Dickens, James L.; Wabash; commissioned 21 Oct 1861, mustered in 13 Dec 1861; named surgeon-in-chief of Veatch's division on 8 March 1865 at Dauphin Island; mustered out with regiment.[2]

Assistant Surgeon:

Mills, James R.; Huntington; commissioned 21 Oct 1861; mustered in 13 Dec 1861; died at Helena, AR, 8 Feb 1863.
Stewart, William J.; Camden; commissioned and mustered in 24 Jul 1862; resigned 10 Dec 1862.
Crosby, Thomas H.; Bluffton; commissioned 25 Nov 1862; mustered in 25 Dec 1862; acquitted of being absent without leave by Military Commission of Inquiry 1 April 1864; mustered out 21 Dec 1864; term expired.[3]
Fitzgerald, David A.; Indianapolis; commissioned 27 Jan1865; died as Hospital Steward 1 Jan 1865.
Regimental Non-Commissioned Staff— all mustered in 13 Dec 1861:

Quartermaster Sergeant:

Wallace, John R.; promoted Captain U.S. Colored Troops.

Commissary Sergeant:

Lemon, Peter H.; Anderson; discharged 1 Sep 1862, disability.

Sergeant Major:

Jennings, Horatio P., promoted 1st Lt. Company C.

Hospital Steward:

Vance, Mark T.; died at Louisville, KY, 25 Feb 1862.

Company A (*Original members mustered in 2 November 1861*)

Captain:

McLaughlin, John A; Indianapolis; commissioned 10 Oct 1861; mustered in 2 Nov 1861; promoted Major.
Moorhous, Albert; Indianapolis; commissioned 22 Apr 1862; mustered in 10 Aug 1862; resigned 18 Oct 1863; re-entered service as captain in the 9th Cavalry.
Sturgis, Elmore Y.; Bluffton; commissioned and mustered in 19 Oct 1862; mustered out 31 Dec 1864; term expired.
Hough, Thomas; Indianapolis; commissioned 1 Mar 1865; mustered in 9 Apr 1865; mustered out with regiment 23 Oct 1865.

First Lieutenant:

Moorhous, Albert; Indianapolis; commissioned 20 Oct 1861; mustered in 2 Nov 1861; promoted Captain.

Wisner, Sharpe; Bluffton; commissioned 22 Apr 1862; mustered in 10 Aug 1862; honorably discharged 3 Oct 1862.

Sturgis, Elmore Y.; Bluffton; commissioned and mustered in 4 Oct 1862; promoted Captain.

Arnold, Eli; Warren; Warren; commissioned and mustered in 19 Oct 1862; mustered out 31 Dec 1864; term expired.

Hough, Thomas; Indianapolis; commissioned 1 Jan 1865; promoted Captain.

Stober, William H.; Murray; commissioned 1 Mar 1865; mustered in 6 Apr 1865; mustered out with regiment 23 Oct 1865.

Second Lieutenant:

Van Horn, Nicholas; Tipton; commissioned 10 Oct 1861; mustered in 2 Nov 1861; resigned 12 Apr 1862.

Moorhous, Hiram; Indianapolis; commissioned 22 Apr 1862; mustered in 10 Aug 1862; neglect of duty charge dismissed by General Court-Martial 1 Sep 1862 at Helena, AR; resigned 30 Oct 1862.[4]

Hough, Thomas; Indianapolis; commissioned and mustered in 19 Oct 1862; promoted 1st Lieutenant.

Lewis, John B.; Reiffsburg; commissioned 1 Jul 1865; mustered out with regiment 23 Oct 1865 as 1st Sergeant.

First Sergeant:

Wisner, Sharpe; Bluffton; promoted 1st Lieutenant.

Sergeants:

Moorhous, Hiram; Indianapolis; promoted 2nd Lieutenant.
Sturgis, Elmore T.; Bluffton; promoted 1st Lieutenant.
Stober, William H.; Murray; promoted 1st Lieutenant.
Dain, Edward T.; Indianapolis; promoted 2nd Lieutenant.

Corporals:

Anderson, William; Bluffton; discharged 4 May 1863, as Sergeant.
Wellinger, Benedict; Bluffton; died at Keokuk, IA, 10 Nov 1862.
Jones, Benjamin; Decatur; veteran; mustered out 23 Oct 1865, as Sergeant.
Moore, Orton; Vera Cruz; veteran; mustered out 23 Oct 1865.
Arnold, Eli; Warren; promoted 1st Lieutenant.
Hough, Thomas: Indianapolis; promoted 2nd Lieutenant.
Miller, Allen L.; Bluffton; wounded at Brown's Plantation, MS, 11 Aug 1862; killed at Champion Hill, MS, 16 May 1863.
Wood, William S.; Bluffton; veteran; mustered out 23 Oct 1865, as Corporal.

Musicians:

Plessinger, James B.; Bluffton; transferred to Non-Com Staff 1 Jan 1862.
Covert, William H.; Bluffton; transferred to Non-Com Staff 1 Sep 1862.

Wagoner:

Stout, Joseph W.; died at St. Louis, 14 Oct 1862.

Privates:

Adams, William; Nottingham; veteran; transferred to VRC; mustered out 9 Oct 1865.
Alspack, Daniel; Bluffton; veteran; mustered out 23 Oct 1865.
Alspack, Elijah; Bluffton; discharged 6 Mar 1863, disability.
Baker, Henry H.; Bluffton; discharged 28 Mar 1863, disability.
Barber, Charles; Lingrove; veteran; mustered out 23 Oct 1865.
Boden, William; Bluffton; veteran; mustered out 23 Oct 1865.
Broannum, Joseph; Bluffton; died at Memphis, 5 Jul 1863.
Burgess, John; Reiffsburg; veteran; mustered out 23 Oct 1865, as Corporal.
Burgess, Richard; Reiffsburg; veteran; mustered out 23 Oct 1865.
Burgess, James; Reiffsburg; veteran; mustered out 23 Oct 1865.
Butterfield, Willard O.; Bluffton; died at St. Louis, 4 Nov 1862.
Covert, William H.; _____; unaccounted for.
Craig, Zebedee; Bluffton; veteran; mustered out 23 Oct 1865.
Crosby, Isaac; Bluffton; veteran; mustered out 23 Oct 1865 as Corporal.
Crosby, Simeon; Bluffton; veteran; mustered out 23 Oct 1865.
Crosby, Thomas H.; Bluffton; transferred to Non-Com Staff 24 Mar 1862; promoted Assistant Surgeon.
Crumley, Thomas I.; Reiffsburg; veteran; mustered out 23 Oct 1865, as Corporal.
Custard, Aaron; Bluffton; mustered out 13 Dec 1864.
Custard, John; Bluffton; died at Helena, AR, 1 Mar 1863.
Davis, Amos; Bluffton; mustered out 13 Dec 1864.
Devoss, Job T.; Nottingham; died at Jefferson Barracks, MO, 4 Feb 1863.
Devoss, John S.; Nottingham; died 17 May 1863 from wounds received at Champion Hill, MS.
Downey, Michael; Bluffton; veteran; mustered out 23 Oct 1865.
Engle [Ingle], Jonas; Liberty; wounded at Brown's Plantation, MS, 11 Aug 1862; died at Jefferson Barracks, MO, 24 Jul 1863.
Faulstick, John; Indianapolis; discharged 7 Mar 1863, disability.
Forchee, Philip; Indianapolis; veteran; mustered out 23 Oct 1865.
Haines, Timothy H.; Nottingham; discharged 7 Mar 1863, disability.
Hale, Madison; Nottingham; died at Memphis, 17 Mar 1863.
Halterman, Jackson; Lingrove; discharged 15 Apr 1862, disability.
Harper, William; Nottingham; veteran; mustered out 23 Oct 1865, as Sergeant.
Higdon, Benedict; Indianapolis; veteran; mustered out 23 Oct 1865.
Higgins, John W.; Camden; died 16 Aug 1862 of wounds received at Brown's Plantation, MS.
Higgins, William N.; Camden; discharged 23 Aug 1862, disability.
Hilton, Daniel; Limber Lost; veteran; mustered out 23 Oct 1865, as Corporal.
Hodgson, Isaac; Bluffton; discharged 22 Sep 1862 of wounds received at Brown's Plantation, MS.
Hodgson, Michael W.; Bluffton; veteran; wounded at Brown's Plantation, MS, 11 Aug 1862; mustered out 23 Oct 1865.
Hovland, Elijah; Camden; mustered out 13 Dec 1864.
Huffman, David; Bluffton; transferred to Invalid Corps, 15 Jan 1864.
Jarrett, Bently; Bluffton; discharged 9 Dec 1862, disability.
Jeffries, William H.; Murray; discharged 7 Mar 1863, disability.
Johnson, Abel S.; Bluffton; died at St. Louis 31 Oct 1862 of wounds.
Johnson, Elbridge; Bluffton; veteran; discharged 14 Jun 1865, disability.
Johnson, Isaac W.; Bluffton; killed at Brown's Plantation, MS, 11 Aug 1862.
Jones, John; Nottingham; died at Tiptonville, TN, 7 May 1862.
Jones, Joseph; Bluffton; veteran; mustered out 23 Oct 1865.
Juday, Andrew J.; Liberty; transferred to Invalid Corps 15 Jan 1864.
Kenedy, John; Bluffton; veteran; mustered out 23 Oct 1865.
Louis, John B.; Reiffsburg; veteran; mustered out 23 Oct 1865, as Sergeant.
Lynch, Chancy W.R.; Bluffton; veteran; dropped as deserter 8 Jul 1865; mustered out 22 Mar 1866.
McGlauglin, Theodore; Reiffsburg; died at Benton, MO, 29 Mar 1862.
McLain, Andrew J.; Indianapolis; veteran; mustered out 23 Oct 1865.
Mechling, Levy; Bluffton; died at Mound City, IL, 21 Sep 1862.
Millikan, Alfred B.; Bluffton; deserted; killed on way to rejoin the regiment.

Moore, Seth; Vera Cruz; veteran; mustered out 23 Oct 1865.
Morgan, Charles H.; Bluffton; veteran; mustered out 13 Dec 1864.
Mountjoy, John; Indianapolis; veteran; mustered out 15 Jun 1865.
Phillips, Evan H.; Bluffton; died at New Orleans 22 Aug 1863.
Phillips, Henry L; Decatur; discharged 21 Aug 1862.
Plessinger, Benjamin F.; Bluffton; veteran; mustered out 23 Oct 1865, as Corporal.
Plessinger, James B.; unaccounted for.
Pronty, Jesse; Nottingham; veteran; mustered out 23 Oct 1865.
Ralstain [Ralston], Smith; Lingrove; veteran; wounded at Brown's Plantation, MS, 11 Aug 1862; mustered out 23 Oct 1865.
Ralstain [Ralston], William; Lingrove; veteran; mustered out 23 Oct 1865.
Reynolds, Charles H.; Indianapolis; discharged 16 Feb 1862.
Rinear, John W.; Bluffton; discharged 7 Aug 1862, disability.
Robbins, James H.; Bluffton; discharged 10 Aug 1862, disability.
Rowney, Joseph; Indianapolis; mustered out 13 Dec 1864.
Rowney, Thomas H.; Indianapolis; died at Helena, AR, 15 Aug 1862 of wounds received at Brown's Plantation, MS.
Runkle, Peter; Bluffton; veteran; mustered out 23 Oct 1865.
Scott, Robert H.; Decatur; died at Memphis 7 Jul 1863.
Snow, John; Bluffton; died at home 21 Oct 1862.
Tate, John; Bluffton; died at Helena, AR, 5 Mar 1863.
Tate, Samuel; Bluffton; veteran; wounded at Brown's Plantation, MS, 11 Aug 1862; mustered out 23 Oct 1865.
Tharpe, William H.; Bluffton; died at Helena, AR, 2 Feb 1863.
Thomas, John; Bluffton; veteran; wounded at Brown's Plantation, MS, 11 Aug 1862; mustered out 23 Oct 1865 as Corporal.
Thrailkill, Elijah; Bluffton; killed at Brown's Plantation, MS, 11 Aug 1862.
Tremain, Benjamin; Bluffton; mustered out 13 Dec 1864.
Updergraft, David; Nottingham; died at home 30 May 1864.
Vandaman, James; Indianapolis; veteran; mustered out 23 Oct 1865.
Vandaman, John M.; Indianapolis; transferred to Invalid Corps 15 Jan 1864.
Wilson, Charles G.; Nottingham; veteran; mustered out 23 Oct 1865, as sergeant.
Watts, Joseph; Nottingham; discharged __ Jan 1862, disability.
Young, James R.; Bluffton; veteran; mustered out 23 Oct 1865.

Recruits:

Alspach, John F.; Bluffton; mustered in 2 Mar 1864; mustered out 23 Oct 1865.
Blackledge, Charles; Nottingham; mustered in 1 Nov 1862; discharged 22 Jul 1863.
Blackledge, James M.; Nottingham; mustered in 2 Mar 1864; mustered out 23 Oct 1865.
Blair, Jacob W.; Reiffsburg; mustered in 16 Oct 1862; mustered out 16 Jul 1863.
Brineman, William H.; Bluffton; mustered in 21 Nov 1862; deserted 24 Jan 1863.
Coe, Christopher N.; Nottingham; mustered in 1 Nov 1862; mustered out 23 Oct 1865.
Cline, Frederick; Indianapolis; mustered in 10 Mar 1864; mustered out 23 Oct 1865.
Cline, Richard; Indianapolis; mustered in 16 Mar 1865; mustered out 23 Oct 1865.
Craig, Harrison; Bluffton; mustered in 22 Aug 1862; discharged 28 Jul 1865; by order, as Principle Musician.
Dawley, Gideon J.; Nottingham; mustered in 22 Oct 1862; transferred to VRC 13 Jan 1864.
Dragoo, Samuel W.; Nottingham; mustered in 1 Nov 1862; mustered out 13 Oct 1865.
Emmons, Ephraim; Nottingham; mustered in 1 Nov 1862; deserted 12 Jul 1865; dishonorably discharged, 18 May 1867.
Frink, John; Nottingham; mustered in 15 Feb 1865; mustered out at general rendezvous, Indianapolis, 24 May 1865.
Furnace, Henry; Nottingham; mustered in 26 Mar 1864; died at New Orleans 25 Jun 1864.
Gardner, George E.; Ossian; mustered in 15 Feb 1865; mustered out 23 Oct 1865.
Hale, James R.; Nottingham; mustered in 1 Nov 1862; mustered out 23 Oct 1865.
Harvey, Robert; Murray; mustered in 15 Feb 1865; mustered out 23 Oct 1865.
Helm, Thomas J.; Bluffton; mustered in 2 Mar 1864; died at New Orleans, 21 Sep 1864.

Hodgson, Isaac; Bluffton; mustered in 21 Mar 1865; mustered out 23 Oct 1865.
Hurst, Thaddeus S.; Nottingham; mustered in 26 Mar 1864; mustered out 23 Oct 1865.
Jones, William; Bluffton; mustered in 2 Mar 1864; mustered out 23 Oct 1865.
Lockwood, John S.; Nottingham; mustered in 2 Mar 1864; mustered out 23 Oct 1865.
McClain, Lorenzo D.; Indianapolis; mustered in 8 Mar 1865; mustered out 23 Oct 1865.
McClain, Robert; Nottingham; mustered in 16 Feb 1865; mustered out 23 Oct 1865.
McClain, William B.; Indianapolis; mustered in 26 Mar 1864; mustered out 23 Oct 1865.
McVey, Newton; Indianapolis; mustered in 20 Mar 1865; mustered out 23 Oct 1865.
Nutter, Levi; mustered in 29 Mar 1864; mustered out 24 Aug 1865.
Priest, George; Nottingham; mustered in 26 Mar 1864; mustered out 23 Oct 1865.
Roby, John W.; Bluffton; mustered in 2 Mar 1864; mustered out 23 Oct 1865.
Rodgers, George W.; Indianapolis; mustered in 6 Mar 1865; mustered out 23 Oct 1865.
Rodgers, John; Thorntown; mustered in 6 Mar 1865; mustered out 23 Oct 1865.
Rodgers, Simpson; Indianapolis; mustered in 6 Mar 1865; mustered out 23 Oct 1865.
Ryan, Felix; Half Way; mustered in 25 Nov 1862; discharged 11 Sep 1863.
Steele, Benjamin P.; Wabash; mustered in 6 Nov 1861; discharged 21 Mar 1865, disability.
Shaw, Elmond B.; Nottingham; mustered in 26 Mar 1864; mustered out 23 Oct 1865.
Shaw, Reed; Nottingham; mustered in 22 Oct 1862; mustered out 23 Oct 1865.
Tharpe, Isaac N.; Bluffton; mustered in 2 Mar 1864; mustered out 23 Oct 1865.
Warner, David; Reiffsburg; mustered in 4 Nov 1864; mustered out 23 Oct 1865.
Wilson, John; Bluffton; mustered in 14 Apr 1864; died at New Orleans 6 Jun 1864.
Wilson, William; Bluffton; mustered in 14 Apr 1864; mustered out 23 Oct 1865.

Company B *(Original members mustered in 15 November 1861)*

Captain:

Goodwin, Lewis; Wabash; commissioned 10 Oct 1861; mustered in 15 Nov 1861; promoted Major.
Rager, Christian B.; N. Manchester; commissioned and mustered in 22 Oct 1862; mustered out 30 Dec 1864, term expired.
Church, Freeman S.; Wabash; commissioned 1 Mar 1865; mustered in 9 Apr 1865; mustered out with regiment 23 Oct 1865.

First Lieutenant:

Henley, William M.; Wabash; commissioned 10 Oct 1865; mustered in 15 Nov 1861; transferred to Co. I; promoted Captain.
Rager, Christian; N. Manchester; commissioned 1 Apr 1862; promoted Captain.
Perry, James F.; Wabash; commissioned and mustered in 22 Oct 1862; killed at Champion Hill, MS, 16 May 1863.
Brown, Henry; Wabash; commissioned and mustered in 17 May 1863; mustered out 31 Dec 1864, term expired.
Church, Freeman S.; Wabash; commissioned 1 Jan 1865; promoted Captain.
Cook, Michael; Liberty Mills; commissioned 1 Mar 1865; mustered in 9 Apr 1865; mustered out with regiment 23 Oct 1865.

Second Lieutenant:

Rager, Christian B.; N. Manchester; commissioned 10 Oct 1861; mustered in 15 Nov 1861; promoted 1st Lieutenant.
Perry, James F.; Wabash; commissioned and mustered 1 Apr 1862; promoted 1st Lieutenant.
Cole, George W.; N. Manchester; commissioned and mustered 22 Oct 1862; killed at Champion Hill, MS, 16 May 1863.

Shuler, John B.; N. Manchester; commissioned and mustered in 17 May 1863; mustered out 31 Dec 1864, term expired.
Porter, Zerah C.; Wabash; commissioned 1 Jul 1865; mustered out with regiment 23 Oct 1865 as Sergeant.

First Sergeant:

Perry, James F., Wabash, promoted 2nd Lieutenant.

Sergeants:

Hoke, Albert W.; N. Manchester, discharged 6 Feb 1862, disability.
McMillan, Jonathan; Wabash; died at Helena, AR, 3 Oct 1862.
Cole, George W.; N. Manchester; promoted 2nd Lieutenant.
Richardson, Isaac; Wabash; died at St. Louis, 3 Jan 1863.

Corporals:

Baer, Manassah N.; Wabash; discharged 6 Feb 1862, disability.
Brown, Henry; Wabash; promoted 1st Lieutenant.
Winger, Jacob; N. Manchester; died at St. Louis 24 Jul 1863.
King, William M.H.; Wabash; discharged 30 Jun 1862, disability.
Frame, David; N. Manchester; discharged 27 Jul 1863, disability.
Shuler, John B.; N. Manchester; veteran; promoted 2nd Lieutenant.
McGuire, James; N. Manchester; veteran; mustered out with regiment as Sergeant 23 Oct 1865.
Ridgley, John B; N. Manchester; acquitted of murder by General Court-Martial 1 Aug 1862 at Memphis; discharged 14 Feb 1865, disability.[5]

Privates:

Baer, Daniel; Laketon; veteran; mustered out 23 Oct 1865.
Baker, John; Wabash; mustered out 12 Dec 1864.
Baker, Joseph; Wabash; veteran; dishonorably discharged by General Court-Martial 20 Sep 1865. (No record found.)
Benge, John; N. Manchester; deserted 21 Oct 1862; mustered out 23 Oct 1865.
Breckner, Aaron; Lagro; veteran; discharged 17 May 1865, disability.
Breckner, Joseph; Lagro; veteran; mustered out 23 Oct 1865.
Breckner, Wilson; Lagro; veteran; mustered out 23 Oct 1865.
Brown, Martin; Wabash; died at Cairo, IL, 8 Sep 1862.
Cable, William P.; Wabash; deserted, 21 Oct 1862.
Clemmons, Benjamin; Liberty Mills; transferred to Non-Com Staff, 1 May 1864; mustered out 23 Oct 1865 as Quartermaster Sergeant.
Cook, Michael; Liberty Mills; promoted 1st Lieutenant.
Cooper, Abraham; Wabash; veteran; mustered out 23 Oct 1865.
Cooper Daniel; Wabash; veteran; mustered out 23 Oct 1865.
Cooper, Isaac; Wabash; veteran; mustered out 26 Jun 1865.
Crow, Wilson H.; Wabash; killed at Champion Hill, MS, 16 May 1863.
Curry, John W.; N. Manchester; died at St. Louis, 6 May 1862.
Cutler, Allen J.; Wabash; died at Memphis, 1 Mar 1865.
Eckman, George W.; N. Manchester; died at Benton, MO, 4 Mar 1862.
Edmonds, William; N. Manchester; veteran; mustered out 23 Oct 1865.
Eller, Henry; Urbana; veteran; mustered out 23 Oct 1865, as Corporal.
Faucett, Randolf; Wabash; deserted 25 Jul 1863.
Flora, Alexander; Wabash; mustered out 12 Dec 1864.
Flora, Edward; Wabash; died 1 Jun 1862 of wounds received at Champion Hill, MS.
Frame, James; N. Manchester; veteran; mustered out 23 Oct 1865, as Corporal.
Freshour, Edward; largo; veteran; mustered out 23 Oct 1865, as Corporal.

Freshour, George: Lagro; veteran; mustered out 23 Oct 1865, as Corporal.
Gardner, Myron D.; Wabash; died 30 May 1862 of wounds received at Champion Hill, MS.
Hensler, George; Wabash; discharged 17 Jul 1862, disability.
Hill, Henry F.; Huntington; mustered out 12 Dec 1864.
Hippenstell, Henry; N. Manchester; discharged 17 Jul 1862, disability.
Huff, John H.; Wabash; discharged 26 Nov 1862, disability.
Ide, Adam; Wabash; veteran; transferred to 1st Missouri Light Artillery 1 Jan 1864.
Jackson, James M.C.; Wabash; veteran; mustered out 23 Oct 1865.
Jackson, Richard W.; Wabash; mustered out 12 Dec 1864.
James, Charles H.; Wabash; mustered out 12 Dec 1864.
Jeffery, Alvin; Wabash; veteran; mustered out 23 Oct 1865, as Corporal.
Jones, Joseph; Wabash; veteran; mustered out 23 Oct 1865.
Jones, Samuel; Wabash; discharged 30 Sep 1862; disability.
Kennedy, Edward; _____; mustered out 23 Oct 1865.
Lautzenhizor, David; Laketon; killed at Port Gibson, MS, 1 May 1863.
Lautzenhizor, Silas; N. Manchester; discharged 24 Jul 1863, disability.
Learman, John; _____; unaccounted for.
Lope, Lee; Urbana; veteran; mustered out 23 Oct 1865, as Corporal.
Long, Josiah; Wabash; died at Indianapolis 1 May 1863.
Lynch, Michael; N. Manchester; veteran; mustered out 23 Oct 1865.
McGuire, John G.; N. Manchester; died at Tiptonville, TN, 5 May 1862.
Messmore, William; N. Manchester; died at St. Charles, AR, 14 Oct 1864.
Michael, Eli; _____; unaccounted for.
Misener, Jasper; N. Manchester; discharged 29 Apr 1862, disability.
Mowrer, Emanuel J.; N. Manchester; discharged 27 Feb 1862, disability.
Mowrer, Jacob; N. Manchester; veteran; mustered out 23 Jul 1865, as Corporal.
Moore, Philip; Urbana; veteran; mustered out 23 Oct 1865, as Sergeant.
Murphy, Hugh J.; Wabash; veteran; mustered out 23 Oct 1865.
Musselman, Thomas B.; Laketon; died at Wabash, IN, 18 Jul 1862.
Myers, John; Wabash; killed at Champion Hill, MS, 16 May 1863.
Nelis, William; Wabash; veteran; mustered out 23 Oct 1865.
Nusebaum, Henry; Wabash; veteran; mustered out 23 Oct 1865.
Nusebaum, Josiah; Wabash; killed at Port Gibson, MS, 1 May 1863.
Porter, Zarah C.; Wabash; veteran; mustered out 23 Oct 1865, as 1st Sergeant.
Powell, Thomas; Wabash; died at Louisville 6 Mar 1862.
Rager, John; N. Manchester; discharged 20 Oct 1862, disability.
Reed, Harrison J.; Liberty Mills; veteran; acquitted of desertion by General Court-Martial 1 Mar 1863; dishonorably discharged 29 Sep 1865.[6]
Ridgley, Jonathan B.; N. Manchester; veteran; mustered out 23 Oct 1865.
St. John, Albert R.; Liberty Mills; killed at Champion Hill, MS, 16 May 1863.
Sampson, Daniel; Wabash; discharged 5 Aug 1863.
Simpson, Richard; N. Manchester; veteran; mustered out 23 Oct 1865.
Sloup, William; Wabash; veteran; mustered out 23 Oct 1865.
Smith, Jacob; Wabash; died at Memphis, 26 Jul 1862.
Southwick, Philip; Wabash; deserted, 1 Jul 1862.
Speicher, Frederick; Wabash; veteran; mustered out 23 Oct 1865.
Speicher, John; Wabash; transferred to VRC 1 Sep 1863.
Steckman, John W.; Wabash; discharged 2 Nov 1862, disability.
Talmadge, Jesse; Wabash; veteran; mustered out 23 Oct 1865.
Talmadge, Thomas; Wabash; discharged 3 Sep 1863; disability.
Truss, Edward H.; Wabash; mustered out 12 Dec 1864.
Truss, Silas; Wabash; mustered out 12 Dec 1864.
Wallace, John; N. Manchester; veteran; supposed to have been murdered in Louisiana.
Wantz, John J.; Liberty Mills; discharged 9 Oct 1863, disability.
Wantz, Levi B.; Liberty Mills; veteran; mustered out 23 Oct 1865.
Watts, Benjamin; Wabash; veteran; mustered out 23 Oct 1865.
Weidner, John B.; N. Manchester; veteran, mustered out 23 Oct 1865, as sergeant.
Wertenberger, William; Laketon; discharged 30 Oct 1862, disability.

Whitesel, Henry; N. Manchester; veteran; mustered out 23 Oct 1865.
Wiezel, Daniel; Wabash; veteran; deserted, 1 Apr 1864.
Winger, Uriah; Laketon; died at Helena, AR, 6 Feb 1863.
Wolf, John; Urbana; veteran; mustered out 23 Oct 1865.

Recruits:

Benham, Michael; Wabash; mustered in 29 Sep 1864; mustered out 23 Oct 1865.
Breckner, Peter; Lagro; mustered in 7 Mar 1864; mustered out 23 Oct 1865.
Broke, James; Wabash; mustered in 12 Mar 1864; mustered out 23 Oct 1865.
Cooper, John; Wabash; mustered in 27 Feb 1864; mustered out 23 Oct 1865.
Cooper, John H.; Wabash; mustered 18 Sep 1862; mustered out 28 Jul 1865.
Foster, Francis H.; N. Manchester; mustered in 5 Mar 1864; mustered out 23 Oct 1865.
Freshour, Andrew C.; Lagro; mustered in 18 Oct 1864; mustered out 23 Oct 1865.
Freshour, Charles H.; Lagro; mustered in 18 Oct 1864; mustered out 23 Oct 1865.
Gatrel, Paton H.; Lagro; mustered in 18 Oct 1864; mustered out 23 Oct 1865.
Gwin, Granville; Wabash; mustered in 26 Mar 1864; mustered out 23 Oct 1865.
Jelleff, Joseph; Wabash; mustered in 6 Apr 1865; mustered out 23 Oct 1865.
Lacy, Charles P.; Wabash; mustered in 24 Mar 1865; mustered out 23 Oct 1865.
Mowrer, Madison; N. Manchester; mustered in 25 Mar 1865; mustered out 23 Oct 1865.
Newsbaum, William; Wabash; mustered in 14 Apr 1864; died at Morganza, LA, 20 Aug 1864.
Reed, Francis M.; Wabash; mustered in 5 Apr 1863; mustered out 23 Oct 1865.
Reed, Hezekiah; Wabash; mustered in 24 Mar 1865; mustered out 23 Oct 1865.
Rickerd, Israel I.; Union city; mustered in 16 Mar 1864; died at New Orleans, 14 Sep 1864.
Sayre, Benjamin F.; Wabash; mustered in 13 Feb 1865; mustered out 23 Oct 1865.
Swank, Peter; Urbana; mustered in 25 Mar 1864; mustered out 23 Oct 1865.
Wallace, Amos C.; N. Manchester; mustered in 2 Feb 1865; mustered out 23 Oct 1865.
Weigel, Henry; Wabash; mustered in 25 Mar 1864; mustered out 23 Oct 1865.
Welsh, Benjamin; N. Manchester; mustered in 13 Feb 1865; mustered out 23 Oct 1865.
Whitebread, Peter; Urbana; mustered in 25 Mar 1864; mustered out 23 Oct 1865.

Company C (*Original members mustered in 29 November 1861*)

Captain:

Dailey, Esaias; Decatur; commissioned 10 Oct 1861; resigned 5 Feb 1862.
Dent, Byron H.; Decatur; commissioned 20 Feb 1862; mustered in 3 Feb 1862; resigned 12 Apr 1862.
Crabbs, Austin; Decatur; commissioned and mustered in 1 May 1862; mustered out 31 Dec 1864; term expired.
Blossom, Ira A.; Decatur; commissioned 1 Mar 1865; mustered in 9 Apr 1865; mustered out with regiment 23 Oct 1865.

First Lieutenant:

Dent, Byron; Decatur; commissioned 10 Oct 1861; mustered in 29 Nov 1861; promoted Captain.
Crabbs, Austin; Decatur; commissioned 1 Apr 1862; mustered in 3 Feb 1862; promoted Captain.
Jennings, Horatio G.P.; Lafayette; commissioned 1 May 1862; mustered in 5 May 1862; mustered out 22 Dec 1864; term expired.
Blossom, Ira A.; Decatur; commissioned 1 Jan 1865; promoted Captain.
Weimer, John T.; Decatur; commissioned 1 Mar 1865; mustered in 9 Apr 1865; mustered out with regiment 23 Oct 1865.

Second Lieutenant:

Weimer, Henry C.; Decatur; commissioned 10 Oct 1861; mustered in 29 Nov 1861; died at Bardstown, KY, 18 Feb 1862.

Hart, Calvin D.; Decatur; commissioned 1 Apr 1862; mustered in 19 Feb 1862; resigned 18 Oct 1862.
Dailey, William A.; Decatur; commissioned and mustered in 19 Oct 1862; resigned 23 Oct 1864.
Lenhart, Jacob; Decatur; commissioned 1 Jul 1865; mustered out with regiment 23 Oct 1865 as Sergeant.

First Sergeant:
Hart, Calvin D.; Decatur; promoted 2nd Lieutenant.

Sergeants:
Crabs, Austin; Decatur; promoted 1st Lieutenant.
Dailey, William A.; Decatur; promoted 2nd Lieutenant.
Kern, John W.; Decatur; died at Riddle's Point, MO, 7 Apr 1863.
Weimer, John T.; Pleasant Mills; veteran; promoted 1st Lieutenant.

Corporals:
Watkins, Wilson G.; Pleasant Mills; died 13 Jun 1863.
Tindall, John C.; Pleasant Mills; discharged 6 Dec 1862, disability.
Teeple, John P.; Pleasant Mills; veteran; mustered out 23 Oct 1865.
Lenhart, Joseph; Decatur; veteran; mustered out 23 Oct 1865, as 1st Sergeant.
Helm, Joseph; Decatur; veteran; mustered out 23 Oct 1865, as 1st Sergeant.
Smith, Samuel; Decatur; died near Rocky Springs, MO, 8 May 1863.
Reichard, Henry H.; Wallshire; veteran; mustered out 23 Oct 1865.
Blossom, Ira A.; Decatur; veteran; promoted Captain.

Musicians:
Baxter, Isaac; Monmouth; killed at Champion Hill, MS, 16 May 1863.
Christian, Godfrey; Monmouth; discharged, 5 Jan 1864, by order.

Wagoner:
Michael, Eli.

Privates:
Alguire, Emanuel; Decatur; killed at Champion Hill, MS, 16 May 1863.
Anders, Dennison; Decatur; discharged 5 Jun 1862, disability.
Ault, John C.; Decatur; veteran; mustered out 26 Oct 1865.
Avery, Daniel; Decatur; veteran; mustered out 26 Oct 1865.[7]
Avery, John; Decatur; died in Louisiana, 5 Nov 1863.
Avery, Lorenzo D.; Decatur; veteran; mustered out 26 Oct 1865.
Baker, Marion; Decatur; veteran; mustered out 23 Oct 1865.
Ball, Frederick; Decatur; veteran; died at New Orleans, 21 May 1865.
Ball, Samuel; Decatur; veteran; mustered out 25 Oct 1865.
Balley, Mahlon; Decatur; veteran; mustered out 25 Oct 1865.
Barkley, Simon; Decatur; veteran; mustered out 25 Oct 1865, as Corporal.
Bates, Henry; Decatur; killed at Champion Hill, MS, 16 May 1863.
Beam, Johnson; Willshire; died 30 May 1863 of wounds received at Champion Hill, MS.
Billman, Jonathan; Pleasant Mills; veteran; mustered out 23 Oct 1865.
Blossom, John M.; Decatur; mustered out 12 Dec 1864.
Bonner, Samuel E.; Pleasant Mills; died at Milliken's Bend, 6 Jun 1862.
Brock, John; Decatur; mustered out 12 Dec 1864.
Brothers, Clark; Decatur; transferred to Invalid Corps, 26 Nov 1863.
Brothers, Edward W.; Decatur; mustered out 12 Dec 1864.
Brown, John M.; _____; mustered out 12 Dec 1864.
Brown, William; Decatur; veteran; mustered out 23 Oct 1865.
Carpenter, Josiah; Decatur; discharged.

Cronan, James; Fort Wayne; veteran; mustered out 23 Oct 1865.
Crosler, Samuel; Decatur; veteran; died 21 March 1865.
Davy, James; Pleasant Mills; veteran; mustered out 23 Oct 1865, as Sergeant.
Dean, John; Decatur; veteran; mustered out 23 Oct 1865.
Denman, John; Pleasant Mills; veteran; mustered out 23 Oct 1865.
Eley, Jacob; Pleasant Mills; veteran; mustered out 23 Oct 1865.
Everett, Joseph; Pleasant Mills; discharged 17 Sep 1862.
Everett, Phillip; Pleasant Mills; veteran; mustered out 23 Oct 1865.
Fordyce, Henry B.; Pleasant Mills; killed at Champion Hill, MS, 16 May 1863.
Fordyce, Jasper N.; Pleasant Mills; transferred to Invalid Corps 15 Feb 1864.
Ganze, Enoch W.; Pleasant Mills; veteran; mustered out 23 Oct 1865.
Ganze, Wilson; Pleasant Mills; veteran; mustered out 24 Aug 1865.
Gilson, James; Decatur; veteran; mustered out 23 Oct 1865.
Gilson, Menassah; Decatur; veteran; mustered out 23 Oct 1865.
Haynes, Isaac N.; New Corydon; veteran; died at Morganza Bend, LA, 23 Aug 1864.
Humes, George; Decatur; transferred to Invalid Corps 19 Aug 1863.
Johnston, James M.; Decatur; veteran; died at Memphis, 30 Nov 1864.
Jones, John; Decatur; veteran; mustered out 23 Oct 1865.
Jones, William I.; Pleasant Mills; veteran; died near Shreveport, LA, 28 Jul 1865.
Lahmon, Dayton; Decatur; discharged 13 Oct 1862.
Learman, John; _____; unaccounted for.
Long, John; Decatur; veteran; mustered out 23 Oct 1865.
Lord, Franklin; Monmouth; discharged 27 Dec 1862.
Lotzenhiser, John; Pleasant Mills; veteran; mustered out 23 Oct 1865.
Major, Milton; Willshire; veteran; mustered out 23 Oct 1865.
Martin, Harmon; Decatur; veteran; mustered out 23 Oct 1865, as Corporal.
Marvin, William; _____; veteran; lost on *Sultana* 27 April 1865.
McLeod, John; Pleasant Mills; veteran; mustered out 23 Oct 1865, as Sergeant.
Middleton, James; Decatur; veteran; mustered out 23 Oct 1865.
Middleton, John; Decatur; discharged 21 May 1865, disability.
Overly, James; Union City; veteran; mustered out 23 Oct 1865, as Sergeant.
Place, George; Pleasant Mills; mustered out 12 Dec 1864.
Porter, William; Pleasant Mills; discharged, 4 Dec 1863 due to leg wound received at Vicksburg.
Railing, Jacob; Decatur; mustered out 12 Dec 1864.
Railing, Martin; Decatur; killed by accident at Helena, AR, 22 Dec 1862.
Ray, John M.; Pleasant Mills; veteran; mustered out 23 Oct 1865, as Corporal.
Riker, Eli; Pleasant Mills; died at Vicksburg , MS, 1 Aug 1863.
Riker, Lafayette; Pleasant Mills; veteran; mustered out 23 Oct 1865.
Ritter, Tobias; Pleasant Mills; deserted 7 Dec 1862; returned; convicted of striking and threatening a superior with violence, conduct prejudicial to good order and military discipline, and desertion by General Court-Martial 1 Aug 1863; sentenced to confinement at hard labor at Fort Jefferson, FL, for remainder of his term of enlistment; released 23 May 1864; returned to duty with regiment.[9]
Roop, William; Pleasant Mills; veteran; mustered out 23 Oct 1865.
Ruby, William; Willshire; died at New Madrid, MO, 19 Mar 1862.
Sackett, Cyrus; Pleasant Mills; veteran; mustered out 23 Oct 1865.
Sackett, William; Pleasant Mills; killed at Champion Hill, MS, 16 May 1862.
Scoles, Andrew W.; Pleasant Mills; killed at Champion Hill, MS, 16 May 1862.
Shell, Levi; Pleasant Mills; veteran; mustered out 23 Oct 1865.
Shrank, Jacob; Pleasant Mills; killed at Champion Hill, MS, 16 May 1865.
Sipes, Peter W.; Decatur; discharged 2 Apr 1862, disability.
Smith, Isaac; Decatur; veteran; mustered out 23 Oct 1865.
Smith, John; Decatur A.; Decatur; discharged 16 Nov 1862, disability.
Smith, Josiah; Decatur; veteran; mustered out 23 Oct 1865.
Snader, Theodore; Decatur; veteran; mustered out 23 Oct 1865, as Sergeant.
Snyder, Samuel C.; Decatur; died at Helena, AR, __ Apr 1862.
Thatcher, John; Pleasant Mills; veteran; discharged 30 Dec 1864; wounds.[10]
Thompson, Robert H.; Decatur; killed while asleep at Vicksburg, MS, 13 Jun 1863.[11]

Troutner, George W.; Pleasant Mills; veteran; mustered out 23 Oct 1865.
Vance, Mark T.; New Corydon; appointed hospital steward; died at Louisville, KY, 24 Feb 1862.
Watkins, Seth W.; Pleasant Mills; died at Commerce, MO, 24 Feb 1862.
Weriner, Henry, Jr.; Pleasant Mills; veteran; mustered out 23 Oct 1865.
Woodward, James; Decatur; veteran; mustered out 23 Oct 1865, as Corporal.
Zediker, Joseph; Decatur; killed at Champion Hill, MS, 16 May 1863.

Recruits:

Ball, Jeremiah; Decatur; mustered in 14 Mar 1865; mustered out 23 Oct 1865.
Blossom, John M.; Decatur; mustered in 14 Mar 1865; mustered out 23 Oct 1865.
Blossom, Simon R.; Decatur; mustered in 23 Feb 1865; mustered out 23 Oct 1865.
Bottenburg, Jay P.; Decatur; mustered in 23 Feb 1865; mustered out 23 Oct 1865.
Bowers, Michael; Decatur; mustered in 18 Jan 1864; mustered out 23 Oct 1865.
Brothers, Oscar; Decatur; mustered in 18 Jan 1864; mustered out 23 Oct 1865.
Cline, George B.; Decatur; mustered in 23 Feb 1865; mustered out 23 Oct 1865.
Colgrill, Thomas J.; Wabash; mustered in 29 Dec 1861; mustered out 12 Dec 1864.
Crabbs, Jacob; Decatur; mustered in 11 Feb 1864; lost on steamboat *Sultana*, 27 Apr 1865.
Davy, Joshua; Decatur; mustered in 4 Dec 1864; mustered out 23 Oct 1865.
Everett, Barney; Pleasant Mills; mustered in 21 Mar 1864; mustered out 23 Oct 1865.
Fordyce, John; Pleasant Mills; mustered in 10 Dec 1862; discharged 17 Oct 1863.
Green, Stephen; _____; mustered in 15 Jan 1864; deserted 16 May 1865.[12]
Hull, George W.; Decatur; mustered in 11 Feb 1864; mustered out 23 Oct 1865.
Jacobs, Charles; _____; mustered in 31 Dec 1861; discharged 26 Aug 1863.
Jones, Zachariah; Decatur; mustered in 11 Feb 1864; mustered out 32 Oct 1865.
Patterson, James N.; Decatur; mustered in 23 Feb 1865; mustered out 23 Oct 1865.
Plocher, David; Decatur; mustered in 12 Mar 1864; mustered out 23 Oct 1865.
Plocher, Jacob; Decatur; mustered in 18 Jan 1864; mustered out 23 Oct 1865.
Purdy, Lewis; Wabash; mustered in 27 Dec 1861; mustered out 23 Oct 1865, as Com. Sergeant.
Teeple, Thomas H.; Decatur; mustered in 26 Mar 1864; mustered out 23 Oct 1865.
Trim, Henry; Decatur; mustered in 12 Mar 1864; mustered out 23 Oct 1865.
Weimer, Benjamin F.; St. Mary's; mustered in 12 Mary 1864; mustered out 23 Oct 1865.

Company D (*Original members mustered in 15 November 1861*)

Captain:

Bruner, James R.; Wabash; commissioned 10 Oct 1861; mustered in 15 Nov 1861; promoted Lt. Colonel of the 130th [Indiana] Regiment.
Siling, Tighlman J.; N. Manchester; commissioned and mustered in 1 Mar 1864; mustered out 31 Dec 1864; term expired.
Rager, Elias M.; N. Manchester; commissioned 1 Mar 1865; mustered in 9 Apr 1865; mustered out with regiment 23 Oct 1865.

First Lieutenant:

Siling, Tilghman J.; N. Manchester; commissioned 10 Oct 1861; mustered in 15 Nov 1861; promoted Captain.
Dain, Edward T.; Indianapolis; commissioned and mustered in 1 Mar 1864; mustered out 29 Dec 1864; term expired.
Rager, Elias M.; N. Manchester; commissioned 1 Jan 1865; promoted Captain.
McGinnis, John A.; Ashboro; commissioned 1 Mar 1865; mustered in 9 Apr 1865; mustered out with Regiment 23 Oct 1865.

Second Lieutenant:

Lines, Conrad H.; Ashland; mustered in 10 Oct 1861; mustered in 15 Nov 1861; resigned 23 Jan 1862.
Dain, Edward T.; Indianapolis; commissioned and mustered in 1 Apr 1862; promoted 1st Lieutenant; testified at the Oct 1863 court-martial of Jonathan Benefiel.
Daily, William F.; Laketon; commissioned 1 Mar 1864; mustered in 30 Mar 1864; mustered out 31 Dec 1864; term expired.
Hutchins, Theodore; Wabash; mustered in 1 July 1865; mustered out with regiment as 1st Sergeant 23 Oct 1865.

First Sergeant:

Daily, William H.; Laketon; promoted 2nd Lieutenant.

Sergeants:

McGinnis, John A.; Ashboro; promoted 1st Lieutenant.
Rager, Elias M.; N. Manchester; promoted 1st Lieutenant.
Fatzinger, Samuel; N. Manchester; mustered out 23 Oct 1865.
Lower, Benjamin F.; Wabash; veteran; mustered out 23 Oct 1865.

Corporals:

Liston, George A.; Wabash; discharged 18 Jun 1862.
Hutchins, Theodore; Wabash; veteran; mustered out 23 Oct 1865 as 1st Sergeant.
Church, Freeman S.; N. Manchester; promoted Captain of Co. B.
Miller, George I.; N. Manchester; mustered out 12 Dec 1864.
Hower, David; Niconza; veteran; mustered out 23 Oct 1865 as Sergeant.
Hamilton, Samuel; N. Manchester; mustered out 12 Dec 1864.
Chinworth, William; Niconza; discharged 9 Jul 1862.
Straw, John H.; Manchester; mustered out 12 Dec 1864.

Musicians:

Sheak, Charles; discharged Aug 1862.
Strausse, Daniel; Liberty Mills; mustered out 12 Dec 1864.

Wagoner:

Davis, Mark; Wabash; veteran; mustered out 23 Oct 1865 as Private.

Privates:

Abbott, Levi; Liberty Mills; veteran; mustered out 23 Oct 1865.
Abbott, Lewis; Liberty Mills; died at Tiptonville, TN, 19 Apr 1862.
Antrim, Caleb; N. Manchester; mustered out 12 Dec 1864.
Argerbright, Abraham; N. Manchester; died at Helena, AR, 1 Sep 1862.
Auhenbaugh, Jacob; died at Helena, AR, 14 Feb 1863.
Badger, David; Wabash; veteran; mustered out 23 Oct 1865.
Baker, James C.; Niconza; died at Nelson Furnace, 22 Mar 1862.
Baker, Michael; Liberty Mills; veteran; mustered out 23 Oct 1865.
Ball, Milton; Claypool; mustered out 12 Dec 1864.
Bloomer, Benjamin; Wabash; died at Helena, AR, 21 Dec 1862.
Brown, George; Niconza; died at home 28 Aug 1862.
Bumgardner, John H.; Liberty Mills; died at Helena, AR, 23 Nov 1862.
Burke, William A.; Liberty Mills; mustered out 12 Dec 1864.

Carper, William; N. Manchester; veteran; mustered out 23 Oct 1865.
Catlin, William; Wabash; died at St. Louis, MO, __ Sep 1862.
Chinworth, John S.; Niconza; veteran; mustered out 23 Oct 1865 as Corporal.
Conde, James E.; N. Manchester; died at Vicksburg, MS, 29 Jul 1865; mortally wounded at Jackson, MS, 10 or 11 July 1863.[13]
Dorrough, James; Liberty Mills; discharged 30 Dec 1862.
Dorrough, Joseph; Liberty Mills; died at Helena, AR, 23 Sep 1862.
Donaldson, Sanford; Wabash; veteran; mustered out 23 Oct 1865 as Corporal.
Dunbar, George H.; N. Manchester; died at Helena, AR, 16 Sep 1862.
Dunbar, Milton; N. Manchester; veteran; died at home 28 May 1865.
Ellis, James L; Liberty Mills; discharged 16 Jan 1863.
Fry, Christopher; Wabash; discharged 29 May 1862.
Fry, John; Wabash; veteran; mustered out 23 Oct 1865.
Hall, William, Liberty Mills; discharged 18 Jun 1862.
Hanley, Thomas; N. Manchester; mustered out 12 Dec 1864.
Hatfield, Samuel; Niconza; veteran; mustered out 23 Oct 1865.
Helvy, George W.; N. Manchester; died at New Orleans, LA, 21 Mar 1864.
Hidy, George; Liberty Mills; died on way home 5 Aug 1863.
Huffman, Martin; Liberty Mills; veteran; mustered out 23 Oct 1865.
Hullbarger, Lewis; Liberty Mills; died at home __ Sep 1863.
Iholtz, George; Liberty Mills; veteran; mustered out 23 Oct 1865 as Corporal.
Jenks, James N.; N. Manchester; veteran; mustered out 23 Oct 1865 as Corporal.
Jenks, Stephen W.; N. Manchester; discharged 29 May 1862.
Johnson, Jonathan; Niconza; veteran; mustered out 23 Oct 1865.
Kerby, Bartlett; Indianapolis; veteran; mustered out 23 Oct 1865.
Kline, Daniel; veteran; mustered out 23 Oct 1865.
Klink, David; Columbia City; discharged 6 Nov 1862.
Krisher, Zera; N. Manchester; veteran; mustered out 23 Oct 1865.
Latta, Silas; Niconza; died at Benton, MO, 6 Mar 1862.
Latta, William A.; Niconza; died at Helena, AR, 26 Feb 1863.
Martin, John L.; N. Manchester; discharged 1 Nov 1862.
McCleery, William; Bluffton; veteran; mustered out 23 Oct 1865 as Corporal.
Moore, John H.; N. Manchester; mustered out 12 Dec 1864.
Moore, William J.; Sommersett; died at Helena, AR, 2 Oct 1862.
Morrow, Nathan C.; Liberty Mills; veteran; mustered out 23 Oct 1865.
Morrow, Simon S.; Liberty Mills; veteran; mustered out 23 Oct 1865.
Moyer, Reuben; Niconza; veteran; mustered out 23 Oct 1865.
Myers, Daniel; Silver Lake; veteran; mustered out 23 Oct 1865.
Parker, Charles; N. Manchester; discharged 30 May 1862.
Pensinger, Jonathan; N. Manchester; veteran; mustered out 28 Oct 1865.
Peck, Martin V.; N. Manchester; mustered out 12 Dec 1864.
Peck, William N.; N. Manchester; mustered out 12 Dec 1864.
Ramey, Jeremiah; N. Manchester; veteran; mustered out 23 Oct 1865.
Reed, Ezekiel; Laketon; veteran, mustered out 23 Oct 1865.
Reed, James H.; Laketon; died at St. Louis, MO, 28 Oct 1862.
Ritter, Emanuel; N. Manchester; died at St. Louis, MO, 20 Oct 1862.
Rogers, John; Sommersett; veteran; mustered out 23 Oct 1865.
Sharp, William H.; N. Manchester; died at Indianapolis, IN, 3 Jan 1862.
Sharp, Wilson; Liberty Mills; veteran; mustered out 23 Oct 1865.
Shetzly, Henry; Wabash; veteran; mustered out 23 Oct 1865.
Shiltz, Franklin; N. Manchester; veteran; mustered out 23 Oct 1865.
Smith, Henry H.; N. Manchester; veteran; mustered out 23 Oct 1865 as Corporal.
Smith, Reuben S.; N. Manchester; died at Champion Hill, MS, 16 May 1863.
Stanley, Leander; Niconza; veteran; mustered out 23 Oct 1865.
Strickler, Abraham; N. Manchester; discharged 13 Dec 1862.
Tillman, David; N. Manchester; discharged 12 Dec 1864.
Tillman, Job E.; N. Manchester; mustered out 12 Dec 1864.
Tridle, Simon S.; Silver Lake; discharged 22 Dec 1862.

Tridle, William; Silver Lake; died at St. Louis, MO, 10 Aug 1863.
Upsall, John; Warsaw; mustered in 16 Oct 1862; died 7 Aug 1863.
Vanduyne, Jasper; Wabash; veteran; deserted 3 Aug 1865; dishonorably discharged 18 May 1867.
Vanduyne, John; Wabash; veteran; discharged 13 Aug 1862.
Waits, Charles; deserted 5 Dec 1861.
Walker, John; Niconza; killed at Port Gibson, MS, 1 May 1863.
Warner, John; Niconza; deserted 5 Dec 1861.
West, Amos L.; N. Manchester; veteran; mustered out 23 Oct 1865 as Sergeant.
Williams, Cyrus W.; N. Manchester; died at Tiptonville, TN, 11 May 1863.
Williams, John H.; Wabash; killed at Champion Hill, MS, 16 May 1863.
Winesburg, Hiram; N. Manchester; mustered out 12 Dec 1864.
Wood, William W.; Wabash; veteran; mustered out 23 Oct 1865 as Sergeant.
Young, Jesse; N. Manchester; veteran; mustered out 23 Oct 1865.
Zintsmaster, David; N. Manchester; mustered 12 Dec 1864.

Recruits:

Archer, James; N. Manchester; mustered in 19 Jan 1864; mustered out 23 Oct 1865.
Allen, Peter; Silver Lake; mustered in 28 Mar 1864; died at home 27 Jul 1864.
Baker, Aaron; Fort Wayne; mustered in 8 Mar 1865; mustered out 23 Oct 1865.
Baker, Josiah; Silver Lake; mustered in 28 Feb 1864; veteran; mustered out 23 Oct 1865.
Ballinger, John H.; N. Manchester; mustered in 20 Feb 1864; mustered out 23 Oct 1865.
Barnhart, Ezra; Warsaw; mustered in 10 Oct 1862; died at Memphis, TN, 2 Jul 1863.
Beetly, Rutherford; N. Manchester; mustered in 6 Feb 1865; mustered out 16 Aug 1865.
Breeding, Benjamin F.; Laketon; mustered in 19 Jan 1864; died at Shreveport, LA, 18 Aug 1865.
Breeding, Henry H.; Laketon; mustered in 19 Jan 1864; mustered out 25 May 1865.
Breeding, Menoah; Laketon; mustered in 20 Oct 1862; discharged 17 Jul 1863.
Breeding, William J.; Laketon; mustered in 1 Oct 1862; mustered out 23 Oct 1865.
Bright, Leroy; Niconza; mustered in 8 Mar 1864; died at Simmesport, LA, 18 May 1864.
Bryner, Benjamin B.; N. Manchester; mustered in 6 Dec 1862; died at Vicksburg, MS, 25 May 1863.
Burtram, William; _____; mustered in 8 Mar 1864; imprisoned by General Court-Martial; discharged Feb 1865 by order of War Dept.[14]
Bush, William; Wabash; mustered in 25 Mar 1864; imprisoned by General Court-Martial; discharged Feb 1865 by order of War Dept.[15]
Chaplin, Noah; N. Manchester; mustered in 21 Oct 1862; deserted 3 Aug 1865.
Clevenger, John A.; N. Manchester; mustered in 18 Mar 1864; mustered out 23 Oct 1865.
Dane, Edward F.; Indianapolis; mustered in 22 Sep 1861; promoted 2nd Lieutenant.
Dunbar, Peter; N. Manchester; mustered in 24 Mar 1864; mustered out 23 Oct 1865.
Elbum, William; Niconza; mustered in 8 Mar 1864; died at Memphis, TN, 13 Jan 1865.
Erb, Joseph; N. Manchester; mustered in 8 Mar 1864; mustered out 23 Oct 1865.
Green, Michael; Wabash; mustered in 25 Mar 1864; deserted 16 Jan 1864.
Hamilton, Chancey; N. Manchester; mustered in 25 Mar 1864; discharged 3 Dec 1864.
Harter, Stephen; Wabash; mustered in 25 Mar 1864; mustered out 23 Oct 1865.
Haskins, Thomas B.; Warsaw; mustered in 16 Oct 1862; died at Vicksburg, MS, 27 July 1863.
Hass, William; Germantown; mustered in 10 Oct 1864; mustered out 23 Oct 1865.
Heck, Thomas M.; N. Manchester; mustered in 25 Mar 1864; mustered out 23 Oct 1865.
Hower, William; Niconza; mustered in 25 Mar 1864; died at New Orleans, LA, 30 Jul 1864.
Howett, John; N. Manchester; mustered in 19 Jan 1864; mustered out 23 Oct 1865.
Howett, William; N. Manchester; mustered in 19 Jan 1864; died at St. Charles, AR, 14 Sep 1864.
Huffman, Jacob; Liberty Mills; mustered in 23 Oct 1862; died at Helena, AR, 7 Mar 1863.
Huffman, Simon; N. Manchester; mustered in 8 Mar 1864; died at home 8 Oct 1864.
Kuffel, Jonathan; Niconza; mustered in 26 Mar 1864; died at New Orleans, LA, 17 Jul 1864.
Long, Edward; N. Manchester; mustered in 19 Jan 1864; mustered out 23 Oct 1865.
Long, William; Warsaw; mustered in 16 Oct 1864; mustered out 16 Jul 1863 [sic] drafted.
Meek, James A.; Lodi; mustered in 20 Feb 1864; mustered out 23 Oct 1865.
Mills, William C.; N. Manchester; mustered in 4 Nov 1862; died at home 29 Apr 1863.
Moore, Jacob T.; N. Manchester; mustered in 7 Feb 1865; mustered out 23 Oct 1865.

Moore, Joseph; N. Manchester; mustered in 25 Mar 1864; mustered out 23 Oct 1865.
Myers, Ephraim; Wabash; mustered in 25 Mar 1864; mustered out 23 Oct 1865.
Oswalt, Jacob T.; Warsaw; mustered in 16 Oct 1862; mustered out 16 Jul 1863; drafted.
Peck, Martin V.B.; N. Manchester; mustered I 6 Feb 1865; mustered out 23 Oct 1865.
Rager, William; N. Manchester; mustered in 26 Mar 1864; mustered out 23 Oct 1865.
Ramsey, John P.; Wabash; 26 Mar 1864; died at New Orleans, LA, 25 Jul 1864.
Rockwell, Thomas; Warsaw; mustered in 16 Oct 1862; died 2 Aug 1863.
Rusman, Daniel W.; N. Manchester; mustered in 6 Feb 1865; mustered out 23 Oct 1865.
Sivihart, Eli; Warsaw; mustered in 16 Nov 1862; mustered out 16 Jul 1863; drafted.
Smith, Emanuel; Niconza; mustered in 8 Mar 1864; mustered out 23 Oct 1865.
Tillman, William E.; N. Manchester; musered in 20 Feb 1864; transferred to VRC 17 Jun 1864.
Tucker, Henry L.; Laketon; mustered in 8 Nov 1862; mustered out 23 Oct 1865.
Tyler, Jesse J.; N. Manchester; mustered in 6 Feb 1863; mustered out 23 Oct 1865.
Upsall, John; Warsaw; mustered in 16 Oct 1862; mustered out 16 Jul 1863; drafted,
Warren, Henry; Warsaw; mustered in 16 Oct 1862; mustered out 16 Ju. 1863; drafted.
Weidner, John; Akron; mustered in 8 Mar 1864; died at home 24 Mar 1864.
Young, John; N. Manchester; mustered in 8 Mar 1864; mustered out 23 Oct 1865.

Company E (*Original members mustered in 13 December 1861*)

Captain:

Wintrode, Jacob; Antioch; commissioned 10 Oct 1861; mustered in 13 Dec 1861; mustered out 15 Dec 1864; term expired.
Payton, Benjamin W.; Roanoke; commissioned 1 Mar 1865; mustered in 11 Apr 1865; mustered out with Regiment 23 Oct 1865.

First Lieutenant:

Swaidner, John; Roanoke; commissioned 10 Oct 1861; mustered in 13 Dec 1861; resigned 26 Jul 1863.
Bullard, Sherman L.; Fort Wayne; commissioned 27 Jul 1863; mustered in 12 Nov 1863; mustered out 30 Dec 1864; term expired.
Payton, Benjamin W.; Roanoke; commissioned 1 Jan 1865; promoted Captain.
Snodgrass, Sylvester W.; Antioch; commissioned 1 Mar 1865; mustered out with regiment 23 Oct 1865.

Second Lieutenant:

Snowden, Elijah; Antioch; commissioned 10 Oct 1861; mustered in 13 Dec 1861; resigned 17 Nov 1862.
Bullard, Sherman L.; Fort Wayne; commissioned 18 Nov 1862; mustered in 17 Nov 1862; promoted 1st Lieutenant.
Hart, Jacob W.; Roanoke; commissioned 27 Jul 1863; promoted 1st Lieutenant in 93rd Colored Regiment.
Payton, Benjamin W.; Roanoke; commissioned and mustered in 1 Mar 1864; promoted 1st Lieutenant.
Stirk, Samuel W.; Fort Wayne; commissioned 1 July 1865; mustered out as 1st Sergeant with regiment 23 Oct 1865.

First Sergeant:

McFarland, Martin; Dora; mustered out 7 Mar 1862; to date 6 Oct 1862.

Sergeants:

Ballard, Sherman L.; Fort Wayne; promoted 2nd Lieutenant.
Elkenbarg, John; Antioch; discharged 5 Jan 1864, disability.
Zent, Henry W.; Fort Wayne; promoted 1st Lieutenant Colored Infantry.
Churchill, Benjamin F.; Antioich; discharged 25 May 1862, disability.

Corporals:

Heath, Seneca; Roanoke; discharged 3 Jun 1862; disability.
Hackett, John; Roanoke; discharged 14 Sep 1862; disability.
Williams, John W.; Antioch; killed at Champion Hill, MS, 16 May 1863.
Adams, Henry; Antioch; transferred to VRC 1 May 1864.
Payton, Benjamin W.; Roanoke; promoted 2nd Lieutenant.
Snodgrass, Sylvester; Antioch; promoted 2nd Lieutenant.
Hart, Jacob W.; Roanoke; promoted 1st Lieutenant Colored Infantry.
Weaver, Wesley; Antioch; veteran; mustered out 23 Oct 1865.

Musicians:

Welker, Thomas; Roanoke; discharged 11 May 1862; disability.
Bash, John A.; Roanoke; veteran; mustered out 23 Oct 1865 as Corporal.

Wagoner:

Shively, Owen; Antioch; veteran; mustered out 23 Oct 1865.

Privates:

Adams, James H.; Antioch; veteran; mustered out 23 Oct 1865 as Sergeant.
Ammerman, Dudley C.; Antioch; discharged 14 Sep 1862; disability.
Andy, William S.; Antioch; killed at Champion Hill, MS, 16 May 1863.
Baker, Abraham; Antioch; killed at Champion Hill, MS, 16 May 1863.
Bambeck, John; Antioch; died at Mound City, IL, 29 Oct 1862.
Beauchamp, Henry; Antioch; discharged 29 Nov 1862l; disability.
Bennett, Isaac; Polk Town; died at Helena, AR, 27 Sep 1862.
Bowen, Alburtes A.; Roanoke; veteran; mustered out 23 Oct 1865 as Corporal.
Brown, Joseph M.; Roanoke; died in Stark Co., OH.
Carpenter, Dimon; Antioch; veteran; mustered out 23 Oct 1865.
Cutshall, Philip; Antioch; discharged 24 Fed 1863; disability.
Davis, Abraham; Roanoke; veteran; mustered out 23 Oct 1865 as Corporal.
Davis, George W.; Antioch; veteran; mustered out 23 Oct 1865 as Corporal.
Davis, James T.M.; Aboite; discharged 21 Aug 1863; disability.
Davis, Spencer W.; Antioch; veteran; mustered out 23 Oct 1865.
Dilly, Eli; Antioch; killed at Champion Hill, MS, 16 May 1863.
Dinius, Eli; Roanoke; killed at Jackson, MS, 12 Jul 1863.[16]
Dinius, Sylvester; Roanoke; veteran; mustered out 23 Oct 1865.
Ellis, Solomon J.; Antioch; veteran; mustered out 23 Oct 1865.
Ellis, Theodore; Antioch; died 2 Aug 1863 of wounds received at Jackson, MS.
Evans, Joseph; Aboite; veteran; mustered out 23 Oct 1865.
Eviston, James; Antioch; discharged 25 Jun 1862; disability.
Eyestone, George; Antioch; discharged 30 Sep 1862; disability.
Fallor, Charles C.; Roanoke; died at Evansville, IN, 24 Jul 1863.
Foosher, Gabriel; Antioch; mustered out 1 Aug 1865.
Gaskill, George W.; Roanoke; mustered out 13 Dec 1864.
Goings, Francis; Roanoke; veteran; mustered out 23 Oct 1865 as Corporal.
Grim; Eli P.; Roanoke; discharged 14 Sep 1862; disability.

Hackett, William; Roanoke; killed at Champion Hill, MS, 16 May 1863.
Harter, Josephus; ____; discharged 18 Jun 1862; disability.
Hatfield, Daniel; Aboite; discharged 15 Sep 1862; disability.
Hier, Robert; Antioch; veteran; deserted 10 Mar 1863; mustered out 23 Oct 1865.
Hobble, George W.; Antioch; veteran; mustered out 23 Oct 1865.
Hollingsworth, Ellis J.; Antioch; veteran; mustered out 23 Oct 1865 as Hospital Steward.
Hull, Jacob; Antioch; veteran; mustered out 23 Oct 1865.
Huston, William R.; Antioch; veteran; mustered out 23 Oct 1865.
Hyatt, Anson J.; Antioch; veteran; mustered out 23 Oct 1865.
Iray, Joseph; Antioch; veteran; mustered out 23 Oct 1865.
James, Martin; Antioch; unaccounted for.
Jeffrey, Reuben O.; Antioch; discharged 20 Apr 1862; disability.
Jennings, Mark W.; Antioch; veteran; mustered out 23 Oct 1865.
Johnson, Cyrus; Antioch; mustered out 13 Dec 1864.
Jones, Robert; Antioch; veteran; mustered out 23 Oct 1865.
Kenaga, Matthias; Roanoke; discharged 11 May 1862; disability.
King, Samuel; Antioch; veteran; mustered out 23 Oct 1865.
Krider, George W.; Roanoke; discharged 11 May 1862; disability.
Lee, Squire C.; Roanoke; veteran; mustered out 23 Oct 1865. [17]
Lockwood, Samuel N.; Fort Wayne; died at Tiptonville, TN, 5 May 1862.
Munford, David; Antioch; transferred to VRC 1 May 1864.
Nivison, George; Antioch; died 28 Jun 1863 from wounds at Champion Hill, MS.
Parrot, Amos; Wabash; died at Helena, AR, 24 Sep 1864.
Parrott, Elias; Wabash; died at Louisville, KY, 22 Feb 1862.
Poinsett, Joseph; Fort Wayne; died at Milliken's Bend 3 Jun 1863.
Reefy, Solomon; Roanoke; deserted 15 Oct 1862.
Reemer, Solomon; Roanoke; veteran; mustered out 23 Oct 1865.
Richards, Hiram; ____; veteran; mustered out 23 Oct 1865 as Sergeant.
Rine, John; Fort Wayne; veteran; mustered out 23 Oct 1865.
Rose, Franklin; Roanoke; veteran; mustered out 23 Oct 1865.
Schammahorn, Isaac; Antioch; veteran; mustered out 23 Oct 1865.
Schroyer, William H.; Antioch; discharged 18 Dec 1862; disability.
Shulse, John; Antioch; died at Milliken's Bend, LA.
Shirley, Joseph; Antioch; mustered out 13 Dec 1864.
Slyter, Thomas; Antioch; died 25 May 1863 from wounds received at Champion Hill, MS.
Snyder, David; Roanoke; veteran; mustered out 23 Oct 1865.
Stevens, Milton J.; Antioch; veteran; mustered out 23 Oct 1865.
Stirk, Samuel W.; Fort Wayne; veteran; mustered out 23 Oct 1865 as 1st Sergeant.
Stirk, Wilmer J.; Fort Wayne; died at Keokuk, IA, 21 Oct 1862.
Sutton, Amos; Antioch; mustered out 10 Feb 1865.
Thomas, Henry; Antioch; veteran; mustered out 23 Oct 1865 as Sergeant.
Tibbals, Edwin; Dora; discharged 11 May 1862; disability.
Troubey, Abraham; Antioch; veteran; mustered out 23 Oct 1865.
Wade, Thomas; Roanoke; veteran; died at Memphis 10 Mar 1865.
Warmuth, Augustus; Roanoke; veteran; mustered out 23 Oct 1865 as Corporal.
Watson, James; Antioch; veteran; mustered out 23 Oct 1865 as Corporal.
Williams, Jersey; Indianapolis; discharged 23 Dec 1862; disability.
Yantis, John; Antioch; veteran; mustered out 23 Oct 1865.
Yeangher, Joab; Antioch; killed at Champion Hill 16 May 1863.
Yost, John; Antioch; discharged 13 Feb 1862; disability.
Zent, Jacob W.; Roanoke; mustered out 13 Dec 1864.
Zent, Thomas W.; Roanoke; veteran; died at Chicago, IL, 3 Mar 1865.

Recruits:

Ager, William M.; Roanoke; mustered in 7 Mar 1864; died at St. Louis, MO, 10 Oct 1864.
Bachtel, Aaron; Roanoke; mustered in 9 Jan 1864; mustered out 23 Oct 1865.
Barger, Elias; Roanoke; mustered in 9 Jan 1864; mustered out 23 Oct 1865.

Beachamp, Henry; Antioch; mustered in 7 Mar 1864; mustered out 23 Oct 1865.
Bennett, Simon P.; Antioch; mustered in 22 Oct 1862; mustered out 23 Oct 1865.
Bishop, Martin; Roanoke; mustered in 9 Jan 1864; mustered out 23 Oct 1865.
Bowman, William H.; Coessa; mustered in 21 Mar 1864; died at Fort Wayne, IN, 27 Oct 1864.
Bremer, John B.; Antioch; mustered in 26 Mar 1864; died at Morganza Bend, LA, 9 Jun 1864.
Buffington, John; Jordon; mustered in 22 Oct 1862; deserted 23 Jan 1863.
Burnside, James S; Roanoke; mustered 9 Jan 1864; mustered out 23 Oct 1865.
Click, Henry; Antioch; mustered in 26 Mar 1864; died at New Orleans, LA, 22 Apr 1864.
Davis, Richard B.; Antioch; mustered out 23 Oct 1865.
Depew, Isaac L.; Roanoke, mustered in 9 Jan 1864; died at New Orleans, LA, 22 Apr 1864.
Ervin, William; Antioch; mustered in 29 Mar 1864; mustered out 23 Oct 1865.
Fisher, John P.; Antioch; mustered in 7 Mar 1864; mustered out 8 May 1865.
Fisher, Milton W.; Antioch; mustered in 7 May 1864; mustered out 5 Aug 1865.
Fitzgerald, David A.; Indianapolis; mustered 9 Jan 1864; died 7 Jan 1865; Hospital Steward.
Galbreath, William; Antioch; mustered in 16 Oct 1862; mustered out 16 Jul 1863.
Gettys, John; Roanoke; mustered in 7 Mar1864; mustered out 23 Oct 1865.
Guise, William; Roanoke; mustered in 7 Mar 1864; mustered out 23 Oct 1865.
Harris, David D.; Antioch; mustered in 26 Mar 1864; died at Mound City, IL, 17 Sep 1864.
Henderson, Alvy W.; Huntington; mustered in 22 Oct 1862; died at Helena, AR, 23 Jan 1863.
Hoffmire, Joseph, Roanoke; mustered in 9 Jan 1864; mustered out 23 Oct 1865.
Johns, Jacob W.; Roanoke; mustered in 21 Mar 1864; mustered out 23 Oct 1865.
Kesselring, Joseph; Antioch; mustered in 25 Jun 1865; mustered out 23 Oct 1865.
Lockwood, Henry; Antioch; mustered in 26 Mar 1864; died at Kokomo, IN, 4 Oct 1864.
Long, Edward; Antioch; mustered in 7 Mar 1864; mustered out 23 Oct 1865.
Moon, John M.; Roanoke; mustered in 9 Jan 1864; died at New Orleans, LA, 18 Jun 1864.
Mortz, Daniel; Roanoke; mustered in 7 Mar 1864; died at Indianapolis, IN, 24 Jul 1864.
Mote, Abraham; Antioch; 26 Mar 1864; mustered out 23 Oct 1865.
Mote, William; Antioch; mustered in 7 Mar 1864; mustered out 23 Oct 1865.
Nichols, Andrew; Roanoke; mustered in 9 Jan 1864; died at New Orleans, LA, 18 Jun 1864.
Osborn, Arthur T.; Antioch; mustered in 10 Mar 1864; mustered out by War Dept. 29 Apr 1865.
Pattenger, Lewis; Pierceton; mustered in 22 Oct 1862; died 29 May 1864 of wounds received at Champion Hill, MS.
Patton, Michael; Collamer; mustered in 22 Oct 1862; mustered out 23 Oct 1865.
Schichter, William H.; Roanoke; mustered in 7 Mar 1864; mustered out 23 Oct 1865.
Steel, Charles; Antioch; mustered in 7 Mar 1864; died at New Orleans, LA, 13 April 1864.
Stuts, Christian; Antioch; mustered in 26 May 1864; mustered out 23 Oct 1865.
Taylor, Lorenzo D.; Mt. Etna; mustered in 22 Oct 1862; died at New Orleans, LA, 22 Aug 1863.
Thurber, Isaac C.; Mt. Etna; mustered in 22 Oct 1862; deserted 23 Jan 1863.
Truax, William T.; Roanoke; mustered in 7 Mar 1864; died at St. Louis, MO, 17 Jul 1864.
Vriers, James R.; Antioch; mustered in 7 Mar 1864; mustered out 23 Oct 1865.
Williams, William T.; Antioch; mustered in 7 Mar 1864; mustered out 23 Oct 1865.
Wise, John D.; Roanoke; mustered in 26 Mar 1864; died at Morganza Bend, LA, 3 Aug 1864.
Yahn, Emanuel; Roanoke; mustered in 9 Jan 1864; mustered out 23 Oct 1865.
Yantis, Thendas; Antioch; mustered in 9 Jan 1864; mustered out 23 Oct 1865.

Company F (*Original members mustered in 3 December 1861; all residents of Huntington County*)

Captain:

Shearer, Sextus H.; commissioned 10 Oct 1861; mustered in 3 Dec 1861; promoted Major.
Slusser, Jefferson F.; commissioned 1 Feb 1865; mustered in 9 Apr 1865; mustered out with regiment 23 Oct 1865.

First Lieutenant:

Hall, Silas S.; commissioned 10 Oct 1861; mustered in 3 Dec 1861; resigned 17 May 1862.
Purviance, Aurelius S.; commissioned 18 May 1862; mustered in 28 Dec 1862; resigned 6 Feb 1863; re-entered service as 1st Lt. in 130th [Indiana] Regiment.
Johnston, James A.; commissioned 7 Feb 1863; mustered in 9 Feb 1863; died 14 Feb 1864.
Beaver, Daniel G.; commissioned 1 Mar 1864; mustered in 30 Mar 1864; mustered out 30 Dec 1864; term expired.
Slusser, Jefferson F.; commissioned 9 Jan 1865; mustered in 10 Mar 1865; promoted Captain.
Whitestine, John; commissioned 1 Feb 1865; mustered in 9 Apr 1865; mustered out with regiment 23 Oct 1865.

Second Lieutenant:

Purviance, Aurelius S.; commissioned 10 Oct 1861; mustered in 3 Dec 1861; promoted 1st Lieutenant.
Johnston, James A.; commissioned 18 May 1862; mustered in 28 Dec 1862; promoted 1st Lieutenant.
Beaver, Daniel G.; commissioned 7 Feb 1863; mustered in 9 Feb 1863; promoted 1st Lieutenant.
Slusser, Jefferson F.; commissioned 1 Mar 1864; promoted 1st Lieutenant.
DeChant, Jeremiah; commissioned 18 Feb 1865; not mustered.
Whitestine, Asa; commissioned 1 Jul 1865; mustered out as Sergeant with Regiment.

First Sergeant:

Johnston, James A.; promoted 2nd Lieutenant.

Sergeants:

Caverly, Phillip D.; died at Helena, AR, 13 Sep 1862.
Holloway, Ceppas M.; discharged 8 May 1862.
Beaver, Daniel G.; promoted 2nd Lieutenant.
Anspach, John P.; mustered out 12 Dec 1864.

Corporals:

Oates, Jacob
Slusser, Jefferson F.; promoted 2nd Lieutenant.
Whitestine, John; promoted 1st Lieutenant.
Davies, Joseph.
Purviance, James; promoted 2nd Lieutenant 130th [Indiana] Regiment.
Galster, Matthias; died at Evansville, IN, 1 Jul 1862.
Smithers, Henry; discharged 12 Jul 1862.
Amaden, Edwin C.; mustered out 12 Dec 1864.

Musicians:

Nellis, Franklin J.; mustered out 12 Dec 1864.
Crabill, Charles; discharged 7 Apr 1862.

Wagoner:

Holder, Daniel; veteran; mustered out 23 Oct 1865.

Privates:

Ager, Daniel; veteran; mustered out 23 Oct 1865 as Corporal.
Allerton, John; died at Evansville, IN, 6 Apr 1862.

Roster of the 47th Indiana Volunteer Infantry 341

Allison, William; discharged 12 Jul 1862.
Andrew, Jefferson; died 2 Oct 1862.
Anglemyre, Jacob; died at Louisville, KY, 11 Mar 1862.
Anglemyre, John; discharged 12 Aug 1862.
Anglemyre, Samuel; veteran; mustered out 23 Oct 1865 as Corporal.
Bateman, Newton; killed at Tallahatchie River, MS, 29 Mar 1863.
Beel, James.
Brandt, Charles; veteran; mustered out 23 Oct 1865 as Corporal.
Brown, Cyrus; killed at Tallahatchie River, MS, 29 Mar 1863.
Carl, John S.; died 21 Feb 1862
Clark, William; died 2 Mar 1862.
Cruca, Enoch; veteran; mustered out 23 Oct 1865.
Cruea, James; veteran; mustered out 23 Oct 1865.
Cruea, William; discharged 13 Nov 1862; accidental wounds.
Culp, John C.; veteran; mustered out 23 Oct 1865.
Darrow, Raphael; mustered out 12 Dec 1864.
Davis, Joseph; killed at Champion Hill, MS, 16 May 1863.
Denning, Humphrey; deserted at Helena, AR, 1 May 1863.
Dougherty, Lemuel; veteran; mustered out 23 Oct 1865.
Duman, Joel; died at Helena, AR, 13 Feb 1863.
Eberding, Philip; veteran; mustered out 15 Jun 1865.
Felzaph, John; veteran; mustered out 23 Oct 1865 as Sergeant.
Fetters, Richard D.; veteran; mustered out 12 Dec 1864.
Farmer, Martin; died 12 Sep 1863; disease.
Frame, John O.; veteran; mustered out 23 Oct 1865 as Sergeant.
Fullhart, Nicholas; died 4 Sep 1862; disease.
Fullhart, Samuel; veteran; died at Baton Rouge 16 Oct 1865.
Garwood, Marcus L.; died 14 Dec 1862.
Griffith, Andrew; veteran; deserted 25 Mar 1864.
Guffin, Walter L.; died at Camp Wickliffe, KY, 15 Jan 1862.
Guminaker, Joseph; veteran; died at Jefferson Barracks, MO, 15 Jul 1865.
Gundy, George W.; mustered out 12 Dec 1864.
Hawkinsmith, Hiram; mustered out 12 Dec 1864.
Hawley, David M.; discharged 16 Oct 1862.
Heckel, David; died 2 Sep 1862; disease.
Hoke, Henry F.; veteran; mustered out 23 Oct 1865 as Corporal.
Hughes, Cyrus; mustered out 12 Dec 1864.
Hummel, John; died 27 Oct 1862.
Hey, Jerome; died 16 Sep 1862; disease.
Hey, Michael; mustered out 12 Dec 1864.
Hill, Benjamin B.; discharged 23 Apr 1863.
Hindall, Samuel; veteran; mustered out 23 Oct 1865 as Sergeant.
Hunt, Samuel; died at New Orleans, LA, 4 Jan 1864; disease.
Hunter, William J.; veteran; mustered out 23 Oct 1865 as Sergeant.
Jones, Josiah M.; mustered out 12 Dec 1864.
King, Emanuel; mustered out 12 Dec 1864.
Koontz, Peter; discharged 5 Aug 1862; disability.
Koontz, Solomon; mustered out 12 Dec 1864.
Kuhlman, Nathan; veteran; mustered out 23 Oct 1865.
Large, Jeremiah; discharged 31 Jan 1863.
Mahon, Alderman D; veteran; mustered out 23 Oct 1865.
Michael, Jacob; killed at Champion Hill, MS, 16 May 1863.
Millner, Eli; transferred to Co. H.
Minehart, Andrew; died at St. Louis, MO, 19 Nov 1862.
Oats, Jacob; discharged 28 May 1862.
Oats, William H.; veteran; mustered out 23 Oct 1865.
Payne, Lewis; died at New Madrid, MO, __ 1862.
Potter, David R.; veteran, mustered out 23 Oct 1865 as Corporal.

Ream, John M.; transferred to Co. H.
Reed, James M.; discharged 26 Mar 1862.
Roaster, William; killed at Tallahatchie River, MS, 29 Mar 1863.
Rose, Eli E.; veteran; mustered out 26 July 1865.[18]
Schnider, Christian; died at Camp Wickliffe, KY, 4 Feb 1862.
Slucker, William J.; veteran; mustered out 23 Oct 1865.
Smith, Daniel; died at St. Louis, MO, 31 Mar 1862.
Stephen, Andrew; veteran; mustered out 23 Oct 1865.
Stephen, Conrad; veteran; mustered out 23 Oct 1865.
Storm, Francis A.; died at Helena, AR, 20 Apr 1863.
Tramell, William H.; transferred to Co. H.
Trovinger, Hiram; killed at Tallahatchie River, MS, 29 Mar 1863.
Tyson, Robert; promoted 2nd Lieutenant of the 92nd U.S. Colored Troops.
Wade, Edwin A.; deserted at Helena, AR, 1 Mar 1863.
Warner, Charles A.; discharged 27 Dec 1862.
Whitacre, George W.; transferred to VRC.
Whitestine, Asa; veteran; mustered out 23 Oct 1865 as 1st Sergeant.
Wiles, Nixon A.; veteran; mustered out 23 Oct 1865 as 1st Sergeant.
Wise, William M.; veteran; mustered out 23 Oct 1865 as Sergeant.
Wohlford, Benjamin F.; died at Helena, Ar, 4 Oct 1862.
Wohlford, Jacob; discharged 17 Apr 1863.
Wohlford, Thomas A.; veteran; mustered out 23 Oct 1865 as Corporal.
Wood, Ozias; died at Helena, AR, 30 Sep 1862.

Recruits:

Ayers, Edwin B.; mustered in 24 Jan 1865; mustered out 23 Oct 1865.
Corrig, James; mustered 31 Jan 1864; mustered out 23 Oct 1865.
Corrig, Patrick; mustered in 24 Jan 1865; mustered out 23 Oct 1865.
Croft, Amzi D.; mustered in 24 Jan 1865; mustered out 23 Oct 1865.
Dechard, Jeremiah; mustered in 24 Jan 1865; mustered out 23 Oct 1865.
Dillon, George W.; mustered in 27 Jan 1865; died 28 Mar 1865 of wounds.
Dougherty, James L.; mustered in 24 Jan 1865; mustered out __ Aug 1865.
Elder, Levit B.; mustered in 25 Jan 1865; mustered out 23 Oct 1865.
Eltzer, Eli; mustered in 18 Aug 1862; mustered out 28 Jul 1865.
Eltzroth, George; mustered in 15 Aug 1862; mustered out 28 Jul 1865.
Freel, William; mustered in 15 Aug 1862; mustered out 28 Jul 1865.
Gawn, George W.; mustered in 26 Jan 1865; mustered out 23 Oct 1865.
Gaynor, Michael W.; mustered in 24 Jan 1865; mustered out 23 Oct 1865.
Hannah, William; mustered in 2 Apr 1864; mustered out 8 Sep 1865.
Hausman, Zachariah; mustered in 26 Jan 1865; mustered out 23 Oct 1865.
Helm, Benjamin F.; mustered in 15 Aug 1862; mustered out 12 Sep 1865.
King, Wesley; mustered in 24 Jan 1864; deserted 28 Jul 1865.
Koontz, Solomon; mustered in 24 Jan 1865; mustered out 23 Oct 1865.
McGuire, Thomas; mustered in 7 Mar 1864; mustered out 23 Oct 1865.
Milton, David A.; mustered in 15 Aug 1862; mustered out 28 Jul 1865.
Milton, John W.; mustered in24 Jan 1865; mustered out 23 Oct 1865.
Pierson, Issacher; mustered in 21 Mar 1864; mustered out 12 May 1865.
Pipenbrink, Ernest; mustered in 28 Jan 1865; mustered out 23 Oct 1865.
Purviance, Francis M.; mustered in 25 Jan 1865; mustered out 23 Oct 1865.
Reaser, George W.; mustered in 26 Mar 1864; killed at Spanish Fort, AL, 27 Mar 1865.
Richmond, Edward F.; mustered in 24 Jan 1865; mustered out 23 Oct 1865.
Ricker, David H.; mustered in 24 Jan 1865; mustered out 23 Oct 1865.
Schoolcraft, Rufus; mustered in 15 Aug 1862; mustered out 28 Jul 1865.
Searls, Jonah H.; mustered in 26 Mar 1864; mustered out 23 Oct 1865.
Shaffer, Daniel F.; mustered in 15 Aug 1862; mustered out 28 Jul 1865.
Shroyer, Benjamin; mustered in 24 Jan 1865; mustered out 23 Oct 1865.

Shueman, George W.; mustered in 20 Mar 1864; deserted 1 Feb 1865.
Sibert, Frederick A.; mustered in 7 Mar 1864; mustered out 23 Oct 1865.
Sibert, John E.; mustered in 20 Mar 1864; mustered out 23 Oct 1865.
Slusser, Andrew N.; mustered in 7 Mar 1864; mustered out 23 Oct 1865.
Springle, Benjamin F.; mustered in 26 Mar 1864; mustered out 23 Oct 1865.
Underwood, William; mustered in 30 Mar 1864; deserted 28 Jul 1865.
Williams, James; mustered in 30 Jan 1865; mustered out 23 Oct 1865.

Company G (*Original members mustered in 9 December 1861*)

Captain:

Robinson, John T.; Anderson; commissioned 10 Oct 1861; mustered in 9 Dec 1861; resigned 2 Feb 1863.
Eglin, John F.; Anderson; commissioned 3 Feb 1863; mustered in 2 Feb 1863; resigned 31 Jul 1863.
Myers, William R.; Anderson; commissioned 1 Aug 1863; mustered in 15 Nov 1863; mustered out 31 Dec 1864; term expired.
Vinyard, Henry M.; Anderson; commissioned 1 Mar 1865; mustered out as 1st Lieutenant with regiment 23 Oct 1865.

First Lieutenant:

Eglin; John F.; Anderson; commissioned 10 Oct 1861; mustered in 9 Dec 1861; promoted Captain.
Myers, William R.; Anderson; commissioned 3 Feb 1863; mustered in 1 Mar 1863; promoted Captain; testified at the Oct 1863 court-martial of Jonathan Benefiel.
Vinyard, Henry M.; Anderson; commissioned 1 Mar 1864; mustered in 30 Mar 1865; promoted Captain.
Bird, Willet E.; Miami; commissioned 1 Mar 1865; mustered out as Sergeant with regiment 23 Oct 1865.

Second Lieutenant:

Woodbeck, William; Huntington; commissioned 10 Oct 1861; mustered in 9 Dec 1861; resigned 24 Jun 1862.
Myers, William R.; Anderson; commissioned 25 Jun 1862; mustered in 24 Jan 1862; promoted 1st Lieutenant.
Harding, Robert N.; Indianapolis; commissioned 3 Feb 1863; mustered in 2 Feb 1863; promoted Captain of Co. K.
Auspach, John; Huntington; commissioned 30 Jul 1863; not mustered.
Wyman, John; Anderson; commissioned 1 Jul 1865; mustered out as 1st Sergeant with regiment 23 Oct 1865.

First Sergeant:

Myers, William R.; Anderson; promoted 2nd Lieutenant.

Sergeants:

Harding, Robert N.; Indianapolis; promoted 2nd Lieutenant.
Bryant, McClue H.; Anderson; died at Indianapolis 16 May 1862.
Vinyard, Henry; Anderson; promoted 1st Lieutenant.
McMullen, Joseph C.; Anderson; discharged 22 Apr 1862.

Corporals:

Waymire, Jacob E.; killed at Riddle's Landing, MO, 22 Mar 1862.
Snelson, Matthias; Anderson; veteran; mustered out 22 Oct 1862.
Sines, Martin; deserted 4 Jul 1862.

Clem, David E.; died at Alexandria, LA, 12 May 1864.[19]
Davis, Docter B.; Anderson; veteran; mustered out 23 Oct 1865 as Sergeant; testified as 2nd Sgt. in the Oct 1863 court-martial of Jonathan Benefiel.
Caster, John M.; Anderson; veteran; mustered out 23 Oct 1865 as Sergeant.
Ingram, Samuel; Huntington; discharged 3 Sep 1863.
Rent, Frederick; Anderson; veteran; mustered out 23 Oct 1865.

Musicians:

Hankey, John M.; Anderson; Principal Musician; deserted 25 Jul 1865; testified at the Oct 1863 court-martial of Jonathan Benefiel.
Jackson, Harrison; Anderson; discharged __ Jun 1862.

Wagoner:

Wyman, John; Anderson; veteran; mustered out 23 Oct 1865 as Sergeant.

Privates:

Anderson, Samuel; Fort Wayne; veteran; mustered out 23 Oct 1865.
Ashby, Daniel; Anderson; discharged 2 Dec 1863.
Ballard, Warren T.; Knightstown; transferred to Non-Commissioned Staff 1 Sep 1862; promoted Regimental Quartermaster.
Beard, William S.; Anderson; discharged 25 Jun 1862.
Benefiel, Johnson [Jonathan]; Anderson; veteran; deserted 15 Feb 1862; apprehended; convicted of desertion and breach of arrest by General Court-Martial, 8 Oct 1863; confined at hard labor for the term of his enlistment, forfeiture of pay, and dishonorable discharge; died 23 Oct 1863 at Ship Island, MS.[20]
Berryman, Hugh; Anderson; veteran; mustered out 23 Oct 1865.
Bird, Willett E.; Miami; veteran; mustered out 23 Oct 1865.
Bodkins, William W.; Anderson; transferred to VRC.
Brown, William; Anderson; veteran; deserted 3 Jan 1865.
Cannon, Moses; Anderson; veteran; deserted 28 Jun 1865.
Cannon, Thomas; Anderson; mustered out 23 Oct 1865 as Corporal.
Carroll, William; Anderson; discharged 20 Nov 1863.
Childers, Franklin; Anderson; deserted 12 Dec 1861.
Church, John; Huntington; deserted 4 Jul 1862.
Clark, Nathan; Anderson; deserted 13 Dec 1861.
Clary, Sylvester; Anderson; transferred to VRC.
Cloud, Andrew; Anderson; died at Bardstown 1 Jan 1862.
Cook, Abraham; Anderson; died at Indianapolis 24 Nov 1861.
Cornelius, John P.; Anderson; discharged 8 Oct 1862.
Costello, Peter; mustered out 23 Oct 1865 as Corporal.
Crum, Abraham; Huntington; killed at Champion Hill, MS, 16 May 1863.
Davis, Marion; Anderson; discharged 27 Jan 1863.
Davis, Meredith; Anderson; deserted 31 Aug 1862.
Davis, Nathaniel; Anderson; veteran; mustered out 23 Oct 1865.
Dougherty, Henry; Anderson; deserted 14 Dec 1861.
Douglass, George; Huntington; killed at Champion Hill, MS, 16 May 1863.
Ellis, Bartholomew; Anderson; discharged 1 Jul 1862.
Ferris, Edmond; Anderson; transferred to VRC.
Foltz, Joseph; fort Wayne; veteran; mustered out 23 Oct 1865.
Hammer, Jacob; veteran; mustered out 23 Oct 1865.
Hardcastle, William; Anderson; transferred to VRC.
Harless, Jacob; Anderson; deserted 31 Aug 1862.
Hatfill, Archibald A.; Anderson; deserted 12 Dec 1861.
Hensley, Joseph; Anderson; veteran; mustered out 23 Oct 1865.

Hinkle, Henry; Anderson; veteran; mustered out 23 Oct 1865.
Hodgson, Reuben; Anderson; discharged 19 Oct 1862.
Holloway, Isaac; Anderson; discharged 22 Apr 1862.
Hour, Dorsey M.; Anderson; killed at Champion Hill, MS, 16 May 1863.
Ingram, William; Anderson; discharged 9 Oct 1863.
Jackson, Isam; Marion; died at New Haven, KY, 24 Feb 1862.
Jarrett, Owen; Anderson; veteran; mustered out 23 Oct 1865.
Jay, Albert; veteran; mustered out 23 Oct 1865.
Jones, John A.; Marion; deserted 4 Jul 1862.
Keller, John; Anderson; mustered out 9 Nov 1866.
Lee, John H.; Anderson; veteran; mustered out 23 Oct 1865; testified as 3rd Sergeant, Co. G at the Oct 1863 court-martial of Jonathan Benefiel.
Lust, Hugh C.; Anderson; veteran; mustered out 23 Oct 1865 as Corporal.
Mabbitt, James B.; Anderson; deserted 14 Feb 1862.
Maynard, WilliamA.; Anderson; deserted 13 Jul 1862.
Miller, John; Anderson; killed at Champion Hill, 16 May 1863.
Moore, William B.; Marion; veteran; mustered out 23 Oct 1865 as Corporal.
Morse, Justes; Anderson; transferred to VRC.
Odam, Michael; Anderson; deserted 4 Sep 1863.
Phillips, Joseph; Andersons; died at Tiptonville, TN, 24 May 1862.
Phillips, William H.H.; Anderson; died 20 Aug 1863.
Pope, William A.; Huntington; veteran; mustered out 23 Oct 1865.
Prillman, John; Anderson; deserted 13 Aug 1863.
Ralph, Wilson; Anderson; drowned 23 Aug 1862.
Randolf, Henry; Byhalia; veteran; mustered out 23 Oct 1865 as Sergeant.
Reed, Athaniel Jr.; Greensburg; veteran; mustered out 23 Oct 1865.
Reed, Athaniel Sr.; Greensburg; discharged 23 Feb 1863.
Reeder, George W.; Anderson; veteran; mustered out 23 Oct 1865.
Riley, George W.; Anderson; deserted 31 Aug 1862.
Scott, Jesse D.; Huntington; transferred to Co. I, 47th [Indiana] Regiment.
Slater, John; Peru; deserted 16 May 1863.
Smith, George A.; Anderson; died at Tiptonville, TN, __ May 1862.
Smith, Oliver; Anderson; mustered out 12 Dec 1864.
Stanley, Andrew; Anderson; veteran; mustered out 23 Oct 1865.
Stevenson, Andrew; Indianapolis; died at Helena, AR, __ Mar 1863.
Stewart, William E.; Huntington; died at Helena, AR, 15 Aug 1862.
Suffield, David T.; Anderson; discharged 17 Sep 1862.
Trump, Jacob; Indianapolis; veteran; mustered out 23 Oct 1865.
Watkins, J.; Anderson; discharged 18 Jul 1862.
Watkins, William H.; Anderson; discharged 30 Oct 1862.
Weir, Joseph; Anderson; veteran; mustered out 23 Oct 1865.
Whitaker, John; Anderson; veteran; mustered out 23 Oct 1865; testified at the Oct 1863 court-martial of Jonathan Benefiel.
White, William E.; Anderson; died at Helena, AR, 15 Aug 1862.
Williamson, George W.; Anderson; veteran; mustered out 23 Oct 1865.
Williamson, Jefferson; Anderson; killed at Champion Hill, MS, 16 May 1863.
Yager, James B.; Bluffton; mustered out 12 Dec 1864.

Recruits:

Bunce, Anson A.; Huntington; mustered in 7 Mar 1864; transferred to VRC.
Carmany, Willliam J.; Columbus; mustered in 2 Mar 1862; died at New Orleans, LA, __ June 1864.
Denton, Daniel S.; Huntington; mustered in 29 Oct 1862; killed at Champion Hill, MS, 16 May 1863.
Ervin, Moses; Huntington; mustered in 8 Nov 1862; transferred to Co. I, [47th Indiana Regiment].
Feighner, William A.; Huntington; mustered in 7 Mar 1864; died at New Orleans, LA, 22 June 1864.
Heatley, Henry; Burlington; mustered in 7 Mar 1864; mustered out 23 Oct 1865.
Hich, James A.; Indianapolis; mustered in 2 Mar 1864; deserted 30 Mar 1864.

Kaylor, Andrew; Huntington; mustered in 7 Mar 1864; mustered out 23 Oct 1865.
Perkins, Adam; Anderson; mustered in 14 Mar 1864; mustered out 23 Oct 1865.
Reilly, Alexander; New York City; mustered in 1 Mar 1864; mustered out 23 Oct 1865.
Rinerson, Hezekiah; Huntington; mustered in 8 Nov 1862; died at home.
Rudy, Daniel; Huntington; mustered in 7 Mar 1864; mustered out 23 Oct 1865.
Shaw, Orange L.; Anderson; mustered in 30 Mary 1864; mustered out 23 Oct 1865.
Stanley, Amos; Anderson; mustered in 20 Mar 1864; died at Cairo, IL, 15 Sep 1864.
Swafford, William H.H.; Huntington; mustered in 8 Nov 1862; mustered out 17 Jul 1863.
Swaine, John W.; Huntington; mustered in 11 Mar 1864; died at Shreveport, LA, 7 Aug 1865.
Trombla, William; Huntington; mustered in 7 March 1864; mustered out 23 Oct 1865.

Company H (*Original members mustered in 13 December 1861*)

Captain:

Keller, Samuel J.; Bluffton; commissioned 10 Oct 1861; mustered in 13 Dec 1861; mustered out 15 Dec 1864.
Spake, John; Bluffton; commissioned 1 Mar 1865; mustered in 9 Apr 1865; mustered out with regiment 23 Oct 1865.

First Lieutenant:

Brinkerhoff, George H.; Huntington; commissioned 10 Oct 1861; mustered in 13 Dec 1861; mustered out 15 Dec 1864.
Spake, John; Bluffton; commissioned 16 Sep 1864; mustered in 10 Mar 1865; promoted Captain.
Wisner, Samuel; Bluffton; commissioned 1 Mar 1865; mustered in 9 Apr 1865; mustered out with regiment 23 Oct 1865.

Second Lieutenant:

Gordon, James; Bluffton; commissioned 10 Oct 1861; mustered in 13 Dec 1861; mustered out 15 Dec 1864; term expired.
Karnes, Oliver; Bluffton; commissioned 1 July 1865; mustered out 23 Oct 1865 with regiment as 1st Sergeant.

First Sergeant:

Vance, William; College Corners; promoted Adjutant.

Sergeant:

Roether, Daniel B.; Rockford; discharged 10 Apr 1863.
Johns, William H.; Bluffton; transferred 21 Dec 1863 to 25th Regiment, CDA.
Sloan, George; Markle; mustered out 13 Dec 1864.
Whitmore, John; Bluffton; promoted 2nd Lieutenant in 25th Regiment, CDA.

Corporals:

Robbins, Charles; Indianapolis; transferred to 1st Nebraska Infantry, 28 Jun 1862.
Caril, John; Knightstown; mustered out 13 Dec 1864.
Larimore, David; Zanesville; killed at Champion Hill, MS, 16 May 1863.
Spake, John; Bluffton; veteran; promoted Captain.
Wisner, Samuel; Bluffton; veteran; promoted 1st Lieutenant.
Karns, Calvin; Bluffton; transferred IC.

Karns, Oliver; Bluffton; veteran; mustered out 23 Oct 1865 as Sergeant.
Johnson, Matthew E.; Bluffton; discharged 4 Dec 1862; disability.

Musicians:

Stewart, William; Indianapolis; veteran; mustered out 23 Oct 1865.
Snyder, Joshua; Ossian; discharged 13 Oct 1862; disability.

Wagoner:

South, Jesse M.; Bluffton; discharged 27 Apr 1863.

Privates:

Ady, Jonathan; Ossian; died at Benton, MO, 2 Mar 1862.
Aspinwall, William; Bluffton; veteran; mustered out 23 Oct 1865.
Ault, Henry; Knightstown; discharged 21 Jun 1862; disability.
Bagby, Elisha; Bluffton; veteran; mustered out 23 Oct 1865 as Corporal.
Becker, George; Huntington; veteran; mustered out 23 Oct 1865.
Bigby, John J.; Bluffton; veteran; mustered out 23 Oct 1865.
Boden, Thomas; Bluffton; convicted of misbehavior in the presence of the enemy at Jackson, MS, by General Court-Martial 1 Aug 1863; sentenced to confinement at hard labor for the term of enlistment, forfeiture of pay, and dishonorable discharge; mustered out 12 Dec 1864.[21]
Bolenbauger, John; Limber Lost; discharged 24 Feb 1863; disability.
Brooks, William; Bluffton; discharged 5 Jul 1862; disability.
Brown, Henry; Bluffton; mustered out 12 Dec 1864.
Buckles, William S.; Bluffton; veteran; mustered out 23 Oct 1865 as Corporal.
Chapman, Moses; Markle; veteran; mustered out 23 Oct 1865 as Corporal.
Clark, Marshall; Bluffton; died at Milliken's Bend, LA, 21 Apr 1863.
Cogan, Benjamin; Huntington; died at Tiptonville, TN, 9 May 1862.
Cooper, Samuel H.; Bluffton; veteran; mustered out 23 Oct 1865.
Cotton, James; Murray; mustered out 12 Dec 1864.
Dewitt, Nicholas; Bluffton; veteran; mustered out 23 Oct 1865.
Dilworth, Richard; Bluffton; discharged 29 Nov 1863; disability.
Dougherty, Francis; Bluffton; veteran; mustered out 23 Oct 1865.
Fairchild, George W.; Bluffton; discharged 29 Nov 1863; disability.
Gilliam, Elias F.; Bluffton; discharged 16 Jul 1862; disability.
Hall, Franklin H.; Danville; mustered out 12 Dec 1864.
Hamilton, Thomas; Bluffton; veteran; mustered out 23 Oct 1865.
Henly, William; Bluffton; killed at Champion Hill, MS, 16 May 1863.
Hixon, James; Bluffton; discharged 7 Jul 1862.
Hoag, Milo; Huntington; died at Helena, AR, 28 Sep 1862.
Hoag, Stephen C.; Ossian; mustered out 12 Dec 1864.
Honsel, Hiram P.; Ossian; veteran; mustered out 23 Oct 1865.
Kimberly, Newell M.; Indianapolis; deserted before muster.
Klingle, Andrew H.; Huntington; died at home 11 Dec 1861.
Klingle, George; Huntington; died at home 11 Dec 1861.
Manning, Albert A.; Markle; mustered out 13 Dec 1864.
Manning, William Z.; Markle; veteran; mustered out 23 Oct 1865.
Mantece, Cornelius; _____; died at Millikan's Bend, LA, 28 May 1863.
Martin, John J.; Bluffton; veteran; mustered out 23 Oct 1865.
Milliner, Eli R.; Huntington; veteran; mustered out 23 Oct 1865.
Myers, James; Rockford; veteran; mustered out 23 Oct 1865 as Corporal.
Nave, Jonathan; Markle; mustered out 12 Dec 1864.
Parkinson, William; Bluffton; convicted of misbehavior in the presence of the enemy at Jackson, MS, by General Court-Martial 1 Aug 1863; sentenced to confinement at hard labor for term of enlistment, forfeiture of pay, dishonorable discharge; mustered out 12 Dec 1864.[22]

Price, Andrew; Bluffton; discharged 3 Feb 1863; disability.
Ream, John M.; Huntington; discharged 14 Oct 1862.
Sallor, William; Markle; discharged 18 Aug 1862; disability.
Schnatterly, Henry J.; Rockford; discharged 17 Sep 1862; disability.
Shire, Jeremiah; Bluffton; veteran; mustered out 23 Oct 1865.
Shoemaker, Jesse; Huntington; veteran; died at Fort Gaines, AL; 26 Mar 1865.
Singleton, Henry; Bluffton; died at Nelson's Furnace, KY, 1 Mar 1862.
Singleton, Josiah; Bluffton; died at Benton, MO, 4 Jan 1863.
Sloan, Albert; Markle; mustered out 12 Dec 1864.
Sloan, Milton; Markle; died 8 May 1864 of wounds received at Alexandria, LA.
Smith, Benjamin; Warren; discharged 27 may 1863.
Sowers, Aaron R.; Huntington; veteran; mustered out veteran; mustered out 23 Oct 1865 as Corporal.
Sowers, Henry M.; Huntington; veteran; mustered out 23 Oct 1865 as Sergeant.
Staunton, John W.; Bluffton; veteran; mustered out 23 Oct 1865 as Corporal.
Stockham, David; _____; veteran; transferred to non-com staff 10 Apr 1865; mustered out 23 Oct 1865 as Sergeant Major.
Stone, Cyrenus; Huntington; mustered out 12 Dec 1864; transferred to VRC.
Sturgis, John E.; Bluffton; veteran; mustered out 23 Oct 1865 as Sergeant.
Thompson, David N.; Bluffton; veteran; discharged 26 May 1865; disability.
Thompson, John W.; Bluffton; veteran; mustered out 23 Oct 1865.
Trammel, William H.; Huntington; discharged 4 Jun 1862.
Wade, George; Bluffton; discharged 1 Nov 1862; disability.
Walker, Robert W.; Bluffton; died 28 May 1863 of wounds received at Champion Hill, MS.
Wire, Andrew; Huntington; mustered out 12 Dec 1864.
Wisner, John; Bluffton; mustered out 12 Dec 1864.
Zink, Elias; Huntington; mustered out 12 Dec 1864.

Recruits:

Bender, David; Bluffton; mustered in 15 Feb 1865; mustered out 23 Oct 1865.
Boyer, Franklin S.; Rockford; mustered in 26 mar 1864; mustered out 3 Jul 1865.
Brice, William A.; Bluffton; mustered in 26 Mar 1864; mustered out 23 Oct 1865.
Croviston, Joseph; Markle; mustered in 26 Mar 1864; discharged 11 May 1865; disability.
Draper, Solomon; Huntington; mustered in 8 Jan 1862; discharged 15 Feb 1862; disability.
Foncannon, Samuel; Bluffton; mustered in 26 Mar 1864; mustered out 23 Oct 1865.
Franklin, Joseph; Huntington; mustered in 10 Mar 1864; deserted 20 Mar 1864.
Harshan, John B.; Philadelphia; mustered in 24 Jul 1862; mustered out 28 Jul 1865.
Hartman, Joseph W.; Decatur; mustered in 2 Jan 1865; mustered out 23 Oct 1865.
Hull, Josephus; Huntington; mustered in 10 Mar 1864; mustered out 23 Oct 1865.
Lehr, William H.; Markle; mustered in 26 Mar 1864; died at Shreveport, LA, 2 Jul 1865.
Lindsey, William; Bluffton; mustered in 26 Mar 1864; mustered out 23 Oct 1865.
Little, John; Markle; mustered in 16 Mar 1864; died 11 Dec 1864.
Little, Joseph; Markle; mustered in 26 Mar 1864; mustered out 23 Oct 1865.
Morgan, Jacob G.; Bluffton; mustered in 26 Mar 1864; mustered out 23 Oct 1865.
Murray, John E.; Huntington; mustered in 30 Jan 1865; mustered out 23 Oct 1865.
Niceby, John H.; Bluffton; mustered in 26 Mar 1864; mustered out 23 Oct 1865.
Pollock, John; Cincinnati, OH; mustered in 4 Sept 1862; deserted 27 Feb 1863.
Sale, Andrew J.; Markle; mustered in 15 Aug 1862; died of wounds received at Champion Hill, MS, 21 Jun 1863.
Sale, Francis M.; Markle; mustered in 15 Aug 1862; mustered out 28 Jul 1865.
Smith, George; Huntington; mustered in 27 Jan 1865; mustered out 23 Oct 1865.
Spese, Franklin; Huntington; mustered in 27 Jan 1865; mustered out 23 Oct 1865.
Strather, George B.; Markle; mustered in 26 Mar 1864; mustered out 23 Oct 1865.
Walker, Sewell D.; Markle; mustered in 15 Aug 1862; mustered out 28 Jul 1865.
Wallace, James; Markle; mustered in 26 Mar 1864; mustered out 23 Oct 1865.
Ward, George W.; Huntington; mustered in 24 Jan 1865; mustered out 23 Oct 1865.

Warren, William; Huntington; mustered in 27 Jan 1865; mustered out 23 Oct 1865.
Witham, Sanford; Bluffton; mustered in 26 Mar 1865; died at Morganza, LA, 21 Aug 1864.

Company I (*Original members mustered in 12 December 1861*)

Captain:

Bowersock, Joshua W.; Laketon; commissioned 10 Oct 1861; mustered in 12 Dec 1861; resigned 6 Feb 1862.
Henley, William M.; Wabash; commissioned 1 Apr 1862; mustered in 5 Apr 1862; mustered out 29 Dec 1864; term expired.
Bender, David S.; Laketon; commissioned 1 Mar 1865; mustered in 9 Apr 1865; mustered out with Regiment 23 Oct 1865

First Lieutenant:

Emory, John; Ashland; commissioned 10 Oct 1861; mustered in 12 Dec 1861; resigned 12 Apr 1862.
Martin, John A.; North Manchester; commissioned 30 Apr 1862; died 15 Dec 1862.
Lindsey, Hiram; Wabash; commissioned and mustered in 28 Dec 1862; resigned 24 Sep 1863; re-entered service as Captain in 11th Cavalry.
Bender, David S.; Laketon; commissioned 1 Jan 1864; mustered in 30 Mar 1864; promoted Captain.
Cox, Robert S.; Laketon; commissioned 1 Mar 1865; mustered in 25 Apr 1865; mustered out with regiment 23 Oct 1865

Second Lieutenant:

Williams, Edward J.; Wabash; commissioned 10 Oct 1861; mustered in 12 Dec 1861; resigned 12 Apr 1862.
Lindsey, Hiram; Wabash; commissioned 30 Apr 1862; mustered in 12 Apr 1862; promoted 1st Lieutenant.
Bender, David S.; Laketon; commissioned and mustered in 28 Dec 1862; promoted 1st Lieutenant.
Cox, Robert S.; Laketon; commissioned 1 Jan 1864; mustered in 30 Mar 1864; promoted 1st Lieutenant.
Lines, Jacob; Wabash; commissioned 1 Jul 1865; mustered out as 1st Sergeant with regiment.

First Sergeant:

Lines, Jacob; Wabash; veteran; promoted to 2nd Lieutenant.

Sergeants:

Cox, Robert S.; Laketon; promoted 2nd Lieutenant.
Shaffer, John; Ashland; mustered out 11 Dec 1864.
Enbody, Joseph; Laketon; mustered out 11 Dec 1864.
Lindsey, Hiram; Wabash; promoted 2nd Lieutenant.

Corporals:

Bender, David S.; Laketon; promoted 2nd Lieutenant.
Hahn, James; Ashland; veteran; mustered out 17 Jul 1865.
Weidner, David; North Manchester; veteran; mustered out 23 Oct 1865.
Kelley, George W.; Laketon; killed at Champion Hill, MS, 16 May 1863.

Stone, Nelson; Wabash; mustered out 23 Oct 1865.
Hummel, Charles; Ashland; veteran; died at Shreveport, LA, 28 Jun 1865.
Sampson, George W.; Wabash; veteran; mustered out 23 Oct 1865 as Sergeant.
Palmer, Hiram; Laketon; veteran; mustered out 23 Oct 1865 as Sergeant.

Musicians:

Lichanwalter, David; Pierston; discharged 15 Oct 1862; disability; Principal Musician.
Bert, Henry L.; Tipton; veteran; mustered out 23 Oct 1865 as Principal Musician.

Wagoner:

Cox, John I.; Laketon; veteran; mustered out 23 Oct 1865.

Privates:

Abbott, William J.; Liberty Mills; veteran; mustered out 23 Oct 1865.
Armstrong, Christopher; Liberty Mills; veteran; mustered out 23 Oct 1865.
Augherbright, Andrew J.; Liberty Mills; discharged 25 Sep 1863; wounds.
Baker, Aaron; Wabash; veteran; mustered out 23 Oct 1865.

Lt. David S. Bender, Co. I (courtesy of Terry C. Smith).

Baker, Henry; Wabash; veteran; mustered out 23 Oct 1865.
Baker, Joseph; Wabash; discharged; disability.
Baker, Josiah; Liberty Mills; transferred to Co. D.
Baugher, Albert; Wilmot; veteran; mustered out 23 Oct 1865 as Corporal.
Baugher, Allen; Wilmot; veteran; mustered out 23 Oct 1865.
Briner, Jacob; Laketon; drowned at Helena, AR, 4 Aug 1862.
Case, Thomas; Ashland; transferred to VRC.
Claxton, Elias; Liberty Mills; discharged 16 Nov 1862; disability.
Comstock, Henry; Liberty Mills; discharged 12 Sep 1862; disability.
Edwards, Jacob; Peru; deserted 23 May 1862.
Egler, John M.; Wilmot; deserted 27 Feb 1862.
Enyart, William; Liberty Mills; veteran; died at Indianapolis 23 Aug 1864.
Garrison, Elihu; Ashland; veteran; mustered out 23 Oct 1862.
Grant, John; Ashland; died at Young's Point, LA, 26 Jun 1863.
Grant, Napoleon B.; Ashland; veteran; mustered out 23 Oct 1865.
Hand, Michael; Indianapolis; discharged 13 Sep 1862; disability.
Hart, Henry; Louisville, KY; deserted 29 Dec 1862.
Howser, David; Ashland; veteran; mustered out 23 Oct 1865.
Howser, Jacob; Ashland; died at Bardstown, KY, 8 Feb 1862.
Kelly, William; Laketon; discharged; disability.
Leach, Almond; Liberty Mills; died at New Madrid, MO, ___ 1862.
Makemson, Alexander; Wilmot; died at Helena, AR, 20 Dec 1862.
Martin, John; Wabash; died 1 Jul 1863 of head wound received at Vicksburg, MS.[23]
Martin, John A.; Liberty Mills; promoted 1st Lieutenant.
McIlvain, John; Ashland; veteran; mustered out 23 Oct 1865 as Sergeant.
Miller, Henry E.; Liberty Mills; died 3 Jul 1863 of wounds [received at Vicksburg, MS].
Muldoon, Arthur; Indianapolis; accounted for as veteran recruit.

Murphy, Hugh J.; Wabash; transferred to Co. B.
Murray, Clinton; Liberty Mills; veteran; mustered out 23 Oct 1865.
Palmer, Henry; Laketon; died at Bardstown, KY, 8 Jan 1862.
Parrish, James; Lagro; deserted 11 Apr 1862; convicted of being absent without leave by General Court-Martial 1 Apr 1863; sentenced to forfeiture of two months' pay and public reprimand at the head of his regiment by the commanding officer.[24]
Pensinger, Jacob; Liberty Mills; discharged 20 Jan 1864; disability.
Phillips, Henry M.; Liberty Mills; veteran; mustered out 23 Oct 1865.
Ramey, David; Laketon; died at Bardstown, KY, 14 Jan 1862.
Reinard, Samuel; Wabash; veteran; mustered out 23 Oct 1865.
Ricard, Daniel; Wabash; veteran; mustered out 23 Oct 1865.
Richardson, Howard; Wabash; died at St. Louis, MO, 26 Oct 1862.
Robbins, Enoch; Liberty Mills; veteran; mustered out 23 Oct 1865 as Corporal.
Rodgers, Samuel; North Manchester; discharged 27 Dec 1862; disability.
Rushton, E.M.; Indianapolis; deserted 13 Dec 1861.
Scott, Jesse D.; Ashland; veteran; mustered out 23 Oct 1865.
Scott, Jesse D.; Ashland; died at Bardstown, KY, 21 Jan 1862.
Shoey, Thomas; Wabash; veteran; mustered out 23 Oct 1865.
Sutton, Sydney A.; Ashland; died at St. Louis, MO, 19 Oct 1862.
Tryon, Lewis; Laketon; died of wounds received at Memphis, TN, 12 Jul 1863.
Tryon, Thomas L.; Laketon; veteran; mustered out 23 Oct 1865.
Washburn, Ellis; Ashland; veteran; mustered out 23 Oct 1865 as Sergeant.
Watkins, Enoch; Liberty Mills; veteran; mustered out 23 Oct 1865.
Watkins, Perry; Liberty Mills; veteran; mustered out 23 Oct 1865.
Watkins, Robert; Liberty Mills; veteran; mustered out 23 Oct 1865.
Watkins, William; Liberty Mills; veteran; mustered out 23 Oct 1865.
White, John; Wilmot; died at Helena, AR, 9 Sep 1862.
White, Samuel A.; Wilmot; veteran; mustered out 23 Oct 1865 as Corporal.
Yeuger, Joel; Wilmot; veteran; mustered out 23 Oct 1865.

Recruits:

Baker, William H.; mustered in 10 Feb 1862; mustered out 9 Feb 1865.
Barritt, Hiram; mustered in 25 Mar 1864; mustered out 23 Oct 1865.
Baugher, Francis; mustered in 25 Mar 1864; mustered out 23 Oct 1865.
Bradley, John M.; mustered in 6 Nov 1862; deserted 22 Mar 1864.
Campbell, Stockton; mustered in 23 Aug 1862; mustered out 28 Jul 1865.
Cayler, Valentine; mustered in 26 Mar 1864; mustered out 31 May 1865.
Dicken, John H.; mustered in 25 Mar 1864; mustered out 23 Oct 1865.
Ervin, Moses; mustered in 8 Nov 1862; mustered out 23 Oct 1865.
Garrison, James O.; mustered in 7 Mar 1864; died at Thibodaux, LA, 4 Jul 1864.
Goshorn, Franklin; mustered in 25 Mar 1864; mustered out 23 Oct 1865.
Goshorn, William; mustered in 25 Mar 1864; mustered out 23 Oct 1865.
Heeter, Reuben; mustered in 28 May 1862; mustered out 23 Oct 1865.
King, Lavinus; mustered in 23 Aug 1862; died at Helena, AR, 27 Aug 1862.
Koch, William; mustered in 25 Mar 1865; mustered out 23 Oct 1865.
Laman, Abraham; mustered in 8 Mar 1864; mustered out 23 Oct 1865.
Lincicum, Nathan; mustered in 28 Mar 1864; mustered out 22 May 1865.
Lower, Mathias; mustered in 8 Mar 1864; mustered out 23 Oct 1865.
Lumaree, Barton W.; mustered in 23 Aug 1862; mustered out 28 Jul 1865.
Lunculum, George; mustered in 3 Mar 1864; mustered out 23 Oct 1865.
Meek, Richard; mustered in 26 Mar 1864; mustered out 23 Oct 1865.
Noggle, Nelson; mustered in 25 Mar 1864; discharged 6 Feb 1865; disability.
Payne, Samuel J.; mustered in 25 Mar 1864; mustered out 23 Oct 1865 as Sergeant.
Pierson, Malon B.; mustered in 25 Mar 1864; mustered out 3 Jul 1865.
Pingsey, David; mustered in 25 Mar 1864; mustered out 24 Oct 1865.
Ramey, George M.; mustered in 3 Mar 1864; mustered out 23 Oct 1865.

Ramey, John S.; mustered in 3 Mar 1864; mustered out 6 Jun 1865.
Rhoads, Carlton; mustered in 21 Mar 1864; mustered out 23 Oct 1865.
Robbins, James; mustered in 8 Mr1864; died at Morganza, LA, 31 Aug 1864.
Scott, Jacob; mustered in 25 Mar 1864; died on hospital steamer 30 Jun 1864.
Slagle, William S.; mustered in 15 Aug 1862; transferred to VRC; mustered out 5 Jul 1865.
Stephens, William; mustered in 25 Mar 1864; mustered out 23 Oct 1865.
Turney, Henry J.; mustered in 3 Mar 1864; died at Morganza, LA, 29 Jul 1864.
Wagner, Alonzo; mustered in 15 Feb 1865; mustered out 23 Oct 1865.
Warner, William; mustered in 23 Mar 1864; mustered out 23 Oct 1865.
Zink, Samuel; mustered in 24 Oct 1862; transferred to VCR 30 Apr 1864.

Company K (*Original members mustered in 13 December 1861*)

Captain:

Hill, Ellison, C.; Tipton; commissioned 10 Oct 1861; mustered in 13 Dec 1861; dishonorably discharged (contumacious conduct) 1 March 1863.
Rumsey, Isaac M.; Tipton; commissioned and mustered in 12 Mar 1863; died 27 Jun 1863.
Harding, Robert N.; Indianapolis; commissioned 30 Jul 1863; mustered in 19 Nov 1863; testified at the Oct 1863 court-martial of Jonathan Benefield; mustered out 31 Dec 1864; term expired.
Paul, Thomas; Tipton; commissioned 1 Mar 1865; mustered out with regiment 23 Oct 1865 as 1st Lieutenant.

First Lieutenant:

Hayford, William H.; Tipton; commissioned 10 Oct 1861; mustered in 13 Dec 1861; acquitted of disobedience of orders, conduct unbecoming of an officer and a gentleman, and breach of arrest by General Court-Martial 1 Aug 1863; acted for the defense in court-martial of Pvt. Jonathan Benefiel; honorably discharged 21 Apr 1864.[25]

Second Lieutenant:

McKinsey, Joseph A.; Normanda; commissioned 10 Oct 1865; mustered in 13 Dec 1861; resigned 12 May 1862.
Paul, Thomas; Tipton; commissioned and mustered in 13 May 1862; promoted 1st Lieutenant.
Carey, Peter; Duck Creek; commissioned 1 Jul 1865; mustered out as Sergeant with regiment 23 Oct 1865.

First Sergeant:

Paul, Thomas; Tipton; promoted 2nd Lieutenant.

Sergeants:

Hamilton, James; Petersburg; discharged 11 Jun 1862; disability.
Weed, Adam M.; Petersburg; discharged 2 Sep 1862; disability.
Pearce, William; Tipton; transferred to Invalid Corps Jan 1862.
Gales, Peter M.; Tipton; transferred to Invalid Corps Nov 1862.

Corporals:

Jackson, Andrew; Duck Creek; died at Helena, AR, 20 Feb 1862.
Kindley, Samuel J.; Jackson's Station; discharged Feb 1862, disability.

Evans, James W.; Normanda; veteran; mustered out 23 Oct 1865 as 1st Sergeant.
Brown, James G.; _____; died at Benton, MO, 12 Mar 1862.
Campbell, James T.; Tipton; died near Columbus, KY, 1 Oct 1862.
Fuller, James O.; Tipton; veteran; mustered out 23 Oct 1865 as Sergeant.
Weed, James M.; Petersburg; transferred to IC 11 Nov 1863.
Overman, Jeremiah; Petersburg; died of wounds received at Champion Hill, MS, 16 May 1863.

Musicians:

Paul, Charles B.; Tipton; veteran; mustered out 23 Oct 1865 as Principal Musician.
Parker, John. S.; Tipton; died at Tiptonville, TN, 27 May 1863.

Wagoner:

Burton, Henry C.; Tipton; veteran; mustered out 23 Oct 1865.

Privates:

Angstadt, Henry C.; Tipton; transferred to IC 18 Sep 1863.
Angstadt, John A.; Tipton, veteran; mustered out 23 Oct 1865.
Ashpaugh, Sanford; Philipsville; died at Helena, AR, 12 Mar 1863.
Barger, Joseph; Tipton; deserted 16 Oct 1862.
Basy, Solomon T.; Tipton; veteran; mustered out 23 Oct 1865.
Basy, William J.; Tipton; discharged 15 Aug 1862; disability.
Bishop, Jacob; Jackson's Station; mustered out 12 Dec 1864.
Brady, John W.; Tipton; killed at Champion Hill, MS, 16 May 1863.
Bunch, Hardin; Petersburg; transferred to IC 26 Sep 1863.
Bunch, Nazareth J.; Petersburg; killed at Champion Hill, MS, 16 May 1863.
Calvert, John W.; _____; veteran; mustered out 23 Oct 1865.
Campbell, Thomas M.; Tipton; killed at Port Gibson, MS, 1 May 1863.
Carey, Peter; Duck Creek; veteran; mustered out 23 Oct 1865 as Sergeant.
Cloud, Thomas H.; Petersburg; died at Cairo, IL, 8 Oct 1862.
Cogswell, John P.; Noblesville; discharged 24 Jun 1862; disability.
Conkling, Joseph; Petersburg; discharged 14 Jan 1863; disability.
Daniels, Jacob; Shielsville; discharged 14 Oct 1863; disability.
Deal, George; Petersburg; mustered out 12 Dec 1864.
Debard, William F.; Tipton; discharged 10 Jul 1862; disability.
Downhower, Samuel; _____; veteran; mustered out 23 Oct 1865.
Dunn, Levi Jr.; Petersburg; died at Grand Gulf, MS, 6 May 1863.
Emchizer, Kenion; Tipton; mustered out 12 Dec 1864.
Endaly, Daniel; Tipton; veteran; mustered out 23 Oct 1865.
Evans, Cyremus D.; Normanda; discharged 19 Mar 1863; disability.
Foster, Andrew F.; Petersburg; veteran; mustered out 23 Oct 1865.
Foster, Silas F.; Normanda; died at Louisville, KY, 21 Feb 1862.
Frazier, James A.; Normanda; discharged 18 May 1862; disability.
Hackleman, Pleasant A.; Shielsville; veteran; mustered out 23 Oct 1865 as Corporal.
Hall, Hiram B.; Tipton; died at Tipton, IN, 19 Dec 1863.
Hall, Ross; Tipton; died at New Orleans, LA, 25 Jan 1864.
Harbst, Frederick; Tipton; veteran; discharged 6 Dec 1864; disability.
Hasket, Newby M.; Tipton; discharged 15 Aug 1862.
Henderson, Samuel; West Kinderhook; died at St. Louis, MO, 5 Jan 1863.
Hillegoss, Samuel; Tipton; deserted 18 Aug 1862.
Hopkins, James; _____; mustered out 18 Jul 1865.
Innis, Jarvis A.; Tipton; died at Tipton, IN, 24 May 1863.
Innis, Joseph A.; Tipton; died at St. Louis, MO, 14 Oct 1862.
Jackson, Presley E.; Duck Creek; mustered out 12 Dec 1864 as Corporal.
Jennings, William H.; Sheilville; veteran; mustered out 23 Oct 1865 as Corporal.

Judd, William; New Lancaster; veteran; mustered out 23 Oct 1865.
Kennear, William W.; Petersburg; discharged 5 Jun 1862; disability.
Knight, Reuben; Quincy; veteran; mustered out 23 Oct 1865.
Lane, Doctrine C.; Tipton; died at Bardstown, KY, 20 Jan 1862.
Law, Francis M.; Normanda; veteran; mustered out 23 Oct 1865.
Law, James H.; Normanda; discharged 14 Aug 1862; disability.
Lemon, Joseph B.; Petersburg; veteran; mustered out 23 Oct 1865.
Lewis, Eli; Normanda; died at Nelson's Furnace, KY, 8 Feb 1862.
Lister, Harrison; Shielsville; discharged 11 Feb 1863; disability.
Martin, Joseph; Normanda; mustered out 12 Dec 1864.
McMurtrie, Harvey L.; Jackson Station; died at Tipton, IN, 18 Oct 1862.
McNeal, George; Tipton; died at Tipton, IN, 15 Sep 1862.
Minick, William, Tipton; died at Grand Gulf, Ms, 20 May 1863.
Mitchell, James T.; Normanda; mustered out 15 Dec 1864.
Moatz, John H.; Tipton; died at Benton, MO, 16 Mar 1862.
Montgomery, John P.; Normanda; discharged 28 Jun 1862; disability.
Osburn, Calvin F.; Tipton; mustered out 23 Oct 1865.
Parker, Christopher C.; Tipton; veteran; mustered out 23 Oct 1865 as Corporal.
Parker, John S.; _____; died at Tiptonville, TN, 27 May 1863.
Pea, Martin; Jackson Station; died at Tipton, IN, 18 Nov 1863.
Phares, Solomon D.; Petersburg; veteran; mustered out 23 Oct 1865.
Phillips, Christopher; Tipton; discharged 1 Mar 1863.
Redman, Hiram; Jackson Station; discharged 25 Aug 1862; disability.
Reed, Norris, Jackson Station; veteran; deserted 22 Mar 1864.
Ridley, Joseph; Sheilville; died at Bardstown, KY, 3 Jan 1862.
Robinson, David P.; Tipton; died at Memphis, TN, 18 Jul 1863.
Smith, Larkin; Petersburg; discharged 2 Dec 1862; disability.
Stewart, John T.; Tipton; died 17 May 1863 from wounds received at Champion Hill, Ms.
Stone, Solomon, Tipton; killed at Champion Hill, MS, 16 May 1863.
Summers, Lewis J.; Sheilville; died at Tipton, IN, 12 Aug 1863.
Tucker, Charles O.; Sheilville; discharged 24 Jun 1862.
Tucker, March; Sheilville; wounded; discharged from Hospital Post at Indianapolis 6 Nov 1863.[26]
Turner, George W.; Tipton; veteran; mustered out 23 Oct 1865.
Vanbuskirk, Joseph Jr.; Sheilville; died at Tipton, IN, 26 Apr 1862.
Wanuell, William; Tipton; promoted Captain U.S. Colored Infantry.
Warford, John; Tipton; veteran; mustered out 23 Oct 1865 as Corporal.
Warley, George; Tipton; died at Tiptonville, TN, 22 Apr 1862.
Wolf, George; Petersburg; discharged 1 Aug 1863.
Wolford, Solomon; Petersburg; veteran; discharged 19 Mar 1863.
Wolford, Valentine; Petersburg; killed at Champion Hill, MS, 16 May 1863.

Recruits:

Arnett, Lindley; Jonesboro; mustered in 21 Nov 1862.
Basey, Jones L.; Tipton; mustered in 26 Feb 1864; mustered out 23 Oct 1865.
Basey, Martin V. B.; Tipton; mustered in 25 Mar 1864; mustered out 23 Oct 1865.
Bockman, Edward F.; Sheilville; mustered in 27 Feb 1862; discharged 27 Apr 1863; disability.
Butler, John; Jonesboro; mustered in 21 Nov 1862; mustered out 6 Jul 1865; drafted,
Campbell, Nathaniel A.; Tipton; mustered in 26 Feb 1864; mustered out 23 Oct 1865.
Carroll, James; Tipton; mustered in 26 Feb 1864; mustered out 23 Oct 1865.
Carroll, Robert; Tipton; mustered in 26 Feb 1864; mustered out 23 Oct 1865.
Cope, Edmund; Tipton; mustered in 26 Feb 1864; mustered out 23 Oct 1865.
Eller, John W.; Sheilville; mustered in 21 Mar 1864; mustered out 5 Jun 1865.
Good, Koontz John; Sheilville; mustered in 1 Mar 1864; mustered out 23 Oct 1865.
Horton, William; Petersburg; mustered in 2 Mar 1864; mustered out 23 Oct 1865.
Howell, Albert; Shelbyville; mustered in 17 Feb 1862; veteran; mustered out 23 Oct 1865 as Corporal.
Jackson, Adam; Tipton; musteredin in 17 Feb 1862; transferred to VRC 16 Sep 1863.

Keen, Charles; Petersburg; mustered in 2 Mar 1864; mustered out 28 Jun 1865.
Lane, Joseph; Petersburg; mustered in 26 Feb 1864; mustered out 23 Oct 1865.
Lester, Phillip; Sheilville; mustered in 26 Feb 1864; died at Tipton, IN, 6 Oct 1864.
Mayer, William B.; Petersburg; mustered in 25 Mar 1864; mustered out 23 Oct 1865.
McNeil, David; Tipton; mustered in 17 Mar 1864; died at Shreveport, LA, 12 Jul 1865.
Morrison, Humphrey H.; Indianapolis; mustered in 10 Mar 1864; mustered out 23 Oct 1865.
Paul, Samuel; Tipton; mustered in 17 Mar 1864; died at home19 Apr 1864.
Sanders, Richard M; Sharpsville; mustered in 2 Mar 1865; mustered out 23 Oct 1865.
Scott, John A.; Indianapolis; mustered in 26 Feb 1862; mustered out 23 Oct 1865.
Scott, Uriah S.; Sheilville; mustered in 7 Mar 1862; mustered out 23 Oct 1865.
Smith, John W.; Normanda; mustered in 25 Jan 1862; veteran; mustered out 23 Oct 1865.
Sumner, Absolom; Sheilville; mustered in 1 Mar 1862; mustered out 23 Oct 1865.
Tharp, William H.H.; Sheilville; mustered in 1 Mar 1864; died at Paducah, KY, 25 Apr 1864.
Thomas, James P.; Tipton; mustered in 17 Feb 1862; discharged 14 Aug 1862; disability.
Thomas, Jesse B.; Tipton; mustered in 17 Feb 1862; discharged 10 Jun 1862; disability.
Tucker, Elias W.; Sheilville; mustered in 17 Mar 1864; mustered out 5 Aug 1865.
Vanbuskirk, Daniel F.; Tipton; mustered in 25 Mar 1864; mustered out 23 Oct 1865.
Wilson, John A.; Normanda; mustered in 21Feb 1862; veteran; mustered out 23 Oct 1865.

Unassigned Recruits:

Barker, Alexander C.; mustered in 6 Jan 1865; unaccounted for.
Carpenter, Benjamin; mustered in 20 Oct 1862.; died at Helena, AR, 11 Jan 1863; disease.
Corrillion, Francis; mustered in 15 Aug 1862; unaccounted for.
Delvin, William T.; mustered in 15 Aug 1862; unaccounted for. [27]
Esrey, William; mustered in 7 Jan 1864; unaccounted for.
Felsopp, Ambrose, mustered in 15 Aug 1862; unaccounted for.
Figart, Jacob; mustered in 22 Oct 1862; unaccounted for.
Hauley, Amos; mustered in 28 Mar 1864; unaccounted for.
Kearns, John; mustered in 15 Aug 1862; unaccounted for.
Kimble, Nathan H.; mustered in 18 Sep 1862; died 11 Jan 1863.
Ogden, Hayden; mustered in 20 Oct 1862; discharged 30 Sep 1863.
Robinson, William T.; mustered in 22 Aug 1864; substitute; mustered out 24 Oct 1865.
Sebiney, James A.; mustered in 20 Oct 1862; unaccounted for.
Sickafos, Daniel J.; mustered in 20 Oct 1862; unaccounted for.
Spigelmeyer, Emanuel; mustered in 22 Oct 1862; died 13 Aug 1863.
Thrushe, Samuel; mustered in 15 Aug 1862; unaccounted for.
Wall, Benjamin F.; mustered in 15 Aug 1862; unaccounted for.
White, Benjamin; mustered in 21 Oct 1862; unaccounted for.

Notes

Preface and Acknowledgments

1. Benson J. Lossing, *A History of the Civil War, Illustrated with Reproductions of the Brady War Photographs* (New York: The War Memorial Association, 1912).

2. Harvey Keagy Rose Papers; Franklin Keagy, *A History of the Kagy Relationship in America from 1715 to 1900* (Harrisburg, PA: Harrisburg Publishing Company, 1899; reprint ed., Salem, MA: Higginson Book Company, n.d.).

3. Hannah was the daughter of Zacharia and Rhoda Penn Jenkins of Burlington County, New Jersey.

4. 1860 Census for Summit County, Ohio; 1860 Census for Huntington County, Indiana; Eli E. Rose Pension and Military Records, National Archives and Records Administration, Washington, D.C.

5. David Williamson, *The Third Battalion Mississippi Infantry and the 45th Mississippi Regiment: A Civil War History* (Jefferson, NC: McFarland & Co., Inc., Publishers, 2004, 2009).

6. Abner James Wilkes, "A Short History of My Life in the Late War Between the North and the South," transcribed from the original by Rear Admiral Ivan Bass (mimeographed, n.d.).

Chapter 1

1. Peaceful separation and the "inherent right to freedom, independence, and self-government," claimed by Jefferson Davis, did not, according to President Lincoln in his first inaugural address, include the right to seize federal facilities in the South like Fort Henry or the $536,000 in the Federal Mint at New Orleans. Roy P. Basler, ed., *The Collected Works of Abraham Lincoln*, 10 vols. (New Brunswick, NJ: Rutgers University Press, 1953–55), IV: 271 (quote); Jefferson Davis, *The Rise and Fall of the Confederate Government*, 2 vols. (Nashville: W.M. Coats, 1881): I: 327 (quote).

The *Indianapolis Daily Journal*, echoing the President, went a step further by charging that the war had been "a long planned scheme" by Jefferson Davis and John B. Floyd, "which ... would have left the Northern States totally unarmed, and carried to the South every gun, pistol, saber and shot in the nation." Many in the North believed, and there was some evidence, that Davis, while Secretary of War and later U.S. Senator, and Floyd, Davis's successor as Secretary of War in the Buchanan administration, had, anticipating secession, conspired to ship heavy guns and small arms to Southern arsenals while weakening the defenses of northern ports. These allegations were fueled by Davis's acceptance of the presidency of the Confederate States and Floyd's acceptance of a commission as brigadier general in the Confederate Army after hightailing it from Washington under a cloud of suspicion. "A New Light on the Disunion Business," *Indianapolis Daily Journal*, 25 May 1861; *The War of the Rebellion: A Compilation of the Official Records of the Union and Confederate Armies*, 4 series, 128 parts (Washington, D.C.: Government Printing Office, 1880–1901), Series III, Volume I, pp. 12–13, 15–17, 30, 44, 52, 60, 321–22, 566, 745, 767, 964 (hereafter cited as O.R., Ser. III, Vol. I).

2. *Ibid.*, Ser. I, Vol. II, pp. 9–21; Ser. II, Vol. I, pp. 569–70, 634, 649–50, 666–677; Ser. III, Vol. I, p. 306; *The Official Military Atlas of the Civil War*, comp. Calvin C. Cowles (New York: Gramercy Books, 1983), Plate CXXXVI (hereafter cited as Atlas Plate CXXXVI).

3. U.S. Congress, House, *Suspension of Habeas Corpus*, H. exdoc. 6, 37th Cong., 1st Sess., 1861, pp. 1–3 (quote); O.R., Ser. I, Vol. LI, pt. 1, pp. 337, 409. The U.S. Constitution, Article I, Section 9, Part 2 reads: "The privilege of the writ of habeas corpus shall not be suspended, unless when in cases of rebellion or invasion, the public safety may require it." As noted by Craig R. Smith, the Constitution is clear that suspension is possible in specific cases, but vague as to who determines when public safety is endangered. Craig R. Smith, "Lincoln and Habeas Corpus—1861–1865," *Center for First Amendment Studies. White Papers*. Also see William H. Rehnquist, *All the Laws But One: Civil Liberties in Wartime* (New York: Alfred A. Knopf, 1998), pp. 36–39.

4. *Ex parte John Merryman*, 17 F. cas. 144 (1861); and for the transcript of Taney's opinion see O.R., Ser. II, Vol. I, pp. 577 (quote), 585 (quote). For discussion and a transcript of the proceedings of *Ex parte John Merryman*, also see Samuel Klaus, ed., *The Milligan Case* (New York: Alfred A. Knopf, 1929; reprint ed., New York: Da Capo Press, 1970, pp. 4–5, 459–73; and Charles Fairman, *Mr. Justice Miller and the Supreme Court 1862–1890* (Cambridge, MA: Harvard University Press, 1939), pp. 69–80, 89–90.

5. U.S. Congress, Senate, *Message of the President to the Two Houses of Congress*, 37th Congress, 1st Sess., S.

exdoc. 1, 5 July 1861, pp. 9–10; Rehnquist, *All the Laws But One*, pp. 33–39.

6. Attorney General Edward Bates gave his opinion on 5 July 1861 to the special session of Congress called by the president to consider the issue of habeas corpus and Chief Justice Taney's opinion in the Merryman case. O.R., Ser, II, Vol. II, pp. 1, 19–30. As noted by Sidney Fisher, Congress did not validate the president's habeas corpus order or Bates's opinion until 3 March 1863, almost one year later. Calling the writ of habeas corpus "the great writ of liberty," Fisher got to the crux of the constitutional crisis when he noted that "the power secretly to hurry a man to jail, where his sufferings will be unknown or soon forgotten, is more dangerous to freedom than all the other engines of tyranny." Sidney G. Fisher, "The Suspension of the Writ Habeas Corpus During the War of the Rebellion," *Political Science Quarterly* 3 (1888): 454–55 (quote), 456.

7. O.R., Ser. II, Vol. I, pp. 563, 608, 637–38; Vol. II, pp. 1, 19–30, 102, 225, 779, 781, 786–87, 793, 795. Fisher, "The Suspension of Habeas Corpus," *Political Science Quarterly*, pp. 456–57. Gov. Hicks denied authorizing the bridge burning and was not arrested. With the arrests, Hicks, an inveterate politician, quickly changed his tune, denounced the bridge burners, and with prodding from the military, led the legislature in its vote to remain in the Union. So thorough was Hicks's transformation, his pro-Union replacement as governor, Augustus W. Bradford, appointed him to the senate seat that came open with the death of Sen. James A. Pearce. In 1864, Senator Hicks endorsed Lincoln's bid for reelection. He died in Washington in 1865. Mayor Brown of Baltimore, Police Marshall Kane, the Baltimore police commissioners, the Maryland legislators, and the Baltimore newspapermen were all imprisoned by the military. Held for 17 months, they were all released without charge or trial from Fort Warren Prison in Boston Harbor on 27 November 1862. O.R., Ser. II, Vol. I, pp. 613–14, 748.

8. *Ibid.*, Vol. II, pp. 40, 56, 82, 496, 500, 505, 666; James G. Randall, "The Newspaper Problem and its Bearing Upon Military Secrecy During the Civil War," *American Historical Review* 23 (June 1918): 303–23.

9. O.R., Ser. II, Vol. II, p. 56.

10. *History of Huntington County, Indiana* (Chicago: Brant & Fuller, 1887), pp. 382, 425, 540 (quote).

11. *Ibid.*, pp. 350–51. Although the derivation of the term "Copperhead" is unknown, on 2 July 1861 in the *New York Times* then Colonel Frank P. Blair Jr. compared the Maryland legislature to "a nest of copperheads." And in their 20 July 1861 edition, the *New York Tribune*'s Baltimore correspondent appears to be the first to label antiwar northerners with the pejorative term "Copper-Heads." The use of the term to refer to antiwar or "Peace" Democrats spread quickly and Republican newspapers frequently published political cartoons depicting antiwar Democrats as copperhead snakes. Pejorative or not, the more militant antiwar Democrats gladly adopted it as their own. "Serenade to Col. Blair," *New York Times*, 2 July 1861, p. 9; "News of the forward movement of 'The Grand Army,' ... electrified our city [Baltimore] yesterday, and the effect was discernable in almost every portion of the town. The 'Copper-Heads' are very irritable, and are growling savagely at the late successes of Major-General McClellan." "News of the Movement of the Army — Its Effect in Baltimore — Bitter Feeling Among the 'Copper-Heads,'" *New York Tribune*, 20 July 1861, p. 7; Charles G. Leland and Henry B. Leland, "Ye Book of Copperheads," pamphlet 38 in Frank Freidel, ed., *Union Pamphlets of the Civil War, 1861–1865*, 2 vols. (Cambridge, MA: The Belknap Press of Harvard University, 1967), vol. 2, pp. 857–71.

12. *History of Huntington County, Indiana*, p. 351.

13. *Ibid.*, p. 352.

14. "Wants to Talk to Sinners," *Huntington Democrat*, 12 September 1861.

15. Lincoln to Fremont, 2 September 1861, quoted in John G. Nicolay and John Hay, *Abraham Lincoln: A History*, 10 vols. (New York: The Century Co., 1914), IV: 418. Two orders in Fremont's 30 August 1861 proclamation caused problems for the Lincoln Administration. The first order ("All persons ... taken with arms in their hands within these lines [from Leavenworth via Jefferson City, Rolla and Ironton to Cape Girardeau] shall be tried by court martial, and if found guilty, will be shot") would, according to the president, cause endless retaliation and any planned executions should be halted immediately. The second order ("The property, real and personal, of all persons in the State of Missouri who shall take up arms against the United States, or who shall be directly proven to have taken an active part with their enemies in the field, is declared to be confiscated to the public use, and their slaves, if any they have, are hereby declared freemen") violated the first and fourth sections of the "Act to confiscate property used for insurrection purposes" approved by Congress on 6 August 1861 and should also be rescinded immediately. Fremont replied, in effect, that the president did not understand the conditions he faced in Missouri or what his proclamation really meant. O.R., Ser. I, Vol. III, pp. 467 (quote), 469 (quote), 477–78.

16. Basler, ed., *Lincoln*, IV: 513, 549; Emmet Crozier, *Yankee Reporters 1861–65* (New York: Oxford University Press, 1956), pp. 166–71; Nicolay and Hay, *Lincoln*, IV: 411–13, 429–33.

17. On 20 May, Governor Magoffin of Kentucky, attempting to prevent his state from becoming a major battleground, proclaimed Kentucky to be neutral and forbade "the march of any forces over Kentucky soil to attack Cairo, or otherwise disturb the peaceful attitude of Kentucky." *Indianapolis Daily Journal*, 21 May 1861; R.M. Kelly, "Holding Kentucky for the Union," in *Battles and Leaders of the Civil*, eds. Robert U. Underwood and Clarence C. Buel (Edison, NJ: Castle Books, 1995), I: 378–79; O.R., Ser. IV, pp. 196–97; in their 12 September 1861 edition, the antiwar *Huntington (Indiana) Democrat* criticized the Lincoln administration for disregarding Kentucky's neutrality by permitting U.S. Grant to take possession of Paducah.

18. On 15 August 1861, the states of Kentucky and Tennessee were constituted as the Federal Department of the Cumberland, with Brigadier General Robert Anderson, late of Fort Sumter, commanding. Two days later, President Lincoln wrote to Secretary of War Simon Cameron to have Anderson offer a commission of brigadier-general of volunteers to Kentuckian Simon B.

Buckner, which was "to remain secret unless and until the commission is delivered." Buckner refused, accepting instead the same commission in the Confederate Army. O.R., Ser. I, Vol. IV, pp. 254-55.

19. *Ibid.*, p. 256.

20. *Ibid.*, p. 257 (quote), 258-59.

21. *Ibid.*, p. 266.

22. *Ibid.*, p. 265.

23. James R. Slack, born in Bucks County, Pennsylvania, 28 September 1818, was educated at the Newtown Academy before his father brought the family to Delaware County, Indiana, in 1837. He assisted his father on his father's farm and taught school in 1838 while reading law. Admitted to the bar in 1840, he moved to Huntington when it was still "a howling wilderness" and was the first practicing attorney in the county. Described as "a young man of little legal experience, but a fine looking blond of the Pennsylvania Teutonic type, of easy manners, of fine social qualities, vivacious, inclining to hilarity," he married Ann P. Thompson of Huntington on 5 October 1843. They had four children, three of whom survived: James R., Jr., born 15 December 1848; Sarah E. "Sallie," born ca. 1853; and Mary Caroline, born ca. 1856. He practiced law and served as county auditor from 1842 to 1851. A Democrat, he was elected to several terms in the state senate before the war. Last elected in 1858, he served until May 1861. During the summer of 1861 he politicked in favor of war. In the fall, he was appointed Colonel of the 47th Indiana Volunteer Infantry and recruited heavily in the Eleventh Congressional District of northeastern Indiana. *History of Huntington County, Indiana* (Chicago: Brant & Fuller, 1887), pp. 383 (quote), 540 (quote), 543; 1860 U.S. Census, Huntington County, Indiana.

24. O.R., Ser. I, Vol. IV, pp. 176, 296-97.

25. Nicolay and Hay, *Lincoln*, IV: 430; Basler, ed., *Lincoln*, IV: 459n; Louis M. Starr, *Bohemian Brigade: Civil War Newsmen in Action* (New York: Alfred A. Knopf, 1954), pp. 70-71; Crozier, *Yankee Reporters*, pp. 170-71; *New York Herald*, 23 March 1862.

26. O.R, Ser. I, Vol. IV, pp. 313-14; Basler, ed., *Lincoln*, IV: 549, 562-63; Nicolay and Hay, *Lincoln*, IV: 430; Crozier, *Yankee Reporters*, pp. 170-71.

27. O.R., Ser. I, Vol. IV, pp. 313-14; Sherman to Halleck, 12 December 1861, quoted in William T. Sherman, *Sherman's Civil War: Selected Correspondence of William T. Herman 1860-1865*, eds. Brooks D. Simpson and Jean V. Berlin (Chapel Hill: University of North Carolina Press, 1999), p. 165; William T. Sherman, *Memoirs of William T. Sherman* (New York: The Library of America, 1990), pp. 218-23, 228-32; Starr, *Bohemian Brigade*, p. 71; Lloyd Lewis, *Sherman: Fighting Prophet* (New York: Harcourt, Brace and Company, 1932), p. 195. .

28. O.R., Ser. I, Vol. III, p. 548; Vol. IV, pp. 313-14; *New York Tribune*, 30 October, 1861; "The War in Kentucky," *Chicago Tribune*, 5 November 1861; Starr, *Bohemian Brigade*, pp. 70-71; Lewis, *Fighting Prophet*, p. 196.

29. O.R., Ser. I, Vol. V, pp. 3, 5, 37-38.

30. Cameron arrived in Washington on 21 October. On 24 October, President Lincoln wrote to Brigadier General S.R. Curtis with the message: "[If], when General Fremont shall be reached by messenger — yourself or anyone sent by you — he shall then have in personal command, fought and won a battle, or shall then be actually in battle, or shall then be in the immediate presence of the enemy in expectation of a battle, it is not to be delivered, but held until further orders. After, and not till after, the delivery to General Fremont, let the enclosure addressed to General Hunter be delivered to him." General Order No. 18 from the War Department of that same date read: "Major-General Fremont, of the U.S. Army, the present commander of the Western Department of the same, will, on the receipt of this order, call Major-General Hunter of the U.S. Volunteers, to relieve him temporarily in that command, when he (Major-General Fremont) will report to General Headquarters, by letter, for further orders." President Lincoln wrote to General Hunter on that same date offering advice on how to handle the situation in Missouri against Sterling Price. A messenger sent by Gen. Curtis finally tracked Fremont down and handed him his dismissal. O.R., Ser. I, Vol. III, pp. 553-54; Vol. IV, p. 314; Nicolay and Hay, *Lincoln*, IV: 433, 435, 437.

31. Following the appearance of Thomas's report in the newspapers, on 4 November Sherman sent Thomas a detailed report of his estimated requirements for military success in Kentucky. Two days later he again telegraphed Thomas with details of his estimate of Confederate strength in Kentucky and closed his message: "Do not conclude, as before, that I exaggerate the facts. They are as stated and the future looks as dark as possible. It would be better if some man of sanguine mind were here, for I am forced to order according to my convictions." From this, it appears the War Department concluded that Sherman had lost faith in his own ability to command with the resources available and relieved him of departmental command. It was not, according to the president's private secretaries, John Nicolay and John Hay, due to the newspaper reports of his alleged insanity. Sherman, *Memoirs*, pp. 223-25, 227 (quote); Nicolay and Hay, *Lincoln*, V: 64.

32. O.R., Ser. I, Vol. III, p.567; Vol. IV, p. 349; Vol. VIII, pp. 369-70.

33. Located at Pineville, Louisiana, the state seminary and academy would eventually move to Baton Rouge and become Louisiana State University, "the Ole War Skul." Sherman, *Memoirs*, pp. 29-30, 164-65, 233-36, 286; Sherman, *Sherman's Civil War*, pp. 1-58 passim; O.R., Ser. I, Vol. VIII, p. 819.

34. Just prior to recalling Sherman to St. Louis and giving him a 20-day leave, Halleck had countermanded Sherman's orders for the concentration of Halleck's scattered forces in western Missouri in anticipation of an attack on the town of Sedalia. Sherman, *Memoirs*, pp. 232-34, 1097-98; O.R, Ser. I, Vol. VIII, pp. 198, 514; Sherman to his wife, Ellen, 1 November 1861, quoted in Sherman, *Sherman's Civil War*, pp. 154-55.

35. Newspapermen had to be careful. On 7 August 1861, President Lincoln invoked the Fifty-seventh Article of War, which allowed military commissions to order the death penalty for any "correspondence with, or giving intelligence to, the enemy, either directly or indirectly." In its 1861 application, this meant that the commander of a military district had prior approval for all

newspaper reports of military affairs (everything from camp life to troop movements) that emanated from his command, and violation carried a possible death sentence. O.R., Ser. III, Vol. I, p. 390; Starr, *Bohemian Brigade*, p. 67.

36. "General William T. Sherman Insane," *Cincinnati Commercial*, 11 December 1861, quoted in Marszalek, *Sherman's Other War*, pp. 64–65. On 12 December, Lancaster, Ohio, lawyer Philemon B. Ewing, Sherman's childhood friend, foster brother, and later brother-in-law, wrote a scathing letter to the *Cincinnati Commercial*, a copy of which he forwarded to Halleck, charging that "every material statement" in the one-paragraph article was false and libelous. Halleck, who had condemned Sherman in a 2 December 1861 report to Commander-in-Chief McClellan, nevertheless replied to Ewing that he, too, believed the charges were slanderous. In a 12 December letter to the *Missouri Democrat*, the Assistant Adjutant-General of Missouri, J.H. Hammond, contradicted Halleck's negative report to McClellan and independently corroborated Ewing's complaint. O.R., Ser. I, Vol. LII, pt. 1, pp. 200–201; Vol., VIII, pp. 198, 441–42; Sherman, *Memoirs*, pp. 13–14, 218–21, 223, 228–36; Sherman, *Sherman's Civil War*, pp. 161–65; "The Case of General Sherman," *New York Times*, 16 December 1861, from the *Missouri Democrat*, 12 December 1861.

37. O.R., Ser. I, Vol. VIII, pp. 818–19. The historian Emmet Crozier believed that Villard, a German native (b. Heinrich Hilgard), may have merely misunderstood American hyperbole and thought that usage of the word "crazy," as in "Cameron thinks he is crazy," literally meant that Cameron considered Sherman to be clinically insane. Crozier, *Yankee Reporters*, p. 177; also see Donald W. Curl, *Murat Halstead and the Cincinnati Commercial* (Boca Raton: A Florida Atlantic University Book, University Presses of Florida, 1980), pp. 27, 148n.

Villard himself claimed in his memoirs that the "sensational information" about Sherman that he sent to Halstead was in a private letter not intended for publication and said that Halstead, to his "painful surprise and great indignation," published a "cruel misstatement." Henry Villard, *Memoirs of Henry Villard: Journalist and Financier 1835–1900*, 2 vols. (Westminster: Archibald Constable & Co., Ltd, 1904), I: 212 (quote).

After Villard's death in 1901, Halstead wrote an obituary praising his late friend as an honest and forthright newspaperman and later financier and railroad magnate. He also mentioned the Sherman insanity story in the obituary, acknowledging that Sherman's assessment of the situation in Kentucky had been correct and that although Sherman "had a way of stating things that stung and stuck," he had never been "crazy" and the whole affair an unfortunate misunderstanding. Halstead neglected to mention, however, that Villard had sent him the story or that it was he himself who had created the brouhaha in the first place by publishing it. Murat Halstead, "Some Reminiscences of Mr. Villard," *American Review of Reviews* 23 (January 1901), p. 63 (quote).

38. In their 14 December 1861 edition, the *Indianapolis Daily Journal* reported: "The Cincinnati *Commercial* published a report the other day [11 December] that General Sherman, late of the Kentucky army, but transferred to the division of the Missouri at Sedalia, has shown unmistakable symptoms of insanity, and has been taken away by his family for treatment. In the *Commercial* of yesterday, a Mr. [P.B.] Ewing, of Lancaster, Ohio, denies the statement…. But, we are not sure, so far as the general's reputation is concerned, that it would not have been better to let the public remain in the belief of his insanity. His conduct in Kentucky was so strange and unfortunate, and insanity so generally believed to be the cause, that the allowance of a full possession of his faculties can only impeach the quality of the faculties." For a reprint of the *Commercial's* special dispatch in a southern newspaper, see "Latest News From Kentucky. A Federal General Insane," *The Natchez (Mississippi) Daily Courier*, 17 December 1861; R.M. Kelly, "Holding Kentucky for the Union," *Battles and Leaders*, I: 380, 385.

39. O.R., Ser. I, Vol. IV, pp. 412–23, 420–21, 431–32, 434; VII, pt. 1, p. 691; Reuben Davis, *Recollections of Mississippi and Mississippians* (rev. ed.; Oxford: University and College Press of Mississippi, 1972), pp. 416–19.

40. Adjutant General's Office, *Report of the Adjutant General of the State of Indiana*, 8 vols. (Indianapolis: Alexander H. Conner, State Printer, 1868), I (Appendix): 4; II: 463–70; V: 429–48; VIII: 215–17; Roger Peckinpaugh, *Rescue by Rail: Troop Transfer and the Civil War* (Lincoln: University of Nebraska Press, 1998), pp. 110, 114; Atlas Plate CLI.

41. Bringhurst and Swigart of the 46th Indiana said the campground near Louisville was "on or near the Oakland race course, a short distance from the city." The 46th Indiana followed the 47th Indiana to Louisville a day later (on 14 December), taking the night train to Madison, Indiana, aboard the Madison & Indianapolis Railroad and transferring to steamers for the trip downriver to Louisville. They arrived at the Louisville campground at 7:00 P.M. on 15 December. Thomas A. Bringhurst and Frank Swigart, comps., *History of the Forty-sixth Regiment Indiana Volunteer Infantry, September 1861–September, 1865* (Logansport, IN: Press of Wilson, Humphreys and Company, 1888), p. 13; Atlas Plate CII, No. 3.

42. Theo. T. Scribner and David Stevenson, *Indiana's Roll of Honor*, 2 vols. (Indianapolis: A.D. Strieght, Publisher, 1866), II: 73; Sawyer's obituary, *Indiana Journal*, 24 May 1902. For Sawyer, Netherland, and Brownlow's exchanges in the *Times*, see: "Why a Minister Left His Church—Brutal Outrages On Slaves," *New York Times*, 17 September 1857; "The Netherland Negro; Statement From Col. Netherland, Concerning the Negro That He Bought of Dr. Ross; Character and Conduct of the Negro," *New York Times*, 25 September 1857; and, "More of Mr. Brownlow. The Netherland Negro Case—Rev. Mr. Brownlow's Lecturing Programme," *New York Times*, 26 September 1857.

By the end of 1861, four years after helping to run Rev. Sawyer out of East Tennessee, "Parson" Brownlow himself would be forced into exile in the North by Confederate authorities for publishing pro-Union and anti–Confederate sentiments in his *Knoxville Whig*. He would travel the North speaking out against Jeff Davis and the Confederacy until his return to Union-held

Nashville in early 1863. Later, a bit prematurely, he returned to Knoxville in September to reopen his newspaper, which he renamed *The Knoxville Whig and Rebel Ventilator*, the first issue of which appeared on 11 November, 1863. About a week later, however, the second issue was rudely interrupted by "the thunder of Longstreet's guns before Knoxville." Brownlow skedaddled temporarily to Cincinnati, telling an audience there: "I did not run out of cowardice, but I will know that if they took me I would have to pull hemp without a foothold. [laughter] So I ran." He returned to Knoxville after Longstreet's withdrawal on 3 December and resumed publication. "Affairs at Nashville," *New York Times*, 23 December 1863 (quote); "Parson Brownlow On Skedaddling," *New York Times*, 27 December 1863 (quote); William G. Brownlow, *Secessionists and Other Scoundrels: Selections from Parson Brownlow's Book*, ed. Stephen V. Ash (Baton Rouge: Louisiana State University Press, 1999), pp. 7, 93–95, 108–29, 137–39; E. Merton Coulter, *William G. Brownlow: Fighting Parson of the Southern Highlands* (Chapel Hill: University of North Carolina Press, 1937), pp. 200, 203.

43. Charles Anderson Wickliffe of Bardstown, Kentucky (b. 8 June 1788; d. 31 October 1869); Governor of Kentucky from 5 October 1839 to September 1840; elected as a Union Whig to the 37th Congress (4 March 1861 to 3 March 1863); unsuccessful candidate for Governor in 1863; delegate to the Democratic National Convention at Chicago, in 1864. U.S. Congress, *Biographical Directory of the American Congress, 1774–1961*, pp. 174, 1812 (hereafter cited as *Biographical Directory of Congress*).

44. Graham N. Fitch, a practicing physician in Logansport and Democratic U.S. Senator from Indiana prior to the war, organized the 46th Indiana Volunteer Infantry. *Ibid.*, p. 891.

45. *Indianapolis Daily Journal*, 27 December 1861.

46. Scott was a Huntington public school teacher from 1857 to 1859. *History of Huntington County, Indiana*, p. 399.

47. "Letter From the 46th," *Huntington Democrat*, 2 January 1862. The vehemently antiwar *Huntington Democrat* used a number of Indiana soldiers, including Scott, as war correspondents, although attrition and growing antipathy in the army to "Copperhead" newspapers would eventually end this practice.

48. "General Dumont's Address to His Brigade," *Indianapolis Daily Journal*, 27 December 1861.

49. *Huntington Democrat*, 2 January 1862. At camp near Bardstown, the 47th Indiana was placed in Brig. Gen. Thomas J. Wood's division of Buell's newly organized Army of the Ohio. Caverly was probably referring to 1st Lt. George H. Brinkerhoff and Corporal John Carl of the 47th Indiana.

50. On 31 March 1862, John Wilkes Booth, after completing this tour of the country, debuted in New York City as a star at "Wallack's Old Theatre" at Broome and Broadway. Englishman Felix A. Vincent, born 4 May 1834, came to the United States as a young man and performed with the James Wallack stock company in New York. In 1860 he went on a "starring tour" with Marion Macarthy and continued until her death in 1865. Miss Marion Macarthy, born in Hull, England, in 1838, came to the United States with her mother in 1853. In 1858, before going on tour with Vincent, she performed with Laura Keane's Company in New York City. In October 1863, while on tour with Vincent, she fell ill. Taken to an asylum in Indianapolis, she lingered until 1 April 1865, when she died of "congestion of the brain." She was the sister of Harry B. Macarthy, who, while performing in Jackson, Mississippi, on 9 January 1861, celebrated the passage of Mississippi's Ordinance of Secession by writing the lyrics of the Confederate marching song "Bonnie Blue Flag" in honor of the blue flag with one white star that was raised over the capitol after the ordinance was passed. Sung to the tune of "The Irish Jaunting Car," the song became so popular that in April 1862 General Ben Butler arrested the song's publisher, A.E. Blackmar of New Orleans, and banned the singing, playing, or even whistling of it in his department. The ban remained in effect as late as March 1866 with the "temporary arrest by military authorities" of Engine Company No. 13's band for playing the tune in a parade honoring New Orleans firemen. Thomas Allston Brown, *History of the American Stage, from 1733 to 1870* (New York: Burt Franklin, 1870; reprint ed., 1969), pp. 37–38, 227, 368; Thomas Allston Brown, *A History of the New York Stage, From the First Performance in 1732 to 1901*. 3 vols. (1903; reprint ed., Benjamin Blom, Inc., 1964), 1:353; "Felix A. Vincent, Old Actor, Dead," *New York Times*, 12 January 1912; Wayne Erbsen, *Rousing Songs & True Tales of the Civil War* (Pacific, MO: Mel-Bay Publications, 2000), pp. 23–24; "From New Orleans. Grand Parade of the Fire Department — Arrest of Musicians for Playing Secessionist Airs," *New York Times*, 7 March 1866.

Chapter 2

1. Captain Charles Wilkes was the great-nephew of John Wilkes, English parliamentarian, antagonist to King George III, supporter of freedom of the press and the American Revolution. Charles was no less a "firebrand" in his own way than was his great-uncle. James A. Rawley, *Turning Points in the Civil War* (Lincoln: University of Nebraska Press, 1966, reprint edition Lincoln: New Bison Books, 1989), pp. 69, 77–78.

2. Besides triggering the *Trent* Affair, Wilkes was convicted twice by court-martial. In September 1842 he was found guilty of overly harsh treatment of his men, which meant something in those days, although he only received a mild public reprimand. In March 1864, he was found guilty on all five charges brought against him by Secretary of the Navy Gideon Welles: disobedience, insubordination, disrespect and disrespectful language to a superior officer, refusal of an order of the Secretary of the Navy, and conduct unbecoming of an officer. Wilkes had taken exception to a report by Welles that called him too old for promotion to the rank of commodore. Wilkes apparently considered Welles's report to be a shot across his bow and returned fire with a broadside of his own. Welles took exception to Wilkes's response and filed the five charges against him. The court-martial found Wilkes guilty on all charges and specifications and suspended him from service for three

years. President Lincoln, however, aware that renowned navigators and audacious commanders were hard to come by, no matter how irascible or insubordinate, quashed the record of the trial and neither it nor the verdict appears in Wilkes's navy records. He retired on 6 August 1866 as a "Rear Admiral on the Retired List." A summary of both court-martial proceedings can be seen in Daniel Henderson, *The Hidden Coasts: A Biography of Admiral Charles Wilkes* (New York: William Sloan Associates, 1953; reprint ed. Westport, CN: Greenwood Press, 1971), pp. 208–12 and 262–69; and as noted by Henderson, for the only published record of the full court-martial proceedings, see U.S. Congress, House, *Commodore Charles Wilkes's Court-Martial*, H. exdoc. 102, 38th Cong., June 29, 1864.

3. The USS *San Jacinto* was a first-class wooden screw steamer, which, at the time, mounted twelve guns: one 11-inch Dahlgren SB; ten 10-inch Dahlgrens SB; and one light 12-pounder SB. It operated as part of the cruiser fleet blockading the southern coast and Florida Keys. After taking their prisoners to Fort Warren, the *San Jacinto* put in for repairs at the Boston Navy Yard and was recommissioned on 1 March 1862 at a cost of $418,835.25. Wrecked on 1 January 1865 at No Name Key, Great Abaco, Bahama Islands, it was sold for scrap on 17 May 1871 for $224.61. *Official Records of the Union and Confederate Navies in the War of the Rebellion*, 2 series, 30 volumes (Washington, D.C., 1894–1927), Series 2, Volume 1, p. 200 (hereafter cited as O.R.N., Ser. 2, Vol. 1).

4. O.R.N., Ser. 1, Vol. 1, pp. 130–42, 145, 147; Martin B. Duberman, *Charles Francis Adams, 1807–1886* (Boston: Houghton-Mifflin, 1961), pp. 278–79; Henderson, *Hidden Coasts*, pp. 235–38.

5. Duberman, *Charles Francis Adams*, p. 282; Rawley, *Turning Points*, pp. 91–92, 94–95; Henderson, *Hidden Coasts*, p. 245. Most of the support for the Confederacy in Great Britain seems to have come from the upper class; the working class seems to have been less impressed. Thomas Stedman, chairman of an unnamed, London-based workingman's association, wrote to Charles Francis Adams, the U.S. Minister to Great Britain, to express the association's antislavery stance and their opposition to Mason and Slidell as representatives of the slavery-based Confederacy, which, he argued, made them "agents of a tyrannical faction now in rebellion against the social and political rights of the working class of all countries." O.R., Ser. II, Vol. II, pp. 1169, 1195–96 (quote); Duberman, *Charles Francis Adams*, p. 282; Rawley, *Turning Points*, pp. 91–92, 94–95; Henderson, *Hidden Coasts*, p. 245.

6. O.R., Ser. II, Vol. II, pp. 196–97, 1122–23, 1137, 1140, 1153–55, 1162–63, 1169–71, 1185–90, 1193, 1195–96, 1199–1200; O.R.N., Ser. 1, Vol. 1, pp. 139, 159–94, 195–202; Duberman, *Charles Francis Adams*, pp. 282–86; Charles Francis Adams, *A Cycle of Adams Letters*, ed. W.C. Ford, 2 vols. (Boston: Houghton-Mifflin, 1920), I: 87, 92; James P. Baxter III, "The British Government and Neutral Rights," *American Historical Review* 34 (October 1928): 15–16, 83–86.

7. *Indianapolis Daily Journal*, 1 January 1862; Kenneth Boune, "British Preparations for War with the North, 1861–62," *The English Historical Review* 76 (October 1961): 600–32.

8. *Indianapolis Daily Journal*, 4 January 1862. In November 1861 the British ship HMS *Fingal* delivered 7,520 Enfield rifles to the Confederates in South Carolina. In December 1861, the U.S. blockading squadron, of which the *Ottawa* was a part, blockaded the *Fingal* and the *Camilla* in Savannah Harbor. At least by September 1862 the *Fingal* successfully ran the blockade and eventually sailed under the Confederate flag as the CSS *Atlanta*. On 17 June 1863, the *Atlanta* was captured in Warsaw [Wassaw] Sound, off Savannah, Georgia, by the U.S. monitors *Weehawken* and *Nahant* and was put into U.S. service about a month later. O.R.N., Ser. 2, Vol. 1, p. 40; Vol. 14, p. 270; O.R., Ser. I, Vol. VI, p. 48; Vol. XXVIII, pt. 1, pp. 1, 189–92; pt. 2, p. 27; Vol. LIII, pp. 188, 190, 759; Ser. II, Vol. III, p. 289; Ser. IV, Vol. I, p. 832; Vol. II, p. 88.

9. *Indianapolis Daily Journal*, 6 January 1862. Secretary of State Seward, although he later changed his tune at Lincoln's insistence, had initially called for war with the British, reportedly hoping in the end to annex Canada, and had urged the governors of the Great Lakes states to fortify their coasts. Rawley, *Turning Points*, p. 83; Helen G. MacDonald, *Canadian Public Opinion on the American Civil War* (New York: Columbia University Press, 1926), pp. 85–88, 98. For a selected view of the opinions of notable Europeans, see Belle Becker Sideman and Lillian Friedman, eds., *Europe Looks at the Civil War* (New York: Orion Press, 1960), pp. 100–12.

10. Printing excerpts from both addresses, the *Daily Journal* reported: "Rev. Mr. Sawyer, Chaplain of the 47th Regiment, Col. Slack, sends us the addresses of himself in presenting, and Col. Slack accepting, a splendid regimental banner, costing $101, from the ladies of Wabash county. They will be read with interest by the many friends of the regiment throughout the State." In his address, Rev. Sawyer noted that their "mutual friend, Mr. T.B. McCarty," had delivered the flag to them. "Presentation of a Regimental Standard to the Forty-Seventh," *Indianapolis Daily Journal*, 13 January 1862; also see Scribner and Stevenson, *Indiana's Roll of Honor*, II: 45–49. Unfortunately, Rev. Sawyer did not describe the flag, nor did Col. Slack in the partial collection of his letters to Ann obtained by the author from the Indiana State Library. For a discussion of the flags carried by the 47th Indiana, see Appendix D, "Flags of the 47th."

11. O.R., Ser. I, Vol. VII, p. 529; Scribner and Stevenson, *Indiana's Roll of Honor*, II: 49.

12. This was probably the camp at Bardstown that Sawyer had originally called "Camp Wickliffe"; it was not the infamous prison camp near Chicago. It is difficult to determine what the camp names really were. Slack, for example, referred to the Bardstown camp as "Camp Wickliffe" and "Camp Morton." James R. Slack to Ann P. Slack, 27 December 1861 and 3 January 1862, James R. Slack Collection, L145, Manuscript Section, Indiana State Library (hereafter cited as James R. Slack to Ann P. Slack). Slack's letters were transcribed verbatim by the author, with his original spelling left intact.

13. General John Pope called Nelson "the most tyrannical, arrogant, and abusive officer to those junior to him in rank that I ever saw.... Indeed he did not appear to make any effort to control his violent temper,

except as it was held in check in the presence of superiors in rank." John Pope, *The Military Memoirs of General John Pope*, eds. Peter Cozzens and Robert I. Giraldi (Chapel Hill, NC: University of North Carolina Press, 1998), p. 102. A large man who lived up to his nickname, "Bull" Nelson would continue to have problems with "free-born" Hoosiers.

14. *Indianapolis Daily Journal*, 13 January 1862; *The Official Military Atlas of the Civil War*, comp., Cowles, Atlas Plate CL.

15. W.B. Hazen, *A Narrative of Military Service* (Boston: Ticknor & Co., 1885), pp. 15–16. When Opdycke was promoted to colonel in command of the 125th Ohio, one of the members of his new regiment wrote from Camp Cleveland on 16 September 1862: "Do you remember in the account we read of the battle of Shiloh, what was said about Capt. Emerson Opdycke, Company A, 41st O.V.I.? I do very well. He was acting as Major, and was wounded, a minnie ball passing through his arm. His regiment had a rough experience, but came out of the fight covered with glory, a result to which Opdycke's heroic conduct and good judgment contributed not a little. He is to be our Colonel." After the Battle of Chickamauga (19–20 September 1863), Brig. Gen. Thomas J. Wood dubbed the 125th Ohio the "Opdycke Tigers" for their conduct during the battle. Promoted to brigadier general, Opdycke showed "good judgment" and decisiveness that would play a leading role in saving Maj. Gen. John M. Schofield's Army of the Ohio at the Battle of Franklin, Tennessee, on 30 November 1864. Charles T. Clark, *Opdycke Tigers: 125th O.V.I.: A History of the Regiment and of the Campaigns and Battles of the Army of the Cumberland* (Columbus, OH: Spahr & Glenn, 1895; reprint ed., Salem, MA: Higginson Book Company, 1998), pp. 2 (quote), 126; Williamson, *The Third Battalion Mississippi Infantry*, pp. 267, 272.

16. Hazen, *Narrative*, p. 18. Privates Walter L. Guffin and Christian Schnider, both of Co. F, died at Camp Wickliffe on 15 January and 4 February 1862, respectively. Eight more died at Bardstown between 1 January and 18 February: 2nd Lt. Henry C. Weimer, Co. C; Privates Andrew Cloud, Co. G; Jacob Howser, Co. I; Henry Palmer, Co. I; David Ramey, Co. I; Jesse Scott, Co. I; Doctrine C. Lane, Co. K; and Joseph Ridley, Co. K. Another five died at Louisville between 21 February and 6 March: Privates Mark T. Vance, Hospital Steward; Thomas Powell, Co. B; Elias Parrott, Co. E; Jacob Anglemyre, Co. F; and Silas Foster, Co. K (Roster of the 47th Indiana). Albert Sidney Johnston's recruits also suffered from disease and exposure in Kentucky. Discussing the fate of the lightly clothed McNair Rifles, one of many companies of recruits who had arrived in Kentucky from southern Mississippi after the freezing weather hit, the 7 February 1861 edition of the *Natchez Daily Courier* reported: "When the company left here (last December) it numbered eighty-four robust, healthy men, while now but fifty only are fit for duty. It is truly a sad record. We trust they may all recover, and prove of service to our glorious cause and an honor to the State": quoted in Williamson, *The Third Battalion Mississippi Infantry*, p. 22.

17. Emerson Opdycke, *To Battle for God and the Right: The Civil War Letterbooks of Emerson Opdycke* (Urbana: University of Illinois Press, 2003), p. 11.

18. In a letter to his wife Ann, Slack noted with some satisfaction that Hazen had taken prized Enfield Rifles from Fitch's 46th Indiana and had given them to his 47th Indiana troops, Fitch's troops receiving Prussian muskets in exchange: "Three days since the Rifles from Col Fitches Regiment were taken from them, and given to us. Our Regt is finely armed with Enfield Rifles, Col Fitch's with the Prussian musket. It is said the officers of his Regt felt very strong about it. It was certainly very flattering to the 47th, and complimentary to the officers. It indicates that we will take the 2nd position in the Brigade. The boys all feel very proud over it. It was a matter of some gratification to me, to know that I was outranking Col Fitch. Our Brigade consists of the 41st Ohio, 6th Kentucky, & 46th & 47th Ind, commanded by Brigadier Genl W.B. Hazen. He is all over a gentleman, pleasant in his intercourse, very communicative, always ready to impart any kind of instruction or information sought." James R. Slack to Ann P. Slack, 13 January 1862.

19. *Indianapolis Daily Journal*, 17 January 1862. In that same edition, the *Daily Journal*, supporting the idea of "colored emigration," printed an article taken from the *New York Tribune* titled "The Haytien Emigration Movement." According to the *Tribune*, "Twenty-five colored emigrants sailed on Friday last for Port-au-Prince in the regular packet, *Joseph Grice*, of Murray's Haytien Line.... Arrangements are being made by Mr. Redpath, the General Agent, by which emigrants will be enabled to sail every month from Boston, New York and Philadelphia. Each emigrant must be provided with a hoe, ax and spade. All must be of the farming class. Persons desiring to avail themselves of the offer of the Haytien Government should address James Redpath, Haytien Bureau of Emigration, New York." The *Tribune* added: "The (Boston) *Pine and Palm*, the organ of the movement, publishes a large number of letters from emigrants, which demonstrate that those who have accepted the offer [of President Geffard] of Hayti have done a good thing for themselves and their children. St. Mark, where nearly all the [1,500] emigrants have settled, presents quite an American aspect. Sunday schools, day schools, churches and a reading room have been established.... Aguin and Cape Hayti have been selected as the next points for settlement." The article enthusiastically called it "the only movement of a practical character, looking to the permanent elevation of the colored race, as a race, that has ever met with any success in the United States."

20. Atlas Plate CL.

21. *Huntington Democrat*, 20 February 1862.

22. O.R., Ser. I, Vol. VII, pp. 159, 164, 254–56; Ser. III, Vol. I, pp. 767, 982. With the Federals approaching, Floyd, apparently fearing that he would be tried as a traitor if captured, transferred command to Pillow, who, for reasons of his own, immediately passed it on to Buckner before skedaddling with Floyd. Buckner, however, remained in the face of similar problems and surrendered to his old friend U.S. Grant. Angry Kentuckians had threatened Buckner with lynching, and an order for his arrest had already been issued by a supe-

rior court in Cairo. Grant, however, kept him out of the hands of the civilian authorities. Assistant Secretary of War Thomas A. Scott ordered Halleck to hold him in military custody and to send him directly to prison at Johnson's Island, Ohio. From there Buckner was transferred to Fort Warren, Boston Harbor, where he remained for about five months until exchanged for Brig. Gen. G.A. McCall. Buckner returned to Kentucky shortly after the war, became editor of the *Louisville Courier*, and was elected governor in 1887. In the national election of 1896 Buckner and former U.S. Brigadier General John M. Palmer ran for vice-president and president, respectively, in the Democratic primary on the "Gold" ticket against William Jennings Bryan and the "Free Silver" platform. *Ibid.*, Ser. I, Vol. VII, pp. 941–42; Ser. II, Vol. III, pp. 269, 333, 355; Ser. II, Vol. IV, p. 437; Ezra J. Warner, *Generals in Blue: Lives of the Union Commanders* (Baton Rouge: Louisiana State University Press, 1964), p. 359; Ezra J. Warner, *Generals in Gray: Lives of the Confederate Commanders* (Baton Rouge: Louisiana State University Press, 1959), p. 38.

23. O.R., Ser. I, Vol. VII, pp. 609, 614, 618, 629.

24. Opdycke, *To Battle for God and the Right*, p. 15 (quote); Bringhurst and Swigart, *History of the 46th Indiana*, p. 15. According to J.Z. Scott, the 46th Indiana "left Camp Wickliffe on the 14th of February, marching 15 miles through deep mud and snow, to within a half mile of Elizabethtown. On the 15th we marched six miles, and on the 16th twenty-two, to a place called West Point, on the Ohio river." *Huntington Democrat*, 27 March 1862.

25. Bringhurst and Swigart, *History of the 46th Indiana*, pp. 15–16; Opdycke, *To Battle for God and the Right*, pp. 14–15; Scribner and Stevenson, *Indiana's Roll of Honor*, II: 49–50; Atlas Plates CLI and CXVII.

26. *Huntington Democrat*, 27 February 1862.

27. Sherman, *Memoirs*, p. 240. Hazen, a regular army officer and West Point graduate, was appointed Colonel to command the 41st Ohio Volunteer Infantry in October 1861. Still a colonel, although commanding a brigade at this time, Hazen recalled in his memoirs: "We here [in Paducah] found General W.T. Sherman in command. I met him for the first time. He detached Fitch's and Slack's regiments from my brigade — by what authority I never knew — and I never saw them again." Indeed, had the 46th and 47th Indiana not been detached from Hazen's brigade, their stories would have been much different. Hazen went on to lead his brigade (including the 6th Kentucky and 41st Ohio) at the battles of Shiloh and Stones River (or Murfreesboro, Tennessee), where they held the bloody "Round Forest" and helped to save Rosecrans's Army of the Cumberland. They also fought at Missionary Ridge, Chickamauga, Pickett's Mill, Kennesaw Mountain and Atlanta. Hazen, *Narrative*, p. 18; O.R., Ser. I, Vol. VII, pp. 78–80, 564–65, 651, 654; Williamson, *The Third Battalion Mississippi Infantry*, pp. 105, 132, 192–95; Peter Cozzens, *No Better Place to Die: The Battle of Stones River* (Urbana, IL: University of Illinois Press, Illini Books edition, 1991), p.15; Wiley Sword, *Shiloh: Bloody April* (Dayton, OH: Press of Morningside Bookshop, 1988), p. 389.

28. Opdycke, *To Battle for God and the Right*, p. 17.

29. *Huntington Democrat*, 20 February 1862, from an article first appearing in the *New York Observer*.

30. *Huntington Democrat*, 20 March 1862. C.F. Smith was injured at Savannah, Tennessee; and Grant, exonerated, resumed command of the Tennessee Expedition on 15 March 1862.

31. Pope's Army of the Mississippi was made up of five infantry divisions under Brigadier Generals David S. Stanley (1st), Schuyler Hamilton (2nd), John M. Palmer (3rd); E.A. Paine (4th); and Joseph B. Plummer (5th), and a division of cavalry under Gordon Granger. O.R., Ser. I, Vol. VIII, pp. 91–95, 589–90. Prior to the arrival of Pope's Federals to the area, Missouri Confederates bivouacked south of Benton at "Camp Hunter," although the exact location is uncertain. Describing their camp near Benton, a soldier of the 43rd Indiana wrote: "On Monday we made an easy march to Benton, in Scott County, where we encamped on the ground formerly occupied by the celebrated Jeff Thompson & Co." *Indianapolis Daily Journal*, 24 March 1862 (quote).

32. "Col. Hunter" may have been Col. Jason H. Hunter, an officer in Thompson's Missouri State Guard, C.S.A.. O.R., Ser. I, Vol. III, p. 140; Ser. I, Vol. VIII, pp. 153–54, 767.

33. Part of the left margin of the article in the *Daily Journal* on microfilm was illegible. Words in brackets indicate calculated guesses on what was missing; the line indicates no good guess could be made. The anonymous soldier had written the *Logansport Journal* shortly after another reorganization had taken place in mid–March in which Fitch and Slack swapped two regiments — Fitch regained his 46th Indiana in exchange for the 34th Indiana, which joined the 47th Indiana in Slack's brigade. Reprinted in the *Indianapolis Daily Journal*, 18 March 1862; O.R. Ser. I, Vol. VIII, pp. 91–93.

34. Bringhurst and Swigart, *History of the 46th Indiana*, p. 20.

35. O.R., Ser. I, Vol. VIII, pp. 589–90; John M. Palmer, *Personal Recollections of John M. Palmer: The Story of an Earnest Life* (Cincinnati: The Robert Clarke Company, 1901), p. 96.

36. Giving his opinion of Palmer, Slack, and Fitch, a soldier calling himself "Raw Recruit" wrote: "Our division commander is from the people, despises 'airs,' and can't be beat in his eager desire to 'let us out' at the chivalry, who are frank enough to say 'the Western soldiers do fight pretty well.' The only fault with Gen. Palmer is that he is not a Hoosier. A Hoosier General should command a Hoosier Division. I can't say too much in praise of our acting Brigadier Generals, Fitch and Slack. They have proved themselves in trying times gallant and brave. They can be approached by a private upon any occasion without their dignity being offended, and they always have an ear open to their wants. They are not Nelsons nor Hazens in any respect. Privates do not have to approach them through their company officers. In short, they are the idols of their men, and worthy of higher positions." *Indianapolis Daily Journal*, 19 April 1862.

37. Atlas Plate X, No. 1.

38. O.R., Ser. I, Vol. III, pp. 681, 704–705, 741; Atlas Plate CLIII.

39. O.R., Ser. I, Vol. VII, pp. 437–38; table show-

ing the distance between towns on the Mississippi River from Cairo to New Orleans: Columbus, KY, to New Madrid, MO = 55 miles. *Indianapolis Daily Journal*, 26 March 1862.

40. O.R., Ser. I, Vol. VIII, pp. 138–45.

41. *Ibid.*, pp. 138–45, 810–11.

42. *Ibid.*, Vol. III, pp. 740–41; Vol. VIII, pp. 81, 126, 162–63, 166, 169–70; "The Opposing Forces at New Madrid (Island Number Ten), Fort Pillow, and Memphis," Johnson and Buel, eds., *Battles and Leaders*, I: 463.

43. O.R., Ser. I, Vol. VIII, pp. 163, 167, 186; Larry J. Daniel and Lynn N. Bock, *Island No. 10: Struggle for the Mississippi Valley* (Tuscaloosa: University of Alabama Press, 1996), p. 157.

44. O.R., Ser. I, Vol. VIII, pp. 81, 184–85.

45. Atlas Plate X, No. 1.

46. Jay Feldman, *When the Mississippi Ran Backwards: Empire, Intrigue, Murder, and the New Madrid Earthquakes* (New York: Free Press, 2005), pp. 170–71; Rear Admiral Henry Walke, U.S.N., "The Western Flotilla at Fort Donelson, Island Number Ten, Fort Pillow and Memphis," in Johnson and Buel, eds., *Battles and Leaders*, I: 437; O.R., Ser. I, Vol. VIII, pp. 142, 704–705; Atlas Plates X, No. 1 and CLIII.

47. O.R., Ser. I, Vol. VIII, p. 80; Atlas Plate CLIII.

48. O.R., Ser. I, Vol. VIII, pp. 102, 571; Pope, *Military Memoirs*, p. 48; John Quincy Adams Campbell, *The Union Must Stand: The Civil War Diary of John Quincy Adams Campbell, Fifth Iowa Volunteer Infantry*, eds. Mark Grimsley and Todd D. Miller (Knoxville: University of Tennessee Press, 2000), p. 29.

49. Campbell, *The Union Must Stand*, pp.29–30; O.R., Ser. I, Vol. VIII, p. 571; Larry J. Daniel and Lynn N. Bock, *Island No. 10: Struggle for the Mississippi Valley* (Tuscaloosa: University of Alabama Press, 1996), p. 41.

50. Detachments from Paine's division set to work on the railroad came from the 10th, 16th, 22nd, 51st and 64th Illinois Sharpshooters. Johnson and Buel, eds., *Battle and Leaders*, I: 463.

51. O.R., Ser. I, Vol. VIII, p. 80, 573, 587, 591, 594, 596, 580, 603; Campbell, *The Union Must Stand*, pp.29–30; Pope, *Military Memoirs*, p. 48.

52. The Federal detachment was from Col. William P. Kellogg's 7th and Capt. Robert D. Noleman's 1st Illinois Cavalry and an infantry detachment from the 10th and 22nd Illinois under Col. James D. Morgan. O.R., Ser. I, Vol. III, pp. 740–41; Ser. I, Vol. VIII, pp. 102, 110–11, 568; Daniel and Bock, *Island No. 10*, pp. 10, 41. The colorful and controversial Thompson, who had aided the Confederate cause in the Missouri State Guard and later did a stint as a POW at Johnson's Island, Ohio, was considered by Confederate authorities to be somewhat cocky and vainglorious, even a comic-opera buffoon, and he was denied a generalship in the Confederate Army. Some Confederates appreciated his efforts, however. Besides Fort Thompson, a Confederate gunboat was named for him, and he and his troopers operated on the gunboats as part of the River Defense Fleet at Memphis. He ended the war with Sterling Price and J.O. Shelby. An engineer by training, he moved to New Orleans after the war to assist with levee building, and he died there of yellow fever. Clement A. Evans, ed., *Confederate Military History*, 12 vols. (New York: Thomas Yoseloff, 1962), vol. 9: *Missouri*, by Col. John C. Moore, pp. 67–68 (hereafter cited as Moore, "Missouri," in Evans, *Confederate Military History*); "'Jeff' Thompson's Unsuccessful Quest for a Confederate Generalship," *Missouri Historical Review* 35 (October 1991): 53–56; Bruce Allardice, *More Generals in Gray* (Baton Rouge: Louisiana State University Press, 1995), pp. 219–20; O.R.N., Ser. I, Vol. 23, pp. 55–57, 700.

53. When the prewar state legislature of Missouri refused to secede, Gov. Claiborne F. Jackson, in conflict with the pro-Union legislature and U.S. authorities, created a shadow pro-Confederate state government in Neosho in the southwest corner of Missouri, along with its military arm, the Missouri State Guard. To replace Jackson, the state legislature set up a provisional government at Jefferson City and St. Louis with Hamilton R. Gamble as governor and the Missouri State Militia as its pro-Union military arm. With Pope's army approaching New Madrid on 3 March 1862, the pro-Confederate state legislature, then meeting at New Madrid, was forced to adjourn downriver about thirty-five miles to Caruthersville under Thompson's guidance. The Confederate military defeat at Pea Ridge, in the northwest corner of Arkansas five days later, along with Pope's incursion into southeast Missouri, effectively ended Confederate legislative authority in the state, although Confederate guerrilla activity continued under such notables as William Quantrill, Jesse and Frank James, Cole Younger and William "Bloody Bill" Anderson. O.R., Ser. I, Vol. VIII, pp. 378, 454–56, 765, 879; Moore, "Missouri," in Evans, *Confederate Military History*, vol. 9: pp. 20–30; Atlas Plate CLIII.

54. O.R., Ser. I, Vol. VIII, pp. 102,125, 171–74. A woman reportedly signaled the steamboat carrying the 47th Indiana as it approached Commerce, preventing Jeff Thompson's troops from capturing it. Scribner, *Indiana's Roll of Honor*, II: 50.

55. O.R., Ser. I, Vol. VIII, pp. 102, 110–11, 171–74, 580–83, 593. Although in his memoirs Pope disparaged Thompson's "artillery," as he put it, he appears to have been more impressed with them in his official report, describing Thompson's 1-pounder light artillery pieces as "breech loading, beautifully rifled, and handsomely mounted on four wheels, drawn by two horses each. They have an ingenious repeating apparatus at the breach, and were undoubtedly made for service in this swampy, low region." *Ibid.*, p. 580 (quote); Pope, *Military Memoirs*, pp. 48–49.

56. James R. Slack to J.S. Keith, 1 March 1863. Slack wrote to Keith from aboard the steamer *Moderator* at Yazoo Pass, Mississippi, and Keith, of Newtown, Pennsylvania, submitted it to the editors of the *Bucks County (Pennsylvania) Intelligencer*. It was published on 31 March 1863 with this introduction from Keith: "Messrs. Editors: I send you some extracts from a private letter written by James R. Slack, colonel of the 47th Indiana Regiment. Make what use of them you see proper. Col. Slack was formerly of Bucks county, a Democrat 'dyed in the wool,' and for many years he has been a subscriber for the *Doylestown Democrat*—he has represented

his district in both Houses of his State legislature, and is well known to many of your readers. J.S. Keith."

57. Pope, *Military Memoirs*, p. 48; Campbell, *The Union Must Stand*, p. 30; Scribner and Stevenson, *Indiana's Roll of Honor*, II: 50; *Huntington Democrat*, 27 March 1862.

58. O.R., Ser. I, Vol. VIII, pp. 81, 102, 583; Campbell, *The Union Must Stand*, p. 30.

59. *Ibid.*, pp. 184–85, 583, 591, 593–94, 603.

60. Pope, *Military Memoirs*, p. 49; O.R., Ser. I, Vol. VIII, pp. 81, 114, 184–85.

61. *Ibid.*, pp. 81–82, 96, 587, 591, 594, 596, 603, 772, 774, 777, 779.

62. D.A. Turren to Miss Pink Willis, 12 March 1862, James R. Slack Collection, L145, Manuscript Section, Indiana State Library.

63. *Indianapolis Daily Journal*, 21 March 1862; *Huntington Democrat*, 27 March 1862; Daniel and Bock, *Island No. 10*, p. 61. On the march from Benton to New Madrid, Slack was given command of the 1st brigade, Fitch the 2nd, with the 46th Indiana transferred to Fitch's 2nd and the 34th Indiana to Slack's 1st brigade. O.R., Ser. I, Vol. VIII, pp. 91–95.

64. *Ibid.*, pp. 127–28, 162–68, 184, 779; O.R.N., Ser. I, Vol. 22, pp. 737–38, 749–50, 757; *Indianapolis Daily Journal*, 21 March 1862; *Huntington Democrat*, 27 March 1862.

65. Campbell, *The Union Must Be Saved*, p. 33; *Indianapolis Daily Journal*, 21 March 1862; *Huntington Democrat*, 27 March 1862; O.R., Ser. I, Vol. VIII, p. 108.

66. *Ibid.*, pp. 83, 96,103–104, 168; Atlas Plate X, No. 1; *Indianapolis Daily Journal*, 21 March 1862; quoted in the *Huntington Democrat*, 27 March 1862.

67. *Ibid.*

68. *Indianapolis Daily Journal*, 21 March 1862. On 17 April 1862, the otherwise antiwar *Huntington Democrat*, reporting the capture of New Madrid, complained that Indiana troops were not being given the credit due them for their part in the exercise, pointing out that five Indiana regiments had taken part, and that the 47th and 34th Indiana of Slack's brigade were the first troops to enter Fort Thompson. The *Democrat* added: "[I]t was Hoosier hands that tore down the secession rag and hung out the Stars and Stripes in its stead, and that rebel rag is now at Indianapolis, sent home as a trophy by Captain John A. McLaughlin, of the 47th."

69. The *Benton* was an old, 200-foot-long and 75-foot-wide, two-hulled "snag boat" redesigned and converted by St. Louis industrialist James Eads into a heavy-draft, 1,000-ton, side-wheel ironclad with casemate plating 3.5 inches thick. It originally carried seven 32-pounder and seven 42-pounder rifled guns, and two 9-Dahlgrens. Two 100-pounder and two 50-pounder rifled guns were added later. Although underpowered, it was considered by Eads to be the most powerful ironclad in the fleet. O.R.N., Ser. 1, Vol. 23, pp. xv, 28; Ser. 2, Vol. 1, p. 44; James B. Eads, "Recollections of Foote and the Gun-Boats," in Johnson and Buel, eds., *Battles and Leaders*, I: 342; John D. Milligan, *Gunboats Down the Mississippi* (Annapolis: United States Naval Institute, 1965; reprint ed., New York: Arno Press, 1980), pp. 16, 28, 109; Fletcher Pratt, *Civil War on Western Waters* (New York: Henry Holt and Company, 1956), pp. 233–34.

70. Naval architect Samuel M. Pook designed the city-class gunboats as relatively shallow-draft vessels for use on the Mississippi River and its tributaries. Built by St. Louis industrialist James Eads, these 512-ton gunboats were 175 feet long and 51 feet wide, carried fourteen heavy guns (mostly 32- and 42-pounder rifled guns), and displaced 6 feet of water when fully laden. They carried 2.5-inch iron plate and were also somewhat underpowered with an upstream speed of only four knots. Named for western cities, they were officially known as "city-class" gunboats; but, because of the designer's name and their appearance in the water, they were soon dubbed "Pook Turtles." Pook designed and Eads built seven city-class gunboats: the *Cairo*, the *St. Louis* (which was renamed the *Baron De Kalb*), the *Cincinnati*, the *Louisville*, the *Carondelet*, the *Mound City*, and the *Pittsburg*. Almost identical, they were identified by markings on their smokestacks. O.R.N., Ser. 1, Vol., 25, pp. xv, xvi; Ser. 2, Vol. 1, pp. 42, 52, 58, 59, 129, 168, 180; Vol. 25, pp. xv, xvi; Pratt, *Civil War on Western Waters*, pp. 232–33; Spencer C. Tucker, *Blue and Gray Navies: The Civil War Afloat* (Annapolis, MD: Naval Institute Press, 2006), p. 41; David Dixon Porter, *The Naval History of the Civil War* (New York: Sherman, 1886; reprint ed., Secaucus, NJ: Castle Books, 1984), pp. 138–39.

71. O.R.N, Ser. I, Vol. 22, pp. 503, 505, 660, 757, 773; O.R., Ser. I., Vol. VIII, pp. 115, 153; Walke, "The Western Flotilla," in Johnson and Buel, eds., *Battles and Leaders*, I: 439.

72. Pope, *Military Memoirs*, p. 53; O.R.N., Ser. 1, Vol. 22, pp. 659–60, 701; O.R., Ser. I, Vol. VIII, pp. 86–87, 620; Walke, "The Western Flotilla," in Johnson and Buel, eds., *Battles and Leaders*, I: 439; Eads, "Recollections of Foote and the Gun-Boats," in *Battles and Leaders*, I: 345; "Latest from Down the Mississippi, Riddle's Point, Mo., March 27," quoted in the *Indianapolis Daily Journal*, 2 April 1862; Bringhurst and Swigart, *History of the 46th Indiana*, p. 22..

73. *Indiana State Sentinel*, 7 April 1862; *Indianapolis Daily Journal*, 28 March and 2 April 1862; Atlas Plate X, No. 1. Palmer wrote: "The point occupied by these troops was one of singular loveliness; around the position was a peach orchard in full bloom, and in the rear were the undulations in the surface made by the great earthquakes of 1818 [1811], following each other in almost regular succession at short distances. The narrow elevations with corresponding depression formed a natural protection for troops at supporting distances from the earthworks and the rifle pits, while the river, here confined within its banks on both sides, flowed south in a rapid but smooth current." Palmer, *Personal Recollections*, p. 97.

74. *Ibid.*, pp. 99–100.

75. *Ibid.*, pp. 100–101.

76. *Ibid.*, p. 97; Daniel and Bock, *Island No. 10*, p. 98.

77. *Indianapolis Daily Journal*, 29 March 1862.

78. *Ibid.*, "The Battle with the Rebel Gunboats," 28 March 1862 (quote); *Ibid.*, "Latest from Down the Mississippi," 2 April 1862 (quote); *Indiana State Sentinel*,

21 April 1862; O.R.N., Ser. I, Vol. 22, pp. 740–41; Palmer, *Personal Recollections*, p. 98; O.R., Ser. I, Vol. VIII, p. 86; Daniel and Bock, *Island No. 10*, p. 99.

79. *Indianapolis Daily Journal*, 28 March 1862 (quote). On 26 March 1862, the *Daily Journal*, noting that "all eyes" were "now turned down the Mississippi River," printed a table of distances between towns on the Mississippi from Cairo, Illinois, to New Orleans, Louisiana. The distance between New Madrid and Memphis was listed as 165 miles.

80. *Indiana State Sentinel*, 7 April 1862.

81. O.R., Ser. I, Vol. VIII, pp. 620, 622–23; Bringhurst and Swigart, *History of the 46th Indiana*, p. 25; Daniel and Bock, *Island No. 10*, p. 99; Atlas Plate X, No. 1.

82. O.R., Ser. I, Vol. VIII, pp. 88, 104, 133, 135, 158, 175–76, 670; Walke, "The Western Flotilla," in Johnson and Buel, eds., *Battles and Leaders*, I: 443–45; Col. J.W. Bissell, U.S.V., "Sawing out the Channel above Island Number Ten," in *Ibid.*, I: 461–62; Pope, *Military Memoirs*, p. 55; *Indiana State Sentinel*, 21 April 1862; Atlas Plate X, No. 1.

83. Walke, "The Western Flotilla," in Johnson and Buel, eds., Battles and Leaders, I: 445; Palmer, *Personal Recollections*, p. 99; *Indiana State Sentinel*, 21 April 1862..

84. O.R., Ser. I, Vol. VIII, pp. 158, 176–77; O.R.N., Ser. I, Vol. 22, pp. 720, 771, 777.

85. O.R., Ser. I, Vol. VIII, pp. 78–79, 89, 98–99, 104, 109–110, 133..

86. *Ibid.*, VIII, pp. 158–59, 176–77. Daniel and Bock estimate that about 1,000 escaped via Reelfoot Lake. *Island No. 10*, p. 136.

87. This was true of Republican newspapers as well. Generally, the only reports that carried bylines were letters from soldiers at the front; reports from their own correspondents were either completely anonymous ("From Our Correspondent") or listed only by initials.

88. *Indiana State Sentinel*, 21 April 1862.

89. O.R., Ser. I, Vol. VIII, p. 682; *Indianapolis Daily Journal*, 8 May 1862.

90. *Indiana State Sentinel*, 21 April 1862.

91. O.R., Ser. I, Vol. X, pt. 2, pp. 121–22, 147; Walke, "The Western Flotilla," in Johnson and Buel, eds., *Battles and Leaders*, I: 446; Scribner, *Indiana's Roll of Honor*, II: 61.

Chapter 3

1. *Indianapolis Daily Journal*, 30 April 1862. For the estimated river mileage see the *Indianapolis Daily Journal*, 26 March 1862.

2. *Huntington Democrat*, 24 April 1862.

3. Atlas Plate CLIII.

4. "B" described Flag Officer Foote as "affable and agreeable — a gentleman as well as a hero, and in this many thousands will agree with me that he differs from some of our fresh fledged Generals whose mushroom honors have made them so boorish that it will take years of civil life hereafter to make them decent pets in society." "Our Army Correspondent — From the Mississippi River," *Indiana State Sentinel*, 28 April 1862; also see Walke, "The Western Flotilla," in *Battles and Leaders*, I: 436, 446. The *Shingiss* hit a snag and sank on 9 July 1862 near Fort Pillow. O.R.N., Ser. I, Vol. 23, pp. 22–23, 255, 257.

5. *Indianapolis Daily Journal*, 2 May 1862. The 1 May 1862 dispatch from the *Tribune* concluded: "Memphis papers of the 26th say that at a convention of cotton planters held at Selma, Alabama, it was unanimously resolved to restrict the production of cotton to five hundred pounds for each hand employed, and advising the cultivation of breadstuffs instead. It was recommended to levy a tax of $25 per bale on all grown over that amount. Martial law has been declared in Eastern Tennessee. The Columbus, Georgia, works were turning out six cannon per day. Gen. Albert Pike has issued an order complimenting his Indian allies for gallantry at Pea Ridge."

6. "Our Army Correspondent — Cairo and the Condition of Affairs on the Mississippi," *Indiana State Sentinel*, 28 April 1862.

7. *Indianapolis Daily Journal*, 8 May 1862.

8. O.R., Ser. I, Vol. X, pt. 1, pp. 897–900; Walke, "The Western Flotilla," *Battles and Leaders*, I: 447.

9. "The Approach of Peace," *Liverpool (England) Post*, 19 May 1862, reprinted in the *Indianapolis Daily Journal*, 10 June 1862.

10. O.R., Ser. I, Vol. X, pt. 1, p. 902; Atlas Plate CLIV.

11. *Ibid.*, pp. 898–900; pt. 2, pp. 262–63; O.R.N., Ser. I, Vol. 23, pp. 3–59..

12. Anthony T. Slack, James R. Slack's brother, operated as a sutler throughout the war. W.W.H. Davis, *The History of Bucks County, Pennsylvania, from the Discovery of the Delaware to the Present Time* (Doylestown, PA: Democrat Book and Job Office Print, 1876), pp. 123–24.

13. *Indianapolis Daily Journal*, 11 June 1862.

14. Commander A.T. Mahan, U.S. Navy, *The Navy in the Civil War: The Gulf and Inland Waters*, vol. 16 of *Campaigns of the Civil War* (New York: Charles Scribner's Sons), 1885, pp. 47–49; O.R.N, Ser. 1, Vol. 1, pp. 129–32, 139–41, 195–202.

15. Captain James R. Bruner, Co. D, 47th Indiana, delivered a copy of the 6 June 1862 *Memphis Evening Argus* to the editor of the *Indianapolis Daily Journal*, and the *Daily Journal* published the *Evening Argus*'s editorial in their 11 June 1862 edition.

16. *Indianapolis Daily Journal*, 17 June 1862; *Indiana State Sentinel*, 16 June 1862.

17. *Indianapolis Daily Journal*, 25 June 1862.

18. *Memphis Daily Appeal*, 9 June 1862, www.uttyler.edu/vbetts/memphis_appeal_grenada.htm (quote); Robert Talley, *One Hundred Years of the Commercial Appeal: The Story of the Greatest Romance in American Journalism, 1840–1940* (Memphis: Commercial Appeal Publishing Co., 1940), pp. 24, 40; Joseph H. Parks, "Memphis Under Military Rule: 1862–1865," *East Tennessee Historical Society's Publications* 14 (1942): 34; Thomas H. Baker, "Refugee Newspaper: The *Memphis Daily Appeal*, 1862–1865," *Journal of Southern History* 29 (August 1963): 328.

19. O.R., Ser. I, Vol. XLIX, pt. 1, p. 494.

20. Thomas H. Baker, *The Memphis Commercial Appeal: The History of a Southern Newspaper* (Baton Rouge: Louisiana State University Press, 1971), pp. 113–14.

21. Sherman, *Memoirs*, pp. 291–92; O.R., Ser. I, Vol. XVII, pt. 2, pp. 116–17; Park, "Memphis Under Military Rule," *East Tennessee Historical Society's Publications* 14 (1942), p. 34. Pvt. J.K. Davisson had also edited a newspaper called *The News-Letter* for the men of the 24th and 26th Indiana Volunteer Infantry at their camp at Otterville, Missouri. The first edition (Vol. 1, No.1) was published on 27 January 1862 at Otterville (Americana Books). Davisson was mustered out as a sergeant (National Park Services Civil War Soldiers and Sailors System).

22. *Memphis Daily Appeal*, 25 July 1862, from uttyler.edu/vbetts; Major General Don Carlos Buell, "East Tennessee and the Campaign of Perryville," in *Battles and Leaders*, III: 35.

23. O.R., Ser. I, Vol. XVII, pt. 2, pp. 13–15.

24. Built in 1861, the 448-ton *Lexington* and 512-ton *Conestoga*, two of the original vessels in the Mississippi Flotilla, were converted side-wheel river steamers. The *Lexington* drafted six feet of water fully laden, and had a maximum speed of seven knots. The White River afforded ten feet of water to Devall's Bluff, 175 miles from the mouth of the river. *Ibid.*, Vol. XIII, p. 35; O.R.N, Ser. 1, Vo. 23, pp. 198–99; Ser. 2, Vol. 1, pp. 65, 126; James Russell Soley, "The Union and Confederate Navies," in Johnson and Buel, eds., *Battles and Leaders*, I: 620..

25. The two 32-pounders had been taken from the CSS *Pontchartrain* and shipped from Little Rock to St. Charles by rail and boat. The last of the Confederate gunboat fleet on western waters, the *Pontchartrain* had fled up the Arkansas River and was burned at Little Rock in September 1862 to avoid capture by Steele's Federal troops. The other Confederate gunboats, the *Van Dorn*, *Polk*, *Livingston*, and *Clark*, were set afire in the Yazoo River on 26 June 1862 and sent adrift downriver against the approaching Federal rams *Monarch* and *Lancaster No. 3*. The *General Bragg*, the *General Curtis* and the *Sumter* had been captured or salvaged at Memphis and sent to Cairo for repairs. O.R.N., Ser. 1, Vol. 23, pp. 140, 162, 195, 198–206, 233–34, 242; Ser. 2, Vol. 1, pp. 259, 263.

26. O.R., Ser. I, Vol. XIII, pp. 35–36, 104–105; James Russell Soley, U.S.N., "Naval Operations in the Vicksburg Campaign," in *Battles and Leaders*, III: 551–53.

27. *Indianapolis Daily Journal*, 28 June 1862.

28. O.R., Ser. I, Vol. XIII, p. 106.

29. *Ibid.*, pp. 36, 108, 835.

30. *Ibid.*, pp 108–109.

31. *Indianapolis Daily Journal*, 17 July 1862.

32. *Ibid.*, 19 July 1862.

33. On 7 June 1862, private citizen William A. Mumford was arrested in New Orleans for tearing down the United States flag from the U.S. Mint building and executed two days later by order of Major General Benjamin F. Butler, which, among other acts, would earn him the sobriquet "Beast." About the same time in Missouri, Col. John L. Owen of the Missouri State Guard (C.S.A.), living at home as a civilian, and under indictment by a Missouri grand jury for murder and bridge burning, was executed without trial by a detachment of the Missouri State Militia (U.S.) when captured near his home. These incidents, plus the erroneous news printed by the *Indianapolis Daily Journal* about Colonel Fitch's supposed execution of civilian hostages, inflamed feelings and brought denials and threats of retaliation from the highest levels of government. O.R., Ser. II, Vol. III, pp. 645, 673, 899; Vol. IV, pp. 134–35, 170, 233–34, 235–36, 350, 792, 808–809; Vol. V, pp. 130, 150, 796–97. The U.S. Congress's amendment of the militia act of 1795 to prohibit military executions without the approval of the president did not go into effect until 17 July 1862. *Ibid.*, Ser. III, Vol. II, p. 280.

34. *Ibid.*, Ser. I, Vol. XV, p. 551.

35. *Ibid.*, Vol. XIII, pp. 106–109, 726–28, 741–43.

36. *Ibid.*, Ser. II, Vol. IV, p. 419; Fitch's resignation from the army was announced in the 20 September 1862 edition of the *Indianapolis Daily Journal*: "Colonel Fitch of the 46th has resigned, for what cause we do not know."

37. James R. Slack to Ann P. Slack, 29 June 1862.

38. *Ibid.*, 6 July 1862.

39. U.S. National Archives & Records Administration, Washington, D.C., "The Court-Martial of Pvt. John B. Ridgley," Record Group 153, Records of the Judge Advocate General's Office (Army), entry 15, Court-Martial Case Files, 1809–1894, File KK284, Box 356 (hereafter cited as Court-Martial Case Files, KK284, Box 356).

40. O.R., Ser. I, Vol. XIII, pp. 103, 118; XVII, pt. 2, pp. 29–31, 54–55; Atlas Plate CLIV. The White River was too low for Fitch's expedition to reach Curtis with the supplies, however, and Curtis returned to Helena in order to be supplied from Memphis. By mid–July, Fitch and his White River Expedition had also returned to Helena and come under Curtis's command, just prior to Fitch's resignation. O.R., Ser. I, Vol. XIII, pp. 462, 470, 477, 560.

41. *Ibid.*, Vol. XVI, pt. 1, pp. 34–36.

42. *Indianapolis Daily Journal*, 15 July 1862.

43. *Ibid.*, 16 July 1862.

44. Confederate cavalryman A.R. Johnson, in his official report of Morgan's raid, said: "I believe we were the pioneer invaders of the Northern soil. We captured 520 muskets, 400 pistols, 150 sabers, and a large lot of commissary and hospital stores. We paroled 180 prisoners. The number of men engaged in this and the Henderson expedition numbered 35." O.R., Ser. I, Vol. XVI, pt. 2, pp. 994–95. Regarding the raid on Newburg, W.R. Holloway, Governor Morton's personal secretary, wrote: "The rebels under Johnson remained ... long enough to steal and destroy all the hospital stores, parole the sick and wounded soldiers, steal a few horses and wagons, then recross to Kentucky. The boys in hospital were armed and wanted to fight, but the surgeon ordered them to lay down their arms. Governor Morton has ordered the arrest of the surgeon. Two citizens of our state, who brought the rebels over and remained after they left, were killed by our citizens.... We have sent a sufficient force to Henderson, under General Love, of our State Militia, to clean out Henderson, Webster, Davis, and Union Counties.... Governor Morton has gone with him." O.R., Ser. I, Vol. XVI, pt. 1, pp. 813–14.

45. *Ibid.*, Vol. XVII, pt. 2, pp. 30–31, 114, 121–23; Sherman, *Memoirs*, pp. 279, 285.

46. Sherman, *Memoirs*, pp. 291–92; also in Sherman, *Sherman's Civil War*, pp. 257–58 and O.R., Ser. I, Vol. XVII, pt. 2, pp. 116–17.

47. The day before Sawyer published Fitch's article in the *Union Appeal*, Sherman sent a letter dated 21 August 1862 to Sawyer as editor of the *Union Appeal* and to the editor of the *Memphis Bulletin* in which he clarified his views about current journalistic practice and libel: "A man who for any reason with holds his signature for publication has some base motive. The publisher of an anonymous article becomes the author and is liable." Sherman, *Sherman's Civil War*, p. 283.

The paragraph written by Chaplain Fitch that led to Curtis's complaint, and to Sawyer's arrest for publishing it in the 22 August 1862 edition, read: "So complete a desolation never met my eye before. Even the Masonic Lodge was despoiled by some ruthless hands of the jewels, its bible torn to pieces on its altar, and its stands broken to flinders scattered over the floor. This latter work is attributed to the barbarian bands composing Osterhaus's division, who, it is said, when passing through with Curtis's army, went for plunder, theft, and indiscriminate smashup of whatever they could lay their hands on." *New York Daily Tribune*, 5 September 1862; see also Marszalek, *Sherman's Other War*, p. 104.

Ironically, on 5 September 1862, the *New York Daily Tribune* published a news dispatch from the peripatetic original *Memphis Appeal* on the same page titled "Extracts from Rebel Sources," from the "Editorial Correspondence of the *Grenada Appeal*," dateline 26 August 1862, Jackson, Mississippi. The news dispatch, subtitled "Rebel Account of the Yazoo River Expedition," dealt with the problems the Confederates were having in defending Vicksburg and the lower Yazoo River from Federal gunboats. Noting that part of the problem was lack of serviceable batteries, the editorial concluded: "But our authorities ought to learn one thing, and had as well make a note of it now as any other time: that raw recruits, particularly *misfits*, who are mostly under inexperienced officers, will not answer for the defense of positions that can be assailed."

Chapter 4

1. "A Secret Treasonable Organization," *Indianapolis Daily Journal*, 11 July 1862; *ibid.*, "A New Form of Secession," 16 July 1862

2. William Dudley Foulke, *Life of Oliver P. Morton, Including His Important Speeches*, 2 vols. (Indianapolis-Kansas City: The Bowen-Merrill Company, 1899), I: 66–67; *Biographical Directory of Congress*, pp. 170, 174, 187, 891, 1041, 1189, 1365; *Indianapolis Daily Journal*, 20 September 1862.

3. O.R., Ser. I, Vol. XVI, pt. 2, pp. 74–57, 729–34; Irving A. Buck, *Cleburne and His Command* (Jackson, TN: McCowat-Mercer Press, 1957; reprint ed., Wilmington, NC: Broadfoot Publishing Company, 1995), p.103.

4. O.R., Ser. I, Vol. XIII, pp. 206–207, 555–56, 560, 572. On 29 August 1862, at Helena, Arkansas, Brigadier General Frederick Steele replaced Major General Samuel R. Curtis in command of the Army of the Southwest; Curtis would assume command of the Department of the Missouri at St. Louis about one month later. *Ibid.*, pp. 5–6.

5. In their 7 August 1862 edition, the *Huntington Democrat* wrote: "Colonel James R. Slack, of the 47th Regiment, arrived here yesterday morning, on a visit to his family. The Colonel looks exceedingly hearty—somewhat rougher than we have been accustomed to see him, but not as rough as he had been represented to us as looking at Memphis. They told us he wore nothing but a shirt collar and boots during the hot weather there, and had a big nigger to fan him. Somebody had one on him, no doubt."

6. *Indianapolis Daily Journal*, 17 September 1862.

7. "The Court-Martial of 2nd Lt. Hiram Moorhouse," Court-Martial Case Files, KK275, Box 355.

8. Buck, *Cleburne*, p. 108; O.R., Ser. I, Vol. XVI, pt. 1, pp. 5–6, 907–916, 932.

9. *Indianapolis Daily Journal*, 4 and 5 September 1862; these Ohio Valley home guards were sometimes referred to as "minute men" and "squirrel hunters." O.R., Ser. I, Vol. XVI, pt. 1, p. 428; pt. 2, pp. 514, 524

10. Of Buell, the editor of the *Daily Journal* wrote that he was being "out-generaled" by Bragg; of Nelson he wrote: "If he does well now [defending Louisville] it will astonish the nation." *Indianapolis Daily Journal*, 23 September 1862.

11. *Ibid.*, 26 and 27 September 1862.

12. Although arrested, Davis was soon released and returned to his command. He never stood trial for Nelson's murder. *Ibid.*, 30 September and 22 October 1862.

13. O.R., Ser. I, Vol. XVI, pt. 2, p. 634 (quote). On 24 October 1862, Brigadier General William Rosecrans superseded Buell and immediately moved the army to Nashville, where Buell's old Army of the Ohio became the reconstituted Army of the Cumberland. The Department of the Ohio, which had been enlarged on 19 August 1862 to include Ohio, Indiana, Illinois, Wisconsin, and Tennessee east of the Tennessee River, including Cumberland Gap, remained under the command of Major General Horatio Wright, carrying, from that time on, the name Army of the Ohio. The "Army of the Mississippi" temporarily lost its distinctive designation when Grant assumed command on 25 October 1862 of the newly constituted 13th Army Corps and the Department of the Tennessee, with districts at Memphis; Jackson, Tennessee; Corinth, Mississippi; and Columbus, Kentucky. *Ibid.*, pp.374–75; Vol. XVII, pt. 1, pp. 4–5; Francis Vinton Greene, *The Army in the Civil War: The Mississippi*. Vol.8 of *Campaigns of the Civil War* (New York: Scribner's Sons, 1885), p. 55.

14. James R. Slack to Ann P. Slack, 9 and 11 September 1862.

15. *Ibid.*, 15 September 1862.

16. *Indianapolis Daily Journal*, 22 October 1862; *Huntington Democrat*, 9 October 1862; "camp fever" was the common term for epidemic louse-born typhus. Lee Goldman and J. Claude Bennett, eds., *Cecil Textbook of Medicine*, 21st ed. (Philadelphia: W.B. Saunders Company, 2000), p. 1767.

17. By November, Generals Carr, Osterhaus, and Washburn were all reported sick. O.R., Ser. I, Vol. XIII, pp. 718–19, 781.

18. *Huntington Democrat*, 30 October 1862.
19. *Indianapolis Daily Journal*, 13 August 1862.
20. *Huntington Democrat*, 16 October 1862.
21. Jerome Ruff, John M. Powers, Rannals Walser, George J. Gottschalk, John Gottschalk, George Dulinsky, William Dulinsky, Matthew Long, Cyrus Marsh, Bennville Sawyer, John A. Sawyer, Amos Gehrett, and E.A. Horton cosigned Dr. Theodore Horton's affidavit. The *State Sentinel*, editorializing about the political prisoners being held in Indiana, wrote an opinion that would eventually be vindicated by the U.S. Supreme Court: "Who two years ago would have anticipated that such arrests would have been made? Who would have thought one year ago that the President would have brought all the people of the United States under martial law, to be administered at his own discretion, and that the magnificent Postoffice building, in a state loyal to the Government and in which the administration of the civil law has never been obstructed, seventeen of its citizens would be confined, deprived of all their civil rights? And what is their offense?... The President may think that the public safety requires these extreme measures, but it gives a power to bad men which may be exercised, and which has been exercised, to injure the best citizens. Wherever civil law can not be administered, martial law may be necessary, but in Indiana no one can doubt that all offenses known to the laws can be punished through judicial tribunals." *Indiana State Sentinel*, 27 October 1862.
22. The Democratic Congressmen elected in 1862 were John Law, James A. Cravens, Henry W. Harrington, William S. Holman, Daniel W. Voorhees, Joseph K. Edgerton, and James F. McDowell; the Republican Congressmen were Godlove S. Orth, Schulyer Colfax, George W. Julian, and Ebenezer Dumont. *Huntington Democrat*, 22 October 1862; *Biographical Directory of the American Congress 1774–1961*, p. 179. Shanks served as colonel and aide-de-camp to Fremont twice between September 1861 and October 1863, mustering out in 1865 with the 7th Indiana Cavalry as a brevetted major general of volunteers. *Ibid.*, p. 1586.
23. *Huntington Democrat*, 22 October 1862; *Indianapolis Daily Journal*, 17 November 1862; O.R., Ser. II, Vol. IV, pp. 746–47.
24. *Ibid.*, pp. 272–73, 316, 476, 492–95, 574, 609–610, 615, 628–29, 634, 664–65.
25. O.R., Ser. I, Vol. XIII, pp. 653 (quote), 768–71. John A. McLaughlin (b. 27 September 1826 at Indianapolis), married Louisa Morehouse at Indianapolis in 1851. An orderly sergeant in the 4th Indiana Infantry during the Mexican War, at the outbreak of the Civil War he first served for three months as 1st Lieutenant of Company K, 11th Indiana Volunteers before he raised the company of volunteers that became Company A of the 47th Indiana. William G. Cutler, *History of the State of Kansas* (Chicago: A.T. Andreas, 1883), p. 29. www.kancoll.org/books/cutleer/shawneeshawnee-co-p29.html.
26. *Indianapolis Daily Journal*, 11 November 1862.
27. O.R., Ser. I, Vol. XIII, pp. 358–60. On 20 November 1862, Slack's 47th Indiana was part of Steele's District of Eastern Arkansas infantry, no divisions listed; on 13 December 1862, the 47th Indiana was listed in C.E. Hovey's 1st brigade, along with the 43rd and 46th Indiana, of A.P. Hovey's 2nd division. The 2nd brigade of A.P. Hovey's division included the 13th Illinois, the 4th Iowa, the 56th Ohio, and the 29th Wisconsin; the 3rd brigade included the 11th, 24th, and 34th Indiana. O.R., Ser. I, Vol. XIII, pp. 808–12; XXII, pt. 1, pp. 831–32.
28. O.R., Ser. I, Vol. XVII, pt. 2, p. 718; Sherman, *Memoirs*, pp. 283–84; Gen. Joseph E. Johnston, *Narrative of Military Operations During the Civil War* (New York: D. Appleton and Co., 1874; reprint ed., New York: Da Capo Press, 1959), pp. 147–52.
29. O.R., Ser. I, Vol. XVII, pt. 2, pp. 274–75, 277–78, 282,333–34, 401, 308502, 849–50; Col. Thomas L. Snead, "The Conquest of Arkansas," in Johnson and Buel, eds., *Battles and Leaders*, III: 451; Richard L. Kiper, *Major General John Alexander McClernand: Politician in Uniform* (Kent, OH: Kent State University Press, 1999), p. 138. McClernand, a longtime Democratic politician and congressman from Illinois, resigned from the Thirty-seventh Congress on 28 October 1861 to accept a commission as brigadier general of volunteers with virtually no military experience. (He had served for three months in 1832 in a militia unit as a private and brigade assistant quartermaster during the Black Hawk War.) *Biographical Directory of the American Congress, 1774–1961*, pp. 1285–86; Francis Vinton Green, "The Mississippi," in *Campaigns of the Civil War*, 4: 59–61. John G. Nicolay and John Hay, Lincoln's private secretaries and confidants, wrote: "After the death of Senator Douglas, there was probably no Democrat in the State of Illinois, except John A. Logan, who could bring such a decided and valuable support to the Union cause as McClernand." Nicolay and Hay, *Abraham Lincoln*, VII: 136.
30. James H. Wilson, *Under the Old Flag: Recollections of Military Operations in the War for the Union, the Spanish War, the Boxer Rebellion, etc.* 2 vols. (New York: D. Appleton, 1912) microform, I: 120–21, 144–45; Snead, "Conquest of Arkansas," in Johnson and Buel, eds., *Battles and Leaders*, III: 451; O.R.N, Ser. I, Vol. 23, pp. 396–97; Kiper, *McClernand*, pp. 142–43. On 24 November 1862, Sherman wrote his brother, Sen. John Sherman: "McClernand is announced as forming a grand army to sweep the Mississippi when the truth is he is in Springfield, Illinois, trying to be elected to the U.S. Senate." *Sherman's Civil War*, p. 337.
31. O.R., Ser. I, Vol. XVII, pt. 1, p. 469.
32. *Ibid.*, pp. 5, 471; pt. 2, pp. 282, 307–8, 502; O.R.N., Ser. 1, Vol. 23, p. 397.
33. O.R., Ser. I, Vol. XVII, pt. 1, pp. 530–32, 892; Atlas Plate CLIV.
34. O.R., Ser. I, Vol. XVII, pt. 1, pp. 528–41; Atlas Plate CLIV.
35. The term "Bohemian" derives from the French word "Boheme" or "Bohemien," which was applied to travelers or wanderers from the east (thought to be from a lower caste in India) and who first appeared in France in the 15th century. The travelers, who referred to themselves as the "Roma" or "Gypsies," traveled through Bohemia, in what is now the Czech Republic, on their way to France. The French mistakenly identified them as originating in Bohemia and called them "Bohemians."

Originally, the Bohemians were considered dangerous outsiders, wanderers without roots, beggars and thieves. By the early 19th century, French writers and poets like Victor Hugo and George Sand had begun to transform the idea of the "Bohemian," at least in literary circles, from "wandering beggar and thief" to "freedom-loving vagabond" at odds with conventional French society, as were they and many other Romantic writers of the period. In turn, "Bohemian" came to refer not to Gypsies, but to the unconventional lifestyle of the young scholars and philosophers who had traveled to Paris from all over Europe since the 13th century to study theology at the University of Paris (La Sorbonne). In the early years, Latin had been their universal language and the neighborhood around the university had come to be known as the "Latin Quarter." As the university expanded to include more faculties than theology, the Latin Quarter came to be inhabited by a wide variety of scholars, writers, and artists known for their unconventional lifestyles. Jean-Paul Clebert, *The Gypsies*, trans. Charles Duff (Baltimore: Penguin Books, 1969), pp. 54, 64, 69, 74, 123–24; Marilyn Brown, *Gypsies and Other Bohemians: The Myth of the Artist in Nineteenth-Century France* (Ann Arbor: UMI Research Press, 1985), pp. 7–8, 22–24

By 1845, the term "Bohemian" was applied primarily to struggling artists and writers in the Latin Quarter who were striving for intellectual and artistic freedom. That year, the French writer Henri Murger, himself penniless and struggling, wrote a series of stories about life in the Latin Quarter for the newspaper *Corsair-Satan*. In 1849, his serialized stories were turned into a successful stage play, and in 1851 they were published in book form under the title *Scenes de la Vie de Boheme*. Murger's work popularized the definition of the "Bohemian" as a struggling but independent artist or writer not only in Europe, but in the United States as well. Arthur Moss and Evalyn Marvel, *The Legend of the Latin Quarter: Henry Murger and the Birth of Bohemia* (New York: Beechhurst Press, 1946), pp. 7–8; Encyclopedia Britannica, 11th ed., s.v. "Murger, Henri."

The idea of a "Bohemian" lifestyle caught on in New York in the 1850s, with its epicenter at Pfaff's beer cellar at the corner of Bleeker Street and Broadway in lower Manhattan. There, a circle of young and aspiring writers and newspaper "reporters" adopted the term to emulate Murger's popularized notion of the struggling denizens of Paris's Latin Quarter. With the outbreak of the Civil War, these self-styled "Bohemians" were among the first war correspondents. Andie Tucher, "Reporting for Duty: The Bohemian Brigade, the Civil War, and the Social Construction of the Reporter," *Book History* 9 (2006): 133 (quote), 139; Starr, *Bohemian Brigade*, pp. 3–11, 62–64; Crozier, *Yankee Reporters*, pp. 167–68.

Most of the new war correspondents to emerge from Pfaff's beer cellar reported to their New York newspapers via telegraph from the eastern front. Others, however, were sent west to cover General Fremont in Missouri, and they took the spirit of Pfaff's beer cellar with them. Western reporters who had never been to New York, or to Pfaff's, quickly identified with the romanticized idea of the "Bohemian" lifestyle and with membership in an unofficial fraternity of reporters. The original western "Bohemian Brigade," those who covered Fremont's movements in Missouri in 1861, included Franc B. Wilkie, hired away from the *Dubuque Herald* to the *New York Times*; Thomas Knox of the *New York Herald*, who would later be court-martialed by Sherman and convicted of "spying" for publishing reports of Sherman's position and troop strength at Vicksburg, and ordered outside the army's lines; Albert D. Richardson of the *New York Tribune*; Junius Henry Brown of the *New York Tribune*; Richard T. Colburn of the *New York World*; George W. Beamon of the *St. Louis Democrat*; Henry Lovie, artist for *Frank Leslie's Illustrated Newspaper*; and Alexander Simplot of *Harper's Weekly*. As the war progressed, this group of reporters and those who would join them became known as the "Bohemian Brigade." While writing for the *Times*, Wilkie wrote under the pen name, "Galway," which he took from the name of the town in Saratoga County, New York, where he lived before going west. Franc B. Wilkie, *Pen and Powder* (Boston: Ticknor and Company, 1888), pp. 16, 18, 23, 38, 51–52, 54, 117; Galway [Franc B. Wilkie], "The War in the West, Progress of Gen. Fremont," *New York Times*, 4 November 1861; also see "The Vault at Pfaff's: An Archive of Art and Literature by New York City's Nineteenth-Century Bohemians," Lehigh University Digital Library; O.R., Ser. I, Vol. XVII, pt. 2, pp. 588, 889–97.

36. Galway [Franc B. Wilkie], "War in Mississippi, Details of the Expedition Under Gen. Hovey," *New York Times*, 18 December 1862.

37. *Ibid*. In his memoir, Wilkie called Hovey's raid into Mississippi "the most outrageous of the war" and added: "A desire to destroy seemed to pervade a large portion of the forces. The torch was applied to everything that would burn. In one house I saw the ruffianly soldiers drag a beautiful piano into the yard and then use it as a block on which to chop beef. In the same house fine pictures were thrust through with bayonets, the mirrors were smashed, the table-ware broken, beds ripped open, and, in fine, every possible form of deviltry perpetrated. Valuable trees were chopped into, the panels of doors driven in with axes, walls were defaced, and finally, when there remained no other form of destruction, the torch was applied to dwellings and outhouses." Wilkie also charged that he sent his story to the *New York Times* "and received a personal letter from Raymond, saying that they had been forced to suppress it, fearing the effect such an account would have on English government opinion." Raymond was Henry J. Raymond, founder (in 1851) and editor/publisher of the *Times*, who had hired Wilkie away from the *Dubuque Herald* to cover the early fighting in Missouri. Curiously, Wilkie made no mention in his memoir, published some twenty-five years later, that Raymond had, in fact, published his highly critical story in a timely manner, apparently without, or in spite of, concern for English government sensibilities. Wilkie, *Pen and Powder*, pp. 214–15.

38. O.R., Ser. I, Vol. XVII, pt. 1, pp. 528–41; Johnston, *Narrative*, p. 153.

39. O.R.N., Ser. I, Vol. 23, p. 397.

40. O.R., Ser. I, Vol. XVII, pt. 1, p. 532; pt. 2, pp.

421–22, 424, 506, 530, 544; William T. Sherman to John Sherman, 14 December 1862, in Simpson and Berlin, eds., *Sherman's Civil War*, pp. 260, 319; *Indianapolis Daily Gazette*, 5 and 6 January 1863.

41. O.R., Ser. I, Vol. XVII, pt. 1, 476; pt. 2, pp. 432–33, 461; Sherman, *Memoirs*, p. 305; Kiper, *McClernand*, p. 149.

42. O.R., Ser. I, Vol. XVII, pt. 1, pp. 477, 508, 515–16; Sherman, *Memoirs*, pp. 317, 441.

43. O.R., Ser. I, Vol. XXII, pt. 1, p. 212 (quotes), 809. Brig. Gen. Alvin P. Hovey commanded the 2nd division; which consisted of Col. James R. Slack's 1st Brigade (the 43rd, 46th and 47th Indiana); Col. Peter Kinney's 2nd Brigade (the 24th and 28th Iowa, the 56th Ohio and the 29th Wisconsin); Col. George F. McGinnis' 3rd Brigade (the 11th, 24th and 34th Indiana); and Capt. Peter Davidson's artillery (the Peoria Light Artillery, the 3rd Iowa and 2nd and 16th Ohio Batteries. *Ibid.*, p. 892.

44. O.R., Ser. I, Vol. XIII, p. 742 (Sherman quotes). On 9 October 1862, Sherman wrote Grant: "Since I caused the destruction of the town of Randolph [Tennessee, about 30 miles north of Memphis], and gave notice if boats engaged in commerce were fired on I should expel rebel families and cause others to take passage on those boats as common targets for the guerrillas, no boats have been molested." *Ibid.*, Vol. XVII, pt. 2, p. 273. Gorman claimed, in defense of Sherman, that Sherman, for the first time in the Federal army, had executed seven Federal soldiers convicted of plundering, marauding, and burning property. *Ibid.*, Vol. XXII, p. 212.

45. *Indianapolis Daily Journal*, 1 January 1863.

46. James R. Slack to J.S. Keith, 1 March 1863, reprinted in the 31 March 1863 *Bucks County Intelligencer*.

47. *Indianapolis Daily Journal*, 1 January 1863.

48. *Ibid.*, 25 December 1862.

49. Originally from Londonderry, Ireland, Matilda Heron (1830–1877) first appeared on the American stage on 17 February 1851 at the Walnut Street Theatre in Philadelphia. Traveling to France in 1854 to study French theatre, she adopted the French style of realism in acting and was drawn to Alexandre Dumas *fils*' play, *La Dame aux Camelias*. Returning to America in 1855, she starred in an adaptation of Dumas *fils*' play in New Orleans called *Camille or the Fate of a Coquette*. Undaunted after flopping in New Orleans, she moved to Wallack's Theatre in New York City in 1857, won immediate acclaim for her performance as Camille, and became a regular among the "Bohemians" at Pfaff's beer cellar. Her realistic and emotional performances in that and other roles would greatly influence American stage performance. Only a month before the start of her tour, a *New York Times* theatre critic called her perhaps the greatest actress ever to appear on the American stage. "In saying that Miss Heron acts *Camille*," he noted, "we do her an injustice. She does not act the character — she lives it." Tice L. Miller, *Bohemians and Critics: American Theatre Criticism in the Nineteenth Century* (Metuchen, NJ: Scarecrow Press, Inc., 1961), pp. 10, 31; "Amusements," *New York Times*, 4 November 1862 (quote); Garff B. Wilson, *History of American Acting* (Bloomington, IN: Indiana University Press, 1966), p, 124; also see "The Vault at Pfaff's."

50. A noted "luminary of minstrelsy," Billy Arlington (Valentine Burnell) gained fame as a performer with George Christy's Minstrels in New York City. In February 1862, in partnership with John B. Donniker, a leading impresario in minstrelsy, he formed his own Broadway-based traveling minstrel company called Arlington and Donniker's Minstrels. By the Indianapolis performance, Arlington and Donniker had added "Leon" (Patrick Francis Glassey) as a partner. The show continued over the next few years, becoming "Arlington, Leon, Kelly, and Donniker's Minstrels." The partnership eventually broke up and "Leon" teamed with vocalist and burlesque comic Edwin Kelly to form a new show. At the turn of the century, Arlington ended his career playing banjo and giving humorous political monologues on the traveling Chautauqua lecture circuit, including a lecture in favor of women's suffrage dressed as Susan B. Anthony. He died in Los Angeles on 25 May 1913 at age 76 while on tour. John B. Donniker, called "one of the oldest as well as the best 'leaders' in minstrelsy," died at age 69 on 17 July 1902 in Penn Yan, New York. Edward Le Roy Rice, *Monarchs of Minstrelsy, from Daddy Rice to Date* (New York: Kenny Company, 1911), pp. 83–84 (quote), 109, 115, 123, 143–44; Billy Arlington's obituary in the *New York Times*, 25 May 1913; Billy Arlington, "Minstrel Reminiscences," 4 pages, ca. 1903, in *Traveling Culture: Circuit Chautauqua in the Twentieth Century* (Redpath Chautauqua Collection. University of Iowa Libraries, Iowa City, Iowa. http://sdrcdata.lib.uiowa.edu/ libsdrc/details.jsp?id=arlington/1).

Chapter 5

1. *Chicago Tribune*, 3 January 1863.

2. *Indianapolis Daily Gazette*, 3 January 1863.

3. The *Democrat* editorial concluded: "We battled against the election of Mr. Lincoln on these principles, and we battle against the prosecution of the war on these principles. We cleanse our hands of the murders that may be hereafter committed in the name of fighting for a servile race." "The War for the Union," *Huntington Democrat*, 1 Jan 1863

4. "Out-Heroding Herod," *Huntington Democrat*, 1 January 1863.

5. William Pitt Chambers, *Blood and Sacrifice: The Civil War Journal of a Confederate Soldier*, ed., Richard A Baumgartner (Huntington, West Virginia: Blue Acorn Press, 1994), pp. 49–50, 245–46; Wilkes, "A Short History of My Life in the Late War Between the North and the South," p. 5 (quote).

6. James R. Slack to Ann P. Slack, 2 January 1863. Rear Admiral Porter also believed the *Blue Wing*'s captain intentionally "ran it onto the bank and delivered it up to the guerilas." Atlas Plate CLIV; Table of Distances between towns on the Mississippi River, *Indianapolis Daily Journal*, 26 March 1862; O.R., Ser. I, Vol. XXII, pt. 1, p. 886; pt. 2, pp. 11; O.R.N., Ser. I, Vol. 24, pp. 93 (quote), 204.

7. O.R., Ser. I, Vol. XVII, pt. 1, p. 5, 612, 700,

709; O.R.N., Ser. I, Vol. 23, p. 398; Vol. 24, pp. 216–17.

8. O.R., Ser. I, Vol. XVII, pt. 1, p. 757; Vol. XXII, pt. 1, p. 218.

9. *Ibid.*, Vol. XVII, pt. 1, p. 5; pt. 2, pp. 545–56, 552–53, 579, 757; Vol. XXII, pt. 2, pp. 32, 43, 70; Vol. XXII, pt. 2, pp. 14–15, 32; Vol. XXIV, pt. 3, pp. 42–43; O.R.N., Ser. I, Vol. 24, pp. 153–60. Lt. Com. James G. Walker commanded the flotilla aboard the *Baron De Kalb*; Lt. Com. George M. Bache commanded the *Cincinnati*. O.R.N., Ser. I, Vol. 24, p. 182. A.P. Hovey's division consisted of Slack's 1st brigade: the 43rd, 46th and 47th Indiana; Kinney's 2nd brigade: the 24th and 28th Iowa, the 56th Ohio, and the 29th Wisconsin; and McGinnis's 3rd brigade: the 11th, 24th, and 34th Indiana. O.R., Ser. I, Vol. XXII, pt. 1, p. 892. Fisk's brigade consisted of the 33rd and 35th Missouri; the 29th, 33rd, and 40th Iowa; the 28th Wisconsin; a detachment from the 10th Missouri Cavalry and Schofield's battery of the 1st Missouri Artillery. *Ibid.*, pt. 2, pp. 20–21, 32. Fisk, a banker and ardent abolitionist, was appointed colonel of the 33rd Missouri on 5 September 1862 and brigadier general on 24 November 1862. After the war he was assistant commissioner of the Freedmen's Bureau in Kentucky and Tennessee and founded the Fisk School for Freedmen in Nashville. In 1867 the school became Fisk University, which he supported financially the rest of his life. Warner, *Generals in Blue*, pp. 154–55.

10. *Ibid.*, Vol. XVII, pt. 2, 553 (quote), 555, 559; Vol. XXIV, pt. 1, pp. 5, 8–11, 12–15; O.R.N. Ser. 1, Vol. 23, pp. 397–98; Grant, *Memoirs*, p. 139.

11. The 190-ton sternwheeler *Signal*, carrying six howitzers, reportedly displaced 22 inches of water aft and 21 inches forward when carrying only crew and battery. The 260-ton sternwheeler *Forest Rose* carried six howitzers and reportedly displaced 5 feet of water fully laden. The 175-ton sternwheeler *Romeo* carried eight 24-pounder howitzers and reportedly displaced 4 feet 6 inches of water fully laden, but only 22" aft and 21" forward when carrying only crew and battery. All armored with metal plate less than an inch thick, they could only withstand small arms and rifle fire and the occasional shot from a small-caliber cannon. The 12- and 24-pounder boat howitzers they carried made them useful as picket or patrol boats on inland waterways like the White River. O.R.N., Ser. 1, Vol. 23, p. 439; Vol. 25, pp. xv, xvi; Ser. 2, Vol. 1, pp. 85, 194, 208; Soley, "The Union and Confederate Navies," in Johnson and Buel, eds., Battles *and Leaders*, I: 621; Tucker, *Blue and Gray Navies*, pp. 213–14.

12. O.R., Ser. I, Vol. XXII, pt. 2, pp. 53–54; O.R.N, Ser. I, Vol. 24, pp. 156–57. Acting Master George W. Brown commanded the *Forest Rose*; Acting Volunteer Lt. John Scott commanded the *Signal*, and Acting Ensign R.B. Smith commanded the *Romeo*. O.R.N., Ser. 1, Vol. 24, pp. 165, 172.

13. *Ibid.*, p. 157–58.

14. O.R., Ser. I, Vol. XXII, pt. 1, p. 218 (quote); pt. 2, p. 54; Atlas Plates XXXII, No. 6 and CLIV.

15. Gorman failed to recapture the *Blue Wing*, and as late as April 1863, Price's Confederates were still using it in Arkansas. O.R., Ser. I, Vol. XXII, pt. 2, p. 210; O.R.N., Ser. I, Vol. 24, p. 155 (quote).

16. O.R., Ser. I, Vol. XVII, pt. 2, pp. 578–79; Vol. XXII, pt. 2, pp. 65, 68, 70. Although Fisk reported to Curtis in February that the expedition up the White River "was worth the cost," in March he wrote to General Ross: "Nearly two hundred new-made [graves] at Helena contain the bodies of men of my command who were murdered outright by crowding them into dirty, rotten transports as closely as slaves in the 'middle passage.' It was a crime against humanity and Heaven, the packing of our brave soldiers on the White River expedition." *Ibid.*, Vol. XXIV, pt. 3, pp, 42–43 (quote), 144 (quote).

17. James R. Slack to J.S. Keith, 1 March 1863, reprinted in the *Bucks County (Pennsylvania) Intelligencer*, 31 March 1863. In his letter to Keith in which he discussed the White River Expedition, Slack also referred to the arrest of the editor of the *Philadelphia Evening Bulletin* for having published a pro-Confederate editorial. Between midnight and 1:00 A.M. on 28 January 1863, soldiers under orders from Maj. Gen. Robert Schenk did, in fact, arrest the *Evening Bulletin*'s editor, Albert D. Boileau, at his home in Philadelphia, imprison him at Fort McHenry, Baltimore, Maryland, and close his newspaper. Boileau's "crime" was the publication in the 20 January 1863 *Evening Bulletin* of an open letter from Confederate President Jefferson Davis entitled "Davis's Message." In the somewhat complicated habeas corpus case that followed, the Pennsylvania state legislature authorized the governor to go to Washington to demand Boileau's release. About a month after his arrest, Boileau was indeed released from prison and permitted to resume publication of his newspaper, but only after he relinquished his First Amendment rights by signing a statement that included his regrets for having published the message from Davis and his promise that he would no longer publish "other articles of like dangerous character." *The American Cyclopaedia and Register of Important Events of the Year 1863*. 1872 ed., s.v. "Habeas Corpus."

18. O.R., Ser. I, Vol. XXIV, pt. 3, p. 609; Grant, *Memoirs*, pp. 136, 138; Sherman, *Memoirs*, p. 326; O.R.N, Ser. I, Vol. 24, p. 479.

Chapter 6

1. O.R., Ser. I, Vol. XXIV, pt. 1, pp. 14, 117–23; Grant, *Memoirs*, pp. 141–43. Rear Admiral Porter had advised against this, believing that the area was too prone to flooding to land infantry troops. O.R.N., Ser. 1, Vol. 24, p. 159; Atlas Plate XXXVI, No. 2.

2. O.R., Ser. I, Vol. XV, p. 590; Vol. XVII, pt. 1, pp. 616–17; Vol. XXIV, pt. 1, pp. 19–20, 44–45; Ser. III, Vol. II, pp. 691–92; Grant, *Memoirs*, pp. 142–44; Warner, *Generals in Blue*, pp. 17–18. On 16 December 1862 Banks, former governor of Massachusetts, replaced Major General Benjamin "Beast" Butler in command of the troops in the Department of the Gulf. E.B. Long with Barbara Long, *The Civil War Day by Day: An Almanac 1861–1865* (New York: Da Capo Press), p. 297.

3. O.R., Ser. I., Vol. XXIV, pt. 3, pp. 39, 55.

4. *Ibid.*, Vol. XXII, pt. 2, 110; Vol. XXIII, pt. 2, p. 151; Vol. XXIV, pt. 1, pp. 250, 391–92.

5. *Ibid.*, Vol. XXII, pt. 2, pp. 133–34. Born in

Strobeck, Saxony (Prussia) in 1826, Salomon had risen to the rank of lieutenant in the army before becoming an architectural student in Berlin. When revolution broke out in 1848, he and his three younger brothers emigrated to the United States. He was appointed colonel of the 9th Wisconsin on 26 November 1861, and made brigadier general on 18 July 1862. Warner, *Generals in Blue*, pp. 417–18.

6. O.R., Ser. I, Vol. XXIV, pt. 1, pp. 8, 13–14, 45; Sherman, *Memoirs*, pp. 326–29; Atlas Plates CLIV and CLV.

7. O.R., Ser. I, Vol. XXIV, pt. 1, pp. 374–75, 388; O.R.N., Ser. 1, Vol. 23, pp. 405–6, 706; Edwin C. Bearss, *The Campaign for Vicksburg*, vol. 1: *Vicksburg is the Key* (Dayton, OH: Morningside Books, 1985), p. 482; river distances estimated from Atlas Plates CLIV and CLV.

8. O.R., Ser. I, Vol. XXIV, pt. 1, pp. 373 (quote), 376, 387; pt. 3, pp. 55–56.

9. *Ibid.*, Vol. XXIV, pt. 1, p. 374; O.R.N., Ser. 1, Vol. 24, pp. 295. 298.

10. O.R., Ser. I, Vol. XXIV, pt. 1, p. 401.

11. *Indianapolis Daily Journal*, 3 March 1863.

12 . O.R., Ser. I, Vol. XXIV, pt. 1, pp. 381, 415, 640–41; LII, pt. 2, p. 456; O.R.N., Ser. 1, Vol. 24, pp. 298–99 (quote); Milligan, *Gunboats Down the Mississippi*, p. 132; Atlas Plate CLIV.

13. *Indianapolis Daily Journal*, 2 March 1863.

14. Disabled in the Yazoo Pass, the *Emma* was replaced by the *Key West*. O.R., Ser. I, Vol. XXIV, pt. 1, p. 397.

15. O.R., Ser. I, Vol. XXIV, pt. 3, p. 62; O.R.N., Ser. 1, Vol. 23, pp. xv, xvi, 405–6; Ser. 2, Vol. 1, pp. 42, 56, 85, 137, 176, 189, 208, 213, 233; Tucker, *Blue and Gray Navies*, p. 228; "'Mosquito Fleet' of '63 Recalled by Governor," *Milwaukee Sentinel*, 20 April 1915, reproduced in Wisconsin Historical Society website, www.wisconsinhistory.org; "Important From the Mississippi," *New York Times*, 28 February 1863. The Northern press had originally used the term in a somewhat disparaging way to describe the wooden Confederate gunboat fleet that had been swept from the Atlantic Coast earlier in the war. "Commodore Lynch's Mosquito Fleet Demolished," *New York Times*, 12 February 1862.

16. The West African kingdom of Dahomey (present-day of Benin) had been a major supplier of slaves.

17. Milton W. Shaw to Alf Giague, 10 March 1863, Collection No. M59, McCain Library, University of Southern Mississippi, Hattiesburg. Part of Quinby's force, Shaw wrote his friend Alf Giague of Birmingham, Iowa, from "On board Von Phul." Shaw, who may have been sending letters anonymously to an Iowa newspaper, concluded his letter rather cryptically: "Write just as usual & if you see any more of the epistolary aspirations of your humble servant send them to me if your conveniance is not greatly hampered thereby. And keep mum, as I dont desire everybody to know everything. Yes but I did mean it for truth. Non campos mentis is the word although I do not desire to hurt the feelings of his parents. Now Alf write often and dont forget that I am realy your friend. Milt." Unfortunately, Shaw was one of about sixty skirmishers from the 5th Iowa who were trapped and captured on 25 November 1863 near the railroad tunnel on the north end of Missionary Ridge. He died at Andersonville Prison on 4 November 1864 and is buried in Grave No. 11789, Andersonville National Cemetery, Georgia. IAGenWeb, Iowa in the Civil War online; O.R., Ser. I, Vol. XXXI, pt. 2, pp. 88, 644, 652, 655; Capt. S.H.M. Byers [5th Iowa], "Sherman's Attack at the Tunnel," in Johnson and Buel, eds., *Battles and Leaders*, III: 712–13; also see Byers's memoir, *With Fire and Sword* (New York: Neale Publishing Company, 1911), for his account of the Yazoo Pass Expedition, pp. 49–53, and the 5th Iowa skirmishers at Missionary Ridge and in captivity, pp. 106–10.

18. James R. Slack to Ann P. Slack, 28 February 1865. Gen. James L. Alcorn, born in Illinois in 1816, was a lawyer, Whig politician, planter and reluctant Confederate who had initially opposed secession prior to acquiescing and voting for the Mississippi Secession Ordinance. Appointed a general in the C.S. Army, he helped to organize Mississippi's first sixty-day companies at Grenada. Following eighteen months' service, however, he returned to his cotton plantation near Yazoo Pass, saving his home and great wealth by selling cotton to the Federals. A noted "scalawag" during Reconstruction, he supported suffrage and education for freedmen and helped found Mississippi's "Black Republican" Party. He was elected to the U.S. Senate in 1865, although, since Mississippi had not yet been readmitted to representation, was not permitted to take his seat. In 1869, he was elected governor of Mississippi. After Mississippi was readmitted on 3 February 1870, he was again elected as a Republican to the U.S. Senate for the term beginning 4 March 1871. Preferring to retain the governorship, however, he did not take his seat until December of that year, serving as senator until 3 March 1877. Returning to his law practice at Friar's Point, Mississippi, he died in 1894 and was buried on his plantation, Eagle's Nest, near Yazoo Pass in Coahoma County, Mississippi. Alcorn State University was named for him. *Biographical Directory of the American Congress 1774–1961*, pp. 193, 464; Richard A. McClemore, ed., A *History of Mississippi*, 2 vols. (Hattiesburg: University & College Press of Mississippi, 1973), I: 444, 524–25, 628; II: 18; William C. Harris, *Presidential Reconstruction in Mississippi* (Baton Rouge: Louisiana State University Press, 1966), p. 244; Atlas Plate CLIV.

19. The steamer *Emma*, disabled near the Coldwater, was replaced by the *Key West*. O.R., Ser. I, Vol. XXIV, pt. 1, p. 421; O.R.N., Ser. 1, Vol. 24, p. 298.

20. Watson Smith reported that he found a receipt for cotton signed by I.N. Brown, C.S. Navy, for cotton for the steamer *St. Mary's* to protect her from the enemy's shot. Smith also reported that the man who sold Brown the cotton still had a few bales left. O.R., Ser. I, Vol. XXIV, pt. 1, pp. 410–11.

21. *Ibid.*, pp. 397, 421; O.R.N., Ser. 1, Vol. 24, p. 299; Bringhurst and Swigart, *History of the 46th Indiana*, p. 48 (quote).

22. *Indiana State Sentinel*, 30 March 1863. Lt. Col. J.H. Wilson, Federal Chief Topographical Engineer, said the *Chillicothe* carried 7-, 9-, 10- and 11-inch guns; Confederate Maj. Gen. W.W. Loring reported that the *Chillicothe* was firing 11-inch shells and 13-inch mortars

at Fort Pemberton. O.R., Ser. I, Vol. XXIV, pt. 1, pp. 379, 415–16.
23. *Indiana State Sentinel*, 30 March 1863.
24. O.R., Ser. I, Vol. XXIV, pt. 1, pp. 388, 395, 398–401; 415–16. O.R.N., Ser. 1, Vol.24, p. 269.
25. O.R., Ser. I, Vol. XXIV, pt. 1, pp. 395,398, 416; O.R.N., Ser. 1, Vol. 24, pp. 246–47.
26. *Ibid.*, pp. 268–70, 272, 693; O.R., Ser. I, Vol. XXIV, pt. 1, pp. 388, 416; Atlas Plate LXVII, No. 2.
27. O.R.N, Ser. 1, Vol. 24, p. 247; O.R., Ser. I, Vol. XXIV, pt. 1, p. 416 (quote); "Give them blizzards," John D. Wright, *The Language of the Civil War* (Westport, CT: Oryx Press, 2001), p. 210; Bringhurst and Swigart, *History of the 46th Indiana*, p. 49 (quote).
28. O.R., Ser. I, Vol. XXIV, pt. 1, p. 416; Warren Ripley, *Artillery and Ammunition of the Civil War* (New York: Van Nostrand Reinhold Company, 1970), p. 256.
29. O.R.N., Ser. 1, Vol. 24, pp. 269, 276–77, 694; Bringhurst and Swigart, *History of the 46th Indiana*, p. 49 (quote).
30. O.R., Ser. I, Vol. XXIV, pt. 1, p. 416; O.R.N., Ser. 1, Vol. 24, pp. 276, 693.
31. *Indiana State Sentinel*, 30 March 1863.
32. O.R., Ser. I, Vol. XXIV, pt. 1, pp. 397, 416–17.
33. James R. Slack to Ann P. Slack, 15 March 1863.
34. O.R., Ser. I, Vol. XXIV, pt. 1, pp. 397–98, 416; O.R.N., Ser. 1, Vol. 24, pp. 247–48, 277, 280 (quote), 694.
35. Grant, *Memoirs*, p. 145.
36. O.R., Ser. I, Vol. XXIV, pt. 1, pp. 397–98, 417 (quote); Grant, *Memoirs*, p.145; Atlas Plate CLIV.
37. O.R., Ser. I, Vol. XXIV, pt. 1, pp. 22, 45–46, 397–98, 407.
38. James R. Slack to Ann P. Slack, 21 March 1863.
39. O.R.N, Ser. 1, Vol. 24, p. 694.
40. James R. Slack to Ann P. Slack, 26 March 1863.
41. No longer extant, McNutt, Mississippi, was located near the intersection of present day U.S. 49E and S.H. 442, about four miles east of Schlater, Mississippi. Named after former Governor Alexander H. McNutt, it was the county seat of Sunflower County in 1863. In 1871, it became part of Leflore County.
42. Although Forrest had been in southwestern Tennessee about three months earlier disrupting Grant's railroad communication with Memphis, these Confederates were not likely to have been from his command. On 24 March 1863, Forrest, not one to sit still, was busy capturing the Federal garrison at Brentwood, Tennessee, near Nashville. O.R., Ser. I, Vol. XXIII, pt. 1, p. 187.
43. O.R., Ser. I, Vol. XXIV, pt. 1, pp. 407–9, 419–20.
44. Privates Newton Bateman, Cyrus Brown, William Roaster, and Hiram Trovinger, of Co. F, were killed. Privates Frank Storm and Jacob Wohlford of Co. F were injured: Wohlford recovered from his injuries sufficiently to be discharged from service on 17 April 1863; Storm died of his injuries at Helena, Arkansas, on 20 April 1863. The *Huntington Democrat* listed Hiram Trovinger, Frank Hall, John Roster (aka John Vance, according to the *Democrat*), and Cyrus Brown as killed instantly; Frank Storm and Jacob Wohlford injured. Both Slack and the *Democrat* named Frank Hall as one of those killed, but the roster lists him as being mustered out on 12 December 1864. *Adjutant General's Report*, "Indiana Volunteers: Roster of Enlisted Men, 1861–1865," II: 463–71, V, 429–48, VIII: 215–17; *Huntington Democrat*, 16 April 1863; James R. Slack to Ann P. Slack, 28 March 1863.
45. O.R., Ser. I, Vol. XXIV, pt. 1, p. 419; "The Court-Martial of Lt. William H. Hayford," Court-Martial Case Files, NN597, Box 1578.
46. *Ibid.*, Vol. XXIV, pt. 1, p. 418.
47. *Indiana State Sentinel*, 20 April 1863.
48. O.R., Ser. I, Vol. XXIV, pt. 1, p. 409.
49. *Ibid.*, Vol. XXIV, pt. 1, p. 419.
50. *Ibid.*, Vol. XXIV, pt. 1, p. 21 (quote), 46; O.R,N., Ser. 1, Vol. 24, pp. 474, 687; James Russell Soley, *Admiral Porter* (New York: D. Appleton and Company, 1903), pp. 286–88.
51. Soley, *Admiral Porter*, pp. 289–90; O.R., Ser. I, vol. XXIV, pt. 1, pp. 458, 463; O.R.N., Ser. 1, Vol. 24, pp. 474–80; Atlas Plate CLV.
52. O.R.N., Ser. 1, Vol. 24, pp. 475, 492–93; Soley, *Admiral Porter*, pp. 290–93. Brig. Gen. Winfield Featherston, C.S.A., reported that Deer Creek's depth ranged from ten to twenty feet, with from six to ten feet between the shore and the boats in the middle of the stream. O.R., Ser. I, Vol. XXIV, pt. 1, pp. 458, 460.
53. *Ibid.*, pp. 458, 460–61, 463, 465–67; Soley, *Admiral Porter*, p. 293 (quote), 294, 296–300; O.R.N., Ser. 1, Vol. 24, pp. 475, 688, 698.
54. *Ibid.*, pp. 477–78, 491–95, 687–88, 698; O.R., Ser. I, Vol. XXIV, pt. 1, pp. 459–61 467.
55. O.R.N., Ser. 1, Vol. 24, p. 478.
56. O.R., Ser. I, Vol. XXIV, pt. 1, pp. 22, 25 (quote).
57. Grant, referring to a diary he read after the war written by a lady who had accompanied Pemberton on his retreat from the Yalobusha to Vicksburg, said he would have taken Sherman's and Porter's advise if he had known the demoralized condition of Pemberton's army on their retreat or the abundance of supplies that were available in Mississippi if he had chosen to march to Vicksburg from Memphis. Grant, *Memoirs*, pp. 136, 140–41; Sherman, *Memoirs*, pp. 338–40; O.R., Ser. I, Vol. XXIV, pt. 1, p. 332, 46–47; O.R.N., Ser. 1, Vol. 24, p. 479.
58. O.R., Ser. I, Vol. XXIV, pt. 1, pp. 5, 21. 23–30, 44–46; O.R.N., Ser. 1, Vol. 24, pp. 474–80, 492; Sherman, *Memoirs*, pp. 334–35; Grant, *Memoirs*, p. 146.

Chapter 7

1. O.R., Ser. I, Vol. XX, pt. 2, pp. 294, 297; Ser. III, Vol. III, pp. 19–20; *Indianapolis Daily Journal*, 3 and 12 March 1863. Carrington, a politically connected Ohio lawyer, originally commanded the 18th United States Infantry Regiment, organized at Columbus, Ohio, in July 1861. During his command of the 18th U.S. Infantry, Carrington and his junior officers were despised for their brutal and inhumane treatment of their soldiers, including one reported death by torture, apparently committed in Carrington's absence while the regiment was commanded by Lt. Col. Oliver L. Shepherd and a Capt. Wood, although with Carrington's approval as he filed no charges against his junior officers.

On 14 April 1862, the Congressional Committee on the Conduct of the War asked for a court of inquiry to investigate the charges of brutality. In spite of voluminous testimony against Carrington and his junior officers, the court of inquiry cleared them all. The brutal treatment of his troops in the 18th U.S. did nothing to dampen his career or hinder his ability to recruit volunteers, and in the summer of 1862, he was posted at Indianapolis to supervise the recruitment and mustering of new volunteer regiments. At Indianapolis he developed close ties with Gov. Morton and began a campaign against antiwar activists in Indiana with, as noted by the *State Sentinel* and other Democratic newspapers, a Constitution-be-damned vehemence that further inflamed already growing antiwar sentiments. Thomas P. Lowry, *Curmudgeons, Drunkards & Outright Fools: Courts-Martial of Civil War Union Colonels* (Lincoln: University of Nebraska Press, 2003), pp. 130–135, citing National Archives Record Group 153, Records of the Judge Advocate General's Office (Army), entry 15, Court Martial Case File, II 985 and "A Chapter on Complaints — Abuse in the Army," *Cincinnati Daily Commercial*, 7 April 1862; Warner, *Generals in Blue*, p. 72; Stephen E. Towne, "'Such conduct must be put down': The Military Arrest of Judge Charles H. Constable during the Civil War," *Journal of Illinois History* 9 (spring 2006), p. 49.

2. The House reference to "the tyrant's plea" comes from 17th-century poet John Milton's epic poem *Paradise Lost*: "By conquering this new World, compels me now to do what else though damned I should abhorre. So spake the Fiend, and with necessitie, the Tyrant's plea, excused his devilish deed." John Milton, *Paradise Lost: A Poem Written in Ten Books: An Authoritative Text of the 1667 First Edition*, trans. and ed. John T. Shawcross and Michael Lieb (Pittsburgh, PA: Duquesne University Press, 2007), 4:393–94, p. 107; *Adjutant General's Report*, I: 245, 246 (quote).

3. "To the Democracy of Indiana," *Huntington Democrat*, 19 February 1863. Slack closed his 1 March 1863 letter to J.S. Keith: "I also send you an address to the Democracy of Indiana, published by a few of us, all of whom are Democrats, and all have been somewhat prominent in our State. Some of the Democratic papers in Indiana have been giving us a great deal of thunder over it." James R. Slack to J.S. Keith, 1 March 1863, reprinted in the *Bucks County Intelligencer*, 31 March 1863; *Adjutant General's Report*, I:21–22.

4. "The Habeas Corpus Act," *Chicago Tribune*, 3, 4 February, 5 March 1863; James G. Randall, *Constitutional Problems Under Lincoln* (Urbana: University of Illinois Press, 1951), p. 130; Smith, "Lincoln and Habeas Corpus — 1861–1865"; Frank L. Klement, *The Limits of Dissent: Clement L. Vallandigham and the Civil War* (Lexington: University of Kentucky Press, 1970), pp. 319–21; *Ex parte John Merryman*, 17 F. Cas. 144 (1861). In contrast, the Confederate Constitution authorized the suspension of the privilege of habeas corpus only when authorized by Congress. Steven A. Smith, "Freedom of Expression in the Confederate States of America," in *Perspectives on Freedom of Speech*, eds. Thomas T. Tedford, et al. (Carbondale: Southern Illinois University Press, 1987), p. 42. Also see William M. Robinson, Jr. *Justice in Grey: A History of the Judicial System of the Confederate States of America* (Cambridge: Harvard University Press, 1941), p. 620; and O.R., Ser. I, Vol. XI, pt. 3, p. 636; Vol. LI, pt. 2, p. 482.

5. Richard Lubinski, *James Madison and the Struggle for the Bill of Rights* (New York: Oxford University Press, 2006), p. 258 (quote), citing George N. Carey and James McClellan, eds., *The Federalists* (Indianapolis: Liberty Fund, 2001), p. 48; Randall, *Constitutional Problems Under Lincoln*, pp. 164–166; Smith, "Lincoln and Habeas Corpus —1861–1865."

6. Robert J. Wagman, *The First Amendment Book: Celebrating 200 Years of Freedom of the Press and Freedom of Speech* (New York: Pharos books, 1991), pp. 46–50.

7. O.R., Ser. I, Vol. XLVII, pt. 2, p. 1250; "Mob Law in Texas — A Methodist Conference Broken Up and Dispersed," *Chicago Daily Press and Tribune*, 29 April 1859; "Slavery Excitement in Texas," *The Semi-Weekly Mississippian*, 4 October 1859. Like "Parson" Brownlow in Knoxville, even seventy-five-year-old United States Supreme Court Justice John Catron, who reportedly supported slavery but opposed secession, was driven out of Nashville for his pro-Union sentiments. Clement Eaton, *Freedom-of-Thought Struggle in the Old South* (New York: Harper and Row, 1964), pp. 376–78; Eaton, "Mob Violence in the Old South," *Mississippi Valley Historical Review* 19 (December 1941), pp. 351–70.

8. *Indiana State Sentinel*, 16 March 1863; "The Conscription Act," *New York Times*, 19 February 1863, also published in the *Indianapolis Daily Journal*, 12 March 1863.

9. Documenting the American South, "A Thrilling Narrative From the Lips of the Sufferers of the Late Detroit Riot, March 6, 1863, with the Hair Breadth Escapes of Men, Women and Children, and Destruction of Colored Men's Property, Not less than $15,000," Academic Affairs Library, University of North Carolina at Chapel Hill, 2001, pp. 3, 11, 15, including accounts from the *Detroit Advertiser & Tribune*, pp. 19–23.

10. *Chicago Tribune*, 10 March 1863; *Indiana State Sentinel*, 23 March 1863.

11. *Indianapolis Daily Journal*, 19 February, 16 March 1863; O.R., Ser. III, Vol. III, pp. 19–20. The term "Butternut" was another pejorative term for northern opponents of the war. It referred to the color of the homespun cloth used in the shirts and pants of many Confederate soldiers in the western theater. The dye, made from walnut hulls, produced a yellow-brown color that today would be called "khaki" or "tan."

12. "Filibusters" were freebooting adventurers or soldiers of fortune caught up in the expansionist and empire-building excitement that followed the war with Mexico. Supported in particular by slave-expansionists, they led unsanctioned raids in the Caribbean, primarily from New Orleans, then considered the "hot bed of filibustering," in order to conquer new territory and reintroduce slavery. The new territory, so the scheme went, would be annexed to the United States as slave states to weaken the growing power of the abolitionist North. Robert E. May, *The Southern Dream of a Caribbean Empire, 1854–1861* (Baton Rouge: Louisiana State University Press, 1973), pp. 3, 100 (quote), 106.

13. *New York Times*, 16 January 1855; Prof. Edwin Freeman, MD, "Biographical Sketch of the Faculty of the Eclectic Medical Institute, 1852–1856," *The Eclectic Medical Journal* 58 (January–December 1898): 156. Eclectic medicine was one of three major competing medical practices (allopathic, homeopathic, and eclectic) in the mid–nineteenth-century United States. Allopathy, the predominant medical practice, whose remedies were supposed to regulate the body's secretions and produce effects different from those produced by the disease, relied on, among other similar invasive treatments, bloodletting and purging by poisonous mercury-based medicines. Homeopathy ("likes cure likes"), the less widely practiced rival, believed that minute quantities of substances that produce symptoms of the disease in healthy persons administered to a sick person would cure the disease. Eclectic medicine emerged in the United States as a competing pragmatic approach, the name "eclectic" referring to the use of whatever remedy worked. Based primarily on botanic medicine and Native American herbal remedies, the eclectics rejected the allopathic practitioner's use of invasive and obviously dangerous remedies. At the turn of the twentieth century, however, allopathic medicine supplanted homeopathy and eclectic medicine in the United States when it adopted the more scientific, evidence-based germ theory of infectious disease developed in Europe by Louis Pasteur and others. Its total dominance followed Abraham Flexner's 1910 report on medical education in the United States for the American Medical Association, funded by the Carnegie Foundation. Flexner endorsed allopathic medicine's late-nineteenth-century adoption of germ theory and scientific, evidence-based research. Flexner also established strict guidelines for medical education, including training in biological and physical science, university affiliations, and rigorous examinations. Flexner's refusal to endorse the less scientifically rigorous practices of eclectic and homeopathic medicine resulted in the decline and eventual closure of their proprietary medical schools in the United States. In the twentieth century, "allopathy" would become synonymous with "modern medicine," while herbal and homeopathic practices would move to the fringes as unscientific and therefore unproven "alternative" therapies. John S. Haller, Jr., *A Profile in Alternative Medicine: The Eclectic Medical College of Cincinnati, 1845–1942* (Kent, OH: Kent State University Press, 1999), pp. 7, 11–12, 16–20; Abraham Flexner, *Medical Education in the United States and Canada* (New York: A Report of the Carnegie Foundation for the Advancement of Teaching, 1910; reprint ed., Arno Press, 1972).

14. C.A. Bridges, "Knights of the Golden Circle: A Filibustering Fantasy," Southwestern Historical Quarterly 44 (January 1941): 287–287, 291, 294, 300, 301; Ollinger Crenshaw, "Knights of the Golden Circle: The Career of George Bickley," *American Historical Review* 47 (October 1941): 24, 26n, 28–29.

15. Nicaraguans backed by Cornelius Vanderbilt, whose shipping interests Walker had threatened, overthrew Walker on 1 May 1857 but allowed him to surrender and return to New Orleans. Attempting to reclaim his position in Nicaragua in 1860, Walker attacked Honduras but was quickly defeated by the Honduran army. Walker surrendered to the British Navy, but the British, who were then in negotiations with President Buchanan to reduce their holdings in the Caribbean, turned him over to the Hondurans and his filibustering days ended in front of a firing squad. May, *The Southern Dream*, pp. 83–85, 89–90, 102, 131, 149; Bridges, "The Knights of the Golden Circle," 288; John McCardell, *The Idea of a Southern Nation* (New York: W.W. Norton & Company, 1979), pp. 268–273. For an example of Bickley's money-raising schemes, see "Filibustering Again. Organization for the Armed Invasion of Mexico — Pronouncements for the Knights of the Golden Circle," *New York Times*, 23 July 1860, originally published as "An Open Letter to the Knights of the Golden Circle," in the *Richmond (Virginia) Whig*; also see Frank L. Klement, "Carrington and the Golden Circle Legend in Indiana During the Civil Ear," *Indiana Magazine of History* 61 (March 1965): 31–52.

16. Jimmie Hicks, "Some Letters Concerning the Knights of the Golden Circle in Texas, 1860–1861," *Southwestern Historical Society Quarterly* 65 (July 1961): 80–86. For early national articles on Bickley, see the *New York Times*, 4, 7, 9 April, 23 July and 2 August 1860; May, *Southern Dream*, pp. 142–43, 149–55; Crenshaw, "The Knights of the Golden Circle," 27–29.

17. O.R., Ser. II, Vol. II, p. 32; "The K.G.C.'s Unmasked," *New York Times*, 5 June 1861, from the *Louisville Courier*; "The Arrest of Gen. Bickley," *New York Times*, 26 July 1863, from the *New Albany (Indiana) Ledger* (quote). For more detail on the K.G.C. and other secret organizations of the era see for example: Frank L. Klement, *Dark Lanterns: Secret Political Societies, Conspiracies, and Treason Trials in the Civil War* (Baton Rouge: Louisiana State University Press, 1984); Mayo Fessler, "Secret Political Societies in the North During the War," *Indiana Magazine of History* 14 (September 1918).

18. O.R., Ser. I, Vol. I, p. 672; Philip Kinsley, *The Chicago Tribune: Its First Hundred Years*, 2 vols. (New York: Alfred A. Knopf, 1943), vol. 1, p. 348; Fessler, "Secret Political Societies in the North," pp. 215, 221; Klement, *Dark Lanterns*, pp. 1, 34–35; Foulke, *Life of Oliver P. Morton*, I: 85.

19. Showing the international reach of Bickley's defunct scheme, the *New York Times*, in their 30 August 1861 edition, published an article taken from the 17 August 1861 *London Spectator* titled "The Knights of the Golden Circle," in which the author worries about the possible success of the K.G.C, or the scheme it represented, and its ties to the Confederacy: "It reads, all this, rather like a dream of some mad slaveholder than a grave and definite project, which nevertheless, we believe it to be.... The whole scheme may be unreal.... But it must not be forgotten that this, whatever the truth as to this society, is one of the designs of the South, and that the plan, which thus boldly stated seems incredibly atrocious, is part of the permanent policy of the Government which has just won its first battle in front of Manassas Gap. The design we fear, if the North succumbs, is at once as possible of execution as it is remorselessly wicked in conception."

20. Frank L. Klement, "Phineas C. Wright, the

Order of American Knights, and the Sanderson Expose," *Civil War History* (18 (March 1972): 9–10; Fessler, "Secret Political Societies," pp. 224–25.

21. O.R., Ser. I, Vol. I, p. 672; Ser. II, Vol. VII, pp. 247, 931–32; Robert Churchill, "Liberty, Conscription, and a Party Divided: The Sons of Liberty Conspiracy 1863–1864," *Prologue* 30 (1998): 297, 300.

22. *Indianapolis Daily Journal*, 20 January 1863; *Indiana State Sentinel*, 4 January, 23 February, 21 April 1863.

23. O.R., Ser. I, Vol. XXIII, pt. 2, pp. 60 (quote), 65, 75; Ella Lonn, *Desertion in the Civil War* (Gloucester, MA: American Historical Society, 1928; reprint ed. Lincoln: University of Nebraska Press, First Bison Books, 1998), p. 204.

24. Towne, "'Such conduct must be put down,'" pp. 46, 48, 50, 56–57, 59–60.

25. O.R., Ser. I, Vol. XXIII, pt. 2, pp. 168.

26. *Indiana State Sentinel*, 30 March 1863.

27. O.R., Ser. I, Vol. XXIII, pt. 2, pp. 237; Ser. II, Vol. V, p. 633.

28. *Ex parte Vallandigham*, 68 U.S. (1 Wall.) 243 (1863); Nicolay and Hay, *Abraham Lincoln*, VII: 336.

29. *Ex parte Vallandigham*, 68 U.S. (1 Wall.) 243 (1863); Michael O. Lacy, "Military Commissions: A Historical Survey," *The Army Lawyer* (March 2002), pp. 42–43; Klement, *Limits of Dissent*, pp. 319–22; *Indianapolis Daily Journal*, 7 May 1863. On 25 May 1863, Vallandigham was escorted under protest by cavalry to the Confederate lines near Murfreesboro, Tennessee, and escorted to Richmond, Virginia, where he reportedly advised the Confederate authorities against an invasion of Pennsylvania, which, he believed, would ruin the chances of the Peace Democrats to remove Lincoln from office via the ballot box. The Confederate authorities did not take his advice. He left Richmond on 22 June for Canada, where he arrived on 5 July 1863, just after Lee's defeat at Gettysburg. He continued to berate the Lincoln administration from Canada and ran unsuccessfully for governor of Ohio while in exile. He returned to the United States via Detroit in June 1864, subject once again to arrest and imprisonment. But Lincoln felt Vallandigham's diatribes against him actually helped the Republican cause and permitted him to remain in the country and continue his antiwar and anti–Lincoln activities. This dismayed many moderate Democrats, who felt that Vallandigham's entry back into the United States was a Republican campaign trick to discredit them and their candidate, General George B. McClellan. Vallandigham attended the Democratic convention, gave a nomination speech for McClellan, and remained in the United States without incident, although this would not be true for everyone who attended the convention. Nicolay and Hay, *Abraham Lincoln*, VII: 339, 354–57, 359–60; John Hay, *Lincoln and the Civil War in the Diaries and Letters of John Hay* (New York: Dodd, Mead and Company, 1939; reprint ed., Westport, CT: Negro Universities Press, 1972), p. 193; Vallandigham: "The peace party of the north would sweep the Lincoln dynasty out of political existence" if the Confederates could hold out one more year and not invade Pennsylvania. Quoted in Nicolay and Hay, citing John B. Jones, *A Rebel War Clerk's Diary, 1810–1866*, 2 vols. (Philadelphia: J.B. Lippincott, 1866), I: 357–58.

30. Nicolay and Hay, *Abraham Lincoln*, VII: 340 (quote).

31. O.R., Ser. I, Vol. XXIII, pt. 2, p. 326; Ser. II, Vol. V, p. 485; Ser. III, Vol. IV, pp. 163, 578; Stephen E. Towne, "Killing the Serpent Speedily: Governor Morton, General Hascall, and the Suppression of the Democratic Press in Indiana, 1863," *Civil War History* 52.1 (2006): 48; Warner, *Generals in Blue*, pp. 72, 214.

32. O.R., Ser. I, Vol. XXIII, pt. 2, p. 369; Ser. II, Vol. V, pp. 723–25; Towne, "Killing the Serpent Speedily," pp. 41–65.

33. O.R., Ser. II, Vol. V, pp. 726, 741; *Indianapolis Daily Journal*, 3 June 1863; Arthur Charles Cole, *The Era of the Civil War, 1848–1870* (Springfield: Illinois Centennial Commission, 1919), p. 304.

34. O.R., Ser. II, Vol. V, pp. 724–25 (quotes); Ser. III, Vol. III, p. 252; Ser. I, Vol. XXIII, pt. 2, p. 386.

35. *Ibid.*, Ser. I, Vol. XXIV, pt. 1, p. 25.

36. *Ibid.*, pt. 3, p. 251; "The Opposing Forces in the Vicksburg Campaign," Johnson and Buel, eds., *Battles and Leaders*, III: 546–48; Warner, *Generals in Blue*, pp. 154, 411, 417.

37. O.R., Ser. I, Vol. XXIV, pt. 1, pp. 32, 46–47; Sherman, *Memoirs*, pp. 339–40; O.R.N., Ser. 1, Vol. 24, p. 479.

38. James R. Slack to Ann P. Slack, 16 April 1863; O.R., Ser. I, Vol. XXIV, pt. 1, pp. 47, 123–24, 139, 188, 490; pt. 3, p. 370; Arthur W. Bergeron Jr., *Guide to Louisiana Confederate Units 1861–1865* (Baton Rouge: Louisiana State University Press, 1989), pp. 62–63, 179. The march down Roundaway Bayou roughly follows present-day State Route 603. Smith's Plantation, near the confluence of Bayous Vidal and Roundaway, was near present-day King, Louisiana. New Carthage, on the Mississippi River two miles south of Smith's Plantation, no longer exists due to excessive flooding and changes in the course of the Mississippi.

39. Judge John Perkins Jr. (1819–1885), former judge of the U.S. Circuit Court for Tensas and Madison Parishes, Louisiana (1851–1861), Democratic representative in the 33rd U.S. Congress, 1853–1855, and member of the Confederate Senate from 1862 to 1865, had burned his mansion about a year earlier to prevent its capture by Admiral Farragut's fleet. *Biographical Directory of Congress*, p. 1446.

40. O.R., Ser. I, Vol. XXIV, pt. 1, pp. 140, 188, 491–94, 601; pt. 2, p. 30; Grant, *Memoirs*, p. 153. Present-day Louisiana SR-603 follows Bayou Vidal westward from its junction with Roundaway Bayou near King, Louisiana.

41. O.R., Ser. I, Vol. XXIV, pt. 1, pp. 140, 188, 490–94, 496–97; Atlas Plate XXXVI, No. 1.

42. O.R., Ser. I, Vol. XXIV, pt. 1, pp. 77, 139–41, 494, 615; pt. 2, pp. 30–31; pt. 3, p. 197; Atlas Plate XXXVI, No. 1.

43. As Raynor put it: "Some incarnate fiends, with a desire for destruction, instigated by abolition devils at home, set fire to every building not watched by an officer. More than a dozen buildings were thus fired today [16 April], generally by the new Iowa troops." Raynor, *Diary*, p. 246. Regarding the destruction on

the march to Richmond, a soldier from one of the Iowa regiments, Cpl. James P. Oxley of the 24th Iowa, noted in his diary, "Nothing important occurred until we reached Knowlands Plantation [on Bayou Vidal]." James P. Oxley, "A History of Co. H. 24th Iowa Volunteer Infantry," (unpublished diary, n.d), p.5.

44. Porter's flotilla consisted of seven ironclads (the *Benton, Lafayette, Tuscumbia, Carondelet, Louisville, Mound City* and *Pittsburg*) and one ram (the *General Price*). Soley, "Naval Operations," *Battles and Leaders*, III: 566; O.R., Ser. I, Vol. XXIV, pt. 1, p. 47.

45. Owen Johnston Hopkins, *Under the Flag of the Nation: Diaries and Letters of a Yankee Volunteer in the Civil War*, ed. Otto F. Bond (Columbus, OH: Ohio State University Press for the Ohio Historical Society, 1961), pp. 51–52.

46. Chambers, *Blood and Sacrifice*, p. 61.

47. William H. Raynor, "The Civil War Experiences of an Ohio Officer at Vicksburg: Diary of Colonel William H. Raynor, 56th Ohio Infantry," ed. Edwin C. Bearss, *Louisiana Studies* 9 (Winter 1970), pp. 247–48; O.R., Ser. I, Vol. XXIV, pt. 1, pp. 47, 141, 490–94, 601; pt. 2, pp. 30–31; Atlas Plate XXXVI, No. 1 and CLV. Present-day Louisiana SR-603 follows Roundaway Bayou to Bayou Vidal.

48. James R. Slack to Ann P. Slack, 17 April 1863. Raynor, referring to the plantations on Roundaway Bayou, wrote: "As yesterday, our route lay through splendid plantations, all of the most extensive scale, each one a perfect town itself, but all deserted except by a few negros too worthless to be removed by their masters. Almost all had been completely ransacked and devastated by our troops." Raynor, *Diary*, p. 247. Osterhaus, the only other officer on this march to mention in his report any destruction done by Federal troops, denied that any of his 9th division troops were responsible, simply stating: "Not a single case of wanton destruction has occurred within the lines of the Ninth Division." O.R., Ser. I, Vol. XXIV, pt. 1, p. 494.

49. *Ibid.*, pp. 521–29; Johnston, *Narrative*, p. 168.

50. Raynor, *Diary*, p. 248.

51. O.R., Ser. I, Vol. XXIV, pt. 1, p. 47 (quote); Grant, *Memoirs*, p. 156.

52. Raynor, *Diary*, p. 249. Noland's Plantation appears on Federal maps where Dunbar's Plantation was said to be located. O.R., Ser. I, Vol. XXIV, pt. 1, p. 188; Atlas Plate XXXVI, No. 1. Bringhurst and Swigart of McGinnis's brigade referred to it as Dunbar's Plantation; Slack and his troops referred to it in various spellings as Noulen's or Knowland's Plantation. Whether these were adjacent plantations or the same one is unknown. Bringhurst and Swigart, *History of the 46th Indiana*, p. 54; Oxley, *History of the 24th Iowa*, p. 5.

53. James R. Slack to Ann P. Slack, 23 April 1863.

54. O.R., Ser. I, Vol. XXIV, pt. 1, p. 601; Atlas Plate XXXVI, No. 1.

55. O.R., Ser. I, Vol. XXIV, pt. 1, pp. 47, 601; pt. 3, pp. 211–12, 370. Lt. Hains, West Point class of 1861, joined the Army Corps of Engineers after the war. He designed and built the Tidal basin in Washington, D.C., and Hains' Point overlooking the Tidal Basin is named for him. Called to active duty in 1916 by a special act of Congress, he was appointed major-general and served as Division Engineer in Washington, D.C., the only Civil War officer to serve in World War I, and, at age 76, the oldest officer in uniform. www.arlingtoncemetery.net/pchains.htm.

56. Hopkins, *Under the Flag of the Nation*, p. 53.

57. Chambers, *Blood and Sacrifice*, p. 62.

58. O.R., Ser. I, Vol. XXIV, pt. 1, pp. 126–27.

59. *Ibid.*, pp. 126–27, 141, 186,188, 601; Raynor, *Diary*, pp. 250–51; Atlas Plate XXXVI, No. 1.

60. Yates (governor of Illinois, 1861–1865) had appointed Grant mustering officer for Illinois and had given him his first commission as colonel of the 21st Illinois regiment. Yates had lost a bid to take the late Senator Stephen A. Douglas's seat in 1862, but ran and won as a "Union Republican" in November 1864 after a series of Federal victories on the battlefield reversed the rising tide of antiwar sentiment in Illinois. His well-timed battlefield tour with Grant's army certainly did not hurt his race for the Senate. He served as U.S. Senator from Illinois from 4 March 1865 to 3 March 1871. *Biographical Directory of the American Congress*, pp. 182, 1856; Grant, *Memoirs*, pp. 28, 32. Horace Greeley, founder and editor of the *New York Tribune*, forced Dana from his position as managing editor of the newspaper over differences of opinion on the course of the war. Courted by Secretary of War Stanton to print pro-administration editorials after his forced resignation, Dana hired on to spy on Grant and report back to Stanton in Washington with regular reports with the cover title "special commissioner of the United States War Department." Harry J. Maihafer, *The General and the Journalists: Ulysses S. Grant, Horace Greeley, and Charles Dana* (Washington: Brassey's, 1998), pp. 102–105; O.R., Ser. I, Vol. XXIV, pt. 1, pp. 63, 65–67, 81; Charles A. Dana, *Recollections of the Civil War: With the Leaders at Washington and in the Field in the Sixties* (New York: Appleton and Company, 1902), p. 41; Kiper, *McClernand*, pp. 215–16. According to Lt. Col. James H. Wilson, "Dana, from the day he joined the staff, conceived a dislike to McClernand, and his dispatches to Stanton throughout the Vicksburg campaign were altogether unfavorable to him." Wilson, *Under the Old Flag*, p. 184.

61. Raynor, *Diary*, pp. 252–53.

62. O.R., Ser. I, Vol. XXIV, pt. 1, pp. 139–40, 188, 571–74; pt. 3, pp. 663, 720, 753–54; Grant, *Memoirs*, p. 157.

63. O.R., Ser. I, Vol. XXIV, pt. 1, p. 80; pt. 2, pp. 30–31; Raynor, *Diary*, pp. 252–53; James R. Slack to Ann P. Slack, 5 May 1863; Grant, *Memoirs*, p. 159.

64. O.R., Ser. I, Vol. XXIV, pt. 1, pp. 524–25, 544.

65. *The Natchez Weekly Courier*, May 13, 1863.

66. O.R., Ser. I, Vol. XXIV, pt. 1 pp. 253–55, 524–26, 544; O.R.N., Ser. I, Vol. 20, p. 89; Atlas Plates CLV and CLVI.

67. O.R., Ser. I, Vol. XXIV, pt. 1, pp. 47–48, 126–27, 142, 490, 601, 615; pt. 3, pp. 238–39 (quote), 240; Bringhurst and Swigart, *History of the 46th Indiana*, p. 55.

68. Solely, "Naval Operations," *Battles and Leaders*, III, 567; O.R.N., Ser. I, Vol. 24, p. 627.

69. O.R.N., Ser. I, Vol. 24, pp. 615, 618–19, 621–22, 625, 628a; Bringhurst and Swigart, *History of the 46th Indiana*, p. 55.

70. O.R.N., Ser. I, Vol. 24, pp. 610–11, 613, 620–22, 630, 706

71. *Ibid.*, pp. 611 (quote), 613, 615, 620–21, 629–30, 706. Companies from the 58th Ohio, detached from Sherman's 15th corps, were the sharpshooters aboard the *Mound City* (A & B), *Benton* (F & G), *Carondelet* (D), *Pittsburg* (H), and *Louisville* (K). O.R.N., Ser. I, Vol. 24, pp. 620, 629–30

72. The total casualties reported by the commanders of the *Benton,* the *Tuscumbia,* and the *Pittsburg* (Lt. Com. James A Greer, Lt. Com. James W. Shirk, and Acting Vol. Lt. William R. Hoel, respectively) were 18 killed and 56 wounded. Acting Rear Admiral David D. Porter reported 24 killed and 56 wounded aboard those three gunboats. O.R.N., Ser. I, Vol. 24, pp. 610, 613, 616, 621; Grant, *Memoirs,* p. 159.

73. O.R., Ser. I, Vol. XXIV, pt. 1, pp. 48, 142, 593; O.R.N., Ser. I, Vol. 20, p. 90; Vol. 24, p. 618 (quote), 627, Grant, *Memoirs,* p. 159.

74. Ephraim McDowell Anderson, *Memoirs: Historical and Personal, Including the Campaigns of the First Missouri Confederate Brigade* (St. Louis: Time Printing Co., 1868, reprint ed. Dayton, OH: The Press of Morningside Bookshop, 1971), p. 293.

75. *Ibid.*, pp. 293–94.

76. O.R., Ser. I, Vol. XXIV, pt. 1, p. 593.

77. Hopkins, *Under the Flag of the Nation,* p. 53

78. O.R., Ser. I, Vol. XXIV, pt. 1, pp. 47–48 (quote), 81–83, 142, 615; Grant, *Memoirs,* pp. 159–60; Hopkins, *Under the Flag of the Nation,* pp. 54–55; Atlas Plate XXXVI, No. 1, and CLV; sometimes spelled De Cheron's, De Shroon's, or D'Shron's. Atlas Plate XXXVI, No. 1.

79. O.R.N., Ser. I, Vol. 24, pp. 610–11, 615, 618, 624, 683–84; Vol. 25, p. xv; Anderson, *Memoirs,* p. 294.

80. Bringhurst and Swigart recalled on the morning of 30 April: "Only one man was seen on the bank. He was supposed to be a spy of General Grant's and was sent on board [the *Benton*]." On the other hand, the log of the *Benton* recorded that they encountered "one rebel and two negroes" at the landing. At any rate, they were unopposed because the Confederate cavalry had been diverted to pursue Grierson's raiders, and Bowen had moved most of his infantry division from Grand Gulf to Port Gibson on the night of 29 April to block the roads to Vicksburg from the best defensible position his infantry could reach in a timely manner. Bringhurst and Swigart, *History of the 46th Indiana,* p. 56 (quote); O.R.N., Ser. I, Vol. 24, p. 684; O.R., XXIV, pt. 1, pp. 142–43. The 56th Ohio crossed on the *Mound City.* Raynor, *Diary,* p. 255.

81. O.R., Ser. I, Vol. XXIV, pt. 1, pp. 142–43, 601; the 22nd Iowa mentioned in Terrence J. Winschel, "Grant's Beachhead for the Vicksburg Campaign: The Battle of Port Gibson, May 1, 1863," *Blue & Gray Magazine,* February 1994, p. 15; Bringhurst and Swigart, *History of the 46th Indiana,* p. 56; Raynor, *Diary,* p. 255.

82. McClernand may have chosen the longer Rodney Road after learning that the flooded James Creek crossed Bruinsburg Road and would have to be bridged. Speculation is that either a patrol sent out by McClernand or slaves at Windsor Plantation gave him this information. Kiper, *McClernand,* pp. 222, 352; Bringhurst and Swigart, *History of the 46th Indiana,* p. 56 (quote).

83. Hopkins, *Under the Flag of the Nation,* p. 55.

84. O.R., Ser. I, Vol. XXIV, pt. 1, pp. 48, 143–44, 663–64, 672; Anderson, *Memoirs,* p. 297; Winschel, "The Battle of Port Gibson," pp. 18–19; Stewart Sifakis, *Compendium of the Confederate Armies: Mississippi* (New York: Facts on File, Inc., 1995), p. 23.

85. O.R., Ser. I, Vol. XXIV, pt. 1, pp. 615, 628, 672.

86. *Ibid.*, pp. 49, 601, 615–16, 625.

87. *Ibid.*, pp. 601–02, 606, 610; James R. Slack to Ann P. Slack, 5 May 1863.

88. O.R., Ser. I, Vol. XXIV, pt. 1, pp. 602, 625–26, 629, 664, 672–73.

89. *Ibid.*, pp. 602, 606, 610–11, 613, 615.

90. *Ibid.*, pp. 610–11; 613, 664, 673.

91. *Ibid.*, pp. 612–13.

92. *Ibid.*, pp. 602–603, 629.

93. *Ibid.*, pp. 602–603, 609, 611, 615, 623–24, 673; Raynor, *Diary,* p. 257 (quote). Capt. Charles of Co. H, 18th Indiana Volunteers, was credited as the first to reach Anderson's Battery and seize a gun. The 18th Indiana was also credited with the capture of the flag and flag bearer of the 15th Arkansas Infantry. *Ibid.*, p. 626.

94. O.R., Ser. I, Vol. XXIV, pt. 1, pp. 607, 609, 664, 673, 675; Chambers, *Blood and Sacrifice,* pp. 63–64 (quote).

95. O.R., Ser. I, Vol. XXIV, pt. 1, pp. 673, 676; Winschel, "The Battle of Port Gibson," p. 49.

96. O.R., Ser. I, Vol. XXIV, pt. 1, pp. 664, 667, 668; Winschel, "The Battle of Port Gibson," pp. 50–52; Anderson, *Memoirs,* p. 296.

97. O.R., Ser. I, Vol. XXIV, pt. 1, pp. 593, 602, 607, 609, 611, 615, 627, 633, 673, 676, 668–69; pt. 2, p. 31; Winschel, "Battle of Port Gibson," p. 52.

98. O.R., Ser. I, Vol. XXIV, pt. 1, pp. 664, 668; Winschel, "Battle of Port Gibson," p. 53.

99. O.R., Ser. I, Vol. XXIV, pt. 1, pp. 603, 607, 611, 613.

100. *Ibid.*, pp. 607, 611, 613.

101. *Ibid.*, pp. 603, 607–08, 612 (quote), 627, 668–69.

102. *Ibid.*, p. 613.

103. Anderson, *Memoirs,* pp. 297–98.

104. O.R., Ser. I, Vol. XXIV, pt. 1, p. 612. Describing this fight to Ann, Slack wrote: "The most stubborn & hard fighting during the day occurred in the afternoon between the 47th Ind, 56th Ohio & 24th Ind, with three rebel regiments. We killed them by scores, piled them up. Their shots were too high or our casualties would have been very heavy. Here we lost most of our men." James R. Slack to Ann P. Slack, 11 May 1863.

105. O.R., Ser. I, Vol. XXIV, pt. 1, pp. 614, 643–44, 653; 677 (quote).

106. Chambers, *Blood and Sacrifice,* p. 66 (quote).

107. *Ibid.*, p. 66; O.R., Ser. I, Vol. XXIV, pt. 1, p. 664, 666–67, 669; Winschel, "Battle of Port Gibson," *Blue & Gray,* p. 55.

108. Wilkes, "A Short History of My Life in the Late War Between the North and the South," p. 5.

109. O.R., Ser. I, Vol. XXIV, pt. 1, pp. 34–35; 254–55; 519–529; *Battles & Leaders*, III: 549–50.
110. James R. Slack to Ann P. Slack, 5 May 1863; O.R., Ser. I, Vol. XXIV, pt. 2, p. 40; Atlas Plate XXXVI, No. 1.

Chapter 8

1. O.R., Ser. I, Vol. XXIV, pt. 1, pp. 258–61, 655–56, 667; pt. 2, p. 114; Grant, "Vicksburg Campaign," *Battles & Leaders*, III: 550. The Southern Railroad of Mississippi is sometimes referred to incorrectly as the Vicksburg & Jackson Railroad on U.S. Army maps. Atlas Plates XXXVI, No. 1 and CLV.
2. O.R., Ser. I, Vol. XXIV, pt. 1, pp. 49–50, 723.
3. *Ibid.*, pp. 49–50.
4. James R. Slack to Ann P. Slack, 11 May 1863; O.R., Ser. I, Vol. XXIV, pt. 1, pp. 49–50, 146–47, 634–36, 752–54; pt. 2, pp. 40–41, 279; Atlas Plate XXXVI, No. 1.
5. O.R., Ser. I, Vol. XXIV, pt. 1, pp. 146–47, 754; pt. 2, pp. 40–41, 118; pt. 3, p. 865. On 12 May, Slack, writing from his "camp on Baker's Creek ... five miles from Edwards Depot ... near the Emely Schoolhouse," told Ann: "The people here are not near so violent in their feelings and expressions as farther north. All seem to be anxious for peace. I hope their anticipation and hopes may be fully realized. We are now to very great extent living off the Country. Get all our meat from the planters. We just walk in and take it. Does look very hard in some cases, but there is no help for it." James R. Slack to Ann P. Slack, 12 May 1863.
6. O.R., Ser. I, Vol. XXIV, pt. 1, pp. 50–51, 147, 260, 637–38,754; pt. 2, p. 115; Atlas Plate XXXVI, No. 1.
7. *The Daily Mississippian*, 12 May 1863. At first, Adams had reported success against the Federals, with a quick follow-up report that he was falling back. O.R., Ser. I, Vol. XXIV, pt. 3, pp. 861–62.
8. O.R., Ser. I, Vol. XXIV, pt. 1, pp. 260–61; pt. 3, pp. 861, 863, 877; "The Opposing Forces in the Vicksburg Campaign," *Battles and Leaders*, III: 549–50; Johnston, *Narrative*, pp. 176, 506.
9. O.R., Ser. I, Vol. XXIV, pt. 1, p. 239; Joseph E. Johnston, "Jefferson Davis and the Mississippi Campaign," *Battles and Leaders*, III: 478–49. Johnston's expectations for reinforcements from the east were due to the relative inactivity in Beauregard's Department and Rosecrans's inactivity at Murfreesboro, Tennessee, following his victory there at the beginning of the year. Braxton Bragg, under little pressure from Rosecrans at the time due to the extended lull in the fighting, was busily establishing his defensive line around Tullahoma, some thirty-five miles to the south. Since it appeared that Rosecrans was not going on the offensive anytime soon, critically needed reinforcements could be sent to Johnston from Bragg's quiescent army without endangering their hold on Tennessee south of Murfreesboro. Johnston, *Narrative*, p. 163.
10. O.R., Ser. I, Vol. XXIV, pt. 1, p. 248; Clifford L. Alderman, *Retreat to Victory: the Life of Nathanael Greene* (Philadelphia: Chilton Book Company, 1967).
11. O.R., Ser. I, Vol. XXIV, pt. 1, p. 147; pt. 2, pp. 41, 116, 118; pt. 3, p. 300; Raynor, *Diary*, pp. 266–67.
12. Johnston, *Narrative*, p. 506.
13. O.R., Ser. I, Vol. XXIV, pt. 1, pp. 239–40, 248, 639, 753; pt. 3, pp. 876–78; Johnston, *Narrative*, pp. 176–78.
14. James R. Slack to Ann P. Slack, 15 May 1863; O.R., Ser. I, Vol. XXIV, pt. 2, p. 41; Raynor, *Diary*, p. 267; Atlas Plate XXXVI, No. 1.
15. O.R., Ser. I, Vol. XXIV, pt. 3, pp. 842, 877 (quote); Robert S. Bevier, *The History of the First and Second Missouri Confederate Brigades 1861–1865* (St. Louis: Bryan, Brand & Company, 1879), p. 185.
16. Johnston, *Narrative*, pp. 180, 187, 506; O.R., Ser. I, Vol. XXIV, pt. 3, p. 876–77, 887–88, 89–92.
17. *Ibid.*, pt. 1, pp. 262–63; pt. 3, pp. 891–92; Johnston, *Narrative*, pp. 178–82; Johnston, "Jefferson Davis," 478–79; S.H. Lockett, "The Defense of Vicksburg," *Battles and Leaders*, III: 487. Grant said that he expected Pemberton to follow Johnston's 13 May order to attack Grant at Clinton, although he, Grant, agreed with Pemberton that they were "impracticable" orders. Grant, "The Vicksburg Campaign," *Battles and Leaders*, III: 507–509.
18. O.R., Ser. I, Vol. XXIV, pt. 1, pp. 50, 261–62,639, 754; XXII, pt. 1, p. 212; Johnston, *Narrative*, pp. 180–81; Grant, *Memoirs*, p. 175.
19. James R. Slack to Ann P. Slack, 15 May 1863; Raynor, *Diary*, p. 268.
20. O.R., Ser. I, Vol. XXIV, pt. 1, p. 148; Atlas Plate CXXXII, No. 8. In a special dispatch to the *New York Times*, a reporter from the *Cincinnati Commercial* described Champion Hill accurately as "an abrupt terminus of a high ridge running north and south, flanked on both sides by deep ravines and gullies, and in many places covered with an impenetrable growth of scrubby with oak brush." "The Great Battle of Baker's Creek," *New York Times*, 26 May 1863. In the 1930s the northwestern slope was excavated for gravel from near the crest, although the original roadway from the Champion House to the southern base of the ridge is still intact. William C. Everhart, "The Battle of Champion Hill, May 16, 1863," Vicksburg National Military Park, MS, National Park Service Handbook Series 21, Washington, D.C., 1954. www.battleofchampionhill.org; www.civilwaralbum.com/vicksburgh/ch_assault.htm. The crest of Champion Hill, 196 feet above sea level, is 75 feet above the surrounding countryside. U.S.G.S, Geographical Names Information System, on Waypoint Information: http://wayhoo.com/ index/a/wdet/wid/821251/gmap/1/.
21. O.R., Ser. I, Vol. XXIV, pt. 1, pp. 148, 150; pt. 2, p. 41.
22. *Ibid.*, p. 148.
23. James R. Slack to Ann P. Slack, 16 May 1863; O.R., Ser. I, Vol. XXIV, pt. 1, pp. 52, 54, 148, 639, 754; pt. 2, pp. 59, 255.
24. The flamboyant Storey, a devoted Copperhead, purchased the *Chicago Times* in 1861 and soon became famous for his directive to his reporters: "Telegraph fully all the news, and when there is no news, send rumors." Franc B. Wilkie, *Thirty-five Years in Journalism* (Chi-

cago: F.J. Schulte & Company, 1891), p. 114, quoted in Starr, *Bohemian Brigade*, p. 241.

25. Storey hired Cadwallader, former editor of the *Milwaukee Daily News*, and sent him to Grant's headquarters, then at Jackson, Tennessee, to cover the western front and to seek the release of his predecessor, Warren P. Isham. Grant had arrested and imprisoned Isham, Storey's brother-in-law and chief correspondent, for fabricating war stories, and for continuing to do so after Grant had warned him to stop. Grant finally had him arrested for fabricating a story about "a formidable fleet of rebel gunboats at Pensacola," and ordered a happy-to-oblige William T. Sherman to convene the court-martial. The military court convicted Isham and sentenced him to imprisonment at Alton (Illinois) Penitentiary "for the duration of the war," although Grant ordered him released after three months. Cadwallader, to his credit, did not follow Storey's famous directive, nor did he send Storey scurrilous tales about Grant's behavior. He, in fact, earned Grant's trust and became a well-respected member of the "Bohemian Brigade." After Vicksburg, he left Storey's *Chicago Times*, became the chief of staff of the *New York Herald*'s war correspondents, and accompanied Grant for the remainder of the war. Sylvanus Cadwallader, *Three Years With Grant, As Recalled by War Correspondent Sylvanus Cadwallader*, ed. Benjamin P. Thomas (New York: Knopf, 1955), pp. 3–5, 10; Wilkie, *Pen and Powder*, p. 208; Starr, *Bohemian Brigade*, pp. 279–86; William Huntzicker, *The Popular Press, 1833–1865* (Westport, CT: Greenwood Press, 1999), pp. 142–43.

26. Cadwallader, *Three Years With Grant*, p. 77.

27. Lockett's engineers completed replacement of the washed-out Raymond Road Bridge over Baker's Creek by 2:00 P.M., O.R., Ser. I, Vol. XXIV, pt. 2, pp. 69–70, 100.

28. *Ibid.*, pt. 1, pp. 50–51, 148–49, 261–63; pt. 2, pp. 31, 75, 90, 93, 99, 126; Anderson, *Memoirs*, p. 310; Johnston, *Narrative*, p. 176–77; Stephen D. Lee, " The Campaign of Vicksburg, Mississippi, in 1863 — From April 15 to and Including the Battle of Champion Hills, or Baker's Creek, May 16, 1863," *Publications of the Mississippi Historical Society* (Oxford: Mississippi Historical Society, 1900), III: 33, 35–36; Atlas Plate CXXXII, No. 8.

29. O.R., Ser. I, Vol. XXIV, pt. 1, pp. 52, 263–64; pt. 2, pp. 29, 31, 41, 79, 82, 94–95, 101, 110, 263–64; pt. 3, pp. 316–19; Grant, "The Vicksburg Campaign," 509–10; Lee, "The Campaign for Vicksburg," III: 36; Atlas Plate CXXXII, No. 8; www.civilwaralbum.com/vicksburg/ch_deploy.htm..

30. O.R., Ser. I, Vol. XXIV, pt. 2, pp. 94–95, 101; Lee, "The Campaign for Vicksburg," III:39; Francis Obenchain to John W. Johnston, 8 January 1903, on file at Vicksburg National Military Park, quoted in Terrence J. Winschel, "The Guns of Champion Hill (Part II)," *Journal of Confederate History* 6 (1990): 98 (quote), 100; Jerald H. Markham, *The Botetourt Artillery* (Lynchburg, VA: H.E. Howard, 1986), p. 38.

31. O.R., Ser. I, Vol. XXIV, pt. 2, pp. 95, 104–105.

32. *Ibid.*, pp. 15, 31, 75–79, 83, 110.

33. *Ibid.*, pp. 42, 53, 101, 104–105: Lee, "The Campaign for Vicksburg," III: 37, 41–42.

34. O.R., Ser. I, Vol. XXIV, pt. 2, pp. 48–49, 53.

35. *Ibid.*, p. 55.

36. *Ibid.*, pp. 48–49, 50, 53, 102; Lee, "The Campaign for Vicksburg," III: 37, 40. Lee's brigade consisted of the 20th, 23rd, 30th, 31st, and 46th Alabama, and Waddell's Alabama Battery.

37. O.R., Ser. I, Vol. XXIV, pt. 1, p. 52.

38. *Ibid.*, pp. 647–48, 709, 717–18; pt. 2, pp. 155–56.

39. *Ibid.*, pp. 647, 709, 717–18.

40. *Ibid.*, pt. 2, p. 42 (quote); Oxley, "History of Co. H 24th Iowa," p. 8.

41. O.R., Ser. I, Vol. XXIV, pt. 2, p. 55.

42. *Ibid.*, pp. 42 (quote), 49, 50–51, 55, 57 (quote), 104.

43. *Ibid.*, p. 50 (quote), 57.

44. *Ibid.*, pp. 100, 102, 106.

45. Ibid,., p. 49. Bringhurst and Swigart, *History of the 46th Indiana*, p. 60.

46. O.R., Ser. I, Vol. XXIV, pt. 2, pp. 49, 55, 57. Cumming claimed that "the battle broke upon us, and without previous intimation received" when McGinnis's troops charged out of the woods near the crest less than fifty yards from their front because his skirmishers had not come up from his "first front," and apparently none of Lee's skirmishers behind the Champion House had made it to his position on the crest. *Ibid.*, p. 105; Winschel, "The Guns of Champion Hill," p. 102.

47. O.R., Ser. I, Vol. XXIV, pt. 2, pp. 42, 46, 49, 55, 57–58, 95, 99–102, 105; T.J. Williams, "The Battle of Champion Hill," *Military Order of the Loyal Legion of the United States (MOLLUS), Ohio* (Cincinnati: The Robert Clarke Company, 1903), V: 206; Scott Walker, *Hell's Broke Loose in Georgia: Survival in a Civil War Regiment* (Athens: University of Georgia Press, 2005), p76–77.

48. O.R., Ser. I, Vol. XXIV, pt. 2, pp. 101–102.

49. *Ibid.*, pt. 1, pp. 229, 647–48, 717, 720. The 7th Missouri remained in the rear to protect the brigade wagon train. *Ibid.*, pp. 717–18; pt. 2, pp. 95, 99–103.

50. *Ibid.*, pt. 1, p. 52 (quote), 147; pt. 2, pp. 32, 41–42, 79, 82, 110, 149, 256; pt. 3, pp. 316–19; Grant, "The Vicksburg Campaign," 509–10.

51. O.R., Ser. I, Vol. XXIV, pt. 2, p. 32.

52. *Ibid.*, pp. 110–111, 116, 119; Anderson, *Memoirs*, pp. 312–14; *Battles and Leaders*, III: 550.

53. O.R., Ser. I, pt. 2, pp. 106, 111, 116, 119; Bevier, *The First and Second Missouri Confederate Brigades*, p. 188; Pvt. A.H. Reynolds, "Vivid Experiences at Champion Hill, Miss.," *Confederate Veteran* 18 (January 1910), pp. 21–22.

54. O.R., Ser. I, Vol. XXIV, pt. 2, p. 55.

55. Williams, "The Battle of Champion's Hill," V: 209 (quote); also see Smith, *Champion Hill*, pp. 260–61; O.R., Ser. I, Vol. XXIV, pt. 2, p. 116 (quote).

56. *Ibid.*, pp. 42, 50 (quote), 111 (quote). The color bearer and two subsequent soldiers of the 57th Georgia who had picked up the fallen flag were killed in Bowen's counterattack, possibly while fighting the 47th Indiana. Walker, *Hell's Broke Loose in Georgia*, p. 81.

57. O.R., Ser. I, Vol. XXIV, pt. 2, pp.43–44, 50, 56; A.P. Hovey, "A War Reminiscence, General Alvin P. Hovey Relates an Experience with Grant at Vicksburg,"

New York Times, 13 March 1885; Smith, *Champion Hill*, p. 282.

58. O.R., Ser. I, Vol. XXIV, pt. 1, pp. 718, 724, 730; Smith, *Champion Hill*, p. 276.

59. *Ibid.*, pp. 640, 730–31; pt. 2, pp. 61–62.

60. *Ibid.*, p. 640; pt. 2, p. 315.

61. *Ibid.*, pp. 44 (quote), 50, 111, 117, 316; Hovey, "A War Reminiscence," from the *Indianapolis Journal*, 8 March 1885 (quote); Lee, "The Campaign of Vicksburg," III: 48; Byers, *With Fire and Sword*, p. 78–80.

62. O.R., Ser. I, Vol. XXIV, pt. 2, p. 44.

63. *Ibid.*, pp. 22, 25, 89 (quote).

64. *Ibid.*, pp. 15, 22 (quote), 89 (quote).

65. *Ibid.*, p. 88.

66. *Ibid.*, pt. 1, p. 265; pt. 2, pp. 111–12, 117. S.D. Lee reported that his troops were the last Confederates fighting north of Jackson Road, which he referred to as "Edwards Depot Road" in his report. Barton's brigade had collapsed on his left, and Bowen's division had collapsed on his right, while the 30th and 46th Alabama were still fighting north or east of Jackson Road. Lee was able to withdraw the 30th Alabama, but the 46th Alabama was captured. *Ibid.*, p. 102; Anderson, *Memoirs*, p. 314. Also see Lee, "The Campaign of Vicksburg," III: 48.

67. O.R., Ser. I, Vol. XXIV, pt. 2, p. 88.

68. *Ibid.*, pt. 1, pp. 264–65, 616; pt. 2, p. 256; Johnston, *Narrative*, p. 183.

69. O.R., Ser. I, vol. XXIV, pt. 1, p. 616; pt. 2, p. 255.

70. *Ibid.*, pt. 1, p. 265; pt. 2, pp. 32, 80, 84, 96, 112, 117.

71. *Ibid.*, pt. 1, pp. 151, 718; pt. 2, pp. 32, 80; Anderson, *Memoirs*, p. 314.

72. O.R., Ser. I, Vol. XXIV, pt. 2, pp. 112, 776–78.

73. *Ibid.*, pp. 44, 58, 640); Grant, "The Vicksburg Campaign," III: 513.

74. *Huntington Democrat*, 11 June 1863. On the Federal side, Hovey's, Logan's, and Crocker's divisions fought the bulk of the battle. Their 15,380 men constituted a little over one-half of Grant's army. Smith, *Champion Hill*, p. 372.

75. O.R., Ser. I, Vol. XXIV, pt. 2, pp. 7–11, 45–46, 57.

76. The day after the battle, Slack wrote: "Well here is Sunday morning, May 17th. We left camp yesterday morning at 7 o'clock. Came five miles, when we heard cannonading two or three miles to our left. At once formed line of battle, sent out six Cos [companies] from my Command as skirmishers. Very soon they engaged the enemy and skirmished till about noon when the battle became general. I thought the battle of Port Gibson was terrific, but it was a mere skirmish in comparison with yesterdays fight. Far from any houses with my own whole Brigade, without the aid of artillery, or any one to help me, I held at bay most certainly five times my number. They walled their forces against me, and I had to give back about a 1/2 mile. We rallied again, reinforcements came also, and we drove the piratical scoundrels from the field and about sun an hour high we were masters of the field, but at a terrible price. My loss is about 700. I occupied the extreme left and had to resist the whole flanking force of the enemy, and well did we do it.

Many of the poor boys from Huntington are laid low. Sergt Joe Davies killed, shot through the head. Jacob Michael killed. John W. Williams, our cook a year ago, shot & killed. John Yantis slightly wounded. Frank Slusser wounded, not severely, a ball cut through his left hand between his thumb and forefinger. Eli Elser [Eltzer], Samuel Emley's son in law, is missing. May turn up this morning. Capt Wintrode is slightly wounded. Sergt Peyton is slightly wounded, Wintrodes Co. Major Goodwin wounded, shot through the thigh, will recover. Capt. Sturgiss shot through the thigh. Lieuts Perry & Cole of Co. B of Wabash Co. were both killed. Co K of the 47th is almost annihilated, also Co. G. Capt Wintrodes Co suffered badly. Capt Shearer had two killed & four wounded. B.F. Helm, of Shearers Co is missing. Oh you can form no just appreciation of the horror of a battle field. I came out without a scratch, although it literally rained and poured leaden hail all round us. Did not get my horse hit, came off clear. I wonder how it did occur." James R. Slack to Ann P. Slack, 17 May 1863. The brigade losses (677) and 47th Indiana losses (143) come from Slack's 20 May 1863 letter to Ann. Four hundred fifty (450) is a rounded number based on the presumption that each of Slack's four regiments in his 1,809-man brigade entered the fight with equal numbers. O.R., Ser. I, Vol. XXIV, pt. 1, pp. 45, 57.

77. *Ibid.*, pt. 2, pp. 106–7, 112–13, 115, 117 (quote); Johnson and Buel, eds., *Battles and Leaders*, III: 550; Smith, *Champion Hill*, pp. 372, 384–85.

78. O.R., Ser. I, Vol. XXIV, pt. 2, pp. 44–45.

79. *Ibid.*, p. 32.

80. *Ibid.*, pt. 1, p. 616; pt. 2, p. 78, 80.

81. Grant, "The Vicksburg Campaign," 513; Johnston, *Narrative*, pp. 183–84; O.R., Ser. I, Vol. XXIV, pt. 2, p. 32.

82. *Indianapolis Daily Gazette*, 25 May 1863.

83. "Military Items," *Indianapolis Daily Journal*, 5 June 1863.

84. O.R., Ser. I, Vol. XXIV, pt. 2, pp. 55–56.

85. *Ibid.*, p. 56; "Captures His Captor," in Walter F. Beyer and Oscar F. Keydel, comps., *Deeds of Valor: How America's Heroes Won the Medal of Honor*, 2 vols., (Detroit: The Perrien-Keydel Company, 1907), I: 184–85; *The Story of American Heroism: Thrilling Narratives of Personal Adventures During the Great Civil War As Told by the Medal Winners and Roll of Honor Men* (Springfield, OH: J.W. Jones, 1879), p. 270–71.

86. Gordon A. Cotton, "Champion Hill Recalled By Indiana Tramp," *The Vicksburg Evening Post*, 27 May 1984. My thanks to Jeff Giambrone and Gordon A. Cotton of The Old Court House Museum, Vicksburg, Mississippi, for a copy of Gordon Cotton's article. For excerpts of "Roving Bill's story, also see H. Grady Howell Jr., *Hill of Death: The Battle of Champion Hill* (Madison, MS: Chickasaw Bayou Press, 1993), p. 19.

87. O.R., Ser. I, Vol. XXIV, pt. 2, pp. 112 (quote).

88. *Ibid.*, pt. 1, pp. 54 (quote), 266–67; Grant, "The Vicksburg Campaign," 514; Johnston, *Narrative*, p. 184; Anderson, p. 317 (quote).

89. O.R., Ser. I, Vol. XXIV, pt. 1, pp. 266–67, 616;

pt. 2, pp. 113, 117; U.S. Grant, "The Vicksburg Campaign," 512; Atlas Plates XXXVII, No. 7 and CXXXV-C, No. 3.

90. O.R., Ser. I, Vol. XXIV, pt. 1, pp. 54, 616; pt. 2, pp. 73, 113, 135; Oxley, "History of Co. H 24th Iowa," p. 10.

91. For a slightly exaggerated version of Kendall's efforts, see "Kendall's Ten Foot Leap," in Beyer and Keydel, comps., *Deeds of Valor,* I: 185–86. Notwithstanding the Beyer and Keydel account, a majority of the commissioned officers of the 49th Indiana were not killed or captured in the charge. Keigwin, in fact, reported that Captain McConahay was the only casualty in the 49th Indiana and it "was the poorest fight I ever saw the rebels make." O.R., Ser. I, Vol. XXIV, pt. 1, p. 23 (quote); pt. 2, p. 137; Samuel D. Pryce, *Vanishing Footprints: The Twenty-second Iowa Volunteer Infantry in the Civil War,* ed. Jeffry C. Burden (Iowa City: Camp Pope Bookshop, 2008), p. 106.

92. O.R., Ser. I, Vol. XXIV, pt. 1, pp. 54, 266–67; pt. 2, pp. 73, 113, 119, 136–38, 142; Anderson, *Memoirs,* p. 317; Chambers, *Blood and Sacrifice,* pp. 71–72.

93. Lockett, "The Defense of Vicksburg," 488; Anderson, *Memoirs,* pp. 318–19; O.R., Ser. I, Vol. XXIV, pt. 2, pp. 73, 119–20.

94. *Ibid.,* pt. 3, p. 888; also see, Johnston, *Narrative,* pp. 187–89.

Chapter 9

1. O.R., Ser. I, Vol. XXIV, pt. 2, pp. 107, 169–70, 329–35, 343–45, 350, 361, 382, 398, 420; Lockett, S.H., "The Defense of Vicksburg," 481; Atlas Plate XXXVII, No. 1.

2. O.R., Ser. I, Vol. XXIV, pt. 1, p. 54, 87, 641, 648–49, 755; pt. 2, p. 168; pt. 3, p. 334.

3. *Ibid.,* p. 617; pt. 2, pp. 17–18, 149–151, 240.

4. U.S. Grant, *The Civil War Memoirs of Ulysses S. Grant,* ed. Brian M. Thomsen (New York: A Tom Doherty Associates Book, 2002); single-volume abridgement of the *Personal Memoirs of Ulysses S. Grant,* 2 vols. (NY: Charles L. Webster & Company, 1885), p. 189; O.R., Ser. I, Vol. XXIV, pt. 1, p. 57, pt. 2, pp. 154, 168.

5. *Ibid.,* pt. 1, pp. 756–57; pt. 2, pp. 18–19, 257, 263–64, 266, 280–81; Bond, ed., *Under the Flag of the Nation,* p. 64; Louis Bir, "Reminiscence of My Army Life," ed. George P. Clark, *Indiana Magazine of History* 101, no. 1 (March 2005): 31 (quote).

6. O.R., Ser. I, Vol. XXIV, pt. 1, p. 617; pt. 2, 240.

7. *Ibid.,* pp. 55, 756; pt. 2, pp. 20–21, 170.

8. *Ibid.,* pt. 1, p. 756.

9. *Ibid.,* p. 710.

10. *Ibid.,* pp. 154–55, pt. 2, p. 240. The 23rd Iowa was detached from Lawler's brigade to guard prisoners and the 130th Illinois of Landram's brigade was assigned to Lawler. *Ibid.,* pt. 1, p. 617.

11. Chambers, *Blood and Sacrifice,* p. 76; O.R., Ser. I, Vol. XXIV, pt. 1, p. 54.

12. *Ibid.,* pt. 2, p. 240.

13. Stone was wounded and Dunlap killed by Confederate sharpshooters while observing the assault from the woods beyond the Confederate rifle pits. *Ibid.,* pt. 1, pp. 140–41, 178, 617.

14. Pryce, *Vanishing Footprints,* pp. 116–118, 123 (quote).

15. O.R., Ser. I, Vol. XXIV, pt. 1, pp. 154–55, 178–80, 619; pt. 2, pp. 142, 181, 242–44, 357–58.

16. *Ibid.,* pt. 1, p. 155.

17. *Ibid.,* p. 617; pt. 2, pp. 33, 140–41, 151, 326–27, 350, 382, 385.

18. *Ibid.,* pt. 1, p. 155; pt. 2, pp. 34, 361, 382, 388; Kiper, *McClernand,* p. 159.]

19. O.R., Ser. I, Vol. XXIV, pt. 2, pp. 388–89.

20. O.R., Ser. I, Vol. XXIV, pt. 1, pp. 154, 177, 320; pt. 2, pp. 140, 181, 238, 242, 244, 357.

21. O.R., Ser. I, Vol. XXIV, pt. 1, pp. 55–56, 154–55; pt. 2, pp. 34, 361, 382; McClernand's dispatch to Grant, sent by messenger at noon on May 22nd: "We are hotly engaged with the enemy. We have part possession of two forts, and the Stars and Stripes are floating over them. A vigorous push ought to be made all along the line." O.R., Ser. I, Vol. XXIV, pt. 1, p.172; Pryce, *Vanishing Footprints,* p. 120.

22. O.R., Ser. I, Vol. XXIV, pt.1, pp. 55–56; Sherman, *Memoirs,* pp. 352–53; Kiper, *McClernand,* p. 161; Vicksburg National Park Map..

23. O.R., Ser. I, Vol. XXIV, pt. 1, p. 154; pt. 2, pp. 141, 244, 344, 354–55, 351, 358; Pryce, *Vanishing Footprints,* pp. 118, 119 (quote), 124.

24. O.R., Ser. I, Vol. XXIV, pt. 1, pp. 177, 179; pt. 2, p. 358. Soldiers who escaped from the parapet prior to Waul's attack saved the 22nd Iowa's two flags, the U.S. flag and the blue regimental banner that Federal regiments typically carried. Graham and the other prisoners were taken to Vicksburg City Jail for the night, then paroled and turned loose in the woods near the river. Pryce, *Vanishing Footprints,* p. 124.

25. O.R., Ser. I, Vol. XXIV, pt. 1, p. 179; pt. 2, pp. 238, 242, 358.

26. O.R., Ser. I, Vol. XXIV, pt. 1, pp. 361, 382.

27. O.R., Ser. I, Vol. XXIV, pt. 1, p. 389.

28. O.R., Ser. I, Vol. XXIV, pt. 1, p. 389.

29. O.R., Ser. I, Vol. XXIV, pt. 1, pp. 617, 732–33; pt. 2, pp. 33–35, 360–61, 382, 339.

30. O.R., Ser. I, Vol. XXIV, pt. 1, pp. 55–56, 180, 617, 732, 776–77; pt. 2, pp. 67–68, 344, 34–35, 361.

31. O.R., Ser. I, Vol. XXIV, pt. 1, p. 389.

32. O.R., Ser. I, Vol. XXIV, pt. 1, pp. 155.

33. O.R., Ser. I, Vol. XXIV, pt. 2, pp. 181, 380–81, 385; Pryce, *Vanishing Footprints,* pp. 119, 121–22, 131.

34. O.R., Ser. I, Vol. XXIV, pt. 1, pp. 55–56, 154–56, 172–73, 179–81, 183, 777; Grant, "The Vicksburg Campaign," 518; Kiper, *McClernand,* p. 261

35. O.R., Ser. I, Vol. XXIV, pt. 1, p. 155; pt. 2, p. 240. Although Landram was in support of McClernand's position, Pryce (*Vanishing Footprints,* p. 122) claimed Landram's brigade had come in support too late to exploit the breach before the Confederates could regroup. McClernand, apparently, did not call up Landram's reserves until 1:30 P.M., and then only to fill the gaps between Lawler's and Benton's brigades and cover the space between the Confederate forts on that part of the line. O.R., Ser. I, Vol. XXIV, pt. 2, pp. 340–41. By 2:40 P.M., Landram reported to A.J. Smith that his men

were holding the flanks of the fort in their front but were under heavy crossfire and the Confederates were "hurling grenades upon us and hurting us considerably in that way." *Ibid.*, p. 341.

36. Hopkins, *Under the Flag of the Nation*, p. 65.
37. O.R., Ser. I, Vol. XXIV, pt. 2, pp. 330–32, 390–91.
38. *Ibid.*, pt. 1, pp. 55–56; Grant, "The Vicksburg Campaign," 518.
39. *Ibid.*, pt. 2, p. 240.
40. William C. Davis and Bell I. Wiley, *Photographic History of the Civil War: Vicksburg to Appomattox* (New York: Black Dog & Leventhal Publishers, 1994), pp. 930, 1100, 1101, 1103, 1145.
41. O.R., Ser. I, Vol. XXIV, pt. 2, pp. 184. Col. Ashbel Smith, describing the sap rollers from his viewpoint in the 2nd Texas Lunette, reported: "The sap-rollers were cylinders of some 7 or 8 feet long and 41/2 [feet] in diameter, and made by rolling a matting woven of wire for the warp and cane for the filling around a central core. Six-[pounder] or 12-pounder shot did not materially damage them." *Ibid.*, p. 391.
42. *Ibid.*, pp. 171–72, 176–77, 184, 391.
43. *Ibid.*, pt. 1, p. 756; pt. 2, pp. 171, 177–78, 397–98, 403. On the night of 7 June, a soldier from the 9th Iowa, Thayer's brigade, was captured by pickets from Shoup's brigade. *Ibid.*, p. 408.
44. *Ibid.*, pt. 2, pp. 172, 281, 332.
45. *Ibid.*, pp. 172, 332, 397–98, 408–410, 413.
46. *Ibid.*, pp. 172, 264, 367.
47. *Ibid.*, pp. 172, 297, 367.
48. *Ibid.*, p. 171.
49. *Ibid.*, pp. 173, 332 (quote), 371; Lockett, "The Defense of Vicksburg," 491n; Grant, "The Vicksburg Campaign," 552.
50. O.R., Ser. I, Vol. XXIV, pt. 2, p. 183.
51. *Ibid.*, pt. 2, pp. 173, 183; Bearss, *The Campaign for Vicksburg*, III: 935–36.
52. *Ibid.*, pp. 174, 240, 343–45, 350–51, Raynor, *Diary*, p. 297n; Bearss, *The Campaign for Vicksburg*, III: 937.
53. *Ibid.*, p. 351.
54. Slack, describing the nighttime mortar boat shelling of the city, added: "In the night you can very distinctly see the shell very soon after it leaves the mortar. Can trace it by the burning fuse which looks for all the world like a fire bug flying through the air." And from his line: "The riflemen shoot whenever they see anything to shoot at. Were you here it would remind you of a hundred men chopping wood in a clearing in the spring a short distance off, in a clear still March morning." James R. Slack to Ann P. Slack, 25 May 1863.
55. O.R., Ser. I, Vol. XXIV, pt. 1, p. 319; pt. 2, pp. 168, 291–92, 345.
56. Diary of Capt. S.J. Keller, Co. H, 47th Indiana, quoted in Henry Lawson Bert, "Letters of a Drummer Boy," *Indiana Magazine of History* 34, no. 3 (September 1938): p. 328.
57. O.R., Ser. I, Vol. XXIV, pt. 2, p. 331.
58. *Ibid.*, p. 331; O.R.N., Ser. 1, Vol. 25, pp. 37–44; Soley, "Naval Operations in the Vicksburg Campaign," *Battles and Leaders*, III: 569.
59. Keller Diary, quoted in Bert, "Letters of a Drummer Boy," p. 328.
60. James R. Slack to Ann P. Slack, 28 May 1863.
61. O.R., Ser. I, Vol. XXIV, pt. 2, pp.331–32.
62. James R. Slack to Ann P. Slack, 6 June 1863.
63. O.R., Ser. I, Vol. XXII, pt. 2, pp. 856–57.
64. *Ibid.*, pp. 856–57; XXIV, pt. 2, pp. 158, 446–49, 467–70; Robert L. Kerby, *Kirby Smith's Confederacy: The Trans-Mississippi South, 1863–1865* (New York: Columbia University Press, 1972), pp. 113–115. For a more detailed discussion of black troops at Milliken's Bend, see Joseph T. Glatthaar, *Forged in Battle: The Civil War Alliance of Black Soldiers and White Officers* (New York: The Free Press, 1990), pp. 130–35.
65. O.R., Ser. I, Vol. XXIV, pt. 2, pp. 460 (quote), 472.
66. *Ibid.*, Ser. I, Vol. XXII, pt., pp. 855–57, 859, 868; XXIV, pt. 2, pp. 449–50; XXVI, pt. 1, pp. 209–10; Kerby, *Kirby Smith's Confederacy*, p. 115.
67. James R. Slack to Ann P. Slack, 11 June 1863; Keller Diary, quoted in Bert, "Letters of a Drummer Boy," p. 328.
68. O.R., Ser. I, Vol. XXIV, pt. 1, p. 57; pt. 2, pp. 149, 158, 168, 174, 533; James R. Slack to Ann P. Slack, 13 June 1863.
69. *Indianapolis Daily Journal*, 26 June 1863.
70. Ibid.
71. Wilkes, "A Short History of My Life," p. 6.
72. Davis and Wiley, *Photographic History of the Civil War*, p. 47; O.R., Ser. I, Vol. XXIV, pt.. 1, p. 295; pt. 2. pp. 345, 352.
73. *Ibid.*, pt. 1, pp. 159–61; pt. 2, pp. 380–81, 385, 388–89.
74. *Ibid.*, pt. 1, pp. 162–64; Sherman, *Memoirs*, p. 353.
75. *Ibid.*, p. 159. Charles Dana wrote to Stanton that it was McClernand's insubordination ("repeated disobedience of important orders") and negative relations with Sherman and McPherson that had led to his dismissal, not his congratulatory address. *Ibid.*, p. 103.
76. *Ibid.*, pp. 158, 166–69; Kiper, *McClernand*, p. 24.
77. O.R., Ser. I, Vol. XXXIV, pt. 2, pp. 378, 400.
78. *Ibid.*, p. 425; pt. 3, pp. 40–41; Kiper, *McClernand*, p. 281.
79. James R. Slack to Ann P. Slack, 21 June 1863.
80. O.R., Ser. I, Vol. XXVI, pt. 1, pp.209–210.
81. *Ibid.*, pp. 210, 217–20; O.R., XXII, pt. 2, pp. 855–57; Atlas Plate CLVI.
82. *Ibid.*, pp. 215–16, 218–19.
83. *Ibid.*, pp. 210, 216–17.
84. *Ibid.*, pp. 47, 202–203.
85. *Ibid.*, pp. 191, 202, 216; O.R.N, Ser. 1, Vol. 20, pp. 325–27, 345–46.
86. Ibid, pp. 47, 190, 202, 605, 621, 630; O.R.N., Ser. 1, Vol. 20, pp. 330, 327; Augustine Thompson (formerly Capt., Co. G., 28th Maine), "History of Donaldsonville," 1 January 1896 to General Seldon Connor, Adj. Gen. State of Maine, Maine State Archives. www.maine.gov/sos/archives/military/civilwar/donald/htm.
87. O.R., Ser. I, Vol. XXVI, pt. 1, p. 47.
88. *Ibid.*, Vol. XXIV, pt. 1, p. 108 (quote), 195; pt. 2, pp. 107, 174, 290–92, 288–89, 345.

89. *Ibid.*, pt. 2, pp. 172–73, 403.
90. Grant, "The Vicksburg Campaign," 527.
91. O.R., Ser. I, Vol. XXIV, pt. 2, pp. 202, 372; Grant, "The Vicksburg Campaign," 527; Lockett, "The Defense of Vicksburg," 491.
92. O.R., Ser. I, Vol. XXIV, pt. 2, pp. 173, 294, 333, 372 (quote), 397, 415–16; Lockett, "The Defense of Vicksburg," 491; Andrew Hickenlooper, Brevet Brigadier-General, Chief Engineer of the 17th Army Corps, "The Vicksburg Mine," *Battles and Leaders*, III: 542.
93. Keller Diary, quoted in Bert, "Letters of a Drummer boy," p. 328.
94. O.R., Ser. I, Vol. XXIV, pt. 2, pp. 172,190, 333, 366–67, 416,420–21; Lockett, "The Defense of Vicksburg," 491.
95. O.R., Ser. I, Vol. XXIV, pt. 2, p. 192.
96. *Ibid.*, pp 185–86.
97. *Ibid.*, pp. 391–92. For the Federal engineers' reports see pt. 2, pp. 173, 183–86.
98. Keller Diary, quoted in Bert, "Letters of a Drummer Boy," p. 328.
99. O.R., Ser. I, Vol. XXIV, pt. 2, pp. 202–203, 334, 377, 416; Lockett, "The Defense of Vicksburg," 491.
100. O.R., Ser. I, Vol. XXIV, pt. 2, pp. 173, 334, 416; Lockett, "The Defense of Vicksburg," 491.
101. O.R., Ser. I, Vol. XXIV, pt. 2, pp. 173, 203, 334, 416; Lockett, "The Defense of Vicksburg," 491.
102. Grant, "The Vicksburg Campaign," 527–28.
103. "We had a fight last night, about 11 o'clock, continued about 2 hours. We had three wounded. John Mohn of Shearers Col, was struck in the abdomen, but not much injured. Capt Bruner was struck in the arm with a gun but not much hurt. One of the 87th Ill was hit in the abdomen, but it was glancing, and only a flesh wound. Was a very keen fight for a while, but we got through, and maintained our position. I had a very interesting dialogue with a reble officer this morning. I gave him as good as he sent." James R. Slack to Ann P. Slack, 3 July 1863; Keller Diary, quoted in Bert, "Letters of a Drummer boy," p. 328; O.R., Ser. I, Vol. XXIV, pt. 1, p. 114.
104. *Ibid.*, pt. 3, p. 460.
105. *Ibid.*, pt. 2, p. 192; Lockett, "The Defense of Vicksburg," 491.
106. O.R., Ser. I, Vol. XXIV, pt. 1, pp. 59–61, 114–116, 283–85; pt. 2, p. 192; pt. 3, pp. 461–63, 465. In a dispatch to Grant on July 3rd, Ord stated that a flag of truce would be raised at 3:00 P.M. where the Jackson Road crossed the Confederate trenches, adding: "The rebel time is forty-eight minutes faster than mine. I will send you my time." *Ibid.*, pt. 3, p. 460.
107. *Ibid.*, pt. 1, pp. 45, 57, 60; pt. 3, p. 460; Grant, *Memoirs*, pp. 202–203.
108. *Ibid.*, p. 411.
109. *Ibid.*, Vol. XIII, pp. 768–71; *Ibid.*, Vol. XXII, pt. 1, pp. 110, 386–87.
110. *Ibid.*, p. 394.
111. Ibid, pp. 392–94, 400.
112. *Ibid.*, pp. 409–410; Col. Thomas L. Snead, "The Conquest of Arkansas," 455–56.
113. O.R., Ser. I, Vol. XXII, pt. 1, pp. 392–93, 400, 413, 417, quote 420, 436.
114. *Ibid.*, pp. 385, 392–93, 400, 408–12, 420, 425, 427413–18. Later, Chaplain Sawyer, who had remained at Helena in charge of the contraband camp, would recall that the battle at Helena was the fiercest he had ever seen. *Indianapolis Daily Journal*, 18 June 1864.
115. O.R., Ser. I, Vol. XXIV, pt. 1, pp. 44, 57 (quote), 61, 284–85; pt. 2, p. 325; Grant, *Memoirs*, pp. 203–204.
116. William Pitt Chambers, "A History of the 46th Mississippi Regiment," unpublished manuscript, 22 September 1904, Mississippi Department of Archives and History, p. 5. Not all stayed home. At least some of the paroled soldiers and officers of the 17th and 31st Louisiana, as well as some from the other paroled Louisiana units, joined E. Kirby Smith's Army of the Trans-Mississippi. O.R., Ser. I, Vol. XXVI, pt. 2, p. 173 and O.R., XLI, pt. 3, p. 966.
117. Wilkes, "A Short History of My Life," p. 6.
118. Compiled Service Record, Pvt. Abner J. Wilkes, Co. B, 46th Mississippi Infantry.
119. Wilkes, "A Short History of My Life," p. 6.
120. *Ibid.*; Chambers, *Blood and Sacrifice*, p. 93; O.R., XXIV, pt. 3, pp. 1002, 1010, 1011, 1048.
121. *Ibid.*, pp. 460–61 (quote); Grant, *Memoirs*, p. 206.

Chapter 10

1. Allen C. Guelzo, "Defending Emancipation: Abraham Lincoln and the Conkling Letter, 1863," *Civil War History* 48 (2002), pp. 320–21; Lottie E. Jones, *Decisive Dates in Illinois History: A Story of the State* (Danville, IL: Illinois Printing Company, 1909; original reproduced online in the American Libraries Internet Archive), p. 218 (quote).
2. Guelzo, "Defending Emancipation," pp. 320–21 Glenn Altschuler and Stuart Blumin, "Limits of Political Engagement in Antebellum America: A New Look at the Golden Age of Participatory Democracy," *Journal of American History* 84 (December 1997), p. 883;
3. Report of the Adjutant General, I: 261–66; Lorna Lutes Sylvester, "Oliver P. Morton and Hoosier Politics during the Civil War" (Ph.D. dissertation, Indiana University, 1968), pp. 205–207; George F. Milton, *Abraham Lincoln and the Fifth Column* (New York: Vanguard Press, 1942), pp. 199–204.
4. *Report of the Adjutant General*, I: 266; Sylvester, "Oliver P. Morton," pp. 206–210; Milton, *Abraham Lincoln*, pp. 204–205.
5. Klement, "Carrington and the Golden Circle Legend," p. 52; Milton, *Abraham Lincoln*, p. 205; Sylvester, "Oliver P. Morton," p. 207; for the Morton-McDonald debates, see Foulke, *Life of Morton*, I: 303–371.
6. O.R., Ser. I, Vol. XXIII, pt. 1, pp. 635, 667–69, 673–75; *Indianapolis Daily Journal*, 8, 10, 13, 14, 21, 24, 25, 27 July 1863.
7. "Another 'Leader' Arrested," *Indianapolis Daily Gazette,* 23 July 1863; "The Arrest of Gen. Bickley, *New York Times*, 26 July 1863; *Indianapolis Daily Journal*, 22 July 1863, cited by Crenshaw, "Knights of the Golden Circle," p. 46; *Indiana State Sentinel,* 21 July 1863, and

the *Indianapolis Daily Journal*, 20, 21 July 1863, cited by Klement, "Carrington and the Golden Circle Legend," pp. 48–52.

8. *Huntington Democrat*, 10 July 1863.

9. *New York Herald*, 12 July 1863; *New York Times*, 12 July 1863; *New York Tribune*, 13 July 1863; Iver Bernstein, *New York City Draft Riots: Their Significance for American Society and Politics in the Age of the Civil War* (New York: Oxford University Press, 1991), p. 18.

10. Due to a split in the Democratic Party, Opdyke was the first Republican elected mayor of New York. He defeated incumbent Mayor Fernando Wood, who had split with Tammany Hall and formed the "Mozart Hall Democrats," named for the building where he and his followers met. Opdyke, who would serve only one term (1861–1863), defeated C. Godfrey Gunther of the "Tammany Hall Democrats" by 613 votes and Wood of the "Mozart Hall Democrats" by 1,213 votes. For the vote totals, see Opdyke's obituary in the *New York Times*, 13 June 1880. For the three parties in the 1861 mayoralty race, see *New York Times*, 15, 22, 27 November 1861; "The Beastly Principles of Greeley," *New York Herald*, 20 October 1862 (quote); also see Albon Man Jr., "Labor Competition and the New York Draft Riots of 1863," *The Journal of Negro History* 36 (October, 1951), pp. 380–811; "Mayor Fernando Wood Recommends the Secession of New York," in Henry Steele Commager, ed., *The Civil War Archive: The History of the Civil War in Documents*, rev. ed. (New York: Black Dog & Leventhal Publishers, 2000), pp. 45–57.

11. "The Right to Work," *New York Tribune*, 14 April 1863. In a prelude to the more widespread violence to come, the longshoremen had hurled "stones and other missiles" until the police arrived and broke up the attack. According to the *Times*, "the only two persons known to be seriously injured were Jas. Agar, one of the ringleaders of the attacking party, and James Olney, one of the colored men. The latter was arrested for firing a pistol at his assailant, but was subsequently discharged by the magistrate on the ground that the act was committed in self-defense." *New York Times*, 14 April 1863.

12. Cecil Woodham-Smith, *The Great Hunger: Ireland 1845–1849* (New York: Harper & Row, 1962), pp. 246–69; Edgar W. Martin, *Standard of Living in 1860: American Consumption on the Eve of Civil War* (Chicago: University of Chicago Press, 1942), p. 174. Douglass, in an address to the American and Foreign Anti-Slavery Society in New York preceding the repeal of the Missouri Compromise in 1854, observed regarding the replacement of black workers by Irish immigrants in the lowest level jobs: "Every hour sees us elbowed out of some employment to make room for some newly-arrived emigrant from the Emerald Isle, whose hunger and color entitle him to special favor." Frederick Douglass, *Autobiographies*, vol. 3: *Life and Times of Frederick Douglass* (New York: Literary Classics of the United states, 1994), p. 740. Similar observations made by Douglass regarding the impact of Irish immigration on black employment are quoted in Charles H. Wesley, *Negro Labor in the United States 1850–1925: A Study in American Economic History* (New York: Vanguard Press, 1927); reprint ed., New York: Russell and Russell, 1967), pp. 61–62; and in Adrian Cook, *Armies of the Streets: The New York City Draft Riots of 1863* (Lexington: the University Press of Kentucky, 1974), p. 205.

13. Man, Jr., "Labor Competition," pp. 377, 386, 392, 394, 396–97; Sterling Spero and Abram L. Harris, *The Black Worker and the Labor Movement* (New York: Columbia University Press, 1931), pp. 13–14. Although unskilled German workers participated in the anti-black draft riots in both New York and Detroit, many of the more highly educated and skilled German immigrants who came to America in the late 1840s actively supported the abolition of slavery. Unlike the unskilled, uneducated, and desperately poor Irish peasant farmers who had fled starvation in Ireland at about the same time, most of these Germans (known as "the Forty-Eighters") were refugees from the liberal democratic revolutions that swept Europe in 1848—in the German case, a failed attempt to unite Germany as a liberal-democratic republic. German refugees tended to be better-educated liberals and socialists who were opposed not only to the chattel slavery of blacks but to "wage slavery" in the so-called "free labor" economy as well—i.e., the absence of workers' rights, the ten- to fifteen-hour workdays at pay insufficient for a decent living or chance for improvement, and the exploitation of children in the workplace. Many of these Germans were active in the abolition movement and formed or served in German regiments in the United States Army during the Civil War. August Willich, an old Prussian "Forty-Eighter," commanded the 32nd Indiana Volunteer Infantry, Indiana's all-German regiment. Joseph R. Reinhart, ed. and trans. *August Willich's Gallant Dutchmen: Civil War Letters from the 32nd Indiana Infantry* (Kent, OH: Kent State University Press, 2006), passim; Spero and Harris, *The Black Worker and the Labor Movement*, pp. 13–14; Herman Schluter, *Lincoln, Labor and Slavery* (New York: Socialist Literature Company, 1913), pp. 34–84; Martin, *Standard of Living in 1860*, passim.

14. Man Jr., "Labor Competition," pp. 396–97. In spite of the devaluation of their already low wages by wartime inflation, the *Times* called the strikers' demands "extortionate" and defended the use of deserters to break the strike. "Deserters Used by the Government," *New York Times*, 14 June 1863.

15 "The Conscription Act," *New York Times*, 19 February 1863; O.R., Ser. III, Vol. III, pp. 199–200.

16. Bernstein, *New York City Draft Riots*, p. 18; *New York Herald*, 12, 13, 14 July 1863; *New York Times*, 12, 14 July 1863; *New York Tribune*, 13, 14, July 1863.

17. Bernstein, *New York City Draft Riots*, p. 18; Cook, *Armies of the Streets*, p. 56; "New York Divided: Slavery and the Civil War," New York Historical Society website, www.nydivided.org. "Black Joke" was reportedly the name of a War of 1812 privateer and was adopted by Engine Company No. 13 when was it was first organized in the 1820s. Competing volunteer fire companies continued until 1865 when legislation abolished them and established the more unified and professional New York Metropolitan Fire Department. *New York Times*, "Metropolitan Fire Department," 26 June; "The Fire Department," 28 September 1865; "Wants to be Discharged. A 'Black Joke' Fireman Before the Court Asking Mandamus," 1 March 1893.

18. *New York Tribune*, 13–18 July 1863; *New York*

Herald, 13–18, 20 July 1863; *New York Times*, 12, 14–18 July 1863; O.R., Ser. I, Vol. XXVII, pt. 2, p. 899; Cook, *Armies of the Streets*, p. 59; Bernstein, *New York City Draft Riots*, p. 22.

19. *New York Times*, 14, 15 July 1863; "Anna Dickinson Sees the Draft Riots in New York City," in Commager, ed. *The History of the Civil War in Documents*, pp. 480–83.

20. *New York Tribune*, 15 (quote), 17 July 1863. Midshipman Adams was sent over by Rear Admiral Hiram Paulding, commander of the New York Navy Yard, to protect the *Tribune* and Printing-House Square. O.R., Ser. I, Vol. XXVII, pt. 2, p. 882.

21. Elmer Davis, *History of the New York Times, 1851–1921* (New York: New York Times, 1921), p. 60; Meyer Berger, *The Story of the New York Times: The First 100 Years, 1851–1951* (New York: Simon and Schuster, 1951), pp. 24–25; also see Cook, *Armies of the Streets*, p. 87.

22. "The Riots in Second-avenue," *New York Times*, 15 July 1863.

23. O.R., Ser. I, Vol. XXVII, pt. 2, pp. 253–54, 275–76, 875–94, 914.

24. The 7th New York National Guard. *Ibid.*, pp. 250; the 8th and 162nd New York National Guard, and the 26th Michigan Infantry. *New York Times*, 17 July 1863.

25. The 74th New York National Guard. O.R., Ser. I, Vol. XXVII, pt. 2, pp. 274–75; *New York Times*, 17 July 1863; Cook, *Armies of the Streets*, pp. 194, 196, 213–18, 310n3.

26. "The Riot," *New York Tribune*, 14 July 1863; "The Poor and the Rich; A Lesson from the July Riots," *New York Times*, 18 October 1863 (quote); "The Draft. Terrible Excitement in the City. Popular Opposition to the Enforcement of Conscription.," *New York Herald*, 14 July 1863.

27. John C. Breckenridge of Kentucky was the vice-president of the United States under James Buchanan and presidential candidate in 1860. He would become the last Confederate Secretary of War. "Red" Jackson's cavalry division consisted of two brigades and artillery: Col. John W. Whitfield's brigade (Lt. Col. J.H. Broocks's 1st Texas Legion; Col. J.S. Boggess's 3rd Texas Cavalry; Col. L.S. Ross's 6th Texas Cavalry; and Col. D.W. Jones's 9th Texas Cavalry); Col. George B. Cosby's brigade (Col. R.A. Pinson's 1st Mississippi Cavalry; Col. James Gordon's Mississippi Cavalry; Col. Peter B. Starke's 28th Mississippi); Ballentine's Mississippi Cavalry (Lt. Col. W.L. Maxwell); Wirt Adams's Mississippi Cavalry; and King's Battery of Clark's Missouri Artillery. O.R., Ser. I, Vol. XXIV, pt. 2, pp. 248, 310; pt. 3, pp. 947, 987–89, 995, 1041.

28. *Ibid.*, pt. 3, pp. 987–88.

29. *Ibid.*, pt. 1, pp. 114, 245; pt. 2, pp. 551–52, 578; pt. 3, p. 557; 11 July 1863; Edwin C. Bearss, *The Battle of Jackson, May 14, 1863; The Siege of Jackson, July 10–17, 1863* (Baltimore: Gatewood Press, 1981), p. 67; E. Chris Evans, "Return to Jackson: Finishing Stroke to the Vicksburg Campaign," *Blue & Gray Magazine* (August 1995): 22; *Battles and Leaders*, III: 550; Johnston, *Narrative*, pp. 203–206. Sherman, *Memoirs*, p. 356.

30. James R. Slack to Ann P. Slack, 11 July 1863; O.R., Ser. I, Vol. XXIV, pt. 3, p. 988.

31. *Ibid.*, pt. 2, p. 620; pt. 3, pp. 987–89.

32. *Ibid.*, pp. 555–57; pt. 3, pp. 987–89.

33. *Ibid.*, pt. 2, pp. 574, 580, 591, 597; pt. 3, pp. 987–88.

34. *Ibid.*, pt. 2, pp. 555–57, 578, 580, 620–21, 989; Fullerton's cavalry brigade: the 2nd Illinois, 2nd Battalion (3 companies); the 3rd Illinois, 3rd Battalion (3 companies); the 4th Indiana (1 company); the 6th Missouri (7 companies); and the 118th Illinois Infantry (mounted), 100 men. Artillery: Capt. C.H. Lanphere, commanding. The 1st Wisconsin Battery (six 20-pounder Parrotts, Lt. Nutting, commanding); 7th Michigan Battery (six 10-pounder Rodmans, Lt. Stillman, commanding). *Ibid.*, p. 580; Atlas Plate XXXVI, No. 1.

35. O.R., Ser. I, Vol. XXIV, pt. 1, p. 245; Johnston, *Narrative*, p. 206; Atlas Plate CLV.

36. O.R., Ser. I, Vol. XXIV, pt. 2, pp. 534, 621; Sherman, *Memoirs*, p. 356; Evans, "Return to Jackson," 22.

37. O.R., Ser. I, Vol. XXIV, pt. 2, pp. 628, 644, 651.

38. *Ibid.*, pp. 578, 580–81, 599 (quote), 603.

39. *Ibid.*, pp. 569, 630, 634, 637.

40. *Ibid.*, pp. 551–52; pt. 3, p. 485. Bussey's cavalry included Maj. Thomas A. Apperson's 5th Illinois; Maj. Oliver H.P. Scott's 3rd Iowa; and Col. Thomas Stephens's 2nd Wisconsin. *Battles & Leaders*, III: 548.

41. O.R., Ser. I, Vol. XXIV, pt. 2, pp. 555–56.

42. *Ibid.*, p. 581.

43. *Ibid.*, pp. 581–82, 586.

44. *Ibid.*, pp. 552, 556.

45. *Ibid.*, pp. 522, 534, 582.

46. *Ibid.*, pp. 557, 561, 563, 568, 570.

47. *Ibid.*, pp. 582, 586, 592; Atlas Plates XXXVII, Nos. 2, 3 and 5, and XXXIX, No. 1.

48. O.R., Ser. I, Vol. XXIV, pt. 2, pp. 578–79, 582, 586, 592, 594; Johnston, *Narrative*, p. 207.

49. O.R., Ser. I, Vol. XXIV, pt. 2, pp. 563, 566.

50. The Confederate pickets included W.J. Cawley's Holcomb Legion, part of Nathan G. Evans's South Carolina brigade. *Ibid.*, pp. 609–12, 657.

51. *Ibid.*, pp. 574, 582, 597, 600–603, 658–59; Atlas Plate XXXIX, No. 1.

52. O.R., Ser. I, Vol. XXIV, pt. 2, p. 602. Describing this movement to Ann, Slack wrote: "As soon as I crossed the creek the rebels opened fire on me from their skirmishers. The balls flew round us quite thick & fast. I had three men wounded, one, Condie [James E. Conde, Co. D, 47th Indiana] of Wabash Co. mortally, shot through the right heart, coming out at the back passing through the right lobe of his lungs. He is living yet, but think he cannot recover. Lieut of the 28th Iowa was shot in the head, just grazing his skull, not serious. One of the 56th Ohio had two fingers shot off. The fight did not last more than a half hour, we drove them in, and then rested on our arms for the night." James R. Slack to Ann P. Slack, 13 July 1863.

53. O.R., Ser. I, Vol. XXIV, pt. 1, p. 245; pt. 2, pp. 522, 597–98, 657–59; Johnston, *Narrative*, p. 207; Atlas Plate XXXVII, No. 5.

54. O.R., Ser. I, Vol. XXIV, pt. 2, p. 602. Describing this movement to Ann, Slack wrote: "About nine o'clock yesterday morning I advanced ... a line of skirmishers across a field in front, and then moved forward

my whole colum in line of battle across the field. It was a beautiful sight. Five Regts in a straight line, all with their Regimental Colors flying, moving steadily forward, and all keeping their line well closed up, and well drilled. The movement was as perfect as though it was being made on a parade ground.... We moved forward into the woods with four Cos. of skirmishers about 100 yards in advance and covering our whole front. Very soon fighting again commenced, but we drove them in and made them take to their entrenchments, and then we halted and there we yet are. Had one man killed, Eli Dinius of Roanoke, Capt Wintrodes Co [E, 47th Indiana], shot through the right breast, died in a very short time. The balls flew quite thick and fast round us, but myself and staff escaped unhurt." James R. Slack to Ann P. Slack, 13 July 1863. During this engagement, Privates Thomas Boden and William Parkinson of Co. H threw down their guns and returned to Vicksburg. Charged at their court-martial with "misbehaving in the presence of the enemy," they pled guilty and were sentenced to confinement at hard labor for the duration of their enlistment and dishonorably discharged. The roster of the 47th Indiana, however, indicates that they eventually returned to duty and were mustered out on 12 December 1864. "The Court-Martial of Privates Thomas Boden and William Parkinson," Court-Martial Case Files, NN597, Box. 1578.

55. O.R., Ser. I, Vol. XXIV, pt. 1, p. 201; pt. 2, pp. 523, 525, 574–75, 598, 603–608, 654–56; pt. 3, pp. 503, 1039. The 33rd Wisconsin Infantry was on reconnaissance toward the Pearl River and was not involved in the charge of Breckenridge's breastworks. The Confederates left behind the wounded Federals who were captured and unable to be moved when they evacuated Jackson; those who were able to be moved remained Confederate prisoners. *Ibid.*, pp. 603, 605. Referring to Lauman's blunder, Slack told Ann: "A very severe fight came off yesterday on our right, by Genl Lauman of Iowa advancing his line without proper caution. He ran into a rebel ambush, and got three of the Regts cut to pieces badly, losing three stand of colors." James R. Slack to Ann P. Slack, 13 July 1863.

56. O.R., Ser. I, Vol. XXIV, pt. 1, pp. 200–207; Johnston, *Narrative*, pp. 211–252.

57. Slack told Ann: "Our provisions and forage have to be hauled from Black river. The distance is 30 miles. From Vicksburgh to Black river we run out in cars. Have two locomotives and about 30 cars in constant use. Had it not been for the burning of Black river Bridge and the tressel work this side, we could now have put the road in order and run to this place." James R. Slack to Ann P. Slack, 16 July 1863.

58. O.R., Ser. I, Vol. XXIV, pt. 2, pp. 526, 535, 595; Johnston, *Narrative*, p. 208.

59. O.R., Ser. I, Vol. XXIV, pt. 2, p. 653.

60. *Ibid.*, pp. 526, 535–36, 540, 552, 618–19, 660–61.

61. *Ibid.*, pt. 1, pp. 235, 246; pt. 2, pp. 540–42; pt. 3, p. 1027; Johnston, *Narrative*, p. 252.

62. O.R., Ser. I, Vol. XXIV, pt. 2, p. 539.

63. *Ibid.*, pp. 529, 536; pt. 3, p. 1008; Johnston, *Narrative*, pp. 208–209.

64. Bir, "Reminiscence," 25.

65. O.R., Ser. I, Vol. XXIV, pt. 3, p. 1008; Atlas Plate XXXVII, Nos. 3 and 5; Johnston, *Narrative*, p. 209.

66. O.R., Ser. I, Vol. XXIV, pt. 2, p. 595.

67. *Ibid.*, pp. 536, 568; Johnston, *Narrative*, p. 209;

68. O.R., Ser. I, Vol. XXIV, pt. 2, p. 529.

69. *Ibid.*, p. 529; Johnston, *Narrative*, pp. 210–211.

70. O.R., Ser. I, Vol. XXIV, pt. 2, p. 528 (quote); Johnston, *Narrative*, pp. 208–210.

71. O.R., Ser. I, Vol. XXIV, pt. 2, pp. 621–25.

72. *Ibid.*, pp. 525, 536 (quote), 559–60, 621–26; pt. 3, pp. 524–25; Sherman, *Memoirs*, p. 357.

73. O.R., Ser. I, Vol. XXIV, pt. 2, p. 537.

74. *Ibid.*, p. 539.

75. *Ibid.*, pp. 526, 539–40 (quotes).

76. James R. Slack to Ann P. Slack, 25 July 1863.

77. O.R., Ser. I, Vol. XXIV, pt. 3, p. 557.

78. *Ibid.*, p. 570.

79. *Ibid.*, pt. 1, p. 551; pt. 3, pp. 1005, 1028; Johnston, *Narrative*, p. 228.

80. O.R., Ser. I, Vol. XXIV, pt. 1, pp. 201, 246; pt. 3, pp. 1027–32, 1033 (quote), 1034–39. The president of the Mississippi Central Railroad complained to Richmond on 24 July that Johnston had ordered $5,000,000 worth of railroad equipment in Jackson to be burned. A week earlier, the president of the Memphis & Charleston Railroad telegraphed President Davis with the same $5,000,000 figure and asked that the order to destroy the railroad property be rescinded. Davis replied that the railroad equipment should be removed as far as possible; and Johnston replied on 2 August that, since the Federals had withdrawn from Jackson, he would protect the Mississippi Central Railroad, which he hoped to use for supplies, if their owners would make the repairs. *Ibid.*, pt. 1, p. 232; pt. 2, p. 235.

Chapter 11

1. O.R., Ser. I, Vol. XXVI, pt. 2, pp. 112–13; Grant, *Memoirs*, p. 213; "Important from Havana. The Case of the English Steamer Blanche," *New York Times*, 26 October 1862.

2. O.R., Ser. I, Vol. IX, p. 674 (quote); Vol. XXVI, pt. 1, p. 657; Ser. III, Vol. III, p. 213. Also see Nicolay and Hay, *Lincoln*, VI: 30–48.

3. "A New Era—Banks and McClernand," *New York Times*, 30 October 1862 (quote); "The Crisis and Cotton," *New York Times*, 24 September 1863; "End of Cotton Famine in England," *New York Times*, 23 October 1863; Ludwell H. Johnson, *The Red River Campaign: Politics and Cotton in the Civil War* (Baltimore: Johns Hopkins University Press, 1958; reprint ed., Kent, OH: Kent State University Press, 1993), pp. 13, 34. Karl Marx, a special columnist on Horace Greeley's *New York Tribune*, noted that the British could not afford to get too belligerent with the United States on the question of the blockade of Confederate cotton and its negative impact on the British textile industry for two reasons: (1) Cotton was not readily available from India due to a lack of transportation and communication there; and (2) the United States was their principal source of corn. Marx urged the British to "emancipate cotton from the slave-

breeding and slave-consuming oligarchies." He added: "As long as the English cotton manufactures depended on slave-grown cotton, it could truthfully be asserted that they rested on a twofold slavery, the indirect slavery of the white man in England and the direct slavery of the black man on the other side of the Atlantic." "The British Cotton Trade," *New York Daily Tribune*, 14 October 1861.

4. "Interesting from Mexico. Election of Alvarez," *New York Times*, 23 October 1855; *ibid.*, "The Latest Revolution in Mexico — How it is Received by the Liberals," 24 January 1859; *ibid.*, "Interesting from Mexico. Proceedings of the French and English Commanders at Vera Cruz. The Rival Presidents of Mexico — Miramon and Juarez," 22 March 1859; *ibid.*, "Important From Mexico. The Recognition of the Juarez Government," 18 April, 1859; *ibid.*, "Important from Mexico. The Decrees Secularizing Church Property," 25 July 1859. For a general discussion, see Charles A. Weeks, *The Juarez Myth in Mexico* (Tuscaloosa: University of Alabama Press, 1987).

5. In another column for Greeley's *Tribune*, Marx called the English, Spanish and French invasion of Mexico "one of the most monstrous enterprises ever chronicled in the annals of international history," done in order to "plunder a bankrupt country." Karl Marx, "The Intervention in Mexico," *New York Daily Tribune*, 23 November 1861. Several weeks later, Marx wrote that British Prime Minister Lord Palmerston had been pushing to intervene in Mexico and was saber-rattling over the Trent Affair in order to gain an advantage over the United States while it was distracted by a civil war. *Ibid.*, Karl Marx, "Progress of Feelings in England," 7 December 1861. By mid-1863, Lord Palmerston had long given up on the idea of intervening in Mexico, and after the fall of Vicksburg and the Confederate defeat at Gettysburg, was no longer willing to recognize the Confederacy.

6. For a general discussion of the French in Mexico see Alfred J. Hanna and Kathryn A. Hanna, *Napoleon III and Mexico: American Triumph over Monarchy* (Chapel Hill: University of North Carolina Press, 1971) and Jasper G. Ridley, *Maximillian and Juarez* (New York: Ticknor and Fields, 1991.)

7. Mexico had abolished slavery by decree in 1829 shortly after having achieved independence from Spain. Before being ousted, however, the Spanish colonial government had issued land grants to Anglo-American settlers to come into the northern Mexican state of Coahuila y Tejas. The newly independent government of the Republic of Mexico honored the land grants, and the Anglo-American settlers, most of them from the southern United States, brought slaves with them at a time when the new republic was too weak to stop them. Eventually, however, the Mexican government tried to clamp down on slavery in the Anglo-Texan settlements north of the Rio Grande by prohibiting the importation of slaves and later banning immigration from the United States entirely. This led to the largely Anglo-Texan revolt in 1835 (putatively a rebellion against President Santa Ana's takeover of power in a *coup d'état*). The Anglo-Texan-led rebellion succeeded in establishing the slaveholding Republic of Texas, which lasted until 1845 when it became, with much controversy, a slave state in the United States. To complete the land grab, in 1848 the Polk administration declared war on Mexico. After Mexico lost the war it was forced to cede about one-third of its territory, about half in all if Texas is included. Their ceded territory now includes the entire southwestern United States. Texas became part of the Confederacy in 1861. On the desire of Texas Confederates to expand slavery into Central American and the Caribbean, see May, *The Southern Dream of a Caribbean Empire*, pp. 162, 233–34.

8. O.R., Ser. I, Vol. XXVI, pt. 2, pp. 144, 147; O.R.N., Ser. 2, Vol. 3, pp. 802–804, 820. The rumor of a French move into Texas and Arizona came at least in part from Leonard Pierce Jr., U.S. Consul at Matamoros, Mexico, in a 6 June 1863 dispatch to Secretary of State Seward: "My own opinion is that Texas and Arizona are to be included in the price paid to the French, but I may be mistaken." O.R., Ser. III, Vol. III, pp. 213. Also see: "The French in Mexico," Message from the President of the United States. S. exdoc. 11, 38th Congress, 1863–1865, pp. 459–60, cited in Johnson, *Red River Campaign*, p. 480. Rumors of a French/Confederate alliance persisted as late as April 1865, including the idea that a "big war" was about to commence in the South, a conflict that would pit the United States, Great Britain, and Russia against France, Austria, and Maximilian's Mexico. Southerners, so the rumor went, would take the oath of allegiance to France as the French army advanced victoriously through the South. Samuel T. Foster, *One of Cleburne's Command: The Civil War Reminiscences and Diary of Capt. Samuel T. Foster, Granbury's Texas Brigade, CSA*, ed. Norman D. Brown (Austin: University of Texas Press, 1980), p. 167, quoted in Williamson, *The Third Battalion Mississippi Infantry*, p. 317; also see Nicolay and Hay, *Lincoln*, VI: 30–48 and VIII: 254–280. Regarding Confederate trade with Mexico, Governor Santiago Vidaurri of the State of Coahuila and Nuevo Leon, a semi-independent caudillo and opportunistic royalist, had refused orders from Juarez in November 1862 to stop trading with the Confederates and opened his part of the upper Rio Grande border to Confederate transshipments. Texas Confederates, though, complained of his high import/export tariffs, reportedly $40 in specie per bale, which they expected to be eliminated when the French took over. O.R.N., Ser. 2, Vol. 3, pp. 900–902; O.R., Ser. I, Vol. XV, pp. 881, 1066.

9. *Ibid.*, pp. 882; Vol. XXVI, pt. 1, pp. 402–409; pt. 3, pp. 144, 292. In September 1863, Zapata was killed in a skirmish with a Confederate force under Santos Benevides. *Ibid.*, pp. 283–84. Juan Cortina, a Texas-Mexican, went on to play a major, if not controversial, role in Juarez's fight, first against the Texas Confederates and later against the French army and its Mexican Royalists allies. *Ibid.*, Vol. I, pp. 577, 631; Vol. XXVI, pt. 1, pp. 399–40; Mexico, Comision Pesquisidora de la Frontera del Norte, *Reports of the Committee of Investigation Sent in 1873 by the Mexican Government to the Frontier of Texas* (trans. from the official edition made in Mexico; New York: Baker and Godwin, printers, 1875), pp. 149–50 (cited hereafter as Mexico, Comision Pesquisadora).

10. O.R., Ser. I, Vol. XXVI, pt. 2, pp. 359–60. J.B. Magruder came to be known "Prince John" for his somewhat extravagant lifestyle and pomposity while an officer in the U.S. Army prior to the war. Paul D. Casdorph, *Prince John Magruder: His Life and Campaigns* (New York: John Wiley & Sons, 1996); Warner, *Generals in Gray*, pp. 24, 207.

11. O.R., Ser. I, Vols. IV, pp. 131–32, 137, 152; IX, pp. 615, 684–85; 704–706; XV, pp. 1016, 1132–34; XXVI, pt.1, pp. 412, 657; pt. 2, p. 898; *The Handbook of Texas Online*, Texas State Historical Association; Claude Elliot, "Union Sentiment in Texas," *Southwestern Historical Quarterly* 50 (1946–1947), pp. 451, 453–55, 460, 465–66. This notice appeared in the *New York Times* on 20 November 1862: "The Texan Refugees. Notice to Texas Refugees. Texas refugees in this city and neighborhood are notified that the First Regiment Texas United States Volunteers in now being organized (under authority from Maj. Gen. Butler) by Judge E.J. Davis, of Texas, who will command as Colonel. This regiment will be furnished with the arms and accoutrements of mounted riflemen, and will be supplied with horses in Texas, as it is inconvenient to ship them from this port. In the meantime, it will act as an unmounted rifle corps. It is understood that a number of Texas refugees have enlisted in other regiments of this Department. All of these who wish to return to Texas may be transferred to this regiment, on sending their names to Col. Davis at Park Hotel, Lafayette Square."

12. O.R.N., Ser.1, Vol. 20, p. 201; O.R., Ser. III, Vol. III, p. 213.

13. *Ibid.*, Ser. I, Vol. XXVI, pt. 1, p. 659.

14. *Ibid.*, Vol. XXIV, pt. 3, p. 584

15. Grant, *Memoirs*, p. 214 (quote); O.R., Ser. I, Vol. XXVI, pt. 1, pp. 652, 664, 666, 672–73, 675.

16. Grant, *Memoirs*, p. 214; O.R., Ser. I, Vol. XXIV, pt. 2, pp. 680–82.

17. *Ibid.*, pp. 661, 685–86.

18. Logan's Confederate cavalry continued operating in the countryside of southwest Mississippi after the Federals left, although in a very disorganized manner, at times trading with the enemy and at others committing depredations against Mississippi civilians. *Ibid.*, Vol. XXVI, pt. 2, pp. 541–42; pt.3, p. 727; Vol. XXX, pt. 4, p. 51–52, 493, 599; Vol. XXXI, pt. 3, pp. 673–74. Regarding the Confederate cavalry operating in southwest Mississippi and a population there anxious for peace, Pvt. William B. Johnston, a soldier in the Army of Tennessee, received three letters from home at the end of the year and one in April 1864 that illustrate this point: (1) From a brother-in-law, David Edwards, recuperating at home in Pike County, Mississippi, 4 December 1863: "Times is very hard here a worse is coming. I hope this cruel war will end so we can git to stay at home.... You wrote for me to stay at home as long as I could. I am going to stay as long as I can. I hope I never will haft to go out in the horble war any more." (2) From a brother, George B. Johnston, 1 December 1863: "Thir is a few cavalry a stealing about here trying to get a few conscripts but it is insane. The Yanks are too close.... The times is very hard and it looks like it is a getting worse. The crops are all a drying up.... some are bad fixed to get on." (3) From his eldest sister, Nancy Johnston Roberts, 8 April 1864: "Times is hard and distressing down here.... [T]he cavalry is still in this part of the country and as for the good they are doing they might as well be home at work trying to make something to live on instead of doing nothing and eating ever thing up that they can get." William B. Johnston Papers, privately held, quoted in Williamson, *The Third Battalion Mississippi Infantry*, pp. 157, 172.

19. Grant, *Memoirs*, p. 214.

20. Alvin P. Hovey returned to Indiana on leave and was replaced in command of the new 3rd division of the 13th corps by Brig. Gen. Albert L. Lee. Slack retained command of the 2nd brigade, which included the 47th Indiana, the 87th Illinois, the 24th and 28th Iowa, the 56th Ohio, the 1st Missouri Light Artillery, and the 2nd Ohio Battery. Due to illness, E.O.C. Ord relinquished command of the 13th corps to Maj. Gen. Cadwallader C. Washburn. O.R., Ser. I, Vol. XXVI, pt. 1, p. 710.

21. James R. Slack to Ann P. Slack, 4 August 1863..

22. The Town of Carrollton, which is today an uptown neighborhood centered on what is now called South Carrollton Avenue and Oak Street, provided a good campground for the Federal troops, with access to water and rail transportation. The town of Carrollton was connected to New Orleans by the Carrollton & New Orleans Railroad, which ran about six and a half miles from the river at Canal Street in the Faubourg St. Mary (the present-day Central Business District, bounded by Iberville Street, Loyola and Howard Avenues, and the river), turned upriver on Baronne to the *Place du Tivoli* (Lee Circle), and continued upriver around the crescent on the *Cours de Nayades* (present-day St. Charles Avenue) to Carrollton and its terminus at the bend of the river (Carrollton Bend) at the base of present-day South Carrollton Avenue. That railroad line became part of what is now the St. Charles Avenue Streetcar Line. Carrollton Avenue and a drainage canal ran northeastward from the river through town and onward through a former cypress swamp that began near present-day South Claiborne Avenue. (Sometimes called "the backswamp," it had been cleared of most of its timber in 1862 for defensive reasons by Ben Butler.) Carrollton Avenue and the canal connected at a right angle with northwestward-running Poydras Street and the New Orleans (or New Basin) Canal in what is today the Mid-City neighborhood. At its junction with Carrollton Avenue in the mid-city swamp, the New Orleans Canal angled northward to Lake Pontchartain, entering the lake near the present-day yacht harbor on West End Boulevard. In addition, the Jefferson & Lake Pontchartrain Railroad ran northward from Carrollton Bend and its junction with the Carrollton & New Orleans Railroad and terminated at a wharf on the lake about one-half mile west of the New Orleans Canal. About a mile and a half north of Carrollton Bend, a spur of the railroad followed Metairie Road westward about a mile to the army supply depot. Richard Campanella, *Time and Place in New Orleans: Past Geographies in the Present Day* (Gretna, LA: Pelican Publishing Company, 2002), pp. 10, 66, 70–71, 95–97, 183; Merl E. Reed, *New Orleans and the Railroads: The Struggle for Commercial Empire 1830–1860* (Baton Rouge: Louisiana State University Press, 1966), pp. 38–39; Benjamin F.

Butler, *The Autobiography and Personal Reminiscences of Major-General Benj. F. Butler: Butler's Book* (Boston: A.M. Thayer, 1892), pp 488–89; Atlas Plate XC.

23. The town of Greenville, which bordered Carrollton's downriver side, was created in 1836 from a subdivision of long and narrow plantation property that also radiated out from the river to the mid-city backswamp. Today an integral part of the Carrollton neighborhood, Greenville ran northeastward from the river to Freret Street, which marked its "lakeside" boundary. Lowerline Street marked its upriver side, adjacent to the town of Carrollton, and Walnut Street its downriver side, adjacent to today's Audubon Park and Tulane University's uptown campus. Broadway was its main thoroughfare. Campanella, *Time and Place in New Orleans*, pp. 95–97, 183; Atlas Plate XC.

24. James R. Slack to Ann P. Slack, 21 August 1863.

25. O.R., Ser. I, Vol. XXVI, pt. 1, pp. 19–20, 286–87. Franklin had been commander of the "Left Grand Division" (the 1st and 6th corps) in Burnside's Army of the Potomac, which was plagued by command problems as it moved toward Richmond. After the 13 December 1862 debacle at Fredericksburg, in a letter dated 20 December 1862, Franklin publicly criticized Burnside's plan of advance. Burnside counterattacked and accused Franklin of disobedience of orders. He blamed him in part for the defeat and relieved him from duty on 23 January 1863. Two days later, however, Burnside himself was relieved of duty and replaced in command of the Army of the Potomac by "Fighting Joe" Hooker. On 25 March 1863, Burnside, in turn, relieved Horatio Wright in command of the Dept. of the Ohio, where it was mistakenly believed that he could do little damage (See Chapter VII above). Franklin's career was revived following the fall of Port Hudson in July, when he was assigned command of the 19th corps in Banks's Dept. of the Gulf. He led the failed attack on the Confederate fort at Sabine Pass, Texas, and then was given command of the land expedition up Bayou Teche, which included Ord's 13th corps. *Ibid.*, Vol. XXI, pp. 868–70; Warner, *Generals in Blue*, pp. 159–60.

26. Lt. R.W. Dowling commanded the Davis Guards and Capt. F.W. Odlum commanded Cook's Texas Artillery. The Federal troop transports were the *Suffolk, St. Charles, Landis, Exact, Laurel Hill, Thomas* and *General Banks*. O.R., Ser. I, Vol. XXVI, pt. 1, pp. 288–89, 294–99, 301, 303; pt. 2, pp. 359–60; O.R.N., Ser. 1, Vol. 20, pp. 527–30, 532–35, 539, 542–49, 557–60, 562.

27. Grant, *Memoirs*, p. 215; James R. Slack to Ann P. Slack, 8 September 1863, James R. Slack Collection, Indiana State Library.

28 O.R., Ser. I, Vol. XXII, pt. 1, pp. 474–77, 520–22.

29. O.R., Ser. I, Vol. XXVI, pt. 1, pp. 18–20, 290, 334–36; James R. Slack to Ann P. Slack, 12 September 1863.

39. Bringhurst and Swigart, *History of the 46th Indiana*, p. 72; Atlas Plate CLVI. Built in the late 1850s, the railroad was intended to connect New Orleans (Algiers) and Opelousas via Bayou Teche and eventually connect Opelousas with eastern Texas. By 1859, the railroad was completed to Berwick Bay and a third-class port with a depth of less than ten feet constructed for steamers plying the Atchafalaya River. The outbreak of the war ended the construction at Berwick Bay, and the railroad was almost completely destroyed during the war. Reed, *New Orleans and the Railroads*, pp. 117–18.

31. James R. Slack to Ann P. Slack, 13, 16 September 1863. "Nutmeg" was a mildly derisive term the residents of south Louisiana applied to the eastern troops of Franklin's 19th corps. The western soldiers of the 13th corps adopted its use to deride their eastern comrades. As with words and phrases, however, one man's derisive epithet is another man's honorific. When the 13th corps followed in the footsteps of the 19th corps, the locals used the (at least for Indianans) complimentary term "Hoosier" to deride all the westerners of the 13th corps. Neither corps was welcome there. Bringhurst and Swigart, *History of the 46th Indiana*, p. 72.

32. *Indianapolis Daily Journal*, 25 September 1863.

33. James R. Slack to Ann P. Slack, 20 September 1863.

34. Grant, "Chattanooga," *Battles and Leaders*, III: 685–87; O.R., Ser. I, Vol. XXX, pt. 2, p. 723; Vol. XX, pt. 1, pp. 621–70, 670–78.

35. Grant, *Memoirs*, pp. 215–17, 223.

36 James R. Slack to Sallie Slack, 29 September 1863, James R. Slack Collection, Indiana State Library (the letter is largely illegible); Bringhurst and Swigart, *History of the 46th Indiana*, p. 74 (quote).

37. O.R., Ser. I, Vol. XXVI, pt. 1, pp. 369, 393; Atlas Plate CLVI. The 1st division, Cadwallader Washburn; 3rd division, George McGinnis (Cameron's 1st and Slack's 2nd brigades); and the 4th division, Stephen G. Burbridge. Francis J. Herron's 2nd division was detached and remained in New Orleans.

38. Due to E.O.C. Ord's illness, Cadwallader Washburn took command of the 13th corps on 20 October 1863. Six days later, Maj. Gen. N.T.J. Dana was assigned command of the 13th corps, but Washburn continued in command of the 1st, 3rd and 4th divisions of the 13th corps and operated under William B. Franklin's command during the Teche Campaign. Albert L. Lee was assigned command of the 13th corps' cavalry division, and George McGinnis assigned to Lee's former command of the 3rd division of the 13th corps. Robert L. Cameron replaced McGinnis in command of the 1st brigade. Slack retained command of the 2nd brigade, but the 87th Illinois was transferred to Lee's cavalry division as a mounted infantry unit. O.R., Ser. I, Vol. XXVI, pt. 1, pp. 334–36, 369; Bringhurst and Swigart, *History of the 46th Indiana*, p. 77.

39. O.R., Ser. I, Vol. XXVI, pt. 1, p. 332.

40. *Ibid.*, p. 393.

41. *Ibid.*, pp. 357, 359, 364, 391, 394; H.A., "*Wisconsin State Journal* Account, New Orleans, La., Nov. 9, 1863," reprinted in Frank Moore, ed., *The Rebellion Record: A Diary of American Events*, vol. 8 (New York: D. Van Nostrand, 1865), p. 151, cited hereafter as H.A., "*Wisconsin State Journal* Account"; Atlas Plate CLVI; Richard G. Lowe, *Walker's Texas Division, C.S.A.: Greyhounds of the Trans-Mississippi* (Baton Rouge: Louisiana State University Press, 2004), p. 138.

42. O.R., Ser. I, Vol. XXVI, pt. 1, p. 364; H.A., "*Wisconsin State Journal* Account," p. 151.

43. O.R., Ser. I, Vol. XXVI, pt. 1, pp. 360–61, 363–64, 372, 394.

44. *Ibid.*, pp. 357–58, 372, 374–75, 394, 721.
45. *Ibid.*, p. 371.
46. Washburn had sent McGinnis's division (Cameron and Slack's brigades), led by Cameron due to McGinnis's illness, from Carrion Crow Bayou. *Ibid.*, p. 358; T.J. Woods, letter, n.d., reprinted in N.N. Hill, comp., *History of Knox County, Ohio* (Mt. Vernon, Ohio: A.A. Graham & Co., Publishers, 1881), p. 324; Bringhurst and Swigart, *History of the 46th Indiana*, p. 78; James R. Slack to Ann P. Slack, 6 November 1863 (quotes). Fonda reported that his cavalry captured forty prisoners at Bayou Bourbeau on 3 November; the remainder were presumably captured in the infantry pursuit mentioned by Slack and T.J. Woods. O.R., Ser. I, Vol. XXVI, pt. 1, pp. 358, 361, 365–66, 371, 378.
47. *Ibid.*, pp. 359, 395.
48. Most of the Confederate casualties were from Roberts's three infantry regiments. They included 21 out of 22 (95 percent) of those killed, 77 out of 103 (75 percent) of those wounded, and 41 out of 55 (75 percent) of those listed as missing. Indeed, 32 out of 41 (78 percent) of the missing infantrymen came from the 11th Texas alone. Green and Roberts both failed to cite how their losses, especially the missing fifty-five, occurred in their easy withdrawal. *Ibid.*, p. 394; Alwyn Barr, "The Battle of Bayou Bourbeau, November 3, 1863: Colonel Oran M. Roberts' Report," *Louisiana History* 6 (Winter 1965): 89.
49. Bringhurst and Swigart, *History of the 46th Indiana*, p. 78.
50. James R. Slack to Ann P. Slack, 6 November 1863.
51. O.R., Ser. I, Vol. XXVI, p. 371.
52. T.J. Woods, letter, n.d., reprinted in Hill, *History of Knox County, Ohio*, p. 324.
53. O.R., Ser. I, Vol. XXVI, pt. 1, pp. 359, 375.
54. *Ibid.*, pp. 396, 435; Comdr. James H. Strong commanded the *Monongahela*; Lt. Comdr. E.W. Henry, the *Owasco*; and Act. Vol. Lt. Charles H. Brown, the *Virginia*. O.R.N., Ser. 1, Vol. 20, p. 643; Atlas Plates LXV, No. 10 and XLIII, No. 8.
55. The Confederates gave two versions of the burning of Brownsville. One version was that an arsonist set the fire; the other was that Bee had ordered it set, but it got out of control. O.R., Ser I, Vol. XXVI, pt. 1, pp. 433–34, 439; Vol. XXXIV, pt. 2, p. 889.
56. O.R., Ser. I, Vol. XXVI, pt. 1, p. 429; Lt. Col. Richard Irwin, Asst. Adjutant General, Dept. of the Gulf, "The Red River Campaign," *Battles and Leaders*, IV: 346. Comdr.
57. Com. Bell explained to the senior British Naval Officer in the Gulf, who protested the seizures, that the British merchant vessels would not have been seized if they had been anchored in Mexican waters. They were, however, in American waters. The United States claimed the belligerent right to inspect and seize and send to prize court any vessel in American waters or on the high seas that appeared to be attempting to run the blockade of American ports. "Report of Commodore H.H. Bell, U.S. Navy, transmitting correspondence with the commanding officer of H.B.M.S. *Galatea* [Capt. Rochfort Maguire], regarding the exercise of belligerent rights off the Rio Grande," 20 November 1863. O.R.N., Ser. I, Vol. 20, pp. 693–94. Capt. Joseph G. Solar, Captain of the Post of Boca Del Rio, Mexico, also protested the seizures. In reply, Comdr. J.H. Strong of the *Monongahela* explained: "We claim the right to capture any vessels anchored in our waters on this coast, as it has all been declared closed to commerce by the Government of the United States. Capture, however, does not necessarily infer condemnation; that is the duty of the court to decide." The Treaty of Guadalupe Hidalgo in 1848 determined the boundary waters between Mexico and the United States to be a line at right angles to the mid-channel or bar of the Rio Grande and three leagues east of the coastline. Mexican waters lay south of this line, American waters to the north. O.R.N., Ser. 1, Vol. 20, pp. 280–81, 460–61, 478, 500, 643, 646, 648, 658–63, 664 (quote), 677, 693–94.
58. O.R., Ser. I, Vol. XXVI, pt. 1, pp. 399–405; pt. 2, pp. 402–409.
59. *Ibid.*, pp. 396, 416–24, 426; Irwin, "Red River," 346; Atlas Plate LXV, No. 10.
60. Worried about Mexican support on the upper Rio Grande, Bee even apologized to Vidaurri for accidentally burning Brownsville and assured the governor that his troops did not prevent civilians from extinguishing the blaze. O.R., Ser. I, Vol. XXVI, pt. 1, p. 437 (quote), 438.
61. *Ibid.*, p. 799; James R. Slack to Ann P. Slack, 17 November 1863 (quote).
62. O.R., Ser. I, Vol. XXVI, pt. 1, pp. 336, 346–49, 370 (quote), 378; Atlas Plate XXIII; Bringhurst and Swigart misidentified Spanish Lake as "Lake Mauripas," *History of the 46th Indiana*, p. 81. Lee's cavalry brigades were led by Col. Thomas J. Lucas of the 16th Indiana Mounted Infantry and Col. Charles J. Paine of the 2nd Louisiana Mounted Infantry (U.S.). Slack did not mention if the four remaining unnamed men of the 47th Indiana were rescued in this raid.
63. James R. Slack to Ann P. Slack, 24 November 1863.
64. Grant, *Memoirs*, p. 254, 260; Johnston, *Narrative*, p. 262.
65. *Indianapolis Daily Journal*, 19 December 1863.
66. *Indianapolis Daily Gazette*, 31 December 1863.
67. *Adjutant General's Report*, I (Appendix), p. 4; Eli E. Rose, Military Records, National Archives Trust Fund, Washington, D.C.; Daniel Hilton Papers (courtesy of Commander Roger L. Johnson, U.S. Navy, retired.)

Chapter 12

1. *Indiana State Sentinel*, 4 January 1864.
2. Klement, *Dark Lanterns*, pp. 101, 105; Robert. S. Harper, *Lincoln and the Press* (New York: McGraw-Hill, 1951) p. 326.
3. Frank L. Klement, "The Indianapolis Treason Trials and *Ex Parte Milligan*," in *American Political Trials*, ed. Michal P. Belknap (Westport, CT: Greenwood Press, 1981), pp. 104–106. The Sons of Liberty council also included Lambdin P. Milligan, Esq., a Huntington, Indiana, attorney and radical Democratic candidate for governor; John C. Walker; Horace Heffrin, Esq., editor of the *Salem (Indiana) Washington Democrat* and

former Lt. Col. of the 13th Indiana Volunteer Infantry; and Andrew Humphreys, member of the Indiana State House of Representatives from Green County. Kenneth Stampp, "The Milligan Case and the Election of 1864 in Indiana," *Mississippi Valley Historical* Review 31 (June 1944): 44–45.

4. Marshall, *American Bastille*, p. 218; Harper, *Lincoln and the Press*, p. 330.

5. Bringhurst and Swigart, *History of the 46th Indiana*, p. 83. Of the 1st brigade, the 46th Indiana remained in Louisiana; the 24th Indiana was on veteran furlough; the 34th Indiana and 29th Wisconsin were sent to Texas to join the remainder of Ord's 13th corps and Corps d'Afrique. McGinnis and the 11th Indiana went to Madisonville, but would soon receive their veteran furloughs and follow the 24th and 47th Indiana home. Brig. Gen. Cuvier Grover commanded at Madisonville, a sub-post in the Defenses of New Orleans. Johnson and Buel, *Battles and Leaders*, IV: 367; O.R., Ser. I, Vol. XXXIV, pt. 2, pp. 194, 198; Vol. XLI, pt. 4, p. 864.

6. *Indianapolis Daily Journal*, 16 February 1864.

7. O.R., Ser. III, Vol. IV, pp. 133–35; Library of Congress, Manuscript Division, *The Abraham Lincoln Papers*, Ser. 1, General Correspondence, 1833–1916, Louisiana Election Returns, 25 February 1864; *Biographical Directory of Congress*, pp. 894–95, 986. Hahn was inaugurated on 4 March 1864 in a ceremony held at Lafayette Square in New Orleans. "The Inauguration Ceremonies," *New York Times*, 6 March 1864.

8. *Indianapolis Daily Journal*, 20 February 1864; *Indianapolis Daily Gazette*, 20 February 1864; Scribner and Stevenson, *Indiana's Roll of Honor*, pp. 72–73. McGinnis and the 11th Indiana were due to come home later in the month via New York City. *Indianapolis Daily Journal*, 27 February 1864.

9. *Ibid.*, 22 February 1864 (quote). The "Family Marketing" section of the 29 March 1864 *Daily Journal* listed potatoes, carrots, and old onions, $1.00 per bushel; new onions, 5 to 10 cents per bunch; dried peaches, 20 cents per pound; turkey, 10 to 12 cents per pound; pan chickens, 50 to 60 cents; choice cuts of beef, pork or mutton, 15 cents per pound; butter 35 cents per pound; eggs, 20 cents per dozen; and wood, $5.00 to $6.50 per cord. In the 29 March 1864 edition, they advertised: "New Spring Styles. Misses' and Ladies' Straw Hats and Bonnets. Trimmed and Untrimmed, Received at Callinan's. No. 28 East Washington Street." And the February and March editions of the *Indianapolis Daily Gazette* regularly advertised: "J.K. Sharpe. Manufacture and Dealer in Boots, Shoes, Leather. No. 90 East Washington Street"; and "John A. Heidlinger. Manufacture and Wholesale Dealer in all kinds of Cigars and Tobacco. No. 3 Palmer's House, Indianapolis."

10. O.R., Ser. I, Vol. XXXII, p. 1, p. 6; Vol. XXXIII, p. 753; Vol. XXXIV, pt. 2, pp. 193, 378, 400, 392, 474 (quote), 512, 545; Kiper, *McClernand*, p. 281.

11. *Battles and Leaders*, IV: 367; O.R., Ser. I, Vol. XXXIV, pt. 1, p. 256; pt. 2, pp. 20,71, 545, 614; Atlas Plate CLVII.

12. O.R., Ser. I, Vol. XXXII, pt. 1, pp. 174–75.

13. *Ibid.*, p. 176 (quote); Sherman, *Memoirs*, pp.452–57; Johnston, *Narrative*, p. 282.

14. O.R., Ser. I, Vol. XXXII, pt. 1, pp. 251, 260–61, 294–95, 302, 351.

15. *Ibid.*, pp. 177, 181, 294–95, 350–55; William T. Sherman to Ellen Ewing Sherman, 10 March 1864, steamer *Westmoreland*, approaching Memphis, in Sherman, *Sherman's Civil War*, p. 605 (quote).

16. O.R., Ser. I, Vol. XXVI, pt. 1, pp. 666, 673; Irwin, "Red River Campaign," 345.

17. O.R., Ser. I, Vol. XXXIV, pt. 1, pp. 169, 171; pt. 2, p. 610; Grant, *Memoirs*, p. 281; Sherman, *Memoirs*, p. 489; U.S. Congress. Joint Committee on the Conduct of the War, vol. 2, pt. 1, *The Red River Expedition*, 38th Cong., 2nd Sess., Feb. 20, 1865, pp. III-XLIX; also see "The Red River Expedition. Minority Report on the Responsibility of Gen. Banks for its Failure," *New York Times*, 25 May 1865. Republican Senator Benjamin F. Wade of Ohio chaired the committee, whose report blamed Banks for the failure of the campaign and essentially exculpated everyone else, from Lincoln and Stanton to Halleck and the other generals (Grant, Sherman, Steele, and Franklin) who were associated either directly or indirectly with its failure. They even concluded falsely that Banks had undertaken the expedition on his own. Unwilling to support the whitewashing of the higher-level politicians and generals by his fellow Republican committeemen, Representative Daniel W. Gooch of Massachusetts, who had been elected to fill the vacancy caused by Banks's resignation, wrote the minority report. Unable to completely exculpate Banks, who was, of course, partly at fault, Gooch at least spread the blame to the others who had contributed to its failure and largely debunked the findings of the committee, including the charge that Banks had interfered with the civilian elections in Louisiana. Although he merely mentioned "Washington's" (i.e., Lincoln and Stanton's) part in the fiasco, he named Halleck and the other leading generals, especially Grant, Sherman, and Franklin, for their part in the failure of the campaign. The members of the committee were: Senator Benjamin F. Wade, R-Ohio; Senator Zacharia Chandler, R-Michigan; Representative George W. Julian, R-Indiana; Representative Benjamin F. Loan, R-Missouri (a Brig. General in the U.S. Army, 1861–1863, elected to the 38th Congress as an "Emancipationist"); and Representative Daniel W. Gooch, R-Massachusetts. *Biographical Directory of Congress*, pp. 680, 954–55, 1142, 1228, 1759.

18. O.R.N., Ser. 1, Vol. 26, p. 29; Thomas O. Selfridge, "The Navy in the Red River," in *Battles and Leaders of the Civil War*, IV: 362.

19. O.R., Ser. I, Vol. XXXIV, pt. 1, pp. 162, 426–28.

20. *Ibid.*, pt. 3, p. 58; Grant, *Memoirs*, pp. 272–74.

21. Grant, *Memoirs*, pp. 274–79; Grant, "Preparing for the Campaigns of '64," *Battles and Leaders*, IV: 97, 103, 179.

22. Grant, *Memoirs*, p. 281; Sherman, *Memoirs*, pp. 489–90; O.R., Ser. I, Vol. XXVI, pt. 1, pp. 610 (quote), 661, 666, 673, 675.

23. *Ibid.*, pp. 303, 315, 562; Irwin, "The Red River Campaign," 351; Atlas Plate LII..

24. O.R., XXXIV, pt. 1, p. 284; Bringhurst and Swigart, *History of the 46th Indiana*, pp. 85–86; Atlas Plates CLV and CLVI.

25. "The Opposing Forces in Arkansas," *Battles and*

Leaders, IV: 368; E. Kirby Smith, "The Defense of the Red River," *Battles and Leaders*, IV: 370

26. Charles H. Coleman and Paul H. Spence, "The Charleston Riot, March 28, 1864," *Journal of Illinois State Historical Society* 33 (March 1940), p. 81; reprinted as "Coles County in the Civil War 1861–1865," *Eastern Illinois University Bulletin* online, p. 6, citing the *Mattoon (Illinois) Gazette*, 3 February 1864. As discussed in Chapter 7 above, Stephen E. Towne noted Coleman and Spence's errors of fact in their discussion of Judge Constable's arrest and detention in 1863; their discussion of the Charleston Riot, however, contains many interesting firsthand accounts and newspaper editorials that contribute to understanding the causes of the 1864 riot. Towne, "'Such conduct must be put down,'" pp. 43–44; "Daring Resistance to Federal Officers in Clark County. Arrest of the Judge and his Accomplices," *Chicago Tribune*, 14 March 1863.

27. *Mattoon Gazette*, 6 April 1864, quoted in Coleman and Spence, "The Charleston Riot," p. 6.

28. Coleman and Spence, "The Charleston Riot," p. 7, citing the Memoirs of Frank T. O'Hair., son of John H. O'Hair, Sheriff of Coles County, Illinois; O.R., Ser. I, Vol. XXXII, pt. 1, p. 636.

29. O.R., Ser. I, Vol. XXXII, pt. 1, p. 633–34; *Chicago Tribune*, 1 and 3 April 1864; also see the *Mattoon Gazette*, 24 February 1864, cited by Coleman and Spence, "The Charleston Riot," p. 7. Milton York had also probably been involved with Co. E of the 66th Illinois, along with Co. E of the 12th Illinois, in a firefight with Copperheads in Paris, Illinois, on or about 5 March 1864 in an attempt to seize guns held by the Copperheads. "The Copperhead War at Paris, Illinois," *Indianapolis Daily Gazette*, 5 March 1864; *Chicago Tribune*, 1, 2, and 3 April 1864.

30. O.R., Ser. I, Vol. XXXII, pt. 1, p. 633–34. Regarding Republican vigilantism, the Republican *Chicago Tribune* reported that George Rust, the special correspondent for the Copperhead *Chicago Times*, was forced to flee from the Essex Hotel in Mattoon on the morning of 1 April by a "committee representing the loyal men of Mattoon." The *Tribune* report also noted that a citizen "foraging party" had gone to Sheriff John O'Hair's farm that afternoon and had returned with five loads of corn. *Chicago Tribune*, 2 April 1864.

31. O.R., Ser. I, Vol. XXXII, pt. 1, pp. 635, 638; *Chicago Tribune*, 1 and 2 April 1864; Coleman and Spence, "The Charleston Riot," pp. 17, 19, citing the Memoirs of Frank T. O'Hair, son of Sheriff John H. O'Hair.

32. *Chicago Tribune*, 3 April 1864; Atlas Plate CLI.

33. O.R., Ser. I, Vol. XXXII, pt. 1, p. 631; James R. Slack to Ann P. Slack, 1 April 1864. The *Chicago Tribune*, citing a special dispatch from Mattoon dated 31 March 1864, reported that "insurgents" at Windsor were going to attack Mattoon in order to release the prisoners being held there, but changed their minds when they learned their "scout" had been arrested. *Chicago Tribune*, 1 April 1864. In a letter home, Pvt. Henry Bert of the 47th Indiana noted: "We captured only two of them but the citizens of Mattoon caught 42 of them." On his way to Cairo with the regiment at "about 10 o'clock" that morning," Bert added: "I don't know what they done with the butternuts but I hope they hung them for I know they need it." Bert, "Letters of a Drummer Boy," p. 330.

34. O.R., Ser. I, Vol. XXXII, pt. 1, p. 643 (quote); *Illinois State Register*, 1 April 1864, quoted in *Mattoon Gazette*, 6 April 1864, cited by Coleman and Spence, The Charleston Riot," p. 19; Cole, *The Era of the Civil War*, p. 308n.

35. *New York Times*, 2 April 1864, quoting the *Chicago Tribune*, 28 March 1864; also see Coleman and Spence, "The Charleston Riot," pp. 24–25. The Republican newspapers in Indiana relied primarily on dispatches from the *Tribune* and the *Charleston Plain Dealer*. In their 30 March 1864 edition, the *Indianapolis Daily Journal* announced that a county sheriff had shot up the court at Charleston, Illinois, during a Copperhead riot. That same day, the *Indianapolis Daily Gazette* gave the first details of the riot.

36. *Indianapolis Daily Gazette*, 30, 31 March 1864; *Indianapolis Daily Journal*, 30, 31 March, 1 April 1864. Brig. Gen. Henry B. Carrington's 30 March 1864 dispatch to Maj. Gen. Heintzelman in Illinois read: "Col. Slack's 47th Indiana, 560 strong, started within half an hour after the receipt of Col. Oake's telegram for Mattoon. Extra ammunition on passenger train." O.R., Ser. I, Vol XXXII, pt. 3, p. 198.

37. *Indianapolis Daily Journal*, 30, 31 March 1864, 1 April 1864. The *Charleston Plain Dealer*'s 28 March 1864 "Extra" was printed in the 1 April 1864 edition of the Daily Journal. It is partially reproduced in Coleman and Spence, "The Charleston Riot," pp. 9–10.

38. *Dayton Daily Empire*, 31 March 1864, and *New York World*, 4 April 1864, quoted in Coleman and Spence, "The Charleston Riot," pp. 24–25; Chicago Times, 1 April 1864, quoted in Cole, *Era of the Civil War*, p. 308n.

39. Forrest, with artillery and a potentially overwhelming cavalry force, had planted a battery and surrounded Fort Anderson with sharpshooters. In a clear example of his method of attack against isolated outposts, Forrest, under a flag of truce, told Col. Stephen Hicks, commander at Fort Anderson: "If you surrender, you shall be treated as prisoners of war; but if I have to storm our works, you may expect no quarter." Hicks respectfully declined the offer. Forrest's artillery opened on the fort and his sharpshooters took possession of nearby houses, putting Hicks troops under an effective fire. Hicks, with only the experienced 122nd Illinois Infantry, the 16th Kentucky Cavalry, and two inexperienced cavalry regiments (the 7th and 13th Tennessee), and a number of black recruits who had not yet been mustered in or paid, defended the fort. With the experienced troops providing leadership and the black recruits skillfully manning weapons, including artillery, Hicks's men held off three separate attacks over two days, but not before squads from the 16th Kentucky Cavalry, sent out by Hicks, burned all houses within musket range of the fort. Three Federal gunboats on the Ohio River assisted in driving off Forrest's cavalry. At Paducah, Forrest received a rare repulse from a Federal outpost during his West Tennessee and Kentucky Expedition and perhaps his heaviest losses (he reported 25 killed, including two high-ranking officers). In his

official report he claimed that he could have stayed, but withdrew out of concern about disease in the area and noted, without mentioning that they were convalescent soldiers in the hospital at Paducah, that he had captured 500 prisoners. He lost, according to the Federal account, 300 killed and over 1,000 wounded. Hicks reported Federal losses at 14 killed and 46 wounded. Forrest, in the meantime, moved his troopers southward toward Ft. Pillow, Tennessee. O.R., Ser. I, Vol. XXXII, pt. 1, pp. 506, 510, 547–49, 551–52, 606, 612; pt. 2, 302; James R. Slack to Ann P. Slack, 6 April, 1864; Bert, "Letters of a Drummer Boy," p. 330.

40. U.S. Congress, Joint Committee, *Red River Expedition*, pp. VI, XXXVII; "The Red River Expedition Minority Report," *New York Times*, 25 May 1865; O.R.N, Ser. I, Vol. 26, p. 50; Irwin, "Red River Campaign," 348, 351

41. O.R., Ser. I, Vol. XXXIV, pt. 1, p. 446.

42. *Ibid.*, pp. 167, 179–80, 264–67, 444–45; O.R.N, Ser. 1, Vol. 26, p. 90..

43. *Ibid.*, p. 610; Irwin, "Red River Campaign," 355–56; Smith, "Defense of the Red River," 372.

44. Bringhurst and Swigart, *History of the 46th Indiana*, p. 90; O.R.N., Ser. 1, Vol. 26, pp. 50–52, 61; Smith, "Defense of the Red River," 373; "From Banks' Department. A Sad Story of his Complete Failure," *Huntington Democrat*, 19 May 1864.

45. O.R., Ser. I, Vol. XXXIV, pt. 1, pp. 550–60, 581, 659–67, 779, 781–82, 788–90, 793, 821, 827, 834.

46. O.R.N., Ser. 1, Vol. 25, p. xv; Vol. 26, pp. 71, 237.

47. *Ibid.*, Vol. 26, p. 52; O.R., Ser. I, Vol. XXXIV, pt. 1, p. 571; Atlas Plate LIII.

48. James R. Slack to Ann P. Slack, 15 April 1864.

49. *Ibid.*, 19 April 1864. Part of the responsibility for the increase in take-no-prisoners "black flag" violence was due to Confederate presidential proclamations and congressional joint resolutions to execute captured white officers of black regiments as soon as they discovered some being organized; blacks captured in arms were to be considered as captured property to be returned to their owners. In 1862, Generals David Hunter in South Carolina, and John W. Phelps and Ben Butler in Louisiana, had, without authorization, started recruiting former slaves and freedmen into the Federal army. In August 1862, President Davis proclaimed Hunter and Phelps felons to be held, if captured, "in close confinement for execution ... at such time and place as the President shall order." O.R., Ser. I, Vol. XIV, p. 599. In December 1862, Davis by proclamation added Ben Butler to his list of felons to be executed if captured for forming the Louisiana Native Guards, and for executing William Mumford in New Orleans for tearing down a United States flag. In his December proclamation, Davis also proposed what he called retaliatory treatment for captured black soldiers and their white officers. *Ibid.*, Ser. II, Vol. V, pp. 795–97. On 1 May 1863, with the Emancipation Proclamation in effect and the official recruitment of black soldiers into the United States Army underway, President Davis, epitomizing the Confederacy's primal fear, signed a Joint Resolution passed by the Confederate Congress, which stated in part that any white officers who commanded "negroes or mulattos in arms against the Confederate States ... shall be deemed as inciting servile insurrection, and shall, if captured, be put to death, or be otherwise punished at the discretion of the court." *Ibid.*, Ser. I, Vol. XXVIII, pt. 2, pp. 235–36. President Lincoln responded "that for every soldier of the United States killed in violation of the laws of war a rebel soldier shall be executed, and for every one enslaved by the enemy or sold into slavery a rebel soldier shall be placed at hard labor on the public works and continued at such labor until the others shall be released or receive the treatment due to a prisoner of war." *Ibid.*, Ser. II, Vol. VI, p. 163. Lincoln's response helped to cool the ardor in Richmond for "retaliation." The fear and loathing of black Federal soldiers and their white officers, and the at least unofficial approval of summary execution, remained ever present in the field, however. This was especially true in the Trans-Mississippi and other border areas, where the cycle of personal violence and revenge made it difficult to determine who started it — except, of course, in the case of violence against black soldiers and their white officers, which originated with President Davis, his War Department, and the Confederate Congress. *Ibid.*, Ser. I, Vol. XXXIV, pt. 3, p. 415; Ser. III, Vol. II, pp. 147–48. Also see Glatthaar, *Forged in Battle*; Noah Andre Trudeau, *Like Men of War: Black Troops in the Civil War 1862–1865* (New York: Little, Brown and Company, 1998; reprint ed., Edison, NJ: Castle Books, 2002); and John Cimprich, *Fort Pillow, a Civil War Massacre, and Public Memory* (Baton Rouge: Louisiana State University Press, 2005).

50. For Forrest's accusations against Bradford and Col. Fielding Hurst of the 6th Tennessee Cavalry (U.S.) of murder and mayhem committed against his men prior to the Fort Pillow assault, see O.R., Ser. I, Vol. XXXII, pt. 1, pp. 592, 612; pt. 3, pp. 118–19. In addition, "Parson" Brownlow's son, Lt. Col. James P. Brownlow, commanding the 1st Tennessee Cavalry (U.S.), reported following a skirmish at Yankeetown, Tennessee, on 30 November 1863 that some of his scouts had driven the enemy away after killing nine and wounding between fifteen and twenty, but concluded his report with the chilling assertion: "I would take no prisoners." *Ibid.*, Vol. XXXI, pt. 1, p. 591; John A. Wyeth, *That Devil Forrest: The Life of General Nathan Bedford Forrest* (New York: Harper, 1959), p. 340. U.S. Congress. Joint Committee on the Conduct of the War. vol. 2, pt. 1, *The Fort Pillow Massacre*. 38th Cong., 1st Sess., May 5, 1864.

51. Letter of Samuel H. Caldwell, CSA, quoted in John Cimprich and Robert C. Mainfort Jr., "Fort Pillow Revisited: New Evidence about an Old Controversy," *Civil War History* 28 (December 1982): 300; "The Massacre at Fort Pillow. Details of the Butchery. A Walk Through the Fort Under Flag of Truce. Scenes and Incidents. Correspondence of the *Missouri Democrat*, *New York Times*, 20 April 1864; O.R., Ser. I, Vol. XXXII, pt. 1, pp. 558, 610 (Forrest quote), 623 (Chalmers quote).

52. For W.R. McLagan's testimony, see U.S. Congress. Joint Committee, *Fort Pillow*, pp. 101–103 and O.R., Ser. I, Vol. XXXIV, pt. 1, p. 557; for William Ferguson's testimony, see U.S. Congress, Joint Committee, *Fort Pillow*, pp. 100–101(quote) and O.R.N., Ser. 1, Vol.

26, pp. 231–32 (quote); Letter of Achilles V. Clark, CSA, quoted in Cimprich and Mainfort, "Fort Pillow Revisited," p. 299 (quote), 300; *Memphis Appeal*, 18 April 1864, cited in Jack Hurst, *Nathan Bedford Forrest: A Biography* (New York: Vintage Books, 1994), pp. 175–76.

53. News of the massacre first appeared in the *New York Times* only four days after the battle. The headlines, which summarize the account, read: "THE BLACK FLAG. Horrible Massacre. Fort Pillow Captured After a Desperate Fight. Four Hundred of the Garrison Brutally Murdered. Wounded and Unarmed Men Bayoneted and their Bodies burned. White and Black Indiscriminately Butchered. Devilish Atrocities of the Insatiate Fiends." *New York Times*, 16 April 1864. Capt. John T. Young, 24th Missouri (U.S.), Provost-Marshall at Fort Pillow, stated in a letter to Gen. C.C. Washburn that while he was a prisoner, Forrest threatened to execute him if he did not endorse Forrest's account of Fort Pillow. O.R., Ser. I, Vol. XXXII, pt. 1, pp. 604–605, 615 (quotes); pt. 3, p. 822; O.R.N., Ser. 1, Vol. 26, pp. 233–35; *New York Times*, 20 April 1864.

54. Forrest became something of a mythical figure in both the North and the South after the war, and toward the end of his life apparently held quite enlightened liberal views on race relations. Still, the Fort Pillow massacre had badly damaged his reputation, and he spent the rest of his life trying to convince at least the Northern public that he was not a monster — his efforts hindered by his immediate postwar dispute with "Parson" Brownlow and his election as the first "Grand Wizard" of the Ku Klux Klan. Brownlow, Chaplain Sawyer's proslavery nemesis in prewar East Tennessee, became the vengeful Radical Republican Reconstruction governor of Tennessee (1865–1869) and quickly got highly punitive, anti–Confederate legislation passed. Among other things, he disenfranchised all known ex–Confederates, including Forrest, while at the same time he organized Liberty or Union Leagues to teach freedmen their rights; in February 1867 got the Radical Republican legislature to pass a Negro suffrage bill. Captain John W. Morton, Forrest's chief of artillery during the war and one of the original Klan founders, claimed that Forrest was recruited and elected the first "Grand Wizard" of the secretive Invisible Empire of the Ku Klux Klan in May 1867 in Nashville to fight Brownlow's usurpation of power and denial of their civil rights, not to mention of course to promote the Klan's opposition to Negro suffrage. Some early members claimed that the Klan only turned violent when their "peaceful" tactic of parading at night as ghostly apparitions in hoods and white sheets failed to scare the freedmen and their radical white allies from exercising their right to vote. Morton, however, noted that the Klan's tactics had included acts of violence from the outset and later claimed: "When the white race had redeemed six Southern States from negro rule in 1870, the Grand Wizard knew that his mission was accomplished, and issued his order to disband." The disbanding of the original Klan by Forrest also coincided with the arrival of Federal troops that Brownlow had requested to quell growing Klan violence and to arrest and prosecute all Klansmen. Not coincidentally, this was also the end of the Brownlow era as governor. Brownlow resigned as governor, perhaps somewhat prematurely, to become a U.S. Senator (1869–1875). He was replaced in the governor's mansion by Speaker of the Senate DeWitt Senter, a less radical Republican who was more acceptable to the ex–Confederates, and who was elected with their support against a Radical Republican candidate in the 1868 election. Coulter, *William G. Brownlow*, pp. 268–69, 272, 330, 334, 353, 395; John Watson Morton, *The Artillery of Nathan Bedford Forrest's Cavalry* (Nashville, TN, and Dallas, TX: Publishing House of the M.E. Church, South, 1909; reprint ed., Kennesaw, GA: Continental Book Company, 1962), pp. 337–41, 345 (quote), 346; Allen W. Trelease, *White Terror: The Ku Klux Klan Conspiracy and Southern Reconstruction* (Baton Rouge: Louisiana State University Press, 1971), pp. 20, 180–81; Andrew Lytle, *Bedford Forrest and His Critter Company*, rev. ed. (New York: McDowell, Obolensky, 1960), pp. 382–83; Hurst, *Forrest*, pp. 284–87, 323, 326–27.

Regarding Forrest's emerging liberal views on race, in March 1869 he reportedly endorsed a policy of encouraging African blacks to immigrate to the South to populate and help rebuild it. "N.B. Forrest: Some Extraordinary View Respecting Negroes," *New York Times*, 15 March 1869.

Two years later, Forrest's credibility suffered when he testified disingenuously before the U.S. Senate that he had no direct knowledge or involvement with the Ku Klux Klan (he had joined the "Pale Faces," a benevolent secretive order like the Odd Fellows or Masons) and blamed "Parson" Brownlow's policies for the Klan's rise in Tennessee and elsewhere. U.S. Congress. Senate. *Testimony Taken by the Joint Select Committee to Inquire into the Condition of Affairs in the late Insurrectionary States — Florida and Misc.: The Ku-Klux Conspiracy*. S. rp. 41, Vol. XIII, 42nd Cong. 2nd Sess., 24 June 1871, pp. 4–35.

Near the end of his life, although his credibility was diminished by his congressional testimony, Forrest showed an emerging liberal enlightenment on the issue of race in a speech to a 4th of July 1875 "gathering of negro societies and clubs" in Memphis. Forrest, who may have been the only high-ranking ex-Confederate in Tennessee who believed this, asserted: "It has always been my motto to elevate every man — to depress none. I want to elevate you to take positions in law offices, in stores, on farms, and wherever you are capable of going." On suffrage he added: "You have a right to elect whom you please; vote for the man you think best, and I think, when that is done, that you and I are freemen." Speaking to the same assembly, Gideon Pillow acknowledged the equal civil and political rights of blacks under the law and encouraged their education (separate but equal), but blamed blacks themselves for the rise of unnamed hostile white organizations. On suffrage he added: "My colored friends, give up politics as a pursuit." "Gens. Forrest and Pillow. Remarkable Scenes at the Celebration in Memphis — The Colored People Hearing and Applauding the Ex-Confederate Generals," *New York Times*, 9 July 1875. Other articles, editorials, and letters about Forrest, including a few letters from Forrest himself, continued to appear in the *New York Times* and other newspapers until his death in 1877.

See, for example, 2 April 1866, 15 October 1867; 22 June, 3, 13, 14, 17 September, 26, 29 October, 7, 12 November 1868; 15 March 1869; 24, 28 June, 2 July 1871; 28 September 1874; 6 July 1875; 30 August, 23 September, 27, 30 October, and 1 November 1877. *New York Times* Article Archives online.

55. O.R., Ser I, Vol. XXXIV, pt. 1, pp. 406–407, 580, 615.

56. *Ibid.*, pt. 3, pp. 253, 269, 296.

57. *Indianapolis Daily Journal,* 16 May 1864.

58. O.R., Ser. I, Vol. XXXIV, pt. 1, p. 634.

59. O.R.N., Ser. 1, Vol. 25, p. xv; Vol. 26, pp. 62–63, 71–79, 81–83, 87–88, 167–68, 176; O.R., Ser. I, Vol. XXXIV, pt. 1, p. 176; Selfridge, "The Navy in the Red River," 364–65.

60. O.R.N., Ser. 1, Vol. 26, pp. 87–88, 167, 169, 176 (quote), 781–82. After the war, Capt. Thomas O. Selfridge of the *Osage* wrote: "The captain, Stewart, three engineers, and all the crew, composed of some 200 negroes, were scalded to death, with the exception of 15." Selfridge, "The Navy in the Red River," 365n.

61. O.R., Ser. I, Vol. XXXIV, pt. 1, pp. 269, 296

62. *Ibid.*, pt. 3, pp. 276, 296–97, 317–18; James R. Slack to Ann P. Slack, 27 April 1864.

63. O.R., Ser. I, Vol. XXXIV, pt. 1, p. 587–88. Slack and the 47th Indiana were forced to abandon their camp on the outskirts of Alexandria with the rest of McClernand's newly arrived troops, but Slack reported that while they were gone his camp had been "securely moved to the rear," and at least his belongings were secure. James R. Slack to Ann P. Slack, 29 April 1864.

64. O.R., Ser. I, Vol. XXXIV, pt. 1, pp. 251, 253. 403.

65. *Ibid.*, Vol. XXXIV, pt. 1, pp. 251, 254; Irwin, "Red River Campaign," 358; O.R.N., Ser. 1, Vol. 26, p. 130.

66. O.R., Ser. I, Vol. XXXIV, pt. 1, pp. 475, 590, 621; O.R.N., Ser. 1, Vol. 26, pp. 102 (quote).

67. O.R., Ser. I, Vol. XXXIV, pt. 1, pp. 211, 474–75, 622; O.R.N., Ser. 1, Vol. 26, pp. 105, 107, 171.

68. *Ibid.*, pp. 117–19, 123–24; O.R., Ser. I, Vol. XXXIV, pt. 1, pp. 211, 474–75, 622–23.

69. *Ibid.*, pt. 1, p. 626.

70. James R. Slack to Ann P. Slack, 6 May 1864. The fight at Graham's Plantation on 5 May 1864 is designated as "Muddy Bayou" on the 47th Indiana's last flag. This may have been a transcription error or simply the name they adopted for "Middle Bayou." Atlas Plate LII.

71. O.R., Ser. I, Vol. XXXIV, pt. 1, pp. 277, 626; Bringhurst and Swigart, *History of the 46th Indiana,* pp. 92–93.

72. O.R., Ser. I, Vol. XXXIV, pt. 1, p. 254; O.R.N, Ser. 1, Vol. 26, pp. 131–32.

73. O.R., Ser. I, Vol. XXXIV, pt. 1, pp. 254 (quote), 255; O.R.N., Ser. 1, Vol. 26, pp. 131–32, 144, 779, 793.

74. O.R., Ser. I, Vol. XXXIV, pt. 1, pp. 254, 405.

75. Pearsall had wanted the 13th corps pioneers to begin working overnight on 10 May. The navy commanders, whose assistance was required, all told him to "wait until daylight." Pearsall thus blamed the navy for what he called a six-hour delay in constructing the upper dam. According to Lt. Com. John G. Mitchell of the *Carondelet,* Banks also complained that the navy wasn't doing anything that night. Mitchell countered that they had worked all that night hauling the *Carondelet* into position over the rocks and "nearly across the lumps in the channel," and implied that other vessels were encountering similar problems. *Ibid.*, p. 255; O.R.N., Ser. 1, Vol. 26, p. 144.

76. O.R., Ser. I, Vol. XXXIV, pt. 1, pp. 251, 254–55; O.R.N., Ser. 1, Vol. 26, pp. 124, 132, 779, 793.

77. O.R., Ser. I., Vol. XXXIV, pt. 1, p. 592. Reporting on the fire at Alexandria, the correspondent of the *New York Times* wrote: "About dusk on of the 12th the army was in motion. There were apprehensions felt that Alexandria might be set afire by some rascal. Gen. Banks gave strict orders, which were executed in the best style by Gen. Grover. Double-guards were kept at all the street crossings and all buildings closed at the setting in of night. Everything went well until about 9 o'clock A.M. on the morning of the 13th, when a fire broke out in a small two-story building on the levee. All troops about town were set to work to extinguish the flames. There were no fire engines that could be used, and no water except in the river. Everything was done to prevent further progress of the flames. Gen. Banks, with his whole staff, were at work. About 10 o'clock the wind got stronger, and set in the direction of the town. The flames became master, and in about five hours two-thirds of Alexandria was laid in ashes. All the roofs being covered with shingles, old and dried to cinder by the long drought, and most of the houses being frame buildings, the flames spread at a fearful rate." "The Red River Campaign," *New York Times,* 5 June 1864.

78. O.R., Ser. I, Vol. XXXIV, pt. 1, pp. 193, 277–78, 399, 593, 631–32; "Red River Campaign," *New York Times,* 5 June 1864. "Union" was referring to the news of Grant's success in battles of the Wilderness and Spotsylvania earlier in the month. News of the extremely heavy losses suffered by Grant's forces in the bloody battles would arrive later.

79. Although listing fewer casualties, Bringhurst and Swigart gave a similar account of the attack on the wagon train: "At 3 o'clock on the morning of the 17th, the division was again on the road, without breakfast. Halted at 7, and made coffee. An attack was made on the rear of the column, but repulsed. The Third Division marched beside the wagon train, with an African brigade in front. A dash was made by the rebels upon the train, ahead of the negroes. They pushed ahead, repulsed the attack, and killed two rebels. One negro was killed and two wounded, and it was said that a rebel captain killed both the wounded men." *History of the 46th Indiana,* p. 94.

80. O.R., Ser. I, Vol. XXXIV, pt. 1, pp. 443, 593 (quote).

81. In his letters to Taylor, Smith cited the presidential order found in General Orders, No. 111, Adjutant & Inspector General's Office, Series 1862. He added, showing that he understood the reluctance in Richmond to cause retaliatory measures to be taken against Confederate prisoners of war: "Should negroes thus taken be executed by the military authorities capturing them it would certainly provoke retaliation. By turning them over to the civil authorities to be tried by the laws of the State no exception can be taken." *Ibid.*, Ser. II, Vol. VI, pp. 21, 22 (quote), 115.

82. *Ibid.*, p. 115 (quote). Due to threats of Federal retaliation, this was true on the eastern front as well where some black prisoners of war were held at Florence, South Carolina, albeit in terrible, disease-ridden conditions that, according to Howard Westwood, rivaled the conditions at Andersonville. Howard Westwood, "Captive Black Union Soldiers in Charleston — What to Do?" *Civil War History* 28 (January 1972): 44.

83. www.archives.gov/education/lessons/blacks-civil-war/images/wood-capture-letter.gif. National Archives and Records Administration Compiled Service Records, Records of the Adjutant General's Office, 1780s–1917, RG 94 (hereafter cited as National Archives: Black Soldiers in the Civil War).

84. National Archives: Black Soldiers in the Civil War. Federal retaliation served to dampen, although not completely eliminate, these prisoner abuses, and the Confederate Congress did not amend the 1 May 1863 joint resolution until 8 February 1865. President Davis approved the amendment, which now merely condemned the employment of Confederate slaves as Union soldiers and authorized the president to retaliate as he thought proper. O.R., Ser. II, Vol. VIII, p. 197. For the October 1864 exchanges between U.S. Grant and R.E. Lee on the issue of retaliation, see O.R., Ser. II, Vol. VII, pp. 990–93, 1010, 1018.

85. Bringhurst and Swigart, *History of the 46th Indiana*, p. 94.

86. O.R., Ser. I, Vol. XXXIV, pt. 1, pp. 193, 311, 320–21, 347, 357, 370, 466–67, 593–95, 624, 631–32; Irwin, "Red River Campaign," *Battles and Leaders*, IV: 360; Bringhurst and Swigart, *History of the 46th Indiana*, p. 95. Brig. Gen. Richard Arnold, Chief of Artillery for the Dept. of the Gulf, replaced Albert Lee in command of the department's cavalry division on 18 April, following Sabine Cross Roads. Lee was sent to New Orleans where he was put in charge of the cavalry depot.

87. O.R., Ser. I, Vol. XXXIV, pt. 3, pp. 211, 294, 646, 648; Atlas Plate CLVI.

88. *Indianapolis* Daily Journal, 18 June 1864.

89. O.R., Ser. I, Vol. XXXIV, pt. 1, p. 6; pt. 3, pp. 490, 543.

Chapter 13

1. *Huntington Democrat*, 21 April 1864; *Indianapolis Daily Journal*, 8, 18, 21 May, and 9 June 1864.

2. *New York Herald*, 5 June 1864. Eight steamers (*Black Hawk, Empire Parish, Meteor, Fawn, Time and Tide, Belle Lee, New Orleans* and *Belle Creole*) and two unnamed schooners were burned in the fire; records do not indicate that anyone was ever arrested or tried in connection with this fire. Coincidentally, at this same time a Confederate plot was uncovered in Havana to capture steamers plying between New York and New Orleans. O.R.N., Ser. 1, Vol. 21, p. 302. The *New Orleans Picayune* did not carry news of the fire because U.S. military authorities temporarily suspended its publication for issuing what they called a bogus presidential proclamation in their 23 May 1864 edition. *New York Times*, 5 June 1864. Resuming publication on 9 July 1864, the editors of the *Picayune* denied publishing "anything that could give just cause of offense to the Government." *New Orleans Picayune*, 9 July 1864.

3. James R. Slack to Ann P. Slack, 29 May 1864.

4. Bert, "Letters of a Drummer Boy," pp. 331–32.

5. O.R., Ser. I, Vol. XXXIV, pt. 1, pp. 959, 964; pt. 4, pp. 387, 530, 653–55. Leander H. McNelly was a noted Texas partisan ranger. Chuck Parsons and Marianne E. Hall Little, *Captain L.H. McNelly, Texas Ranger: The Life and Times of a Fighting Man* (Austin, Texas: State House Press, 2000).

6. E.J. Davis' cavalry included: the 1st and 2nd Texas, the 3rd Maryland, the 1st Louisiana, the 87th Illinois Mounted Infantry, the 2nd New York, 4th Wisconsin, 6th Massachusetts, and the 2nd New Hampshire. O.R., Ser. I, Vol. XXXIV, pt. 4, p. 614. Jacob Sharpe's infantry brigade included the 38th Massachusetts and the 128th, 156th, 175th, and 176th New York. *Ibid.*, p. 570.

7. Atlas Plates CXXXV-A and CLVI.

8. O.R., Ser. I, Vol. XXXIV, pt. 1, pp. 961–64.

9. *Ibid.*, pp. 961, 963.

10. *Ibid.*, p. 961. False River is a twelve-mile long oxbow lake on the west bank of the Mississippi about twelve miles east southeast of Morganza and about thirty miles northwest of Baton Rouge that was formed in the eighteenth century when the Mississippi River changed course. Its upper and lower ends, although not navigable at the time of the Civil War, were about five miles apart and still connected to the Mississippi by the old channels. Today, False River is separated from the Mississippi by a levee, its upper end about five miles from the river, its lower end about ten miles from the river. Atlas Plate CLVI.

11. James R. Slack to Ann P. Slack, 2 June 1864.

12. O.R., Ser. I, Vol. XXXIV, pt. 1, pp. 956, 959, 961, 963 (quote), 964–65; Theo Noel, *A Campaign From Santa Fe to the Mississippi: Being the History of the Old Sibley Brigade From its First Organization to the Present Time* (Shreveport, LA: Shreveport News Printing Establishment, 1865; reprint ed. Raleigh, NC: Charles R. Sanders, Jr., 1961), p. 90.

13. David Barrow (1805–1874), head of the Barrow family, owned extensive plantation lands in Pointe Coupee Parish. David, whose main residence was at Afton Villa in West Feliciana Parish on the east bank of the Mississippi, had given El Dorado Plantation, on the west bank of Bayou Maringouin in Pointe Coupee Parish several miles south of Livonia, to his son, Barthalameau "Batt" Barrow, Major and Asst. Adjutant-General on J.P. McCown's staff, as a wedding present in 1856. National Register of Historic Places: Louisiana, www.crt.state.la.us/hp/nhl; David King Gleason, *Plantation Homes of Louisiana and the Natchez Area*. Baton Rouge: Louisiana State University Press, 1982, p. 94.

Major "Batt" Barrow had been captured by Col. Frederick A. Boardman's 4th Wisconsin Cavalry following a skirmish on Bayou Grosse Tete in February 1864, and he was held in New Orleans until at least 18 November 1864. In May 1864, Richard Taylor identified Ratliff as "Captain W.B. Ratliff, a scout whom I left on the Grosstete." As late as March 1865, Ratliff, in command of a Confederate force in Point Coupee Parish, sent civilian Alexander Barrow to negotiate a temporary cease-fire with Capt. Patrick Donnelly of the gunboat *Nymph*, operating on the Mississippi around Pointe Coupee, and with Maj. Gen. Francis J. Herron, commanding U.S. Forces at Baton Rouge, so that his force could clear out "Jayhawkers" (in this case, deserters from the Confederate Army) who had been firing on workers repairing the levee. Herron agreed to let Ratliff operate without interference between Bayou Plaquemine to the south and Morganza to the north for ten days commencing 16 March 1865 to clear out the "Jayhawkers." O.R., Ser. I, Vol. XXXIV, pt. 1, pp. 585–86 (quote); pt. 2, p. 247; Vol. XLVIII, pt. 1, pp. 1085–86, 1137; Ser. II, Vol. VII, pp. 764, 1139.

14. *Ibid.*, Ser. I, Vol. XXXIV, pt. 1, pp. 961–64.

15. *Ibid.*, pp. 962–64; Gleason, *Plantation Homes of Louisiana*, p. 106.

16. James R. Slack to Ann P. Slack, 2 June 1864; O.R., Ser. I, Vol. XXXIV, pt. 4, pp. 653–54.

17. *Ibid.*, pt. 1, p. 964. While Davis and Crebs reported one man killed and two wounded in this action, Noel claimed "eight Yankees were killed and fifteen wounded." Following this action, McNelly, who was erroneously reported killed in the fighting, was sent with his company of scouts westward to the Calcasieu in southwestern Louisiana, near the Texas border, to hunt jayhawkers and deserters. McNelly survived the war and returned to Texas, where he worked for Davis, his erstwhile enemy and former commander of what his Confederate troopers had called the "First Texas Traitors." Davis, 12th District Judge before the war, became the Republican reconstruction governor of Texas, and in the early 1870s, McNelly helped him reorganize the Texas Rangers for use as the state police. Noel, *Old Sibley Brigade*, pp. 90–91; O.R., XLI, pt. 2, pp. 473, 549; Walter Prescott Webb, *The Texas Rangers: A Century of Frontier Defense*, 2nd edition (Austin: University of Texas Press, 1982), pp. 219–20.

18. James R. Slack to Ann P. Slack, 5 and 26 June 1864.

19. *Ibid.*, 29 June 1864; O.R., Ser. I, Vol. XXXIV, pt. 4, pp. 304, 617; XLI, pt. 1, p. 180.

20. *Ibid.*, p. 611; XLI, pt. 2, pp. 5, 17, 34, 663.

21. James R. Slack to Ann P. Slack, 8 July 1864.

22. Bert, "Letters of a Drummer Boy," p. 332.

23. In April 1864 at Matamoras, Mexico, Cortina had made a deal with John A. McClernand and Francis J. Herron to close the border to Confederate trade in exchange for refuge from the approaching French Imperial and Mexican Royalist forces. McClernand was then in command at Brownsville prior to his departure for the Red River Campaign, and Francis J. Herron commanded the 2nd division of the 13th corps at Brownsville prior to his departure for Baton Rouge. O.R., Ser. I, Vol. XXXIV, pt. Pt. 2, pp. 73–74, 87–88; pt. 4, p. 560; Kiper, *McClernand*, pp. 285–86..

24. O.R., Ser. I, Vol. XXXIV, pt. 2, p. 890; pt. 4, pp. 276, 559–60; XLI, pt. 1, pp. 211–12; pt. 2, p. 581; pt. 3, p. 973 (quote).

25. *Ibid.*, pt. 2, pp. 646–50; pt. 3, p. 963; pt. 4, pp. 646–50, 655; XLI, pt. 3, p. 963; pt. 4, p. 1005.

26. *Indianapolis Daily Journal*, 8 August 1864. Chaplain Simmons was the Rev. John T. Simmons, the Methodist chaplain of the 28th Iowa. John W. Brinsfield, William C. Davis, Benedict Maryniak, and James I. Robertson Jr., eds., *Faith in the Fight: Civil War Chaplains* (Mechanicsburg, PA: Stackpole Books, 2003), p. 194. The Rev. Dr. Newman was John Phillip Newman, who had been sent recently to New Orleans by Bishop Edward R. Ames to reestablish the Methodist Episcopal Church in Louisiana, Texas, and Mississippi. The statement in support of Col. Slack was signed by Lt. Col. John McLaughlin, Major Lewis Goodwin, Adjutant William Vance, Chaplain Samuel Sawyer, Asst. Surgeon J.H. Crosby, and thirty other officers from each company of the 47th Indiana.

27. O.R., Ser. I, Vol. XLI, pt. 2, pp. 56, 555; Bert, "Letters of a Drummer Boy," p. 333.

28. O.R., Ser. I, Vol. XLI, pt. 1, pp. 122, 179; pt. 2, pp. 473, 549, 970; Bert, "Letters of a Drummer Boy," p. 333; Noel, *The Old Sibley Brigade*, p. 91. Ullmann's U.S. Colored Troops included in the 1st brigade the 73rd, 75th, 84th, and 92nd U.S.C.T. and the 62nd, 65th, and 67th U.S.C.T. in a provisional brigade.

29. Brig. Gen. Daniel Ullmann was a New York lawyer who had run unsuccessfully in 1851 as a Whig candidate for state attorney general and in 1854 as a Know-Nothing candidate for governor of New York. Warner, *Generals in Blue*, pp. 517–18. Ullmann's claim to fame was his early advocacy of black combat regiments and his command of the U.S. Colored Troops at Morganza from 23 June 1864 to 26 February 1865. Ullmann continued his advocacy of black combat troops after the war, and in an 1868 speech to the Soldiers' and Sailors' Union of New York, answered questions about the ability of black troops in combat by referring to a Mr. William Craft, "an educated African gentleman." Craft had addressed the British Association for the Advancement of Science in response to an anthropological essay published by the association that asserted the "inferiority and incapacity for improvement of all negro races." Ullmann scoffed at claims of black inferiority by quoting Craft's admonition to the British scientists: "The common error in judging Blacks is to look at them as a unit, as a whole, as being all alike—the inferior specimens ... selected as samples of all." To this Craft had added the rhetorical question: "How would white races stand such a test?" Ullmann related that Craft had adroitly and cogently answered his own question by telling the assembled British scientists: "Since I have been traveling in England, I have perceived that there are differences and inequalities even here, and have particularly noted that all Englishmen are not Shakespeares." Daniel Ullmann, "On the Organization of Colored Troops and the Regeneration of the South," Address Before the Soldiers' and Sailors' Union of the State of New York, delivered at Albany, New York, 5 February 1868, Daniel A.P. Murray Pamphlet Collection 1818–1907, Rare Book and Special Collections, Library of Congress online, pp. 5–6. William Craft and his wife Ellen had escaped slavery in Georgia in 1848 and lived in Boston until the passage of the Fugitive Slave Law in 1850. Nearly captured that year, they fled to England, where they attended the Ockham School for three years and raised five children. Remaining active in the abolitionist movement, they lectured in England and Scotland and published a memoir of their escape from slav-

ery and life as abolitionists. They returned to Georgia in 1870. Barbara McCaskill, "William and Ellen Craft (1824–1900; 1826–1891)," *New Georgia Encyclopedia* online; William and Ellen Craft, *Running a Thousand Miles for Freedom: The Escape of William and Ellen Craft from Slavery* (London: W. Tweedle, 1860; reprint ed. Athens: University of Georgia Press, 1999).

30. *Indianapolis Daily Journal*, 23 August 1864.
31. O.R., Ser. I, Vol. XLI, pt. 2, pp. 682, 759, 968.
32. *Ibid.*, pt. 4, p. 27; Vol. XLV, pt. 1, p. 1234.
33. *Ibid.*, pt. 2, p. 884; pt. 4, p. 27; Atlas Plates CLV and CLVI.
34. O.R., Ser. I, Vol. XLI, pt. 1, pp. 216–18.
35. *Ibid.*, pt. 2, pp. 817–18.
36. *Ibid.*, pt. 1, pp. 274–75, 277–79; pt. 2, p. 970; Atlas Plate CLVI.
37. O.R., Ser. I, Vol. XLI, pt. 1, pp. 274–76.
38. *Ibid.*, Vol. XXXIV, pt. 2, pp. 817–18, 977–78; pt. 4, pp. 646–50; XLI, pt. 3, p. 963.
39. *Ibid.*, pp. 817–18; XLI, pt. 2, pp. 1023–24, 1085–86; Robert E. Shalhope, *Sterling Price: Portrait of a Southerner* (Columbia: University of Missouri Press, 1971), pp. 261–62.

Chapter 14

1. O.R., Ser. I, Vol. XLIII, pt. 2, p. 930; Klement, "The Indianapolis Treason Trials," p. 106. A lawyer and Democrat politician, Thompson was born and educated in North Carolina and began his law practice in Pontotoc, Mississippi. Elected to Congress in 1835, he served as a represented from Mississippi until 1851 and as Secretary of the Interior in the Buchanan administration from 1857 to 1861, when he resigned to join the Confederate Army. He served as special Confederate commissioner to Canada from May 1864 to the end of the war; he died in Memphis, Tennessee, in 1885. *Biographical Directory of Congress*, p. 1708.

2. "Speech of H.H. Dodd," *Indianapolis Daily Journal*, 28 June 1864, from the *Indiana State Sentinel*, 25 June 1864; "Speech of C.L. Vallandigham at the Democratic Convention of Hamilton, Ohio, June 15, 1864," *Indianapolis Daily Journal*, 17 June 1864.

3. O.R., Ser. I, Vol. XLIII, pt. 2, pp. 931, 935; Klement, "The Indianapolis Treason Trials," p. 935; William A. Tidwell, *April '65: Confederate Covert Action in the Civil War* (Kent, OH: Kent State University Press, 1995), pp. 21, 33, 118, 128–29, 235n44.

4. O.R., Ser. II, Vol. VII, pp. 371–73; Klement, *Dark Lanterns*, pp. 154–55; Klement, "Indianapolis Treason Trials," p. 107. Dodd allegedly promised to assist Thompson in his plan to foment an uprising to seize and hold "the three great Northwestern States of Illinois, Indiana, and Ohio." Under this plan, Thompson believed the people of Missouri and Kentucky would follow and the war would end in sixty days. In conjunction with his agreement with Dodd, Thompson had arranged a plan to release prisoners from Camp Douglas near Chicago, Rock Island, Illinois, and Camp Morton at Indianapolis. Separate plans existed to disrupt shipping on Lake Erie and the rescue of Confederate officers imprisoned on Johnson's Island, Ohio; to disrupt the gold market in New York; and to finance various acts of incendiary sabotage. O.R., Ser. I, Vol. XLIII, pt. 2, pp. 930–36.

5. Benn Pitman, ed., *The Treason Trials at Indianapolis Disclosing the Plans for Establishing a North-Western Conspiracy* (Cincinnati, OH: Moore, Wilstach & Baldwin, 1865), p. 121; Klaus, ed., *The Milligan Case*, p. 328; O.R., Ser. I, Vol. XXXIX, pt. 2, p. 237; Ser. III, vol. IV, pp. 162–63. The antiwar faction of the Democratic Party took advantage of the fact that many Northerners had become despondent and war-weary in June following the carnage of Grant's troops at Cold Harbor and Petersburg, Virginia, and at Kennesaw Mountain, Georgia, where Sherman seemed to be making little progress against Joe Johnston's Army of Tennessee. Lincoln's 30 June acceptance of the resignation of Secretary of the Treasury Salmon P. Chase, who had presidential ambitions of his own, seemed to presage the disintegration of Lincoln's administration. To make matters worse, this was followed in turn by Jubal Early's advance into the suburbs of Washington, D.C., and great resistance to Lincoln's mid-July call for 500,000 more troops. Melancholy about his prospects for reelection, on 28 August 1864 Lincoln acknowledged the probability of his defeat at the polls when he delivered a memorandum to his cabinet, which read: "This morning, as for some days past, it seems exceedingly probable that this Administration will not be re-elected. Then it will be my duty to co-operate with the President elect, as to save the Union between the election and the inauguration; as he will have secured his election on such ground that he can not possibly save it afterwards." Nicolay and Hay, *Abraham Lincoln*, IX: 244–46; Roy P. Basler, ed., *The Collected Works of Abraham Lincoln*, 8 vols. (New Brunswick, NJ: Rutgers University Press, 1953–55), VII: 514; William F. Zornow, "Indiana and the Election of 1864," *Indiana Magazine of History* 45 (March 1949): 13–38.

6. Stidger's career path took him from a short stay in the 15th Kentucky Vol. Infantry (U.S.), to clerk at divisional headquarters, to a discharge based on a feigned illness, to civilian clerk; then, when he learned of the much higher pay for spies, to "special agent" in the District of Kentucky provost-marshal's office. At Governor Morton's behest, Stidger was "loaned" to Carrington to replace an agent who had bungled an assignment in the Kentucky-Indiana area. Klement, *Dark Lanterns*, pp. 156. Although his sworn testimony was suspect at best, Stidger denied soliciting anyone to join the Sons of Liberty. Felix G. Stidger, ed., *Treason History of the Order of the Sons of Liberty, Formerly Circle of Honor, Succeeded by the Knights of the Golden Circle, Afterwards Order of American Knights: The Most Gigantic Treasonable Conspiracy the World Has Ever Known* (Chicago: By the Author, 1903); Pitman, *The Treason Trials at Indianapolis*, pp. 106, 140; Kenneth M. Stampp, "The Milligan Case," 46–47; Fessler, "Secret Political Societies in the North," 258–59; O.R., Ser. I, Vol. XXXIX, pt. 2, p. 237.

7. At a Peace Democrat political rally at Fort Wayne on 13 August, Milligan railed against the Lincoln administration for its usurpation of power, suppression of free speech, arbitrary arrests, and use of force against states that Milligan believed had the right to secede,

and he asserted the right to resist the draft because the war itself was wrong. The Peace Democrat meeting adopted ten resolutions along these lines, emphasizing opposition to the draft and immediate peace based on restoration of the Union as it was before the war. Pitman, *Treason Trials*, pp. 151–57; "Large Copperhead Meeting. Resolutions Passed to Resist the Draft — Rebellion to be Inaugurated in Indiana," *Chicago Tribune*, 16 August 1864; "Treason in Indiana," *New York Times*, 22 August 1864.

8. Klement, *Dark Lanterns*, pp. 102, 132, 158; Stidger, *Treason History*, pp. 18, 64–65; Stampp, "The Milligan Case," p. 47; O.R, Ser. II, Vol. II, pp. 341–42.

9. Foulke, *Life of Oliver P. Morton*, I: 300, 303–371; "Indiana Politics: The Democratic State Convention," *New York Times*, 19 July 1864; "From Goshen, Indiana," *Chicago Tribune*, 14 August 1864.

10. Stampp, "The Milligan Case," citing the *Indianapolis Daily Journal*, 30 July and 1, 2, 10 August 1864, and the *Indianapolis Gazette*, 30 July and 13 August 1864, p. 47n. Also see 29 July 1864 dispatches from the *Daily Journal* to the *New York Times* and the *Chicago Tribune*: "Treason in Indiana. Expose of the Sons of Liberty — Official Report of Gen. Carrington — Interesting Details," *New York Times*, 2 August 1864. The *Tribune* first mentioned the expose in brief in their 30 July 1864 edition and used seven front-page columns to publish the expose in their 2 August 1864 edition, also titled "Treason in Indiana."

11. Klement, "Indianapolis Treason Trials," p. 108; Klement, *Dark Lanterns*, p. 163.

12. Stidger, *Treason History*, pp. 101–102, 112–116, 123, 137, 173; "The Louisville Arrests," *Chicago Tribune*, 13 August 1864; Stamp, "The Milligan Case," p. 49; Klement, *Dark Lanterns*, pp. 157–58; O.R., Ser. I, Vol. XLIII, pt. 2, p. 931.

13. *Ibid.*, Vol. XXXIX, pt. 2, pp. 211, 215, 238; "The Correspondence," *New York Times*, 25 August 1864. In the same edition, the *Times* published Voorhees's brief written complaint about the raid and Carrington's lengthy response in "Hon. D.W. Voorhees and the O.A.K.'s — Sharp Letter from Gen. Carrington."

14. Klement, *Dark Lanterns*, p. 164.

15. *Ibid.*, pp. 165–66; Churchill, "Sons of Liberty Conspiracy," p. 300, citing the *Indiana State Sentinel*, 15 August 1864.

16. Carrington to Heintzelman, 9 August 1864, O.R., Ser. I, Vol. XXXIX, pt. 2, pp. 236–38 (quote); Klement, *Dark Lanterns*, pp. 166–67.

17. O.R., Ser. I, Vol. XXXIX, pt. 2, p. 295 (quote); "Treason in Indiana" and "The Dodd Papers," *Indianapolis Daily Journal*, 22, 23 August 1864; "Treason in Indiana," *New York Times*, 25 August 1864.

18. Hines had led an unsuccessful raid into southern Indiana about a month prior to Morgan's July 1863 raid in which 62 of his men were trapped and captured on Blue River Island, near Leavenworth, Indiana. Hines and two others escaped and participated in Morgan's July raid. Captured with Morgan near Salineville, Ohio, they escaped with Morgan from the Ohio Penitentiary in Columbus, Ohio, and returned to Confederate service. *Report of the Adjutant General*, I: 161–65; O.R., Ser. I, Vol. XLIII, pt. 2, p. 934.

19. Klement, *Dark Lanterns*, p. 194

20. *Ibid.*, p. 209; O.R., Ser. II, Vol. VIII, pp. 87, 369, 511, 519, 704.

21. Charles R. Wilson, "McClellan's Changing Views on the Peace Plank of 1864," *American Historical Review* 38 (April 1933), p. 498; *New York Times*, 1 September 1864.

22. Virtually all of Thompson's plans failed, including, on 19 September 1864, a plan to seize the USS *Michigan*, then guarding prisoners at Johnson's Island in Lake Erie, and an elaborate attempt in November 1864 to use delayed-action liquid phosphorous incendiaries ("Greek fire") to burn several hotels and the Barnum Museum in New York City. So skeptical of conflicting and contradictory requests for reimbursement for "property ... destroyed by burning" by other saboteurs, Thompson refused to recognize or pay any further claims without proof, noting especially that conflicting and contradictory claims were made for fires in St. Louis, New Orleans, Louisville, Brooklyn, Philadelphia, and Cairo. On 19 October, ex-Confederate soldiers from Canada made a successful bank-robbing raid on the town of St. Albans, Vermont, but Thompson claimed to have not known about it until after it had transpired. O.R., Ser. I, Vol. XLIII, pt. 2, pp. 932, 934. One of the New York saboteurs, Robert Cobb Kennedy, was convicted in military court and hanged at Fort Lafayette on 25 March 1865; the others escaped. For a reasonably accurate description of the St. Alban's Raid and the incendiary attack on New York City by a participant, see John W. Headley, *Confederate Operations in Canada and New York* (New York: The Neale Publishing Co., 1906), pp. 256–83. Although Headley accepted and repeated Hines and Castleman's exaggerated tales of Chicago, the known record of events substantiates his firsthand account of the attempted sabotage in New York City. See "The Plot. Full and Minute Particulars," *New York Times*, 27 November 1864, 28 November 1864, and 26 March 1865.

23. O.R., Ser. I, Vol. XXXIX, pt. 2, pp. 281, 303. Interestingly, the *Daily Journal* sided with Carrington and Heintzelman that the civil courts had jurisdiction. *Indianapolis Daily Journal*, 23 August 1864.

24. Klement, *Dark Lanterns*, pp. 155, 172; Fessler, "Treason Trials in Indiana," p. 257. Although demoted, Carrington remained in Indiana in charge of new recruits and the supply of new regiments to George H. Thomas's garrison at Nashville. O.R., Ser. I, Vol. XLV, pt. 1, p. 1105; XLIX, pt. 1, p. 761.

25. James R. Slack to Sarah E. Slack, 2 September 1864.

26. O.R., Ser, I, Vol. XLI, pt. 1, pp. 625–26, 641–42, 702; Atlas Plate XLVII, No. 1.

27. *Ibid.*, pp. 191–92, 280–88, 642. The *New York Herald* reported that the White River country was "alive with guerillas, who fire into passing boats," and that on 23 August, Shelby's "rebel gang attacked the forces boarding the railroad between Duvall's Bluff and Little Rock, and captured nearly all the Fifty-fourth Illinois, occupying three stations" and were now threatening Duvall's Bluff and St. Charles. "The War in the Southwest," *New York Herald*, 2 September 1864. For a highly exaggerated firsthand account of Shelby's brigade, see

John N. Edwards, *Shelby and His Men* (Cincinnati: Miami Printing & Publishing Co., 1867).

28. O.R., Ser. I, Vol. XLI, pt. 1, pp. 307, 318, 320; Wiley Britton, 6th Kansas Cavalry, "Resume of Military Operations in Missouri and Arkansas, 1864–65," *Battles and Leaders*, IV: 376.

29. James R. Slack to Ann P. Slack, 8 September 1864; Eli E. Rose, Pension Records, National Archives Trust Fund, Washington, D.C.

30. "Glorious News. Gen. Sherman Occupies Atlanta," *Indianapolis Daily Journal*, 3 September 1863; "Letter of the Committee," and "Reply of Gen. McClellan," *New York Times*, 9 September 1864. The *New York Times* charged that McClellan was evasive about what he accepted or did not accept of the Democratic Platform. "McClellan's Letter of Acceptance," *New York Times*, 10 September 1864; Wilson, "McClellan's Changing Views," pp. 498–504; James R. Slack to Ann P. Slack, 8 September 1864.

31. *Ibid.*, 11 and 12 September 1864 (quote). In his official report, Slack accused the *Pringle's* pilot of trying to sink the boat. O.R., Ser. I, Vol. XLI, pt. 3, pp. 152–53

32. *Ibid.*, 12 September 1864 (quote).

33. *Ibid.*, 16, 18, and 25 September 1864.

34. *Indianapolis Daily Journal*, 20 December 1864. Brownlow, as noted previously, became the highly controversial Reconstruction Governor of Tennessee; James R. Slack to Ann P. Slack, 28 September 1864.

35. O.R., Ser. I, Vol. XXXIX, pt. 3, p. 160; Ser. II, Vol. VII, p. 1215; Klement, *Dark Lanterns*, p. 176; James D. Horan, *Confederate Agent: A Discovery of History* (New York: Crown Publishers, 1954), p. 150. Built in 1860 at 45 North Pennsylvania Avenue at the southeast corner of Market Street, the Federal Building, better known as the Post Office Building, "was three stories tall and seventy feet wide by ninety feet long." The Post Office occupied the basement and ground floor, with government offices and courtrooms on the second and third floors. www.insd.uscourts.gov/History/ct_hist_OldFedBldg.htm. Early in 1862, the second and third floors were fitted with special cells for political prisoners, and as early as 2 October 1862, seventeen civilians, the most notable being a Dr. Theodore Horton, were arrested at a political meeting in Wells County, Indiana, and charged with "discouraging enlistments." With *habeas corpus* suspended, they were confined in the Post Office Building in Indianapolis without benefit of counsel or trial. Describing the cells of the seventeen prisoners, the *State Sentinel* noted: "Three of the prisoners have very comfortable quarters, but fourteen are confined in cells built for criminals. In one cell, a small room, nine are confined, and in a still smaller one are five. Neither of them have side windows, but light and air comes through the skylight in the roof. Here they eat, sleep and live, shut out from the world, and only permitted to see the light of heaven through the small opening in the roof. Under no circumstances are they permitted to leave their cells, and before the iron-grated door of their prison house, securely fastened, armed sentries, day and night, watch them." "Political Prisoners," *Indiana State Sentinel*, 27 October 1862. Dodd's "mitigated confinement" was apparently in one of the "comfortable quarters" on the second floor.

36. O.R., Ser. I, Vol. XXXIX, pt.3, p. 295; Ser. II, Vol. VII, pp. 939, 1214–17, Fessler, "Secret Political Societies," p. 258; Klement, *Dark Lanterns*, pp. 172–73.

37. Stampp, "Milligan Case," pp. 52–53; Fessler, "Secret Political Societies," p. 259.

38. Milligan claimed that he had been taken from his home in the middle of the night of 5 October 1864 when he was known to be "sick, helpless and prostrate." Meanwhile, "a large number of armed ruffians" surrounded his house, stole his clothes from the line and carried away his roosting poultry before seizing him and imprisoning him for twenty-four hours in a boxcar of the Toledo, Wabash & Western Railroad that was "foul with whiskey and tobacco smoke." He was then transported by rail to Indianapolis, where General Alvin P. Hovey handed him over to his subaltern, A.J. Warner, who marched him through the streets "in the presence of an excited mob of thousands of rude and insolent persons." Milligan also claimed that Warner, like Hovey, abused him and incited the mob to threaten him, "to wit: 'hang him ... on a lamppost; he is a traitor, a rebel sympathizer, and has no rights that loyal persons are bound to respect.'" He was then delivered to "an unhealthy and filthy prison called a hospital at the Soldiers Home" at Indianapolis. *Lambdin P. Milligan v. James R. Slack, et al.*, State of Indiana, Huntington County Court of Common Pleas, May Term, 1865, pp. 3–4, 28, 42. A copy of the original transcribed by the author, courtesy of the Lilly Library, Indiana University, Bloomington, Indiana (hereafter cited as *Milligan v. Slack*). Also see Marshall, *American Bastile*, pp. 73–74.

39. Klement, *Dark Lanterns*, pp. 176 (quote), 177; Fessler, "Secret Political Societies," p. 261, quoting the *Indianapolis Daily Journal*, 8 October 1864. Foulke noted that Heffren and Slack had been political allies in 1859. Foulke, *Life of Oliver P. Morton*, I: 109.

40. O.R., Ser. II, Vol. VII, p. 1214; Klement, *Dark Lanterns*, pp. 177–78; Fessler, "Secret Political Societies," p. 261; Stampp, "Milligan Case," pp. 54–55. As many have noted, Sherman's occupation of Atlanta on 1 September was undoubtedly the major reason for the Republican electoral success in October and November.

41. O.R., Ser. II, Vol. VII, pp. 1214–1217; Klement, *Dark Lanterns*, p. 178; Fessler, "Secret Political Societies," pp. 261–62.

42. *New York Times*, 13 October 1863. The Democrats' 7 to 4 majority in the 38th Congress was turned into an 8 to 3 majority for the Republicans in the 39th Congress. The Republican majority was increased to 9 to 2 when staunch Copperhead Daniel W. Voorhees, who had won reelection in a close contest, lost a challenge from his opponent, Henry D. Washburn. Washburn took his seat on 23 February 1866. *Chicago Tribune*, 15 October 1864; *Biographical Directory of Congress*, pp. 179, 183.

43. James R. Slack to Ann P. Slack, 19 October 1864.

44. As Shalhope notes, on 1 October 1864, as Price's columns approached St. Louis, John H. Taylor, who called himself the "Supreme Commander of the O.A.K. in Missouri," issued a call-to-arms to all the O.A.K. members in Missouri to aid Price, but his call failed to produce large numbers of recruits. Finding St. Louis and Jefferson City too well protected, Price redirected

his columns westward. Shalhope, *Sterling Price*, p. 267n; O.R., Ser. I, Vol. XLI, pt. 3, pp. 975–76.

45. *Ibid.*, pt. 1, pp. 632, 662. The notoriously bloodthirsty Confederate partisan, Captain William "Bloody Bill" Anderson, who operated in western Missouri loosely under Price's command, was assigned by Price to attack the North Missouri Railroad. At Centralia, Missouri, on 27 September 1864, Anderson and his company stopped a passenger train at the depot, captured and murdered 24 unarmed Union soldiers, mostly from Sherman's army going home on medical leave, and a number of civilians. Major A.V.E. Johnston's 39th Missouri militia (111 militiamen) went in pursuit of Anderson with single-shot, muzzle-loading rifles. Forced to dismount to fire and reload their weapons, Johnston and most of his militia were killed when Anderson's mounted company charged and routed them. Galloping into Centralia, Anderson's men killed most of Johnston's 36 militiamen who had been left behind, for a total killed of 124 out of 147. Anderson was killed about a month later in a skirmish with troops from the 33rd and 51st Missouri militia under Lt. Col. Samuel P. Cox. *Ibid.*, pt. 1, pp. 417–18, 442; pt. 3, 420–23, 455. For accounts of Anderson's actions in the northern press, see the *New York Times*, 2 October and 20 December 1864. Other notables in Price's expeditionary force included Colonel William C. Quantrill, notorious for the 21 August 1863 sacking of Lawrence, Kansas, and the soon-to-become postwar outlaws Jesse and Frank James, among others, who rode with him. Quantrill joined Price in western Missouri after operating under Price's orders on the Hannibal & St. Joseph Railroad. Price reportedly ordered Quantrill and his men to leave his army after receiving word that Kansas troops were executing prisoners from Shelby's command when they learned that Quantrill and his men were riding with Price. Quantrill and at least some of his men made their way to Kentucky, where they continued to plunder until 10 May 1865 when Quantrill was killed in a fight with a Federal force under Edwin Terrill. John McCorkle, *Three Years with Quantrill: A True Story Told by His Scout, John McCorkle*, ed. Herman Hattaway (Norman: University of Oklahoma Press, 1995), pp. 163, 165, 173–76, 179, 207, 223n.

46. Pleasanton's cavalry consisted of three Missouri brigades (Sanborn's, Brown's, and McNeil's), and one brigade (Winslow's) from A.J. Smith's force. O.R., Ser. I, Vol. XLI, pt. 1, pp. 320–23, 340, 573; pt. 4, p. 145; Wiley Britton, "Resume of Military Operations in Missouri and Arkansas, 1864–65," *Battles and Leaders*, IV: 374–77.

47. O.R., Ser. I, Vol. XLI, pt. 1, pp. 340–41, 389, 636–37, 646, 659, 681–84; pt. 4, p. 110, 134, 159; Atlas Plates LXI, nos. 106, 8 and XLVII, no. 1.

48. *Ibid.*, pp. 314, 321–23, 337, 392, 491, 496, 504–10, 577, 393, 638, 646, 661, 685; pt. 4, pp. 1076–77; Shalhope, *Sterling Price*, pp. 272–74. Atlas Plate XLVII, No. 1.

49. Dennis was busy sending Dornblaser's brigade from the mouth of the White River to Memphis due to an erroneous dispatch from C.C. Washburn that Nathan Bedford Forrest "will probably attack Memphis in heavy force very soon." O.R., Ser. I, Vol. XXXIX, pt. 3, pp. 357, 377, 394; XLI, pt. 4, pp. 72 (quote), 73, 75–76, 106–7, 177.

50. Following Price's raid into Missouri, Thomas C. Reynolds, the state's exiled Confederate governor, denounced him for his mismanagement of the campaign and the misconduct of his troops, especially the recruits picked up in Missouri, who had looted and pillaged through the center of the state and had thereby made it difficult for any of them to be welcomed back home. Thompson told Price he would not make these charges public, nor air the evidence he had that Price's son Edwin was a traitor to the Confederacy, if he would resign his commission in the army and cease to have anything further to do with the military or political affairs of the Confederate government. (Edwin, a general in the CSA, had returned to Missouri in 1863 after having been captured, had signed the loyalty oath, and was accused of having aided the Federals in Missouri.) Price responded by sending Kirby Smith a copy of the *Texas Republican*, which had published Reynolds's accusations and asked Smith to appoint a court of inquiry at Shreveport so that he could clear his name. Price was forced to leave active duty in order to attend the court, but the war ended before the court issued its findings. Price, who apparently had second thoughts about returning to Missouri himself, fled to Mexico with a number of other Trans-Mississippi Confederates. *Ibid.*, pt. 1, pp. 701–29; pt. 4, pp. 1123, 1318; XLVIII, pt. 1, p. 1181; Shalhope, *Sterling Price*, pp. 275–76, citing the *Texas Republican*, 23 December 1864.

51. According to Klement, Judge Advocate Burnett refused to allow Yeakel to testify because he did not want Stidger's testimony discredited by someone who had direct knowledge of his activities in the S.O.L. To protest Burnett and what he considered a sham trial, Yeakel wrote and distributed a pamphlet titled "To the People of Indiana," in which he rebutted Stidger's testimony and criticized Burnett's handling of the trial. Klement, *Dark Lanterns*, pp. 179, 181, citing Yeakel's pamphlet, "To the People of Indiana;" Marshall, *American Bastille*, pp. 76–77.

52. O.R., Ser. II, Vol. VII, pp. 951–52.

53. Pitman, *Treason Trials*, p. 121; O.R., Ser. III, Vol. IV, pp. 162–63.

54. *Ibid.*, pp. 120–122, 244–48; Klement, *Dark Lanterns*, p. 183.

55. Klement, *Dark Lanterns*, p. 181.

56. Pitman, *Treason Trials*, pp. 123, 128, 140; *Chicago Tribune*, 5 November 1864.

57. *Huntington Democrat*, 3 November 1864.

58. O.R., Ser. I, Vol. XLV, pt. 1, pp. 1077–80; Ser. II, Vol. VII, pp. 102, 428; Klement, *Dark Lanterns*, p. 202.

59. *Ibid.*, pp. 191–92, 239.

60. *Ibid.*, pp. 190–92, 192n16, 197–99; U.S. Congress, House, *Message of the President on the Case of George St. Leger Grenfel [sic: Grenfell] Imprisoned at Dry Tortugas*, H. exdoc. 50, 39th Cong., 2nd Sess., ser. 1290, 1867, pp. 21–22, 196, 214, cited hereafter as U.S. Congress, House, *Grenfel*. The *Harvard Alumni Directory* online lists: "Ayer, Isaiah Winslow [m 1842–45]." No degree is indicated and he admitted under cross-examination that he had not graduated. The *Tribune*

introduced the threat of a "guerilla raid" on Chicago in the 6 and 7 November editions, and published Bross's "expose," along with the false and inaccurate information about the prominent citizens arrested in the 8 November 1864 edition. *Chicago Tribune*, 6, 7, 8 November 1864. The headlines of the Republican *Indianapolis Daily Gazette* blared on Election Day: "The Chicago Conspiracy! Discovery of a Plot to Release Rebel Prisoners at Camp Douglas and Burn The City! Capture of the Ringleaders, Citizens and Rebel Officers. The Conspirators Harbored by 'Peace Democrats.' Seizure of Arms and Ammunition! Several Hundred Imported Guerillas and Bushwhackers Captured." The editors assured their readers that "the military and police constantly scouring the city have picked up hundreds of them." *Indianapolis Daily Gazette*, 8 November 1864. Receiving national coverage, the "expose" also appeared in the 6 and 8 November editions of the *New York Times*.

61. *Indianapolis Daily Gazette*, 9 November 1864.
62. Pitman, *Treason Trials*, p. 241.
63. *Ibid.*, pp. 9, 74, 150–57.
64. *Ibid.*, pp. 238–48.
65. *Ibid.*, pp. 195–237.
66. *Ibid.*, p. 266.
67. O.R., Ser. II, Vol. VIII, pp. 8–11, 543–49; Klaus, *The Milligan Case*, p. 38.
68. Among those rounded up in Sweet's dragnet were former judge of the Seventh Judicial Circuit in Illinois and outspoken critic of the war, the Hon. Buckner S. Morris, and his wife, Mary, who was subsequently released. Marshall, *American Bastille*, pp. 97–106, 624–28; *Chicago Tribune*, 7 January 1865; U.S. Congress, House, *Grenfel*, p.4.
69. Bert, "Letters of a Drummer Boy," p. 334; O.R., Ser. I, Vol. XLI, pt. 4, pp. 574, 583, 638–39.
70. *Ibid.*, pp. 361, 574, 655, 702, 711, 765 (quote), 838, 904, 972–73.
71. A detachment from the 47th Indiana and the 29th Wisconsin, commanded by Captain Elmore Y. Sturgis, Co. A, 47th Indiana, had been sent back to Little Rock. Upon arrival at Little Rock on 22 December, they were immediately ordered to rejoin their regiments at Memphis. *Ibid.*, p. 915.
72. *Ibid.*, pp. 765, 901–905; XLV, pt. 1, p. 865.
73. *Ibid.*, pp. 869–71, 1001–1002; XLV, pp. 844–47.
74. *Ibid.*, Vol. XLIX, pt. 1, pp. 951–52; Chambers, *Blood and Sacrifice*, pp. 185–86, 195–97, 201.
75. *Indianapolis Daily Journal*, 2 January 1865.
76. *Ibid.*, 24 October 1864.
77. *Ibid.*, 25 October 1864.
78. *Ibid.*, 24 December 1864.

Chapter 15

1. O.R., Ser. II, Vol. VIII, p. 11 (quote). 543–49.
2. Stampp, "The Milligan Case," p. 56; Klement, *Dark Lanterns*, pp. 184, 224; Marshall, *American Bastille*, pp. 76–77. In their 4 January 1865 edition, the *Chicago Tribune* complained: "The military commission which tried Bowles & Co., has been dissolved by an order from District headquarters. Various rumors are rife as to what the findings and sentences of the Commission were in respect to the individuals tried, but nothing official has yet been promulgated." They concluded hopefully, although incorrectly, that "a day or two will disclose something reliable."
3. A fourteenth prisoner, Canadian John Maugher, was sent from Camp Douglas on 7 January, but was not indicted. In the days before the trial, Maugher, Mrs. Mary B. Morris, and four others were released from custody. The eight indicted were: the Hon. Buckner S. Morris, former judge in the 7th Circuit Court of Illinois; Charles Walsh, a Chicago Democratic leader; Vincent Marmaduke, incorrectly supposed to have been a colonel in the Confederate Army; Richard T. Semmes, a Chicago lawyer; Charles T. Daniel, an ex-Confederate who worked in Chicago and who dated one of Walsh's daughters; George E. Cantrill, a Kentucky drifter who lived in Chicago, supposedly an ex-Confederate, who also dated one of Walsh's daughters; Benjamin M. Anderson, a Confederate deserter from Kentucky; and English adventurer and former Confederate cavalry officer George St. Leger Grenfell. Klement, *Dark Lanterns*, pp. 207–8; Horan, *Confederate Agent*, p. 123; Marshall, *American Bastille*, pp. 97–106; U.S. Congress, House, *Grenfel*, pp. 2–20; *Chicago Tribune*, 7, 10 January 1865.
4. O.R., Ser. I, Vol. XLVIII, pt. 1, p. 618; Vol. XLIX, pt. 1, pp. 91–92.
5. Johnston, *Narrative*, p. 371.
6. O.R., Ser. I, Vol. XLVIII, pt. 1, pp. 409–10; O.R.N., Ser. 1, Vol. 27, p. 296.
7. "From New Orleans," *New York Times*, 26 January 1865.
8. Although their pay did not arrive while they were in New Orleans, which made it unlikely that Bert was able to purchase the books he wanted, Don Russell, the editor of Bert's letters for the *Indiana Magazine of History*, notes that Bert studied the Bible and ancient history after the war and became a local preacher in the Methodist Episcopal Church. Bert, "Letters of a Drummer Boy," pp. 335–36.
9. O.R., Ser. I, Vol. XLIX, pt. 1, pp. 92–93; Richard B. Irwin, "Land Operations Against Mobile," in Johns and Buel, eds., *Battles and Leaders*, IV: 410–11.
10. Lt. Col. Frederick W. Moore would command the 3rd brigade from 15 March through the battles at Spanish Fort and Fort Blakely in April.
11. O.R., Ser. I, Vol. XLVIII, pt. 1, pp. 729–30, 738, 1022.
12. The *Peabody* carried the brigade headquarters, the 47th Indiana, and the 21st Iowa; the *Belvedere* carried the 99th Illinois, 29th Wisconsin, and the ambulance corps. *Ibid.*, p. 738.
13. From the French "rigole" meaning "channel" or "rivulet." They also could have taken Chef Menteur Pass (French for "Chief Liar") from Lake Pontchartrain to Lake Borgne. Chef Menteur was an equally navigable but longer pass about ten miles south of the Rigolets that wound its way from Fort Macomb (sometimes called Fort Wood) into the southern part of Lake Borgne. The early explorers are said to have called it the "Chief Liar" because it gave the false impression that it flowed directly into the Gulf of Mexico.

14. A navigable passage along the Mississippi and Alabama coasts separated from the Gulf by, from west to east, Cat, Ship, Horn, Petit Bois, and Dauphin Islands, averaging eight to ten miles wide and about twelve feet deep. http://chps.sam.usace. army.mil.

15. Pass a l'Outre means "Pass Beyond" in French. It was dredged in late 1858 to a depth of 18 feet and a width of not less than 300 feet and a lighthouse installed. Early in the war, the Federals removed the lighthouse's Fresnel lens and Confederates burned the lighthouse keeper's house, but the lens was put back into service on 20 April 1863 and operated throughout the remainder of the war. Pass a l'Outre has since silted over and the lighthouse has almost completely sunk into the marshland. U.S. Congress, House, "Action of the War Department for Removal of Obstructions in the Mouth of the Mississippi River," 28th Cong., 2nd Sess., H. exdoc. 5, Dec. 5, 1860, pp. 94, 201, 210; "Pass a l'Outre, LA," http://www.lighthousefriends.com.

16. O.R.N., Ser. 1, Vol. 16, p. 620–22; Vol. 27, p. 118; O.R., Ser. I, Vol. XLVIII, pt. 1, p. 801; Atlas Plate CLVI.

17. O.R., Ser. I, Vol. XLVIII, pt. 1, p. 738; Vol. XLIX, pt. 1, pp. 118–19.

18. *Ibid.*, pp. 772, 1018, 1021, 1240; Atlas Plate LXIII, No. 6.

19. James R. Slack to Ann P. Slack, 15 February 1865.

20. O.R., Ser. I, Vol. XLVIII, pt. 1, pp. 910; Vol. XLIX, pt. 1, pp. 116–35, 771, 782.

21. *Ibid.*, pt. 2, pp. 5–6, 92, 233–34; O.R.N., Ser. 1, vol. 22, p. 66; Benjamin C. Truman, "Where Fish River Is — Movements of Our Troops," *New York Times*, 7 April 1865; Atlas Plate CX.

22. Granger's column included some 13,200 troops and artillery from the 1st and 3rd divisions and Bertram's 1st brigade from Andrews's 2nd division, 2,500 troops from Joseph Bailey's engineer brigade (the 96th and 97th U.S. Colored Troops and the 1st Company of Pontoniers), and 1,200 troops in the artillery siege train (the 1st Indiana Heavy Artillery and the 18th Battery, New York Light Artillery). O.R., Ser. I, Vol. XLIX, pt. 1, pp. 91–92, 105–107, 109, 141; Irwin, "Land Operations Against Mobile," 411; Atlas Plate CX.

23. O.R., Ser. I, Vol. XLIX, pt. 1, pp. 141, 279, 158, 160, 165, 168, 170; Donald C. Elder III, ed., *A Damned Iowa Greyhound: The Civil War Letters of William Henry Harrison Clayton* (Iowa City, IA: University of Iowa Press, 1998), p. 158; Irving J. Dungan, *History of the Nineteenth Iowa Infantry*, transcribed for the Internet by Norma Jennings, http://iagenweb.org/civilwar/regiment/infantry/19th/hist19thxi_xiv.htm, p. 163; Bvt. Maj. Gen. C.C. Andrews, *History of the Campaign Against Mobile: Including the Co-operative Operations of Gen. Wilson's Cavalry in Alabama*, 2nd ed. (New York: D. Van Nostrand Company, 1889), pp. 33–35.

24. Steele's column numbered 13,200, including 5,200 in Spicely's and Moore's brigades detached from Andrews' 13th corps division, 5,500 troops from John P. Hawkins's division of U.S. Colored Troops, and 2,500 troopers from Thomas J. Lucas's cavalry division. O.R., Ser. I, Vol. XLIX, pt. 1, pp. 92, 108–109.

25. *Ibid.*, p. 165.

26. *Ibid.*, pp. 141, 216, 234, 237, 239, 313; Truman, "Where Fish River Is," *New York Times*, 7 April 1865; Dungan, *History of the Nineteenth Iowa*, p. 163; Andrews, *Campaign Against Mobile*, p. 35.

27. From the 1697 French fairy tale, "La Maistre Chat ou Le Chat Botté" ("The Master Cat or the Booted Cat") by Charles Perrault, translated into English as "Puss in Boots." According to P.D. Stephenson, Fifth Company, Washington Artillery: "Our commander was Dabney H. Maury, 'every inch a soldier,' but then there were not many inches of him. The soldiers called him 'puss in boots,' because half of his diminutive person seemed lost in a pair of the immense cavalry boots of the day." Stephenson also noted that Maury "was a wise and gallant soldier." P.D. Stephenson, "Defense of Spanish Fort: On Mobile Bay — Last Great Battle of the War," *Southern Historical Society Papers* 39 (1914): 119.

28. Soley, "Land Operations Against Mobile," in *Battles and Leaders*, IV: 411; O.R., Ser. I, Vol. XLIX, pt. 1, pp. 1046–47.

29. *Ibid.*, pp. 282–83, 317; pt. 2, p. 1204; Andrews, *Campaign Against Mobile*, pp. 44, 60; Segrex, "The Siege of Mobile," *New York Times*, 21 April 1865; Roger B. Hansen, "Blakeley Battlefield Self-Guided Tour," Historic Blakeley Authority of the State of Alabama, Spanish Fort, AL (n.d.), www.blakeleypark.org; Atlas Plates LXI, No. 6, LXXI, Nos. 13, 14, and CX.

30. The ironclad *Nashville* drafted 10'9" of water and mounted three 7-inch Brooke rifles and one 24-pounder howitzer; the floating batteries *Huntsville* and *Tuscaloosa* had four large guns each; the ironclad ram *Baltic* drafted 8' and mounted six large guns; and the wooden *Morgan* drafted 7'2" and mounted six large guns, including 6- and 7-inch Brooke rifles and two 32-pounder Parrotts. O.R.N., Ser. I, Vol. 22, pp. 59–60, 227; Ser. II, Vol. 1, pp. 248, 256, 260, 261, 269.

31. Atlas Plates LXXI, No. 13, XCI, No. 5, and CX; Andrews, Mobile Campaign, pp. 62, 70–71. Maps then and now differ on which names should be used to designate these waterways.

32. Gibson, a graduate of Yale College (1853) and the University of Louisiana law department (1855), practiced law in New Orleans after the war. He served as a Democrat from Louisiana in the U.S. House of Representatives from 1875 to 1883 and as U.S. Senator from 1883 to his death in 1892. He was philanthropist Paul Tulane's agent in reorganizing the public University of Louisiana as the private Tulane University of Louisiana and served as the first president of the Board of Administrators of the Tulane Educational Fund from 1882 to 1892. Tulane's Gibson Hall is named after him. *Biographical Directory of the American Congress*, p. 942; http://Tulane.edu.

33. O.R., Ser. I, Vol. XLIX, pt. 1, pp. 314, 1046–47; pt. 2, p. 1136–38, 1144, 1146, 1149; Segrex, "Department of the Gulf. Defenses of Mobile Statements of Deserters. Forces Garrisoning the Defenses," *New York Times*, 26 March 1865; Atlas Plates CXLVII and CXLVIII.

34. In 1860, 36-year-old Lt. Artemus O. Sibley, an overseer before the war, lived next door to 76-year-old mill owner Cyrus Sibley, who was the father of Pvt. Walter H. Sibley, also of the 15th Confederate Cavalry. Twenty-five-year old Lt. Origen Sibley Jr. was the son

of 66-year-old planter Origen Sibley Sr., whose mill was about four miles north of Cyrus Sibley's Mill. Mill owners Cyrus and Origen Sibley Sr. appear to be kin, although their relationship is unknown. U.S. Census, Baldwin County, Alabama, 1830–1860; O.R., XLIX, pt. 2, pp. 1120, 1128–29, 1141, 1149–50, 1153–54, 1158 (quote), 1176.

35. Andrews, *Campaign Against Mobile*, pp. 35–36.

36. O.R., Ser. I, Vol. XLIX, pt. 1, p. 161.

37. *Ibid.*, p. 165.

38. *Ibid.*, pp. 141, 158, 161, 164, 165–66 (quote), 168, 170, 220, 313; pt. 2, p. 1149 (quote); 1153.

39. *Ibid.*, pp. 314, 158, 161, 166, 228; Andrews, *Campaign Against Mobile*, p. vii; Atlas Plate CX.

40. Col. Morgan H. Chrysler's brigade consisted of the 1st Louisiana, 31st Massachusetts Mounted Infantry, and the 2nd New York Veterans; Lt. Col. Andrew B. Spurling's brigade consisted of the 1st Florida, the 2nd Illinois, and the 2nd Maine Cavalry. *Ibid.*, p. 109.

41. Pvt. Thomas Riley of the 1st Louisiana Cavalry (U.S.) received the Medal of Honor for capturing the flag of the 6th Alabama Cavalry at Bluff Springs. *Ibid.*, pp. 105, 280, 303, 308, 313; pt. 2, p. 1153; Segrex, "The Attack on Mobile," *New York Times*, 9 April 1865.

42. O.R., Ser. I, Vol. XLIX, pt. 1, pp. 281 (quote); pt. 2, p. 1153.

43. *Ibid.*, pp. 142, 156, 158, 228, 233–34.

44. *Ibid.*, p. 142, 314; pt. 2, pp. 1142, 1162; Andrews, *Campaign Against Mobile*, pp. 48–49, 60 (quote); Atlas Plate LXXIX, No. 7.

45. Gibson reported that he had "four heavy guns" in Old Spanish Fort (Redoubt No. 1). O.R., Ser. I, Vol. XLIX, pt. 1, p. 314. Maj. Gen. Dabney H. Maury (C.S.A.) in "Defense of Spanish Fort: Some Comment by the Confederate Commander on Mr. P.D. Stephenson's Article," *Southern Historical Society Papers* 39 (1914): p. 133, said he had "constructed there a heavy six-gun battery of Brooke rifles." After the surrender, Segrex ("The Siege of Mobile") reported that Spanish Fort contained two 6.4-inch Brooke rifles and three 8-inch Columbiads. According to Andrews (*Campaign Against Mobile*, p. 48), Redoubt No. 1 was armed with 7-inch Columbiads and 30-pounder Parrotts.

46. O.R., Ser. I, Vol. XLIX, pt. 1, pp.142, 314; pt. 2, p. 1204; Andrews, *Campaign Against Mobile*, pp. 48–49, 71–72.

47. O.R., Ser. I, Vol. XLIX, pt. 1, p. 317; Stephenson, "Defense of Spanish Fort," p. 126 (quote); Maury, "Defense of Spanish Fort: Commentary," pp. 130–31; Atlas Plates LXXIX, No. 7 and LXXI, Nos. 13, 14; XC, No. 11; XCI, No. 5.

48. "Each frame or section consisted of four heavy timbers parallel to each other and a few feet apart, tied together by cross timbers. At the head of each timber is bolted a cast-iron torpedo ... containing about 27 lbs. of gunpowder, with a fuse presented so that it would come into contact with the bottom of any advancing vessel." Supports kept it at the proper angle and weights, anchors, and chains kept it in position and connected to other frames. Lt. Com. J.S. Barnes, *Submarine Warfare, Offensive and Defensive, Including a Discussion of the Offensive Torpedo System, its Effects Upon Iron-Clad Ship Systems, and Influence Upon Future Naval Wars* (New York: D. Van Nostrand, Publishers, 1869), p. 66.

49. "The barrel was strapped with a rope, and to a span underneath were attached a weight to keep it upright, a mooring line to keep it at the proper depth below the surface, and a line to connect it with another torpedo." Barnes, *Submarine Warfare*, p. 70. For more discussion of the Confederate torpedoes in Mobile Bay, see Chester G. Hearn, *Mobile Bay and the Mobile Campaign: The Last Great Battles of the Civil War* (Jefferson, NC: McFarland & Company, Inc. Publishers, 1993), pp. 33–40.

50. O.R.N., Ser. 1, Vol. 21, pp. 568–69; Vol. 22, p. 86; Maury, "Defense of Spanish Fort: Commentary," p. 134.

51. O.R., Ser. I, Vol. XLIX, pt. 1, pp. 94, 142, 233, 314; Atlas Plate XCI, No. 5.

52. O.R., Ser. I, Vol. XLIX, pt. 1, pp. 156, 161, 167, 169, 185.

53. *Ibid.*, pp. 161, 166, 314–15, 1046; pt. 2, pp. 1162, 1164, 1174; Andrews, *Campaign Against Mobile*, pp. 49–50.

54. O.R., Ser. I, Vol. XLIX, pt. 1, p. 166.

55. James R. Slack to Ann P. Slack, 28 March 1865; Eli Rose, Pension Records, National Archives.

56. O.R., Ser. I, Vol. XLIX, pt. 1, pp. 185, 314–15; pt. 2, p. 1162.

57. *Ibid.*, pt. 2, pp. 140, .314; O.R.N., Ser. I, Vol. 22, p. 70.

58. Stephenson, "Defense of Spanish Fort," p. 121.

59. O.R.N., Ser. 1, Vol. 22, pp. 70–73; Segrex, "Operations at Spanish Fort — The Loss of Our Monitors," *New York Times*, 9 April 1865.

60. Stephenson, "Defense of Spanish Fort," p. 122 (quote); O.R., Ser. I, Vol. XLIX, pt. 1, p. 96.

61. Stephenson, "Defense of Spanish Fort," p. 122.

62. "Clyde-built" (Glasgow, Scotland) steamers, the *Red Gauntlet, Heroine, Virgin*, and *Mary* had been very effective blockade-runners that the army now used as picket boats and transports on Mobile Bay. O.R.N., Ser. I, Vol. 22, pp. 60, 263; Atlas Plate CX.

63. O.R., Ser. I, Vol. XLIX, pt. 1, p. 166.

64. *Ibid.*, pp. 161, 166, 179, 180 (quote), 315. On 29 March, Gibson reported to Liddell that he had at Spanish Fort "2,688 total present; aggregate present, 2,888; number of guns, 2,325; 24 public and 10 private negroes. Our casualties up to this evening are 30 killed, 119 wounded, and 1 missing." O.R., Ser. I, Vol. XLIX, pt. 2, p. 1174.

65. O.R., Ser. I, Vol. XLIX, pt. 1, pp. 95, 159, 281; Atlas Plate CX.

66. On 4 April, Marshall's brigade returned to McArthur's division line on the right and Benton's division shifted to the left to fill the gap on the Spanish Fort line. During those four days Marshall reported that his troops were placed "in front of the high fort (Fort Alexis, I believe)" on the line just evacuated by Veatch's troops and his men "advanced the parallels 150 yards, and almost to the rifle pits of the enemy's sharpshooters outside of the fort." O.R., Ser. I, Vol. XLIX, pt. 1, pp. 107, 142, 242 (quote).

67. *Ibid.*, pt. 1, pp. 95, 142, 161–70.

68. Holtzclaw's Brigade consisted of the 18th, 32nd

and 58th consolidated, 36th, and 38th Alabama Infantry; Ector's Brigade consisted of the 29th and 39th North Carolina, and the 9th Texas Infantry and the 10th, 14th and 32nd Texas Cavalry (dismounted). O.R., XLIX, pt. 1, pp. 315, 1046; pt. 2, p. 1180.

69. Stearns and his men were taken as prisoners to Mobile, then sent to Meridian and Jackson, Mississippi, and finally to parole camp near Vicksburg. *Ibid.*, pp. 142, 158, 161, 218, 225–26, 233–34, 267, 316.

70. *Ibid.*, pt. 1, pp. 315, 1046; Hansen, "Blakeley Battlefield Self-Guided Tour."

71. O.R., Ser. I, Vol. XLIX, pt. 1, p. 282, 311; Chambers, *Blood and Sacrifice*, pp. 210–11, 227–29.

72. Wilkes, "A Short History of My Life," pp. 16–17.

73. O.R., Ser. I, Vol. XLIX, pt. 1, pp.201, 209, 215, 283, 287–88, 291,295; Atlas Plates LXI, No. 6 and CX.

74. O.R., Ser. I, Vol. XLIX, pt. 1, pp. 157, 161(quote), 174–75, 185, 248, 283; Atlas Plate LXI, No. 6.

75. O.R., Ser. I, Vol. XLIX, pt. 1, pp. 159, 162, 164, 166, 171, 185.

76. *Ibid.*, p. 96; Stephenson, "Defense of Spanish Fort," p. 122.

77. O.R., Ser. I, Vol. XLIX, pt. 1, pp. 96, 275, 278.

78. *Ibid.*, p. 278.

79. *Ibid.*, pp. 275, 277–78; Elder, ed., *Damned Iowa Greyhound*, p. 161.

80. *Ibid.*, pp. 316–18.

81. Stephenson, "Defense of Spanish Fort," pp. 125–26.

82. Gordon Granger merely reported: "On the 8th ... all batteries and light batteries on my line opened fire at 5:30 P.M., continuing for one hour, under cover of which the left of the enemy's line was carried by the troops of Major-General Smith's assault. During the night the enemy evacuated his position, withdrawing by his left and escaping across the marsh to transports in the vicinity of Batteries Tracy and Huger, abandoning all his artillery, ordnance stores, and supplies." O.R., Ser. I, Vol. XLIX, pt. 1, pp. 143 (quote), 207, 315–18; pt. 2, p. 1174; O.R.N., Ser. 1, Vol. 22, p. 101; Andrews, *Campaign Against Mobile*, pp. 161–62.

83. O.R., Ser. I, Vol. LXIX, pt. 1, pp. 267–68, 275, 277–78.

84. *Ibid.*, pp. 96, 162, 164, 166, 169, 171.

85. Andrews, *Campaign Against Mobile*, pp. 202, 220–21 (quote); O.R., Ser. I, Vol XLIX, pt. 1, pp. 97, 143, 160, 171, 249, 283, 287, 289.

86. *Ibid.*, pp. 209, 214, 287–90; Andrews, *Campaign Against Mobile*, p. 202.

87. Wilkes, "A Short History of My Life," p. 17. For an annotated roster of the Confederate prisoners of war sent to Ship Island, including Pvt. Wilkes's comrades from the 46th Mississippi, see Teresa Arnold-Scriber and Terry G. Scriber, *Ship Island, Mississippi: Rosters and History of the Civil War Prison* (Jefferson, NC: McFarland & Company, Publishers, 2008).

88. O.R., Ser. I, Vol. LXIX, pt. 1, pp. 247–48, 252–53.

89. *Ibid.*, pt. 1, pp.157, 175–76.

90. *Ibid.*, pp. 247, 252–53, 322 (quote); O.R.N., Ser. 1, Vol. 22, pp.101 (quote), 102.

91. Bert, "Letters of a Drummer Boy," pp. 336–37.

92. O.R., Ser. I, Vol. XLIX, pt. 1, p. 207.

93. Although there were no official reports of escapes from Fort Blakely or guards being shot or killed by prisoners, Abner and his fellow 46th Mississippi comrades did in fact escape. They made it to their homes in and around Williamsburg, Covington County, Mississippi (near present-day Collins) after an arduous trek of roughly 300 or more miles, which saw them travel eastward across the Perdido River swamp, northward on the Escambia River, and westward across the Alabama River at Oven Bluff. Crossing the Tombigbee, they continued westward to Shubuta, Mississippi, about 75 miles northeast of Williamsburg. At Shubuta, they prudently chose to bypass Jones County, which stood in their path to Williamsburg, for fear "the deserters would kill us if we had any showing from the government." On the last leg of their journey they moved westward above the northern end of Jones County before they "struck out" southward for Williamsburg, "the spot we started from." Jones County, the legendary "Free State of Jones," a hotbed of anti–Confederate activity, was located in the piney woods region and populated largely by poor, non-slaveholding whites who had no interest in fighting a war for the benefit of the slave-holding oligarchy. Led by Captain Newton "Newt" Knight, a band of local pro-Union partisans and deserters who had the temerity to reject involuntary subjugation to the Confederacy engaged in guerrilla warfare from hideouts in the pine forests and swamps of the Leaf River Valley. Calling Jones County an "*imperium in imperio*," in March 1864, Dabney Maury had sent "Harry" Maury's 15th Confederate Cavalry and Robert Lowry's 6th Mississippi Infantry on a black-flag expedition to wipe out Knight's anti–Confederate partisans. Although they were unable to track Knight's "company" in the Leaf River swamps and soon left the area, they captured and executed several of Knight's men, which only served to increase the bitterness and hostility. Abner and his friends were wise to avoid Jones County, Mississippi. Wilkes, "A Short History of My Life," pp. 17 (quote), 18–19, 20 (quote), 21; Dabney H. Maury, *Recollections of a Virginian in the Mexican, Indian, and Civil Wars* (New York: Charles Scribner's Sons, 1894), pp. 200, 247 (quote); Victoria E. Bynum, *The Free State of Jones: Mississippi's Longest Civil War* (Chapel Hill: University of North Carolina Press, 2001, pp. 4, 112, 157; O.R., Ser I, Vol. XXXII, pt. 1, p. 499; pt. 3, pp. 632, 662, 711; Vol. XXXIX, pt. 2, p. 777; Vol. LII, pt. 2, pp. 657; Atlas Plate CLV.

94. O.R.N., Ser. 1, Vol. 22, pp. 95, 102, 139, 178; Ser. 2, Vol. 1, pp. 256, 269; Annual Report of the Chief of Engineers, U.S. Army, to the Secretary of War, Doc. No. 446, Office of the Chief of Engineers, August 11, 1913, p. 681.

95. O.R., Ser. I, Vol. XLIX, pt. 1, p. 98, 162.

96. Maury, "Defense of Spanish Fort: Commentary," p. 136; Andrews, *Campaign Against Mobile*, p. 223.

97. Sometimes called Catfish Point, it is listed as Dog River Point on Canby's campaign map. Atlas Plate CX.

98. O.R., Ser. I, Vol. XLIX, pt. 1, pp. 143–44, 146, 162; pt. 2, pp. 348–49; O.R.N., Ser. 1, Vol. 22, pp. 93–96; Benjamin R. Cox, "Mobile in the War Between the States," *Confederate Veteran* 24 (1916): 210; a copy of an original letter from a resident of Mobile to his sis-

ter describing the day of surrender and a copy of the front page of the 16 April 1865 *Mobile Sunday News*, giving the local newspaper account of the surrender of the city, in Delaney Caldwell, *Confederate Mobile: A Pictorial History* (Mobile: Haunted Bookshop, 1971, pp. 320–21; Hearn, *Mobile Bay*, p. 201; Atlas Plate CV, No. 1.

99. James R. Slack to Ann P. Slack, 15 April 1865; O.R., Ser. I, Vol. XLIX, pt. 1, pp. 162, 164, 166, 169, 171. Catfish Point is called Dog River Point on Canby's campaign map. Atlas Plate CV, No. 1; "Hotel Arrivals — Battle House," *Mobile Sunday News*, 16 April 1865, in Delaney, *Confederate Mobile*, p. 322..

100. O.R., Ser. I, Vol. XLIX, pt. 1, pp. 143, 169; James R. Slack to Ann P. Slack, 15 April 1865; Bert, "Letters of a Drummer Boy," p. 339.

101. O.R., Ser. I, Vol. XLVIII, pt. 2, pp. 400, 1284; Joseph H. Parks, *General Edmund Kirby Smith, C.S.A.* (Baton Rouge: Louisiana State University Press, 1954), pp. 456–57. On 21 April 1865, the *Daily Telegraph* of Houston, Texas, on the same day it printed news of Lee's surrender to Grant, also printed the concluding paragraphs of E. Kirby Smith's Address to the Army of the Trans-Mississippi in which Smith urged them to fight on: "You possess the means of long resisting invasion. You have hopes of succor from abroad. Protract the struggle, and you will surely receive the aid of nations, who already deeply sympathize with you." Smith concluded by asserting that, if they stood by their colors, they would be able to secure terms they could accept with honor, even to the point "of securing the final success of our cause." Smith's attempt to boost morale was needed because, as news of Lee's surrender spread, many Trans-Mississippi soldiers simply put down their arms and went home. Eric C. Caren, comp., *Civil War Extra: A Newspaper History of the Civil War from 1863 to 1865*, 2 vols. (Edison, NJ: Castle Books, 1999), II: 325.

102. O.R.N., Ser. 1, Vol. 22, pp. 99–102, 176–78, 180, 213–14, 228; O.R., Ser. I, Vol. XLIX, pt. 1, p. 319; Stephenson, "Defense of Spanish Fort," p. 128; Maury, "Defense of Spanish Fort: Comment," p. 136; Maury, *Recollections*, pp. 232–33; Annual Report of the Chief of Engineers, U.S. Army, to the Secretary of War, War Department Doc. No. 446, August 11, 1913, p. 681; Atlas Plate CX.

103. In March 1865, Maj. Gen. Lew Wallace, then commanding the Middle Department, 8th corps, at Baltimore, Maryland, had received permission from Grant to go to Brazos Santiago in anticipation of a Confederate surrender in the east to negotiate a secret truce agreement with Confederate General James E. Slaughter, commanding at Brownsville. Wallace's proposal, although complicated, essentially called for a cessation of hostilities and avoidance of needless bloodshed until the question of war and peace could be settled in the east. Slaughter and "Rip" Ford accepted it, but Maj. Gen. John G. Walker, commanding Confederate forces in Texas, and Kirby Smith at Shreveport, rejected it outright. Following the surrender of the Confederate forces in the east in April, Col. Robert B. Jones of the 34th Indiana was reportedly ordered not to make any military move against Brownsville in order to let news of the loss in the east spread and give Confederates in the Trans-Mississippi opportunity to quit fighting on their own, especially with reliable reports coming in of widespread desertions and refusal to obey orders by many of the Trans-Mississippi Confederate soldiers. At any rate, whether or not he was aware of Jones's orders or the unofficial "understanding" with Slaughter and Ford, there was no need at that time for Barrett to take such a weak force to attempt a military move against Brownsville or any of its outposts. O.R., Ser. I, Vol. XLVIII, pt. 1, pp. 512, 1275–79; 937, 1166, pt. 2, pp. 458–63, 1277, 1289, 1313; Jeffrey W. Hunt, *The Last Battle of the Civil War: Palmetto Ranch* (Austin: University of Texas Press, 2002), pp. 50–51, 169–71.

104. O.R., Ser. I, Vol. XLVIII, pt. 1, pp. 266–69, 1457; pt. 2, p. 517; Hunt, *The Last Battle*, pp. 55–56, 59.

105. Ford, *Rip Ford's Texas*, p. 391; Hunt, *The Last Battle*, pp. 99–100, 169–71; O.R., Ser. I, Vol. XLVIII, pt. 1, p. 266

106. O.R., Ser. I, Vol. XLVIII, pt. 1, pp. 265–69; Hunt, *The Last Battle*, pp. 107–9, 112–16, 119; John Salmon Ford, *Rip Ford's Texas* (Austin: University of Texas Press, 1963), p. 391.

107. O.R., Ser. I, vol. XLVIII, pt. 2, pp. 1308, 1309, 1313. On 11 June, under the headline "Military Insubordination in Texas," the *New York Times* quoted Confederate commissioners Col. Ashbel Smith and W.P. Ballinger, Esq., on the disintegration of Confederate forces in Texas. Smith and Ballinger had been sent from Texas to New Orleans to discuss surrender terms with Canby. *New York Times*, 11 June 1865, from the *New Orleans Times*, 21 May 1865

108. O.R., Ser. I, Vol. XLVIII, pt. 1, pp. 189–93; pt. 2, p. 457; Parks, *Kirby Smith*, pp. 462–65, 468, 470.

109. O.R., Ser. I, Vol. XLIX. pt. 1, p. 100; XLVIII, pt. 2, pp. 300, 476 (quote), 643.

110. During an eight-day recess at Cincinnati in February, Daniel escaped custody (he was found guilty in absentia but never sentenced) and Anderson committed suicide. Cantrill became mentally ill, was separated from the proceedings, and was never brought to trial on the charges. Judge Morris and Marmaduke were acquitted on both charges and released on their oaths of allegiance. Based on the highly dubious testimony of the commission's two star witnesses, Shanks and Langhorn, three defendants were found guilty on both charges. Walsh was sentenced to five and Semmes to three years' hard labor at the Ohio Penitentiary; both, however, were pardoned after serving only a month or two of their sentences. Grenfell, on the other hand, convicted principally on Shanks's testimony without any direct evidence against him, received the death penalty. As in the Milligan case, the death penalty raised a protest from many respectable people, including Republicans, who were concerned about military jurisdiction, the weak evidence presented, and the fact that none of the defendants had been convicted of committing any overt acts. Even Republican Speaker of the House Schuler Colfax wrote Judge Advocate General Holt that he mistrusted the summary hearings and "could not hang a cat" on evidence that relied so heavily on testimony from the likes of Shanks and Langhorn. His death sentence commuted to life at hard labor

on 22 July 1865, Grenfell was remanded to military prison at Fort Jefferson on Dry Tortugas, Florida. U.S. Congress, House, *Grenfel*, pp. 24, 272–73, 396–99, 418, 423, 454–80, 573–75, 618, 640, 645–49, 652–53; Stephen Z. Starr, *Colonel Grenfell's Wars: The Life of a Soldier of Fortune* (Baton Rouge: Louisiana State University Press, 1971), pp. 273–74, 286, 290, 324–26; Klement, *Dark Lanterns*, pp. 197–99, 213, quoting Colfax to Holt, 20 January 1865, in the Joseph Holt Papers, Library of Congress), 216–17; *New York Times*, 27 June 1865; Atlas Plate CXLVI.1

111. Slack, who did not learn of the President Lincoln's assassination until late on the night of 20 April, had come to believe that President Lincoln would commute the death sentences. James R. Slack to Ann P. Slack, 21 April 1865; O.R., Ser. II, Vol. VIII, pp. 523, 525.

112. *Ibid.*, pp. 543–48; Klement, "The Indianapolis Treason Trials," p. 116; Klaus, ed., *The Milligan Case*, pp. 39–40.

113. Morton to Pres. Johnson, 12 May 1865, Telegram Dispatch Books, Oliver P. Morton, 1861–1865, Archives Division, Indiana State Library; Klement, *Dark Lanterns*, pp. 44, 226; Klement, "The Indianapolis Treason Trials," p. 115, citing the *Indianapolis Daily Journal*, 13, 14 May 1865. A letter to the editor complained of the *Daily Journal*'s (and the governor's) change of editorial opinion regarding the death sentences. *Indianapolis Daily Journal*, 6 June 1865; Klaus, *The Milligan Case*, p. 40, quoting Foulke, *Life of Oliver P. Morton*; Marshall, *American Bastille*, p. 80.

114. O.R., Ser. II, Vol. VIII, pp. 587–88. As Klement points out, not only had Judge Davis and Governor Morton pressured President Johnson for commutation of the sentences, but also the previous March "both houses of the U.S. Congress had passed by large margins resolutions challenging the trial of civilians by military tribunals." Citing the Congressional Globe, 38th Cong., 2nd Sess., pp. 1323–30, Klement quotes a pertinent resolution on p. 1323, to wit: "No person shall be tried by a military commission in any State or Territory where the courts of the United States are open." Klement, *Dark Lanterns*, p. 226.

115. O.R., Ser. I. Vol. XLVIII, pt. 2, pp. 581, 591; "The Surrender of the Trans-Mississippi. S.B. Buckner in Reply to Gen. Sheridan — His Defense of Kirby Smith," *New York Times*, 10 January 1867, from the *New Orleans Crescent*.

116. O.R., Ser. I, Vol. XLVIII, pt. 2, pp. 581, 648–49, 675–76, 715–16, 1319; O.R.N., Ser. 1, Vol. 22, pp. 199, 205–207.

117. O.R., Ser. I, Vol. XLVIII, pt. 2, pp. 533, 579–81, 591, 600–603, 675–76, 727–28.

118. Parks, *Kirby Smith*, pp. 474–75, quoting the Smith Papers, 30 May 1865, and the *Galveston Tri-Weekly News*, 5 June 1865.

119. "The Explosion in Mobile," *New York Times*, 8 June 1865, from the *Mobile News*, 26 May 1865; Atlas Plate CV.

120. James R. Slack to Ann P. Slack, 28 May 1865.

121. O.R., Ser. I, Vol. XLVIII, pt. 2, pp. 476, 525–26.

122. *Ibid.*, Ser. II, Vol. VIII, pp. 583–84, 638–39; Klement, *Dark Lanterns*, pp. 226–27.

Chapter 16

1. O.R., Ser. II, Vol. VIII, pp. 578–80.

2. *Ibid.*, Ser. I, Vol. XLVIII, pt. 1, p. 193 (quote), 1358; pt. 2, pp. 727–28, 1292–93; Parks, *Kirby Smith*, p. 481; Kerby, *Kirby Smith's Confederacy*, p. 428.

3. Disgusted with the French Imperialist officers in Matamoros, Ford quickly returned to Texas after being persuaded by Lt. Richard Strong of Steele's staff, a cousin of Mrs. Ford's, who conveyed Steele's wishes that he return to Texas and convince others to return with him. Steele, in fact, offered Ford the position of parole agent for the Rio Grande. Knowing that Frederick Steele was a cousin of ex-Confederate General William Steele and therefore a "gentleman," Ford agreed to return and Steele appointed him parole commissioner on the Rio Grande. Ford, *Rip Ford's Texas*, pp. 401–404.

4. O.R., Ser. I, Vol. XLVIII, pt. 2, pp. 813–14, 827–28, 858, 1015, 1313; Hunt, *The Last Battle*, p. 139; "The Mexican Border. The Capture of Brownsville," *New York Times*, 18 June 1865.

5. James R. Slack to Ann P. Slack, 1 June 1865.

6. O.R., Ser. I, Vol. XLVIII, pt. 2, pp. 813–14, 903 (quotes); Kerby, *Kirby Smith's Confederacy*, pp. 423, 425, 428–29; Casdorph, *Prince John Magruder*, pp. 296–97; "Texas. Military Insubordination in Texas," *New York Times*, 21 May 1865.

7. Philip H. Sheridan, *Personal Memoirs of Philip Henry Sheridan: General United States Army*, 2 vols. (New York: C. Appleton and Company, 1902), II: 208, 218–19 (hereafter cited as Sheridan, *Memoirs* II).

8. General Orders No. 22, O.R., Ser. I, Vol. XLVIII, pt. 2, p. 749.

9. *Ibid.*, pp. 749, 854–55.

10. At the mouth of the Rio Grande, Brazos Santiago Island would be the staging area for Steele's force, but with no water except the 6,000 gallons per day that could be condensed from salt water, few troops could stay there. *Ibid.*, pp. 841–42; James R. Slack to Ann P. Slack, 18 June 1865.

11. James R. Slack to Ann P. Slack, 5 June 1865; O.R., Ser. I, Vol. XLVIII, pt. 2, p. 902 (quote), 910.

12. *Ibid.*, p. 929.

13. *Ibid.*, pp. 970, 1027.

14. *Ibid.*, pp. 854–55, 929.

15. James R. Slack to Ann P. Slack, 21 June 1865; O.R., Ser. I, Vol. XLVIII, pt. 2, pp. 931, 1140, 1156.

16. James R. Slack to Ann P. Slack, 25 June 1865; O.R., Ser. I, Vol. XLVIII, pt. 2, p. 918.

17. *Ibid.*, pt. 1, pp. 11, 303; pt. 2, pp. 656, 910, 1003–4.

18. *Ibid.*, pt. 1, pp. 787, 847, 1084–86, 1137.

19. By July 1865 Mexican Royalist and French Imperialist control of the Rio Grande had diminished greatly and the Liberals had begun to take control of the border. John N. Edwards, Shelby's adjutant and publicist, wrote a highly romanticized and exaggerated tale of Shelby's derring-do. Edwards's tale, his elaborations and exaggerations taken with a grain of salt and accompanied by reliable accounts, official and otherwise, has Shelby's entourage lowering their flag in the Rio Grande at Eagle Pass, crossing to Piedras Negras, Mexico, and selling their artillery for much-needed specie to the

Hon. Andres Viesco, the Juarista governor of Coahuila. After rejecting Viesco's offer to join Juarez's Liberals, Shelby and his entourage were permitted to retain their horses and sidearms and travel southward to Imperialist-held Monterrey. From there, they were ordered by the French commander Pierre Jeanningros to continue on to Mexico City, where Maximilian, worried about reaction from the United States, turned down their offer of military assistance and offered them a subsidized exile and colonization plan instead, which they accepted. John N. Edwards, *Shelby's Expedition to Mexico: An Unwritten Leaf of the War* (Kansas City: Kansas City Times Steam Book and Job Printing House, 1872; reprint ed., Fayetteville: University of Arkansas Press, 2002), pp. xvii, xxiii, 31–41; also see Edwards, *Shelby and His Men*, pp. 545–51; O.R., Ser. I, Vol. XLVIII, pt. 2, pp. 1077, 1147–48; Carl Coke Rister, "Carlota, A Confederate Colony in Mexico," *Journal of Southern History* 11 (February 1945), pp. 36–41; U.S. Congress, House, "Southern Immigration to Mexico," in *Message of the President of the United States of January 29, 1866, Relating to the Present Condition of Mexico*, 39th Cong., 2nd Sess., H. exdoc. 76, pp. 500–28.

20. O.R., Ser. I, Vol. XLVIII, pt. 2, pp. 1053, 1067.

21. *Ibid.*, pp. 1068, 1077 (quotes).

22. *Ibid.*, p. 1092.

23. James R. Slack to Ann P. Slack, 19 July 1865.

24. U.S. Congress, House, *Difficulties on Southwestern Frontier. Message of the President of the United States* [James Buchanan], H. exdoc. 52, 36th Cong., 1st Sess., 1860, pp. 69–82; Arnoldo De Leon, *They Called Them Greasers: Anglo Attitudes Toward Mexicans in Texas, 1821–1900* (Austin: University of Texas Press, 1983), p. 54.

25. Armando C. Alonzo, *Tejano Legacy: Rancheros and Settlers in South Texas, 1734–1900* (Albuquerque: University of New Mexico Press, 1998), pp. 146–48; Frank H. Dugan, "The 1850 Affair of the Brownsville Separatists," *Southwestern Historical Quarterly* 61 (October 1957), pp. 273–75; Frederick Law Olmstead, *A Journey Through Texas, or, A Saddle-trip on the Southwestern Frontier* (microform; New York: Dix, Edwards, 1857); David J. Weber, ed., *Foreigners in their Native Land: Historical Roots of the Mexican American* (Albuquerque: University of New Mexico Press, 1998), pp. 207, 231–34.

26. Fort Brown was established in 1846 by Gen. Zachary Taylor at the outset of the war with Mexico to solidify by force of arms the U.S. claim that, with the annexation of Texas into the United States, the Rio Grande was the international border between Mexico and the United States, not the Nueces River. Stillman and the other Anglo businessmen on the Rio Grande and their lawyers were part of a group petitioning the U.S. Congress to establish a territory separate from the State of Texas between the Nueces and the Rio Grande. The Nueces River had been the original southern boundary of the Mexican State of Tejas, about one hundred and fifty miles north of and roughly parallel to the Rio Grande, separating it from Coahuila. Stillman and his Anglo business partners argued in their petition to the U.S. Congress that the Nueces River should be declared the southern border of Texas and that the land between the Nueces and the Rio Grande should be made a separate U.S. territory. Dugan, "Brownsville Separatists," *Southern Historical Quarterly* 61 (October 1957): 273–76; Alonzo, *Tejano Legacy*, pp. 146–48.

27. U.S. Congress, House, *Impeachment of John C. Watrous, United States District Judge for the District of Texas*, 34th Cong., 3rd Sess., H. rp. 175, Ser. 913, February 2, 1857, pp. 19–20; Dugan, "Brownsville Separatists," *Southern Historical Quarterly*, 61 (Oct 1957), pp. 273–75; Alonzo, *Tejano Legacy*, pp. 146–48.

28. *Rafael Garcia Cavazos et al. vs. Charles Stillman et al.* in U.S. Congress, House, *Impeachment of Judge John C. Watrous of Texas*, pp. 19–23, 156, 166; Watrous's enemies, including the defendants in the Cavazos case, petitioned the House Judiciary Committee four times for his impeachment. Watrous was cleared the first three times. On the fourth try, Texas seceded from the Union and the case was dropped. Watrous left Texas during the war, returning in 1866 to resume his position as federal district judge. He was disabled three years later, and Congress authorized his retirement at full pay for life. He died ca. 1873. William M. Robinson Jr., review of *The Case of John C. Watrous, United States Judge for Texas: A Political Story of High Crimes and Misdemeanors*, by Walace Hawkins, in *Journal of Southern History*, 17 (1951): 262–63. The House Judiciary Committee also ruled that there was no evidence of malfeasance by Judge Watrous in the Cavazos case. U.S. Congress, House, *Case of Judge John C. Watrous*, 36th Cong., 2nd Sess., H. rp. 2, 27 December 1860; Dugan, "Brownsville Separatists," 275.

29. U.S. Congress, House, *Difficulties on the Southwestern Frontier*, pp. 70–82; U.S. Congress, House, *Troubles on Texas Frontier*, H. exdoc. 81, 36th Congress, 1st Sess., May 3, 1860, pp. 2–14; Dugan, "Brownsville Separatists," 275; Alonzo, *Tejano Legacy*, pp. 146–48; Weber, ed., *Foreigners in their Native Land*, p. 233.

30. U.S. Congress, House, *Troubles on Texas Frontier*, pp. 2–14; U.S. Congress, House, *Difficulties on the Southwestern Frontier*, pp. 66, 70–72, 79–82; Alonzo, *Tejano Legacy*, p. 45; De Leon, *They Called Them Greasers*, p. 54.

31. U.S. Congress, House, *Difficulties on the Southwestern Frontier*, pp. 64–69, 76, 82.

32. *Ibid.*, *Troubles on Texas Frontier*, pp. 4, 12, 63, 101–103; U.S. Congress, House, *Difficulties on the Southwestern Frontier*, pp. 53, 70–72, 76, 79–82, 145; "Governors' Messages. Inaugural Message of Sam Houston," *New York Times*, 13 January 1860. Major Samuel P. Heintzelman became a Major General in the U.S. Army and toward the end of the Civil War commanded the Northern Department at Columbus, Ohio, in charge of the Federal prison for Confederate officers at Johnson's Island, Ohio. Captain John S. "Rip" Ford became a colonel of cavalry in the Confederate Army, operating on the Rio Grande. At the end of the war, William G. Tobin also operated on the Rio Grande as a captain, commanding a company of the 2nd Texas Cavalry (CSA); and Colonel Robert E. Lee, of course, became "Ole Marse," commander of the Confederate Army of Northern Virginia.

33. Weber, ed., *Foreigners in their Native Land*, pp. 207, 232.

34. Mexico, *Comision pesquisidora*, pp. 148–49; Pedro Pruneda, *Historia de la Guerra de Mejico desde 1861 a 1867* (Madrid: Elizalde y Compania, 1867; facsimile reprint ed., Mexico City: Fundacion Miguel Aleman, A.C.; Fondo de Cultura Economica, c1996), p. 334.

35. Jesus de la Serna's election in 1861 as governor of Tamaulipas was contested and triggered a rebellion before he could take office. In order to calm the civil strife there, Juarez declared a state of siege and appointed Gen. Manuel Ruiz as military governor. Mexico, *Comision Pesquisidora*, pp. 148–49; Jose R. del Castillo, *Juarez, la intervencion y el imperio: Refutacion de la obra "el verdadero Juarez," de Bulnos* (Mexico: Herrero Hermanos, editores, 1904), p. 360; O.R., Ser. I, Vol. XVI, pt. 1, p. 438; Vol. XXVI, pt. 1, pp. 399–409, 823, 839, 841; Vol. XXXIV, pt. 1, pp. 81–84; pt. 2, pp. 415, 888–90; Vol. LIII, p. 594.

36. Mexico, Comision Pesquisidora, pp. 149–50; O.R., XXXIV, pt. 2, pp. 7, 9, 39–40, 92–93, 218, 224.

37. *Ibid.*, pp. 223–24, 536; Castillo, *Juarez*, pp. 368, 370, 372–73.

38. O.R., Ser. I, Vol. XXXIV, pt. 2, pp. 223–24; pt. 3, p. 736–37; Vol. LIII, pp. 980–81.

39. Cortina worked out the deal with Major General John A. McClernand, recently returned to active duty by President Lincoln, and Francis J. Herron, who commanded the 2nd division of the 13th corps at Brownsville. O.R., XXXIV, pt. 3, pp. 73–74, 87–88; pt. 4, p. 560; Kiper, *McClernand*, pp. 285–86.

40. O.R., Ser. I, Vol. XXXIV, pt. 2, p. 834; pt. 3, p. 835; Vol. LIII, pp. 1001–1002; Mexico, *Comision Pesquisidora*, p. 151.

41. U.S. Congress, House, *Message of the President of the United States* [Andrew Johnson], *of March 20, 1866, Relating to the Condition of Affairs in Mexico*, 2 parts, 39th Cong., 1st. Sess., H. exdoc. 73, March 20, 1866, I: 34–35; O.R.,Ser. I, Vol. XXXIV, pt. 4, pp. 559–60; Vol. XLI, pt. 1, pp. 185–86, 211–12, 1088; pt. 3, p. 973.

42. Castillo, *Juarez*, pp. 380, 416; Pruneda, *Historia de la Guerra*, pp. 333–35, 401; O.R., Ser. I, Vol. XLI, pt. 1, pp. 957–59.

43. *Ibid.*, pt. 3, pp. 99–100, 957–59, 973–74.

44. *Ibid.*, pp. 100–101, 931–32, 956, 972.

45. Echarzaretta's troops numbered 13 officers and 290 men. They turned over to Day twenty-seven .69-caliber muskets, one hundred ninety-five .58-caliber Enfield rifles, twenty-four .58-caliber Whitney muskets, twenty-two cavalry horses with equipment, ten mules, three 6-pounder rifled brass guns, 1,200 rounds of assorted caliber cartridges, and seventy-six rounds of assorted ammunition. *Ibid.*, pt. 3, pp. 184–85, 721–22, 947, 973; U.S. Congress, House. *Condition of Affairs in Mexico*, I: 320, 323–24; Mexico. *Comision Pesquisidora*, pp. 152–53.

46. In a letter to Sec. of State Seward, dated 19 October 1865, the head of the French legation, the Marquis de Montholon, charged that the U.S. had violated neutrality by permitting Cortina to operate as a "guerila" against "the Imperial authorities." Specifically, Montholon charged that Cortina was permitted to operate from Texas with impunity, resupplying and recruiting "many American colored persons" to the Republican cause, his men able to "walk around in the streets of Brownsville with ribbons in their hats," as well as being permitted to use Brownsville as a base to attack and capture in July 1865 a shipment of cotton bound for Matamoros on the steamer *Senorita* and to attack a convoy of goods on its way to Monterrey. U.S. authorities, of course, denied the charge. In his letter to Seward, Montholon does not mention that Cortina had ever operated for Maximilian and the Empire. See Montholon to Seward, O.R., Ser. I, Vol. XLVIII, pt. 2, p. 1241; also see, *Ibid.*, pp. 18, 106, 814, 1053, 1067–68, 1148, 1174, 1253–54; LIII, p. 1021; U.S. Congress, House, *Condition of Affairs in Mexico*, I: 338–40.

47. Under increasing pressure, the French stopped bringing in Nubian troops and began recruiting Spanish-speaking Austrian volunteers to replace the withdrawing French army, assuring Seward, to no avail, that they would be enrolled in Maximilian's Mexican Royalist Army and would be expected to become Mexican citizens. U.S. Congress, House, *Condition of Affairs in Mexico*, II: 331, 335, 481(quote), 484–86, 492.

48. Sheridan, *Memoirs* II: 216–19; O.R., Ser. I, Vol. XLVIII, pt. 2, pp. 1068, 1077; U.S. Congress, House, *Condition of Affairs in Mexico*, II: 68, 333; Pruneda, *Historia de la Guerra*, pp. 334, 401; Castillo, *Juarez*, pp. 425.

49. "Among the Liberal leaders along the Rio Grande during this period there sprang up many factional differences from various causes, some personal, others political, and some I regret to say, from downright moral obliquity — as for example, those between Cortinas [sic] and Canales — who, though generally hostile to the Imperialists, were freebooters enough to take a shy at each other frequently, and now and then even to join forces against Escobedo, unless we prevented them by coaxing or threats." Sheridan, *Memoirs* II: 219.

50. James R. Slack to Ann P. Slack, 24 July 1865; Hunt, *The Last Battle*, pp. 152–53, citing the court-martial of Robert G. Morrison, Judge Advocate General's Court-Martial Case Files, RG 153, microcopy 594, National Archives and Records Administration, Washington, D.C.

51. John M. Ray Diary, Manuscript Section, Indiana State Library. Transcribed by the author from a copy of the original; O.R., Ser. I, Vol. XLVIII, pt. 2, pp. 804, 956.

52 Ray Diary, Indiana State Library.

53. O.R., Ser. I, Vol. XLVIII, pt. 2, pp. 1148 (quotes).

54. About a month after Shelby's entourage crossed, Cortina reportedly stopped and disarmed Terry's ex-Confederates on the upper Rio Grande, but also allowed them to proceed to Monterrey. David S. Terry, Esq., had been a justice on the California Supreme Court from 1855, the year he stabbed an opponent in the neck with his Bowie knife, to 1859, when he resigned as Chief Justice after he shot and killed U.S. Senator David Broderick in a duel. Born in Kentucky in 1823 and raised in Texas, he returned to Texas early in 1864 with a commission to recruit a cavalry brigade of New Mexico, Arizona and California volunteers to open the road from California to El Paso. Having failed to open that road, at the end of the war Terry commanded a regiment of dismounted cavalry in H.P. Bee's infantry brigade. After

a short exile in Mexico, he returned to California. In the end, known more for his knife fights than for his cogent legal opinions, he, not surprisingly, was killed in 1889 during a scuffle with the bodyguard of U.S. Supreme Court Justice S.J. Field. *Ibid.*, p. 1174, 1192 (quote), 1291; Vol. XLI, pt. 4, p. 1009; Vol. L, pt. 2, p. 1078; Vol. LIII, p. 962; Ser. IV, Vol. III, pp. 76, 960; Charles S. Potts, "David S. Terry: The Romantic Story of a Great Texan," *Southwest Review* 19 (April 1934), pp. 295–34; *New York Times*, 28 July, 4, 30 August 1856.

55. Kirby Smith, having more trouble with ex-Confederates in Mexico than he cared to handle, moved to Cuba, where he met former Confederate Secretary of State Judah Benjamin. About to accompany Benjamin to England, on 14 November 1865 Smith returned to the United States after receiving assurances of safety from U.S. Grant and took the oath of allegiance. Murrah and Allen died in Mexico in August 1865 and April 1866, respectively, and Moore returned to the U.S. in January 1867 after having received a full pardon from President Johnson. Even before Maximilian's downfall, armed Liberals attacked and ransacked the holdings of ex-Confederate colonists at Carlota who had tried to force Indian laborers to fulfill their work contracts after a protest and work stoppage. After this, many ex-Confederates, now convinced that Maximilian's troops were unable to effectively protect them, decided to return to the United States. Many more would return to the United States in 1867 after Juarez's triumph was accompanied by a wave of xenophobia so strong that Juarez, as popular as he was, was unable to bow to intensive diplomatic pressure to commute Maximilian's death sentence. Reynolds returned to Missouri in 1868 and resumed government service as an elected state legislator and later with a U.S. commission on commerce with South America. Shelby returned to Missouri following Maximilian's downfall and was eventually appointed U.S. Marshall for Western Missouri by President Cleveland. Parks, *Kirby Smith*, pp. 481–84, 492; Kerby, *Kirby Smith's Confederacy*, p. 428; Rister, "Carlota," 36–37, 49; U.S. Congress, House, *Present Condition of Mexico*, pp. 169, 516–17, from the *New York World*, 22 June 1866; card from Sterling Price to the *Nashville Union & American*, 10 October 1866, printed in the *New York Times*, 2 November 1866; "Later From Mexico ... The Colony of Southern Exiles Broken Up," *New York Times*, 10 December 1866; "Mexican Intelligence. Particulars on the Execution of Maximilian," *New York Times*, 3 July 1867; George D. Harmon, "Confederate Migration to Mexico," *Hispanic American Historical Review* 17 (November 1937), pp. 458–87. For details of Reynolds's suicide, see *New York Times*, 30 March 1867; for Shelby's obituary, see *New York Times*, 14 February 1897.

56. Ray Diary, Indiana State Library.

57. *Ibid.*

58. *Ibid.*

59. Slack's troops included the 7th Vermont Veteran Volunteers, the 77th Ohio, the 27th, 28th and 35th Wisconsin, the 28th Illinois, the 26th New York Battery, a pioneer company and train. O.R., Ser. I, Vol. XLVIII, pt. 2, pp. 517, 1140, 1156; Hunt, *The Last Battle*, p. 163.

60. Dr. J.E. Bright, D.D., President of the Minden Female College, 1862–1871; Bell I. Wiley, ed., *This Infernal War: The Confederate Letters of Sgt. Edwin H. Fay* (Austin: University of Texas Press, 1958), pp. 153, 452.

61. James R. Slack to Ann P. Slack, 23 August 1865.

62. The 47th Indiana ended service having added 344 recruits and 18 unassigned recruits to the original 980 officers and enlisted men. They lost 8 commissioned officers and 304 non-commissioned officers and men either killed in battle or died of disease, with 20 from all ranks unaccounted for, and 62 deserters. *Adjutant General's Report*, I (Appendix): 4.

Epilogue

1. "Arguments for the United States," *Ex parte Milligan* 71 U.S. (4 Wall) 2 (1866), reprinted in Klaus, ed., *The Milligan Case*, pp. 84–92.

2. *Ibid.*, pp. 42–43.

3. "Argument for the Petitioner," *Ex parte Milligan*, reprinted in *Ibid.*, pp. 93–94, 122, 150.

4. "Order of the Court," *Ex parte Milligan*, reprinted in *Ibid.*, p. 224 (quote). The Habeas Corpus Act of 1863 required that arrested persons be indicted by a grand jury in the district in which they were held and tried in civil, not military, court. If not indicted by the time the grand jury adjourned, they were to be released from custody. Rehnquist, *All the Laws But One*, pp. 129–31.

5. The majority justices were: David Davis, who wrote the majority opinion; Stephen J. Field; Samuel Nelson; Nathan Clifford; and Robert Grier. Dissenting justices were: Chief Justice Salmon P. Chase, who wrote the dissenting opinion; Samuel Miller; Noah Swayne; and James Wayne. Charles Warren, *The Supreme Court in United States History*, 2 vols. (Boston: Little, Brown and Company, 1926), II: 426.

6. "Opinions of the Court," *Ex parte Milligan*, reprinted in Klaus, ed., *The Milligan Case*, p. 246 (quote).

7. *History of Huntington County*, p. 515 (quote); Marshall, *American Bastille*, quoting "local newspapers," presumably the *Huntington Democrat*, pp. 87–91; also cited by Klement, *Dark Lanterns*, pp. 230–31.

8. Although the first grand jury failed to indict Milligan and the others during its term as required in the Habeas Corpus Act of 1863, after Milligan filed for habeas corpus and it appeared likely that he and the other petitioners would be released, prosecutors convinced the next grand jury to issue indictments. These indictments were kept alive while the petitioners were in custody. The stipulation of Milligan's release that he be turned over to the circuit court for trial by jury or be discharged altogether was based on that later indictment. According to Klaus, on 8 January 1867 in federal district court at Indianapolis, "nolle prosequis were entered as to Milligan, Heffren, Bullitt," and on 29 May for the rest. Klaus, ed., *The Milligan Case*, p. 45; O.R., Ser. II, Vol. VIII, p. 897.

9. "Opinions of the Court," *Ex parte Milligan*, reprinted in Klaus, ed., *The Milligan Case*, p. 235. Former Supreme Court Chief Justice William H. Rehn-

quist referred to the majority opinion regarding the right of Congress as an *obiter dictum*, a judicial opinion "not pertinent to the decision of the point in question." Congress, he noted, had not enacted a law establishing the military commissions, and the case was decided when the Court unanimously agreed that Milligan's rights had been violated according to the Habeas Corpus Act of 1863, which rendered further opinion unnecessary. Rehnquist, *All the Laws But One*, pp. 134, 136 (quote).

10. "Opinions of the Court," *Ex parte Milligan*, reprinted in Klaus, ed., *The Milligan Case*, p. 250.

11. *Ibid.*, pp. 235, 237.

12. *Ibid.*, p. 234; also see Rehnquist, *All the Laws But One*, p. 129; and Peter Irons, *A People's History of the Supreme Court*, rev. ed. (New York: Penguin Books, rev. ed. 2006), 188–89.

13. The 2 January 1867 *Indianapolis Daily Journal*, for example, typical of the radical Republican response, editorialized that the Milligan decision had created "misgivings in the minds of the patriotic people who had saved the Nation from destruction at the hands of rebels," quoted in Warren, *Milligan Case*, pp. 420; also see pp. 429, 435–37. The 3 January 1867 *New York Times* echoed those sentiments by charging that the Court had thrown "the great weight of its influence into the scale of those who assailed the Union." Breaking ranks with the radicals, the otherwise staunchly Republican *Chicago Tribune* agreed that the decision was correct, and that the prisoners should be released and turned over to the civil courts in Indiana for trial, as ordered in the decision. *Chicago Tribune*, 3 January 1867.

14. Those fears would subside somewhat with the passage of the first Reconstruction Act on 2 March 1867, which, among other things, divided the South into five districts ruled by the military, restricted the rights of ex-Confederates, enabled freedmen to vote and hold office, and abolished the right to jury trial for those who violated any provisions of the act, although it permitted habeas corpus petitions to be heard in the district circuit courts. The Republican Congress quickly eliminated that problem by amending the first Reconstruction Act to remove the appellate jurisdiction of civil courts in habeas corpus cases in the South and thus paved the way for military rule in the former Confederacy. See *Ex parte McCardle*, 74 U.S. (7 Wall.) 506 (1869), a Reconstruction-era habeas corpus case filed by an ex-Confederate colonel and racist newspaper editor arrested by Maj. Gen. E.O.C. Ord essentially for using his newspaper to incite white Mississippians against Reconstruction.

In the end, however, Reconstruction would fail to weave the freedmen into the fabric of Southern society, not because of the *Milligan* decision, but because Congress, although it had guaranteed freedmen suffrage in the Fifteenth Amendment, turned its back on the poor by allowing poll taxes and literacy tests to determine eligibility and by failing to provide adequate protection for the voting rights of all citizens who could otherwise pass those tests but who faced organized violence and intimidation to keep them from the polls. By 1876, the "Black Republican" abolitionists had been eclipsed in the party, and the deal that brought Republican Rutherford B. Hayes the disputed presidency that year would also bring an official end to Reconstruction. Thus enabled, the white ex-Confederate oligarchy returned to power in the South. For a discussion of pre- and post–Reconstruction voting rights and *Ex parte McCardle*, see William H. Rehnquist, *Centennial Crisis: The Disputed Election of 1876* (New York: Alfred A. Knopf, 2004), pp. 81, 105–7, 127–28; Stanley I. Kutler, "*Ex Parte McCardle*: Judicial Impotency? The Supreme Court and Reconstruction Reconsidered," *American Historical Review* 72 (April, 1967), pp. 835–51. For newspaper accounts of the *McCardle* case, see for example, McCardle's newspaper, the *Vicksburg Times*, 24, 25, 28, 29 January 1868; 4, 12, 16 February 1868; and 3 January 1869; the *New Orleans Daily Picayune*, 13 April 1869, and the *New York Times*, 27 March 1869.

15. Marouf Hasian Jr. also makes this observation in his book, *In the Name of Necessity: Military Tribunals and the Loss of American Civil Liberties* (Tuscaloosa: University of Alabama Press, 2005), p. 9.

Although former Chief Justice William Rehnquist noted that the *Milligan* decision was "justly celebrated for its rejection of the government's position that the Bill of Rights has no application in wartime," subsequent administrations, aided by compliant and sometimes ideologically driven congresses and courts, would rely on the "plea of necessity" to circumvent the *Milligan* ruling on the Bill of Rights and due process.

See, for example, the ideologically driven Sedition and Espionage Acts of 1917 and 1918, respectively, in which the First Amendment rights of political dissenters were abrogated in civil courts in very much the same way that rights of Vallandigham, Milligan, and others were illegally abrogated by military commissions during the Civil War on the "plea of necessity." Following the war, this ignited peacetime domestic labor and political strife that came to be known as "the Red Scare." *In Schenck v. United States*, 249 U.S. 47 (1919); *Frohwerk v. United States*, 249 U.S. 204 (1919); and *Debs v. United States*, 249 U.S. 211 (1919), all were found guilty for expressing antiwar opinions that, if the Supreme Court had followed the *Milligan* ruling, would have been protected by the First Amendment of the Bill of Rights. For a more in-depth discussion, see David M. Kennedy, *Over Here: The First World War and American Society* (New York: Oxford University Press, 1980), pp. 84–86; also see Rehnquist, *All the Laws But One*, pp. 174, 179.

And, of course, there was President Roosevelt's Executive Order 9066 during World War II that ordered the forced relocation of peaceful, law-abiding Japanese-American citizens to military-run concentration camps, which Constitutional scholar Edward S. Corwin called "the most drastic invasion of the rights of citizens of the United States that had thus far occurred in the history of our nation." Quoted in Paul L. Murphy, *The Constitution in Crisis Times: 1918–1969* (New York: Harper & Row, 1972), p. 91; Rehnquist, *All the Laws But One*, pp. 188–211, 223; see, for example, *Hirabayashi v. United States*, 320 U.S. 81 (1943) and *Korematsu v. Untied States*, 323 U.S. 214 (1944).

Regarding the *Milligan* decision and subsequent military commission trials, the World War II case *Ex Parte Quirin* at least reinforced the supremacy of the civil justice system over the military established in *Milligan*. In June 1942, eight specially trained German saboteurs, one of whom was a United States citizen, entered the United States — four at Amagansett Beach, Long Island, New York, and four at Ponte Vedra Beach, Florida. The eight would-be saboteurs were soon arrested in New York and Chicago, and President Roosevelt appointed a military commission to try them. Found guilty and sentenced to death, they appealed to the Supreme Court for jurisdictional review. Citing the *Milligan* decision, they argued that that jurisdiction belonged in the civil courts. The Court ruled against them, however, stating that because they were agents of the enemy military and not civilians, as required in *Milligan*, the military had jurisdiction and they, to their chagrin, were quickly executed. Their appeal, however, helped to bolster the Court's ruling in *Milligan* that military commissions in wartime, where the civil courts were open and operating, remained subject to review by the Supreme Court — although in this case, the review was unfavorable to the appellants. *Ex parte Quirin*, 317 U.S. 1 (1942); Murphy, *The Constitution in Crisis Times*, p. 243; Rehnquist, *All the Laws But One*, pp. 136–37; Hasian Jr., *In the Name of Necessity*, pp. 187–249

For the House Un-American Activities Committee assault on the Bill of Rights prior to and following World War II and the constitutionality of President George W. Bush's apparently perpetual war on terror, see Gore Vidal, *Imperial America: Reflections on the United States of Amnesia* (New York: Nation Books, 2004), p. 15; Stefan Kanfer, *A Journal of the Plague Years: A Devastating Chronicle of the Era of the Blacklist* (New York: Atheneum, 1973), passim; Eric Bentley, *Thirty Years of Treason: Excerpts from Hearing before the House Committee on Un-American Activities, 1938–1968* (New York: The Viking Press, 1971), passim.

16. Klement, *Dark Lanterns*, p. 228, citing the 19 February 1867 *Indianapolis Daily Journal*. Although Humphreys lost a close race for a state senate seat to a Republican in 1868, he retained enough of his popularity as a politician and farmer in southern Indiana to defeat a Republican for a seat in the state senate 1874. He resigned his seat after one term and was elected to the 44th Congress (5 December 1876 to 3 March 1878). Again resigning after one term, he was elected to the state senate in 1878 and served one term before retiring to his farm. Persuaded to come out of retirement at age seventy-four, he was again elected to the state senate in 1896. He died on 24 June 1904. Klement, *Dark Lanterns*, pp. 229–30; *Biography of Congress*, p. 1095.

17. Klement also noted that in 1866, Congress, effectively endorsing the "doctrine of necessity," had already amended the Indemnity Act of 1863 to prohibit those seeking damages for arbitrary arrests and wrongful imprisonment from suing state or federal officials in state courts. *Dark Lanterns*, p. 229 (quotes), citing the *Indiana House Journal*, 1867, II: 684, 834; and William H.H. Terrell, *Report of the Adjutant General of Indiana*, 8 vols. (Indianapolis: Indiana State Government, 1869), I, Appendix, pp. 267–68.

18. Two hundred thousand dollars' damages for false imprisonment and sentence of death and mistreatment resulting in ill health and injury to his good name; $50,000 libel for Pitman's book *Indiana Treason Trials*; $100,000 libel for the copy of Pitman's book *Trial for Treason at Indianapolis*; and $500,000 essentially for the continual slander of his good name by the defendants. State of Indiana. Huntington County Court of Common Pleas, May Term 1868. *Lambdin P. Milligan vs. James R. Slack, et al.* (Milligan v. Slack), courtesy of the Lilly Library, Indiana University, Bloomington, Indiana, pp. 2 (quote), 30–32, 36; Klaus, ed., *The Milligan Case*, p. 45; Klement, *Dark Lanterns*, p. 236, citing G.R. Tredway, *Democratic Opposition to the Lincoln Administration in Indiana* (Indianapolis: Indiana Historical Bureau, 1973); also see Klaus, ed., *The Milligan Case*, Appendix A, pp. 251–458 for an accurate transcription of the Indianapolis trial, including Zumro's testimony on being recruited by Slack to spy on Milligan and others, p. 328; also in Pitman, *Treason Trials at Indianapolis*, p. 121.

19. Those listed who were dropped from the suit with Slack were: William Bickle, Joseph Holt, Oliver P. Morton, Thomas J. Lucas, Henry L. Burnett, Ambrose A. Stevens, Ausel D. Wass, Albert Heath, Benjamin Pitman, Samuel Place, James S. Frazier, Robert Gregory, James A. Dean, William Arnold, and William R. Holloway. *Milligan v. Slack*, p. 1; *Milligan v. Hovey*, Circuit Court D. Indiana, 3 Biss. 13; Fed. Cas. 9605.

20 Milligan v. Slack, p. 1; *History of Huntington County*, pp. 360, 453; "L.P. Milligan's Suit for Damages," *New York Times*, 23 March 1868, from the *Indianapolis Journal*, 19 March 1868.

21. Klaus, ed., *The Milligan Case*, p. 45

22. *Ibid.*, p. 46, quoting Thomas R. Marshall (1854–1925), Indiana lawyer, friend of Milligan, Democratic governor of Indiana (1909–1913), and vice-president of the United States under Woodrow Wilson (1913–1921). *Biographical Directory of Congress*, p. 1266; Klement, *Dark Lanterns*, p. 232, citing the 31 May 1871 *Indianapolis Daily Journal*, and quoting the 22 December 1899 *Huntington Herald*.

23. Crenshaw, "Knights of the Golden Circle," p. 47, citing Harvey Wickes Felter, *History of the Eclectic Medical Institute, Cincinnati, 1845–1900* (Cincinnati: n.p., 1902), p. 111; Klement, *Dark Lanterns*, p. 219.

24. *Ibid.*, p. 222, citing Wright's account in Marshall, *American Bastille*, p. 231.

25. Klement, *Dark Lanterns*, pp. 233–34.

26. *Biographical Directory of Congress*, p. 1708.

27. E. Polk Johnson, *A History of Kentucky and Kentuckians* (Chicago and New York: The Lewis Publishing Company, 1912), 3: 1445; Horan, *Confederate Agent*, p. 272; Headley, *Confederate Operations*, p. 460.

28. Basler, ed., *Collected Works of Abraham Lincoln*, vol. 8, p. 123; Charles Kerr, ed., *History of Kentucky*, 5 vols. (Chicago: The American Historical Society, 1922), vol. 3, pp. 24–25; Horan, *Confederate Agent*, p. 270; Headley, *Confederate Operations*, p. 462.

29 ."The Chicago Conspiracy," *Atlantic Monthly*, July 1865, pp. 108–21; Thomas H. Hines, "The Northwestern Conspiracy," *Southern Bivouac*, June 1886 to May 1867, pp. 506–510. See Klement, *Dark Lanterns*, pp. 154n4, 194n20, 239n74, and 252 for a well-documented discussion of this issue.

30. Starr notes that General Order No. 46, which,

following *Milligan*, released political prisoners from military custody who had served more than six months, specifically excluded the prisoners remaining on Dry Tortugas. Judge Advocate Holt and Secretary of War Stanton were also instrumental in keeping President Johnson, by then beleaguered with impeachment proceedings, from releasing Grenfell to the British consul. Starr, *Colonel Grenfell's Wars*, p. 290; U.S. Congress, House, *Grenfel*, pp. 645–56.

31. Starr, *Colonel Grenfell's Wars*, pp. 324–26; Klement, *Dark Lanterns*, pp. 233–34.

32. *Biography of Congress*, p. 1648; *History of Huntington County*, p. 542 (quote).

33. 1860 U.S. Census, Indianapolis, Indiana, 1870 and 1880 U.S. Census for Topeka, Ancestry.com;

34. Courtesy of Maureen Frei.

35. *Biographical Directory of Congress*, p. 1531.

36. Dixon Wecter, *When Johnny Comes Marching Home* (Cambridge, MA: Houghton Mifflin Company, 1944), pp. 172, 182; Todd DePastino, *Citizen Hobo: How a Century of Homelessness Shaped America* (Chicago: University of Chicago Press, 2003), p. 45, 51; Kenneth Kusmer, *Down and Out on the Road* (Oxford: Oxford University Press, 2002), 59, 124.

37. After the war, the Rev. John James McCook, a former 2nd Lieutenant in the Union Army, studied at Trinity College, Connecticut, became a deacon in the Episcopal Church, a social reformer, and later a professor at Trinity College, where he began his tramp studies. Tim Cresswell, *The Tramp in America* (London, UK: Reaktion Books, 2001), pp. 182, 191.

38. DePastino, *Citizen Hobo*, pp. 51, 55 (photo of Roving Bill taken at a photographic studio in Bennington, Vermont, 8 July 1893), 56–58; Cresswell, *Tramp in America*, pp. 192, 194 (1893 photo of Roving Bill), 195 (photo of Connecticut Fatty); Kusmer, *Down and Out on the Road*, pp. 141–43.

39. *Ibid.*, p. 1377.

40. County History Preservation Society, http://www.countyhistory.com/ doc.cass/517.htm; Roster of the 47th Indiana Volunteer Infantry.

41. Courtesy of Bob Cooper.

42. Samuel Hardin, *Those I Have Met, or Boys in Blue* (Anderson, IN, 1888). Courtesy of Mark Davis.

43. Courtesy of James Manning.

44. Eli E. Rose Pension and Military Records, National Archives and Records Administration, Washington, D.C.; Harvey Keagy Rose Papers; Franklin Keagy, *A History of the Kagy Relationship in America from 1715 to 1900* (Harrisburg, PA: Harrisburg Publishing Company, 1899; reprint ed., Salem, MA: Higginson Book Company, n.d.), pp. 66–67; Zacharia and Rhoda Penn Jenkins, Ancestry.com., courtesy of Joe Means. Walter Burroughs Rose was 31 years old in 1863 when he enlisted as a private in the 130th Indiana Volunteer Infantry. He died on 29 June 1864 in Knoxville, Tennessee, of unreported causes and is buried in the Chattanooga National Cemetery, Section E, Site 11520. Ancestry.com., US Veterans' Gravesites ca. 1775–2006. Of Eli's three other brothers, Jesse, then 23 years old, enlisted as a private in the 19th Ohio Volunteer Infantry on 9 October, 1861, transferring to the 5th Veterans' Reserve Corps (the old Invalid Corps) in March 1864; 36-year-old John W. enlisted as a private in the 10th Ohio Cavalry on 20 December 1863 and mustered out on 15 May 1865 at Nashville, Tennessee; and 18-year-old William P. enlisted as a private in the 10th Ohio Cavalry on 28 December 1863 and mustered out on 14 June 1864 at Louisville, Kentucky. Ancestry.com., Headstones Provided for Deceased Union Civil War Veterans.

45. Courtesy of Keith Hudson.

46. Courtesy of Kevin Lindsey.

47. Courtesy of Dewey Jones.

48. Daniel Hilton Papers (courtesy of Commander Roger L. Johnson, U.S. Navy, retired); Death Records, Indiana Works Progress Authority, Book H-14, p. 85, Ancestry.com.

49. Henry S. Adams Papers (courtesy of Dan Nelson).

Appendix A

1. *Indianapolis Daily Journal*, 4 June 1863.

2. McLaughlin/Jordan Family Papers, Indiana Historical Society, Collection # SC 1030; Thornton Family Notebook, Indiana Historical Society, Collection # BV 1749. Courtesy of Maureen Frei.

3. *Ibid.*, Collection SC 1030. Courtesy of Maureen Frei.

4. Indiana Historical Society, Digital Image Collection.

5. *Ibid.*

6. *Ibid.*, McLaughlin/Jordan Family Papers, Indiana Historical Society, Collection SC 1030. John died 15 April 1890 in Topeka, Kansas. Henry died "before 1889 in the south." Thornton Family Notebook, Indiana Historical Society, Collection # BV 1749. Anna Erving died on 14 December 1919 according to her obituary in the *Newburgh (New York) Daily News*, 15 December 1919. Letter and genealogical information courtesy of Maureen Frei.

Appendix B

1. The introductory paragraph is paraphrased from a typewritten paragraph by an unknown author at the bottom of the page on which the printed lyrics of Zent's song appear: "This is a copy of a regimental song written by H.W. Zent of Huntington County while his regiment was stationed at Memphis, Tenn. This valuable historical paper gives us the names and ranks of all the staff officers and company officers except for lts. and even includes the regimental sutlers who were generally unloved by the common soldier. The sergent [*sic*], in a unique moment, even listed the companys [*sic*] by the way they stood in line of battle, left to right, and not alphabetically." Courtesy of James C. Taylor, Huntington County History Society, Inc., Huntington, IN.

Appendix C

1. Adjutant General's Report, I (Appendix): 161; Philip Katcher, *Flags of the American Civil War*, 3 vols. (London: Osprey, 1993), II: 7.

2. *Ibid.*

3. Donna M. Schmink, Collections Manager, Indiana War Memorials Commission.

4. Adjutant General's Report, I (Appendix): 162;

"Fight for the Colors: The Ohio Battle Flag Collection," Ohio Historical Society Exhibits, http://ohsweb.ohiohistory.org/ exhibits.

5. David I. McCormick, comp., *Indiana Battle Flags and Record of Indiana Organization in the Mexican, Civil and Spanish Wars* (Indianapolis: Battle Flag Commission, 1929), pp. 298–99.

6. Adjutant General's Report, I (Appendix), p. 162.

7. *Ibid.*, p. 161.

Appendix D

1. Record Group 153, Records of the Office of the Judge Advocate General's Office, Court-Martial Case Files, 1809–1894, File LL2038, Box 668, National Archives and Records Administration, Washington, D.C., cited hereafter as File LL, Box 2038, NARA.

2. O.R., Ser. I, Vol. XLIX, pt. 1, p. 867.

3. File LL2038, Box 66, NARA.

4. File KK275, Box 355.

5. File KK285, Box 356.

6. File LL373, Box 456

7. Reportedly wounded severely in the thigh on the Red River Expedition. *Indianapolis Daily Journal*, 22 June 1864.

8. *Ibid.*, 26 June 1863.

9. File LL961, Box 530, NARA.

10. Reportedly died of wounds received on the Red River Expedition. *Indianapolis Daily Journal*, 22 June 1864

11. *Ibid.*, 26 June 1863; James R. Slack to Ann P. Slack, 15 June 1863.

12. Reportedly deserted on the Red River Expedition. *Indianapolis Daily Journal*, 22 June 1864.

13. James R. Slack to Ann P. Slack, 13 July 1863.

14. No court-martial records found.

15. *Ibid.*

16. James R. Slack to Ann P. Slack, 13 July 1863.

17. Reportedly wounded in the shoulder on the Red River Expedition. *Indianapolis Daily Journal*, 22 June 1864.

18. Wounded accidentally by gunshot to right shoulder while at mouth of White River, Arkansas, September or October 1864 by Pvt. Harvey Oats; 27 March 1865, wounded by musket ball to left knee at Spanish Fort, Alabama; left leg amputated above knee at 1st Division (13th Corps) Hospital; transferred to Sedgewick Hospital, Greenville, Louisiana, 1 Apr 1865; mustered out 26 Jul 1865. Eli E. Rose Pension Records, NARA; O.R., Ser. I, Vol. XLVIII, pt. 2, p. 148.

19. Reportedly died of disease on the Red River Expedition. *Indianapolis Daily Journal*, 22 June 1864.

20. File NN513, Box 1569, NARA.

21. File NN597, Box 1578.

22. *Ibid.*

23. *Indianapolis Daily Journal*, 26 June 1863.

24. File LL283, Box 444.

25. File NN597, Box 1578.

26. *Indianapolis Daily Gazette*, 9 November 1863.

27. Reportedly died at Helena, Arkansas, 11 March 1863 after receiving his discharge. James R. Slack to Ann P. Slack, 26 March 1863; *Huntington Democrat*, 16 April 1863.

Bibliography

Official Documents and Records

Adjutant General's Office. *Report of the Adjutant General of the State of Indiana.* 8 vols. Indianapolis: Samuel M. Douglass, State Printer, 1866.

Library of Congress, Manuscript Division. *The Abraham Lincoln Papers*, Ser. 1, General Correspondence, 1833–1916, 20 to 25 February 1864, No. 39, Louisiana Election Returns, 22 February 1864, certified by S. Wrotnowski; No. 65, Cuthbert Bullitt to Abraham Lincoln, 23 February 1864, online.

Mexico; Comision pesquisidora de la frontera del norte. *Reports of the Committee of Investigation sent in 1873 by the Mexican Government to the Frontier of Texas.* Translated from the official edition made in Mexico. New York: Baker and Godwin, 1875.

U.S. Congress. *Biographical Directory of the American Congress, 1774–1961.* Washington, D.C.: U.S. Government Printing Office, 1961.

U.S. Congress. House. "Action of the War Department for Removal of Obstructions in the Mouth of Mississippi River," H. exdoc. 5, 38th Cong., 2nd Sess., 5 December 1860.

———. *Case of John C. Watrous.* H. rp. 2, 36th Cong., 2nd Sess., 20 December 1860.

———. *Commodore Charles Wilkes's Court-Martial*, H. exdoc. 102, 38th Cong., June 29, 1864.

———. *Difficulties on the Southwestern Frontier. Message from the President of the United States James Buchanan*, H. exdoc. 52, 36th Cong., 1st Sess., March 29, 1860.

———. *Impeachment of John C. Watrous, United States District Judge of the District of Texas.* H. rp. 175, Ser. 913, 34th Cong., 3rd Sess., 2 February 1857.

———. *Message of the President of the United States [Andrew Johnson] of January 29, 1866, Relating to the Present Condition of Mexico.* 2 vols. H. exdoc. 73, 39th Cong., 2nd Sess., March 20, 1866.

———. *Message of the President on Case of George St. Leger Grenfel, Imprisoned at Dry Tortugas.* H. exdoc. 50, 39th Cong., 2nd Sess., Ser. 1290, 1867.

———. *Message of the President [Andrew Johnson] on Mexican Affairs, 1865–66*, H. exdoc. 76, 39th Cong., 2nd Sess., 29 January 1867.

———. *Suspension of Habeas Corpus*, H. exdoc. 6, 37th Cong., 1st Sess., 1861.

———. *Troubles on Texas Frontier. Letter from the Secretary of War John B. Floyd*, H. exdoc. 81, 36th Cong., 1st Sess., May 3, 1860.

U.S. Congress. Joint Committee on Printing. *Biographical Directory of the American Congress 1774–1961.* Washington, D.C.: Government Printing Office, 1961.

———. Joint Committee on the Conduct of the War, vol. 1, *The Fort Pillow Massacre.* 38th Cong. 1st Sess., 5 May 1864.

———. Joint Committee on the Conduct of the War, vol. 2, pt. 1, *The Red River Expedition.* 38th Cong., 2nd Sess., 20 February 1865.

U.S. Congress. Senate. *Message of the President to the Two Houses of Congress*, 37th Congress, 1st Sess., S. exdoc. 1, 5 July 1861.

———. *Testimony Taken by the Joint Select Committee to Inquire into the Condition of Affairs in the late Insurrectionary States—Florida and Misc.: The Ku-Klux Conspiracy.* S. rp. 41, Vol. XIII, 42nd Cong. 2nd Sess., 24 June 1871.

U.S. National Archives & Records Administration. Washington, D.C., Records of the Judge Advocate General's Office (Army), entry 15, Court-Martial Case Files, 1809–1894.

U.S. War Department. *The War of the Rebellion: A Compilation of the Official Records of the Union and Confederate Armies.* 4 series, 70 volumes, 128 parts; Washington, D.C.: Government Printing Office, 1880–1901.

———. *Official Records of the Union and Confederate Navies in the War of the Rebellion.* 2 series, 30 volumes, Washington, D.C.: Government Printing Office, 1894–1927.

Legal Citations

Ex parte John Merryman, 17 F. cas. 144 (1861).
Ex parte Milligan, 71 U.S. (4 Wall.) 2 (1866).
Ex parte Vallandigham, 68 U.S. (1 Wall.) 243 (1863).
Milligan v. Slack, State of Indiana, Huntington County Court of Common Pleas, May Term, 1865; *Lambdin P. Milligan v. James R. Slack, et. al.* Courtesy of the Lilly Library, Indiana University, Bloomington, Indiana.
Milligan v. Hovey, Case No. 9,605, Circuit Court, D. Indiana, 17 F.Cas. 380; 1871 U.S. App. LEXIS 1740; 3 Biss. 13; 14 Int. Rev. Rec. 20; 3 Chi. Leg. News 321; 4 Am. Law T. Rep. U.S. Cts. 136.

Maps

Cowles, Calvin C. comp. *The Official Military Atlas of the Civil War*. New York: Gramercy Books, 1983.

Newspapers

American Tribune (Indianapolis)
Bucks County (Pennsylvania) Intelligencer
Chicago Tribune
Columbia (South Carolina) Democrat and Planter
Daily Mississippian (Jackson)
Daily Telegraph (Houston)
Daily True Delta (New Orleans)
Huntington (Indiana) Democrat
Indianapolis Daily Gazette
Indianapolis Daily Journal
Indianapolis State Sentinel
Liverpool (England) Post
London (England) Spectator
Mattoon (Illinois) Gazette
Memphis Daily Appeal
Memphis Evening Argus
Memphis Union Appeal
Milledgeville (Georgia) Recorder
Milwaukee Sentinel
Natchez Daily Courier
New Orleans Era
New Orleans Picayune
New York Daily Tribune
New York Herald
New York Times
Savannah (Georgia) News
Shreveport Gazette
Topeka (Kansas) Weekly Leader
Vicksburg Evening Post
Vicksburg Whig

Letters and Diaries

Daniel Hilton Papers, courtesy of Commander Roger L. Johnson, U.S. Navy, retired.
Harvey Keagy Rose Papers, privately held.
Henry S. Adams Papers, courtesy of Dan Nelson.
Oxley, Corporal James Pryor. "A History of Company H. 24th Iowa Volunteer Infantry." Unpublished diary, n.d. http://home.fuse.net/oxley/CivilWarDiary3.htm.
Shaw, Milton W. to Alf Giague, 10 March 1863. Collection No. M59. McCain Library, University of Southern Mississippi, Hattiesburg, MS.
Slack, James R. Collection of Letters, L145. Indiana State Library, Indianapolis, IN.
Slack, James R. to J.S. Keith, 1 March 1863. Reprinted in the *Bucks County (PA) Intelligencer*, 31 March 1863.
William B. Johnston Papers, Diary and Letters of Private William B. Johnston, Co. E., 3rd Battalion Mississippi Infantry, privately held.
Woods, T.J., Letter, n.d., reprinted in N.N. Hill, comp., *History of Knox County, Ohio*. Mt. Vernon, Ohio: A.A. Graham & Co., Publishers, 1881, pp. 322–24.

First-Person Accounts

Adams, Charles Francis. *A Cycle of Adams Letters: 1861–1865*, ed. by W.C. Ford, 2 vols. Boston: Houghton-Mifflin, 1920.
Alderman, Clifford L. *Retreat to Victory: The Life of Nathanael Greene*. Philadelphia: Chilton Book Company, 1967.
Anderson, Ephraim McDowell. *Memoirs: Historical and Personal, Including the Campaigns of the First Missouri Confederate Brigade*. St. Louis: Times Printing Co., 1868; reprint 2nd ed., with Notes and Forward by Edwin C. Bearss, Dayton, OH: The Press of Morningside Bookshop, 1972.
Andrews, C.C. Bvt. Maj. Gen. *History of the Campaign Against Mobile: Including the Co-operative Operations of Gen. Wilson's Cavalry in Alabama*, 2nd ed. New York: D. Van Nostrand Company, 1889.
Arlington, Billy. "Minstrel Reminiscences," ca. 1903. *Traveling Culture: Circuit Chautauqua in the Twentieth Century*. Redpath Chautauqua Collection. University of Iowa Libraries, Iowa City, Iowa. http://sdrcdata.lib.uiowa.edu/libs-drc/details.jsp?id= arlington/1.
Barnes, Lt. Com. J.S. *Submarine Warfare, Offensive and Defensive, Including a Discussion of the Offensive Torpedo System, its Effects Upon Iron-Clad Ship Systems, and Influence Upon Future Naval Wars*. New York: D. Van Nostrand, Publishers, 1869.
Barr, Alwyn. "The Battle of Bayou Bourbeau, November 3, 1863: Colonel Oran M. Roberts' Report." *Louisiana History* 6 (Winter 1965): 83–91.

Basler, Roy P., ed. *The Collected Works of Abraham Lincoln*. 10 vols. New Brunswick, NJ: Rutgers University Press, 1953–55.

Bert, Henry Lawson. "Letters of a Drummer Boy." Don Russell, ed. *Indiana Magazine of History* 34, no. 3 (September 1938): 324–39.

Bevier, Robert S. *The History of the First and Second Missouri Confederate Brigades 1861–1865*. St. Louis: Bryan, Brand & Company, 1879.

Bir, Louis. "Reminiscence of My Life in the Army." George P. Clark, ed. *Indiana Magazine of History* 101, no. 1 (March 2005): 17–57.

Bissel, Josiah W. "Sawing Out a Channel above Island Number Ten." In *Battles and Leaders of the Civil War*, I: 460–61. Edited by Richard U. Johnson and Clarence C. Buel. Edison, NJ: Castle Books, 1995.

Bringhurst, Thomas H., and Frank Swigart. *History of the Forty-sixth Regiment Indiana Volunteer Infantry: September 1861–September 1865*. Logansport, IN: The Press of Wilson, Humphreys & Co., 1888.

Britton, Wiley. "Resume of Military Operations in Missouri and Arkansas, 1864–65." In *Battles and Leaders of the Civil War*, IV: 374–77. Edited by Richard U. Johnson and Clarence C. Buel. Edison, NJ: Castle Books, 1995.

Brownlow, William G. *Secessionists and Other Scoundrels: Selections from Parson Brownlow's Book*. Edited by Stephen V. Ash. Baton Rouge: Louisiana State University Press, 1999.

Buck, Irving A. *Cleburne and his Command*. Jackson, TN: McCowat-Mercer Press, Inc., 1957; reprint ed., Wilmington, NC: Broadfoot Publishing Company, 1995.

Buell, Don Carlos. "East Tennessee and the Campaign of Perryville." In *Battles and Leaders of the Civil War*, III: 31–51. Edited by Richard U. Johnson and Clarence C. Buel. Edison, NJ: Castle Books, 1995.

Butler, Benjamin F. *The Autobiography and Personal Reminiscences of Major-General Benj. F. Butler: Butler's Book*. Boston: A.M. Thayer & Co., 1892.

Byers, Samuel H.M. "Sherman's Attack at the Tunnel." In *Battles and Leaders of the Civil War*, III: 712–13. Edited by Richard U. Johnson and Clarence C. Buel. Edison, NJ: Castle Books, 1995.

———. *With Fire and Sword*. New York: Neale Publishing Company, 1911.

Cadwallader, Sylvanus. *Three Years With Grant, As Recalled by War Correspondent Sylvanus Cadwallader*. Edited by Benjamin P. Thomas. New York: Knopf, 1955.

Campbell, John Quincy Adams. *The Union Must Stand: The Civil War Diary of John Quincy Adams Campbell*. Edited by Mark Grimsley and Todd D. Miller. Knoxville: The University of Tennessee Press, 2000.

Cannon, J.P. *Bloody Banners and Barefoot Boys: A History of the 27th Regiment Alabama Infantry CSA: The Civil War Memoirs and Diary Entries of J.P. Cannon, M.D.* Edited by Noel Crowson and John V. Brogden. Shippensburg, PA: Burd Street Press, 1997.

Chambers, William Pitt. *Blood and Sacrifice: The Civil War Journal of a Confederate Soldier*. Edited by Richard A. Baumgartner. Huntington, WV: Blue Acorn Press, 1994.

———. "A History of the 46th Mississippi Regiment." Jackson, MS, 22 September 1904. (Mimeographed.)

Clark, Charles T. *Opdycke Tigers 125th O.V.I.: A History of the Regiment and of the Campaigns and Battles of the Army of the Cumberland*. Columbus, OH: Spahr & Glenn, 1989; reprint ed., Salem, MA: Higginson Book Company, 1998.

Cox, Benjamin R. "Mobile in the War Between the States," *Confederate Veteran* 24 (May 1916): 209–13.

Craft, William, and Ellen Craft. *Running a Thousand Miles for Freedom: The Escape of William and Ellen Craft from Slavery*. London: W. Tweedle, 1860; reprint ed., Athens: University of Georgia Press, 1999.

Dana, Charles Anderson. *Recollections of the Civil War: With the Leaders at Washington and in the Field in the Sixties*. New York: Appleton and Company, 1902 (c. 1898). (Microform.)

Davis, Jefferson. *The Rise and Fall of the Confederate Government*, 2 vols. Nashville: W.M. Coats, 1881.

Davis, Reuben. *Recollection of Mississippi and Mississippians*, revised ed. Oxford: University and College Press of Mississippi, 1972.

Documenting the American South. "A Thrilling Narrative from the Lips of the Sufferers of the late Detroit Riot, March 6, 1863, with the Hair Breadth Escapes of the Men, Women and Children, and Destruction of Colored Men's Property, not less than $15,000." Chapel Hill: University of North Carolina Academic Affairs Library, 2001. Electronic Edition: http://docsouth.unc.edu/neh/detroit.html.

Dungan, J. Irving. *History of the Nineteenth Iowa Infantry*. Davenport, IA: Publishing House of Luse & Griggs, 1865. Transcribed for the Internet by Norma Jennings. http://iagenweb.or/civilwar/refgiment/infantry/19th/hist19thxi_.htm.

Eads, Captain James B. "Recollections of Foote and the Gun-Boats." In *Battles and Leaders of the Civil War*, I: 338–346. Edited by Richard U. Johnson and Clarence C. Buel. Edison, NJ: Castle Books, 1995.

Edwards, John N. *Shelby and His Men*. Cincinnati: Miami Printing & Publishing Co., 1867.

_____. *Shelby's Expedition to Mexico: An Unwritten Leaf of the War*. Kansas City, MO: Kansas City Times Steam Book and Job Printing House, 1872; reprint ed., Fayetteville: University of Arkansas Press, 2002.

Elder, Donald C., III, ed. *A Damned Iowa Greyhound: The Civil War Letters of William Henry Harrison Clayton*. Iowa City, IA: University of Iowa Press, 1998.

Ellet, General Alfred W. "Ellet and His Steam-Rams at Memphis." In *Battles and Leaders of the Civil War*, I: 453–459. Edited by Richard U. Johnson and Clarence C. Buel. Edison, NJ: Castle Books, 1995.

Evans, Clement A., ed. *Confederate Military History*. 12 vols. Vol. 8: *Tennessee*, by James D. Porter. Vol. 9: *Missouri*, by Col. John C. Moore. New York: Thomas Yoseloff, 1962.

Felter, Harvey Wickes. *History of the Eclectic Medical Institute, Cincinatti, 1845–1900*. Cincinnati: n.p., 1902.

Ford, John Salmon. *Rip Ford's Texas*. Ed. with commentary by Stephen B. Oates. Austin: University of Texas Press, 1963.

Freeman, Edwin, M.D. "Biographical Sketch of the Faculty of the Eclectic Medical Institute, 1852–1856." *The Eclectic Medical Journal* 58 (January–December 1898): 156.

Freidel, Frank, ed. *Union Pamphlets of the Civil War, 1861–1865*. 2 vols. Cambridge, MA: The Belknap Press of Harvard University Press, 1967.

Grant, Ulysses S. *The Civil War Memoirs of Ulysses S. Grant*. Edited by Brian Thomsen. New York: A Tom Doherty Associates Book, 2002; abridged ed. of *Personal Memoirs of Ulysses S. Grant*. 2 vols. New York: Charles L. Webster & Co., 1885.

_____. "The Vicksburg Campaign." In *Battles and Leaders of the Civil War*, III: 493–539. Edited by Richard U. Johnson and Clarence C. Buel. Edison, NJ: Castle Books, 1995.

Halstead, Murat. "Some Reminiscences of Mr. Villard." *American Review* of *Reviews* 23 (January 1901): 63.

Hamilton, Maj. Gen. Schuyler. "Comment [on Col. J.W. Bissel] by General Schuyler Hamilton, Major-General, U.S.V." In *Battles and Leaders of the Civil War*, I: 462. Edited by Richard U. Johnson and Clarence C. Buel. Edison, NJ: Castle Books, 1995.

Harper, Annie. *Annie Harper's Journal: A Southern Mother's Legacy*. Denton, TX: Flower Mound Writing Company, 1983; reprint ed., Hattiesburg, MS: University of Southern Mississippi Publication and Printing Services, 1996.

Hay, John. *Lincoln and the Civil War in the Diaries and Letters of John Hay*. New York: Dodd, Mead and Company, 1939; reprint ed., Westport, CN: Negro Universities Press, 1972.

Hazen, Gen. William B. *A Narrative of Military Service*. Boston: Ticknor & Co., 1885.

Headley, John W. *Confederate Operations in Canada and New York*. New York: The Neale Publishing Company, 1906.

Hopkins, Owen Johnston. *Under the Flag of the Nation: Diaries and Letters of a Yankee Volunteer in the Civil War* [Pvt. Owen Johnston Hopkins, 42nd Ohio V.I.]. Edited by Otto F. Bond. Columbus, OH: Ohio State University Press for the Ohio Historical Society, 1961.

Hovey, Alvin P. "A War Reminiscence, General Alvin P. Hovey Relates an Experience with Grant at Vicksburg." *New York Times*, 13 March 1885. Originally published in the *Indianapolis Journal*, 8 March 1885.

Irwin, Richard B. "The Capture of Port Hudson." In *Battles and Leaders of the Civil War*, III: 586–97. Edited by Robert U. Johnson and Clarence C. Buel. Edison, NJ: Castle Books, 1995.

_____. "Land Operations Against Mobile." In *Battles and Leaders of the Civil War*, IV: 410–11. Edited by Robert U. Johnson and Clarence C. Buel. Edison, NJ: Castle Books, 1995.

_____. "The Red River Campaign." In *Battles and Leaders of the Civil War*, IV: 345–68. Edited by Robert U. Johnson and Clarence C. Buel. Edison, NJ: Castle Books, 1995.

Johnson, E. Polk. *A History of Kentucky and Kentuckians*. Chicago and New York: The Lewis Publishing Company, 1912.

Johnson, Robert U., and Clarence C. Buel, eds. *Battles and Leaders of the Civil War*. Edison, NJ: Castle Books, 1995.

Johnston, Joseph E. "Jefferson Davis and the Mississippi Campaign." In *Battles and Leaders of the Civil War*, III: 472–82. Edited by Robert U. Johnson and Clarence C. Buel. Edison, NJ: Castle Books, 1995.

_____. *Narrative of Military Operations During the Civil War*. New York: D. Appleton and Co., 1874; unabridged reprint edition, New York: Da Capo Press, 1959.

Jones, John B. *A Rebel War Clerk's Diary, 1810–1866*. 2 vols. Philadelphia: J.B. Lippincott, 1866.

Kellogg, Capt. J.J. [John Jackson]. *War Experiences and the Story of the Vicksburg Campaign from Milliken's Bend to July 4, 1863: being an accurate and graphic account of campaign events taken from the diary of Capt. J.J. Kellogg, of Co. B, 113th Illinois volunteer Infantry*. Washington, IA: Evening Journal, c. 1913. [Microform.]

Kelly, R.M. "Holding Kentucky in the Union." In *Battles and Leaders of the Civil War*, I: 378–79. Edited by Robert U. Johnson and Clarence C. Buel. Edison, NJ: Castle Books, 1995.

Kinney, John Coddington, "Farragut at Mobile Bay." In *Battles and Leaders of the Civil War*, IV: 379–400. Edited by Robert U. Johnson and Clarence C. Buel. Edison, NJ: Castle Books, 1995.

Klaus, Samuel, ed. *The Milligan Case*. New York: Alfred A. Knopf, 1929; reprint ed., New York: Da Capo Press, 1970.

Lee, Stephen D. "The Campaign of Vicksburg, Mississippi in 1863 — From April 15 to and Including the Battle of Champion Hills, or Baker's Creek, May 16, 1863." *Publications of the Mississippi Historical Society*, III: 21–53.

Lockett, S.H. "The Defense of Vicksburg." In *Battles and Leaders of the Civil War*. III: 482–492. Edited by Robert U. Johnson and Clarence C. Buel. Edison, NJ: Castle Books, 1995.

Longley, Charles L. "Champion's Hill." Military Order of the Loyal Legion of the United States MOLLUS-Iowa. Des Moines: Press of P.C. Kenyon, 1893; I: 208–214.

Lossing, Benson J. *A History of the Civil War 1861–65 and the Causes that Led Up to the Great Conflict*. New York: The War Memorial Association, 1912.

McCaskill, Barbara. "William and Ellen Craft (1824–1900; 1826–1891)." *New Georgia Encyclopedia* online.

McCorkle, John. *Three Years with Quantrill: A True Story Told By His Scout, John McCorkle*. Edited by Herman Hattaway. Norman: University of Oklahoma Press, 1995.

Maury, Dabney H., Maj. Gen., C.S.A. "Defense of Spanish Fort: Some Comment by the Confederate Commander on Mr. P.D. Stephenson's Article." *Southern Historical Society Papers* 39 (1914): 130–36.

_____. *Recollections of a Virginian in the Mexican, Indian, and Civil Wars*. New York: Charles Scribner's Sons, 1894.

Memminger, Maj. R.W. "The Surrender of Vicksburg — A Defense of General Pemberton." *Southern Historical Society Papers* 39 (1914): 352–60.

Moore, Frank, ed. *The Rebellion Record: A Diary of American Events*. New York: D. Van Nostrand, 1865.

Moore, Col. John C. "Missouri." In *Confederate Military History*. Vol. 9: 20–30. Edited by Clement A Evans. New York: Thomas Yoseloff, 1962.

Morton, John Watson. *The Artillery of Nathan Bedford Forrest's Cavalry*. Nashville, TN and Dallas, TX: Publishing House of the M.E. Church, South, 1909; reprint ed., Kennesaw, GA: Continental Book Company, 1962.

Nelson, Michael, ed. *The Evolving Presidency: Addresses, Cases, Essays, Letters, Reports, Resolutions, Transcripts and Other Landmark Documents, 1787–1998*. Washington, DC: CQ Press, 1999.

Noel, Theo. *A Campaign from Santa Fe to the Mississippi: Being the History of the Old Sibley Brigade from its First Organization to the Present Time*. Shreveport, LA: Shreveport News Printing Establishment, 1865; reprint ed., Raleigh, NC: Charles R. Sanders, Jr., 1961.

Olmstead, Frederic Law. *A Journey through Texas, or, A Saddle-trip on the South-western Frontier*. New York: Dix, Edwards, 1857. (Microform.)

Opdycke, Emerson. *To Battle for God and the Right: The Civil War Letterbooks of Emerson Opdycke*. Urbana: University of Illinois Press, 2003.

Palmer, John M. *Personal Recollections of John M. Palmer: The Story of an Earnest Life*. Cincinnati: The Robert Clarke Company, 1901.

Pitman, Benn, ed. *The Treason Trials at Indianapolis Disclosing the Plans for Establishing a North-Western Conspiracy*. Cincinnati, OH: Moore, Wilstach & Baldwin, 1865.

Pope, John. *The Military Memoirs of General John Pope*. Edited by Peter Cozzens and Robert I. Giraldi. Chapel Hill, NC: University of North Carolina Press, 1998.

Porter, David Dixon. *The Naval History of the Civil War*. New York: Sherman, 1886; reprint ed., Secaucus, New Jersey: Castle Books, 1984.

Porter, James D. "Tennessee." In *Confederate Military History*. Vol. 8: 3–348. Edited by Clement A. Evans. New York: Thomas Yoseloff, 1962.

Pryce, Samuel D. *Vanishing Footprints: The Twenty-second Iowa Volunteer Infantry in the Civil War*. Edited by Jeffry C. Burden. Iowa City: Camp Pope Bookshop, 2008.

Raynor, William H. "The Civil War Experiences of an Ohio Officer at Vicksburg: Diary of Colonel William H. Raynor, 56th Ohio Infantry." Edited by Edwin C. Bearss. *Louisiana Studies* 9 (Winter 1970): 246–300.

Reinhart, Joseph R., ed. and trans. *August Willich's Gallant Dutchmen: Civil War Letters from the 32nd Indiana Infantry*. Kent, OH: Kent State University Press, 2006.

Reynolds, Pvt. A.H. "Vivid Experiences at Champion Hill, Miss." *Confederate Veteran* 18 (January 1910): 21–22.

Segrex. "Department of the Gulf. Defenses of Mobile — Statements of Deserters — Forces Garrisoning the Defenses." *New York Times*, 26 March 1865.

_____. "Operations at Spanish Fort — The Loss of Our Monitors." *New York Times*, 9 April 1865.

_____. "The Attack on Mobile." *New York Times*, 9 April 1865.

_____. "The Siege of Mobile." *New York Times*, 21 April 1865.

Selfridge, Thomas O. "The Navy in the Red River." In *Battles and Leaders of the Civil War*. IV: 362–66. Edited by Robert U. Johnson and Clarence C. Buel. Edison, NJ: Castle Books, 1995.

Sheridan, Philip Henry. *Personal Memoirs of Philip Henry Sheridan: General United States Army*. Edited by Michael V. Sheridan. 2 vols. New York: Appleton and Company, 1902.

Sherman, William T. "Grand Strategy of the Last Year of the War." In *Battles and Leaders of the Civil War*, IV: 247–59. Edited by Richard U. Johnson and Clarence C. Buel. Edison, NJ: Castle Books, 1995.

_____. *Memoirs of General William T. Sherman*. New York: The Library of America, 1990.

_____. *Sherman's Civil War: Selected Correspondence of William T. Sherman: 1860–1865*. Edited by Brooks D. Simpson and Jean V. Berlin. Chapel Hill & London: The University of North Carolina Press, 1999.

Smith, E. Kirby. "The Defense of the Red River." In *Battles and Leaders of the Civil War*. IV: 369–74. Edited by Robert U. Johnson and Clarence C. Buel. Edison, NJ: Castle Books, 1995.

Smith, Steven A. "Freedom of Expression in the Confederate States of America." In *Perspectives on Freedom of Speech*. Edited by Thomas T. Tedford, et al. Carbondale: Southern Illinois University Press, 1987.

Stephensen, Philip D., Fifth Company, Washington Artillery (Piece Four). "Defense of Spanish Fort: On Mobile Bay — Last Great Battle of the War." *Southern Historical Society Papers* 39 (1914): 118–29.

Stidger, Felix G., ed. *Treason History of the Order of the Sons of Liberty, Formerly Circle of Honor, Succeeded by Knights of the Golden Circle: The Most Treasonable Conspiracy the World Has Ever Known, 1864*. Chicago: By the Author, 1903.

The Story of American Heroism: Thrilling Narratives of Personal Adventures During the Great Civil War as Told by the Medal Winners and Roll of Honor Men. Springfield, OH: J.W. Jones, 1879.

Terrell, William H.H. *Report of the Adjutant General of Indiana*. 8 vols. Indianapolis: Indiana State Government, 1869.

Thompson, Augustine. "History of Donaldsonville." 1 January 1896 to General Seldon Connor, Adj. Gen. State of Maine, Maine State Archives. www.maine.gov/sos/ archives/military/civilwar/donald.htm.

Time-Life Books. *Voices of the Civil War: Vicksburg*. Alexandria, VA: Editors of Time-Life Books, n.d.

Truman, Benjamin C., "Where the Fish River Is — Movements of Our Troops." *New York Times*, 7 April 1865.

Ullmann, Daniel. "On the Organization of Colored Troops and the Regeneration of the South." Address before the Soldiers' and Sailors' Union of the State of New York, delivered at Albany, New York, 5 February 1868. Daniel A.P. Murray Pamphlet Collection 1818–1907. Rare Book and Special Collections, Library of Congress online.

Underhill, Joshua Whittington. *Helena to Vicksburg: A Civil War Odyssey—The Personal Diary of Joshua Whittington Underhill, Surgeon, 46th Regiment Indiana Volunteer Infantry 23 October 1862–21 July 1863*. Edited by Christopher Morss. Lincoln Center, MA: Heritage House, 2000.

Vallandigham, Clement Laird. "The Great Civil War in American." Pamphlet 30 in *Union Pamphlets in the Civil War, 1861–1865*. Vol. 2, pp. 697–738. Edited by Frank Freidel. Cambridge, MA: The Belknap Press of Harvard University Press, 1967.

Villard, Henry. *Memoirs of Henry Villard: Journalist and Financier 1835–1900*. 2 vols. Westminster: Archibald Constable & Co., Ltd., 1904.

Walke, Rear Admiral Henry. "The Western Flotilla at Fort Donelson, Island Number 10, Fort Pillow, and Memphis." In *Battles and Leaders of the Civil War*, I: 446. Edited by Richard U. Johnson and Clarence C. Buel. Edison, NJ: Castle Books, 1995.

Wiley, Bell I., ed. *This Infernal War: The Confederate Letters of Sgt. Edwin H. Fay*. Austin: University of Texas Press, 1958.

Wilkes, Abner James. "A Short History of My Life in the Late War Between the North and the South." Transcribed from the original by Rear Admiral Ivan E. Bass. (Mimeographed, n.d.)

Wilkie, Franc B. *Pen and Powder*. Boston: Ticknor and Company, 1888.

_____. *Thirty-five Years in Journalism*. Chicago: F.J. Schulte & Company, 1891.

Williams, T.J. "The Battle of Champion's Hill." *Military Order of the Loyal Legion of the United States (MOLLUS), Ohio*. Cincinnati: The Robert Clarke Company, 1903, V: 204–212.

Wilson, James Harrison. *Under the Old Flag: Recollections of Military Operations in the War of the Union, the Spanish War, the Boxer Rebellion, etc*. 2 vols. New York: D. Appleton, 1912. (Microform.)

Secondary Sources: Books and Articles

Adams, Henry C. Jr., comp. *Indiana at Vicksburg*. Pub. Pursuant to an act of the sixty-sixth General Assembly by the Indiana-Vicksburg Military Park Commission. Indianapolis: W.B. Buford, 1910.

Allardice, Bruce S. *More Generals in Gray.* Baton Rouge: Louisiana State University Press, 1995.

Alonzo, Armando C. *Tejano Legacy: Rancheros and Settlers in South Texas, 1734–1900.* Albuquerque, NM: University of New Mexico Press, 1998.

Altschuler, Glenn, and Stuart Blumin. "Limits of Political Engagement in Antebellum America: A New Look at the Golden Age of Participatory Democracy." *Journal of American History* 84 (December 1997): 855–85.

American Annual Cyclopaedia and Register of Important Events of the Year 1863. 1872 ed. S.v. "Habeas Corpus."

Arnold, James R. *Grant Wins the War: Decision at Vicksburg.* New York: John Wiley & Sons, Inc., 1997.

Arnold-Scriber, Theresa, and Terry G. Scriber. *Ship Island, Mississippi: Rosters and History of the Civil War Prison.* Jefferson, NC: McFarland & Company, Inc., Publishers, 2008.

Ash, Stephen V. *Middle Tennessee Society Transformed 1860–1870.* Baton Rouge: Louisiana State University Press, 1988.

Baker, Thomas H. *The Memphis Commercial Appeal: The History of a Southern Newspaper.* Baton Rouge: Louisiana State University Press, 1971.

_____. "Refugee Newspaper: The *Memphis Daily Appeal*, 1862–1865." *Journal of Southern History* 29 (August 1963): 326–44.

Baxter, James P., III. "The British Government and Neutral Rights." *American Historical Review* 34 (October 1928): 9–28.

Bearss, Edwin C. *The Battle of Jackson, May 14, 1863; The Siege of Jackson, July 10–17, 1863.* Baltimore: Gateway Press, 1981.

_____. *The Campaign for Vicksburg.* 3 vols. Dayton, OH: Morningside Books, 1985.

Belknap, Michal P., ed. *American Political Trials.* Westport, CN: Greenwood Press, 1981.

Bentley, Eric. *Thirty Years of Treason: Excerpts from Hearing before the House Committee on Un-American Activities, 1938–1968.* New York: The Viking Press, 1971.

Berger, Meyer. *The Story of the New York Times: The First 100 Years, 1851–1951.* New York: Simon and Schuster, 1951.

Bergeron, Arthur W., Jr. *Guide to Louisiana Confederate Military Units: 1861–1865.* Baton Rouge: Louisiana State University Press, 189.

Bernstein, Iver. *New York City Draft Riots: Their Significance for American Society and Politics in the Age of the Civil War.* New York: Oxford University Press, 1991.

Beyer, Walter F., and Oscar F. Keydel, comps. *Deeds of Valor: How America's Heroes Won the Medal of Honor.* 2 vols. Detroit: The Perrien-Keydel Company, 1907.

Biographical Record and Portrait Album of Tippecanoe County, Indiana. Chicago, IL: Lewis Publishing Co., 1888. www.rootsweb.com/~intippec/Bio_JRCoffroth.html.

Boune, Kenneth. "British Preparations for War with the North, 1861–62." *The English Historical Review* 76 (October 1961): 600–32.

Bridges, C.A. "The Knights of the Golden Circle: A Filibustering Fantasy." *Southwestern Historical Quarterly* 44 (January 1941): 287–302.

Brinsfield, John W., William C. Davis, Benedict Maryniak, and James I. Robertson Jr., eds. *Faith in the Fight: Civil War Chaplains.* Mechanicsburg, PA: Stackpole Books, 2003.

Brown, Marilyn. *Gypsies and Other Bohemians: The Myth of the Artist in Nineteenth-Century France.* Ann Arbor: UMI Research Press, 1985.

Brown, Thomas Allston. *History of the American Stage Containing Sketches of Nearly Every Member of the Profession that has Appeared on the American Stage, from 1733 to 1870.* New York: Burt Franklin, 1870; reprint ed., 1969.

_____. *A History of the New York Stage, From the First Performance in 1732 to 1901.* 3 vols. New York, 1903; reprint ed., Benjamin Blom, Inc., 1964.

Burgess, John W. *The Civil War and the Constitution, 1859–1865.* 2 vols. Charles Scribner's Sons, 1901.

Burton, Shirley, and Kellee Green. "Defining Disloyalty: Treason, Espionage, and Sedition Prosecutions 1861–1946." *Prologue: Quarterly of the National Archives* 21 (1984): 215–221.

Bynum, Victoria E. *The Free State of Jones: Mississippi's Longest Civil War.* Chapel Hill: University of North Carolina Press, 2001.

Caldwell, Delaney. *Confederate Mobile: A Pictorial History.* Mobile: Haunted Bookshop, 1971.

Campanella, Richard. *Time and Place in New Orleans: Past Geographies in the Present Day.* Gretna, LA: Pelican Publishing Company, 2002.

Caren, Eric C., comp. *Civil War Extra: A Newspaper History of the Civil War from 1863 to 1865.* 2 vols. Edison, NJ: Castle Books, 1999.

Carter, Samuel. *The Final Fortress: The Campaign for Vicksburg, 1862–1863.* New York: St. Martin's Press, 1980.

Casdorph, Paul D. *Prince John Magruder: His Life and Campaigns.* New York: John Wiley & Sons, 1996.

Castillo, Jose R. del. *Juarez, La Intervencion y El Imperio: Refutacion A La Obra "El Verdadero Juarez," de Bulnes.* Mexico: Herrero Hermanos, Editores, 1904.

Catton, Bruce. *Grant Moves South.* Boston: Little-Brown, 1960.

Churchill, Robert. "Liberty, Conscription, and a

Party Divided: The Sons of Liberty Conspiracy 1863–1864." *Prologue* 30 (1998): 295–303.

Cimprich, John, and Robert C. Mainfort Jr. *Fort Pillow, a Civil War Massacre, and Public Memory*. Baton Rouge: Louisiana State University Press, 2005.

_____. "Fort Pillow Revisited: New Evidence about an Old Controversy." *Civil War History* 28 (December 1982): 293–306.

Clebert, Jean-Paul. *The Gypsies*. Translated by Charles Duff. Baltimore, MD: Penguin Books, 1969.

Cole, Arthur Charles. *The Era of the Civil War, 1848–1870*. Springfield: Illinois Centennial Commission, 1919.

Coleman, Charles H., and Paul H. Spence. "The Charleston Riot, March 28, 1864." Coles County in the Civil War 1861–1865. Eastern Illinois University Bulletin, reprinted from *The Journal of Illinois State Historical Society* 33 (March 1940): 78–112.

Commager, Henry Steele, ed. *The Civil War Archive: The History of the Civil War in Documents*. Rev. ed. New York: Black Dog & Leventhal Publishers, 2000.

Cook, Adrian. *The Armies of the Streets: The New York City Draft Riots of 1863*. Lexington: The University Press of Kentucky, 1974.

Cotton, Gordon A. "Champion Hill Recalled By Indiana Tramp." *The Vicksburg Evening Post*, 27 May 1984.

Coulter, E. Merton. *William G. Brownlow: Fighting Parson of the Southern Highlands*. Chapel Hill: University of North Carolina Press, 1937.

Cozzens, Peter. *No Better Place to Die: The Battle of Stones River*. Urbana, IL: University of Illinois Press, Illini Books edition, 1991.

Crenshaw, Ollinger. "The Knights of the Golden Circle: The Career of George Bickley." *American Historical Review* 47 (October 1941): 23–50.

Cresswell, Tim. *The Tramp in America*. London, UK: Reaktion Books, 2001.

Crozier, Emmet. *Yankee Reporters 1861–65*. New York: Oxford University Press, 1956.

Curl, Donald W. *Murat Halstead and the Cincinnati Commercial*. Boca Raton: A Florida Atlantic University Book, University Presses of Florida, 1980.

Curry, Richard O. "The Union as it Was: A Critique of Recent Interpretations of the 'Copperheads.'" *Civil War History* 13 (March 1967): 25–39.

Cutler, William G. *History of the State of Kansas*. Chicago: A.T. Andreas, 1883.

Daniel, Larry J., and Lynn N. Bock. *Island No. 10: Struggle for the Mississippi Valley*. Tuscaloosa: University of Alabama Press, 1996.

Davis, Elmer. *History of the New York Times, 1851–1921*. New York: *New York Times*, 1921.

Davis, William C., and Bell I. Wiley. *Photographic History of the Civil War: Vicksburg to Appomattox*. New York: Black Dog & Leventhal Publishers, 1994.

Davis, W.W.H. *The History of Bucks County, Pennsylvania, from the Discovery of the Delaware to the Present Time*. Doylestown, PA: Democrat Book and Job Office Print, 1876.

De Leon, Arnoldo. *They Called Them Greasers: Anglo Attitudes Toward Mexicans in Texas, 1821–1900*. Austin: University of Texas Press, 1983.

DePastino, Todd. *Citizen Hobo: How a Century of Homelessness Shaped America*. Chicago: University of Chicago Press, 2003.

Douglass, Frederick. *Autobiographies*. Vol. 1: *Life and Times of Frederick Douglass*. New York: Literary Classics of the United States, 1994.

Duberman, Martin B. *Charles Francis Adams: 1807–1886*. Boston: Houghton-Mifflin, 1961.

Dugan, Frank H. "The 1850 Affair of the Brownsville Separatists." *Southwestern Historical Quarterly* 61 (October 1957): 270–87.

Eaton, Clement. *Freedom-of-Thought Struggle in the Old South*. New York: Harper and Row, 1964.

_____. "Mob Violence in the Old South." *Mississippi Valley Historical Review* 19 (December 1942): 351–370.

Elliott, Claude. "Union Sentiment in Texas: 1861–1865." *Southwestern Historical Quarterly* 50 (1946–1947): 449–477.

Erbsen, Wayne. *Rousing Songs & True Tales of the Civil War*. Pacific, MO: Mel Bay Publications, 2000.

Evans, E. Chris. "Return to Jackson: Finishing Stroke to the Vicksburg Campaign." *Blue & Gray Magazine* (August 1995): 9–63.

Everett, Donald E. "Benjamin Butler and the Louisiana Native Guards, 1861–1862." *Journal of Southern History* 24 (1958): 202–217.

Everhart, William C. "The Battle of Champion Hill, May 16, 1863." Vicksburg National Military Park, MS. Washington, D.C.: National Park Service Handbook Series 21, 1954.

Fairman, Charles. *Mr. Justice Miller and the Supreme Court 1862–1890*. Cambridge, MA: Harvard University Press, 1939.

Feldman, Jay. *When the Mississippi Ran Backwards: Empire, Intrigue, Murder, and the New Madrid Earthquakes*. New York: Free Press, 2005.

Fessler, Mayo. "Secret Political Societies in the North During the War." *Indiana Magazine of History* 15 (September 1918): 183–286.

Fisher, Sidney G. "Suspension of the Writ of Habeas Corpus During the War of the Rebellion." *Political Science Quarterly* 3 (1888): 454–488.

Flexner, Abraham. *Medical Education in the United States and Canada*. New York: A Report of the Carnegie Foundation for the Advancement of Teaching, 1910; reprint ed., New York: Arno Press, 1972.

Foster, Samuel T. *One of Cleburne's Command: The Civil War Reminiscences and Diary of Capt. Samuel T. Foster, Granbury's Texas Brigade, CSA*. Ed. Norman D. Brown. Austin: University of Texas Press, 1980.

Foulke, William Dudley. *Life of Oliver P. Morton, Including His Important Speeches*. 2 vols. Indianapolis-Kansas City: The Bowen-Merrill Company, 1899.

Glatthaar, Joseph T. *Forged in Battle: The Civil War Alliance of Black Soldiers and White Officers*. New York: Free Press, 1990.

Gleason, David King. *Plantation Homes of Louisiana and the Natchez Area*. Baton Rouge: Louisiana State University Press, 1982.

Goldman, Lee, and J. Claude Bennett, eds. *Cecil Textbook of Medicine*. 21st ed. Philadelphia: W.B. Saunders Company, 2000.

Greene, Francis Vinton. *The Army in the Civil War: The Mississippi*. Vol. 8 of *Campaigns of the Civil War*. New York: Charles Scribner's Sons, 1885.

Guelzo, Allen C. "Defending Emancipation: Abraham Lincoln and the Conkling Letter, 1863." *Civil War History* (2002): 313–337.

Haller, John S., Jr. *A Profile in Alternative Medicine: The Eclectic Medical College of Cincinnati, 1845–1942*. Kent, OH: Kent State University Press, 1999.

Hanna, Alfred J., and Kathryn A. Hanna. *Napoleon III and Mexico: American Triumph over Monarchy*. Chapel Hill: University of North Carolina Press, 1971.

Hansen, Roger. "Blakeley Battlefield Self-Guided Tour." Historic Blakeley Authority of the State of Alabama. Spanish Fort, AL, n.d.

Harper, Robert S. *Lincoln and the Press*. New York: McGraw-Hill, 1951.

Harmon, George D. "Confederate Migration to Mexico." *Hispanic American Historical Review* 17 (1937): 458–87.

Harrington, Fred H. *Fighting Politician: Major General N.P. Banks*. Philadelphia: University of Pennsylvania Press, 1948.

Harris, William C. *Presidential Reconstruction in Mississippi*. Baton Rouge: Louisiana State University Press, 1966.

Hasian, Marouf Arif. *In the Name of Necessity: Military Tribunals and the Loss of American Civil Liberties*. Tuscaloosa: University of Alabama Press, 2005.

Hawkins, Walace. *The Case of John C. Watrous, United States Judge for Texas: A Political Story of High Crimes and Misdemeanors*. Dallas: University Press of Dallas, 1950.

Hearn, Chester G. *Mobile Bay and the Mobile Bay Campaign: The Last Great Battles of the Civil War*. Jefferson, NC: McFarland & Co., Inc. Publishers, 1993.

Henderson, Daniel. *The Hidden Coasts: A Biography of Admiral Charles Wilkes*. New York: William Sloan Associates, 1953; reprint ed., Westport, CN: Greenwood Press, 1971.

Hicks, Jimmie. "Some Letters Concerning the Knights of the Golden Circle in Texas, 1860–1861." *Southwestern Historical Society Quarterly* 65 (July 1961): 80–86.

History of Huntington County, Indiana. Chicago: Brant and Fuller, 1887.

Hoehling, A.A. *Vicksburg: 47 Days of Siege*. Englewood Cliffs, NJ: Prentiss-Hall, 1969.

Horan, James D. *Confederate Agent: A Discovery of History*. New York: Crown Publishers, 1954.

Hollandsworth, James G., Jr. *The Louisiana Native Guards: The Black Military Experience in the Civil War*. Baton Rouge: Louisiana State University Press, 1995.

_____. *Pretense of Glory: The Life of General Nathaniel P. Banks*. Baton Rouge: Louisiana State University Press, 1987.

Horan, James D. *Confederate Agent: A Discovery of History*. New York: Crown Publishers, 1954.

Howell, H. Grady. *Hill of Death: The Battle of Champion Hill*. Madison, MS: Chickasaw Bayou Press, 1993.

Hunt, Aurora. *The Army of the Pacific, 1860–1866*. Mechanicsburg, PA: Stackpole Books, 2006; originally published: Glendale, CA: Arthur H. Clark Co., 1951.

Hunt, Jeffrey W. *The Last Battle of the War: Palmetto Ranch*. Austin: University of Texas Press, 2002.

Huntzicker, William. *The Popular Press, 1833–1865*. Westport, CT: Greenwood Press, 1999.

Hurst, Jack. *Nathan Bedford Forrest: A Biography*. New York: Vintage Books, 1994.

Irons, Peter. *A People's History of the Supreme Court: The Men and Women Whose Cases and Decisions Have Shaped Our Constitution*, rev. ed. New York: Penguin Books, 2006.

"'Jeff' Thompson's Unsuccessful Quest for a Confederate Generalship." *Missouri Historical Review* 35 (October 1991): 53–56.

Johnson, Ludwell H. *Red River Campaign: Politics and Cotton in the Civil War*. Baltimore: Johns Hopkins University Press, 1958; reprint ed., Kent, OH: Kent State University Press, 1993.

Joiner, Gary D. *One Damn Blunder from Beginning to End: The Red River Campaign of 1864*. Wilmington, DE: Scholarly Resources, 2003.

Jones, Lottie E. *Decisive Dates in Illinois History: A*

Story of the State. Danville, IL: Illinois Printing Company, 1909; original reproduced online by the American Libraries Internet Archive.

Kanfer, Stefan. *A Journal of the Plague Years: A Devastating Chronicle of the Era of the Blacklist.* New York: Atheneum, 1973.

Katcher, Philip. *Flags of the American Civil War.* 3 vols. London: Osprey, 1993.

Keagy, Franklin. *A History of the Kagy Relationship in America from 1715 to 1900.* Harrisburg, PA: Harrisburg Publishing Company, 1899; reprint ed., Salem, MA: Higginson Book Company, n.d.

Kennedy, David M. *Over Here: The First World War and American Society.* New York: Oxford University Press, 1980.

Kerby, Robert L. *Kirby Smith's Confederacy: The Trans-Mississippi South, 1863–1865.* New York: Columbia University Press, 1972.

Kinchen, Oscar A. *Confederate Operations in Canada and the North.* North Quincy, MA: The Christopher Publishing House, 1970.

Kinsley, Philip. *The Chicago Tribune: Its First Hundred Years.* 2 vols. New York: Alfred A. Knopf, 1943.

Kiper, Richard L. *Major General John Alexander McClernand: Politician in Uniform.* Kent, Ohio and London: Kent State University Press, 1999.

Klement, Frank L. "Carrington and the Golden Circle Legend in Indiana during the Civil War." *Indiana Magazine of History* 61 (March 1965): 31–52.

_____. *The Copperheads in the Middle West.* Chicago: University of Chicago Press, 1960.

_____. *Dark Lanterns: Secret Political Societies, Conspiracies, and Treason Trials in the Civil War.* Baton Rouge and London: Louisiana State University Press, 1984.

_____. "The Indianapolis Treason Trials and *Ex Parte Milligan*." In *American Political Trials*, pp. 101–127. Edited by Michal P. Belknap. Westport, CN: Greenwood Press, 1981.

_____. *The Limits of Dissent: Clement L. Vallandigham and the Civil War.* Lexington: University of Kentucky Press, 1970.

_____. "Phineas C. Wright, the Order of American Knights, and the Sanderson Expose." *Civil War History* (18 (March 1972): 9–10.

Kusmer, Kenneth. *Down and Out on the Road.* Oxford: Oxford University Press, 2002.

Kutler, Stanley I. "*Ex Parte McCardle*: Judicial Impotency? The Supreme Court and Reconstruction Reconsidered." *American Historical Review* 72 (April, 1967): 835–51.

Lacy, Michael O. "Military Commissions: A Historical Survey." *The Army Lawyer* (March 2002): 41–47.

Leland, Charles Godfrey, and Henry P. Leland. "Ye Book of Copperheads." Pamphlet 38 in *Union Pamphlets in the Civil War, 1861–1865*. vol. 2, pp. 857–71. Edited by Frank Freidel. Cambridge, MA: The Belknap Press of Harvard University Press, 1967.

Lewis, Lloyd. *Sherman: Fighting Prophet.* New York: Harcourt, Brace, and Company, 1932.

Long, E.B., with Barbara Long. *The Civil War Day by Day: An Almanac 1861–1865.* New York: Da Capo Press, 1971.

Lonn, Ella. *Desertion in the Civil War.* Gloucester, MA: American Historical Society, 1928; reprint ed., Lincoln: University of Nebraska, First Bison Edition, 1998.

Lowe, Richard. *Walker's Texas Division: Greyhounds of the Trans-Mississippi.* Baton Rouge: Louisiana State University Press, 2004.

Lowry, Thomas P., M.D. *Curmudgeons, Drunkards & Outright Fools: Courts-Martial of Civil War Union Colonels.* Lincoln: University of Nebraska Press, 2003; originally published as *Tarnished Eagles: The Courts-martial of Fifty Union Colonels and Lieutenant Colonels.* Mechanicsburg, PA: Stackpole Books, 1997.

_____. *The Story the Soldiers Wouldn't Tell: Sex in the Civil War.* Mechanicsburg, PA: Stackpole Books, 1994.

Lubinski, Richard. *James Madison and the Struggle for the Bill of Rights.* New York: Oxford University Press, 2006.

Lytle, Andrew. *Bedford Forrest and His Critter Company*, rev. ed. New York: McDowell, Obolensky, 1960.

MacDonald, Helen G. *Canadian Public Opinion on the American Civil War.* New York: Columbia University Press, 1926.

Mahan, A.T. Commander, U.S. Navy. *The Navy in the Civil War: The Gulf and Inland Waters.* Vol. 16 of *Campaigns of the Civil War.* New York: Charles Scribner's Sons, 1885.

Maihafer, Harry J. *The General and the Journalists: Ulysses S. Grant, Horace Greeley, and Charles Dana.* Washington: Brassey's, 1998.

Man, Albon, Jr. "Labor Competition and the New York Draft Riots of 1863." *The Journal of Negro History* 36 (October 1951): 375–405.

Markham, Jerald H. *The Botetourt Artillery.* Lynchburg, VA: H.E. Howard, 1986.

Marshall, John A. *American Bastille: A History of the Illegal Arrests and Imprisonment of American Citizens During the Late Civil War.* Philadelphia: Evans, Stoddart & Co., 1870.

Marszalek, John F. *Sherman's Other War: The General and the Civil War Press.* Memphis: Memphis State University Press, 1981.

Martin, David G. *The Vicksburg Campaign, April 1862–July 1863.* Mechanicsburg, PA: Stackpole Books, 1994.

Martin, Edgar W. *Standard of Living in 1860: Amer-*

ican Consumption on the Eve of the Civil War. Chicago: University of Chicago Press, 1942.

May, Robert E. *The Southern Dream of a Caribbean Empire, 1854–1861.* Baton Rouge: Louisiana State University Press, 1973.

McCardell, John. *The Idea of a Southern Nation.* New York: W.W. Norton & Company, 1979.

McClemore, Richard A., ed. *A History of Mississippi.* 2 vols. Hattiesburg, MS: University & College Press of Mississippi, 1973.

McCormick, David I., comp. *Indiana Battle Flags and Record of Indiana Organization in the Mexican, Civil and Spanish-American Wars.* Indianapolis: The Indiana Battle Flag Commission, 1929.

McPherson, James M. *Battle Cry of Freedom: The Civil War Era.* New York: Oxford University Press, 1988.

Miers, Earl S. *The Web of Victory: Grant at Vicksburg.* 2nd ed. New York: Knopf, 1984.

Miller, Tice L. *Bohemians and Critics: American Theatre Criticism in the Nineteenth Century.* Meduchen, NJ: Scarecrow Press, Inc., 1961.

Milligan, John D. *Gunboats Down the Mississippi.* Annapolis, MD: U.S. Naval Institute, 1965; reprint ed., New York: Arno Press, 1980.

Milton, George F. *Abraham Lincoln and the Fifth Column.* New York: Vanguard Press, 1942.

Milton, John. *Paradise Lost: A Poem Written in Ten Books: An Authoritative Text of the 1667 First Edition,* trans. and ed. John T. Shawcross and Michael Lieb. Pittsburgh: Duquesne University Press, 2007.

Moss, Arthur, and Evalyn Marvel. *The Legend of the Latin Quarter: Henry Murger and the Birth of Bohemia.* New York: The Beechhurst Press, 1946.

Murphy, Paul L. *The Constitution in Crisis Times: 1918–1964.* New York: Harper & Row, 1972.

Nicolay, John G., and John Hay. *Abraham Lincoln: A History.* 10 vols. New York: The Century Co., 1886 and 1890.

Parks, Joseph H. "A Confederate Trade Center Under Federal Occupation: Memphis, 1862–1865." *Journal of Southern History* 7 (August 1941): 289–314.

_____. *General Edmund Kirby Smith, C.S.A.* Baton Rouge: Louisiana State University Press, 1954.

_____. "Memphis Under Military Rule: 1862–1865." *East Tennessee Historical Society's Publications* 14 (1942): 31–58.

Parsons, Chuck, and Marianne E. Hall Little. *Captain L.H. McNelly, Texas Ranger: The Life and Times of a Fighting Man.* Austin, Texas: State House Press, 2000.

Peat, Wilbur D. *Portraits and Painters of the Governors of Indiana, 1800–1978.* Revised and edited with new entries by Diane Gail Lazarus, Indianapolis Museum of Art. *Biographies of the Governors by Lana Ruegamer,* Indiana Historical Society. Indianapolis: Indiana Historical Society and Indianapolis Museum of Art, 1978.

Peckinpaugh, Roger. *Rescue by Rail: Troop Transfer & the Civil War.* Lincoln: University of Nebraska Press, 1998.

Pershing, Marvin W. *Tipton County, Indiana History.* 2 parts. Kokomo, IN: Selby Publishing & Printing, 1914; reprinted 1985.

Potts, Charles S. "David S. Terry: The Romantic Story of a Great Texan." *Southwest Review* 19 (April 1934): 295–34.

Pratt, Fletcher. *Civil War on Western Waters.* New York: Henry Holt and Company, 1956.

Pruneda, Pedro. *Historia de la Guerra de Mejico desde 1861 a 1867.* Madrid: Elizalde y Compania, 1867; facsimile reprint ed., Mexico City: Fundacion Manuel Aleman, A.C.; Fondo de Cultura Economica, c. 1996.

Randall, James G. *Constitutional Problems Under Lincoln.* Urbana: University of Illinois Press, 1951.

_____. "The Newspaper Problem and its Bearing Upon Military Secrecy During the Civil War." *The American Historical Review* 23 (June 1918): 303–23.

Rawley, James A. *Turning Points of the Civil War.* Lincoln: University of Nebraska Press, 1966; reprint ed., Lincoln: University of Nebraska, New Bison Book Edition, 1989.

Reed, Merl E. *New Orleans and the Railroads: The Struggle for Commercial Empire 1830–1860.* Baton Rouge: Louisiana State University Press, 1966.

Rehnquist, William H. *All the Laws But One: Civil Liberties in Wartime.* New York: Alfred A. Knopf, 1998.

_____. *Centennial Crisis: The Disputed Election of 1876.* New York: Alfred A. Knopf, 2004.

_____. "Civil Liberty and the Civil War: The Indianapolis Treason Trials." Speech delivered at the Indiana University School of Law, Bloomington, IN, on Monday, 28 October 1996, published in the *Indiana Law Journal* 72 (Fall 1997).

Rice, Edward Le Roy. *Monarchs of Minstrelsy, from "Daddy" Rice to Date.* New York: Kenney Company, 1911.

Ridley, Jasper G. *Maximillian and Juarez.* New York: Ticknor and Fields, 1991.

Ripley, Warren. *Artillery and Ammunition in the Civil War.* New York: Van Nostrand Reinhold Company, 1970.

Rister, Carl Coke. "Carlota, A Confederate Colony in Mexico." *Journal of Southern History* 11 (February 1945): 35–50.

Robinson, William M., Jr. *Justice in Grey: A History of the Judicial System of the Confederate States of America.* Cambridge: Harvard University Press, 1941.

_____. "Review of *The Case of John C. Watrous, United States Judge for Texas: A Political Story of High Crimes and Misdemeanors*, by Walace Hawkins." *Journal of Southern History* 17 (1951): 262–63.

Schluter, Herman. *Lincoln, Labor and Slavery*. New York: Socialist Literature Company, 1913.

Scribner, Theo. T., and David Stevenson. *Indiana's Roll of Honor*. 2 vols. Indianapolis: A.D. Streight, Publisher, 1866.

Shalhope, Robert F. *Sterling Price: Portrait of a Southerner*. Columbia: University of Missouri Press, 1971.

Sideman, Belle Becker, and Lillian Friedman, eds. *Europe Looks at the Civil War*. New York: Orion Press, 1960.

Sifakis, Stewart. *Compendium of the Confederate Armies: Mississippi*. New York: Facts on File, Inc., 1995.

Smith, Craig R. "Lincoln and Habeas Corpus—1861–1865." *White Papers: Center for First Amendment Studies*. California State University, Long Beach. www.csulib.edu/ ~crsmith/lincoln.html.

Smith, Timothy B. *Champion Hill: Decisive Battle for Vicksburg*. New York: Savas Beatie, 2004.

Snead, Col. Thomas L "The Conquest of Arkansas." In *Battles and Leaders of the Civil War*. III: 451. Edited by Robert U. Johnson and Clarence C. Buel. Edison, NJ: Castle Books, 1995.

Soley, James Russell, U.S.N. *Admiral Porter*. New York: D. Appleton and Company, 1903.

_____. "Land Operations Against Mobile." In *Battles and Leaders of the Civil War*. IV: 411. Edited by Robert U. Johnson and Clarence C. Buel. Edison, NJ: Castle Books, 1995.

_____. "Naval Operations in the Vicksburg Campaign." In *Battles and Leaders of the Civil War*. III: 551–570. Edited by Robert U. Johnson and Clarence C. Buel. Edison, NJ: Castle Books, 1995.

_____. "The Union and Confederate Navies." In *Battles and Leaders of the Civil War*. I: 611–31. Edited by Robert U. Johnson and Clarence C. Buel. Edison, NJ: Castle Books, 1995.

Spero, Sterling, and Abram L. Harris. *The Black Worker and the Labor Movement*. New York: Columbia University Press, 1931.

Stampp, Kenneth. "The Milligan Case and the Election of 1864 in Indiana." *Mississippi Valley Historical Review* 31 (June 1944): 41–58.

Starr, Louis M. *Bohemian Brigade: Civil War Newsmen in Action*. New York: Alfred A. Knopf, 1954.

Starr, Stephen Z. *Colonel Grenfell's Wars: The Life of a Soldier of Fortune*. Baton Rouge: Louisiana State University Press, 1971.

Sword, Wiley. *Shiloh: Bloody April*. New York: William Morrow and Company, 1974; reprint ed., Dayton, OH: Press of Morningside Bookshop, 1988.

Sylvester, Lorna Lutes. "Oliver P. Morton and Hoosier Politics during the Civil War." Ph.D. dissertation, Indiana University, 1968.

Talley, Robert. *One Hundred Years of the Commercial Appeal: The Story of the Greatest Romance in American Journalism*. Memphis: The Commercial Appeal Publishing Co., 1940.

Tidwell, William A. *April '65: Confederate Covert Action in the Civil War*. Kent, OH: Kent State University Press, 1995.

Towne, Stephen E. "Killing the Serpent Speedily: Governor Morton, General Hascall, and the Suppression of the Democratic Press in Indiana, 1863." *Civil War History* 52.1 (2006): 41–65.

_____. "'Such conduct must be put down': The Military Arrest of Judge Charles H. Constable during the Civil War." *Journal of Illinois History* 9 (Spring 2006): 43–62.

Tredway, G.R. *Democratic Opposition to the Lincoln Administration in Indiana*. Indianapolis: Indiana Historical Bureau, 1973.

Trelease, Allen W. *White Terror: the Ku Klux Klan Conspiracy and Southern Reconstruction*. Baton Rouge: Louisiana State University Press, 1971.

Trudeau, Noah Andre. *Like Men of War: Black Troops in the Civil War 1862–1865*. New York: Little, Brown and Company, 1998; reprint ed., Edison, NJ: Castle Books, 2002.

Tucher, Andie. "Reporting for Duty: The Bohemian Brigade, the Civil War, and the Social Construction of the Reporter." *Book History* 9 (2006): 131–157. (Project Muse: http://muse.jhu.edu/journals/book_history/index.html.)

Tucker, Spencer C. *Blue and Gray Navies*. Annapolis, MD: Naval Institute Press, 2006.

"The Vault at Pfaff's: An Archive of Art and Literature by New York City's Nineteenth-Century Bohemians." Lehigh University Digital Library.

Vidal, Gore. *Imperial America: Reflections on the United States of Amnesia*. New York: Nation Books, 2004.

Wagman, Robert J. *The First Amendment Book: Celebrating 200 Years of Freedom of the Press and Freedom of Speech*. New York: Pharos Books, 1991.

Walker, Scott. *Hell's Broke Loose in Georgia: Survival in a Civil War Regiment*. Athens: University of Georgia Press, 2005.

Warner, Ezra J. *Generals in Blue: Lives of the Union Commanders*. Baton Rouge: Louisiana State University Press, 1964.

_____. *Generals in Gray: Lives of the Confederate Commanders*. Baton Rouge: Louisiana State University Press, 1959.

Warren, Charles. *The Supreme Court in United*

States History. 2 vols. Boston: Little, Brown and Company, 1926.

Webb, Walter Prescott. *The Texas Rangers: A Century of Frontier Defense*. 2nd ed. Austin: University of Texas Press, 1982.

Weber, David J., ed. *Foreigners in their Native Land: Historical Roots of the Mexican American*. Albuquerque, NM: University of New Mexico Press, 1996.

Wecter, Dixon. *When Johnny Comes Marching Home*. Cambridge, MA: Houghton Mifflin Company, 1944.

Weeks, Charles A. *The Juarez Myth in Mexico*. Tuscaloosa: University of Alabama Press, 1987.

Wesley, Charles H. *Negro Labor in the United States 1850–1925: A Study in American Economic History*. New York: Vanguard Press; 1927; reprint ed., New York: Russell and Russell, 1967.

Westwood, Howard C. "Captive Black Union Soldiers in Charleston — What to Do?" *Civil War History* 28 (January 1982): 28–44.

Williamson, David. *The Third Battalion Mississippi Infantry and the 45th Mississippi Regiment: A Civil War History*. Jefferson, NC: McFarland & Company, Inc., Publishers, 2004, 2009.

Wilson, Charles R., "McClellan's Changing Views on the Peace Plank of 1864." *American Historical Society* 38 (April 1933): 498–505.

Wilson, Garff B. *History of American Acting*. Bloomington, IN: Indiana University Press, 1966.

Winschel, Terrence J. "Grant's Beachhead for the Vicksburg Campaign: The Battle of Port Gibson, May 1, 1863." *Blue & Gray Magazine* (February 1994): 9–60.

_____. "The Guns of Champion Hill (Part II)." *Journal of Confederate History* 6 (1990): 94–104.

_____. *Triumph & Defeat: The Vicksburg Campaign*. Mason City, IA: Savas Publishing Co., 1999.

Wood, Gray. *The Hidden Civil War: The Story of the Copperheads*. New York: Viking Press, 1942.

Woodham-Smith, Cecil. *The Great Hunger: Ireland 1845–1849*. New York: Harper & Row, 1962.

Woodworth, Steven E. *Jefferson Davis and His Generals: Failure of Command in the West*. Lawrence: University of Kansas Press, 1990.

Wright, John D. *The Language of the Civil War*. Westport, CT: Oryx Press, 2001.

Wyeth, Andrew J. *That Devil Forrest: The Life of General Nathan Bedford Forrest*. New York: Harper, 1959.

Zornow, William F. "Indiana and the Election of 1864." *Indiana Magazine of History* 45 (March 1949): 13–18.

Index

Numbers in ***bold italics*** indicate pages with photographs.

"A. Hoosier" (correspondent to the *Indiana State Sentinel*) 39–40
Adams, Charles Francis 16; importance of the Rio Grande 194, 362
Adams, Henry S. (47th Indiana Infantry) ***309***, 310
Alabama Artillery: Lumsden's Tuscaloosa Battery 271; Waddell's Battery 131, 134
Alabama Cavalry: 6th 269; 8th 266; 16th 266
Alabama Infantry (CS): 1st Reserves 266; 2nd Reserves 266; 3rd 266; 6th 266; 8th 266; 20th 118, 134; 21st Reserves 266; 23rd 118–19, 134, 151, 157, 162; 27th 135, 151; 30th 118; 31st 118, 134; 32nd & 58th, consolidated 268; 35th 113, 135, 137, 323; 37th 150, 152; 42nd 150, 152; 46th 118, 134; 54th 135
Albert, Prince Consort 16; *see also* Queen Victoria
Alcorn, James L. 88, 374
Alcorn State University 374
Alexandria, Louisiana ***208***, 212, 223, 398
Algiers, Louisiana 165, 196, 208–9, 238–39, ***262***
Algiers Methodist Church 239
Alspack, Daniel (47th Indiana Infantry) ***80***
Alspack, Elijah (47th Indiana Infantry) ***80***
American Cavalier (Baltimore, Maryland) 102
Ames, Edward R. 400
Anderson, Ephraim (2nd Missouri, CSA): attack on Grand Gulf 115; on charge of Cockrell's Brigade 121
Anderson, Robert 9, 10–11
Anderson, William (47th Indiana Infantry) ***80***
Andrews, Christopher C. 265, 268–69, 275
USS *Antona* 283
USS *Arizona* 196
Arkansas Artillery (CSA): Owen's Battery 270

Arkansas Cavalry (CSA): 1st Battalion 127, 135
Arkansas Infantry (CSA): 2nd 183; 4th 183; 9th 135; 11th 27; 11th Mounted 195; 12th 27, 41; 12th Battalion Sharpshooters 135; 15th 117; 21st 117, 135; 19th 135; 20th 135; 21st 135
Arkansas Post, Arkansas 79
Arlington, Billy (Arlington, Leon & Donniker's Minstrels) 76, 372; *see also* George Christy's Minstrels
Armistead, Charles C. 266, 268
Army Corps (USA): Parke's 9th 160, 179, 194; Granger's 13th 265; McClernand's 13th 74, 79, 82, 124; Ord's 13th 162, 179, 195; Sherman's 15th 74, 79, 124; Steele's 15th 179–80, 187; Hurlbut's 16th 74; Smith's 16th 265; McPherson's 17th 74, 124, 185, 194; Emory's 19th 235; Franklin's 19th 195–96, 199, 212; Reynolds' 19th 238; Reynolds' Reserve Corps 258
Army of Central Kentucky (CSA) 8, 21, 24
Army of Mississippi (CSA) 43, 45, 63
Army of Tennessee (CSA) 65, 79
Army of the Cumberland (USA) 79
Army of the Mississippi (USA) 24
Army of the Ohio (USA) 10, 23–24, 43, 57, 60, 107
Army of the Potomac (USA) 10, 107
Army of the Southwest (USA) 30, 60
Army of the Tennessee (USA) 43
Arnold, Eli (47th Indiana Infantry) ***80***, 308
Arnold, Richard 229
Asboth, Alexander: desertion in Illinois 104
Aspinwall, William "Roving Bill" (47th Indiana Infantry): account of Battle of Champion Hill 142–43, 305
Atchafalaya River, Louisiana ***234***, 240

Ayer, Isaiah W. 256

"B" (reporter for the *Indiana State Sentinel*) 45–49
Bagdad, Mexico 239, 293
Bailey, Joseph 224, 226
Baldwin, W.E. 121–23, 165
Baltic (CS ram) 268, 280, 406
Baltic (US marine boat) 263
Baltimore, Maryland: *American Cavalier* 102; newspapers *Daily Exchange* and *The South* 6; riots 3–6, 358
Bankhead, Capt. Smith P. 27
Banks, Nathaniel 82, 194, 203, 211, 291; blamed for failure of the Red River Expedition 394
Bardstown, Kentucky ***4***, 12, 13, 14, 18, 21
USS *Baron de Kalb* 80, 81, 87, 90–92
Barrett, Theodore H. (34th Indiana Infantry) 281, 409
Barrow, Alexander 288, 399
Barrow, Barthalameau "Batt" 399
Barrow, David 237, 399
Bates, T. Jeff (Waddell's Alabama Battery) 131
Batesville, Mississippi 92
Baton Rouge, Louisiana ***234***, 243, 288
Baylor, George W. 225, 229
Bayou Bourbeau (Grand Coteau), Louisiana ***191***; battle of 200–3
Bayou Cortableau, Louisiana 191, 200
Bayou Fordoche, Louisiana ***234***
Bayou de Glaise, Louisiana ***208***, 229
Bayou Grosse Tete, Louisiana ***234***, 237
Bayou La Fourche, Louisiana 165
Bayou Maringouin, Louisiana ***234***, 237
Bayou Teche, Louisiana ***191***, 196, 199, 212
Bayou Vidal, Louisiana ***98***, 108; spanning 111

431

Index

Bazaine, Francois Achilles 292, 294
Beal, James (47th Indiana Infantry) 272
Beauregard, P.G.T. 45, 51, 63
Bee, Hamilton P. 193, 204, 226, 291, 393
Bell, H.H. 204, 393
Bell, William B. (8th Iowa Infantry) 276
Belvedere (US transport) 264
Bender, David S. (47th Indiana Infantry) *350*
Benevides, Santos 292, 294, 390
USS *Benton* 35, 47; attack on Grand Gulf 114–16, 366
Benton, William P. 265, 280, 284, 287
Benton, Missouri 25, 28
Bert, Henry L. (47th Indiana Infantry) 235, 238, 240–41, 258, 263, 395, 405
Berwick City, Louisiana 212
"Betsy" 36–37
Bickley, George W.L. 101–2, 174, 302; *see also* Eclectic Medicine; Knights of the Golden Circle;
Big Black River Bridge, Mississippi *125*, 143–44, 162
Bill of Rights 100, 376, 414–15
Bingham, Joseph J. 41, 43, 246, 248; arrested 253; released 254; witness for state 257; *see also Indiana State Sentinel*; Indiana Treason Trials
Bir, Louis (93rd Indiana Infantry) 186
Bird's Point, Missouri 28, 30
Bissell, Josiah W. 28, 30, 35, 82
CSS *Black Diamond* 280
"black flag" fighting 220–21, 396, 408
Blackhawk (US steamer) 220, 234
Black soldiers and their white officers: Confederate policy towards 228–29; Federal policy of retaliation 229
Blair, Montgomery 6
Blossom, Ira A. (47th Indiana Infantry) 295
Blue Wing (US supply boat) 79–80, 372
"Bohemian Brigade" 72, 359, 370, 371, 382
Bonez, R.G. 295
Boomer, George E.: at Champion Hill 136; death 153
Booth, John Wilkes 15, 361; *see also* Wallack's Old Theatre
Bowen, John S. 113, 117, 134–38, 167
Bowles, William A. 207, 246, 254, 261, 282, 284; *see also* Indiana Treason Trials
Bowling Green, Kentucky *4*, 11, 13, 22
Bragg, Braxton 63, 65–66, 79
Brashear City (Morgan City), Louisiana 164, 197
Brayman, J.M 229

Brazos Santiago Island, Texas 203, 239, 281, 285–87, 410
Breckenridge, John C. 59, 64, 179, 388
Brent, Joseph L. 223
Bright, J.E. 296
Bringhurst, Thomas A. (46th Indiana Infantry) 90, 140, 200, 202, 360, 380
Brinkerhof, George H. 15
Bross, William "Deacon" 256, 405; *see also Chicago Tribune*
Brown, George W. (USS *Forest Rose*) 84, 87
Brown, George W. (mayor of Baltimore) 3
Brown, Isaac N. 84, 88
Brown, John 24
Brown, Dr. S. Clay 313
Brown, Susan Louise McLaughlin 313–15
Brownlow, James P. 396; *see also* Forrest, Nathan Bedford
Brownlow, William G. "Parson" 12, 252, 360, 396
Brown's Plantation, Mississippi: skirmish at 64–65
Brownsville, Texas 193, 203, 211, 238, 243, 290, 296, 411
Bruinsburg, Mississippi *98*
Buckner, Simon 8, 12, 13, 19, 22, 283, 363–64
Bucks County, Pennsylvania 74
Buehler, Theodore (67th Indiana): attack on Grand Gulf 116; at Bayou Bourbeau 201
Buell, Don Carlos 10, 23, 24, 43, 60, 66
Bullen, Joseph D. (28th Maine): defends Fort Butler, Donaldsonville, Louisiana 164
Burbridge, Stephen G. 141, 201–2
Burnell, Valentine 372; *see also* Arlington, Billy
Burnett, Henry L. 252–53, 255, 257–58, 282
Burnside, Ambrose 105, 107
Bush, William S. (*Cincinnati Gazette* reporter) 257; *see also* Indiana Treason Trials
Butler, Benjamin F. 5, 45, 82, 361, 368, 396

Cadwallader, George 5
Cadwallader, Sylvanus (*Chicago Times* reporter) 130, 382
Cairo, Illinois 8, 21, 24, 49, 297
Cairo & Fulton Railroad 28
Camden, Arkansas 219–20, 287
Cameron, Robert L. 51, 85, 140, 205, 211, 218, 228, 231
Cameron, Simon 6, 9, 10
Camp Douglas, Illinois: conspiracy 248, 256; military trial at Cincinnati 258
Camp Sullivan, Indiana 11–12
Camp Wickliffe, Kentucky *4*, 12, 14, 18, 19, 20–23

Canby, E.R.S. 10, 232, 238, 260–61, 263, 265, 274–76, 279–80
Carey, James L. (1st Indiana Cavalry) 131
Carle, John 15
Carlota, Mexico: ex–Confederate colonists at 412
USS *Carondelet* 35, 40 42, 95, 114–16, 227
Carr, Eugene A. 107, 113, 144–45, 214, 276–77
Carrington, Henry B. 97, 101, 104–6, 208, 246, 375
Carrion Crow Bayou, Louisiana *191*, 199, 202
Carrollton & New Orleans Railroad 391
Carrollton, Louisiana: Slack's brigade in camp at 195, *262*, 391
Castleman, John B. 248–49, 303
Catterson, W.S. (1st Battalion Arkansas Cavalry) 127
Cavazos, Rafael Garcia 289–90, 411
Caverly, P.D. (47th Indiana correspondent to the *Huntington Democrat*) 14, 23, 31–32; death 67
Chalmers, James R. 221; *see also* Fort Pillow, Tennessee
Chambers, William Pitt (46th Mississippi Infantry): on Grierson's raid 111; on the second Federal assault at Vicksburg 149, 170; on watching the Federal fleet run the Vicksburg batteries 109
Champion Hill, Mississippi *125*, 129; battle 132–38; casualties 140; described 381
Champion No. 3 (US pump boat) 223
Champion No. 5 (US pump boat) 223
Charleston, Illinois 214
Charleston (Illinois) *Plain Dealer* 217
Chef Menteur Pass, Louisiana *262*
Chicago, Illinois 245
Chicago Times (Wilbur Storey) 107, 217
Chicago Tribune (William "Deacon" Bross) 10, 48, 101, 216, 261, 405; on emancipation 78; on *Ex parte Milligan* 414
Chickasaw Bayou, Louisiana 79
USS *Chillicothe* 86–87, 90–92, 227, 374
USS *Choctaw* 160
Chretien Point, Louisiana *191*, 200
Chrysler, Morgan H. 236
Churchill, Thomas J. 218
USS *Cincinnati* 80, 95–96, 158
Cincinnati, Ohio 65, 249
Cincinnati (Ohio) *Commercial* (Murat Halstead) 6, 10, 141, 360
Cincinnati (Ohio) *Enquirer* 104
Cincinnati Treason Trial 258, 282; indicted 405; verdicts 409
Circleville (Ohio) *Watchman* 6

Citronelle, Alabama: Confederate surrender 280
City Belle (US transport) 225
Clarendon, Arkansas *46*, 61, 64
Clark County, Illinois 104
USS *Clifton* 196, 204
Clinton, Louisiana: expedition to 242–44
Cockrell, Francis M. 108, 120–22; at Big Black River Bridge 144, 167, 274, 278; at Champion Hill 135–36
Coffroth, John R. 7; defends Milligan 257
Coldwater River, Mississippi 83, 88
College of Indiana 12
Columbia City (Indiana) *News* 106
Columbiana, Ohio 1
Columbus, Kentucky 26; flooding 48
Commerce, Mississippi *46*; sacking of 74
Commerce, Missouri 24–25, 28
Conde, James E. (47th Indiana Infantry) 388
USS *Conestoga* 57
Confederate Cavalry (Armistead's): Henry Maury's 15th 266; Spence's 16th 266, 268
"confidential agents" (US) 103, 208, 246, 255
"Connecticut Fatty" 305
Conscription Act (USA) 100, 104
Constable, Judge Charles H. (Illinois Fourth Judicial Circuit) 104, 214
Contrabands 75, 82, 86–87
Cooper, Abraham (47th Indiana Infantry) 306
Cooper, Bob 2
Cooper, John H. (47th Indiana Infantry) 306
Cope, Edmond (47th Indiana Infantry) 241
Copperheads 7, 195, 217, 256, 358
Corinth, Mississippi 26
Corps de Afrique Engineers: engineer brigade 212; 3rd 224; 5th 224
Corps de Afrique Infantry: 1st 203; 16th 203
Corps de Belgique 103
Cortina, Juan N. 193, 204, 238, 288–95; "Cortina's War" 290–91
Cotton, Gordon 2
USS *Covington* 225–26
Cox, Elijah (11th Indiana): death 86
Crabbs, Austin 49
Craft, William: "all Englishmen are not Shakespeares" 400; *see also* Ullman, Daniel
Craig, Zebedee (47th Indiana Infantry) *80*
Crebs, John M. 236
USS *Cricket* 223
The Crisis (Columbus, Ohio): destroyed by mob of soldiers 101
Crittenden, George B. 21

Crocker, Frederick: gunboats attack Fort Griffin 196
Crocker, Marcellus M. 130; at Champion Hill 136
Crosby, Isaac (47th Indiana Infantry) *80*
Crosby, Simeon (47th Indiana Infantry) *80*
Cumming, Alfred 131; at Champion Hill 133–34, 382; on Confederate line at Vicksburg 154
Cunningham, James M. (34th Indiana Infantry) 85
Curtis, Samuel R. 30, 60, 61; Price's raid 253
Custard, Aaron (47th Indiana Infantry) *80*
Custard, John (47th Indiana Infantry) *80*

Dahlia (US tug) 96
Daily Mississippian (Jackson): on skirmish at Fourteen-Mile Creek 126
Daily Telegraph (Houston, Texas) 409
Dana, Charles 111, 165, 379, 385
Dana, Napoleon J.T. 203, 211, 258
Dannelly's (Danby's) Mill, Alabama *267*, 268–69
Dartmouth College 210
Dauphin Island, Alabama 242, 264; *see also* Fort Gaines, Alabama
Davis, Antoine (92nd USCT) 228; *see also* "black flag fighting"
Davis, Charles H. 50, 53
Davis, David (US Supreme Court Justice) 106
Davis, Docter B. (47th Indiana Infantry) 306
Davis, Edmund J. (1st Texas Cavalry, USA) 193–94, 235, 240, 391
Davis, Jefferson 3, 99, 126, 186, 357
Davis, Jefferson C. 66; *see also* Nelson, William "Bull"
Davis, Mark 2
Davisson, Joseph K. (24th Indiana Infantry) 57; *see also Memphis Union Appeal*
Day, Henry M. 293
Dayton (Ohio) Daily Empire 217
Deer Creek, Mississippi 96
Deer Creek, Ohio 6
Dennis, Elias 159, 243, 264, 278, 280, 294
Department of Tennessee (USA) 71, 74
Department of the Cumberland (USA) 10
Department of the Missouri (USA) 10
Department of the Ohio (USA) 10, 104
Detroit, Michigan: Lafayette Street Unitarian Church 101; *see also* Hunting, Rev. S.S.
Detroit (Michigan) Advertiser & Tribune: the Detroit Riot 101

De Valls Bluff, Arkansas *46*, 80–81, 250, 254
Devlin, William T. (47th Indiana Infantry): death 93
Diligent (US packet) 48, 50
Dill, Benjamin F. 56
Dingess, R.A. 77
Dinius, Eli (47th Indiana Infantry) 389
District of Arkansas (CSA) 58, 64
District of Eastern Arkansas (USA) 74, 80, 82
District of West Tennessee (USA) 60
Dodd, Harrison H. 207; arrest 250; conspiracy 245–48, 252, 303, 401; military trial 252; *see also* Indiana Treason Trials
Donaldson, Louisiana 164
Donniker, John B. 372; *see also* Arlington, Billy
Dornblaser, Benjamin 243
Douglass, Frederick 175; on Negro/Irish labor competition 387
Drew, Charles W. 275
Dumont, Ebenezer 12, 13, 14
Dyersburg, Tennessee 41

Eagle Pass, Texas: Confederate exiles enter Mexico 288–89, 412
USS *Eastport* 223
Eaton (Ohio) *Register* 101
Eclectic Medicine 101, 377; *see also* Bickley, George W.L.
Edwards, David 391; *see also* Johnston, William B.
Edwards Depot, Mississippi *98*, *125*, 128
Eglin, John F. (47th Indiana Infantry) 132
Elk Ridge Railroad 4
Ellet, Charles 53
Emancipation Proclamation 78; *see also* Lincoln, Abraham
USS *Emma* 87, 222, 225
Emory, W.H. 235, 238
Enterprise, Mississippi 113
Eustis, George 16
Evergreen, Louisiana *208*, 228
Ewing, Hugh 168

Fagan, "Bully" 60; *see also* Memphis, Tennessee
Fagan, J.F. 169, 214, 219; Price's raid 250
False River, Louisiana *234*, 236, 399
Farragut, David G. 45, 242
Featherston, Winfield S. 95–96
Ferguson, Samuel W. 95
HMS *Fingal* 18
Firehammer, Mrs. Sara 2
Fisher, Sidney G.: on the writ of habeas corpus 358
Fisk, Clinton 80, 83, 107, 373
Fisk University 373
Fitch, Charles (Chaplain of the 24th Indiana Infantry) 61, 369
Fitch, Graham N. 12, 18, 22, 35,

42, 44, 49, 53, 54, 57–59, 63, 361, 368
Flags of the 47th 319, **320**
Florida & Alabama Railroad 268–69
Florida Cavalry (USA): 1st 407
Florida Infantry (CSA): 3rd 185; 4th 185
Florida Infantry (USA): 1st 274
Floyd, John B. 22
Fonda, John G. 201
Foote, Andrew H. 35, 44, 367
Ford, John S. "Rip" 239, 281, 291–93, 409, 411
USS *Forest Rose* 81
Forest Queen (US transport) 109
Forrest, Nathan Bedford 57, 60, 74, 211, 215, 220–21, 217; at Fort Pillow 395–96; postwar life 397
Fort Blakely, Alabama 266, **267**; capture 277
Fort Butler, Louisiana 164; see also Bullen, Joseph D.; Green, Thomas
Fort De Russy, Louisiana **208**, 225
Fort Donelson, Tennessee 22–23
Fort Gaines, Alabama 264
Fort Griffin, Texas 195–96
Fort Henry, Tennessee 21
USS *Fort Hindman* 223
Fort Huger, Alabama 268, 273, 279
Fort Jackson (US steamer) 285
Fort Pemberton, Mississippi **46**, 90, 92–93
Fort Pike, Louisiana **262**, 264
Fort Pillow, Tennessee 45, 47–48, 51; massacre 220
Fort Randolph, Tennessee 45, 48
Fort Thompson, Missouri 27, 28, 30; capture 39–40
Fort Tracy, Alabama 268, 273, 279
"the Forty-Eighters" 387
Foster, James D. 86, 92–93
Fourteen-Mile Creek, Mississippi **125**; skirmish at 126
Franklin, William B. 195, 205, 212, 392
Franklin, Louisiana 199
Franklin, Tennessee 1
Freebooters (Filibusters) 102, 376
Freedom of the Press 6, 107
Frei, Maureen 2
Fremont, John C. 8, 9, 10, 102, 358–59
Freitag, Charlotte Rose 2
Freitag, Thomas 2
Fullilove, Thomas R. 295
Fulton (US mortar boat) 88

Gamron, Elizabeth 104
Gamron, James 104
Gantt, E.W. 27, 35
Garrett, Isham 120, 157; killed at Vicksburg 162
Geddes, James L. 276
General Price (US ram) 116
General Banks (US transport) 279
George Christy's Minstrels 372

George Peabody (US transport) 264
Georgia Artillery (CSA): Massenberg's Light 270; Van Den Corput's Cherokee Battery 134
Georgia Infantry (CSA): 34th 131, 134; 36th 131; 39th 130; 40th 131; 41st 131; 42nd 130–31; 43rd 131; 47th 185; 52nd 131; 56th 131, 134; 57th 131, 134, 165, 382
German Workingmen's Association (Chicago): "life blood of a poor man" 100
Gibson, Randall L. 268–69, 271–72, 274–77, 281; see also Tulane University
Glassey, Patrick Francis "Leon" 372; see also Arlington, Billy
Glendale (US transport) 23, 24, 28
Glenn, W.W. 6
Giambrone, Jeff T. 2
Goodwin, Edward (35th Alabama Infantry): at Champion Hill 137–38
Goodwin, Lewis H. (47th Indiana Infantry) 75, 141, 205, 243
Gorman, Willis A. 74, 80, 83, 87, 107
Graham's Plantation, Louisiana **208**, 226
CSS *Grampus* 35
Grand Ecore, Louisiana 213
Grand Gulf, Mississippi **98**, 109; attack on 114–16; battery on Point of Rocks 113
Granger, Gordon 242, 261, 264, 265, 279–80; Juneteenth 287
USS *Granite City* 196
Grant, Ulysses S. 8, 9, 21, 22, 24, 43, 51, 60, 71, 74, 80, 82, 96, 107, 115, 153, 162–63, 165, 167, 196, 199, 213, 232, 286, 375
Gray, A.B. 26
Great Mingo Swamp, Missouri 28
Green, Martin 166
Green, Thomas 164, 199, 212
Greene, Martin E. 117; at Champion Hill 135; at Big Black River Bridge 144; at 2nd Texas Lunette 152–53
Greene, William A. (29th Wisconsin Infantry) 243
Greenville, Louisiana 195, 392
Grenada, Mississippi 51, 56, 92
Grenfell, George St. Leger 304, 404–5; remanded to Fort Jefferson, Dry Tortugas, Florida 410, 416; see also Cincinnati Treason Trial
Grierson, Benjamin H. 110, 113, 259
Griffith, Joseph E. (22nd Iowa Infantry) 149
Griswold, Lt. D.B. 29
Griswold, Elihu 1

"H" (11th Indiana correspondent to the *Indianapolis Daily Journal*) 86–87
habeas corpus (CSA): 99–100, 376

habeas corpus (USA): 5, 7, 68, 99–100, 104, 106, 282, 299, 357–58, 376, 403, 413
Hahn, Michael (governor of Louisiana, USA) 210
Hains, Peter C. 110, 156, 379
Hall, Thomas W. 6
Halleck, Henry W. 10, 11, 24, 43, 44, 45, 71, 96, 359
Halstead, Murat (*Cincinnati Commercial*): on Sherman' "insanity" 10–11, 360
Hamburg, Tennessee 44
Hamilton, Schuyler 28, 31, 33, 35, 43
Hannibal & St. Joseph Railroad 404
Hardeman, William P. 228–29
Hardesty, John (34th Indiana correspondent to the *Indianapolis Daily Journal*) 58
Harrison, William H. 254; see also Indiana Treason Trials
Hascal, Milo: replaced by Willcox 107; replaces Carrington 106
Hawes, Richard (governor of Kentucky, CSA) 66
Hawkins, John P. 275; capture of Fort Blakely 277
Hayford, William H. (47th Indiana Infantry) 93
Haynes, Isaac (47th Indiana Infantry) 241
Hazen, William B. 18–20, 22–24
Hebert, Louis 165, 167
Heffren, Horace 254; see also Indiana Treason Trials
Heinel, Samuel (47th Indiana Infantry) 241
Heintzelman, Samuel P. 248, 411
Helena, Arkansas **46**, 63; Mrs. Cogswell's silverware 240; Sterling Price's attack on 168–70
Helena (Arkansas) *Shield* 75
Hendricks, Thomas A. 63
Henry Clay (US transport) 109
Henry Von Phul (US transport) 88
Heroine (CS transport) 273
Heron, Matilda 76, 372
Herron, Francis J. 160, 165, 211, 238, 243, 286, 288, 291, 400
Hey, Michael (47th Indiana Infantry) 241
Hickenlooper, Andrew 165, 167
Hickman, Tennessee 45; flooding 49
Hicks, Thomas H. (governor of Maryland) 3
Hilton, Daniel (47th Indiana Infantry) **308**, 309
Hindman, Thomas C. 58, 64
Hines, Thomas H. 248–49, 303, 403
Hodgenville, Kentucky **4**, 18
Hodgson, Michael W. (47th Indiana Infantry) **80**
Hogane, James T. 29
Hollins, George N. 27, 44
Holmes, Theophilus 168–70
Holtzclaw, James T. 274, 276
Hooker, Joseph "Fighting Joe" 107

Index

Hopkins, Owen Johnston (42nd Ohio Infantry) 109; attack on Grand Gulf 116; on Grant's generalship at Vicksburg 154; running Vicksburg's batteries 111
US transport *Horizon* 113, 116
Horsey, Stephen A. 254, 261, 282, 284; *see also* Indiana Treason Trials
Hovey, Alvin P. 60, 64, 70, 71–73, 74, 80, 83, 86, 99, 107, 113, 121, 137, 140, 154, 157, 183, 197, 249, 255, 257; *see also* Indiana Treason Trials
Howard, F. Key 6
Howell, Grady 2
Hudson, Keith 2
Hudson, Ohio 1
Humphreys, Andrew 208, 248, 254, 261, 415; *see also* Indiana Treason Trials
Hunter, David 10
Hunting, Rev. S.S. (Lafayette Street Unitarian Church, Detroit) 101
Huntington County Historical Society 2
Huntington, Indiana 7; casualties at Champion Hill 383
Huntington (Indiana) *Herald* 69, 302
Huntington (Indiana) *Democrat* 7, 13, 14, 21, 23–24, 32, 45, 67, 97–98, 139, 174; arrests of Indiana dissidents 69; Camp Douglas conspiracy trial begins at Cincinnati 258; on emancipation 78–79; Indianapolis trials end 258; on Slack 233; on the treason trials 255–56
Huntsville (CS floating battery) 268, 406
Hurlbut, Stephen A. 74
Hutchens, John B. 227

Illinois Artillery (USA): 1st Light 129, 132; 2nd Light 121; Chicago Mercantile 129, 139, 150; Peoria Battery 74, 122; Waterhouse's Battery E., 1st 187; Waterhouse's Battery E., 2nd 50, 129
Illinois Cavalry (USA): 2nd 50, 108, 110, 129, 181, 243, 274–75, 407; 7th 29; 8th 132; 10th 159; 17th 214
Illinois Infantry (USA): 8th 132, 134, 243, 264, 274, 278; 10th 30; 11th 243, 264, 274, 147 165; 16th 30; 20th 132; 26th 29; 28th 185, 287; 29th 114, 258, 263–64; 30th 132; 31st 132; 32nd 387; 41st 185, 216; 45th 165; 46th 243, 264, 278; 53rd 185, 274; 54th 50, 214 216, 250; 55th 166; 66th 215; 76th 243; 77th 148, 150; 81st 132, 134; 87th 108, 157, 196, 224, 236, 399; 91st 293; 93rd 136, 153; 97th 148; 99th 251, 264, 269, 272, 275, 280; 108th 148, 118th 224, 243; 119th 278; 124th 134; 130th 104, 150

Indiana Artillery (USA): Klauss's 1st 118; 21st Battery 210
Indiana Cavalry (USA): 1st 104, 131, 169
Indiana Elections 69
Indiana Historical Society 2
Indiana House of Representatives: "the tyrant's plea" 97, 376
Indiana Infantry (USA): 8th 240; 11th 71, 74, 86, 99, 107; 23rd 132, 157, 165, 202, 224, 240; 24th 61, 71, 81, 86, 99, 107, 121, 131, 157, 202, 224; 31st 104; 34th (Morton Rifles) 19, 24, 25, 31, 34, 39, 40, 43, 44, 50–52, 56, 58, 60, 69, 84, 107, 110, 119, 281, 287; 38th 152; 43rd 24, 25, 39, 43–44, 49, 56, 57, 60, 83, 99, 169; 46th 12, 13, 18, 22–25, 39, 43, 49–50, 52, 57, 83, 93, 117, 132, 157, 202, 208, 211; 48th 12, 152; 49th 12, 108, 137, 148, 224; 51st 12; 53rd 185; 54th 157; 59th 24–25, 43; 60th 182, 187, 201; 67th 182; 69th 224; 93rd 148, 186; 118th 210
Indiana State Library 2
Indiana State Sentinel 39, 41, 43, 45, 49, 54, 69, 72, 100, 104, 105, 207, 246, 248, 252, 254, 370, 403; *see also* Bingham, Joseph J.
Indiana Treason Trials: arrests 250, 252; the indicted 254
Indiana University, Lilly Library 2
Indiana War Memorials Commission 2
Indianapolis, Indiana *4*, 12, 208
Indianapolis Daily Gazette 206, 217, 256, 297–98, 405; Battle of Champion Hill 141; on emancipation 78
Indianapolis Daily Journal 6, 11, 12, 15, 18, 33, 37, 45, 48, 51, 54, 59, 60, 64–65, 67, 68, 69–70, 76, 84, 101, 104, 141, 205, 209–10, 217, 222, 247, 260–61, 282, 311–12, 357, 362, 364, 394, 414
Invalid Corps (USA): 1st Battalion 176
Iowa Artillery (USA): Griffith's Battery, 1st 118
Iowa Cavalry (USA): 3rd 56; 9th 250
Iowa Infantry (USA): 3rd 185; 4th 187; 5th 88, 136; 8th 276; 9th 187; 10th 136; 12th 274; 17th 136; 21st 118, 144, 148, 150, 152, 263–64, 270–71, 275; 22nd 117, 144, 148–49, 150, 154; 23rd 144, 159; 24th 108–9, 120, 132, 134, 157, 196, 208, 211, 224, 226, 236, 238, 240; 26th 187; 28th 72, 108–9, 120, 132, 157, 196, 208, 211, 231, 238, 240; 29th 83; 30th 187; 33rd 83, 169; 34th 224; 35th 274; 36th 83; 56th 108
Island No. 10 (New Madrid) 16, *17*, 26, 40

Jackson, William H. "Red" 57, 178, 186, 188–89
Jackson, Mississippi 56, 126, *173*; destruction of 187; mayor's committee 188
Jefferson & Lake Pontchartrain Railroad 264
Jeffersonville Railroad (Indiana) 11
Jennings, Lt. Horatio P. 49
Jennie Whipple (US transport) 296
John D. Perry (US transport) 54
John H. Dickey (US transport) 258
John H. Groesbeck (US transport) 222
John Kilgore (US transport) 297
John Warner (US transport) 225
Johnson, Andrew 282, 286
Johnson, A.R. (Morgan's Cavalry, CSA) 368
Johnson, Elbridge **80**
Johnson, George W. (governor of Kentucky, CSA) 11
Johnson, Roger L. 2, 308
Johnson's Island, Ohio 323
Johnston, Albert Sidney 8, 11, 24, 26, 43
Johnston, George Benton "Bent" 391; *see also* Johnston, William B.
Johnston, John W. (Botetort's Virginia Battery) 131
Johnston, Joseph E. 127–28, 145, 178, 186, 213
Johnston, William B. (great-great-grandfather of Brenda Perrott Williamson) 391
Jones, Benjamin (47th Indiana Infantry) **308**, 309
Jones, Dewey 2, 309
Jones, Joseph (47th Indiana Infantry) **80**
Juarez, Benito 192, 204, 286, 291, 390
Jones County, Mississippi: "Free State of Jones" 408; *see also* Wilkes, Abner
USS *Juliet* 223

Kansas Infantry (USA): 1st USCT 214; 2nd USCT 214
Keigwin, James 148, 181, 226
Keim, William H. 5
Keller, S.J. (47th Indiana Infantry) 158–60, 166, 231
Kendall, Wendall Wesley (49th Indiana Infantry): Medal of Honor at Big Black River Bridge 145
Kenner, Louisiana *262*, 263
Kent, Lauren 264
Kentucky Artillery (CSA): Cobb's Battery 184
Kentucky Infantry (CSA): 3rd 135; 7th 135
Kentucky Infantry (USA): 6th 18, 19, 20, 21, 22, 23; 19th 148, 211; 22nd 157
Key West, Florida 18
USS *Kineo* 164

436   Index

"Kizer" (43rd Indiana correspondent to the *Indianapolis Daily Journal*) 37
Knight, Newton "Newt" 408; *see also* Jones County, Mississippi
Knights of the Golden Circle 63, 101–3, 217, 377, 401
Knoxville Whig and Rebel Ventilator 360; *see also* Brownlow, William G. "Parson"

labor issues in the North 175–76, 387
Lady Pike (US transport) 23
USS *Lafayette* 114, 219–20
Lafayette, Louisiana *191*, 199
La Grange, Tennessee 74, 79
Lake Pontchartrain, Louisiana *262*, 264
Landis (US transport) 280
Landrum, William J. 211, 218
Lane, Sen. Henry Smith: deal with Gov. Morton 63
Laurel Hill (US transport) 250
Langhorne, Maurice 256
Lauman, Jacob 165; at Jackson 183, 185
Lawler, Michael 144–45, 149, 200, 236, 258, 263
Lee, Albert L. 205, 213, 218, 243
Lee, Robert E. 213, 291, 411
Lee, Stephen D. 131; at Champion Hill 133, 138; at Vicksburg 149, 151, 154; Vicksburg report 157
Leggett, Mortimer 165
Lewis, Merrill 2
USS *Lexington* 57, 160, 220, 368
Library of Hattiesburg, Petal, and Forrest County, Mississippi 2
Liddell, St. John 266, 278
Lincoln, Abraham 3, 4, 5, 6, 7, 8, 18, 22, 68, 103, 106, 193–94, 314, 357, 401
Lindsay, Robert H. 271
Lindsey, Hiram (47th Indiana Infantry) 18, 39, 49
Lindsey, Kevin 2, 307
Lindsey, William (47th Indiana Infantry) *307*, 308
USS *Lioness* 87
Little Rock, Arkansas 214
Liverpool (England) Post 51
Livonia, Louisiana *234*, 236–37
Lobdell's Landing, Louisiana *234*
Lockett, Samuel H. 145, 156, 158, 167
Lofton, Ted and Teresa 2
Logan, John 129, 167, 189–90, 195, 391
Logan's Cross Road, Kentucky 21
Logansport (Indiana) *Journal* 25
London (England) *Spectator* 377
Long, Thomas (1st Indiana Cavalry) 104
Loomis, John M. 29
Loring, William W. 81, 85, 92–94, 113, 124, 139, 211
Louisiana Artillery (CSA): 22nd 268, 270; Cornay's Battery 223–24; Pointe Coupee Battery 27; Scott's Appeal Battery 166; Washington 184–85, 270, 272;
Louisiana Cavalry (CSA): 1st 242; 2nd 213, 228; 9th 243; 13th Battalion 160; 15th Battalion 108, 112
Louisiana Cavalry (USA): 1st 202, 269, 399
Louisiana Infantry (CSA): 3rd 156; 4th 183; 9th Battalion 243; 12th 135, 137; 17th 120, 152; 28th 152; 31st 120; Gibson's Brigade 268
Louisiana Infantry (USA): 1st 164, 407; 8th (African descent) 160; 9th (African descent) 134, 159; 11th (African descent) 159–60; 13th (African descent) 159
Louisiana Plantations: Barrow's *234*; Bennett's *98*, 110; Dawson's *98*, 110; Disharoon's 116; Dunbar's *98*, 108; Graham's *208*, 226; Holmes's *98*, 110; James's 108; Noland's *98*, 110; Perkins's Somerset *98*, 108, 111; Smith's *98*, 108; Winn's *208*; Woolfolk's *234*, 237
Louisiana State University 359
USS *Louisville* 95–96; attack on Grand Gulf 114–16
Louisville, Kentucky *4*, 9, 10, 11, 13, 65
Louisville & Nashville Railroad 12
Lyne, W.H. 225

Ex parte McCardle 414
Macarthy, Harry B.: "Bonnie Blue Flag" 361
Macarthy, Marion 15, 76, 361; *see also* Wallack's Old Theatre
Mackall, William W. 27, 41
USS *Madison* 217
Madison, George T. 235
Madison, James: on the Bill of Rights 100; *see also* Bill of Rights
Madison & Indianapolis Railroad *4*, 360
CSS *Magenta* 88
Magruder, John Bankhead "Prince John" 193, 283, 285, 292
Maine Cavalry (USA): 2nd 274–75, 407
Maine Infantry (USA): 13th 203; 15th 203; 28th 164
Manning, Albert Augustus (47th Indiana Infantry) 306
Manning, James 2
Manning, William Ziba (47th Indiana Infantry) 306
Manship, C.H. (mayor of Jackson, Mississippi): plea to Sherman from mayor's committee 188
Manson, Malone D. 65
Mansura, Louisiana 228
Marland, William (2nd Massachusetts Battery) 203
Marmaduke, John S. 170, 214; Price's raid 250
USS *Marmora* 87
Martin, John A. (47th Indiana Infantry) 49; death of 76
Marx, Karl 389–90
Mary (CS transport) 273
Maryland Cavalry (US): 3rd 237, 399
Mason, James M. 16
Massachusetts Artillery (USA): 2nd Battery 201, 203, 205; 4th Battery 264; 7th Battery 237, 264, 278; 15th battery 263
Massachusetts Cavalry (USA): 6th 236, 399
Massachusetts Infantry (USA): 31st mounted 407
Matamoros, Mexico 239, 285, 288–95
Mattoon (Illinois) *Gazette* 214
Mattoon, Illinois: violence in Coles County 214–15, 395
CSS *Maurepas* 57
Maury, Dabney 261, 266, 406, 408
Maury, Henry "Harry" (15th Confederate Cavalry) 266, 408
Maxey, Samuel B. 219
Maximilian 281, 289, 292, 295, 390, 413
Maynadier, Capt. Henry C. 47–48
McClanahan, John R. 56
McClellan, George B. 10, 11; Democratic presidential candidate 207, 243, 249, 251
McClernand, John A. 60, 71, 74, 79, 80, 83, 135, 153, 156, 162–63, 210, 222, 225, 370
McCook, Alexander 66
McCook, John James 305, 416; *see also* Aspinwall, William "Roving Bill"
McCown, John P. 26
McCulloch, Benjamin 8, 102
McCulloch, Henry E. 159
McDonald, Joseph E. 246
McFarland, J.E. 16
McFarland, John (31st Indiana Infantry): 104
McGinnis, George F. 87, 97, 99, 107; at Champion Hill 135–36, 139; line at Vicksburg 154, 197, 205, 287
McLaughlin, Henry B. "Harry" (35th Alabama) 139, 304, 311
McLaughlin, John A. 34, 49, 70, *72*, 75, 107, 119, 121, 140, 205, 243, 251, 264–66, 269, 272–73, 304, 311–12, 370
McLean, William E. 97, 99
McNaught, Peter 52
McNelly, Leander H. (Texas Scouts, CSA) 238, 400
McPherson, James B. 74, 83, 16
Means, Joe 2
Mejia, Tomas 285, 288, 293–94
Melville, Louisiana *234*
Memphis, Tennessee 41, 45, *46*, 56, 263
Memphis & Charleston Railroad 57, 60, 389

Index

Memphis & Ohio Railroad 41
Memphis Argus 53–56
Memphis Appeal 55–56, 221, 369
Memphis Avalanche 54–55
Memphis Evening Bulletin 162
Memphis Union Appeal 57, 61–62
Meridian, Mississippi 56; destroyed 211
Merriam, Henry (73rd USCI) 277–78
Merryman, John (*Ex parte John Merryman*) 5, 99, 104
Messenger, N.C. (22nd Iowa) 149
Methodists: churches 239; ministers 109, 239, 376, 400
Mexico 102; abolition and reintroduction of slavery 390; French invasion 192–93, 204; "War of the Reform" 192;
Michigan Artillery (USA): DeGolyer's Battery, 7th 181; 8th Light 50, 122, 132, 136
Michigan Infantry (USA): 2nd 183; 7th 129; 11th 12
Mickle, Samuel S. (47th Indiana Infantry) 49–50
Middle Bayou, Louisiana **208**, 226, 230; *see also* Graham's Plantation
Mill Bayou, Louisiana **98**, 108
Milligan, Lambdin P. 7, 208, 246, 254–55, 257, 261, 282; on his arrest 403; and Bill of Rights 414; *Ex parte Milligan* 284, 299–301; *Milligan v. Hovey*, et al. 302; *Milligan v. Slack*, et al. 302, 415; *see also* Indiana Treason Trials
Milliken's Bend, Louisiana 96, **98**, 108, 160
Mills, Mrs. James R. 50
Mills, S.S. 6
Minden (Louisiana) Female College 296
Milwaukee (US monitor) 272
Minnesota Infantry (USA): 4th 152; 7th 274
Miramon, Miguel 192; *see also* Mexico
Mississippi Artillery (CSA): 1st Battery 184; 1st Light 95, 130, 134, 268; Hudson's Battery, Pettus Flying 117
Mississippi Cavalry (CSA): 15th 408; 22nd 95; 28th 388
Mississippi Central Railroad 72, *173*, 186, 188, 259, 389
Mississippi Infantry (CSA): 4th 120, 122; 6th 119–20, 408; 23rd 95; 28th 95; 43rd 165; 46th 1, 109, 111, 120, 122–23, 149, 170, 275
Mississippi & Tennessee Railroad 51, 72, 92
Mississippi Plantations: Doyal's 243; Hill's 96; Moore's 96; Windsor 117
Missouri 8
Missouri (US steamer) 222
Missouri Artillery (CSA): Guibor's Battery 120; Landis's Battery 120, 137
Missouri Artillery (USA): 1st 108, 121, 130, 136, 211, 236; Schofield's Battery A, 1st Light 119, 122, 136; 33rd
Missouri Cavalry (CSA): 3rd 135; Clark's Light 181
Missouri Cavalry (USA): 6th 181, 243; 8th 250; 9th 250
Missouri Infantry (CSA): 1st 108, 135; 2nd 115, 135; 3rd 120, 135; 5th 120, 122, 135; 6th 120, 135; 7th 170; 10th 170
Missouri Infantry (USA): 7th 243; 8th 96; 10th 136; 11th 29; 26th 136; 30th 243, 264; 33rd 83; 35th 83
Missouri State Guard (CSA) 25
Mitchell, Eliza Kimberly McLaughlin 312
Mitchell, Dr. T.G. 312
USS *Mittie Stevens* 251
Mobile, Alabama 190, **267**, 279, 283
Mobile (Alabama) *News* 113, 211, 283
Mobile & Great Northern Railroad 268–69, 274
Mobile & Ohio Railroad 51, 211, 259, 280
Mobile Bay, Alabama **267**
Mobile Point Peninsula, Alabama **267**
Moderator (US transport) 87, 92
Monette's Ferry (Cane River Crossing), Louisiana 221
USS *Monongahela* 203
Monroe, John (mayor of New Orleans) 45
Monroe County, Arkansas 58–59
Monroe, Louisiana 219
Montgomery, Alabama 56
Montholon, Marquis de 412
Monticello, Mississippi 242
Moon Lake, Mississippi 84
Moore, John C. 152–53
Moorhous, Albert (47th Indiana Infantry) 64
Moorhous, Hiram (47th Indiana Infantry) 49, 64
CSS *Morgan* 268, 273, 279–80, 406
Morgan, Charles H. (47th Indiana Infantry) **80**
Morgan, James D. 30
Morgan, John Hunt 60, 174, 368
Morgan's Ferry, Louisiana **234**, 235
Morganza, Louisiana **208**, 230, 232, **234**, 240, 250, 288
Morton, Oliver P. (governor of Indiana) 8, 9, 11, 52, 63, 97, 104, 107, 172, 174, 208, 246, 255, 282, 313
Morrison, Humphrey (47th Indiana Infantry) 241
Morrison, Robert G. (34th Indiana) 281, 294, 296
"Morton Rifles" (34th Indiana correspondent to the *Indianapolis Daily Journal*): on the Yazoo Pass Expedition 84–85

"Mosquito Fleet" (US) 87
USS *Mound City* 35, 57–58, 95, 114, 227
Mouton, Alfred 164, 199, 212, 218
Munfordville, Kentucky **4**, 19
Murfreesboro, Tennessee 60, 79
Mustang (US transport) 265
Myers, William Ralph (47th Indiana Infantry) 305

N. Longworth (US transport) 238
Nanna Hubba Bluff, Alabama: surrender of Confederate fleet 281
CSS *Nashville* 268, 273, 278–80, 406
Natchez, Mississippi 194
Natchez (Mississippi) *Weekly Courier* 112, 124
National Zeitung (New York City) 6
Navigator (US transport) 297
Nelson, Dan 2, 309
Nelson, William "Bull" 18, 19, 21, 23, 24, 65–66, 362
Netherland, Col. 12, 369; *see also* Sawyer, Samuel
New Hampshire Cavalry: 2nd 236
New Iberia, Louisiana 199–200, 204–6
New Madrid, Missouri 16, *17*, 24, 26, 43; flooding 48
New Orleans, Louisiana 45, 209, 214, 222, 233, **262**, 263, 283, 391
New Orleans, Jackson & Great Northern Railroad 113, *173*, 184, 187, 189
New Orleans, Opelousas & Great Western Railroad 165, 196, 238, 392
New York Artillery (USA): 21st 241; 26th 244, 287
New York Cavalry (USA) 178, 236, 242, 243, 399, 407
New York City: "Bohemians" at Pfaff's beer cellar 371–72; draft riots 175–78; labor issues 175–76; Metropolitan Fire Department 387; politics 387
New York Daily News (Benjamin Wood) 207
New York Herald (John Gordon Bennett) 72, 175, 177, 178, 233
New York Infantry (USA): 161st 264, 272
New York Journal of Commerce 6
New York National Guard 178
New York News 6
New York Times (Henry J. Raymond) 72, 175, 177, 178, 216, 227–28, 263, 266, 371, 377, 398, 391
New York Tribune (Horace Greeley) 9, 10, 72, 175, 177–78; and C.H. Dana 379; and Karl Marx 389
New York World 107, 217
Newburg, Indiana 60
Newman, John Phillip 239, 400; *see also* Algiers Methodist Church

Nichol, George (47th Indiana) 52, 75
Noble, John H. 56
North Central Railroad 3
North Missouri Railroad 404
Northwest Conspiracy 245, 249, 252
"Nutmegs" 196, 392
USS *Nymph* 400

Oats, Harvey (47th Indiana Infantry) 250, 417
Odd Fellows 7
O'Hair, John 214–16; *see also* Mattoon, Illinois
Ohio Artillery (USA): 2nd 108, 121, 129; 3rd 129, 132, 211; 5th Battery 184–85; 6th 108, 129; 11th 130; Murdock's 16th Battery 121, 136, 183; 17th 129, 201
Ohio Infantry (USA): 6th 23; 16th 157, 224; 41st 18, 19, 22; 42nd 109, 114th 117, 137, 157; 43rd 24, 29; 45th 23; 48th 148, 152; 56th 119, 121, 132, 157, 208, 225, 238; 58th 114, 116, 380; 63rd 40; 77th 287; 78th 185; 83rd 201, 278; 93rd 278; 96th 201, 203; 114th 224; 120th 243, 251, 258; 128th 313
Okalona, Mississippi 211
Opdycke, Emerson 20, 23, 24, 363
Opdyke, George (mayor of New York City) 175; defeats Fernando Wood 387
Opelousas, Louisiana *191*, 200, 203
Ord, E.O.C. 162, 182, 210–11, 414
Order of American Knights 103, 106, 207, 244, 403
Order of the American Cincinnatus 247
USS *Osage* 220, 273
Osceola, Arkansas 44
Osterhaus, Peter J. 61, 107, 113, 134, 144–45, 180, 283
USS *Ottawa* 18
USS *Owasco* 203
Owen, Richard 187
Owensboro, Kentucky 9
Oxford, Mississippi 73–74

"P" (anonymous 47th Indiana correspondent to the *Indianapolis Daily Journal*): on the Vicksburg siege 161
Paducah, Kentucky *4*, 8, 9, 23, 24, 217
Paine, E.A. 28, 41
Paine, H.E. 59
Palmer, John M. 24, 25, 28, 33, 36, 42
Palmerston, Lord 16, 390
Palmetto Ranch, Texas 281
Pannabaker, William E. 29
Parke, J.G. 160
Parsons, Mosby M. 218
Paul, Benjamin G. (24th Iowa Infantry) 236

Paul, Charles (47th Indiana Infantry) 305
Paul, Thomas (47th Indiana Infantry) 305
Pea Ridge, Arkansas 30
Peace Democrats 7
Pearsall, Uri B. 224, 226
Pemberton, John C. 71, 73, 84, 127–28; surrenders Vicksburg 167
Pensacola (US steam sloop; West Gulf Blockading Squadron) 204
Perry, James F. (47th Indiana Infantry): at Champion Hill 141
Perryville, Kentucky 66
USS *Petrel* 87
Phares, Soloman (47th Indiana Infantry) 241
Phelps, John W. 396
Philadelphia, Wilmington & Baltimore Railroad 3
Phillips, Evan (47th Indiana Infantry) 65
Pile, William A. 275
Pillow, Gideon 22, 26
Pineville, Louisiana **208**
USS *Pittsburg* 35, 41, 95; attack on Grand Gulf 114–16
Pittsburg Landing/Shiloh, Tennessee 3, 45
Pleasant Hill, Louisiana 218
Plummer, Joseph B. 29
Plymouth (Indiana) *Democrat* 6
Point Pleasant, Missouri 26, 36; flooding 49
Pointe Coupee Parish, Louisiana **234**, 237
Polar Star (US transport) 222
Polignac, Camille de 219, 229, 235
Polk, Leonidas 8, 26, 43, 66, 211
CSS *Pontchartrain* 57, 368
"Pook Turtles" 35, 40, 80, 366
Porter, David D. 71, 80, 82, 96, 115, 212, 219
Porter, Ed E. 84, 88
Pope, John 24, 25, 28, 29, 33, 42, 44, 45, 282
Port Gibson, Mississippi **98**, **112**, 118, 120
Portsmouth (Ohio) *Times* 45
Prentiss, Benjamin 107; defense of Helena, Arkansas 168–70
Presbyterians 12–13, 117, 252; *see also* Sawyer, Samuel
USS *Price* 95
Price, Sterling "Old Pap" 8, 71, 168–70, 194, 214, 243, 250, 254, 286, 288, 404
Prime, Frederick 82
USS *Princess Royal* 164
Princeton University 12
USS *Pringle* 251
Pronty, Jesse (47th Indiana Infantry) 241
Providence (Rhode Island) *Post* 100

Queen Victoria 16
Quinby, Isaac F. 44, 50, 51, 57, 92–94, 130
Ex parte Quirin 414–15

Railing, Martin (47th Indiana Infantry) 76
Ransom, Thomas E.G. 194, 204, 211–12
Rapier, Mr. 19
Ratliff, W.B. 237, 288, 399
USS *Rattler* 87
Ray, John M. (47th Indiana Infantry) 294–96
Raynor, William H. 109, 140, 211, 225, 231, 378
Red Gauntlet (CS transport) 273
Reed, Athaniel, Jr. (47th Indiana Infantry) 306
Reed, Athaniel, Sr. (47th Indiana Infantry) 306
Reelfoot Lake, Tennessee 27, 41
Rehnquist, William 414; *see also* Milligan, Lambdin P.
Republican Watchman (Greenport, Long Island) 6
Reynolds, Joseph J. 214, 238
Richmond (Indiana) *Jeffersonian* 101
Richmond, Louisiana **98**, 109
Riddle's Point, Missouri 26, 36, 40–41
Ridgley, John B. (47th Indiana Infantry) 60
The Rigolets **262**, 264, 405
HMS *Rinaldo* 18
Risor, George (47th Indiana Infantry) 272
Roberts, Nancy Johnston 391; *see also* Johnston, William B.
Robinson, George D. 224, 226
Robinson, Milton S. (47th Indiana Infantry) 20, 24, 34, 50, 52, 70, 304
Rodney, Mississippi **98**
USS *Rodolph* 273
Rogersville, Tennessee: Second Presbyterian Church 12; *see also* Sawyer, Samuel
USS *Romeo* 81
Rose, Charles Warren **307**
Rose, Eli E. (47th Indiana Infantry) v, 250, 272, **306**, **307**, 417
Rose, Eli E., Sr. 1, 306
Rose, Hannah Jenkins 1, 306
Rose, Harvey Keagy v, 1, **307**
Rose, James William **307**
Rose, Josephine Kirkbride v
Rose, Mary Keagy v, **306**, **307**
Rose, Walter Burroughs 1
USS *Rose Hambleton* 258
Rosecrans, William S. 71, 79, 104
Ross, Leonard F. 83, 87, 90, 92
Rosedale, Louisiana **234**, 237
Runkle, Peter (47th Indiana Infantry) **80**
Russell, Lord John 17
Ryan, Carol 2

Index

USS *S. Bayard* 88
Sabine Cross Roads, Louisiana 218
USS *Sachem* 196
St. Albans, Vermont 402
St. Charles, Arkansas **46**, 57, 80, 251
USS *St. Louis* 35, 57
St. Louis Democrat 48
St. Louis, Missouri 8, 244, 253, 282
St. Mary (CS transport) 88
Salineville, Ohio 402
Salomon, Frederick 83, 107, 169, 214, 374
Sanborn, John B. 136
USS *San Jacinto* 16, 362
Sawyer, Samuel (chaplain of the 47th Indiana Infantry and correspondent to the *Indianapolis Daily Journal*) 12–13, 20, 33–35, 49, 51, 57, 61, 70, 74, 75, 86–87, 209, 210, 222, 230–31, 239, 240, 241, 251–52, 360, 369; *see also* Presbyterians
Saxon, Rufus 78
Scott, John S. (1st Louisiana Cavalry, CSA) 242
Scott, Joseph "J.Z." (46th Indiana correspondent to the *Huntington Democrat*) 13, 21–22, 67–68, 139, 364
Scott, Thomas A. 8
Scott, Thomas M. (12 Louisiana Infantry, CSA): at Champion Hill 137
Scott, Winfield 4, 20
Scovill, Edward A. 313; *see also* Johnson's Island, Ohio
Seddon, James 228
Seward, William 16, 17, 245, 286, 294, 412
Shanks, John T. 256
Shaw, Milt (5th Iowa Infantry): on the Yazoo Pass Expedition 88, 374
Shelby, Joseph O. "J.O." 244, 250–54, 286, 288–89, 295, 410–11, 413
Sheppard, Francis E. 84
Sheridan, Philip 284, 288, 294–95, 412
Sherman, William T. 9, 10, 11, 23, 43, 60, 61, 71, 74, 83, 96, 162, 186, 188, 211–13, 251, 359, 360, 369, 382
The "Shillito" flag **19**, 319; *see also* Flags of the 47th
USS *Shingiss* 45, 47
Shoup, Francis A. 166
Shreveport, Louisiana 212, 286
Sibley, Artemus O. (15th CSA Cavalry) 268, 269, 406
Sibley, Origen, Jr. (15th CSA Cavalry) 268, 269
USS *Signal* 81, 87, 225–26, 373
Sikeston, Missouri 28
Silver Cloud (US steamer) 221; *see also* Fort Pillow, Tennessee

USS *Silver Wave* 109
Simmesport, Louisiana **208**, 228–30
Simmons, John T. (28th Iowa Infantry) 239, 400
Slack, Ann P. 50, 60, 67, 75, 88, 92–93, 110, 157, 159, 179, 188, 195–96, 198, 202, 226, 235–36, 250, 253–54, 272, 280, 289, 359, 363, 380–81, 383, 385–86, 388, 392
Slack, Anthony 52
Slack, James R. 3, 7, 9, **10**, 19, 21, 25, 28, 31, 34, 42, 43, 44, 53, 60, 66, 67, 74–75, 88, 90, 92–93, 97, 107, 110, 122, 133, 135, 154, 157, 159, 179, 183–84, 188, 195, 196–99, 198, 202, 205, 220, 222, 224, 226, 230, 233, 235, 236, 238, 240–42, 243, 250, 251, 253–54, 258, 264, 265, 269, 270, 272, 277–78, 280, 283, 286, 289, 304, 359, 363, 380–81, 383, 385–86, 388, 392
Slack, Sarah E. "Sallie" 199
Slane, Amos (34th Indiana Infantry) 85
Slaughter, James 282, 285, 409
slaves 8, 12, 27, 35, 73, 85, 154–55, 167, 193, 266, 294, 407
Slidell, John 16
Sloan, Milton (47th Indiana Infantry) 231
Slough, Robert H. (mayor of Mobile) 279
Smith, Andrew J. 107, 113, 144–45, 150–51, 166–67, 212, 253–54, 259, 265, 276
Smith, Ashbel 150, 153, 166, 282–83, 385, 409
Smith, C.F. 24
Smith, E. Kirby 65, 159, 163, 193, 212, 228, 239, 243, 280, 282, 285, 409, 413
Smith, Giles 96, 166, 168
Smith, J.L. Kirby 29
Smith, M.L. 146
Smith, Terry C. 2, 350
Smith, Watson 83, 87, 90
Smith, William Sooy 211, 216
"Snacky" (correspondent to the *Indianapolis Daily Journal*) 197
Sons of Liberty 207, 245, 247
South Bend (Indiana) *Forum* 106
Southern Railroad of Mississippi **98**, 113, **125**, 129, **147**, **173**, 211
Spanish Fort, Alabama **267**, 268, 270, 274; capture 276
Spicely, William T. 71, 81, 97, 99, 140, 183, 197
Spring Hill, Alabama **267**, 280
Stanley, David S. 28, 29
Stanley, Katherine 2
Stanton, Edwin M. 107
Starke's Landing, Alabama **267**
Starlight (US transport) 222
Stedman, Thomas 362
Steele, Frederick 69, 71, 74, 168,
212, 214, 219, 250, 265, 274, 282; to Texas 284
Steele's Bayou, Mississippi 95
Stephenson, P.D. (Washington Artillery, CSA) 272–73, 276, 406
Stevens, Thaddeus 79
Stewart, A.P. 27
Stewart, R.A. 27
Stidger, Felix 246, 248, 401; *see also* Indiana Treason Trials
Stillman, Charles 289–90, 411; *see also* Brownsville; Cavazos, Rafael Garcia
USS *Stockdale* 272, 279
Stoner, Noah (34th Indiana Infantry) 85
Storey, Wilbur 107, 381–82; *see also* *Chicago Times*
Sturgis, John E. (47th Indiana Infantry) 142
Sullivan, Henry 96
Sutcliffe, Eliza Edna Rose **307**
Sutcliffe, Henry **307**
Sweet, Benjamin J. 256
Sweetser, J.N. 76

Tallahatchie River, Mississippi 83, 88, 90
Taney, Roger 5, 6, 99, 104
Tate, John (47th Indiana Infantry) **80**
Tate, Samuel (47th Indiana Infantry) **80**
Taylor, Richard "Dick" 159, 163, 199, 212, 218, 224, 229, 243
Tennessee Artillery (CSA): Bankhead's Battery 27; Phillips' Battery 270; Upton's Battery 27
Tennessee Cavalry (USA): 1st Battalion 220
Terre Haute, Indiana 104
Terre Haute & Richmond Railroad 172
Terry, David S. 295, 412
Terry, Mississippi 189
Texas Artillery (CSA): Cook's 196; Daniels's Battery 201; Edgar's Battery 213; Moseley's Battery 226; Valverde Battery 164, 200; West's Texas/Arizona Battery 225
Texas Cavalry (CSA): Chisum's 2nd Partisan Rangers 225; 3rd 235; 6th 388; 7th 205; 9th 388; 12th 226; 13th 160; 19th 226; 21st 226; Green's 200; McNelly's Scouts 238, 400
Texas Cavalry (USA): 1st 193–94, 203, 236–37; 2nd 281
Texas Infantry (CSA): 2nd 150; 3rd 235; 11th 200; 15th 200; 18th 200; Davis Guards 196; Waul's Texas Legion 86, 90, 151–52
Tharpe, William H. (47th Indiana Infantry) **80**
Thatcher, H.K. 272
Thayer, John M. 214
Thibodaux, Louisiana 165, 238, 240

Thirty-fifth Parallel (CS transport) 88
Thomas, Lorenzo 9, 10
Thompson, Egbert 41
Thompson, Jacob "Jake" 245, 248–50, 303, 401–2
Thompson, Meriwether "Jeff" 25, 28, 29, 365
Tiger (US tug) 57
USS *Tigress* 110
Tiptonville, Tennessee 17, 26, 28, 30, 43, 45, 49
Toledo, Wabash & Western Railroad 403
Topeka (Kansas) Weekly Leader 304
Toronto, Canada 245
Tracy, Edward D. 118
Trans-Mississippi: Confederate economy in 244
Treat, Samuel H. (US District Judge): 105
Trent Affair 16–18, 24
Trinity College 416
Tulane University 210, 406
Turren, D.A. 31
Tuscaloosa (CS floating battery) 268, 406

USS *Tuscumbia*: attack on Grand Gulf 114–16
USS *Tyler* 168–69
"the tyrant's plea of military necessity" 97, 376, 414; *see also* Indiana House of Representatives
Ullman, Daniel 240, 400
CSS *Uncle Ben*: at Fort Griffin, Texas 196
Union City, Tennessee 60
Union Theological Seminary (New York City) 12
United States Artillery: Battery F, 1st 236
United States Artillery (Colored Troops): 6th 220
United States Cavalry: 4th 215
United States Infantry: 12th 178
United States Infantry (Colored Troops): 46th 287; 62nd 281; 73rd 277–78; 92nd 228; 97th 224–25; 99th 224–25
United States Military Academy at West Point 19, 67
Universe (US transport) 222
University of Paris 371
University of Southern Mississippi 2

Vallandigham, Clement L. 105, 217, 245, 378
Van Dorn, Earl 30, 71, 74, 81
Veatch, James 265, 271–74, 280, 294
Vermont Infantry (USA): 2nd 34; 7th 164, 274, 287
Vicksburg, Mississippi **147**; Confederate positions 147; Federal positions 147–48; first Federal assault 148; second Federal assault 148–54; siege 154–68

Vicksburg News 161
Vicksburg Times 414
Vicksburg Whig 124
Victoria (r. 1837–1901) 16; *see also* Albert, Prince Consort; Queen Victoria
Vidaurri, Santiago 292, 390
Villard, Henry (*Cincinnati Commercial* reporter) 10–11, 360
Villepigue, John B. 51
Vincent, Felix A. 15, 361; *see also* Wallack's Old Theatre
Virgin (CS transport) 273
USS *Virginia* 203
Virginia Artillery (CSA): Botetort's 118, 131, 133
von Sheliha, Victor: "frame torpedoes" in Mobile Bay 271, 407
Voorhees, Daniel W. 217, 247, 403

Wade, William 115
Walke, Henry 40, 113
Walker, John G. 218, 409
Walker, L.M. 27
Walker, William 102
Wall, James W. 247
Wall, T.N. 90
Wallace, Lew 43, 55, 57, 60
Wallack's Old Theatre (New York City) 361
Warren, Indiana 7
Warrior (US transport) 280
Warsaw (Indiana) Express 106
Washburn, Cadwallader C. 71, 83, 200, 204, 210
Washburn, Henry D. 204
Watrous, John C. (Judge, US District Court of Texas) 290, 411; *see also* Cavazos, Rafael Garcia; Stillman, Charles
"W.C.F." (correspondent to the *Indiana State Sentinel*): on failure to capture Fort Pemberton 94; gunboats at Fort Pemberton 91; on the Yazoo Pass Expedition 89–90
Weitzel, Godfrey 284
Wells, D.S. 295
West Point, Kentucky **4**, 23
West Point, Mississippi 211, 259
West Virginia Infantry: 4th 168
Wharton, John A. 226, 235, 237
"Whistling Dick" 159
White River, Arkansas **46**, 78–81
Whitmore, J.W. (47th Indiana Infantry) 142
"Wide Awakes" 102
Wiles, Greenburg, F. (78th Ohio Infantry) 185
Wilhelm, George (56th Ohio Infantry): Medal of Honor 142
Wilkes, Abner (46th Mississippi) 1; attitude toward parole 171; on capture 278–79; on escape 408; on Pemberton's surrender 170; on siege at Fort Blakely 275; on siege at Vicksburg 162
Wilkes, Charles 16, 18, 361

Wilkeson, Sam 9, 10
Wilkie, Franc B. (*New York Times* reporter, "Galway") 72–73, 371
Willcox, Orlando B. 107
Williams, Thomas 64
Williamsburg, Mississippi 408; *see also* Wilkes, Abner
Williamson, Brenda Perrott v, 1, 2; *see also* Johnston, William B.; Wilkes, Abner
Williamson, David, Sr. v
Williamson, Mary Kathryn Rose v, 1
Willis, Miss Pink 30
Wilson, James B. 254; *see also* Indiana Treason Trials
Wilson, James H. 56
USS *Winnebago* 273
Winn's Plantation, Louisiana **208**, 226
USS *Winona* 164
Winschel, Terry 112
Winter, Sam F. (*Huntington Democrat*) 7
Wisconsin Artillery (USA): 1st 129; 1st Battery 224; 6th 130; Dillon's 6th Battery 136; 12th 130
Wisconsin Cavalry (USA): 4th 399
Wisconsin Infantry (USA): 4th 224; 8th 73; 11th 144; 18th 152; 23rd 150; 27th 287; 28th 83, 93, 201, 271, 287; 29th 107, 121, 132, 157, 202, 238, 240, 241, 243, 251, 258, 264, 269, 272, 275, 280; 35th 287
Wohlford, Thomas J. (47th Indiana Infantry) 241
Wood, Fernando (mayor of New York City) 175; *see also* Opdyke, George
Wood, Thomas J. 9, 15, 18, 363
Wood, Dr. T.J. (surgeon, 96th Ohio Infantry) 203
Woodville, Mississippi 242
Wright, Edward (24th Iowa Infantry) 141
Wright, Horatio 104
Wright, Phineas C. 103, 207, 208, 302; *see also* Order of American Knights

Yale College 406
Yalobusha River, Mississippi 86
Yates, Richard (governor of Illinois) 172, 379
Yazoo Pass Expedition **46**, 82–96; troop transports 87
Yazoo River, Mississippi 83
Yeakel, David T. 208, 254; *see also* Indiana Treason Trials
Yellow Bayou, Louisiana **208**, 229–30
Yoist, John 225,
Young's Point, Louisiana 82, 109

Zent, Henry W. (47th Indiana Infantry) 316
Zollicofer, Felix 21
Zumro, Henry L. 246, 257; *see also* Indiana Treason Trials